DATE DUE

Ja. 9			

GAYLORD　　　　　　　　　　　　PRINTED IN U.S.A.

The Larger Hope

The Owen D. Young Peace Tower, Universalist National Memorial Church, Washington, D.C.

The Larger Hope

*The Second Century
of the Universalist Church
in America
1870-1970*

Russell E. Miller

Unitarian Universalist Association
Boston

©1985 by Russell E. Miller
All rights reserved
Printed in the United States of America
ISBN 0-933840-00-4 (v.2)

Contents

Section I Setting the Stage for the Second Century

Chapter 1 The Evolution of an Organization: A Retrospective Glance 3
      2 Inventory and Self-Assessment 9

Section II The State of the Denomination After 1870

Chapter 3 "That Little Company Called Universalists:" The Statistical Record 19
      4 Administering and Financing the Denomination 30
        Financing the Denomination
      5 From Expansion to Contraction 47
        "A World Church for World Service"
        The Universalist National Memorial Church
        A Denomination with an Uncertain Future

Section III Theology for a Changing World

Chapter 6 Testing the Winchester Profession 65
        The Bisbee Heresy Trial
        Standing the Test of Time
        The Declaration of 1899
      7 Science and Religion: A Debate Avoided 94
      8 The Bond of Fellowship and Statements of Faith (1935) 109
        The Challenge of Humanism
        Forging a New Profession

Section IV The Search for a Wider Fellowship

Chapter 9 The International Scene 119
        The World's Columbian Exposition and the World's Parliament of Religions
        International Religious Liberalism
     10 The National Scene 130
        The Congress of Liberal Religion and the "New" Universalism
        The National Federation of Religious Liberals

Section V Institutional Activities and Organizations

Chapter 11 Clergy and Laity 153
        The Clergy
        Adjusting the Rules of Fellowship
        The Fraters
        The Laity
     12 The Church and Its Youth 174
        The Young People's Christian Union and Its Successors
        The General Sunday School Association
     13 Summer Institutes: Combining Religion and Recreation 217

14	Publications and Scholarship *The Universalist Publishing House*	230
15	Secular Education in Other Hands *Lombard College* *Throop Polytechnic Institute* *Southern Industrial Institute*	253
16	Theological Education: Ryder and Canton *Ryder Divinity School* *Canton Theological School*	274
17	Theological Education: Crane Theological School	302
18	Quillen Hamilton Shinn, The "Grasshopper Missionary"	341
19	The Norfolk and Suffolk Missions in the South	361
20	In the Mountains of North Carolina	372
21	The Association of Universalist Women	379
22	Denominational Pioneering Overseas: The Scottish Mission	400
23	The Field is the World: "The Establishment of the Japan Mission, 1890-1915 *Paving the Way* *Launching the Mission* *Struggling to Survive*	412
24	The Japan Mission Between Two Wars	447

Section VII Universalism, Social Issues, and Social Service

Chapter 25	Facing a World of Change	463
26	Clarence R. Skinner and the Social Gospel *The Community Church of Boston*	493
27	"Not Your Creed, But Your Need:" Social Service and Benevolences *The Universalist Service Committee*	510

Section VIII Interdenominational Relations

Chapter 28	Edging Closer Together: Universalist-Unitarian Relations, 1870-1925	533
29	An Enlarged "Household of Faith"? Aborted Union with the Congregationalists	553
30	Half-way Steps Toward Union: Universalist-Unitarian Relations, 1927-1937	583
31	"God's Stepchildren:" The Rebuffs of the Federal Council of Churches, 1939-1947	608
32	Universalism at the Crossroads *A Temporary Reprieve* *Beyond Christianity* *Toward a World Religion*	624
33	"And Flow on Together:" Universalist-Unitarian Consolidation, 1937-1961 *"Union by Installments:" The Council of Liberal Churches* *The Joint Merger Commission* *The Final Steps*	648

Notes		667
Bibliography		725
Appendices		
	A. Universalist Declarations of Social Principles	733
	B. Constitution and Bylaws of the Unitarian Universalist Association Ratified in 1961	745
Index		752

Illustrations

	Page
The Owen D. Young Peace Tower, Universalist National Memorial Church, Washington, D.C.	Frontispiece
John Coleman Adams (1849-1922), Universalist minister and prolific author	21
Church membership certificate, Murray Anniversary Crusade	48
Herman Bisbee (1833-1879), subject of a heresy trial	69
Orello Cone (1835-1905), a leading Universalist scholar	102
Marion D. Shutter (1853-1939), Universalist champion of evolution	105
Clinton Lee Scott, signer of the Humanist Manifesto	110
Frederic W. Perkins (1870-1943), distinguished Universalist clergyman and scholar	113
Henry Blanchard (1833-1918), an exponent of the "New" Universalism	142
A Fraters ritual	166
A representative group of Fraters	166
Owen D. Young (1887-1962), Universalist businessman and diplomat	170
Victor Friend (1871-1952), a leading Universalist layman, and one of his enterprises	172
Harry Adams Hersey (1870-1950), a veteran YPCU'er on his bicycle	179
The National YPCU Convention of 1895 in the Church of the Unity (Boston)	179
Mary Grace and Harry L. Canfield (1860-1942, 1864-1946), noted for their Universalist youth work	182
"Aunty"Lucinda Brown (1822-1917), beloved friend of many youth groups	192
A product of YPCU effort: Shinn Memorial Church, Chattanooga, Tennessee	199
Sixtieth National Universalist Youth Fellowship in Norway, Maine, 1948	209
George E. Huntley (1870-1950), President of the General Sunday School Association	213
A Universalist picnic in Tacoma, Washington with Q. H. Shinn	218
Memorial Church at Murray Grove, New Jersey	221
The "Quillen," Ferry Beach, Maine, in 1906	224
Memorial Day at Ferry Beach in 1902	226

Quillen Hamilton Shinn and Isaac Morgan Atwood at Ferry Beach	228
The Universalist Publishing House building at 359-61 Boylston Street in Boston	239
Frederick A. Bisbee (1855-1923), editor of the *Leader* for twenty-five years	243
John van Schaick (1873-1949), editor of the *Leader* for almost a quarter of a century	246
Emerson Hugh Lalone (1899-1960), editor of the *Leader* and Universalist author	250
Joseph Mayo Tilden (1873-1928), indefatigable President of Lombard College	257
Ryder Divinity School in Chicago	278
Fisher Hall at St. Lawrence University	285
Heads of the Canton Theological School, (1856-1965)	287
Students and faculty at Canton Theological School about 1908	291
Frank Oliver Hall, Professor of Homiletics at the Crane Theological School, 1919-1929	313
Dean McCollester at his New Hampshire farm	319
The Crane Theological School complex. The Fischer Arcade, flanked by Miner and Paige Halls and the Crane Chapel	321
Lee S. McCollester and Clarence R. Skinner, Deans of the Crane Theological School (1912-1933 and 1933-1945, respectively)	323
The Shinn family as he was embarking on his missionary career	343
Announcing Shinn's appearance in West Virginia	345
Quillen Hamilton Shinn (1845-1907), Universalism's best-known circuit rider	351
Thomas E. Wise. a Universalist minister and his son in Norfolk, Virginia	364
Headquarters of the Suffolk Mission in Virginia	365
Joseph Fletcher Jordan (1863-1929), Universalist minister in Suffolk, Virginia	366
The mission in Western North Carolina	375
Presidents of the Women's Centenary Association, 1869-1905	381
Presidents of the Women's National Missionary Association, 1905-1921	387
The summer institute of the Women's National Missionary Association at Ferry Beach, Maine, in 1928	389
President of the Women's National Missionary Association, 1921-1939	391
Presidents of the Association of Universalist Women, 1939-1955	394
Aerial view of the Clara Barton Camp, North Oxford, Massachusetts	396
Issac Wallace Cate (1862-1908) and George L. Perin (1854-1921) with Japanese theological students in 1892	426

Tenth anniversary celebration of the graduates of the Midori kindergarten, 1918	440
The Japan mission at its greatest extent, 1906	442
The Shizuoka Church in 1920	449
Georgene Bowen teaching a men's Bible class in 1926	451
Levi M. Powers (1864-1920) at his desk in Somerville, Massachusetts in the 1890s	495
Clarence Russell Skinner (1881-1949), prophet of the social gospel	497
Bethany Union, Boston	515
The Chapin Home on Long Island, New York	518
The Doolittle Home	522
Award to the Universalist Service Committee by the Dutch Government, 1947	525
Carleton Fisher, associated with the Universalist Service Commitee from 1944 to 1953	528
Robert Cummins, leader in Universalist affairs, with his son John, also a Universalist minister	616
The Universalist church in Hollywood, California	627
The historic Charles Street Meeting House in Boston	644
The interior of the Charles Street Meeting House	646
Newly elected members of the Council of Liberal Churches in 1957	652
Robert Cummins (Universalist) and Frederick May Eliot (Unitarian) in 1953	653

Foreword

When Christopher Gist Raible wrote the Foreword to Volume I of *The Larger Hope: 1770-1870*, he suggested that the first century of the history of Universalism in America truly is a larger hope, but that "the second century of the Universalist Church is a story of decline and disappointment." The second volume of *The Larger Hope: 1870-1970* actually is the story of a century of decline of Universalism from one of the major religious denominations of America to a small sect of some 40,000 persons before the merger with the American Unitarian Association in 1961.

But the story is the history of the decline of a denomination which in great part had lost its reason for existence. Universalists had been so successful in promulgating their doctrines that Universal ideas became commonplace in many of the larger Protestant churches of America. As Universalist ideas were more and more adopted by persons in other denominations, and fewer pulpits were preaching special salvation, and as the hold of Calvinistic ideas lessened, there was almost no need to establish and even to maintain churches that were explicitly Universalist. No denomination should hang its head if it has made such progress in disseminating its ideas, that others take up their banner and march with it. This history of Universalism is the story of the rise and fall of human institutions. Few institutions can perpetuate their ideas after they are adopted by many others. The aim of many human institutions is to work so hard that they work themselves out of existence. The Universalists were so successful that they almost accomplished this feat.

Until the publication of Volume I of *The Larger Hope* very little work had been done in recent times on the first century of the history of Universalism in America. Almost nothing has been done on the second century until Russell Miller set aside a large part of his life to do the research necessary to write this account.

Need I say that the officers, the Board of Directors, and the members of the Unitarian Universalist Historical Society are delighted to see the completion of this ambitious project, for now the whole story has been told. The Universalist Church of America ceased to exist as such in 1961 when it merged with the American Unitarian Association to become the Unitarian Universalist Association. And it has become a merged group. We now have more diversity than we did in 1961. Any pangs that merger brought about did not come because there were struggles between Unitarians and Universalists. Most of us have forgotten which side of the merger we came in on.

Walter Donald Kring
President, Unitarian Universalist Historical Society
July, 1984

Preface

This work is the second half of a two-volume history of the Universalist Church in America from its eighteenth-century origins up through its consolidation with the American Unitarian Association in 1961 to form the Unitarian Universalist Association. The combined denominations continued to maintain their headquarters in New England (specifically Boston), the historic center of both Universalism and Unitarianism.

The author has followed generally the same pattern that prevailed when the first volume was published in 1979. The aim is to provide as comprehensive and as accurate an institutional history of the denomination as possible. This entails a degree of detail which, it is hoped, will provide, without unduly overwhelming or burdening the reader, a reference source as well as an interpretive narrative of a small but important segment of American religious history.

One major departure has been made from the *schema* announced originally for the second volume. The continuation of the state-by-state coverage has been abandoned. Instead of presenting a somewhat dreary (and somewhat depressing) recital of organized Universalism, which was confined within the nation to twenty-eight states and the District of Columbia at the time of consolidation, the author has seen fit to select those geographical areas which seemed most important in denominational history. They serve to illustrate most clearly those basic features of Universalism which accounted for its persistence and, on occasion, its success as a small denomination comprising considerably less than one percent of the total religious configuration of the nation.

This volume, with occasional overlap with the first in the interests of continuity, concentrates on the ninety years embracing the history of the denomination since the celebration of its centennial in 1870. Between 1871 and 1961 Universalism, long characterized by its loose organization and emphasis on congregational autonomy and theological freedom for the individual, became almost as institutionalized and bureaucratized as most of its contemporary Protestant counterparts. This was illustrated by the growing power of its central body, the General Convention, which in 1942 became the Universalist Church of America (UCA), with its legislative body designated as the General Assembly.

Simultaneously, as many of its basic teachings, including its once-distinctive tenet of the ultimate salvation of all humanity in the spiritual realm, were adopted either implicitly or explicitly by other religious groups, it gradually but steadily lost ground as a denomination, and its official membership declined at its lowest point, to less than 40,000. Its constituency became more or less reconciled to a minor position in the American religious spectrum although they continued to hope that their philosophy of non-creedalism and human brotherhood would eventually prevail.

As Universalist numbers declined, the focus shifted, for the majority, from a traditionally Christian orientation to a version of theistic humanism which stressed social service and a version of world-wide religion which underplayed denominationalism and brought most Universalists closer to the Unitarians and eventually played an important part, after much backing and filling, in their eventual organic union. Even when united, the combined denominations, claiming a formal membership of less than 200,000 in the 1980s, still conceived of themselves as the true champions of religious liberalism whose mission it was to propagate a concept of world brotherhood and service yet to be achieved in a troubled world.

Throughout their history as a separate denomination Universalists represented one of the many ironies and paradoxes in the diverse history of the nation. While both professing and attempting to practice the historic ideals of voluntarism, individualism, and freedom which epitomized the very essence of the American ethos, for the most part they remained largely outside the religious mainstream, often because their conceptions were in advance of those of their contemporaries or were considered in other ways too unorthodox by their neighbors. By the time they ceased their separate denominational existence—and possibly because of it—history seemed to a great extent to have caught up with them.

A word of explanation should be injected about the use of such purportedly sexist verbiage as "man," "mankind," "brotherhood," and "layman" which may distress or even antagonize some readers. An effort has been made to substitute neutral language where possible, but the constraint imposed by the need for historical accuracy requires that if such words occur in direct quotations they be left unchanged. To alter the language arbitrarily in order to conform to present usage would distort the record. The past must be taken on its own terms.

The writer is indebted to the officers of the Unitarian Universalist Historical Society, sponsor and principal financial supporters of this publication, for unfailing support in all respects, including complete freedom to make his own mistakes. A special acknowledgement must be made to the staffs of the Andover-Harvard Theological Library of the Harvard Divinity School and of the Nils Y. Wessell Library of Tufts University for making their resources available. Particular mention should be made of the invaluable assistance of Alan Seaburg, Curator of Manuscripts at the Harvard Divinity School, whose contributions to this book went far beyond the call of duty; and to Carl Seaburg, former Information Officer of the Unitarian Universalist Association, whose meticulous editing of the manuscript has prevented the author from falling into many a trap. He is absolved from all responsibility for whatever mistakes may have slipped through his dragnet.

The Larger Hope

Section I
Setting the Stage for the Second Century

Chapter 1

The Evolution of an Organization: A Retrospective Glance

In September 1870 a mass of humanity, estimated at 12,000, most of whom were associated with the Universalist Church, crowded into a tent city in the Massachusetts seacoast town of Gloucester, where the first church of the denomination had been organized. They were there to attend a three-day series of meetings to celebrate the 100th anniversary of the first sermon preached in America by the Englishman John Murray, and to conduct denominational business.

They could and did look with immense satisfaction and pride at what they had accomplished in the course of a century. They had met and to a large degree had surmounted obstacles of almost every kind, and their optimistic doctrines of God's universal love, the inevitability of Christian salvation, the efficacy of good works, and ultimate holiness and happiness for all, had been embodied in a Profession of Faith adopted in 1803. Their beliefs had "leavened the religious mind of the age [and had] compelled recognition and respect where it has not found hospitality."[1] The denomination could claim some 700 ministers, with churches in all the Northern and nearly all of the Midwestern and Southern states. In numbers it was presumed to rank sixth among American Protestant denominations, although no one seemed to know for sure how many members there were or how large their constituency actually was.

Universalists in 1870 could boast of three institutions of higher education under their sponsorship, the largest and most prosperous of which was Tufts College which straddled two Boston suburbs; two theological schools; and a sizeable number of academies and secondary schools concentrated in but not confined to New England. The denomination had, like most others, been caught up in the reform fervor of the pre-Civil War period and, although it operated more or less independently of others, had taken its stand against slavery and had made its mark in temperance, prison reform, and the innumerable other attempts to improve the world.

The denomination, full of confidence and determination, firmly rooted in the Christian tradition, had committed itself to raising a then unprecedented fund of $200,000 in order to extend its missionary work and to make it, if not the largest, then certainly one of the most influential religious bodies in the nation.

The editors of the *Universalist,* writing on the eve of the centennial celebration, expressed confidence that "God had selected the Universalist Church as the instrumentality through which He would work out the religious destiny of this continent. It commands all the promises of the future. Its idea will surely dominate the Church in the coming generations. Why, then, shall not the Universalist Church, the institution in which these ideas are organized, become the largest and foremost Christian sect?"[2]

Yet there were some sobering facts to be considered. The question of whether it should be much larger than it then was, had to be decided, and decided soon. This was especially important because many other denominations were assimilating Universalist ideas while Universalism as a denomination was being almost completely ignored. One alternative was to "crystallize around our present centers of influence, and prepare to occupy the place of a 'small but respectable' sect." Much more desirable was another route: "a mighty missionary impulse." The great opportunity was "a grand Centennial Celebration" as Universalism entered its "Providential epoch."

Murray and his contemporaries had never intended to organize a separate denomination, but to present a religious interpretation which would somehow prevail when their fellow Americans saw the logic and inevitability of their position. But historical circumstances had dictated otherwise.

Reluctant as they were to create a formal organizational structure, Universalists from their beginning as a sect in the late eighteenth century had seen the merit of banding together to promote their common purposes. The earliest attempt had been made at Oxford, Massachusetts, in 1785. A principal object had been mutual protection; as Murray put it, "for the purpose of deliberating upon some plan to defeat the designs of our enemies, who aim at robbing us of the liberty wherewith the Constitution has made us free." There was also a growing feeling of fraternity and desire for fellowship among the few Universalists who knew of each other's existence. No organization had resulted immediately from the first attempt to unite the brethren, but acquaintance and exchange of fraternal sentiments had been accomplished.

Another endeavor had been made in Philadelphia in 1790, nearly five years later. A call was issued by Universalists in the area to "the brethren in different parts of the continent" to attend a conference. The announced purpose was to plan "one uniform mode of divine worship, one method of ordaining suitable persons to the ministry; one consistent way of administering the Lord's Supper, or whatever else may appear desirable to any when such Convention meets." Of the seventeen who attended, seven were preachers. Murray was the sole representative from New England. Out of the two-week meeting had come the first Universalist Profession of Faith and a plan of church government based on a congregational system of polity allowing virtually complete independence for local units.

Lacking the aid needed from the Northeast, the Philadelphia Convention lasted only until 1809. Meanwhile, the New Englanders had met again at Oxford, this time in 1793. Out of their deliberations had come the Convention of the New England States and Others in 1803, which included New York State. In 1833 this central ecclesiastical body became the Universalist General Convention, although not yet a truly national organization. A parallel development had been associations made up of Universalists in neighboring societies. Some of these regional organizations, such as the Western Association in New York State, evolved into state conventions while others subdivided into new associations as the denomination grew in numbers and strength. The idea soon prevailed that state lines were the most natural and convenient boundaries, although regional associations cutting across two or more states did occasionally appear.

By about 1860 agitation had begun for a more coherent and compact union than had earlier prevailed, and after tentative steps had been taken the convention was incorporated in 1866. The organization that came out of it in 1870, after "many long years of study, labor, and experience," and known officially as the Universalist General Convention, was given, at least on paper, legislative authority to promote unified action, cooperate in missionary work, and secure uniformity in fellowshipping, ordination, and discipline. This administrative arrangement set the general pattern for the remainder of Universalist history as a separate denomination, although the name was changed to the Universalist Church of America in 1942 and a General Assembly, meeting biennially, became the legislative body.

Two somewhat antagonistic tendencies had already become evident by 1870 in the evolution of organized Universalism. One stemmed from a desire for liberty and what appeared to be the threat of "ecclesiastical tyranny." Jealous of their freedom and chronically suspicious of authority, Universalists wrote into their compacts and covenants their determination to be as independent and as free from outside restraint as possible.

Each religious society or church was to be sovereign in its temporal affairs. The other tendency was toward centralized authority, an influence reflecting in part the more highly structured denominations from which converts to Universalism had come, but including many with denominational antecedents like Elbridge Gerry Brooks, Richard Eddy, William H. Ryder, Thomas J. Sawyer, and Hosea Ballou 2d. They, as well as many lay members, saw both the necessity and desirability of devising an organization clothed with definite and real powers, restricted as they might be in reality.

Of the two tendencies it was the latter which eventually won out, but only after discussion and debate which lasted for decades. The plan worked out by 1870 and expressed in the revised constitution of the General Convention adopted that year, was roughly analogous to that of the national structure of federalism in the secular realm. The existence of separate jurisdictions and populations was recognized, with state conventions made up of delegates from local churches and parishes. Each convention had certain executive and legislative powers defined in a written constitution, and unorganized religious territories were placed under the jurisdiction of the central body. The functions earlier exercised by the associations were vested in appropriate state conventions, and most associations gradually disappeared after 1870, functioning only as non-legislative organizations.

The crucial question came at first to be the nature and degree of authority to be vested in the state conventions. In the beginning all authority had resided in the local religious societies and/or churches. But in the process of development part of it had been yielded, first to the associations, and then in turn by the latter to the state organizations. Some individuals, such as William S. Balch, were alarmed at such a transfer of power, considering it a threat to liberty; others remained indifferent; while the majority saw the advantages and favored the centralizing movement as long as it remained within certain carefully circumscribed bounds.

Then the key question became the relation of the state conventions to a central authority. Logic alone seemed to call for an agency to coordinate the activities of the state bodies and assure that "a more perfect union" would not be jeopardized by a score or more of unregulated and sometimes discordant authorities, each vested with supreme powers. The way out of the dilemma was the General Convention which had been a national assembly of some value and importance but which had no legal standing or authority, and advisory powers only. It was, in effect, "a great gathering of Universalist clans" which heard sermons and committee reports, passed innumerable resolutions, discussed many subjects, and gave advice, but had no real authority to enforce its recommendations or make its counsels prevail.

The logic of the situation did indeed result in some action. The General Convention was made the supreme executive and legislative body to whose laws and enactments state conventions and other church organizations were expected to conform. It was a sweeping, even radical, change, from the days of "primitive independency," and not all had become reconciled to it, even after many decades of operation.

There were admittedly, according to Isaac M. Atwood who evaluated the structure of the denomination soon after the turn of the twentieth century, some "incidental evils" which had appeared.[3] They reflected not so much any basic flaw in the plan of organization as the assumptions which had accompanied its evolution and refinement over the years. One was the growth of a feeling that, once established, the organization could be depended on to maintain itself automatically and somehow to be self-realizing. It was people, not the system, who were to blame when things went wrong. Another evil was the confusion of means with ends; the fact was lost sight of that the system existed for the benefit of the denomination and not the reverse. There was too much of a tendency to concentrate on the machinery itself, with insufficient attention to the ends it was intended to serve.

This, too, became a subject of prolonged discussion and debate, indulged in for the most part by the denominational leadership over the years rather than by the rank-and-file, who could not have cared less as long as their local interests were not adversely affected. It was this exaggerated sense of localism and individualism that continued to permeate the denomination throughout its history.

Scarcely a decade after the celebration of the denominational centennial, the trustees of the General Convention detected, with great optimism, two signs that were becoming visible in Universalism and were stressed in their annual report in 1879. One was the growing sense of "organic unity," and the other was an increasing commitment to evangelism. "It is only for nine years that we have lived under an ecclesiastical polity which is capable of organizing and concentrating our strength; but already this system, which was at first received with distrust and some dislike, finds cordial assent far and near."[4] Whether this sweeping generalization could be supported was left up in the air.

There was also pointed reference not only to the renewed determination to propagate the faith but to do so in the name of Christ, both individually and as a church.

There was, at the same time, the clear implication that the church was nearing the accomplishment of its original and historic mission. "We find each year less and less need to stand for that great truth which gave us our name, because the fulness of time seems come for that truth to assert itself in all the churches." This in no sense meant closing up shop. Universalists had all the more obligation to set an example for the rest of the Christian world and to make their church "a presentment... of the largest liberty of understanding, utterly indifferent to venerable error, with the most fervent and loyal devotion to the person of Christ."[5]

A considerable amount of surprise was expressed in 1901 when it was announced that the Universalist church in Reading, Pennsylvania, proposed to mark the new century with a series of revival services.[6] This constituted such a major departure from the historic opposition of the denomination to such activities that the pastor, A.G. Rogers, was interviewed by the secular press. He explained that the trustees of the General Convention had called for "aggressive spiritual work" but had left it largely up to individual ministers to determine what form it should take.

He elected to use gospel meetings and revival sermons not so much to bring unrepentant sinners into the fold as to quicken the spiritual life of those already within the Christian churches but who had become too apathetic and neglectful. The mere acceptance of Christ and union with a church were not sufficient. Rogers admitted another, more pragmatic purpose in conducting revivals in the Universalist church. Quickened spiritual awareness would result in increased donations wherewith to open new fields for denominational work. Universalists could thereby contribute to a new sense of dedication which he discerned in all churches, regardless of creed or faith. The possibilities were almost unlimited.

The call by the trustees and voiced by Rogers for "aggressive spiritual work" was one of the attempts common to most denominations periodically to infuse themselves with renewed strength and vigor. Among Universalist precedents many years earlier had been the efforts of Elbridge Gerry Brooks (1816-1878), himself a trustee and a member of the committee which had prepared the original draft of the constitution and bylaws adopted in 1870.[7] He had served briefly as General Secretary for one year (1867) and during his short tenure had attempted to bring a semblance of order to denominational affairs, which he found in "a chaotic state." In 1874 the Universalist Publishing House had issued *Our New Departure; or the Methods and Work of the Universalist Church of America, as it enters on its Second Century.*[8] It was a plain-spoken rebuke by Brooks to Universalists for their loss of true Christian spirituality. He offered a gloomy picture, putting much of the blame for denominational failings on Hosea Ballou's "death and glory" teaching which erroneously seemed to absolve Universalists of all responsibility for their spiritual welfare on earth; instead, true spirituality had to be actively sought and striven for. Brooks, in detailing denominational shortcomings, also had harsh words for Universalists because they had failed to develop a coherent and effective administrative structure.

It appeared that they were not very far into their second century before some were convinced that the entire denomination needed reassessment.

Chapter 2

Inventory and Self-assessment

An opportunity to assess the state of the denomination came a decade after the centenary of Murray's preaching in the first Universalist meeting house in America had been recognized. The denomination lost on 26 December 1880 one of its best-known ministers, Edwin Hubbell Chapin. This prompted a feature article on the history and state of Universalism which appeared in the *Boston Sunday Herald* on 2 January 1881.[1] After acknowledging Chapin's contribution, as an individual who had "done more than any one else to make this denomination of Christians popular in this country" and had been "the first pulpit orator in America," the author (or authors) reviewed the contributions of Murray in tempering the harshness of Calvinism and of Hosea Ballou in promoting unitarian theology. The article reviewed briefly the evolution of American Universalism, giving it credit as "a religious body which has certainly broken the back of orthodoxy in New England."

The authors came to the conclusion that as a denomination Universalism had passed its peak and was perceptibly on the decline. The first half-century had been "its noblest and best period. It then had a positive work to do." But it had, after a halcyon period of abnormally rapid growth between 1830 and 1850, not only come to a standstill but was exhibiting signs of "ultimate extinction."

Given this rather dramatic and categorical assertion, it was incumbent upon the writers of the article to support it, and so they did. According to the analysis, the paramount reason for the decline was that Universalism's adherents were "unfaithful to the system." It had set up ideals impossible of realization. They were unwilling "to accept the responsibilities of Christian people. They want to be saved without the personal effort for righteousness, which is called rightness of life. The doctrine is too good for the people who hold it."

There were other factors accounting for the decline. The denomination was weakened because it attracted happy-go-lucky opportunists who were satisfied to be told that there was no hell and assumed that personal responsibility stopped then and there. Universalist preaching had been "too much a mere protest against orthodoxy, not a positive teaching of Christianity, not a teaching which recognized the fact of sin in the world, and the exceeding sinfulness of sin in itself." This was compounded by the absence of a creed which "could have compelled a moral life as the condition of belief." There was "nothing to lean back on." This, in turn, brought to the surface another factor which flawed Universalism. It was not at base a theological denomination. It had yet to produce even one great theologian who had been able to postulate a *bona fide* system. True, about 1880 there were those who were theological in tendency and direction, but they had had no discernible influence outside the denomination. Among them were Thomas B. Thayer, editor of the *Universalist Quarterly;* William H. Ryder, pastor of St. Paul's Universalist Church in Chicago; Elmer H. Capen, president of Tufts College; and Charles H. Leonard, on the faculty of the Tufts Divinity School. A. St. John Chambré, considered at least the intellectual equal of these individuals, had in 1880 left the Universalist church to become an Episcopalian.

As to Chapin, according to the article his great contribution had been to personify the "great broad churchman" who was mentally much like Phillips Brooks, although superior to the latter as an orator. Chapin was more evangelical, more sympathetic toward Christ, and more spiritual than most Universalists. He was able to transcend the narrow interests of sectarianism. Chapin was, in short, "the light of Universalism, and its best, most spiritual tie with the great Christian world." But a theologian he was not.

What had happened to Universalism by 1880? It had begun to decline because other denominations had appropriated in some degree its distinctive teachings. All Christians had "stepped down from high Calvinism to a more rational belief." Meanwhile, Universalism as a religious organization, "without an ecclesiastical polity, without a creed, without a vigorous connection with historical Christianity, has allowed itself to drift further and further away from the vigorous activity of the great evangelical bodies of Christian people, instead of demanding to be received as one of them, drifting, in fact, into what is called a hopeless rationalism, where religious fervor is petrified, and where to stand still is to part with influence and power." It had to show for its denominational efforts only a handful of inadequately endowed schools, one feeble and struggling foreign mission in Scotland, and no evangelical enthusiasm.

Here were some serious challenges to the entire undergirding of Universalism that demanded answers, particularly because the authors of the article insisted that they were voicing the opinions of denominational leaders themselves and not their own personal prejudices. Replies from Universalists were not long in coming; two rejoinders appeared in a matter of days. The first came from G.H. Emerson in an essay somewhat longer than the piece to which he was responding; and the second took the form of a sermon preached by Alonzo A. Miner on 9 January 1881 to his Boston congregation, entitled "Universalism Not Declining."[2]

Emerson defended Hosea Ballou and his generation for their attacks on orthodoxy and their concentration on doctrinal debate, given their need not only to spread their version of religious truth but to survive the onslaughts they faced, often reaching bitter proportions. Emerson did admit that contentiousness and protest had become a habit among many Universalists and had survived beyond any real need in a later day. He admitted also that Universalism embraced all too many who were merely anti-orthodox rather than truly spiritual-minded. When pressures from orthodoxy receded, hastily assembled congregations melted away. Emerson sensed that since about 1860 the Universalists had settled down, and that "sober, systematic, Christian work" had largely replaced temporary enthusiasm and controversy. Order and stability, with salaried missionaries, had begun to replace the uncoordinated activities of individualistic itinerants operating largely on their own.

Emerson did not disagree with the authors' roster of theological leadership, except to add the names of Hosea Ballou 2d and T.J. Sawyer. As to the assertion that the denomination had, according to some of its own spokesmen, no future to which to look forward, Emerson disagreed completely. He denied that a single individual had made or supported such a statement and, further, that no one was omniscient in any case. It was true that there were currents of thought abroad in the land that obscured or even threatened the spiritual realm — "the 'cold wave' of secularism, the enthusiasm born of marvellous discoveries in the physical world, the disintegrating and revolutionary character of many inventions." But these affected unfavorably all denominations, not the Universalists alone. Perhaps, on balance, Universalist promotion of "righteousness" was nothing to boast of; still, "in the greatest reform of the age, that of temperance," Universalists ranked second only to the Methodists.

The statements in the article that the denomination was "without vigorous connection with historical Christianity" and was drifting into "a hopeless rationalism" were, according to Emerson, an utter misapprehension of the facts and an absolute perversion of the record. From the days of Murray until the death of Chapin, Universalism had remained firmly planted on the rock of Christ and his apostles. Whenever the issue of rationalism had arisen, it had "been met firmly and effectually." Whatever the mistakes or foibles of Universalists, rationalism was not one of them. At the risk of uttering a "Boston conceit," Emerson cited the quantitative advance of the denomination in the very center of American culture and education which, by coincidence, was also the Mecca of Universalism. And finally, he wrote triumphantly, was it not Universalism as an idea as much as an ecclesiastical body that was most important in the final analysis?

Miner went over much the same ground as did Emerson, emphasizing the solidity, the refinement of organization, and the augmented resources of the denomination in 1880 as contrasted with its early days. Miner emphatically denied the allegations that Universalists had no church polity and had separated themselves from historic Christianity. Even the constitutional structure of Universalism, from local parishes to the General Convention, paralleled the political structure of the nation, in the same way that the equality of man before God matched the secular principle of the equality of man before the law. The Universalist church therefore breathed the American spirit in its form and its teachings, opening "the doors of hope to all the children of God." The denomination was undeniably an American church in every sense, and a part of the American mainstream.

Neither Emerson nor Miner addressed himself directly to all of the questions raised either explicitly or by implication by the *Boston Herald* article. They remained silent on the matter of a creed, and in their defense emphasized the physical attributes of the denomination and its quantitative rather than qualitative aspects. Their replies to the article were greeted with great approbation by the editors of the *Leader* who considered them together as "the greatest missionary document yet printed."[3] Extra copies were printed because of anticipated demand.

A.J. Patterson also made the *Herald* article the occasion for a sermon in the Roxbury church on 9 January 1881. His defense of Universalism was fully as energetic as those of Emerson and Miner. He pointed out that the denominational statistics given in the article itself contradicted the theme of decline.[4] The stock argument that Universalism lacked the sanction of morality was completely fallacious; in fact, Universalists were possibly too rigid in their moral standards and held too tight a rein on the individual.

Spiritual strength and enthusiasm in the decade prior to 1880 were even greater than before, judging from congregational participation in such religious rituals as Communion services. Monetary contributions to denominational expenses had been impressive, and the value of church property had doubled between 1850 and 1880. In the same period the denomination had founded no less than five colleges and universities as well as numerous academies. No other denomination had done so much in proportion to numbers and resources. True, not all were well endowed or attended, partly because Universalists had undertaken to found too many in too short a time, but both endowments and patronage were increasing. Admittedly the past record of the denomination in missionary work and church extension had not been impressive, but efforts were being made with greater seriousness and more efficient organization than ever before, and were certainly not in decline.

The theological contributions of Miner, Sawyer, and Atwood may not have been as profound or esoteric as scholars in other denominations, but their influence was surely as great and as positive as those. Patterson also denied the implication that Chapin had not been sufficiently appreciated by Universalists, and offered as proof the numerous testimonials at the time of his death.

Miner had acknowledged that the Universalist church was too good for most of those who belonged to it, and Patterson agreed. After all, only Christ could claim that distinction. But there was no reason why Universalists should not have an ideal to which to aspire.

The meeting of the General Convention in Meriden, Connecticut, marked a quarter-century since the centennial convocation in 1870, and Henry B. Metcalf, a leading layman, reviewed in a major address the progress of the denomination in the intervening years.[5] He noted that many of the leaders, both clerical and lay, had by then passed off the scene — Alonzo A. Miner, Israel Washburn, E.H. Chapin, William H. Ryder, E.G. Brooks, Horace Greeley, and many others. It was nonetheless gratifying that of the 116 delegates at the 1870 convention, nearly three-fourths were still serving the denomination in 1895, and that only two had left the church.

In a wider field, Universalists had won acceptance as a religious body greater than at any other period in American history, despite occasional evidences of suspicion, opposition, and unwillingness to break down the barriers of hostility. One unhappy example was the continued refusal of the YMCA to admit Universalists to its ranks. That organization had formally proscribed Universalists in 1872; had refused to rent their hall in Philadelphia for the use of the General Convention meeting in 1882 because of their "utter unworthiness"; and its national constitution had specifically excluded Universalists as well as Unitarians, Jews, and Roman Catholics.[6] Lee S. McCollester, pastor of the church in Detroit, Michigan, had allowed representatives of the YMCA to speak in its behalf in his church even though he was himself prohibited from becoming a member.[7]

But this policy of the YMCA was the exception, Metcalf believed, rather than the rule. Universalism, whether acknowledged by others or not, had been a chief promoter of a theological and ecclesiastical revolution which was transforming Christianity at large into the humane and reform-minded religion visualized by its founders.

Yet Metcalf and many another committed Universalist were disappointed at the tangible results, if measured in columns of figures and other statistical data. But he took comfort in believing as did the founders of the denomination that the establishment of their truths was ultimately more important than any formal measurement in numbers or wealth. Within the confines of organized Universalism there was growing "strength, power, and progress." For example, in 1870 foreign missions were scarcely dreamed of; by 1895 more than $60,000 had been raised and expended for propagating the Universalist version of Christianity in Japan. All of this, and much more, had been attained in a quarter of a century.

However, Metcalf felt strongly that not all was well. At base was the unwillingness of the denomination to support its own activities once they were launched — a complaint repeated by every succeeding generation of Universalists. Above all was the failure to support the General Convention which, by the mandate of the denomination itself through its representatives, was given responsibilities which it was unable to carry out. Metcalf had harsh words for a denomination which permitted the creation of more or less autonomous organizations which headed off in their own directions, with little or no regard for existing machinery which overlapped, duplicated, or even competed. This too was a recurrent complaint. He singled out the women's groups and the various youth groups which, at least in the past, had, with the best of intentions, diluted and dispersed denominational strength and had seriously weakened the very body (the General Convention) which had been created to strengthen church polity.

The General Convention which met in Chicago in 1897 was a particularly significant occasion in several respects. The largest number of delegates (125) since the centennial assembly of 1870 attended.[8] At a ministers' meeting preceding the formal proceedings nearly everyone present rose and pledged loyalty and subordination to "the appointed authorities of the Church." Out of this came the "Ministers' Covenant" (also referred to as the "Chicago Covenant"), signed by some seventy clergy at the convention and subsequently circulated among all Universalist clergy and signed by about 500. It was strictly voluntary, and in effect meant a reaffirmation of the ordination vows that each had taken earlier. At the same time it signified more than this: It was a tangible way of demonstrating allegiance to a denomination which seemed to suffer chronically from an excess of centrifugal movement.

The fact that there was a general feeling of anxiety and uncertainty about the future of the denomination was pinned down by Anthony Bilkovsky (Beresford) in 1904.[9] An address by Samuel A. Eliot at the second International Council of the Unitarian and Liberal Religious Thinkers and Workers held in Amsterdam prompted Bilkovsky to warn Universalists against giving up their denominationalism in the belief that they no longer had a message or a mission, and could find satisfaction only in a larger and broader arena than their church provided, under such a vague designation as "liberalism."

Bilkowsky's reply left no room for doubt. Universalists should not only renew their faith in the value of organization but develop an "unfaltering loyalty" to their denomination. Apologizing for smallness, for their very existence, and talking of some mirage called "Christian unity" was quite the wrong strategy for Universalists to follow. Denominationalism was an indispensable organizational form by which moral conviction was united; it was the custodian of a given body of truths and ideals for which there was no substitute. Further, the time for protest, criticism, and reform had long since passed. The task was frankly to spread and expand Christian Universalism, a positive way of "entering upon our rightful possession."

The same determination to expand was expressed by the Committee on the State of the Church when it made its formal report and recommendations in 1871. "The chief business of the General Convention and of all its subordinate bodies, for the next quarter of a century, will be to create and foster the missionary spirit among our people."[10] Strengthened by its new constitution, the denomination could devote itself to "the propagation of the faith [and could] move as one grand and well-disciplined army."

And so the denomination committed itself to expansion. Did the statistics bear out this decision? They did not. Looking back in 1872, Abel C. Thomas of Philadelphia noted that, "after the endeavors of one hundred years, we are numerically, in the sense of organization, a small people."[11] And as such the Universalists remained.

Section II

The State of the Denomination After 1870

Chapter 3

"That Little Company Called Universalists": The Statistical Record

How large was the Universalist denomination when it celebrated in 1870 the centennial of John Murray's arrival in America? No one really knew. The last compendium published before the Civil War had listed 1,202 organizations (societies and churches) and 693 preachers. Not even an approximation of either actual membership or attendance had been attempted in 1860, and what figures were given were later considered "optimistic guesswork."[1] In 1865 a post-war inventory had been attempted, but with little success. Addresses for clergy listed in 1860 were available for only about 500, and after two years of effort, less than 350 had responded. It was obvious also that the number of organizations listed in 1860 had been grossly exaggerated. The figures had included places where Universalism was preached only occasionally and where it was impossible to verify church rolls.

Bowing to the actualities of the situation, the *Universalist Register* carried only estimates between 1861 and 1870, and not even these for the South. The editors of the *Register* for 1871, covering the previous year, warned readers that the returns were "imperfect, inconsistent, and meagre" and that the information as to the number and conditions of churches and societies was so "scanty and imperfect" that they would not even be published for that year.[2] The numerous gaps and discrepancies derived from at least three deficiencies: failure to distinguish between parishes and churches; the tendency to add to previous lists new parishes and/or churches without removing those which had become extinct, dormant, or provided only part-time services; and failure to make any report at all.

The compilers of the United States Census for 1870 reported that their own staff had found figures for Universalism actually "much below" those given in official denominational sources such as the *Register*. According to the government statistics, which were checked independently in the field by district marshals, there were 719 Universalist organizations in 1870, while the *Register* listed more than 900, including those in Canada. Part of the discrepancy was accounted for by the different base lines used. Government census takers counted only organizations with full-time, permanent pastors, while the Universalists counted all organized parishes, regardless of the presence or status of clergy. For the sixteen organizations reported for Missouri, the census officials indicated that there was only one person in the state in 1870 who devoted full time to the ministry. In fact, the census takers reported that the Universalists had a larger proportion of congregations without permanent pastors than any other denomination in the United States.[3] No membership, either by family or individuals, was listed in either governmental or denominational statistical sources.

In 1871 the number of clergy, after rigorous pruning of the list, was recorded in the *Register* as 633, and the number of members as less than 25,000, a total "doubtless below the fact." There were, said the *Register*, grounds even then for optimism if the approximations given for 1871 were compared with those of thirty-seven years earlier (1836), when the *Register* had first been published. Statistics available to the trustees of the General Convention in 1871 listed 22,929 families, with a total of 43,608 adult members. Even then, these figures were considered "conspicuous for their incompleteness."[4] The Committee on the State of the Church that year confirmed this by referring to "the comparative worthlessness of our statistics."

A decade later the situation gave little cause for optimism. The *Register* for 1881 listed 736 ministers serving an estimated 43,000 members; but the officers of the General Convention reported only 620 clergy for the same year.[5] The *Christian Leader* came up with even a third set of figures. It listed 42,500 families but only 37,965 communicants. The number of families, by that computation, included both those registered but having only "nominal membership" and those unregistered who lived in areas without parishes.[6] There were only two points on which all seemed to agree: About two-thirds of all Universalists in 1880 were residing in New England and New York State; and, compared to such grups as the Methodists and Baptists, Universalists were very much a minority denomination. By 1890 approximately 1 out of every 400 Protestants was a Universalist.[7]

As the nineteenth century drew to a close it brought a general stock-taking of church membership and resources, so far as they could be determined. Even allowing for imperfect records which made accurate comparison with 1870 well nigh impossible, the denomination in 1895 could point to 782 clergy in fellowship, 993 parishes of record, 44,351 families in fellowship, 47,800 church members, and 58,604 Sunday

John Coleman Adams (1849-1922), Universalist minister and prolific author

school pupils reported.[8] Parish property was estimated at $5,000,000 in 1870, and in actual returns, nearly $9,000,000 in 1895. Parish expenses and contributions had been $600,000 in 1870, and had exceeded $1,000,000 twenty-five years later. The value of property of Universalist schools and colleges had more than doubled, to nearly $4,000,000, in the same period. Convention funds, state and national, had grown from $100,000 to almost $700,000.

Comparative statistics published in the *Independent,* a religious weekly, for 1889-1890 and 1899-1900, brought forth much protest from Universalists. According to its figures, Universalists had declined to less than 47,000 within a decade, with a corresponding decline in number of clergy. There was no agreement within the denomination as to the accuracy of the statistics. According to the General Secretary's records, there were 52,177 members in 1899-1900, a total of 5,655 more than given for that year in the *Independent,* which did not indicate the source for its figures. On the other hand, Richard Eddy, then editor of the *Register,* reported 46,767, only slightly more than the *Independent*'s figures.[9] The *Leader* suggested rather pointedly that the various reporting agencies within the denomination should get together on their statistics in order to avoid both confusion and embarrassment.

In 1899 the *Independent* carried a special feature summarizing the state of churches in America in relation to total population, and included a statement from each denomination.[10] Of the more than 84 million Americans, almost 28 million were church members, a substantial increase over the previous decade. The editor concluded that it had been, overall, "a good year" for religious bodies. The Roman Catholic membership had skyrocketed to more than 8 million, followed by the Methodists, with almost 6 million; and the Baptists, with more than 4 million. The Unitarians, reporting 552 clergy and 460 churches, rounded out their membership in 1899 at 75,000.

Isaac M. Atwood, in his official capacity as General Superintendent, supplied the information for the Universalists. He reported the existence of organizations in thirty-four states, territories, and provinces, which included Canada; eleven state superintendents, 776 churches, 760 clergy; 1,003 parishes, 47,411 families, 52,177 church members, 59,179 Sunday school pupils, parish property (less debts) worth slightly below $10 million, and parish expenses and contributions at slightly more than $1,100,000. According to the report of the General Secretary, quoted by Atwood, it was not until 1884 that reasonably accurate statistics had become available. Comparing that year with 1899, the increases for each statistical category indicated above represented, in percentages, significant increases over the fifteen-year period. However, if comparisons were made on a broader base, namely with other religious groups, it was clear that the denomination was falling behind. According to the statistics compiled by the *Independent,* the Universalists were losing in an absolute as well as a relative sense, at least in the short run. They experienced a net loss of over 1,700 members between 1898 and 1899; this represented a decrease of 3.7 percent in a one-year period. The *Leader* attributed this to a more accurate tabulation rather than to an "actual reduction" in membership.[11]

Part of the discrepancy was finally explained by the fact that the *Independent* had compared the number of *parishes* in 1890 with the number of *churches* in 1899-1900, which of course skewed the statistics significantly. Universalists had traditionally measured their strength by the number of parishes (societies) — almost always a much larger figure than churches.[12] It was also discovered that the *Independent* had reported its statistics on the basis of the "constituency" — average church attendance rather than actual membership for some denominations. One such case was the Unitarians. By using this criterion the Universalist total for 1900 should have been 113,207 rather than less than 50,000.

Regardless of that inconsistency, it was realized that there was indeed lack of uniformity within the denomination in compiling statistics. The *Register* obtained its figures as of 1 October each year, based on whatever information was furnished by individual clergy. But the trustees depended, through the General Secretary, on figures furnished through state conventions. Further, the statistics used by the trustees were based in part on the calendar year previous to those appearing in the *Register;* i.e., nine months earlier.[13] The results were admittedly incomplete in both cases.

It was not until 1906, when the federal Department of Commerce and Labor inaugurated a ten-year (diennial) census of religious bodies in the United States, that the Universalists were prodded into making the state conventions responsible for gathering denominational statistics and reporting them to the General Secretary. The trustees came to the unhappy conclusion that "some mysterious incapacity appears to affect our officials in the matter of statistics."[14]

The difficulty in compiling completely reliable and accurate statistics was compounded because of the differing formulas used by the federal government in arriving at census totals. The person in charge of the Division of Churches for the Eleventh Census (1890) determined the "religious population" of the nation by using church attendance rather than membership for Protestant churches. The figures were arrived at by multiplying actual membership by 3½.[15] Universalist strength for 1890, by this computation, was 172,179. Bisbee, editor of the *Leader,* reckoned the constituency at 300,000 in 1910.[16]

For the special religious census of 1906 the federal government collected its own statistics independently of denominational sources. By using its enumeration formula adopted for other religious bodies, there were 64,158 Universalists, some 12,000 more than denominational records indicated.[17] It was finally determined in 1911 that a single set of figures was to be furnished for the denomination by the General Secretary and delivered to the Universalist Publishing House which was responsible for publishing the *Register.* This would presumably minimize if not eliminate the divergent statistics within the denomination.

Eddy, as did his successors, periodically pruned the parish statistics in the *Register* by dropping inactive organizations.[18] This brought the total into greater conformity with the records in the General Secretary's office, but discrepancies continued to appear. His reports almost invariably showed smaller figures than those appearing in the *Register.*

The trustees in 1909 recommended that statistics be gathered biennially rather than annually, thus coinciding with meetings of the General Convention.[19] As a consequence, no official statistics were reported for 1910. But there was so much objection to that policy that the General Convention refused to follow the trustees' recommendation and continued to require reports annually until 1936.

Gathering reasonably complete and accurate statistics continued to be a problem at both the federal and denominational levels. When the second of the biennial national censuses of religious bodies was being assembled for 1916 the Universalists were identified as among the least cooperative, and a reminder notice had to be sent by the Census Bureau listing the delinquent churches.[20] So many parishes failed to report to the General Secretary by way of their state conventions in 1917 that the trustees refused to release any statistics at all that year.[21] Ten years earlier, Q.H. Shinn had considered the lack of an accurate count of Universalists to be "our most serious problem."[22] He had, probably with some exaggeration, estimated a gain of about 3,000 a year, the bulk of whom had never been reflected in official figures.

Unitarians had about as much difficulty with statistics as did the Universalists, and complained about the alleged inaccuracy of federal census figures. The 1926 Census of Religious Bodies indicated a decrease of 27 percent in Unitarian membership during the previous decade. The

Christian Register called the figure "preposterous" and asserted that no systematic attempt had even been made prior to 1920 to compile accurate statistics.[23] The Unitarians claimed a membership in 1926 of 63,690, compared to 51,156 in 1920, and a constituency which had increased from 103,936 to 131,240 during the same period.

One Universalist clergyman, Frank L. Masseck, was very impatient with those who persisted in equating the statistics of Universalist church membership with Universalism. He felt strongly that the effort to count the number of members or determine in purely quantitative terms the size of the denomination was "one of the most unwise, foolish, and useless proceedings in which we may engage."[24] Despite all efforts, the statistics were incomplete as well as inaccurate; size, strength, and influence were not in any sense identical or even comparable. As he wrote after the 1926 Federal Census of Religious Bodies was made public, "if incorrect reports were fatal the Universalist church would have perished several decades ago."[25] It was much more rewarding to preach, teach, and practice Universalism than to wring one's hands over the statistics and apologize for the numerical shortcomings of the denomination.

However the statistics might vary in particular, no one could deny that the number of centers of Universalist preaching was steadily declining. The federal census had reported 956 churches in 1890; 811 in 1906; 643 in 1916; and 498 in 1926. The 1928 denominational yearbook, covering 1927, listed 600 in the continental United States (excluding seven in Canada and six in Japan). Roger Etz, the executive secretary of the General Convention, made an unrelievedly pessimistic report at the end of 1928.[26] Facts had to be faced, unpleasant as they might have been. His office had sent out letters to all clergy in fellowship earlier that year, with a follow-up in the fall, attempting to ascertain the general state of the denomination.

The prevailing tone was one of depression and discouragement. Many replies came from old and prominent churches as well as small and isolated ones. What were the explanations for the unrelieved gloom? Changed conditions in community life constituted one important factor; churches formerly located in strategic centers found members of their congregations moving elsewhere, and but few people replaced them. Universalists lacked "missionary foresight and zeal often displayed by other denominations."

Changed economic conditions comprised another factor. All too few local church budgets reflected changes for ten years or more; there was too much of a tendency to operate on a year-to-year basis, and not even then to take into account the fact that salaries were advancing and other expenses were increasing. Insufficient effort had been made to secure financial support commensurate with these changed conditions. Too little use had been made of such agencies as the national laymen's committee, one of whose functions was to assist churches in preparing workable financial plans. Or even if long-range plans were attempted, there was a tendency to carry them out for one or two years and then to abandon them.

Agitation for church unity was offered as another reason for the aggravation of local problems. The report of the Joint Commission in 1927 had been seized upon by some churches as an excuse for withdrawing support; local mergers were often effected precipitately; and the increasing popularity of dual fellowship seemed at least to some to be a weakening factor in promoting church solidarity. There was mounting feeling that the Universalist church was "going out of business."

Etz reported that there appeared to have been an almost deliberate attempt to avoid building up a spirit of denominational loyalty. Neither the General Convention nor the state conventions had much meaning to either clergy or laity. Both the caliber and the commitment of ministerial leadership were other questions that needed some sort of confrontation and resolution. The greater appeal of churches, both inside and outside the denomination, which offered far more in the way of equipment, religious education, and even social life, had to be taken into account.

What was to be done to bolster the lagging denomination? From Etz's vantage point, it was the responsibility of the General Convention to generate "a new sense of mission" comparable to what had accompanied the Million Dollar Drive, the Christ Crusade, and the Murray Anniversary Crusade. But another crusade was not the answer. Instead, Universalists had to be infused with a spirit that confronted living issues and required inspiration to "sacrificial service" which would simultaneously reward society and fulfill the individual.

Two statistical analyses covering approximately the same half-century (1900-1950) were made in the 1950s in an attempt both to document the changing organizational structure and status of the denomination at the state and local levels, and to account if possible for the steady decline in numbers and strength in two key states: Massachusetts and New York. The authors of the two studies, David MacPherson and Richard Woodman, respectively, also offered suggestions for reversing or at least slowing the process of decline.[27]

In the case of Massachusetts the primary purpose in reorganizing and incorporating the state convention in 1859 had been to promote missionary activity and church extension both inside and beyond the state. From 1859 to 1868 several clergymen were employed in different parts of the state as missionary agents. J.H. Chapin was elected as financial agent in 1868 and for nearly three years devoted his entire time to raising the state's quota of $50,000 for the Murray Fund. Thereafter, beginning in

1872, the energy and resources of the convention were focused on work within the state. Until 1877 there was someone in the field at all times, devoted to home missionary activity.

For eighteen years of the convention's existence (1859-1877) the office of secretary had been solely that of a recording officer. The executive committee then decided to request the secretary to take charge of missionary work as an additional duty. For over fifteen years W.A. Start served in that capacity, and in 1891 made a retrospective report of his work.[28] The tangible results were most promising. When he undertook his work in 1877 there were ninety-five active parishes on the roll, and nearly the same number of Sunday schools, with sixty-nine settled pastors. The parishes were contributing about $3,000 a year for outside purposes, and the mission fund was only $19,000. By contrast, in 1891 there were 121 parishes with 90 settled pastors, 110 Sunday schools, and parish contributions of more than $5,000 a year for mission work. The permanent funds by then amounted to more than $56,000 and the ministerial relief fund, which had totalled less than $4,900, had nearly doubled fifteen years later. Statistics were not only complete but more accurate than ever before, despite the fact that changes in pastors and pastorates had been both frequent and widespread. Only four ministers in 1891 served the same churches as they had in 1877; only twelve, including these four, were pastors in the state fifteen years later.

During the same fifteen-year period, twenty-six new parishes had been created, representing either new organizations or revivals of old ones. During the same time, twenty-five new churches had been built and six remodelled. Sixty-two parishes had received aid from the state convention, totalling over $40,000. Almost half (thirty) had become self-sustaining. In 1876 the state convention adopted the policy of having church property deeded to it and then redeeded to the parish in order to save the property and bind the parishes more closely to the convention. By 1891 this arrangement had been made with forty-one parishes, and the General Convention as well as other state conventions followed the example of Massachusetts.

Beginning in 1902 the secretary of the state convention, whose responsibilities had already been enlarged, served also as state superintendent. One of the most visible was Charles Conklin who served from 1903 until 1914, and among his other activities was responsibility for establishing the Doolittle Home for Aged Persons. A system of district superintendents existed at the turn of the century, with twelve in operation. They conferred with the state superintendent and made periodic reports which comprised much of the statistical information available. They received no financial compensation for their work.

In Massachusetts the number of parish organizations (churches and societies) dropped from 128 in 1900 to 78 in 1950; the number of churches having full-time pastoral services declined from 95 to 49 in the same period; and the number of clergy shrank from slightly over 100 to little more than half that number. The two new churches organized in the 1940s scarcely made up for the fifty-two that had legally ceased to exist during the half-century or had become dormant and had closed their doors.

Much the same story of decline had to be told for New York State, which entered the twentieth century with more than 125 parish organizations, of which 89 were active, and little more than fifty years later had less than 50, of which only 32 maintained regular full-time services. During the same period the number of clergy dropped from more than seventy to less than thirty.[29] Fifteen new churches or societies had been organized in New York since 1900 but only five of these still existed by the mid-1920s. Only two new churches were organized between 1925 and 1954, and one of those was a community church with summer services only.

More important than statistical evidence for decline were the reasons given, where known, or assumed, in the absence of any record.[30] The authors came to substantially the same conclusions, and also ran into the common problem of missing, incomplete, and sometimes inaccurate records.

Among the recurrent general reasons given by MacPherson (some actually symptoms rather than causes) were changes in population make-up, numbers, and distribution which made conditions unfavorable; internal conflicts; mergers; financial difficulties; and failure of the state convention to serve local constituencies adequately and effectively. In the case of New York, for which the causes were analyzed in considerably more detail and depth than for Massachusetts, the following factors accounting for decline were offered: failure to enlarge functions and to expand into areas of growth; shortage of clergy, especially in rural parishes (in which the greatest number of churches in the state had historically been located); inconsistent as well as inadequate aid to churches unable to be self-supporting (although money alone did not necessarily solve the problem); and the general failure of the church circuit system.

The problems of urban churches in New York received even greater emphasis after World War II than those of rural churches, including greater financial aid. Changing neighborhoods was the factor most often stressed — a problem shared with rural areas but aggravated by the problem of shrinking congregations in parishes with church buildings too large and too expensive to maintain, or inadequately structured for such activities as religious education and community service.

In his analysis Woodman also found defects in the organizational structure at the state level, such as the overburdening of the superintendents; and in those weaknesses deriving from the very nature of Universalism, stressing as it did an attitude of independence. This resulted in particularism, jealously guarded local autonomy, and misplaced priorities. The failure at both the state and local level to do long-range planning and to follow consistent policies were also contributing factors, seen in aid to local churches both rural and urban.

Another important factor was what the author called "ideational changes." He cited the fear of George D. Walker, the state superintendent in 1927, that old-line Universalists, both clerical and lay, were out of step with changing times and were still too much prone to think in terms of theological battles long since won or settled, and not enough in terms of social awareness and community welfare. Many churches had lost their "unique or distinctive message" and had not found another to replace it.

The dreary list of deficiencies and shortcomings, based on statistical evidence presented in the two studies, somehow had to be confronted at the national level as well. The fact that some other denominations had experienced the same sort of decline in the same period, and for much the same reasons, was not a source of much comfort. The depressing actuality of steady decline, in spite of brief spurts of growth, continued to prevail up to consolidation with the Unitarians in 1961.

Inventories made in 1946 and 1947 continued to give the lie to the optimistic hopes of General Superintendent Robert Cummins who, after three years of aggressive leadership and devotion to the cause, had pointed in 1941 to a dramatic increase to 82,000 Universalists by the end of that year.[31] In longer perspective, the denomination was still losing out, both absolutely and relatively, both in terms of clergy and number of active churches. Between 1936 and 1946 there had been only 61 ordinations, and a minimum of 100 were needed within the next ten years merely to hold the line.[32] Over 30 percent of the clergy were in their fifties and sixties, with an average age of fifty-two instead of the generally accepted average of forty-three. The denomination was experiencing a steady net loss of almost twenty clergy a year, and those that remained shifted pastorates at an alarming rate, making for instability and lack of continuity. Of the 448 churches listed in 1947, only 258 were active. The membership was officially 46,443; it was estimated by the General Superintendent that four out of every ten who were counted in the total Universalist constituency were not even members of the church.[33]

In 1941 R. S. Kellerman, Universalist pastor in Blanchester, Ohio, had offered a whole series of reasons for the decline of the church, some shared by other denominations but some either unique to or most evident in Universalism.[34] It had started out as a denomination with only one basic aim in mind—to refute or deny endless punishment and to preach the world-wide salvation of all, broadened to include the fatherhood of God and the brotherhood of man. The denomination seemed to thrive on opposition, and great numbers were at first attracted. But insufficient advantage was taken of the opportunities, and the potential membership was not organized into churches, remaining too loosely knit, often with little more in common than the denial of endless punishment.

The church lacked authority to enforce the laws and decisions of its various units, and was too democratic, lacking both efficient government and discipline. There was chronic doubt in some quarters about its truly Christian character, and it thus failed to secure the sympathy and cooperation of other denominations. Its strength in rural areas was being steadily eroded, not only because of population shifts beyond its control, but because it consistently failed to attract clergy both able and willing to live on miniscule salaries. The church had come to rely too much on the intellectual side of religion and consequently lacked "color, action, pageantry, incense, vestments, incidents and attributes that appeal to the senses. The services have been too staid, sober, dignified and dull to hold the mass of people that once attended." The findings of the natural sciences had created doubt and confusion, had seemed in some instances to contradict parts of the Bible, and appeared "to cast a shadow on the very existence of an eternal and creative God." Religious faith had been seriously weakened, and Universalists had done all too little to rebuild it.

Finally — and this was paramount in Kellerman's estimation — twentieth-century developments had created a new and changed world in which the need for religion itself had seemingly diminished; religion in the traditional sense was being crowded out. "What is the remedy? How can we arrest the decline in Universalist churches, and turn the tide toward greater success both of numbers and of churches and greater influences?" Neither Kellerman nor his contemporaries seemed to have a ready answer, and the tide never turned. As the denomination concluded its final negotiations in 1960 to consolidate with the Unitarians, there were only 36,864 members in 244 active Universalist churches.[35] It was but the pitiful remnant of a church with such great promise.

Chapter 4

Administering and Financing the Denomination

As the responsibilities of the General Convention grew after 1870, so did the variety and complexity of the business it transacted. The details of administration and the oversight of activities between convention meetings were placed in the hands of an executive committee which served as a board of trustees. The secretary of the convention, who was made a member of the board, was the only officer employed to devote his full time to the work, and by the nature of the situation carried on the day-to-day administrative functions of the convention.

The office of secretary, which had been created in 1867 and was first occupied a year later, suffered at first from rapid turnover of personnel. E. G. Brooks (1816–1878) served in 1868 for less than a year, resigning for reasons of health, as did his successor, Asa Saxe (1827–1908), who resigned in 1871. William H. Ryder had been selected to take his place but he declined because of the complications resulting from the destruction of his church in the great Chicago fire; he declined a second time in 1877.[1] So in 1872 the trustees themselves served for the remainder of the year. Royal H. Pullman (1826–1900) held the office until 1876, when he too resigned. One of his complaints was that he was expected to attend all state conventions — an absolute impossibility in view of the fact that in 1873, to cite one instance, five were convened during the same week.[2] At last some measure of continuity and stability was provided in the person of G. L. Demarest (1816–1909) who served for nearly thirty years in this capacity.

Even with the invaluable work done by the convention secretary, there was much that needed to be undertaken beyond absorption in administrative and clerical detail. A separate officer was required to devise and execute plans for fostering the growth of the denomination, encouraging spiritual development, and increasing the vitality and efficiency of the work being done. In response to these needs the office of General Superintendent was created in 1898, followed by the establishment of state superintendencies and then regional or district offices embracing more than one state. The latter two positions were the ones actually authorized to perform administrative functions; it was the province of the General Superintendent only to advise and not actually to create or carry out programs at the state or regional level. The fact that he had no real power was to be a long-standing source of difficulty. The effectiveness of the office came to depend more on the personality of the occupant and denominational circumstances at any one time than on any grant of authority inherent in the office.

The policy of encouraging state conventions to provide missionaries, agents, or superintendents had been enunciated several times in the 1870s, but the idea of creating a general superintendent for the entire denomination was at first ruled out on the ground that the office would compete with other jurisdictions.[3] However, the idea would not die. In 1893 the Massachusetts Convention recommended the creation of such an office, the holder to serve as a "spiritual counselor" for the whole church.[4] In 1897 seventy clergy recommended the creation of the post of General Field Secretary to oversee the work of state officers who together would comprise a Council of Administration. The proposal was favorably received.[5]

The immediate impetus for creating the office of General Superintendent came from Willard C. Selleck, who presented the idea in an address to the New England Conference in the Congress Square Universalist Church, Portland, Maine, in the fall of 1896.[6] It attracted considerable favorable attention, notably from Isaac M. Atwood in the *Leader*. A statistical analysis based on information derived from the *Universalist Register* convinced Selleck that a pressing need of the denomination was an individual who could provide "a fostering oversight" and spiritual sustenance and encouragement on a national scale to the smaller, isolated churches of thirty members or less which made up more than 40 percent of the Universalist constituency, scattered as it was over a vast territory. Such churches were especially vulnerable "to stress and strain, weakness and failure, through losses, discouragement, or dissension," and needed "every possible help toward coherence and perseverance." To Selleck the position would emphasize in particular inspirational and basically religious functions rather than such mundane but necessary responsibilities as money-raising.

Even greater centralization had been recommended in 1897 by Edgar Leavitt, missionary in Japan, after his review of the proceedings of the General Convention that year.[7] Memorials had been presented from both the Vermont and Quebec, and the Connecticut Conventions recommending the appointment of bishops who would have served as overseers in districts into which the country would have been divided. The term "superintendent" might have been preferred by some, but the term "bishop" was a proper word comparable to "parish" instead of "society," or "church" in preference to "meeting house."

The plan to create "a Bishopric of the Universalist Church," as the Vermont and Quebec Convention recommended, would clearly have been revolutionary if carried out, for Universalists, as Leavitt pointed out, were historically "the most independent and individualistic of Congregationalists." The very word "bishop" conjured up all kinds of images of hateful and tyrannical ecclesiasticism. Nonetheless, he detected a growing sentiment in the direction of episcopacy among those Universalists who were convinced that the conditions of the time required a tighter organization than had existed earlier. Leavitt was among the first to admit that even if Universalists ever seriously considered such a step, it would never have unanimous support. Of course if the word "superintendent" were substituted for "bishop" much of the opposition would dissolve, even though operationally there might be little or no distinction. Certainly leaders like James H. Tuttle in Minneapolis, Alonzo A. Miner in Boston, and other individuals might have been even more effective if they had presided over a state or a region rather than over a single church.

If an episcopal organization were actually adopted, Leavitt saw no need for a radical reorganization of the church. The bishops could preside over conventions which might (and should) be organized flexibly to include any area, from part of one state to a region embracing one or more states. There was no need to be circumscribed, as was then the case, by political and/or geographical lines. Bishops could be elected by conventions, and their powers and responsibilities delimited and delegated by constitutions and by the conventions themselves.

There would need be no basic change in the customary means of raising funds for denominational purposes, and such funds could be allotted as appropriate for the support of the bishop and his activities. Among his functions would be oversight of pastors in his jurisdiction, including selection, removal, and supervision, all with the concurrence of the parishes involved. The South and West could be made into missionary jurisdictions, with individuals like Q. H. Shinn in charge. Leavitt made it quite clear that his experiences in Japan, as well as those of other denominations engaged in foreign missionary work, had led him to advocate greater centralization of authority. What he advocated was admittedly far from pure democracy, but that did not exist anywhere, even in the United States. But it did represent "democratic republicanism" of a representative character which provided both leadership and responsibility.

Almon Gunnison agreed with Leavitt. Universalism's heterodoxy was becoming the nation's orthodoxy by the late 1890s. The challenge was no longer theology but creating effective administration of what Universalists already possessed.[8]

The arguments in favor of creating the position of General Superintendent were sufficiently persuasive to result in the selection by the trustees of Isaac M. Atwood (1838–1917) to fill the new position which they had created. The title of "bishop" was summarily rejected even though the New Jersey Convention considered it "more dignified" than "General Superintendent."[9] Some individuals such as Henry I. Cushman, who thoroughly approved the creation of enlarged central authority, insisted on referring to the new General Superintendent as "Bishop Atwood."[10]

The duties of the new superintendent were

> to supervise the spiritual interests of our Church, and to promote its prosperity, by using his influence to stimulate the zeal and activity of our people; to secure unity and continuity of action on the part of our parishes; to encourage weak parishes; to revive dormant parishes; to remove causes of disaffection between pastors and parishes; to foster the apointment of State Superintendents and District Superintendents; to help pastors in their difficulties; and, so far as possible, to utilize all of our ministerial forces, that our Church may do its share of Christ's work in the world.[11]

It was a large and rather ambiguous order, and Atwood set out to fill it, but with some private trepidation.

Atwood had been selected for the new position because he was one of the best known and most widely respected leaders in the denomination, and seemed to be a natural choice. He had been born on 24 March 1838 in Pembroke, New York, the product of an impoverished farm family.[12] After his family moved to Lockport he was bound out to another farmer, served as a driver on the Erie Canal, and attended Lockport Academy. His plans to attend Yale University were frustrated by poverty, so he taught in a rural private school where he boarded with a Universalist family.

He had been reared as a Baptist but decided at the age of nineteen to enter the Universalist ministry and was ordained at Clifton Springs, New York, in 1861. That same year he was married. Five children were born to the Atwoods. One was John Murray Atwood, who in his later years followed very much in his father's footsteps. After serving two full-time pastorates between 1867 and 1872, the senior Atwood shared his time between a part-time pastorate and as editor of the *Universalist* in Boston. For two years he edited the *Christian Leader* (New York), and returned to the Greater Boston area as pastor of the church in North Cambridge.

Atwood accepted the presidency of the Canton Theological School at St. Lawrence University in 1879, where he served for some twenty years, until called to the new office, a position he held until 1907. After serving seven years as General Secretary, he returned in 1912 to the theological school as Professor of Theology and Philosophy and pastor of the local church. After his retirement in 1915 he lived with his daughter Alice in Washington, D.C., where he died on 26 October 1917 at the age of seventy-nine.

The new General Superintendent was quite aware of what was happening to his denomination at the end of the nineteenth century. He believed that clergy and laity alike were beginning to realize that "they must be up and doing if they are not to witness the rebuking phenomenon of more Universalism preached and more Universalists made in other churches than their own. For it is precisely at this point that the denomination has encountered in recent years its most insidious and availing competition."

Atwood left the presidency of the Canton Theological School with the understanding that he would retain a nominal connection with the school for one year, but that his time and energies would be devoted primarily to his new work.[13] His assignments as a denominational officer actually lasted until he finally relinquished them in 1912.

The new General Superintendent found the task neither easy nor "altogether agreeable." His strength lay in preaching and teaching rather than in administration.[14] He travelled a phenomenal 32,000 miles during his first year, visiting Universalists in thirty-one of the thirty-four states in which the deonomination was organized.[15] The most discouraging phenomenon encountered in his travels about the nation was the disposition of churches to operate on niggardly contributions and to settle for the "cheapest" preacher, regardless of merit. This represented to the General Superintendent an unwarranted policy of negativism and retreat at the very time the decision had been made to expand.[16]

Atwood carefully avoided much of the South in his travels so as not to conflict with the work of Shinn, who was officially appointed as Southern Missionary in 1900. There was much territory still to be covered, and Atwood looked after (and into) churches and preaching stations from Canada to California. He regretted that he "could not multiply himself by two or three, and sometimes by ten."[17]

Among other accomplishments during his term was the growth of a system of state superintendents, of which Illinois had created the first, in 1880. There were fourteen such offices by 1900.[18] A National Council of Superintendents was also authorized in 1899 and held its first informal meeting in Chicago a year later in order to improve communication and exchange experiences.[19] It was formally organized at Philadelphia in 1907.[20]

Regional or district superintendents had also begun to appear, such as those of the tri-state district authorized for Wisconsin, Iowa, and Minnesota in 1903, but not fully operational until 1907 because of lack of funds.[21] The idea of dividing the United States into districts cutting across state lines can be traced as far back as 1868 (recommended by the Iowa Convention), but nobody heeded it at the time, and had long since forgotten such arrangements which had existed before the Civil War, in practice if not in name.

After two years of experimentation with the office of General Superintendent it was pronounced a success, and Atwood recommended its continuation.[22] He received much support from Marion Crosley, who considered it a worthy step in creating "a denomination in the true sense of the word, — something more than a rope of sand."[23]

But the denomination was by no means united on this. Frederick W. Hamilton, later to become president of Tufts College, was absolutely opposed both to the creation of the office and to its continuation.[24] He claimed that it violated historic congregational church polity; had too much of a centralizing tendency; involved interference in local affairs; was too costly for the denomination to afford; and was "utterly repugnant to the genius of our people, and would not be tolerated by them if voted by twenty Conventions. Universalists are individualists of a very pronounced type and in the last resort always do as they please with but little regard for advice and none at all for authority." The editor of the *Leader* countered by telling Hamilton and those who thought as he did that they were twenty years behind the times.[25] Organization and growth were synonymous. It was lack of cooperation with the General Superintendent, not the office itself, that was to blame if there were any shortcomings.

Atwood added a postscript to his earlier report urging that the position be given "legislative sanction" and be made independent of trustee control.[26] An attempt in 1903 to have the General Superintendent elected by the General Convention was defeated, as was an attempt two years later to make the superintendent not only a member of the trustees but their chairman.[27] There was also prolonged but indecisive debate for many years over whether the functions of the office could be assumed by the General Secretary.

To compound the situation, the trustees had created the position of Field Secretary in 1903 with ill-defined functions, many of which overlapped those of the General Superintendent. At the very same meeting the trustees had been instructed to undertake no new projects until existing obligations had been met.[28] The idea had ostensibly been to have the Field Secretary supervise and encourage church expansion, especially in the Mississippi Valley, and to raise funds.

C. Ellwood Nash (1855–1932) resigned from the presidency of Lombard College to accept the position. He had become well known in the denomination and had a reputation as "a perpetual fountain of enthusiasm" as a fund raiser, and that seemed to make him an admirable choice for the position.[29] But he soon regretted his decision. His presence was often resented because he personified "dictation" from above; his duties and responsibilities were never adequately defined; and within a year after his appointment he was in the unhappy position of listening to a debate on the floor of the General Convention over whether to continue his office.[30] According to the treasurer's reckoning, expenses still exceeded the income collected by the Field Secretary, plunging the denomination even more deeply into debt.[31]

The post of Field Secretary was abolished in 1906, much to Nash's disappointment and chagrin. He felt that he had received too little credit for his efforts, and that the position had not been given a fair trial. The denomination was making a basic mistake in eliminating a "missionary secretary" indispensable to extending Universalism.

The administrative confusion and uncertainty were worse confounded by debate over whether even to continue the General Superintendency. A majority of the trustees recommended in 1905 that after Atwood's term was over the office should be eliminated and its functions absorbed by the General Secretary. But the General Convention agreed with the minority instead, and after much discussion voted by a narrow margin to continue it.[32] Such division of opinion was certainly not conducive to building or maintaining Atwood's morale, but he resolutely defended the office because it performed a useful function, even though it carried no authority with it, and it met with widespread resentment as well as indifference.[33]

Atwood intended to relinquish his labors in 1905 but was persuaded to continue until 1907. Meanwhile, Demarest had decided to retire (at the age of eighty-eight) as General Secretary, after more than a quarter of a century of service. Atwood took over the position while continuing temporarily as General Superintendent. The decision to retain the office resulted in the appointment of William H. McGlauflin (1856–1927), and Atwood continued to serve as General Secretary until 1912.

McGlauflin was preeminently a missionary, with an impressive record as a recruiter for the denomination and as a money-raiser, having been instrumental in organizing Universalism in Harriman, Tennessee, and Atlanta, Georgia. At the time of his appointment as General Superintendent he had been busy since 1904 bringing into full operation the tri-state superintendency in the Midwest, with headquarters in the Church of the Redeemer in Minneapolis. In effect he was attempting simultaneously to fill the shoes of the ill-fated Field Secretary, the Southern Missionary (Shinn having died in 1907), and the General Superintendency. McGlauflin led a hectic life in that position for an entire decade (1907–1916) until he resigned to take a less demanding position as pastor of the church in Scranton, Pennsylvania, until his death only a year later.[34]

McGlauflin was able, despite a demanding schedule as General Superintendent, to produce a considerable denominational literature, all with a distinct missionary flavor. Aside from numerous pamphlets, he wrote two books: *What the Universalist Church is Doing* (1909), and a biography of Shinn (1912). He intended to publish a monthly missionary journal but the expense was prohibitive and he had to settle for a page each week in the *Leader*.[35]

There continued to be so much opposition to the very idea of a General Superintendent that supporters of McGlauflin found it advisable to extract votes of confidence at General Convention meetings from time to time. They were able even to have the position of Assistant General Superintendent authorized in 1915, but no one was ever appointed because there was no money provided to finance the position.[36]

In the midst of McGlauflin's tenure as General Superintendent the editor of the *Leader* warned Universalists that, even though the national missionary was doing his utmost, the church would never be a growing or influential institution until it had "a real, executive head."[37] The General Superintendent was in reality only a "field officer," with no official connection with the trustees beyond his appointment, and had no direct responsibility to the General Convention. It was unfortunate that "the idea of any one directing any one else in this independent Church of ours is the rankest heresy!"[38] Perhaps, according to the editor, the General Secretary or the president of the General Convention might be the chief executive officer instead of a General Superintendent.

In 1908 the position of the president of the General Convention had undergone a review and transformation. An amendment to the constitution was proposed by which the presiding officer was made *ex officio* not only a member of the board of trustees but its chairman. This represented a significant departure from past practice and signified a basic change in the philosophy which had hitherto prevailed. When the organic law of the convention had been originally formulated its presidency had been deliberately designed as a largely ceremonial and honorary office, shared by both clergy and laity. Its basic function had been to provide parliamentary guidance and a moderator for business sessions. Presidents had been chosen on account of their prominence in the denomination, with rotation to provide recognition of various geographic sections and individuals as the convention assembled in different locations within the nation.

The policy of separating the presiding officer from the trustees had been intended to guard against the suspicion or temptation of making the convention subservient to either his interests or those of the trustees. There was also a practical consideration. A person active in business or some other secular profession could not be expected to devote the time and effort donated by individuals serving as trustees. The convention could not command the services of such a person as a salaried officer because there was no money to pay such an individual. On the other hand, there was much merit in having a person thoroughly conversant with the work of the trustees and the affairs of the denomination who could represent it at public events, serve as an executive officer, and exercise general administrative leadership.

Marion D. Shutter, pastor in Minneapolis of one of the most flourishing churches in the denomination, was the first to be elected to the enlarged office, in 1911. He served for two years, followed by Lee S. McCollester, pastor of an equally large and influential church in Detroit. They served as advisers to the various committees and commissions of the General Convention and otherwise provided visibility for Universalists. It also became the responsibility of the president to provide periodic reports on the state of the denomination.

The resignation of McGlauflin as General Superintendent in 1916 was made the occasion for a general review of the entire administration of the denomination, urged by McCollester. He noted that, using a biological analogy, the church had evolved from a single- to a multi-celled organism that needed a coordinating officer or executive committee both to hold the organization together and to prevent needless competition and duplication among its components.[39] A special trustee committee was appointed to look into the matter, but its work was interrupted by the intrusion of World War I and very little was actually accomplished beyond confirming the idea that the convention president was to be considered the chief executive and administrative officer, on a part-time basis and without pay, even though "titular head of the denomination"; the General Superintendent was to be the officer in the field.

But their respective lines of responsibility were still blurred, and the situation was further complicated by a suggestion that the offices of president and General Superintendent be combined. McCollester even offered to resign as president to make this possible.[40] This the editor of the *Leader* opposed, arguing that both offices be continued, and made coequal. Together with the General Superintendent, the president would constitute the executive arm of the trustees.[41] There was no consensus on this, just as there was no actual acknowledged "head" of the denomination throughout its history although many sought to be the official spokesman. This ambiguity was quite consistent with Thomas Whittemore's assertion made in 1833 that "no individual, however eminent, could speak for the denomination.... It is not to be expected that Universalists will consent to accept the opinions of any one as the standard of the whole."[42]

The General Superintendent's powers were enlarged in 1917 when he was given membership on the trustees, but many more steps had yet to be taken before his authority was actually strengthened.

Financing the Denomination

The year 1870 marked a significant turning point in the history of the Universalist Church, a transition from a scattered theological movement interested chiefly in spreading the optimistic doctrine of a world's salvation to a better organized and "a more inclusive Christianity."[43] It represented "a new departure," a church "with a capital 'C' " which required a more businesslike approach than had existed earlier. New and extended commitments were made in such fields as financing theological education, church extension, and conducting denominational affairs. How were all of these, and many other activities befitting a full-fledged church, to be financed?

Down to 1870 very little had been accomplished in establishing funds or making contributions for the general business of the denomination. What had been done was centered in local churches, schools operated by Universalists, and meager domestic missionary activity by a few state conventions. The principal contributions to denominational expansion had been made by individuals operating very much on their own. But with the celebration of their centennial Universalists seemed to sense the opening of a new era, with new and greatly increased financial responsibilities. Could they meet the challenge?

There were basically three potential sources of income: Capital fund drives, parish contributions, and special gifts and bequests. The overall goal in 1870 had been the raising of the then unprecedented sum of one million dollars from all sources. The first and largest single commitment had been undertaken by way of the Murray Centenary Fund of $200,000, created in 1869. The campaign to raise this amount represented more than ten times the total raised by or on behalf of the General Convention from 1801 to 1870.[44]

In 1863, several years before the centennial, a "General Aid Association" had been proposed and incorporated in 1870 into the general plan of organization. For the first time in denominational history it was mandated that every parish in the fellowship of the General Convention was to make an annual contribution to the general fund. This was written into the constitution and by-laws of the General Convention in 1870, and called for contributions amounting to 2 percent of the operating expenses of each parish. The third major source of income, most of it earmarked for special projects, was uncertain from year to year and could not be counted on to provide a steady flow of funds but was continuously solicited.

The record of giving to support the General Convention and its activities had never been satisfactory. In fact, "all attempts to raise money . . . had simply humiliated us by their results."[45] The failure to support adequately the work of the denomination beyond the locality was a long and painful story. The first solicitation for funds had been made at the meeting of the New England Convention in Swanzey, New Hampshire, in 1801. There had been no response whatever to the call for aid. Two years later, only fourteen of the forty societies then in fellowship had contributed a grand total of less than $33. As recently as 1865, when the General Convention had met in Middletown, Connecticut, receipts for the year had totalled $161.20, with a balance remaining of $4.51.[46] What little revenue had been received otherwise had been expended from special funds. In the years intervening up to 1870, while the number of societies had increased to some 1,000, the General Convention had not raised "one tenth of the sum now proposed [in 1870] as the work of a single year."

With this unenviable record confronting him, the General Secretary visited Universalists in eight states, canvassing through the state conventions and financial agents appointed for each. By 1870 there had been $129,000 pledged to the Murray Fund, and the Woman's Centenary Aid Association had raised more than $21,000, with additional contributions yet to come. The largest individual contribution had been $31,000 to establish Buchtel College in Ohio. When solicited by the General Convention the Ohio Convention had asked to be excused from making further contributions on the ground that the college project was to stand as its main effort.

Almost $950,000 of the total goal had been pledged by the time the great centennial convocation had been held. Perhaps the denomination had turned the corner and reversed its earlier record. But this was not to be the case. After the euphoria of the events of 1870 had begun to wear off, the denomination was again confronted with an unhappy financial prospect. Pledges and actual payments were not the same thing. Only $116,000 of the Murray Fund had actually been paid in by 1871, and for many years subsequently, few if any contributions at all were made to it in spite of the fact that the deadline was repeatedly extended. By 1873 only five states had paid their quota in full.[47]

An indebtedness of $31,000 hung over the General Convention by 1871, and money had to be borrowed to carry on its work. A total of $17,500 had been tied up in the combined gift and loan program for promoting theological education by then. There were, in addition, other commitments to carry out plans to assist struggling parishes in the church extension program.

The editors of the *New Covenant* (Chicago) accused the trustees of gross mismanagement for such a state of affairs. "It should never have been permitted. Under a judicious management it would never have been allowed."[48] An indignant reply was immediately forthcoming from Asa Saxe, the General Secretary. In the first place, the centenary year had opened with a commitment made by a former board of $4,000 to assist the church in Clinton, New York. Second, a canvass for the Murray Fund had been made with no provision whatever for paying the expenses involved, which amounted to approximately $15,000.[49] In addition, all the resources of the General Convention were siphoned off into the Murray Fund, and not one cent was provided for the general treasury. There was only one alternative to abandoning the whole fund-raising machinery, and that was to incur an indebtedness. Loans from three individuals and one from the New York Convention had to be negotiated. Otherwise, aid to theological students would have had to be cut off; assistance to the church in Des Moines, Iowa, would have been cancelled after a firm commitment had been made, and the church would in all probability have had to be closed.

Despite the policy of retrenchment announced in 1871, annual operating expenses of the General Convention could not possibly have been reduced below $15,000. In 1870 and 1871 the work of the General Convention was actually carried out with less than $5,000 annual income. The treasury was in such a sad state in 1871 that the convention had to default on its pledge to assist the Clinton church. The trustees were obliged to mortgage the church to the amount of the appropriation in order to meet their liabilities.[50]

A special fund of $40,000, one quarter of it to reduce the indebtedness, was authorized in 1871, apportioned among the states, with one-half to be retained by them for local work. The assessments for Massachusetts and New York State were the largest, totalling $10,000 each; that for Kansas was $50.[51] Less than half the goal had been reached by 1875.[52] Convention expenditures of almost $23,000 were called for in 1872, less than half of which was to be devoted to theological scholarships and missions combined. Appropriations totalling in excess of $20,000 were also made for 1873, all in blithe disregard of where the revenue might come from to cover such expenditures. Deficit financing became the order of the day, the General Convention being frequently dredged out by temporary loans endorsed by individual trustees.

Annual collections from parishes were a source of continuing disappointment. Contributions from that source came almost to a halt in 1873, and the collections from missionary boxes, first provided in 1870, were less than $3,000 in 1876. Annual contributions had fallen from more than $5,000 in 1876 to less than $4,000 four years later, with a corresponding decline in receipts from missionary boxes. How could a denomination survive financially with such a record?

It was not only "indolence and indifference" but the annoying burden of constant appeals, both national and local, and the ever-present question of establishing priorities that prevented larger contributions.[53] Until 1871 there was no penalty at all for non-payment of parish quotas; in that year the returns had been so small that the trustees threatened to cut off all disbursements if payments were not made.[54] Even that seemed to have had but minimal effect, for in 1889, when the total was set at $15,000, only Rhode Island and Ontario Universalists contributed 100 percent of their allocated pledges; only 138 out of more than 700 parishes made any contribution at all that year.[55]

Because so many parishes were failing to support the General Convention, ministers at a retreat in Galesburg, Illinois, recommended in 1899 a rather drastic step. If a parish were delinquent for as many as three years it (or its minister) should be suspended from fellowship.[56] Another penalty, seldom invoked, was to refuse to seat delegates at convention meetings if their parishes had not made "some" contribution. In practice, however, appeals from the floor almost always brought seating for the delegates in question.

In the competition for funds as among the parishes, the state conventions, and the General Convention, it was invariably the latter that lost out. Time after time Universalist officials criticized the lack of liberality in financial support, particularly for the denominational propensity for embarking on projects for which there were few or no dollars. Isaac M. Atwood observed that there was "too much steeple for our meeting house."[57] He also believed that, with few exceptions, Universalists in the West had never really supported the General Convention, and offered as proof the fact that of 340 parishes in 6 Midwestern states, only 48 had made contributions in 1875.[58] The total received from them was not sufficient to cover even stationery and postage.

There was also the problem of which General Convention officer (if any one) was responsible for fund raising. The trustees decided that the office of General Secretary should be "financially productive."[59] R. H. Pullman, the incumbent in 1876, was "unwilling to make money-raising the main business of his office," and resigned. In order to economize, the services of the General Secretary were temporarily dispensed with, and expenditures for missions were reduced to $2,000 by 1880.

Eliminating the General Convention debt became an overriding consideration for many years, for progress in that direction was markedly slow. It remained in excess of $25,000 until after the economic recovery of the nation had been achieved following the panic and depression of 1873. A five-person committee was appointed at the 1877 convention to launch a drive to extinguish the debt, but had raised only $1,200 by the following year. The members of the committee were so completely discouraged that they asked to be discharged.[60] The General Convention refused to comply. The trustees even considered borrowing $26,000 from the Murray Fund, which amounted by 1877 to slightly more than $120,000, but that would have so reduced the principal that support of theological education would have had to be abandoned. It was not until 1880 that the indebtedness was reduced to less than $12,000.[61]

Prospects looked much brighter in the 1880s than during the "hard times" of the 1870s. Receipts went up, the Murray Fund reached more than $123,000 by 1883, and the indebtedness shrank below $3,000, and by 1887 had been "swept away."[62] But the $200,000 goal of the Murray Fund was never attained; at its maximum if fell some $60,000 short. Many Universalists by the turn of the twentieth century had forgotten or did not even realize that the fund existed unless they scrutinized with care the intricacies of the treasurer's report, which most did not.

Richard Eddy, the denominational historian, estimated that by 1885 working resources amounted to more than $350,000, over half of which was held by state conventions.[63] The trustees were administering thirteen special funds by 1892.[64]

The greatest difficulty seemed to be the persistent failure of parishes to heed requests for contributions. "Representation without taxation is about as bad as taxation without representation."[65] The largest parish contribution so far in the entire history of the General Convention was made in 1890, when $6,540 of the $15,000 sought was actually received from that source.[66] Even then the trustees were far from satisfied, and made some rather acid comments in 1892. Among the reasons they found for the relatively poor returns were: procrastination to "a more convenient season" which never came; a tendency of ministers "to become guardians not only of the parish treasuries but also of those of their parishioners"; and the disposition "never [to] do today what . . . can [be] put off till tomorrow."[67] The Massachusetts Convention blamed the failure of the contributory system on insufficient awareness of convention needs, and placed the primary responsibility on the clergy.[68]

After debating for more than a decade the expediency of appointing a special "missionary secretary" to raise funds for church extension, Henry W. Rugg, a trustee, was appointed in 1894 to secure funds and at the same time attempt to coordinate and consolidate the numerous requests for financial assistance.[69] A "Cent-a-Day" plan was adopted the same year to try to reach parishioners with modest means by personal appeal.[70]

The freedom from indebtedness that had been hailed with such satisfaction in 1887 did not last very long. The denomination was again in the red to an amount just short of $23,000 by 1896, and the deficit was steadily increasing, largely because of expansion of missionary work both at home and abroad. It was time for the trustees to realize that they had been "living on faith; and faith does not pay bills, nor support missions, nor carry on new churches."[71] The initial plan was to liquidate the indebtedness by withdrawing money from the theological scholarship fund.

It was appropriate that another major fund-raising campaign be initiated, timed to signalize the beginning of a new century. The new financial effort was the brainchild of Frederick A. Bisbee, editor of the *Leader*. Work on attaining the goal of $200,000 over a two-year period for what was called the Twentieth Century Fund was begun by the *Leader* in the fall of 1898; there was no public appeal until the fall of 1900.[72] George L. Perin, who had had great success in raising money to start the Japan mission, succeeded Rugg as missionary secretary and was appointed chairman in 1899.[73] The original intention had been to use the income for church extension, but when the General Convention endorsed the drive no restrictions were placed on its use; it was made a permanent fund in 1899. There were so many demands for financial assistance that the trustees were forced to establish priorities. The Japan mission came first, followed by parish contributions and then the Twentieth Century Fund.

Progress in raising the fund in 1900 was heartening, for the full $100,000 to be raised during that year, and representing half of the grand total, had been pledged by the time of the biennial convention in 1901. But pledges were not enough. Only $85,000 had actually been paid in by 1904. So the convention voted that the canvass be "continued without cessation" until the full amount was actually in hand. No salaried official was to be employed for this specific purpose, although the missionary secretary was expected to be involved as part of his regular duties. The emphasis was not only on the raising of money but on "the evangelization and denominationalization of the Church."[74]

It was, in the eyes of Universalists, an eminently respectable record, despite its shortcomings, in a period of consolidation rather than of spectacular growth. The number of parishes, churches, and adherents had increased by only a barely perceptible percentage between 1870 and about 1900. What was significant about the denomination, institutionally speaking? It had finally "acquired a coherency, a compactness, unity of aim and action, and a habit of giving, that amounted to a revolution." A truly radical transformation had taken place, comparatively speaking, in a rather short time. If Universalists had not done as well as they might, and there was still much room for improvement, there was no justification for discouragement, disparagement, or serious complaint.

This sort of General Convention rhetoric was self-deluding, for the brute facts indicated otherwise. Between 1866 and 1905 more than $100,000 in direct aid had been rendered to 155 churches, including one-time grants, grants from two to five years, and continuous subsidies. Only slightly more than half receiving aid (82) were still alive in 1905, and many of those were accused of having developed a "dependency complex."[75] The creation of the office of Financial (Field) Secretary in 1903 to supervise and encourage collections had not worked out. It was clear to the trustees by 1907 that "neither the financial returns nor the spiritual results" seemed to have justified the expense.

The position was abolished and the General Secretary was given the impossible task of combining the responsibilities of both offices with that of the General Superintendent until the latter position was filled later the same year. The trustees had created separate committees on investments and finance in 1900, but these had apparently done little to solve the problem, for expenditures had exceeded income by nearly $42,000 by the close of 1905.[76] Donations to the General Convention were $10,000 less in 1901 than in the previous year. The fact that almost all other denominations were experiencing a similar "diminution of religious zeal" during this period was no great comfort.[77]

With an average collection of less than one-third of the $15,000 annual amount expected from parishes, the General Convention voted an increase to $25,000 in 1903, presumably with the idea in mind that larger expectations would bring larger returns.[78] At the same meeting the delegates simultaneously instructed the trustees to undertake no new ventures until existing obligations were met, and authorized the new position of Financial (Field) Secretary. This somewhat contradictory mandate increased the indebtedness by almost $5,000. Twentieth Century Fund collections by 1906, instead of reaching the anticipated $200,000, amounted to less than $92,000. It was no larger in 1912.

Business depression between 1905 and 1907 reduced market values of investments substantially; the value of the Murray Fund dropped by almost $30,000.[79] No more than half of all Universalist individuals and parishes made even a token contribution in 1907; one parish contributed 32 cents.[80] The indebtedness had reached $32,000 the same year. The General Convention in 1911 adopted a resolution entitled "Living Within Our Income" as "the fixed policy of the Convention."[81] Resolutions or not, the convention persisted in authorizing expenditures for which there were no funds. General Superintendent McGlauflin, in exasperation, asked: "Are we merely at play in religion? Do not Universalists have any sense of responsibility or duty?"[82]

But the great majority of Universalists paid little or no attention to financial matters over which their national officers were agonizing. They were much more interested by 1914 in making plans for the great "Missionary Convention" to be held on the West Coast the next year which coincided with the Great San Francisco Exposition as an added attraction.

The meeting of the General Convention in Pasadena, California, in 1915, was a particularly noteworthy event in denominational history and demonstrated, at least on the surface, that "organic unity" so hopefully expressed by the trustees in 1879. It was the first national denominational meeting held on the Pacific side of the Rocky Mountains. It was notable also for the number of anniversaries it celebrated. The year 1915 was the 100th anniversary of the death of John Murray. It was the 50th anniversary of the legal incorporation of the General Convention. It was the 25th anniversary of the founding of the mission in Japan. And a new precedent was set: It was the first time in Universalist history that the General Convention and its three auxiliary national organizations — the Women's National Missionary Association, the Young People's Christian Union, and the General Sunday School Association — had ever been all convened at the same time and place.

A special cross-country train was chartered to transport hundreds of Universalists to California. One of the two sections originated in the East, and a second section was added in Chicago, with a stop farther west at Salt Lake City.[83] A special seal was designed for the "United Universalist Conventions," displaying a cross, a Bible, and the motto "Christ Will Conquer."

The church body met first in Los Angeles, where a new church was dedicated, and then proceeded to Pasadena and San Francisco, where a "Universalist Day" was celebrated at the exposition then in progress. Lee S. McCollester delivered the keynote address there on behalf of the denomination, and received a commemorative bronze medal from the commissioner of the exposition.[84]

The Universalist proceedings in Pasadena were concluded with a ringing farewell address by Marion D. Shutter, the first president of the General Convention, as he completed his two-year term of office. He called on Universalists to "rebuild the world"; after all, as Shutter reminded his audience of the oft-repeated expression, "the word 'Universalism' is the biggest word in the dictionary."[85]

Chapter 5

From Expansion to Contraction

"A World Church for World Service"

The years 1919 and 1920, in the eyes of Universalist leadership, marked the beginning of a "new epoch."[1] World peace had been permanently restored (or so it was thought) and the denomination could enter a period of unparalleled prosperity. In a great burst of resolve and activity, a Million Dollar Campaign was launched with great fanfare, with the double slogan of "A Greater Universalist Church" and "A World Church for World Service."

It was John Smith Lowe (1878–1954), successor to McGlauflin in 1917 as General Superintendent, who was responsible for both the "World Service" slogan and the idea of conducting the drive for one million dollars over a three-year period.[2] It was also during his administration, which lasted until his resignation in 1928 to return to the parish ministry, that the denomination celebrated the 150th anniversary of John Murray's arrival in America, and completed the planning for and much of the construction of the Universalist National Memorial Church in Washington, D.C. Every signpost seemed to point toward a glowing future.

Joseph M. Tilden, president of Lombard, volunteered to conduct the fund drive in the Midwest.[3] Many local churches were strengthened, some debts were paid, new buildings were erected, and the financial resources of the General Convention were strengthened to the amount of some $350,000, supplemented by $100,000 from the successful completion of the Jubilee Fund Drive of the WNMA.

Receipts from the quota system and the Cent-a-Day plan exceeded $10,000 in 1920 — the largest amount yet obtained from these sources.[4] Total funds held by the General Convention were almost $626,000, a

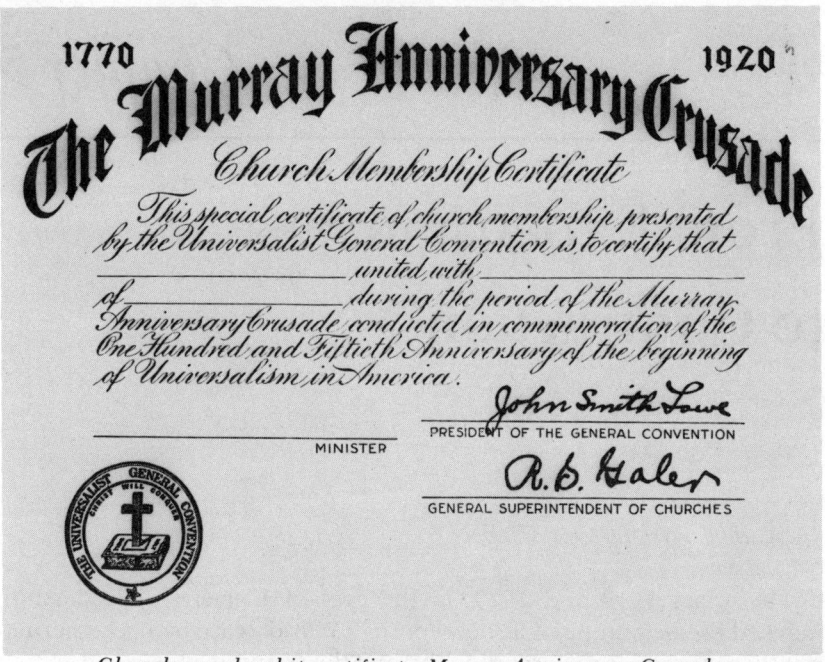

Church membership certificate, Murray Anniversary Crusade

substantial increase over the previous year. An even more encouraging record was achieved in 1923, when 333 churches paid all or part of their quotas.[5] Laymen under the leadership of Victor Friend, a prominent Boston-area businessman, were largely responsible for these gratifying returns.[6] With these encouraging signs in mind, and in anticipation of the exhaustion of the proceeds from the Million Dollar Drive, parish quotas were raised from 2 percent to 5 percent in 1923.[7]

Two-thirds of the more than $1,200,000 pledged in the total campaign remained in local church treasuries. Of the funds raised for disposition by the trustees, a system of apportionment was worked out among a dozen church organizations and activities, to be allocated over a five-year period. A Midwestern office which had existed in Chicago in the late nineteenth century (and which had published the *Universalist* there from 1884 to 1897, when the office was closed) was reopened in 1921 with funds from the Million Dollar Campaign.[8] It also became the regional headquarters of the Midwestern superintendent.

The year 1920 marked the 150th anniversary of the landing of Murray and was appropriately recognized throughout the denomination. The focus was on special meetings at both Good Luck, New Jersey, and Gloucester, Massachusetts.[9] At the Good Luck site the YPCU and the GSSA held conventions which brought together large contingents of Universalists from all over the country. Each convocation extended over several days in August, and men and women prominent in the church addressed the numerous assemblages. A special event at the Good Luck celebration was the dedication of the newly enlarged Murray Grove House, a hotel available for church gatherings.

At Gloucester, where the activities were scheduled with a one-day interval after the close of the Good Luck celebration to allow attendance at both, the climax of the four-day meeting was a great pageant depicting the origin of American Universalism and Murray's part in it. The Gloucester celebration was patterned roughly on the centennial held in the same community in 1870, including the use of a large tent erected for the purpose in Stage Fort Park overlooking the ocean. Meetings and services were also held in the local church, of which J.C. Lee was pastor, and in the Sargent-Murray House which was in the process of rescue from neglect.

Among the activities was a meeting of the Layman's League, with the largest gathering of the men of the church in the history of the denomination.[10] One outgrowth of the Gloucester celebration was the recommendation by the convention trustees that Gloucester be considered a national shrine and as headquarters for annual meetings of the entire denomination. To that end a drive for an initial endowment of $25,000 and an eventual fund of $50,000 for perpetual maintenance of the church and the house where Murray had lived was announced; $7,000 was immediately pledged in a burst of temporary enthusiasm, but that was about as far as the plans ever went. There was also the announcement of a Murray Anniversary Crusade, begun in 1920, to double church membership — a goal never reached. The drive was intended "to put Universalism into action and action into Universalism," under the supervision of the General Superintendent.[11] Universalists were more successful in coining catchy slogans than in carrying them out.

Still another means of increasing membership was initiated by the General Convention in 1921 as a follow-up to the Anniversary Crusade, and was known as the "Christ Crusade."[12] It reaffirmed the concept of the brotherhood of all, adherence to the Golden Rule, and the consecration of the denomination to the social gospel of Jesus. It was intended both to reinvigorate the spiritual thrust of the denomination and to double membership, beginning on Christmas Day in 1923 and to last for four years. Again the General Superintendent was placed in charge, and again it failed.[13] The overburdened General Superintendent already had too much to do.

One trustee project that was begun with high expectations but had a continuous history of less than a decade was the John Murray Lectureship established in 1919 largely through the efforts of Lee S. McCollester, as a sort of "spiritual memorial."[14] Its particular goal was frankly propagandistic. "The plain fact is that we are not reaching the multitudes at the present moment."[15] It was in part an answer to those who felt that Universalists had failed to spread their message effectively. At the General Convention meeting in 1919 the Committee on Resolutions frankly advocated an "aggressive advertising campaign" to make Universalism more widely known.[16] The trustees even considered hiring an advertising expert to get Universalism into public consciousness.[17]

As originally conceived, the plan for the Murray Lectureship was roughly comparable to the Board of Lectureship of the Christian Science Church and the outreach activities of the Unitarian Layman's League. One individual was to be put into the field who would circulate around the country spreading Universalist ideas and doing, on a more modest scale, what Shinn had attempted to accomplish. F. O. Hall was initially selected but was unable to accept because of a multitude of other responsibilities, and because he could not devote even a month's time to it.[18] So the decision was made to put several individuals at work on a series of nation-wide circuits simultaneously, all pastors released temporarily from their churches.

Between 1920 and 1923 such men (mostly from Massachusetts) as Ulysses S. Milburn (Salem), Leroy Coons (Haverhill), Stanley Manning (Boston), Frederick A. Bisbee (former editor of the *Leader*), and Vincent E. Tomlinson (Worcester) delivered more than 500 lectures, addresses, and sermons in all sections of the Union. Tomlinson delivered forty addresses in thirty days; Bisbee, who had relocated to Miami, was responsible for establishing a church there.

But the effort was too much for the limited financial resources of the trustees, even though those clergy who participated received no compensation beyond their travelling expenses. In addition, the need for arranging released time from their churches caused disruption and other difficulty. Valiant as were the efforts of those who gave of their time and energy, the Murray Lectureship was "not sufficient for the task." As Hall reported in 1923, while serving simultaneously as the chairman of three committees and commissions (including the Murray Lectureship itself), there was a greater need for more settled pastors and preachers than for a system of "temporarily drafting able men from their regular work." Some other device would have to be found.

In 1923 the trustees of the General Convention, headed by McCollester, presented for its biennial meeting a wide-ranging suggested program for the denomination, representing a blend of generalized objectives and specific proposals. Most of the blueprint was enacted or at least approved in principle.[19] The program was based on three general guidelines: emphasizing the "furthering of God's Kingdom on earth" rather than on a future life; increasing relations with like-minded (liberal) Christians everywhere, stressing "a community of ideals and purposes rather than uniformity of belief and ... theological agreement"; and strengthening the ties of brotherhood of all humanity, demonstrated in social service leading to peace and justice on both national and international fronts.

The strengthening of the church itself was also high on the agenda. Organizationally, a realignment of departments and responsibilities was called for as a result of growing complexity which had resulted in overlapping of effort and conflicts of jurisdiction — an all too familiar recital of denominational experience. At the hub was to be the General Convention, from which all agencies and activities would radiate, to be operated "in line with the best modern systematic and scientific organization of corporate functions," for which careful budgeting was indispensable.

McCollester was confirming what Isaac Smith had said in 1919, when he had called for "a central business administration" which the denomination had lacked. "The genius of our church lies in the fact that it positively refuses to be organized, each church choosing rather to live in splendid isolation."[20] Until existing machinery was made more effective, resolutions to strengthen the church remained "a waste of breath and paper."

If the ambitious program they envisaged, both internally and externally, were to be carried out, largely increased funding was presupposed. But another financial drive coming on the heels of the Million Dollar Drive, and authorized by the General Convention to begin on 1 January 1923, was not considered advisable by the trustees. They recommended instead that the work of the church be financed by consistent and continued giving rather than by spasmodic drives. The ideal was to have each church give as much to others as they raised for themselves. In practical terms this meant that, besides gifts and bequests for special objects, the principle of an every-member canvass was to be extended to the entire church, with a simultaneous campaign throughout the denomination.

After the General Convention meeting in Providence, Rhode Island, in 1923 the trustees made a determined effort to reconcile the conflicting signals they had received as to the financial support of the denomination and its growing list of activities. They had recommended a general canvass to do away with separate special drives for special projects. The convention had simultaneously, and with complete inconsistency, both approved the idea and instructed the trustees to continue separate campaigns for three major special projects — the Japan mission, the building of a national memorial church, and the implementation of a contributory ministerial pension fund. These were all in addition to raising funds for the normal operating budget. In all, they amounted to $760,000 for a two-year period, a total considered "too much to ask our churches and our people to contribute at once."[21]

After much consideration the trustees adopted a so-called "Five Year Program" to spread out the financial commitments which amounted to an even one million dollars. Apportionments were worked out which meant almost 25 percent of the local budget for each church or parish. A

National Laymen's Committee was put in charge of the campaign in 1924. By the end of the first year less than one-third of the churches (141) had agreed to contribute about one-half of the total projected. The campaign lagged so noticeably that in 1926 the committee employed Frank W. Merrick, a former Congregational minister who held lay Universalist fellowship, as a financial adviser.[22] The appointment produced very few results, for the convention deficit continued to mount, returns were meager, and Treasurer A. Ingham Bicknell pronounced the entire plan to raise funds a failure in 1927.[23] Vincent E. Tomlinson, for several years a member of the trustee finance committee, complained that furthering interdenominational comity had occupied center stage while unpaid bills were piling up in General Convention offices.

The trustees responded by deciding finally to operate on a budget, first put into effect for the fiscal year 1927-28.[24] Sources and amounts of probable income were identified in advance; appropriations were then made within these limits rather than following the previous practice of trusting to luck that income and expenditures might somehow balance. The recommendation made in 1923 had finally been adopted.

The trustees had also created in 1923 a Special Gifts Fund to cover the expenses of the Five Year Campaign and to carry out simultaneously a grandiose plan of committing one million dollars to the "Golden Rule World Service Fund." It had been inspired by the model of Arthur Nash, a Cincinnati manufacturer of men's clothing and active Universalist. Much had been made of his principle of shared management as a factor in financial success. The trustee commitment to further good causes beyond the denomination was not idle talk.

Even though not a member of the Federal Council of Churches, Universalists helped its Industrial Relations Committee to put a worker in the field. The convention also voted to contribute funds for the building of a nondenominational chapel at Fort Snelling, Minnesota, and to the Walter Hines Page School of International Relations at the Johns Hopkins University, sponsor by Universalist Owen D. Young. The General Convention likewise provided a Universalist chaplain for a three-year period at the Mayo Clinic in Rochester, Minnesota. Universalists cooperated officially with the International Committee of the YMCA in establishing Turkish-American clubs for boys and young men in the nation reconstituted after World War I. The "spirit of larger things" of which Universalists often spoke was really coming to pass even though there was almost no money to support that spirit.

The Five Year Program came officially to an end in the fall of 1929, with almost $100,000 in pledges unpaid.[25] All churches which had paid their regular quota and their part of the apportionment for the Japan mission and the memorial church were excused from contributing further. There were too many projects under way and too many financial claims on unwilling Universalists to assure even a minimum of success.

There had been so much confusion about the relationship of quotas, special projects, and capital fund drives that the decision was made in 1929 to work out a comprehensive and coherent plan for financing the denomination adequately.[26] But the stock market crash and the ensuing economic depression put an end to that plan. Even then the total funds held by the General Convention surpassed the one million dollar mark in 1931, at least on paper.[27]

The General Convention continued to struggle along with totally inadequate resources during the period of the Great Depression. Judge Robert W. Hill of Salem, Massachusetts, in 1932 placed as much of the responsibility on Universalists themselves as on national economic conditions for the consistently poor showing. "Our history has been a story of individualism carried and glorified to the extreme."[28] It was high time that Universalists acted "as a united and loyal Church" and cease following their own selfish interests.

Some Universalists did respond to Hill's criticism. After it had been announced in the fall of 1933 that only fifty-seven churches had paid their quotas in full, the Universalist Loyalty Fellowship was created, with membership at $10 each, recommended at the General Convention session that year.[29] Of the 200 subscribers sought among the 357 delegates, 75 responded. The deficit had reached more than $78,000 that year. It was charged off against unrestricted general funds, leaving total assets of little more than $700,000 and total available funds of $458,000.[30] Quotas were reduced from 5 percent to 3 percent in 1934 for a two-year period in an effort to make the financial burden more bearable.[31] There seemed to be no alternative but extra careful husbanding of resources and a policy of living within denominational means even though it meant retrenchment on every hand until better times returned.

Vividly illustrative of the straitened circumstances under which the denomination was forced to operate was the case of Roger F. Etz (1886–1950). He had begun his service as General Secretary in 1919 following a career in the parish ministry, and after Lowe's resignation in 1928 was designated as Executive Secretary and as Acting General Superintendent unofficially. The two offices were formally combined in 1930 because the trustees felt that they could not afford a replacement for Lowe. Etz, overwhelmed with administrative details, could do little more than conduct a holding operation until his resignation in 1938.

In his very first report of his work, made in 1929, Etz voiced his impatience with a denomination that had such high expectations and had so little to show for them. "If I had my way, I would ask this Convention ... to rescind the recommendations and resolutions of the past which have been largely ignored in practice [and] which we mainly forget after the Convention [is over]."[32] In 1932 he took a 10 percent reduction in salary in order to help keep the General Convention financially afloat.[33]

Etz's comments that the Universalist reach and grasp did not coincide were reminiscent of an editorial by Bisbee written in the *Leader* in 1913.

> It has been the unfortunate fate of the Universalist Church to be, or seem to be, unable to stick to any one purpose or plan for more than one session; we have started splendid enterprises which would take years for completion, and at the very next session torn them up or down and started something else in their place, until it has been a shame to us that we had to recognize our lack of stability and continuity of purpose.[34]

One administrative development during Etz's tenure in office, and partly through his efforts, was the creation in 1935 of a Council of Executives composed of staff members representing both the General Convention and its affiliated organizations.[35] This move to centralize management and improve coordination of programs paved the way later for a Central Planning Council and eventually a Committee on Survey and Reorganization.[36] Another recommendation was made in 1937 to unify the denomination by changing its corporate name to "The Universalist Church"; under existing practice the term "General Convention" signified to many merely an auxiliary organization rather than the chief executive and legislative body it had become.[37]

A further step to increase "efficiency" was taken the same year by a trustee decision to separate again the offices of General Secretary and General Superintendent. Denominational policy had changed considerably since Selleck had made his plea in 1896 that a General Superintendency be established to assist smaller churches struggling for existence. One half of them had disappeared by 1938, and the denomination, both by force of circumstance and to meet its own needs, had concentrated on the much fewer and larger churches in urban and suburban centers; yet the paper work had increased rather than diminished.

A questionnaire distributed by the editor of the *Leader* in 1939 (with a 25 percent return), indicated a desire for stronger central leadership and "a greater sense of responsibility" at the top. Authority was requested to give the General Superintendent the power even to step in and resolve conflicts between congregations and their ministers, and terminate their pastorates. Such a recommendation would have been unheard of only a few decades earlier.

The atmosphere of the early 1920s had been radically different from the pessimism of the 1930s, with hopes and expectations running high. There was an abundance of plans for expansion on the drawing board. One of the more prominent was the construction of a church of cathedral proportions in Washington, D.C., which would serve as a symbol of denominational contributions to the life of the nation, and at the same time memorialize individual Universalists and their work. It was to be, as General Superintendent Etz later described it, "the greatest single enterprise the Universalist Church has ever undertaken."[38]

The Universalist National Memorial Church

The idea for a church that would represent the entire denomination in the nation's capital was discussed in 1868, at the General Convention meeting in Baltimore, a year before a permanent society had even been formed in Washington, D.C. Nothing was accomplished toward providing such a church until after World War I, when it was announced that the Murray Universalist Church (later redesignated as the Church of Our Father), first used in 1883, was to be replaced by a "cathedral church." The first intimation that such would actually take place had come in 1921.[39] The original plan was two-fold: to erect a building which would memorialize Universalists who had served overseas during the Great War or who had "proved themselves worthy of a national memorial"; and to provide increased strength and stability for the local society, which was leading a marginal existence, having been without a settled pastor since the death of Levi Powers in 1920.[40]

The proposal to raise $200,000 was presented to a meeting of the Universalist Comrades, an organization of laymen, at the biennial meeting of the denomination in Detroit in 1921, and met with an enthusiastic response.[41] Plans were even drawn up for a colonial style edifice with a tall, slender steeple and Greek columns, and flanked by two smaller columned buildings — one for religious education activities and the other for community events.[42] The finished product, however, bore no resemblance to the original plans, and the financial projection approached $500,000, over twice the first estimate.

A snag developed immediately. Not only was there opposition to the proposal, particularly from the Midwest, but a prolonged argument over priorities. Objections poured in, based on every conceivable ground.[43] The project appealed to "a narrow group of people" who were supporting a "sentimental program" with no real value to the denomination. In short, the money that would have to be committed to build it would be misspent. It was much better to use the funds to support churches by developing "their own shrinking work." Up to fifty small churches could be supported with such funds. Let local churches establish their own memorials. Why not use the money for a decent pension system to attract and retain clergy?[44] If the anticipated half a million dollars were expended on this project — "the most ill-judged which was ever foisted upon our denomination" — the result would be "disaster."

As to priorities, a drive had already been started to build the Perin-Cate Home for Boys in Japan, comparable to the existing Blackmer Home for Girls. Could the denomination finance both? Then a disastrous earthquake in Japan intervened, and priorities had to be reordered. At least $100,000 was needed immediately to finance reconstruction there. Support for the memorial church had to be reduced to $300,000. Clarence E. Rice, then the minister of the Washington church, was understandably dismayed by the turn of events, and reluctantly scaled down his expectations to $200,000.[45] He had expected $85,000 from the sale of the old church, but it was actually only $60,000.[46] The convention trustees recommended that the memorial church project be suspended temporarily, but the General Convention voted to raise both funds simultaneously.[47]

The decision, in perspective, was ill-advised, for the Japan project was never carried out, and the plans for the Washington church were much delayed. Less than $20,000 of the anticipated cost, set at $300,000, had been raised by the fall of 1923. Much of General Convention President Atwood's efforts were taken up with attempting to quiet the doubts and fears of those who thought the plan too visionary, impractical, and expensive. He reassured them by stressing the fact that, in supporting the idea of a national church, the convention had no intention of building "a beautiful, expensive cathedral church which will be a white elephant on our hands and involve us in limitless expense for all time."[48] Instead, the goal was "a creditable, serviceable church" which would strengthen the local parish, eventually become self-supporting, and at the same time enhance the Universalist presence in the nation's capital.

The property of the old church was sold in 1925 to the Christian Scientists and, after one change of site, a new location was selected on 16th Street for the new edifice. There was much discussion over whether Frederic W. Perkins, pastor of the Lynn, Massachusetts, church, would accept a call to Washington, but all doubt was removed when he agreed to come, beginning in January 1927. By that time over half of the $300,000 had been subscribed, and the trustees had already planned to have the General Convention meet there in 1929 even though the building was not expected to be completed.

A bill was filed in Congress in 1928 to obtain a national charter, as befitted the primary purpose of the church. The Attorney General of the United States, John G. Sargent, very circumspectly refused to be an incorporator because his office had to review all such applications, and he was himself a Universalist.[49]

Funds to finance the memorial church came in with agonizing slowness, with little more than $175,000 raised by the fall of 1927, so the expedient was tried, beginning in 1928, of selling symbolic building stones for $10 each. Each subscriber was furnished with a miniature paper replica carrying the message "I Am a Building Stone in the Memorial Church."[50] Contributions were solicited from every organization and individual in the denomination to memorialize friends and relatives, and the *Leader* periodically published the names of both the donors and the individuals being honored. Some $30,000 was raised in this fashion.[51] The 3,000-mark for building-stone contributions having been achieved, a new goal of 5,000 was set in 1930.[52] Although this was never reached, scattered contributions were still being received many years after the church was actually opened. In 1944 a music room was dedicated as a memorial to Emilie F. Libby by the Massachusetts Convention which had received a bequest from her estate.[53] Substantial contributions were received from organizations such as the WNMA, which subscribed funds to provide a clerestery window.[54] Sunday school pupils contributed a memorial in honor of Charles H. Leonard, founder of Children's Day.[55]

Sufficient funds had been accumulated by 1928 to start construction that fall, and a temporary Commission on Church Architecture had been established to coordinate the planning between the pastor and the architect Charles Collens, of the Boston firm of Allen and Collens.[56] Perkins, as both the pastor of the church and as chairman of the one-person Commission on Architecture, reported wryly in 1927 that "conferences between the two officers have been made easy and expeditious, and so far they have found themselves in entire accord." The Washington parish met for three years in the Ambassador Theater while the new church was being constructed.

The building, of combined Gothic and Romanesque design, was to have been an all-stone structure, but financial limitations required some modification. A combination of gray stone and gray-buff brick had to be substituted as an economy measure.[57] It was still a most impressive structure, combining dignity, massiveness, and grace.[58]

The cornerstone of the new church was laid on a rainy 28 April 1929, and later in the year the tower of the church was dedicated to the ideals of international brotherhood and world peace, the first such memorial in the city. It was named the Young Tower of World Peace in honor of Owen D. Young, one of the denomination's better known members, a high-ranking businessman and diplomat who had recently formulated a plan for settling the German reparations problem. He was unable to be present because he was attending the dedication by Madame Curie of a new science building at St. Lawrence University, his *alma mater*.[59] The first services in the completed building were held on Palm Sunday in April 1930, with a congregation overflowing the seating capacity of 500. The dedication took place on 27 April.[60]

It had been a long struggle, and the timing could not have been worse in terms of finances. John Smith Lowe, who had been principally responsible for raising money, as General Superintendent, resigned in 1928, and a replacement had to be found immediately. By good fortune, Charles H. Emmons, who, after serving several pastorates, had achieved prominence as a fund raiser for Near Eastern relief, was available to take charge of completing the canvass.[61] Then came the stock market crash, with all of the economic crises which accompanied and followed it. The cost overrun on the church amounted to $150,000, making a grand total expenditure of almost half a million dollars. The trustees were forced to take out a mortgage to complete construction.[62]

The denomination was at least able to dedicate the Peace Tower free of debt by virtue of an emergency plea to the General Convention then in session.[63] The same device had been used in financing the tower as the main church building — the solicitation of memorial gifts. Among the prominent Americans so memorialized in 1929 was Eugene V. Debs, the nationally known and controversial labor leader.[64]

There was a sense of real accomplishment in spite of all the difficulties that had surrounded the building of the church. It was, as convention president Frank D. Adams expressed it at the cornerstone laying, "the fruition of a long, long dream." As if to dramatize the time-span that had elapsed between the expressed hope for a "national temple at the heart of the nation" and its transformation into actuality, among those present was a single individual — Edwin C. Sweetser — who had attended the meeting in 1868 when the idea had been born.

The church immediately became a very lively and significant part of the religious life of Washington under Perkins' leadership which lasted until his resignation in 1938. It attracted hundreds of visitors, and within a year after it opened it achieved widespread attention with its National Capital Choir which in 1931 gave a concert of Christmas music broadcast over a combined hook-up of the National and Columbia Broadcasting Systems.[65]

After Perkins' retirement a parish search committee surveyed the field for a successor; among the choices were Cornelius Greenway (Brooklyn), Ellsworth Reamon (Syracuse), Clarence R. Skinner (Dean of the Crane Theological School at Tufts), and Seth R. Brooks (Malden, Massachusetts).[66] Brooks was selected. He was completing the eleventh year of a highly successful pastorate in the historic First Parish Church (Universalist) in Malden, after having received both his undergraduate and theological degrees from St. Lawrence (1922, 1924) and having served the church in Little Falls, New York, for six years. The search committee visited the Malden church without Brooks' knowledge and was impressed with both him and his record. When they reported their choice both the General Superintendent and the trustees of the Universalist Church of America (UCA) concurred.[67]

The new pastor immediately became deeply involved in both secular and religious affairs in Washington, and he did his utmost to provide visibility for the church. Behind the scenes, however, there was an unremitting struggle to keep the church on a sound financial footing. Although it held onto a membership in excess of 400 into the 1950s, fewer than 300 were permanent members in residence, and the church had to depend largely on limited endowment and occasional gifts to provide adequate financing.[68]

When Brooks succeeded Perkins in 1939, more than $175,000 in General Convention funds were tied up in the church and were not income-producing.⁶⁹ Since 1922 the responsibility for the fiscal affairs of the church had been shared by the local parish and the UCA. After 1950 the parish assumed an increasing share of support. The appropriation from the UCA was only $1,745 in 1953, and during the financial crisis experienced in the mid-1950s was reduced to a token $1.00.⁷⁰ At the suggestion of the parish itself the UCA trustees voted in 1956 to cut all financial links with the church and place the entire responsibility on the local organization.⁷¹

Why had all of this happened? Brooks, in looking back over the history of the church after his retirement and placing it within the perspective of the entire denomination, concluded that the whole Universalist philosophy and state of mind had been responsible. Universalists were not "a church people [and] never had that sense of organizing and pulling ourselves together because we thought we had to go out and save other people by bringing them into our movement."⁷² They had for the most part lacked an evangelical commitment, and that in turn had been reflected in failure to provide adequate financial support. "We had nothing to frighten people, we had nothing to threaten people, we made few demands."

Yet the hopes of the founders remained, as the Universalist National Memorial Church itself remained, a monument to the denomination under the leadership of a new generation.

A Denomination with an Uncertain Future

Even as Universalists had been celebrating their centennial in 1870 a few voices had been occasionally heard casting a shadow of doubt and uncertainty about the future of the denomination. Had it achieved its main purposes? Was it ready "to close up shop," as one individual put it? The challenge was offered again by the editor of the *Leader* on the eve of the General Convention which met in Chicago in 1913. "Shall we have a Universalist Church or shall we not? . . . . We are not making any marked impression on the world to-day because we are not big enough, strong enough, and enough in earnest to command the support with which to serve."⁷³ The machinery was there but the spirit and will were lacking.

The evidence of decline was becoming noticeable even to those outside the denomination. An editorial in the *Boston Herald,* commenting in 1914 on the destruction of the historic Columbus Avenue Church (the Second Society) by fire in Boston, noted that only one Universalist church remained in New York City (Divine Paternity).⁷⁴ Why should the Universalist Church continue to exist? Its major teachings had been generally adopted by others. It could be of more service if it threw in its lot with other Christian churches and cease to remain an anachronism left over from a "bygone controversy."

A sprightly defense was immediately forthcoming from Frederic W. Perkins of the First Universalist Church in Lynn, Massachusetts, who pointed out that Universalists still had to be the principal catalysts in bringing about a unified Christendom.[75]

Walter Rauschenbusch, the eminent exponent of the Social Gospel who gave an address at the Massachusetts Convention in 1914, echoed the same sentiments as those expressed in the *Boston Herald*. It was generally acknowledged that Christians as a whole had absorbed Universalist ideas. 'If true, what is your mission? Unless you get another job, you must go out of business!'[76]

Isaac M. Atwood, who viewed with consternation in 1915 the comparative shrinkage in parish rolls and ministerial rosters, called for a grand inventory of the denomination and where it stood.[77] It had to be not only thorough and honest, for most reports were unrealistically and misleadingly optimistic to the point of inaccuracy. Universalists were deluding themselves in paying too much attention to putting their best foot forward. Atwood's recommendation was coolly received. There were more important tasks confronting the denomination than making surveys, and most of the information was already available in central files, it was said.[78] W. H. Skeels, the General Secretary at the time, threw cold water on the whole idea of taking inventory. He had already sent out questionnaires and had gotten almost no response; many refused to reply to questions because they were somehow considered an invasion of privacy.[79]

F. O. Hall, who resigned in 1919 from the Church of the Divine Paternity to accept a lectureship at the Crane Theological School, put much of the blame for decline on Universalists themselves. "Nine-tenths of the people of our own country, to say nothing of the rest of the world, never heard of our Church or its message. It is time they did hear, if [it] is worth hearing. If it is not, then let us go out of business."[80] Another Universalist, writing to the *Leader,* agreed completely. If nothing were done to arrest the decline "it will not be long before our greatest local need will be cemeteries."[81]

From the late 1920s into the late 1930s the voices of concern for the future of the denomination were becoming more numerous and more strident. The president of the General Convention, Frank D. Adams, delivered at the meeting in Washington, D.C. in 1929, one of the most jolting presentations that had been heard by Universalists in many a day.[82] He took them to task for their loss of pioneering spirit and the challenge of being different. They had lost their sense of unique mission, had found nothing to take its place, and had become overly concerned with what the orthodox denominations thought of them. Where had the spirit of adventurousness gone? The blame for apathy, smugness, limited vision, and self-satisfaction rested on laity and clergy alike. Nobody had the courage to change. An "impalpable wall of conservatism" had been built that was stifling the denomination.

No clearer example of paradox could be found, he told his startled listeners, than the reluctance, or even hostility of a vocal minority to establish closer relations with other religious groups without at the same time losing their own identity. Universalists had complained for generations about their lack of acceptance by others, yet when opportunity for recognition came, by way of the Unitarians and more particularly the Congregationalists, some Universalists saw a threat to their history, their traditions, and to their presumed distinctiveness, and balked at the idea of joining the mainstream of American Protestantism represented by the Congregationalists. That was no way to be "different."

Adams found other instances with which to castigate the denomination for its contradictions and inconsistencies. The General Convention unthinkingly approved all kinds of commitments, such as the National Memorial Church and the Japan mission, yet with seeming perversity refused to support them. The trustees were constantly being blamed for carrying out (or failing to carry out) policies that they had not necessarily been responsible for initiating. They were the creatures of the denomination, not its masters.

The solution to these and a myriad of other problems was not a more elaborate or coercive organization or even greater church discipline. The answer was very simple and perfectly consonant with the spirit and practice of Universalism, with its emphasis on localism and congregational autonomy. The ultimate responsibility for the welfare of the church rested on the individual minister and the parish, working through the local church. The clergy had to be willing to be pioneers again, using the liberty, freedom, and courage bequeathed by earlier generations. It would be easy, but the very survival of the denomination was at stake. Did Universalists want to fold up their tents and disappear into the crowd, or did they want to stand up and be counted?

After a moment of stunned silence most of the assemblage gave Adams a standing ovation. A few remained in their seats, unwilling or unable to accept the indictment of their denomination by one of its own members. There was momentary talk in the corridors of the Mayflower Hotel preceding the choice of officers for the next biennium that the president be defeated for reelection, but that mood passed, and the General Convention proceeded with its business. There was no question that the address had been provocative. It was greeted as "prophetic" by the younger generation, but was received in stony silence by many elder statesmen in the church.[83]

The "new epoch" so confidently expected after World War I was not as easily entered as the Universalist leadership had so optimistically anticipated.

Section III

Theology for a Changing World

Chapter 6

Testing the Winchester Profession

> We believe that the Holy Scriptures of the Old and New Testament contain a revelation of the character of God, and of the duty, interest and final destination of mankind.
>
> We believe that there is one God, whose nature is Love, revealed in one Lord Jesus Christ, by one Holy Spirit of Grace, who will finally restore the whole family of mankind to holiness and happiness.
>
> We believe that holiness and true happiness are inseparably connected, and that believers ought to be careful to maintain order and practice good works; for these things are good and profitable unto men.

The year 1903 was important for the Universalist denomination, for it marked the 100th anniversary of the adoption of its profession of faith in Winchester, New Hampshire, quoted above. The event was commemorated with addresses, sermons, and special services at such widely separated locations as the church in which the Profession had been adopted; a special assembly in Rome City, Indiana; and the General Convention which met in the nation's capital in the fall of 1903.[1]

One of the most significant of the presentations was an historical address delivered in whole or in part at all three locations by J. S. Cantwell of Chicago. His conclusion was simply stated: The Profession had "stood the test of time." There had been almost no dissent from its statement of doctrine; there had been no impeachment of its general principles. "The Profession anchored us in the beginning and the anchor holds to this day." It was in no way a limiting creed, or even a confession but an affirmation. It was "compact in expression, clear as crystal and luminous in simplicity." The three articles were not "susceptible, by any turn or twist of the phraseology, of expressing anything but what is clearly intended by their authors."

None of the developments in philosophy, Biblical criticism, or sociology had yet endangered the Profession or the faith it expressed. On the contrary, they might very well "enrich, enlarge and re-establish it for the benefit of future generations." The Scriptures still contained "the word of truth"; humanity would always need restoration to divine favor as long as there were sinners in the world. God would still be transcendent; just as nature was the expression of the divine immanence, Christ would "remain as the translation of God in the terms of human experience." The vision was still "the Universal harmony of a reconciled universe."

Had the authors of the Winchester Profession committed any errors? Yes, one. They had unwisely declared that there was never to be an alteration of any part of the Profession. They seemed to have ignored the fact that any form of a written creed might "prove inadequate in future years of the church to the needs of an expanding Christianity." There could be no finality in creeds. The Profession would be rewritten "whenever it is no longer recognized as the fittest expression of the Universalist belief, or when the need exists for a new emphasis on any point of doctrine or the religious life in the more advanced development of a Christian society." But the time was not yet, nor was there any sign of its coming, in Cantwell's estimation.

A glance at the record of the first century of the Profession would indicate that indeed the wording had remained unchanged. Although an occasional voice had been raised about both its terminology and its status in the denomination, there had been almost uniform acceptance as it originally stood. Many societies and churches between 1803 and 1870 had exercised the option of adding their own statements in accordance with the "liberty clause" which had accompanied the Profession when it had been adopted.

> Yet while we adopt a general profession of belief . . . we leave it to the several churches and societies or to smaller associations of churches, if such should be formed, within the limits of our General Association, to continue or adopt within themselves, such more articles of faith . . . as may appear to them best under their particular circumstances, provided they do not disagree with our general profession or plan.

Most Universalists referred to their denomination as a "creedless religion," and took the Profession for granted as merely a theological statement which bore no resemblance in its form or obligation to the more or less elaborate and binding creedal pronouncements of other denominations, such as the Westminster Confession, the Apostles' Creed, or the Thirty-Nine Articles of the Church of England. William S. Balch went so far as to argue that for over half a century the Profession had had no force or authority whatever, and that belief in it, either expressed or implied, was not even needed as a condition of fellowship or ordination.[2]

The Profession did not become a subject for discussion in the General Convention until 1867, when a Declaration and Interpretation was adopted. It set forth the "evident intention of the authors . . . to affirm the divine authority of the Scriptures and the Lordship of Jesus Christ." This in itself actually represented no new or radical interpretation of the Profession, but a somewhat redundant paraphrase and explanation of part of it. The significant fact about the explanatory statement was not so much that it was adopted by a vote of 49 to 1, as that the interpretation was considered essential to a "sincere acceptance of our fellowship."

What had made the reaffirmation necessary at all? The answer was to be found in the report of the Committee on the State of the Church in 1867. It had detected a growing religious skepticism in the denomination that bordered on disbelief. The committee recommended passage of a resolution "that in order for one to become a Christian minister, or a member of a Universalist Church, he or she shall believe in the Bible account of the life, teachings, miracles, death and resurrection of our Lord Jesus Christ; and any interpretation of the Winchester Confession of Faith that makes it compatible with a denial of that account is a false one."[3] The committee recommended that the constitution of the convention be so amended as to include this statement. The convention had responded by refusing to take such a formal step, but had settled for the reaffirmation mentioned above.

There was still nothing mandatory about the Profession, and assent could still be assumed as well as expressed explicitly. There is no evidence that the Declaration of 1867 provoked any controversy or even attracted much attention. A scattering of ecclesiastical bodies like the Vermont State Convention officially approved the interpretation adopted by the General Convention, but most apparently considered no action necessary.[4] It was an elaboration of the obvious.

While the Unitarians in the 1860s were engaged in a protracted debate over whether to adopt a creed at all, Universalist John Greenleaf Adams sided with those favoring the adoption of some statement of belief. Indiscriminate denunciation of creeds was an unwise policy. "A faith in the unseen that is most in accordance with nature, human intuitions, sound philosophy and the Word of God, is the one after which all souls may rightfully seek."[5] By good fortune, wrote Adams, Universalists had just such a statement in the Winchester Profession. It was an eminently reasonable document, serving as both a positive declaration and as a call to a virtuous life.

The Winchester Profession came closest to achieving the status of a compulsory creed in 1870. As a climax to the drive for denominational unity and organizational efficiency the General Convention that centennial year adopted a revised constitution in which the Profession was incorporated as part of its body of organic law. Although its wording was not changed, explicit consent to the Profession became for the first time a specific condition of fellowship. In the course of the discussions concerning the adoption of the new constitution in 1870, a delegate moved to strike out that part of the report of the revision committee which required "expressed assent" to the Profession as a condition of fellowship. But when the question was put, only he voted for it.[6]

Cantwell admitted in 1903 that, in removing the "liberty clause," the General Convention had deviated from the intention of the original framers. But it had reinforced the doctrinal as well as legal position of the denomination and had notified the world that "we were not a church of all outdoors, but that American Universalism had a creedal incarnation, with a heritage of recognized beliefs, from the beginning of the century."[7] It should be remembered that Cantwell uttered these words almost forty years after the Profession had been cloaked with a new aura of authority and had undergone what one Universalist clergyman of a later day dubbed "canonization."

In 1945, little more than forty years after Cantwell had declared that the new status accorded the Profession in 1870 was "a wise action at the time," Frederic William Perkins was unsparing in his criticism of the "spiritual aberration" that had taken place when the "liberty clause" had been left out.[8] According to Perkins, from the perspective of almost three-quarters of a century, ecclesiastics of that earlier day had, with the best of intentions, forgotten "the genius of our faith" and had transformed the Winchester Profession into "the very sort of compulsory creedal test which its framers explicitly stated it was not. The unity of spiritual freemen was exchanged for the lockstep of the theological drill master. The letter of the church's law was thrown into irrepressible conflict with its historic spirit." Two of the by-products and consequences had been the most noted "heresy" trial in the denomination, and a persistent but ultimately unsuccessful attempt that lasted for almost twenty-five years to tinker with the phraseology of the Profession. What had started out as a statement of religious principle had become, in Perkins' view, at the least the equivalent of a formal creed to which adherence was required as evidence of ecclesiastical good standing.

The Bisbee Heresy Trial

The first real test of the Winchester Profession came in 1872, only two years after it had been written into the constitution of the General Convention, without the "liberty clause." Herman Bisbee (1833-1879) was tried by the ecclesiastical procedures provided by the denomination, and was disfellowshipped. He was at the time the pastor of the St. Anthony Universalist Church in the community of that name which was later incorporated into the city of Minneapolis, Minnesota.[9]

Bisbee was born 29 October 1833 in Springfield, Vermont, one of eight

Herman Bisbee (1833-1879), subject of a heresy trial

children, who were raised on a farm in West Derby (Newport). After marriage in 1853 to Mary Phelps Sias, and some years' experience as a farmer, he took his wife and two children to Canton, New York, where he graduated from Canton Theological School (St. Lawrence University) in 1864. An ardent Universalist, he preached in Malone, New York, while still a student, and was ordained there.

In the spring of 1865, with a wife and family of three children, Bisbee moved to St. Paul, Minnesota, where he organized a parish the same year. He became acquainted with Seth Barnes, the pioneer Universalist preacher in nearby St. Anthony. When Barnes died in the summer of 1866 Bisbee replaced him.[10] Bisbee served briefly in Quincy, Massachusetts, but in 1869 returned to Minnesota and resumed his pastorate in St. Anthony.

Until his trip East, there seems to have been nothing unusual about Bisbee's Universalist teachings, and in his biography of Barnes had been uncritical of his subject's traditional evangelical Universalism. But after his return to the Midwest Bisbee showed mounting sympathy for the transcendentalism of men like Ralph Waldo Emerson. The young pastor had also been exposed to Boston Unitarianism while at Quincy, and particularly the radical wing which showed enthusiasm for "natural religion" and for the Free Religious Movement which had surfaced in the 1860s and had appeared in Minneapolis by 1871 in the person of William Denton. Denton had lectured in Minneapolis on such subjects as Darwinism, evolution, and science.

Denton's lectures had resulted in an elaborate reply from James Harvey Tuttle, pastor of the Universalist church in Minneapolis, who delivered a series of public lectures announced in January 1872. These in turn brought responses from Bisbee and William G. Haskell, who had recently arrived from Illinois and was pastor of the Universalist church in Stillwater, Minnesota. The public addresses became known as the "Minneapolis Radical Lectures," of which two were delivered by Haskell. The first of the seven comprising the series was delivered on 6 February and all were reported in detail in the local press, including the *Minneapolis Tribune*. One of the byproducts of the interest generated by the lectures was the organization of the New Radical Society, headed by L. K. Washburn, a Unitarian clergyman.

Almost two years before Bisbee had inaugurated his series of controversial lectures he had addressed the subject of "natural religion." He had delivered a sermon on the subject at Pence Opera House in Minneapolis in which he defined the term as "the effort which man makes to perfect himself, not the effort that God makes to perfect him." He argued that Jesus taught natural religion, without creed or ceremony, emphasizing such verities as goodness, on which Christians had no monopoly.

The lecture which put Bisbee on a collision course with Tuttle and eventually with many of the spokesmen for the denomination was a review of one of Tuttle's discourses on natural and supernatural religion. In it Tuttle had justified Christian belief in miracles, including the resurrection of Christ, accounting for them by 'an interposition of divine power.' He likewise attributed the origins of all forms of life to some manifestation of the miraculous, beyond human explanation. Bisbee flatly denied the existence or possibility of miracles, claiming that those recounted in the Bible had "no significance whatever" and averred that Tuttle had gone beyond the information furnished and claimed by science in explaining the origins of natural phenomena. Neither did the great wisdom existing in the Bible in itself prove the existence of miracles. In fact, the infallibility of the Bible itself was an unsupportable myth. This did not mean a wholesale discarding of the Scriptures but the securing of a more rational reading and interpretation of them.

The reaction to Bisbee's lectures in the denominational press was both immediate and uniformly negative. In fact, he was, in effect, tried and convicted before his case was even reviewed by an ecclesiastical tribunal. He had first attracted the attention of the *Universalist* (Boston) in the spring of 1871, when his decision had become known to return to Minnesota after his brief pastorate in Quincy. It was understood in Boston that he would no longer engage in the ministry, and there was speculation about whether he was even still in fellowship.

The *Universalist* immediately denounced Bisbee in no uncertain terms. Judging from reports of his discourses delivered in St. Anthony, as to fellowship, "he ought not to hold it."[11] He was represented in Minneapolis papers "as taking the most ultra Radical ground, was discoursing in the high and oracular fashion of our Boston Free Religionists. He discards the Bible 'as a foundation,' and puts Christianity among 'the religions,' and makes 'humanity' the 'eternal foundation' of religion." Universalists had no objection to his program "provided he does not implicate the

Universalist Church in it. Evidently he is no longer in sympathy with our denomination. We hope he does not, either in form or in fact, pretend to be."

Bisbee replied that he had returned to St. Anthony "for the express purpose of engaging in the ministry, at the urgent invitation of the First Universalist Society of that city."[12] He replied furthermore that he was in fellowship and had never been called before any tribunal "to answer heretical or other charges." He had urged his society to contribute funds to the denomination and to participate in it in every way. He was himself "in sympathy with Universalism. I am a Universalist, I did not know that I was regarded as being other than a Universalist clergyman."

Bisbee objected to being considerd in the denominational press as unworthy of fellowship until the question was decided. He should be heard before being condemned. He called upon the *Universalist* for a statement of particulars as to what was necessary to believe; then he would indicate whether he could accept it. He felt that the majority of readers would concede that he was "so far sound in the faith, as to be worthy to retain my letter." The *Universalist* had condemned him without ever having learned or even asked him for his religious opinions, and not having even hinted previously that his views were suspect.

In reply the *Universalist* refused to retract any of its assertions. The reports in the papers were presumed to be reliable and Bisbee had made no effort to disclaim them. Until evidence was produced to the contrary, the paper repeated "with added emphasis" that "he has no right to pass himself as a Universalist minister or to claim to represent the Universalist denomination." As to the matter of pronouncing a premature judgment, the *Universalist* would have taken the complaint more seriously if it had not come from an individual who had shown "an entire disregard of the obligations of fellowship by preaching and publishing sentiments subversive of the very foundations on which he ostensibly stands." Anyone who "stands up before an assembly to advocate 'the radical movement,' to disparage the Christian Religion and scout all 'supernatureal religion,' and to pour contempt on the Bible as containing things 'coarse, cruel and unbelievable,' is one whose plea for indulgence and consideration at the hands of a Universalist paper, cannot carry great weight with anybody."

The *Universalist* deplored the fact that Bisbee had chosen to throw whatever influence he had "in the scale against the authority of the Bible and Christianity" and considered it unfortunate, to say the least, that a man holding such opinions should be a representative of Universalism anywhere. A few days later the author of an editorial used even stronger language. He was amazed at Bisbee's "effrontery in continuing to hold the fellowship of a Christian denomination, and fill a professedly Christian pulpit; while he is doing his utmost to discredit both."[13] Bisbee was described as "a thoroughgoing infidel" who had ridiculed the Bible, scoffed at Christianity, and shown contempt for the entire Christian faith. The writer called for prompt and decisive action; namely, disfellowshipping by the Minnesota State Convention. "The Universalist Church is a Christian Church, unqualifiedly such. No man has any business in its ministry who is not also a Christian, in faith as well as in character."[14] The *New Covenant* (Chicago) joined in the attack, noting that Bisbee apparently considered all religions, including Christianity, as "only amiable superstitions."

Bisbee replied promptly and unequivocally, pointing out that he had entered the Universalist ministry with the definite understanding that it did not require acceptance of the Bible as an infallible document. He had checked this out with Ebenezer Fisher, then head of the Canton Theological School where Bisbee had been a student, and had been assured that it was sufficient to accept the Bible as containing a revelation, without any reference whatever to literal interpretation or complete acceptance of its contents.

Bisbee admitted that he was making a conscious effort during his ministry to counteract the "extreme conservative tendencies" which had surfaced among some leaders of the Universalist church. Attempts to make the Winchester Profession more specific, delimiting, and creedal, were self-defeating, in his estimation, for they merely promoted the sectarianism to which he had become increasingly opposed as he continued in the ministry. He believed he saw a leaning of many Universalists toward the orthodox and evangelical churches which he could not accept. Liberalism, as preached and taught by Universalists, was the watchword. As to the Winchester Profession and the intent of its authors, Bisbee argued not only that the ambiguities were deliberate but that the document was a tribute to the wisdom of those who had composed it. "The creed is a broad statement, broad enough for the whole liberal element to stand upon." Liberty of interpretation was a cornerstone of the religious freedom for which the denomination had always stood and which had made it historically unique.

Attacks on Bisbee in the Universalist press continued for several months. He replied by protesting that he had never ridiculed the Bible, but had attempted only to expose its imperfections in order "to destroy the dogma of infallibility"; that he had never shown any kind of contempt for the Christian faith or cast aspersions upon Christian churches; and that he had the same right as others to interpret Universalism. He further protested that he was being tried editorially in the press rather than by the proper official route.

Possibly in response to Bisbee's claim, the *Universalist* pulled in its horns. In the fall of 1872, after Bisbee had already been disfellowshipped, the paper admitted that the denominational press, the *Universalist* among them, had all been guilty of trying his case in their columns, and had committed a breach of judicial propriety. The newspapers should not have meddled.[15] This was, of course, an admission after the damage had been done.

Bisbee could take some comfort from at least one other fact: His parish supported him unanimously. At its annual meeting in February 1872 he read the correspondence which had been exchanged, beginning in the fall of 1871, with the Committee on Fellowship, Ordination and Discipline of the Minnesota Convention. The parish concluded that serious procedural errors had been made; among them, that Bisbee had never been able to obtain a copy of the charges brought against him, yet had been ordered to surrender his letter of fellowship without a fair hearing. As to the identity of the complainants, the record indicated only that they were "various persons, members of the Universalist Societies in Minneapolis, St. Paul, and other parishes."

The Minnesota Convention duly met in Mankato in June 1872, at which time the Committee on Fellowship and Discipline presented a report charging Bisbee with "unministerial conduct." More specifically, "in the name of Christianity and Universalism Mr. Bisbee had uttered doctrines subverting Christianity, and entirely contrary to the principles of the Universalist Church." The committee, consisting of Moses Goodrich, Russell Blakely, and Paris Gibson, had then recommended that the state convention withdraw Bisbee's fellowship. After discussing the case for the better part of a day, the convention adopted the resolution by a vote of 47 to 23.

What was meant by "unministerial conduct"? A few days after the convention adjourned Bisbee was furnished with an explanatory statement from J. C. Chaney, standing clerk of the convention. "The issue was one of *religious doctrines,* simply — a charge of *teaching doctrines not in accord with those held and taught* by the *Universalist denomination.*"[16] Chaney made clear that the vote to disfellowship had no reference whatever to Bisbee's character, morality, or integrity. It was a matter only of relieving both the convention and denomination "of all responsibility for whatever of error may be taught" by Bisbee.

It is impossible to determine precisely the influence of personal considerations on the convention's decision to disfellowship Bisbee, but some evidence can be adduced to support the conclusion that more than purely doctrinal conflicts entered into the judgment of both the Committee on Fellowship and Discipline, and on the vote of the convention.[17] Among those members of the committee who had reasons of their own to wish Bisbee's removal was Russell Blakely, a prominent businessman and president of the Minnesota Convention. He had never gotten along well with Bisbee from the time the latter arrived in St. Paul in 1865 and had organized a society over Blakely's opposition. Blakely seemed to have been the chief prosecutor when Bisbee's case came before the convention.

Tuttle, one of the best known and most highly respectd clergymen in the Minneapolis area, was unquestionably upset by Bisbee's public attack on his religious beliefs.[18]

Until 1873 the records of the General Convention remained curiously silent about the whole Bisbee affair, despite the fact that the controversy had been aired in the press for nearly two years; the Minnesota Convention had disfellowshipped him; and an appeal had been filed with the General Convention by the aggrieved minister. There was no mention at all, even as a matter of information, in either the minutes of the convention or in reports of committees at the 1872 convention. The fact that an appeal had been filed was noted only in part of the denominational press, the *Star in the West,* published in Cincinnati, where the convention had met.

The Bisbee case was officially brought to the denomination's attention when the General Convention met in Washington, D.C. in 1873. By then a Board of Appeal had been appointed by the trustees and had made a decision upholding the action of the Minnesota Convention.[19] The report of the board, consisting of W. H. Ryder, E. L. Rexford, Richmond Fisk, Jr., M. R. M. Wallace, J. S. Dennis, and R. H. Pullman, was presented in extraordinary detail, and covered more than a dozen pages of small print. Roughly two-thirds of the board proceedings consisted of a lengthy introduction in which the responsibilities of the board were spelled out; and the evolution, status, and nuances of interpretation of the Winchester Profession were presented in discursive fashion.

As to the nature of the complaint of "unministerial conduct," it comprised two specifications: "preaching heretical doctrines" and "unbrotherly conduct." The first was amply supported, in the view of the board, by extracts from Bisbee's printed sermons and lectures. Nothing more was needed, in fact, than his discourse on natural religion, extracts from which were read into the proceedings. The board did not confine itself to specific addresses or extracts, however, in making its determination, but condemned Bisbee for "the general drift of doctrine and statement apparent in all. . . . a sustained sentiment . . . which is antagonistic to the conviction and express belief of the Universalist Church, and subversive of the integrity and influence of the denomination."

The circumstances surrounding the delivery of the Radical Lecture series supported, according to the board, the second charge — that of "unbrotherly conduct." The very existence of the lectures indicated not only "an unfraternal feeling toward the Universalist parish in that city" but very strongly confirmed the judgment that Bisbee's teachings were "opposed to the denominational welfare, and harmful thereto." Bisbee's attacks on Tuttle's religious position, within the jurisdiction of the latter's own bailiwick, "must have compromised the character of the Universalist denomination as a Christian body" as well as humiliated Tuttle, "our faithful pastor in Minneapolis." The lectures therefore had an adverse effect on both the effectiveness of Tuttle's ministry and on the denomination as a whole. Theologically, Bisbee's position in his "unbrotherly" lectures "was inconsistent with his public professions of faithful adhesion to the Winchester Profession of Faith." So he had erred on at least two counts.

Bisbee tendered his resignation both as a Universalist minister and as a pastor of the St. Anthony church in June 1872, following his disfellowshipping by the state convention. On the request of his parish he remained until the end of the church year. In the fall he received a unanimous request from the church trustees to remain another year, or as long as his "health and sense of duty shall permit." The parish redesignated itself as the "First Independent Universalist Society," thereby indicating its willingness to withdraw from denominational jurisdiction if necessary.

The disfellowshipped pastor resigned from St. Anthony in the fall of 1872, giving ill health as the reason, and in response received a unanimous vote of confidence from the parish, and an open-ended invitation to return if and when he wished. Instead, Bisbee returned to the Boston area, where he enrolled in the Harvard Divinity School, followed by a year at Heidelberg University in Germany. After serving briefly in a church in London's East End in the spring of 1874 he returned to the United States to serve as minister of the Hawes Place Unitarian Church in South Boston. His wife having died in 1872, he married Clara Maria Babcock, the daughter of a Unitarian minister, in 1874. Bisbee died on 6 July 1879.

A significant postscript was added to the Bisbee episode in 1889, long after the details had been forgotten.[20] A great debate took place in the denominational press that year over the alleged threat of a rationalist wing which had ostensibly appeared within Universalism. It took the specific form of prolonged discussions of whether the Bible was a divinely inspired document, and more particularly whether Universalists believed literally in the miracles reported to have been performed by Christ as recorded in the New Testament. The debate was made even more acute when W. S. Crowe, pastor in Newark, New Jersey, published in the local church paper a list of some thirty Universalist clergy whom he identified as rationalists, meaning that they either denied the existence of miracles or were sufficiently ambivalent to raise suspicions about the extent of their commitment to the entire Christian drama.

The *Universalist* (Chicago), considering the heresy trial of Herman Bisbee pertinent at that point, saw fit to dredge up the report of the Board of Appeal printed in the General Convention proceedings in 1873 and adopted by that body. One of the alleged motives in reprinting the report was to justify "the claim of some that under the precedents of our church as thus shown, all those among us who are rated as 'rationalists' should go out, or be put out."

This in turn brought forth an explanation of the background of the report from Richmond Fisk, Jr., of Watertown, New York, who had served as secretary of the board and was the author of the preamble and resolutions in which the charges against Bisbee were sustained.[21] According to Fisk's account, Rexford had thought the resolutions too harsh, and had offered a substitute to the effect that the action of the Minnesota Convention should have been disapproved and that Bisbee should only have been censured for his position. That was "all the case would justly warrant." After discussion, Rexford withdrew his substitute but declined to vote. According to Fisk, two drafts of the report were submitted, one by the board chairman (Ryder), and one by Fisk. Fisk's version was considered "too elaborate and as entering too far into an analysis of the Profession of Belief." So Fisk withdrew his statement "in the interest of harmony," and Ryder's briefer version had been adopted. But it was the much more elaborate and detailed printed document which appeared in the 1873 General Convention proceedings. Fisk, Rexford, and Pullman claimed in 1889 that none of them had ever seen the version that was printed.

What had apparently happened was as follows: The final meeting of the board (23 June 1873) was called to meet in Chicago; only Ryder, Wallace, and Dennis resided there, so when Fisk received his notice it included the statement that the meeting would be 'a mere matter of form' and only those living in Chicago would actually be expected to attend. There was no record known to have been made of what took place at the rump meeting. There was no quorum present, the secretary was absent, and he was never informed of what had transpired at the Chicago meeting.

Fisk was frank to say that at the time of the trial and report, the preamble and resolutions expressed his own convictions and those of a majority of the board. But he had become convinced during the intervening years that the adoption of Rexford's statement "would have been more wise and just, and not inconsistent with the spirit and liberty of opinions we, as a church, have permitted under the Winchester Profession of Faith, since 1803." If Bisbee had not "brought himself into personal conflict with our church interests at this time, in Minneapolis, his position theologically would have doubtless passed without formal ecclesiastical challenge, as that of others did at the time, and has ever since." The board was convinced that Bisbee "had placed himself in the attitude of antagonism to organized Universalism and the church in Minneapolis."

From the very start the board had been divided over the scope of the Profession, and "the question of denominational interference with opinions of interpretation." Fisk was also positive that the lengthy arguments printed in the report would never have received the endorsement of the full board, for discussions were included over which they were honestly divided, and many of the points argued in the report were already taken for granted; they were therefore unnecessary and inappropriate, and should never have been included. He stated categorically that the printed report was "not the document to which our names were appended." As to the resolutions, they were in themselves a compromise. Ryder had warned the board that they could not go before the denomination with a divided report. So he requested Rexford to take the papers to his hotel room and write out what he would be willing to endorse, which he did. The report, as adopted by the final meeting of the board on 8 May 1873, was thus worded "to secure harmony."

In a very real sense Bisbee had become the victim of the very sectarian rigidity he had been so anxious to avoid, as well as of the expedience of the board which had sat in judgment on him. The irony was that he had found it within his own denomination, which did not officially catch up with his thinking for a quarter of a century.

In 1873 the editors of the *Register* published a brief essay entitled "The Universalist Faith," comprising a review of the adoption of the Winchester Profession and a plea for maintaining a statement of faith as a means of holding the denomination together as a Christian body. The essay may very well have been sparked by the Bisbee episode. "No doctrine which is not plainly taught in the Bible, or not fairly deducible therefrom forms any part of our faith as Universalists. Here we stand as a people, and here we have ever stood." This belief had "remained unmodified to this day, the accepted symbol (sign, token, test, standard) of our faith as Christians. The circumstances of the times demanded it." It had "proved to be a bond of unity and peace, and a source of power to us as a Christian denomination, and no serious attempt has been made either to supplant it or to improve upon it."

After quoting the Profession "in its authentic form," together with most of the prefatory and explanatory remarks of the committee which had drafted it, the author went on to note that "the great problem now awaiting practical solution in Christendom [was] how to unite freedom with order, liberality with stability, growth with permanency." The writer concluded "that creeds are not only safe, as long as they are subject to periodic revision, but they are salutary, nay, even necessary, as landmarks of growth and progress, necessary as a bond of union, fellowship and cooperation among large bodies of men. A church without a creed is smitten with paralysis, is in a false position before the world, and will be inefficient for great and critical emergencies." It is worthy of note that the author, in making allowance for "periodic revision" of creeds, omitted that part of the explanatory remarks accompanying the Profession which prohibited any future change in its wording.

Standing the Test of Time

For over seventy years after its adoption by the New England Convention in 1803 the wording of the Winchester Profession remained unchallenged, although it was considered from time to time at denominational gatherings. It had been a topic of discussion at the General Convention in 1867, when debate had been rather heated.[22] After the General Convention in 1870 had deleted the "liberty clause" which had accompanied the Profession, its phraseology became the subject of scrutiny, then controversy, which became more and more serious as the years wore on. At first the issue centered on a single word in the last clause of the second article, and was then extended to include other parts of the clause and indeed the entire Profession as the debate waxed in warmth and intensity. The clause in question expressed the belief that God would "finally restore the whole family of mankind to holiness and happiness." The most troublesome word at first was "restore."

Abel C. Thomas of Philadelphia appears to have been the individual who opened what became a theological Pandora's box. In 1875 he wrote a letter to the *Universalist* objecting to the wording "finally restore" in the Profession because it expressed an idea not held by "any Universalist in the land."[23] It was, he thought, an anachronism left over from an earlier day and had no place in any official Universalist statement. By the same token, Thomas considered the name "Church of the Restoration" in Philadelphia completely inappropriate. The edifice, serving the Second Parish, had been so designated when it had been constructed in 1872. According to Thomas, the doctrine of restoration was neither preached by its pastor, B.F. Bowles, nor believed in by the congregation.

Edwin C. Sweetser, in charge of the Third Parish in New York City at the time Thomas raised the question, immediately joined in the discussion and advocated a change in line with Thomas' expressed dissatisfaction with the wording. Sweetser recommended the substitution of the word "bring" for "restore," and in a series of articles in the *Christian Leader* and speeches on the floor of the General Convention he marshalled a host of arguments in favor of the change of wording. Inasmuch as the Profession was an integral part of its constitution (Article III, section 2, paragraph 3), an amendment was required in that document as well as in the Profession itself if any change took place.

It was Sweetser who took the initiative in attempting to pilot the change through the necessary constitutional steps. At the General Convention in Chicago in 1877 he offered a resolution calling simply for striking out the word "restore" and substituting "bring." A special committee consisting of Sweetser, J.W. Hanson, and E.L. Conger was appointed at the meeting and reported unanimously in favor of adoption. But the convention was nearing its close, and there was insufficient time to discuss the matter fully; so there was no vote. The proposal was laid over to the next convention. Even if adopted, the recommendation would have laid over for a year, in accordance with the provisions of the constitution. At the 1878 convention the recommendation was defeated by a vote of 25 to 31.[24]

Sweetser, who in 1879 became pastor of the Church of the Messiah in Philadelphia, determined to keep the proposed change of wording alive. On the eve of the next convention he wrote a lengthy article advocating the change. His principal argument was that the word "restore" in no sense represented the actual belief of the great majority of Universalists. They had never been "holy or happy" in the sense used in the Profession, any more than they had been a "fallen race" because of Adam's disaster in Eden. So how could something be restored that never existed? Sweetser carefully reviewed the arguments against the change, and countered each one.

The most frequently expressed argument against change was that the acceptance of one alteration might open the door to others. Furthermore, changing the wording would be a mark of disrespect for the founding fathers of the denomination. The word "restore" was used in the Bible and was therefore legitimate and allowable. And no better word could be found. In reply, Sweetser pointed out that ultra-conservatism, brooking no change, would stultify the denomination and prevent advancement. Universalists would be showing true reverence for the past by adhering to the spirit rather than blindly clinging to the letter. The Scriptures were not originally written in English, and even if they had been, "bring" was much more Scriptural than "restore."

Sweetser's efforts bore but little fruit. At the General Convention in 1879 a new verbal complication was introduced. Israel Washburn, Jr. attempted to substitute "lead" for "bring." The whole matter was referred to the trustees for report in 1880. One Universalist after another joined in the debate between convention meetings. One recommended that use of the word "come" or "attain" would solve the problem; A.B. Grosh defended the original wording; Sweetser defended his proposed change; Grosh disagreed with any change at all.[26] Some objected because no direct quotation from the Bible was included in the Profession.

The trustees made their report in 1880 and the majority recommended that the entire final clause be recast, so that the article would read: "We believe that there is one God, whose nature is Love, revealed by one Holy Spirit of Grace in one Lord Jesus Christ, through whom the whole family of mankind will finally attain holiness and happiness."[27] But another change was then introduced from the floor calling for transposition of some of the wording, and the entire question was indefinitely postponed. The convention was forewarned, however, that the battle over the Profession was just beginning. E.L. Rexford and Sweetser gave notice that they would offer substitute motions at the next annual meeting.

As the debate had progressed, the word "holiness" as well as "restore" was being brought into question. It was argued that the word "holiness" should probably not have been included in the Profession in the first place, for that state of being was an achievement of a strictly personal character. The responsibility for achieving it rested with the individual rather than with God.

Sweetser again brought the subject of the wording of the Profession to the attention of Universalists just prior to the 1881 General Convention by way of an article in which most of his earlier arguments were repeated.[28] He insisted that the word "restore" could be defended on neither etymological nor Biblical grounds. Further, "We are Universalists, not Restorationists. Let us make the language of our creed conform to what we really are, and to what we believe." For those who did not take the wording seriously and considered the debate little more than an exercise in semantics, Sweetser called attention to the seriousness of the situation for prospective clergymen. No persons could receive a letter of license unless they signed a printed application form. It required not only expressed assent to the Profession but included a declaration that the assent and pledge bound the individual, so long as fellowship was held, "without reservation or explanation to be in honest agreement with the above named Confession."[29]

When Sweetser's motion to substitute "bring" for "restore" came up for discussion at the 1881 convention it generated much discussion but little support. One who advocated the change was Elmer H. Capen. A substitute motion was also offered which would have worded the last clause to read: ". . . [God], who will finally save the whole family of man from sin, and thus through his love and truth produce universal holiness and happiness."

William H. Ryder, with growing impatience over the entire proceeding, delivered a sermon at the 1881 convention in which he emphasized the fact that the Profession was never intended to be a complete theological structure but provided only corner-stones. The filling in was left to personal conviction and individual conscience. Universalism was itself a system of religious thought and not simply "the dogma of the world's salvation."[30] Universalists, according to Ryder, were wasting their time over picayune details and mere verbalism by attempting to reword the Profession.

But some Universalists did not agree with Ryder. The entire subject was referred to a committee of nine which was given a free hand to reword the entire Profession as it saw fit, subject of course to convention approval. L.J. Fletcher, who made the motion, asked that he not be placed on the committee, and his request was honored. Sweetser, however, was among those appointed.

The committee, for which Henry W. Rugg served as chairman, immediately decided that its responsibility could be best carried out by personal conference rather than by mail. But for that very reason it was never able to meet at full strength. Seven members, including Sweetser and Isaac M. Atwood, who served as secretary, did manage to assemble in New York City. After devoting an entire day to the subject of the Profession, they concluded that the best strategy was to have each one submit a draft to the chairman, who would then convene another meeting. It was never held, and by the time the General Convention assembled in the fall of 1882, only five members were present. Four reached substantial agreement on a revised version immediately before the convention met, but the exact wording had not yet been perfected and the sentiments of the entire committee were still lacking. So there was no alternative but to ask for additional time.

Faced with this inconclusive result and, like Ryder, impatient with the whole matter, Charles Caverly moved that the committee be discharged, thus finally disposing of the entire question.[31] He was possibly influenced by a memorial from the Miami Association (Ohio) presented to the convention protesting any change at all in the Profession. The committee was not only continued but the president of the convention was authorized to fill any vacancies that might exist. One of the replacements immediately required was for Washburn, who had died.

In anticipation of the possibility that there might actually be an alteration in the Profession at the 1883 General Convention, a motion was made at that meeting that any such change would require assent of two-thirds of the state conventions. It was defeated. The precaution, even if it had been taken, was unnecessary, for again nothing was done. The special committee, which was never able to meet as a group because the members lived too far apart, concluded that no general revision of the creed was yet required. The Profession expressed "beyond question . . . in substance the fundamental beliefs of Universalists." The committee did, however, recommend some changes, including the substitution of the word "save" for the troublesome word "restore." The recommended alterations received support from little more than one-third of the delegates. The denomination was not yet converted to the need for modification, and certainly not to a wholesale revision.[32] After a discussion of whether to appoint a new committee and start all over, the report was recommitted. One irritated delegate thought there were more urgent matters needing attention than rewording the Profession.

The committee duly made its report in 1884. Both the phrase "holiness and happiness" and the word "restore" were dropped, so that the last clause of Article II of the Profession read "save the whole family of mankind." However, there was insistence from the floor that "holiness and happiness" be retained. The editor of the *Leader* insisted that God's purpose was clear and undebatable; but agreement broke down as to the methods and procedures employed by God to achieve the final holiness and happiness of all. Nobody seemed to know.[33]

Alonzo A. Miner tried the same tactic in 1885, again unsuccessfully, that he had used the previous year; namely, to table indefinitely all attempts to revise the Profession. He was more interested in obtaining resolutions advocating total abstinence and the outlawing of war than in rewording the Universalist document. On a motion by Sweetser a three-man committee, of which he was one, was created to consider amending the Profession.

The only action taken in 1886 was the granting of further time to the special committee. The reason for the delay was obvious when its report was presented in 1887. The committee had decided that, rather than attempt to amend the Profession "in some particulars," it was proper to frame an essentially new statement that would most adequately express a "living faith." The committee offered the following, as amended from the convention floor:

> 1. I believe that the Holy Scriptures of the Old and New Testaments contain a revelation from God to mankind.
> 2. I believe in one God, the Father Almighty, Maker of heaven and earth; in Jesus Christ, His Son, who is the Revealer of God and the Saviour of the world; and in His Holy Spirit, the Comforter, through which all disciples of Christ are united in one spiritual body.
> 3. I believe in the necessity of personal regeneration; in the forgiveness of sins; in the certainty of retribution; in the immortality of the human soul; and in the final holiness and happiness of all mankind.
> 4. I believe that the opportunities, obligations and rewards of religion are in their nature eternal, and of such immediate urgency that I ought to strive earnestly for present salvation, by repenting of my sins and diligently using the means of grace which, in His mercy, God has provided for me.[34]

The committee admitted that the wording may have been the result of compromise, but that Universalist truths, as they saw them, were correctly and adequately expressed. The committee made a plea for "brotherly concession" as to phraseology so that the whole matter could be laid to rest. But the delegates refused to comply and proceeded to make no less than six changes of wording from the floor.

The report of the committee in 1887 had precipitated an animated discussion which lasted almost three hours.[35] As Miner pointed out, a controversy which had begun over the single word "restore" had by 1887 developed into "a profound revolution — a complete reconstruction" which was not at all to his liking. He considered the entire structure of the revised statement "clumsy, wholly lacking in the wisdom which constructed the old Profession." The word "Christian" was not even included. Atwood expressed a completely opposite viewpoint. A new creed was inevitable, for the 1803 statement was woefully out of date; there had to be an end to forcing modern interpretations into an anachronistic framework. But the drift of the debate was clear. As T.J. Sawyer stated it, the time for a new creed had not yet come.

After verbal amendments were accepted, the proposed statement was laid over for further consideration at the next convention. It appeared to be an endless process, for the revised Profession fared no better at the 1888 convention, by which time the proposed new document had been expanded to five articles. Back it went to a reconstituted committee of five. One member had died in the meantime. Equipped with a new three-paragraph version submitted by Orello Cone, the committee's only instructions were to "report at a subsequent session of the convention."

Although debate over revision dominated the proceedings of the 1889 session, again nothing was accomplished. The committee presented a unanimous report recommending a five-article statement of faith, to which assent was to be required for fellowship. But before the session was over, the committee produced another version, this time reduced to three articles. It was referred to the next session of the convention which became biennial beginning in 1891. At the 1889 session the General Convention did reaffirm its position, held from the very beginning, that the church "rests on and believes in the historical veracity of the New Testament records of the life, and words, and works of our Lord Jesus Christ."

As the denomination prepared for its convention in 1891 many Universalists had come to at least two conclusions: The Winchester Profession could never be amended so as to satisfy the entire church; and no statement could be devised to replace the Profession on which all Universalists could agree.[36] One way suggested out of the dilemma was to allow each society or church to formulate its own statement. The only restriction would be that whatever was adopted had to be consistent with the "general consensus of our Church."

By the time the whole question had again been postponed (until 1893), revision of the creed had become a sore point. Tempers had become ragged and patience short. One clergyman, Walter Dole of Vermont, reported that the stalemate had created actual hostility and bitterness, and a reluctance on the part of many even to discuss the matter. He was dismayed that, at three different state convention sessions, he had been prevented from speaking on the subject. Either he had been declared out of order, or the topic had been immediately tabled.[37] He detected an unfortunate polarization in the denomination. At one extreme were the younger clergy who professed complete indifference or looked with amusement or ill-disguised contempt on efforts to revamp the creed. At the other extreme were the older, more conservative clergy who would brook no change whatever. Caught in the middle were those sincerely trying to modify — and presumably improve — the existing Profession to make it coincide more closely with denominational realities.

The extremes were illustrated by Miner, representing the older generation, who did his best to block every effort to change a single word; and Julian S. Cutler, ordained in 1885 and pastor of the church in Melrose, Massachusetts. He considered the entire agitation as an exercise in futility because the days of creed-making had long since passed. Such documents were as obsolete as the warming-pan, the tallow candle, and the stagecoach.

The prolongation of discussions about the Winchester Profession brought mounting criticism from clergy and laity alike. A.N. Alcott, pastor of the church in Elgin, Illinois, noted that the Profession had become "a sort of battle-ground where microscopic criticism and finical niceties, rather than the salvation of men, absorb too much energy and time in our biennial gatherings."[38] Other Universalists put their concern into a larger context. One was afraid that many Universalists would desert the denomination and be driven into the Unitarian camp. Another feared that public knowledge of the controversy would make the denomination ridiculous in the eyes of others as they frittered away their time in heated arguments over mere wording.[39]

In 1893 the revision committee, which by this time had been reduced to three individuals, took a long, hard look at the entire question in their report to the convention, and came to two conclusions: There was a clear indisposition to stop with any mere verbal amendments; and there was an equally clear disposition to find an equally brief substitute. As to the first, it seemed obvious that every conceivable substitute for the much-criticized word "restore" had been considered and had been decisively discarded. There seemed no alternative but to recommend an entirely new profession. The committee thereupon submitted an even briefer statement than the original one, substantially the same as another committee had presented eight years earlier.

A new complication was introduced in 1893 when the very right and power of the General Convention to tamper with the Profession was challenged. Some delegates thought that changes of any kind could be made only by state conventions or even by individual churches and parishes, although nothing seemed clear on that point. The result of the debates on the Profession in 1893 was easily predictable. The committee report was referred to the next session. Nonetheless, the matter would not be downed. At the 1893 session a resolution was referred to the trustees which foreshadowed later developments. A statement was proposed to the effect that, while Universalists recognized the Winchester Profession as the basis of general church fellowship, each parish and church should be free to adopt its own version so long as it was consistent with denominational religious principles.

The action of the General Convention which met in Meriden, Connecticut, in 1895, was completely unexpected and caught almost everyone off guard. After various amendments to the creed proposed by the committee in 1893 had been made from the floor, the revised Profession was adopted by a vote of 69 to 15, more than the necessary two-thirds required to amend the constitution of the convention.

The revised creed, heavily freighted with Biblical language reflecting the King James version, read as follows:

> 1. We believe in the universal Fatherhood of God and in the universal Brotherhood of Man.
> 2. We believe that God, who hath spoken through all His holy prophets since the world began, hath spoken to us by His Son, Jesus Christ, our Example and Saviour.
> 3. We believe that Salvation consists in spiritual oneness with God, who, through Christ, will finally gather in one the whole family of mankind.

The new version had been drafted by Sweetser and Charles W. Tomlinson. Cone, the third member of the committee, later admitted that he had had no part in drafting it, and had not really considered the wording with sufficient care before signing it.[40]

Sweetser had tried for eighteen years to have the word "restore" deleted from the Winchester Profession and the word "bring" substituted. The debate in the General Convention had begun in 1877 and the proposal for a simple word change had broadened year by year into a full-blown argument that went far beyond a single word, to new clauses, then new paragraphs, and finally wholesale substitution. Was this what the denomination really wanted?

At first the *Christian Leader,* so far as its editors had expressed themselves in print, had supported the idea of change. But after almost two decades of fruitless debates, proposals, and counterproposals by individuals, committees, and conventions, the denominational paper changed its stance. The editors had become exasperated by 1894 and lectured Universalists on the absolute impossibility of compressing the full theology of an entire denomination into three articles of three or four lines each.[41] According to their interpretation, the authors of the original Profession had consciously sought "to see how little else they could say." They had deliberately left all the details "to self-expansion, developments, growth."

Over a decade earlier, Miner had expressed much the same idea. In an explication of "The Doctrines of Universalism" he had quoted the Winchester Profession in a footnote and had added the comment that "the Universalist Church congratulates itself on the brevity, simplicity, and comprehensiveness of its Confession of Faith."[42]

By 1895 the *Leader* could no longer endorse change. The entire character of the Profession had been so basically altered that the paper could do nothing else than oppose what amounted not to a revision of the original but its displacement by another version.[43] It proceeded to publish an extended analysis which carried over into several issues. Not surprisingly, Sweetser had replied with a long rebuttal, followed by a counter-reply.

After the unexpected turn of events at Meriden, the *Leader* predicted that eventual acceptance of what in effect was an entirely new Profession would be equally unexpected. The proposal for a new Profession created a torrent of correspondence to the *Leader*, nearly all of which was opposed to the change. One communicant summarized the whole matter by pointing out that almost everyone had a version to present — at least 1,000; only modesty saved 999 of them from being offered. Another correspondent, who saw no logic or reason for a new three-point creed, put his version into one sentence: "We believe in the Universal Fatherhood of God, the universal brotherhood of man, the leadership of Jesus, the inspiration of Scripture truth, and the ultimate righteousness of all mankind."[44]

Discussion and debate over the revised Profession were lively, to say the least. At a meeting of the New England Conference of Ministers (Universalist), Frank Oliver Hall and Richard Eddy each presented a paper on the subject "Do We Need a New Creed?" Hall spoke for the affirmative and Eddy for the negative. One advocate of the revised statement insisted at a symposium at the Connecticut Convention that the 1803 declaration had all the earmarks of Calvinism, was trinitarian in its implications, unmistakably implied the dogma of the fall of man, and was commercial in its ethics.[45] This interpretation naturally provoked disagreement, but the discussion at least provided "a very entertaining, possibly an instructive, evening's service."[46]

At a meeting of the Union Association (Massachusetts) in 1896 a resolution was offered recommending the adoption of the new version. It was overwhelmingly defeated. The sentiments of one laywoman were expressed in unequivocal terms: If the new version were adopted, there would be, in effect, two competing creeds for those who had been reared on the 1803 statement. "I'd as soon take something out of my Bible as to give up the old creed."[47] The suggestion was made that every proposed change of creed be submitted to the members of each church and determined by popular vote. The matter would thus be settled by a completely democratic process.

The Declaration of 1899

The months preceding the biennial meeting of the General Convention in 1897 were especially busy ones for those interested in what was to happen to the "creed question." The editors of the *Leader* did their best to keep the denomination informed, and even published a "creed issue" which provided a forum for all viewpoints.[48] Some felt that the entire future of the church depended on retaining the Winchester Profession unaltered. One Universalist predicted that the denomination would break up in the course of a few months if a vote prevailed to change the Profession in any way. The editors of the *Leader,* after printing dozens of communications in numerous issues, finally begged for mercy.

The fate of the Profession was unquestionably the paramount concern of the 124 delegates as they assembled in St. Paul's Universalist Church in Chicago in 1897. Memorials had been received from state conventions in all parts of the nation expressing one sentiment or another. The Vermont and Quebec Convention urged sufficient amendment to the 1803 Profession to make it "conform to the actual belief of our Church." The Georgia Convention went on record "emphatically in favor" of the existing Profession. Fifty members of the historic church in Winchester, New Hampshire, where the Profession had been adopted, expressed their firm belief in the original document exactly as it stood. They predicted that if the General Convention insisted on any change, calamity would result, with withdrawal of numerous parishes from the denomination.[49]

T.E. Ballard, a delegate from Indiana, then presented on the floor of the convention a memorial from his state convention protesting the revised version. It was contended that the proposed rewording of the creed constituted "such a sweeping and radical change in the fundamental articles of faith" that the denomination would jeopardize, as a result of judicial interpretation, its possession of thousands of dollars of church property. The promulgation of what the Indiana Convention considered "a substantially new and different faith" would make the action of the General Convention illegal and null and void, by creating, in effect, a new doctrinal base and hence a new denomination.

A procedural snag immediately developed over whether to proceed immediately to a roll-call vote, without discussion, on the revision which had been so substantially supported two years earlier. Ballard, speaking on behalf of the Indiana Convention, insisted that any vote without opportunity for discussion was out of order. Charles L. Hutchinson, the presiding officer, ruled that the revised creed adopted at Meriden in 1895 was to be considered exactly as worded, without amendment and without discussion. The convention sustained his judgment.

How much influence the remonstrance from Indiana had in determining the outcome is a moot question. But there was no ambiguity about the vote. The revised profession of faith adopted in 1895 went down in resounding defeat, 1 in favor and 102 against. One of the seven delegates from Pennsylvania cast the sole affirmative vote. It was the solitary voice of Sweetser.[50]

However, the "creed question" at the convention was by no means settled. Under a suspension of the rules, a proposal known as the "Boston Plan" was presented on behalf of a group of Massachusetts clergy and endorsed by several state conventions. It was discussed and amended by one delegate after another. Everyone was so caught up in the deliberations that two delegates scheduled to deliver addresses waived the privilege and postponed them. In the midst of it all, Eddy dramatically produced the original copy of the Profession, in the handwriting of Walter Ferriss, the principal framer of the document, and presented it to the convention.

Then a delegate from Indiana who wanted no change at all, and knowing very well what the fate of his proposal would be, moved that a twenty-five person committee be created from among those who wanted change of some sort. If they could make a *unanimous* report, then he would accept the changes. The disposition of that motion was not difficult to predict.

The so-called Boston Plan had been the outgrowth of discussions early in 1897. The Boston Ministers Association, not satisfied with the 1895 statement, had decided to try their hand at revision of the creed and had appointed a special committee headed by George T. Knight, a member of the faculty of the Tufts Divinity School. He had already decided that people were "becoming disgusted with the long delay."[51]

Knight's first step had been to send out questionnaires to churches in the Boston area soliciting information about what creeds, if any, were then in use. Forty-one churches produced twenty-two different versions, ranging from one article to seven. The only common denominators were the principles of the fatherhood of God, the leadership of Jesus, and the ultimate salvation of all.[52] Other churches replying required subscription to no creed at all as a condition of membership or fellowship. Given the state of affairs which seemed to prevail among Universalists regarding the Profession and its status, the Boston-area ministers had then decided to recommend to the forthcoming General Convention both the retention of the Winchester statement without amendment, and the adoption of an alternate statement which might be equally acceptable. This would give Universalists a choice.

The vote for the Boston Plan was at first lost (76-32), being six votes short of the two-thirds majority required. Reconsideration was then voted. The author of the account in the *Leader* noted that the marked feature of the discussion preceding that vote "was not its ability in considering the question at issue, but the introduction of all sorts of motions and points of order that kept the audience in a continual state of wonder." The proposal was debated for more than an hour, with numerous amendments from the floor. It was then adopted by a vote of 94 to 30, all of the delegates voting. At least a semblance of unity had somehow prevailed over diversity. Ratification at the 1899 session was the next step.

The "Chicago Declaration," as the new statement came to be known, no longer required acceptance of the Winchester Profession as a condition of fellowship. It was offered as an alternative. A new article (III) was to be added to the convention constitution, worded as follows:

"Creed and Conditions of Fellowship"

1. The Profession of Faith adopted by this body at its session at Winchester, N.H., A.D. 1803, is as follows: [Here the words of the original Profession.]
2. The conditions of fellowship in this Convention shall be as follows:
  I. The acceptance of the essential principles of the Universalist faith, to wit: The Universal Fatherhood of God; the spiritual authority and leadership of His Son Jesus Christ; the trustworthiness of the Bible as containing a revelation from God; the certainty of just retribution for sin; the final harmony of all souls with God. The Winchester Profession is commended as containing these principles, but neither this, nor any other precise form of words, is required as a condition of fellowship, provided always that the principles above stated be professed.
  II. The acknowledgement of the authority of the General Convention and assent to its laws.

After the experience at Chicago there were few predictions recorded about the outcome of the next vote on the Profession. There was, in fact, very little discussion in the denominational press concerning the entire matter until the weeks immediately preceding the convention. The denomination, after almost a quarter of a century of struggle, was apparently ready to accept what had been hammered out in 1897. There was, too, a general feeling of satisfaction with the way in which a troublesome problem had been resolved.

The Congress of Liberal Religions, consisting predominantly of Unitarians, greeted the action of the General Convention with tolerant amusement. Jenkin Lloyd Jones, one of the leaders in the Liberal Congress, noted that the Winchester Profession had finally become "an abandoned relic . . . [to] be preserved for archeological purposes."[53] Universalists had finally realized that belief had become a matter of private judgment rather than of ecclesiastical determination.

Rodney F. Johonnot, Universalist pastor in Oak Park, Illinois, and active in the Liberal Congress, greeted the adoption of the Chicago Declaration with great satisfaction. This action marked "the dawn of a new day for this denomination."[54] It had not only put an end to a controversy that had wasted Universalist energies for more than twenty years but had put the denomination on a purely non-creedal basis. In so doing Universalists had brought themselves into harmony with "the pronounced tendencies of the age."

There was one Universalist, Ballard of Indiana, who recorded his dissatisfaction on the eve of the 1899 convention. However, it was with only one of the "Five Principles" and not with the new Declaration as a whole. It was he who had presented at the Chicago session in 1897 the memorial from his state convention opposing the proposed Declaration, and who had challenged the ruling that no discussion was to be allowed.

The principle to which he objected was the fourth, "the certainty of just retribution for sin." It had not been a part of the Declaration as originally presented, but had been added on the floor of the convention, by unanimous vote. No objection had been raised to it at the time except from those who opposed any change whatever in the wording of the Profession itself.

Ballard argued that the fourth principle sounded retaliatory and more reminiscent of "partialist" (orthodox) beliefs than Universalist, and was completely out of harmony with denominational precepts.[55] Ballard was strongly supported by J.W. Hanson, who in addition contended that the implication that the Winchester Profession contained all of the five principles was not only misleading but false. Nowhere in it was there any declaration about retribution, either expressed or implied.[56] Furthermore, according to Hanson, the reference to the Holy Spirit was entirely missing from the Declaration of Principles. Ignoring the wording of the original Profession would put the Universalists in the unenviable position of being the only Christian denomination to omit reference to the Holy Spirit in their official statements of belief. This was in reality rejecting "the divine dynamics of Christian progress." Hanson apparently misread the whole intention of the Declaration; namely, to provide an acceptable alternative to the Profession rather than to replicate it.

Sweetser, who had seen so many of his own recommendations ignored, sidetracked, or defeated, defended the inclusion of the fourth principle. He thought it would be "a great pity" if any attempt were made to prevent its adoption.[57] He did, however, agree with Hanson regarding the desirability of including a reference in the new Declaration to "the sanctifying influence of the Holy Spirit" as a Universalist principle. Sweetser made a fruitless attempt at the 1899 meeting to amend the Declaration accordingly.[58]

In anticipation of what was already being described as "the great Historic Convention of 1899," the Universalist Publishing House prepared half-tone facsimilies (11" by 16") of the original Profession which sold at 15 cents. G. L. Demarest, secretary of the convention, prepared a history of the many attempts to amend the Profession from 1877 through 1897, which was published in the *Leader*.[59]

The Boston meeting of 1899 represented a high point in the history of the denomination. The number in attendance surpassed even that of the great centennial convocation in Gloucester in 1870. There was an overflow at almost every session. In sharp contrast to the conventions of 1895 and 1897, the adoption of a new statement of belief passed so routinely that it was anti-climactic. The motion to amend the convention constitution and ratify the action of the Chicago meeting was made by Henry B. Metcalf of Rhode Island. Of the members present and voting, 132 favored ratification and only 10 were opposed; 104 votes had been necessary. The convention had proceeded at once to a roll-call vote. There was no discussion, no debate, no quibbling over terminology or phraseology. The Chicago Declaration of 1897 had become the Boston Declaration of 1899 with none of the turmoil that had accompanied and followed most of the earlier efforts at revision.

The widespread feeling that the denomination had finally gotten what it had desired for so many decades was confirmed. The *Leader* had greeted the Chicago Declaration with great enthusiasm. The logjam had at last been broken. Universalists could now get about their business with a renewed sense of purpose. "The Universalist Church has been reborn."[60] This sense of confidence had been reinforced in 1899. The Winchester Profession had become a document of "historic interest . . . a symbol to which there is a strong sentimental attachment . . . revered for its associations and its accumulated history."[61]

Universalists, theologically speaking, had seemed finally to have achieved the best of both worlds. They had retained unchanged the original Profession which many Universalists considered sacred. They had also kept the faith with the old New England Convention which, after adopting the Profession, had specified that "there is no alteration on any part of the three articles that contain the Profession of our Belief ever to be made at any future period." The convention in 1899 had simultaneously returned the Profession to its pre-1870 status by restoring the idea of the "liberty clause." At the same time, it had offered an alternative — "the essential principles of the Universalist faith." No one thereafter need feel compromised in any way; everyone was free to follow either or both paths.

The *Leader* thenceforth carried the Five Principles on the masthead of every issue, and in 1923 the General Convention instructed the Universalist Publishing House to include the "liberty clause" as well.[62]

Writing within the context of the 175th anniversary of the denomination in 1920, Frederic W. Perkins noted that the twenty-five year battle over phraseology had not been the real issue. Outwardly it may have seemed to be a controversy over wording, but actually the issue was not the adequacy of this or that creedal statement but whether "any creedal statement had a right to fix the official form in which the Universalist faith must be expressed."[63] The stalemate had been broken by the restoration of a freshly worded "liberty clause." Creeds, he wrote, were not to be considered as "tests, but as testimonials, as voices, confessedly inadequate, of the larger, living faith behind them." It "set up a charter of Christian liberty, a statement of principles intended to rally believers rather than to expel heretics." Here was an express repudiation of the mind-set that had resulted in the disfellowshipping of Herman Bisbee in 1872.

The *Leader* commented editorially on the significance of the new declaration and Perkins' interpretation of it with the assertion that Universalists had finally recovered their own heritage as "free members of free churches."

There were lingering doubts in the minds of a few, and some misunderstanding about what the denomination had done. A small number of clergy who had been received into the church exclusively on the basis of the Winchester Profession were hesitant and dubious about their status as well as that of the Profession itself. One went so far as to interpret the action of the General Convention as legislating him out of the denomination.[64] He was assured that the Profession remained absolutely unchanged and that his status as well as that of others like him, had in no way been altered. Merely another choice had been provided for those unwilling to accept every word of the original statement.

There were also some who lacked understanding outside the denomination about what the Universalists had done. The press, both secular and religious, had given the revised statement national publicity.[65] Many papers erroneously referred to the Boston Declaration as a "new creed." One Universalist clergyman tried to set the record straight by pointing out that what had been adopted was neither new nor a creed.[66] The Universalists had consciously avoided the term "creed" when the Winchester statement had been originally adopted, as had the authors of the alternate statement.

The Declaration of 1899 represented no change of belief but merely the culmination of a lengthy effort to express with greater clarity existing beliefs. There was no novelty in the Five Principles. The Declaration taken as a whole signified the fact that the church, from its very beginning, had been "a developing church, an organism steadily unfolding from an imperishable germinal principle to larger and fuller belief and life." Universalism had turned no abrupt corners but had exhibited continuous growth since it had issued its "Declaration of Religious Independence" in 1803.[67]

It was in this manner that the Universalist Church adapted to theological change for the remainder of its existence as a separate and independent denomination. The Winchester Profession was never officially repealed, repudiated, or replaced. It coexisted with, and was incorporated into, the Chicago Declaration of 1897, and later existed side by side with the Washington Declaration of 1935 (the Bond of Fellowship and Statement of Faith).

J.S. Cantwell, in his address delivered as part of the centennial celebration of the Profession in 1903, had asserted that nothing in the course of a century had endangered "the ancient Winchester Faith."[68] In 1916 John Coleman Adams had been even more confident about the durability of the Profession. It was still standing that year "as the historic and official statement of faith of the Universalist Church in America." The very adoption of the "saving clause" in the form of an alternative set of principles in 1899 had only strengthened the statement of 1803. "Thus the spirit of the historic Profession is preserved and a new and perennial lease of life conferred upon it."[69]

Writing in 1921, Lewis B. Fisher, long-time dean of the Ryder Divinity School in Chicago, somewhat cynically characterized the Five Principles as "a truce of fatigue rather than the victory of any particular faction."[70] As he looked back to the twenty-five years in which the General Convention meetings were admittedly "gladiatorial arenas," F.W. Perkins in 1923 took somewhat more elevated ground than had Fisher. Perkins referred to the restoration of the "liberty clause" as "a charter of Christian liberty," and reaffirmed the Universalist principle that "our living bond of union is loyalty to a faith, not assent to a creed."[71]

The relevance of at least part of the original Profession for a later day was underscored in the fall of 1978 by Dorothy Tilden Spoerl, a Unitarian Universalist minister, in a keynote address delivered in the Winchester, New Hampshire, church on the occasion of the 175th anniversary of the adoption of the Profession.[72] After reviewing the circumstances under which the document had been composed, and after linking it to the centennial of 1903, Spoerl placed the admonition in the third paragraph of the Profession—to "practice good works, for these things are good and profitable unto men" — in the context of twentieth-century efforts to achieve "the good society."

While much of the literal meaning had long since given way to modern scholarship and thought, there was still an aura of timelessness about the three articles adopted in 1803.[73] It remained an enduring monument to a liberal religious faith.

Chapter 7

Science and Religion: A Debate Avoided

Universalists in general took a keen interest in science long before the Civil War, and the modern tone of much of the thought and writing of the first half of the nineteenth century impressed at least one mid-twentieth century scholar. An editorial in a Universalist newspaper written in 1837, entitled "Science and Christianity," "could almost as well have been written a hundred years later."[1]

Although submerged much of the time, there was a persistent rationalistic tendency in the denomination in the nineteenth century. And the widely asserted belief of Universalists in freedom of interpretation made acceptance of, or at least adaptation to, the rapidly changing currents of modern science more than a possibility. Hence, in spite of some doubts or even a few protests, Universalists could and did, for the most part, find intellectually satisfactory ways of meshing and modifying traditional and inherited belief with rapid and sometimes bewildering and even contradictory changes of the latter half of the nineteenth century.

Taken as a group, Universalists also had an attitude or mind-set which made them receptive to new ideas, and allowed them to keep abreast, if not ahead of, their times in responding to the intellectual currents of the day. This relative openmindedness was expressed succinctly in 1874 by Elbridge Gerry Brooks (1816-1878). Universalists, by their very nature, must be

> open, receptive, inquiring. . . . A true religion has nothing to fear from any true science. Science is the knowledge of God's doings demonstrated to our reason; religion is the knowledge of the same God revealed to our faith. Let science explore and demonstrate wheresoever or whatsoever it may, then, the religion that has God's truth in it can possibly come to no harm. . . . We should welcome discovery, therefore, and keep abreast of the most advanced knowledge, that we may see how all truth harmonizes.[2]

One of the early primary concerns among pre-Civil War clergy was to harmonize if possible the Biblical account of creation with the findings of historical geology.[3] The conception of evolution and of development over time could of course be traced back as far as the ancient world, but had not created the potential for disagreement or conflict until they directly challenged the Old Testament version, with its cataclysmic interpretation of instant creation by divine intervention. Beginning with the first half of the nineteenth century, when the science of historical geology began to take on modern attributes, the problem of explaining and reconciling its evidence with the Mosaic account became more and more pressing.

One of the more sophisticated arguments by a Universalist showing the evolutionary nature of the universe and of man, based on geological records, was published in a denominational paper in 1843.[4] The unidentified writer declared that there was nothing in the findings of geology that ran counter to the Mosaic account because the "days" referred to in the Old Testament actually meant "epochs," "ages," or "generations." Therefore both the earth and its inhabitants had evolved over a long period of time, the span for human development having been at least 6,000 years. Much the same argument was offered in the 1840s by the author of an article in the *Universalist Quarterly,* the denominational scholarly journal in which most of the articles dealing with science appeared, entitled "Geology and Scripture."[5]

Thomas Starr King, heralded as both a Unitarian and a Universalist denominationally, in a day before such association was generally acceptable, no doubt startled some of his readers when, in an article published in 1847, he presented a pantheistic interpretation of the relation of science and religion.[6] He stated that "there is hardly a tenet of the Christian Scriptures that has not been unfolded or confirmed by the researches of science," and went on to say that the findings of scientists like Copernicus, Kepler, Newton, and LaPlace enlarged one's views of the grandeur of the universe while simultaneously "measuring the grandeur of the Deity." King found that "a delicate correspondence connects every beast, and bird, and tree, and flower, with some type of thought, or passion, or emotion, present in the Creator's mind at their formation, and of which they are the organized exponents." Even "the boldest speculations of modern science, which tell us that men have risen by gradual development from inorganic matter," were to be found at least hinted at in Christian revelation.

In 1851 a combined review in the *Quarterly* of Edward Hitchcock's *The Religion of Geology and its Connected Sciences* and John Pye Smith's *On the Relations between the Holy Scriptures and Some Parts of Geological Science* was generally favorable. The two works confirmed the belief that "the teachings of geology, rightly understood, do not conflict with the statements of Revelation, rightly interpreted."[7] The reviewer's main criticism of both works was that they were "tinctured with . . . Calvinist views of theology."

Another author presented an extended review of Hugh Miller's *The Testimony of the Rocks; or, Geology in its Bearings on the Two Theologies, Natural and Revealed* (1857), and found no conflict. Findings in science became only one more manifestation of the unfolding of the divine plan and purpose as a form of progressive revelation.[8] The Middlesex (Massachusetts) Sabbath School Union sponsored discussions of the relation between science and religion in 1859, and all of the speakers urged the study of science to correct errors of ignorance and superstition.[9] One commended the work of Alexander von Humboldt, the German naturalist, for furthering the partnership of science and the New Testament, while another stressed the need to study science as a means of achieving "a better understanding of the works of God."

Between the end of the Civil War and the turn of the twentieth century a series of intellectual developments ushered in what one scholar has called a "critical period" in American religious history, when the traditional certainties were being challenged by new theories, new methodologies, and exciting new findings.[10] Among the most dramtic and far-reaching was the theory of biological evolution offered by the British naturalist Charles R. Darwin (1809–1882) and buttressed by a massive array of supporting evidence. Another development, with origins in the early nineteenth century, which had a profound and unsettling effect, although not as well known outside the scholarly community, was a series of studies of the Bible embraced under the term "Higher Criticism."[11]

A third development which resulted in a basic rethinking of the Christian tradition was the emergence of the study of comparative religion. James Freeman Clarke's *Ten Great Religions*, first published in 1871 and which went through numerous editions, opened the door for the American reading public to the intriguing field of non-Christian religions. He jolted many by revealing that Christianity was syncretic and derivative rather than unique, and that it shared many common denominators with other religions.[12]

These new findings were brought into sharp focus for many by the World's Parliament of Religions in 1893, attended by thousands, and in which Universalists were actively involved.

Darwinian evolution substituted constant change in animal life for a static conception of creation, and explained the process in natural rather than in theistic terms although the possibility of a First Cause was not completely ruled out. Added to the shock of these challenges to the prevailing Biblical account of creation were the results of textual criticism which turned what was thought to have been a divinely inspired document of infallible authority into a compilation of history, folklore, literature, and prophecy, all assembled over a period of hundreds of years by an undetermined number of very human beings in a series of identifiable historical contexts.

Darwin's *On the Origin of Species by Means of Natural Selection,* published in 1859 with an American edition in 1860, eventually aroused a storm of controversy in the nation at large. Although the application to the human race was not spelled out until the *Descent of Man* (1871), the implications in the earlier work were clear.[13]

The findings of science in the post-1865 period, and particularly the Darwinian challenge to the Bible account of creation, inevitably posed problems for Universalists who had historically put great trust in the Scriptures and had made a place for the Bible in both the Winchester Profession of 1803 and the Declaration of Principles of 1899, although in neither case did they call for a literal interpretation which gave so much trouble to other Protestant denominations.

In an article published in 1854 and entitled "The Bible a Sufficient Revelation from God to Man," a Universalist pointed out that

> as a denomination, Universalists have heretofore been distinguished among the various Christian sects for their strong attachment and fidelity to the Bible. It is the armory from which all the weapons of our successful warfare have been drawn. . . . they depended wholly on the sacred Scriptures, interpreted by enlightened reason, to refute the arguments of their opponents, and to sustain the great principles of the doctrine they inculcated. . . . and the unparalleled success which attended their labors can be attributed to no other cause than their strong attachment to the Bible, and their faithful application of its sanctifying truths.[14]

Any deviation from this, including attempts to substitute "the lights of science and philosophy," would result in the diminution of "the cause of truth."

Universalists had been cool toward, if not actually repelled by, the pre-Civil War transcendentalist movement so popular among Unitarians, and the vast majority had rejected what had been called "the Great Rationalist Craze: 1840–1855."[15] G. T. Flanders, who had no use for those among his fellow Universalists who questioned the divine authority of the Scriptures, including accounts of miracles, identified fourteen members of the denomination who had become rationalists or propagated rationalist ideas during the period. Jonathan Kidwell of Indiana led the list, which included Josiah Upson, O. D. Miller, Andrew Jackson Davis, S. B. Brittain, William Fishbough, and Thomas L. Harris. Harris was at one time pastor of what became the Church of the Divine Paternity in New York City. Horace Greeley had been an admirer and patron of Harris until the latter "became so baldly rationalistic [that] Mr. Greeley felt compelled to give him up."[16]

The burden of Flanders' reminiscences (written in 1889) was that all of the mid-nineteenth-century rationalists had either come to no good end in their professional or personal lives, or had, as was the case with Harris, returned to belief in the supernatural inspiration of the Scriptures. Flanders reminded Universalists that rationalism had reared its ugly head long before and had met within the denomination the fate he thought it deserved — a thorough and complete discrediting. The rationalist of a later day was "simply keeping a theological junk-shop and retailing second-hand goods. It is a dismal business that don't [sic] pay; and the sooner it is closed up the better it will be for all parties concerned."

But rationalism, regardless of the form it might take, would not be downed. A. R. Abbott told the readers of the *Trumpet* in 1863 that the Bible was not to be taken literally.[17] The purpose of Revelation was "entirely foreign" to that of mere physical science. "A scientific account of creation is about as far as anything could well be imagined from the purpose of the first chapter of Genesis." The instruction provided in the Bible was intended to show that heavens and earth owed their existence to God; i.e., its teachings were moral and religious, not scientific. The "drapery" in which religious ideas were presented was admittedly a bit dramatic, if not fanciful at times, but "do not reject this great corner-stone of all religious belief because it does not come measured and squared by the line and compass of physical science."

Readers of Scripture must get rid of "the preposterous assumption that the Bible *must* be our teacher in all departments of science as well as in morals and religion. It matters not whether the creation took place six thousand years ago, or six millions." The drama of creation was expressed in figurative and symbolic terms in order to get an important idea across and was not to be taken word-for-word. This was a somewhat more enlightened explanation than the one attributed to the evangelist Dwight L. Moody, who dismissed all such arguments because the Bible was not meant to be understood anyway.

Much the same interpretation that Abbott had offered almost a decade earlier, appeared in 1872. George S. Weaver (1818–1908), a Universalist clergyman long interested in geology and astronomy, was the author of some fourteen books. In one he intended to demonstrate that the Mosaic account of creation, perceived through a series of visions, metaphors, and allegories, and the scientific account, were in substantial agreement.[18] He presented the earth's evolution in a series of stages. Volcanic action, as part of a lengthy cooling-off period, was followed by vegetable and then animal creation, to which geology testified. Each of the six days of creation was carefully explained in logical sequence; all was part of the grand design of the Deity, each order higher in the cosmic scale, with human beings as "the key-stone of the arch of the creation."[19] It was an exciting and exhilarating tableau in which God was "creating a home for a family of immortals . . . [an] aspect of the creation . . . sublime beyond expression.

... [the] last and lord of all. ... the crowning excellence of the Creator's work on earth."[20]

Advocates of women's rights could take unqualified satisfaction from Weaver's interpretation of the allegory of Adam and Eve in the Garden of Eden that "no superiority is given to either. They are the equal parts of the human creation," two balanced parts of a single unity.[21] The account of the fall of man which became a staple ingredient of Calvinism and its successors, was to be considered as a parable, not to be taken literally; it was never "intended for rational belief." Sin originated with humankind, not with God or a non-existent devil, and it was only human nature to find a scapegoat and blame something or somebody else. Each is responsible for his or her own acts. Even the account of the great flood, familiar to so many generations of Sunday school pupils, was subject to a natural (and therefore rational) explanation.

In one respect at least, Universalist reaction to Darwin followed closely the national pattern. The full implications of his theories were neither realized nor discussed in detail until after 1870, and the flood tide was reached in the 1880s and 1890s.[22] Darwin's two major works were never reviewed in detail in the *Quarterly* although a reference to him occurs in an article on "Animal Instinct and Reason" published in 1860, and several works discussing his ideas were reviewed from time to time.[23] The editor at the time Darwin's works were published, Thomas B. Thayer, promised a review of *The Descent of Man* but it apparently was never published.[24] The closest to a review apeared in 1878, written by John Moore, a Vermont-born clergyman. He was extremely critical of Darwin, not because the scientist challenged prevailing religious views but because he failed to demonstrate the existence of any intermediate stages in the evolution of man, and had to depend on conjecture rather than on facts. Darwin was therefore not a true scientist.[25]

The first article addressed specifically to the question of the origin of the human race which referred to Darwin (among others) was written in all probability by Isaac C. Knowlton, and appeared in 1863.[26] The author answered the question of human origins by considering two explanations: The "development theory" — evolution from "inferior animals" which was hinted at by Darwin rather than clearly stated before 1871; and creation by "a superhuman intelligent agency." Until additional information was available, Knowlton rejected the former and accepted the latter. The idea of the evolution of humans from one or more lower orders was "humiliating..., unreasonable.... [and] mere hypothesis." Until "some plausible proof" were introduced, development theory had to be rejected as "absurd and false. The book of Genesis contains the best, plainest and most self-consistent history of the creation of man ever written. We shall believe that until we find a better."

It should be emphasized that Knowlton carefully left the door open:

"We guess rather than know, that man was created by Deity." Given the uncertainty in answering that question, there was one point on which there was no real disagreement: The human race was "progressive," having evolved by slow stages from barbarism, savagery, and ignorance, "into its present lofty position and attainments" which had yet to reach the climax of ultimate perfection. "Give us one or two hundred thousand years, and we shall rise into a very respectable race."

Whatever uncomplimentary things Knowlton had to say about the theory of development, he did wholeheartedly subscribe to Darwin's principle of natural selection based on the survival of the fittest. After citing numerous examples, including the decline of the American Indian at the hands of the white man, Knowlton predicted the ultimate extirpation of the Negro. Even the superior Anglo-Saxon might eventually be subjected to the same fate by "some higher tribe." The law of competition was one of those absolutes built into the cosmology of the universe.

Edwin C. Bolles took a special interest in science and wrote a number of articles and reviews dealing with the subject in the *Quarterly*. He praised Louis Agassiz' *Methods of Study in Natural History* for his attention to the classification of species, which became a means of providing "the grandest of all confirmations of a Superintending Goodness in the world."[27] Bolles greeted Sir Charles Lyell's *Geological Evidences of the Antiquity of Man* with cautious approval although he was critical because "the subject [was] harnessed with Mr. Darwin's theory of the Origin of Species."[28] The returns were not all in by any means, and it was dangerous to jump to conclusions. Nonetheless, as he told Tufts Divinity School students, in 1873, it was the duty of prospective Universalist clergy to keep in touch with scientific developments.[29]

Thayer, who presided over the *Quarterly* for more than twenty years (1864–1886) and was a theologian of some note, was cautiously sympathetic to the findings of science; he opened the columns of the magazine to all shades of opinion, and wrote many of the reviews dealing with science. Typical was his essay "Science the Helpmate of Religion," which appeared in 1876, and was more positive about science than he had been in an earlier essay.[30] He came to the same conclusion as did Edwin C. Sweetser, who was then pastor of the Bleeker Street Church in New York City.

> Universalism has no fear that the truths of science will in any way conflict with the truth of the Bible but, contrariwise, it feels assured that science will enable men to interpret the Bible much better than before, and that the more they learn of God in nature, the more they will believe in his changeless purpose to reconcile all things to himself.[31]

One of the recurrent themes developed by Universalists to minimize if not deny completely the alleged conflict between science and religion was that they dealt with different areas or levels of existence — the material and the spiritual. T. C. Druley, a clergyman in Belpre, Ohio, criticized John William Draper, author of the *History of the Conflict between Religion and Science* for, among other things, confusing the two.³² "Both came from the same Divine Power; each rules in its own realm."

Universalist clergy in the 1870s were in no sense unanimously convinced that evolution was the wave of the future. Alonzo A. Miner, who had just stepped down from the presidency of Tufts College to devote full time to his ministry in Boston, was still skeptical in 1876. Darwinian evolution was, in his eyes, still only a theory. Not until it became a "verified science" would he accept it completely.³³ Meanwhile, he saw no inherent conflict with religion and insisted that his belief in God remained unshaken.

Almost as soon as knowledge of Darwinism had become public property there were attempts, by analogy, to apply biological evolution to society. Herbert Spencer (1820–1903), the English philosopher and sociologist, found documentary support in Darwin for his theory of social evolution, and the idea promptly became popular in America, with William Graham Sumner (1840–1910) of Yale University as a leading exponent of what became known as Social Darwinism. Competition in economic and social realms was beneficial because it resulted in the survival of the fittest by eliminating the weak and furthering material (and therefore moral) progress.

Not as much was written by Universalists about Spencer and Social Darwinism as biological Darwinism, although Spencer's *Data of Ethics* was reviewed in the *Quarterly* in 1880.³⁴ Sumner's dog-eat-dog philosophy did not particularly appeal, partly because it denied the historic American principle of equality and conflicted with the Universalist conception of the brotherhood of man; however, his pseudo-scientific vocabulary assuring an optimistic future became part of the verbal currency of Universalists. The idea of progress was more congenial than cut-throat competition, although the doctrine of self-help had its exponents among Universalists. Part of the explanation for the sketchy and incomplete treatment of Spencerianism and Sumnerianism lay in the fact that for many decades after the *Quarterly* went out of business in 1891 there was no vehicle for reviewing scholarly publications. *To-Day*, intended to be at least semipopular, lasted less than three years (1894–1896), and the *Leader* did not introduce a literary section until well into the twentieth century.

At the end of the nineteenth century Universalists continued to tell each other that all was right with a world in which Darwinism was steadily acquiring a foothold. John Coleman Adams found that "the doctrines of Darwin have multiplied the evidences of intelligence, purpose, design in creation a hundred-fold."³⁵ When he wrote the introduction to the fourteenth edition of Ballou's *Treatise on Atonement,* published in 1902, Adams was careful to explain that Ballou was not to be expected to have had the

Orello Cone (1835-1905), a leading Universalist scholar

point of view which would "include the ideas of the Divine Method which have been made possible by the doctrines of the evolutionists." Adams simultaneously found points of intersection between the ideas of Ballou and those of John Fiske, a well-known popularizer of Darwinism.

Charles E. Perkins, pastor in Clifton Springs, New York, argued that both science and religion — the human and the divine — could coexist as parts of a larger whole.[36] F. W. Sprague delivered a sermon on "Evolution and Christianity" in which he concluded that, instead of making for conflict, science had made theology "broader and more reasonable," presenting a system of religious belief "closely allied to the doctrines of Universalism. . . . at many points in substantial or exact agreement with the same."[37]

It was Orello Cone (1835–1905), the leading Universalist scholar at the end of the nineteenth century, who most thoroughly and effectively reconciled science and religion on a theistic basis and added the support and authority of Biblical criticism. Cone was born on 16 November 1835 in the town of Lincklaen (Chenango County), New York, and grew up on a farm. After exhausting the limited educational facilities of Woodstock and Cazenovia Academies he began teaching at the age of eighteen, and in 1855 and 1856 was principal of the Union School in Manlius, New York. He then became principal of the preparatory department and assistant professor of Latin and Greek in St. Paul's College, an Episcopal institution in Palmyra, Missouri. After it suspended operations in 1861 because of the outbreak of the Civil War he entered an Episcopal theological seminary with a view toward becoming a clergyman. He found its ideas uncongenial and returned to New York State in 1862, where he was invited to preach. After delivering his first sermon in Cazenovia, he began preaching in neighboring towns and established a small circuit.

He was then fellowshipped as a Universalist and was ordained in 1864 in his first pastorate, at Little Falls, and a church was organized with the counsel and assistance of Universalist veteran Dolphus Skinner. Cone's scholarly proclivities, particularly his competency in both ancient and modern languages, were immediately recognized, and in 1865 he accepted the Professorship of Biblical Language and Literature in Canton Theological School, where he remained for fifteen years. He became an expert in New Testament criticism and contributed almost thirty articles to the *Universalist Quarterly*, relating mostly to Biblical scholarship. His achievements were recognized by award of an honorary D.D. from Lombard College in 1877.

Cone was called to the presidency of Buchtel College in 1880, where he remained until 1886. Finding scholarly pursuits more congenial and rewarding than college administration, he resigned for a year's study in Berlin, Paris, and London, where he became deeply involved in the Higher Criticism, in which the Bible was subjected to rigorous examination based on the findings of such auxiliary sciences as philology.

The Biblical scholar felt as much at home among Unitarians as among Universalists, and served the Unitarian church in Lawrence, Kansas, from the time of his return to the United States until he accepted the Richardson Professorship of Biblical Theology at the Canton Theological School, a position which he held for the six years before his death in 1905. In submitting his resignation to the AUA he expressed pleasure in his fellowship with the Unitarians, hoping to retain it for the remainder of his life, and esteeming the association with that denomination "a high honor."[38] He also taught in the Harvard Summer School of Theology in 1902.[39]

By the 1890s Cone had achieved international as well as national recognition for his Biblical scholarship. His major work on the subject, which immediately attracted attention outside the denomination, was *Gospel Criticism and Historical Christianity,* published in 1891 and assessed almost half a century later by a prominent social and intellectual historian as "the ablest work in its field from an American pen."[40] Among Cone's other book-length contributions were *Gospel Criticism and Its Earliest Interpreters* (1893); *Paul, the Man, the Missionary and Teacher,* published in 1898 while Cone was studying in London; and *Rich and Poor in the New Testament* (1902), in which he challenged the view that Jesus was a social reformer with a definable social program.

Throughout his professional career Cone sought to apply the "scientific spirit" to theology, which meant discarding such errors as the "magic" associated with the Atonement.[41] It was how Christ lived and what he taught that was most important. Cone would undoubtedly have agreed with John D. Gaylord, a Universalist layman, who caused no end of controversy at the California State Convention in 1895 when, in a program devoted to Sunday schools, he called for the elimination of anything partaking of the miraculous as an explanation for any of Christ's activities.[42] All of the myths surrounding Christ should be dispensed with, for they were "impossible and unscientific notions."[43]

Cone saw no conflict whatever between science and religion.[44] Science dealt with the facts and phenomena of the physical world, religion with "the facts and relations of the spiritual life." Both were mutually supportive aspects of truth, operating in different domains. The alleged conflict which so excited and disturbed so many had "arisen from the opposition of priests and theologians to the conclusions of scientific investigation," and had compiled an unenviable record for the church, which attempted to suppress the search for truth.[45]

Far from being injured, the interests of religion had been furthered by science. As science had "unveiled the hidden secrets of nature [it had] revealed the grandeur of the universe and its wonderful economy, its order, harmony and laws"; it made more rather than less secure the foundations of religion. Scientific inquiry did not necessarily produce an exclusively materialistic or atheistic view of either nature or life. There was still room for a theistic ("supersensible") interpretation of the universe. All that science did was to demonstrate the method of creation, not the force behind creation itself. The doctrine of ultimate design remained unchallenged, as did a First Cause.[46]

It was a testimony to Cone's influence that in 1894 the editor of the *Leader* reported "with a grateful welcome to Biblical Criticism — whether the Lower or the Higher — we conjoin a growing belief that Evolution is here to stay."[47]

As the nineteenth century drew to a close, Marion D. Shutter, then pastor of the Church of the Redeemer, the largest Universalist church in Minneapolis, added the final touches to the debate (muted as it was among Universalists, to the point of avoidance) over science and religion. He delivered a series of Sunday evening lectures in which he set out to explain and popularize the teachings of modern science and particularly the theory of evolution. It was, according to Shutter, the first such effort made by anyone in the city. His audiences were large — from 1,000 to 1,200 — and there were numerous requests that the lectures be published. Among those who urged their appearance in book form was John Fiske at Harvard, who since 1869 had delivered several lectures supporting the theory of evolution, and to whom Shutter had submitted the manuscripts of his lectures. Shutter, in fact, dedicated his work to Fiske.[48]

Shutter's complete and unqualified support of the theory of evolution was made crystal clear in his introductory lecture. There was, according to the Universalist clergyman, not only no real conflict between science and

Marion D. Shutter (1853-1939), Universalist champion of evolution

religion, but "religious thought, so far from suffering disaster at the hands of science, has been the actual gainer." Science had substituted facts for wishful thinking, taught the value of evidence rather than dogma, replaced superstition with reason, and enlarged man's conception of the universe in space and time.

Shutter summarily rejected the concept of special creation and supernatural intervention and the Biblical account of the fall of man, which had receded "into the twilight of fable," and stressed the steady evolution of religious ideas from primitive and inchoate beginnings. The evolutionary climax was to be found, more than coincidentally, in the Universalist conception of a God of love.

The evidence of history and morality, and conspicuously of science, demonstrated conclusively, said Shutter, that man "has risen and not fallen; that he did not begin perfect and deteriorate; but that he began low and imperfect, and has been slowly but surely gaining in character and moral power. Everything points to the conclusion that man began at the very bottom, and has since been struggling painfully towards the summit."[49] Shutter found nothing but encouragement and hope for man in a yet unfinished and ever-enlarging world encompassed within an all-embracing God. Jesus, in this context, became an historical personage whose origin and development were "entirely natural and human" and whose great contribution was to serve as an ideal model for humankind, a culmination of the process of moral and spiritual evolution comparable to evolution in the biological world. He was, in terms of mission, the climax of "the religious genius of the Jewish nation . . . its highest example and illustration." The man and the times coincided. Shutter, it should be noted, made no mention in his lecture, "Jesus and Evolution," of the supernatural characteristics attributed to him by many Christians. Herman Bisbee, convicted of heresy in 1872, would have thoroughly approved, and James H. Tuttle, one of his protagonists, would have been greatly perturbed by such a sacrilege.

Shutter was convinced, by his own day at least, that Nature's ultimate purpose had been achieved; namely, "the production and perfection of man" as a biological being. The capacity to invent and to tame the environment had made further evolution in any physical sense unnecessary. What remained was the further development of the human mind and spirit. This would take many forms — a higher sense of social justice for all, the substitution of cooperation for ruthless competition. Within the Christian context, it would mean following the precepts of Jesus. This was the real and true salvation.

Shutter tackled the problem of the relation of God to the new conceptions of the expanding universe and the relation of life to it by positing the idea that evolution was one of the methods by which the Divine was manifested and realized. Shutter rejected completely the idea of God as the master mechanic who, once having set the cosmos in motion, left it to its own devices. God was not external to nature but was inside of it; man is himself a part of nature; ergo, "we must find God also in him, predominantly in him."[50] All outward phenomena such as the laws of gravitation and of evolution were but the manifestation of "the divine method of originating and developing the universe itself."

In his effusive tribute to science, in which the distinction between natural and supernatural was "utterly and forever abolished," the idea of God was equated with "a real universe, that is, a system of things pervaded by unity and order . . . the universality of law, [and] the continuity of the processes of nature." These had "abolished the old form of the argument from design." Science had provided "a larger and grander teleology . . . an aim and plan of wider sweep and more majestic conception." The capstone was God, defined by Shutter as the "Eternal Goodness."

Shutter's interest in the relation of science and religion, and especially the subject of evolution, remained undiminished throughout his life, and on several occasions he delivered lectures or sermons on the subject. One, presented in 1927 in his home church, dealt with "The Church, the State and the Teaching of Science."[51]

Twenty-five years after his book on evolution had been published and had long since gone out of print, Shutter reminisced about the circumstances under which he had written it. He also noted the upheaval it had caused in the mind of at least one reader in the midst of the Fundamentalist-Modernist controversy which raged in the 1920s, climaxed by the Scopes trial in Dayton, Tennessee, in 1925.[52] Shutter's book was unsparingly condemned by a Baptist clergyman, John William Porter (1863–1937) of Lexington, Kentucky, in a work entitled *Evolution A Menace,* published in 1922 by the Baptist Book Concern in Louisville. In it he had attacked Shutter's work for containing "well nigh blasphemous utterances."[53]

Shutter's book prompted Porter to appear before the Baptist State Board of Missions in Kentucky and secure adoption of a resolution opposing Darwinism.[54] Porter went a step farther by launching a campaign to seek legislation prohibiting the teaching of the theory of evolution in the tax-supported schools of Kentucky. Such a bill was introduced in the state senate in 1922 but was buried in committee. The version of the bill debated in the lower house was defeated by only one vote.

Shutter was much amused by this entire episode, commenting that "I suppose I must take my share of responsibility in starting the 'fundamentalist' controversy." He erred, however, in two respects. The controversy, although it reached major proportions after 1922, had already started to brew several years earlier.[55] However, it is true that the attempt to stop the spread of evolutionary ideas in public schools by state legislation did make its first appearance in Kentucky, albeit unsuccessfully.

Shutter also erred in making light of the entire battle over evolution, considering it "only a passing fancy" because the theory had already been so widely accepted and documented. In actuality, "monkey bills," as they were popularly known, restricting or prohibiting the teaching of evolution had become law in eight (Southern) states by 1928, and in 1925, in the very year that Shutter was minimizing the importance of the whole debate, the famous (or infamous) Scopes trial took place.[56] If Shutter had lived into the 1970s and 1980s to witness the resurgent battle between creationists and evolutionists he would have been confronted with the undisputed fact that the matter was by no means "only a passing fancy."

Universalists attending the General Convention meeting in 1923 were told that the Bible was to be interpreted "as any other literature . . . in the light of experience and by the human reason" and that there could be no conceivable conflict between science and religion.[57] In his annual report for 1925, with the Scopes trial undoubtedly fresh in mind, General Superintendent Lowe praised developments in science, which he equated with reason, and called for a partnership between science and religion. "There is," he said, "in the nature of things, no excuse for faith and reason to walk in different paths and toward opposite goals."[58]

The *Leader* reported in much detail the great debate that raged in the 1920s over evolution, emphasizing the struggles in other denominations over creationism versus biological evolution. The paper reflected the preponderant pro-evolution stance among Universalists and reported that they were "aghast" at the action of the North Carolina State Board of Education in forbidding the teaching of evolution in the public schools.[59] Hannah Powell, busy with her missionary work in the western part of the state, reported in 1926 that a young school teacher had been forced out of her position because she was not only a Universalist but had dared to say that she believed in Darwinian evolution.[60]

When one Charles Winter, a Fundamentalist itinerant evangelist, held a series of revival meetings in Morristown, New Jersey, in 1924, and burned copies of several religious publications (including the *Leader*) as "infidel," the editor of the Universalist paper responded by offering to any resident of that New Jersey community a one-month free trial subscription.[61]

The results of Biblical criticism had been widely accepted in Universalist circles by the 1920s, despite a few isolated protesting voices. The Committee on Publications of the General Convention considered the advisability of reprinting some older theological works, including those of J. W. Hanson, a prolific writer who had died in 1901. The commission decided in the negative "because Biblical scholarship has made so many advances since the date of these books that they are practically obsolete."[62]

Yet there were still Universalists who clung in the 1920s to the traditional belief in the Bible as a plenary account. F. O. Hall prepared an article in which he presented "a sane and sensible view" of the Bible. He rejected its alleged infallibility and pictured it as a treasure-trove of literature and inspiration, not in any way supernatural but as "a record of noble thoughts of noble men, to be intelligently studied, conscientiously questioned, [and] carefully criticized."[63] One reader was so shocked that he questioned the propriety of publishing such an article in an ostensibly religious journal and claimed that Hall was destroying a "priceless heritage." After listening to Hall in the pulpit "one feels like a stranded shipwreck with no anchor of hope or of faith to cling to."

The editor of the *Leader* not only defended his decision to publish the article by pointing out that Hall was merely expressing "the commonplaces of modern thinking" but thought so highly of it that he kept the type intact so that the article could be published in pamphlet form.[64]

Half a century after Orello Cone had assured Universalists that Biblical criticism and evolutionary ideas had reinforced rather than weakened religion, Lee S. McCollester, Dean of the Crane School of Religion, was triumphantly making the same claim.

> Always the genius of Universalism has looked frankly and searchingly at the new and general knowledge and at the researches and conclusions of Science, and has tried to readjust these religious and scientific deductions to its working scheme or to readjust itself to the new facts thus revealed. Evolution is not an enemy seeking the destruction of religion, but a wonderful helper leading to more thrilling and satisfying conceptions of God and His dealings with men, and of man's destiny of eternal progress.[65]

Chapter 8

The Bond of Fellowship and Statements of Faith (1935)

The Challenge of Humanism

In mid-1933 there appeared a widely publicized document entitled "A Humanist Manifesto," signed by thirty-four leaders in the movement of which it was a climax. It contained the names of many nationally prominent Americans, including John Dewey, the philosopher and educator. The great bulk of the signatories were Unitarian clergy (thirteen) and laity.[1]

The Manifesto, centered on fifteen propositions, called for a new, all-embracing definition of religion as "those actions, purposes, and experiences which are humanly significant. . . . [anything] that is in its degree expressive of intelligently satisfying human living." There could no longer be a distinction between the sacred and the secular. Traditional revealed religion, which partook of the supernatural or depended on it in any way for its existence or support, was summarily rejected. Faith was placed in human thought and action. The universe was considered self-existing rather than created over time; humankind was the result of a lengthy developmental process which operated without divine intervention of any kind.

The crux of the document was the concluding statement that "man is at last becoming aware that he alone is responsible for the realization of the world of his dreams, that he has within himself the power for its achievement." There was no room for the concept of God, however expressed.

The publication of the Manifesto had been immediately preceded by a lively debate which had been sparked shortly after World War I by a small group of Unitarian clergy, and in which a few Universalists eventually

Clinton Lee Scott, signer of the Humanist Manifesto

became involved. By the late 1920s and early 1930s the religious press, particularly that of the Universalists and Unitarians, had reflected a veritable flood of discussion and controversy. Several issues of the *Leader* in 1930 consisted almost exclusively of articles about humanism, and the column of "letters to the editor" was full of commentary.

Clinton Lee Scott, then the pastor in Peoria, Illinois, represented the only exclusively Universalist clergyman who signed the Manifesto.[2] There were others formally affiliated with the Universalist church who signed the document and who also held fellowship in one or more other denominations. J. A. C. Fagginger Auer, engaged in academic life at the time rather than in the active ministry, held fellowship in both the Unitarian and Congregational churches as well as the Universalist.[3] Charles Francis Potter, founder in 1929 and leader of the First Humanist Society of New York, one-time minister of the Church of the Divine Paternity (Universalist) in New York City, held both Universalist and Unitarian fellowship.[4] Potter called for "a greater faith than the God concept."[5]

In many senses, all Universalists shared in some degree the humanistic beliefs of liberal religionists. They were convinced of the sanctity of every human personality and believed that human life was of supreme worth; that the utmost capacity of every human being should be developed; and that eventually all evil would be abolished. These were all to be reflected in the Bond of Fellowship and Statements of Faith adopted two years after the Manifesto had been published. But whether all this was to be accomplished with or without the presence, assistance, or involvement of a supernatural power, labelled God or otherwise, was the crucial question, and on this the humanist movement divided.

The great majority of Universalists parted company with the nontheistic humanists who believed there was no hope other than through exclusively human channels; that there was no need for God; that humankind was entirely self-sufficient; and that, in fact, there was no God at all.

For the most part, those Universalists who took sides as a matter of record came down on the side of theistic humanism. They did not conceive of God, as did such non-theistic humanists as Unitarian Gordon Kent, as "a superfluous third party" who had to be eliminated before a really vigorous religion could be established.[6] Kent formed a humanist society in Sioux City, Iowa, and announced his intention of dropping his subscription to the *Leader*.[7]

The editor of the *Leader* took up the cudgels on behalf of not only theistic but specifically Christian Universalists, and in 1930 and 1931 was so vociferous (and so repetitive) that his readers begged for mercy. Time after time van Schaick asserted his unswerving belief in God and insisted that no individual could find complete satisfaction exclusively within the realm of the known. He made so bold as to act as a self-appointed spokesman for the entire denomination when he stated unequivocally that "there is not the slightest danger of humanism getting any hold in the Universalist Church.... Always there will be faith in God or there will be no Universalist Church."[8]

Editor van Schaick was roundly criticized by such humanists as Potter for statements such as these, and was held responsible for turning the *Leader* into a rigid defender of "supernaturalistic theism."[9] But the indomitable editor stuck to his guns, and in so doing probably reflected the thinking of most Universalists who were not as articulate or as outspoken as he was.

Long after the verbal battle over humanism had subsided, Scott noted wryly that even though he had signed the Manifesto he was apparently still in the good graces of most Universalists, for he was reelected as a trustee of the General Convention by "a sizable majority."[10] Yet the general mistrust and suspicion of non-theistic humanists by Universalists persisted and surfaced many times. When the creation of the Free Church Fellowship was being discussed in 1932 several individuals suggested that Unitarians who were humanists should separate from their denomination and establish their own societies; otherwise, Christian Universalists would be unwilling to be associated with Unitarians in the proposed organization.[11]

The Christian heritage and character of Universalism was emphatically asserted and repeated in the unsuccessful attempts to obtain full membership in the Federal Council of Churches in the 1940s. The establishment of the Charles Street Universalist Meetinghouse in Boston in 1949 under the auspices of the Massachusetts Convention precipitated a spirited controversy when six ministers in the state protested that the pastor was an avowed humanist and was automatically 'outside the Christian frame of reference.'[12] The granting of fellowship to the church by the state convention was delayed until 1952.

Belief in a purely secular humanism continued to comprise a significant portion of liberal religious thought although it was not again expressed formally until 1973 in Humanist Manifesto II.[13] Seven of the initial signatories were identified as pastors of Unitarian churches, three of Unitarian Universalist churches, and one of a Universalist church. Scott, who had signed the 1933 Manifesto, and in the meantime had retired from the active ministry, also signed Manifesto II. Khoren Arisian, another signer and a product of the Crane School of Religion at Tufts, had — at the time — left the pastorate of a Unitarian church to become an officer in the Society for Ethical Culture in New York City.

The lengthy seventeen-point Manifesto II, in a prefatory statement, considered the 1933 document "far too optimistic" but renewed the determination of the secular humanists to put their entire effort and faith for a better world in human hands. The call for citizenship in a world community in the concluding section was echoed approvingly by the *UU World* (the combined denominational successor to the *Leader*) when it reprinted excerpts. Some detected a note of desperation in the Manifesto that reflected the parlous state of the world at the time it was formulated.

Forging a New Profession

In 1923, as part of a series of "Present Day Objectives of the Universalist Church," the Five Principles adopted in 1899, with the "liberty clause" attached, were reaffirmed "as fundamental to our church and as an adequate expression of faith for the world."[14] Little more than a decade later (in 1935) they had been supplemented by a Bond of Fellowship and Statements of Faith, known for short as the "Avowal of Faith," the last formal religious declaration made by Universalists as a separate denomination, and amended only once after its adoption.

The agitation which had resulted in a revised statement originated from a complex of sources, partly from within the denomination itself, and partly from intellectual forces at work in the larger society which reflected dramatic developments in science and technology, the battle over the Darwinian version of evolution, new insights derived from Biblical criticism, the Social Gospel movement, and the growing influence of humanism.

The desirability of change had been voiced by J. M. Atwood, outgoing president of the General Convention, in his farewell address in 1927. He asserted that, in the spirit of the Joint Statement of the Universalists and Congregationalists made public that year, the conditions of Universalist fellowship should be liberalized so that they would be "simply a declaration of a purpose to live the Christian life."[15] Subscription to a statement of principles should not be required as a condition of church membership although it should be retained for those who wished it. "It ought not to be more difficult to join the Universalist branch of the Christian Church than

Frederic Perkins (1870-1943), distinguished Universalist clergyman and scholar

it is to enter the Kingdom of God." He was echoing the vote of the first meeting of the United Liberal Churches in Florida which requested in 1927 that the General Convention amend Article II of its constitution by deleting the statement "provided that the faith thus indicated be professed."[16] Assent to this or any other statement should no longer be required, "either in word or in substance." The restrictive clause was "wholly unnecessary and ... probably confusing" and was a contradiction of the traditional Universalist devotion to liberty of interpretation.[17]

One by one other suggestions for change were added. At the General Convention meeting in 1929 a resolution by students at the Canton Theological School was presented calling for reconstruction of the entire 1899 statement.[18] H. L. Canfield declared in 1931 that "the entire profession is outmoded, and absolutely at variance with modern thinking and understanding."[19] Perkins agreed. "We need a new statement. We shall need another statement ten years from now. The Universalist faith is a living spirit, not a stereotyped code."[20] The YPCU deleted "For Christ and His Church" from the masthead of *Onward* and memorialized the convention in 1931 to start a movement to revise the statement of faith 'in the direction of the universals and unities of world religion.'[21]

The Ministerial Association which assembled prior to the General Convention meeting in 1931 was so determined to update the 1899 statement that a committee consisting of Atwood, Kapp, and Perkins was appointed to do so.[22] The mood at the convention was such that a resolution to appoint a commission to prepare a revised version was unanimously adopted, to the surprise of many. The trustees immediately named a seven-member body which included the three members of the Ministerial Association committee, with Perkins as chairman.[23] They were instructed to bring to the next biennial meeting "a new statement of faith or covenant of fellowship more in harmony with the religious position of our church to-day, and with the principle of religious liberty which has been our guide in the past."

But little appeared concerning the proposed revision in the denominational press prior to the meeting in 1933 except for a preliminary report of the commission itself.[24] The authorship was largely that of Perkins. The commission, after disavowing any intention of producing anything savoring or a "creedal spirit," presented a statement of purpose binding all together. It played down "abstract theological speculations" and placed the emphasis on love as "the motive-power," based on "the inherent worth of the human personality," with the realities of the present rather than "a vision of future splendor" in the forefront, and with a social as well as a personal thrust. The new statement was clearly theistic, with avowal of faith in God and in the spiritual leadership of Jesus, although all reference to the Bible was omitted. It frankly recognized the inevitability of change which would "progressively establish the kingdom of God" and the power "to overcome all evil."

In explaining the draft statement much attention was paid to its broad and voluntary character. The way was left open to use the venerable Winchester Profession as well as the Five Principles, although neither was mentioned in the draft of the new statement. The commission made no attempt to formulate a short form adaptable to repetition as part of public worship, leaving that to local discretion.[25]

As finally adopted, the Bond of Fellowship and Statements of Faith read as follows:

> 1. The bond of fellowship in this Convention [church] shall be a common purpose to do the will of God as Jesus revealed it and to co-operate in establishing the kingdom for which he lived and died.
>
> To that end we avow our faith in God as Eternal and All-Conquering Love, in the spiritual leadership of Jesus, in the supreme worth of every human personality, in the authority of truth known or to be known, and in the power of men of good-will and sacrificial spirit to overcome all evil and progressively establish the kingdom of God. Neither this nor any other statement shall be imposed as a creedal test, provided that the faith thus indicated be professed.
>
> 2a. [Winchester Profession of Faith]
>
> 2b. [The Declaration of Faith adopted in 1899]
>
> 2c. These historic declarations of faith with liberty of interpretation are dear and acceptable to many Universalists. They are commended not as tests but as testimonies in the free quest for truth that accords with the genius of the Universalist Church.
>
> 3. The conditions of fellowship in this Convention [church] shall be acceptance of the essential principles of the Universalist faith and acknowledgement of the ecclesiastical jurisdiction of the Universalist General Convention.

Two amendments were made from the convention floor. The first was the addition of the adjective "All-Conquering" preceding the reference to God as Love — a change accomplished by "unanimous consent." The second was the insertion, verbatim, of the 1803 Profession and the 1899 statements as "indicative of the historic development of our faith." The vote to adopt the new statement did not carry when the original draft was presented without them; the convention wanted assurance that the past was not being summarily abandoned. A revised version, including the two earlier professions, together with an explanatory statement, was presented and adopted unanimously (263 to 0, out of a total delegate body of 350).[26]

The Bond of Fellowship was ratified unanimously in 1935, with only 91 of the 125 delegates voting, and with a minimum of discussion and no debate. Perkins was so amazed that the revised statement had gone through two convention sessions without a dissenting vote that he suggested the fact be inscribed on his tombstone.[27] The almost perfunctory way in which the 1935 statement was adopted bore no resemblance whatever to the quarter-century of agonizing over the wording of the Winchester Profession and the debates over the Declaration of 1899.

The General Convention in the 1930s did not go as far as one Universalist wanted. He favored "a statement that shall be non-theological in character; that shall make no mention of God, of Jesus, of Christianity, the Bible, punishment or salvation. An expressed aspiration and a pledge of loyalty to the best as we understand it, is enough."[28] Another thought that the "common purpose to do the will of God as Jesus revealed it" was a theologically debatable anachronism left over from the nineteenth century.[29] But the commission's endeavor "to express for the church as a whole our Christian purpose and our Universalist faith, in general and inclusive terms" seems to have satisfied the majority. The critics of the new statement were few and far between.

In 1946 the Ohio Convention made an unsuccessful attempt at the General Assembly to amend the Bond of Fellowship by substituting for the avowal of "our faith in God as Eternal and All-Conquering Love, in the spiritual leadership of Jesus. . . ." a statement of "faith in the Universal Fatherhood of God, in the spiritual leadership — not deity — of Jesus." The proposal was unanimously rejected (0 to 122).[30] Cummins had urged this action in his biennial report. The proposal, which would have had the effect of excluding Trinitarians, was too creedal for his liking and would have denied the very inclusiveness of Universalism which had appealed to him when he joined the denomination.[31]

The Bond of Fellowship put into official form what the editor of the *Leader* had articulated a decade earlier. Universalists were among the "more practical Christians. The application of Christ's principles here and now, the Christianizing of institutions and men, the abolition of war, the establishment of social justice, the relief of misery, the uniting of races and nations in constructive work, take the time and strength of modern Universalists much more than speculations about the hereafter."[32] Or, as Lewis B. Fisher had written in 1921, "we are afraid of nothing but finalities."[33]

Universalism had evolved over the years from a gospel of individual salvation to "a social proclamation of the Kingdom of God."[34] In spite of changing emphases, the theistic character of the denomination was once again asserted, and secular humanism was rejected. "We cannot have the Kingdom of God and leave God out."[35]

The last exposition and analysis of the four professions of belief adopted by Universalists while a separate denomination, published in 1940, was prepared by Perkins. It represented a cogent summary of the changing theology of Universalism over time, and served as a fitting monument to the historic liberal Christian interpretation which most Universalists still shared.[36]

Section IV

The Search for a Wider Fellowship

Chapter 9

The International Scene

The World's Columbian Exposition and the World's Parliament of Religions

The year 1893 was a memorable one for American religious history. The city of Chicago played host that year to the fifth international exposition held in the nineteenth century, known officially as the World's Columbian Exposition and unofficially as the Chicago World's Fair of 1893. The pattern had been set by the Crystal Palace Exhibition in London in 1851; a smaller imitation in New York City in 1853, which had been largely a failure; one in Paris in 1855; and the Centennial Exposition in Philadelphia in 1876, commemorating a century of American independence.

The Chicago exposition, celebrating the annniversary of the discovery of America by Columbus in 1492, was the most elaborate yet held, including everything from carnival shows to exhibits of the material and cultural progress of the nation, from the Pullman Palace railroad car to the electric light, and the linotype. An instant city of temporary buildings was built for the occasion in Jackson Park, on the south side of Chicago.[1] The classic designs of the white plaster and stuccoed buildings, constructed under the direction of Daniel H. Burnham, with the collaboration of Frederic Law Olmsted, the first professed landscape architect, influenced civic architecture for many decades to come.

Probably the most unique and dramatic event associated with the exposition was the holding of the first World's Parliament of Religions. For the first time in recorded history, representatives of almost every known religious faith, sect, and denomination throughout the world were brought together and given an opportunity not only to learn of faiths other than their own, but to review and assess their own in a formal way. It marked, as one contemporary observed, "the highwater-mark of human civilization."[2] It was the first truly ecumenical religious council ever assembled on such an enormous scale; an estimated 150,000 individuals attended its various sessions. It was assuredly "the greatest religious event of the nineteenth century."

What became the World Parliament of Religions was the brainchild of Charles Carroll Bonney (1831–1903), a prominent educator, lawyer, and social reformer then residing in Chicago. When the Columbian Exposition was planned, he conceived the idea of holding auxiliary congresses divided into twenty "departments" into which human thought and activity were classified for purposes of supplementing the exposition. Religion was one of these. Among the others were music, literature, art, science, and commerce and finance. A complex super-organization was created for each department, with the sanction and recognition of the United States Government, and with dozens of subordinate committees and an advisory council.

In the Department of Religion each denomination operated both independently as a part of the World's Congress of Religions, including a World's Parliament of Religions distinct from the Congress and holding plenary sessions. Universalists were not only among the forty-one faiths and denominations that held their own meetings, but were officially represented in the overall coordinating organization. A. J. Canfield, pastor of St. Paul's Universalist Church in Chicago, was on the original planning committee and Augusta J. Chapin chaired the separate Women's Committee of the entire Department of Religion. She was also responsible for appointing a committee of seven to serve for the separate Universalist Congress. The chairman of the original planning committee for the Parliament later called special attention to the committee which Chapin headed, and noted their success in securing "the presence and participation of some of the most distinguished women of our time."[3] Among them was Mrs. Julia Ward Howe, author of the "Battle Hymn of the Republic."

The Universalist section of the Congress in the complicated and interlocking arrangement was headed by Canfield. He, in turn, appointed a Universalist committee to make the necessary arrangements. It consisted of nine ministers and six laymen in the Chicago area. The Chapin committee and the Universalist committee held several joint sessions during 1892. Eight major topics were outlined, each with numerous subdivisions, and speakers were selected. The agenda served the dual purpose of providing a survey of the history of the church as well as a statement of Universalist beliefs, including the arguments by which they were sustained. An additional advantage to the denomination was the fact that the complete proceedings of all components of the Columbian Exposition were to be published. The sessions were formal, as provided in the general rules of the coordinating committee, and consisted only of presentation of papers prepared for the occasion by representative members of the denomination; there was no provision for debate or discussion, or for the transaction of business.

An extraordinary amount of consultation, correspondence, and negotiation had gone into the planning for the World's Parliament. Altogether, more than 10,000 letters and 40,000 documents were sent out all over the globe. It had all begun with a "Committee of Organization" created in the spring of 1891, consisting of sixteen leading clergymen in the Chicago area, including Canfield. John Henry Barrows, of the First Presbyterian Church, served as the chair.

More than 3,000 copies of a "Preliminary Address" were sent out to religious leaders in thirty countries to sound out the possibility of holding the Parliament. The reactions were overwhelmingly favorable. Almost all Christians and non-Christians in the United States were likewise amenable to the idea of a grand ecumenical conference, although a few dissenting voices were raised. Somewhat ironically, in view of Barrows' key role on the coordinating committee, the General Assembly of the Presbyterian Church, at its meeting in 1892, emphatically disapproved of the Parliament. But the bulk of that denomination, including one of the secretaries of their Board of Foreign Missions, served on the advisory council which eventually totalled more than 3,000 church leaders.

The opposition of the Sultan of Turkey to the idea of holding a Parliament surprised no one, but the negative reaction of the Archbishop of Canterbury was quite unexpected. These were exceptions, however, and plans proceeded for convening the Parliament. There is no evidence that Universalists took a negative view, and their participation at every level indicated their favorable response. John Coleman Adams welcomed the Parliament as "an expression of the hospitality of nineteenth century Christianity" and considered it "an expression of the soul of the church in modern days."[4]

Symbolic of the unprecedented confluence of many religions was the attendance of the Buddhist delegation at services in the First Presbyterian Church where the assemblage listened to a sermon on "Christ the Wonderful." H. Adler, acknowledged as the "Chief Rabbi of the British Empire," furnished as the motto of the Parliament the words of the Hebrew prophet Malachi: "Have we not all one Father? Hath not one God created us?" No believing Universalist could have questioned the appropriateness of that passage from the Old Testament.

After a great debate over whether the exposition should be open on Sundays (it was, most of the time), the World's Parliament of Religions was formally opened on Monday, 11 September 1893, before an audience of more than 4,000 in the Hall of Columbus in the Art Palace. It remained in session for seventeen days. Bonney, president of the World's Congress

Auxiliary, presided at the first and last meetings, as well as at several others. The opening ceremonies set the tone of the Parliament. After James Cardinal Gibbons, Roman Catholic Archbishop of Baltimore, led the assembly in the "universal prayer," which turned out to be the Protestant version of the Lord's Prayer, Bonney outlined the three parts of the program to follow the general convocations. There were presentations by representatives of the various religions; separate congresses of individual faiths and denominations; and meetings of specialized organizations such as the YMCA and a group known as the Evolutionists who, for reasons not clear, did not meet in the Department of Science as originally scheduled.

After extended remarks by Barrows at the opening session, Patrick A. Feehan, Archbishop of Chicago, spoke in the name of the Roman Catholic Church, and Cardinal Gibbons responded to the addresses of welcome. Augusta J. Chapin, in her capacity as head of the Women's Committee, then spoke. She made the point that fifty years earlier, one-half of the religious world (the women) could not have been directly represented. Their presence would not have been either thought of or tolerated, and they were too weak, too timid, and too unschooled to have taken advantage of the opportunity even if it had been offered. By 1893 the situation, fortunately, was quite otherwise.

Greetings then followed from such diverse personages as the pastor of the Shepard Memorial Church (Congregational) in Cambridge, Massachusetts; the Archbishop of Zante (Greece); a representative of the Brahmo-Somaj (India); the First Secretary of the Chinese Legation in Washington, D.C.; a representative of Shintoism (Japan) and four Buddhist priests (also from Japan); and the Anglican Archbishop of New Zealand. The Parliament was indeed an event that "attracted the attention of mankind all over the earth."

The meetings lasted for the remaining sixteen days allotted. Universalists were represented on the fourth day, when Everett L. Rexford delivered an address on "The Religious Intent."[5] Olympia Brown, another Universalist representative, presented a brief paper on "Crime and its Remedy" on the twelfth day.[6] Quite fittingly, it was Chapin who read a paper prepared by Antoinette Brown Blackwell on "Women and the Pulpit," and later presided over a session at which two of the three papers had been prepared by women.

The audiences heard papers not only on aspects of different religions but on such topics as comparative theology and comparative study of world religions. The only major disruption in an unusually harmonious Parliament occurred when some listeners objected vociferously to certain points made in a paper on Islam by an American convert, Alexander Russell Webb. The two most controversial passages concerned the propagation of religion by the sword and the approval of polygamy.

With great even-handedness, Barrows presented memorials from Armenians requesting relief from oppression in the Ottoman Empire, and from a society for the restoration of Buddhist holy places in Japan. Hindus were given an opportunity to reply from the floor to an attack by an aggressively Christian Englishman on the alleged immorality of Brahmin practices. A group known as the Brotherhood of Christian Unity outlined its plan for "the federation of the world upon a Christian basis." After the World's Parliament was over, the Brotherhood set about organizing branches in various states. In 1895 they held a meeting in Rochester, New York, for the purpose of organizing a New York State Parliament of Religions patterned after the Chicago model. Clerical representatives from four Protestant faiths and a Jewish rabbi were among those present. Asa Saxe was to have been the Universalist representative but was unable to attend.[7] The Methodists and Episcopalians stood aloof.

While the Parliament was in session there were devotional meetings sponsored by the Brotherhood of Christian Unity; receptions, both private and public; and visits to various events at the exposition. More than 7,000 persons were crowded into the Art Palace for the closing sessions of the Parliament. Portions of the ceremonies had to be repeated in an adjoining hall because one would not contain the throngs, and tickets of admissions were exchanged and sold at exorbitant prices.

In her closing remarks on the last day of the Parliament, Chapin expressed the euphoria of the occasion with a fervent reference to the final reality of "the Fatherhood of God, the Brotherhood of Man, and the solidarity of the human race." She had used almost identical language at the first session of the Universalist Congress which opened the same day as the general sessions of the Parliament. Instead of repeating the phrase "solidarity of the human race" she referred to "the common destiny of the race."

The Universalist Congress proved to be a five-day affair (11–15 September). The sessions were considered, with one exception, to be a "numerical success" so far as attendance was concerned. An average of fifty clergy attended, as well as many lay persons and other interested observers.[8] The Universalist meetings were exceeded in size of audiences only by those of the Lutheran and the Theosophical Congresses.

A. J. Canfield, chairman of the Universalist committee, presided at the first session. The first speaker was John Coleman Adams (Brooklyn, New York), who presented a paper on "Holiness and Happiness the Final Result of God's Government." The address prepared by E. H. Capen, president of Tufts College, was delivered in his absence by Hanson, editor of one of the several collections of papers presented at the Parliament. Capen's paper dealt with the three-fold theme of "Punishment Disciplinary; the Atonement; Life a School." The third and last paper of the first (morning) session, prepared by J. Smith Dodge (Stamford, Connecticut) and read by Cantwell, was on the topic "Man; Intellect; Aspirations; Affections."

At the second session, on the afternoon of the first day, Rufus A. White of Englewood, California, read the paper prepared by Edgar Leavitt of Santa Cruz, California, on "Divine Love, Justice, Power and Wisdom." The general topic of Edwin C. Sweetser (Philadelphia) was "Universalism the Doctrine of Nature." Rexford's address, delivered extemporaneously but later published, was on "The Intrinsic Worth of Man."

The first session the following day was opened with a paper by George H. Emerson (Salem, Massachusetts), read by G. A. Sahlin, which took almost an hour to present, and bore the title "The Bible: Inspiration and Revelation." Charles H. Eaton (New York City) selected "Christ, and the Nature of Salvation" as his topic, and Massena Goodrich (Pawtucket, Rhode Island) explored the findings of Biblical scholars regarding the "Higher Criticism."

The venerable T. J. Sawyer of Tufts College was unable to be present, so his paper was read by James H. Swan of St. Paul's Church (Chicago). It dealt with the "History of Universalism in the Early Church." The next paper was on "Peace, War and National Honor," delivered by the author, Henry Blanchard (Portland, Maine). Olympia Brown (Racine, Wisconsin), who also read a paper at a session of the Parliament, presented an address dealing with three of her major concerns — "Crime, Capital Punishment, and Temperance."

The sessions of the third day were the most sparsely attended of any, due presumably to an oppressively sultry day and the poor ventilation of the hall, and not to the speakers or the subjects covered. Hanson read the paper prepared by George L. Perin, then in Tokyo, reviewing the foreign missionary work of the church in glowing and enthusiastic terms. The second presentation of the day was on "Christian Ethics and Business and Political Successes," read by the author, A. N. Alcott of Elgin, Illinois.

The diminished audience the afternoon of the third day was undoubtedly relieved to hear that not all of the five scheduled papers were actually to be heard. Hosea W. Parker, a prominent Universalist layman of Claremont, New Hampshire, had prepared an address dealing with three topics: Denominational Organization and Policy; the Position of Women in the Church; and Sunday School Work. It was read by title only. Canfield had been unable to complete his paper on the leavening influence of Universalism on other denominations and on religious thought. He was excused and, by the only formal vote taken in the Universalist Congress, was permitted to finish the paper for later publication.

Two papers on the activities of Universalist women were presented, one by Mrs. M. R. M. Wallace of Chicago on women's state missionary organizations, of which Illinois had been a pioneer; and one by Mrs. Cordelia A. Quinby of Augusta, Maine. Her topic was the history of the Woman's Centenary Association, of which she was then the president. Nehemiah White of Lombard University concluded the session with a rather abstract paper on "Love, the Basis of Education."

The climax of the Universalist Congress came in the final sessions, designated as Presentation Day, with several hundred in attendance. There were papers by Alonzo A. Miner of Boston, then a veteran of eighty, on "Universalism the Doctrine of the Scriptures," followed by an historical address on Universalist doctrine over five centuries, delivered by Hanson. Stephen Crane (Earlville, Illinois) discussed Universalism as a theological system, and Isaac M. Atwood of St. Lawrence University spoke on the receptivity of Universalism to science and its methods. C. Ellwood Nash (Brooklyn, New York) provided a "most abstruse and metaphysical discussion" on divine and human will, and human redeemability. James M. Pullman gave an abbreviated address under the heading of "The Contributions of Universalists to the Faith of the World."

Taken as a whole, the presentations comprised the most complete inventory of Universalism, both theologically and organizationally, that had been made since the centennial had been observed in 1870. Could the Universalists claim the same advantages to themselves as did the Congress of the much smaller United Brethren in Christ, which met for only one day at the Parliament? Their meeting "advertised favorably the denomination, directed public attention to its work, and awakened among its own people a deeper feeling of churchliness, increased hope for the triumph of Christianity, and greater zeal for the prosperity of their own religious denomination."[9] Was the state of Universalism at the end of the nineteenth century a source of satisfaction or did it bode ill for its future?

International Religious Liberalism

As the Universalist Church matured and regularized its domestic outreach and maintained its commitment to the mission in Japan, increasing attention was given after 1900 to the international aspects of liberal religion. A Commission on Foreign Relations was created at the session of the General Convention in Philadelphia in 1907, a development which coincided with the involvement of the denomination in various organizations and movements which extended beyond national lines.

The first was with the International Congress of Unitarian and other Liberal Religious Thinkers and Workers (soon shortened to the International Congress of Religious Liberals) which had been organized in Boston in 1900, with headquarters at 25 Beacon Street. Its goal was to establish "the federation of nations, the brotherhood of mankind, and the peace of the world." The Congress met biennially in London, Amsterdam, and Geneva, and the fourth meeting was scheduled for Boston in 1907.

In 1905 the General Convention meeting in Minneapolis received a cordial invitation to send delegates and to participate in the planning. F. C. Southworth, president of the Meadville Theological School, addressed the convention and issued the official invitation. The pastor of the Unitarian church in St. Paul was also present and delivered an address of welcome. J. Coleman Adams responded for the Universalists, pointing out the common goals of the Universalists and Unitarians, and calling attention to "the increasing spirit of fellowship in Christ growing up between these two denominations."[10] The invitation was accepted by the convention by resolution after considerable discussion, with a reference to the Universalists and Unitarians as "natural allies." Only one of the ten Universalists nominated as delegates, Edwin C. Sweetser, declined to serve.

The *Leader* greeted the Boston meeting with great enthusiasm, explained no doubt in part by the fact that the editor, Bisbee, was on the International Council of the Congress. The five-day meeting was planned by a committee consisting of Universalists, Unitarians, and Congregationalists, and was compared in its importance to the World's Parliament of Religions of 1893.[11] The Universalist invited guests at the sessions were Shutter, Hall, and Frederick W. Hamilton, president of Tufts College.

The Congress, considered a "glorious success," was attended by an estimated 7,000 individuals, with fifteen nations and more than thirty faiths and denominations represented.[12] Paid-in membership by then amounted to 2,500. Shutter delivered one of the keynote addresses, which was virtually a repetition of a sermon delivered six years earlier in his Minneapolis church, calling for "A United Liberal Church." In it he emphasized the identity of Universalists and Unitarians as to "thought, spirit, and aim," and identified their mission to lay the foundations of "a new household of faith."[13]

At the General Convention in 1909 the commitment of the denomination to religious liberalism was reaffirmed and in fact Universalism and religious liberalism were officially made synonymous.[14] Bisbee, who had earlier been associated with the Liberal Congress, continued to serve as the Universalist representative on the executive board of the International Council. Five delegates or more were authorized to attend the next meeting, to be held in Berlin in 1910, and Bisbee was instructed to provide "adequate representation" of Universalists on the official program. Thirty representatives of the denomination attended as delegates, five of whom were clergy who did indeed occupy prominent places on the program.

One of the highlights was an address delivered by Effie McCollum Jones, pastor of the church in Waterloo, Iowa, and a champion of women's rights.[15] In her capacity as one of the three representatives of the

WNMA she spoke on women in the ministry. She pointedly called attention to the fact that women had but recently been invading an historically exclusive male domain, and defended the emergent role of women in the professions against their critics and opponents.[16]

Bisbee also gave an address, and the denominational Commission on Foreign Relations reported with great satisfaction that the Universalists, "instead of being simply a small and obscure church," had finally become "part of a great world movement which has for its object religious freedom and human progress."

The international organization, which by 1910 was being called alternatively the "World Congress of Free Christianity and Religious Progress," held its next session in Paris in 1913, with five Universalists serving as delegates: Shutter, then president of the General Convention; McGlauflin, the General Superintendent; McCollester, dean of the Crane Theological School at Tufts College; Bisbee, editor of the *Leader;* and C. Guy Robbins, pastor of the church in Lawrence, Massachusetts. Shutter delivered (in French) an address on "The Universalist Idea."[17] Over thirty different nationalities were represented and the enthusiasm for what the Congress stood for was so evident that the Commission on Foreign Relations felt justified in asking for authority, which was granted by the General Convention, to solicit funds. They were used to assist in defraying the costs of the Congress and those of the denominational representatives at its next session, and to provide Universalist literature to be distributed at its meeting.[18] W. C. Selleck of Rhode Island was selected to participate in a tour of religious liberals around the world, but just as arrangements were being made for the trip and literature for foreign distribution was being prepared, war broke out and the project was postponed indefinitely. Likewise, plans for a meeting in London in 1914 had to be suspended.[19] However, a meeting of religious liberals was scheduled for the summer of 1915 in San Francisco, and Hall was selected as the Universalist representative.

Organizations to foster international religious liberalism after the First World War went through a prolonged period of uncertainty and readjustment that reflected the vast changes in state and religious relationships that had occurred. After peace returned the International Congress of Religious Liberals resumed its sessions, although not on a biennial schedule. A small meeting, "of a tentative character," was held in Boston in 1920, but the next one held in Europe did not gather until 1922, when it convened in Leyden, the Netherlands, and where the Congress went through one of many reorganizations.[20] At the meeting in Prague in 1927, Shutter represented the Universalists among the 150 delegates of various nationalities who attended, and was elected as one of the ten vice-presidents. William Howard Taft, a Unitarian and at the time Chief Justice of the United States Supreme Court, became the new president.

In 1930 sixty-five representatives from twelve countries met in

Arnheim, the Netherlands, and attempted yet another reorganization. Roger Etz, who was serving as both the General Secretary of the General Convention and General Superintendent, represented the Unitarians as well as the Universalists.[21] The other Universalist delegates were Walter H. MacPherson, who was in the midst of arranging a denominational good-will tour of Europe; and J. A. C. Fagginger Auer of Harvard, who held dual fellowship and was serving part-time on the faculty of the Crane Theological School. He was one of the speakers.

At the Arnheim meeting the International Association for the Promotion of Liberal Christianity and Religious Freedom was created, with a permanent secretariat in Amsterdam. This organization was the successor to the International Congress, with many of the same personnel involved. The General Convention authorized $750 to assist in financing it.

A meeting of the reconstituted organization was originally scheduled for 1931 but economic stringency and other factors necessitated a postponement. A small meeting, with only the delegates, among them six Universalists, convened in St. Gall, Switzerland. Copenhagen became the locale for the next full meeting, held in 1934.

There were other channels for international cooperation among religious liberals besides those already noted. The Commission on Foreign Relations had been created in 1907 by the General Convention originally in response to an invitation from clergy in Great Britain to exchange pulpits and otherwise to establish closer relations with American Universalists and other religious liberals.

In 1909 arrangements were made to have John Hunter, pastor of Trinity Congregationalist Church in Glasgow, Scotland, visit selected Universalist churches in America. He had been friendly with the Universalist church in Glasgow, and had often preached in it.[22] His trip to the United States was considered a golden opportunity to bring many churches "out of the local obscurity and isolation they [had] heretofore experienced" and make them aware that they were part of a larger religious configuration. The Hunter visit, made in 1910 and widely advertised, opened the way for informal conversations between religious liberals in England and Universalist delegates en route to the meeting of the International Congress of Religious Liberals in 1910.[23]

Joseph Fort Newton, from the church in Cedar Rapids, Iowa, began service in 1916 as the "ambassador and interpreter of America and Universalism" in the pulpit of the City Temple in London, known as "the cathedral of non-conformity" (Congregational). His tenure there, which lasted four years, together with his appearances in Scotland and Wales, earned for him a widely heralded reputation as an effective speaker.[24] From 1921 until 1925 he was pastor of the Church of the Divine Paternity in New York City and then served in the Protestant Episcopal Church of St. Paul in Philadelphia. Many Universalists raised their eyebrows when he announced that he would retain both Universalist and Congregational as well as Baptist fellowship. He was quite accurately described as a "liberal evangelical" in a "common Christianity" divorced from sectarian division. Newton was considered by a *Christian Century* poll to be one of the twenty-five leading clergy in the United States. His numerous writings included a collection of sermons (*Things I Know in Religion,* published in 1930), articles in the *Atlantic Monthly,* and books on Masonry.

The General Convention trustees, in 1929, sanctioned the idea of a good-will pilgrimage to Europe to foster closer relations among religious liberals.[25] There was much doubt about whether the tour would ever take place, in the face of disastrous economic depression. The goal was nonetheless set at fifty participants.[26] There was some complaint that the money expended should be used for domestic projects, but the answer was that it would be at small cost to the General Convention if private and local church financing could be arranged.

The tour did, in fact, take place, but on a scale drastically reduced from the original plan. Twenty-two Universalists actually made at least part of the trip, with MacPherson and his wife, of the church in Joliet, Illinois, as leaders, and Stanley Manning of Augusta, Maine, as the recorder who made periodic reports published in the *Leader.*[27] They attended liberal (mostly Unitarian) churches, met with kindred souls at various points, and returned to report a modicum of success in their mission.

Another token of international good will was the appointment in 1929 of Mrs. Stella Marek Cushing, of Southeastern European heritage, as the official delegate of the General Convention to the peoples of Czechoslovakia, Jugoslavia, and Albania.[28] She also served, while a resident of Montclair, New Jersey, on the Commission on Foreign Relations.

The General Convention even authorized in 1929 the appointment of a Commission on World-wide Free Religious Fellowship. Its mandate was "to survey the possibilities of religious fellowship and cooperation [with] liberals in non-Christian fields."[29] However, nothing was done at the time, and the main concern in overseas affairs remained the elusive goal of alleviating, if not solving, the chronic problem of deficits in the financing of the Japan mission.

Chapter 10

The National Scene

The Congress of Liberal Religion and the "New" Universalism

There had emerged by the early 1890s a distinct and identifiable progressive or liberal wing in the Universalist Church which made many of the more conservative members uneasy and even provoked a species of antagonism. The relatively small but articulate leadership of this liberal wing was concentrated in the Midwest, although by no means confined to that area, and included a significantly high proportion of women clergy. It comprised those who questioned to some degree the basically Biblical Christian orientation of the denomination, looked with favor on the findings of science, accepted with enthusiasm the theory of evolution, favored a scientific approach to religion, including the Higher Criticism, and put their faith increasingly in the ability to shape one's own destiny. Some went so far as to admit to an unabashed rationalism and to propagate a version of humanism that sounded surprisingly like that voiced half a century later by a growing segment of Universalists.

Exponents of what came to be labelled the "New" Universalism rejected narrow denominationalism, sectarianism, and religious dogmatism of all kinds, and called for closer relations among all religious liberals, particularly with Unitarians. There were even preliminary steps taken to form a "United Liberal Church" comprising representatives primarily of the two denominations although the door was open in some degree to others. A skeleton organization was created to this end during the simultaneous summer grove meetings of Universalists and Unitarians at The Weirs in New Hampshire in 1893.[1]

A similar organization, known as the Universalist League, was organized in 1894 in Boston, with thirty-eight members and with Henry Blanchard as its president.² Among its purposes were closer fraternity with the Unitarians, Ethical Culturists, and Reformed Jews; support of the Higher Criticism; and the study of comparative religion. After a second meeting in 1895, with Blanchard, J. M. Pullman, and Mary A. Livermore as the featured speakers, the group apparently ceased to exist, although many such individuals later joined other comparable organizations which had longer histories.

These two tentative and local movements appear not to have had any immediate results, but there was one organization which did attract a small but important group of Universalists at the end of the nineteenth century. It was what became at first the American Congress of Liberal Religious Societies and eventually the Congress of Religion. The American Congress, incorporated in Illinois in 1894 and inspired by the World's Parliament of Religions, had had its origins in a series of informal meetings in the 1870s attended largely by Unitarian clergy in the Midwest. Among the leading figures in the movement was Jenkin Lloyd Jones who was associated with the Western Unitarian Conference.³ In spite of its name, originally there was to have been no representation from churches as such, and the members were to participate strictly in their individual capacities.

Several members of the group began publishing a series of missionary tracts in 1878, known as the "pamphlet mission for freedom, fellowship and character in religion." After six months under that rather awkward title, it was renamed *Unity*, with the subtitle "A Quarterly Review of Religion, Ethics and Theology."⁴ The publication carried religious articles of various kinds, and items of interest primarily to Universalists and Unitarians from their denominational presses. Articles for early issues were solicited from several Universalist clergy in the Chicago area, including William H. Ryder.

Jones, who served on the original publishing committee and became managing editor of *Unity* in 1880, was also responsible for organizing the program devoted to Unitarianism at the World's Parliament of Religions.⁵ It was out of the planning for the 1893 meeting that the idea of a formal Congress of Liberal Religious Societies emerged, with both annual national meetings and periodic gatherings at the state level. *Unity*, which was designated as one of the two official publications of the Congress, was retitled the *New Unity* between 1895 and 1898, after which the former name was resumed.⁶

In a "salutatory" in 1895 Jones affirmed that the enlarged publication represented "an actual co-operation already begun of Jews, Unitarians, Universalists, Ethical Culturists, Independents and Outsiders."⁷ He announced that he would seek, as editor, to prove that such religious bodies as those mentioned, as well as individuals, could "work together without destroying their individuality or sacrificing any valuable autonomy now existing." At the same time, the vision of religious harmony and cooperation was to be universal, literally embracing the world. To emphasize this point, a seal adopted in 1895 was carried on the masthead of the *New Unity* which pictured a globe with the word "Humanity" printed across it in large letters. Here was the articulation of a truly world religious concept which was to capture the imagination of many of the supporters of the "New" Universalism that had by then become visible.

The suggestion for convening a meeting of religious liberals from all over the United States had been made at an informal conference of four men in 1893 in Chicago, while the World's Parliament of Religions was still in session. Winfield Scott Crowe, pastor of the Church of the Redeemer (Universalist) in Newark, New Jersey, was one of the four. An *ad hoc* committee, including E. L. Rexford, at the time pastor of the Universalist church in Roxbury, Massachusetts, agreed to formulate plans for a national gathering.[8] Over 1,000 individuals responded to the call for the meeting, expressing their interest and/or support. A number of Universalist names were to be found on the list, including Charles H. Eaton of the Fourth Universalist Church in New York City; Henry Blanchard of Portland, Maine; and Orello Cone, then president of Buchtel College.[9]

The organization meeting, held in Sinai Temple in Chicago in 1894, included more than 20 Universalist clergy among the total of more than 200 who attended. However, some who had been active in the preliminary planning, such as Rexford, Crowe, and Marion Shutter, were absent. Shutter was to have given the opening address which was to have indicated the relevance of the Congress for Universalists. Charles Fluhrer (Michigan), A. N. Alcott (Illinois), and Rufus A. White (Illinois), who served a term on the editorial board of *Unity*, were among the Universalist clergy who were present.

The American Congress of Liberal Religious Societies, officially designated thus by its charter in 1894, was usually referred to as the Liberal Congress in its early years, and then simply as the Congress. The idea of changing the designation in order to broaden the appeal of the organization and to reemphasize its non-denominational character was first suggested in 1895, when the name "Liberal Congress of Religion" was proposed.[10] At the annual meeting in 1898 the name "Congress of Religious Unity" was considered.[11] But after the membership was polled the following year, the name finally chosen in 1900 omitted the word "liberal" and the title became simply the "Congress of Religion."

The claim that the Congress was to be a "church of humanity" transcending existing denominational and sectarian arrangements was explicitly stated in the Articles of Incorporation of the new organization. Its aim was "to unite in a larger fellowship and co-operation, such existing societies and liberal elements as are in sympathy with the movement toward undogmatic religion; to foster and encourage the organization of nonsectarian churches and kindred societies on the basis of absolute mental liberty; to secure a closer and more helpful association of all these in the thought and work of the world under the great law and life of love; to develop the church of humanity, democratic in organization, progressive in spirit, aiming at the development of pure and high character, hospitable to all forms of thought, cherishing the spiritual traditions and experiences of the past, but keeping itself open to all new light and the higher developments of the future."[12]

The creation of the Congress immediately raised the question of whether its members were expected to sever their existing denominational ties. Could members stay within their traditional religious organizations and simultaneously belong to a new one under the rather ambiguous banner of "liberalism"? The leaders of the movement expressed no hesitation in replying that an individual could easily belong to both. An alternative rather widely followed, however, was for the clergy to establish their own independent congregations, without any denominational designation. Jones followed this system with his own church (All Souls) in Chicago in 1895. Others on his list of seventeen members of the "Fraternity of Liberal Religious Societies" in Chicago were the Independent Liberal Church and the People's Church.[13] Jones included the six Universalist churches in the city as members of his "Fraternity," together with three Unitarian churches, the Ethical Culture Society, a Friends (Quaker) society, and three Jewish congregations.

The Universalist press would have none of this. Both the *Universalist* (Chicago) and the *Christian Leader* (Boston) made it clear that they would not support or promote in any way a movement such as the Congress represented.[14] It was interpreted not only as a rival and a threat to existing denominations and a potentially divisive force, but as an opening wedge for weakening and diluting Christianity itself. The point was made that Jones had even renounced the Unitarian name — and who could go farther left, theologically, than that?

Bisbee, long-time editor of the *Leader,* was at first very skeptical of the Liberal Congress, particularly if it became a separate denomination. He described it as "a Krupp gun aimed at a canary bird," and pointed out that creating a "non-sectarian sect" and yet another religious bureaucracy was completely unnecessary.[15]

The *New Unity* quite correctly perceived the undisguised hostility of the Universalist press toward the Congress, but was considerably wide of the mark when it asserted that the organization was "made up largely of Universalists."[16] The majority of Universalists probably reacted in the same negative way as did their press, but it was also true that many clergy in the denomination either took an active part in the Congress or at least sympathized openly with its aims. Shutter, Crowe, and White, all Universalist clergymen, were at one time or another on the board of directors of the Liberal Congress, and Alcott was at one time its authorized missionary.

Shutter, pastor of the Church of the Redeemer in Minneapolis, one of the largest and most prosperous Universalist churches in the Midwest, was an active supporter of the Liberal Congress. His published sermon entitled "Liberal Unity" was widely circulated in 1896. In it he called for greater Universalist cooperation with other religious liberals, especially Unitarians, for which he was commended by members of the Congress.[17] Shutter's ideas were further elaborated in a sermon in 1901 entitled "A United Liberal Church" which was delivered in substantially the same form in Boston in 1907.[18]

Shutter saw in the union of Universalists and Unitarians the best possible starting-point for his larger goal of uniting all Christendom in one religious family. Even though there were differences of origin, history, and institutional development, the line of social and intellectual demarcation between the two denominations was growing fainter and fainter. Whatever differences of opinion existed were to be found more in individuals and in local churches than between the main bodies themselves.

He insisted that, however they may have started, the two groups in the final analysis were essentially the same — "the same in thought, in spirit, and in purpose." There was, accordingly, no real obstacle to maximum fraternity and fellowship. The statements of faith of the Universalists, as ratified in 1899, and of the Unitarians, as expressed by James Freeman Clarke before his death in 1888, were almost identical. By a judicious selection of representatives of each denomination, Shutter demonstrated, at least to his own satisfaction, that there were no significant theological differences.[19]

Both denominations, according to Shutter's interpretation, were hospitable to new truths, thoroughly humanitarian in spirit, and had the same aims: The emancipation of the human mind, the building of individual character, and the realization of the kingdom of heaven on earth. In short, in the things that really counted, there was nothing to keep the denominations apart. The differences between the two kinds of liberal religionists were "as futile and shadowy" as those that kept Methodists and Baptists apart among themselves. Why denounce sectarianism and then proceed to practice it?

Shutter did not expect any immediate union of the two denominations; but it would come, he thought, in due course, "by growth and not by manufacture." How was this to be achieved? He offered some practical suggestions: Universalists and Unitarians should become better acquainted; Unitarians should get rid of their "snobbery" on the one hand and Universalists of their "bigotry" on the other (the quotation marks were Shutter's). "There are some Unitarians in whose presence I feel like a 'poor worm in the dust'; and there are some Universalists who make me resolve to go back to orthodoxy and preach nothing but 'hell' all the rest of my natural life." Another step in the right direction was to engage in joint projects at the local level such as the union of liberal women, a Sunday school union, a liberal ministers' club, and a joint settlement house movement in St. Paul and Minneapolis. Joint meetings of the state organization of the two denominations in Minnesota were being planned. Combination of forces in rural areas and small communities was another desirable step. The name of the church did not really matter. Why perpetuate prejudices left over from an earlier and less enlightened day?

Crowe was one of the leaders of the Congress from its very beginning, as were Rexford and Shutter, and can be considered as one of the principal spokesmen for the liberal wing of the denomination.[20] He saw in the Congress an unparalleled opportunity for free fellowship on the widest possible basis. It could include "as many brave Orthodox brethren as we can reach, and just as many good agnostics as we can reach."[21] Universalists must slough off their provincialism and denominational emphasis. "Whoever cares more for Universalist traditions and attitudes than for human fellowship and the progress of truth is not a Liberal and has no place in any such union."[22]

In the winter of 1891 and the spring of 1892 Crowe delivered a course of lectures to his congregation on the main principles of religious thought and feeling in America.[23] To his summary of Universalist thought he appended a postscript entitled "The New Universalism." In it he outlined the "wonderful change" that had come about in the church. While maintaining the basic Universalist principle of the final good outcome of all things, the younger and more progressive elements in the denomination were adding new dimensions and enlarged insights. The "New Universalism" no longer rested upon the Bible as God's miraculous word, but treated it as inspirational literature. God's word was to be found instead in "man's moral sense, in the principles of right that have been established by experience, in the demonstrated laws of life, and in the essential results of conduct."

The key word in the lexicon of the New Universalism was "character," according to Crowe. Individuals entered the next world with the goodness or badness in which they died. None were saints, none were devils. Salvation was not achieved by "going to Heaven" but by the development of good character, the results of which were a human and not a divine responsibility. The old theological scheme, incorporating in it the mythological fall of Adam, was being replaced by the theory of evolution. The chief distinction of the New Universalism was its emphasis "on the present and on methods, not on promises and faith." Faith was worth only what it produced in the way of good conduct. The preacher's greatest mission was no longer the effort to prove that all will finally be happy. The duty nearest at hand was, rather, to labor for the present good, not to speculate and dogmatize upon the events of eternity. Debates over the divinity of Jesus were a waste of time; he was important because he was "the greatest of moral teachers and the purest of human examples."[24]

W. H. Lyon, a Unitarian, greeted Crowe's lectures with enthusiastic approval. In a review of the *Columbian Congress of the Universalist Church*, consisting of addresses delivered at the World's Parliament of Religions in 1893, Lyon noted that the volume was "as near a formal statement of the belief of the denomination as any to be found."[25] However, he did not believe that the papers represented the "braver and more progressive life of Universalism to-day." That was reflected, instead, in Crowe's "bright and energetic lectures on the subject."

Rodney Fuller Johonnot, pastor of the Universalist church in Oak Park, Illinois, and sympathetic with the aims of the Congress, used a somewhat different approach but with the same conclusions. He believed that *Unity* could perform an important service in educating Unitarians about Universalism and thereby do much "to help on the course of coming unity between these two denominations" by devoting increased attention to Universalism.[26] Unitarians would discover that, for the most part, Universalists were just as up-to-date and forward-looking as they. In most Universalist pulpits, clergy could speak freely upon "evolution, salvation, miracles, the Higher Criticism, the nature of Jesus, without any offense, and will find the utmost freedom encouraged, and the largest thought welcomed." Why did Unitarians fail to realize "that this has been the position of Universalism or at least a great number of its exponents for forty years?"

Johonnot placed part of the blame for ignorance of Universalism on lack of communication between the two denominations. For one thing, Universalist newspapers were rarely to be found on the tables of Unitarian clergy. But even if they were, a "true conception" of Universalism was not presented in the press. Why not? "The official press of the church is far behind the real thought of the church.... It is an open secret among us that our clergymen are not satisfied with the theological attitude of our denominational press."

Johonnot's contention that there was lack of definite knowledge on the part of each denomination of the religious position of the other was supported by Charles E. Perkins, minister of the Unitarian church in Iowa City, Iowa, in 1894. He had held a pastorate of three years in a Universalist church and had served two Unitarian churches, and could thus speak from experience.[27] In a brief review of the histories and beliefs of the two denominations he chose to stress their similarities and affinities. He applauded movements for closer union, with each making its own contribution. There was, he thought, too much in common to justify antagonism. If they could not become one in outward organization, Universalists and Unitarians should, at the very least, follow a policy of close cooperation. He hoped for the day when the spiritual descendants of Ballou and Channing could join forces.

One of the clearest and most comprehensive statements of the New Universalism came from A. N. Alcott, pastor of the church in Elgin, Illinois. According to Johonnot, it was Alcott who best expressed "the real position of the Universalist church, and the trend of thought within it."[28] Alcott centered his discussion around what he conceived to be three "great fundamental working principles" which had always governed Universalism. The first was "the endless expansion of religious knowledge," to be found historically in the Bible but going far beyond it. The second principle was the pursuit of truth, wherever it might lead, "no matter what the traditional, denominational doctrine might happen to be." The third was "the perfect autonomy of each soul in religion"; freedom was the watchword, and hence speculative theological doctrine was minimized if not completely eschewed. Universalism was "a republican religion in that it recognizes the autonomy and liberty of each soul in the religious life, as our nation does that of each citizen in political life."

Hosea Ballou was invoked by Alcott as one who tested and found wanting such doctrines and teachings as the Trinity, vicarious atonement, "the infinite demerit of sin," the justice of endless punishment, the widely held belief in a personal devil, and the existence of a physical hell. A combination of proper Scriptural interpretation and enlightened reason, for Universalists at least, had swept away much of the underbrush that had impeded true progress in religion.

The Winchester Profession adopted in 1803 fitted the noncreedal pattern of Universalist thought with admirable consistency by deliberately avoiding dogmatic pronouncements and elaborate theological schema. Unlike the creeds of orthodox denominations, the Profession was eminently flexible. Consequently, the progress of scholarship and science could easily be fitted in, and if truth required it, God's rule and providence could be accommodated solely according to the laws of nature. So far as a creed was concerned, Universalists, clerical and lay alike, had perfect liberty to hold whatever views they wished on such debatable subjects as miracles, the supernatural, revelation, the Higher Criticism, and the laws of evolution. There was no *ex cathedra* doctrine on any of them. Therefore it would be impossible to say that a Universalist who upheld one belief or another was right and one holding the opposite was wrong. "We cannot have heresy outside of the bounds of our creed."

Alcott admitted the existence of two wings in the Universalist church, conservative and liberal. But he played down the importance of the division. It was no more serious than the historic debates over trinitarianism or vicarious atonement. It was the liberal and progressive wing that would eventually win and clear the religious atmosphere of the obfuscations and obsolete traditions that lingered in the denomination. The inevitable triumph, for example, of the principles of the Higher Criticism was producing a new and scientific interpretation of the Bible as a whole. This in turn was producing multiple truths derived from enlarging knowledge.

Religious ideas and truths must be studied in the context of the environment in which they were created. Hence it was quite in order to apply to the Bible the tests appropriate for any piece of literature — authorship, authenticity, credibility, dates, and contents. The result was a progressive (therefore better) Bible. Each part of it, at the time of its origin, was "natural, helpful and practicable. Each succeeding age provided its own truths and rites out of the divine sources." This progressive revelation of religious truth was a clear example of the workings of evolution. Ultimate perfection, overseen by God, "the cosmic workman," was to be the final step.

Alcott was confident that the views he expressed represented the prevailing attitude of the Universalist church. He was even more specific than Johonnot in his criticism of the denominational press. Those who dissented from the ideas he expressed, so he thought, were concentrated on the staff of the Universalist Publishing House in Boston. They were, in "spirit and stage of development, from ten to fifteen years behind the body of our people, and still farther behind the needs of the age." They were, in short, laggards in the evolutionary process. He was sure that "many of our ministers and laymen . . . desire larger social and cooperative relations than they at present have with all other liberal Christian bodies." He was most assuredly among those who sought a broader faith. He was also one of the advance guards of Universalism, speaking to and for generations that were to follow.

Alcott had no easy time in finding acceptance for his ideas among more conservative Universalists. He had become so deeply involved in the work of the Liberal Congress by the end of 1894 that he applied for and was granted a year's leave of absence by his parish. He served as secretary and missionary of the Congress, effective 1 January 1895. Less than six weeks later he was suspended from fellowship by the Illinois Convention because he had chosen to engage "in professional services to a religious organization not in fellowship with the Universalist denomination."[29] He was informed that his action was "in direct violation of the vows of ordination, and such policy if generally pursued would result in the total disintegration of the Universalist denomination."

Alcott immediately protested, considering the action of the fellowship committee not only unjust but unconstitutional, on the ground that the rule applied only to individuals who entered into ministerial labor in another denomination. The Congress, he said, was in no sense another denomination, but was analogous to the YMCA or any other organization with membership drawn from a variety of sources to do supplementary missionary work. He compared his activities in the Congress to those of an evangelist in orthodox churches who worked with several religious groups. The only difference was that he was working among religious liberals who had no church homes in their communities.

The fact that Alcott was also active in the Free Religious Association undoubtedly contributed to his fall from ministerial grace. He was the delegate of the Liberal Congress to the annual meeting of the association in 1895 and suggested to the assemblage that Illinois would be a promising field for the organization of free societies or churches among scattered liberals.[30]

The Alcott case became something of a *cause célèbre* in Universalist and Unitarian circles in 1894, particularly in the Midwest. After a conference with the state fellowship committee failed to change their decision, Alcott appealed to the General Convention. But no action was taken by its Committee on Fellowship and Discipline, of which two members of the *Universalist* editorial staff were members. His case was buried in the committee and was never reported out. Thereupon Alcott elected "to take an independent position in the Universalist ministry."[31] He declared himself no longer under ecclesiastical authority but continued to adhere to Universalism. He accused the denomination of having an organization that was oligarchic, capricious, and arbitrary, and the editors of the denominational press of being arrogant and tyrannical and of suppressing the liberal wing of the church. He likewise accused the editors of the *Universalist* of making war on the Unitarians.[32]

Alcott's disfellowshipping was roundly condemned not only by members of the Congress but by the Stewart Avenue Universalist Church, on the south side of Chicago, which commended the Elgin church for supporting its pastor. The Chicago church likewise commended its own pastor, R. A. White, for "advocating the broadest toleration and fellowship regardless of the limitations of creed or confession"; and for advocating the universal brotherhood of man.

After carrying a notice, without explanation, that he had been disfellowshipped, the *Universalist* published two communications severely criticizing Alcott, one from an influential former parishioner. However, the paper refused to publish a letter of support for Alcott from his parish, representing over 300 members. Thereupon Crowe wrote an open letter to the trustees of the General Convention accusing the editor of the *Universalist* of "Star Chamber" tactics. Crowe's letter was refused publication by the *Universalist,* ostensibly on the ground that the paper did not allow criticism of cases of ecclesiastical discipline to be discussed in its columns.

The Elgin parish also filed a formal complaint with the Universalist

Publishing House because the *Universalist* had allegedly treated Alcott unfairly. The directors of the publishing house refused to overrule a decision of the editor of the *Universalist* not to publish the Elgin letter. It is noteworthy that none of the Universalist papers published any of the foregoing correspondence. The documentation was reproduced in full, however, in the *New Unity,* which took delight in castigating the Universalist establishment for its narrow denominationalism and curbs on freedom of speech.[33] In the meantime the disfellowshipped Alcott carried out his announced intention of devoting his full efforts to the Congress, serving as its state secretary and missionary in Illinois.[34]

J. S. Cantwell, editor of the *Universalist,* continued to oppose the Liberal Congress and the individuals associated with it. In 1894 the trustees of the moribund Universalist parish in Dixon, Illinois, allowed the Congress to use their vacant church building for a meeting to organize a People's Church. Cantwell immediately accused the Congress of attempting "to overthrow and disintegrate the Universalist parish."[35] The trustees protested, pointing out that for a number of years spasmodic attempts had been made to keep the church alive, but to no avail. Both the church and the parish had been dead for two years. If the Universalists could not succeed, and some other liberal church could, the trustees not only saw no objection but in fact encouraged it.

There were several other Universalist clergy besides those already mentioned who found much to commend in the idea of the Liberal Congress, and participated actively in its work. The conception of an organization cutting across denominational lines appealed to Howard MacQueary, controversial pastor of the Universalist church in Erie, Pennsylvania. The former Episcopal minister had been tried for alleged heresy because he questioned certain aspects of the divinity of Christ, and had become a licentiate in the Universalist church in 1891 after "renouncing" his Episcopal ministry.[36] MacQueary was among those who had assembled in the Art Building in Chicago in September 1893, out of which meeting the Liberal Congress had emerged.

MacQueary held a combined celebration of his church's semicentennial and a three-day meeting of the Liberal Congress in 1894.[37] Members of both Unitarian churches and Reformed Jewish synagogues attended, as well as many Universalists. The purpose was to promote fraternal feelings and to break down the barriers among faiths that MacQueary found among religious liberals. Among the Universalist speakers were Rexford; Isaac M. Atwood, president of the Canton Theological School; Bisbee; Cone; and Professor A. B. Curtis of the Tufts College Divinity School, who delivered a paper on the Hebrew idea of God. Among others on the program was Rabbi Moses J. Gries of Cleveland, Ohio, who spoke on the relation between Reformed Judaism and liberal Christianity, emphasizing the concept of universal brotherhood.

Although Cone never held an office in the Congress he frequently expressed sympathy for and support of its work.[38]

R. A. White, pastor of the Stewart Avenue church in Chicago, who had defended Alcott, was an active member of the Liberal Congress. A graduate of Tufts College and its divinity school, he had had a settlement of eight years in Newton, Massachusetts. He moved to Chicago in 1892 and took up the work of Florence Kollock, a Universalist minister who had married Joseph H. Crooker, a Unitarian clergyman. Both were also active supporters of the Congress, and Crooker served as a director in 1898.

White dreamed of a "civic church" in which ministers would be trained in sociology as well as theology, with social service an integral part of the church program. He envisioned a "seven-day" church, with lectures, industrial and domestic training, settlement house work, libraries, and youth reading rooms. He incorporated all of these into the activities of his own church, which in its social emphasis had a counterpart in George L. Perin's Every-Day Church in Boston. Within his first three years in Chicago, White became deeply involved in community affairs, including membership in the Civic Federation and on the board of directors of the National Children's Home Society. He also served on the board of directors of the Liberal Congress and on the staff of the *New Unity*.[39] He delivered a paper at the third annual meeting of the Congress in Indianapolis in 1896 on the role of the institutional church in the inner city.[40]

White vigorously supported the liberalism represented by the New Universalism, insisting that the ideology was not a series of negations but a positive affirmation that discarded such outworn doctrines as belief in hell and endless damnation, and stressed brotherhood and progress.[41] He was accused by the *Universalist* of disloyalty to his denomination because he actively supported the Congress.[42] He replied that the organization was not the antagonist of Universalism, Unitarianism, or any other religious group. The Congress was intended to supplement existing liberal religious bodies, but without a denominational tag. White estimated that there were over forty cities of 19,000 or more inhabitants west of the Ohio River that had no Universalist churches at all, and Unitarians had reached but few of the population. Why should not the Liberal Congress fill the void? If Universalists could or would not accept the challenge of these unexploited fields, then why not support a movement that would? He saw nothing incompatible with holding first allegiance to his own denomination and welcoming and supporting other liberal religious efforts. Even if the Congress became a new denomination, White would welcome it. Neither Universalism nor Unitarianism had "a monopoly of this liberal religious business."

The later history of White's church, of which he was the pastor for forty-four years, bore out the philosophy which he espoused. It became the People's Liberal Church of Englewood, with a Unitarian affiliation in

Henry Blanchard (1833-1918), an exponent of the "New" Universalism

1938 by way of the Chicago Unitarian Conference, and with a formal association with the American Unitarian Association during the pastorate of Donald Harrington (1939–1944), as the suburban Beverly Unitarian Fellowship in 1942.[43]

Among other Universalist supporters of the Congress was J. H. Palmer, pastor of the church in Cedar Rapids, Iowa. He was the organizer of a conference of the Iowa Liberal Congress for which his church was the host in 1898.[44] He also served on the executive committee of the state organization. Two Universalist ministers, Sophie S. Gibb of Boone, Iowa, and Mary Garard Andrews of Omaha, Nebraska, were on the program.

Henry Blanchard was another Universalist clergyman who belonged unmistakably to the progressive wing of the denomination. In fact, during the late 1870s he had temporarily deserted Universalist ranks and had become pastor of the Unitarian church in Worcester, Massachusetts, because he had at first found Universalism to have become too narrowly focused. In 1880 he decided, however, to return to his Universalist allegiance.[45] He attempted to build his own bridge between traditional Universalism and a wider field of liberal religion in general while pastor of the church in Portland, Maine. He called in 1893 for the organization of the Universalist League previously mentioned, which included fraternal relations with Unitarians and others who had advanced beyond a strictly Christ-centered version of religion. He was identified with such Universalists as Crowe, Rexford, White, Alcott, and Johonnot.[46]

Some Universalist organizations as well as individuals supported the Liberal Congress. At its meeting in 1895 the Wisconsin Convention adopted resolutions expressing 'sympathy with all efforts of the Liberal Congress to bring about a closer feeling among liberal churches.'[47] Universalists also participated in state-level meetings of the Congress which had been planned when it was created in 1894. Three Universalists (not identified) attended the Wisconsin Congress in 1900.[48] The Church of

Our Father (Universalist) in Chicago united in 1900 with the neighboring Independent Religious Society to form the North Side People's Church.

On a few occasions the denomination lost its clergy completely to the "ultra liberal" wing. A. K. Beem, Universalist pastor in Osage, Iowa, who had attended the meeting of the Congress in Chicago in 1894, preached the occasional sermon on "The Denominational Situation" before the state convention that year.[49] He had nothing but praise for the idea behind the Congress, calling it a "magnificent movement." He expressed dismay that his own denomination, which professed to believe "in a heaven large enough for all God's children," did not cooperate in encouraging undogmatic religion. With a thinly veiled reference to the *Universalist* of Chicago, Beem noted that if the denominational press were actually voicing the general sentiment of Universalists, he was much discouraged. It seemed "strangely sad to see any of us who have even asked to be recognized as liberal to get on our 'war paint' when there is an opportunity [instead] 'for brethren to dwell in unity.' "

Beem finally became so dissatisfied with Universalism that in 1901 he resigned his pastorate at Benton Harbor, Michigan, withdrew from the fellowship of the state convention, and established himself as a religious independent.[50] He organized a "Temple of Humanity" and held services in the local opera house. He had attempted earlier to transform the Universalist church in Lapeer, Michigan, into a "Church of Humanity." He was forced to resign, but his departure resulted also in the closing of the church.

Rexford, long associated with the Liberal Congress and its principles, and for forty-two years a Universalist minister, resigned from the pastorate of his church in Columbus, Ohio, in 1907, and left the denomination.[51] He organized his own "unsectarian, undogmatic, and ultra-liberal" All Souls Church in Columbus.

Ironically, the denomination also lost support in some quarters because its presumably liberal tendencies were more than some organizations and individuals could stomach. How much was due directly to Universalist involvement in the Liberal Congress and how much to general tendencies in the denomination is impossible to determine. But there was some backlash of which there is a record.

The Indiana Convention reacted decisively and negatively to what was conceived to be attacks on the Bible by a coterie of left-wing Universalists. In 1896 it condemned all clergy in the denomination who belittled the Bible as "an infallible authority in religion," expressed skepticism, or endorsed the Higher Criticism or any form of rationalism.[52] The officers of the convention were instructed to use their influence to prevent the employment or fellowshipping of any such clergy in the state, on the ground that 'no kind of rationalism is in any sense Universalism.'

Readers of the *New Unity* were assured that the dominant spirit at the

Western Universalist Conference held at the Oak Park church in Illinois several weeks later was "broad, rational, [and] progressive," in complete contrast to the sentiments expressed at the Indiana Convention. The latter gathering was in no way representative of prevailing Universalist thought, according to the Congress.[53]

The conservatives in the Indiana Convention were defeated at the meeting in 1901. A resolution committing that body to a belief in the Bible account of the life, teaching, miracles, death, and resurrection of Christ was tabled by a vote of 51 to 10.[54] But that did not deter individuals from taking their own action.

T. E. Ballard of Crawfordsville, Indiana, severed his connection with Universalism in 1901, after having been an ordained minister for more than twenty-five years. He could not accept what he believed was a "virus [which] has now poisoned the entire body of our once devout and pious Church."[55] This consisted of a disavowal of belief in supernaturalism, and denial of the Bible as final authority in matters of religious faith and practice. This skepticism and rationalism, a radical departure from the established doctrines of the church, was justified on the spurious ground of "progress" in religious thought. It amounted to nothing less than infidelity, in his opinion. To make matters worse, the creedal substitute for the Winchester Profession voted by the General Convention in 1895 (but not adopted) had made no mention of the Bible.

The second annual meeting of the American Congress of Liberal Religious Societies in 1895 was held, like the first, in Sinai Temple in Chicago. Invitations to send delegates had been sent out to all potentially interested groups, including the Universalist General Convention.[56] Some forty minister were present, as well as some lay people. At least eight Universalist clergy were there. There were three delegates from the Illinois Convention. The New Jersey Convention had elected delegates but they apparently failed to appear. Among the twenty churches or societies represented were the Ryder Chapel in Chicago; the First Universalist Church of Englewood, a suburb of Chicago, which furnished seventeen delegates; and the society in Elgin, with eight representatives. No delegate had been appointed by the General Convention. Alexander Kent, who for many years had been pastor of the church in Washington, D.C. and who had left the denomination to establish his own "People's Church," was also present.

In the absence of Shutter, J. M. Pullman of Lynn, Massachusetts, spoke for the Universalist delegation. He repeated an often-quoted challenge, variously attributed, that "you Universalists have squatted on the biggest word in the English language. Now the world is beginning to want that big word, and you Universalists must either improve the property or move off the premises."[58] Orello Cone presented a paper on "The Higher Criticism and Its Ethical Relation," and Pullman delivered an address on the "Ethical Emphasis on the Liberal Faith."[59]

A proposal which provoked considerable discussion but no immediate action was made by Arthur M. Judy, a Unitarian clergyman from Davenport, Iowa. He felt that the proper course of the Congress was to let the denominations themselves take action rather than have a self-constituted body such as the Congress attempt to speak or act for them. He recommended that, instead of creating non-sectarian churches and attempting to establish yet another organization drawn from existing denominations, the Congress should sponsor a federation of all liberal denominations in America. It was to be called the "Liberal Church of America."[60] The proposal was considered "premature" and was referred to the board of directors for further consideration.[61]

Johonnot, who was at the meeting, prepared a report of the proceedings for the *Christian Register* which was generally restrained in tone.[62] He noted that the attendance was considerably less than in 1894 and that the enthusiasm which marked the first meeting was missing. He attributed this to growing mistrust of the whole movement and to mounting fear that the final outcome of the Congress would be the creation of yet another liberal denomination rather than enhanced cooperation among existing ones. What had started as a spontaneous and informal fellowship of kindred souls was rapidly becoming a highly structured body complete with officers, treasury, a committee system, and a twenty-three-person board of directors. Indicative of the changing character of the Congress was the provision in the by-laws, a set of which had been adopted in 1895, specifying that the Congress was to be composed primarily of churches and societies rather than of individuals. Participation for the latter was provided under the category of "fellowship" membership.

Johonnot opposed the pledge built into the constitution of the Congress to organize non-sectarian churches, feeling that this would create rivalries and alienate existing denominations. This was precisely what the *Leader* had earlier predicted would happen. Eventual unity among like-minded liberals, if it came at all, had to come by natural growth and not in forced-draft fashion.

The editor of *New Unity* (Jones) was very unhappy with the choice of Johonnot who had reported the proceedings of the Congress for the *Christian Register*. Jones criticized both that paper for publishing a "biased" report, and Johonnot for his lack of real commitment to the principles of the Congress.[63] This stemmed from the fact, said Jones, that Johonnot was admittedly a denominationally oriented Universalist/Unitarian, and this limitation naturally constricted his vision. It was those who were Universalists and Unitarians in spirit, whether or not a denominational label was pasted on them, to which the Congress wished to appeal.

Johonnot was indeed both a Universalist and a Unitarian officially. He held simultaneous fellowship, a somewhat unusual arrangement at the time, and was listed in both the *Universalist Register* and the *Unitarian Yearbook*. He had been fellowshipped as a Unitarian in 1886 and as a Universalist in 1890, and had received an honorary Doctor of Divinity degree from Lombard College in 1898. As might have been expected, he replied to the allegation in the *New Unity* that he did not favor the principles of the Congress. He insisted that he did indeed believe in and work for it.[64]

It was only as to the policy to be followed and the tactics to be used by the Congress with which he differed from Jones. Johonnot's contention was that the organization should restrict itself to the promotion of fraternity among liberal societies and denominations. He was positive that it would be an impossibility at the time, much as he supported the idea, to bring the Universalists and Unitarians together in one body. That might happen sometime in the future, but he did not care to make a prediction.[65]

Howard MacQueary was also a strong supporter of the idea of a federation of existing liberal denominations but, like Johonnot and Judy, opposed Jones' idea of recruiting members from them in order to create new non-sectarian churches.[66] MacQueary did his best to disabuse people of the mistaken idea that the intent of the Liberal Congress was to become itself a new sect.[67] He insisted that it was literally an assembly of societies of different names holding different opinions but organized, like the Congress of the United States, to consider matters of common interest. Similarly, the non-sectarian religious societies called for by the Congress's articles of incorporation were left completely free to affiliate with any denomination they saw fit, or with none at all. So far as he could see, this would neither injure any existing denomination nor build up one at the expense of another. The ideal, of course, would be for all the liberal denominations to form the Congress and lay aside their jealousies and rivalries. Each would mutually benefit from association with the others.

The third annual meeting of the Liberal Congress convened in Indianapolis in 1896. Of the thirty-four ministers in attendance, five were Universalists. Two others scheduled to appear on the program, Shutter and Canfield, were absent.[68] An international flavor was added by the presence of a Buddhist and a Brahmin. The dropping of the word "American" and the change of name to the "Liberal Congress of Religion" was therefore a most appropriate action at the meeting. The omission of the reference to "Liberal Religious Societies" in the new title reflected an attempt at direct appeal to individuals both in and out of churches.

The questions provoking the greatest discussion were the extent to which the Congress should pursue its missionary work, and the possibility of creating a new denomination. The consensus was that it was inexpedient to undertake an aggressive campaign because the organization had neither the money nor the personnel to do so. The opposition of existing denominations was also certainly a contributing factor to the decision not to expand the propaganda campaign in behalf of establishing non-sectarian churches. Rexford was among those who believed that the organization should not be burdened with the responsibilities associated with creation of a new denomination, and the controversy that would probably ensue if such a step were taken.[69] There was, instead, a plan never completely effected, to create a non-denominational "revolving ministry."[70]

The Liberal Congress ventured in 1897 into the Upper South for its annual meeting. It was timed to coincide with the Tennessee Centennial Exposition held in Nashville, and represented a miniature edition of the Chicago Exposition of 1893. R. A. White of Chicago and Amos E. Dolbear, a Universalist layman on the faculty of Tufts College, were among the thirty-two speakers.[71] Dolbear's topic was "Science and Theism."[72]

The participation of Universalists in the Congress was documented in part when its publication, *Unity,* celebrated its twentieth anniversary in 1898. Letters of congratulation and good wishes were reproduced from many sources, including communications from such Universalists as Ada C. Bowles (Gloucester, Massachusetts); Rexford, then in Columbus, Ohio; L. J. Dinsmore of Augusta, Wisconsin; Augusta J. Chapin (Mt. Vernon, New York); and Florence Kollock Crooker of Troy, New York.[73]

The national meeting of the Liberal Congress originally scheduled for the fall of 1899 had to be postponed until the following April because it conflicted with too many other meetings in various parts of the country in which the members were involved. It was held in Boston in 1900 and F. O. Hall, then pastor of the Universalist church in Cambridge, Massachusetts, was on the committee on local arrangements. Among the other Universalists attending were Perin of the Every-Day Church; Richmond Fisk of St. Lawrence University; Crowe of Newark, New Jersey, who presented a personal manifesto; and Cone of Buchtel College, who delivered a paper on New Testament scholarship.[74]

At the meeting in 1900 the word "Liberal" was deleted from the official name of the organization, which became simply the "Congress of Religion."[75] It adopted a somewhat revised statement of principles which reinforced the idea that it had no intention of forming a separate denomination, a fear expressed from the very beginning by many doubting Universalists. The Congress was intended to be literally an assembly point for members of every denomination with similar ideas. It was, as its statement indicated, a means of uniting "in fraternal conference those of whatever name who believe in the application of religious principles and spiritual forces in the present problems of life . . . it simply seeks to provide a medium of fellowship and co-operation."[76]

With such a vague and amorphous declaration, and with no real organizational focus, the Congress after 1900 gradually faded away. It held its annual meeting in Buffalo in 1901, with only a handful present. The time and place of meeting had been deliberately chosen to coincide with the Pan American Exposition then taking place there. The idea was to attract people to the Congress, but the presence of two competing attractions had the opposite effect.[77]

By the early twentieth century the Congress had outgrown its original constituency. That segment of the Jewish community at first involved in it turned increasingly to the Society for Ethical Culture.[78] The Congress continued to meet occasionally at the state level, but seems to have appealed principally to Congregationalists. Unitarian and Universalist support was no longer being solicited. At meetings in 1903 in Rockford, Illinois, and Ithaca, New York, neither denomination was represented on the program.[79] *Unity,* the organ of the Congress, did continue to be published after Jenkin Lloyd Jones' death in 1918. A few Universalists who had been active in the Congress or at least sympathetic to its ideals continued to keep its principles alive. In 1905 Rexford sponsored a two-day "Liberal Conference" in Columbus, Ohio, at which four Universalists, four Unitarians, and a rabbi delivered addresses.[80]

Even though the Liberal Congress as an organization with that name may have disappeared on the domestic front, the ideas on which it was based did not, and in fact were kept alive and their scope expanded. The concept of an International Congress of Religious Liberals, likewise launched under the aegis of Unitarians, appealed to many Universalists who had considered the Congress of (Liberal) Religion congenial to their tastes.

The National Federation of Religious Liberals

One of the by-products of the International Congress of Religious Liberals which had met in Boston in 1907 was a recommendation that a national federation of liberal religionists in the United States and Canada be created.[81] A private meeting to accomplish this was held in Philadelphia in December 1908, at a meeting house of the Society of Friends. The organizational model was the (then) Federal Council of the Churches of Christ in America, organized a few months previously, in which Universalists had not been invited to participate. Universalist representatives were, however, members of some federations at the state level; e.g., Massachusetts and Rhode Island.[82] They also participated in some of the Council's activities, both domestic and foreign.

An extensive correspondence among religious liberals had followed the Philadelphia meeting. Among the forty-five individuals who originally gave their support to the idea of a national federation were seven Universalist clergy: John Clarence Lee, J. Lonsdale Dowson, L. S. McCollester, F.

W. Hamilton, F. A. Bisbee, F. W. Perkins, and F. O. Hall. Lee acted as secretary at the first meeting. The organization which emerged was designated as the "Federation of Religious Liberals of America," intended "to promote the religious life, by united testimony for sincerity, freedom and progress in religion, a fellowship of the spirit beyond the lines of sect and creed, and by social service." Three articles of a Plan of Association were adopted, one of which provided for a council of twenty-five to serve as a governing body. Two persons were to come from each fellowship participating in the Federation, but would not represent any particular church. Individuals were to be responsible for their own opinions alone.[83] Charles W. Wendte (Unitarian), at the time the general secretary of the International Congress of Religious Liberals, was to serve as coordinator.

The first official meeting of the Federation convened in Philadelphia in April 1909, and about 1,000 individuals paid the one-dollar membership fee.[84] There was a deliberate attempt to appeal to liberals beyond Universalists and Unitarians. Hicksite Quakers and Reform Jews were encouraged to join, and a copy of the bulletin of the first meeting was issued as a special supplement to the publications of each denomination.[85] The Federation intended to "co-operate with every agency which endeavors to uplift the national character and invigorate it with high ethical and social aims." It was affiliated with the International Congress and was originally to have met alternately with that organization, although circumstances sometimes dictated otherwise. Wendte served as the direct link between the two bodies. Although not officially represented, the Congress of (Liberal) Religion obviously had similar aims, and consideration was given to consolidating the three groups, among which there was much duplication of membership.[86]

More than twenty Universalist clerics attended the first meeting in 1909, with Hamilton and Hall among the speakers. When the third meeting was held (in New York City) in 1911, the number of delegates was 400, with a small turnout of Universalists. Among the resolutions adopted was one which caused considerable controversy. It volunteered the services of the executive committee to arbitrate differences between Universalists and Unitarians "in place of the present often irrational and wasteful methods and misguided denominational rivalries."[87] Betts, a dedicated Universalist, emphatically denied the need for such services.

At its meeting in 1913 the Federation met jointly with the Free Religious Association.[88] A representative of the Federal Council of Churches gave one of the speeches. The Federation thereupon adopted the entire social program of the Council.[89] Isaac Atwood was the principal spokesman for the Universalists. When the Federation met in Philadelphia in 1915, in close proximity to Billy Sunday's tabernacle, the well-known evangelist consigned the entire organization to hell, although it refused to go.[90]

The Federation continued to meet annually until 1918, when the World War required a postponement. The International Federation meeting for 1917, to have been held in London, was postponed indefinitely because of war in Europe, but the National Federation held two sessions that year, the first in Pittsburgh and the second in Boston, for the first time.[91] McCollester, who was one of the vice-presidents, was on the program of the first meeting that year.[92]

Meetings were resumed in 1919, with official support from the General Convention, the AUA, the General Conference of the Society of Friends, and the Central Conference of American Rabbis.[93] The Universalist contribution was a token $50 a year. Universalists continued to be represented in both the Federation council and among the officers as well as on programs. Among those not previously mentioned were Judge Roger S. Galer, chairman of the trustees of Lombard College, who was elected president of the Federation in 1927 and served for five years; L. Ward Brigham, his successor as president; Joseph M. Tilden, president of Lombard; Shutter, pastor in Minneapolis, who was an honorary vice-president; and Henry R. Rose of Newark, New Jersey.

Like the earlier Liberal Congress, which had ventured into the South at the end of the nineteenth century, the Federation held sessions there after the First World War. Known as the Mid-Southern Federation of Religious Liberals, it had originated independently, but in 1929 voted to merge with the National Federation.[94] At the regional conference in 1931, held at Soddy, Tennessee, four Universalists active in the South were among the participants.

The National Federation met for the last time in 1932, in Joliet, Illinois, where the main topic of conversation was the proposed Universalist-Unitarian merger.[95] At its meeting in June 1933 the council voted to discontinue the entire organization.[96] For one thing, its treasury had been virtually wiped out by bank closings. Most importantly, the Free Church had been organized, with a structure and functions almost identical to those of the Federation. Further, there was no purpose in continuing when even the personnel of the two groups overlapped to a significant extent. The Federation, although not as successful as its founders had hoped, might now find a larger arena under a new name in which to serve the cause of liberal religion and take advantage of the contacts already made.

Section V

Institutional Activities and Organizations

Chapter 11

Clergy and Laity

Universalists followed substantially the same general pattern as did other Protestant denominations in regard to the status of both their clergy and their laity. Ministers were to be properly educated, fellowshipped, and ordained, and to provide the spiritual leadership demanded of their office. They also experienced, possibly in an exaggerated way, most of the problems faced by other religious groups — chronic imbalance in supply and demand, relatively low economic standing and lack of security, and a tendency to desert the ministry for more promising secular professions. These, and other difficulties, seemed on occasion to overbalance the positive side — the many who were dedicated and constructive in their service, professionally competent and experienced, with enviable records as contributors to their churches and to their communities. But a realistic assessment requires an honest review. Further, leadership was often associated with strictly personal qualities impossible to measure on any objective scale.

Universalists had always emphasized the importance of lay involvement; in fact, such missionaries as Q. H. Shinn had assumed without question that the scores of churches which he organized in the course of his many travels would be both led and sustained by extensive lay participation both before and after ministers could be found. In theory at least, clergy and laity were intended to provide a partnership; they were co-workers in a common endeavor. The Washington Association (Ohio) expressed this ideal in a resolution adopted in 1874. The minister was "to be regarded only as the leader and inspirer of work and worship, and *not* as the one from which all work and worship are to be expected."[1] Lay as well as ministerial responsibility was presupposed, and the very success or failure of an individual church or the welfare of its constituency depended on both the nature and extent of lay participation.

Clergy

Maintaining an adequate and stable supply of properly trained clergy after the Civil War became a problem of growing dimensions as the denomination expanded.[2] A special Committee on Pastoral Settlements reported to the General Convention in 1880 and did not like what they found. They discovered that, on average, parishes without full-time pastors were without any ministerial services one year out of every three. The average length of a pastorate was less than two and one-half years; over 40 percent were for no more than a year; and less than 5 percent of the clergy held pastorates for as long as five years.[3] A partial remedy was thought to be supervision by state conventions of "candidating" in their jurisdictions to cut down excessive shopping about by parishes and much "blind, aimless shifting" by clergy.

The trustees responded by recommending that committees on pastoral settlement be created to oversee placement and dismissal but warned that they could be no more than advisory bodies, with no authority of any kind. No parish would allow itself to be dictated to in any degree; neither would a clergyman accept direction as to what parish was to be served. Such attempts would produce nothing short of rebellion, "for both the history and temper of Universalists would forbid it."

In order to alleviate the problem of shortage of clergy, lay preachers were authorized in 1873.[4] They were subject to the same discipline as regular clergy, but were considered lay individuals for purposes of representation at General Convention meetings. They could conduct religious services and perform routine pastoral duties, but were not allowed to administer the ordinances recognized by most Universalists. Theological schools were urged in 1921 to create intensive short courses for lay people who planned to engage in missionary and extension work, and to supply pulpits temporarily.[5] The practice of licensing preachers and providing a minimum probationary period of one year prior to ordination had become well established by 1880, but licentiates were not authorized to administer ordinances until 1946.[6]

Recruitment of candidates for the ministry was urged time after time, and some efforts were made, but almost always with minimal results.[7] The blame for lack of success tended to shift, but ultimately seemed to rest on the clergy in the field. Lee S. McCollester, dean of the theological school at Tufts in the 1920s, supported that view, and insisted that it was not the responsibility of deans of such schools "to run up and down the country seeking students."[8] The problem remained unresolved despite all efforts, and was reflected in the generally small enrollments in denominational theological schools.

The economic status of Universalist clergy was a subject which received no systematic review by the denomination between 1870 and 1900. There was a general feeling that salaries were too low both in relation to other professions and within clerical circles themselves, but there was no documentation to support it. It was not until the national Census of Religious Bodies was published in 1906 that anything approximating an inventory of the salaries of Universalist ministers was made which indicated both the wide range within the denomination and a comparison with other Protestant religious organizations. Although the reportage was far from complete, at least some information was collected and published which gave a rough indication of the economic state of the profession so far as it pertained to Universalists.

Of the 846 churches and parishes reported to have existed in 1906, 373 responded to the request for salary data. The average was $1,238, the third highest among denominations reporting. Universalists had dropped to fourth place a decade later.[9] There was a great variation between urban and rural areas, with 25 salaries averaging $2,363 in cities of 300,000 or more, down to 271 salaries averaging $987 in communities of less than 25,000.

W. H. Skeels, General Secretary in 1912, made a study that year of sixty-six Universalist churches in the countryside or in communities of less than 3,000 and found that the average was $600 and the highest $900.[10] It was no wonder that rural preachers were forced to supplement their clerical income with secular employment.

A government study in 1916 estimated that an annual income of $700 was the minimum for an "average" family expecting to live at a "decent" level. The national average salary for all Protestant ministers that year was $663.[11] Skeels used this grim statistic as a justification for recommending in 1917 that the denomination raise at least $500,000 for relief of aged clergy.

The Ohio Convention resolved that same year that it was "inconsistent with present economic conditions that any church or circuit of churches in Ohio should expect to secure the services of a minister at less than $1,200 per year or its equivalent." The National Council of Superintendents broke down the stipend a bit further by unanimously endorsing in 1918 the recommendation of the Massachusetts Convention that the minimum scale be set at $1,200 for unmarried clergy; $1,500 and a parsonage or equivalent in rent for those married; and $1,500 and a parsonage or equivalent for those married with families, with $200 addition for each child.[12] Those clergy supplying more than one parish should also be paid travelling expenses. One itinerant preacher in the South, Thomas Chapman (grandson of Giles Chapman, a Universalist pioneer in South Carolina) did not meet all the specifications. As late as 1935 he was ministering to twenty-one churches and missions in half a dozen states. His salary that year consisted of $537.85 in free-will offerings, supplemented by $305 from the General Convention.[13]

Achieving a generally acceptable minimum standard of compensation remained an unattainable dream, considering the infinite number of variables involved and the customary reluctance of the denomination to break the historic tradition that the clergy should provide services at little or no cost to their clientele. Of 225 churches active in 1937 — during a period of severe economic recession — only 42 paid as much as $2,000, and 183 paid less than $1,000, even though many ministers were serving more than one parish.[14]

The situation had improved somewhat by the end of World War II. The average salary for all Protestant denominations had been slightly more than $1,800 in 1941; the highest paid were Presbyterian, Episcopal, Unitarian, and Universalist. By 1946 it had risen to $2,400 and to slightly less than $2,800 a year later.[15] The continuing tendency of clergy to move frequently was as evident after 1945 as before. Some 100 Universalist ministers had changed parishes within one year during 1946-1947, and lent credence to the picture of "a perambulatory clergy displaying characteristics of the hummingbird."[16] A sociological study of the Universalist ministry made at St. Lawrence University in 1947 supported this assessment. Of those serving short-term pastorates (less than three years), over one-third had been employed by more than four churches during a three-year period.[17]

The average salary of the sixty-five Universalist clergy in Massachusetts who responded in 1950 to a questionnaire was $2,952.84.[18] The General Assembly recommended in 1959 that the minimum salary be $4,000, plus parsonage, and with annual increases, but of course it was up to the local parish to set the actual amount. So there continued to be a wide variation in stipends actually paid.

Intimately associated with the economic status of Universalist clergy was the matter of pensions for those who had retired from active service. A long-range and systematic plan for providing a measure of economic security in the form of pensions was a long time in coming. It was not really accomplished until the eve of World War II, and even then was far from adequate. The closest equivalent, the Harsen Fund, had been established in 1845, but was limited to clergy and their families resident in New York State, and was intended more for the survivors of those deceased than for the building of a financial nest-egg during the lifetime of the minister.

Nothing came of a proposal made in 1863 by the General Convention to create a "General Aid Association." It was not until 1873 that a special bequest from John G. Gunn of $8,000 was actually received to assist needy individuals; but it was intended for "the relief of disabled clergymen" rather than to provide pensions as such.

The custom began in 1878 of augmenting the Gunn Ministerial Relief Fund by taking up collections at sessions of the General Convention. Approximately $1,600 had been added in this manner to the principal by 1900.[19] Small sums were also collected at district conferences and at meetings of state conventions, and solicited from local parishes, although with indifferent success. Meanwhile, some state conventions, like the one in Massachusetts, established their own relief funds for clergy within their boundaries. The Gunn Fund amounted to $15,000 in 1917, supplemented by resources at the state level which varied greatly in amount.[20] The great bulk of the payments out of both national and state funds were to meet financial emergencies only.

The first of many efforts to establish a denomination-wide pension system was made in 1911, when the General Convention instructed the trustees "to outline some plan that will furnish a reasonable support in age for our worn out ministers."[21] The intent was to consolidate with the Gunn Fund the numerous relief funds of state and local constituencies and provide some degree of uniformity.[22] But actually carrying out the idea was much more difficult and involved than passing resolutions on the subject. The trustees were unable to report a workable plan in spite of repeated calls by the presidents of successive convention meetings and pointed reference to the fact that almost all other denominations had made some provision for support of retired clergy. Even "the great corporations" were doing something for their employees.

One attempt was made in 1915 by the ministers themselves to create a voluntary pension fund. An *ad hoc* "Ministers' Fellowship" was created and managed by the General Secretary. It was to have been a temporary expedient until a permanent system could be provided, but only one-quarter of the clergy paid anything into the fund.[23] Further, it was intended primarily for the beneficiaries of deceased clergy rather than for retired ministers still living.[24]

The General Convention voted in 1919 that financial aid to aged ministers was to be undertaken "immediately" by the trustees, but again nothing was done. So in 1921 the trustees were instructed to present to the next convention "a definite and complete plan of action."[25] General Superintendent Lowe called for pensions of at least $1,000 a year for the balance of the lives of retired clergy.[26] The plea for trustee action seemed to have fallen on deaf ears, for in 1923 they were again authorized to raise funds and put into effect a contributory plan applicable to all ministers and other salaried workers.[27]

No one seemed to know what size the pension fund should be. The trustees had been instructed in 1917 to raise a total of $500,000 for the purpose, but in 1923 the goal had been pared down to $200,000. A ministerial pension fund was actually created by the trustees in 1924 and $25,000 was set aside out of general funds to underwrite it, with additional money to be acquired during the next five years.[28] The decision was based on the results of a questionnaire indicating that 78 of the 141 who responded would participate.[29] But the returns were so meager and there was so much grumbling and outright opposition to the contributory feature that it had to be rethought. So the General Convention reversed itself and rescinded the contributory plan in 1927.[30] The estimated cost of a properly funded system rose immediately to more than one million dollars.

The first pension payments under the revised plan were mailed out in the spring of 1928 to the fifty-seven who qualified according to eligibility standards set by a committee appointed to determine them. Any clergy in fellowship who had attained the age of sixty-eight who had served in the Universalist ministry at least twenty-five years would receive an annual pension of $130, paid in quarterly installments, regardless of need and regardless of whether they were still active in the ministry.[31] Many returned their checks, to be added to the principal, which by then comprised $135,000 and consisted of a combination of funds from numerous sources, including income from some state convention pension funds. The Massachusetts Convention in 1928 provided to the General Convention $1,800 for eligible clergy residing in the state. This was done by using funds earmarked for ministerial relief rather than for pensions, as was the $1,500 given in 1937.[32]

Difficulties immediately surfaced. The General Convention in 1927 had authorized payment of pensions to all clergy who qualified, including those already eligible for, or actually receiving pensions elsewhere. When the plea for a comprehensive and coordinated pension plan involving the individual states had been made, the New York Convention, which had the most generous plan, had refused to enter the system until all pensionable clergy received as much as those in the state.

The convention-sponsored payments actually made went down slightly instead of upward. Between 1928 and 1937 an average of sixty-eight clergy were eligible for pensions each year, and were receiving only $125 each. The principal of the central pension fund amounted to less than $86,000 in 1937, and only the income, drastically reduced by economic depression, could be used. It had to be supplemented by dipping into the Gunn Fund. The fact that clergy were ineligible for Social Security benefits under the legislation enacted originally in 1935 did nothing to help matters.

The onset of the Great Depression in the 1930s was an economic disaster for dozens of Universalist clergy, particularly in small parishes. Congregations continued to dwindle, and pastoral salaries were either cut or not paid at all. One of the most extreme cases reported in the public press involved Lewis Roy Lowry who, with his sixty-five-year-old father (also a clergyman), worked on a pick-and-shovel detail in a road gang under the supervision of the Civil Works Administration, a federal agency created in 1933 to provide work for the unemployed.[33]

So little had been accomplished in the 1930s at the denominational level that Seth R. Brooks, pastor of the Malden, Massachusetts, church, and William Wallace Rose, in neighboring Lynn, founded the Universalist Ministers Retirement Society to provide some sort of program, but it was far from national in scope.[34]

Yet another attempt was made by the convention trustees in 1937 to provide both adequate retirement income and a financially dependable source of funds. A special committee was appointed to formulate a contributory plan and submit it to all clergy and local church trustees at least six months prior to the 1939 convention. After many lengthy sessions and consultations with actuarial experts a plan was developed and presented to the General Convention.[35] It included both parish ministers and lay denominational employees, and provided for voluntary enlistment. Everyone who entered the plan was to contribute 3 percent of annual salary, supplemented by a 5 percent contribution from the employing church or organization. The members had several options upon reaching the retirement age, which was reduced to sixty-five in line with federal legislation. The plan was to be administered by a convention pension board. Emerson Lalone, who was a member of the committee which presented the plan, vehemently urged support and pointed out how ridiculous it would be for the denomination to prolong any further its policy of comparative inaction in providing for a decent retirement stipend.[36] The General Convention, after years of delay, finally approved in 1940 what appeared to be a workable plan which was to go into effect in January 1941 if a sufficient number of ministers and staff approved it.

Clergy and churches were so slow in responding, and showed such minimal interest despite repeated reminder notices, that in November 1940 the entire plan was shelved. Of 183 churches, only 16 agreed to the plan; only 19 of 95 clergy who responded agreed to the proposal.[37] Even then, there were sufficient funds by 1942 to increase payments to $200 a year, a sum still considered "wholly inadequate."[38]

Another attempt was made in 1946 to pool all funds, both state and national, and to provide an allocation through the United Appeal. At the time, five state conventions had their own separate pension funds.[39] As proposed, payments were to begin at age sixty-five, with the goal of $800 annually and $600 as the immediate objective, beginning in 1948. The Universalist Retirement Service Society was created in 1948 to administer the pension program, but the payments from UCA sources amounted to only $400 in 1949.[40]

The pension payment was raised to $500 in 1950, with twenty-five years in the Universalist ministry as a prerequisite for eligibility.[41] It was not until 1958, ten years after the goal of $600 had been set, that that amount was actually paid.⁴² The situation improved dramatically after consolidation with the Unitarians, but prior to the 1960s a generous retirement and pension program certainly was not offered as an inducement to enter the Universalist ministry.

Adjusting the Rules of Fellowship

If Universalists and members of other denominations were to mix and mingle more freely than before, as all the declarations about Christian unity indicated in the 1920s and 1930s, one problem that had to be solved was that of dual and/or reciprocal fellowship of both clergy and parishes; i.e., simultaneous fellowship in two or more denominations. A proposal had been made at the General Convention in 1909 to provide interchangeable fellowship between Universalists and Unitarians, but it had been buried in committee.⁴³

Until 1917 there had been no attempt to amend the convention constitution and by-laws which had prohibited such arrangements by Universalist clergy. According to denominational rules, clergy from outside had to relinquish their fellowship in order to become Universalists — a provision which obviously worked to the disadvantage of the denomination. For several years the prohibition against dual fellowship had been evaded or disregarded. The president of the General Convention estimated in 1917 that more than thirty Universalist clergy held such fellowship in spite of the rules.⁴⁴ So, at the 1917 session it was proposed to legalize the practice, with dual Unitarian fellowship particularly in mind. By a vote of 187 to 38 (with 38 abstentions) Universalist clergy were permitted to hold simultaneous fellowship in other denominations but were not allowed to vote or hold office in other conventions if serving other than a Universalist church.⁴⁵ The same provisions were assumed to apply to clergy in other denominations seeking fellowship with Universalists.

However, through an inadvertence, a provision that such clergy were to be exempt from the one-year probationary period required of Universalist clergy was omitted from both the minutes of the convention and the updated laws of fellowship which were printed and distributed. Edwin C. Sweetser was opposed as a matter of principle to any kind of reciprocal fellowship. "We could never take the place of the Unitarians if we would, and God forbid that we should try!"⁴⁶

As the self-appointed watchdog of legal niceties in the conduct of convention business, he insisted that the entire amendment in 1917 authorizing dual fellowship should be considered null and void because a provision about the probationary period had been omitted from the records; because there was alleged ambiguity about the rights of clergy from other denominations; and because the revised by-laws presumably conflicted with some parts of the constitution.⁴⁷ When he filled out a personnel questionnaire for the General Convention records in 1921, Sweetser had responded to the question of whether he also held fellowship with any other denomination by writing: "Of course not. That would be a violation of the laws of our Church, to which I have pledged my loyalty."[48]

Cosmetic changes were made in the laws of fellowship in 1923, but the matter of dual fellowship and the other problems raised by Sweetser were not directly addressed.[49] While he kept the issue of the legality of dual fellowship for clergy alive almost single-handedly, the problem of reciprocal fellowship for churches and parishes had yet to be confronted. Both matters came to a head in 1924, when the trustees had received a memorandum from All Souls Universalist Church in Cleveland, Ohio, asking that they consider the problem of dual fellowship for parishes created by the union of groups previously belonging to different denominations. The Cleveland church was contemplating merger with the Mayflower Congregational Church under the joint leadership of their pastors. The convention trustees had approved the plan in principle but had not considered the details or legal implications.[50]

The Commission on Comity and Church Unity to which the matter was referred also received a request from the Pennsylvania Convention asking for an amendment to the by-laws making it possible for the Universalist church to grant fellowship to ministers in other churches who desired and applied for such fellowship.[51] The commission thought an amendment to the by-laws was unnecessary in view of the 1917 legislation, but admitted that there was no provision for churches or parishes to hold joint fellowship. The entire subject needed review and clarification.

Another case in point had arisen in 1924 when Norman D. Fletcher accepted a call to the Haverhill Universalist church in Massachusetts while he was still a student in the Canton Theological School. He was not eligible for ordination under Universalist rules because he had not been licensed for at least a year. This restriction was neatly bypassed by having him ordained in the Universalist church by a special council of Unitarian clergy called by King's Chapel in Boston.[52] Fletcher, having thus been ordained under somewhat unusual circumstances, obtained Universalist fellowship under the reciprocal agreement of 1917.

In 1924 the inadvertent omission of 1917 concerning the probationary period was finally corrected, and when copies of the laws of fellowship were distributed at the General Convention meeting in 1925 the waiver of the requirement of a one-year probationary period for any ordained clergyman seeking Universalist fellowship was included.[53]

There was so much confusion and uncertainty about joint fellowship that the trustees in 1925 were instructed to review the entire convention constitution and its by-laws and propose amendments that would clarify and harmonize them. Sweetser, who served as a consultant to the special committee appointed for that purpose, was adamantly opposed to any provision that would have given voting rights in the General Convention, either implicitly or explicitly, to those of other denominations, either individually or collectively, who also held Universalist fellowship. Such a provision, he thought, would "falsify" denominational statistics because of double counting; allow "outsiders" the same convention privileges as tried and true Universalists; enable individuals trained in Universalist theological schools and at least partially at denominational expense, to become pastors in other communions; complicate such matters as determining the probationary period for clergy; and would, in effect, create "an ecclesiastically bigamous sort of relationship" which would in no way promote interdenominational comity.

At the 1925 convention the trustees had recommended an addition to the by-laws "to provide for official recognition of such federated parishes as now exist or which may hereafter be formed to which a parish now in our fellowship may be a party."[54] The proposed amendment was worded as follows: "Any federated, union, or other parish formed by the combination of two or more denominational organizations, one of which has been in the Universalist fellowship, may be granted fellowship by the Convention having jurisdiction upon the recommendation of its Committee on Fellowship, and the parish receiving such fellowship shall be entitled to all the rights and privileges of full fellowship, provided all other legal requirements are fulfilled." Sweetser still questioned the legality of the entire proposal on the ground that the constitution of the General Convention gave no such authority.[55]

The proposed amendment came up, together with numerous others, at the 1927 convention, with its wording unchanged. After it had been unanimously adopted (178-0), all others dealing with fellowship were tabled and turned over to a three-person committee to consider. Any possibility that voting rights would be specifically extended to clergy from other denominations was averted, much to Sweetser's relief. He had been appointed to the special committee to present to the next convention (in 1929) "a revision of all the Laws of Fellowship, Government and Discipline in an attempt to eliminate some of the seeming conflicts and also to define more closely some of the provisions of these laws."[56] However, the committee's report was delayed, for Sweetser had died on the eve of the meeting, after more than sixty years in the Universalist ministry.

A reconstructed and enlarged committee (increased from three to five) made its report at the 1931 convention. Among the recommendations was the creation of four categories of fellowship for clergy, one of which was to have been "associate," without voting privileges. This would have included those holding Universalist fellowship who were engaged in the service of other denominations. But the General Convention refused to accept the idea of categories of fellowship, as well as several other committee recommendations.

Regardless of the technical questions involved, sufficient Universalist clergy held joint fellowship by the fall of 1926 to justify identifying them in the official list of ministers. Fifty-six that year held fellowship also with the Unitarians and six with the Congregationalists. By the time the 1928 yearbook appeared, a total of seventy-eight held dual fellowship but only thirty were serving Universalist churches. This raised the question in the minds of some Universalists like Vincent Tomlinson of whether such arrangements created divided interests and loyalties and weakened the church.[57] Whether it did or not, dual fellowship continued to be popular. In 1932, one year after the Unitarians had proposed merger, sixty-five Universalist clergy held dual fellowship with Unitarians and twenty with Congregationalists.[58] As of 1934, about 20 percent of Universalist clergy (129) held fellowship also with Unitarians, and 23 with Congregationalists; there were four Universalist clergy holding fellowship in both.

After amendment to the laws of fellowship in 1939 which further clarified reciprocal arrangements, there were 100 clergy serving other denominations who had availed themselves of Universalist fellowship.[59] Editor van Schaick, the great exponent of breaking down denominational barriers, waited until 1935 to obtain associate membership in the Union Congregational Church (Boston) and until 1936 to hold fellowship with the Unitarians.[60]

The system of granting reciprocal fellowship with Unitarians, suspended temporarily in 1952, had been resumed by 1957, but was again suspended in 1959, pending the outcome of negotiations for uniting the two denominations.[61] By 1955 there were 122 clergy holding reciprocal Universalist-Unitarian fellowship.[62] The necessity for a system of reciprocal fellowship as between Universalists and Unitarians was automatically eliminated in 1961 when consolidation was achieved.

The incident which provoked the greatest amount of debate about dual fellowship was the ordination in 1928 of Clarence E. Rice which took place in St. Paul's Episcopal Church in Boston, with several Universalist clergy present. He had originally been ordained in the Universalist ministry in 1883 and had never relinquished it. Several questions arose: Why was it necessary to be ordained a second time in another Christian church? Was not the Universalist ordination legitimate, proper, and recognized? Why was he apparently abandoning Universalism for orthodoxy? Would Rice now be put in the awkward position of attempting to serve two masters? These and related questions were raised and discussed for several months and at great length in the *Leader*. Most of these questions were never answered so far as they involved Rice, for he died less than two years after his reordination.[63] He did, however, preach in both denominations although he held no regular pastorate in either.[64] Among the things he missed in Universalism was sufficient attention to liturgy.

Much less stir resulted when George R. Longbrake, a captain in the United States Army, was reordained as an Episcopalian in 1930 without relinquishing his Universalist fellowship.[65] His motive was to enlarge the scope of his activities as a military chaplain.

The whole matter of fellowship and ordination for clergy was reviewed at length by a special committee of the General Convention in 1931. The committee had the alternative of patching up the existing code or preparing an entirely new one, and chose the latter course. The plan called for the centralization of the entire system, which would have replaced the fellowship committees of the various state conventions with a five-member central fellowship committee elected by the General Convention. But that body refused to authorize such an arrangement and instructed the committee to present a more acceptable set of regulations at the next biennial meeting.

A satisfactory compromise was worked out in the laws of fellowship adopted in 1933. The central committee, to consist of seven individuals, was retained, but so also were those of the states. The main functions of the central committee were to establish and maintain uniform standards for fellowship, ordination, and discipline, and to hear appeals.[66] Even then, some Universalist clergy, suspicious or fearful of centralized authority, like Fred C. Leining, insisted that in some cases the action of the central committee should be subject to ratification by the state conventions.[67]

The idea of four categories of clerical membership, which had been rejected in 1931, was revived in 1937, but action was indefinitely postponed because of opposition to it.[68] The denomination solved the problem by providing two broad categories: Full fellowship and associate fellowship for those who had ceased to serve in a full-time capacity.[69]

The Fraters

Among traditional activities in which many Universalists, especially the clergy, participated or held membership over the years were various organizations intended to provide closer fellowship, offer an opportunity to exchange experiences, or otherwise keep in touch. Some were purely local or regional in character, and some were intended largely or exclusively for ministers and took the form of periodic retreats. Such was the Idlewild Fellowship, organized in 1928 and comprising mostly Universalists, with a scattering of Unitarians and Congregationalists. Membership was drawn for the most part from the Greater Boston area. They met annually at a farm in Dunstable, Massachusetts.[70] After the Idlewild Inn burned in 1933 on the eve of the conference scheduled there, the fellowship met for several years at Senexet, a retreat house owned by the Unitarians and located in a Connecticut village.

Senexet consisted of a thirty-room mansion on a forty-acre estate near

South Woodstock, and in 1931 was remodelled to serve as a retreat headquarters.[71] Universalists were invited to share the facilities which were used for all kinds of conferences attended by laity as well as clergy. The Mission Brotherhood, a joint Universalist-Unitarian preaching order, was organized in Senexet in 1932.[72]

One indication of the growing sense of professionalism among younger Universalist clergy was the organization in 1929 of the Universalist Ministers Association.[73] It was intended "to promote closer fellowship and mutual helpfulness," serve as a channel for ministerial opinion, and to draw up a code of ethics for the profession (finally accomplished in 1951).[74] The Association also published an occasional journal, *Teamwork*. The organization was among the first to be consolidated with its Unitarian counterpart, in May 1961. The combined association terminated its existence in 1964.[75]

Of all the organizations among Universalist clergy in New England, the oldest, the one with the most sought-after membership and with the longest continuous history, was the Fraters of the Wayside Inn.[76] It was created to meet a felt need among ministers for "spiritual and physical renewal" preceding the Lenten season. The tradition was started by James F. Albion (Malden, Massachusetts) and Vincent E. Tomlinson (Worcester, Massachusetts), who sent personal invitations to a number of clergy within "easily accessible distance" to assemble for a three-day retreat. Eight responded positively, and ten individuals, including Charles F. Andrews, a Tufts Divinity School student, attended the first retreat in February 1903. It was considered so successful that it became an annual event by consensus. Membership was at first limited to fifteen but was increased to twenty in 1915 and to twenty-one after 1958. The maximum number was governed by the availability of accommodations.

The facilities, located in South Sudbury, Massachusetts, were ideally suitd for the purposes of a retreat. The original building had been started in 1683 and completed in 1685. The inn was located in a quiet rural setting, and was steeped in colonial and early national history. Known for many years as the Red Horse Tavern, it had been immortalized by Henry Wadsworth Longfellow in *Tales of a Wayside Inn* (1863) and the original structure had been carefully preserved under a series of private owners and opened to the public in 1897. Meetings took place in either the parlor or in front of the fireplace in the spacious kitchen, the oldest part of the building. The Fraters took over the entire inn during their retreats.

The same schedule was followed without major deviation for almost half a century after the Fraters had been established. The retreat was held from Sunday night through Wednesday in mid-winter, usually in late January or early February. Many clergy developed the habit of arriving in the late afternoon or early evening of the Sunday preceding. Several papers were read during the three days, with free discussion. There was

A Fraters ritual

A representative group of Fraters

also opportunity for walks in the woods or some other outing or relaxation if weather permitted. Periods of general sociability were also provided for "the merry monks at the Wayside Inn," as one of the members called the group, but the tone of the meetings, as well as the intent, was basically serious — a time for contemplation, reflection, and spiritual renewal. A Communion service was invariably held sometime during the retreat, as well as devotional services.

The organization was simple and uncluttered, and the rules were minimal and carefully observed. There was no constitution or by-laws. Regular membership was limited to active clergy.[77] The connection was automatically dissolved if any member of the Fraters entered secular pursuits (as some of them did). Membership was by invitation and election only, and only after attendance as a guest at least once. The officers were an abbot or prior to serve as coordinator, rotated on the basis of seniority; a scribe; and a treasurer. The group usually met informally for several years in Boston preceding each retreat to plan the program.

Average attendance during the first decade was thirteen; the smallest was seven and the largest seventeen. There were twenty-six active members in 1912, although not all were able to attend each year, so the maximum of twenty was not exceeded. There was so much interest in the Fraters by 1916 that the experiment was tried of holding two retreats each year. A second group (of eight) was organized that year, chaired by Levi M. Powers, but it met with so little response that the idea was immediately abandoned. Instead, the maximum membership was reaffirmed at twenty. There were almost always one or more guests at Frater meetings. In 1917 three seniors from the Crane Theological School at Tufts were invited guests at the fifteenth anniversary celebration. The intent was not to enroll them as members but to give them some insight into how ordained clergy conducted themselves as professional ministers.

One of the elements that gave continuity to the growing tradition of close association between the Fraters and the Wayside Inn was the part played by Henry Ford. When word had been received early in 1924 that the widow of the owner, and the long-time hostess of the inn, had sold it to the automobile magnate, there were many misgivings. But there was great relief in the ranks when it was discovered that no policy changes would affect the cordial relations between the inn and the Fraters. In fact, Ford developed not only a sympathy for their activities but a real affection for them, and followed the custom of sending them a telegram of greeting and welcome for each session. With this encouragement the Fraters even temporarily increased their membership limit to twenty-four in 1930.

By 1929 ninety-seven clergy had attended the retreat at one time or another.[78] The meetings that year might be considered typical. There were eighteen ministers and their guests; three of the clergy had been original members, two of them with unbroken attendance records. Papers were presented on "Effective Preaching" and "The Value of the Christian Tradition," with discussion both during and after the reading of the papers. Book reviews of works on philosophy and theology were added later.

The Fraters continued their tradition of annual meetings without interruption throughout the Great Depression, World War II, and into the 1950s and beyond. Only the personnel changed, as generations of clergy changed, but there were always continued links with the past. Tomlinson's record of unbroken attendance since 1903 was not interrupted until 1935, when he was absent on a world tour. Frederic W. Perkins' perfect attendance record of forty-two years extended even beyond his eleven years as pastor of the Universalist National Memorial Church in Washington, D.C., and was not broken until his death in 1943. Fred Leining (1886–1973) was the first Frater to have been a member for half a century.

It was not until 1951 that there was a break in continuity. Because the inn began to be closed during the winter as a fuel economy measure a later date had to be set (in April), and the retreat was reduced to one day. Time and age had taken their toll, but had not dimmed the determination of the Fraters to continue. "We are the thin minority, the living. We shall cherish the memory, keep the faith, redeem the tradition, and hold fast. . . ." There was a certain irony in the fact that it was on the fiftieth anniversary of the founding of the Fraters in 1952 that they were unable, for the first time, to meet in their beloved inn. Because of the expense of opening and heating the building during the winter months, and because the Fraters were insistent that the pre-Lenten meeting date of late January or early February be restored for their retreat, twelve Fraters met in the Congregational Retreat House in Framingham, Massachusetts, for several years, "with renewed confidence and cheerful hope." But there was yet another break with the traditional association with the Wayside Inn, for it was badly damaged by fire in 1955 and the Fraters were not able to resume their meetings there until after 1958. The innkeeper, Francis Koppeis, was the second individual to have been made an honorary member. Pleasant memories of earlier days could not be extinguished, and many of the papers took the form of reminiscences. As one long-time scribe had noted in the minutes many years earlier, "it was good to have been there," for an enduring comradeship developed over the years.

The practice of inviting speakers from outside the denomination developed after World War II, but an understanding was reached that such individuals be limited to those holding fellowship. There was some discussion in the 1950s about whether to open membership to those outside the denomination, but the consensus was to restrict it to Universalists. It was not until consolidation with the Unitarians that the latter were admitted. The Fraters remained one of the last strongholds of exclusively Universalist clergy.

The Laity

Although literally hundreds of Universalist laymen had made significant contributions to the denomination as individuals and as mostly unpaid officers of organizations, it was not until the early twentieth century that a systematic effort was made to organize the males on a national scale comparable to that of the women, represented by the WNMA.[79] Even then, organized participation by the men of the church had an erratic and uncertain history, characterized by spasmodic revivals and disappearances. The complaint about inadequate lay commitment and cohesion was of long standing. In 1830 the editor of the leading denominational journal had complained that "Universalists fail, and have always failed, in this one point, that they do not bring sufficiently into exercise the gifts of their laymen."[80]

The first organization of laymen on a national scale was created in 1907 as the National League of Universalist Laymen. It had been proposed the previous year by Frank J. Tanner of Buffalo, New York, vice-president of the state convention, who was concerned about the comparative lack of involvement of men in church affairs. The idea was well received, and Tanner agreed to contact others and to serve as temporary secretary. An anonymous donation of $25 provided paper and postage.[81] The first positive steps were taken at a meeting sponsored by the New York Universalist Club and attended by seventy-five men from seven states, at which preliminary plans were drawn up.[82]

Frank P. Bennett, president of the General Convention, strongly supported the plan, and arrangements were made to meet in conjunction with the convention in Philadelphia in 1907. Three hundred men assembled, and out of the meeting came the League, which was "to utilize the manhood of the Universalist Church in the solution of its problems . . . [and be] devoted to a positive and constructive work for Universalism in its best and largest aspects." Edmund Millen of Middletown, New York, was elected as the first president. Many state and local men's groups had already been created earlier, and they were encouraged to combine. Typical was the Universalist Club, the oldest such organization, created in Boston in 1873, with membership limited to thirty.[83] A Laymen's League organized in Chicago prepared a handbook, with model constitutions, and a banquet in Boston had drawn 400 individuals.[84] When organized nationally, there were approximately 6,000 members drawn from local groups; an unattainable membership goal of at least 60,000 was set.[85]

The League had no specific program beyond the general charge to assist in strengthening the denomination, and a few branches were spontaneously created in local parishes. But the organization faded away within a decade, to be replaced by the Order of Universalist Comrades, organized in 1917 with sixty-three charter members who met in Worces-

Owen D. Young (1887-1962), Universalist businessman and diplomat

ter, Massachusetts, at the time of the General Convention sessions. The leadership was assumed by Louis Annan Ames of New York City, as its first president. First known by its full name as "Universalist Comrades in Service," its purpose was to enroll each man for a dual commitment: A special project within his own church, and involvement in general community service.[86]

This effort was much more successful than its predecessor. Although not all of its plans materialized, it did at least undertake a series of specific tasks. In 1919, during a church-wide financial drive, a national committee of 50 of the Comrades was created to assist, with some 350 individuals taking part. Out of this came plans for a permanent group of laymen who would serve as the male counterpart of the WNMA. One responsibility (never carried out) was to have financed the construction of a boys' home in Tokyo as part of the Japan mission.

More successful was the introduction of national Laymen's Sunday in 1922, which Universalists claimed to have been the first to have been held among Protestant churches. The group also rendered valuable assistance in raising funds for the National Memorial Church. At the General Convention meeting in Detroit in 1921 the Comrades spontaneously pledged more than $30,000 in a matter of minutes.[87] The Comrades were so active by 1923 that a full-time field worker was considered necessary although one was never appointed.[88]

Originally, membership in the Comrades was to have been limited to those who had "rendered valuable service to the Universalist Church." But determining who was eligible raised delicate questions of judgment, so membership was quickly extended to those desirous of making special contributions, and then to all Universalist laymen.[89] Membership soared to 5,000 by 1920, with Massachusetts contributing the largest number — nearly 1,200.[90] When the 150th anniversary of the denomination was celebrated in 1920, a mass meeting of lay members was held in Gloucester, Massachusetts, with some 1,500 present. By 1922 there were six state chapters and nearly sixty local groups.[91] An elaborate organization was created, even with a unique emblem: A red, white, and blue rosette symbolizing Courage, Peace, and Hope respectively.

Like so many other Universalist organizations, the Order of Universalist Comrades originated with no official connection with the General Convention. In 1924 it did receive an appropriation of $3,000.[92] It operated simultaneously, and in largely uncoordinated fashion, with other groups in which men were involved in such special activities as fundraising campaigns. In 1924, in an effort to consolidate all of the general and special financial drives in what became the Five Year Program, the trustees created the National Laymen's Committee to take charge, at the suggestion of Victor A. Friend.[93] Robert W. Hill, a prominent Massachusetts lawyer, was made the chairman. Under the circumstances the Comrades disbanded as an organization in 1925 and its activities were dispersed among others in which men participated.[94] The new national committee was thus made a permanent organization as an administrative unit of the General Convention, with local chapters continuing on an optional basis.[95] Some continued to exist after the committee itself ceased operation in 1929.

In 1931 men of the church were urged to organize again as part of activities sponsored by the denomination, and a standing Committee on Men's Work was established in 1933.[96] It sponsored a Laymen's Institute at Ferry Beach in 1935, and the Men's Club, organized in Providence, Rhode Island, the same year, helped support the Clara Barton Diabetic Camp.[97] A regional League of Universalist Men was created in 1935 for Universalists in Massachusetts, Rhode Island, and New Hampshire, but its operations were suspended in 1943 because of wartime conditions.[98]

The last attempt before consolidation with the Unitarians to organize the men of the church on more than a local or regional scale came in 1951 under the leadership of Harold S. Latham, as the National Association of Universalist Men. At their organization meeting in 1950 in Washington, D.C., they discussed such diverse topics as possible service projects, ministerial salaries, church finances, and the appropriateness of discussing political, social, and economic matters in the pulpit.[99] There was no agreement on this. A three-point program was adopted in 1952: Provision of a recreational and educational plan for boys in every community in which there was a Universalist church; recruitment for the ministry; and "support in all ways" for the *Christian Leader*.[100]

At their meeting in Portland, Maine, in 1956, the Association labored mightily but not very successfully to formulate a definition of Universalist faith upon which all could agree. The closest to a consensus was that it was "intellectually impossible" for an honest atheist, or even an agnostic, to be a Universalist and still subscribe to the 1935 Bond of Fellowship and Statements of Faith.[101]

But turning the National Association of Universalist Men into a viable

172 / *Institutional Activities and Organizations*

FRIEND'S BRICK OVEN
- - - BAKED BEANS - - -

**1630—
   1930**

Back to the days of the founding of the Massachusetts Bay Colony goes the tradition of beans baked in the old brick ovens of Puritan households. In this Tercentenary year, Friend Brothers still carry on the age-old practice. The slow-baked beans from Friend's great brick ovens give you the authentic flavor that has made Boston baked beans a by-word the country over. However well you like baked beans, you'll like Friend's Beans better.

A baked bean meal is hardly complete without Friend's Brown Bread. Try it, too!

FRIEND BROTHERS

Melrose Sta.   Boston, Mass.

Victor Friend (1871-1952), a leading Universalist layman, and one of his enterprises organization somehow missed fire, and paid-up membership had shrunk to 300 by 1958. One of its last projects before losing its separate identity and combining with the Unitarian Laymen's League was to arrange for supply ministers for churches otherwise closed during the summer months.[102]

National organizations among Universalist men never achieved the continuity or strength of the Unitarian Laymen's League. This group had offered in 1936 to reorganize as a Liberal Laymen's League so as to include Universalists but received no reply to their suggestion.[103] Universalist men insisted on going their own way until denominational consolidation was achieved.

Chapter 12

The Church and its Youth

The Young People's Christian Union and Its Successors

"On Tuesday last there was inaugurated a movement which is destined to have deep and lasting influence upon the Universalist church."[1] The editor of the *Gospel Banner* (Maine) was referring to the first national young people's convention of the Universalist church which met in Lynn, Massachusetts, on 22–23 October 1889, immediately preceding and overlapping the sessions of the General Convention which also met there. Out of the youth meeting, originally advertised as the "Convention of Young People's Societies," came the National Young People's Christian Union of the Universalist Church (YPCU).[2] A total of 131 delegates, representing 56 societies and 13 states, had attended that inaugural session.[3]

When it celebrated its fiftieth anniversary in 1939 the YPCU had compiled a record of contributions to the Universalist church which was nothing short of phenomenal. It had either assisted in or been primarily responsible for building five churches; and there were, as well, "the scores of men and women we have given to our ministry, the hundreds of laymen we have trained, the thousands of youth we have enrolled in mission study classes... the nearly one hundred thousand dollars we have raised for missionary projects... the misssionary vision and enthusiasm we have engendered, the long, long line of those who were always among the good and the true, and often among the beautiful."[4]

The object of the new organization was "to promote an earnest Christian life among the young people of the Universalist Church, and the sympathetic union of all young people's societies, in their efforts to make themselves more useful in the service of God." The goal was "the development of the spiritual life of the young people, and the advancement of the spiritual work or our church." The primary focus was clearly devotional; it was to be a union of religious organizations as distinct from literary and social gatherings, an emphasis affirmed in the constitution drawn up at the organization meeting and repeated many times afterward.[5] The religious rather than social emphasis as the "paramount feature" was strictly adhered to, at least in the early days. The Ballou Association of Nashua, New Hampshire, was denied membership in 1891 because its religious activities were considered secondary and there was no provision for worship in their constitution.

One or more Communion services were a regular feature of every YPCU national meeting and of most state meetings, and private devotions were encouraged by the establishment in 1915 of the "Comrades of the Quiet Hour" which at one time enrolled nearly 1,000 members.

The YPCU was the denominational expression of a larger movement to bridge the gap between Sunday school and adult church membership which had originated in 1881 with Frances E. Clark, pastor of the Williston Congregational Church in Portland, Maine, as the Young People's Society of Christian Endeavor. By the opening of the twentieth century the movement had mushroomed into an international organization, with most evangelical Protestant denominations represented, and thousands of local societies in existence. Although intended to be interdenominational, various groups used their own identification; so the Methodists organized Epworth Leagues, and the Baptists and other denominations had their own young people's unions. Universalist youth were attracted to the idea, and between 1881 and 1889 had organized thirty-eight Christian Endeavor societies.

At the time the national YPCU was created there were slightly more than 120 young people's societies "of the religious sort" affiliated with Universalist churches, bearing a great variety of names, and widely scattered. Besides those with a Christian Endeavor identification, there were about twenty other societies with such assorted titles as "Christian Union," "Christian Culture," and "Christian Work." Very few had a distinctive denominational label or association, except for Chapin Clubs, consisting largely of young women. There were also a few Young People's Missionary Associations which had been organized locally in an attempt to maintain contributions to the Murray Centenary Fund which had lagged after the great push of the 1870s. When the first systematic effort to organize Universalist youth, provide some measure of uniformity, and link them together was made in 1884, there was a nucleus of seven such organizations which had grown to sixty-three when the Missionary Association was replaced in 1889.

This first proposal to create a national network had been made by Mrs. George B. Marsh of Chicago, the first woman to serve as a General Convention trustee.[6] Her plan, unanimously adopted by her fellow trustees, complete with a model constitution and by-laws prepared jointly by the Committee on Missionary Boxes and the Committee on Missions, was to form the "Young People's Missionary Association of the Universalist Church," with branches in each parish, to serve as auxiliaries to the state conventions.[7] Membership was to be open to all young people in the denomination throughout the country aged twelve "and upwards." There was no maximum age limit. With such a potentially heterogeneous clientele it was obvious that the organization would have to be supervised (if not dominated) by adults.[8] The idea was to stimulate "missionary spirit" and loyalty to the church as well as to serve as fund-raising agencies and, secondarily, to provide social opportunities (carefully supervised, of course).

The plan was submitted to the state conventions and was unanimously approved by churches in Chicago (St. Paul's being the first); Augusta, Maine; Providence, Rhode Island (Church of the Mediator); Dubuque, Iowa; and Watertown, New York.[9] More than twenty such organizations had been created within a year, but the plan failed to appeal to the vast majority. Nearly 100 youth groups, when approached, declined to be associated, preferring to maintain their basically social and/or literary character.[10] So this first attempt to organize Universalist youth on a national scale faded away. The second effort was more successful.

The idea of having youth societies with a distinctively Universalist designation and a primarily religious focus was revived by Stephen H. Roblin, pastor of the church in Bay City, Michigan, who had been ordained in 1882 and, after serving briefly in western New York State, had settled in Michigan in 1885. Within his parish were Albert C. Grier, at the time principal of the Bay City high school, and Alfred J. Cardall, both of them active in the local Christian Endeavor society which Grier had organized and of which he was the first president.[11] He was succeeded by Cardall, who attended the organization meeting in Lynn. A third young man, James D. Tillinghast, then a twenty-three-year-old lawyer and president of the youth society in the Buffalo church as well as of a regional society for western New York, and the first national secretary, had begun publishing in 1887 the monthly *Universalist Union* as the organ of societies connected with Universalist churches in the area.[12] Also involved had been Lewis B. Fisher, then a young pastor in Rochester, New York, ordained in 1881, and later to be prominently associated with a number of Universalist educational institutions and to write a brief history of the denomination intended for young people.

The quartet, using the paper as a channel of communication, contacted in February 1889 all Universalist young people's societies of which they had any knowledge, and publicized the proposal of a national organization. The result was the meeting in Lynn in 1889 and the creation of the YPCU. Every young people's society, regardless of name, had been invited to send delegates.

The constitution and by-laws which were drawn up by the young people in 1889 (with adult assistance) and were approved by the trustees of the General Convention the following year, provided for the customary set of officers, including an executive board. Presidents of state and provincial unions were to serve as vice-presidents in order to strengthen links between the two levels. After a period of confusion and misunderstanding over the relationships among local and state unions, and with the national organization, the constitution was amended to provide that membership in the state unions carried automatic membership in the national YPCU.

There were at first no limits on the terms of any officer (elected annually) but a limit of three consecutive terms was later stipulated. Meetings were to be held annually, and each society was entitled to three delegates.[13] In sharp contrast to the relatively detailed constitution of the national union and those of most state unions, that of the Rhode Island YPCU, organized in 1894 and later consolidated with the union in Massachusetts, consisted originally of a single compound, complex sentence.[14]

Loyalty to the church was not only pledged in the constitution but was reaffirmed periodically, partly to allay the fears of many adults who believed that the new organization would be a divisive, rival force and therefore weaken the church by heading off in its own direction. Henry W. Rugg was delegated as a representative of the General Convention to sit in on the very first conference of the organizing committee to see to it that "nothing dangerous was done." Elders were conspicuous at the first national convention, including Asa Saxe and Edwin C. Sweetser, who gave one of the addresses. Both had been ordained for more than a quarter of a century.

Frederick W. Hamilton registered his opposition to the YPCU on the ground that it was not only unnecessary but antagonistic to the best interests of the church.[15] No intermediate organization should come between the church and the people. This brought a vigorous defense from Lee E. Joslyn of Bay City, Michigan, who was elected the first president of the YPCU and held that office until 1892. Lack of encouragement and support, if not actual opposition, of some clergy, was either a deterrent or an actual obstacle for many Universalist youth groups.

The same uneasiness and concern about the relationship to the General Convention that had existed until 1874 with the national women's organization, recurred with the YPCU. Technically, it was an independent organization, especially after it was incorporated, and with its own constitution and by-laws. The point was emphasized repeatedly that the youth group not only had to be adequately supervised but that it should be listed officially as a subsidiary of or as an auxiliary to the General Convention.[16] Annual reports to that body were begun in 1894. The sense of operating apart from the other components of the church was somewhat reduced in 1903, when at the annual YPCU meeting in Akron, Ohio, General Superintendent Atwood welcomed them as a partner in denominational affairs.

The YPCU had all the trappings of a distinctive organization, complete with official colors (light blue, signifying Truth; and white, signifying Purity) adopted in 1894; a motto ("For Christ and His Church"), adopted in 1897; a national hymn ("Follow the Gleam"); and the watchword "Onward."[17] The first hymn written especially for the YPCU, the "Young People's Missionary Hymn," composed by Clara B. Adams to the tune of "Home, Sweet Home," was sung in closing the first national convention in 1890. A membership pin was devised, and in 1892 even the gavel used in the conduct of meetings, presented by W. H. Luden, had special Universalist significance, having been designed of wood from both the DeBenneville home at Oley, Pennsylvania, where he first preached Universalism, and from the original pew benches in the Potter church in New Jersey, contributed by James Shrigley. Banners, generally on a rotating basis, were provided as awards for such accomplishments as the union with the largest attendance at conventions, and the greatest growth during the year.

What was somewhat extravagantly described as the "first literary work devoted wholly to the interests of the young people's movement of the Universalist Church" was a Young People's Birthday Calendar, designed in 1891. It consisted of appropriate sentiments printed on slips of paper for each day of the year and sold at 50 cents each, the proceeds to be donated to the YPCU.

Even roughly estimating the total membership on a national scale at any given time is a hazardous business and yields only general trends rather than exact figures, for the generations of the youth population changed constantly, as did the age spread. After junior unions were created, there was much overlapping membership, the older youngsters sometimes belonging simultaneously to senior unions. Harry A. Hersey, who knew from long and close experience, considered the average duration of individual membership from only six to eight years. In the 1940s and thereafter, when the membership tended to reflect predominantly those of senior high school age, the length of affiliation with the YPCU became even shorter. The ideal, seldom achieved, was to balance membership lost by drop-outs or "graduation" into full church membership, by constant recruitment from younger ranks.

The national organization started with a local individual membership totalling somewhat less than 3,000. By the time the first annual convention was held in Rochester, New York, in 1890, sixty-seven local societies reported approximately 3,200 members.[18] The number of member unions had grown to 147 by the summer of 1891, and a year later had risen to 222. Participating state unions, which were eventually given equal delegate status with local organizations, had risen from nine in 1891 to thirteen a year later; total membership had grown from more than 4,000

Harry Adams Hersey (1870-1950), a veteran YPCU'er on his bicycle

The National YPCU Convention of 1895 in the Church of the Unity (Boston)

to 9,000 within the next year, with the largest concentrations in Massachusetts and New York State. It had become such an important body that when it convened in Washington, D.C., in 1893 it attracted national attention. The YPCU was tendered a reception at the White House, where President Grover Cleveland shook hands with every one of the delegates.[19]

The largest membership ever reached was achieved in 1895, when 436 unions reported 15,400 members, including junior unions organized nationally the previous year. This high point was reflected in the annual convention held in Boston in 1895, attended by 606 official delegates, with more than 1,000 registered and 27 states represented. The assembly exceeded by far the capacity of George L. Perin's Every Day Church and overflowed into the neighboring Church of the Unity (Unitarian). The speakers had to be shuttled between the two so that no one would miss any part of the program.

The total individual membership had declined to less than 1,800 by 1934, with a corresponding decrease in the number of unions to less than 100.[20] The shrinkage reflected in general the declining fortunes of the denomination, although other factors were also at work. Even though the number of unions had doubled by the time of World War II, the total was less than half that of the late nineteenth century.

As befitted an organization of national scope the annual meetings were rotated among various locations; the YPCU held its first convention in the Midwest (Chicago) in 1898.[21] Summer meetings and institutes became a fixed feature of YPCU activities from the very first. Even before it was organized on a national scale a Youth Day had been held in New Hampshire, at The Weirs on Lake Winnepesaukee, in the summer of 1889, a few weeks before the organization meeting in Lynn. In 1911, ten years after Ferry Beach, on the southern coast of Maine, had been acquired as a summer meeting place for various organizations in the denomination, the YPCU held its first annual convention there. At first there was much hesitation because there were thought to be too many other diversions nearby to secure full attendance, and because the accommodations were believed to be inadequate. But those fears turned out to be unfounded, and more conventions had been held there by 1948 (eight) than at any other location.[22]

Beginning in 1919 the YPCU, together with other church organizations using the Ferry Beach facilities, assumed the obligation of organizing, financing, and conducting its own special summer institutes. They usually lasted a week, with an organizing theme for each. Young people also organized in 1937 the Beachcomber Society which served as a student governing council and published a daily newspaper. One offshoot of the YPCU summer activities held at Ferry Beach was a special leadership conference for older young people, the first held in 1927 and continued until 1930.

After 1939 the policy of enlisting members with a wide age spread was still continued, so youth were organized at Ferry Beach summer institutes into a series of branches which included one for junior high school youngsters (Camp Seabreeze) and one for young adults which began as an informal Labor Day weekend conference and lasted until World War II brought an end to the program in 1942. The summer programs, almost always well attended, provided a judicious blend of recreation and serious religious activity and inspiration which fully justified the time, energy, and money expended on them.

Until 1894 the organization held its national convention in the fall of the year, at the time of General Convention meetings. The first national convention met in connection with the General Conference which for several years alternated with biennial General Convention meetings. However, in 1893 it was decided that youth meetings ought to be held separately and in the summer in order not only to attract larger numbers by avoiding conflict with school schedules but to meet as a separate and distinct organization, with enlarged responsibility for their own activities.[23]

One of the early tasks of the national YPCU was to convince local unions to adopt the new name so that the organization would be "characteristically Universalist." This meant redesignating the majority of the local groups, which bore the name "Christian Endeavor."[24] Richard Eddy, editor of the *Universalist Register,* gave up in despair in his attempt to sort out the names of the various youth organizations. In the 1891 edition he attempted to list them separately but noted that it was "impossible to ... draw the line" between societies connected with the YPCU and those independent of it; the longest list was headed "Miscellaneous." Some progress was made, however; of the 433 youth organizations reported in the *Register* in 1896, only 8 were listed as "unaffiliated." The problem was never completely solved, for as recently as 1935 there was a sizeable number of youth groups associated with Universalist churches which persisted in maintaining not only their local autonomy but their own names. A concerted effort was made that year to remedy the situation.[25]

The campaign to wean away Christian Endeavor societies and induce them to declare denominational allegiance by adopting the YPCU name was a source of considerable friction and ill will between the two organizations in spite of professions of cordiality by the Universalists. According to an account in the public press, when the YPCU and Christian Endeavor held simultaneous conventions in Boston in 1895, the Universalist youth group asked to be allowed to attend the Christian Endeavor convention while retaining their separate identity, but the request was refused because the Universalists were not an evangelical denomination. So the YPCU decided to hold its own.[26] Written greetings by the YPCU were

Mary Grace and Harry L. Canfield (1860-1942, 1864-1946), noted for their Universalist youth work

coolly received by the Endeavorites, who merely acknowledged their receipt without reciprocating. Isaac Atwood defended the YPCU on the ground that its primary allegiance was to the denomination and not to any other religious group.[27]

A basic goal of the YPCU in its early days was to involve every possible age group — a policy which created some serious problems of coordination and articulation. Little attention was paid to making any distinction based on age for several years after the organization had been created. At the 1891 convention there was some discussion about the appropriate age for delegates, and a constitutional amendment was drawn up (but never adopted) that would have specified that all such be between the ages of fifteen and thirty-five. But the Unioners were reluctant to confine themselves even to that twenty-year spread.

In 1893 consideration was given to forming a system of junior unions, the first having been organized at Seneca, Kansas, in 1890. In 1894 they were formally recognized as a branch of the national union, largely through the efforts of Mrs. Mary Grace Canfield, who became their first national superintendent. She immersed herself in promoting junior unions with a devotion that knew no bounds. The age range was considered to be roughly between seven and fifteen, with flexibility at both ends.[28] The government and conduct of business was modelled on the senior unions, and the children served as officers, with adults present to "exercise a gentle supervision." Junior unions participated in annual conventions, at least at the state level. When the Vermont YPCU, which had fifty-two unions in 1894, held its convention that year, one of the speakers was the nine-year-old son of the pastor in Rutland.[29] Mrs. Canfield, in her undiminished enthusiasm, wished to extend junior unions as far back as kindergarten, and urged the organization of pre-school groups under the name "Buds of Promise."[30]

The idea of forming junior unions was immediately popular. Within a year the number had grown to forty in almost a dozen states, with an enrollment of about 1,200. Mrs. Canfield arranged for the adoption of a national emblem (a "Junior Star") which also became the title of a song and service book which she compiled and for which in 1898 she assumed complete financial responsibility. The first 1,000 copies paid for the cost. The "Star" song book earned enough to place a window in the church in Atlanta and contribute to its organ fund.

The number of junior unions had risen to 112 by 1903, with more than 2,600 members, and there was even a special category of "Junior at Large" for isolated children, created in 1900 with its own superintendent. There was, however, a noticeable decline in numbers after 1906 which Hersey, the historian of the YPCU, attributed to "the refusal of good women of suitable age and ability to become local superintendents."[31]

Mrs. Canfield resigned as superintendent of the junior unions in 1899 and was succeeded by Miss Lillian Hosely of Friendship, New York, who served five years, and many other individuals who devoted themselves to the work. The objective of the junior unions was defined in the motto displayed on one of the banners at the Atlanta convention in 1900: "Gather, Educate, Graduate."

Among those counted as locally associated with Universalist youth organizations was the King's Daughters and Sons, of which there were known to be at least eight local contingents connected with Universalist churches in 1890.[32] It was one of the many offshoots of the Chautauqua movement in the post-Civil War period, and had been founded in 1886 as a non-sectarian and interdenominational Christian service organization "for the development of spiritual life and stimulation of Christian activities" such as summer camps for youth, and work in homes for the aged and in hospitals.[33] The organization, still active in the 1980s with headquarters at Chautauqua, New York, encouraged the creation of both state and local groups. They were organized among Universalists as "Hand-in-Hand Circles." Fifty-three members met at Murray Grove in 1911 while the YPCU was in session there in 1911.[34] It operated within the Murray Grove Association, and among its activities sold post cards (for five cents) illustrated with a portrait of John Murray. The object was to raise money to restore the Potter homestead.[35]

Among the inducements used to attract the younger male generation to the YPCU was the formation of "Boys' Battalions," complete with military drill, uniforms, and guns. Each was under the command of a regular United States Army officer. Boys and young men, aged twelve to twenty-one, were eligible. One such unit was organized in Chicago by Rufus A.

White, a Universalist clergyman residing in Englewood, Illinois.[36] A "Boys' Brigade" was organized in Norwalk, Ohio, in 1894. Funds to purchase uniforms and equipment were raised by selling honorary memberships at $2.00.[37]

The Boys' Brigade was described as "a military organization with a religious purpose." This somewhat anomalous if not contradictory denial of the teachings of Jesus as "the Prince of Peace" which youth were pledged to support, was rationalized with the explanation that religious exercises opened every drill. Such exercises were held on Sunday afternoons at the Cross Street Universalist Church in Somerville, Massachusetts, in the 1890s.[38] The military flavor which was evident in the YPCU in its early years was undoubtedly at least a partial reflection of Q. H. Shinn's experiences as a soldier in the Civil War which remained vivid to him throughout his life. Although military matters tended to be associated with "manliness" in the late nineteenth century, it was a young lady, Etta Wallace Miller, who contributed "The Battle Hymn of the Christian Union" to the YPCU repertoire.

At the other end of the age scale among youth there were YPCU groups which appeared more or less spontaneously among Universalist college students in the late nineteenth century. There was such a group at Tufts College by 1894.[39] One of the departments of the early YPCU was the Pauline Brotherhood, an organization of young men in the church and the outgrowth of a local social group organized informally by seven students of the Canton Theological School, and known as the "Seven Club."[40] Two of its members decided to organize a fraternity in the fall of 1891 known as the Pauline Brotherhood, based on the life and teachings of St. Paul. By 1892 it had an elaborate ritual and a club house. The state misssionary in New York, Daniel Wright, heard of the group and suggested to the pastor of the church in Auburn that a branch be organized there. The fraternity was roughly comparable to the Brotherhood of St. Andrew in the Episcopal church.

A convention of Universalist young men in New York State was held in Syracuse in 1893, with about fifty in attendance. They voted to affiliate with the state YPCU. The success of the branch organized in Auburn was so great that when O. M. Hilton, the pastor, reported its activities to the national YPCU at its meeting in Utica in 1894, that body recognized the Brotherhood as a department within it.

Most of the attempts to organize Universalist youth among college students had brief histories, partly because of the transient character of the membership. One of the early attempts had been made following World War I under the leadership of Stanley Manning, but providing pastors for such students was beyond the financial capabilities of the denomination, and most of the organizations soon disappeared.[41] By 1941 there were Universalist-sponsored student programs at almost a dozen institutions.[42] The first real effort to bring together the almost 300 Universalist college students enrolled in the unusually large concentration of institutions in the Greater Boston area was made in 1941, when Nils Y. Wessell, Dean of Liberal Arts at Tufts College (and a Unitarian), gave the opening address to an assembly of young people.[43] Much of the impetus to organize as the "Universalist Student College Association for Greater Boston" came from Douglas Frazier, who had become Director of Youth Activities for the church earlier in 1941.

After World War II another attempt was made to serve the denominational needs of college students with the establishment in 1948 of the Murray Foundation. But the budget of $100 did not go very far, and the movement was much weakened by American involvement in the Korean conflict. Even the activities of the organization known as Student Religious Liberals on college and university campuses, operated by the combined Universalist and Unitarian youth groups after their merger in 1953, met with only indifferent success; it was dissolved in 1978 and enlistment of college students had to await a new effort.

Many youth organizations rose (and fell) without any formal affiliation with the YPCU. Such was the Order of Universal Brotherhood organized in the church in Malden, Massachusetts, in 1904 for young men fifteen to twenty-five years of age.[44] It had all the components of an adult fraternal order, complete with a ritual, grip, insignia, and password. The idea became so popular that a second "lodge" was organized in Everett, Massachusetts, and then in other churches in the Greater Boston area.[45] A Grand Lodge was established at the Malden church in 1911, with a constitution and provision for subordinate lodges and annual conventions. Some members of the Grand Lodge had not only the attributes of the original local organization but even provided for ceremonial regalia.

The purpose of the organization and its subsidiaries was primarily to promote the general welfare of and interest in the church among teenagers, by retaining their allegiance through basically social activities. In 1916 the Grand Lodge established a scholarship for a theological student at Tufts College.[46] In the following year it created a similar one for the Canton Theological School. Instead of recommending that the organization affiliate with the YPCU the General Convention, at its meeting in 1915, for some reason officially recognized it as an auxiliary to that body.

Early conventions were dominated by adults such as C. Ellwood Nash and Quillen Hamilton Shinn, aided and abetted by younger adults who had recently entered the ministry; Harry L. Canfield, one of these, had been ordained just a year before the YPCU was organized. It was he who had suggested the first major mission project (at Harriman, Tennessee) in 1890. Sometimes the youth had to be pushed into taking assignments of which they had but little understanding or appreciation, but were considered by their elders to be of great importance. Occasionally the practice of being treated as miniature adults — prevalent everywhere in the late nineteenth century — brought mild protests. Patterning the YPCU on adult organizations and procedures was not always to their liking. The executive committee was requested in 1892 to "put as few clergymen upon the programme as possible." Fewer sermons and formal papers were to be replaced by greater opportunity for discussion and general sociability.

Many years later Hersey recalled that General Convention meetings were dominated by an "oligarchy of graybeards," and there was neither a youth presence nor meaningful participation of the younger generation in convention assemblies until 1911.[47] Much to the delight of the YPCU, the General Convention strongly endorsed it in 1895 as "a power for good and the most hopeful sign of the perpetuity of our Church."[48] The pleasure was tempered, however, when the request of the YPCU that time at General Convention meetings be assigned for discussion of young people's work went unheeded for many years.

Whether males tended to dominate the top positions in the YPCU, as some intimated, is a moot question, for young women held national office from the beginning. Nannie Jenison of Lynn, Massachusetts, was the first treasurer, and three of the four members of the first executive board were women. Eleanor Bisbee was the first young woman to serve as national president (1918–1919) and Dorothy (Tilden) Spoerl was the second (1929–1930). Ann Postma was elected to that position in 1943.[49] There was, at least in the early days, an aversion by women to presiding at meetings; in 1892, when the president was absent, five of the women who were vice-presidents, declined, in turn, to serve, and a male had to be selected as chairman.

The canons of proper behavior and social morality, as conceived in the late nineteenth century and into the twentieth, were drummed into YPCU members and mirrored prevailing adult standards (if not actually adhered to in all respects by either group). These were repeated by convention resolutions for many years. Strict observance of the Sabbath was called for; and in 1893 the YPCU urged that the World's Fair, then being held in Chicago, be closed on Sundays. The double standard of sexual morality was condemned in 1895 and, following the official Universalist policy of the adults, the convention opposed capital punishment.

Eradication of the "degradation . . . [of] drink and alcohol habits" was pledged at the very first national convention. The influence of Shinn, whose opposition to the use of tobacco and alcohol amounted almost to an obsession, was evident in 1892, when the organization announced that no Universalist admitted to theological school or ordained was to use tobacco in any form. Water only was to be used in Communion services; even "unfermented wine" was disapproved of; and the liquor traffic was roundly condemned as a menace to American institutions. When revisions to the constitution were being considered in 1894 it was proposed that it contain a statement that every individual wishing to become a member had to abstain from use of all intoxicating beverages. Army canteens operated by the federal government and continued after the mobilization associated with the Spanish-American War were of special concern to the YPCU because liquor was made available at these installations. The youth called for their abolition, the existence of such being considered an "unclean and unpatriotic agency."

The YPCU plunged immediately into a host of projects, most of them suggested by adults. One of the earliest was to create visibility for Universalist youth, accomplished in part through the celebration of Young People's Sunday in local churches, first held in January 1892. Suggested topics for local programs had to be arranged and published in advance. A hymn and service book had to be prepared, as well as a "Manual of Faith and Duty" patterned on adult equivalents.[50]

The idea of a Post Office Mission, known as "the black missionary," to distribute denominational literature was suggested by Shinn, who swept into the YPCU orbit like "a benevolent conflagration." The mission, authorized in 1892 and in operation within a year, had distributed more than 5,000 leaflets in twenty-five states and territories by 1894, together with copies of the *Leader,* the *Myrtle,* and *Onward.* There were 1,500 on the mailing list in 1914.

More than 100 local agents were appointed in 30 states to advertise Universalism. It also sponsored a booth at the Cotton States and International Exhibition in Atlanta in 1895 and provided a similar display at the Tennessee Centennial Exposition in Nashville in 1897. The Post Office Mission also established a lending library which had exceeded 200 volumes by 1896. All of these activities were supported by uncertain voluntary funding, so the Universalist Publishing House actually defrayed much of the expense. Another related means of propagating the denomination was an illustrated lecture on Universalism prepared by Almon Gunnison and lent to parishes. It was updated and improved from time to time.

Both interest in and support of the Post Office Mission had declined to such an extent that it lost its separate identity in 1921 and was merged with the Union at Large which had been reestablished in 1901 for isolated Universalist youth.[51]

A paid "National Organizer," patterned on the position of the General Secretary of Christian Endeavor, was sought almost immediately, but until Shinn assumed the position in 1893, no one had been willing to accept. He was to receive an annual salary of $2,000 plus travelling expenses; the YPCU was to be responsible for $1,200, and he was to raise the balance through his own efforts.

On Shinn's recommendation William H. McGlauflin was appointed as

Southern Missionary in 1894, with the YPCU responsible for paying $750 toward his salary. Even after Shinn resigned as National Organizer in 1895 to become General Missionary for the General Convention he continued to organize local YPCUs at a furious pace wherever he went.

Within two years after the first convention had been held, the organization had developed an elaborate network of standing committees to perform various tasks, to which others were added. The number had grown to eleven by 1899. A Lookout Committee was established originally to seek recruits for the ministry. The YPCU committed itself in 1892 to provide a $100 scholarship at each of the three denominational theological schools, at the suggestion of Jonah F. Rice, a minister in Ohio. The committee's responsibilities were soon extended to rounding up potential union members as well. Even a National Union at Large was organized in 1892 for individuals unaffiliated with local unions, but that activity was taken over after one year by the WNMA as a part of its own church extension program, and not reestablished until 1901.

A Denominational Reading Committee was created in 1891 to encourage study groups where serious discussions could take place. A Devotional Committee was established to prepare and publish suggested religious topics for local meetings. However, it did not have a continuous history and had to be reconstituted several times after it lagged in its responsibilities or even disappeared temporarily. As part of an effort to revitalize the organization, which had suffered in membership, morale, and leadership during World War I, it was revived as a Devotional Department in 1919, with a superintendent in charge.

There was also a Charitable Committee to report benevolences and to suggest community social service projects. And of course there was a Missionary Committee to carry out one of the responsibilities of the organization. A Mission Study Department was created in 1905 which worked with the local women's Mission Circles. There was also a Social Committee, with an Entertainment Bureau later added, to make suggestions for recreational programs. A Department of Good Citizenship came into being in 1894, redesignated "Christian Citizenship." It was replaced in 1910 by a Social Service Commission.

The *Universalist Union,* used originally to communicate with youth societies in western New York State, became the first YPCU paper, and a full report of the Lynn meeting in 1889 was printed and distributed in 2,500 copies. Tillinghast continued to publish it, largely on his own responsibility, until 1893, when it was taken over by the YPCU, which was insistent that there should be a weekly successor to the monthly *Union,* and be a larger and more representative paper. The denominational publishing house appeared to be the logical vehicle, although the YPCU somewhat defiantly announced that if the Universalist Publishing House would not agree to publish such a paper, the new organization would produce its own independently. So negotiations were commenced in 1893, and after "tedious delays," arrangements were worked out to publish an eight-page bi-weekly to be named *Onward*. The two parties were to have an equal voice in management, with equal distribution of profits or losses. During the transition period in 1893, before the publishing house took over joint responsibility, the first three issues, beginning in December 1893, were published by the firm of Bisbee and Whitcomb in Philadelphia.

The initial joint editors were Omer G. Petrie and Arthur W. Grose, who at the time were students in the Tufts Divinity School and subsequently held pastorates in adjoining Massachusetts parishes. Beginning in 1895 the national secretary became simultaneously the editor and was paid a small salary.

Onward never became self-supporting in spite of attempting almost every known expedient over the years. Not a single national convention passed which did not include pleas for additional subscriptions at fifty cents a year (later increased to seventy-five cents). The original subscription list was 2,700, with the ambitious goal of 10,000. The deficit by the end of the first year was $700, and the YPCU owed the publishing house almost $1,000 in 1898. The subscription list increased to 3,400 by mid-1896, but the deficit was almost as large as in the first year. It was estimated that a subscription list of 5,000 was necessary if the paper were to pay its own way, but in 1907 it was acutally only 1,795 and "the usual deficit" amounted to more than $870.

The officers of the publishing house were never enthusiastic about taking on what was obviously going to be a financial liability, and as early as 1896 expressed doubt as to whether it should continue to publish the paper.[52] The entire financial responsibility for *Onward* was assumed by the YPCU at the end of that year, and a charge for services was paid to the publishing house.

Throughout its life *Onward* led a precarious existence, with innumerable readjustments of relationship with the publishing house. Much time and energy were expended in periodic debates over the fate of the young people's paper, as well as whether it would be a weekly, a bi-weekly, or a monthly. Conflicts over printing schedules were a source of considerable dissatisfaction on the part of the YPCU. *Onward* was, in its estimation, given too low a priority; copy had to be submitted so far in advance that much of it was out of date when it finally appeared.

One step taken long after *Onward* began publication was to discontinue in 1924 the *Myrtle* as an economy measure; it had first appeared in 1851 for Sunday school use and had been edited for more than thirty years, beginning in 1875, by a minister, Mrs. E. M. Bruce, who died in 1911.[53]

One of the reasons for the difficulties which beset *Onward*, especially in the early years, was the attempt to appeal to a constituency representing widely disparate age groups extending from elementary Sunday school youngsters to senior unioners and even college-age students. A Children's Department was provided at first. When Canfield and his wife became editor and associate editor, respectively, in 1895, *Onward* became a four-page weekly, with a junior union department included, but with the bulk of the space devoted to material intended to appeal to senior high school students. Beginning in 1898 the experiment was tried briefly of publishing a Youth Department in both the *Leader* and *Onward*.[54] The *Leader* claimed that space limitations precluded such an arrangement, but a Young People's Department was still carried, under various names, in the denominational journal.[55]

A treasury was of course indispensable to the successful operation of the YPCU, and the financial commitments from almost the very beginning far exceeded the resources. The rather staggering sum of $10,000 had to be raised from various sources by 1892 if all commitments were to be honored. At first the organization depended on voluntary donations, with a predictably small return. The first appeal for funds (in 1890) garnered slightly over $100, contributed by thirty-two societies. The largest single amount came in 1892 from individuals and local unions in Massachusetts, totalling $84.53; California contributed $1.10. Altogether, the treasury amounted that year to the not very promising sum of $512.85. Annual dues were levied, beginning in 1894, based on a per capita assessment of five cents for each individual union member, with a weekly pledge card to encourage systematic giving and to develop a sense of fiscal responsibility. The amounts were to be forwarded monthly to the state unions; one-half of the receipts were to be retained by state unions and one-half forwarded to the national office. Youth were thus introduced to the intricacies of bookkeeping and finance.

The system of assessments did augment the treasury, although contributions varied widely. At the end of the first year of dues-levying, the income was almost $1,000. Of the 242 assessments made, 121 paid in full; 17 in part, 99 were not heard from; and 5 defied the national union and refused to pay.

The most widely known source of revenue and the one touching youth most directly was the "Two-Cents-a-Week for Missions" plan. The idea of continuous giving, in addition to raising mission funds for special purposes, was planted in 1890, introduced by Miss Louie Rose, encouraged by C. Ellwood Nash, and in operation by 1894. One-fourth of the income so derived was to be returned to the state unions (on request), the remainder to be used to assist in financing missionary projects. A total of 170,000 envelopes had been distributed by 1895, with the hope that the receipts would pay the expenses of the Southern Missionary authorized by the YPCU. A permanent interest-bearing missionary fund was created in 1900 and eventually amounted to nearly $2,500. It went through a bewildering series of name changes until 1929, when it became the Permanent Church Extension Fund.

The ranks of the YPCU were somewhat thinned after 1895, when the five-cent per capita assessment was doubled and then raised to twenty cents in 1898. A cent-a-day pledge for support of the General Convention was added in 1896. Annual receipts rose from about $2,500 in 1895 to more than $7,000 two years later, in spite of considerable grumbling and the failure of some local unions to pay their increased assessments. In 1896 it was voted that all two-cent-a-day surpluses beyond financing missionary work in the South were to be added to the General Convention fund for aiding theological students; $400 was turned over for that purpose in 1897. The sum may seem to have been small, but it provided assistance for at least three students under the formula for support then being used. The largest cash balance in the history of the YPCU was $900, achieved in 1911.

The original Two-Cents-a-Week for Missions was abandoned after 1910 and replaced briefly by "Five Cents a Week for Everything," which meant the consolidation of dues, support of *Onward,* and missions, into one obligation. The financial responsibility for missions was again separated in 1917, first as "Home Missions," and within the same year as the Legion of the Cross. In 1928 it was redesignated as the Church Extension Fund, the financial wing of the Department of Church Extension.[56] A permanent administrative fund was created in 1906 to defray the expenses of the steadily increasing activities of the national union which had been borne by assessments on state YPCUs.

The first permanent fund started by an individual to help finance the YPCU was a $5.00 donation made in 1894 by Lucinda White Brown, widow of a Universalist minister in Perry, New York, who had died less than a decade after their marriage. She was the great-granddaughter of an early Universalist preacher in Maine and had been born in a log cabin.[57] After her husband's death she resumed the teaching career which she had begun at the age of seventeen, and accumulated sufficient funds to make a trip to Europe, including a winter in Italy.

At the time of the Civil War she taught at Clinton Liberal Institute, where she remained for thirteen years. She took much interest in young people, and worked for a time at a school for orphaned boys. After the institution closed because of financial difficulties she started for California, but never arrived. She stopped in Akron, Ohio, where she met John R. Buchtel, chief benefactor of the college bearing his name, and was offered a partly furnished house in exchange for serving as housemother to eight male college students in 1878.

Lucinda Brown, known affectionately to many generations of Buchtel College students as "Aunty Brown," lived for many years in her residence, known as the "old shoe." One of the students, in response to a toast in her

"Aunty"Lucinda Brown (1822-1917), beloved friend of many youth groups

honor, amended the old nursery rhyme by referring to her as 'the old woman who lives in a shoe, and with her many children she knows just what to do.'[58]

The annual income from the Aunty Brown Fund, as her small donation was dubbed, was to assist a divinity school student. It eventually amounted to more than $5,000 after it was augmented by her bequest to the YPCU, the largest individual gift ever made to that organization.

A campaign to raise an endowment fund of $200,000 was planned in 1920, the interest to pay the administrative expenses of the organization. The goal was never completely realized; instead, the YPCU came to depend increasingly on assistance from the General Convention which amounted between 1920 and 1929 to about $20,000. The permanent funds of the YPCU had become so intricate by 1929 that they were placed in the care of the General Convention.

It was at the very first YPCU convention in 1890, under the aggressive leadership and careful guidance of Nash and Canfield, that the fledgling organization undertook what seemed to many a rather audacious missionary project: To organize a parish, finance the construction of a church in Harriman, Tennessee, and to employ a minister for it for which the YPCU would be in part financially responsible. It was indeed a daring undertaking which was being launched even before the organization had been completed and stabilized, or any real experience had been accumulated in handling a relatively large financial obligation.

What had precipitated this rather dramatic series of events, and why had this particular community, of which almost no one had ever heard, been selected for such an ambitious program? Tennessee had never been a propitious field for Universalism. Although many communities had been visited by such itinerants as D. B. Clayton and Thomas Abbott, they had left no permanent impression. William Hale, a country physician licensed by the Georgia Convention, was the only preacher in eastern Tennessee in 1880 and had organized that year the only church in the area (Free Hill, in Washington County).

Until February 1890 the town of Harriman did not even exist, consisting as it did of a single farmhouse and outbuildings somewhat ostentatiously known as the "Byrd Mansion" in Roane County, on Emory River, a tributary of the Tennessee. Two years later it had a population exceeding 2,000 and a name, and within three years had grown to about 4,000 and was still expanding. What had happened?

A group of businessmen, most of whom were from the North and East, had been attracted by what had appeared to be an abundance of coal, iron, timber, and limestone resources, and had organized the East Tennessee Land Company to exploit the economic possibilities.[59] The community was named for General Walter Harriman (1817–1884), an officer during the Civil War, three-time governor of New Hampshire (his native state), and a Universalist clergyman for eleven years.[60] After serving two pastorates in New England, where he had been ordained about 1844, he had decided to enter political and military life, and in 1853 had been sent by President Franklin Pierce to investigate the troubles in Kansas over slavery.[61] When the Civil War broke out he had raised a New Hampshire regiment and was commissioned a colonel. His son, Walter C., became a resident of Harriman and a strong supporter of a Universalist mission there.

Nash had visited the new community in the fall of 1890 in the interests of the denomination, had delivered a sermon, and had appealed for funds to build a church.⁶² The community had been selected as a mission site not only because it had numerous Universalists but because it had a promising future and Universalists could be in the vanguard instead of trailing along as late-comers.⁶³

Another reason the new town appealed was its attitude toward the liquor question. Its charter explicitly prohibited the presence of alcohol within its boundaries; there were to be no saloons; and a clause was included in all land deeds by which the owners agreed not to traffic in alcohol in any way. It was to be a model community, unencumbered by the evils of "the demon rum."

The town was even to have its own institution of higher learning, which was chartered as "The American Temperance University," a nondenominational school financed largely by the East Tennessee Land Company and offering facilities for 200 secondary and college students.⁶⁴ The institution actually opened in the fall of 1893, and Mrs. Lucy McGlauflin, the first wife of the first Southern missionary, served as its instructor in elocution and oratory. Her husband, who was enrolled as a special student, earned an MA from the institution in 1895 and was awarded an honorary DD in 1896.

Nash's appeal for funds attracted the attention of Ferdinand Schumacher of Akron, Ohio, a German immigrant who had made a fortune as a miller and was known as the "oatmeal king."⁶⁵ He was a dedicated temperance advocate who for a quarter of a century served as a trustee of Buchtel College. He pledged $1,000 for a church, provided at least $4,000 could be subscribed in addition.⁶⁶

With most of these events as a background, Nash transmitted to the YPCU meeting in 1890 the information that the East Tennessee Land Company had donated two lots, worth about $3,000, on which a church was to be constructed within two years. Nash's scheme was to have the youth undertake the raising of as much of the $4,000 as possible, and pictured in glowing terms the bright future of the Harriman project; $1,000 was pledged within an hour.⁶⁷ This seems to have been a typical performance of the charismatic Nash, who was described by Hersey as a person who "could make youth see visions. He could magnify opportunity, minimize difficulties, grow eloquent over possibilities, and keep silent as to obstacles."⁶⁸

McGlauflin, then residing in Rochester, Minnesota, was promptly selected to organize a parish in Harriman and arrange for building a church. He preached his first sermon in the summer of 1891, and a year later had gathered a congregation of about 100 and had organized a church with a membership of 34 and a Sunday school of 75.⁶⁹ A building was constructed with great dispatch, the cornerstone having been laid in December 1891; the structure was first occupied and dedicated on Easter Sunday in 1892. It was built at a total cost of $8,500, including furnishings.⁷⁰ The expense beyond the allotted $5,000 was borne by the congregation. It was an imposing Gothic edifice, considered the finest of the five Protestant churches which had been built in the community within less than three years. The church was graced by two special windows, one placed by Walter C. Harriman in honor of his father, and the other dedicated to Nash in recognition of his contributions. It was most appropriate that the YPCU held its fifth annual convention at the Harriman church, with sixty-four delegates, and thereby introduced some Universalist youth to the South. The membership in the church had grown to 100 by 1895.⁷¹

The rush of activities at Harriman had placed a heavy burden on the infant YPCU treasury, and as was the case many times in its history, their funds had to be supplemented by denominational appeals. A building fund had been immediately established when the commitment had been made in Harriman, and part of it had to be used in 1892 to meet the salary obligation to McGlauflin which the YPCU had blithely undertaken, and which by then amounted to almost $1,900. That was too much for the organization to carry, so in 1894 the responsibility was reduced to one-half ($750) of his annual salary. Even then, two loans totalling $350 had to be negotiated that year in order to pay their share of the missionary's salary.

McGlauflin's activities as the Southern Missionary were not confined to Harriman, although the plan was to make it a rallying point for the denomination in the South. He visited many other communities in Tennessee, considering Knoxville and Chattanooga among the more promising locations for the extension of Universalism.⁷² He was prepared even to organize a church at Crossville, some thirty-five miles west of Knoxville, using a single Universalist family there as a base. After a YPCU had been organized in Knoxville, a church with twenty members was established in 1895.⁷³ But after his departure later that year for Atlanta, his missionary efforts were not consistently followed up and most of them failed to take root.

It seemed by 1895 that Grace Universalist Church in Harriman was so prosperous under McGlauflin's leadership, with a parish of 140 members, that it could safely be left to another. As McGlauflin himself optimistically assessed the situation for the benefit of the YPCU meeting in 1896, they had every reason to be proud. Universalists had a debt-free church worth $10,000, with the most conspicuous and handsome religious building in the town. "Many of the prominent citizens [were] in its fellowship and [it] has its full share of the brain, the heart, the culture, and the pocket books of the community." The deed to the church was triumphantly presented to the General Convention at its meeting in 1897. So in 1895 the YPCU decided to open a second mission in the South, with Atlanta as the headquarters, and to place McGlauflin in charge.

The subsequent unfortunate history of the Harriman church clearly illustrates the fact that by no means all of the blame for the decline or disappearance of Universalist churches could be laid directly at the door of the denomination. In 1896, on the surface at least, the prospects looked almost limitless, but the mushroom growth of Harriman had been abruptly checked by the economic upset of 1893, largely the victim of unplanned over-expansion. For a time it became virtually a ghost town, although it slowly revived on a modest scale some years later. A few Universalists believed, mostly with the wisdom of hindsight, that McGlauflin's obvious willingness to transfer his activities to Atlanta was explained by his realization that Harriman's limits had been reached and that the time was ripe to desert a sinking ship.

In any event, those individuals who had flocked into the town thought to be a model community soon became disillusioned. Expectations were not met, property values tumbled, and people expecting to make money quickly had their hopes dashed. There was close to a mass exodus in a very short span of time. A high proportion of those who returned to former homes or sought other locations were Universalists.

The church membership decreased rapidly after 1896, with the loss of population and of McGlauflin's leadership. Then another misfortune befell the ailing church. Harry Lawrence Veazey, a product of the Harriman church, and his wife, were tragically drowned in New York State in 1899 before he had had an adequate opportunity to become well established in his new pastorate as the successor to McGlauflin. Charles R. East, the next pastor, did his best but the results were so disheartening that he left. By early 1903 even Shinn, the eternal optimist, admitted that the church was dead.

Nonetheless, J. M. Rasnake, an ex-Baptist minister converted to Universalism who had preached in Tennessee with Shinn in 1902, accepted the challenge and attempted to revive what by then had become a moribund organization.[74] It seemed to him too great a retreat to give up the effort and admit failure in view of all the time, energy, money, and zeal that had gone into the Harriman church. There were a few Universalist families still remaining, some of whom had children that needed at least a Sunday school. But Rasnake too became so discouraged that he resigned in 1904 to become the state missionary in South Carolina.[75] The church remained dormant for over a decade.

After World War I the WNMA took over briefly the missionary work in Tennessee, but its financial resources were too thinly spread to be of much effect. William E. Manning Todd of Greenfield, Indiana, was employed by them for a short time, and he included Harriman on his missionary circuit in 1920–21. But the prospects were so gloomy that the WNMA voted to dispose of the Harriman church in 1923; the property was sold by the General Convention trustees in 1927 for $2,500. The bright future so confidently expected for Harriman in the late nineteenth century had come to an ignominious end, and organized Universalism ceased to exist in that Tennessee community.

But in 1895, emboldened by their apparent success in Harriman, the YPCU transferred its efforts to Atlanta, with the goal of making it rather than Harriman the eventual center for Southern Universalism. McGlauflin, selected to oversee it with the same arrangements for his salary as at Harriman, conducted his first services there in September and had organized a church which, within a year, claimed seventy members. The YPCU then took a further step in 1897 and pledged to contribute $4.00 for every $1.00 raised by Atlanta Universalists toward the construction of a church building. The $2,500 mortgage on a building lot acquired earlier was paid off in 1899 and the property was deeded to the YPCU. Construction of the structure was begun that year, with a cost originally set so as not to exceed $6,500, but actually much more elaborate than first planned, and costing more than $12,000. The YPCU, unable to assume that much of a financial obligation, was forced to call on the General Convention for assistance; it furnished $2,500, and the women's organization contributed $200. Altogether, the YPCU invested more than $16,000 in the Atlanta effort. The property was subsequently transferred to the state convention. Joint services were conducted by the time of World War I with the Unitarians, using the latter's building. So the Universalist property was returned to the YPCU in 1919 and immediately transferred to the General Convention for disposal.

The YPCU held its annual convention in Atlanta in 1900, and the high point of the proceedings was the dedication of the new church, with the principal sermon delivered by General Superintendent Atwood.[76] There was a total registered attendance of 220 from 23 states and, as one individual observed, Northern members of the YPCU discovered that the South was not a foreign country after all.

McGlauflin continued his duties in Atlanta until 1904, when he resigned to become regional superintendent in the Northwest. The position of Southern Missionary had come to an end in 1900 with his settlement in Atlanta. Clarence J. Harris, a convert from Congregationalism through McGlauflin's efforts, became the latter's successor in Atlanta — the fourth minister who had come into the denomination from that mission.

One YPCU idea which came to nothing regarding the South was to have McGlauflin investigate the possibility of doing missionary work among Southern Negroes.[77] He reported to the annual meeting in 1897 that no effort should be made to admit Negroes to local Universalist Sunday schools or YPCUs, for it would have the same effect upon whites as "a lighted match [in] a powder magazine."[78] Further, the YPCU was told that Negroes in the South were much happier fraternizing with their own kind than with whites. McGlauflin did acknowledge that there were some

Universalists among the black population of Atlanta and that they were welcome as visitors to public services.

The YPCU had not one but four opportunities to establish new churches after the Atlanta project had gotten under way. All were subject to the approval of the General Convention, which gave its blessing to two. Montgomery, Alabama, and Richmond, Virginia, were ruled out as not sufficiently promising, so St. Paul, Minnesota, and Little Rock, Arkansas, remained for consideration after Shinn had investigated the situation. St. Paul was the more successful of the two, with a total investment, beginning in 1901, exceeding $16,000, involving almost total support of a minister and the construction of a church building.

Organized Universalism in St. Paul had had a rather long but erratic history before the YPCU became involved. A society had been established by 1865 and plans were under way then to build a church.[79] Until a church was dedicated in 1872 the group met in public halls.[80] After a rapid turnover of clergy with short pastorates the society had to relinquish its building and virtually disappeared but had been revived by 1887. Services were resumed, with a congregation of twenty, in a partially dismantled chapel abandoned by the Baptists.

The organization had grown rapidly under the ministry of W. S. Vail and plans had been developed in 1891 for a more adequate structure.[81] The society was reorganized as a mission in 1899, with assistance subsequently from the large and prosperous Church of the Redeemer in Minneapolis. At the time the YPCU entered the picture there were twenty families in the parish and nine church members.[82] By 1905 the membership had grown to sixty-nine, with Henry B. Taylor as the pastor, supported by the YPCU until his departure in 1908. L. A. Ames, president of the YPCU in 1903, described St. Paul as "the missionary marvel of the Northwest." A handsome church of stone was dedicated in 1909 as part of the YPCU convention activities which took place in Minneapolis that year.

The mission at Little Rock, authorized in 1901 simultaneously with the one at St. Paul, was operated under several handicaps. It was established in a community dominated by religious orthodoxy and hence met much resistance, and the resources of those to whom Universalism appealed were limited. The first sermon had been preached there in 1895 by Shinn on one of his whirlwind tours.[83] Typically, after a series of religious services he had organized in 1896 a church of ten members from a nucleus of twenty families, and had created a Ladies' Aid Society of fifteen which he made responsible for raising a building fund of $1,000. There was difficulty in both obtaining and retaining a pastor. F. L. Carrier, to whose salary the YPCU contributed $500 a year, resigned in discouragement in 1904, to be succeeded by Mrs. Athalia L. J. Irwin, a native of the state who held several pastorates in the South. The chapel so long planned for, and for which a lot had been purchased, was finally provided

A product of YPCU effort: Shinn Memorial Church, Chattanooga, Tennessee

in 1905, a modest frame structure which in no way resembled a traditional church building. The total YPCU investment in Little Rock, including assistance with the pastor's salary, amounted to $6,207.

The small society continued to struggle along for almost thirty years. Shortly after the last settled minister, H. C. Ledyard, departed for Hutchinson, Kansas, in 1930, the property was sold and the organization disbanded, most members electing to attend the Second Presbyterian Church.[84] The church was reestablished in 1950 and became officially the Unitarian Universalist Church of Little Rock.

The fifth and last church financed in part by YPCU funds was in Chattanooga, Tennessee, where the groundwork had been laid many years earlier by McGlauflin. After the church in St. Paul had been completed in 1909 it became the next mission point. A start toward the building of a church had already been made in 1908 by Southern Universalists, with the establishment of the Shinn Memorial Fund, although the final location had not yet been determined. The YPCU contributed over half the $10,000 still needed after Chattanooga had been selected as the location.

The Shinn Memorial Chruch was dedicated as part of the proceedings of the youth group which held its annual convention there in 1917, and was the climax of the investment of more than $9,000 in the parish. One of the by-products of the Chattanooga project was the establishment in the 1920s of a tri-state youth federation known under the acronym "Tennalaga," consisting of unions in Tennessee, Alabama, and Georgia. It conducted summer institutes for young religious liberals in the South. Both Universalists and Unitarians attended sessions at Chattanooga and at Camp Hill, Alabama, each of which became the headquarters at different times. At a joint meeting in Atlanta in 1935 the Southern Religious Young People's Federation was organized by Tennalaga and held a series of annual meetings such as the one in Mississippi in 1937.[85]

After the lapse of many decades, when the earlier church-building efforts of the youth group had become to most only a memory, the YPCU resumed in 1944 its church extension activities by planning to raise $6,000 toward the construction of a mission church.[86] It was to have been a memorial to William Wesley Cromie, a young minister accidentally killed in 1943 while engaged in pastoral work. The church was never built, but an outdoor chapel in his name was erected in 1950 at the Elliott P. Joslin Camp for Diabetic Boys in Charlton, Massachusetts.

Other domestic missions to which the YPCU committed funds were in Florida and Texas, although they did not, unlike other efforts, involve the construction of church buildings. The sum of $300 was voted in 1908 to advance church work in Pensacola, Florida. The first call from Texas for help had come in 1893 from James Billings, who, with his wife Mary, was attempting the well-nigh impossible job of maintaining and spreading Universalism in the huge expanses of the Lone Star State. But the YPCU had already undertaken more than enough projects to strain the treasury beyond its limits, and so aid was not officially rendered until 1920 as part of a temporary burst of missionary activity following World War I. It was accompanied by a surge of membership and increased revenues.

The YPCU had many other projects to undertake besides helping to establish or support domestic mission points. Some were quite local and "in-house," while others had a broader significance beyond the boundaries even of the nation as the organization grew rapidly in size and influence. The first local union outside the United States to join the national organization was in Moe's River, Quebec, in 1893, with twenty-five members.[87] A YPCU was organized in Japan in 1896 with seven young men; membership had risen to twenty-eight a year later. Membership in it represented a certain amount of courage in a nation where a sharp line was drawn between Christians and non-Christians, and notably when Universalists comprised a minority within a minority.

Support of foreign missionary activity also fell within the province of the YPCU. At its very first convention in 1890 it offered its resources to George L. Perin, busy operating the mission in Japan, as a recruiting agency for missionaries, and in the following year recommended "that we take an interest in the Japan mission and lend a prompt and ready response to its appeals." Plans were outlined by Lillian Hosely in 1900 to finance the education of one or more Japanese girls on behalf of the junior union. The "Suye Fund" was created for the benefit of a Japanese youngster by that name, and amounted seven yars later to more than $400. The junior union project was broadened in 1907 to include all unioners as the Blackmer Home Fund, with an annual contribution of $50.

The existence of far-away Japan was made vivid at the annual meeting in 1903 by the presence of Kiyoshi Satoh and Miss Tame Imai, two students educated at Universalist colleges who were preparing to return to their native land. This visit spurred the YPCU to further activity, for in 1904 it began to pay part of the salary of Sempo Ito in Shizuoka. A record $1,000 was raised for the Japan mission in 1919, and in the following year enthusiasm for the overseas mission was heightened by the visit of Chujiro Kawabata, pastor of the Central Church in Tokyo, at the convention held in Murray Grove.[88] The YPCU also contributed small amounts to medical missionary service in Korea before World War I. A major contribution to the Japan mission came in 1922 with assistance in financing Clifford and Margaret Stetson and their work in Shizuoka, an activity which came to an abrupt end when they were recalled in 1931 because of inadequate support. Almost $12,000 had been provided by union money for the Japan mission. Closer home, the YPCU gave some assistance to J. C. Orito, a Japanese student in the Crane Theological School at Tufts, who in 1916 established a small Japanese church, with services conducted in Boston.

The YPCU supported for two and one-half years (1931–1933), largely through the influence of Stella Marek Cushing, a program in Albania to provide scholarships for the training of youth of that nation in modern agricultural methods. In 1930 the organization contributed $500 toward the financing of the National Memorial Church which took the form of assisting in paying for a fireplace in the structure. Five years later the organization began contributions to the operation of the Clara Barton Fresh Air Camp which amounted to more than $2,000. Funds of varying amounts were also committed to such denominationally related organizations and institutions as the *Universalist Herald*, published in Georgia; and the Franklin Square House in Boston and Unity House in Minneapolis. Some projects, such as aid in subscription drives for the *Leader*, involved no direct financial expenditure.

The YPCU had other international contacts and interests besides Japan, Korea, and Albania. An International Association of Free Christian and Free Religious Youth had been founded in 1923 and reorganized at Copenhagen, as the youth component of the International Association for Liberal Christianity and Religious Freedom of which both the Universalist General Convention and the American Unitarian Association became members.[89] The reorganized group, deriving its name from the location in Holland where it had met, was known for a time as the Leyden International Bureau of Liberal Youth, and had been created to combat rising totalitarianism in Europe by promoting international friendship and spreading a liberal version of Christianity.

In 1935 the YPCU voted to join with its Unitarian counterpart as co-host of a meeting of the international youth group, to be held at the Unitarian summer conference center at Star Island the next year. The national union pledged $500 to assist in defraying expenses, supplemented by a contribution from the General Convention.

The conference, attended by 220 young people, 54 of whom were Europeans from 6 nations, was pronounced an unqualified success, with the theme "The Function of Religious Freedom in a World of Rising Authorities."[90] Another conference was held in Oxford, England, in 1937, with fourteen Universalist delegates, including Benjamin Hersey who returned with a detailed report.[91] Financing was provided by a variety of denominational contributions.

A similar meeting was held in Leersum, Holland, in 1938, where the name of the organization was changed to the International Religious Fellowship. The theme that year was "The Unity of Liberal Religion."[92] The outbreak of war cut short for the time being the activities of the organization, of which Jeffrey W. Campbell, a Universalist, had been elected president in 1939. They were resumed after the conflict had ended.

A World Youth Conference was held in London in 1945. Out of it came the World Federation of Democratic Youth in which both Universalist and Unitarian youth participated. Ann Postma was the Universalist representative, and after her return to the United States was made a special field worker to keep Universalists apprised of international developments on the youth front.[93] The Universalists withdrew in 1948 when the organization became, in their judgment, too deeply involved in the ideological conflict associated with the Cold War. The International Youth Fellowship was revived in 1946 and met in Switzerland the following year. Universalist youth continued to participate after an American branch had been established.

The YPCU came close to the brink of financial disaster more than once in its history, and had to be rescued by the General Convention. It had already become obvious as early as 1898 that the youth group had seriously over-committed itself, partly by the over-enthusiastic influence of Shinn who maneuvered the organization into levying per capita assessments which experience readily proved to be largely uncollectible. So, in 1898 the national convention meeting in Chicago decided to discontinue the practice of paying the secretary and editor of *Onward* a salary, small as it was. But dependence on completely voluntary help made the situation worse, and that course was abandoned.

If the YPCU were continued at the pace demanded, some kind of paid field representative had to be provided, and in 1910 Roger Etz, elected national secretary that year, served until 1912 as a roving field worker on a part-time basis. The experiment was so successful that the YPCU voted in 1919 to employ a full-time Director of Young People's Work, financed mostly by the allocation of funds from the denominational Million Dollar Drive begun that year. In actuality, when Stanley Manning, who had served as national YPCU president from 1912 to 1914, was selected, half his salary was paid by the General Convention which claimed part of his services. The employment simultaneously of a Young People's Missionary to serve in the name of the YPCU was too ambitious a plan to have been carried out at the time.

Manning's field work, even though part-time, was so successful that when his assignment came to an end in 1924 the YPCU voted to obtain a full-time field secretary. But financial considerations again prevented its immediate realization, and the youth group suffered a period of serious decline after the office of Director of Young People's Work was temporarily abolished in 1929.[94] An accumulation of problems in the 1920s and 1930s threatened the very existence of the organization. A gloomy picture was painted in 1935 by the national secretary: "A lack of vital program, a lack of active interest and support by ministers and officials of the denomination . . . a lack of organized field work, low attendance at summer institutes and conventions, no executive head to direct the work of the organization, a decreased age level of the members resulting in decreased income, a financial debt that threatened to increase, and a lack of adult advisorship."[95] This pessimistic assessment was unfortunately borne out by the facts.

The lowest total individual membership — less than 2,000 — in the history of the organization was reported in 1933, with less than 100 unions, including only 10 junior unions.[96] The organization had an indebtedness of $2,000. It seemed that the YPCU was beset by a general malaise, evident on every hand. The average size of those local unions which were still active had dropped to less than twenty. The publication and distribution of *Onward,* still plagued by chronic deficits, had been transferred temporarily in 1924 to the Courier Press in Winchendon, Massachusetts, because the facilities of the Universalist Publishing House were so inadequate and overcrowded.[97] The organization of new junior unions was discontinued in 1929 and only twelve had been reported to have existed in the entire denomination in 1932, with ages ranging from nine to fourteen.[98]

Unlike most previous YPCU conventions, the forty-first annual meeting, held in 1929 in the United Liberal Church in Atlanta, was "one of tension and crisis from beginning to end" in its business sessions.[99] The very life of the organization was at stake. Decline in membership over the past seven years, a serious deficit in operating expenses, the problem of restructuring, the question of merger with their Unitarian peers, and the fate of *Onward* were among the issues to be faced.

Nothing was accomplished regarding union with the YPRU. The assembly did endorse, at the urging of President Adams of the General

Convention, the formation of a Department of Religious Education, but only after the YPCU was assured that its autonomy would not be compromised and that it would not be made an appendage of the General Convention.

The problem of the future of *Onward* received much attention. The sixteen-page publication had incurred a deficit of more than $1,000 the previous year, much larger than earlier. It was decided that, beginning in the fall of 1929, it would be reduced to a monthly of four pages and made more of a news bulletin and less of a vehicle for "abstract articles . . . little read and little used."

The Legion of the Cross, the missionary arm of the organization which was currently supporting Universalists in Texas and the Japan mission, was renamed the "Church Extension Department," with the same responsibilities as before. A movement to withdraw all financial support for missionary work and to concentrate on local unions was defeated. This would have meant a turning inward and a narrowing of horizons thought to be imcompatible with the purposes of the organization. Missionary fervor for both foreign and domestic projects, once providing such vitality and sense of purpose, did almost disappear when most of the activities of the Japan mission had been all but given up by the early 1930s after they had been transferred to other hands. Support of Texas Universalists ended in 1929, and field work virtually came to a halt. Interest in national meetings themselves had in fact declined. At the poorly attended Philadelphia convention in 1926, blame had been placed in part on the competition from summer institutes.

One of the most controversial issues at the 1929 convention was a new constitution which provided for biennial rather than annual sessions, largely on economic grounds. This possibility had been discussed for at least three years.[100] The document was adopted by the narrow margin of two votes (23 to 21), but was subject to ratification the following year. Opposition to biennial sessions was strong, the main argument being that such a change would further weaken the already struggling group.

There was a glimmer of light in the midst of the gloom in 1929. There were pledges to meet the operating deficit, and a new slate of officers was elected which showed unusual promise of leadership. Dorothy Tilden, then of Bath, Maine, thoroughly acquainted with the affairs of the organization and author of a weekly Young People's column in the *Leader,* was elected president. She was the second woman in the history of the YPCU to have been chosen for that office.

The Massachusetts YPCU may be taken as fairly typical of the nationwide rise and decline of the organization.[101] The *ad hoc* board of the state group, organized as the Universalist Young People's Union, held its first meeting at the Universalist Publishing House in Boston in June 1889, at which a constitution was drawn up and 200 copies prepared. A series of three public meetings was held in as many locations, the first in Worcester.

Organization proceeded rapidly, with a nucleus of seventeen local young people's groups then in existence, promptly enrolled. The formation of additional unions was made an early order of business, and by the end of the first year thirty-three groups had joined. A survey indicated in 1891 that there were some seventy churches in the state without a youth group.

The possibility of conflict with the national YPCU which had been organized only a few weeks after the Massachusetts group had taken shape, was almost inevitable. The first disagreement had come in 1890, when the national organization solicited membership directly from local unions and was informed that the duty was to interest young people first at the state level; the state union therefore refused at first to join.

When the second annual meeting convened, eighty-eight delegates attended, representing twenty-two societies. Among the resolutions passed was one suggesting that membership of local unions should be through the state organization and not directly with the national. A conflict of jurisdictions was immediately created, and not remedied until the national constitution was so amended as to provide both state representation at the national level and the permission of the state organization before a local union could join the national. The secretary of the national YPCU made an unsuccessful attempt to have the Massachusetts union bypass the state superintendent and appoint its own missionary.

Sixty-one unions with a membership of more than 2,500 were affiliated with the state YPCU by 1893 and Massachusetts was divided into a number of districts, with their own meetings.

Financing the state YPCU was a problem of long standing. The treasury, dependent at first on solicitations, had a balance of $3.50 in 1893, so a system of assessments was introduced the next year of $5.00 per union, with twenty-five cents allocated to the state organization for each local member.

A junior union was first organized in the state at the Somerville church in 1893, and the first convention extending more than one day was held in 1894 at Plymouth. A new record was achieved, with 105 delegates and 38 unions represented, with a constituency of approximately 3,000. Another record was set in 1895 at the annual meeting in Salem, with 182 delegates representing 51 unions, which coincided with the record attendance and membership of the national YPCU attained that year. The 1895 meeting was also important because state colors (gold and white) were adopted, together with a codfish as the emblem.

There had been much informal contact with the Rhode Island YPCU, a much smaller organization, for several years, and in 1898 the first formal arrangement was negotiated when arrangements were made to have a single agent arrange transportation to the national YPCU meeting in Chicago. The state YPCU claimed a membership exceeding 2,200 in 1901, with 203 in Rhode Island; Massachusetts membership declined to below 2,000 in 1902, with Medford Hillside claiming the largest number — sixty-eight; it was still the largest in the state in 1904.

After "dead wood" was pruned out in 1907, state membership stabilized at about 1,750, with 54 unions, but a period of decline set in which was never reversed. The Rhode Island YPCU had begun to decline correspondingly, when in 1913 the largest union in the state (at the Church of the Mediator, Providence) affiliated with the Massachusetts state union. It was not allowed, however, to vote at annual conventions because the Massachusetts YPCU constitution prohibited full recognition for organizations outside the state. The state union in Rhode Island was dissolved in 1926 and the six local unions formed the Rhode Island League and petitioned for membership in the Massachusetts group. This was officially accomplished in 1929, after the Massachusetts constitution was amended to allow full privileges for those outside the state.

The decline of the state organization in both membership and vigor paralleled that of the national YPCU in the 1920s. Very little business was actually transacted, and most of the time at conventions was spent in making plans for the next meeting or revising the constitution. Not more than half the unions were represented at most meetings.

Very early in its history the state YPCU fell behind in paying its assessments to the national body, and with the steady shrinkage in the membership base the problem became serious. There was in Massachusetts, as in most other states, a reluctance to "be dictated to" by the national YPCU. Resentment became so evident in 1934 that state board members were prohibited from expressing "any opinion against the national organization." The number of unions had declined to little more than forty by the late 1920s, and the number of delegates to the state convention held in Norwood in 1929 was down to thirty-five. In the same year a banquet to be held by the western division had to be cancelled because of insufficient interest.

Dorothy Tilden Spoerl, who for many years conducted the youth column in the *Leader,* noted in 1929 the phenomenon of general decline and raised the question of whether the YPCU had outlived its usefulness.[102] One organizational solution offered by the General Convention trustees in 1929 was to create a department of religious education which would presumably effect a more efficient coordination of all youth activities.[103] Harold A. Lumsen, long involved in YPCU activities, agreed with the action of the trustees, considering the youth group cumbersome and over-organized, operating non-productively and consisting mostly of machinery. He concluded that the existing state and national unions were "a waste of time, money, and effort," and that the sooner they were allowed to die the better.[104] A general Department of Religious Education, with work confined to the local level, was considered sufficient.

Prospects looked much brighter after 1935. The office of Executive Secretary was created as a full-time position which included part-time field work. More stimulating programs were developed. The General Convention had come to the aid of the organization not only financially but with an advisory committee after the YPCU, in desperation, sought its advice and support. Twenty-five new unions were reported at the convention even in 1935, a well-attended affair held at Ferry Beach as a combined summer institute and annual meeting, and at which the national secretary had made such a depressing report.

The number of local groups had risen to 134 by the end of the decade, and to more than 230 on the eve of World War II, although still far below that of an earlier era. If war had not intervened the rebuilding of youth organizations might well have continued apace. The national group experienced a period of general revival even during the conflict, handicapped as it was by departures for military service. A determined effort was made to keep in touch with them, with a mailing list exceeding 4,500 by the spring of 1943.[105] The leadership of such individuals as Alice Harrison was a major contributing factor in keeping youth activities alive. She had begun her career of association with Universalist youth in Lynn, Massachusetts, in 1936, and a decade later became national Director of Youth Activities in the Department of Education, with special attention to both junior and senior high school membership. She served also as Associate Director for High School Programs for the combined youth groups until her resignation in 1957.

Two major responsibilities undertaken by the YPCU early in its history were recruitment for the ministry and encouragement to join the church. In both regards it was a resounding success. Tillinghast estimated as early as 1895 that " two-thirds of the [theological] students are to some extent influenced by the YPCU." Hersey, challenged by reports of the alleged decline in the appeal of the ministry as a vocation, polled in 1895 all who had entered Universalist theological schools since 1889 to find out what had prompted them to enroll. Fifty-eight percent of the replies indicated that the YPCU had been either directly responsible for their decision or had been a contributing factor. More than 90 percent of those joining the church in 1905 had been YPCU members.[106] Some 12,000 members of the church between the ages of thirty-one and fifty in 1905 had been members of the youth group. A record for recruitment for the ministry was set in 1911, when nine yong people, at the national convention in Portland, Maine, pledged themselves to enter the ministry.

In order to make sure that theological students were made aware of the YPCU it recommended in 1919 that the history, organization, and methods of the youth group be incorporated into the curricula as part of the required denominational course work. Some references were made to it in courses dealing with religious education.

Hersey updated his statistics regarding the relation between fellowshipped clergy and the YPCU on its fiftieth anniversary in 1939, when eighteen individuals were present who had been union members in 1889 and/or had attended the organization meeting that year. Of the almost 250 from whom usable replies were received, 62 percent attributed their decision to enter the ministry either directly or indirectly to membership in the YPCU. Among those directly influenced were John Smith Lowe, for eleven years the General Superintendent; two state superintendents (George A. Gay and Fred C. Leining); Hazel I. Kirk, a missionary in Japan; and Stanley Manning, Director of Young People's Work from 1919 to 1924. Participation in the YPCU had influenced, among others, Roger Etz, General Secretary and General Superintendent for many years; Hannah J. Powell, missionary in Western North Carolina; Luther R. Robinson of Chattanooga, Tennessee, a convert through the Post Office Mission; and Benjamin B. Hersey, soon to become pastor of the Church of the Divine Paternity and later dean of the Crane School of Religion.

The same story could be told for large numbers of lay leaders such as A. Ingham Bicknell, long-time treasurer of the General Convention as well as an officeholder in the Massachusetts State Convention. He had been the youngest person ever to serve as the YPCU national secretary. One-half of the General Convention trustees in 1943 had been YPCU presidents.[107] The organization indeed had served as "The Manual Training School of the Universalist Church."

Cooperation with youth groups of "partialist" churches was recommended "wherever a good cause may be advanced," but the YPCU gravitated immediately toward their Unitarian counterpart, the Young People's Religious Union (YPRU), organized in 1896. Like the Universalists, there was no denominational identification in the name. When they were both reorganized in 1941 the Universalists identified themselves denominationally as the Universalist Youth Fellowship (UYF), dropping their designation as "Christian," while the Unitarian group added their denominational label for the first time, as the American Unitarian Youth (AUY). Both were merged as Liberal Religious Youth (LRY) in 1953, the first organization within either church to anticipate by official designation the consolidation of the two denominations eight years later.

A further step in achieving closer relationships with both local churches and fellowships and with the central organization was taken in the summer of 1982 when LRY was transformed into Young Religious Unitarian

Sixtieth National Universalist Youth Fellowship in Norway, Maine, 1948

Universalists (YRUU) after two years of planning and discussion. The age span remained almost as broad as it had been for Universalists almost a century earlier, and adult participation was officially provided.

The first exchange of greetings between the youth of the two denominations originated with the Universalists in 1895, a year before the Unitarian young people had organized nationally. There was recognition by the YPCU from the very outset that the YPRU's "field of liberal Christian effort... in so many ways is similar to our own." In 1897 the Universalists recommended that other liberal churches (meaning basically the Unitarians) schedule their meetings at the same time and place as the YPCU so that "union" meetings could be held. Cooperation regarding citizenship training and local charity work was also encouraged. Exchange of "fraternal delegates" at annual conventions was begun in 1897 and was interrupted only briefly by World War I. The first "double union" rally was held in Boston in 1897.[108]

Such goings-on were heartily disapproved of by Sweetser, the great apostle of denominational separateness who put an end (so he thought) to talk of joint conventions at the Detroit meeting that year. In 1923 the practice of holding joint non-legislative meetings in the Boston area, interrupted by war, was resumed. Granville Hicks, later a prominent and controversial journalist who conducted for several years the young people's column in the *Leader,* thoroughly approved, commenting that "the older people have something to learn."[109]

Denominational lines as between the two groups were further blurred with joint participation in the Student Federation of Religious Liberals which had been organized on Unitarian initiative in 1923 and lasted only four years. It held its second conference at Mt. Holyoke College in 1924, with Atwood and Skinner prominent on the program.[110] Hicks, at the time editor of *Onward,* was elected president that year.

The Unitarian youth group had recommended in 1899 that a conference committee be appointed to devise plans for closer cooperation, a step in which the YPCU readily concurred. This was duly reported to the General Convention.[111] Nothing concrete was done, however, for over a quarter of a century. A joint conference of the two sets of national officers on matters of common interest was held in 1928 but nothing conclusive resulted.

The first official tie between the two youth groups came in 1933, when a Joint Commission on Social Responsibility, created in 1930 and adopted a few weeks earlier by the YPRU, was ratified by the Universalist group at their annual convention.[112] The YPCU had had no comparable group previously except a Social Service Department which in 1930 had issued a pamphlet outlining mostly local community projects. Co-chairmen were appointed, with an equal number from each group to constitute the commission. At the time, the YPRU claimed four times as many members as the Universalists, with the numer of local groups far exceeding theirs.[113]

There was talk of some kind of federation or even of merger between the two groups in the 1930s, during the presidencies of Max A. Kapp (Universalist) and Dana M. Greeley (Unitarian), but nothing came of it. The ill-fated Free Church Fellowship urged closer relations between the two, and the YPRU even established its own committee on interdenominational relations and recommended the establishment of parallel commissions to cooperate in the proposed Free Church.

The majority of adult leaders of the two denominations were not prepared for such a move. The editor of the *Leader* insisted that the two youth organizations "by nature . . . do not belong in one ecclesiastical body, and those whom God has not joined together, let no man haul together by the scruff of the neck."[114] The prevalence of such sentiments in either the YPCU or the YPRU was vigorously denied by their officers, and they continued to cooperate in various projects. Universalist youth joined with Unitarians in 1934 in a peace caravan in which the latter had first participated in 1930, sponsored by the American Friends Service Committee.[115]

The first official action calling for outright merger, if the Universalists so desired, came from the Unitarians in 1935. The first preliminary report of the AUA Commission of Appraisal had urged merger, the desirability of which was confirmed in its second report. It asserted confidently "that the young people of the two denominations will yet achieve this purpose."[116] Leining and Etz, representing an *ad hoc* General Convention advisory committee which had been established to assist the ailing YPCU to dredge itself out of its many difficulties, attended their annual meeting at Ferry Beach in 1935 to map out a course of action.

There were two issues at stake. The first was to revive the youth organization by broadening its base and enlarging its activities. A more inclusive name than YPCU was suggested, such as "Murray Fellowship," comparable to the Pilgrim Fellowship among Congregationalists.[117] The committee also recommended the appointment of a full-time executive secretary, part of whose responsibilities was to engage in field work. It also recommended that the temporary advisory committee be made a permanent body to provide continuous adult involvement nationally.

The second issue to be resolved was merger, and this the adults firmly opposed. The YPCU was an important part of the "denominational set-up" and should not be abandoned. The YPRU had a no more adequate program to meet youth needs than did the YPCU. Further, the YPCU itself was too badly divided to make such a move desirable. So the YPCU bowed to the wishes of the advisory committee representatives and voted (46 to 6) to defer action on the Unitarian proposal for one year.

The deferral was actually much longer than that. Although discussion of the possibility and feasibility of merger took place sporadically after 1935, no definitive action resulted until after World War II. The two youth fellowships continued, however, to cooperate, and collaborated in the publication of *Youth for Action,* dealing with social service. The two groups tried the experiment of a joint publication, the *Young Liberal,* beginning in the fall of 1945, as a bi-monthly, and *Onward* came to an end. The first editor of the *Young Liberal,* Robert H. MacPherson, a Universalist, was at the time a student in the Tufts School of Religion and later served as president of what had become, by a change of name, the Universalist Youth Fellowship. The experiment lasted only two years, when the Universalists brought it to an end "for the purpose of strengthening our organization." There were only 200 subscribers when the *Young Liberal* became an exclusively Unitarian publication.

The Unitarian group announced its regret at the loss of UYF co-sponsorship, considering it "one of the most encouraging signs of growing AUY-UYF unity," and at its next annual meeting expressed the hope for "the eventual union of our two organizations."

The first issue of the *Youth Leader* (Universalist) appeared in December 1947 and changed its format several times. When it was published as a tabloid in 1950 it carried the sub-title "The Journal of Liberal Youth." The name *Youth Leader* was retained after the denominational consolidation, and before its end in 1964 had become a digest and clearing-house for topics of current interest to youth federations around the nation rather than a news medium.

A joint convention of the successors of the YPCU and YPRU was held for the first time in 1951 at Lake Winnepesaukee, New Hampshire, where the Universalist young people had convened in the summer of 1889 just prior to their organization as a national body. The 1951 meeting was considered of sufficient importance to have been attended by Cummins, the General Superintendent of the Universalist Church of America and Eliot, President of the American Unitarian Association.

Resolutions favoring organic union were adopted in 1951 by both youth groups, a tentative constitution was approved the following year, and the negotiations which had begun in 1935 were finally completed at a joint convention at Hanover College in Indiana in 1953, with a vote of 47 to 4 among Universalists made unanimous in joint session. The two organizations combined as Liberal Religious Youth (LRY) which had finally come into being after almost twenty years of on-and-off attempts. Clara Mayo, a Unitarian, became the first president. The new organization, incorporated under Massachusetts law, was given authority, by special legislation in 1956, to meet outside the state just as had the YPCU when it was reincorporated in 1898. The youth of the two churches had been able to accomplish what the adults had debated for an even longer time and were yet to achieve almost a decade later.

The General Sunday School Association

Although there had existed, both before and after 1870, the feeling that the denomination should take "an aggressive stand" in regard to its Sunday school activities, little was done on a national scale until the very end of the nineteenth century. The Sunday school movement was disorganized and localized, and existed without a semblance either of uniformity or professionalism, using only untrained and unpaid volunteers and whatever teaching materials and techniques came to hand.

In fact, Universalist Sunday schools had experienced a period of actual decline in numbers, size, influence, and even respectability which lasted into the early twentieth century. The International Sunday School Association, in estimating the general "efficiency" of such organizations, had placed Universalist Sunday schools below those of almost every Protestant denomination, low as many of them were.[118]

A five-member Sunday School Library Commission had been created in 1883 to recommend suitable books, with more than 2,000 titles on the list by 1891.[119] A Sunday School Superintendents' Bureau of Exchange to provide some measure of communication had been established in 1886, but lasted only four years.[120] There was desultory talk about the possibility of establishing a national Sunday school secretaryship, a Sunday school department, and a Sunday school association, but it failed to move beyond the discussion stage until 1899, when an *ad hoc* Commission on Sunday Schools was finally created by the General Convention and made "permanent" in 1900.[121] But by 1909 either the commission had become inoperative or the General Convention had a collective short memory, for in that year the recommendation was made that a "permanent Commission on Sunday Schools" be created.[122] However, this time it was also recommended that a salaried Sunday school secretary be employed to bolster lagging interest, and that increased attention be paid to the subject in theological schools as well as to more adult Bible classes. The idea of a paid Sunday school secretary financed by the General Convention went down to defeat in 1911.[123]

The idea of having a nationwide organization was first brought forward in definite form at a conference called by the Sunday School Commission

George E. Huntley (1870-1950), President of the General Sunday School Association

which met in Chicago in 1912, with representatives from the Universalist Publishing House, the General Convention, and the theological schools. Of the some sixty individuals present, the only vote in favor of establishing a national Sunday school organization was cast by the maker of the motion.

Not to be deterred, the proponents of the plan called a second conference which met in conjunction with the YPCU in 1913, prior to the sessions of the General Convention. The presiding officer at the meeting concerned with Sunday schools, called away at the last moment, gave a parting injunction to a colleague to kill any such organization. But the motion to create a national Sunday School Association prevailed. A provisional constitution was drawn up and temporary officers were selected, to serve only three months. Instead, George E. Huntley (1870–1950), the first president, served as its executive head for sixteen years.

The majority of the trustees opposed the creation of the Association, and their report to the General Convention in 1913 recommended against it. It was argued that religious education could be carried on just as well by the existing Sunday School Commission. Bisbee, editor of the *Leader,* argued that there were already too many organizations in the denomination already. Even the Sunday School Commission, which sponsored the idea, was not unanimous. C. Neal Barney dissented from his four colleagues, believing that the supervision of Sunday school activities should remain at the state level.[124] There was also hesitation about giving national recognition to a denominational activity that obviously overlapped the YPCU.

Thanks to the persistence of Judge Brayton A. Field and Joseph L. Sweet, trustees sympathetic to strengthening the Sunday school movement, their fellow trustees reluctantly withdrew their opposition and the General Convention created the General Sunday School Association of the Universalist Church (GSSA) in 1913.[125] It was only after much difficulty that the spokesman for the plan had received permission to speak from the floor for five minutes. The brief plea was so effective that the convention overcame the reluctance of the trustees and approved the move.

One of the principal trustee objections to organizing the Association had been that there was already too much of a tendency in the denomination to break up into special interest groups, and that the creation of yet another organization needing financial support would only worsen the situation. So it was made clear that the new Association was to be closely affiliated with the convention as a dependent auxiliary, not an autonomous organization. A trustee committee on Sunday schools was created to monitor its operations.

The GSSA was incorporated in 1914 under the laws of New York State and was divided into seven departments, with a superintendent for each.[126] Huntley, whose dedication to the Sunday school movement was instrumental in keeping the GSSA alive, resigned from the faculty of the Canton Theological School in 1917 to devote full time to the work.[127] When he retired in 1928 and was replaced by John M. Ratcliff, the GSSA, by then a part of the new Department of Religious Education, had fully vindicated itself after its shaky start sixteen years earlier.[128] When it had been organized in 1913 almost one-third of the denominational Sunday schools had been disbanded and almost 40 percent of the membership had disappeared. It had begun with no financial resources at all but by 1922 had a biennial operating budget of $23,000, and only once in that time (1927) had it shown a deficit.[129]

In less than twenty years the decline in Sunday school activities had been reversed in spite of the fact that the denomination as a whole had experienced numerical shrinkage instead of expansion. Teacher training institutes had been established and, beginning in 1921, a field supervisor was made responsible also for leadership training. Miss Harriet G. Yates served for many years in that capacity.[130] Even in the midst of economic depression in the 1930s there were 360 active Universalist Sunday schools with 32,000 pupils registered.[131]

An important impulse which had resulted in the creation of the GSSA had come from chronic dissatisfaction over choice of curricular materials. The trustees of the General Convention had adopted the Bible-centered International Uniform Sunday School Lessons, widely used by Protestant churches and introduced in 1873. The lessons were published in the *Universalist Helper* (usually known simply as the *Helper*) which had been started in 1870 in Chicago by Samuel A. Briggs. After a brief sojourn in New York City it had been transferred to Boston, where it was published first as a monthly and then as a quarterly. It had a circulation of about 3,200 in 1873.[132]

Universalists, by the late 1870s and early 1880s, were complaining that some of the material, reflecting orthodoxy, was not appropriate for denominational use, and called for material prepared by Universalists.[133] Nothing was done, however, for many years to solve the problem. Dissatisfaction continued to be expressed about the appropriateness of the Uniform Lessons, but a special commission reported in 1889 that their use should be continued in preference to any that might be prepared by Universalists. It was agreed that they might be accompanied by interpretations acceptable to the denomination. James M. Pullman was commissioned to provide them.

The suggestion was made in 1899 that methods in Sunday school instruction be improved by dividing classes into five grade levels, from kindergarten through a senior department (beyond the age of fifteen), with specially prepared study manuals. The result was a series of Murray Graded Lessons, first made available for optional use in 1901, prepared by Universalist clergy and laity, and issued by the Universalist Publishing House. They ran parallel to the Uniform Lessons and were edited for many years by John Coleman Adams, who also edited the *Helper*. He was described as "one of the best friends the Sunday schools ever had."[134]

The Murray Graded Lessons were supplemented by pamphlets on special topics such as one on temperance by Harry Adams Hersey. Miss Mary L. Ballou devoted many years to preparing material for the intermediate classes. The lessons, last updated as of 1910, ceased to be recommended when the GSSA observed its twentieth anniversary in 1933, and most of them had by then gone out of print.[135] Some Universalist Sunday schools continued to use material from other denominations and from publishers other than their own. Reluctance to be tied down to any one set of curricular materials characterized denominational Sunday schools from the start.

Cooperation between Universalists and Unitarians in religious education had a long history. An early example was the organization in 1910 at a meeting in Petersham, New Hampshire, of the Channing-Murray Sunday School Union.[136] It originally comprised representatives of eight churches in western Massachusetts, and by the early 1930s had been expanded to fifteen. During that same decade two representatives of the GSSA served on the curriculum committee of the Unitarian Department of Religious Education, and when the federation of the two denominations was approved in 1953 as a prelude to union, it was their departments of education that were, together with the youth groups, the first actually to carry out the plan. A year later they were amalgamated as one body under the Council of Liberal Churches, with a staff drawn from each denomination. Literature common to both was provided by the *New Beacon Series in Religious Education*.

Both the strength and programs of the GSSA were seriously weakened by "five years of grinding war" in the 1940s. But even then a surprising amount of good had been accomplished with limited staff and even more limited income. Sunday school pupils contributed several thousand dollars to three "Friendship Offerings," both foreign and domestic.[137] When Miss Susan M. Andrews resigned in 1945 after fourteen years as executive director and submitted her final report to the General Assembly the following year, she received an official expression of gratitude "for her years of outstanding work in religious education."[138] She was prevailed upon to continue service, and was granted a year's leave of absence, until September 1947; Miss Margaret Winchester served as acting director.

The GSSA was officially dissolved as a corporate entity in 1949 as part of the reorganization of the central administration and the creation of a consolidated Department of Education which took over its functions; its assets were transferred to the church. An era in the history of Universalist Sunday school efforts came to a close with Huntley's death in 1950. Like the YPCU, the GSSA had served an invaluable purpose in both strengthening the denomination and in maintaining its outreach.

Chapter 13

Summer Institutes: Combining Religion and Recreation

The tradition of summer relaxation and recreation away from home base has been carried on by hundreds of thousands of Americans over the years at lake, mountain, or seashore. Many have summer residences owned, rented, leased, or lent, ranging from the most primitive to the most palatial. Among the latter was the elegant residence on one of the Thousand Islands in the St. Lawrence River, built in 1887 by the Universalist railroad equipment tycoon, George M. Pullman, and opened on his mother's eightieth birthday.[1] The newest and finest of the Pullman summer homes on two-acre Pullman Island was christened "Castle Rest" and was used by Pullman's brothers and sisters and their families. Summer hospitality among the wealthy of the so-called Gilded Age was legendary; in 1872 the Pullmans had been hosts in a former residence on their island to Generals Ulysses S. Grant and Philip H. Sheridan of Civil War fame.

But there were other configurations of summer activity in the 1870s and 1880s than the purely recreational and social. In 1874 John H. Vincent, a Methodist Sunday school teacher, and Lewis Miller, a manufacturer and fellow Methodist, established a summer Sunday School Teachers Assembly on the shore of Lake Chautauqua, New York, out of which emerged possibly the best known adult education movement in the United States.[2] The experiment was so successful that all kinds of features were added in the summers following, including public lectures, musical programs, and elaborate recreational activities, all open to the general public. By the late 1880s other denominations became participants, and branches of Chautauqua were widely established in the United States and Canada.

In 1875, only a year after the first program had been offered, the

A Universalist picnic in Tacoma, Washington with Q. H. Shinn

suggestion was made by a small group of Universalists that they establish one or more denominational summer resorts and/or camping grounds, preferably near the seashore. Three years later the "Ocean Home Association" was organized in Boston, with Isaac M. Atwood as the first president. A site was selected at Menauhant, on Vineyard Sound near Falmouth, Massachusetts, on Cape Cod.[3] The officers were authorized to negotiate a lease, and William A. Start, secretary of the state convention, made the necessary arrangements. The location, which included a grove of trees for outdoor religious meetings, was already being developed, and half a dozen cottages were soon under construction, occupied by Universalists as summer homes.

The first summer meeting, advertised in the denominational press in Boston, was held for three days and was pronounced a great success. Those attending had been instructed to pitch their own tents and bring their own hymnals.[4] Fourteen clergymen were among those present. Thus was born the idea out of which came the most popular and long-lasting annual summer meetings at Ferry Beach, Maine.

Quillen Hamilton Shinn is credited with establishing the summer sessions which became a permanent annual feature of denominational activity. According to his reminiscences, recorded a year before his death in 1907, the idea of a summer encampment in New England for Universalists was first planted when he read of "basket" meetings of Universalists in the Midwest, as reported in the *Star in the West*. These were occasions when summer picnics and outings were held.[5] It occurred to him that such meetings might also be held in New England, and he visited several possible sites. He had joined the summer association organized by Start at Menauhant in 1878, but in 1881 Shinn moved from Massachusetts to Plymouth, New Hampshire. With the idea of a series of summer meetings still in mind, he attended "grove meetings" that summer in West Rumney, New Hampshire, in which he assisted H. S. Fiske.[6] Later that same summer of 1881 he visited a meeting conducted by Unitarians at The Weirs, on Lake Winnepesaukee, New Hampshire, and decided to hold a Universalist meeting the next summer at the same location.

Shinn's proposal met with an enthusiastic response, and he dubbed the forthcoming assembly "The National Universalist Grove Meeting." The brochure he prepared outlined three objectives: To bring together Universalists from all over the country in order to get acquainted and to share ideas and experiences; to afford people of other communions and those without any church affiliation an opportunity to hear about Universalism; and, most important, to inspire Universalists to renew their own faith and to generate a desire to engage in missionary work, particularly in the South and West.

The first meeting, which was held in August 1882 on a plot owned by the Methodist Camp Meeting Association on Lake Winnepesaukee and for the use of which a fee of $75 was charged, was a resounding success, consisting of a series of sermons, addresses, and discussions. A. J. Patterson delivered the first sermon, followed by E. C. Bolles and numerous others, over a three-day period. One of the tangible results of this first summer meeting was the raising of $2,000 toward the construction of a church in Plymouth, New Hampshire, one of Shinn's earliest missionary projects. At the meeting in 1883 sufficient funds were obtained to complete the church.[7]

The success of the 1882 meeting, aided by Shinn's infectious enthusiasm and administrative ability, made The Weirs meetings annual events. The scope of activities was steadily broadened, combining recreation and fellowship with religious programs. In 1884 excursions were organized into the neighboring White Mountains. In the same year laymen held their first assembly, and in 1885 systematic instruction was begun for Sunday school workers. Fourteen states were represented at the 1886 meeting, when Frederick W. Betts became the first Universalist minister to be ordained at such an assemblage. It was at the 1888 session that Henry W. Rugg made a plea, heeded two years later, to organize a mission to Japan. Beginning in 1889 a Youth Day was inaugurated, the outgrowth of agitation to create a national organization of Universalist young people which was accomplished the same year. In 1891 three days were set aside specifically for missionary meetings, Universalist youth, and children's meetings respectively. Shinn's goal was to provide the maximum opportunity for the involvement of all members of Universalist families.

One activity traditionally associated with camp meetings was a series of revivals or "conference meetings." These were tried experimentally at The Weirs but were not successful. They appealed to but few. Universalists as a group still avoided the old idea of "bearing testimony" as part of the emotionally intense expression of religious experience. It was soon decided that Universalist meetings could not be conducted "on the Evangelical plan."[8]

While The Weirs summer meetings were becoming a fixture and steadily expanding, members of the denomination were active elsewhere in the field of summer programs. Grove meetings lasting several days were held in Queen City Park in Burlington, Vermont, beginning in 1885, while summer gatherings took place for several years at a lakeside near Rome City, Indiana, drawing participants from four neighboring states.

Of all the summer meetings held by Universalists, the oldest one in point of time had been held at Good Luck, New Jersey, at the site of John Murray's landfall in 1770. What became the first summer conference at Murray Grove had been held in May 1833, when four discourses were delivered, and Abel C. Thomas had provided "a plain marble monument" in memory of Thomas Potter.[9] The meeting was intended to be the first in an annual pilgrimage to the spot although the tradition was not maintained continuously until afer 1887. In the late nineteenth century Murray Grove played host to various church groups for one or more weeks during the summer. Among these were the YPCU which held three of its annual meetings there, as well as the GSSA and numerous special institutes. The thirty-second meeting of the YPCU was held at Murray Grove in 1920 as the first part of a pilgrimage celebrating the 150th anniversary of the denomination. The pilgrimage had ended in Gloucester, Massachusetts.

The establishment of Murray Grove as both a summer headquarters and as a proposed centerpiece for the denomination dated back to 1868. In anticipation of the celebration of the centennial of Universalism in America in 1870 the Murray Grove Association was organized in order to purchase a Methodist church which had been erected on the site of the original Potter meeting house. That plan failed after a Good Luck religious society, formed in 1872 in order to secure funds, had been unsuccessful in that attempt. However, an acre of land adjoining the Potter grave was acquired and a decision was made to erect a memorial church. The idea was proposed by Caroline A. Soule in 1874 at a conference in the Jersey City Universalist Church.[10] Phebe Hanaford, the pastor, made the first contribution ($1.00) to a Potter Memorial Fund established to raise money to build the church. Engraved certificates were issued to each individual who contributed $1.00 or more.

Funds came in only in driblets, but after much delay the cornerstone of the memorial church was laid on 28 September 1876. By that date less than $1,700 had been collected of the estimated $3,000 needed. The

Memorial Church at Murray Grove, New Jersey

discouraged treasurer, D. L. Holden of New York City, remarked in 1878 that he was "getting older every day, and he would like to see this work completed during his natural life. It was not projected like St. Peter's of Rome, to be finished by posterity."[11] The effort proceeded so slowly that the church was not dedicated until 15 October 1885.

Gilbert W. Barnes (1819–1897), who preached part-time at Waretown (Wiretown), had charge of the memorial church until his death.[12] He was buried in the small cemetery at Good Luck, near Potter's grave.

In order to retain and expand the memorial to Murray and Potter the Murray Grove Association was reorganized and its first meeting, which extended to a week, took place beginning 20 August 1887. The Association was incorporated under the laws of New Jersey on 20 January 1891. In the 1880s the New Jersey Convention frequently met at Murray Grove, and in the 1890s a rambling three-story frame hotel known as the Murray Grove House was provided for summer meetings. The building was destroyed by fire in 1955 and a year later was replaced by two smaller buildings and in 1958 by a third.[13]

The property comprising the Good Luck Memorial was acquired piecemeal, over a long span of years. A "memorial boulder," transported from the vicinity of Princeton, New Jersey, was dedicated at the site in 1902, with an inscription marking the Potter-Murray meeting in 1770. Sufficient money had been raised by 1905 through the state convention to acquire a large farmhouse and other buildings, and fifteen acres of land nearby from Caroline M. Jeffrey.[14] The main building, dating from before the Civil War, was christened "Ballou House." A valuable gravel bed was discovered on the premises and the contents were sold to the state highway commission, thus substantially reducing the cost of the property.

The most extensive acquisition, in 1909, was the old Potter homestead, consisting of a group of neglected buildings and 202 acres of land. The property, which had been acquired by Potter in 1753 and had been sold by the executors of his estate in 1789, had passed through many hands by the time it was obtained by the Universalists. T. Glenn Phillips, City Park Commissioner for Detroit, Michigan, and a Universalist, volunteered his services to survey the land and make recommendations for its use.[15]

Sufficient funds had been collected by 1912 to pay for the Potter property which was deeded to the General Convention in 1913.[16] Among the devices used to acquire money was the sale of "John Murray stamps" to be affixed to mail.[17] A drive to establish a $25,000 fund for maintenance and improvement of the Murray-Potter property was proposed in 1915, in observance of the centennial of Murray's death.[18]

An addition was made in 1922 with the dedication on Memorial Day of the Universalist National Cemetery, a plot of land on the west side of the Potter church, as a burial place for "the soldiers of freedom in religion."[19] The cemetery had been the idea of Mrs. Frederick A. Bisbee, wife of the editor of the *Leader,* when she visited Murray Grove during the 150th anniversary celebration of the denomination in 1920. The Murray Grove Association approved, the Bisbees purchased the first lot, and Mrs. Bisbee became the first occupant; her husband was interred there in 1923. Among other Universalists buried in the cemetery were Edwin C. Sweetser of Philadelphia and his wife; and Charles E. Petty and Mrs. Petty.[20] A Cemetery Association was incorporated in 1924, with funds from the sale of lots to be administered by the trustees of the General Convention.

One of the most consistent supporters of the Murray Grove Association was George A. Friedrich, who died in 1957. A well-known Universalist layman and long-time member of All Souls Church in Brooklyn, New York, he took on the work of the Association as a special benevolence.[21] One of his consuming ambitions was to make Murray Grove a great center of the denomination, and to that end he prepared a detailed history of John Murray's part in establishing Universalism in America, drawn largely from Murray's autobiography. Friedrich's hope was that his history, written in semi-dramatic form with much improvised dialogue, might appear first in book form, and that the proceeds from its sale would endow Murray Grove. His ultimate aim was to have the book made into a movie.[22]

Although Murray Grove never achieved the public prominence that Friedrich hoped for, it remained both a visible and a durable part of the Universalist heritage.

Star Island, part of a cluster of small islands ten miles off the mainland, with jurisdiction divided between Rye, New Hampshire, and Kittery, Maine, was considered in 1896 as a possible meeting place for Unitarian summer conferences. The Isles of Shoals Summer Meeting Association (later known as the Isles of Shoals Association, Unitarian-Universalist) was organized and the first conference was held there in mid-July 1897. It was intended to be interdenominational, and in 1914 the Congregational Summer Conference Association was formed to conduct such meetings. The Star Island Corporation was organized in 1915, including both Unitarians and Congregationalists. Star Island was purchased for $16,000 in 1916 and by 1929 the corporation also owned 95 percent of neighboring Appledore Island.[23] Universalists held their first summer conference on Star Island in 1905; the meeting seems not to have lessened attendance at denominational meetings elsewhere.[24]

In the tradition of the original Chautauqua movement, Universalists began to conduct summer school Bible study classes at Bonaparte Lake in the Adirondacks (New York State) in 1896.[25] Universalists frequently appeared on Chautauqua programs, such as Mary A. Livermore and Edwin C. Bolles; in fact, The Weirs summer meetings were often referred to as the "Universalist Chautauqua."[26] At the center campgrounds at Lake Chautauqua various churches operated "denominational houses." In the 1920s a combined Universalist-Unitarian facility was one. The Unitarians had established a summer headquarters there shortly before World War I, and in 1926 extended an invitation to the Universalists to join forces.[27] A precedent for this type of cooperation had been set at the county level with the creation in 1907 of the Chautauqua Association of Liberals, with the ministers of both denominations serving as an executive committee.[28]

Throughout the steadily growing and increasingly popular summer sessions at The Weirs could be seen the hand of Shinn, planning the next summer's activities even before the current sessions were over. P. T. Barnum, when placed in charge of the entertainment for the meetings in 1889, announced that he had, as a showman, only one rival — Q. H. Shinn.[29]

The Universalists convened for the last time in their original series at The Weirs in 1897, having been informed by the Methodists that they needed the facilities. So Shinn made plans to meet at Oak Orchard, on the shore of Lake Ontario about forty miles from Niagara Falls.[30] But the

The "Quillen," Ferry Beach, Maine, in 1906

space provided was inadequate, and only two weeks before the meetings were to take place, the location was switched to Saratoga Springs, New York. In spite of the short notice, some 200 individuals attended.[31] The summer sessions were held there for the next two years.

Shinn then cast about for a location closer to the Universalist concentration in New England and decided on Ferry Beach. The area had long appealed to many Universalists as a summer retreat. Camp meetings, complete with preaching, had been held there under Universalist auspices as early as 1879.[32] Ferry Beach was destined to become the summer headquarters for thousands of Universalists and Unitarians over the years.

Ferry Beach Park, a beachfront area of approximately ninety acres located in the city of Saco, Maine, and dominated by a larger grove of huge pines and hemlock, had been laid out in 1882 and had been operated by the Boston and Maine Railroad to attract patrons to a branch line opened in 1880 and running between Old Orchard Beach to the North and the Saco River to the South. The train, known affectionately as the "Dummy," ceased to run in 1923. Universalists eventually owned about twenty-five acres of the park, acquired in installments.[33]

Housing facilities were totally inadequate for the hundreds who flocked to the summer meetings beginning in 1901, and those who attended were forced to scatter themselves up and down the coast in tents or rented quarters. In 1904 Shinn acquired, at considerable personal risk, the Ferry Beach House, a twenty-three room structure on the property, which by 1900 was owned by a group of residents in Biddeford and which became the administrative headquarters known as the Quillen in his honor. In order to make the down payment on the building, which cost $1,600, he borrowed $400 on a life insurance policy, for which he was eventually reimbursed. The cost was later shared by twelve Universalist families who each put up $100 and in return were each assigned a room during meetings.[34] One of the contributors used the same room for forty seasons. Many lots were also sold to individuals and later deeded to the General Convention.

Attendance had increased to such an extent by 1911 that tents were provided for a small fee for those planning to stay only a few days, and a sixteen-room cottage was constructed, named the "Underwood" in honor of Miss Carrie P. Underwood, a benefactress. In 1916 part of the pine grove and sandy stretch between it and Saco Bay on which a pavilion and a bowling alley stood, were acquired from the railroad. The bowling alley was converted into a dormitory for males, and was known facetiously as the "Belmont." A large cottage was also used between 1918 and 1931, and again in the 1940s, as a dormitory. The pavilion was razed in 1932. The entire property had been placed under the control of the General Convention a decade earlier.

Shinn's plan to finance Ferry Beach was outlined in 1901, at the very first meeting at the new location. An association was formed, with Shinn as president. Membership was to cost between $1.00 and $10.00, and the Summer Meeting Association came into existence when the membership reached 100. Articles of Association were drawn up in 1905 for the governance of Ferry Beach, with minimum dues set at $1.00 for annual members and up to $100 for life members. The organization was incorporated in 1909 as the Ferry Beach Park Association of Universalists, and much of the funding for housekeeping and other improvements was provided by the Ferry Beach Ladies Aid Association, established in 1909 under the leadership of Mrs. Shinn.

Unfortunately, the documents relating to incorporation emphasized business rather than religious and educational aspects, and the Association engaged in a protracted controversy with the city of Saco over taxation of the property. Even though it was held by a religious organization and was used basically for religious purposes, it did maintain lodgings, charge fees, and provide other services of a social nature comparable to those carried on by commercial resorts. After having paid $346 in taxes in 1922, more than doubled by 1925, suit was brought against the city for total abatement. But only partial relief was obtained, and that was cancelled out by the construction in 1927 of a combined school building and dormitory, Rowland Hall (named after a past president of the Association), and financed by a mortgage of $10,000, cancelled in 1936. The new building was assessed for tax purposes at $5,000. In addition, thirteen of the fourteen acres then occupied by the Universalists were taxed, at a total sometimes exceeding $1,000 annually.

Memorial Day at Ferry Beach in 1902

One of the most serious administrative problems was the seasonal use of the property, the facilities remaining vacant and unused for a high proportion of the year even though some 700 persons were registered in each of the summers of 1935 and 1936, with six different church organizations using Ferry Beach in succession. An attendance record of nearly 1,000 was set in 1941.[35] Lengthening summer sessions and intensifying publicity to obtain even larger attendance were both used to ameliorate if not to solve the problem. Further, the property had deteriorated by the mid-1930s to such an extent that much repair work had to be done, financed in part by receipt of a substantial pledge made years earlier. A campaign was announced in 1940 to wipe out the total indebtedness which amounted to approximately $2,500.

The Association was reincorporated in 1936, with all but a few privately owned cottages deeded back to the General Convention. This was done in part to achieve some tax relief by emphasizing the basically religious character of the organization. After some fourteen years of litigation the Universalists won the suit, and their property was declared tax exempt as a benevolent and charitable organization by the Maine Supreme Court in 1939. The last segment of territory acquired to obtain both an unobstructed view of the ocean and a secure right-of-way to the beach was the donation of land in front of Quillen House in 1940 by Mrs. Theodore A. Fischer of New Haven, Connecticut, as a memorial to her husband.

The Ferry Beach summer meetings were greatly expanded in both variety and scope since their origins at The Weirs. At first, under Shinn's leadership, they had been mostly occasions for preaching and were devoted primarily to missionary purposes — the extension of Universalism which paralleled the expansion of the nation at the end of the nineteenth century. Many of the sessions which became standard offerings almost every summer, like the preaching missions, were extended to become ministers' institutes, and new ones were added. Formal mission study was introduced in 1907, sponsored at first by the YPCU and expanded by the WNMA in 1910, after the Japan mission had been firmly estblished. After its creation in 1913 the GSSA held many of its national conventions at Ferry Beach.

The names and responsibilities of the organizations participating in Ferry Beach activities shifted with changes in both the denomination and in the larger world. After the Department of (Religious) Education was established, many of the activities involving youth were consolidated within its jurisdiction. The Laymen's Institute and the WNMA institutes became identified with the Institute of Churchmanship organized in 1939, and in turn with the United Christian Adult movement. An Institute of World Affairs was established in 1935, and its successor in 1941, the Institute of International Relations, was operated for many years, sponsored by the Commission on Social Action in the midst of World War II.[36]

The location became so popular and the number and variety of activities appealed to so many that the summer session was eventually lengthened to include almost the entire summer, from early June to early September, although in 1943 the sessions had to be abbreviated to four weeks because of restrictions imposed by war.[37] The operation of Ferry Beach had become so complex and expensive even by the time of World War I that the Ferry Beach Association in 1919 had turned over to the many groups using it, the responsibility for conducting and financing their own institutes and other programs.

Organizations outside the denomination also used Ferry Beach, such as local Boy Scout groups. In 1942 the use of the summer conference property at Star Island by the Unitarians was prohibited by the federal government for reasons of national security because of proximity to the Kittery naval base. Carl Seaburg, active in denominational affairs and national president of the UYF in 1948–1949, promptly suggested that Unitarians be offered the use of Ferry Beach as a good will gesture.[38] The annual convention of the American Unitarian Youth was held there in 1944.[39] Both Quakers and Congregationalists used Ferry Beach in 1945.

This rather bare recital of the facts gives but little intimation of the human side of Ferry Bech, with its combination of excitement, inspiration, education, interesting and important personalities, and plain sociability, and of the significant contributions made not only to individual but to denominational welfare. Reunions of many who had participated in Ferry Beach activities became an annual tradition in 1912 for those living

Quillen Hamilton Shinn and Isaac Morgan Atwood at Ferry Beach

in the Greater Boston area. They were held at various churches in the fall, and offered an opportunity to exchange pleasant memories. Reunions were also held in at least five other states. The celebration of the seventy-fifth anniversary of the first New England grove meeting organized by Shinn took place at The Weirs in 1957, using the same Methodist facilities as in 1882. Special reunion meetings were also held during sessions of the General Convention, beginning in 1923, interrupted only by World War II.

The summer meetings at Ferry Beach had indeed grown "from a shoe-string organization dominated by one man into a many-sided enterprise of co-operative effort reflecting . . . the denomination as a whole and furnishing the inspiration and training for new leadership and renewed effort."[40]

Although Ferry Beach was the largest, best known, and most elaborate of all the summer facilities operated by the Universalists, there were several others besides those mentioned, mostly regional in nature and conducted either by the denomination or some part of it, or in which Universalists participated. Summer institutes were conducted in the South, originating after World War I under the auspices of the church in Chattanooga; and at Shelter Neck, near Burgaw, North Carolina, on property deeded by the Unitarians in 1932, and the outgrowth of the White Lake Institute organized in the same state in 1928 by F. B. Bishop; its property had likewise been deeded to the Universalists in 1932.[41] The Shelter Neck Institute was still active in the 1980s.

The Midwest Institute, held at various locations, met at first in 1925 at Camp Kenmore, operated by the church in Joliet, Illinois, and included sponsorship of a YPCU Institute each summer. After four years at that location it met until 1938 at the 1,200-acre Turkey Run State Park near Marshall, Indiana, and then at Shakamak State Park, in the southwestern part of the state, near Jasonville. It convened at Bridgman, Michigan, in the 1940s. A California summer institute met at the Barton School, Topanga Canyon, under Unitarian auspices. By 1938 ten different summer gatherings all over the nation were either planned or in operation.[42] Unirondack, on the shores of Beaver Lake near Lowville, New York, became in 1951 the denominationally owned site of a series of summer institutes sponsored by the state convention. By 1943 the Buckeye summer meetings had been added in Ohio. Summer activities had indeed become a national phenomenon, providing a change of pace for the hundreds who participated and adding an important dimension to denominational affairs.

Chapter 14

Publications and Scholarship

Anton Titus, in the course of reviewing in 1919 the history of Universalist writings after 1870, commented that there had been for almost half a century no "expression of great themes" comparable to Thomas Baldwin Thayer's *Theology of Universalism* published in 1862.[1] The closest approximation had been Elbridge Gerry Brooks' *Our New Departure* (1874), inspired by the centennial four years earlier, but it had not been sufficiently appreciated by the denomination. It had not been welcomed by the clergy and was almost unknown to the laity.

True, Alonzo A. Miner's *Old Forts Taken,* consisting of five lectures, had been published in 1878, and *The Latest Word of Universalism,* essays by thirteen clergy, had appeared the same year. But such publications represented "days of retreat and change, and not so much of aggressive advance." The "latest word," in Titus' view, had soon become dated. What Miner and the other clergy had done was produce statements, not inspiration and a larger vision. "Universalism became a conclusion rather than a process of living and character building. Perhaps our denomination was too content with the 'Forts Taken,' and not sufficiently interested in the great thoughts for better appeals, scholarship and leadership."

For better or worse, according to Titus, it was in the addresses, reports, pamphlets, and editorials which never appeared in book form that the most vital expressions of Universalism were to be found. Such were the "Manuals of Faith and Duty," eleven in number, appearing between 1888 and 1895; the "Essays, Doctrinal and Practical," fifteen in all published in 1889; and the twenty-five essays prepared for the Columbian Congress in 1893.

At a meeting of Universalist ministers in the Boston area in 1895 George T. Knight, Professor of Church History in the divinity school of

Tufts College, came to substantially the same conclusion that Titus later expressed. He regretted that no scholarly attempt had been made to formulate a systematic exposition of denominational theology according to the "scientific method" so popular by the end of the nineteenth century.[2] True, there had been attempts in the pre-scientific era, representative of which had been Thayer's work. But not until J. Smith Dodge's *The Purpose of God* had appeared in 1895 had there been a "substantial contribution toward that end"; but even that was not sufficiently comprehensive to fill the need; its readership was minimal and the work was soon forgotten. It did, however, have some of the features lacking in Thayer's methodology: Dodge's work was scientific in its formulation — "orderly, systematic, sequential in the presentation of Universalist thought." What was needed, in short, was an organically unified presentation and a distinctively Universalist theology.

Isaac M. Atwood disagreed. What was needed was not another exposition and defense of Universalism, but Universalist scholars contributing larger works within a broadly Christian frame of reference.[3] The era of religious controversy and apologetics had passed. The Universalist Church had reached the stage of "autonomy." The time had come "to construct theology on larger lines than bounded a denomination." It was time, instead, for not so much another book about Universalism as books on theology written by Universalists. But they were not forthcoming in any significant numbers.

Probably the greatest denominational contributions to religious scholarship in the late nineteenth century were made by Orello Cone in the field of Biblical criticism. George H. Emerson, in *The Bible and Modern Thought,* published in 1889, made a good case for modernism in religion, but his work never attracted much attention, among fellow Universalists at least. The same fate befell the *Universalist Quarterly and General Review* which came to an end in 1891, the victim of too limited an audience. There was a gap of half a century before Universalists sponsored another scholarly publication, the *Journal of the Universalist Historical Society,* which first appeared in 1959 and in 1978 was melded into a similar Unitarian publication which had been started in 1925. The *Crane Review,* which lasted for a decade (1958–1968), came to an end when the Crane Theological School at Tufts, its principal sponsor, was closed.

After World War II a small group of Unitarians launched the *Journal of Liberal Religion* and invited Universalists to contribute when the publication first appeared in 1945.[4] Universalist participation consisted largely of the appointment of one of their number as an associate editor and the inclusion of the Universalist Ministerial Association on the masthead as co-sponsor.

Another attempt to provide a forum for exploring "the social and philosophical problems of free religion" appeared in 1953. Known as *The Edge,* it was issued by the Meeting House Press in Boston, the publishing arm of the Charles Street Universalist Meeting House, during Kenneth Patton's ministry.[5] Each issue was to be devoted to a single theme such as "Naturalism and Worship." One, "Education for the Liberal Ministry," was scheduled originally for an early issue but was postponed so often that it was never published. Only three issues of *The Edge* appeared over a two-year period.

In the final issue Carl Seaburg, then the minister of the Universalist church in Norway, Maine, chided his colleagues for their scanty contributions to and respect for scholarship. The clergy were "too often content with a Norman Vincent Peale approach to theology and a Fulton Lewis, Jr., intellectual attitude. Their Bible is the *Readers Digest*. . . . The Universalist ministry needs scholars today more than it needs salesmen or repair men with their specialties of 'parish management,' public relations, business administration, and constant high-cost renovations on the church plant."[6]

Seaburg's strictures went largely unheeded. As John van Schaick, editor of the *Leader,* explained it, Universalists were more interested in doing good for their fellows on earth than in immersing themselves in abstruse theological questions. This argument was but a reiteration of the same philosophy (or lack of it) that had dominated the Universalist thinking of a century earlier. It was a latter-day expression of the theme of "practical Christianity" without any elaborate intellectual underpinnings or theorizing to accompany it. Universalism continued to be as much or more a religion of the heart than of the mind.

The great monument to nineteenth-century denominational historical scholarship was the major work issued by the Universalist Publishing House in the 1880s. It was the two-volume history of the denomination by Richard Eddy (1828–1906), the first volume of which appeared in 1884 and the second, two years later.[7] The trustees had determined by 1880 that sufficient income was available in the Publication Fund to undertake the project.[8] The two substantial volumes (554 pages and 634 pages, respectively), sturdily bound in brown buckram, retailed for $1.50 and $2.00, respectively, postage paid.[9] No records have been found indicating the size of the press run, but the book had become a collector's item by the 1980s.

Universalism in America was a magisterial work, scrupulously accurate, replete with factual and biographical details not readily available elsewhere, and representing a prodigious amount of research extending over more than a quarter of a century. The first volume, comprising seven chapters, carried the story from 1636 to 1800, and the second, of six chapters, from 1801 through 1885. With only one major exception in each volume, the work was arranged strictly chronologically, with dates instead of chapter titles; e.g., "1636–1770," "1770–1778." In the first volume Eddy interrupted his otherwise year-by-year account to devote the fourth chapter to the Restorationist controversy of the 1830s, for which he interviewed as many of the surviving participants as possible.[10] In the second volume the final chapter was devoted to Universalist educational efforts from 1814 to 1886.

The two volumes, as they were finally organized, did not reflect Eddy's original plan. The first volume was to have been a completely chronological narrative, to have been followed by a topically arranged second volume with separate chapters on such subjects as Sunday schools, hymnology, and periodical literature. But he abandoned this approach as "impracticable." The materials on hymnology and periodical literature had to be confined to references in his comprehensive bibliography, and a mere "brief notice" was given to the history of the Universalist Sunday school movement. Only the chapter on education reflected his original plan for the second volume. According to Eddy it was lack of space rather than paucity of materials that was to blame for the omissions.[11]

One part of his history carried out as originally projected was the inclusion of a chronologically arranged bibliography of every item he could uncover that dealt with Universalism, including data on every denominational periodical ever published up to the date of his own work. Needless to say, the bibliography, with its own index, is still an indispensable source for any student of nineteenth-century Universalist history.

Eddy's history, especially the first volume, is heavily weighted down with extended extracts from primary sources. In the second chapter of the first volume ("1770–1778"), much of which is quite appropriately devoted to John Murray, forty-two of the sixty-nine pages consist of quotations from Murray's autobiography and letters.

The man responsible for this major contribution to Universalist history and scholarship was born in Providence, Rhode Island, on 21 June 1828, and died in Gloucester, Massachusetts on 15 August 1906.[12] He combined fifty-seven years as a minister with a long and distinguished career as a denominational editor and writer. A product of Providence public schools, he never attended college although he received an honorary STD from Tufts in 1883 in recognition of his services. He learned the bookbinding trade as a youth, but in 1848, at the age of twenty, decided on the ministry as a career and prepared at Clinton Liberal Institute under T. J. Sawyer.[13]

Eddy interrupted a pastorate at Canton, New York, to serve as a Union chaplain during the Civil War, and subsequently wrote a history of the 60th New York Volunteer Infantry Regiment (1864) with which he served. After returning to civilian life in 1863 as pastor of the First Universalist Society in Philadelphia, he was simultaneously librarian of the Historical Society of Pennsylvania between his election in 1865 and his resignation in 1868. While in Philadelphia he spent one morning a week talking with and comparing notes with Abel C. Thomas, long-time Universalist pastor there and himself a chronicler of Universalist history. It was while in Philadelphia that Eddy conceived the idea of writing a history of the denomination, using in part the resources of the historical society there.[14]

When the Universalist Historical Society met in Lynn, Massachusetts, in 1876, in conjunction with the annual meeting of the General Convention, and issued a call for someone to update and complete Thomas Whittemore's *Modern History of Universalism,* it was not surprising that Eddy volunteered.[15] He was, at the time of publication of his work in 1884–1886, president of the Universalist Historical Society and an active member of both the Historical Society of Pennsylvania and that of his native state of Rhode Island.

Eddy became assistant to Thomas B. Thayer, editor of the *Universalist Quarterly,* in January 1885, and succeeded him when Thayer died the following year. Eddy served as editor until the discontinuance of the *Quarterly* in 1891. In 1887 he also became editor of the *Universalist Register* and held that position until his death nineteen years later. It was Eddy who contributed that part of the volume dealing with Universalism which comprised the tenth volume of the American Church History series published in 1894. He likewise wrote articles on Universalism for several encyclopedias, and in 1898 published a history of Universalism in Gloucester, Massachusetts.

The temperance movement was another of Eddy's special interests. He served for many years as head of the Independent Order of Good Templars in Massachusetts, and delivered almost 2,000 lectures on behalf of total abstinence. He was also the author of two major works on the general subject, *Alcohol in History* (1887) and *Alcohol in Society* (1888).

Eddy's ample knowledge of and interest in organized Universalism was reflected likewise in such denominational organizations as the General Convention, in which he held a number of offices; he was Standing Clerk between 1861 and 1867. He was pastor of the Gloucester church when the centennial gathering of the denomination took place in that community in 1870. Much of the responsibility for planning the celebration fell to him, and it was his administrative ability that contributed greatly to its success. His life and contributions to denominational scholarship in many respects paralleled those of Hosea Ballou 2d over half a century earlier.

There was talk from time to time of updating Eddy's history, but nothing was ever done on the scale of his work while the Universalist Church remained a separate denomination. In 1923 the publications committee of the General Convention made such a suggestion.[16] A similar proposal came from the Pennsylvania State Convention in 1934, and Lee S. McCollester was to have headed up a commission to bring the history of Universalism up to date.[17] Each state convention was to appoint a historian.

Yet another plan to provide an updated history was worked out in 1940. Thomas Butler, who had collected great quantities of primary sources dealing with the history of Universalism primarily in Pennsylvania and later donated his manuscripts to the Historical Society of Pennsylvania in Philadelphia, visited Tufts College that year.[18] After a conversation with Alfred S. Cole, on the Crane Theological School faculty, a division of labor was planned betwen the two. Butler would contribute a section on Universalist origins in America and carry the story up to the appearance of Hosea Ballou. Cole would then complete the history up to about 1940. But that plan likewise was never carried beyond the discussion stage.

The last attempt to write an "official" history of Universalism before consolidation with the Unitarians in 1961 was made in the early 1950s, when the Department of Education of the UCA commissioned Clinton Lee Scott to prepare a history. A combination of circumstances prevented the carrying out of the project as originally envisioned. Instead, a 124-page summary was prepared, and published by the Universalist Historical Society with the cooperation of the Meeting House Press of the Charles Street Universalist Church in Boston.[19] Brief as it was, Scott's work was still considered too long to attract most readers; it was recommended that it be condensed as a twenty-page pamphlet "designed to influence large numbers of people."[20] The "more definitive history of Universalism" to have been prepared by Scott never appeared.

Elmo A. Robinson, a long-time Universalist clergyman and college professor, published *American Univeralism: Its Origins, Organization and Heritage* in 1970. However, the author made no claim to comprehensiveness. His main theme was "the Universalist General Convention, with illustrative supplementary material."[21] In addition, part of the work was as much a personal manifesto as a conventional historical study.

The most recent work which attempts to remedy some of the deficiencies thought to exist in earlier historical treatments of the denomination is the present book, of which this is the second volume. The project was undertaken under the sponsorship of the Universalist Historical Society, which invested a large proportion of its treasury in the endeavor. The first volume, covering the first century of the denomination in America (1770–1870) was published in 1979 and became a much larger and more detailed volume than was originally planned. Financing of its publication was provided by a combination of denominational organizations, and groups and individuals with Universalist and Unitarian associations and interests.

The Universalist Publishing House

There were twelve periodical publications sponsored, controlled, and published by the Universalist Church as its second century opened in 1871. Most emanated from Boston, the unofficial headquarters of the denomination, although there was a branch office opened in Chicago in 1884. Six of the publications were newspapers, one was a scholarly journal, one a "literary and religious monthly for the home circle," one a statistical annual first published in 1836, and three were for Sunday school use.[22]

By 1960, ninety years after the Universalist centennial, all but two of the newspapers had disappeared, as had the scholarly journal, the literary and religious monthly, and all of the Sunday school publications, at least in their original formats.[23] Some others had taken their places, but the great era of journalistic activity was over. The publishing house in Boston, founded in 1862, was struggling to survive a century later, and lost its identity exactly 100 years after it had been established.

The twenty-fifth anniversary of the establishment of the Universalist Publishing House was celebrated with much fanfare in 1887, including lengthy speeches and musical selections by a male quartet, at the Shawmut Avenue Universalist Church in Boston.[24] The presiding officer was Alonzo A. Miner, president of the board of directors since 1867, and the individual who had first suggested the establishment of a centralized denominational publishing house.

Richard Eddy presented one of the major speeches, in the form of a paper detailing the history of the organization. What he offered had been a success story almost from the very beginning, despite early trials and tribulations. In 1862 the new publishing house, with initial subscriptions by seventy-one individuals, and exceeding the amount of stock originally intended (250 shares at $20 each), began its career with only $3,236 of its capital paid in, and obligations of $28,850. They included the acquisition of the property of James M. Usher at 37 Cornhill Street in Boston; Thomas Whittemore's *Trumpet,* begun in 1819 as the *Universalist Magazine;* Sylvanus Cobb's *Christian Freeman* (the two combined in 1862 and renamed the *Universalist* in 1864); and the *Myrtle,* a Sunday School paper which lasted until 1924.

In 1865 the publishing business of Abel Tompkins, next door to Usher, and the meeting-place of many in the denomination for several years after the Civil War, was purchased. This brought under the control of the publishing house the *Ladies' Repository* and the *Universalist Quarterly.* This transaction, together with acquisition of the plates and copyrights of several books, had cost $7,855.78. The *Christian Repository,* the long-established organ of Universalism in Vermont, was added in 1870, and its list of subscribers merged with that of the *Universalist.*

By 1871, after less than nine years, all obligations had been discharged. With the growth of its operations the publishing house was rechartered in Massachusetts in 1872. This act of incorporation eliminated individual ownership, and the stockholders transferred their holdings to a board of twenty-one trustees elected by the state conventions of the six New England states; fourteen were from Massachusetts. All properties, then valued at almost $40,000, and all profits, were to benefit the church, and the corporation was authorized to receive gifts and bequests and to hold real and personal assets not exceeding $200,000.

In 1871 the *Universalist Register* published a complete catalogue of books, pamphlets, and tracts carrying the imprint of the Universalist Publishing House. The publications, divided into over a dozen categories and including biographies, sermons, doctrinal tracts, and Sunday school materials, totalled 113 titles.

The great Boston fire in November 1872 deranged all of the business of the city, but by good fortune the publishing house office on Cornhill escaped serious damage and the *Universalist* did not miss a single issue.[25] But a month late a fire did result in losses to the publishing house in excess of insurance. Nonetheless, the agent was able to report a net profit of almost $750 in 1873 as well as legacies of over $2,500 invested in a permanent fund. In the same year the publishing house acquired the *Sunday School Helper* for $1,000 from M. K. Pelletrau of New York.[26] The *Ladies' Repository,* which had appeared under variant titles, was discontinued in 1874. It had been carried at a loss for several years, and the multiplication of magazines of a similar character seemed to make its existence no longer necessary.

The *Christian Leader,* published in Utica, New York, was purchased in 1875 and united with the *Universalist,* which became a quarto of eight pages. The redesigned paper became the *Christian Leader,* which carried new departments, including church news from New York as well as New England. This necessitated a change in the by-laws and the election of a trustee from New York State. The business office of the publishing house soon outgrew its cramped quarters on Cornhill Street, and in 1878 was relocated on Bromfield Street, in rented quarters. The press run for the four periodicals being published in 1880 totalled almost one and a half million copies.[27]

One of the goals of the publishing house was to provide Universalist materials at or below cost. In 1875 Thomas B. Thayer lamented the fact that there was no publishing fund that would make this possible.[28] He called attention to the fact that the AUA had published a new and complete edition of William Ellery Channing's writings and had sold the 930-page work (sent postage paid) for $1.00. Such a fund was indeed created by the publishing house in 1875, with a gift from the widow of Sylvanus Cobb as the nucleus.[29] By 1880 it amounted to over $16,000. One of the legacies in 1892 was from P. T. Barnum, and a special fund was established in his name.[30] One of the pamphlets printed by the publishing house which became a best seller was Barnum's *Why I Am a Universalist.*

Within a few months after its appearance in 1890 there were three printings totalling 30,000 copies, and 70,000 three years later.[31]

Many of the important publications of the firm of Williamson & Cantwell (Cincinnati, Ohio) were acquired in 1881. Two years later the *Star and Covenant,* published in Chicago, together with books and plates owned by J. W. Hanson, were acquired. The Midwestern paper was continued as part of the "Western Book Establishment" and was published under the name *Universalist,* beginning in 1884.[32] The format was identical to that of the *Leader.* The denominational press in Chicago bore the name "Universalist Publishing House, Western Branch," and at its height published more than thirty titles, few of which duplicated those of the parent office in the East. The Western branch never paid its own way, and had cost the publishing house $40,000 by 1897, when the publication of the *Universalist* was suspended. The proliferation of local parish papers was blamed for the steady decline in readership and subscriptions. The publications of the book establishment became less and less numerous, and by the time of World War I the Chicago office had become only a distributing agency for Universalist materials published in Boston.

The assets of the Boston headquarters of the publishing house were enlarged in 1884 by acquiring property on Tremont Street, and in the same year the firm received a bequest of $10,000 from Mary T. Goddard, set aside as a special fund. For the first time in its history the publishing house was able to own the property in which it operated. In 1899, after eleven years on Bromfield Street, a new headquarters was obtained at 30 West Street, financed with proceeds from the sale of the Goddard home which had been bequeathed to it. The publishing house took another upward step in 1909, when a new headquarters was constructed specifically for its purposes at 359-61 Boylston Street.[33] The handsome six-story brick and steel building boasted white marble trim.[34] From 1910 to 1921 it served also as the headquarters of the denomination, unofficially at first and officially after 1916. The publishing house made two more moves before it was consolidated with the Beacon Press in 1962. From 1922 to 1933 its headquarters were at 176 Newbury Street. After that property was sold, the operation was moved to 16 Beacon Street, acquired from the AUA, and sold by the consolidated denominations in 1962. Throughout its history the publishing house had stayed in the heart of downtown Boston.

When the publishing house was created, its first efforts were concentrated on strengthening the position and enlarging the circulation of the combined *Trumpet* and *Christian Freeman* rather than immediately increasing its book business. The first book under its imprint had appeared in 1866 and was a hymnal known as the "Portland Collection." Five volumes of Sunday school library books were also issued that year. During its first quarter-century, 84 new books and pamphlets were issued, and 136 new

The Universalist Publishing House building at 359-61 Boylston Street in Boston

editions of existing titles appeared. By 1887 the publishing house issued and owned the titles and copyrights of 150 volumes and 6 periodicals, and in 1910 the Murray Press was established as part of the firm.[35]

The business receipts of the publishing house had increased dramatically in its first twenty-five years, rising from less than $10,000 in 1862 to almost $75,000 in 1887. The assets in the latter year totalled $70,000. It was clear that the undertaking had met with success which "far exceeded the most sanguine expectations of those who inaugurated it" and warranted a round of self-congratulation on the part of the denomination. The greatest lack was an adequate endowment, and a campaign was begun in 1910 to raise $100,000.[36]

Although the publishing house was historically the principal outlet for denominational material, it operated until 1914 quite separately from the General Convention, with its own trustees and board of directors. The suggestion had been made in 1871 that the resources of the publishing house be placed "to some extent under the control of the General Convention," thus making it a truly national endeavor. But discussion of that possibility by the convention was ruled out as "inexpedient."[37] However, the publishing house was considered sufficiently relevant as an "educational institution" to include its activities in the annual reports of the convention trustees.[38]

It was reported in 1895 that there were many not in sympathy with the publishing house and considered it "distant, remote, out of touch."[39] The fact that the General Convention had no direct voice in its management brought the recommendation that the publishing house be bought up by the convention. After a two-year delay a committee was appointed in 1897 to consider the idea. It found that the organization of the publishing house was such as to make it impossible to include a formal representative from the General Convention. Its charter forbade any officer of the convention to serve as a trustee.[40] And even if it had been possible it was considered neither necessary nor desirable. The publishing house was "already entirely devoted to the Universalist Church" and no further steps were required to bring about closer relations.

But the matter was not yet settled, for in 1913 the convention voted to request the trustees of the publishing house "so to broaden their membership as to include the members of the Board of Trustees of the Universalist General Convention."[41] In accordance with this action, consultations took place, and in order to avoid legal changes it was decided that the convention trustees be asked to attend all meetings of the publishing house trustees, with the privileges of the floor; and that the convention trustees appoint one of their members to attend meetings of the directors, with similar privileges. The invitation was accepted, and Frank Oliver Hall was selected, followed by Frederic W. Perkins, editor of the *Leader*.[42]

Because it paid no dividends but was to devote any profits it might accumulate to the reduction of the prices of its publications or to their free distribution, the publishing house was considered "a worthy object of benevolence" and solicited bequests or other gifts.[43] The creation, in effect, of an organization "of public character" immediately elicited protests from other Universalist publishing interests, on the ground that it represented an attempt to establish a monopoly and to squeeze out private entrepreneurs in the denomination.

The publishing house officers, sensitive to these attacks, presented a detailed defense.[44] They protested that the existence of a publicly controlled publishing house intended to benefit the entire denomination did "not stand in the way of private enterprise," and that Universalists elsewhere in the nation were quite free to set up similar concerns. Meanwhile, New England Universalists had followed this route with clear success, and there was, in their view, no justification for attacking the organization. The idea of "one gigantic national book concern for Universalists is, in our judgment, impracticable and unwise. We hope it will never be attempted." Instead, the field should be divided up into convenient sections. Merging all Universalist publishing establishments to create "one overshadowing monopoly" was the last thing to be desired.

Yet that very phenomenon had occurred. One by one, denominational publications continued to fall under its control, and by 1898 the *Leader* carried on its masthead the sub-title "The National Universalist Paper." Only one major denominational newspaper, the *Universalist Herald*, remained outside the direct control of the Boston-based publishing house.

Pressure continued to mount to integrate more closely the General Convention and the publishing house, and to broaden denominational representation on its board of trustees. So in 1920 its board of directors took the initiative and effected a reorganization which enlarged the corporate body from twenty-one to thirty. Instead of being elected for life the trustees were to be chosen for three-year terms and at least one General Convention trustee was to serve on the board of directors.[45] Both the Ohio and Illinois Conventions were given representation.[46] The trustees of the General Convention created in 1920 a Commission on Literature which reviewed material for publication and attempted to avoid or at least to minimize the ever-present problem of duplicated publications by the various denominational organizations.[47]

After Isaac M. Atwood's retirement from the editorship of the *Leader* in 1872 and the incorporation of the publishing house that year, George H. Emerson (1822–1898) had become editor of the denominational newspaper in Boston. A native of Roxbury, Massachusetts, he had grown up in a Baptist home but became a convert to Universalism while clerking in a hardware store in Lowell and attending the Universalist church of which Abel C. Thomas was pastor.[48] It was Thomas who persuaded Emerson to prepare for the ministry. While serving as a preacher in the Midwest he became editor of the *Ohio Universalist and Literary Companion*.

After returning to his native state in 1849 he became the agent of the

Massachusetts Universalist Home Missionary Society. From 1858 to 1864 he edited the *Universalist Quarterly,* to which he was a frequent contributor, and between 1862 and 1864 assisted Cobb in editing the *Trumpet and Christian Freeman.* After the name was changed to the *Universalist* in 1864 he was its editor for three years, when he moved to New York City to edit the *Christian Leader.* From 1872, when he returned to Boston, until his death in 1898, he presided over the *Universalist* as it underwent several changes of name.

Like many another prominent Universalist in the nineteenth century, Emerson was largely self-educated, but a literate and capable writer. He was the biographer of Ebenezer Fisher, first head of the Canton Theological School at St. Lawrence University, and of Alonzo A. Miner, second president of Tufts College, as well as of two books on religious thought.

After Emerson's death Frederick Adelbert Bisbee (1855–1923) became the editor. He was born in Coopersville, New York, on 28 February 1855. After a childhood in Portage, his family moved to Binghamton, where his father continued his occupation as a miller. The young Bisbee's first religious contacts were rather casual. After sampling both the Methodist and Nazarite (Nazarene) churches as a youth, he attended Universalist services, found them congenial to his tastes, and drifted into the denomination in part through the influence of a maternal uncle.[49]

At the age of fourteen Bisbee's physically active regimen was cut short when he was stricken by what was probably inflammatory rheumatism which resulted in a bone disease and left him bedridden for almost two years and a cripple for life. He whiled away the seemingly interminable hours by omnivorous reading and the writing of adventure fiction at which he became not only successful but quite proficient. When he achieved some degree of mobility in his body he was employed as a reporter for a local newspaper and was launched on a successful career in journalism.

He was determined to acquire more formal education than he had obtained but was so lacking in the fundamentals that he had to be admitted to the Tufts divinity school as a special student, through the intercession of William G. Tousey, a faculty member and friend of the family. Bisbee's classmates included such future Universalist notables as Charles H. Eaton; Warren S. Woodbridge, who became a member of the faculty; and H. S. Whitman, who later became president of Westbrook Seminary in Maine.

Bisbee's goal at first was not the ministry but the obtaining of an education by taking advantage of the small grant provided by the General Convention. Grimly determined to make a go of it, the poverty-stricken and crippled youth gradually fell into the choice of the ministry as a career, largely through the influence of fellow students. Like them, he began to preach in vacant pulpits in the neighborhood of the school in

Frederick A. Bisbee (1855-1923), editor of the Leader *for twenty-five years*

order to gain experience and supply much-needed funds. Bisbee found the experience so personally rewarding that he decided on the ministry as a profession.

Both before and after receiving his divinity degree in 1877 and ordination the same year, he held a pastorate in Spencer, Massachusetts, in the meantime having married Hannah Bradley, a member of his first congregation. After six years of involvement in the church and in civic affairs he moved to Philadelphia in 1883 as pastor of the Universalist Church of the Restoration. In 1892 the church structure was extensively remodelled in order to serve as a social service as well as a religious center.

His life was saddened by the death of his wife in 1886 and he was given the additional responsibility of rearing a young daughter. His lameness became worse and necessitated constant hospitalization and bouts with excruciating pain, although he remained outwardly cheerful and optimistic. In 1891 he married Matty Gally, a nurse in a hospital where he was being treated. Two children were born to this marriage before his second wife died in 1921.

While serving the Philadelphia church Bisbee was secretary of the state convention from 1885 to 1898, and in 1897 received an honorary degree from his *alma mater*. He had kept up his interest in writing by publishing a monthly church magazine and then founding, with Merrick Whitcomb, a "popular literary, economic and social review" known as *To-Day*. It lasted less than three years, a financial disaster, and was consolidated with the *Leader* in 1896, but not before Bisbee had attracted much favorable attention as a writer.[50] He became associate editor and, after the death of Emerson, was offered the chief position in 1898 and moved to Boston, where he served the denominational paper for twenty-five years.

During his long tenure as its editor, the content of the *Leader* became less theological and more organization-oriented, stressing domestic and foreign missions and the broadening range of church activities. He fought religious sectarianism, counseled harmony, peace, and cooperation, believing that the mission of the Universalist clergy was to influence character in the direction of brotherhood rather than to become involved directly in such social and economic issues as the struggle between capital and labor. He considered himself in no sense an expert on such problems and refused to use his position as a platform from which to propagate any particular ideology. Reform of society could be accomplished only by reforming the individual first. Men and women shaped their environment, not the reverse. This was the burden of many editorials he published and many speeches and sermons he delivered over the years. To him, the primary duty of the minister was to inspire the businessmen in the congregation to Christianize the social order rather than attempt the task themselves. True brotherhood would "stop every war, it will settle every strike, it will equalize possessions, it will abolish poverty, disease, ignorance and sin."[51]

After the death of his second wife Bisbee spent the two remaining winters of his life in Miami, Florida, with his eldest daughter. By then he was a complete invalid. He died 15 November 1923 after an active career in religious journalism and a lifetime devoted to promoting Universalism.

Between 1864 and 1917 five Universalists served as agents (business managers) of the publishing house, three of whom were also clergy. Russell A. Ballou, for several years editor and publisher of the *Gospel Banner*, was the first to hold the managerial office. Benton Smith, another clergyman, succeeded him in 1868 and served until 1873. Two laymen, Charles Caverly and Eugene F. Endicott, were the next managers. Caverly, who served for twenty years (1873–1893), had been clerk of the publishing house corporation. Endicott was a mayor of Chelsea, Massachusetts, and was also a treasurer of the Universalist Historical Society and of the General Convention. Melville S. Nash, who died in 1916, followed Endicott and had been a high school principal and state legislator as well as minister. Beginning in 1917, Harold Marshall, another clergyman, held the office.

Even though the assets of the publishing house exceeded a quarter of a million dollars in 1913 it was increasingly difficult to break even. In 1918 the organization was forced to borrow more than $32,000 to meet operating expenses.[52] The market for biographies was poor, and in 1913 the revenue from *Leader* subscriptions amounted to little more than the cost of production.[53] It had a circulation of approximately 7,300 in 1915.[54]

The end of World War I brought inflation, labor unrest, and so many uncertainties that no major new publications were attempted. The *Leader* subscription price of $2.00 a year paid only two-thirds of the expense of publishing it in 1920.[55] Trust funds were used to make up deficits. Marshall, the business manager, noted that the publishing house was "a cross between a business enterprise and a charitable institution."⁵⁶ But in spite of the uncertainties of the time he claimed that it was the only religious publishing house which neither lowered the quality of its output nor raised the price of its publications. No less than 276,000 tracts and leaflets were produced for free distribution in 1920–21, three times the volume of the previous year. This was made possible in part by the receipt of $12,000 from the one million dollars denominational fund drive conducted earlier. Marshall predicted optimistically in 1923 that the operation would be completely self-supporting within five years. A campaign by and for the *Leader* to increase its readership had brought many new subscribers by 1924.⁵⁷

The early 1920s also brought a change of editorship of the *Leader* and ushered in an era of exceptionally high quality religious journalism under the guiding hand of John van Schaick (1873–1949), known affectionately to generations of Universalists as "Doctor John." He was born in Cobleskill (Schoharie County), New York, on 18 November 1873, of Dutch ancestry. His father, John van Schaick, Sr., a member of the Dutch Reformed Church, was a lawyer, state senator, and political leader.⁵⁸ After education in the local schools, young van Schaick became a teacher while in his teens in the local district school for two terms and then attended Union College in Schenectady, enrolling in 1891 and graduating three years later. Always interested in history, law, and politics, he campaigned for Grover Cleveland during the summer of 1892 and tried his hand at political journalism.

Following his graduation from college in 1894 van Schaick became principal of the Sharon Springs Academy, where he remained for two years. He arrived at his Universalism independently while in college and met Charles H. Eaton, then pastor of the Church of the Divine Paternity in New York City. It was he who urged van Schaick to enter the ministry, although the final decision was yet to be made.

In 1896 the young van Schaick went west to Kansas to become a teacher of history and English in Emporia College. It was while there that he became the lifelong friend of William Allen White, editor of the *Emporia Gazette* who became nationally known as a journalist and political commentator. Eaton had meanwhile kept up a correspondence with van Schaick, and he was invited to come east to study with the minister. He accepted the invitation, and between 1898 and 1900 acted as Eaton's assistant while pursuing his studies. It was while in the city that he became acquainted at first-hand with the lives of the slum dwellers of New York's East Side through Brevoort House, a mission sponsored by the church.

In 1900 he became pastor of the Church of Our Father in Washington, D.C., to which he had been called in 1899. He was ordained in 1901. His pastorate was an immediate and unqualified success, imbued as he was with a generous spirit and great sensitivity to human problems of all

John van Schaick (1873-1949), editor of the Leader *for almost a quarter of a century*

kinds. Like so many of his ministerial contemporaries, he was a strong advocate of the Social Gospel, with its emphasis on applying what were conceived to be Christian principles to everyday living. He plunged almost immediately into community work and was soon active in the National Tuberculosis Association. He helped to provide summer outings for city children, assisted in Red Cross work and in the activities of the local Associated Charities to which he was elected general secretary but declined, preferring to devote most of his energies to the parish ministry. His distinction as a minister was rewarded by receipt of an honorary DD from St. Lawrence in 1910. While attending Commencement that year he substituted at the last minute for Charles W. Eliot, president of Harvard, who was unable to deliver the scheduled Phi Beta Kappa oration. In 1909 van Schaick married Julia Asenath Romaine, a woman of broad culture and an accomplished linguist.

The Washington pastor took a leave of absence from his church in 1915 in order to serve in Europe for the Rockefeller Foundation War Relief Commission and became its representative in Holland. His administrative ability, already evident, was demonstrated on a large scale while supervising relief for war refugees. His responsibilities also involved work in both Germany and occupied Belgium. His contributions were so notable that, upon return to the United States, he was offered a choice of high positions in the American Red Cross but turned them down in order to return to his ministry. His tenure was brief, for he was called again after American entrance into World War I in 1917 to serve the Red Cross as Commissioner to Belgium.[59] Mrs. van Schaick's linguistic skills made her an invaluable member of the delegation as an interpreter and translator. Among van Schaick's rewards received in Europe for his relief service were membership in the Order of Leopold bestowed by the King of Belgium, a medal of honor from the University of Brussels, and an honorary MD from the University of Liege. An honorary DD from his *alma mater* (Union College) and a patriotic service medal from the National Institute of Science testified to his recognition in the United States.

His next assignment after return to America and resignation from his pastorate was the presidency of the Board of Education of the District of Columbia. It was a demanding assignment, for he became embroiled in a controversy over the replacement of the superintendent of schools which resulted in much recrimination and many accusations. The Board of Education and van Schaick were not only eventually vindicated but were able to effect important reforms in the school system. The Universalist clergyman was a fighter as well as a minister who preached and practiced on behalf of the downtrodden.

While the fight over the superintendency was still in progress van Schaick was appointed Commissioner of the District of Columbia by President Woodrow Wilson but was not confirmed by the Senate. Much of the failure had to be laid at the door of those senators who opposed his attempt to reform and rebuild the District's school system.

The next stage in van Schaick's career brought him into much closer contact with the denomination than had his public service responsibilities. In 1922 he became the acting editor and then editor of the *Leader*, a position which he held for twenty-three years, until his retirement in 1945. He had attracted the favorable attention of the directors of the Universalist Publishing House by both the articles which he frequently contributed and by the publication of his report on the relief work done in Belgium. He came to the paper first as an associate of Bisbee, who was nearing the end of his career as editor, and by 1922 was doing most of the editor's work.

The new editor had a well-developed appreciation of the power of the printed word, and he used it liberally to fight everything from narrow religious orthodoxy to the absolute prohibition on the manufacture and use of alcoholic beverages. His broad experience on many fronts, his willingness to speak his own mind while listening carefully and respecting the opinions of others and, above all, his flair for communicating on a high literary plane, made him one of the most influential editors in the long history of the *Leader*. His quick wit and sense of humor were often misinterpreted as a lack of seriousness — an assessment very wide of the mark. His warmth and sincerity as a human being shone through his long and sometimes controversial career as a religious journalist. Lest this should read too much like an uncritical eulogy it should be pointed out that van Schaick was often high-handed in his dealings, exhibited more than a tinge of racism, and was often theologically conservative to the point of losing step with the more progressive elements in the denomination.

Much of van Schaick's literary talent was expended in a series of highly personalized essays appearing both in the *Leader* and in book form as five volumes of *Cruisings,* with variant subtitles, which made him popular with a wide circle of readers. One of his most important contributions to American literary history was *Characters in Tales of a Wayside Inn,* a thoroughly researched and delightfully written study of the characters in Henry Wadsworth Longfellow's famous work.[60]

The editor's faith in the existence of a wise and benevolent personal God remained unshaken throughout his life. His love of nature as a manifestation of the divine comes through unmistakably in his writings. His attacks on non-theistic humanism brought sharp rejoinders from Albert Dieffenbach, editor of the *Christian Register* (Unitarian).[61] The attack was sufficiently serious to bring forth an official apology from the trustees of the *Register.* It also heightened van Schaick's already strong loyalty both to Christianity and to the Universalist denomination. He had changed the name of the *Universalist Leader* to the *Christian Leader* in 1926, and in 1931 added the subtitle "A Journal of the Universalist Fellowship."

During his editorship he was acknowledged to be one of the best in the field of religious journalism, and consistently maintained high standards for the denominational paper. With other Protestant newspapermen like Guy Emery Shipler, editor of the *Churchman* and known as the dean of religious journalists, van Schaick helped establish the Associated Church Press, known originally as the Editorial Council of the Religious Press. He used his pen, on a more localized level, to support Universalist and Congregational cooperation and the movement to bring Universalists and Unitarians together.

In 1945, beset with failing eyesight and tired from his labors of many years, van Schaick resigned from the editorship of the *Leader* and retired to his beloved Little Hill farm near Cobleskill. He died on 16 May 1949 in Washington, D.C. There was a certain appropriateness in the location in view of his many years of service to Universalism in that city, and to the city itself. With equal appropriateness the memorial services were held in the Universalist National Memorial Church in the nation's capital.

One of van Schaick's unattained goals during his long association with the *Leader* had been to increase both the subscription list and the circulation. One device was to send the publication to some 400 college and university libraries.[62] By 1926 only one-half of the subscriptions were in active parishes, and the deficit that year was $20,000.[63] The editor derived no comfort from the fact that publications of other denominations, including the Methodist, were experiencing the same difficulties. The subscription list declined from about 7,000 in 1929 to one-half of that figure a decade later.[64] Economic depression brought a serious cash flow problem. As economy measures the *Leader* was published every two weeks instead of weekly during the summer months, beginning in 1932, and the staff that year received half-pay.[65]

There was much talk in the 1930s of combining the *Leader* and the

Register, which was having its own serious financial difficulties. There was even consideration given to combining both, together with *Unity,* with *Advance,* the Congregational publication.[66] In 1933 the *Leader* took over temporarily the printing of the *Register,* but van Schaick opposed any permanent combination, and the Unitarian Commission on Appraisal agreed.

The fortunes of the publishing house, so intimately related to those of the *Leader,* languished through the "most trying years" of the Great Depression in the 1930s. Capital had to be used to make up deficits, which by 1932 amounted to more than $110,000. A most serious blow to the publishing house was dealt in the summer of that year by the death of Harold Marshall, business manager since 1917. Broken in health and in serious financial straits because of unwise speculation with funds, some of which had been intended for denominational purposes, he committed suicide.[67] Of the denominational funds involved, $2,050 were from the publishing house. The editor of the *Leader* assumed Marshall's job in addition to his editorial duties and served in that dual capacity until 1937, when Emerson H. Lalone became the new business manager. The financial management of the publishing house was consolidated with that of the General Convention in 1936, with A. Ingham Bicknell as the treasurer for both.[68] The long-standing linkage between the two organizations was continued, with an annual appropriation from the General Convention to publishing house expenses.

Shrinkage in both the number and volume of publications was obvious by the late 1930s. Three new books appeared in 1939 under the publishing house imprint in 1939, and only one in 1941. For several years in the 1940s and 1950s no new titles at all were published. The *Helper* was discontinued as a quarterly publication in 1941 and the *Universalist Register* was no longer printed by the publishing house after 1941. The *Leader,* which had been a weekly for most of its history, was issued only twice a month, beginning in November 1941, and became a monthly in 1948.[69] The composing room was closed in 1941, and both the *Leader* and the *Register* were printed by a commercial press. Paid circulation of the *Leader* had dropped to 3,200 by 1944.[70]

A serious financial crisis was averted in 1944 with an advance of $1,000 by Victor Friend, and by that year there was an accumulated deficit of more than $70,000.[71] Charles A. Wyman relinquished a pastorate paying $4,000 a year to become business manager at a substantially reduced salary in 1944, replacing Lalone who was serving as associate editor of the *Leader.*[72] Wyman lent the publishing house $1,000 to buy a second-hand car for business use. He returned to the parish ministry in 1951 and Lalone took over his duties.[73] The publishing house by the 1950s had become a marginal and makeshift operation.

Another era in the history of the *Leader* began in 1945 when van Schaick

Emerson Hugh Lalone (1899-1960), editor of the Leader *and Universalist author*

retired from the editorship after serving since 1922. Lalone, for seven years the business manager of the publishing house and an associate editor, assumed the task of piloting the paper through another critical period. Meanwhile, the publishing house underwent a modest renaissance after World War II. Use of the trade name "Murray Press" which had been suspended for many years, was resumed in 1946, and four new book titles were published in 1945 and 1946, including Clarence R. Skinner's *Religion for Greatness* (reprinted in 1958). Although only 15 percent of denominational book business came from the area west of Ohio, a second outlet was planned besides the one in Chicago.[74]

After considerable discussion over a period of years the name *Christian Leader* was changed back to *Universalist Leader* in 1953, a designation which had been abandoned in 1926. The change was made without a word of editorial comment from Lalone, but several reactions were received from observant readers. One thought that "the sudden emphasis on denominationalism" was ill-timed in view of negotiations then in progress for some kind of federation with the Unitarians.[75] The ostensible reason for the change was the "need for a journal which stands by name as our representative before the world."[76]

By the early 1950s the *Leader* had become but a pale and anemic reflection of what had been an example of the robust journalism of the van Schaick period. The size of issues had shrunk from thirty-two to less than twenty pages. Instead of a "journal of generalized, liberal religious opinion" it had been narrowed down to a newssheet confined almost exclusively to denominational affairs.[77] It was costing almost $20,000 a year to produce; only $6,300 was received from subscriptions in 1953.[78]

While there seemed to be expansion of the activities of the publishing house in some areas there were signs of continued retrenchment in others in the post-World War II period. The publishing house ceased in 1951, for the first time in its history, to serve as an agency for denominational books and supplies. That function was taken over by the Department of Business Administration.[79] The financial picture continued to be a depressing one. From 1951 until it merged with the Beacon Press (Unitarian) a decade later, the indebtedness was reduced from year to year only by selling off securities from trust funds. A note of hesitation as to the fate of the *Leader* was injected in 1955, after the creation of the Council of Liberal Churches, a joint Universalist-Unitarian experiment. There was again talk of merger with the *Register*, but not even a quorum of directors could be secured to make a decision.[80] Only ten responded to a mail ballot, and although seven voted in favor, three of them registered "negative protests." Nothing was done. The subscription list continued to stand at less than 3,500.[81]

The death of Lalone in 1960 brought another series of changes, complicated by denominational consolidation. Raymond J. Baughan, a minister and Crane Theological School alumnus, became the editor. The masthead, which had described the *Leader* as "A Journal of Liberal Christianity," was changed to "The Free Church of the Universalist Church of America." Baughan returned to the active ministry after little more than a year, and Albert F. Ziegler, another Universalist minister and Crane alumnus, and president of the publishing house since 1958, became co-editor with Victor Bovee, a Unitarian, but almost immediately dropped out.

Consolidation of the Universalist and Unitarian denominations brought a confusing set of changes of name to the *Leader* during the transition period between 1961 and 1963. The directors voted that it would be published jointly as a monthly with the *Register*, with a hyphenated name, as recommended by the Joint Unitarian-Universalist Committee on Publications.[82] The first combined issue, published in May 1961, was called the *Unitarian Register-Universalist Leader*, described as "probably the longest and clumsiest title in use in today's magazine publishing world."[83]

Production costs were first allocated proportionately, with 74 percent borne by the *Register* and 26 percent by the Universalist Publishing House. The nomenclature was improved slightly when the publication beame, in October 1962, the *Unitarian-Universalist Register-Leader,* a title which lasted until 1968. After the interim name *UUA Now* (1968–69) was used, the designation finally decided upon was *Unitarian Universalist World (UU World)*, the title of which had been derived from a column in the first issue of the combined papers in 1961.

Before Universalist-Unitarian consolidation took place in 1961 there were prolonged discussions over what would happen to the publishing house. There were several choices: It could vote itself out of existence, consolidate with the UCA, become part of the joint publication department, or join forces with the Beacon Press. Books under the AUA imprint had been published initially in 1854. The Beacon imprint and colophon were first used after Livingston Stebbins became publishing agent in 1902.[84]

Robert Cummins, former UCA General Superintendent, wanted all of the trustees appointed by the UCA board so that the publishing house would be an integral part of the UCA rather than a semi-independent affiliated body when consolidation did take place.[85] Associate membership in the combined denomination was rejected. The publishing house was to be kept in Universalist hands as long as possible. The directors voted to follow Cummins' plan.[86] Consolidation with the UCA took place, and in turn that body joined the Unitarians to form the Unitarian Universalist Association.

Nothing was published after 1960 but the *Leader* and paperback reprints of five books. After 1946 the publishing house had produced fewer and fewer titles and had confined most of its efforts to preparing pamphlets and brochures.[87] When an inventory of Universalist publications in stock in Boston was prepared in 1961, 5,608 copies of thirteen titles were turned over to the UUA.[88] Total assets by then amounted to less than $60,000.[89] The year before consolidation with Beacon Press took place officially (March 1962) as a part of the UUA Department of Publications, the publishing house had been so strapped for funds that a new office typewriter had had to be purchased on the installment plan.[90]

The Universalist Publishing House, which had lived a life of exactly 100 years, had come to an ignominious end after a career of invaluable and sometimes distinguished service to the denomination. Of the ten regional and state newspapers sponsored within the denomination in 1944, only a tiny handful survived into the 1980s.[91] Another era had come to a close as the Universalist denomination had become a minority within a minority.

Chapter 15

Secular Education in Other Hands

A year after the denominational centennial had been celebrated in 1870 there were three institutions of higher education in operation that had been founded and supported by Universalists: Tufts College, straddling the Greater Boston communities of Medford and Somerville, Massachusetts, chartered in 1852 and opened in 1854; Lombard University (College) in Galesburg, Illinois, chartered in 1852 as an academy but transformed into a college with a new charter in 1857; and St. Lawrence University in Canton, New York, chartered in 1856 and opened first as a theological school. In addition, two other colleges with denominational sponsorship were projected or in process of construction: Smithson College in Logansport, Indiana, incorporated in 1867 but not yet opened; and Buchtel College, located in Akron, Ohio, chartered in 1870 as a part of the centenary celebration, and opened in 1872.

Universalists in 1871 possessed two theological schools, with a third in prospect — one at St. Lawrence, opened in 1856; and the other at Tufts, commencing operation in 1869. The one opened in 1881 at Lombard was relocated to Chicago in 1912. A start had also been made with secular professional education by 1871. A civil engineering department had been established at Tufts the same year the divinity school was opened, and a law department had been created as part of St. Lawrence by the state legislature in 1868.

Seven academies with Universalist origins or connections also existed in 1871, and an eighth had been projected. Clinton Liberal Institute, founded in 1831 and located in Clinton, New York, was the oldest in terms of date of opening, followed by Westbrook Seminary, near Portland, Maine, which had been chartered in 1830 but not opened until 1834. Green Mountain Liberal Institute, chartered and opened in South

Woodstock, Vermont, in 1848, was renamed Green Mountain Perkins Academy in 1870. Green Mountain Central Institute, later redesignated as Goddard Seminary, incorporated in 1863, was opened in Barre, Vermont, in 1870. The least prosperous of the three academies in Vermont in 1871 was Orleans Liberal Institute, located in Glover and opened in 1852; it closed twenty years later. Jefferson Liberal Institute, in Jefferson, Wisconsin, was incorporated and opened in 1866, although it was destined to last only about a decade. More successful was Dean Academy in Franklin, Massachusetts, chartered in 1865 as a feeder for Tufts College and the best endowed of all Universalist secondary schools. An academy, Mitchell Seminary, projected in 1870 but not yet opened, was the last to be established by Universalists; it was not incorporated in Mitchellville, Iowa, until 1872, and lasted less than ten years.

Universalists, as they entered their second century, could claim sixteen educational institutions either in operation or on the drawing board, employing eighty teachers, and with assets approaching two million dollars. Small as they were in numbers and limited as they were in resources, they had made significant contributions to American education in a period of great expansion.

Little more than half a century later the situation had changed radically. A denominational Commission on Educational Institutions created to offer advice and wisdom had gone out of business. When the *Leader* published an Education issue in 1922 not a single school or college remained under direct Universalist control although some still had Universalist associations. Six educational institutions with a Universalist heritage remained, and one of them (Lombard) existed only as a corporate organization on paper, the charter alone remaining to remind later generations of its earlier existence. Buchtel College had become part of the Municipal University of Akron. Ten schools and colleges had disappeared completely. Three of the old academies which continued to exist (Westbrook, Goddard, and Dean) had become, or were about to become, independent colleges or junior colleges.

Only Tufts and St. Lawrence retained their original names and character as liberal arts institutions, although each had a denominational theological school attached to it, with different circumstances of origin. Even the Crane Theological School at Tufts was part of an "entirely undenominational" corporate organization, the officers of which were known officially as the "Trustees of Tufts College." Year by year Universalist presence at Tufts diminished. Although there were still fourteen Universalists among the thirty trustees in 1932, the number declined steadily thereafter.[1] The Tufts charter had been amended in 1907 to enlarge the board from twenty to thirty in order to provide formal alumni representation for fixed terms. The remaining twenty continued to be self-perpetuating. The last active Universalist clergyman to serve as a trustee had been John Coleman Adams, who served for more than forty years until his death in 1922. He was not replaced. He had attempted without success to resign in 1914, feeling alone, "out of place and embarrassed."[2] The last Universalist on the board to have been at one time a clergyman was Thomas O. Marvin (1867–1952), an alumnus of the theological school (1888). But he served only briefly in the ministry and had long since given it up when he became a member and then chairman of the United States Tariff Commission. Tufts awarded its last honorary DD to a clergyman in 1968, by coincidence the year that its theological school was closed.[3]

The Universalists, as a denomination, chartered no new schools or colleges after 1871, although individual Universalists were responsible for the creation of three institutions after that date. None originated as full-fledged liberal arts colleges. Two evolved into institutions of higher education long after their Universalist origins had been forgotten; and the third, intended as a college, became an industrial school and later a military academy.

One educational institution founded by the Universalists prior to 1871, Lombard College in Galesburg, Illinois, was closed in 1930. Its history might be instructive to the student of American higher education, and particularly to those interested in church-related colleges founded in the nineteenth century, regardless of their denominational connections. In its seventy-nine-year history this particular college met a need that became less and less urgent as other collegiate institutions evolved in the Midwest which were larger and more generously supported, most notably the land-grant public universities. And public secondary education encroached increasingly and unrelentingly on the potential clientele of the private academy.

Lombard College

Founded in 1851 as a secondary school (Illinois Liberal Institute) and authorized two years later to give collegiate-level instruction, Lombard University (College) had begun to reach a critical stage in its history by 1912, with declining enrollments and a completely inadequate endowment. Contributions were too small in number and size to make up a chronic deficit. In 1907 a faculty committee had suggested a way out of the institution's difficulties by union with Knox College, in the same community. There was too much opposition among Universalists to such a drastic step when it was suggested again in 1912.

Among those who opposed any such move, which would result in a loss of denominational identity, was Almon Gunnison, president of St. Lawrence University. He considered such a step "out of the question." It would have been an admission of defeat on the part of Universalists.[4]

There was, he argued, still room for a small college such as Lombard, and he campaigned for its continuance. "Save Lombard" became the slogan.

The struggling college had to abandon its preparatory (secondary school) department in 1912 because of lack of patronage. In the same year it lost the leadership of Lewis B. Fisher, who resigned from the presidency to become dean of the Ryder Divinity School which had been transferred from Lombard to Chicago that year. Enrollment at Lombard dropped to less than 100. In desperation the trustees put H. W. Hurt, a member of the faculty, into the presidency, hoping that his previous employment by the Prussian government would bring an efficient administration to bear on Lombard's problems. A vocationally and scientifically oriented program was immediately introduced which included a department of "household economics," courses in industrial chemistry, and a two-year sequence in mathematics and engineering, as well as curricula in journalism and business administration, agriculture, and forestry. This attempt to infuse new life into the institution had necessitated a reorganization "from cellar to garret."[5]

A widely advertised open house celebration was held in 1914, with representatives from six Midwestern states present to view "the New Lombard."[6] Enrollment had tripled (to 190) since the dark days of 1912. Franklin J. Drake, a physician and president of the Iowa Convention, was hired as the field agent to raise funds and assist in reorganizing the institution. But the gloomy financial picture refused to brighten. Hurt resigned the presidency after three years of strenuous effort, and was replaced temporarily by Dean Ralph M. Barton. The services of Drake had to be dispensed with because of the expense. Even the organization of the Lombard Loyal League to raise funds did but little good.[7]

One of the most significant events in the history of Lombard occurred in 1916, when Joseph Mayo Tilden (1873–1928) was elected president.[8] When he became president the college was operating on a budget of $30,000; only $5,000 of the annual income came from interest on the endowment and $10,000 came from tuition and fees.[9] In 1913 Lee S. McCollester, president of the General Convention, had served as a one-person Educational Commission, and before Tilden had assumed office, visited Lombard and reported that it was at a "crisis point."[10] It was not only deficit-ridden but suffered from intense competition from neighboring Knox College and from an apathetic denomination hesitant to support it.

Tilden's greatest challenge was to raise an adequate endowment for the institution, and his efforts up to the time of his sudden death were nothing short of heroic. His magnetic personal qualities made him a phenomenal success as a fund-raiser, although in perspective the money he secured was not sufficient to save from eventual collapse a school which in some ways was being overtaken by the currents of modern education.

Joseph Mayo Tilden (1873-1928), indefatigable President of Lombard College

Tilden was born on 12 March 1873 in Worcester, Massachusetts, the son of Charles Houghton and Ann Maria (Mayo) Tilden. He graduated from Worcester Polytechnic Institute with a BS in 1895, and in 1897 married Gertrude Estelle Bennett of Worcester who had graduated the same year from the Massachusetts State Normal School. Tilden earned a Master's degree from New York University in 1906 and a Doctor of Laws ten years later from Northern Illinois University. He received an honorary Doctor of Humane Letters from St. Lawrence in 1918.

Between 1895 and 1898 he was an instructor in the agricultural department of Harvard College and from then until 1920 was instructor and assistant to the principal of Erasmus Hall High School in Brooklyn, New York. During this period he served also as lecturer on architecture for the New York City Public Lecture System and from 1910 to 1915 as advertising and sales manager for the American Sanitary Works in New York. His many professional and academic memberships and activities brought him election to the presidency of Lombard, and while in that position he served as a trustee of the General Convention for three consecutive four-year terms, beginning in 1919. He was also secretary of the Illinois Convention for two terms, and as a prominent Universalist was much in demand as a speaker. He died in 1928 in Concord, New Hampshire, after having been stricken while attending the General Convention which had met in Hartford, Connecticut.

Tilden had immediately plunged into his work at Lombard. He set three goals for himself, and by 1919 had achieved every one: to raise in cash or pledges $100,000 for endowment; elevate the educational standing of the school; and double the size of the student body.[11] He tried almost every expedient to raise money. He urged patriotic Universalists during World War I to buy Liberty Bonds and make them over to the college.[12] He encouraged students of all religious persuasions to enroll; and by 1917 less than 40 percent of the student body were Universalists. Only a third were Universalists by 1922.[13] By that year the college was a member of, or accredited by, four important professional organizations: The University of Illinois (1918), the North Central Association of Colleges, the American Council on Education, and the Illinois State Department of Instruction. His aim was "a well-organized, efficient, small college," solvent of course, with a maximum of 300 students.[14]

President Tilden was an undisguised champion of church-supported colleges on a denominational basis. He told the General Convention in 1919 that he had little use for "that class of religious thinkers (otherwise rational) who advocate a union of all Churches, a federation of religious beliefs, a veritable trust of denominations."[15] He was convinced that the growth of Universalism in the Middle West depended "more upon Lombard College than any one thing."[16]

The school received an important stimulus psychologically as well as materially when it was allocated $12,000 from the proceeds of the denominational Million Dollar Drive in 1922.[17] It represented a vote of confidence in the college's future, as did a grant of $5,000 from the trustees of the General Convention in 1923.[18] The latter sum was undoubtedly obtained as the result of a special plea by Judge Roger S. Galer, a prominent lawyer in Mt. Pleasant, Iowa, and president of both the General Convention and the college's board of trustees. He told the General Convention that "to lose Lombard would be to strike the keystone from the arch of western Universalism."[19]

The possible loss of Lombard weighed heavily on Galer. In 1926 he wrote Roger Etz, the General Superintendent, that "Lombard College is in a most critical condition."[20] Its trustee executive committee seriously considered closing the institution either at the end of the first semester or at the end of the current school year. The college was "greatly behind" in its finances, owed a large amount at the bank, and was running behind by about $25,000. There seemed to be no way to cut down expenses and prevent the deficit.

The school had "everything except money" — a capacity student body of 350, a fine faculty, and good academic standing. It was "heartbreaking" to think of closing the school under those circumstances. But the actual endowment in hand was less than $100,000, and in spite of the stupendous efforts of President Tilden the problem remained apparently insoluble.

The institution, already in serious distress, saw its problems multiply. During the academic year 1927–28 Lombard lost its membership (accreditation) in the North Central Association of Schools and Colleges because of insufficient endowment. Then another misfortune befell the college:

Tilden, its president since 1916, died in February 1928, necessitating the acting presidency of Dean Charles M. Poor. Tilden had increased the number of students from 100 to almost 300, had raised the standards of the school, and had, with undiminished enthusiasm and hard work, rallied both students and alumni to support the institution. At the time of his death he had secured almost $200,000 in pledges toward a goal of $500,000, but it was not cash in hand. Something had to be done immediately to save the school, and Galer took on the responsibility.

The judge proposed that the Unitarian denomination "should interest itself in the support and future management" of the school.[21] Galer invited Curtis W. Reese, secretary of the Western Unitarian Conference and executive chairman of the National Federation of Religious Liberals of which Galer was president, to sit in with the board at a meeting in Chicago in January 1928.[22] Immediately after the meeting Reese travelled to Boston and outlined the situation to the directors of the AUA. Consideration of Galer's proposal to involve the Unitarians lasted two months, during which time Reese and George G. Davis, executive secretary of the AUA since 1926, made "a careful study of the entire situation."

The directors of the AUA promptly committed the annual income from $250,000 (amounting to $15,000) to help pay the operating expenses of the school. In March the Lombard trustees were reorganized to enable them to take advantage of the Unitarian offer. The twenty-five person board was divided between representatives of the two denominations, with the chairmanship of the reconstructed board to be a Universalist (Galer). The president who succeeded Tilden was to be a Unitarian. In accordance with the agreement the majority of the board (thirteen) were Unitarians, including Louis C. Cornish, president of the AUA. The president of the Universalist General Convention, Frank D. Adams of Detroit, Michigan, was also on the reconstructed board. Reese became the president of Lombard and David was made secretary and treasurer in charge of financial affairs. There was to be no significant change in the conduct of the school and the full-time faculty of twenty-five were to continue at their appointed tasks.

One source of additional strength was the publicity furnished by the *Christian Register* which started its own campaign for "the new Lombard" with an illustrated feature article which included a brief history of the institution.[23] The presentation brought a letter of commendation from Galer for the "admirable" coverage.[24]

The news of the arrangement was greeted with jubilation, for it appeared that the college had been saved and its future assured. A reinvigorated institution would be born — not only "a new day" for Lombard but also for the cause of liberal education as well as liberal religion in the Midwest. Albert C. Dieffenbach, editor of the *Register*, greeted the new regime with enthusiasm and high hopes, noting that

"Unitarians are thus with a single stroke, in time of necessity, more closely bound with their Universalist friends in religious and educational unity than they have been through all the efforts at external union of these recent years."[25] The first joint meeting of the Illinois Universalist Convention and the Illinois State Conference (Unitarian) was held in the Universalist church in Galesburg in 1928 and endorsed the new plan.[26]

At the time the Unitarians became directly involved in Lombard's affairs there were 300 students (exactly the number which had been preferred by Tilden), of whom 263 were degree candidates.[27] The majority of students were from a seventy-five-mile radius and less than 10 percent were Universalists or Unitarians.[28] Registration for the fall term in 1928 totalled 275.[29]

After Reese took charge, improvements were authorized for several buildings and the treasurer was able to report that by May 1928 all "floating indebtedness" had been wiped out.[30] In addition, efforts were successfully made to restore Lombard's membership in the Illinois Intercollegiate Athletic Association. Several years earlier the institution had been dropped from the so-called "Little 19" Conference of the Middle West for alleged irregularities in the conduct of its athletic program. Two unsuccessful efforts at reinstatement had previously been made, but Davis assured the organization that the first step had been taken to adopt a rule whereby freshmen were barred from intercollegiate competition during the first year of residence.[31] Voluntary weekly assemblies were substituted for biweekly compulsory chapel, and other changes were introduced.

Soon after assuming the presidency Reese was absent for several months in the course of a trip to Calcutta, India, as a representative of the Unitarians, and Davis served as acting president. Reese resigned in June 1929 after little more than a year in office and became chairman of the executive committee of the trustees. He had taken the presidency in the first place with the proviso that his services would be temporary.[32] In his letter of resignation he indicated that "the fine condition of the college" and his obligations to the Western Unitarian Conference made his action "both desirable and suitable." Davis, an active Unitarian layman, successful lawyer and businessman, was optimistic about the future of the college.

Harold Marshall, manager of the Universalist Publishing House, also gave an optimistic report of the institution. He attended the Commencement of 1929 and watched the second largest class in the institution's history receive their degrees and diplomas.[33] The entering class was reported to be of excellent quality, including the valedictorians of a large number of high schools, Galesburg among them. The net deficit had been reduced from $28,000 in 1928 to $5,000 and the trustees had approved plans for a financial campaign in 1930 to liquidate the entire deficit and provide a more adequate endowment.

The *Register* announced with great satisfaction, as Lombard opened its seventy-fourth year in the fall of 1929 with a slight gain in registration, that it was "in better condition, and with better prospects and higher hopes than ever before."[34] There was a certain sad irony in the fact that the Universalist Year Book for 1930 covering the activities of the previous year, carried resolutions of the General Convention in 1929 approving the joint administration "on equal terms for the common liberal cause" and listing Lombard as "one of the strongest of the smaller colleges of the Middle West."[35]

But this presumably happy situation was not to continue. The stock market crash of 1929, the grim economic depression that ensued, and the inability to raise working capital aggravated the loss of endowment income and exacerbated the problem of deficit financing. The failure of the anticipated union of Universalism and Unitarianism in the late 1920s also played a major part in the decision to close the school. The last class graduated in 1930. Lombard lost its remaining Universalist identity as Knox College and the town of Galesburg absorbed the remnants of the institution and its physical plant.

However, both the name and corporate existence of the institution were preserved. The Ryder Divinity School, located originally at Lombard in Galesburg and moved to Chicago in 1912, had been transferred to the Unitarian theological school there in 1928. The combined institution became the Meadville/Lombard Theological School. The college charter was never revoked and memories of Lombard were kept alive by its surviving graduates.

The first of the three educational institutions established by individual Universalists after 1871 was Bradley University in Peoria, Illinois, chartered originally as Bradley Polytechnic Institute, and opened in 1897 to teach watchmaking and mechanical trades.[36] The benefactress who made the institution possible was Lydia Moss Bradley (1816–1908), a Universalist and widow of Tobias Bradley, a wealthy businessman who had died in 1867. She had offered both land and money to Lombard College in 1884 if it would move from Galesburg to Peoria and change its name to Bradley University. The offer was discussed by Lombard officials but no action was taken on the offer because the school was already too well established in Galesburg to be uprooted. Bradley Polytechnic Institute was reorganized as Bradley University in 1946 and continued to exist as an accredited, coeducational, and privately controlled institution without Universalist ties.

The two other educational institutions established by Universalists had much more complex and longer Universalist associations than did Bradley, and neither became what the founders had originally intended.

Throop Polytechnic Institute

One educational institution which began at least theoretically "under the patronage and control of Universalists" but which soon lost both its denominational character and its original purpose was Throop Polytechnic Institute in Pasadena, California. It was the brief and imperfect fruition of a dream expressed by the California State Convention which in 1860 encouraged the establishment of a combined college and theological school to serve the denomination on the Pacific coast.[37] The convention went so far as to solicit bids for a site. This was all brought to the attention of the General Convention, which in 1861 reported that prospects were encouraging for establishing a denominational school in California under the leadership of "a recent student of Lombard University."[38]

Nothing came of the plan, but the dream did become at least a partial reality at the end of the nineteenth century. The person responsible was Amos G. Throop (1811-1894), a wealthy businessman and active Universalist layman who moved to the West Coast from Chicago in 1880.

Throop was born in Madison County, New York, in 1811, and spent his boyhood on a farm.[39] He moved to Michigan in 1832, where he engaged in the lumbering business which became the basis for a substantial fortune. In 1843 he located in Chicago, where he prospered as a businessman specializing in real estate and became active in local civic affairs. He served on the City Council from 1849 to 1853, and between 1876 and 1880, was sufficiently well known as an alderman to have had a street named after him. He was also a charter member and officer of the Chicago Board of Trade.

While residing in Chicago he was a member of the Church of the Redeemer (Universalist) and was one of the three lay delegates to the General Convention from Illinois in 1862.[40]

Throop enlarged his holdings by investments in California where he lived first in Los Angeles and then in Pasadena, beginning in 1887. He was a major contributor to Universalist organizations, and in 1890 made a gift of $20,000 to endow the Throop Professorship of Systematic Theology at the divinity school of Lombard; the money came from proceeds from real estate sales in Chicago. Throop was a long-time friend of William H. Ryder, another benefactor of the school.[41]

Throop's plans for financial assistance to Universalism on the West Coast seemed to have gone through several changes during his lifetime. According to his correspondence, he originally intended to use his money to start church work in San Francisco, but his plans miscarried and he decided to donate $50,000 to Universalism in general, presumably through the state convention: $30,000 to endow a Universalist theological professorship; and $20,000 for missionary and church extension work to be undertaken by Q. H. Shinn.[42] By 1891, after Shinn elected not to move to the West Coast, Throop changed his priorities. He was still committed to assisting the Universalist cause, but decided to devote part of his resources to establishing an educational institution, the plan for which he presented to the city of Pasadena.[43]

He provided $200,000 and a site for what was known originally as Throop University. The original board of fifteen trustees, of whom two were women, consisted largely if not exclusively of Universalists. The coeducational school opened in the fall of 1891, advertised ambitiously as a combined preparatory school, liberal arts college, law school, art school, and technical school providing teacher, business, and manual training.[44] James H. Tuttle, pastor of the largest Universalist church in Minneapolis, who spent many of his winters in Pasadena, was to head the new school.[45]

The institution in 1892 enrolled sixty-five students, with plans to spread over eight divisions including such diverse departments as the collegiate and one for the industrial training of women, which included sewing and cooking classes.[46] The president was Charles H. Keyes from Wisconsin rather than Tuttle, who was reluctant to relinquish his pastorate in Minneapolis. Sixteen other individuals comprised the faculty. The manual training department, which became the most numerously populated segment of the "university," was opened in September 1892 with 171 students in a leased forty-room facility known as the "Wooster Block." A building known as "Polytechnic Hall" was erected the same year and in 1893 another building was added.[47] In the same year the school became "Throop Polytechnic Institute," with an enrollment of 175.[48] The curriculum included such disparate practical subjects as stenography, typewriting, cooking, botany, biology, and carpentry.[49]

The institution continued to exist and to bear his name long after Throop's death in 1894. It became primarily a technical and trade school, and in 1914 was renamed "Throop College of Technology." In 1920 the name of the founder was dropped and the school became the California Institute of Technology (known popularly as "Cal Tech"). The individual who saw the possibilities of transforming Throop College into a major center of scientific and engineering research was George Ellery Hale, an astronomer who established the Mt. Wilson Observatory near Pasadena. Together with Arthur Amos Noyes, a chemist, and Robert Andrews Millikan, a physicist, Hale arranged for the change of name and a revised curriculum. Although not officially created as a denominationally controlled school, what had evolved as a vocational school and later as a distinguished university, represented another contribution of Universalists to American educational diversity.

Even though the idea of theological training as a part of the original Throop University was never carried out, the donor continued to express an interest in the education of prospective Universalist clergy on the West Coast. Among his bequests in 1894 was $20,000 to the California Convention to provide for such training, contingent on the raising of a matching $20,000 within two years. Stanford University invited the state convention to establish a professorship of theology in connection with that institution if and when the funds were secured.[50] The California Convention had no such resources, so called upon the General Convention for assistance. After protracted discussion, the trustees ruefully decided that it was "entirely inadvisable" to make an appeal on behalf of such a cause.[51] Too many other projects were under way, and there were insufficient funds even for these. The trustees did consider borrowing from the theological scholarship fund, but time was too short in view of the fact that the assets were in investments rather than in cash. Further, the authority of the trustees to take such a step was considered questionable. So the opportunity went glimmering.

A Universalist church was, however, organized in Pasadena in 1886 as a visible reminder of Throop's generosity by way of a gift of $16,000 in 1890.[52] An impressive Gothic edifice, dedicated in 1923 as the Throop Memorial Church, was yet another reminder.[53] The Universalists never established the theological training facility envisaged by Throop, but ten years after his death the Pacific Unitarian School of the Ministry was established. This school, which later became the Thomas Starr King School for Religious Leadership, provided the preparation for clergy in the liberal church which the Universalists had been unable to undertake.

The Southern Industrial Institute

For many years Universalists particularly interested in the South were distressed by the lack of opportunity for young men in rural areas and with limited resources to train for the denominational ministry. They had no means of attending existing Universalist theological schools, which were all located in the North and Midwest. Q. H. Shinn was among those who sought to provide such facilities in the South, and in 1897 proposed an "evangelistic training school."[54]

Shinn had in mind an institution which would offer not only theological training but basic education in the "common branches" as well as an opportunity for students to earn sufficient money to pay their way. He intended to reverse the usual sequence in divinity schools of formal instruction followed by preaching, by making preaching an integral part of the training from the very first. Shinn was, in effect, calling for a return to old-fashioned evangelism, but with at least token recognition of the need for formal instruction. His goal was an eminently pragmatic one: To furnish practically trained young men and women to serve rural parishes in the South. Their education might be less academic than that offered by the divinity schools of the North, but they would begin their careers with both some experience on which to build, and freedom from the indebtedness which most theological students accumulated. Hence their salary expectations would be modest and their services more affordable. "Shepherds, rather than scientists, pastors and not philosophers were what Dr. Shinn proposed to send forth."[55]

Shinn discussed his proposal with William H. McGlauflin, minister of the Universalist church in Atlanta, and suggested that McGlauflin take on the responsibility for providing the theological training.[56] McGlauflin was reluctant to assume what might have overloaded an already busy schedule, but he otherwise supported Shinn's proposal. The idea was then presented to the trustees of the General Convention at their meeting in New York City in January 1898. They approved a plan to open a theological class in Atlanta to be conducted by Richard M. Smith, who would also serve as an assistant to the pastor in Atlanta. Shinn was authorized to solicit $1,000 in subscriptions for Smith's salary. As soon as the amount had been subscribed, the Missionary Committe of the General Convention was to employ Smith for one year and generally supervise the work.

Shinn immediately set out to procure jobs in the Atlanta area for prospective students. A building formerly used for a private school, and an adjoining dwelling house, were temporarily rented to house the school and its students. The subscription for Smith's salary was raised and he was duly engaged as the teacher. But then Shinn changed his plans. He concluded that if the products of the school were to serve country parishes it would be better that they receive their training in a rural rather than an urban environment. He also broadened his conception of the school to admit young people who could be trained in secular business and trades and work their own way through school.

At this juncture Lyman Ward (1868–1948), another Universalist clergyman, became involved in the planning. He was destined to head what became the Southern Industrial Institute for forty-four years, until a few years before his death in 1948. Ward was born in Hounsfield (Jefferson County), near Watertown, New York, on 17 April 1868, and died on 17 December 1948 in Camp Hill (Tallapoosa County), Alabama.[57] After graduating from high school in Watertown in 1886 he attended St. Lawrence University, from which he received a BS degree in 1892. His *alma mater* conferred on him an honorary DD in 1926.

Ward was ordained in 1894, while serving for one year as a circuit preacher in Washington County, New York. After three years as pastor of the Second Universalist Church in New York City, he moved in 1897 to Camp Hill, where he served at first as a visiting minister in the local Universalist church, and then as its regular pastor. It was in that community that he spent the remainder of his life.

Ward married Mary Louise Smith of Smith's Basin (Washington County), New York, in 1898. From that year until her death in 1944, she spent her life in Alabama. A graduate in 1883 of Clinton Liberal Institute, then located in Fort Plain, New York, she also attended the New England Conservatory of Music in Boston and earned a considerable reputation as a vocalist. It seems that it was she who urged her husband to settle in Camp Hill, and it was she who was at least partially responsible for the permanent location of the school.

Mrs. Ward was actively involved both in the operation of the school and in the local Universalist church as well as in the community. A mission circle was organized in her home, and she served as its first president. She was also a Sunday school teacher, and at the time of her death was chaplain of the Auburn, Alabama, chapter of the Daughters of the American Revolution.

Like Shinn, Ward saw at first hand the need for enlarging educational opportunity for the impoverished children of the rural areas in the South. They had first become acquainted in 1892, with an exchange of correspondence arising out of Shinn's frequent communications in the *Gospel Banner* (Maine) while the latter was serving pastorates in New England.[58]

Ward and Shinn vigorously canvassed the South, soliciting gifts of all kinds, and created sufficient enthusiasm to result in the opening of the school in the fall of 1898. The hope and dream of a denominationally sponsored school in the post-Civil War South had finally been realized, or so it seemed, for its character as Shinn had originally visualized it was soon altered to such an extent that by 1901 he had severed any official connection with it.

The early history of the institution was a confused and unhappy one, a bootstrap operation that somehow managed not only to come into existence but to survive. It was a story of struggle, with almost no resources except hope and determination; it was handicapped by an ambivalent official relationship to the denomination; and its difficulties were exacerbated by a conflict of wills between the two men most responsible for the creation of the school. Yet in many ways it was not only a courageous undertaking in itself but an educational institution that performed an incalculable service for several generations of Southern white youth who might not otherwise have had any schooling or vocational training at all.

The first official act which resulted in the establishment of the school was taken early in 1898 at the third annual meeting of the Alabama State Conference held in Friendship Church near the community of Waverly. The Conference voted, at Ward's urging, that an industrial school be "at once located in the South."[59] Until the question of a permanent location could be settled, it was decided that the town of Camp Hill, where Ward was then preaching, would be the best temporary location. George M. Slaughter, who made the first pledge, of $100, was also a resident of that community. Within six weeks Ward had received additional pledges of nearly $2,000.

The institution was first designated as the "Universalist Industrial School," but when the school was incorporated as the "Southern Industrial College" in March 1899 it did not carry the name of the denomination. Shinn was the chairman of the original eleven-person board of trustees; Ward was the president of the school and served also as secretary of the trustees. As a member of the faculty he was somewhat grandiosely designated as Professor of Philosophy and Ethics. All of the remaining trustees were from the South.[60] The original faculty consisted of Ward, L. Andrews Trimble of Presley, Alabama, who was to teach mathematics and serve also as a trustee; and Richard M. Smith, who had been engaged to teach prospective theological students; none having appeared when the school opened, he taught a variety of other subjects.

In the meantime Universalists were contacted elsewhere in the South and several offers of land were received.[61] J. M. Bowers of Canon, Georgia, was willing to donate ten acres for a site. Isa B. Eberhart of Chicago, owner of a plantation in Georgia, offered 1,000 acres in Montgomery County, provided the school was located there; he subsequently modified his original offer to provide an unconditional gift of 250 acres, and 500 if located in Georgia; and the full 1,000 acres if located on his plantation. The most attractive offer came from John G. Tucker, of Mt. Jefferson, Alabama, who was willing not only to donate 100 acres in Opelika but to contribute $100 toward the building of a church. Ward considered this the best possibility.[62] But after consultation he and Shinn agreed that there was neither the time nor the money to build a school on the property. So in May 1899 the trustees settled on Camp Hill after being assured of a site and at least fifty students.[63] An old plantation was acquired, consisting of 521 acres, largely abandoned but with much tillable land. In order to meet the needs of families with limited resources, part of the land was subdivided into small farms which could be rented by parents willing to move to Camp Hill, cultivate the land, and board their own children.

The school was intended, as the first catalogue described it, "to fit young men and women for the work of life, whether in manual training or in literature and art," and there was to be no infringement on either the religious or political liberties of the students. It was further intended that "a theological department shall always be maintained for the training of young men for the work of the Universalist ministry." Shinn, who was adamantly opposed to the use of either intoxicating liquor or tobacco in any form, was undoubtedly responsible for the provision that no teacher using either was ever to be employed by the institution.

The school was established specifically for poor and needy whites; Shinn felt strongly that it should be a model of "rational charity" in the best and literal sense. Tuition was set at $20 a year, with board available at less than $10 a month. No student was to be graduated or honorably discharged who had not paid every cent of college charges. Likewise, no student was to be turned away, no matter how poor in the world's goods. Somehow a way would be found, but self-support was to be the watchword both in school and out. Industrial training was considered the key to self-reliance, and whatever was needed was eventually to be offered in the way of instruction. The school promised it "to any student, at any age, and would provide the way for him to gain such instruction." Carpentry and printing were the first to be provided, and farming was added the second year. After a printing press was acquired the school published its own monthly newspaper, the *Industrial Student*, beginning in 1900.

Classes began in September 1898, but because there were at first no training facilities for young women, the students during the first year were all males. Beginning in the fall of 1902 courses in laundering, sewing, cooking, and weaving were introduced for the young women.

The theological department that Shinn had planned was to be open, tuition free, to any young man or woman interested in the work of the Universalist ministry. There were only two requirements for admission: Good character and assent to the Winchester Profession of Faith and the Declaration of 1897 (ratified in 1899 as The Essential Principles of the Universalist Faith). The course of study was intended to be "about the same as that in the other Universalist theological schools."

There were twenty-five students enrolled when the school opened but only sixteen were still in school at the end of the academic year.[64] Enrollment increased to more than fifty in 1899–1900 but the attrition rate continued to be high. Assets were listed as $5,000 in 1899.[65] There had been no theological students when the school opened, but by mid-year of 1899–1900 there were four, with two more expected.[66]

Students had every conceivable educational background, from almost none at all to those presumably ready for the college course.[67] Academic classification of students became an almost impossible task. This difficulty had been anticipated in part, for there were no entrance examinations, and the level of each student had to be determined after matriculation. A high proportion of the entering students were found to be completely unqualified for even high school work and were enrolled in a special "fitting school" program that ran the gamut of grade levels. Examinations were provided only after progression was to be made from one grade to another. No examinations were expected at first for those whose previous training had been "scant or neglected," which turned out to be an understatement for the majority. The assignment of students to classes was made doubly difficult by both the lack of high schools in the area and the fact that those which did exist were completely ungraded. As a result, no curriculum at all was worked out during the first two years.[68]

The educational facilities of the new school were as limited as the academic level of most of the students. The original library, consisting mostly of donations amounting to 300 books, was miscellaneous in character and lacked even an encyclopedia. Because the school was intended to serve the entire community, its library, limited as it might have been, was open to any resident of Camp Hill while school was in session.

The physical facilities consisted of a motley assortment of buildings, new and old. The young men occupied old slave cabins, the young women lived in a rented house off-campus. The plantation mansion, known as the "Haunted House," was renovated by the students to serve as a residence for the Ward family. A new frame building was constructed in 1899–1900 which housed classrooms, an auditorium, and the library. The lumber was donated by a local farmer, with the construction work done by the students. They likewise did their own cooking, and paid what they could afford.[69] The main building, insured for $4,000, was destroyed by fire in 1925 and was replaced by a fireproof structure at a cost of approximately $25,000.[70]

Ward, enthusiastic about the work on which he had embarked, attended the sessions of the annual Tuskegee Negro Conference in 1900 to learn how other industrial schools operated. He was warmly received, and was described by one of the trustees of Tuskegee as "a white Booker T. Washington."[71] Ward was a life-long admirer of Washington and his work.[72] Ward also held in 1900 what was announced as the first of a series of annual educational conferences on the advantages of industrial education, urging public schools to add trade courses to their basically classical curricula.[73]

The struggling new school went through a critical period in 1900–1901 which made its continuing existence doubtful. Ward and Shinn had disagreed on the primary mission of the school even as it was admitting its first students in 1898. Ward envisioned an industrial and vocational school, with theological training as a sideline, if included at all; Shinn wanted primarily a theological school, with secular training a necessary but strictly secondary consideration. Ward recognized the need for ministerial training, but insisted that top priority should be given to basic education for both those planning to enter the ministry and those who did not. The Alabama State Conference had unanimously adopted a resolution supporting the Ward concept. But in deference to the strongly expressed wishes of Shinn the prospectus for the school which appeared in the *Universalist Register* provided for a combination of academic, industrial, and theological training.

A crisis over the nature and future of the school came to a head in 1900–1901 when it faced a deficit of $8,000 and the rift between Shinn and Ward widened. The upshot of the disagreement was the decision to turn the entire school over to Ward with the understanding that it would be entirely secular, with no theological department. All officers who disagreed were given the opportunity to resign; Shinn did so immediately. All who had contributed to the school because it was originally to have been a Universalist-sponsored institution were to have their money refunded on demand over a two-year period.

In order to attract more students from families suspicious of Universalists and to obtain greater support, several of the trustees, including Ward, set out to make the school completely undenominational. Shinn adamantly opposed such a decision, and was supported by a minority of trustees. The majority voted in 1901 to sever any official connection that the school might have with the denomination.[74] Although the school was supported by a variety of Universalist individuals and organizations, its establishment was never officially authorized by the church. In fact, the trustees of the General Convention refused to endorse it on the very practical ground that other financial commitments and the limitation of funds made it impossible.[75] The institution was very much the personal concern of Ward and Shinn, and all appeals for denominational support came ultimately from them.

A new board of trustees was constituted, with a revised charter. The enterprise, so far as the church was concerned, became "a thing of the past," except insofar as it appealed to the humanitarian instincts of Universalists. Shinn was rebuked in no uncertain terms by the *Leader* for embarking on a project such as the school completely without authority or approval, and the denomination was warned not to become involved in such activities without first counting up the cost.

Shinn hastened to reply, defending both the idea of the school and his own actions.[76] He knew of no Universalist school that had been fostered by or had the formal sanction of the General Convention. (In this he was mistaken.) It was individuals, he claimed, who started educational institutions, with the work then taken up by state conventions.[77] Shinn insisted that the trustees of the General Convention had indeed supported the school in Camp Hill, at least at the beginning, when Smith had been employed to teach theological students in Atlanta. Before he began his work, however, the Alabama Conference had voted to start an industrial school with a theological department. Smith had therefore been placed in the school so that students could receive both ministerial and industrial training.

Every state convention and conference in the South had passed resolutions supporting the school and many had raised money for it. In addition, both the WNMA and the Massachusetts Woman's Missionary Society not only "sanctioned" the school but supported it with both money and donations of equipment. Hence, Shinn contended that the Southern school had "had as much if not more authority from the church, as any other Universalist institution." He insisted that the school had not failed; there was not only sympathy among some Universalists for keeping the school alive but there were still students anxious and willing to enter.

Shinn blamed the unfortunate turn of events squarely on Lyman Ward. It was he, said Shinn, who "made it undenominational by incurring without authority or advice, debts that Universalists felt under no obligation to pay." Ward made the fatal mistake of hiring four teachers from orthodox denominations and ignored the theological department. Ward allegedly went so far in turning the school into an undenominational affair that the trustees felt the wisest course of action was to turn the entire school over to Ward, debts and all. The trustees, the minority of whom resigned, then intended to open another school, this time under Universalist sponsorship, and to be financed with the money which was to have been returned.

Supporters of a Southern Universalist school immediately set about planning to open one in Winder, Georgia, the residence of Thomas Chapman, the state missionary. Shinn announced in 1901 that there was definitely going to be a theological department, and that a teacher had already been engaged. Nothing ever came of this.

The *Leader,* in response to Shinn's explanation of what had happened to the Camp Hill school, reiterated the point that, desirable as such a school was, it was nothing short of folly for the denomination "to attempt more than we can carry through."[78] It was also pointed out, regarding the role played by the General Convention in educational efforts in the past, that when other denominational schools had been established, the General Convention had been merely a shadow of what it had later become, and whether it had officially sanctioned schools was irrelevant. But now the situation was different. The time for a "go-as-you-please policy" had long since passed; no scheme or pet project should be undertaken on individual initiative alone, without the express authority and consent of the entire denomination unless Universalists wanted to invite disaster by dividing their forces and working at cross purposes.

The *Universalist Register* promptly dropped its description of the school as "under the patronage and control of Universalists" and it was never mentioned again. Ward continued, however, to operate the school, and in order to devote all of his time to it, resigned his pastorate in the Camp Hill church in 1901. It had for Ward the unfortunate financial effect of making him ineligible for a pension because he had served in a Universalist church for less than the number of years of continuous employment required. After having been replaced by Chapman he still preached occasionally in the Camp Hill church, the last time from 1942 to 1946 while the regular pastor, Leonard C. Prater, was serving as a military chaplain. Ward was so well known and so highly regarded in Alabama that in 1946 he was nominated for the governorship by the Republican Party.[79]

After less than two years' experience with the school it was obvious that neither the educational level of the students nor the state of finances could justify collegiate-level offerings. So such plans were abandoned and the

Southern Industrial College became the Southern Industrial Institute in 1901 by a change in the charter. A two-track curriculum was introduced, literary and manual/industrial, divided into elementary and secondary. In 1904–1905 there were twenty-six students in the elementary level of the literary curriculum (twelve boys and fourteen girls) and a total of forty-four at the secondary level.[80] Thirty-two pupils were enrolled in the manual/industrial division. Expenditures that year were reported as $3,600.

Ward continued to receive support from Universalist organizations and to solicit assistance. In 1905 he recieved a grant of $70 from the WNMA for a scholarship.[81] He announced a drive in 1907 for $20,000, to which the same group contributed $100. Prospects for the school brightened considerably when it became a state-approved school in 1912 and was hence eligible for several thousand dollars of public aid.[82] In 1914 a four-year assistance grant of $3,000 annually gave much promise, but there were insufficient funds in the state treasury to pay it when due; the school therefore accumulated a deficit but was still able to maintain itself by rigorous economies and the continued receipt of donations from various sources.[83]

By 1920 the enrollment was nearly 140 and the school, together with the local church, continued to be a center of Universalist influence way out of proportion to the size of either the town or the church; the latter remained the largest in the denomination in the entire South. The children of several Universalist clergy, including those of Ward himself, attended the school, his daughter Mary among them. After graduating from college she returned to teach in the school, as did her husband Crawford Rose, a graduate of Auburn University. A. G. Strain, a minister who spent his entire life in his native South, sent two of his children to the Institute.[84]

In 1930 the cornerstone was laid by Governor Bibb Graves for a new administration building financed by the state in recognition of the great service rendered by the school.[85] The physical plant was simultaneously being expanded by construction of a new gymnasium financed by alumni donations.

Ward retired as head of the school in 1942 and was succeeded by Joseph B. Kirkland, a graduate of the institution.[86] Ward remained as chairman of the board of trustees until his death in 1948. At that time the raising of a 50th anniversary fund was in progress, intended to provide $50,000 for a new dormitory. An anonymous gift of that amount for a boys' residence promised several years earlier had never been made, having been a casualty of economic depression.[87]

The school added a military training program in 1955 and was henceforth known as the Lyman Ward Military Academy. By the late 1960s the enrollment had increased to 250. Although it had long before sloughed off its Universalist origins it retained Ward's ideals of Christian philanthropy and self-reliance.[88]

Universalists, throughout the history of their involvement in educational affairs, showed their sensitivity to changing needs and demands, and responded in a variety of ways. This continued to become evident in the field of theological as well as secular education.

Chapter 16

Theological Education: Ryder and Canton

During its existence as a separate denomination the Universalist Church founded three theological schools to educate individuals for its ministry. The first was located in Canton, New York, and was opened in 1858; it preceded the establishment of St. Lawrence University which was authorized by the same charter in 1856, and was located on the same campus. The Canton Theological School, as the institution was known for many decades, closed its doors in June 1965, after awarding 419 Bachelor of Divinity (BD) degrees to both men and women, and issuing 67 certifications in religious education during a history extending across 107 years of actual operation. The majority of specialists in religious education were women; some who earned the BD, both men and women, were also certified in religious education.

The second such school had been opened in 1869 as a department of Tufts College, which had been chartered in 1852. It was known originally as the Tufts Divinity School; as the Crane Theological School from 1906 to 1925; and as the Tufts School of Religion — Crane Theological School until it closed in June 1968, after a history of ninety-nine years. During that period it had graduated 281 BD's (some in religious education), 152 Bachelors of Sacred Theology (STB), and 2 Masters of Religious Education, a total of 435.

The last theological school to have been organized under Universalist auspices, the smallest, and with the briefest history, was the Ryder Divinity School, opened in 1881, located first at Lombard College and then moved to Chicago in 1912. It was the first of the three theological schools to lose its separate Universalist identity (in 1928), after a history of less than fifty years.[1]

Taken together, the three schools, during their periods of operation between 1858 and 1968, awarded degrees to somewhat over half of the clergy ordained in the denomination in the 110-year period. The others were either educated at other theological schools, were ordained without completing degree requirements, or earned no theological degree at all. The situation at Tufts was typical. Of the 151 men who were enrolled between 1947 and 1952, 80 were non-graduates; of the 33 women who attended during the same period, 14 were non-graduates.[2] The high proportion who never completed the program was accounted for partly by the fact that some registered with no intention of doing so. They enrolled as pre-theological undergraduates only in order to take advantage of the generous financial assistance offered, and dropped out as soon as they had received their bachelor's degree.

Administratively, no two of the schools were alike. The theological school at St. Lawrence *was* the university until a College of Letters was organized in 1861 and its first student received a degree in 1865. Until 1910 all parts of the university were served by a common board of trustees. In that year, by an amendment to the charter, the theological school began to be operated by its own board of trustees elected by the New York State Convention. This arrangement lasted until the school was closed. The ties to the denomination were much closer, with a relationship that lasted much longer, than was true of either of the other schools.

The Tufts Divinity School, although it shared with the Canton Theological School the common purpose of training individuals for the Universalist ministry when it opened, was throughout its history under the jurisdiction of the trustees of the entire institution and was never more than semi-autonomous. Furthermore, like the parent institution, the theological school was established by Universalists but had no official denominational connection, either state or national. In its later years it became non-denominational in both theory and practice.

The Ryder School at Lombard, like Tufts, was a "department of instruction," but after its relocation became affiliated with the University of Chicago Divinity Schools, and then with Meadville School of Theology (Unitarian), also located by 1928 in Chicago.

In spite of differences, there were obvious similarities among the three schools. Not one was under the direct control of denominational headquarters or the General Convention. All were attached to other institutions in some degree of relationship. The enrollments at all three were distressingly small through most of their histories. Not one was ever accredited by the American Association of Theological Schools. Endowments were pitifully inadequate, the problem aggravated by unceasing requests (and expectations) for financial aid from generally impoverished students, and the inability and/or unwillingness of the denomination to meet these ever-pressing needs. Not a single theological school was in any sense self-supporting; all were deficit operations, no matter where located or how large. Theological faculty salaries usually lagged far behind those of their colleagues in other divisions of the institution with which they were associated, and teaching loads were generally much heavier. The excessive dependence on part-time faculty, and grossly inadequate library and research facilities were problems particularly evident at both St. Lawrence and Tufts.

The question may well be asked: Why did the three schools survive for so long? Part of the answer lay in the devotion and sacrificial spirit demonstrated by a majority of the faculty and administration who were imbued with a combination of idealism and determination which sometimes bordered on stubbornness. Most were proud of their denominational heritage and wanted both to preserve and extend it to the best of their ability. They were also sufficiently loyal to Universalism to do all in their power to prevent the responsibility for educating their clergy from falling into other hands. It was in part a measure of their will to survive that accounted for the rather unrealistic attempt to maintain three schools when one would have probably done as well or better, as more than one Universalist pointed out.

There were also those who blamed denominational weakness on the lack of a highly educated clergy. They found much ammunition to support their argument in a statistical analysis prepared in 1924 and summarized in the denominational press.[3] A survey was made of the personnel records of 242 Universalist clergy, comprising more than half on the active list. Of that number, 64 percent had had less than four years of college or theological school; 33 percent had had four years of college or some theological school training; and only 4 percent had completed both four years of college and three years of theological school. The Universalists lagged conspicuously behind both the Unitarians and the Congregationalists in the number of college graduates in their ministry.

A situation approaching crisis proportions had developed regarding denominational theological schools after World War II, and was brought to a head after Universalist-Unitarian consolidation had taken place. Far-reaching decisions had to be made by the early and mid-1960s as to the fate of the five schools that were considered training grounds for liberal religionists. There seemed to be neither justification nor financial resources for attempting to maintain so many schools for so few. Some had to be closed.

It was the fate of this decision that those closed were the two remaining Universalist schools. The education of liberal clergy was left primarily in the hands of those institutions with historic Unitarian ties, sponsorship, and associations. From a narrowly denominational viewpoint, the Universalists had lost out. The Starr King School for the Ministry, Meadville/Lombard, and the Harvard Divinity School (technically non-denominational but with strong Unitarian ties out of its past) had the major responsibility for educating the future Unitarian Universalist ministry. The Canton Theological School and the Tufts School of Religion were no more; they remained only as fading memories of a past never to be recaptured.

The Ryder Divinity School

Almost forgotten by Universalists in the East was the third and last theological school to be directly associated with the denomination. It had opened at Lombard College in 1881 and in 1890 had been designated the Ryder Divinity School in recognition of its major benefactor, William H. Ryder. The school had been transferred to the University of Chicago in 1912 as part of its divinity school complex, in order to take advantage of the educational facilities there. Lewis B. Fisher (1857–1936), who had been president of Lombard for seven years, became the dean of the relocated theological school and served until his resignation in 1923.

The decision to relocate the divinity school had been precipitated by one of the many financial crises that beset Lombard during much of its history. "Save Lombard" had become the rallying cry of Midwestern Universalists, and a crisis was averted by last-minute contributions from alumni and friends.[4] This in turn had produced a lengthy discussion among Universalist officials about the future of the divinity school, aggravated by the refusal of the Carnegie Corporation to allocate funds to any educational institution which had a theological school attached.[5] One solution was to establish direct control over all three of the existing Universalist theological schools by separating them from the institution to which they had been attached, complete with their own boards of trustees, as was then the case at St. Lawrence, but not at Tufts or Lombard.[6]

Another alternative for the Universalists was to consolidate all three theological schools into one, and the General Convention trustees were instructed in 1915 to investigate the possibilities.[7] Enrollments at the Tufts and St. Lawrence theological schools were only twelve and fourteen respectively, in 1913, and so the idea seemed to have some merit.[8] However, no action resulted.

The Ryder Divinity School at the University of Chicago was located first in a building known as Universalist House, but in 1917 the trustees of the General Convention pledged $5,000 towards construction of a building for the school which when completed in 1918 was named Ryder Divinity House.[9] It was to have been part of Universalist center which would serve also as the Midwestern headquarters of the denomination. It was to consist of four buildings — a relocated St. Paul's Church, a library, a community center, and a combined residence for the dean and a dormitory with a capacity of fifteen students, all to cost an estimated $150,000.[10]

278 / Institutional Activities and Organizations

Ryder Divinity School in Chicago

In order to comply with the regulations of the University of Chicago Divinity School, only those holding a college degree could be accepted as candidates for the BD. So Fisher had spent the summer of 1912 attempting to identify as many Universalist students as possible in Midwestern colleges. He discovered sixty-five, exclusive of those in the one Universalist-sponsored institution remaining in the Midwest (Lombard).[11] So few who were interested in the ministry could meet the degree requirement that the dean was immediately forced to admit a high proportion as special students (non-degree candidates). Of the six students who entered in 1912, two dropped out and of the four remaining, none had a bachelor's degree or its equivalent. Those who did remain were mixed in with approximately 200 theological students representing a dozen denominations.

Even with the potential attraction of the resources of the University of Chicago, a curriculum tailored to meet individual needs, free tuition for college graduates and half-tuition remission for those in a combined degree program, enrollment in the theological school remained the smallest of the three Universalist schools. The largest number at the Ryder Divinity School reported in any one year was fourteen.[12]

Fisher was completely discouraged by the unpromising results of his labors, but when the suggestion was made in 1915 that a consolidation of schools might be the solution, he opposed it, possibly because his own position would have been at stake. He made a report tinged with bitterness in reply to the General Convention's lack of action in 1915. He argued that the denomination had neither the money nor the potential faculty, even if combined in one place, to make even "one first rate modern theological school."[13] Universalists had gone so long without any educational standards for their ministry that an adequate supply of competent teachers would have been well nigh impossible to assemble. The only solution, in his mind, was to create four theological schools, all under the direct control of the General Convention, with one for each quadrant of the nation. They would be attached to large, well-established nonsectarian institutions, with a dean for Universalist students at each, modelled on the system at the University of Chicago. If educational standards were raised, as Fisher urged, the small number of theological students would probably be reduced even farther, possibly down to none at all for a brief period. But eventually students of the caliber he hoped for would be recruited and the denomination would achieve the standing and respect it then lacked.

Isaac M. Atwood, dean of the theological school at St. Lawrence, challenged Fisher's low opinion of the quality of Universalist clergy, and produced a list of twenty prominent clergy to prove his point.[14] Dean Lee S. McCollester at Tufts' Crane Theological School also replied, arguing that the divinity school there was actually doing on a small scale exactly what Fisher was calling for.

The Commission on the Ministry felt that consolidation of theological schools was neither practicable nor desirable, and in fact called for the opening of one in either or both the South and the Far West.[15] The commission pointed out that, ideally, all Universalist theological schools should be autonomous, each with its own trustees, rather than operating under the control of secular institutions. A conference was even recommended between the trustees of the General Convention and those of Tufts and Lombard to consider charter modifications to provide increased autonomy. But this was never done; the closest that the Crane Theological School ever came was to separate its faculty from the general faculty in 1962, but that lasted only briefly. The school was too integral a part of the university community to make such separation workable; furthermore, the possible loss of support of the school by the Tufts trustees would have meant financial disaster for it.

When Fisher resigned in 1923 from the deanship of the Ryder Divinity School, the denominational Commission on the Ministry feared that the school would be forced to close. A much more desirable alternative was to continue the school and to have at least one individual installed as professor or dean to rank with the rest of the staff of the Chicago divinity school.[16] This expedient was followed, and the school hung on under the deanship of L. Ward Brigham (1865–1959), with an enrollment in 1924 of three.[17]

Some decisions about the faltering school had to be made, and by the

1920s a solution appeared on the horizon. The Meadville Theological School (Unitarian) had moved in 1926–27 from Pennsylvania to join the divinity school complex at the University of Chicago and a new campus was under construction.[18] Why not join forces?

Franklin C. Southworth, president of Meadville, had approached Fisher as early as 1917, when a move to Chicago had been contemplated by Meadville authorities, and suggested that the two theological schools be combined there.[19] But the Lombard trustees had demurred, feeling that they were not yet prepared for such action. Southworth renewed the suggestion in 1928, in his last annual report as head of Meadville before his retirement. This time, with Lombard College in dire financial straits and on the verge of closing, both Dean Brigham and the Lombard trustees endorsed the idea.

After the Unitarians joined the Universalists in 1928 in a final attempt to rescue Lombard, the divinity school in Chicago was to be under the control of a special five-person committee of Lombard trustees, of whom one was to be the president of the college and the other four were to be Universalists.[20] One possibility again suggested by the Unitarians had been to effect "some sort of merger" of Ryder with the Meadville school. A fund would be created to provide scholarships for Universalists, and an endowed chair would be occupied by a Universalist. This was accomplished by the creation of the Ryder Chair of Parish Administration. The Ryder Divinity House was sold in 1928 to the University of Chicago.

The Ryder School had always remained a small and struggling organization. When the Lombard campus in Galesburg was closed in 1930 there were only two theological students and a faculty of two at the Chicago location.[21] The Meadville school tended to attract Unitarians rather than Universalists, and in 1941 there were only two students enrolled from Universalist backgrounds.[22] A year after four theological schools (including Meadville) associated with the University of Chicago were federated in 1943, of the 283 students registered, 18 were Unitarians; no Universalists at all were reported in the total student body.[23] There were so few Universalists enrolling in the school that in 1959 a recommendation that Meadville be listed in all official lists as a Universalist theological school was tabled by the Universalist trustees.[24] In short, the Ryder Divinity School, during its rather tangled and uncertain history, contributed but minimally to alleviate the shortage of clergy of which Universalists complained so frequently.

One curious legal arrangement was made that resulted in much confusion for those not familiar with the situation. After Lombard was closed in 1930 the charter was retained, and so there existed two sets of trustees — one for Meadville and the other for Lombard, many of the same individuals serving on both. Complete merger was voted by the Meadville trustees in 1964, with the corporate name the "Meadville Theological

School of Lombard College" shortened in popular usage to Meadville/Lombard. Another reminder of Lombard's continued legal existence was the retention of the old college colors (gold and olive) on the hoods of Meadville graduates.[25]

And so the last of the three theological schools to be founded by the denomination became the first to lose its distinctive Universalist identity and to close as a separate institution.

Canton Theological School

Universalists in upstate New York had been much disappointed when Tufts College was opened in 1854 as a liberal arts institution without a theological school or curriculum. So they determined in 1855 to open their own. Almost as an afterthought they decided to establish a college "in connection with the theological school" because there was no such institution to serve what was called the "North Country."[26] The village of Canton in St. Lawrence County was selected as the site of the new school.

Even though there was some fear that they might have overextended themselves by pursuing such a course, the New York Convention had voted in 1855 to raise a permanent fund of $50,000. Some had hesitated because the state convention had already gone into debt to construct a building for the "Female Department" at Clinton Liberal Institute. Others, like T. J. Sawyer, felt that the Universalists had made "a great mistake" in locating the school such "a great distance from the principal centers of the denomination, out of sight and much out of mind of those who have the means." The perpetual struggle of the school throughout its history to obtain both students and financial support bore witness to the wisdom of Sawyer's observations.

The "St. Lawrence University and Theological School" had been chartered in 1856, the college as unsectarian and the theological school "especially intended and organized for the preparation and training of persons for the ministry of the Universalist Church." The two parts of the institution shared a common board of trustees, but their funds were to be kept separate.[27]

Construction of the first building (Richardson Hall) was begun in the spring of 1856 and the cornerstone, containing a tin box with the name "Canton Theological School" and other memorabilia deposited inside it, was laid that summer. William S. Balch, a clergyman who had been active in the Universalist Education Society responsible for raising the money, had delivered an address on that occasion. He made the point that the idea of a College of Letters was purely local in origin and was not part of the plans of the Society. There were to be two departments in the university rather than a theological school alone.

A year after the charter had been secured a petition was filed with the state legislature for a grant toward endowment, and $25,000 was appropriated on a matching basis, the other half to be raised by subscription. This $50,000 for "general education" became the financial foundation of the College of Letters and Science.

Ebenezer Fisher (1815–1879), a largely self-taught scholar who was called from a pastorate in South Dedham (Norwood), Massachusetts, opened the theological school with four students in the spring of 1858.[28] A year later, John Stebbins Lee, active in denominational education in Vermont, joined Fisher to conduct a preparatory department for the proposed college and instruct the theological students in Greek. The student body had reached nine by the winter of the first year, and in 1861, three years after the school opened, five graduated. In that same year one of the four entering students was Olympia Brown, the first woman to receive a divinity degree and to be regularly ordained in the American Protestant ministry. An Olympia Brown Scholarship Fund was started a century later to mark her graduation and ordination in 1863. The 100th anniversary was celebrated by Recognition Day and a bronze portrait tablet was installed in the theological building.

Fisher, originally designated as principal of the theological department and then as president of the Canton Theologial School, was the entire staff of the school until 1860. He served at a salary of $1,100 — modest even for those days. Massena Goodrich was called to a second professorship (Biblical Languages and Literature), after having first declined the appointment, but he stayed only two years. Fisher was forced to spend much of his time attempting to raise a $20,000 endowment for another professorship which was finally filled in 1865 with the appointment of Orello Cone. Fisher was experiencing difficulty enough in raising the promised $26,000 endowment to finance his own salary.

Students admitted to the Canton school represented every conceivable type of preparation — or lack thereof. It was an overwhelmingly undergraduate school in which much of the time of the teaching staff was spent in imparting the rudiments of the English language and drill in the art of expression. For its first half-century the school offered a three-year course leading technically to a diploma or certificate of proficiency rather than a college or professional degree. If a student were a college graduate, which was occasionally the case, only one year of additional training at first entitled the enrollee to a BD degree. In 1916 a combined three-year college and two-year divinity program was introduced, much like that at Tufts. The idea of requiring both a college degree and three years of additional training for the BD had to be abandoned as soon as it was suggested. Otherwise, the school would have lost most of its students.

Besides testimonials of good character, the only other requirement for admission was "belief in the Holy Scriptures [and] fixed determination to devote themselves to the Christian ministry."[29] Diversity was encouraged. As the Committee on Education reported to the General Convention in 1867, the Canton school did "not turn out ministers like coins from a mint, all bearing the same stamp, and speaking in the same tones, and working in the same way." Students in 1870 were entitled to a grant of $180 a year from the trustees of the General Convention if they were "worthy and indigent."

The number of graduates never matched the number enrolled. The school had produced thirty-seven clergy by 1863, but only twenty-six had completed the entire course.[30] By the year of Fisher's death in 1879, 201 students had attended the theological school; 149 of these were also students in the college. Taking a longer view, 445 students had been enrolled up through the year 1915, but only 295 had graduated, yet 360 had been ordained in the Universalist ministry.[31] The completion of degree requirements was obviously not a fixed requirement for ordination. The school nonetheless made its positive contribution to the work of the denomination, turning out college presidents, three deans of theological schools, a superintendent of the Japan mission, and two general superintendents of the entire denomination as well as two of its presidents.

Midway during the Civil War (1863–64), with a sharp drop in enrollment, the plight of the Canton school became so serious that the suggestion was made that it be transferred to Tufts, which at the time offered no theological instruction.[32] But the idea was greeted with enthusiasm in neither Massachusetts nor New York State. There was no assurance that more generous funding would be available farther east, and it would strain Tufts' limited resources even more. Further, removal of the theological school would be a severe blow to the struggling new university in Canton which had not been able even to offer collegiate-level academic instruction until 1861.

Both the theological school and the college, on the verge of foundering, were rescued by a gift of $50,000 from John Craig of Rochester, New York. The funds were used to establish a third professorship in the theological school, held by Lee who had returned from a trip abroad. He held the Craig Professorship of Ecclesiastical History and Biblical Archeology in the theological school until his death in 1902, after a total of forty-two years at St. Lawrence.

The situation at the theological school looked much more promising by the late 1860s than earlier, with a faculty of three and an increase in Fisher's salary to $1,500 in 1866 and to $2,500 by 1871. The Canton school almost lost its senior professor to Tufts when its divinity school was opened in 1869 and T. J. Sawyer, its first head, was casting about for faculty. Fisher's services for the Canton school were retained by hastily raising several thousand dollars to increase the endowment of his chair. George A. Dockstader of New York City, a benefactor also of the Tufts school, gave the largest amount ($5,000), and the Dockstader Professorship of Moral Science and Systematic Theology was established by the trustees.[33] Fisher, the beloved president of the Canton school, died in 1879, and a new era in its history began.

The second president of the Canton Theological School, who served for twenty years (1879–1899), was Isaac Morgan Atwood (1838–1917), as dominating a figure at St. Lawrence as his predecessor had been. He had already achieved much visibility in the denomination as editor of the *Leader* from 1867 to 1872, as an editorial contributor since then, and at the time of his appointment, the pastor of the Third Universalist Church in Cambridge, Massachusetts. He was surprised to have been selected for the presidency, for he was not known primarily as an educator, and at first refused to be considered. But three alumni of the school, including Almon Gunnison who himself later became president of St. Lawrence, were personal (and persuasive) friends and prevailed on him to accept. He was inaugurated in June 1879 and took office that September.[34]

Both the theological school and the College of Letters and Science still shared Richardson Hall, the original building, which also housed most of the theological school students. The chapel of the college was at one end of the building and that of the theological school at the other. The combined college and theological school libraries totalled 5,500 volumes, largely the result of the gifts of two private libraries; the book budget was $200 a year. The presidents of the two coordinate departments of St. Lawrence — Atwood and Absalom G. Gaines — functioned harmoniously under the same roof. Both were already acquainted, and both had received honorary DD's from Tufts — Gaines in 1874 and Atwood in 1879. This sort of "familial" relationship between St. Lawrence and the theological school lasted until almost the end of Canton's existence.

Richardson Hall was released for the exclusive use of the college when Fisher Hall was erected between 1881 and 1883 for the use of the theological school, as a memorial to its first president. It was financed on the initiative of alumni. Atwood played a key part in seeing the building through to completion. Fisher Hall remained the headquarters of the theological school until the structure was destroyed by fire in 1951. Completion of the original building was delayed for many months because most of the contributions came in small sums and collections were often difficult. Even then, the cost of the building was only $17,000. It was a massive and spacious structure, intended to accommodate many more students than ever attended at any one time. In 1908, in a plea for greater patronage, it was pointed out that the facilities were being underutilized. Fifty students could be as easily housed and taught as the fourteen in attendance that year.

Only one year after Atwood's arrival it was found necessary to replace Coné, who had been called to the presidency of Buchtel College. He

Fisher Hall at St. Lawrence University

returned in 1900 to serve until his death in 1905. His successor in 1880 became Henry Prentiss Forbes of Danvers, Massachusetts, who served until 1913 as Professor of Biblical Languages and Literature and became the first dean of the theological school in 1899, replacing Atwood. Forbes was a specialist in the New Testament. Atwood, the last president of the theological school under the original designation of its head, became a trustee of the university in 1880, a position confirmed by the New York Convention which continued until 1910 to be legally responsible for the entire institution.

    Atwood, placed as he was in a position making him knowledgeable about the financial affairs of both the college and the theological school, was unhappy to discover that the productive funds of the latter were only little more than $70,000 and those of the college even less. The college was able to supplement its limited income with a small tuition charge, but the theological school, which charged no tuition at all, had to depend exclusively on interest income and gifts, which were generally small and most uncertain. For almost a decade of his presidency of the theological school he was hesitant to solicit funds for his own school while the college was in such dire need. So he confined his efforts at fund-raising to that portion of the university. Even then, the theological school fared reasonably well in the early 1880s. A bequest by Miss Sarah A. Gage amounted to more than $37,000.

The college was confronted with another financial crisis in 1886; its productive funds had dropped to $50,000. Appeals to a variety of potential donors had brought no substantial results, and a quorum was not even present at the annual meeting of the trustees that year. The closing of the institution appeared to be imminent. So a rescue mission headed by Atwood set out to raise at least $50,000. By dint of efforts little short of heroic, he, the faculty, and the theological students saved the College of Letters by raising nearly $52,000. In 1888, only two years after financial disaster had been averted, the school received a bequest of $30,000 from William H. Ryder which enabled it to establish in 1891 a chair of Pastoral Theology and Sociology. Lewis B. Fisher of Bridgeport, Connecticut, of the Canton class of 1881, was the first occupant, and held it until 1904, when he was called to the presidency of Lombard College.

When Atwood resigned in 1899 to become the first General Superintendent of the denomination the trustees voted to elect one individual to head the entire university, and Almon Gunnison, of Worcester, Massachusetts, a divinity school graduate (1868), was made its first president. Henry P. Forbes became the first dean of the theological school, a position which he held until his death in 1913.

Throughout the history of both parts of the institution, inbreeding was a pronounced characteristic of academic personnel, most of whom were fiercely loyal both to St. Lawrence and to the denomination. J. S. Lee, on the faculty from 1859 to 1902, enrolled all five of his children (three sons and two daughters) in St. Lawrence.[35] By 1916 two of the presidents of the college (A. B. Hervey and Lee) had been graduates of the theological school, and the first president of the entire university after administrative reorganization was likewise a theological school product.

Much of the faculty had to be replaced in the early twentieth century because of deaths and resignations. Lee had died in 1902, Cone in 1905, and Fisher departed for his new assignment in Illinois in 1904. The policy of hiring none but their own graduates was continued. Every one of the replacements was either a St. Lawrence or a Canton graduate, or both. John Murray Atwood of Portland, Maine, who had been an instructor in 1898–99, became Richardson Professor of Sociology and Ethics in 1905 and in 1906 Professor of Biblical Languages and Literature. In 1905 George Ezra Huntley of Oneonta, New York, and a leader in the Universalist Sunday school movement, became Ryder Professor of Homiletics and Pastoral Care and offered the first courses in religious education in 1905. After Forbes' death in 1913 Atwood became dean and Herbert Philbrick Morrell, for many years pastor of Grace Universalist Church in Buffalo, took over his endowed chair. Many in both the college and the community found his pacifism during World War I obnoxious, and he suffered from much verbal abuse.[36]

Heads of the Canton Theological School, (1856-1965)

Ebenezer Fisher, President
1856-1879

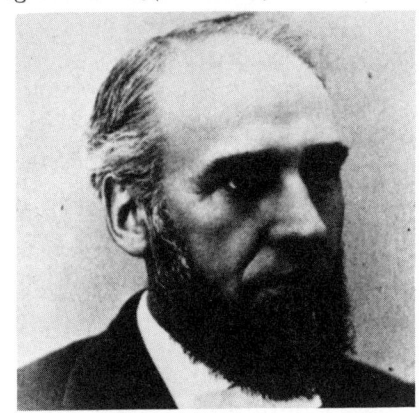

Issac Morgan Atwood, President
1879-1899

Henry Prentiss Forbes, Dean
1899-1913

John Murray Atwood, Dean
1914-1951

Angus Hector MacLean, Dean
1951-1960

Max Adolph Kapp, Dean
1960-1965

Only one additional faculty member of professorial rank was employed during the World War I period. Edson Russell Miles (1875–1958), a St. Lawrence graduate (1900), began his service as professor of Homiletics and Practical Religion in 1917 and remained for thirty-one years. Like many another theological school faculty member, he taught both there and in the college, and his duties, both academic and extracurricular, extended far beyond his official title. He was still teaching freshman English in 1955–56, and for twenty-four years directed the college dramatic society.[37] A memorial reredos in his honor was designed by William C. Pizzo of Stoneham, Massachusetts. The mosaic mural, which was installed in 1960 in Hale Chapel in Atwood Hall, was a semi-abstract rendition of the theme of religious unity and universality.

John Murray Atwood (1869–1951), one of the leading figures in the school's history, had been born on 25 September 1869 in Brockton, Massachusetts, the son of Isaac M. Atwood, the well-known Universalist clergyman, editor, second president of the Canton school, and the first General Superintendent of the denomination. The son received his AB from St. Lawrence in 1889 and his BD in 1893, a Master's degree from St. Lawrence by 1900, and an honorary DD from Lombard in 1906.

He had served his first pastorate between 1893 and 1895 in Clifton Springs, New York, during which time he married Addie B. Ford of Middleville. He was the minister of the Church of the Redeemer in Minneapolis from 1895 to 1898, and then of the Church of the Messiah in Portland, Maine, which he had left in 1905 to rejoin the Canton faculty. In 1913, a year before he assumed the deanship, he was made Gaines Professor of Philosophy. After a total of forty-six years of association with the college and the theological school — thirty-six as a dean and teacher — he was made emeritus in 1951 but died less than a month after his retirement.

The son was by no means as prolific a writer as his father had been. The latter had published seven books in all, the best known of which were *Have We Outgrown Christianity?* (1870), *Latest Words of Universalism* (1879), and *Walks About Zion* (1882), a collection of essays. But J. M. Atwood was as active as the father had been in national denominational affairs, serving two terms (1923–26) as president of the General Convention.

An important legal move had been taken in 1910 that was to cause no end of confusion and misunderstanding in later years. In order to make the college faculty eligible for Carnegie pensions by reasserting its nonsectarian character, and to attract additional funds, the charter of the institution had been amended. One tangible result was a gift of $50,000 from the General Education Board. The Canton school was incorporated separately as "the Trustees of the Theological School of the St. Lawrence University," with its own nine trustees appointed by the New York Convention.[38]

The endowment of the school at the time was listed as $160,000, supplemented by a small amount received from the income of the investments of the Clinton Liberal Institute. The Institute, opened in 1831 as a Universalist-sponsored and financed secondary school, had been moved to Fort Plain, New York, from Clinton, but had been destroyed by fire in 1900. The school no longer existed as a physical entity, but the corporation was neither dissolved nor merged with St. Lawrence, but its remaining assets were assigned to it.[39]

Members of the Clinton board of trustees, like those of the Canton school, were appointed by the New York Convention; as a consequence, many individuals served on both. Whether the funds were to be used by the college or by the theological school or both was left up in the air when an attempt was made to clarify the situation.[40] Over the years the allocation of the bulk of the income had tended to shift from the college to the theological school, but there was nothing in the records to indicate that this was official policy. By the mid-1930s the invested funds from which the income was derived amounted to about $90,000.[41] The funds were used partly to provide five annual awards of $100 each (the McClevey Prizes).

The change in the legal status of the theological school had made no difference whatever in the close relations between it and the college. Students continued, as they always had, to mix and mingle in social organizations, athletics, and use of the college library. The Canton school students took courses in anthropology, psychology, economics, social ethics, and sociology in the college, and many of the faculty, such as the Atwoods, taught in both divisions of the institution.[42] Until 1955, when a department of religion was established in the college, undergraduates took courses with theological school students.

By the 1920s the theological school had shifted from indoctrination in Universalist theology to a broadened conception of the liberal ministry, and students from other denominations began to appear on its rolls with increasing frequency. However, when it came to financial aid, Universalists were given preference, and it was not until the final decades of the school's history that the historic Universalist majority in the student body began to give way to representatives from other denominations, notably the Unitarian. When it closed in 1965 the school was the only remaining ministerial training facility associated with the UUA whose administration and funding were completely under the jurisdiction of Universalists.

Throughout its history it tended to recruit its student body primarily from New York State and upstate New England in spite of the efforts of those like Fisher to stress the fact that the school was intended to serve the entire denomination. It was in particular intended to equip preachers for country churches where, in his view, the strength of Universalism really lay.[43] Fisher's successor, Isaac M. Atwood, felt the same way. He believed that the secret of denominational success was the cultivation of the rural parishes; this was "the most imperative work for the Universalist Church."[44] He believed it would be a mistake to follow the Unitarian policy of concentrating on cities and large towns. The General Convention followed his advice and authorized the cancellation of loan repayments for all ministers who served at least three years in rural parishes after completing their theological education.[45] In the quarter-century between 1926 and 1952, 37 of the 155 clergy who were ordained in the Universalist ministry were Canton graduates, and the majority served rural or small-town parishes.[46]

During the Great Depression of the 1930s, income from all sources was greatly reduced, and Atwood vigorously protested the plan of the General Convention to cut annual student subsidies for Universalists below $150 in loans and to place more responsibility on the theological schools. He reported in 1930 that nine-tenths of the student body had applied for aid, and needed it desperately.[47] By then the college had far outstripped its "parent" (the theological school) in both enrollment and resources. The Canton school needed at least $100,000 in additional endowment and $25,000 to rehabilitate Fisher Hall.[48] A concerted effort was started in 1930 to raise money, the first since 1880 when funds had to be raised to build Fisher Hall.[49] But the results were most disappointing.

The student body had reached thirty by 1939, twenty of them Universalists.[50] Of the ten new students that year, eight were undergraduates, but many dropped out because of economic necessity, changes in plans, and wartime conditions after 1941. Between 1942 and 1945 only ten individuals were awarded theological degrees. A visiting committee had inspected the school in 1942–43 and had found conditions generally favorable but the student body entirely too small. They urged more concrete steps than merely passing resolutions about the need for more active recruitment, and suggested that the fellowship committees of state conventions be utilized in the search for students.

A renewed effort was made to raise $100,000 for endowment, and by the close of World War II the drive to contribute to what was known as the John Murray Atwood Fund, in honor of its long-time dean, reached the half-way point. The UCA contributed $1,000, and by 1947 the goal had been met.[51] Yet this was by no means sufficient, for by 1950 it was estimated that each student cost the school $5,000 for the six-year program.[52] As an economy measure the long-standing policy of furnishing free textbooks had to be abandoned the same year, and a loan policy substituted, with the option to purchase. There was still, however, no tuition charge. Students were responsible only for an annual assessment of $75 in fees. The budget was further strained after a petition from the faculty in 1950 for salary increments resulted in a 10 percent increase the following year. Salaries had been reduced by 10 percent with the onset of

Faculty-student picture, c. 1908. In front row, left to right: Prof. George E. Huntley, Dean Henry Prentiss Forbes, and Prof. John Murray Atwood.

Students and faculty at Canton Theological School about 1908

the economic depression of the 1930s and had never been completely restored. An appeal for funds had to be made to all alumni serving Universalist and Unitarian churches to help pay for the salary increases and to employ a full-time secretary for the school.[53]

The year 1951 was an eventful one for the Canton Theological School. The largest class since 1894 (nine) graduated. Atwood retired from the deanship after thirty-six years of service. And Fisher Hall, home of the school since 1883, was destroyed by fire on 11 December. Very little of its contents could be salvaged, but only one school day was lost, and the veterans' housing project ("Vetsville") became the temporary home of the burned-out school. The trustees voted unanimously, on 4 January 1952, to rebuild, and the state convention promptly ratified the action. A $300,000 drive was announced — $200,000 to replace the building and $100,000 to underwrite faculty salaries.[54] Eugene G. Bewkes, president of St. Lawrence, thought the decision to rebuild was too hastily arrived at, and doubted that such sums could be raised.[55]

Preliminary conversations about possible merger with the Crane School at Tufts or with some other theological school had already taken place but had gotten nowhere. One possibility suggested in 1949 but never acted on was to reorganize both Crane and Canton so that one would concentrate on graduate instruction and the other on undergraduate work.[56] None of the assignment of actual responsibilities as between the two schools was ever worked out.

The decision to rebuild the school at St. Lawrence brought forth another flurry of discussion about the possibility of merger with Tufts. The executive committee of the New York Convention took the initiative by inviting the Crane School to relocate at St. Lawrence in anticipation of new and enlarged quarters. The secretary of the state convention pointed to the $440,000 endowment, plus $100,000 in anticipated bequests and the $110,000 raised for the Atwood Fund.[57] The school had also received $82,000 in insurance payments for Fisher Hall. But these arguments were not sufficiently persuasive, and nothing further happened for a decade concerning merger at either Tufts or St. Lawrence.

While discussions about merger came to a standstill the plans for a new structure at St. Lawrence continued to mature. The building was to be named Atwood Memorial Hall in honor of the father-and-son team who had been associated with the school for so many years. At the time the cornerstone was laid on 9 October 1954 the building fund still lacked $30,000 but construction proceeded without major interruption.[58]

By the time Atwood Hall was occupied in the fall of 1955 the school seemed to be on the verge of a new era of expansion. There had been six graduates in 1952, five of whom entered the Universalist ministry.[59] There had been thirty-three students enrolled in 1952, eighteen of them Universalists. Over a dozen rural churches in upstate New York were being served on a part-time basis by either faculty or students. Undergraduate (pre-theological) students were permitted to preach, beginning in their junior year. This was as much a matter of economic necessity as it was an attempt to provide the internship training urged by the General Assembly.[60]

Prospective ministers could follow any one of three routes: If college graduates, students could enroll in a three-year course leading to the BD, for which a thesis was required; take a six-year combined course which included two years of training in the theological school; or one year of intensive graduate study, including field work, leading to the BD in Religious Education. Tuition of $400 a year was being charged by 1954, but up to $250 was available in scholarships to help offset the charge. The great majority of graduate students had done their undergraduate work at St. Lawrence, where pre-theological scholarships were available. Of the nine holding bachelor's degrees in 1954, six were St. Lawrence graduates.

Although the 1954 catalogue stated that "all denominations are welcome" and that the school did not "seek to emphasize any exclusive sectarianism," the Universalist heritage and associations of the school were stressed in all of its literature and fund-raising efforts. Although there was no separate course in Universalist history as such in the curriculum, by 1961 the school was offering courses in Humanism.⁶¹ At the very same time that the Universalist tie was being emphasized at the New York school, the Crane School at Tufts was advertising its completely nondenominational character.

In perspective, Universalist strength was gradually being whittled away year by year if theological school attendance was any indicator. Of the 140 clergy in active fellowship among those entering the Universalist ministry between 1937 and 1949, only 15 percent (21) had attended Canton and 31 percent (43) had attended Tufts. No less than 54 percent had attended non-Universalist institutions.⁶²

Like the theological school at Tufts, the Canton school was never accredited by the American Association of Theological Schools although there was increasing talk in the 1950s of attempting to meet the requirements. The full-time faculty, which numbered four in 1952 and in 1960 still remained one member short of the minimum required for accreditation, had remained very stable. Only two had been added in the 1920s — Bruce W. Brotherston, who taught religious education and ethics, beginning in 1924, and left six years later to accept an appointment at Tufts; and Angus H. MacLean, whose specialty was religious education, and was first employed in 1928 and succeeded Atwood to the deanship in 1951. Only two full-time faculty members of professorial rank in the entire history of the school served for less than three years.⁶³

When the decision was made in 1952 to rebuild the school, plans were announced to increase the full-time faculty from four to six and to make the school a completely graduate operation.⁶⁴ Dean MacLean presented to the trustees in 1954 the results of a study made by the faculty concerning the academic future of the school. The trustees unanimously endorsed the plan to provide a transition to an exclusively graduate base by the fall of 1957.⁶⁵

MacLean (1892–1969) was thoroughly acquainted with the school and its problems, having been on its faculty for twenty-three years when he became the dean. He had had a variegated career prior to his association with the Canton school. He had been born on Cape Breton Island, Nova Scotia, and after only one year of high school had enlisted in 1910, at the age of seventeen, in a crusade conducted by the Canadian Presbyterian Missionary Society to recruit ministers for Western Canada.⁶⁶ His training for the assignment had lasted for all of one afternoon. He resumed his interrupted education at Westminister Hall Seminary in Vancouver, British Columbia, enrolled in McGill University, and then had served during World War I in the medical corps for four years. After demobilization he attended the University of Edinburgh for one term. Returning to Canada, he completed the work for his AB degree at McGill, and for three years attended the Montreal Cooperative Theological College. He was awarded a fellowship to Teachers College, Columbia University, in New

York City, in the fall of 1923 and earned his PhD degree in 1930, serving meanwhile as an instructor. It was from this position that he was called to the Canton school in 1928. During his days as a faculty member he wrote two books on religious education (1930, 1936) intended primarily for Universalist and Unitarian use.

At the time of his appointment as dean, MacLean held the Richardson Professorship of Religious Education and Psychology, and took office only a few months before the Fisher Hall fire. He was both a realist and a determined individual who saw the need for increased scholarship funds and augmented resources. During his administration a Development Office was established (1957) to strengthen the financial position of the school. Like other administrators in its history, MacLean was underpaid and carried a heavy teaching load in addition to his other duties. His thirty years of service to the school were recognized by a celebration in 1958.[67] Sensitive always to the needs of both the faculty and his students, he stressed the "practical ministry" rather than theological scholarship and fought to eliminate an unfavorable salary differential between his faculty and that of the rest of the university.

His conception of the mission of the school was very much in accord with that of the General Convention, which in 1923 had placed preparation for pastoral duties on an equal footing with academic training in denominational theological schools. He also held to the same philosophy as his predecessor (Atwood), who had told a group of clergy in Boston that the three prime requisites for a successful minister were "grace, gumption, and grit."[68]

MacLean retired from the deanship in 1960, just as the denomination had decided to consolidate with the Unitarians. Simultaneously, the need arose for a reassessment of the direction of theological education and the making of major decisions regarding the future of the school. In his last report to the trustees he reported that he had found the arduous work of the dean engrossing and satisfying, except that it had "nearly wrecked me as a teacher and a scholar." His term of office had begun "in disaster" but both he and the school had survived. His two greatest disappointments were that he had failed to solve the critical financial problem and to increase the size of the student body.

He was also unhappy about the state of the theological library. It had comprised less than 2,000 volumes in 1954 and exceeded 5,000 volumes when MacLean retired, but even when supplemented by the holdings of the new Owen D. Young Library opened at St. Lawrence in the fall of 1959, the resources were completely inadequate in most fields for any research in depth. The theological library comprised slightly more than 7,000 volumes when the school closed and the library was dispersed. No professional theological librarian was ever appointed in the history of the school. The total endowment of Canton on the eve of MacLean's retirement was still less than half a million dollars, including the assets of the old Clinton Liberal Institute, and the enrollment was only seventeen.

The individual chosen to succeed MacLean, Max Adolf Kapp (1904–1979), had to confront these and other problems. It was he who presided over the last and in many ways the most hectic period in the school's history. Like his predecessor, Kapp had the advantage of thorough familiarity with the school, based on long association with it. A native of Herkimer, New York, he attended both St. Lawrence and its theological school, receiving his BD in 1928. He pursued postgraduate work at the Harvard Divinity School, from which he received a Master's degree, and was awarded an honorary DD by his *alma mater* in 1943. He had, like MacLean, been active in the national affairs of the Universalist Church, having served as president of the YPCU and the GSSA.[69] He had joined the faculty in 1942 and had become assistant dean in 1951, and led an exceptionally busy life. He served as Ryder Professor of Homiletics and Church History, and also journeyed each Sunday to Carthage, New York, where he was the supply pastor of the Universalist-Congregational Church.[70]

One of the immediate problems the new dean of the school had to face was to counter faltering morale in the student body. Uncertainty regarding the future of the school was aggravated by what was considered to be excessive faculty turnover and lack of continuity. Somehow the impression was abroad that Canton "was about to crumble." The enrollment had dropped to fourteen by 1960. Actually, with such a small faculty even one change was immediately noticeable. The retirement of MacLean in 1960 probably called to mind the fact that the school had lost in 1955, by resignation, the services of both Myles W. Rodehaver, who had been hired in 1947 and who taught sociology, and Ellis E. Pierce, Professor of Biblical Languages and Literature, who had joined the faculty in 1948. Morton S. Enslin replaced Pierce in 1955, after having engaged in considerable correspondence with Dean Benjamin B. Hersey of the Crane School the previous year about possible employment there. Enslin was one of the more productive scholars on the faculty, and was, besides publishing two major works in Biblical history, the editor of the *Journal of Biblical Literature*.[71]

Two new faculty besides Enslin were appointed during MacLean's deanship: Robert B. Tapp, in 1952, who taught theology and left in 1960 to join the Scripps College faculty in Claremont, California, and Robert L. Cope, who was employed in 1957 and was Professor of Religious Education at the time of his departure in 1960. He had been the minister of the Universalist church in Buffalo and was instrumental in merging it with the local Unitarian church.[72] After MacLean's retirement and Cope's resignation the curriculum in religious education, which was advertised as a specialty of the school, had to be taught temporarily by visiting lecturers, many furnished by the Division of Education of the Council of Liberal Churches.

Between the beginning of Kapp's deanship and the closing of the school, four new faculty members were appointed, but none represented a net increase; all were replacements. Alfred P. Stiernotte was employed in 1960 to teach theology but left in 1964. David B. Parke taught church history from 1960 to 1965. Hugo J. Holleroth, the first holder of the Angus H. MacLean chair of Religious Education, beginning in 1961, had been a Minister of Religious Education in Paramus, New Jersey, and was a PhD candidate at the University of Chicago. Carl H. Voss was the last individual to join the faculty full-time. He taught theology and history of religions during the final year. A grand total of twenty-four full-time faculty of professorial rank served in the 109-year history of the school. In addition, there were numerous part-time appointments from time to time. Kapp exerted every effort possible to strengthen the school and to keep its constituency aware of its many needs. However, the student body remained disappointingly small, with only sixteen enrolled during the academic year 1960–61. Eight of them were married, and six had from one to four children, which made financial aid an absolute necessity. It was estimated in 1961 that at least forty-five ministers were needed to fill liberal pulpits, but the five theological schools that were counted on to educate them produced only twenty that year.[73] Canton contributed one-third of that number.

The largest single gift from an individual in the history of the school came in 1961, when Thomas F. Peterson, an industrialist in Cleveland, Ohio, offered $25,000 a year for ten years in unrestricted funds; the two-fold use was to improve faculty salaries and increase scholarship aid. This brought the total resources of the school to slightly more than $412,000 by 1962. Of the total school budget of $63,450 in 1961, $14,500 was used to finance the Office of Development and Recruitment. But its efforts were so unsuccessful that it was closed in 1962 and its functions became part of the dean's many responsibilities. Receipts from all sources totalled less than $30,000 that year.

One traditional source of funds was redirected and correspondingly diminished, beginning in 1962–63. With the creation of a Joint Fund for Theological Education by denominational headquarters, individual churches were no longer to be solicited for money. As a consequence, some churches, particularly in New York State, which had always donated to Canton, reduced their contributions because they were reluctant to see the funds spread among many schools. It was for them a matter of purely local support. Many New York Universalists refused to aid any school outside their own boundaries. Kapp had tried to conduct a special drive for funds in 1961 but the UUA refused to approve it because it had not been funneled through the proper channels — namely, the United Appeal.⁷⁴ Theological schools were no longer to solicit funds independently.

The year 1961 ushered in a period of confusion and crisis for the Canton school from which it never recovered. There was nothing new about this series of crises, as Dean Kapp reported to the trustees in 1962. For more than a century of its operation, but few years had been "free from anxiety and uncertainty."⁷⁵ Finances, a problem always uppermost in the minds of those responsible for conducting the school, had reached such a parlous state that year, with an anticipated deficit of $20,000, that it was necessary to dip into endowment. Tuition had had to be raised to $500, and every student had had to be given scholarship aid in 1961–62 as a result.⁷⁶

Kapp proposed in 1962 a capital fund drive of $1,250,000 and suggested that Clinton Liberal Institute be merged completely into the theological school so that its funds could be added to Canton assets.⁷⁷ Dissolution of the Institute's board of trustees had been discussed from time to time, and had been recommended in 1925 but no action had been taken. The sole reason for its separate existence had been the provisions of the McClevey gift of $40,000 to the school in 1917. The income, part of which was used for prize money, was to continue only as long as the Institute remained in existence.⁷⁸

Denominational consolidation in 1961 brought a host of unanswered questions. If the New York Universalist Convention went out of existence, as many assumed would be the case, who would elect the theological school trustees? It was recommended that if regional districts were substituted for the state conventions, the New York Convention could continue but only as a corporation to administer funds.⁷⁹ Should the denominational theological schools be consolidated, and if so, which ones would join with what others? The denomination could no longer support four schools. Recruitment was "the most critical problem, not only of this School [Canton], but of all our schools, and of the entire denomination."⁸⁰ If consolidation were to take place, some decisions would have to be made, and those soon, or "students, donors, faculty members, and morale will melt away."⁸¹

The situation was made worse in 1962 with the publication of the Taylor Report which unreservedly criticized the school in almost every respect. According to the findings of Harold Taylor, the outside consultant who had been employed by the denomination's Committee on Theological Education in 1961, the curriculum was anachronistic, was too "historical" and not sufficiently geared to modern and contemporary developments in theological education. Classes were too formally conducted and the lecture method was used excessively for such small classes. As to accreditation, Taylor suggested that all efforts in that direction be abandoned and that the school should set "new standards" of its own.

The Taylor Report was discussed at a special meeting of the theological school trustees in the fall of 1962.[82] Kapp had nothing good whatever to say about it. He accused Taylor of prejudging the school, based on a hurried and superficial visit. The report was entirely inadequate and contained "inaccuracies, if not misrepresentations, which ought not to be allowed to circulate." Taylor had failed to note the school's involvement in and commitment to religious education, neglecting to point out that the school had been a pioneer in this field and that the first certification had been issued as early as 1927. Taylor had denigrated the contribution of the faculty to religious scholarship, and had alleged that the "personal growth" of the students had been ignored by the faculty. Kapp registered an official protest with both the UUA and the Committee on Theological Education regarding Taylor's critique of the school, and the dean attended a meeting of representatives of other theological schools who voiced many of the same complaints about the report."

The Taylor Report also had its effect on the student body, which by the academic year 1961–62 had declined to twelve. There was, as the dean reported to the trustees, "an undeniable restlessness among our students."[83] Using the Fisher Society (the student organization) and a questionnaire distributed by the faculty as forums for expressing their dissatisfaction, they sided with the Taylor Report in its severe indictment of the school. Thirteen of the fourteen students enrolled in 1962–63 considered the program inadequate and eleven found their educational experience to be in some degree "discouraging and oppressive." The "genuine fellowship" promised in the catalogue did not exist, and the school was not truly liberal because it discouraged "freedom of the mind."[84]

In response to the Taylor Report the faculty did make some effort to improve the school. The curriculum was reviewed and teaching methods were reassessed "with a view to initiating as soon as possible desirable changes to bring . . . programs into firmer alignment with its own educational philosophy and the needs of the modern ministry."[85] An "experimental year" was introduced in 1963 which included more tutorials and increased opportunity for independent study.[86] The student reaction was "still not enough." They wanted abandonment of all lecture courses, the substitution of "prolonged discussions by the entire student body, [and] less enforced attention to academic coverage." Accordingly, academic achievement had fallen noticeably below faculty expectations by June 1964.[87]

The Taylor Report also brought into prominence the question of the future of the school. The creation of a large center for liberal religion on the east coast had been among its recommendations, with the possibility that Tufts would become part of it. It was clearly implied that there would need to be a major rethinking of the role of the Canton school in such an arrangement. The theological school responded by agreeing to cooperate in the establishment of "a new School of Religion in the Eastern part of the

United States at an appropriate location."[88] There was to be no change in the conduct of the school until June 1964 "at the earliest."

Between 1962 and 1964 much of the time of the Canton school dean and its board of trustees was spent in conferences with others exploring various possibilities. An all-day conference took place in 1962 between representatives of Canton and Tufts in Albany, New York, to discuss merger at either location. The results were inconclusive. President Wessell of Tufts informed Wallace Fiske, president of the Canton trustees, that if merger took place at Tufts there would be but "little possibility" of a separate board of trustees for the combined theological schools. The trustees of the entire university would be in charge, and the autonomy enjoyed by the Canton school would no longer exist.[89]

The theological school trustees also discussed the feasibility of locating the proposed religious center in New York City under the auspices of the Community Church.[90] This idea had been suggested for consideration by denominational headquarters in 1962 and the theological schools were likewise requested to consider it. But the consensus of all concerned was that it was beyond the financial capabilities of the UUA, and both Tufts and Canton discarded it. After that alternative was ruled out, the possibility of merger with Meadville/Lombard was considered by the Canton trustees.[91] All the while the trustees received a stream of protests from Universalist interests in New York State who opposed the merger of "their" school with any other, or any action which required moving it out of the state.[92] The school was *their* property.

Kapp displayed a hands-off attitude regarding merger and refused to express any preference as to either location or arrangements. For this he was roundly criticized for failing to exert the leadership expected.[93] The closest that he came to an expression of sentiment was his recommendation to the trustees that the charter of the Canton school be amended to free it from the authority of the state convention and make them a self-perpetuating board.[94] This proposal was made on the assumption that the state convention would be dissolved and would be replaced by one or more Unitarian Universalist districts. Perhaps this might increase the potential for greater financial contributions than the state convention was able to make. Support from that source had averaged only a few hundred dollars a year, although it reached $1,000 in 1963.[95] A final effort was made by the convention to assist the school when it voted $5,000 to establish the John Murray Atwood and Addie Ford Atwood Memorial Fund to aid needy students and their families.[96]

The decision about the fate of the school remained up in the air until the summer of 1964. The prolonged uncertainty about its future had taken its toll in the meantime. Of the fourteen who were expected to enroll in 1963–64 only eleven were actually in attendance in the middle of that year. Two had dropped out to enroll in Unitarian-associated schools.

The final blow came at the meeting of the General Assembly in the summer of 1964 when it was voted that both the Tufts and the St. Lawrence theological schools consider consolidation with some other institution, subject of course to the approval of their respective boards of trustees. Meadville/Lombard and the Starr King School of the Ministry were the only ones to be salvaged. Cooperation with Harvard was to continue.

There seemed to be no other path to follow than to close the school. After several motions were defeated to close it and to merge with Meadville/Lombard or Starr King, the trustees voted on 5 June 1964 to terminate instruction at the end of the next academic year (June 1965).[97] It was also voted to continue discussions with Tufts. Dana Greeley, the UUA representative on the Canton board, cast the single negative vote on this motion.

The decision to close the school was an agonizing one for the board to make, but realities had to be faced. The UUA could promise no more than token support, and other sources of income seemed to be drying up. The school received an allocation of less than $4,000 from the Joint Fund of the UUA in 1964–65.[98] Every item of expense seemed to be increasing, from faculty salaries to the cost of library materials. Stiernotte, who had resigned from the faculty a year before the school closed, wrote that "the Theological School of St. Lawrence University has no tangible reason for continued existence, with fewer and fewer students and very little opportunity for practical work for students in the ministry."[99] He recommended merger with some other theological school affiliated with a large university with the proper resources.

Many Universalists were disillusioned and even bitter about the recommendation of their national legislative body, with the approval of the UUA trustees, that Canton be closed. Robert J. Jeffries, a Canton trustee, was "shocked and resentful" at the action, and seventy Unitarian Universalists from ten churches met in Syracuse, New York, in December 1964 to protest the decision and to urge the maintenance of a theological school on the East Coast in addition to Harvard.[100]

There seemed to be two possibilities remaining. One was to merge with another institution, with Tufts as the most likely possibility. Or the trustees could vote to continue its work by way of a foundation to administer its funds so that theological and religious education for the liberal ministry could honor the spirit of the founders of the school. These alternatives had been voted in June 1964, at the same meeting at which the closing of the school had been decided.

The trustees took the second route, voting by a narrow margin in October 1964 to establish the St. Lawrence Foundation for Theological Education as the successor to the school.[101] Sentiment for merger with another school had been first tested by a series of straw votes, and one by one all but Tufts were again eliminated. When the final vote of record was taken, merger with the Crane School was defeated in favor of establishment of a foundation by one vote (6–5). One trustee preferred Meadville/Lombard because it still had a denominational identification which Tufts did not.[102] The trustees then voted $5,000 toward the cost of establishing the foundation. It was evident that the majority of the trustees never contemplated or desired a complete merger of their funds with those of another school.

Then came the sad task of closing a school over a century old. The last graduating class consisted of five who received their BD's and six who received certificates in Religious Education, three of them also recipients of BD's. Of the remaining students, three transferred to the Crane School. The sum of $8,800 was appropriated to assist students in completing their studies elsewhere.[103]

The thirteen-person board of trustees of the St. Lawrence Foundation was headed by Kapp, who exchanged his deanship for the position of executive director, and was elected a trustee by the state convention in 1967. Seven of the board were nominated by the state convention, two by the UUA, and two each by the St. Lawrence and Metropolitan Unitarian Universalist Districts. The Canton trustees had recommended that there be two alumni of the school on the board but this was not done.[104] At the time the school closed, its assets had a market value of $1,136,156, to which were added the endowment of the old Clinton Liberal Institute which amounted to $98,643.38 in 1965, and receipts from the sale of books and equipment. The total assets were approximately $1,250,000. The plan was to distribute the available income for scholarships to Crane, Meadville/Lombard, Starr King, and Harvard, with eligibility limited to Unitarian Universalist students.[105] Four scholarships of $800 each were provided from the McClevey Fund from Clinton assets, with six prizes of $100 each.

Thus had come to an end the historic first attempt of the Universalists to provide an educated ministry by establishing a school for that purpose. Beset as the Canton school at St. Lawrence had been with adversities of all kinds throughout most of its history, it had held on doggedly, developed its own traditions, its own loyalties, and its own mystique, and made its own contributions to the larger cause of the liberal ministry.

Chapter 17

Theological Education: Crane

The second divinity school under denominational auspices had been opened in 1869 at Tufts College fifteen years after the institution had admitted its first students.[1] Begun with a student body of four, the new program had its own faculty, curriculum, and degree requirements, but was only semi-autonomous, for it did not, unlike its counterpart at St. Lawrence, have at any time during its history its own board of trustees, and had to depend extensively on the rest of the college for its sustenance, from housing to financial support. The close relations with Tufts, partly from choice and partly from necessity, lasted until the doors of what had become the Tufts School of Religion (Crane Theological School) were closed in 1968, after a history of ninety-nine years.

The foundation on which the divinity school was built was a bequest by Silvanus Packard, the most generous early benefactor of the college. He had died in 1866 with the stipulation that part of his estate, of which a total estimated at $300,000 was to go to Tufts, be used to establish a Professorship of Christian Theology.[2] The trustees then decided to establish a divinity school "in connection with Tufts College," with its own faculty and degree program.[3] It was up to the entire denomination to use the Packard bequest as a nucleus for the school.[4]

The Tufts trustees complied with Packard's requirement, and offered the chair to Thomas J. Sawyer (1804–1899), who had served the denomination in many ways for some forty years, urging the establishment of educational institutions in season and out, and was already sixty-five years of age.[5] While principal of Clinton Liberal Institute in New York State, he had offered religious instruction on the side to more than thirty students, the denomination having lacked a theological school at the time. When such a school had been opened at St. Lawrence in 1858, he had served as president of the board of trustees of what was at first only a theological school and later a university. After some indecision, Sawyer decided to accept the Tufts offer, even though it meant something of a financial sacrifice.[6] He had earlier declined the presidencies of three Universalist colleges: Tufts, St. Lawrence, and Lombard.

The second faculty member to be selected for the new school before it actually opened was Charles H. Leonard (1823–1918) who had been one of Sawyer's students at Clinton for two years and had held a pastorate in the Church of the Redeemer in Chelsea, Massachusetts, for almost a quarter of a century. He was appointed Goddard Professor of Sacred Rhetoric and Pastoral Theology, a chair underwritten by funds donated to the college by Thomas and Mary Goddard.[7] He had been elected a Tufts trustee in 1862, but in accord with his "own sense of what is proper" and in compliance with a recently adopted rule, he resigned when he became a member of the faculty.[8] His past services were recognized in 1869 when Tufts conferred on him an honorary MA degree, and in 1905 an honorary LL.D. Leonard replaced Sawyer as head of the divinity school faculty after the latter's retirement in 1884, although he was not officially made the dean until 1892, when Sawyer was made emeritus.

The enrollment in the divinity school had increased to twelve by 1871, with twenty-one applicants for admission the following year, so Sawyer requested additional staff. William G. Tousey (1842–1930) was employed as Instructor in Psychology and Natural Theology in 1871, the year he had replaced Leonard in Chelsea and had also received his BD. A Tufts alumnus (1869), he had been a member of the first class in the divinity school. When he retired in 1917 as Professor of Philosophy he donated his library to the school. It bore his name as the "Tousey Philosophical Library."

Tufts, like many another educational institution founded as a hilltop college in the nineteenth century, was at first very provincial and ingrown, and depended to a great extent on its own graduates to staff its faculty. The next individual to join the divinity school staff, George T. Knight (1850–1911), followed this pattern. He had graduated in 1872 (after winning plaudits as the best baseball player in the college), had entered the divinity school, and received a BD in 1875. He was immediately appointed Instructor in Rhetoric and Church History. He also taught Biblical history and Greek during his first year, and by the end of his career in 1910 had taught, either regularly or as a substitute, almost every subject offered. He also served as secretary of the theological faculty from 1883 to 1904.

The professional career of George M. Harmon (1842–1926) had a distinct resemblance to that of his other colleagues, except that, after graduating from Tufts in 1867, he was in the active ministry for five years before returning to the college to earn his BD in 1875. After serving as both pastor of the local church and on the faculty of the newly established theological department at Lombard College in Galesburg, Illinois, beginning in 1882, he returned to Tufts two years later and inherited the courses once taught by Sawyer.

The first faculty member appointed after the divinity school opened who was not a Tufts alumnus was Anson B. Curtis. Born in 1863 and a graduate of the University of Michigan in 1887 and of the Meadville Theological School in Pennsylvania (1889), he earned a PhD degree from Allegheny College. He was the first divinity school faculty member to hold such a degree, awarded in 1890, the year he joined the faculty as Instructor in Hebrew and Old Testament.

The last full-time appointment to the divinity school faculty in the nineteenth century, Warren S. Woodbridge (1851–1914), was both a Tufts alumnus (1874) and a divinity school graduate (1877). He joined the school in 1894 as the first occupant of a chair of Applied Christianity established by his father, Samuel F. Woodbridge.[9] The son spent a year of study in Europe before beginning his teaching duties. Like most other divinity school faculty, Woodbridge was deeply involved in denominational affairs. He had contributed articles to Universalist publications; served as a trustee of the Massachusetts Convention and chairman of its missionary committee; and for eight years was a trustee of the Universalist Publishing House.

Very early in the school's history, members of the faculty of the Tufts College of Letters (later designated as the School of Liberal Arts) shared teaching responsibilities at the divinity school. The divinity school also took advantage of both denominational and non-denominational resources in the Greater Boston area as well as outside by way of visiting lecturers.

The requirements for the Bachelor of Divinity (BD) degree went through a multitude of changes, both major and minor, over the years. Two prerequisites originally required of all were testimonials of Christian character and a commitment to enter the Christian ministry.[10] These requirements were generally enforced, although the trustees in 1883 deferred for one year the awarding of the degree to a candidate who suddenly announced that he did not believe in Christianity, and the faculty refused to recommend him.[11] He received the degree only after a clergyman who had known him interceded in his behalf.[12]

A three-year academic program was provided, without entrance examination, for college graduates. Those who could not fulfill this requirement were examined by the faculty, placed in an appropriate class, and received certificates instead of diplomas after completing the three-year course. So many applied who held no undergraduate degree that an informal fourth year of supervised individual study was introduced in 1871–72 for such students. The entire entering class that year elected this route.¹³ A "partial course" was authorized the same year for those unable or unwilling to attend the full four years.¹⁴ Part-time, non-degree students ("Specials") were enrolled throughout the history of the theological school.

The curriculum was heavily weighted at first with Hebrew, Greek, and Biblical history and exegesis, as well as with other traditional theological subjects. Sullivan H. McCollester (1826–1921), the first president of Buchtel College and the father of Lee S. McCollester who was later to become dean of the theological school at Tufts, had no qualms about its curriculum. He described the school as "thoroughly Christian and Biblical, and therefore Universalist."¹⁵

Modern languages such as French and German, as well as other electives, were available through the regular college curriculum. The students were given training during their second year in preparing and delivering sermons to each other at the required daily devotional services and weekly prayer meetings.

Until construction of the two buildings provided specifically for the divinity school was completed in 1892, its students used existing college facilities. A recitation room was provided in the all-purpose main building, known until 1892 simply as "the College Edifice" and thereafter as Ballou Hall in honor of the institution's first president. When a new men's dormitory was built in 1872 (West Hall), half of it was set aside for the use of divinity school students, including housing accommodations and a chapel.

Divinity school students at first paid neither tuition nor room rent; they were charged only the same board as that furnished to other students. In 1897 divinity school students began to be charged the same tuition ($100 a year) as other students, but they continued to be housed in rent-free rooms.¹⁶ If they were unable to live in the dormitory they were charged half tuition.

The decision to charge tuition was based on both principle and necessity. Free tuition created a "privileged" group which did not always appreciate its advantages; and the denomination had not provided the financial resources expected. In fact, the theological school was self-supporting at no time in its history. It was estimated that by 1896 the divinity school had cost the college more than $180,000.¹⁷ Divinity school income that year was only $5,000, while its operating expenses were estimated at $11,000, and had increased the college deficit accordingly.

Even with the provision for and expansion of systematic theological training, the relatively low educational level of students, coupled with continuing small enrollments, remained matters of serious concern at all three of the theological schools operated for the benefit of the denomination in the 1890s. Time after time the Tufts trustees expressed a desire to raise "ministerial scholarship" in the divinity school, sharing a concern which much of the denominational leadership had for the same problem.

Paralleling this was a chronic shortage of clergy which had prompted the General Convention in 1883 to create a special Committee on the Increase of the Ministry.[18] A survey made in 1890 divulged the disturbing fact that, of 160 prospective candidates for the ministry that were identified, only 40 were college graduates and only 50 of the remainder had even a high school diploma.[19]

The formal four-year program introduced at Tufts in 1873–74 for those who did not possess college degrees still failed to attract an adequate number of candidates. Sawyer reported regretfully in 1881 that there were only twenty students enrolled in the divinity school.[20] A committee of the Tufts trustees had considered in 1877 cutting back the four-year program to three as an economy measure, and simultaneously raising admission standards, but nothing was done regarding either of these recommendations for several years.[21]

Enrollment had continued to decline to only eighteen two years after Sawyer had called attention to the problem, and after the promotion of Knight to a professorship in 1883 it was recommended that the resulting vacancy in the instructorship which he had held, not be filled.[22] The faculty insisted otherwise, and Harmon was appointed. A rather drastic step was taken to finance his position. The salaries of both Tousey and Sawyer were reduced in order to make up Harmon's salary, leaving both close to the poverty level. Sawyer protested, but with no results.[23]

Sawyer's salary was further reduced when he was relieved of all academic duties in 1884. All that remained for his use was a rent-free house owned by the college and badly in need of repair, and a salary not much larger than the one he had received when he began his ministerial career in New York City more than half a century earlier. It was a sad commentary on a denomination to which he had given a lifetime of service.

Student financial aid had been absolutely necessary when Universalists had established their theological school at St. Lawrence because the vast majority of students were too poor to finance their own education in its entirety. Sawyer had called attention to this when he first arrived at Tufts. This situation continued to prevail from the time the divinity school had been opened. The General Convention had first assumed the responsibility in 1865 for providing scholarships for those planning to enter the Universalist ministry and by 1870 had awarded fifty-five at $180 a year.[24] Some state conventions and local churches as well as regional organizations such as the Northwest Conference had attempted to provide funds, but the amounts varied widely and most organizations had been unable to contribute anything at all in spite of repeated requests for donations. The General Convention had been forced to reduce the aid to $160 by 1870.

Simultaneously with the reduction in financial aid the Tufts divinity school determined that need alone was not sufficient to award financial assistance, and in 1871 the requirement was added that all candidates for such aid pass an examination demonstrating adequate academic preparation. Each candidate was required also to affirm acceptance of the Winchester Profession.[25] By 1889, with theological students now in three denominational schools, the convention allocation had been reduced to $150 per student per year.[26]

The semi-autonomy of the divinity school was recognized from the very beginning. The faculty was considered to be separate from the general faculty, kept its own records, and made its recommendations for degrees directly to the trustees. Separate financial accounts of the divinity school were kept, beginning in 1897. It had its own Visiting Committee, established by the trustees when the school opened. It had its own curriculum and offered a distinctive degree. Even the academic calendar differed at first from that of the College of Letters, but was abandoned after one year. Divinity school students had their own literary club and alumni association, organized in 1873.

Sawyer complained frequently that the hoped-for financial support from the denomination was not forthcoming, and that the divinity school had no funds apart from those of the college. However, many of the monetary contributions to the institution were designed for the special use of the divinity school. The Greenwood Prize Scholarship was established in 1878–79 as the result of a bequest by Mrs. Eliza M. Greenwood, with income from $1,000 to reward excellence in oratory as determined by the faculty. The income from a gift of $500 in 1882 was provided by John Vannevar, a Universalist clergyman, to purchase books for the Department of Homiletics.[27] The Dockstader Fund (originally $6,000) was established in 1889 by George A. Dockstader of New York City to provide financial assistance to needy students. The fund, which was to be kept "in perpetuity," amounted, with subsequent gifts, to $10,000 by 1896, with income of approximately $600. The Benjamin H. Davis Scholarship was provided in 1894 for students who agreed to take the regular college course and then enroll in the divinity school.[28]

While the existence of the divinity school was being recognized by gifts earmarked for it, there were many relationships shared with the rest of the college. They operated under a common board of trustees, many of whom were themselves Universalists. Divinity school students shared the same campus, including living and dining accommodations, and used the same library facilities. The considerable holdings of the Universalist Historical Society which Sawyer had brought with him in 1869 were to a confusing extent intermixed with but greatly strengthened the inadequate resources of the college library. A separate theological collection was not provided until after space was made available in 1892 in spite of repeated requests earlier by the Visiting Committee. Students were used at first to perform library services which were minimal at best.

The desire for a separate building for the divinity school was so strong that in 1889 the students and alumni met in Boston to formulate plans to raise $60,000 for the purpose. Former President Alonzo A. Miner, who continued to serve on the board of trustees until his death in 1895, agreed that a separate building was essential. It was not so much a matter of anticipating a substantial increase in the enrollment of the divinity school as alleviating the pressure for space by other parts of the college. Further, "a wider separation of the School of Theology from the other departments of the institution [was] on many grounds greatly to be desired."[29] It was Miner himself who provided most of the money for a separate classroom and office building in 1891, with the proviso that $12,000 be raised to provide a separate dormitory for divinity school students. Both were constructed within the next year.

Miner Hall was named in honor of the individual who had contributed $40,000 for its construction, and in whose presidential administration the school had been opened. The dormitory was named for Lucius R. Paige (1802–1896), then the oldest living Universalist clergyman by date of ordination (1825).[30] Much of the credit for raising the funds for the dormitory went to President Capen and Dean Leonard. Local parishes were invited to contribute $100 each to furnish the rooms.

The cornerstone of the academic building of the divinity school was laid on 25 October 1891, and the structure was dedicated on 13 June 1892 and first occupied in September. The building included, besides classrooms and offices, space for a library, a chapel, a reception room, and a room for faculty use. There was but little at the time to be deposited in the room reserved for the library, for there were no appropriations to buy books, and the school had to continue to depend on the facilities of the college library and on donations, largely from ministerial libraries.

The year 1892–93 was notable not only for the completion of two much-needed buildings which gave the divinity school the most commodious quarters on the campus, but because, like the rest of the college, it was opened to women for the first time.[31] One of the three women admitted in 1892 was a regular student, the other two were special (part-time) students; none received a degree. One became the wife of a classmate, James D. Tillinghast, who received his BD in 1895 and became prominent as a founder and officer of the Young Peoples Christian Union (YPCU), the first national youth group in the denomination.

No one woman could claim the distinction of having received the first BD at Tufts. It was shared instead by three, all of whom were awarded degrees in 1897: Augusta Gertrude Earle, Isabella Stirling MacDuff, and Nancy Wiley Paine Smith. When the announcement was made with great fanfare that the Harvard Divinity School would be opened to women beginning in September 1955, the Universalist press observed that women had not only been admitted to the Tufts divinity school more than half a century earlier, but had received degrees as well.[32]

There were forty-four students enrolled in 1892–93, representing twelve states. When the school's twenty-fifth year had been reached, it could boast of an enrollment of forty, contrasted with the four students originally enrolled. It was many years before such a glowing picture could be painted again.

Three serious problems continued to confront the school: lack of endowment, elevating the standards of both admission and academic performance, and increasing the number of students. The enrollment after 1895 declined steadily, dropping to less than twenty annually for several years. The Visiting Committee had also detected by 1898 "a lack of spiritual earnestness in the atmosphere of the School." There were so few students occupying Paige Hall that there was talk of closing it and accommodating students in other dormitories. Instead, the dormitory was opened to non-divinity school students. The only bright spot had been the fact that, in the entering class of eight in 1900, all had college degrees or their equivalent; hence there was no need that year for a "sub-junior" class.[33] Only one new student was enrolled in 1906–1907, and in the following year the total enrollment was only nine.

Tufts officials sometimes compared notes with their sister institution at St. Lawrence to see how theological education was faring there, and usually found the same unhappy situation. In response to an inquiry from the Tufts president to President Almon Gunnison of St. Lawrence in 1910, it was discovered that the two institutions shared the same problem: There were only ten theological students enrolled at Tufts that year, while at St. Lawrence there was but one new student. This was a situation that President Hamilton considered "very serious."[34]

All kinds of explanations were offered to account for the decline. Leonard blamed the lack of enrollment on influences largely outside the denomination: The increasing secularism in American society, the failure of organized religion to adjust to new conditions, waning interest in the narrowly technical aspects of theology, and the failure of theological schools to offer a broad, humane education. An obvious cause was the increased appeal of professions other than the ministry.[35] Gunnison blamed the problem on the church itself. There was insufficient financial inducement to enter the ministry. Church janitors were being paid more than the clergy. Further, "our church is in a state of suspended animation but the suspension more in evidence than the animation."[36]

The divinity school made many attempts to broaden the scope of its training program in spite of financial difficulty. One was the offering of special courses, beginning in 1895, for those preparing as pastor's assistants or to serve as Sunday school superintendents or teachers.[37] Religious education, which comprised a major emphasis in the program up to the very end of the school, thus had a long history.

There was also a conscious effort to keep students abreast of developments outside the strictly religious field. Amos Dolbear, one of Tufts' better known scientists, delivered a series of lectures on molecular physics.[38] Leonard wanted to train future clergy to "do something besides write and preach fine sermons."[39] J. C. Snow, chairman of the Visiting Committee in 1897, applauded the establishment of a chair of Applied Christianity (Christian Ethics). "The mass of the students in the School are in preparation not for a scholastic life in the grateful quiet of academic shades, but for the stirring scenes and bustling activities of the outer world." Opportunity for benevolences in Boston was abundant for providing practical work experience. Lucius M. Bristol was the first to be appointed to the new chair, in 1910, and served for four years. Offerings in the field of Applied Christianity were augmented between 1911 and 1913 by the appointment of Adolph A. Berle.

Leonard suggested training in settlement house work and courses in what was then the new academic discipline of sociology. President Capen also offered a course in Political Economy required of all divinity school students. New courses in parish administration and "The Application of Psychology to the Work of the Christian Ministry" were added in 1907–1908.[40]

Hamilton, who had assumed office in 1905 as the last Universalist clergyman to occupy the Tufts presidency, promoted the idea of introducing one or more courses in what a later generation would call psychotherapy and psychosomatic medicine.[41] He recommended in 1908 a course open only to divinity school students, with the basic course in psychology as a prerequisite. Some of the trustees were dubious about such a new-fangled idea, but approved it by an 8 to 7 vote.[42] The students commuted to the Tufts Medical School in Boston twice a week to attend the lectures of Morton Prince, and spent part of a day in a clinic at the Boston City Hospital.

The problem of establishing an endowment had dogged the divinity school from the start, and was aggravated by declining enrollment. A few special funds had been received up to 1900, but even when totalled up, were not adequate to meet the expenses of the school. A bequest of $60,000 from Mary Goddard in 1899 had helped somewhat, but half of it was earmarked for the use of the College of Letters, and the principal could not be touched.[43] The burden of operating the school was "causing a permanent disablement of the other departments."[44] More than half the operating loss of the college in 1899–1900 was attributed to the divinity school.

The first sizable endowment came in 1906, the gift of Albert Crane of the Class of 1863, as a memorial to his father Thomas, a Tufts trustee from 1852 until his death in 1875, and a close friend of Sawyer. The $100,000 benefaction was immediately accepted by the trustees and the suggestion was promptly made that the divinity school be named in honor of the father as the Crane Theological School.[45] The son agreed. The gift, welcome as it was, only alleviated rather than solved the financial problem, for the entire college was experiencing one of its most serious economic downturns. It was estimated that at least another $100,000 was required to make the newly designated Crane School self-supporting.[46]

The matter of admission standards also continued to be a serious problem. In 1876, only one year after Capen had become president of Tufts, he was disturbed to discover that, of the eleven students who had entered in 1876–87, not one was a college graduate.[47] There had been no graduates at all in 1874 because the students themselves had found the work so demanding and their academic background so deficient that they had petitioned that the course of study be extended from three to four years.[48] Capen was very much afraid that the academic standards and reputation of the entire college would suffer when it undertook "to give a second degree to those who could not take a first degree."

The college was trapped in the dilemma of maintaining standards and at the same time meeting the demands of the denomination for a greatly increased ministerial supply. The problem was at least partially solved in 1903, when a new combined degree program was introduced which made it possible for a student to secure both the AB and BD degrees in five years, done at Capen's insistence.[49] The number of AB degree holders in the divinity school always remained small, partly because, until 1913, students were expected to have studied Greek as undergraduates. During the transition period, five of the fifteen theological students then enrolled were under the old program; seven were enrolled in the new program; and three were already AB degree holders.

The combined degree program, with one brief interlude, remained an acceptable and popular route for half a century, with only superficial changes; it was not until after 1953 that the decision was made to turn the Crane School into an (almost) exclusively graduate division. Under the combined degree program the students were required, in theory at least, to meet the admission standards of the College of Letters and complete four years of undergraduate work.

The new curriculum was hailed as ushering in a new era for the divinity school. Closer integration than had ever existed between it and the regular college students was now assured, and Capen's ideal, shared by Leonard, of breaking down departmental barriers, was nearer to achievement. Crane School courses were to be open to other students as well.[50] There were other advantages. Not only would the new program articulate more closely with the rest of the college, but it would turn a higher proportion of prospective clergy into college-educated individuals. Theological students would receive a much broadened preparation and eliminate or minimize overlapping and duplication of course offerings in such fields as philosophy and psychology. At the same time, a distinctive program for ministerial candidates would be provided during the fifth year. The shortening of time between receipt of the AB and the divinity degree would also be accomplished, thus meeting more fully the insistent denominational demands for a formally educated clergy.[51]

In spite of administrative shifts and a temporary increase in enrollment, however, the Crane School was faring badly. Hamilton called the student body "pitiably small," and with much justification. There was not a single student in the class scheduled to enter in 1911. The school continued to be a financial burden in spite of the Crane gift and other smaller benefactions. The five-year combined course had to be extended one year in 1907 because students could not complete the shorter program satisfactorily.[52] Only one new professorship (the chair of Hebrew and Old Testament Exegesis) had been created by 1910, the first in many years. It was for ten years held by Hinckley G. Mitchell, who had been expelled from the faculty of Boston University for holding allegedly "heretical" ideas. The Woodbridge Professorship was vacant after the incumbent had resigned.[53] Dean Leonard was more than ready for retirement, after forty-one years of continuous service, and Knight, who had been on the faculty since 1875, was seriously ill.[54]

The trustees reviewed the situation and authorized the use of part-time faculty to fill in the gaps. Henry I. Cushman was employed as Instructor in Homiletics and Pastoral Care to replace Leonard, and served for a decade. President Hamilton himself agreed to do the administrative work until a successor to Dean Leonard could be found.[55] A committee was appointed to confer with officers of the Universalist Church about the whole future of the school, and suggestions were solicited.[56]

Frank Oliver Hall, a divinity school alumnus (1863), a trustee of the Canton Theological School, and a clergyman prominent in the denomination who was to serve later on the Crane faculty, suggested consolidation of the three denominational theological schools as the best long-range solution.[57] His plan was to close the schools at both St. Lawrence and Lombard and consolidate them with the Crane School at Tufts. The idea of concentrating three schools into one was shared by many others. Cushman recommended that all Protestant theological schools in New England be "coordinated under one management," with Harvard as the natural centerpiece.[58] In 1910 President Gunnison of St. Lawrence noted that one school could easily take care of Universalist students, and that attempting to operate three was the height of financial foolishness. "But we have our endowments and traditions and any attempt at consolidation would be regarded as high treason."[59]

President Hamilton was torn between conflicting problems by 1912. The attempt to keep the men and women segregated at Tufts, which meant duplicate classes, staff, and other facilities, together with the depressed state of the national economy and the state of college investments following the financial panic of 1907, brought the institution close to

Frank Oliver Hall, Professor of Homiletics at the Crane Theological School, 1919-1929

financial disaster. Endowment funds had to be used to meet operating deficits, and considerable property bordering the college buildings had to be sold to meet expenses. The continuing problems of the Crane School bore heavily, exacerbated by constant complaints from Universalists about the low caliber of the student body and the poor quality of the ministers being produced.[60] Hamilton thoroughly agreed with the negative assessment and came close to losing his temper over the sad state of affairs.

The theological school, in Hamilton's view, was being "crushed" by the weight of the college and at the same time was collapsing internally. "A great many of the Theological students are looked down upon by the academic students, and they deserve the contempt they get. It is not because they are theological students. It is because they are weak, badly prepared, hampered by personal peculiarities which do not commend them to healthy minded young men, and coddled through their classes by a Faculty which cannot bear to lose a student, and has unlimited time to devote to lame ducks. It is openly said by the other students that nobody ever failed a course in the Theological School, no matter how much of a duffer he was."[61]

There were only thirty students in the three denominational theological schools in 1911. Of the ten at Tufts only one was a college graduate and four did not have even high school diplomas and had to be admitted as special students. By 1912 the school had reached its lowest ebb in point of numbers, and Hamilton seriously considered closing it but was deterred by Bisbee, editor of the *Leader,* and Harold Marshall, business manager of the Universalist Publishing House.[62] One factor which probably influenced Hamilton in his plan to close the school had been the news that possible merger of the three Universalist theological schools was to be discussed at the Massachusetts Convention.[63]

Hamilton, in spite of all of his criticisms of the school, was reluctant to close it. No one could really entertain such an idea. "We remember... that the School is intimately related to the original purpose of the founders of the College, and that its graduates have been among its most active, enthusiastic and efficient supporters. If the influence of the Universalist ministry were withdrawn the College would suffer severely."[64]

Only a few weeks after he had made his uncomplimentary remarks about the Crane students in 1911 and had lambasted them for their deficiencies, Hamilton submitted his resignation — frustrated, unpopular, and completely discouraged — and left the problems of the college for others to solve.

One of Hamilton's last acts before he left office was to invite, on the urging of Crane School alumni, Lee Sullivan McCollester (1859–1943) to become the dean. The man chosen to succeed Leonard was an alumnus of Tufts and of the divinity school, having received an AB in 1881 and his BD in 1884. McCollester was born in Westmoreland, New Hampshire, on 5 June 1859, in the community where his father was then the minister of the Universalist church. After attending Melrose Seminary in Brattleboro, Vermont, and doing college preparatory work in Nashua, New Hampshire, he had started his college career at Buchtel, where his father was serving as president. The son transferred to Tufts at the end of his sophomore year. After serving his first pastorate in Claremont, New Hampshire, he accepted a call from the Church of Our Father in Detroit. He had served there with distinction for twenty-three years before accepting the Crane deanship in 1912.

During his busy career he also served in many denominational capacities, including membership on the trustees of the General Convention (1906–23), of which he was chairman for twelve years, and president of the General Convention for four. Even before his appointment as dean he had received an honorary STD from Tufts (1899), as well as similar degrees from other denominational schools, and served as librarian of the Universalist Historical Society.

McCollester hesitated before accepting the deanship. He held an eminently successful and well-paid post in a large urban church noted for its community and social service work, and had become well acquainted with Henry Ford, the automobile magnate. He was reluctant to take on a new set of responsibilities for a theological school with a depleted staff, four students, and an uncertain future.

McCollester accepted the challenge nonetheless, after assessing the potentialities of the school and after heeding the importuning of alumni. He made it very clear, however, that he would accept only under certain conditions on which he would not compromise. He was to have a completely free hand to carry out any policies he considered essential to the rehabilitation of the school within the limited financial resources available. He was to have freedom from outside work in the denomination to recruit students, create an interest in both the school and the ministry, and to assist churches whenever called upon. He refused to be only "a recluse teacher of theology."

Hamilton and the trustees accepted the conditions set down by McCollester, but the president laid down two of his own. The Crane School was to remain on the Tufts campus, and it was not to be merged with any other institution.[65]

The new dean immediately set to work, and in his first annual report announced that he had been planning a new program to be made public the following year. The changes that he contemplated would, he told the trustees, give the Crane School "a new place among professional schools in the training of men for efficient religious leadership."[66] He had confidently pledged upon becoming dean that only those "with full college training" would be admitted, and announced the suspension of the combined degree program.[67] But he soon discovered that very few could meet the collegiate requirement, so he promptly restored the combined program and encouraged students to work at least for the AB before undertaking graduate work. Parish and social settlement involvement were emphasized in the final year.

Two revised curricula were introduced in 1913–14 — one for undergraduates and one for graduates; both emphasized the practical rather than the strictly academic. As stated in the catalogue that year, they were intended "to turn out, not men distinguished for varied and curious learning, but men thoroughly informed as to the problems of the hour, in sympathetic touch with modern needs, trained and equipped for moral and religious leadership in the seething life about us." In the three-year course for college graduates substitutions were allowed for the traditional Greek or Hebrew. The undergraduate BD course was to be five years, with increased emphasis on strictly professional subjects.

McCollester, in his own thinking, attempted to instill in students a conception that the church's primary mission was to deal "with the problems of the souls of man." The social responsibilities of the church were not to be neglected, but neither were they to be unduly stressed. There should be a balance.

For several years the school experimented with variations in the undergraduate degree program in which the great majority of the students were enrolled. The old AB-BD course became a six-year program, with the first year designated as a "try-out" or "professional guidance" period. An aggressive recruitment campaign announced in 1913 increased the enrollment only slightly. There were fifteen students registerd on the eve of World War I; then in the years immediately after 1916 the school almost disappeared.

Hermon C. Bumpus, former business manager of the University of Wisconsin, had been recruited for the Tufts presidency in 1914 in an attempt to dredge the institution out of its financial morass. He was the first chief executive officer, either lay or clerical, who had not been a Universalist.[68] He at first accepted the Crane School as part of the institution but became increasingly disenchanted with it because it harbored on its faculty Clarence R. Skinner, who had been appointed in 1914 and was an openly avowed and uncompromising pacifist.

Bumpus was an ardent supporter of American involvement in World War I and spent part of his time in Washington aiding the war effort. He was primarily responsible for the installation on the campus of a unit of the Student Army Training Corps (SATC). He was so caught up in the fear of a German invasion of New England that he armed the male students with Indian clubs borrowed from the college gymnasium to ward off possible attacks by spies and saboteurs. Bumpus considered Skinner a subversive character, and relations between the president and Dean McCollester became strained because of Skinner's presence. The latter was quite aware of Bumpus' perturbation. In a friendly letter to the president written just a few months after the United States declared war on Germany, Skinner expressed hope that Bumpus could get some relaxation from college cares and responsibilities. "I doubt not that I have been one of these causes of worry," and signed the letter "your pacifist friend."[69]

The Crane student body was badly depleted by the war. Although entitled to exemption from conscription, several insisted on serving as chaplains, in the YMCA, in the ambulance corps, or in the Red Cross.[70] The school survived largely through the determined efforts of the dean, who held classes in the living room of his home after the theological facilities had been assigned to military units during the war. The handful of students dispossessed from Paige Hall lived, appropriately, in the home once occupied by Leonard, the second dean of the school. Plans for expansion had to be postponed until the mid-1920s, when renewed hope for an enlarged school, both in numbers and in buildings, could be made into a reality. Tufts' first professional school had by World War I become its feeblest, even though McCollester had done his best to adjust to circumstances largely beyond his control.

The theological school returned to peacetime conditions after 1919 with hope and confidence for the future. Until McCollester's retirement in 1932 the school under his leadership not only survived the war but grew and prospered, comparatively speaking. The enrollment had grown to twenty-four in the fall of 1923 — the largest since he had taken up his duties in 1912. Relations with the rest of the institution had become so close that the school was in reality, as described in its literature, "a department of Tufts." The instructional staff taught some classes open to all students, and a few of the faculty of the School of Arts and Sciences such as William F. Wyatt, chairman of the Department of Greek, offered special courses for the benefit of Crane students. J. A. C. Fagginger Auer was added to the Crane faculty in 1923–24 as Professor of Church History and Philosophy of Religion, and also taught in the Department of Modern Languages in the School of Liberal Arts. Bruce W. Brotherston, who resigned from the St. Lawrence faculty to join the Tufts staff in 1930, taught courses in philosophy in both the theological school and the college.

Identification with Tufts became even closer in 1925 with the redesignation of Crane as the "Tufts School of Religion, Crane Theological School."[71] The change had come after an alumni conference in the fall of 1924 and the Visiting Committee had recommended it.[72] President Cousens also favored the change of name as a formal recognition of close relations. The growing emphasis on social service work and on religious education also made a more comprehensive description than "theological" appropriate.[73] Offerings in religious education were greatly expanded when John M. Ratcliff joined the faculty in the fall of 1927.

Students from denominations other than Universalist had begun to appear in the school in appreciable numbers by 1926. Although most of those enrolled in 1928–29 intended to enter the Universalist ministry, several were preparing for Unitarian assignments. There was one student each intending to enter the Episcopal, Methodist, and Congregational ministry. By the 1930s Baptists and Quakers were added to the list. As of 1943, twelve Episcopalians were known to have attended Crane.[74] This tendency to deemphasize denominationalism became even more evident after Skinner succeeded to the deanship. In many instances in the later history of the school Universalists actually found themselves a minority in the student body. More and more Unitarians attended the school, and Skinner's relations with that denomination were even more cordial than those of his predecessor. In 1942 Skinner received a letter of commendation for his work from Crane alumni who had entered the Unitarian ministry.[75]

Housing for the Crane School and its students was a sore point for many years after World War I, for Miner and Paige Halls were diverted to other uses when the college was turned over largely to military purposes and were not returned to the school after the war. The school headquarters remained in Packard Hall until 1927 and in the mid-twenties Paige Hall became temporarily a women's dormitory. Male Crane students were housed in Dean Hall, on the western edge of the campus.

Both the dean and the Visiting Committee to Crane were strongly in favor of having a new building constructed for the exclusive use of the school.[76] Instead of a new building, the School of Religion received, between 1927 and 1929, the first floor of a renovated Miner Hall, a chapel attached to Paige Hall, and an arcade connecting the two main buildings. The addition of the wing housing the Crane Chapel made possible the utilization of the ground floor for the theological library which had been housed in Packard. The dean had earlier proposed that the theological collection be located in the main college library and that no distinction be made in the rules governing the use of books. This was another expression of the fact that Crane was an intimate part of the college.

The School of Religion, housed in rehabilitated and enlarged quarters, and appealing increasingly to individuals outside the denomination, prospered in the 1920s under McCollester's leadership. The enrollment had climbed to thirty-six by 1928-29, and it was not considered necessary to raise tuition for new students (from $250 to $300) until 1931.[77] The makeup of the faculty underwent but few changes. In 1931 Alfred S. Cole replaced Frank Oliver Hall in the Department of Homiletics, and remained on the faculty for a quarter of a century. Relations with the School of Liberal Arts remained generally satisfactory, although the Crane faculty, after reviewing its own curriculum, found that there were still areas of pre-ministerial preparation at the undergraduate level that needed more attention than was possible by adhering strictly to the AB requirements. Consideration was given in 1928-29 to creating a distinctive undergraduate degree (PhB) for the Crane School's undergraduates, while continuing to award the STB for those completing the professional course.

With an eye toward strengthening the work of the school in new directions and developing new programs, the trustees created the office of vice-dean in 1929, on McCollester's recommendation, and elected

Dean McCollester at his New Hampshire farm

Skinner to the new post.[78] The dean left no doubt that he was grooming the new vice-dean to take his place eventually, and Cousens added his blessing by noting that the elevation of Skinner was "wise and necessary and desirable."[79] An affiliation was also worked out in 1930 with the Harvard Divinity School which enabled Crane students to take courses there without charge.[80]

McCollester considered his work done by 1931 and was ready to retire from the deanship at the age of seventy-three. But President Cousens, who was a close personal friend as well as a congenial and supportive colleague, would not hear of it. So the dean repeated his request a year later, and this time it was honored.[81] But the retired dean by no means severed his connection with the institution. It was to last until after 1940. He retained the title of Professor of Religious Literature and the post of college chaplain which he had held since 1919. He was granted a six-month leave of absence by the trustees at full salary in 1937, and two years later his eightieth birthday was recognized by a testimonial dinner at the Wayside Inn, in the restoration of which his friend Henry Ford had taken a special interest. McCollester continued to lecture to the entire Tufts community in his popular course on the English and Hebrew Bible as Literature until 1941, when the infirmities of age made it impossible for him to continue.[82] Rolland Emerson Wolfe, who had joined the Crane faculty in 1934, taught McCollester's courses in Biblical Literature in the school, including those concerned with the Old Testament. He remained on the faculty until 1946.

Dean McCollester could retire with a feeling of great satisfaction for his contributions to both the theological school and the college. A man of warmth, friendliness, and attractive personality, he had rescued the Crane School from threatened oblivion and had made it an increasingly respected and important part of the Tufts community both academically and in terms of brick and mortar. He had, in his own words, "paid his way."[83] The enrollment had increased during his administration from four students in makeshift quarters to forty-five, housed in buildings intended for them. The outlook for the school looked bright indeed.

Among MCollester's accomplishments in the physical realm was the acquisition of funds to construct the Fischer Arcade connecting Miner and Paige Halls and to provide the new wing for Paige Hall.[84] Before the new wing was constructed McCollester had spent an entire summer in the British Isles studying church architecture. The design of the Crane Chapel edifice was an adaptation of a building in Oxford, and the oak paneling was cut from the Warwich Forest in England.

The entire building complex, both new and rehabilitated, was dedicated in June 1930. By 1929 about thirty-five Unitarian clergy had received their theological education at Crane. As their contribution to the improvement of the physical facilities, twenty of those then living in the Greater Boston area donated the furnishings for a suite in Paige Hall known as the Channing Room for the use of visiting Unitarian ministers and lecturers.[85]

A flight of fifty-five steps leading from the street had also been added. They were financed from sources other than from Crane, and commemorated those associated with the institution whose lives had been lost in wars. The memorial steps thus completed the much-photographed official front entrance to the college.

In recognition of McCollester's services to Tufts the school created the Lee S. McCollester Professorship of Biblical Literature, with the individual so honored as the first incumbent. It had been proposed by Dean Skinner and approved by the trustees in 1935.[86] The professorship was intended to serve the entire institution and to promote and sustain interest in the literature of both the Hebrew and Christian traditions — fields which were McCollester's special province and were considered indispensable to a liberal education. The original intent had been to raise a fund of $100,000 in time for the Commencement season in 1937. This goal proved to be utterly unrealistic; even the greatly reduced target of

The Crane Theological School complex. The Fischer Arcade, flanked by Miner and Paige Halls and the Crane Chapel

$20,000 by June 1938 proved to be completely unattainable, only $13,000 having been raised by January of that year. The intervention of the Great Depression, followed by another world war, meant one frustration after another before sufficient funds were provided.

If enrollment had been the sole criterion, the Tufts School of Religion would have been experiencing a period of unprecedented prosperity when Carmichael became president of the college in 1938. There were sixty students enrolled in Crane in 1937-38, the largest number in the history of the school up to that time and a dramatic reversal of a previous sharp decline. The trustee executive committee even considered the advisability of curtailing enrollment.[87] At the same time, denominational representation in the student body had continued to broaden. Of the forty-five students registered in 1935, twenty-eight were Universalists or Unitarians; five other denominations were represented.[88] In 1942 individuals from seven different religious bodies were enrolled, including one individual of the Greek Orthodox faith.[89] This was quite in harmony with Dean Skinner's desire to promote a universal religion that excluded no one.

President Carmichael viewed the school with a much less enthusiastic eye than did some of its supporters, and found it deficient in several respects. It posed a continuing financial problem for the college, and in 1939 the president told the trustees that the school involved "a deficit which may be inconsistent with its accomplishment." He was also critical of the curriculum, and called for increased attention to "scientific social work" and similar "technical studies." His most serious doubt concerned the continued admission of undergraduates to the school. He might have noted also, as did the Visiting Committee in the fall of 1937, that although eight faculty members were teaching in the school, in that year there was only one who was actually full-time, and four were teaching half-time in the School of Liberal Arts.[90]

The School of Religion fared as well as did other parts of the institution during World War II. It followed the rest of Tufts in switching to a three-semester program, beginning in July 1943, which meant in effect year-round operation. In contrast to the World War I period, tensions between the school and the rest of the institution were notably absent. Although enrollment was somewhat depleted, the school emerged from the war period in much better condition than in 1919.[91]

Theological students were deferred from military service by law, although about one-fourth of those at Crane left their studies to volunteer in some capacity. Paige Hall was taken over by the Navy and the remaining Crane students were housed temporarily in a residence adjacent to the campus.[92] During and immediately after the war the school's greatest losses were in the faculty. Dean Emeritus McCollester died, and Bruce Brotherston, who taught half-time in the school, retired. The Crane Alumni Association petitioned the Tufts trustees not only to fill the vacancies as promptly as possible but to secure individuals who could serve Crane exclusively and preferably on a full-time basis.[93] The Association also outlined for the trustees their suggested qualifications for a new dean to replace Skinner, who had announced his retirement as of 1945. He was to be, above all, a Universalist.[94] In spite of repeated efforts to retain his services, Rolland E. Wolfe resigned to accept a position elsewhere. After Cole temporarily replaced Skinner as acting dean, Ratcliff was elected dean.

The school emerged in 1945 from the war period with thirty-four students, but with only one full-time faculty member and one serving half-time. The three remaining faculty gave but a single course each. The McCollester Professorship, the funds for which had still not been fully raised, remained unfilled, and the school was farther than ever from meeting the standards of minimum staff strength established by the American Association of Theological Schools, which required at least four full-time faculty for accreditation.[95] The situation was little better four years later. The school commenced the academic year 1949-50 with thirty-eight students, and Eugene S. Ashton, who had joined the faculty in 1947 as Associate Professor of Biblical Literature, had been appointed to the McCollester chair. By then, only $26,000 of the proposed $100,000 had been raised to finance it.[96] He and Dean Ratcliff still comprised the only full-time faculty. The school had seldom operated with so small a full-time staff.[97]

The curriculum was kept at a respectable level during Dean Ratcliff's tenure only by the expedient of using part-time faculty to offer courses in alternate years. Among those with the longest such association and who contributed greatly to it were J. A. C. Fagginger Auer, who served as Professor of Church History from 1924 until his retirement thirty years later, and Rabbi Beryl D. Cohon, a Visiting Lecturer secured through the

Lee S. McCollester and Clarence R. Skinner, Deans of the Crane Theological School (1912-1933 and 1933-1945, respectively)

Jewish Chautauqua Society, who taught from 1947 through 1961. Students were beginning to desert the school because it had so few faculty and such meager course offerings. Ironically, one of the reasons was the renewal in 1943 of the cooperative arrangement with the Harvard Divinity School made in 1933, whereby Crane students maintaining a high academic average could take without charge two courses there.[98] When some of the Crane students saw the opportunities at Harvard they transferred.

The school even lost the residence facilities for its students when Paige Hall, to have been returned to it after the war, became a women's dormitory in 1946 and was not again made available for theological students until 1954. Until then, dormitory accommodations were provided for the displaced Crane men in Fletcher Hall. University housing for neither female nor married theological students was ever provided in spite of repeated requests.

Only one systematic study is known to have been made of the alumni of the School of Religion.[99] Although intended primarily to measure the adequacy of the curriculum to meet ministerial needs, the elaborate questionnaire, which had the blessing of Dean Skinner and involved several faculty members in an advisory capacity, garnered much additional information regarding the educational and vocational background, salaries, initial placement, and other data for graduates between 1921 and

1940. Of the sixty-six questionnaires distributed, twenty-seven were returned.

Average initial salaries were $1,700 by 1940, and the average peak salary during initial pastorates was $2,000. Most still active in the ministry had improved their salaries by 1941 to an average of $2,200, representing improvement not only within the profession, but for over half of the respondents, higher economic status compared to their earlier employment. None went very far afield. Only two of the twenty-seven first settled outside New England; the greatest concentration was in Massachusetts. Half the respondents had been gainfully employed for an average of five years prior to their enrollment in the school. In terms of educational level, eight had only high school diplomas upon entrance, and less than half engaged in formal advanced study after graduation from theological school.

The author of the study, after a review of the publication records of the graduates, came to the rueful conclusion that they had "little flair for writing, much less serious research." The evidence seemed to be clear that the Tufts school was serving best as a training facility for the "practical ministry," although even there some gaps existed if the questionnaire responses were to be believed.

Ideologically and politically, the respondents revealed a wide spectrum of belief and allegiance. Several listed themselves as "Independents" and nine favored socialism or had socialist leanings, while the majority of the parishes to which they ministered were Republican and basically conservative. Theological diversity was the keynote among the graduates, with several gradations between deistic-theistic and humanist; none listed themselves as atheists.[100] Half of the respondents listed themselves as deists/theists, and two as "deistic, humanistic theist." No one could claim that the Tufts School of Religion turned out identical assembly-line products.

In the fall of 1952 the trustee executive committee approved a set of revised degree requirements for the combined AB-STB program of the school. They went even farther by requiring the completion of a four-year undergraduate degree for admission to the BD program.[101] Ratcliff did not live to see the working out of the new scheme, for death cut short his career on 23 February 1953, a few weeks after Carmichael had departed to take over the secretaryship of the Smithsonian Institution in Washington, D.C. Ashton, an ordained Congregational minister, continued as college chaplain and served as acting dean until a successor to Ratcliff could be chosen.[102] When this was accomplished, Ashton was appointed chairman of the undergraduate Department of Religion and ceased his administrative responsibilities and faculty status in Crane. It was left to the new head of the school to see if a successful transition could be made to the status of a full-fledged graduate operation.

The identity of the individual selected to succeed Ratcliff in September 1954 was revealed at Commencement that year by President Wessell. He was Benjamin Butler Hersey (1903-1971), a native of Salem, Massachusetts, born 19 March 1903, and a graduate both of Tufts (BS) and its School of Religion (STB) in 1935. While a special (part-time) student he had defrayed part of his expenses by working as a fireman on the Boston-to-Portland run of the Boston and Maine Railroad. By economic necessity the work for the combined degree had to be extended from six years to ten.

Hersey had had extensive experience as a parish minister, and had served his first pastorate (1929-34) in the village church at Annisquam, Massachusetts, where he was ordained in 1931 while still a student. Between 1935 and 1943 he occupied the pulpit of the Congress Square Universalist Church in Portland, Maine. It was a church beset with many problems, and Hersey in effect rebuilt its membership, morale, and finances. While there he served as chaplain of Westbrook Junior College, which had been founded by Universalists as an academy in the nineteenth century, and as faculty lecturer at the Maine General Hospital School of Nursing.

His ministry between the time of his installation as pastor of the Church of the Divine Paternity in New York City in January 1944 and his departure for Tufts in 1954 was likewise exceptionally constructive, serving it as he did in much of the difficult war period and its aftermath. His work was recognized by his *alma mater* in 1944, when he received an honorary DD. His wife, Laura Ruth Smith Hersey, an alumna of Jackson College (Tufts) in 1926, was president of the AUW in the year of her husband's choice as dean and as Professor of Ministerial Practice. He became the Woodbridge Professor of Applied Christianity in 1958.

Hersey, like his wife, had held several offices in the denomination. He had been president of the national denominational youth fellowship (1936-39), and had served two terms as a UCA trustee (1943-51) as well as on the board of the New York Convention, of which he was both a trustee and president from 1948 to 1952. With a record of solid if not spectacular accomplishment before his appointment to the deanship, he was destined to be the last to hold that position in the history of the school.

On the eve of Hersey's election to the deanship, Acting Dean Ashton made a study of the school and submitted it for the information of Acting President Nils Y. Wessell. Ashton reported that it was "not in a particularly healthy state."[103] The curriculum was neither fish nor fowl, attempting as it did to serve as an undergraduate department of religion as well as a professional graduate training facility. It had consistently failed to satisfy the first four of the nine standards established by the American Association of Theological School for accreditation.

The basic minima to which the Crane School aspired were: Exclusively graduate-level instruction; i.e., all degree candidates were to possess a bachelor's degree at the time of admission; adequate instruction to be provided in at least four fields, with a total of no less than four full-time faculty; and an adequate library. When Ashton made his report in 1953, not one of the requirements had been met by Crane, although plans were under way with the tacit approval of the trustees to meet all of them.

Income from endowment could not support even two full-time faculty. The alternative was to close out Crane as a degree-granting institution and substitute for it a department of religion which would serve as an undergraduate service agency, and would include the chaplain's office; or embark on a program of "purposeful expansion" to fulfill Crane's potential. Following the latter course would take both determination and money. Of the six entering students in 1953-54 all but one were receiving financial aid, and this constant drain on resources had somehow to be reduced if not eliminated.

The decision to make the transition to an exclusively graduate school and to create a separate undergraduate department of religion coincided with Hersey's arrival on campus in 1954. No first-year pre-theological undergraduates were admitted in the fall of 1954. The six-year combined AB-STB program was to be eliminated by 1960, and earlier if possible, provided undergraduates then registered in the program elected to take the seven-year course leading to the BD. There were twice as many graduates in the student body (fourteen) in 1954 as in the previous year, and eight of the entering students in 1954 were BD candidates, four of them Tufts graduates. Of the total enrollment of thirty-one in 1954-55, seventeen were undergraduates.

President Wessell told the trustees triumphantly in 1956 that, at long last, a "fundamental change" in the character of the Crane School had taken place. It would not only operate entirely on a graduate level and in this way would approach national standards in theological education, but could now concentrate its pesonnel and resources "within more carefully defined and more appropriate limits." For the first time that anyone could remember, not a single one of the twenty-five students enrolled in 1956 was simultaneously registered in the undergraduate School of Liberal Arts. Perhaps the awkward (and sometimes embarrassing) combined degree program was to be a thing of the past. Although the conversion to graduate status was being accomplished by 1956, Provost Mead called attention to other pressing needs. More generous financial support and accreditation were both "essential for survival."[104]

Three years after his appointment as dean, Hersey made a progress report to the Tufts president. The prospects were encouraging but far from bright. Prior to 1954, graduates of Crane had been awarded the STB after completion of a six-year course of combined undergraduate and graduate study. The transition to a graduate school had been largely completed by 1957, and the BD was being awarded for completion of three years of study beyond the undergraduate level. Six such students had been enrolled in 1954. The total number of full-time students had risen to twenty-two by 1957, and the number of course offerings had grown from twenty-one to twenty-eight. The library, which had received special attention, was being used more extensively than ever before.[105]

But raising the school to accreditable standards had not yet been achieved. The goal of adding one new full-time faculty member each year until the minimum of four had been reached, had not yet been attained. Two such appointments had been made by 1956 but the unexpected resignation of one in the spring of 1957 had again reduced the number of full-time faculty to one, plus the dean, with five teaching part-time. Hersey thought that, under the circumstances, two full-time appointments in 1958 were necessary, and an additional one by 1959. It was essential that the school offer educational facilities at least equal to those of other theological schools.

Dean Hersey took pride in the fact that all of the eight new students admitted in 1957 possessed bachelor's degrees; none was from Tufts that year.[106] Of the twenty-four students, Unitarians outnumbered Universalists three to one, and the great majority of the student body continued to come from New England. The dean continued the policies of his predecessors in admitting students from all denominations intereted in liberal religion.[107] Enrollment in the 1950s continued to remain fairly constant at between twenty and thirty. The basically non-denominational admissions policy encouraged by Hersey was fully supported by President Wessell. It was reinforced by a glance at the makeup of the Crane student body in 1954-55; of the thirty-one students, eleven were Universalists, twelve were Unitarians, six were Congregational, and one each were Presbyterian and Episcopal.

Another opportunity for inventorying the school in terms of its needs came between 1956 and 1958 with an intensive and extensive self-study of Tufts financed by a grant from the Carnegie Corporation.[108] The self-study brought forth a dreary and all-too-familiar recital of deficiencies and weaknesses. In curricula, supervised field work was "non-existent" although listed in the catalogue. Clinical training in general and mental hospitals was inadequate. There were no courses in religious art, and insufficient use was being made of university resources such as the Graduate School for elective courses. Offerings were "grossly inadequate" in such fields as Applied Christianity, Philosophy of Religion, and theology. Twenty-eight semester courses were being offered in eight fields, taught by the dean, one full-time faculty member of professorial rank and five others who served only part-time.

In order of priority the three most urgent needs were accreditation, an augmented full-time faculty, and a more adequate library. Two representatives of the American Association of Theological Schools had made a three-day visit the very year the self-study was completed, and the school was informed that the minimum number of full-time faculty required for accreditation had been raised from four to six, that the same individual could not teach courses in both Old and New Testament, and that part-time faculty could not be totalled up and counted as full-time equivalents.

Very few of the part-time faculty taught for more than a year or even more than one semester. The turnover was frequent even among those who became full-time, as did Charles S. Milligan, who was employed in 1956 as Associate Professor of Philosophy and Theology after serving briefly on a part-time basis; he departed after one year. Howard E. Hunter, who was the only full-time, tenured faculty member when the school closed, started out as a part-time instructor and was made full-time in 1958; he resigned in 1961 but returned later. The goal of six full-time faculty was almost achieved in 1959, but the school was still one member short. The number was certainly more than sufficient for a student body of only twenty-three that year.[109] Many of the faculty, such as Gene A. Reeves, who was hired in 1962, were themselves working on advanced degrees; he was a doctoral candidate at Emory University at the time of his employment at Crane.

Great strides had been made in providing more adequate theological library materials and service with the employment of Alan Seaburg, a Tufts alumnus who had earned his BD in 1957 and subsequently a library degree at another institution. He divided his time between the Crane library and various bibliographical projects under the supervision of the university librarian. The accreditation team recommended a full-time librarian with faculty status and a greatly increased budget for library materials. An annual expenditure of at least $3,200 was specified, while only $750 was budgeted for Crane in 1958. The book and periodicals budget was increased to $1,100 the next year, but was still far from adequate. The collection comprised about 7,000 volumes, exclusive of the holdings of the Universalist Historical Society which were slowly being catalogued with part-time aid. Much distance had to be traversed before Crane met all of the specifications, but by 1960 the school had complied with recommended standards of admission, length of training, requirements for graduation, and balance of curriculum.

The school extended the scope of its activities in the late 1950s and into the 1960s with several special programs and institutes. In 1959 it hosted a successful colloquium on science and religion which attracted widespread attention, and in the fall of 1963 had held a conference on the ministry attended by forty clergy.[110] Ministerial education was the subject of a meeting of the sixteen district executives of the UUA held at Tufts in 1965 to which all theological faculty were invited.[111]

On the recommendation of Dean Hersey the trustees approved two new Crane degrees in 1961: A three-year program leading to a BD in Religious Education, and a two-year Master of Religious Education program.[112] A new faculty member, R. John Waka, was employed to offer courses leading to the new degrees.[113] The primary purpose was to attract more students by offering enlarged opportunities. But the effort had no positive effect whatever on enrollment. In fact, the school experienced what the president called an "alarming" drop of degree candidates in the next four years (from thirty in 1960 to a low of seventeen in 1964). He warned the trustees that the future status and role of the Crane School had to be a matter of "careful scrutiny."[114]

Wessell had already (in 1963) forewarned them that denominational policy might call for the merger of Crane with a theological school such as Meadville/Lombard in Chicago. The question of what Tufts could do most appropriately for theological education needed reexamination. The most promising possibility that he saw was to bring Crane "into a close and intimate relationship of some kind with the Graduate School of Arts and Sciences." Besides raising standards, such a relationship would enhance academic opportunities, especially for those interested in the Universalist and Unitarian ministry, by giving them increased access to graduate-level courses in such fields as psychology, sociology, economics, and education. Prospective clergy could therefore have the best of both worlds — professional training and opportunity for a liberal arts education offered by the university.

One result of this policy was the reunion of the Crane faculty with the Tufts Faculty of Arts and Sciences; the theological school faculty had disassociated itself in 1962 and reported directly to the trustees. The original intent had been to elevate Crane to the rank of a separate professional graduate school.[115] However, the Crane faculty had soon realized that the school did not have the resources to lead even a quasi-independent existence. Rejoining the combined faculties was accomplished in 1965, when the new program was instituted. It called for increased involvement of university faculty in the instruction of Crane students, so the step was a logical one.

After denominational consolidation had been officially accomplished in 1961 an attempt had been made by UUA headquarters to provide a central fund each year which would be allocated to the five theological schools which enrolled most of its students. A Joint Fund for Theological Education of $89,000 was budgeted for 1962, although that amount was never actually raised. During its first year Harvard and Meadville/Lombard endorsed the idea but agreed not to draw on the fund.[116] The Tufts and St. Lawrence theological schools received the least, the lion's share going to the Starr King school.[117] In 1964 the legislative body of the denomination voted that theological schools be included in the regular annual budget.

Even more significant for the future of Crane and Canton was the report of a UUA Committee to Study Theological Education headed by Raymond B. Johnson, formerly director of the Unitarian Department of the Ministry. The report, made in 1962, set in motion a series of events which had a profoundly unsettling impact on the two denominational theological schools in the East.

The committee to review the state of theological education had grown directly out of an inquiry as to how that portion of the Unitarian Development Fund designated for theological education could be used most effectively. An even more comprehensive and long-range study was almost immediately authorized by the AUA Board of Directors, and the committee had met over a dozen times since the summer of 1959. With the consolidation of the two denominations the former UCA had been brought into its deliberations which ranged far and wide, and included the services of many consultants both inside and outside. Among the latter was Harold Taylor, a professional educational consultant and former president of Sarah Lawrence College (1945-1959) who had raised considerable controversy over his so-called "advanced" ideas about education. The results of his investigation, embodied in the Taylor Report, caused no end of discussion, and provoked an uproar in the two historically Universalist theological schools in particular.

The UUA committee, in what was known as the Johnson Report, concurred with the recommendations of the Taylor Report which provided for three religious educational centers: One on the East Coast, one on the West Coast (Starr King), and one in the Midwest (Meadville/Lombard).[118] On the East Coast the Canton and Crane schools were to be combined on the Tufts campus as part of an enlarged religious center, and would include collaboration with the interdenominational divinity school at Harvard. This plan met with Hersey's complete approval, for it meant that the Universalist heritage and identity would not be lost.

If consolidation of the St. Lawrence school with the one at Tufts were not possible for any reason, they should both be closed and UUA efforts should be concentrated on Starr King and Meadville/Lombard. Starr King, in Taylor's estimation, was by far the best of all the schools then being operated in the name of the combined denomination. However, he hoped the closing would not take place, for it would destroy his prized "continental concept."[119]

A variation on this plan was favored by Greeley and by C. Conrad Wright, Professor of Church History, who was the Harvard Divinity School representative at many of the numerous meetings which took place. Greeley pointed out that there were five Unitarians on the faculty in 1963 who would furnish the necessary denominational representation in the school. He saw the possibility of a religious center adjacent to the divinity school which would also house the merged Crane and Canton schools as well as a center for scholarly research.[120] Wright (one of the Unitarians on the faculty) prepared an elaborate plan for an Institute of Advanced (Religious) Studies in which Universalists and Unitarians would participate, and which would have available the vast and unparalleled resources of Harvard.[121]

The case for locating the center at Tufts was contained in "A Brief Summary of Tufts University as a Possible Location for Merged Theological Schools or as a Unitarian-Universalist Educational Center," prepared early in 1964 as a basis for discussion. Wessell was quick to point out that if either alternative came to pass, the ultimate control would rest with the Tufts trustees.[122] The sober fact was also noted that the full cost of the center would be at least $750,000 annually. Where would the money come from?

When the contents of the Taylor Report had been made public in 1962 neither the Crane faculty nor the dean was especially happy over his findings. Taylor had determined after a brief personal visitation that tests and examinations at Crane were "continual, and sometimes punitive." Old-fashioned pedagogical techniques such as the lecture method were employed excessively and contradicted the traditional Unitarian Universalist emphasis on individualism, open discussion, and freedom of expression. Students were treated too paternalistically and not as adults.[123] Taylor could not, on the other hand, have accused the students and alumni of excessive theological conservatism. In 1962 fourteen signed a "Liberal Manifesto" stating their values and beliefs.[124] It was written by Ira Blalock, Jr., and Robert W. Gardiner and bore an interesting resemblance to the Humanist Manifesto of 1933.[125]

Taylor had other criticisms to offer. He failed to find sufficient interaction between the theological students at Crane and the rest of the academic community, and no meaningful connection between the Crane curricula and the rest of the university. Taylor was even more critical of the Canton Theological School.

There was so much dissatisfaction with Taylor's negative comments regarding the denominational theological schools that a meeting was arranged between the deans or their representatives and Taylor in 1963.[126] It was charged that Taylor was unduly biased; that his report was not only grossly inaccurate but presented almost a caricature of Crane and Canton.[127]

The majority of Crane students supported the recommendations of the Johnson and Taylor Reports which were also endorsed by a special committee of the Crane Alumni Association.[128] The criticisms of the school were of much less import to them than the question of its future. As to the directorship of the proposed eastern center, Kapp ruled both

Hersey and himself out of consideration. Neither had "the stature which is expected" and Hersey did not contradict or challenge his judgment.[129]

As soon as the Johnson and Taylor Reports had been made available a liaison committee headed by Joseph Barth was appointed by the UUA trustees to keep in touch with the theological schools. The UUA trustees had received the reports "with enthusiastic appreciation."[130] The reports were also placed on the agenda of the Senexet Conference on Theological School Standards which had been meeting annually for nine years previously, and convened in Chicago in February 1963 to discuss them.[131] After the heads of the schools agreed in principle to the formation of the three recommended committees, the Conference discussed every possible alternative for combining the schools.

As a result of a meeting on the Tufts campus in the spring of 1964 preceding that of the General Assembly in San Francisco, an Implementation Committee replaced the liaison committee, with Barth continuing as chairman. Provost Leonard C. Mead served as the Tufts representative on the committee. It investigated comparative costs for one, two, or three schools. The only consensus at first seemed to be that the denomination could in no way support four.

It was initially decided that financial support from the UUA for theological education was so limited that the four denominational schools had to be consolidated into one. But this possibility was rejected, and yet another set of alternatives was finally recommended at a committee meeting on the eve of the General Assembly. After approval in principle by the UUA trustees they were unanimously voted at the General Assembly without discussion.

The recommendations made no one happy: That the Crane School was to "consider seriously" the transfer of its assets either to Starr King or to Meadville/Lombard, and that Canton was to do the same. The resources of the Harvard Divinity School were to continue to be used by mutual agreement. The relocation of Crane and Canton, if approved by the appropriate officials at both schools, was to be under way by September 1964. The UUA was to adopt a plan of subsidizing theological education totalling $100,000 for each of three years; $125,000 for the next three; and $150,000 for the succeeding four. None of these financial projections was ever met.

Those critical of the recommendations (principally Universalists) were quick to point out that neither the Pacific Coast nor the Midwest was, unlike the East, a center of denominational strength and that there would be no more historically Universalist theological schools. It was a bitter pill for Universalists to swallow.

After months of deliberation and some agonizing, Tufts officials decided in 1964 to disregard the recommendations of the UUA and continue the Crane School even if it meant reduced aid, or no further aid at all, from the denomination. After all, the school was under the direct control of the Tufts trustees and not the UUA. Hersey was instructed by President Wessell to state that Crane would continue, whether or not merger with Canton was effected. Crane would continue "to exist as long as Tufts was in existence."[132] Wessell respected Universalist and Unitarian traditions, but the Crane School had to be capable of offering even the PhD to any qualified applicant, regardless of denominational affiliation.

There was, in Wessell's view, both a historical and moral commitment to continue the school; it had the potential for receiving both increased support and an improved student body. And a ministry trained in a broad university liberal arts environment was indispensable to a well-educated clergy.[133] Mead added the practical consideration that if the school were closed its endowment, small as it was, might be lost.

The Tufts trustees were encouraged from many directions in their decision to continue the school. The Massachusetts Bay UUA District applauded the effort to maintain the school.[134] The AUW promised increased scholarship aid and the Massacusetts Association of Universalist Women continued to provide funds for the same purpose.[135] Gifts to Crane had doubled in 1964 over preceding years, and exceeded $10,000. Letters of encouragement and support poured in advocating a renewed and strengthened Crane.[136]

So the trustees and administration made one more attempt to put the School of Religion on a viable footing in 1964–65, with approval of a plan in the fall of 1964. The publicity called it "a new Crane." Wessell made a determined effort to seek advice from liberal clergy in eastern Massachusetts by arranging a conference to discuss the school. An accelerated effort was made to recruit students, secure additional funds, enlarge the full-time faculty, increase scholarship assistance, and revamp the entire curriculum. Frederick A. Pope, Jr., an outside professional consultant from the Episcopal Theological Seminary of the Southwest in Austin, Texas, was employed in 1964 to review the curriculum.

Robert L'H. Miller, who had first joined the Crane faculty in 1952 as a part-time instructor, was made an associate dean in 1965 to supervise the production of a revised course of study. Plans for a frankly experimental program emphasizing an interdisciplinary approach were sent to a trustee committee for their information, and 7,000 flyers were distributed to recruit students. Miller even submitted a detailed set of recommendations for refurbishing the Crane School buildings in anticipation of an enlarged faculty and student body.[137]

The Crane library was transferred to enlarged quarters in the new Wessell library shortly after it was opened in September 1965, and a search was begun for another professionally trained librarian to service the theological school library, Seaburg having resigned to accept a pastorate in Boston.

There was talk of either dissolving the Universalist Historical Society or consolidating it with its Unitarian counterpart (finally accomplished in 1978). If dissolution took place there was the possibility that the unique and valuable Universalist library could be placed on permanent deposit at Tufts, thus greatly strengthening the still inadequate theological collection. Instead, it was transferred to Harvard in 1975.

As part of the plan for an enlarged faculty, James D. Hunt was employed in 1965–66 as Assistant Professor of Religion and Society, and William R. Shealy, Jr., as Assistant Professor of Church History. Full-time faculty to teach Biblical Studies and religious education seemed to be the only important gaps in 1965–66 to round out a balanced total academic offering. It appeared that the requisite number of full-time faculty for accreditation had finally been reached. The renovation of existing buildings would provide facilities for fifty students.

Plans were under way in 1964 to replace Dean Hersey as part of the "new look" promised for Crane. Provost Mead recommended that the dean take early retirement by 1965 and that in the meantime an administrative assistant be hired to conduct a vigorous recruiting and fundraising campaign.[138] But the search for a new dean was ordered temporarily suspended by the trustees, for the president had submitted his letter of resignation on 17 June 1965, effective September 1966.[139]

The findings and recommendations of the Johnson and Taylor Reports naturally interjected a note of uncertainty into Crane operations. Enrollment dropped to seventeen degree candidates in 1964, and many of the faculty had already started to make plans to transfer elsewhere. Half the Crane operating budget of $90,000 in 1964 had to be made up from general university funds in order to balance it.[140] Confusion was compounded after the General Assembly met in 1964 and it had been erroneously reported in the press that the assembly had unanimously voted to close both Crane and Canton. Hersey spent much time and effort reassuring all concerned that such was not the case. In a letter sent to each Crane alumnus in the summer of 1964 enclosing a copy of the Barth committee recommendations, Mead informed them that no decision had yet been reached about the future of Crane and that in any case it was up to the trustees and no one else to make the final determination.

There was a general sense of outrage and a feeling of betrayal among Crane alumni that the recommendations of the Johnson and Taylor Reports regarding the fate of the schools had been disregarded by the Barth committee. Kenneth Patton, minister of the Charles Street Meeting House in Boston, reported that its trustees had unanimously voted that the General Assembly action was "not in the best interest of the liberal movement," and that Crane should continue.[141] Cole, who had resigned from the Crane faculty a decade earlier, wrote a letter of strong support for continuing the school, addressed to the president, claiming that it would be "disastrous" to allow the influence of Crane to fade away.[142]

With the fate of both Crane and the St. Lawrence school in more doubt than ever, the question of possible merger which had been considered off and on for years, was raised again. Hersey and Kapp had discussed it informally in 1961, but the matter had lain dormant until after the Johnson and Taylor Reports had been made public. The Crane Alumni Association urged that the Canton school be combined at Tufts, with a new name such as the "Hosea Ballou School for the Ministry."[143] At Provost Mead's request Hersey even drew up a tentative annual operating budget for the combined school. The dean set the figure at $350,000 for thirty students and $362,000 for fifty students.

The future of the Crane School, so far as enrollment was concerned, looked most promising after 1965. There were thirty degree candidates in 1965–66 — the largest number since becoming a graduate school little more than a decade earlier. In addition, there were six "specials" who were registered on a part-time basis who were not degree candidates; most were taking one or more courses in religious education. There were thirty-three degree candidates a year later, the largest number of graduate students yet registered. If the four special students in 1966–67 were added, there were twenty-seven men and ten women comprising the student body. That academic year was described by the dean as "one of the best and most promising years in the history of Crane." The "new look" approved by the trustees in 1964 had apparently begun to pay dividends.

There continued to be considerable faculty turnover up to the very year the school was closed. Cassara and E. Palmer Clarke resigned at the end of the academic year 1965–66 and Hunter returned as Associate Professor of Religious Literature after a five-year absence. Walter H. Clark served as Visiting Professor of Psychology of Religion in 1966–67, and Mrs. Eugene Meyer was employed as Instructor in Religious Education for 1967–68. Peter A. Baldwin, who had served as an instructor (part-time) in 1964–65, was employed as a full-time assistant professor the following year. His primary task was to supervise field education, although he resigned after one year. Reeves likewise resigned at the end of the 1966–67 academic year.

Solving the long-range problem of the Crane School had become sufficiently pressing by early 1967 to result in the creation of an *ad hoc* trustee study committee comprising the chairmen of all standing committees. They investigated the budgetary problem and Acting President Mead reviewed with the trustees in detail the operating expenses of the school over a period of several years. Annual deficits seldom fell below $50,000 and frequently exceeded that amount. Not counted was the non-funded investment in Paige Hall and Wessell Library which housed the theological library and provided other services to the school.[144]

The trustee committee made its report in the late spring of 1967. They estimated that annual support amounting to $250,000 was needed to provide a school worthy of accreditation, based on an enrollment of fifty students. But how could such a sum be raised each year? Closing the school seemed to be the only alternative, for financial projections "made it appear not practical to continue [it] as presently structured." The trustee executive committee concurred and recommended in April "the eventual removal of Crane Theological School from the campus or its liquidation." A committee was appointed to work out the details. Financial considerations were listed as the governing factor leading up to the recommendation. However, when the full board voted in June 1967 "that the program of instruction at Crane Theological School be terminated as of June 1968" no mention was made of finances as a reason. Instead, the school had "not maintained its place of considerable distinction in theological education."[145] Mead and Charles E. Stearns, dean of the College of Liberal Arts, reported the trustee decision to the Crane alumni at a meeting a few days after the vote was taken.

Even though the announcement of the closing of the school cast "a long shadow" over all of its activities, the necessary work was carried on by the twenty-six degree candidates and five faculty members up to the time of closing. Twelve were graduated in 1968 — the largest number in any one year since 1897. Nine of the remaining students elected to continue as candidates for the Tufts degree at other institutions, and five transferred to other theological schools.[146] Four of the faculty (none of them tenured) were able to secure positions elsewhere; the single tenured faculty member continued as a member of the Faculty of Arts and Sciences and headed the undergraduate Department of Religion.

As soon as the decision had been made to close Crane the trustees adopted a policy of ensuring that all of the theological students who continued their studies at some other institution would receive financial assistance in the same amounts as those granted to them by Crane while they were enrolled there.[147] A settlement totalling $24,000 was made to those students still enrolled when the school closed. The reimbursement covered both financial aid and moving expenses.[148] The last Crane degree was awarded in 1971. The following year a Crane alumnus brought to Tufts' attention the fact that several theological schools were allowing their graduates who held BD's or STB's to exchange them for Master of Divinity (M. Div.) or Master of Sacred Theology (STM) degrees. In 1978 the Tufts trustees authorized holders of Crane degrees to make an exchange if they wished.

Litigation regarding disposition of the assets of the school was expected. In order to forestall it, President Burton C. Hallowell, who had become president in 1967, was to be given authority by the state courts to carry out such plans as in his judgment would "most nearly carry out the intention of the donors."[149] This effectively blocked any attempt on the part of either the UUA or the donors to retrieve any funds.[150] After court approval in 1968 the university established a so-called Crane Program Fund which was to be used for support of the Department of Religion; the university chaplaincy; scholarships for those enrolled at Tufts who intended to enter the liberal ministry, religious education, or social welfare work; and community social service programs.[151] The total of the fund amounted to $213,000 in 1972, comprising 1 percent of all university funds available for investment.

The Tufts School of Religion/Crane Theological School was no more, and all that Hersey could do was accept the decision with "deep regret."[152] This was probably an understatement of the dean's true feelings; it was a blow from which he never recovered. He retired officially from the deanship in 1968, which coincided with the closing of the school, having been given emeritus status by the trustees the previous year. It was a sad occasion when the Crane faculty, at its last meeting on 29 April 1968, adopted resolutions on his retirement, after fourteen years of service — some satisfying and full of hope for the future but ending with trying and difficult final years.

Hersey's retirement was brief. He became pastor of the small Universalist church in Essex, Massachusetts, but died on 6 January 1971 at the age of sixty-seven, grievously disappointed that the end of the Crane Theological School had come during his deanship.

The eventual demise of the school was made almost inevitable by a combination of circumstances which, taken separately, might not have been responsible for its closing. If they had not been present, the life of the school might have been prolonged but by no means guaranteed. By 1967 the Tufts trustees were facing an operating deficit of more than half a million dollars, and every division of the university that was not paying all or most of its own way was a candidate for severe retrenchment if not actual elimination. Crane was the most likely casualty.

Both Wessell and Mead were personally committed to liberal religion, and were sympathetic to the aims of the Crane School. Both were themselves Unitarians in religious affiliation. Both were likewise committed to a nondenominational theological school, as both announced repeatedly. Mead had leaned so far over backward to maintain the nondenominational stance of the institution that when the Massachusetts Bay District of the UUA requested a list of Unitarian and Universalist faculty members, Mead refused to supply it. Such an act, he believed, would give a religious coloration denied by the charter of the institution.[153] Wessell's decision to resign just as negotiations were reaching a critical stage likewise played a part. Mead had been appointed acting president (effective September 1966) and had accepted the new responsibility as a strictly temporary measure, with the full knowledge that a new president might be appointed at any time.[154]

Officials of the UUA also faced the practical problem of attempting by 1964 to subsidize to some extent four theological schools with totally inadequate funding. Something had to give. Greeley had not been at all enthusiastic about Tufts' plans for an enlarged and rehabilitated "new Crane," much preferring to give support to a more strictly Unitarian Universalist school such as Meadville/Lombard or Starr King.[155]

There was the undisputed fact, painfully clear to both the Tufts administration and UUA officialdom, that Crane had never achieved the standing of a first-class theological school in spite of all the good work it had accomplished, and that great quantities of money which neither could afford would need to be poured into the school. Still, it had rendered just one year short of a century of service to the liberal ministry, and that was no small contribution.

Section VI

Church Extension, Domestic and Foreign

Chapter 18

Quillen Hamilton Shinn: The "Grasshopper Missionary"

"When the history of the Universalist Church is written in truth, the name of Q. H. Shinn will shine among the founders and builders whom future generations shall delight to honor."[1] These words were penned little more than a week after the death of the individual preeminently associated with the domestic missionary activities of the Universalist denomination after the Civil War. His work, particularly in the South, was quite correctly compared to the pioneer efforts of earlier generations of Universalist missionaries in the North and Midwest, operating as he did in "almost untouched territory."[2]

For sixteen years, during which he held no regular pastorate, Shinn roamed far and wide, spreading Universalist ideas and organizing parishes and churches wherever he went. His missionary enthusiasm earned for him several appellations, both admiring and derogatory. He was often referred to as "the St. Paul of the Universalist Church."[3] S. H. Roblin, associate pastor of the Columbus Avenue Church in Boston under Alonzo A. Miner, described Shinn as "the John Wesley of Universalism." He was characterized as a "nomad," and one critic in 1893 called him derisively "the grasshopper missionary" because he travelled so constantly and landed so briefly at any given point that permanent results were impossible.[4]

Shinn (1845–1907) was born on 1 January 1845 in Bingamon (Harrison County) in what in 1863 became the state of West Virginia. His father Elisha, who died in 1847, was a pioneer farmer in what was then frontier country.[5] Shinn's widowed mother, Mary (LeFevre) Shinn, then married a widower, Jacob H. Fortney, a physician with a large family of his own. Shinn grew up in the agricultural settlement of Shinnston, where he led an active outdoor life, bcame an expert horseman, and developed a love of nature that was reflected in many of the reports which he made later as a missionary.

After a minimum amount of formal education Shinn enlisted in the Union Army at the age of sixteen. He first served for eight months in the Third Virginia Infantry from which he was discharged. He reenlisted in the late summer of 1862 in the West Virginia Volunteer Infantry, with which he remained until the close of the Civil War. After having been wounded by a sharpshooter he was taken prisoner by the Confederates in 1863 but was paroled near Richmond, Virginia, shortly thereafter and rejoined his military unit. He participated in twelve military engagements, including the battle of Appomattox Courthouse as hostilities were drawing to a close in 1865, and where he witnessed Robert E. Lee's surrender. In his widespread travels many years later Shinn took every opportunity possible to visit the scenes of his military days and to look up former associates. He was discharged with the rank of corporal and set out to resume his interrupted schooling. He attended a Methodist academy in Mount Union, Ohio, and taught school briefly.

Shinn had been born into a Presbyterian family, and his mother had named him for the preacher of that faith who had baptized him. She intended that the son become a minister in that denomination. Her expectations were at least partially realized, for he became a clergyman, but in another faith. Her second husband was a Universalist who had been converted through the writings of George W. Quinby and Thomas B. Thayer. Two of Shinn's half-brothers also became Universalist clergymen. Shinn himself was also introduced to the denomination by way of Thayer's *Theology of Universalism*.[6] As a young man Shinn had at first written for information to the only Thayer whose name he knew — William M. Thayer, a Congregational minister in Franklin, Masachusetts, who edited a temperance paper and whose name was familiar to Shinn through the Good Templars.[7] It was this minister who referred Shinn's inquiry to the Universalist Publishing House for a reply.

Shinn was also influenced by Andrew Willson, a Universalist minister whom he had heard preach in Kent, Ohio, in 1867. As a strong opponent of the use of alcoholic beverages while a youth, Shinn became a temperance lecturer and effective speaker while still in school, and was encouraged by one of his hearers to enter the ministry. He thereupon decided in 1867, over the opposition of some members of his family, to attend Canton Theological School, part of Universalist-operated St. Lawrence University.

En route to the school in upstate New York, he stopped in Baltimore long enough to attend the General Convention then in session, and was so distressed by the debates over the Winchester Profession that he violated parliamentary protocol by speaking extemporaneously and vigorously from the floor without delegate status. He is reported to have said that

The Shinn family as he was embarking on his missionary career

"the Universalist ministers could write better than they could talk," and that he was tempted to give up on the spot his plans to prepare for the ministry and return to West Virginia.[8] The "Baltimore bedlam" was then reported to have turned suddenly into "a love feast" as a result of Shinn's plea for harmony.

Shinn was persuaded by A. J. Patterson, who delivered a sermon at the convention, to carry out his original plan. The eager young Universalist graduated from theological school in 1879, in a class of twelve. Never pretending to be a scholar or even a bookish person, Shinn compiled an undistinguished academic record. As a student he gave forceful and doctrinally centered sermons characteristic of his entire ministerial career. While at St. Lawrence he was much more interested in assisting the poor and unfortunate and in giving temperance lectures than in concentrating on his studies.

Shinn was fellowshipped by the Vermont Convention and was ordained in Gaysville, his first pastorate, in 1870. Like many of his contemporaries, he held a series of brief ministries in his early career; but unlike most of them, he never really settled down. His last regular assignment was in 1890.

Shinn's enthusiasm for missionary work was apparent from the first, as was his religious enthusiasm. His fierce loyalty to Universalism was strikingly reminiscent of that of Thomas Whittemore of an earlier generation. To Shinn's undying devotion to Universalism was added his considerable organizational ability, an outgoing personality, and a talent for fund-raising, although not all of his efforts met with unqualified success. He returned briefly to West Virginia in 1872, and failed in an attempt to organize a church in Wheeling. He then migrated to Massachusetts, where he served in 1873 as a travelling agent for the Universalist Publishing House.[9] In 1876 he married Maria S. Burnell of Portland, Maine, in the Congress Square church in that city. Three of their four sons lived to adulthood and all three at some time attended Universalist schools, although none followed in their father's ministerial footsteps.

Between 1874 and 1889 Shinn held four short pastorates in various Massachusetts communities (Tyngsboro, Lynn, Foxboro, and Mansfield) and served numerous churches in other parts of New England, including New Hampshire, Maine, and Vermont. During his stay of less than four years in Plymouth, New Hampshire, beginning in 1881, he was responsible for building a new church there as well as serving as a correspondent for the denominational *Gospel Banner* published in Augusta, Maine.

Never content to serve but one church at a time, he organized his own circuits wherever he went. In 1882, while pastor in Plymouth, he established no less than fourteen preaching stations on his own initiative and organized a series of summer meetings which he had begun informally the previous year at The Weirs on Lake Winnepesaukee, a tourist resort.[10] The National Summer Meetings, as they were called, became an annual denominational event, although not always held in New Hampshire. A church edifice was erected in Westbrook, Maine, during Shinn's brief ministry there. By 1889 he had attracted sufficient attention to receive an invitation from Amos G. Throop, a wealthy Universalist layman in California, to settle on the West Coast.[11] But Shinn elected to remain in New England, at least temporarily. While serving a nine-month interim appointment in Rutland, Vermont, in 1889, he assisted in raising $6,000 for a new church which he dedicated.

Shinn's unique fitness for missionary activity had already been recognized by others. In 1883 Nathaniel R. Wright, after a visit to Waterloo, Province of Quebec, saw a fertile field for missionary activity, and recommended Shinn. "He would look well on Canadian snowshoes. Eight days in them might weary him a little, but not much. Young, vigorous, faithful, and deeply earnest, he would make a most excellent missionary."[12] Shinn did not need to be told that there was a need for aggressive denominational work; he had already seen it. So he departed from New England and hastened off to Omaha, Nebraska, to serve the Universalists there. Typically, a building (the Church of the Good Shepherd) was erected during a ministry which lasted less than two years.[13]

The Omaha pastorate was to be Shinn's last settlement, for after the church was dedicated in 1891 he went on the road. By the time of his death at the age of 62 he had preached in every state then in the Union, and at many points in Canada as well. When he signed the register at the Ferry Beach summer session in 1904 he quite appropriately listed his address as "Everywhere."[14]

UNIVERSALISTS!

Under the Auspices of the

Universalist Society,
OF CHARLESTON,

A Special Series of Meetings will be conducted by

Rev. Q. H. SHINN, D. D.,
OF BOSTON,

September 23rd to 30th, 1900.

IN THE SUPREME COURT ROOM, CAPITAL.

Subjects:

SUNDAY, SEPTEMBER 23.

11:00 A. M.—"Spiritual Growth."

8:00 P. M.—"Universal Fatherhood of God."

MONDAY, SEPTEMBER 24.

8:00 P. M.—"Spiritual Authority and Leadership of Christ."

TUESDAY, SEPTEMBER 25.

8:00 P. M.—"The Bible."

WEDNESDAY, SEPTEMBER 26.

8:00 P. M.—"The Certainty of Just Punishment for Sin."

THURSDAY, SEPTEMBER 27.

8:00 P. M.—"The Final Harmony of All Souls with God."

FRIDAY, SEPTEMBER 28.

8:00 P. M.—"What is Religion? Can we get it? Can we lose it?"

SATURDAY, SEPTEMBER 29.

8:00 P. M.—"Death, Immortality, Heaven."

SUNDAY, SEPTEMBER 30.

11:00 A. M.—"Christ's Atonement."

8:00 P. M.—"Garden of Eden. Origin of Evil. The Galveston Flood."

Dr Shinn will answer each evening any questions that may be handed to him.

☞ "PROVE ALL THINGS. HOLD FAST THAT WHICH IS GOOD."

Announcing Shinn's appearance in West Virginia

During his lifetime, Shinn's name was probably more familiar to Universalists in more sections of the United States than that of any other individual. He literally darted from one end of the nation to the other, spreading his "good tidings" wherever he went.[15] He ferreted out Universalists wherever they were to be found, from isolated rural areas (the "piney woods" of the South were among his favorite haunts) to urban centers, organizing new churches or attempting to strengthen those that were lagging.

He also had ambitious plans to reach scattered Universalists and bring them into the national mainstream. He outlined a grand design in 1897 whereby the entire country would be divided into four missionary departments, with a full-time administrator and financial solicitor in each.[16] He produced an even more grandiose plan in 1900 to organize a "missionary skirmish line" marching from the Atlantic to the Pacific by holding at least one Universalist meeting in every precinct or neighborhood in the United States.[17] Another of Shinn's suggestions was to obtain a pledge from every Universalist minister to serve a term as a missionary.

His presence had become so pervasive that in 1895 he was appointed General Missionary by the General Convention, at an annual salary of $3,000. In that same year St. Lawrence University conferred on him the honorary degree of Doctor of Divinity in recognition of his services.

As his work progressed, more and more of it was devoted to the South, which as early as 1883 he had singled out as the most important field in the nation for missionary activity.[18] The General Convention, bowing to his wishes, appointed him as Southern Missionary in 1900, a title which he bore at the time of his death. He assumed the position with the understanding that he would give full time to that assignment, except for two months during the summer in order to conduct meetings in the North. In addition, he was appointed in 1893 as the national organizer of the Young People's Christian Union which, in turn, established under his guidance what was known for many years as the Post Office Mission to spread Universalism.

Shinn's last trip, the report of which comprised the last one published in the denominational press, was made to the four churches in South Carolina in the summer of 1907.[19] He died of rheumatic fever at his home in Medford Hillside, Massachusetts, on the edge of the Tufts College campus, on 6 September 1907. Funeral services were held in the college chapel, with thirty-five clergy among those present. He was interred in Evergreen Cemetery, Portland, Maine. Memorial services were held all over the country, including one at the General Convention meeting in Philadelphia, for this one-man "missionary army." Tributes poured in from every corner of the nation.

Within a matter of days after Shinn's death Southern Universalists attending the General Convention met to discuss ways in which to carry on his work and to secure a successor. The idea of constructing a great memorial church in his name, to be located somewhere in the South, was projected. The suggestion was also made that a permanent fund be established, the income of which was to support a Southern lectureship or to finance a missionary to succeed Shinn. Charles P. Hall, who had known Shinn for almost twenty years and had worked with him in the South, thought that an endowed lectureship would be more appropriate than a church building.[20]

Both suggestions were eventually carried out, spread over a period of several years. In 1907 the *Leader* sponsored a campaign to raise funds for a lectureship which amounted to more than $1,600 within a year.[21] The first lecturer, selected in 1909, was unable to serve and that plan was temporarily shelved, although a Shinn Memorial Lectureship Fund continued to exist and exceeded $2,000 by 1915. Frederick A. Bisbee, then editor of the *Leader,* made a grand tour of much of the South in 1912 under the lectureship, including all states except the Carolinas.[22] He gave an address at Tuskegee Institute on the invitation of Booker T. Washington, whom he had known for several years.

A Shinn Memorial Fund for a church to bear his name was created in 1908 and more than $2,300 had been contributed by 1909.[23] Southern delegates again assembled at the General Convention in 1909 and formed an association to raise additional money. Probably no single individual was responsible for originating the idea, although it was attributed to W. H. McGlauflin, Shinn's long-time associate in the South. It was McGlauflin who headed the association.[24] The plan was originally to construct an edifice to cost at least $25,000, with half of the expense to be borne by the General Convention. But it was subsequently modified to provide that $10,000 be raised by subscription, with the equivalent of $15,000 to be donated by the town or city selected as a site for the church. Cash in excess of $2,700 had been paid in by the spring of 1911, consisting mostly of small sums (from $1.00 to $10.00), with every Southern state represented.

McGlauflin offered to donate all of the proceeds above expenses received from a biography of Shinn which he prepared and which was published in 1912. Mrs. Emma E. Bailey of Mansfield, Pennsylvania, donated 100 copies of her autobiography, the proceeds from the sale of which she contributed to the memorial fund.

Rivalry for the location of the proposed church was keen. Houston, Texas; Little Rock, Arkansas; Chattanooga, Tennessee; Winder, Georgia; and Rocky Mount and Kinston, North Carolina, were among the early contenders.

Difficulty immediately arose both in conducting the canvass and in raising the requisite money. McGlauflin had already arranged a series of itineraries which he felt obligated to carry through. He was accordingly unable to fulfill immediately the goals of the memorial association that he headed. There was also considerable competition for the limited funds available in the South. There were still efforts to reduce the deficit of the

General Convention; there were pleas on behalf of the reconstruction of the memorial church in Winchester, New Hampshire; and the Murray Grove Association was attempting to raise an endowment fund. Nonetheless the idea was kept alive, and at its biennial session in 1911 the General Convention passed a resolution expressing approval of the continued efforts of Southern Universalists to erect a memorial church in his name, and pledged $1,000 the following year.[25] The national YPCU, which in 1911 was busy organizing a mission in Chattanooga, proposed that the church be located there as a part of their church extension activities. The memorial association agreed, and the location of the church was endorsed by the General Convention in 1913.[26]

The church in which the first services were held in the summer of 1916 had the distinction of being the only one both sponsored by the entire denomination and named in honor of one of its ministers. Of the $10,000 secured in pledges, well over half the total had been raised by the YPCU; $4,000 came from the South.[27] It was a proud day for the youth organization when it held its national convention in the new church in 1917.[28]

One of Shinn's lifetime ambitions, largely thwarted earlier by the change of direction at the Southern Industrial Institute in Alabama under Lyman Ward, was at least partially realized after Shinn's death. A "School of Evangelism" was opened in the Chattanooga church in 1917 for "special training for the ministry for those unable to attend the regular theological schools of the Universalist church." It lasted into the 1930s, but the exact number of those it trained is not known.

The Shinn Memorial Church also became the headquarters for many years of what, beginning in 1919, was originally known as the Southern Universalist Young People's Institute. The summer programs were intended to train workers especially for service in Sunday schools, young people's societies, and missionary organizations. The Institute was at first a joint project of the General Sunday School Association, the YPCU, and the WNMA, with some financial assistance from the General Convention. In 1920 the YPCU turned its missionary work there over to the WNMA and concentrated its attention on Texas.[29]

When the pastor of the Chattanooga church, George A. Gay, moved to Camp Hill, Alabama, in 1925, the Institute moved with him, redesignated as the Southern Universalist Association. In 1930 it returned to Chattanooga, where it offered a summer program for all Southern religious liberals. In that year eleven students attended, from four Southern states.[30] Shinn would probably have enthusiastically approved the establishment of the School of Evangelism, but would have been more hesitant to have endorsed the Southern Universalist Association, partly because it was described in the official church literature as intended for "religious liberals," and more particularly because Unitarians were included.

Although many of the notes for Shinn's sermons and addresses were too fragmentary to allow reconstruction exactly as he delivered them, he kept a diary and documented his missionary career with extraordinary regularity and detail. Weekly, monthly, and yearly reports were made available through the columns of the denominational press and periodically to the trustees of the General Convention. He wrote them in all kinds of places — in railroad waiting rooms, on trains, in carriages, in backwoods cabins, and in hotel rooms during or after journeys amounting more than once to as much as 700 miles a week, much of it often on horseback or on foot. His hand luggage invariably bulged with denominational literature, his extensive correspondence, notes for his reports, railroad timetables, and schedules of forthcoming appointments.

The accounts appearing in the papers were almost always permeated with enthusiastic optimism, heavily weighted with statistics of his activities, and reflective of his passionate and single-minded devotion to his religious convictions and his determination to spread them at almost any cost to himself.[31] In 1901, after preaching for several days in Durham, North Carolina, to unresponsive audiences, his reaction was puzzlement rather than discouragement. He simply could not understand why he could not convert people "to the glorious faith" when it was so self-evident to him.[32]

Shinn followed an easily discernible pattern which amounted to a formula, in his missionary work. He was a firm believer in the policy of organizing a church and constructing a building as soon as one or more Universalist families could be gathered. He considered the most effective device both for recruitment and retention of allegiance to be formal church membership. Likewise, church structures were visible evidence of religion. Even the smallest and humblest household was entitled to a church home. After determining to plant or spread Universalism in a given community, he would arrange to deliver one or more sermons, usually having determined in advance whether any Universalists resided there. The fact that there were none known did not deter him in the least. If one or more were identified, or identified themselves, or anyone was even sympathetic to him and to his ideas, he would organize a ladies' aid group, a committee to start a building fund, and a young people's organization. He would then designate one or more individuals to lead or coordinate activities. On a follow-up visit, weeks, months, or even years later, he would attempt to organize a parish and/or church, leaving the organization and conduct of religious services in the hands of laity until a minister could be found. If clergymen could be obtained who could visit a Universalist group as frequently as once a month, Shinn considered this a signal accomplishment.

On the state level, Shinn's technique, which came to be known as the "Missouri Plan," was to concentrate all the missionary efforts in a state on building at least one church a year. The plan, begun in 1893 in Missouri, was carried out successfully for several years. The first three churches there were located in rural areas.³³ The practice was followed, with more or less consistency, in all the Southern states. Between 1896 and 1902 six church buildings were erected in Georgia. Shinn dedicated four in the state in 1897 alone.³⁴ Of the eleven churches existing in Alabama in 1902, all but two had their own structures.³⁵

To make his system work, Shinn had by the nature of the situation to depend almost exclusively on lay leadership from the start. He was completely confident that a combination of self-reliance, enthusiasm, and inspiration would be sufficient to carry the day. In this he was more often than not a victim of wishful thinking, for the momentum that he initially generated by his great personal magnetism and devotion to the Universalist cause often did not last.

There is no completely accurate way of measuring Shinn's permanent accomplishments, even in quantitative terms, but there is no question that he recruited hundreds of individuals, was responsible for building churches by the dozens (at least forty), and was responsible for almost thirty additions to the ministry.³⁶ As many Universalists were insistent on emphasizing, it was the spirit that was engendered by such persons as Shinn, and not the statistical evidence, that was ultimately important.

Like most Universalist clergy in earlier times, Shinn preached and conducted services wherever he could, regardles of the physical setting. If other church buildings were barred to him, as they sometimes were, he used courthouses or schoolhouses or even a natural amphitheater. If the number of potential hearers was too few to justify larger quarters, or other facilities were not available, he met in private homes. He often conducted services in lumbering camps or industrial establishments. In 1902, while in Banner, Mississippi, he held two Easter services in a blacksmith shop, using a turning-lathe covered with newspapers as an altar. The congregation sat on planks freshly milled for framing a Universalist church yet to be built.³⁷

A typical report during his first year as General Missionary (1895) illustrates Shinn's almost frenetic missionary activity.³⁸ He preached during the year eighteen sermons in six states, from Kentucky to Vermont; he delivered thirteen addresses; travelled 3,569 miles; attended the state convention in Kentucky and organized a YPCU in that state; while in Missouri, created a building fund for Atlanta, Georgia; conferred with the parish in Kansas City, attended the state convention, and assisted in one ordination; in Virginia he assisted in the ordination of Thomas E. Wise, the second Negro minister in the denomination, and organized a Negro YPCU. He substituted for Sweetser in Philadelphia; addressed the General Convention in Meriden, Connecticut; assisted in missionary work in New York State, including the start of a building fund on Staten Island; and addressed the Vermont YPCU in Brattleboro. That was only the beginning.

Quillen Hamilton Shinn (1845-1907), Universalism's best-known circuit rider

In 1897, at the General Convention in Chicago, Shinn made his first biennial report as General Missionary as of February 1895.[39] It was an amazing record. In little less than three years he had labored in thirty-four states, the District of Columbia, and the two Canadian provinces of Quebec and Ontario, and had travelled more than 15,000 miles. Much of his energy was expended in fostering movements he had started before his official appointment. All told, he had organized eight churches, four state conferences, two state YPCU's, twenty-five local YPCU's, six Ladies' Aid societies, and three mission circles. He averaged almost one sermon or address a day, received 350 into church membership, christened innumerable children, and had attended meetings of almost every kind. Considerable time was spent in organizing a total of seven summer meetings at The Weirs in New Hampshire and Sebago Lake in New York. The parishes for which he started church building funds were almost without number. He was also responsible for adding directly more than $14,000 to the financial resources of the denomination, exclusive of the value of church properties.

In the two years of 1904 and 1905 Shinn delivered 453 sermons in twenty-two states; travelled more than 38,000 miles, an estimated 900 of them on horseback or on foot; and assisted in building seven churches, five of which he dedicated.[40]

Shinn was unabashedly a "Bible Universalist" from his early youth until his death. His theological ideas, once set, never changed. He was a doctrinal preacher from beginning to end, a person who had no use for such intellectual sophistications as the Higher Criticism or the brand of religious liberalism which he believed the Unitarians professed. While a soldier he had carried a Bible in his knapsack and committed passages of scripture to memory. Later, in his ministerial career, he could repeat entire chapters. This familiarity with the Bible often stood him in good stead as a missionary, especially when he engaged in verbal tilts with members of other denominations.

In 1889 Shinn issued an unambiguous religious manifesto of his Universalist beliefs. They were: The Bible; God; man as the child of God, including immortality of the soul; Christ and his divinity, with a distinct personality derived from God; salvation; and the certainty of punishment for sin. "There is no hell for any of us to fear outside of ourselves."[41]

While the denomination was involved in a seemingly never-ending debate over the phraseology of the Winchester Profession and especially over the word "restore," Shinn saw absolutely no reason to change what had been originally written. If any word was to be substituted, he would suggest "win," so that the sentence in the second article would read: "God will finally win all men to holiness and happiness."[42] This would have been quite in keeping with Shinn's missionary enthusiasm to make converts.

Throughout his life Shinn distrusted the word "liberalism" as applied to religion. "I am afraid of liberalism. It is apt to be too nebulous for crystallization."[43] He refused to refer to Universalism as a liberal religion, not because it was necessarily illiberal, but because the word had become associated with Unitarianism which Shinn described as the " 'go-as-you-please church.' "[44]

He expressed his dislike of Unitarians in even stronger language on another occasion. Noting in 1897 that the so-called liberal society in Yankton, South Dakota, contained both Universalists and Unitarians, he labelled it a "mongrel movement," and part of a conspiracy on the part of Unitarians to preempt a field properly belonging to Universalists.[45] Unitarians had allegedly canvassed Universalists and had explained that there was no real difference between the two denominations. This the Unitarians "always do when they want our people." It is a certainty that Shinn would never be a party to building any bridges between the two groups.

The Universalist missionary had no objection whatever to being labelled old-fashioned. He was very unhappy that the younger generation of Universalist clergy lacked first-hand knowledge of the Bible. Mere lectures on the subject were no substitute for actually reading and understanding the Scriptures. Entirely too many were talking about "liberalism" and "the larger hope," neither of which was true Universalism.[46] Traditional doctrinal preaching was what was needed above all else.

Shinn was a traditional Universalist in another respect. He refused to use blood-and-thunder revivalist techniques and considered "sensationalist" preaching undesirable.[47] They all carried too much of the connotation of emotionalism and backsliding associated with the vocabulary of orthodox religions and frontier revivalism.

While known principally for his missionary work, there were other aspects of Shinn's career and thought deserving mention. Some of them unquestionably complemented and contributed to the respect and esteem with which he was regarded in the denomination.

Shinn was not only an outspoken Universalist but an American patriot of the first order. His military service during the Civil War had produced a record of which he could always be justifiably proud. As a Union veteran he was active in the Grand Army of the Republic, and was chaplain of several local units while serving various pastorates. At the same time he urged an attitude of understanding and good will toward those who had served in the Confederacy. He lectured frequently on patriotic subjects and the duties of American citizenship, stressing the importance of national unity and strength.

He was uncompromising on three issues: temperance, use of tobacco, and profanity. He had become a total abstainer from alcohol at the age of sixteen, while in the army, and had taken a triple pledge against the use of intoxicants, tobacco, and profanity to which he consistently adhered throughout his life. The pledge was engraved on a medal which he had worn during military campaigns. As a dedicated foe of the saloon and the liquor traffic, he joined the Prohibition Party and was a member of the strictly abstemious Good Templars which he joined soon after his discharge from the army. He adamantly refused, as a clergyman, to serve wine at Communion services. While living in the frontier atmosphere of Omaha he suffered physical as well as verbal abuse for advocating prohibition.

Shinn delivered numerous lectures on the evils of alcohol and tobacco, and in an address at Foxboro, Massachusetts in 1875, asserted that he was "against the ordination of any young man who uses tobacco."[48]

The field of penology interested Shinn for much of his life. As an unremitting enemy of capital punishment he delivered a paper at the General Convention in 1897 on prison reform. It was followed by the adoption of a resolution against the use of the death penalty and the appointment of a committee on penology of which Shinn served as chairman.[49] He was horrified in 1899 to discover that in a straw vote taken at a meeting of Boston-area Universalists ministers, five of the twenty-four present had voted in favor of capital punishment. It was "the most mortifying thing I have read since I have been in the Universalist ministry."[50]

He was active in the National Prison Association and was a speaker at one of its conventions, held in New Orleans in 1899.[51] He was very quick to call attention to the fact that Ellen O. Johnson, a member of the Columbus Avenue Universalist Church in Boston, was a long-time superintendent of the Massachusetts Women's Prison in Sherburne. Clara Barton, another Universalist, had been her predecessor in that post. Mrs. Johnson served for fifteen years, until her death in 1899 while attending an international conference of the Women's Congress in London at which she had delivered an address of prison reform. Shinn was a strong supporter of women's rights, particularly suffrage, and was very proud of the part he played in converting to Universalism Mrs. Athalia L. J. Irwin, the first ordained woman minister of the denomination in the South.

Shinn's great missionary services to Univeralism bore no resemblance to the small expenditure his activities entailed. Hundreds of dollars were donated directly to him by such supporters of his work as J. W. Anderson, Latimer W. Ballou, and Albert and Henry B. Metcalf. Shinn made special acknowledgement of the financial contributions as well as moral support of Mrs. Mary T. Goddard, and Mrs. Eleanor P. Townsend of Sycamore, Illinois. It was Shinn, according to McGlauflin, who first suggested, in 1892, that the Woman's Centenary Association change its official title to the "Women's National Missionary Association of the Universalist Church" in order to emphasize their important role in activities such as his.[52]

In the single year 1899 Shinn obtained contributions for the denomination which, when credited against his salary of $3,000, left a net cost of only $753.90.[53] By that year he had had a hand in making possible the building of twenty-six churches and had personally raised $80,000 toward their construction at no cost to the General Convention.

Shinn's role as a self-appointed missionary was at times a controversial one. Dedicated unreservedly to the dissemination and organization of Universalism everywhere, he provoked a prolonged debate over denominational policy. Should Universalists concentrate their efforts and resources in a relatively few strategic urban centers and strengthen well-established churches; or should they expand and disperse by attempting to plant the denomination in every nook and cranny of America and hope that an admittedly calculated risk would pay off? There was no doubt about Shinn's answer to that question.

Shinn was quite well aware that there was considerable criticism of his policy of attempting to organize churches wherever he found two or more isolated Universalists. But he wanted no opportunity to pass in spreading the faith, and hoped that the laymen on whom he had to depend at first would eventually have settled pastors. This was, he was forced to admit, seldom the case. There were not sufficient ministers both willing and able to engage in new mission fields — a source of grievous disappointment. What should be done posed a real dilemma for him. Refusing to organize Universalists whom he found was painful to him. The denomination could not stand still. If it elected to call a halt and refused to make the commitments Shinn believed necessary, Universalism would die on the vine.

In 1892, scarcely a year after Shinn had announced that he would commit his entire efforts to missionary work, the *Leader* observed wistfully that the denomination would be in a splendid position if only it were pssible to provide pastors to match the preaching stations he had already begun to create in the South and Midwest. If pastors were not found, much of his energy would have been dissipated in vain.[54]

Mary T. Goddard, who donated more than $2,000 directly to Shinn to further his missionary plans, suggested to him in 1894 that he devote his efforts to fostering churches already established rather than to organizing new ones. He should "strengthen the roots of the trees already planted and leave the seeds thrown broadcast to take on form bye and bye."[55]

At a meeting of the Boston-area Universalist Ministers' Association, missionary work was discussed at much length; some thought that church extension had been "scattering too much."[56] Although Shinn was not mentioned by name, he assumed that the criticism was aimed at him and retorted that almost all Universalist churches had been the result of missionary effort.

In 1902 Anthony Bilkovsky (Beresford), pastor of the church in Baltimore, reviewed the domestic missionary policy of the denomination and found much wanting.[57] He discussed in some detail the merits of concentrating on a few large churches and the demerits of attempting to expand everywhere without the resources or the will to sustain what was started. Dispersal of effort, given the advancing state of communication, he considered anachronistic and faulty. Concentration was the order of the day. There was no need at all to attempt to make Universalism formally visible in every state, county, city, and hamlet in the nation.

Bilkovsky argued that the larger and more prosperous denominations had long since abandoned such a policy, or had not ever attempted it in the first place. Where was the "natural clientele" of the church? It was to be found in metropolitan areas of the North, East, and West, and in those urban centers of the South where Northerners had settled. Churches grew most rapidly wherever they were already strongest. Multiplication by division was not the proper route. The denominational press had already been largely consolidated and eventually the three divinity schools then operated by Universalists would by logic and necessity be combined into one. All too many state conventions were aiding parishes that had no future, but merely existed, and usually because they were being propped up from the outside by resources better expended elsewhere.

The missionary policy, "by pathetic mistake called 'Our Mission Field,' " in the South, was "altogether out of date." Without mentioning Shinn by name, Bilkovsky referred to "a nomad scurrying over half a continent," who was the embodiment of the opposite of what should be done. " 'Scrap' the Southern missionary policy." A hundred churches of great strength would be far superior to "a myriad of feeble parishes scattered up and down forty-five states." Andrew Carnegie had learned the secret of consolidation and A. T. Stewart and Marshall Field had offered the retail department store as evidence that "the day of little things has gone." The church had better follow suit and keep up with the march of time and change. The time had come for "a frank denominational self-examination, a candid reconsideration" of the path Universalists should take.

This was strong medicine for many Universalists to swallow. One Canadian, applying Bilkovsky's principle to his portion of North America, saw only disaster if a policy of concentration were followed exclusively.[58] According to the Dominion census of 1901, there were 2,589 Universalists in Canada, but only 446 were church members. The combined membership of their five small churches in the province of Ontario was 165. There was only one church in all of the Maritime Provinces (Halifax, with a membership of 110). Only 171 individuals belonged to Universalist churches in the province of Quebec. And what about the 8,993 who claimed no denominational connection of any kind? Thee was certainly room for expansion as well as concentration. The latter policy seemed not to have worked; in fact, it appeared to the Canadian that "with a little more 'Concentration' we will have reached the vanishing point."

Shinn's reaction to Bilkovsky's proposal could easily be anticipated. The indignant Southern missionary was positive that the minister in Baltimore had no understanding at all of either the missionary policy of the General Convention, which had been "concentrating" for years, or that of the state conventions through the system of superintendents.[59] Shinn then listed numerous specific examples. He doubted that concentrating denominational papers was the best way, believing that locally produced publications had much merit. Consolidation of theological schools would further deplete an already scarcely populated ministry. Adopting the "Carnegie Steel Trust system" or the department store plan would be unthinkable.

There was not, according to Shinn, a single city in the Union where a consolidated church was established that did not depend in some way on the countryside. If young men and women from small rural churches had not come in to Kansas City, Atlanta, or Birmingham, there could have been no urban churches. Never in all his life had he seen a more suicidal theory than Bilkovsky's. Shinn used the Red Hill church in North Carolina as an example of what could be done even with a country church. In 1902 it had a membership of 192 even though it had no resident pastor.[60] Furthermore, it had sent Universalists into other states, such as South Carolina, and was the parent church of a growing congregation established at Oak Grove, a rural community thirty-five miles north of Red Hill.

The controversy aired in the press between Bilkovsky and Shinn continued on a rather personal level for some time. Bilkovsky accused Shinn of possessing "intemperate zeal" and of rushing in prematurely before surveying adequately the possibilities. He pointed out that merely organizing a church and providing a building were not "finalities" but only starting points.[61] The existence of neither was a guarantee of success, particularly if they were left to fend for themselves.

Rodney F. Johonnot added his voice to the debate over concentration versus expansion and came down on the side of concentration. He believed that compactness was superior to dispersion. With a transparent reference to Shinn's statistic-laden reports, Johonnot argued that denominational success was not to be measured by the number of miles travelled by railroad or the distances between mission stations and preaching posts.[62]

The debate brought forth reactions from other Universalists which for the most part supported the indomitable Shinn. When the term "grasshopper missionary" had been first applied to him in 1893, several individuals had come to his defense, favorably comparing his conributions to those of earlier missionaries.[63] Ada C. Bowles, writing from Kinston, North Carolina, was positive that Shinn was overcoming the two main obstacles to denominational prosperity in the South: The failure to obtain adequate financial support, and the lack of disciplined organization.[64]

One of Shinn's most loyal supporters, Mrs. Irwin, blamed the denomination as a whole rather than any weaknesses inherent in his system for the inability to keep churches going.[65] It was the failure of the organization "which authorized him to do those things to keep alive that which he started."[66] She emphasized another contribution made by Shinn and not sufficiently appreciated; namely, that not until he worked among Southern Universalists did it occur to most of them that they were parts of a larger organization as well as members of local constituencies.

In Shinn's defense it should be pointed out that he did not favor the rural South entirely at the expense of urban centers. He aimed for towns and cities as well as hamlets, crossroads, and isolated countrysides. He planted, or attempted to plant, Universalism in such key centers as Durham, North Carolina; Columbia, South Carolina (the state capital); Jacksonville, Florida; Montgomery, Mobile, and Birmingham, Alabama;

Nashville and Chattanooga, Tennessee; Little Rock, Arkansas; Houston, Texas; and Charleston, West Virginia, the largest city in that state as well as the state capital. As he put it, "My way is to go wherever a hungry soul calls for our message."[67]

In the course of carrying out his plan to build a church a year in each state, Kansas City and St. Louis had just as much a place on his schedule in Missouri as did the rural communities of Archie, Elmer, and Knob Noster. Near the close of his life Shinn decided to travel less widely than in the past, and to devote increased attention to the urban centers to which so many rural youth had migrated.

Shinn repeatedly and quite accurately pointed out in the course of his missionary travels over the years that the South was basically a rural rather than an urbanized section of the nation; hence it was logical to organize Universalism where the real strength of the population seemed to be. He was at least partially vindicated when the *Leader* in 1915 came out strongly in favor of spreading Universalism in rural communities and establishing country and small-town missions rather than in large urban centers.[68]

Hannah Powell, from her vantage point as a missionary in the mountains of western North Carolina in the 1920s, was impressed by the vitality of country churches. She felt that Universalists made a mistake in attempting to organize in Southern cities. "If I had money for church extension, I would spend it all at the country cross roads."[69] At almost the same time, the General Superintendent was instructed by the trustees of the General Convention to follow a policy of "concentrating money and men on hopeful points instead of scattering resources."[70] The debate over whether to concentrate in rural or urban America was never resolved, and it would probably hve been too much to expect otherwise. The denomination pursued both paths as best it could.

The demarcation of Shinn's official relationship to the central authority of the denomination was a source of much difficulty and even embarrassment at times after 1895. When he was made General Missionary that year he reported directly to the trustees and was given freedom to schedule his own activities and determine his own priorities with a minimum of oversight. This system worked very well until the office of General Superintendent was created in 1898. It was obvious that there would be much overlapping and duplication of effort between the two offices as well as questions of jurisdiction and accountability. The General Convention, after hearing the annual report of the first General Superintendent, Isaac M. Atwood, voted in 1899 to transfer to his office all missionary work previously overseen by the trustees.[71] This left Shinn in a rather ambivalent position, compounded by the fact that Atwood had cautioned against establishing churches where there was no prospect of permanency.[72] He also warned against spreading the denomination too thinly over too extended an area. Both of these comments by Atwood bore directly on Shinn's own work.

Atwood had expressed his views on church extension many years earlier, and was only repeating them. In 1891 he had doubted the advisability of establishing a large number of new parishes when the supply of ministers was so uncertain, and many rural churches were languishing or closed because of lack of clergy. He had recommended that new ones be organized only in such strategic urban centers as Denver, Omaha, and Duluth.[73]

In the course of his first year as General Superintendent, Atwood had traversed much of the same ground as Shinn himself had covered, and on which the latter had reported in so much detail in separate reports. In 1899 a partial solution of the problem of overlapping activities was temporarily effected when Atwood, in supervising missions from Canada to California, carefully avoided trespassing on Shinn's domain in the South except to attend convention and conference meetings on special invitation. The dilemma was at least alleviated when the General Convention created the special position of "Missionary to the Southern States" in 1900 for Shinn's benefit, and so as to retain his increasingly valuable services in the location of his first choice. Shinn's position was made semi-autonomous; he reported directly to the General Convention.

But the device of creating a special office for Shinn merely complicated the situation by making a financial commitment, small as it was, that the General Convention could ill afford. The official relation of Shinn to the General Superintendent was left unresolved. There was not enough money to support both a General Superintendent and a missionary to one section of the nation, particularly when one of the former's duties already called specifically for supervision of missionary work.

The problem came to a head within a year. The *ad hoc* convention committee to which all reports were routinely referred for recommendation to the main body, advised the General Convention in 1901 to discontinue the office of Southern Missionary. Abolition of Shinn's post was narrowly averted when Thomas Chapman of Georgia, a member of the committee and a person with first-hand knowledge of Shinn's contributions to Southern Universalism, submitted a minority report.[74] He commended the missionary for his outstanding work and recommended that Shinn's office be continued. The committee's report was then amended to recommend continuation of the post of Southern Missionary as Chapman advised. However, it was provided that Shinn would be "under the direction of the General Superintendent." The convention accepted the arrangement, as did Shinn.

A second attempt was made, in 1903, to abolish Shinn's position and replace it with a financial secretary who would operate on a national level and be responsible to the General Superintendent.[75] But there was such a chorus of praise at the meeting for Shinn and his work, led by Mrs. Irwin and the venerable D. B. Clayton, and such a flood of testimonials on his behalf, that Shinn's office was rescued again. The position came to an end with Shinn's death in 1907.

W. H. McGlauflin, who succeeded Atwood as General Superintendent, took over the general oversight of the area previously covered by Shinn.[76] However, this interim arrangement could not be continued because of McGlauflin's multitude of other duties, and he was unable to visit the South as often as he wished.

By 1908 many Southern states, like those in other parts of the nation, had created state and district superintendencies which took over many of the responsibilities exercised previously by Shinn, and the incumbents served in actuality as missionary pastors. The office of Southern Superintendent was finally created in 1920; F. B. Bishop, for five years previously the state superintendent in Ohio, was the first incumbent. He used Montgomery, Alabama as his headquarters, and concentrated his activities in Alabama and Florida.[77]

Assistance and encouragement continued to come also from other denominational organizations, notably the Women's National Missionary Association which sponsored its own personnel in North Carolina and attempted to continue the work of the beloved "grasshopper missionary," even though concentrated in one state.

Shinn had also become involved in what was later described as "the only project for Negroes sponsored by our denomination." The reference was to the Norfolk and Suffolk missions in Virginia.

Chapter 19

The Norfolk and Suffolk Missions in the South

Within a year after the conclusion of the Civil War occasional references were made by Universalists to the need for schools and teachers in the South to lift the newly emancipated Negro "in the scales of civilization."[1] A resolution adopted by the Vermont Convention in 1867 called for equal treatment of the races and applauded the educational work of the Freedmen's Bureau which had been established in 1865 as a government-sponsored agency to assist the Negro.[2]

In 1867 Henry Summer of Newbury, South Carolina, had addressed a series of six articles in the *Universalist Herald* "To the Universalists of the South and North" in which he made an impassioned plea for the fair and just treatment of the Negro. To Summer, education was crucial to accomplish his goal of elevating the Negro to a position of political and economic equality with whites, which he believed the freedman deserved as a part of his birthright as a human being. By education Summer meant training in all branches of learning, and not a narrow vocationalism confined to physical labor and the industrial arts. The Negro needed, as well, inculcation of good habits and moral instruction, so that he could "feel and act like a freeman, with all the responsibilities of a freeman."[3] Here was the golden opportunity for Universalists to practice "works of benevolence and charity," and to prove that indeed they held "the enlarged faith."

But the rhetoric of Summer, whose sincerity was no doubt as genuine as his Southern birth and upbringing, and the resolutions of ecclesiastical bodies in the North, remained for some twenty years so far as the denomination was concerned, only paper declarations of good intent. Whatever the will, the way was lacking. There were fugitive references in the records to individual Universalists who journeyed south to teach school or to assist in charitable activities after 1865, but their numbers were few and their influence unknown.

After a brief visit to Missouri and attendance at two Negro church services in 1890, Isaac M. Atwood wrote a lengthy editorial on "The Negro Problem."[4] He identified it as primarily one of finding a way for whites and Negroes to live harmoniously in the same community as political equals. He found that the races were basically distinct in their relations in almost every respect, that the whites were politically dominant, and that socially there was no movement whatever toward a blending of the races. He did, however, detect "an approach to obliteration of race lines in the schools."

A correspondent (J. K. Street) in the *Leader,* writing from Waco, Texas, immediately challenged Atwood's statement and warned outsiders not to jump to conclusions derived from inadequate information and based only on a passing trip through parts of the South.[5] A few years' residence in the South would change preconceived notions about the desirability of giving equal political and social rights to the Negro. Atwood's comment about the schools was "wholly unsupported by the facts. Mixed schools in the South are unknown and not desired by either race." Social and political equality of the two races would (and should) never come to pass. No enactment of law could ever force such a result, for the laws of nature would always prevail. Street believed that giving the franchise to the Negro was the worst mistake ever made; he should be relegated "to his true position with other inferior races, such as the Chinaman, which the settled policy of this government declares unfit for citizenship."

The question was voiced occasionally of why so few Negroes were members of Universalist churches in either the North or the South. Part of the blame for their absence seemed to lie in the lack of vigorous missionary programs such as those conducted by other denominations.[6] Why not combine missionary work on behalf of Universalism with the establishment of educational opportunities for the Negro?

The first known attempt by Universalists to provide such facilities was made in the Midwest rather than in the South, and was far from comprehensive. The women of William H. Ryder's church in Chicago conducted for several years "St. Paul's Universalist Industrial School."[7] Opened in 1879 for Negro children who were not welcome at existing schools, the Universalist-sponsored project used the facilities of the (Negro) Olivet Baptist Church. The school, which concentrated on teaching sewing and domestic skills to young girls, attained an enrollment of more than seventy but was strictly local in character and was operated by a single church.

It was in the late 1880s that the denomination became directly involved in the dual task of assisting in the education of Southern Negroes and in the propagation of Universalism among them. It was an ex-Baptist Negro minister who actually took the initiative in establishing what came to be known as the Norfolk and Suffolk missions.

Joseph Jordan (1842–1901) was born in West Norfolk (Norfolk County), Virginia, and died in Huntersville, the black community in

Norfolk, on 3 June 1901. He was converted to Universalism largely through the writings of Thomas Whittemore, Alonzo A. Miner, and Thomas B. Thayer.[8] He had occasion in the late 1880s to visit Philadelphia, where he heard Universalism preached by Edwin C. Sweetser, pastor of the Church of the Messiah. Jordan was received into the fellowship of the Philadelphia church and in 1889 became the first ordained Negro minister in the denomination.[9] The ceremony took place in Sweetser's church.

An enthusiastic supporter of his new faith, Jordan set out to establish a mission in his native community. The congregation which he had begun to assemble in 1887 was admitted to the fellowship of the General Convention at the same time Jordan was fellowshipped by that body in 1889.[10] By 1891 he had organized, with an assistant, a day school, a Sunday school, and a church of eighteen members which met in a private home.[11]

Through arrangements made by Sweetser, Jordan delivered an address at the General Convention when it met in Washington, D.C., in 1893. Entitled "Our Mission Among the Colored People," his plea for financial assistance to construct a chapel in Norfolk brought pledges of more than $2,600 while the convention was still in session.[12] Shortly thereafter the Woman's Centenary Association pledged $100.[13] A small frame building was erected which served as a combination chapel on Sundays and secular school on weekdays.

Shinn, who by 1894 had become a full-time roving missionary in the South, organized a Young People's Christian Union among the Negro youth, and preached his first sermon in the new building in September 1894. The structure was dedicated as the First Universalist Church of Norfolk (Huntersville Section) in November, with the principal sermon delivered by Sweetser.[14]

The venture was an immediate success. A sizable congregation was assembled (much larger than the actual church membership), and the day school soon had an enrollment of nearly 100, although the average daily attendance was much lower. Assistance was obtained in the person of Thomas E. Wise of Ocean View, Virginia. He was one of Jordan's Negro converts and was fellowshipped in 1895. It was Wise who was responsible for the idea of establishing a second Universalist mission among the Negroes.

The second mission was located in Suffolk, Virginia, twenty miles south of Norfolk. Wise had preached occasionally to Negroes in Suffolk in the 1890s and had earlier taught school in the Negro community there. Shinn immediately saw the possibilities for a second mission, and in the summer of 1897 raised at a meeting at The Weirs in New Hampshire, more than $500 to establish it.[15] This sum was augmented by a donation of $50 by the Universalist Missionary Society of Massachusetts (a women's group), and contributions from various individuals.

The result of this effort was the construction in 1898 of a small two-story white frame building, with a total estimated value of $1,000, including the building site. It was located in the shadow of the Planters Peanuts processing plant, where many of the Negroes were employed. A schoolroom with a capacity of 200 persons was provided on the first floor, a portion of which was later set aside as a chapel. Wise, who was put in charge of the mission, eventually lived with his wife and one child in four rooms on the second floor.[16] Wise assisted the black contractor with the finish work on the building, which became the property of the General Convention.

Even before December 1898, when the mission's quarters were formally opened by Shinn, he and Wise had arranged for a school of sorts, and Shinn had organized both a Sunday school and a youth group, all of which met at first in a hired hall. The school, intended to provide basic

Thomas E. Wise, a Universalist minister and his son in Norfolk, Virginia

Headquarters of the Suffolk Mission in Virginia

industrial training for boys and domestic instruction for girls, had opened in 1897 with eleven students. There were also classes in the rudiments of the three R's and religious services on Sunday, conducted by Wise.

With the opening of the new facilities in the winter of 1898 school enrollment jumped to sixty-five and assistance had to be obtained. Miss M. E. French, a young Negro who had been among the first to attend the mission school, and who had received some normal school training, was employed as a teacher in 1901. She conducted a sewing class and supervised both the Sunday school, which by then had an enrollment of fifty, and a youth group of sixty. In 1901 there were 275 pupils on the roll of the school, with a monthly average attendance of 96.

After Joseph Jordan died in 1901, Wise was placed in charge of both the Norfolk and Suffolk missions, under the general direction of the missionary committee of the trustees of the General Convention. Wise at first commuted between the two communities, preaching at each on alternate Sundays and teaching classes whenever practicable. However, shortly after Jordan's death, Wise left the denomination to become a Methodist, followed by eight members of the mission.[17] Wise put George W. Watson, who had attended the Norfolk mission school, in charge of that operation, assisted by Jordan's widow. The total annual cost to the denomination of the two missions in 1901 was less than $600.[18]

The Norfolk mission withered away after Wise's departure; the school had closed by 1904 although the church organization continued to exist; most of the members had migrated northward.[19] In 1913 C. W. Jones, a Negro minister previously ordained in the Methodist church, and residing in Suffolk, was licensed for one year to work in and around Norfolk and attempt to keep the remnants of the church together, but was unsuccessful.[20]

The name most often associated with the Suffolk mission was that of Joseph Fletcher Jordan (1863–1929), another Negro convert to Univer-

Joseph Fletcher Jordan (1863-1929), Universalist minister in Suffolk, Virginia

salism. He was not related to the founder of the Norfolk mission (Joseph Jordan) but was frequently confused with him, for obvious reasons. The second Jordan had been born in Gates County, North Carolina, in that part of the Dismal Swamp known as "Pocoson," on 6 June 1863. He was born of slave parents, William and Anne Jordan. His first association with organized religion had come through the Baptist church, although he never joined it.[21] At the age of fourteen he was apprenticed to a white Methodist in order to learn bricklaying and plastering. He also served as janitor of a white Methodist church, where he was required to attend church and Sunday school, an experience which probably led to his becoming a preacher in the African Methodist Church.[22] He served in that capacity for twelve years, after which he practiced law.

Jordan was a graduate of the state normal school for Negroes at Plymouth, North Carolina, at the age of twenty-two. He was twice married and widowed; his first wife died in 1916 and his second in 1926.

While residing in Durham, North Carolina, he read of preaching by Shinn, who was responsible for Jordan's conversion to Universalism. After a year's study at Canton Theological School (St. Lawrence University) as a special student, arranged by Shinn, Jordan joined the Universalist church in Norfolk. Jordan was licensed in 1903 and fellowshipped in 1904 after taking charge of the Suffolk mission. He was active in the temperance movement, served as a correspondent for the *New York Age* and the *Guide and Journal* (Norfolk, Virginia). He also published at irregular intervals the *Colored Universalist*.[23] He received an honorary Doctor of Divinity degree from Barretts College, North Carolina, in 1900.

Jordan was associated with the Suffolk mission from 1904 until his death on 1 May 1929. The "St. Paul Mission School," as Jordan designated the Suffolk school, almost disappeared after Wise's departure, but Jordan attempted not only to reorganize it but hoped to elevate it into the "Suffolk Industrial College."[24] By 1904 the school had seventy-four students on its roll, "of all colors, sizes, and ages," from five to twenty-two. But there was no money or other support forthcoming, and Jordan predicted that the school might be forced to close at the end of 1904. But somehow it managed to survive. Within a year Jordan had built the day school from "almost nothing" to 186 — more than its normal capacity.[25] In 1909 it was reported to have an enrollment of 129.[26] At the same time Jordan designated it as the "Shinn Universalist Mission School" in honor of the well-known missionary.

The religious organizations at Suffolk seemed also to have been prospering this year, with fifty families in the parish, twenty-three church members, a Sunday school of forty-four, and a youth group of twenty-one. This was in sharp contrast to the situation Jordan had found when he arrived in 1904; there had been only one member left in the church. Here was visible evidence that Jordan's efforts were meeting a genuine need, both religiously and educationally.

Jordan encountered opposition from Negroes as well as whites because of his Universalist affiliation, particularly those who belonged to fundamentalist denominations (as did the majority). However, Negroes did not hesitate to take advantage of the opportunity to send their children to his school. Religious organizations and services were consequently never as well populated as were the school classes. While the congregation in the parish which Shinn had organized seldom reached fifty, and the Sunday school and youth group averaged between twenty-five and thirty, there were seldom less than seventy-five attending the school at any one time. Students were about equally divided between boys and girls. Over the twelve-year period from 1899 to 1911, some 1,400 had received instruction of some kind.

Isaac M. Atwood visited the Suffolk mission in 1906 and was much impressed with the "civilizing and humanizing influences" of Jordan and his school, and commented on his "heroic work on very slender resources."[27] The school desperately needed enlarged quarters, having an enrollment of 158 the year of Atwood's visit.[28]

By 1912 enrollment in what was known by then as the "Suffolk Normal Training School" exceeded 200. One of the staff of four was J. W. Wilson, a native of Africa who had come to America as a youth and had been educated in a Presbyterian school, supplemented by correspondence courses taken through the University of Chicago. A convert to Universalism, he served as Jordan's assistant.

Instruction by 1912 was offered from kindergarten through the first year of high school. In 1911 night classes were being provided for boys and young men in a variety of fields, including such diverse subjects as carpentry and bookkeeping. Some even studied Latin and Greek.[29] Tuition in the school, which had no endowment of any kind at the time, was 5 cents a week for regular day courses and up to 50 cents a week for certain night courses. The tuition charge by 1915 had been raised to 10 cents a week for each student, with an average collection of $5.65; only half of the students were able to pay anything.[30] The staple curriculum for the girls centered around what was then called "domestic science," emphasizing the development of sewing and cooking skills.

The school, bulging at the seams, was brought personally to the attention of the General Convention by Jordan, who attended its session in 1911. His plea for help brought an authorization to conduct a canvass to secure $6,000.[31] The full amount was never raised but sufficient money was obtained to enlarge the building slightly, with improvements costing $1,400. It was valued at about $3,500 in 1912.[32] Even then the accommodations were inadequate; in 1915 the students had to be divided into two groups and attend on alternate days.[33]

The school continued to be supported by small grants from the General Convention, various Universalist organizations, and private donations. For a time before World War I it received regular contributions from the Union Baptist Church (Colored) in Cambridge, Massachusetts.[34] It became in 1917, at the request of the General Convention, one of the projects supported by the General Sunday School Association. The Sunday school contribution the first year amounted to $440.[35] An annual appeal for $1,000 was begun in 1922, known at first as the "Suffolk Offering." It became, in turn, the "American Missionary Offering" and then part of an enlarged "American Friendship Offering."[36]

The closest approximation to an endowment was a bequest by Jordan to the General Convention of property worth $1,200. It was transferred only after prolonged litigation.[37] In 1917 the Mary Louise Lisbon Fund was established for the purpose of supporting Negro education.[38] However, the income from a principal of $616.53 did not go very far; it amounted to $24.66 in 1920.[39]

There is no question that the Suffolk mission performed a valuable community service from the very beginning, especially in a racially segregated city where between 50 and 60 percent of the population was Negro and schooling for them was grossly inadequate. William H. McGlauflin, who had visited the school and had talked with the townspeople, reported in 1911 that the structure which housed the school, inadequate as it was, was considered the best school building in the city.[40] According to both the city and county school superintendents, if the mission closed, the one public school for Negroes would have been unable to accommodate the children. The school also served Negroes outside the corporate limits of the city. Two-thirds of the students in 1917 came from the surrounding countryside.[41]

Jordan seems to have been able to maintain good relations with whites as well as Negroes, in spite of what most whites considered his questionable religious choice. The school was highly endorsed by both the mayor and the chief of police for "promoting the intelligence, good order, sobriety and general usefulness of the Negro population."[42] Jordan, in addition to his other responsibilities, served for a time as the probation officer for an estimated 700 Negro juveniles in Suffolk.[43] It was reported that no Negro who had attended the school had ever been arrested.[44] This may have sounded like a somewhat left-handed compliment, but given the circumstances which existed, it was a tribute to both Jordan and his school.

Shinn, who played a decisive role in the establishment of both the Norfolk and Suffolk missions, was among those who saw the possibilities of spreading Universalism among Southern Negroes. He was responsible for converting such isolated Negroes as Henry Holmes of Henderson, Tennessee, who became a licensed minister and eked out a living with odd jobs which included janitorial services for the local white Methodist church.[45] However, Shinn's greatest efforts among Negroes were concentrated on the two Negro missions in Virginia. When the Suffolk mission moved into its own building in 1898, he decided that there would be sufficient additional space to build a theological school to train prospective Negro clergy.[46] This was a facility "which our Church must in a few years establish." This, like many of Shinn's ambitious plans for the denomination, never materialized. Neither did another mission effort among Negroes which Shinn considered briefly, and which adds an interesting footnote to the Norfolk and Suffolk missions.

Shinn had become acquainted with one J. A. Murphy, a Negro convert to Universalism, in the rural community of Bartow (Jefferson County), Georgia, about eighty miles northwest of Savannah.[47] Murphy, in turn, had converted three other Negro clergy, and two small church organizations and a Sunday school had been established. The church headed by Murphy had sixteen members. Shinn visited the community in 1901, on instruction from the convention trustees, conferred with the four ministers, and heard each of them preach in succession at a conference he arranged. Hopeful as he always was of adding Universalists to the ranks, wherever found, he had to confess that not all met his specifications. Nonetheless, here was the raw material for another mission.

A Baptist church vacated by whites was available for $300 and could be paid for in installments. Murphy could serve as the leader. If, as Shinn pointed out, Universalists could go to the other side of the globe and contribute thousands of dollars to a mission in Japan, certainly they could support a home mission among Negroes in one area of one state. "I suppose the only question with us is this: Is the soul of the Negro worth as much as the soul of a Japanese or Chinaman?"

Shinn was forced to admit that the obstacles to establishing a mission in Bartow, Georgia, were almost insurmountable. There was so much opposition to Universalism among whites as well as Negroes in the community that it might be the better part of wisdom for the Negroes not even to undertake anything in the Universalist name. Further, the Negroes were so poverty-stricken that they could probably do little by themselves, and would never be able to make a church self-supporting. Nevertheless, it was a challenge which the denomination had to face if it felt any obligation at all "to the colored race." So far as the records indicate, this particular challenge in Georgia was never met.

The trustees of the General Convention did go so far as to appoint a committee to review the situation of the three Negro missions, but only minimal financial support was ever given to the Norfolk mission which had disappeared by the time of World War I. The one in Georgia never officially came into existence; and the Suffolk mission had to struggle on with little more than rhetorical encouragement from national headquarters, although it doggedly held on.

After Jordan's death in 1929 the church organization at Suffolk which had achieved a membership of forty-eight the previous year, was dissolved.[48] The school, however, continued. Mrs. Annie B. Willis, Jordan's daughter, and a teacher in the school, continued as principal, assisted by her daughter Dorothy and Miss Ethel Whack. The staff was augmented to a total of four or five by the end of the 1920s, although there was considerable turnover of personnel because of inadequate salaries.[49]

The school barely weathered the economic depression of the 1930s, and its already shabby and outgrown facilities deteriorated even farther while enrollment had continued apace. There were 210 students in the fall of 1938 while the staff had been reduced to three by necessity. General Superintendent Cummins visited the Suffolk school in the summer of 1938 and was shocked at its deplorable physical condition.[50] He found many of the children sitting on the floor because there were no desks for them. The library was "made up of books which could not command a place on the 5 cent shelf in front of a second-hand bookstore." Something had to be done. So a plea for increased support was issued, and in the fall of 1938 the Young People's Christian Union voted to join with the GSSA in making the school one of its service projects. The women's group continued to lend token support, constricted as its treasury was. Simultaneously, changes were being considered that radically changed the character of the Suffolk mission.

Since the establishment of the mission school greatly improved public education for Negroes had been provided, so the offering of classroom instruction had become much less pressing. In 1939 it was decided to phase out academic instruction and concentrate on social service and kindergarten work. The four upper grades were dropped that year, followed by the lower four in 1940.[51]

The school had also diversified its functions by the late 1920s to include a pre-natal and well-baby clinic. A decade later both state and city public health departments expanded their activities and provided both equipment and personnel for a mothers' clinic and other medical services, all housed in the school building which had been partially rehabilitated after Cummins' visit. It was therefore appropriate in 1939 that the Suffolk facility be renamed the Jordan Neighborhood House to emphasize its new role in the community. At the same time Universalists established a day care center and nursery school for working mothers. The change in the type of activity from school work to social work was approved by the General Convention in 1941.[52]

In the midst of World War II there were seventy-five pupils in the kindergarten and more than fifty older children in recreational and club groups.[53] During the 1940s a reminder of the religious origins of the old Suffolk school was demonstrated by the conduct during the summer months of a popular vacation Bible school which had a waiting list almost every year. Part of the financing of the summer activities was made possible by the national Universalist youth group by way of its Legion of the Cross.[54]

General oversight of Jordan Neighborhood House continued to be provided by Universalist headquarters under a variety of administrative designations such as the Universalist Service Committee which had been created in 1945, and the Department of Service Projects established four years later. Financial support was provided by a network of sources which included the Association of Universalist Women which had had a long-standing interest in the Suffolk mission. Of the budget of almost $7,500 authorized for 1951–1952, almost half ($3,500) was provided by the women's organization.[55] The AUW also committed itself to provide $3,000 annually for three years toward the salary of a full-time staff member to asist Mrs. Willis, who continued her long association with the Suffolk mission.

During the 1950s and 1960s Jordan Neighborhood House continued to fulfill its many community responsibilities. It quietly but effectively did its part in the delicate and often painful transition in race relations precipitated by the epochal Supreme Court school desegregation decisions. It was a pioneer in operating the first Head Start program for pre-school children in the region in the mid-1960s.[56]

The last denominational ties were cut when the Unitarian Universalist Service Committee, which had been responsible for the project after denominational consolidation, ceased financial support in 1969. By the time of Mrs. Willis' death in 1977 the pre-school activities had been assumed by the Southeastern Tidewater Opportunity Project and the Neighborhood House had become the Jordan Community Center. Only the name of the individual who had kept the old Suffolk mission alive, remained as a reminder of its Universalist origins.

Chapter 20

In the Mountains of Western North Carolina

Tucked away along the Pigeon River Valley some 3,000 feet above sea level in the Blue Ridge Mountains of Western North Carolina (Haywood County), eleven miles from the nearest town of any size (Canton), there existed in the nineteenth century a small community of fiercely independent farmers of Scotch-Irish, English, and German heritage who had been converted to Universalism in the mid-1860s by Benjamin F. Strain, a saddlebag preacher operating out of Georgia.[1] Among the converts was Jonathan Plott.[2]

Plott, who had been licensed as a Universalist preacher, presumably by Strain, was among those who organized the First Universalist Church of Haywood County, North Carolina, in July 1868, after an initial meeting in 1865.[3] The next step was to find a settled minister, and James Anderson Inman was Plott's choice. Inman sought the advice of John C. Burruss of Notasulga, Alabama, on how ordination could be conferred, and was informed that because of "our scattered condition in the South we must work according to the exigencies of the circumstances that surround us."[4] Imman followed Burruss' instructions and was ordained shortly after the church was organized, by prayer and the laying on of hands by three men in the group. He was also baptized in a stream near the Plott home — a requirement not specified by Burruss. Strain, who signed the ordination certificate, was the moderator for the occasion.

Inman (1826–1913) was the son of a tenant farmer just across the border in Tennessee, and had moved to Pigeon River at age seventeen. He and his wife had first lived in the Plott home and, like most of his neighbors, became a farmer. He had a numerous family — seven daughters and three sons — and remained the preacher for forty-five years, almost up to the time of his death at the age of eighty-seven. There is no record that he left the community for as much as overnight or travelled a radius of more than ten miles by mule to hold Sunday school classes.

Until 1902 there was no building except private residences in which to hold services, and this lack had been made known to the state conference, organized in 1896 in the eastern part of the state, and which became the state convention in 1905. One of the first acts of the conference, in 1897, was to pledge assistance in constructing a church. Aid was also provided by Q. H. Shinn, who first visited the settlement in 1902. He secured cash subscriptions totalling $4.00 and donations of eighty hours of labor.[5] He pitched in himself and helped saw the foundation blocks from the donated lumber for what became Inman's Chapel, dedicated in 1903 by Shinn as a tribute to the seventy-seven-year-old Universalist preacher. Inman, who himself did much of the actual construction, refused to allow one cent of indebtedness, and sold off part of his holdings to raise money.[6]

On the eve of Inman's death in 1913 the WNMA assumed responsibility for supervision and support of denominational activities in North Carolina, and in 1912 authorized the expenditure of up to $150 toward a minister's salary for Inman's Chapel.[7] But nothing was done to provide regular preaching for several years and the tiny Universalist enclave in the midst of old-fashioned Southern Calvinistic orthodoxy almost disappeared from sight. Mrs. Minnie J. Ayres, president of the WNMA, had the existence of the Pigeon River community called to her attention in 1915 and discovered that the small wooden chapel, which had been deeded to the General Convention, was being used by a group of Methodists.[8]

The WNMA then instructed J. L. Everton, serving in the eastern part of the state, to assess the situation and report on the feasibility of providing ministerial service. His report in 1916 was so unenthusiastic that nothing was done for five years. In 1921 Harry L. Canfield and his wife, Mary Grace, made a similar journey and returned with the strong recommendation that the chapel be reopened under Universalist auspices as both a religious and social service center. This time, because the advice was more positive, Hannah Jewett Powell (1866–1854) was selected as the denominational representative in that remote mountain region.

Probably no better choice could have been made for the assignment than Miss Powell, who for fifteen years remained at Inman's Chapel, admired for her tireless energy and beloved for her dedicated service with minimal material resources, and for her ability to overcome the suspicion of outsiders in a poverty-stricken and largely unlettered community of proud mountaineers mostly isolated from the rest of America. The area was aptly described by her successor as "this land of doing without."[9]

Powell had in her own background, in at least one respect, an experience shared by the inhabitants of the settlement in Western North Carolina. She had come of a family poor in material goods. She was born in

Clinton, Maine, on 6 October 1866, her father a logger struggling to support children of whom only she survived to adulthood. Her longstanding ambition to receive an education and to become a ministerial missionary was realized only after much struggle. She attended Coburn Classical Institute, a boarding school in Waterville, Maine, and later attended Colby College. She received a divinity degree from Tufts in 1899, the only woman in her graduating class of seven, and was ordained the same year. She was employed by the Sea Coast Mission in Maine for five years (1899–1903), working with residents on the islands.

After refusing an offer of marriage to the skipper of the cargo ship servicing the offshore islands, Powell did occasional preaching in various Maine communities, taught in public schools, travelled widely as a money-raiser for the WNMA, and served as a lecturer for the YWCA during World War I. She was selected by the WNMA to work in the Pigeon River community and arrived in September 1921, in the midst of economic depression following the war. Pigeon River was especially hard hit by the closing of the extensive operations of the Suncrest Lumber Co. which had built a saw mill near a railroad spur known as Sunburst. Inhabitants of the area had used lumbering activities to supplement their meager incomes from subsistence farming. The community was virtually isolated from the outside world, six miles from the nearest paved road, and suffering from all the ills of rural poverty.

Powell tackled with determination the multitude of problems she found, convinced that something should and would be done, and by the late 1920s had literally accomplished miracles. Besides conducting regular church services she concentrated on the youth of the community. Within a year she had opened a Sunday school of sixty and started the first Universalist-operated kindergarten in the state, with an initial enrollment of seventeen, aged four through seven.[10] Between her arrival in 1921 and 1934 not a session of the Sunday school was missed, winter weather and travel in the mountains notwithstanding.[11]

Quarters were so cramped by the mid-1920s that another building was needed to serve as both the minister's residence and as a community center. A half-acre of land adjoining the chapel was purchased for $25, from Pingree Inman in 1924, and another one-third of an acre was acquired the following year.[12] An appeal for funds by the WNMA had to be supplemented by a short-term loan, but in 1927 the goal of additional housing had been realized. Known as "Friendly House," it was still in operation when Universalist sponsorship ceased after World War II. The nine-room building cost $6,000 and was used for a wide variety of purposes.

Powell had come to depend increasingly on older girls for assistance in conducting Sunday school and other youth activities and in 1927 obtained through the WNMA the services of Miss Ruth G. Downing, who remained

The mission in Western North Carolina

until transferred to the Japan mission in 1929. She held a ministerial license issued by the state convention at the time of her arrival and was periodically renewed. She worked especially with the Negro children in the abandoned saw mill village of Sunburst and thus kept up the tradition of Father Inman, who had preached to Negroes as well as to whites in his congregation.

The editor of the *Leader,* after a visit in 1928, was so impressed with the work being done that he pledged $100 a year to assist, and issued a call for $1,000 to establish an educational fund.[13] The denomination-wide plea for aid brought immediate results, although not enough to provide the school facilities on the scale desired by Powell. Typical was a donation of $150 from the women's mission circle in Malden, Massachusetts.

Powell had started a summer school which in 1930 had an enrollment of more than sixty, and offered academic subjects as well as courses in woodworking, sewing, weaving, health and home care.[14] The school expanded from a series of adult education classes begun in 1929 with an average attendance of twenty-five to thirty, with two evening sessions a week, and known as the "Pioneer Night School." The hard-working missionary was, as one Universalist described her, "a whole social service organization" in herself.[15]

The activities at Inman's Chapel grew by leaps and bounds in the 1920s, which represented the high point of Universalist activities under Powell's leadership. She spread information at meetings of the state convention about the constructive work being done, and issued periodic reports which were published in the *Leader* by its sympathetic editor. She visited churches in the North to enlist aid and to publicize the cause, and obtained additional personnel to assist her from time to time, drawing on Universalist churches in Eastern North Carolina.[16]

Hannah Powell, the tireless Universalist worker, immersed herself in the life of the community, steadily gaining their confidence and trust. She conducted the funeral in 1926 of James Ballou Inman, a son of the first preacher, who had earlier been doubtful about female preachers but had become completely reconciled to Powell's presence shortly before his death.[17] With a combination of tact, diplomacy, and great determination, she introduced successfully such Universalist organizations as the Young People's Christian Union, a mission circle for women, and a Clara Barton Guild for girls whose assistance was indispensable for her many social service projects.

The missionary announced plans in 1936 to retire to the Sunset Home in Waterville, Maine, but she was reluctant to leave and was prevailed upon to stay on for many months. She was replaced by George Boorn and his wife, from Pennsylvania. For seven years they carried on the work as best they could, faced with the obstacles of chronic economic depression, the withdrawal of much of the financial support once supplied by the WNMA, and the experience of another world war. The situation had been made more uncertain than ever by the announced intention of the WNMA in 1937 to relinquish by 1940 its responsibility for supervising denominational activities in North Carolina and providing sharply reduced financial support, which included Inman's Chapel and Friendly House. In 1939 the organization reconsidered its decision and allocated $1,800 of the $5,500 designated for North Carolina to the Pigeon River settlement.

One of Boorn's accomplishments was the addition to the staff in 1941 of Miss Rowena Melhuish, a member of the church in Binghamton, New York, and a nurse who served the medical needs of the community which Powell had long since sought to meet. A cabin with living facilities became a medical center, known as Collins House after its previous inhabitants. It was a historic structure, one of the last of the authentic mud-daubed log cabins known to exist in the area. It had been moved, after great difficulty, from its almost inaccessible original site in the mountains while Powell was still in charge; she had been determined to preserve a relic of old-time mountain life. It was located adjacent to Friendly House and served as both a dispensary and as a day nursery for working mothers.[18] The cabin was removed in the 1950s by a member of the Inman family and relocated to assure its preservation.

Unfortunately for the Pigeon River community, the Melhuish tenure lasted only a few months, for she found a larger field of service as a county nurse. She was replaced temporarily by Mrs. Florida Perkins, a native North Carolinian and a registered nurse, and then by Miss Ora Cox Gaskins, a native of South Carolina, also a registered nurse, and assigned to the North Carolina post under AUW auspices.[19] Medical services were about to be abandoned in 1943, when the AUW made provision for limited financing.[20] But the situation was not as critical as it had been earlier, for a new highway connected the valley with Waynesville, and public health services had been greatly expanded.

One project planned by the AUW was the development of an agricultural program for the community in 1944, with additional land to have been acquired by purchasing an adjoining farm.[21] A fund to have totalled $2,000 was to have been started by the Men's Club of the church in Haverhill, Massachusetts, but the plan was never carried out.

Lyman I. Achenbach was selected to replace Boorn after the latter's resignation in 1943 to accept a pastorate in Towanda, Pennsylvania, but he remained less than a year.[22] A native of the community, Mrs. Donald Plott, attempted to maintain the activities on a restricted basis until 1945. There seemed to be no alternative but to recall Powell from her retirement and resume her work at Inman's Chapel and Friendly House. Powell had retained her ties with the state convention from the very beginning, and was its guest at the meeting at Outlaw's Bridge in 1940.

Powell accepted the task early in 1945, as articulate and as forceful as ever at the state convention meeting that year, but reflecting an aura of the past never to be completely recaptured. Mrs. Verna Mitchell Taylor, who first met the matriarch of Inman's Chapel at the 1945 state convention, left this vivid description:

> Suddenly this towering figure swept down the aisle of the church — wearing a long flowing black skirt, just barely off the floor, a long sleeved shirtwaist, fastened at the neck with a large jeweled brooch — her graying hair pulled straight back and fastened in a tight bun — her jaws set with determination — her eyes blazing with a fire that compelled the attention of every soul in that house. Her voice rang out loud and clear about the conditions at Inman's Chapel and what could be done and must be done about it.[23]

Enthusiasm was so spontaneous and so great that not only was a generous donation received but a recently widowed young woman, Mrs. Lillie Belle Brummit, immediately volunteered to serve as Powell's assistant, continuing the long-standing North Carolina Universalist tradition of serving at that mountain outpost for limited periods.

After serving several months, Powell returned to Waterville to resume her life as a retiree, and made her last trip to the scene of her many years of labor in 1951. She died in 1954.

For three years after Powell's departure in 1946, Mrs. Rosalie A. West, a convert to Universalism and a member of the church in Oak Park, Illinois, was licensed as a lay minister and served at Inman's Chapel. A graduate of McGill University, she had been a missionary for the United Church of Canada.[24] One of her activities was to arrange a youth rally at Inman's Chapel in 1947, attended by about seventy individuals.[25] But she was not happy in the South, and rural work was unfamiliar to her.[26] She resigned in 1949 to bcome executive director of the AUW.

Ordell Bryant, who had retired after sixteen years on the Clinton circuit in Eastern North Carolina, and had settled in the western part of the state, served the parish of Inman's Chapel until his death in 1948 — the last regular minister of the mountain community.

The AUW voted in 1947 to discontinue the work at Friendly House because it was "no longer a fertile field for Universalist work, and . . . no significant service can be performed in that area."[27] This decision was confirmed by a detailed report from Mrs. West who had recommended that it be closed out. This meant also the closing of Inman's Chapel, which by 1947 had only twelve church members. A plea by three ministers in North Carolina to delay the closing in hopes that the state convention could keep it alive was unsuccessful. The convention was unable to continue the work. Boorn, who had spent seven years in the area, protested the abandonment, but to no avail.[28] The last vestige of organized religious liberalism in Western North Carolina had disappeared.

Inman's Chapel and Friendly House, scarcely known even to many Universalists within North Carolina, gradually faded from their consciousness. The leadership was gone, not to be replaced, and generations and circumstances had changed. The fellowship of the state convention was withdrawn in 1957 because the church no longer met the requirements. After much consideration, the property on which Friendly House had stood for more than half a century, and which in 1927 had been deeded to the state convention at its request by the General Convention, was sold at public auction for $2,300.[29] It was the end of one small and little-known facet of denominational history.

Powell's accomplishments as a missionary were soon forgotten and her name became only a memory even to those few who knew of her and her work. On the eve of her death at the age of eighty-eight, she had wistfully hoped that the institution from which she had received her divinity degree in 1899 would award her an honorary degree in recognition of her contributions, but it was not forthcoming.[30]

When the pastor of the church in Waterville conducted Hannah Powell's funeral three years after his arrival in that Maine community, he had to be instructed to mention in the memorial service her contribution to Universalism in North Carolina, for he had never heard either of Friendly House or Inman's Chapel. She had expressed the hope in 1928 that somehow the history of Universalist activity in an obscure mountain settlement in the South would be recorded for posterity.[31]

Chapter 21

The Association of Universalist Women

If there had ever been any doubt as to the contributions of the women in the denomination, who comprised the majority of its membership after 1870, a review of the record would certainly dispel it. They embarked on a series of missionary and church extension projects and contributed thousands of dollars and hundreds of hours of devoted service to maintain and to further Universalist interests whenever and wherever duty called or opportunity beckoned. They likewise experienced most of the changes of fortune which the denomination encountered over the years; there were failures as well as successes to record.

The organization which became successively the Woman's Centenary Aid Association (WCAA) (1869–1871), the Woman's Centenary Association (WCA) (1871–1905), the Women's National Missionary Association (WNMA) (1905–1939), the Association of Universalist Women (AUW) (1939–1963), and after consolidation with its Unitarian counterpart (1963–), the Unitarian Universalist Women's Federation (UUWF), became so deeply involved in so many ways that its history is impossible to separate from the denomination with which it was associated.[1] It had originated in anticipation of the celebration of the centennial of the denomination in 1870. The newly formed body, which claimed to be the first national organization of church women in America, was created "for special work independent of the general assembly of the church," and conducted an active canvass for member and funds in nearly every state then in the Union. The effort resulted in a membership of 13,000 and a contribution in excess of $35,000 to the Murray Centenary Fund under the aggressive and dedicated leadership of Mrs. Caroline A. Soule who served as its president for eleven years.[2]

In 1871, after success far beyond the hopes and expectations of the founders, it was reorganized on a permanent basis as the "Woman's Centenary Association of the United States." The organization took on both a more denominational character and a more extended jurisdiction in 1882 when, by a new act of incorporation in the District of Columbia and a new constitution and by-laws, it became the "Woman's Centenary Association of the Universalist Church" and included the British provinces in Canada.[3]

The Association was financed by annual dues of $1.00, with life memberships at first available for $50, later reduced to $25, and the title of "patron" for contributors of $100 or more at any one time. By 1902 there were 209 life members and a permanent fund of almost $21,000. It had collected and disbursed $300,000 by that year. In 1884 Sunday schools were first asked to take up annual collections to augment the WCA treasury.

There was also a category of honorary membership. The first such member had been a three-year-old girl who had been adopted by a Universalist family in Cincinnati, Ohio, and had been inducted by Soule. In 1874 she allowed six young men at the Clinton Liberal Institute to become honorary members, but without either voting or office-holding privileges.[4] Men were made eligible for honorary membership in 1882, when the WCA obtained a new act of incorporation, but with the same restrictions. It was not until 1923 that the constitution was amended so that men could become "associate" (non-voting) rather than honorary members.

At first, one-half of the regular membership fee went into the national treasury for general work. After deductions for expenses out of the other half, the balance was appropriated to the state in which it was raised and was used in the missionary work of that state.[5] Beginning in 1902 two-thirds of the dues went either to state organizations or mission circles. A "Missionary Day" was declared throughout the denomination, the first in 1891, to raise money for WCA projects.[6]

All power was originally vested in a president and in an executive board, with a vice-president in each state and an agent in each parish. Sixteen vice-presidents were immediately elected. Until 1903 there was no limit set on the number of terms the officers could serve. Thereafter, none except the treasurer could be reelected more than once to the same office. The maximum term was set at four years. The first three presidents had served for eleven years each. Mrs. M. Louise Thomas, the second president, had served for two terms as president of Sorosis, an organization headquartered in New York City which marked the beginning of the Women's Club of America.[7]

Over the years state missionary societies were organized, some independently of the Association as local needs dictated. The WCA undertook, first in 1895, to bring all of these into its province, and all women of

Presidents of the Women's Centenary Association, 1869-1905

Rev. Caroline A. Soule
(1869-1880)

M. Louise Thomas
(1880-1891)

Mrs. Cordelia A. Quinby
(1891-1902)

each parish under the banner of united missionary endeavor auxiliary to the General Convention. A further step toward consolidation was then taken, calling for the organization of state societies under Association auspices and the creation of mission circles at the parish level. Another link was provided with the creation of four regional corresponding secretaryships, with the incumbents serving on the executive board.

There was much discussion in the 1880s over whether state organizations could carry out the objectives of the WCA as effectively as the national office, and in some states (such as Iowa) the women's groups were disbanded in the belief that they were incapable of realizing the goals of the national organization.[8] But a division of funds was agreed upon, and most of the state auxiliaries were revived or expanded.

In many ways the most successful of all the state organizations was the Women's Universalist Missionary Society of Massachusetts, chartered in

1886 with a potential membership of 8,000 in the 116 parishes then existing.[9] Although its objectives were substantially the same as the national, the Massachusetts group did not become a member of the WCA until 1901. It had been made an auxiliary to the General Convention when it was created, after negotiations extending as far back as 1893. Thenceforth the Massachusetts group held membership in both organizations. As in so many other instances in denominational history, particularism prevailed over nationalism, resulting eventually in a species of federalism that balanced the two extremes.

The activities of the Massachusetts organization were by no means limited by the state boundary. Their goal of aiding Universalism everywhere was indicated in their statement of purpose, which was "to extend our faith, awaken a new interest among our people, and establish new churches in the unoccupied portion of our country."[10] One of their earliest projects was to aid the parish in Tarpon Springs, Florida, and they answered appeals for help in states as far away as Kentucky and Texas.[11] Aid was granted in all such cases with the stipulation that the property be deeded to the General Convention. The organization announced a policy in 1900 of encouraging and supporting only those missions and parishes that showed promise of becoming self-supporting rather than starting new movements — a policy quite the opposite of that followed by Q. H. Shinn, the denomination's best-known roving missionary. The state organization also assumed the financial responsibility for educating a young woman at Booker T. Washington's Tuskegee Institute in Alabama.[12]

There were representatives from seven state missionary societies and a number of mission circles in 1894, and the practice of an annual meeting was instituted in 1897, with one mission circle delegate for every nine members. By 1902 the number of state societies had risen to ten and the number of mission circles to more than 100 in 19 states.[13] The next step, urged by the national president, Mrs. Cordelia A. Quinby, was to nationalize missionary work by arranging to have the state organizations become part of the central body as auxiliaries, working in turn locally through mission circles.

Although there were an estimated 50,000 women in the church, the bulk of the missionary work fell on the shoulders of only about 2,000. A persistent difficulty was the inclination of local societies to be "perfectly independent," and some state missionary associations, like the one in Illinois, voted in 1903 against uniting with the WCA because "the time is not ripe."[14] Even then, twenty-one state organizations had become affiliated by 1909, and the number had grown to twenty-five by 1914, with an individual membership of more than 5,000 and more than 200 mission circles.[15]

The Association, from its beginning until 1895, held its meetings at the same time and place as the General Convention assemblies, although in separate sessions. The officers of the convention complained in 1893 that the simultaneous WCA meetings interfered with their business, so the women obligingly changed their time of assembly to precede the General Convention. It was accomplished "without prejudice, wounded feeling or aught of [sic] perfect loyalty."[16] But they found the time allotted inadequate for reports, discussions, and action; so, for the next several years the representatives of the organization met independently. But at the meeting in 1902 the decision was made, for practical reasons, to resume the original practice of meeting at the same time and place as the General Convention, which by then had become biennial. Allocating sufficient time for the conduct of business remained a chronic bone of contention.

Relations between the WCA and the General Convention were strained for many years. The battle was over the autonomy of the WCA, which had been separately chartered and incorporated in 1873 and maintained its own treasury. Affairs had reached a critical stage by the time of their sessions in New York City in 1874. A special committee of the convention had been appointed and had conferred in Maine with Mrs. Soule during the preceding summer. At the convention the committee presented five resolutions lauding the Universalist women for their contributions to the denomination and declaring that all offices in the convention should be open to both sexes. It was further declared to be the policy of the convention "to encourage the existence of no organization composed exclusively of men or women." The WCA was cordially invited to enter directly into the work of the convention and to share in both its deliberations and its labors. State conventions were therefore encouraged to elect delegates to the convention without regard to sex, and the trustees were to take into account in making appointments the proven capacity of the women to awaken religious interest and to solicit funds.[17]

An animated debate followed the presentation of the resolutions, and tenseness was very evident, even though "the prevailing sentiment was entirely favorable to the resolutions."[18] The equal rights of women to participate in all aspects of Universalist affairs was acknowledged, and it was affirmed that such rights should be officially recognized. There should be "no discarding of half the force of the Church, nor any division of the Church against itself."

But at first, there was no agreement. D. C. Tomlinson spoke emphatically in favor of permitting the women "to do their work in their own and separate way." Then there was much discussion over whether to allow Soule to speak before the convention in her capacity as president of the WCA. J. M. Pullman argued vigorously that there was no more appropriate person than she to make a case for the organization and demonstrate that it was not a rival of the General Convention. His argument prevailed, and Soule addressed the convention.

Soule was not in a happy frame of mind, and made her dissatisfaction known. According to the account in the denominational press she "spoke with much feeling, and seemed to rest under a sense of injury." Among other things, she objected strenuously to the procedure that had been followed in attempting to resolve the differences between the two organizations.

Earlier in the year a committee consisting of Governor Sidney Perham of Maine and R. H. Pullman, representing the General Convention, had consulted informally with Soule and other members of the WCA in Cleveland, Ohio, to try to arrange some plan for preserving the unity of church work.[19] At the formal meeting a few months later, four propositions were offered by Perham and Pullman as a basis for discussion, the burden of which was to recognize the WCA as a subservient arm of the General Convention, and made accountable to it. The trustees subsequently accepted this solution as the only practicable one. Otherwise, the operation of two organizations roughly parallel in aims was in direct competition, rivals if not actual antagonists. The unfortunate consequence was not only the appropriation by the WCA of functions belonging exclusively to the convention, but a conflict of loyalties and diversion of efforts and funds which seriously weakened the church. The trustees had no definite plan to offer, but left the solution up to the convention itself.

Soule objected to the fact that the WCA had never been formally consulted. No agreement had come out of the informal meeting, and she felt that she had been put in a false position, appearing to have yielded without any consultation with her organization. Further, she had told the two representatives of the trustees that "We will not give up our name, we will not give up our money, we will not give up our charter, but we will divide the work." She did not recognize the General Convention as the supreme head of the church; only Jesus Christ held that position. But she would bow, albeit reluctantly, to the General Convention as "the chief ecclesiastical body," in the interests of harmony, and the resolutions hammered out at the meeting in Maine, in which she had participated, were acceptable to her.

After all the verbal fireworks the resolutions recognizing the WCA as an integral part of the General Convention passed unanimously. Working out the actual terms of their "mutual relations" was left to the women's organization and the trustees. The WCA officially accepted "the hand of fellowship" offered by the General Convention, and a major crisis was thus averted. The first woman to serve on the board of trustees (Mrs. George B. Marsh of Chicago) was elected in 1877 and served until 1885 and again between 1889 and 1893. There was a long gap before another woman became a member, despite repeated requests by the WCA for representation.

General Convention-WCA relations were reviewed again in 1884 by a joint committee after the WCA reluctantly agreed, and the supremacy of the convention was reasserted.[20] All special projects were to be determined by joint consultation and a detailed accounting by the WCA was to be made each year of all receipts and disbursements. The WCA dutifully complied.

The objects of the Association, according to its first constitution and by-laws, were "to assist weak parishes, foster Sunday schools, help educate worthy young students for the ministry, relieve the needs of disabled preachers, ministers' wives and orphans, distribute denominational literature, and to do both home and foreign missionary work." By the time President Soule submitted her annual report in 1879 the organization had succeeded in some measure in everything it had undertaken. The general purpose, as she pointed out that year, of promoting "the interests of the Universalist Church," had already been achieved.

The first tract had been issued in 1873, and in 1879 alone, 304,100 pages had been distributed, and 500 books and 5,000 papers had been gathered for use in Scotland.[21] The plan to assist denominational colleges and other institutions of learning could be verified by inspecting the records of the treasurer. There was tangible evidence of assistance to local churches in reducing indebtedness and building new houses of worship as well as aiding struggling parishes and Sunday schools. Assistance was being given to young people in obtaining theological education, and indigent ministers and their families. It was the WCA which had started foreign denominational missionary work in Scotland in 1874 and had sent the first missionary less than five years later. In all of its first ten years the Association had remained free of debt and had never failed to meet a financial obligation when due.[22] Even in its very first year under its charter of 1873 the WCA had raised more than $25,000 toward such projects as the construction of a women's dormitory at Lombard College and the endowment of a professorship at Buchtel College.

Universalist missionaries financed in whole or, more frequently, in part, by the WCA fanned out over most of the United States and some parts of Canada in the late nineteenth century. Typical was a mission in Texas operated by James Billings, formerly of Connecticut, and his wife, and supported partially by the WCA, beginning in the 1880s, and by its Connecticut branch. Other special projects included the establishment in 1874 of a fund to purchase the Potter meeting house at Good Luck (Murray Grove), New Jersey. The first dollar, contributed by Phebe Hanaford, was donated in the name of the WCA.[23] The women's group accepted the responsibility in 1895 of employing Asa M. Bradley as a missionary on the West Coast, and paid his annual salary of $1,500, plus travelling expenses. His assignment lasted until he resigned two years later, and the mission had to be suspended. Decisions to extend church activities uniformly outran resources.

A new era of enlarged activity had begun in 1905 when the WCA became "The Women's National Missionary Association of the Universalist Church." The practice of using this designation had begun as early as 1894 in order to call attention to its principal purpose.[24] The women's group, by the early twentieth century, had raised more than a quarter of a million dollars devoted to mission work of various kinds, which included a revolving church building and loan fund instituted in 1902 which replaced the policy of making outright gifts.

The organization, from its origin in 1869, sought to affiliate to some extent with groups outside the denomination, both nationally and internationally. A representative was selected in 1883 to attend the World Peace Conference in Paris, and in 1889 contributed toward the expenses of a delegate. Membership in numerous organizations associated with foreign missions logically paralleled their interest in missionary activity outside the United States. Dues were paid, beginning in 1893, to the international Board of Missions. The WCA joined the Women's Council, an interdenominational group, in 1890, with which it was affiliated until 1903; and in 1888 became an institutional member of the National Council of Women but was forced to drop out ten years later "on account of the expense."[25] Mrs. Quinby served as a delegate to the national convention of the Women's Christian Temperance Union in 1900, and Mrs. Marion D. Shutter represented Universalist women at the International Congress of Religious Liberals in Paris in 1913. During World War I the organization supported both the international temperance movement and the prohibition movement in the United States as well as the enfranchising of women.[26]

Much of the financing of missionary activities was provided by the successful raising of a "Jubilee Fund," set originally at $20,000 and then increased to $100,000, $95,000 of which had been raised by 1925. The fund had been established to celebrate the fiftieth anniversary of the organization. No better illustration of the jealousy with which they guarded their own funds was the indignant demand of the Association for the return of Jubilee funds transmitted in error to the General Convention in 1921.[27]

The WNMA became directly involved in Sunday school work in 1911, and a new department was created to supervise such activities. One goal was to introduce mission studies into their curricula as well as to solicit funds for the Japan mission.[28] The General Sunday School Association took over fund soliciting in 1921 but it had to pay $1,250 a year to the women's group in exchange.[29] The WNMA also recommended in 1913 the introduction of systematic study of missions as part of the curricula of denominational theological schools. George E. Huntley, then on the faculty of the Canton Theological School, responded positively, and the

Presidents of the Women's National Missionary Association, 1905-1921

*Emma Foster
(1905-1909)*

*Theresa A. Williams
(1909-1913)*

*Minnie J. Ayres
(1913-1917)*

*Marietta B. Wilkins
(1917-1921)*

WNMA promptly donated $100 for educational materials. The WNMA simultaneously promoted mission study groups within their own ranks and in the summertime held institutes on the subject at Ferry Beach, the first in 1910. Dues-paying participation in the Foreign Missions Conference began in 1919, as was the case also with the Women's Board of Foreign Missions.

Foreign mission study was of course conducted by many organizations outside the denomination, among them the Northfield Conference which met in Western Massachusetts as an outgrowth of Dwight L. Moody's student summer conferences in the late nineteenth century. Even though Mrs. Marietta B. Wilkins, who served as president of the WNMA from 1917 to 1921, was rebuffed after her first appearance at the conference in 1913 when it was discovered that she was a Universalist, she insisted on Universalist participation and by 1916 sixty women in the denomination attended its meetings.

The first Universalist summer meeting at Northfield, organized as Camp Murray, was held in 1916, its primary purpose to provide missionary training for girls and young women. One outgrowth was the organization that year of junior groups known as Clara Barton Guilds, devoted to social service, with a wide range of ages represented, extending far beyond the young people for whom they were originally intended. Guilds were subsequently organized all over the nation but had an uneven existence. They seemed to have almost disappeared during the economic depression of the 1930s, for a recommendation was made in 1949 that they be reestablished.[30]

An attempt was made to keep Universalist women informed of developments by publication of a *Bulletin,* begun in 1913 as a monthly during the church year, and by a *Yearbook,* the first in 1941.

The women's group considered the South as a promising field for cultivation in spite of its size, its scattered and largely rural population, the predominance of religious fundamentalism, and the devastation which had accompanied the Civil War and from which Universalism recovered but slowly. The first serious interest by the WCA in that section of the nation had been manifested when President Quinby attended the Alabama Conference in Camp Hill in 1899, where she delivered several addresses.[31] It was the first time that most of her listeners had heard a woman speak in public. One of her accomplishments there was to organize a mission circle of seventeen members.

During the same year a delegation of clergy working in the South, including Lyman Ward who had just opened a school in Camp Hill, visited Boston and requested aid in the form of ministers and money.[32] Small donations to the Camp Hill school were made by both the WCA and its successor, the WNMA.

The WNMA turned next to Universalists in Eastern North Carolina

The summer institute of the Women's National Missionary Association at Ferry Beach, Maine, in 1928

which Thomas Chapman had been attempting to cover in a series of preaching stations as state superintendent since 1904. The first missionary in the South with which the national women's group had become involved was Ada C. Bowles, who had travelled to several locations beginning in 1902. An arrangement had been worked out whereby she was responsible to the General Convention but the WCA and the women's missionary group in Massachusetts paid part of her salary. Her support, which had been sporadic and largely unfocused, was made a matter of official policy in 1906.

The determination to provide expanded missionary service to North Carolina was strengthened in 1907, when a Universalist from Durham made an impassioned two-hour plea for aid.[33] With the resignation of Chapman in 1911, and at the request of the North Carolina Convention which had been created in 1905, the WNMA took on a major financial and administrative responsibility by agreeing to assume the superintendency of the entire state. The General Convention, with but few resources itself upon which to draw, readily acquiesced. The arrangement was to last forty years.

A series of circuits was established, and Willard O. Bodell, from Ohio, became the first of three missionaries whose salaries, totalling $3,600, were paid by the WNMA. When he began his service he had to spread himself rather thin; he was the only minister for fourteen parishes and an even greater number of "mission points."[34] He used Kinston as his base, and the others were located at Clinton and Rocky Mount; however, the circuits were changed constantly, in an attempt to keep up with population changes and parish needs.

The WNMA commitment to North Carolina paid dividends; between 1908 and 1916 the number of organized churches in the state increased from five to fourteen.[35]

The frequent changes of personnel, however, were a source of basic weakness in carrying out WNMA plans for the state, and the number of clergy fluctuated widely. After Bodell resigned in 1919 to accept a pastorate in the Midwest there was for a brief time only one minister in Eastern North Carolina. But the WNMA not only continued its support but had increased it to $6,000 a year by 1920 and had placed four clergy in the field, soon increased to seven. By 1923 one-third of its entire operating budget was being spent in North Carolina.[36] This included partial support of Hannah J. Powell in the Western part of the state.

Among those clergy who did have long tenure in North Carolina were Harry L. Canfield (1860–1942) and his wife Mary Grace Canfield (1864–1946) who, after serving briefly in Kinston, spent more than a decade (1923–1936) in Greensboro, where they became deeply involved in community affairs and did much to overcome the suspicion of Northerners in general and of Universalists in particular.[37] The Canfields had considerably greater success in maintaining good relations with orthodoxy than did George Wood, minister of the Kinston circuit in 1925. He reported ruefully that Universalists had "no standing at all" and were forbidden to join the local ministerial association.[38] Similarly, Leon P. and Martha G. Jones encountered opposition in Clinton, where they established a free public library of some 5,000 volumes, after much difficulty.

Canfield was a strong supporter of the idea of establishing a state-wide denominational paper. This was accomplished with the creation of the *Tar Heel Universalist* in 1932. He served as its first editor until his retirement. The paper, a sprightly twelve-page publication, was first printed in a woodshed on the property of the parsonage occupied by Ordell E. Bryant in Clinton, on equipment which he owned.[39] Bryant remained on the Clinton circuit for sixteen years, the longest of any minister receiving support from the women's organization.[40] The paper had a continuous history into the 1980s, although it had shrunk to about two pages of mimeographed material by 1982, when its fiftieth anniversary was acknowledged.[41]

In the same year that a state publication was provided, North Carolina Universalists acquired property at Shelter Neck, near the community of Burgaw, as a headquarters for summer institutes encouraged by the WNMA. It had been owned originally by the Unitarians as part of a movement to expand the denomination in the state. In 1900 a church was dedicated there, and three other Unitarian churches were organized in the state. A school under Unitarian auspices had been founded at Shelter Neck in 1902, and in 1911 had been incorporated as the "Carolina Industrial School." But it was closed after the expansion of the public

President of the Women's National Missionary Association, 1921-1939

Ethel M. Allen
(1921-1925)

Grace Valentyne
(1925-1929)

Alice T. Walker
(1933-1937)

Rev. Hazel I. Kirk
(1929-1933)

Madelyn H. Wood
(1937-1939)

school system, and in 1928 the Unitarians largely abandoned both their religious and educational efforts in the state. In 1932 they deeded the Shelter Neck property as well as other church properties to the Universalist state convention. The forty-four acre holding contained at the time a cluster of buildings consisting of the church, a five-room schoolhouse, and a twelve-room dwelling.[42] The first use by Universalists was made of it in May 1932, and continued into the 1980s.

WNMA-financed missionaries by 1923 claimed twenty Universalist churches in the state.[43] There was even a plan in 1924 to establish and finance a chair of theology at either Duke University or the state university at Chapel Hill, but there were no funds forthcoming from national headquarters to support it, and the idea was dropped.[44]

Universalist strength in North Carolina, which had apparently reached a high point in the early 1920s, had entered a period of slow but steady decline by the end of the decade, a decline for which the WNMA was only partially responsible. The Association did have increasing difficulty in financing state activities, partly because membership in the organization itself had begun to decline. In 1928 the WNMA employed Francis B. Bishop as the state superintendent in an attempt to halt the downward movement within the state. They had to discontinue the office in 1931 and all clergy were requested to take a voluntary 10 percent reduction in salary.

The decline was by no means confined to the Universalists but was shared by other Protestant denominations that claimed largely rural constituencies.[45] Country cross-roads churches had probably been appropriate when the rural population flourished and adequate transportation facilities were unavailable. But the pervasive rural-to-urban movement, the attraction of increasing industrialization in larger towns and cities, and the revolution associated with the automobile, all products of the post-World War I era, had begun to have their full impact by the late 1920s.

The number of country churches had become excessive in proportion to population, and there was needless multiplication and duplication. Of the eleven Protestant denominations to be found in largely rural Lenoir County in 1929, the Universalists were listed as seventh in size. Their church in Woodington (subsequently closed) had to compete with both a Free Will Baptist and a Methodist church.[46] In predominantly rural Wayne County, Universalists ranked seventh in numbers among the ten denominations found there that year. In the 1980s the only Universalist church that remained active in that county was at Outlaw's Bridge. Relocation and consolidation were among the solutions offered, and were recommended by Bishop in his first annual report to the state convention. Some consolidation did in fact take place. The congregations of two country churches in the vicinity of Rocky Mount were merged with the church there in 1928.

One internal administrative problem continued for several years to create a certain amount of tension if not ill-will. Relations between the WNMA and the state convention and its constituencies were often strained. There was a tendency, especially during the financially desperate 1930s, for the national women's organization to make policy decisions affecting North Carolina Universalists without sufficient consultation with the state and local organizations or first-hand knowledge of local conditions. There was so much complaint that a decision was made in 1933 to create a joint WNMA-state convention committee to coordinate state planning, but even then communication was frequently imperfect and otherwise unsatisfactory.

In 1934 North Carolina Universalists were informed that the promotion of liberal religion in the state was no longer to be the sole responsibility of the WNMA but was to be shared by a host of other denominational organizations, including the General Convention, the AUA, and the council of the Free Church Fellowship.[47] While Universalists in the state were still digesting this rather bewildering information they were informed that no more money could be contributed to maintain several circuits. Their support would have to be provided locally, and at a time when it was most difficult to provide.

A further step, reflecting the financial exigencies both nationally and denominationally, was taken in 1937. The WNMA voted to relinquish to the General Convention by 1940 the superintendency in North Carolina when the last contracts with ministers would expire. The WNMA rescinded its decision, however, in 1939, and offered assurance that Universalists in the state would not be abandoned afer all. When it was discovered that the Committee on Church Extension had no funds to continue the work, the WNMA committed $3,500 a year, to be supplemented by $2,000 from other sources.[48] Unfortunately, all of these arrangements were made without consulting either the state convention or the local churches, which were left in a haze of uncertainty. Only the mission circles were informed of the plans before they were made public.[49]

The Association also confronted another problem in the 1920s and 1930s which had no direct reference to North Carolina but which did affect indirectly the ability to sustain its work there. National membership had been registered at 8,000 in 1921; by 1937 it had declined to less than 3,000, with almost half of it confined to Massachusetts.[50] President Ethel M. Allen had been concerned about declining membership in the mid-1920s, and had suggested a single organization of all Universalist women be created, disregarding state and national boundaries, downplaying its historic missionary purposes. Direct individual representation in national meetings was to replace the delegate system originally provided.[51]

The Olinda mission circle in Ontàrio also suggested that the word "National" be dropped from the name of the organization so that Canadian Universalist women could continue to be included; they suggested

394 / Church Extension, Domestic and Foreign

Presidents of the Association of Universalist Women, 1939-1955 (not including Helen Hamlin, 1955-1959, and Edna Whippen, 1959-1963)

Madelyn H. Wood
(1939-1941)

Corinne H. Brooks
(1941-1945)

Jeannette C. Mulford
(1945-1949)

Marjorie L. Springall
(1949-1953)

Laura S. Hersey
(1953-1955)

substitution of the word "General."[52] The officers considered it inexpedient to make the change at the time, and the adoption of the more inclusive name, "Association of Universalist Women," was delayed until 1939, when the organization was reincorporated.[53] A broad-gauged program was also announced, with much of the planning done by Miss Ida M. Folsom, who served as the chief executive officer from 1940 until her resignation in 1947 to become an assistant to the General Superintendent.

The newly renamed organization continued to debate into the 1940s the future of financial support for Universalists in North Carolina, who numbered but slightly more than 500 in 1943.[54] The AUW was grimly determined not only to continue support but to expand it — clearly beyond its financial capabilities.[55] The trustees of the Universalist Church refused in 1946 to accept the financial responsibility for activities in the state as long as the AUW insisted on maintaining its own treasury and declined to join in a unified financial appeal on behalf of the entire denomination.[56] And so direct subsidization of North Carolina churches gradually disappeared, and they were told that self-support had to be the direction of the future. In 1948 the Universalist Church began to replace the AUW in North Carolina, with scaled-down support by the women to end in 1951.[57]

Of all the instrumentalities for securing financial support, it was on the mission circles that the national women's organization had depended to the greatest extent. They had been the backbone of missionary activities in North Carolina since the first circle had been organized at Kinston by Ada Bowles in 1903. A state mission circle had been created in 1906 and a local unit had been organized in every church within a few years. In fact, North Carolina was the only state in which 100 percent of the churches reported mission circles in 1947.[58] It was to their work that national presidents or their representatives paid particular attention when they visited the state.

Although the dwindling number of churches in the state did not all become self-supporting as the AUW and other Universalists had hoped, the state mission circles contributed to every major project in which the national organization was involved, including support of the Blackmer Home in Japan and the camps for diabetic children in Massachusetts, the one for girls opened in the midst of the Great Depression of the 1930s.[59] The state AUW continued to be involved in the national organization long after official financial ties with North Carolina had been severed.

One of the many series of projects undertaken by the AUW under its various names was the establishment of memorials marking milestones in the history of the denomination. The first such had been the establishment of a fund in 1874 to finance the acquisition and maintenance of the Potter meeting house in New Jersey where Murray had preached his first sermon in America. The second was an interest in acquiring the colonial

Aerial view of the Clara Barton Camp, North Oxford, Massachusetts

house in Gloucester, Massachusetts, occupied by the family of Murray's wife, Judith Sargent. Very little was actually accomplished to further that end until 1916, when Levi M. Powers (1864–1920), minister of the church in Gloucester, was given approval by the convention trustees to raise $50,000 to purchase and restore the residence in anticipation of the celebration of the 150th anniversary of Murray's arrival in America.[60] The Gilman House Association was incorporated in 1919 as a non-profit organization to raise the money, the name having been derived from one of the various owner-occupants. It was known from then on as the Sargent-Murray-Gilman House.[61]

The most widely known of all the memorials for which the WNMA assumed responsibility was the Clara Barton home in Oxford, Massachusetts, at which a summer camp for diabetic girls was established, the first such facility in the nation and a model for others. The idea of acquiring the birthplace had first been discussed in 1920, when it became known that the property was up for sale. It was to be considered as both a denominational shrine and a community center project for the Clara Barton Guilds of young women which had been organized at the time of World War I.

The property, consisting of more than ninety acres and a house with barn, was to be purchased for approximately $6,100 from its owner, Carl O. Carlson, and restored, the total to cost about $15,000.[62] The property was duly acquired in 1921, and the house was dedicated that fall. Mrs. Marietta B. Wilkins, president of the Association, took formal possession of the homestead on the 100th anniversary of the birth (25 December 1821) of the famous Universalist founder of the American National Red Cross. The Clara Barton Memorial Association was immediately created to raise the necessary funds.[63]

Custodians were employed in 1921, with the understanding that the home would be open all year, but the financial condition of the WNMA and the slowness with which money came in were so discouraging that it was voted in 1922 to close the historic home until more money was forthcoming. A compromise was worked out in 1923 to keep the property open to the public during the summer months only.[64] It had become evident by 1926 that an endowment fund was needed to maintain as well as to improve the property, so $50,000 was sought and a campaign begun that year to provide it.

From the first it was determined that the homestead would be used as a service facility of some kind, and in 1922 a plan was devised to work with small children. The first summer fresh-air camp was projected for 1925 as a joint activity, with the state youth group and the Clara Barton Guilds furnishing volunteer assistance. It actually opened in 1926, with facilities provided for fourteen girls, aged eight to eleven. Extension to two two-week periods made possible the attendance of twenty-eight girls.[65] The camp was an immediate success, and by the summer of 1931 the capacity was exceeded as word spread of the good work being done for underprivileged children. Financial support furnished originally by the state YPCU was augmented in 1935 when the national youth organization took over a share of the responsibility.[66] Part of the funds contributed went into the construction of an administration building, dedicated in 1938.[67]

The moving force behind the decision to use the camp for diabetic girls was Mrs. Alice Enbom Taylor, who served the WNMA from 1921 until her retirement in 1955, and was active in its fund-raising campaigns.[68] Mrs. Taylor was much impressed by an article in the *Boston Transcript* by Dr. Elliot P. Joslin, on the staff of the New England Deaconess Hospital in Boston, and an internationally known expert on diabetes. In the article he made several proposals for treating diabetic children, including the desirability of establishing summer camps for such individuals as "islands of safety." Mrs. Taylor immediately thought of the Clara Barton summer camp as a possibility and brought it to the attention of the Association. President Wilkins had also seen the article and lent her ready support to the idea of offering the campsite in Oxford.

Representatives of the WNMA and the other organizations involved in the camp, met with Joslin, and he promptly accepted their offer. An understanding was reached that he would select the girls, and that they would be admitted to the program without regard for race, creed, or nationality.[69] The WNMA would provide the physical facilities, including those for a laboratory, and Joslin would provide the medical service, which included two nurses from the Deaconess Hospital staff, together with a dietician and laboratory technicians for the summer.

This adventure in social service was enthusiastically received, and the Clara Barton Birthplace Camp for Diabetic Girls, as it was officially known, began operations in the summer of 1933. The partnership between a church and a medical unit was eminently satisfactory, and immediately attracted national attention. By 1943 it was providing services for 112 girls on a staggered schedule, 50 for four weeks or more. They were organized into three groups according to age, and came from eleven states, with all major religious faiths represented.[70] The campers in 1947, housed in small cottages, came from twenty-two states and three foreign countries. The camp that year attracted physicians from five foreign countries besides many from the United States.

By the mid-1930s pressure had begun to build to provide similar services for boys. A precedent of sorts had been set in the summer of 1934 when Unitarians, in cooperation with Joslin, had opened a summer camp at the Prendergast Preventorium for those suffering from tuberculosis.[71] It had become a boarding school by 1935, with year-round operation. Two years later, facilities were provided in Winthrop, Massachusetts, for eighteen boys, underwritten by the Boston Tuberculosis Association.[72]

In 1947 Joslin offered to equip a camp for diabetic boys, to be operated on the same plan as the one for girls. A sixty-acre site (for which additional acreage was acquired in 1949) was purchased by Joslin in the adjacent community of Charlton, financed by the Diabetic Fund and a $30,000 gift from Dr. and Mrs. George G. Averill of Waterville, Maine.[73] Arrangements were worked out to have the AUW furnish non-medical equipment and management personnel. The medical work, as in the case of the girls' camp, was to be provided by Joslin and his associates at the George F. Baker Clinic of the Deaconess Hospital. The Elliot P. Joslin Camp for Diabetic Boys was dedicated and opened in the summer of 1948, with Leonard Carmichael, president of Tufts College, as the principal speaker.[74]

The camp for boys was as successful as the one for girls, with 116 enrolled the first year and 176, aged five to fifteen, in 1955.[75] Commitment to support of the two camps by Universalist women had become a matter of course by the 1950s. Of the total AUW budget of nearly $100,000 for 1953–54, $65,000 was allocated to them, and in 1959 the goal of $25,000 as a special twenty-fifth anniversary fund, was reached; this, together with other gifts, totalled more than $45,000.[76] Arrangements were made in the summer of 1955 for both camps to attend nondenominational religious services in the historic Oxford church, advertised as "the oldest Universalist Church building in the world."[77] By 1959 camping facilities were being provided for 450 children each summer.

When the AUW voted in 1961 to consolidate with the Alliance of Unitarian Women (accomplished in 1963), continued involvement in the Barton camp was high on the list of AUW activities. Financial responsibility for the boys' camp was eventually turned back to the Joslin Fund, and in the 1980s only the girls' camp was being supported by the UUWF. The historic association of Universalists with establishing and maintaining the Clara Barton camp was one of the signal successes of the denomination.

Relations between the AUW and the church at large, which had on occasions degenerated into actual friction over the years, tended to become closer during the 1950s. A departmental organization for the AUW had been provided when a new constitution had been adopted in 1941, and paralleled to a large extent a similar structure adopted by the Universalist Church later in that decade. Both had Departments of Social Action (Service), Education, and Publications. The AUW requested representation on the UCA board of trustees, a practice once followed, but for many years had to settle for one of the vice-presidencies, which did not carry voting privileges. The women did obtain membership on various departmental boards of the national organization and contributed, after many years of abstention, through the Unified Appeal to the overall budget of the church, while still maintaining its own treasury.

When the Unitarian Univeralist Association was created in 1961 the AUW was recognized as an associate member. This status was continued when the Universalist and Unitarian women's groups become the Unitarian Universalist Women's Federation in 1963.

The contributions of the women to so many of the church's activities and strengths for almost 100 years were excelled by no other auxiliary body in the Universalist Church.

Chapter 22

Denominational Pioneering Overseas: The Scottish Mission

One of the commitments made by the Woman's Centenary Association (WCA) when it became a permanent organization in 1871 was the conduct of foreign as well as domestic missionary work. The first such opportunity came only a year later when, with the co-sponsorship of the General Convention, the association became the principal financial supporter of a mission to Scotland which lasted for twenty years and which became intimately associated with the name of Caroline Augusta Soule, first president of the WCA.

Universalism had been known to exist in Scotland in the early 1700s and American Universalists after 1800 had had occasional communication with their Scottish counterparts. By 1755 a group of small congregations in the Merse (Berwickshire) in the Borders Region which had been associated with the Reformed Presbytery (an offshoot of the Scottish Covenanters) declared their belief in Univeralism. James Purves (1734–1795) became their pastor in 1769. He ministered, starting in 1776, to a group of less than ten families from the Merse who had migrated to Edinburgh and thus became the individual considered the first public preacher of the faith in Scotland. It was this group that became the antecedents of St. Mark's Unitarian Church which observed its bicentennial in 1976.[1]

Purves' congregation adopted in 1792 a declaration of belief, of which he was probably the author, and designated themselves as "Universal Dissenters." By 1814 the group was generally known as Unitarian, and the congregation was housed, beginning in 1835, in what was then known as St. Mark's Chapel.

By 1830 there were at least six societies in Scotland, including one in Glasgow. Neil Douglas (1750–1823), a convert about 1800, and known as "the father of Universalism in Scotland," had a congregation of 130 in Glasgow at the time of his death. Douglas, with a reputataion as a powerful and outspoken preacher, was tried for sedition in an Edinburgh court for allegedly making "wicked," false, and slanderous assertions regarding certain British officials.[2] There was no conclusive evidence in the transcript of the proceedings of religious prejudice, but Douglas' Universalism might have played a part in precipitating the episode.

William Worrall, who studied under Douglas, succeeded him. Worrall spent considerable time urging increased contact among Universalists on both sides of the Atlantic, and corresponded with T. J. Sawyer and Stephen R. Smith in America.[3] Worrall used a hall as a church; it was fitted with a pulpit and seats at a cost of £200. The pulpit was later used by another Scottish Universalist congregation.[4]

After Worrall's death in 1838 the membership of the Glasgow church declined sharply because of frequent turnover of preachers, most of them laymen; as a result the congregation was forced to move into smaller quarters. Very little was known in the United States about the Scottish church until 1852, when a small link was forged with the visit of Abel C. Thomas, who travelled in the British Isles and preached in Glasgow several times.

In the 1850s P. H. Waddell, who had studied for the ministry in the Church of Scotland but who had refused to sign its required confession of faith, created much excitement in southwestern Scotland because of his oratorical ability and universalist ideas. Waddell was invited in 1860 to form a church in Glasgow for believers in universal restoration and was an immediate success in what was known as "The Church of the Future." John Mitchell, who was the pastor of the struggling congregation which had been organized earlier, was among the first to recognize Waddell as a Universalist, and persuaded his own church to merge with Waddell's. A new building, with a capacity of 1,800, was constructed, but financial difficulties required its sale. So the combined congregation returned to the hall previously used by Waddell. Shortly thereafter he was admitted to the Established Church, but without renouncing his Univeralism. He merely signed the required confession "with mental reservations."

The individual who took over the leadership in Scotland in the 1860s was James Ure Mitchell (1833–1905), who served at first as a junior pastor in Glasgow and preached extensively in neighboring communities. He was among those who participated in debates with the defenders of orthodoxy in the Glasgow Universalist Controversial Society which had been organized in 1857.[5] At Stenhousemuir, Larbert, an independent group had been organized in 1866 by laborers from the Carron Iron Works. After he and R. S. Bowie held meetings in nearby Falkirk, a parish was organized at Larbert in 1867.[6]

Mitchell delivered a series of lectures on Universalism at Dunfermline in 1871, where he had organized a parish in 1869. By 1873 there were reported to be seven lay preachers serving several other communities besides those already mentioned, including Dundee and Falkirk.[7] Mitchell attempted to tie all of these congregations together with the Scottish Universalist Missionary Association which he had started in Glasgow in 1862 and which was reconstituted as the Scottish Universalist Convention in 1874.[8] A Universalist book and tract center was opened in Dunfermline in 1873.

Mitchell first brought Universalist activities in Scotland to the attention of the American denomination in 1871, when he issued a plea for financial assistance, noting that the strength of Universalism in Scotland was "precisely the same as it was in America about fifty years ago."[9] He pointedly noted also that Universalism in that part of the United Kingdom could not survive on good wishes alone. Mitchell then decided to make a visit to the United States and plead for the Scottish cause in person.

His way was paved by J. S. Cantwell, who delivered an address on the subject at the General Convention in 1872. He had vacationed abroad during that summer and had been urgently solicited by Mitchell to see "the only Universalist Church building in Great Britain." When they arrived at the church at nearly 11 o'clock at night, great excitement prevailed and the bell was rung to assemble the parishioners in the neighborhood to meet the American Universalist.[10] Although the speech at the convention brought no immediate aid, as neither the convention nor the WCA was in a position at the time to provide money, the idea had at least been planted, and took concrete form after Mitchell's visit.[11]

Mitchell arrived in the United States in 1873 and attended the General Convention, which met in Washington, D.C. that year. He was fellowshipped and was recognized as an "honorary" delegate. He also travelled and preached extensively while in America, bringing word of the situation in Scotland. His efforts immediately yielded more than $800, part of which was used to pay his travel expenses, and part to carry on his work. Mitchell also induced Donald Fraser (1850–1925), a member of his Larbert congregation, to come to America to study for the ministry. Fraser attended St. Lawrence University and remained in the United States where he held various pastorates for forty years.[12] Mitchell's son Ure also served in the United States.

In the spring of 1874 the WCA undertook the responsibility of organizing a Scottish mission and assisting with regular contributions. The initial sum of $250 was raised in about a month's time, with the largest contribution from Massachusetts and with donations also from New Hampshire, New York State, and Pennsylvania.[13] The funds were administered by Mitchell.

The original plan was to concentrate on establishing a mission station at

Edinburgh, but the money was used in such communities as Kilmarnock, Glasgow, Galashiels, and Selkirk when it was discovered that most Universalists in Edinburgh were associated with St. Mark's. After a conference between the trustees of the General Convention and the president of the WCA in November 1875 it was decided to continue the mission, with the WCA furnishing the funds. By then the Scottish Universalists had organized a convention, so the WCA dealt with that body rather than with any individual. The first quarterly installment of the $250 provided under this arrangement was sent on 1 January 1876, with the understanding that the WCA would contribute the same amount annually.

Caroline A. Soule (1824–1903), who was to be closely associated with Scotland as the first foreign missionary in the denomination, became involved in 1875.[14] She had already established a reputation as a teacher, writer, editor, and poet, and in 1869 had become the first president of the WCA, an office she held until 1880. She travelled constantly through the United States in that capacity and followed such a rigorous and exhausting regimen that she was forced in 1875 to seek relief by way of a change of pace and scenery in Europe. By then she had been widowed for more than twenty years.

In the course of her travels abroad she made a point of visiting Scotland for several months, the WCA having already contributed to the Universalist cause there. She immediately plunged into the work she felt needed to be done among the few, scattered, and largely poverty-stricken Universalists who had sought assistance. She visited almost every community in the vicinity of Edinburgh and Glasgow, as well as Universalists in these two cities, delivering sermons and temperance addresses to those who would listen. She met opposition not only because she was a Universalist but because she was a woman. She was not allowed for that reason to use the facilities of the Catholic Apostolic Church in Selkirk when it was discovered that the preacher was a female. As she reported ruefully to the WCA, "Why wasn't I made a man!"[15]

Typical of the other challenges she faced was the situation in Stenhousemuir, Larbert, where at the time of her arrival the first and only church building owned by Scottish Universalists existed. In 1867, the year they organized, the small congregation had decided to construct a temporary wooden house of worship. Money was limited because the majority were of the working class, making only minimum wages.[16] Many donated their labor, and kept the cost down to about $400. Services were conducted by laymen such as James Graham, a convert from the Baptists, who departed for Glasgow about 1875.

The building constructed at such sacrifice was neglected and in disrepair by the time of Mrs. Soule's arrival. During rainy weather, worshippers had to move from pew to pew to find a dry spot in which to worship. In January 1875 large piles of snow inside the church had to be shovelled before a fire could be lit. The alternative was to give up the meetings or make "a grand effort" to build a new church. Under the leadership of J. M. Cunningham, an experienced lay preacher and temperance lecturer from Glasgow, they took the latter course and undertook to build on the site of the old one a substantial brick edifice with a capacity of 300. It was still unfinished, and with an indebtedness until after 1880 because of the inability of the congregation to raise the estimated $250 needed to complete it.[17] Nonetheless, it was dedicated by Mrs. Soule in 1875 as the Church of the Redeemer.

In the fall of 1875 the doughty American Univeralist returned to the United States, fully as exhausted as when she had arrived in Scotland, and only partially recovered from serious illness which had delayed her departure. After a period of recuperation she preached in Elizabeth, New Jersey. It was while there that in 1876 the WCA received a request from Scottish Universalists to provide a missionary for a two-year period. Mrs. Soule, after considerable hesitation, agreed to serve at a beginning annual salary of $650 provided by the WCA. The organization formally committed itself to the plan at its meeting in 1877, with Mrs. Soule to begin her duties the following year.

The WCA missionary, who had greatly impressed the Scottish Universalists with her abilities and her devotion to the cause, was greeted warmly when she arrived, but she soon uncovered a serious problem in Dunfermline which had become the unofficial headquarters, with Mitchell in charge. The congregation had split into two groups, one under the leadership of J. U. Mitchell, and the minority headed by R. S. Bowie, who had been assisting since 1871.[18] Bowie's congregation met in the storeroom of the town music hall and theater, surrounded by flags, banners, swords, guns, brass helmets, and tin teapots.[19] As he was quick to point out, such an environment was not conducive to a worshipful attitude. Bowie's Church of the Messiah (Universalist) did receive temporary assistance from the British and Foreign Unitarian Association in London, including funds to rent more suitable quarters. But in 1877 the association was forced to withdraw its support. It recommended the union of the two congregations as a means of obtaining increased resources. Mrs. Soule endeavored to reunite the two groups, but before the work had been completed she moved her headquarters to Glasgow in 1878, much discouraged by the slow progress being made.

At a special meeting which she called soon after her arrival in Glasgow, she discussed the weaknesses as she perceived them, based on an analysis of what she had learned of the history of Scottish Universalism prior to her appearance; and on her admittedly brief first-hand experience.[20] As a "theory," Universalism seemed to be spreading satisfactorily, but in organized form it was weak and ineffective. She considered the most pressing need to be the development of a few strong centers, such as one in

Glasgow, rather than numerous scattered and feeble missionary stations which faded away almost as soon as they had been established. They were too loosely organized and unstable — "a myth rather than a reality" — with insufficient discipline and lay leadership.

Having delivered herself of these sentiments, she proceeded in 1879 to reorganize, as St. Paul's Universalist Church, the informal congregation which had been gathered in Glasgow in the early 1870s under the lay leadership of J. M. Cunningham. He also served as secretary of the Scottish Convention until succeeded by Mrs. Soule. She preached several times every Sunday, organized what was known locally as "the American woman's Sunday school," created a Bible class, and established a library comprising books, tracts, and other Universalist literature which she solicited constantly from the United States. The WCA took the major responsibility for furnishing her with denominational material of all kinds which she distributed in Scotland until the very end of her life. One estimate placed the total at more than thirty barrels.[21] She added Communion to the church rite, with silver service donated by C. F. LeFevre of Milwaukee, Wisconsin.[22]

One of her other contributions was to overcome, at least partially, the traditional Scottish aversion to singing hymns. She also introduced Christmas celebrations for children in both the Dunfermline and Glasgow churches. This raised some eyebrows, for most natives of Scotland considered Christmas a "popish festival" to be avoided.

Whatever her views might have been as to the uncertain or questionable utility of mission stations, she continued to visit them regularly and used as much local talent as she could muster. James Paterson of Dunfermline, a lay preacher, had graduated from the Canton Theological School in 1878 and returned to his native land as one of the few professionally trained Universalist clergy in Scotland.[23] While residing in Scotland Mrs. Soule also visited northern Ireland, the Isle of Man, and England as a lecturer.

All told, Mrs. Soule's missionary work was deemed a success, although there were some who had doubts about either the necessity or appropriateness of her presence in Scotland, especially while still serving as president of the WCA. In recognition of her services to Scottish Universalism, Mrs. Soule was ordained by the Scottish Convention in March 1880, thus becoming not only the first and only person to be so recognized in the Universalist church in Scotland but the first woman in all of Europe known to have gained such status.[24]

In 1881 her tour of duty was extended a year as a result of the importuning of the congregation at St. Paul's.[25] The church grew steadily, if not dramatically. Fourteen individuals had signed the constitution in 1879; the membership had risen to forty-two little more than a year later, with twenty-three families represented, and attendance frequently numbering more than 100.[26] The membership had reached almost sixty by 1881. Mrs. Soule's salary, still the responsibility of the WCA and made up in part of special gifts, was increased over the years, and by 1884 had reached $1,600.[27]

There was frequent mention after 1881 of the desirability of having the General Convention share part of the financial responsibility for the mission, but some Universalists were either hesitant about or actually opposed to such a commitment. Israel Washburn, Jr. was very cool toward the entire idea of sending a missionary to Scotland, on the ground that the essential truths of Universalism were already being taught through other churches there, and that it was an unnecessary diversion of effort and resources.[28] He thought that the Broad Church element within the United Presbyterian Church was already serving Universalist purposes sufficiently in Scotland.

Isaac M. Atwood disagreed, citing the case of David Macrae, pastor of one such church who was tried for heresy for attempting to obtain ecclesiastical authority to allow his church members to be exempted from the requirement of professing faith in the doctrine of endless torment.[29] Macrae, who preached in the Congregational Church in Dundee in 1883, expressed publicly his opposition to the doctrine but did not openly profess Universalism.[30] Such ideas as Macrae expressed were considered by the authorities to be a direct challenge to the Westminister Confession and Catechism.

Mrs. Soule was herself a conservative "Bible Universalist" within the framework of the denomination, and was gratified to discover that Unitarianism and Universalism in the British Isles were virtually interchangeable. It was a source of satisfaction to her that Unitarians in the United Kingdom did not identify themselves with their American counterparts who had discarded their belief in revealed religion.[31]

Official relations between the General Convention and the Scottish Universalists were always ambivalent because of a technical problem. The jurisdiction of the Universalist Church in America did not of course extend to churches overseas. Consequently the Scottish Convention could not be fellowshipped and its representatives could not serve as voting delegates to the General Convention. That was the reason Mitchell had been designated as an "honorary" delegate when he attended in 1873.

The question of the legal relationship between the two bodies had arisen several times after 1873. Sullivan H. McCollester, who had visited Mrs. Soule in Scotland in 1879 and had been much impressed by what he saw and heard, was designated to represent the Scottish Convention at the General Convention that year. But he felt that it was improper, and nominated J. W. Hanson in his stead. Hanson was thereupon given a seat "out of sympathy with the purposes of [the] organization in Scotland."[32] But that did not solve the problem either, so in 1880 the trustees of the

General Convention neatly resolved the dilemma by extending "*moral fellowship*" to the Scottish body and by making members of the mission honorary delegates "by special order."[33] Once decided upon, this rather unconventional arrangement never had to be used again because there is no record of any missionaries from Scotland after 1887 who required such recognition. The General Convention left matters in the hands of the WCA.

Even though Mrs. Soule had resigned the presidency of the WCA in 1880, her services on its behalf were still much needed at home, and she had been away a year longer than originally planned. The WCA therefore decided that as soon as at least $1,000 in gifts, in addition to the continuing annual appropriation of $250, could be provided, a successor would be appointed.[34]

A male, Marion Crosley, pastor in Utica, New York, accepted the position. He inherited only two churches — Glasgow and Larbert — a few preaching stations, and an amorphous body of unorganized Universalists, the exact size of which was unknown. There was a certain irony in the fact that St. John's Universalist Church, reorganized in 1879 to serve the communities of Carluke and Braidwood, ceased to exist after 1882 because much of its constituency had emigrated to America.[35] Yet if Mrs. Soule had not taken over the leadership in Scotland, no organized Universalism might have survived at all, as was pointed out in a tribute to her services.[36]

When Crosley completed his assignment in 1884 he urged that the mission be continued and supported from America.[37] However, there were delays in making a replacement and doubts about the value of the mission. Crosley was succeeded temporarily by H. W. Smith, ex-chaplain of the Edinburgh Poor House, until a missionary from America could be found. Issac Atwood raised the question of whether the WCA was misdirecting its efforts by concentrating on the Scottish mission when there was so much to be done in the Southern and Western United States. He saw no real future for the mission, and predicted that if it survived at all it would continue to be "humble and uninfluential."[38]

Mrs. M. Louise Thomas, who had succeeded Mrs. Soule to the presidency of the WCA, objected strongly to Atwood's pessimistic remarks and argued that the mission was not disproportionately expensive in relation to other WCA projects, where most of its resources were still being expended.[39] She showed her determination to continue the mission by announcing in 1884 that J. W. Hanson would take charge of it as soon as sufficient funds could be raised. Atwood remained unconvinced and went so far as to remind Mrs. Thomas that the WCA itself was at the time an anomaly in the organizational structure of the church and that its constituents had no official representation; neither was it responsible to any other body; there was no other way of dealing with it than by direct appeal.[40]

Hanson's service in Scotland was delayed until 1886 because of a combination of factors. The WCA had difficulty in providing the salary of $1,000 which he had been promised; then he fell ill, and to make matters worse his wife died before his planned departure.[41] When he did arrive at his post, at which he remained until mid-1887, he sent back reports full of gloom and discouragement.

The long delay in replacing Crosley had resulted in a "retrograde" situation, and the uncertainty surrounding Hanson's tenure beyond a year had a disheartening effect. The lack of a church building was another negative factor, for the members were reluctant to use a hired hall because it gave not only too secular a character to church services but too much of a temporary appearance. At the same time, the parishioners did not have the financial ability to purchase a lot or construct their own building. This situation had existed from the very start. When St. Paul's had been organized by Mrs. Soule the congregation had moved from a small, uncomfortable hall to larger and more convenient quarters in the center of the city, but it was still considered far from ideal.

Yet Hanson felt that the Glasgow mission should be continued, not only for the direct benefit of the few faithful, but for the indirect leaven that it provided for all Universalists — the sense of involvement in a broad spiritual movement that transcended national boundaries.

Hanson was greatly relieved and the Universalists in Glasgow were jubilant when word was received that Mrs. Soule was to return in 1886. She had been preaching and working on behalf of the WCA during her five years in America, but decided to make another visit to the country whose land and people she had grown to love. She was enthusiastically welcomed upon her arrival to resume her work. During the winter of 1886–1887 she served the Unitarian church in Dundee, of which Henry Williamson (1839–1925), a Unitarian and close friend, was the pastor.[42] He had been largely responsible for raising the funds for the church constructed in 1879 in which Mrs. Soule preached; he served what became the Williamson Memorial Church for sixty years.[43] He had participated in the dedication of the Stenhousemuir church in 1875.

Mrs. Soule agreed at first to preach in Glasgow only from March to May 1887, but in fact served the church until her retirement in 1892. She was, like Hanson, made an honorary president of the Scottish Convention, and her modest salary was supplied for the most part by the WCA. The church population during the remainder of her active career remained relatively stable, with about forty families, a membership of about 150, and a Sunday School of forty.[44] At long last, a small chapel was built in 1891. Mrs. Soule contributed 20 percent of her salary toward its construction.[45] For the first time during her connection with the Scottish mission she asked directly for money; it was to assist in constructing the church.[46] Up to that time her requests had been confined to the donation of Universalist literature. Her goal was to raise $2,000 for the church, a figure somewhat unrealistically raised to $10,000 by the trustees of the General Convention. The estimated cost was first set at $1,250 but when completed the actual expenditure was somewhat in excess of $2,000. The church was valued at $2,500.[47]

Charles A. C. Garst, a graduate of Lombard College, was selected in 1892 by the WCA to replace Mrs. Soule. The organization was forced to dip into its permanent fund to provide the $1,000 to transport him and his wife and child to Scotland.[48] Garst had accepted a three-year assignment, but he resigned in 1894 after less than two years, discouraged by the poor prospects and beset by ill health.[49] The WCA made no attempt to provide a replacement; the "leading topic" at the annual meeting in 1894 was the feasibility of continuing the mission, and it was decided in the negative.[50]

After the guiding hand of Mrs. Soule was removed in 1892 and divisions appeared in the ranks, the membership of the Glasgow church declined precipitately to only fifteen families and forty members by 1894, which was the last year any report was received.[51] The only course seemed to be the sale of the church property, the proceeds of which were to be used to pay the WCA's indebtedness of $1,100 to its permanent fund incurred by the Scottish mission.[52] But the WCA was unable to take the money out of Scotland and the internal debt had to be made up out of any unappropriated funds that might become available.

It was a rather unhappy ending for a mission that had been started with such hope and sacrifice on the part of a small number of dedicated people. Between 1873 and Mrs. Soule's return to Scotland in 1886, the WCA had contributed more than $12,000 from all sources.[53] The net cost to the denomination for the six years from 1878 to 1884 had been a mere $6,500, excluding gifts.[54]

After Mrs. Soule's retirement she remained in Scotland for the remainder of her life. She died on 6 December 1903, with the funeral address delivered at her residence by her old friend Williamson. At her request, she was cremated, and in 1905 a stained glass window was placed in her honor in the Glasgow Crematorium by James F. Currie, one of her parishioners.[55] She had served long and faithfully and had become well known and highly esteemed in Glasgow, notwithstanding "the harsh Scottish prejudice against woman preachers."[56] Another of her generation, J. U. Mitchell, and a pioneer Scottish Universalist leader, passed off the scene in 1905, at the age of seventy-two.[57]

The Scottish mission may have come to an end with the collapse of the Glasgow congregation, but the one remaining church, at Larbert, resolutely held on. About twenty families in their small brick church valued at $620 in 1893, continued to meet under the lay leadership of Andrew and George Ure, two of four brothers who had been converted to Universalism in 1866. George Ure had been one of the first Scottish Universalists Mrs. Soule had met when she made her first trip in 1875. He was president of the church at the time of his death in 1901. In 1908 E. T. Russell, a Scottish Unitarian missionary, visited the church and in 1910 it became affiliated with the Scottish Unitarian Association, with the distinct understanding that the Universalist name would be retained.[58]

The existence of the Larbert church was called to denominational attention from time to time. In 1912 Henry Williamson, the Unitarian minister in Dundee, suggested that American Universalists continue to support the church, and called attention in 1912 to the fact that Mrs. Soule had left a $500 legacy for its use. Although individuals from the United States occasionally visited the church, such as Frederick A. Bisbee in 1913, there is no record that direct, official relations were ever reestablished. When its fiftieth anniversary was celebrated in 1917, American Universalists were asked not to forget the church. In the early 1920s Williamson, still at Dundee, was urging Universalists to send denominational literature to a mailing list he was willing to provide.

Among the last to visit the Stenhousemuir church was Noble E. McLaughlin, pastor of the church in Wausau, Wisconsin, on the eve of the celebration of its sixtieth anniversary, in 1927.[59] Two years later the attendance had fallen away to such an extent that it was considered "quite hopeless to continue."[60] The church was closed in 1929, the property disposed of, and the membership dissolved. The first foreign missionary venture of the denomination had probably faded from the memory of most American Universalists by then, but there were those who could find and recall the name of Caroline A. Soule in its annals.

Only one other overseas missionary effort among Christians was ever attempted by the denomination, although it never in any sense achieved the status of a mission comparable to that in Scotland. In 1901 Isaac M. Atwood, the first General Superintendent, announced a plan to establish a mission in Cuba.[61] The idea had been planted by Jacob Straub (1835–1917), a Universalist clergyman from Chicago who moved to the American colony of Columbia (La Gloria Bay, Camaguey Province), on the northeastern coast of the island, in search of a warm climate.[62]

Straub, born in Marion, Ohio, in 1835, had served various pastorates in Michigan and Illinois. His family had been long associated with the Ryder Memorial Church in Chicago and his sister, Mary A. Straub (1837–1914), was briefly a minister but was best known as a hymnologist.[63] He studied science and medicine and was the author of *The Consolation of Science* (1886) and *Prophecy and the Prophet; or, the Laws of Inspiration and Their Phenomena* (1887). Straub received an honorary Doctorate of Divinity from Lombard College in 1890.

Upon arrival in Cuba, Straub began preaching to a varied group made up largely of Protestant Americans, with a few English-speaking Cubans and Spaniards. The unofficial "co-operative church" held services at the hotel operated by Straub's daughter and son-in-law, and in 1902 Straub organized an undenominational Sunday school.[64]

Plans were made for constructing a union church building and Straub suggested to Atwood that the Universalists establish a mission as a nucleus. The General Superintendent thereupon made an investment of $100 on behalf of the General Convention. Straub journeyed to a meeting of the Murray Grove Association in Good Luck, New Jersey, where he described with great enthusiasm the possibilities of propagating Universalism in Cuba.[65]

There is no evidence that anything was ever done, and the ambitions for a Cuban mission came to an end with Straub's death in 1917.

Chapter 23

"The Field is the World": The Establishment of the Japan Mission, 1890–1915

Paving the Way

In 1890 the Universalist Church took an epochal step in its history by establishing, in Japan, outposts in a predominantly non-Christian land. Proposals to work among the "heathen" had been made from time to time, the first over half a century earlier. In 1819, in the "General Epistle" which accompanied the proceedings of the New England Convention, reference was made to the fact that the Universalists were "destitute of a sufficient number to supply the regular organized societies in our connexion, without having any to send on heathen missions." Henry Bowen, publisher of the *Universalist Magazine* in 1821, had received an inquiry from a correspondent soliciting his views about engaging in foreign missionary activities. Bowen had promptly replied that he saw no justification whatever for sending missionaries abroad when so much needed doing at home. "Surely the soul of a native American ought to be as precious in our view, as the soul of a native of Hindoostan or the Sandwich isles."[1]

Universalists were taunted some thirty years later by the "orthodox" for their refusal to engage in foreign missionary efforts to convert the heathen. One Universalist interpreted this as an underhanded way of prodding his denomination into diverting its energies into foreign fields and thus weakening its efforts to spread the faith in America. This would mean lessened competition on the home front.[2]

The most positive expression before 1870 of the desirability of Universalist-sponsored foreign missions had come from Sylvanus Cobb, editor of the *Christian Freeman*. B. Bowser, an American Negro Universalist, had settled in Cape Palmas, West Africa, in the 1850s, and had sought aid in establishing a religious mission. This prompted Cobb to express the wish that the denomination could "send a band of well qualified Universalist missionaries into heathen lands."[3] But no such aid was forthcoming, so Bowser joined the Episcopal Church in Africa because he could not do the task single-handedly, and it had offered assistance.[4]

The Boston Association in 1869 seems to have been the first official denominational group to have discussed the then-novel possibility of Universalist foreign missions to non-Christians. However, the consensus at the time was that it would have been impossible to have engaged in such an undertaking because of the multitude of other projects then on hand.[5] Preparations for celebrating the denominational centennial in 1870 were under way and activities abroad would have to await future consideration.

There appears to have been no further mention of the subject until 1879, when the suggestion was made that the explorations of Henry M. Stanley and David Livingstone in Africa might open the way for Universalist missionary activity on that continent.[6] That was as far as denominational involvement in that part of the world ever went, although the idea received some support.[7]

The individual who first brought the entire subject of foreign missions in non-Christian countries to Universalist attention was Thomas B. Thayer, editor of the *Universalist Quarterly*. In 1881, in the course of reviewing a work on Protestant foreign missions among non-Christians, he raised the question of why his own denomination had not yet appeared on the scene.[8] Even the Unitarians had a mission in India dating back to the 1820s.[9] Where was the Universalist sense of stewardship? There was only one Universalist missionary abroad in 1881 (Caroline A. Soule in Scotland), and she was working among Christians. Thayer then proceeded to summarize the impressive foreign missionary record of other denominations.

There was indeed a considerable backlog of experience accumulated by the early 1880s. The pioneer organization had been the American Board of Commissioners for Foreign Missions, which had grown out of an organization among a group of Williams College students in Massachusetts in 1808.[10] Their object was "to effect in the persons of its members a mission, or missions to the heathen." Two years later the General Association of Congregationalists in Massachusetts had created the board, which was incorporated in 1812. Their first mission had been established in India, where five missionaries were sent that year.

Denominational lines were not strictly followed in the early years of the board, and by 1831 the Congregationalists were outnumbered by Presbyterians, who split in 1837 into "Old School" and "New School," with the latter continuing to support the board. After the two wings of the Presbyterian Church were reunited in 1870, they were no longer represented, and the board became an exclusively Congregational body. The American Baptist Missionary Union was organized in 1814 after two of the missionaries sent out by the Congregationalists in 1812 became Baptists while en route to India.[11] Missionary groups were likewise organized in rapid succession by other Protestant denominations.

As of 1880 the Methodists had 184 missionaries in the foreign field; the American Board of Foreign Missions (Congregational) had 144 ordained missionaries; the Presbyterians had 122; and the Baptist Missionary Union (Boston) had 141 missionaries in Asiatic lands alone.[12] Universalists had as much a duty as others of "teaching and civilizing these ignorant and wretched barbarians who, nevertheless, are our brothers." Universalists were needed to "go among these degraded and superstitious idolaters." Thayer predicted that, like the Unitarians, the Universalists would soon have at least one foreign mission among the heathen.

Other Universalists soon joined Thayer in pointing out the possibilities for missionary endeavor and the remissness of the denomination in not taking advantage of the opportunities before it. More and more mention of foreign missions began to appear in the denominational press after 1880. Universalists were told that their church could not become strong and efficient unless foreign missions were established and Universalism exerted influence in other parts of the world. The church was not for English-speaking peoples only; the Scottish mission was not sufficient.

At first there was no focus suggested, and some Universalists made no distinction at all between Christian and non-Christian peoples. Mexico, Japan, India, Africa, England, and France were among those suggested as profitable fields.[13] The General Convention expressed an interest specifically in establishing missions in London and Paris, but the Woman's Centenary Association did not consider that a judicious move, particularly after Mrs. M. Louise Thomas, in her capacity as "vice-president at large," agreed to investigate personally. The possibility of establishing a mission in Sweden was raised, but the general feeling seemed to be that it would be more feasible to include the entire Scandinavian population of the American Northwest instead, with work to be centered in Minnesota where there was a considerable concentration.[14]

In 1898, almost a decade after the Japan mission had been established, one California Universalist noted that the newly acquired area of Hawaii would make an excellent mission field, but was forced to admit that the lack of means and workers prevented its establishment.[15] The Middle East was also suggested as a missionary field. B. M. Peshdimaljian, a student in the Tufts Divinity School, announced his intention of returning to his native Armenia as a Universalist missionary. While in the Boston area he spent considerable time and energy speaking to young people's groups urging them to assist in starting a mission in Turkey. Evaristo Hurtado, a former Roman Catholic who studied for a year at St. Lawrence, recommended that Mexico would be a good field for Universalist effort.[16]

The Massachusetts Convention was the first body in the denomination to devote a special session to the topic of foreign missions. In 1882 Thayer, the principal advocate of the idea, offered to be the first contributor to a special foreign missionary fund.[17] J. G. Adams, at the same meeting, suggested the publication of a monthly missionary journal and the introduction of foreign missions into the curricula of theological schools.

Whenever the subject of foreign missions was discussed, the ever-present problem of money was raised. A proposal was made that, because Universalists would never have sufficient resources to engage in such work, any funds raised for the purpose should be turned over to the American Board of Foreign Missions. Congregationalists, so it was said, with their vastly greater wealth and experience, could do the work much more effectively than could the Universalists.[18] There was also the chronic fear that Thayer's enthusiasm for foreign missions might divert attention and sorely needed funds from domestic missionary needs. The "true field" was at home, not abroad.[19] What about the problems of the tenement, the neglected child, and the evils of the grog shop? They should be given top priority.

The first official action in the name of the entire denomination to establish foreign missions was taken at the General Convention meeting in Philadelphia in 1882. The trustees expressed the view that "the time has come for our Church to look toward the establishment of missions to heathen lands."[20] Resources were not yet available, but some Universalists were already desirous of making contributions toward that end. The delegates responded by authorizing the trustees to receive donations. Four years were to elapse before a positive commitment was made, but at least the movement was beginning to take shape.

After 1882 the subject of foreign missions continued to attract attention, but the signals were not always clear. In 1883 the trustees expressed disappointment that "the subject of missions to heathen lands" had not awakened the interest it deserved.[21] Several individuals spoke during the Anniversary Week meetings in Boston in 1883 in favor of foreign missions. A recurrent justification was the Universalist belief in "the oneness of the human family." One spokesman was sure that the denomination was "destined to be a great missionary church."[22] Henry W. Rugg, an enthusiastic supporter of missionary activity, devoted his Occasional Sermon at the General Convention in 1883 to the need for Universalist involvement. Vincent E. Tomlinson placed foreign missionary work in an even broader context. Using as his Biblical text Matthew xiii: 38, "The field is the world," he delivered a sermon on the subject in 1887. "If anything is clearly taught in the Bible it is that the Christian religion is to become the religion of the whole earth."[23]

But there were dissenting voices. Alonzo A. Miner was unenthusiastic about foreign missions. Universalists, he argued, had challenges aplenty at home. He was worried about "so much heathenism coming to our shores" by way of immigrants that mission stations were needed in American cities much more than in foreign lands.[24] One Universalist who addressed the Niagara Association at Rochester, New York, in 1887, found no justification whatever for Universalist involvement in foreign missions.[25] If converting and helping souls were the work of the church, Universalists could do more good among "enlightened people" than among savages. Two civilized people could be helped for every one savage. Further, there were already too few Universalist clergy in relation to domestic needs; sending them abroad would only worsen the situation. As long as there were vacant parishes at home, their needs should come first. But a growing number of Universalists were beginning to think otherwise.

The first official step by Universalists specifically to establish one or more missions in non-Christian parts of the world and which actually resulted in action, came in 1886, on the initiative of the Rhode Island Convention. At its meeting in June of that year C. W. Tomlinson had submitted a resolution, unanimously adopted, that the General Convention consider the subject of extending the mission work of the church "not alone at home and among Christians, but into heathen lands."[26] It was proposed that a special committee be created "to consider this subject with respect alike to its advisability, its methods, and the fields most favorable to the enterprise." The subject was considered sufficiently urgent to demand immediate attention. The work should not be "left entirely with other branches of the Christian Church." The Massachusetts Convention echoed the same sentiments in a memorial presented to the same session in 1886.

The recommendation regarding missions was presented on behalf of the Rhode Island Convention by Rugg, and was endorsed by the convention. A special committee, including Rugg and Capen, was appointed to consider the subject in detail. Their elaborate report was presented at the 1887 session. They had concluded that it was the duty of the church "to engage in a work of Foreign Missions."

The committee also recommended that a special fund be immediately created and that as soon as a sufficient sum had been received and pledged, the trustees were to establish the mission. The recommendations were unanimously adopted, the motion to do so having come from Q. H. Shinn, the denomination's most enthusiastic apostle of domestic missions.[27] From that time forward the projected mission was urged with growing vigor.

The decision having finally been made to enter the foreign mission field, the question of why Universalists had been so slow to respond to the challenge was raised repeatedly both within and outside the denomination. Because the step was unprecedented in the annals of the church, the committee recommending the mission had seen fit to place the proposal in historical context. With an almost apologetic tone it had pointed to the fact that until the late 1880s conditions within the denomination had not been favorable to missionary work in distant lands. But with growing attention to church exension by way of home missions, and with consolidation and increase of strength there was enhanced appreciation of the denomination's obligation "to do its part in the evangelizing of the world."

Just prior to the meeting of the General Convention in 1887 the editor of the *Independent,* an interdenominational publication, pointed out that Universalists had no foreign missions among non-Christians and ascribed this to the fact that there was no need for them inasmuch as all would finally be saved anyhow, according to Universalist teachings.[28] T. J. Sawyer took issue with this explanation, acknowledging meanwhile that Universalists indeed had done nothing as yet among "Chinamen, Japanese, or the Islanders of the Pacific."[29] The reasons were obvious. The denomination, after feeble beginnings, had had to spend three-quarters of its first century struggling to survive and the last quarter-century in founding and endowing sorely needed institutions of learning. All of this had taken place in an uncongenial and inhospitable environment, under "a constant and often unscrupulous opposition." But Universalists by the 1880s no longer had to devote their main efforts to gaining and holding a recognized position in the Christian world. They were now ready to push ahead on another front.

Sawyer could not resist aiming a shaft at the opposers of the denomination. If Universalists had "converted no savage tribes to the religion of Christ" they had at least done something towards converting "a savage theology" (Calvinism) into a semblance of the true gospel. It was in part through Universalism's largely unacknowledged influence that "heaven has been becoming year after year broader and more populous, while hell has been shrinking correspondingly." Neither could Sawyer refrain from pointing out that the Congregational churches had existed in America almost twice as long as had the Universalist before organizing a foreign missionary society, and that their first efforts had been weak and hesitant.

The editors of the *Leader* offered almost the same explanations as had Sawyer in accounting for the tardiness of the denomination in entering the foreign missionary field. They emphasized the need for a new spirit of unity. Universalists had been "educated in demolition, not construction [and their] wild horse rioting in independence had to be broken to harness."[30] They were now ready to take the next step, of "applying Universalism to the work of evangelizing foreign peoples." They had overcome their excessive particularism and their need to be so defensive and so negative. However, "conversion by circular" was not enough. Individuals were needed not only to establish missions abroad but to educate Universalists at home to the need for such overseas activity. There had to be "a conversion first of the converters."

The decision to establish at least one foreign mission among non-Christians, representing as it did a giant step on the part of the denomination, was made with great deliberation and careful review of the implications. There were several tasks to be performed and questions to be answered. Those who favored the idea had to keep constantly before the denomination the need for Universalist involvement; had to be sure that the country chosen was the most propitious location for mission activity; and had to provide the money, personnel, and facilities for such an undertaking. It was also necessary to explore, if possible, the experiences of other denominations.

The choice of Japan as the missionary field seems to have been almost a foregone conclusion. It appeared to be more hospitable to Christianity than at any time in the history of that nation, as was pointed out by the special committee on missions when it made its report in 1887. Japan welcomed Westerners, other denominations had already paved the way, and first-hand information was available about their prospects and problems.

Admittedly, very few Universalists probably knew much about that part of the world. Few, if any, knew that in 1860, when the Japanese Embassy left the United States that year, the only books both proffered by various denominations and accepted, had been Universalist publications. This had been accomplished through the efforts of James Shrigley, then pastor in Richmond, Virginia.[31] One member of the embassy staff had also heard Edwin H. Chapin preach in Washington.

In 1887 another Universalist clergyman, James H. Chapin, Professor of Geology and Mineralogy at St. Lawrence University, and a member of the General Convention board of trustees, made a trip to Japan and other Asiatic countries. He was appointed a representative of the Universalist Church while abroad, although his instructions were "simply to observe, inquire, and report."[32] It was clearly indicated that his trip was a private arrangement, made at no cost to the convention, and was in no way intended to affect any action that the convention might want to take regarding establishment of a mission in Japan.[33]

There were, of course, serious and practical questions to be raised and answered. Did the denomination have the financial means and the personnel requisite for such a commitment? It appeared to the committee which made its report in 1887 that the expense of maintaining a mission in Japan need not exceed $5,000 a year; and if such a sum could be guaranteed for at least two or three years, surely the staffing of such a mission would not be difficult.

The committee attempted to anticipate another inevitable question: Would not a foreign mission divert resources from other activities to which the church was already pledged? The committee replied that foreign missions would have the opposite effect; they would actually strengthen and solidify efforts at home by increasing a sense of commitment and the will to extend the blessings of Christianity (Universalist version) to all. The machinery was already available. All that was needed was to test the idea by making an appeal for special contributions.

By the time of the next convention, in 1887, several supporters of the mission movement had volunteered annual subscriptions over a five-year period, provided the total of $5,000 was pledged for each of the five years.[34] Nine individuals had made pledges ranging from $50 to $200 a year, including one by "a friend" in Bridgeport, Connecticut, easily identified as P. T. Barnum, a strong supporter of foreign missions. The editor of the *Gospel Banner* (Maine) had proposed in 1887 that 1,000 individuals give $100 apiece. Barnum offered to give $1,000 to complete the sum, and was confident that at least half a million could be raised in six months. The editors of the *Leader* suggested that it would be even nicer if he made the $1,000 the first rather than the last contribution.[35]

The very first pledges had already come in 1886 from the Sunday school in Stamford, Connecticut, and from the Young People's Missionary Association of the Church of the Messiah in Philadelphia, the two contributions totalling slightly more than $100.[36] There had also been pledges from several other organizations. The Rhode Island Convention was the first statewide body to make a pledge ($500).

It was clear by 1888 that the denomination was serious about establishing a mission in Japan. The trustees added to their standing committees one for foreign missions, and appointed to it Rugg, Sweetser, and G. L. Demarest.[37] In compliance with the action of the 1887 convention the trustees established a special foreign mission fund in 1888. It was understood that after the immediate needs were met, a permanent foreign mission fund would be created.

By the time the convention met in 1888 more than $7,000 in pledges and gifts had been received. Meanwhile, supporters had been busy on both the platform and in the press. Rugg had spoken enthusiastically on the subject at a denominational summer conference. And at the convention itself, no less than three major addresses were devoted to the subject.

Universalists by 1889 had access to a considerable body of information about the prospects in Japan, and the experiences of other American denominations in that part of the world. Particular attention was paid to those of the Unitarians who, in 1887, had sent Arthur M. Knapp to Japan to assess the prospects of establishing a mission, but not before they had been given some realistic advice. At a farewell meeting for Knapp in the Second Church in Boston before his departure, a native of Japan, Stejiro Fukuzawa, addressed the assembly.[38] He told his audience that if the object of the missionaries was to transform Japan into a Christian nation they were probably doomed to failure. Missionaries had established some schools and had done some good in other respects. But their efforts to propagate Christianity had been far from successful; the number of genuine converts was "hopelesly small." Most such converts were poor and uneducated; orthodox Christianity did not appeal to the upper class.

Fukuzawa laid much of the blame on the missionaries themselves, who generally lacked sympathy for the Japanese people. This in turn rested on the assumption by the missionaries that, as a people, the Japanese were "a degree below them, — a swarm of poor heathen." Consequently, Westerners expected to find nothing good in Japanese ideas and customs. "Therefore they simply want us to throw away all our religion, philosophy and morals, and take of *theirs* instead." Ceremonies honoring ancestors were considered foolish by Westerners, for the dead were probably all in hell anyway. Such an attitude on the part of the missionaries naturally provoked indignation, for it was difficult if not impossible for an individual to understand why deceased parents were "doomed to eternal damnation for apparently no reason." Missionaries were also considered excessively pious, and seemed to have no interest in the "heathen" except to convert them and enroll them as members of churches. Japanese could not be treated as were Fijians or Hottentots. The educated classes, in fact, were "rather bored by missionaries." What such Japanese wanted was "broad-minded Christians" who could meet and talk with non-Christians "without feeling the necessity of calling their attention to the danger of their future salvation."

According to Universalist Richard Eddy, who wrote an editorial based on the Unitarian report, the field for Universalists was therefore a most inviting one, for in spite of all obstacles, they represented the broad-minded Christianity that other denominations lacked. Further, there was a practical advantage possessed by Japan in contrast to other "distant localities" because the English language was already being taught in Japanese schools. All religions were also on about the same footing and the nation seemed to be making great strides "towards the highest civilization." This would make the work of Universalists that much less difficult.

The general situation in Japan did indeed appear propitious for Universalists as well as for other Western faiths and denominations, even though there might be some difficulties. The nation was in the process of rapid Westernization which led to the boast that Japan would do in a generation what had required centuries to accomplish in English-speaking lands. Feudalism had been officially abolished in 1871 and a limited monarchy promised by the emperor was in the process of establishment, with a parliament scheduled to convene in 1890. Anti-Christian laws had been repealed in 1872, when only a handful of converts existed; by 1889, while Universalists were gathering support for a mission, there were nearly 29,000 Protestant Christians in Japan, and the Roman Catholic and Greek Orthodox churches had 39,000 and 16,000 respectively.[39] It was hoped, and even predicted, that Japan would be thoroughly Christianized by the end of the century. This was quite in line with the motto of a student volunteer movement for Christian missions adopted when it was organized in 1880: "The evangelization of the world in this generation."

The door to Christianity had been thrown wide open with the promulgation of the constitution of 1889, the twenty-eighth article of which read: "Japanese subjects shall, within limits not prejudicial to peace and order and not antagonistic to their duties as subjects, enjoy freedom of religious belief." The ground was thus cleared for free competition of religions, and both Americans and Europeans were taking full advantage of it. Christianity had not only gained approved status but had secured legal equality with other religions, including Shintoism and Buddhism.

Indications were that Protestant Christianity in Japan was making considerable progress in the late 1880s in a very short span of time. When J. H. Chapin visited Japan in 1887 he reported 193 churches, 215 missions, and 14,000 Christianized Japanese.[40] Two years later the numbers had risen to 250 churches and slightly more than 25,000 adherents, of whom 2,000 were children.[41] There were reported to be 443 missionaries, both native and foreign, in 1889. Not only was the number of converts growing, but their financial contributions were impressive. Most of the preaching was done by Japanese ministers, with the missionaries serving as advisers. There were 142 native clergy, 40 more than in 1888, and in a few instances they had developed self-sustaining congregations.

A high proportion of the missionaries were engaged in education. In 1889 there were fifteen boarding schools for boys and thirty-nine for girls, with forty-seven coeducational day schools, with a total enrollment of over 9,500. The goal of most of the schools was not to provide general education but to train church leaders.[42]

There were skeptical voices raised among Universalists about whether the sudden hospitality to foreign ideas and institutions might just as suddenly evaporate, but the majority of the missionaries of all denominations seemed to assume otherwise. In view of the complexities of international relations and national policies, and with the wisdom of hindsight, some of the expectations were undoubtedly unrealistic and simplistic. With almost twenty years of first-hand experience in Japan, one veteran Universalist missionary, Isaac W. Cate, wrote a year before his death in 1908 that the palmy days of missions were the five years prior to the time the Universalists appeared, and that one of the periodic nationalistic reactions to foreigners had already begun to set in although most missionaries had failed to realize it.[43]

Christians were indeed confronted by one of the reactions against Europeanization in general and Christianity in particular; this was reflected in the relatively small numerical gains made by Protestants between 1890 and 1900. The number of converts who became church members increased from 28,977 in 1889 to 42,454 in 1900.[44] This was the situation that confronted the Universalists when they arrived and started their mission. Within the next decade the reaction had given way to steady, although by no means spectacular, progress. The number of Protestant Japanese had risen by the end of 1905 to a total in excess of 55,000.[45]

During the period of Christian missionary expansion in the 1880s the greatest complaint voiced by the missionaries was the uncoordinated increase in missionary societies which resulted in two or more denominations frequently operating in the same community or neighborhood. Such wasteful duplication of efforts and resources, it was thought, could be avoided by cooperation rather than competition, and by consolidation on both an inter- and intra-denominational basis. Two-thirds of the native Protestant Christians were in churches organized by either the Congregationalists or Presbyterians. There were no less than eight branches of the latter denomination, each operating according to its own polity and government until seven of them organized as the United Church of Japan.

A move was under way by 1889 to form "The Associated Church of Christ in Japan" as an interdenominational effort emphasizing the autonomy of the local congregations. Episcopal missionaries from various nations had already united their congregations under the name of "The Holy Church of Japan" and intra-denominational unions of other groups were in various stages.

Unitarians and others had been much heartened by the report of Knapp, who had returned in 1889. Although he organized no churches and gathered no congregations, he was cordially received and had had space placed at his disposal in the two leading Tokyo newspapers. He was much in demand as a speaker, but noted that there was almost total indifference among prominent Japanese to "the Gospel as ordinarily presented." There was, he thought, a great opportunity for liberal Christians from Britain, Germany, and the United States to cooperate in mission work.

The possibility of a Universalist mission to Japan was discussed at some length during the meetings of Anniversary Week in Boston in the spring of 1889. Rugg had reported that Universalists were assured that representatives would be welcomed. He was confident that a complete mission could be installed for $5,000 a year, consisting of a minister and his wife, a physician, a school teacher, and an interpreter and translator.[46]

Eddy took a more cautious approach than did Rugg and called attention to the fact that there would be serious problems. Universalists would be obligated to "stand alone, with neither sympathy nor encouragement from those already in the field, nor from those who may soon enter it."[47] The growing sentiment for union among the evangelical churches would virtually guarantee the exclusion of Universalists. Further, there was no assurance that Universalists would be recognized by or receive cooperation from the Unitarians in view of "the history of their attitude toward us." If the "rationalistic side of their house" should dominate their missionary movement in Japan, sympathy from them, even if it were demonstrated, would do more harm than good.

Then there were all the problems inherent in getting actual missionary work under way. Rapid results could not be expected; one or more schools would have to be established. Special training of the Japanese would be imperative. Whoever was selected to get the mission under way would need special skills and talents. Because the Japanese revered antiquity, someone exceptionally well-versed in the history of Christianity and the origins of the doctrine of universal salvation had to be chosen. The reported decay of Buddhism in Japan was no sure indication that Christianity was destined to take its place.

Capen was among those who undertook to convince Universalists that the operation of foreign missions should be one of their primary obligations. In 1889 he prepared an article on the subject and developed two themes: That historical Christianity was by nature a missionary religion and was "essentially aggressive. . . . so long as souls are ignorant, degraded, unreconciled, unregenerate, it must go after them, and must seek them out whatever their habitation may be."[48] He argued further that Universalists had been on the domestic front, "as truly moved by the missionary impulse as any church in Christendom." But they could no longer confine their activities to home ground. In a burst of literary dramatics he wrote that "ours is the flag that is to conquer the world. If we are to continue to grasp this sceptre we must go forth and help to gather the nations into the fold of God."

Launching the Mission

After almost a decade of discussion, debate, reports, and resolutions, the idea of a mission to Japan became a reality in the fall of 1889.[49] As the Committee on Official Reports expressed it, "the time is now ripe for a beginning." On their recommendation, the trustees were instructed "to indicate as soon as possible what missionary force we can command to initiate the enterprise." The financing of the mission seemed not to be a problem at all. Calls for pledges and cash went out in 1889, based on a five-year projection suggested by J. H. Chapin. By the end of the year over $20,000 had been committed by individuals and organizations such as the WCA which promised $100 a year for five years.

The individuals to staff the mission were selected with a minimum of delay. All accepted the invitation to participate, and all signed five-year contracts. The three were George L. Perin, who agreed to head the mission, accompanied by his family; I. Wallace Cate, and Miss Margaret

C. Schouler, who were to serve as his assistants. Perin (1854–1921) had been for many years a strong supporter of the foreign mission concept and at the time of his appointment had been for several years the popular pastor of the socially activist Shawmut Avenue Church in Boston. He was born near Newton (Jasper County), Iowa, on 31 July 1854, the son of Caleb and Mary J. Perin of New England background.[50] The family had soon joined the great trek to the Far West, where they settled in Oregon. Perin's rather sketchy formal education at a district school in Iowa and a Willamette College preparatory course in Oregon was alternated with labor on the family farm.

His decision to enter the Universalist ministry had been influenced by E. L. Rexford. Perin had earned his way through the Canton Theological School, from which he was graduated in 1878, by working in a local cheese factory and by reading to a blind student, H. N. Couden, who later became chaplain of the United States House of Representatives. Perin also met while in school his first wife, Vinnie Danforth, daughter of Abbie E. Danforth, a Universalist minister in Ohio who served briefly in Japan in 1893 as an unpaid volunteer assistant.[51]

Upon graduation Perin had been ordained in Kent, Ohio, in 1878, and held two brief pastorates in the state. In 1882 he gave an address on theological education at the Ohio Convention which attracted the attention of Demarest, then secretary of the General Convention. He arranged to have Perin speak on the same subject at the General Convention when it met that fall in Philadelphia. Perin made such a favorable impression on the Massachusetts delegation that they invited him to take charge of the Shawmut Avenue Church in Boston in 1883. In the seven years in Boston he had revitalized the church which was being adversely affected by changing population patterns, noticeably a movement to the suburbs, and had introduced numerous social service activities welcomed and utilized by the local community.

Isaac Wallace Cate (1862–1908), born in Calais, Vermont, on 30 July 1862, held a bachelor's degree from Tufts College (Class of 1889) and was in the midst of preparing for the ministry in the Tufts Divinity School at the time he was asked to join the mission. Before departing for Japan he was ordained as both a minister and missionary. A precedent was set not only in the purposes of the ordination but in the sponsoring agency. It was the first time in Universalist history that a minister had been ordained directly under the auspices of the General Convention in a jurisdiction where a state convention existed.[52] The ordination was a special occasion in another way. John Coleman Adams, who delivered the principal sermon, noted that by establishing the mission the Universalist church had finally "attained its majority" by assuming "the last of the great functions of a Christian body."[53]

Margaret Schouler, a wealthy member of Perin's church and Sunday school, had been for a number of years a teacher in the Franklin grammar school in Boston. She had considerable musical talent and was a painter who used the New Hampshire hills as one of her favorite subjects.[54]

As soon as the appointments were announced, cash and additional pledges poured in, largely as a result of Perin's personal enthusiasm. The last Sunday of his pastorate in January 1890 was observed as "Japan Sunday" throughout the denomination, with almost 200 parishes collecting special offerings. A spirited campaign which he led had produced, together with previous contributions, a grand total in subscriptions and cash, in excess of $62,000. This was thought to be more than enough to finance the mission for the first five years, as the missionaries departed for their new and challenging assignment.

The three missionaries landed in Japan on 22 April 1890. They were surprised and delighted to be welcomed at the port of Yokohama by Hizedo Yoshimura, a recent graduate of Doshisho University (Kyoto), an institution sponsored by the Congregationalists. He had read of their impending arrival in the local press. Yoshimura later visited the United States. He also served as the first interpreter when preaching began in Tokyo.

The missionaries immediately set to work after living quarters were obtained in Tokyo with the assistance of Knapp, the Unitarian missionary who had preceded them. Within a few weeks Cate was teaching English daily in a Buddhist school and Schouler was similarly occupied in a girls' school.

Perin had considerable difficulty in securing suitable rental quarters for the mission at a reasonable price, so he determined to erect a headquarters with accommodations for a school as well as a place of worship. This arrangement was not only more economical in the long run but gave the mission a more permanent appearance than rented facilities. A lot was obtained in the center of the city, in the Iidimachi section, and a simple two-story frame building complete with a picket fence was erected in a short time, with a chapel seating about 300 on the second floor; rooms with movable partitions were provided on the floor below.

The first public service was held in mid-December and the church was dedicated on Christmas day, with participation by other denominations.[55] The church narrowly escaped destruction in 1892 when the building immediately back of it burned to the ground and the fence separating the two lots was completely destroyed.[56]

Regular preaching was begun early in 1891, with services every Sunday, and with an average attendance of about sixty. Individuals were contacted in every province of the empire informing them of the mission, a church was organized with ten baptized members, a Sunday school with twenty children was opened, and a Bible class was started.

The head of the mission realized from the very beginning that the

Issac Wallace Cate (1862-1908) and George L. Perin (1854-1921) with Japanese theological students in 1892

secret of missionary success lay in training native clergy. They had to be the mainstay of every preaching station. In 1889, even before he had embarked on the mission, Perin had declared that "I shall aim to multiply just as fast as possible through men who can speak the Japanese language. We must have Japanese preachers. I fancy the success or failure of our missionaries hinge here."[57] He therefore immediately opened a theological school with two students who received four hours of formal instruction each day in an old dwelling on the same lot on which the church was built.[58] Both students were already Christians when converted to Universalism.[59]

The theological school most certainly had an ideal faculty-student ratio at the beginning, with the number of teachers (Perin and Cate) equalling the number of students. Clarence E. Rice, who arrived in the fall of 1892, comprised the third faculty member, and in 1893 H. Hoshino was added. From time to time other Japanese were invited to give lectures, and W. I. Laurence, of the Unitarian mission, also participated.[60]

Perin made it clear that the main task of the theological school was to convert non-Christians and to try to get distinctively Universalist principles across as effectively as possible. "We shall not begin our work by trying to make these intelligent Japanese believe that their ancestors are now in hell for the simple reason that we did not happen to come along a little sooner. I shall try to present the love of God . . . and to let hell take care of itself."[61]

Perin immediately called on American Universalists for financial aid in training native missionaries. The first to respond was Henry Nehemiah Dodge, who agreed to support one, specifying that the recipient make periodic reports detailing his experiences.[62]

The theological school, which lasted until 1900, had a total registration of twenty-seven, eight of whom were eventually graduated. Four of the five Japanese active in the Universalist mission in 1906 were among the graduates.[63] The theological school held its first Commencement in 1894, in the midst of an earthquake which did little appreciable damage.[64] The first graduate was Akashi Shigataro, a transfer from a German-operated theological school.

One of the early graduates, Kiyoshi Satoh, who had been among Schouler's first students, served as superintendent of the Tokyo Sunday school and later attended Lombard College and had taken special courses at Tufts College. He was the first Japanese Universalist to be ordained in America, at the Every-Day Church in Boston where Perin had served.[65] Satoh returned to his native land as a missionary.

One difficulty shared by the missionaries and the Japanese which had to be met and surmounted was the language barrier. There seemed at first to be no words to describe properly the concept of Universalism. It was tentatively identified in 1890 as *Uchu Shinkyo,* meaning "Universal Reaching Theism" (pantheism).[66] But there was increasing dissatisfaction with that Japanese terminology, which could also be translated as "universe religion," which implied the religion of the globe, or somehow connoted a connection with astronomy. So *Uchu Shinkyo* was dropped in 1906 and the English words "Universalist Church" were used until some other designation could be found. Those words, being completely foreign and therefore meaningless to the Japanese, had to be discarded, and in 1909 a new name was decided upon which met with the unanimous approval of the Japanese Universalist ministers, namely *Nippon (Nihon) Dojin Christo (Kirisuto) Kyok(w)ai.* This was translated either as "Japanese Impartial Love Christian Church" or, more euphoniously, as "Japanese Christian Church of Impartial Love."[67] The new name had been suggested by Hoshino.

The confusion over terminology was not finally eliminated until 1926, when the Universalist Church in Japan was registered with the Ministry of Education as *Kiristoyko Kojin (Dojin) Shadan* ("The Corporation of Christian Universalists"). This was shortened in unofficial use to *Dojin Shadan* or the *Sadan.* The key word was *Dojin,* meaning "all people," thereby carrying out the Universalist principle of embracing all of humanity.

Then there was the problem shared by all three of the first missionaries, and most of those who followed, of mastering the language or at least achieving sufficient proficiency to communicate reasonably well. Perin struggled valiantly but with only indifferent success to learn Japanese, and in the frequent reports back home, he was disarmingly frank about learning a language which he considered "awful."[68] He was mystified by how Japanese children mastered it so easily, and estimated that over five years of study and practice were needed for individuals like himself before proficiency was achieved. Cate reported much the same experience, and wrote about the need for "thinking backward" and the difficulty in learning the idiom.[69]

Perin was forced from the time of his arrival until his departure to address Japanese audiences through an interpreter. The two American assistants spent much of their first year learning Japanese by teaching English. Plans were soon under way to establish a school of English so that Cate and Schouler could teach in their own facility. Because of the opposition of the Japanese to the education of women, extreme caution had to be used in selecting pupils and considerable negotiation had to take place. A "School of Liberal English" was opened in the fall of 1890, with five women attending morning classes and a somewhat larger group of men attending in the afternoon.[70] There were no women enrolled at all during the first part of the second year. This was undoubtedly a reflection of the objection by Japanese males to having their women Americanized and possibly elevated in status.[71] An understanding of this phenomenon illustrated one of the many adjustments required of American missionaries. By 1891, when the mission had its own building, up to forty students attended although the enrollment fluctuated widely and unpredictably.

The missionaries soon discovered that the Japanese were avid readers, regardless of their social class or economic status. Even though they might not enter a Christian church, they would read Christian literature. So the distribution of Universalist materials immediately became an important activity. Donations of books and pamphlets were sought from the United States, and a reading room was provided. The first tract translated into Japanese was P. T. Barnum's "Why I Am a Universalist"; part of the expense was defrayed by the author.[72] Before the end of the second year three more tracts had been added and distributed widely, and a steady flow was provided thereafter. Between 1909 and 1916, fifteen titles were prepared for Japanese circulation, and more than 800,000 copies were distributed, averaging 5,000 a month.[73] Perin considered the Englishman Thomas Allin's *Universalism Asserted* the most valuable work available for those particularly interested in theology.[74] It was translated into Japanese in 1893.

The most ambitious plan for disseminating Universalism by means of the written word took the form of a monthly newspaper first published in 1892. It was initially called the *Liberal Christian* and then the *Universalist*. After suspending publication for a time, it was resumed in 1904 as a sixteen-page paper with a press run of more than 5,000 copies; there were 330 paid subscriptions that year, and the remainder were distributed free of charge. For a time the paper was published at the mission station in Nagoya but was later moved to Tokyo. Twenty-one issues had appeared by the fall of 1906.[75] Perin spent much of his time and energy throughout his stay in Japan, and particularly during the first year, in answering scores of inquiries and in explaining to numerous callers the mysteries of *Uchu Shinkyo.*

The first effort to extend Universalism outside the metropolis was made early in 1891. A movement was started in Shizuoka, a city of 40,000 southwest of Tokyo. A native pastor, Takeo Sagara, was placed in charge and prospects of establishing a church seemed hopeful. It was he who made the first special appeal from a native Japanese (in 1892) to the WCA for funds; they were to be used for the purpose of establishing a girls' school at Shizuoka.[76] He was also the first Japanese Universalist to be ordained in the Universalist ministry.[77]

A society of nineteen members was organized in 1891 in Sendai, the largest city in northern Japan, by Hizedo Yoshimura. He and Perin had their first serious setback in Nagoya, a stronghold of Buddhism, where their appearance sparked a small but well-orchestrated riot led by about fifteen youths. The missionaries had to be escorted to safety by the police.[78]

Perin was both an optimist and a realist regarding missions in Japan. Christianizing the Japanese was "no mere holiday task [but] a long, slow, hard work."[79] He fully realized the implications for native Japanese of being a Christian. After little more than a year's experience he noted that for many it meant complete religious separation from relatives, possible social ostracism, and the forsaking of centuries of tradition.

He reported to the trustees of the General Convention that the total number of converts to Christianity by 1891 amounted to about one for every 4,000 inhabitants. But considering the demands on a person who became a Christian, almost any numerical showing would be encouraging. Aside from this there was the general influence for good in the various contacts made by the missionaries, even though impossible to quantify. Nevertheless, Perin forged ahead as best he could. A mission outpost was established in 1892 at Osaka, a major trading center southwest of Tokyo. It was headed by Yasujiro Abe who, before becoming a Universalist, had been trained in a Presbyterian theological school.[80]

Establishing a working relationship with other denominations already in the field was one of Perin's concerns. He appears to have done as well as could have been expected under the circumstances, considering the fact that Universalists were relative latecomers. He reported that the reaction of orthodox missionaries to their arrival was divided; most still looked upon Universalists as semi-heretical at best.[81] There were about fifty Protestant congregations representing ten denominations in Tokyo when the Universalist mission arrived in 1890. The largest number (twenty-one) were associated with the United Church, through which the German (Liberal) Reformed and the Presbyterians cooperated.[82] The Methodists had thirteen and the others had from one to five. The Unitarians had the use of a hall but did not begin regular services until the fall of 1890.

The Universalist missionaries were much impressed with the "excellent work" being done, and Perin thought the educational activity was especially worthy of note. His relations with the Unitarian missionaries, W. I. Laurence and Clay MacCauley, were so harmonious that Perin recommended that the Universalists combine forces with them and create a single mission. F. O. Hall presented a resolution to that effect on Perin's behalf at the General Convention in 1891, suggesting that the eventual union of the two denominations might very well begin in Japan. There was immediate objection to the idea. It was feared that the Unitarians, who concentrated on theological education rather than the establishment of mission stations, did not yet have a fully developed mission even in Tokyo, and might exploit the work already being done by the Universalists. Miner considered the proposal of a jointly operated mission "absurd and preposterous."[83] Even with this rebuff, Perin continued while in Japan to urge a union of efforts. But he was unsuccessful, and whatever cooperation existed remained at an informal and personal level.

In the United States, Universalists were willing, after their mission in Japan had been established, to keep officially in touch with the efforts of other denominations in the mission field. In 1894 the second conference of representatives of the Protestant Missionary Societies of the United States and Canada was held in New York City. The Universalist General Convention was one of the nineteen organizations which sent delegates. Although no Universalists were on the formal program, there were five delegates present, including Demarest, the convention secretary.[84]

In 1891, after slightly more than a year of operation, Perin outlined a fifteen-year projection for the Universalist mission. It had started with a subscription of nearly $12,000 annually for the first five years, and he estimated that all of it would be used. For the second five years, an annual income of $15,000 would be needed. The maximum expenditure, of $16,000 to $17,000, would come in the third five-year period. Thereafter the appropriation ought to decrease gradually until it would finally cease. The operation would have become self-supporting in all respects, and American missionaries could then begin operations on the Asian mainland.[85] Perin was enough of a realist to admit that much might be accomplished with less money than he had projected, but he strongly urged maximum assistance in the critical period of the first five years.

By the time the third year of operation of the mission began, the trustees of the General Convention were unabashedly optimistic. Tangible evidence of progress was beginning to accumulate, and actual success had "exceeded the anticipation of its friends."[86] Two converts who had been in the theological school for nearly two years had been ordained in 1892 (Takeo Sagara and Hizedo Yoshimura). They were assigned to Shizuoka and Sendai, respectively, with hopes of permanent organizations in the near future. In Tokyo, six students were preparing for the ministry, regular preaching services were well attended, and inquiries about Universalism were increasing. The school for girls in Tokyo, planned when the mission was established, had been opened in 1892 under the supervision of Schouler, and with an enrollment of nine. Her assistant was Miss Tame Imai, who became Mrs. Satoh, and was well known among Universalists both in Japan and America. The school lasted until 1908, and the school opened in Shizuoka in 1892 lasted a decade.

The total missionary force in 1892 stood at seven, counting a licentiate, Yasujiro Abe. The original American contingent of three had been unofficially augmented in 1891 with the arrival of Miss Ella Stimson of Medford, Massachusetts. She and Cate were married by the United States consul in Yokohama upon her arrival.[87] The staff was officially increased by the appointment of Clarence R. Rice (1860–1930). A native of Watertown, New York, Rice was the son of a Universalist clergyman (Luther Rice). He had received a Bachelor of Divinity degree from the Tufts Divinity School in 1883. After having been ordained the same year, he served several churches before arriving in Japan in 1892; he remained until 1899. Early in 1893 Schouler was forced to return home because of impaired health and until her place was taken by Miss Catherine M. Osborn (1859–1925), a Sunday school teacher from Avon, Illinois. She was destined to serve in the Japan mission for twenty-seven years. Mrs. Cate supervised the girls' school in Tokyo.

After almost five years of arduous service, Perin resigned in 1894 while on a trip to the United States. Cate, who was re-engaged for a second five years, was placed in charge. Perin returned to his Shawmut Avenue pastorate in Boston which was later merged with the First Universalist Church in Brookline to form the Beacon Universalist Church.

After his resignation from the Japan mission Perin continued to share his enthusiasm with others in numerous speeches and articles. When in 1894 Henry W. Rugg edited a series of fifteen papers written by as many clergy "treating of principles and ideas relative to Christian missions . . . with special reference to the Universalist Church," an article by Perin on the Japan mission was included.[88]

In 1894 Edgar Leavitt joined the mission, with a tenure of six years. A native of Farmington, Maine, he was a nephew of Zenas Thompson, a pioneer Universalist clergyman in that state. After preaching for a time in Maine, Leavitt held a succession of pastorates in Wisconsin. He presented one of the papers at the Universalist Congress at the Columbian Exposition in Chicago in 1893. In 1890 he had settled in Santa Cruz, California, and established the church there and engaged in considerable domestic missionary work. While on the Pacific coast he published and edited a semi-monthly, the *Evangel*.[89]

With increased and enthusiastic staff support and leadership the Japanese mission expanded steadily. There were eight stations by 1893, including one in the Shiba section of Tokyo, about three miles from the parent church.[90] A year later, there were nine stations, and the need had become evident for an administrative and governing structure that would tie them together and regularize their activities.

The groundwork for what became in 1895 the Universalist National Convention of Japan was laid in 1893 with the meeting of the first Japanese Universalist Conference in Tokyo. Each church was represented by its minister and one lay delegate; seven groups participated. It was there that the plans for a general church body in Japan were formulated.

The organization which resulted reflected the fact that Universalism in Japan was organized somewhat differently from that in the United States, emphasizing by the nature of the situation a less democratic and more closely articulated arrangement than prevailed at home.[91] There were three levels of administration: the local church; the association; and a national convention. Overall supervision was provided by a mission board. There was no distinction made between a parish or society, and a church, all communicants being church members. The business of each church was in the hands of a council of five, elected by the church. The pastor, appointed by the national convention, was the presiding officer at both council and church meetings, and was responsible both to the appropriate association and to the convention.

Associations corresponded roughly to state conventions in the United States and were composed of an equal number of ministerial and lay members, headed by a superintendent chosen by the national convention. Every ordained minister was a member of the convention, with equal lay representation from the associations. The convention was also the ordaining authority and placed all new ministers. The convention was headed by a general superintendent, who also chaired all standing committees and served on the board of overseers of all schools. An executive committee corresponded to the board of trustees of the General Convention. The overall organization was such that a direct relation with each church was provided, with a clear delineation of the authority and responsibility of each level.

While Cate was serving in Japan the arrangements seemed far superior to those in America, avoiding "the lamentable disconnectedness which seems to dampen the interests of the people and to paralyze the arms of the officers in our American organization." He was, of course, overlooking or minimizing the quite different magnitude and nature of Universalist activity and organization on the home front.

The convention organization, as later pointed out by one of the missionaries, was entirely too elaborate and complex for such a small and inexperienced body, and soon "fell by its own weight into disuse."[92] For several years Japanese ministers were not in fellowship with any organized body in the church. This deficiency was remedied in 1911 when the Japan Mission Board was given authority to confer fellowship, subject to the review and approval of the fellowship committee of the General Convention.

It seemed that Universalists had, by the late 1890s, established a firm foothold in Japan. The mission stations and the central church in Tokyo were supervised by either an ordained minister or licensed preacher educated especially for the work. A Sunday school with between fifteen and fifty pupils was connected with each mission; a day school was also provided at most mission outposts, at which English was taught. A kindergarten had been opened at the Tokyo church in 1895. There were, in addition, two schools for girls with a total of approximately sixty in attendance.

The students received daily instruction in the Bible and in Universalism, the older ones trained as potential Christian teachers and "Bible women." A Home and Industrial Class, with about ten students, was also conducted in connection with the girls' schools in Tokyo to offer instruction in homemaking or what the nineteenth century called "domestic economy." The theological school had three students enrolled in 1897, the number limited by the resources available to employ them at mission stations. The denomination also conducted two night schools with a total enrollment of almost fifty; activities included Bible instruction and religious services. Another department comprised the Post Office Mission which distributed Japanese translations of Univeralist literature. Among the recipients were some 500 orthodox Christian native ministers. The total annual expense of the Japan mission was $6,500 in 1897, considerably less than the $10,000 projected when the mission was begun.

Struggling to Survive

There were, besides accomplishments, many disappointments and frustrations which had appeared by 1900; some were to plague the mission throughout much of its history. One was strained relations with other denominations operating in Japan. Rice was very unhappy because of the opposition encountered from orthodox Protestant missionaries. Universalists were considered by some to be "emissaries of evil" intent on "poisoning" the minds of the Japanese.[93] At one union meeting a clergyman rose and "prayed that the Lord would send out more missionaries, but that Universalists might not be among the number." Rice reported that Universalists were "inadvertently" invited to participate in a summer missionary training school for kindergarten teachers. When it became known to the Southern Presbyterian representatives that Universalists were to be included, they announced that if Universalists had any part in the proceedings, the Presbyterians would withdraw.[94] The Universalist young ladies retired as gracefully as possible.

Universalists were conspicuously absent from a conference of Protestant missions in Japan convened in Tokyo in 1900.[95] They were allowed to attend, but not to participate or hold membership in the Japan Evangelical Alliance which was ostensibly open to all "Christian workers," lay as well as clerical.[96] When the fiftieth anniversary of the coming of Protestant Christianity to Japan was celebrated in Tokyo in the fall of 1909, the Universalists were not invited.[97]

Gideon I. Keirn, who had become head of the mission in 1909, fared somewhat better than most of his predecessors with the other Protestant missionaries. In 1913 he was one of the five foreign missionaries at the National Conference of Religion held in Tokyo under the auspices of the Minister of Education. Keirn gave an address, on invitation, with one of the Japanese Universalist ministers serving as interpreter.[98]

Another source of unhappiness by the end of the first decade of the mission was the disappointingly small number of converts and church members. Although there was increased interest in the study of English, the Japanese appeared to be more attracted to commercial and industrial schemes and financial and military expansion than to religion. Another wave of strongly nationalistic and anti-foreign sentiment had also appeared, notably in the schools, and Christianity was under considerable attack. Instead of adapting the Japanese to Christianity, there seemed to be a move on foot to amalgamate Shintoism, Buddhism, and Christianity and hence make Christianity more of a hybrid religion than most missionaries were willing to accept.

The Universalist kindergarten in Tokyo had to be suspended temporarily in 1898 because of government edicts requiring all foreign teachers to hold special certificates, and because the physical facilities did not meet safety and other requirements.[99] Christian schools operated by other denominations met the same fate. A ruling from the Japanese educational department in 1899 forbade religious instruction in private schools teaching pupils from six to ten years of age.[100] It was evidently aimed at Christian missionary endeavors and directly affected the Universalist schools in Tokyo. The mission did succeed in "salvaging" ten children in the upper classes (those aged eleven and twelve) by getting permission to teach them under the name of an "English school." Rice, after his return to the United States to become pastor of the church in Watertown, New York, told the General Convention in 1899 that "our future as a Church depended largely on our foreign missions." If that were the case, the prospects were certainly not very bright.[101]

Another adverse influence, aside from "the dead weight of about 43,000,000 non-Christians," was the tendency of the Japanese to adopt the materialistic culture of the West but to discard the spiritual, and to propagate agnosticism. But the Universalist missionaries took comfort from their belief that this was but a transient phase in the religious development of the nation, for "the Christianity of the New Testament is bound to conquer the whole earth." What was happening in Japan was only a series of "pauses in the Divine procedure." Like other non-Christians, the Japanese would eventually realize that Christianity was "the only way for the world's temporal and eternal salvation."

It should be realized that the depressed state of missionary enthusiasm was in no way confined to the experience of Universalists. Their entrance into the foreign mission field had seemed to coincide with a great burst of activity shared by most evangelical churches. A pamphlet had been circulated entitled "The Immediate Evangelization of Japan." The discrepancy between the rather naive prophecy in the title, and actual fulfillment, was evident after 1900. For more than a decade after 1890, Japanese Christianity had scarcely held its own. Cate reported that, according to the best estimate, there was fewer than one Christian for every 4,000 members of the population — the same proportion Perin had estimated ten years earlier.

There was no question that the Universalists had been caught up in the enthusiasm of the 1890s. Cate recollected that many in the denomination had confidently expected their work in Japan to be so successful that in a quarter of a century at the longest, Universalism would be so well established that the Japanese themselves could take over.[102] True, only twelve of the twenty-five years projected had passed at the time he wrote, but Cate believed that the expectation was completely unrealistic. The oldest missions in Japan had labored for over half a century, yet felt it necessary to maintain a full complement of missionaries. Why should the Universalists expect to do otherwise? It was natural to demand tangible results from a project which had already required an expenditure of $100,000, and indeed there were some evidences of accomplishment. Like Perin, Cate took refuge in the belief that most of the results were not of the kind that could easily be tabulated or otherwise measured.

If one reviewed the recent history of Universalism in the United States, according to Cate, the same conclusion had to be reached. In the year 1900 alone, more than one million dollars had been expended in the states for the maintenance and propagation of Universalism; yet, so far as statistics were concerned, the church stood close to the bottom in numbers as compared with others, and was "scarcely a drop in the bucket." Placed on a local basis, how many Universalist clergy could boast of overflowing membership in their churches? Some were called upon to bury many more members than they baptized. But did this mean that the work was not deserving of support? The Japan mission should be judged by the same standards that applied to any church. Why should greater success be anticipated in Japan than in America?

The American Universalist missionaries, like other foreign religious bodies, also had to review their strategy for making converts. Their original plan had been to ignore class divisions, but the Japanese Christians recommended otherwise. It was best, they said, to convert the middle and upper classes first; then the lower classes would follow their example.[103] Class stratification in Japan was much more of a reality than most Americans realized. The difficulty was compounded by the fact that Christianity seemed not to appeal to the upper classes, most of whom were "utterly indifferent." The majority of Universalist recruits were from the emerging middle class whose ancestors had been *samurai*, knight retainers of the historic feudal lords.[104] Most contact with the so-called lower classes came by way of the day schools and kindergarten.

One obstacle connected with the primary goal of the mission and faced throughout its existence, had to do with administration. It was difficult to convince the Japanese to take responsibility for their own religious work. The native leaders, both clerical and lay, were prone to assume that all responsibilities rested in the mission staff; hence the idea of assessing themselves to support the minister and the church was difficult if not impossible to convey. Even the appeal to raise money to provide their own buildings often fell on deaf ears.[105]

A chronic problem was finance. After the first flush of enthusiasm for the mission had subsided, raising sufficient funds in the United States became a constant source of worry. The publication of the *Universalist* (Japan) had to be suspended in 1897 for reasons of economy. A high proportion of Japanese converts were young, and unable to support the churches financially; therefore it was difficult, if not impossible, to make them self-supporting in a short period of time.[106] Other resources had to be found.

Aside from WCA commitments to recruit and support the missionaries, at first there were no really assured sources of income, and even the WCA was often hard pressed to do its self-appointed share. In 1895 the proposition was offered in the General Convention that a quota system be established among the parishes to raise the necessary mission funds. But the delegates refused to comply and voted decisively to continue to depend on free-will offerings, the number and amount of which could not be estimated from one year to the next. Pleas for assistance were made on every hand, with completely unpredictable results.

In its special "Japan Mission" issue each year the *Leader* published the names of contributors in an effort to keep the mission in the forefront of Universalist consciousness. The basic theme of the special issue for 1902 was a gloomy one — the failure of Universalists to support the work adequately. The denomination was admonished for its lack of sincerity and earnestness, and was told that failure to support it would make Universalism "an anomaly in the Christian world." It was even hinted that it might be advisable to consider cooperation with other denominations to the extent of some kind of federation. One recommendation (never acted on) was "to ally ourselves with the Missionary Education movement of the united churches, organized by the Foreign Mission Boards of the United States and Canada, and use, as far as possible, their literature and their methods."[107]

The temporary decline in interest in the Japan mission after 1891 can easily be documented by a glance at the statistics of support, although there was encouragement in the financial picture by 1898. After a struggle, $7,000 was pledged in 1895 but not all of it was actually paid in. A special canvass netted less than $2,500 in 1897, and a total of only $6,000 was actually raised of the estimated $9,000 needed that year. However, the situation was measurably improved after 1897. A Permanent Missions Fund was established that year with a gift of $2,000 from Lucian Blackmer, who also contributed $4,000 to the Murray Fund.[108] The General Convention made the Japan mission the top priority for 1900, and as a result almost $1,500 in gifts and pledges was received at the meeting in the fall of 1899.

Keeping staff support up to full strength in Japan was, like the matter of finance, a difficulty constantly to be met. In the spring of 1897 Cate had been forced to resign because of his health and that of his family, so a replacement had to be provided. It was hoped that Luther Weston Attwood of South Weymouth, Massachusetts, who had visited Japan in 1897, might join the staff, but he had returned to the United States after only nine months.[109] At least three reinforcements were then thought to be needed — one man, and two women with teaching capabilities. Instead, the number of American personnel in the Japan mission reached one of its lowest points at the turn of the century. Within less than two years (1899–1900), Leavitt returned to the United States; Osborn, who had arrived in 1895, was on furlough; and Rice resigned to resume preaching in the United States. He caused considerable stir two years before his death in 1930 by invoking a seldom-used concordat in the Protestant Episcopal Church and being ordained in that denomination also.[110] For the remainder of his life he served churches in both denominations and was listed in the *Universalist Year Book*. In 1900 Gideon Isaac Keirn (1854–1922), who had arrived in January 1899 to replace Rice, was left for a time as the sole missionary from America, and he returned to the United States in 1901 — temporarily, as it turned out.

Keirn was born in 1854 near Columbia City, Indiana, and from ages seventeen to twenty-two had alternated as a student, teacher, and farm worker.[111] After meeting a Universalist clergyman, Marion Crosley, and being informed of the Canton Theological School, he decided to prepare for the ministry, a vocation in which he had been interested for some time. He graduated in 1879 and held brief pastorates in New York State, Indiana, and Massachusetts. Desirous of a college education, after eight years in the ministry he enrolled in Tufts College, from which he graduated in 1891. Three years later he was called to the church in Charlestown,

Massachusetts. At the time of his assignment to the Japan mission he was vice-president of the Massachusetts Convention and head of its mission committee, but he had had no first-hand missionary experience. It was thanks largely to the native preachers and teachers that the mission was able to operate with a fair degree of success during the transition period, but the time had not yet come to leave it in native hands. This would have been construed, according to the trustees of the General Convention, as an admission of failure.[112] The work had to go on.

Keirn, who resigned in 1901 because of the state of his wife's health, was constantly asked to report on the achievements of the mission to various church groups, and echoed the same theme developed earlier by Perin and Cate. The value of the work was not to be determined by numbers and figures alone. Being a friend, counselor, and pastor could in no way be measured by external results. The very presence of a Christian family which practiced the precepts of their religion was important, even though the members in no way engaged directly or formally in missionary activity.

Cate, who was prevailed upon to replace Keirn, left his parish in Machias, Maine, in 1901, and for the second time set sail for Japan. His budget was $2,000 less than the $7,000 anticipated.[113] Yet there were positive aspects to be considered. Cate was familiar with the mission and was, like all of the Universalist missionaries, dedicated to his work and willing to sacrifice his own welfare, if need be, to further the cause to which he was committed. He was destined to serve until his death in 1908.

Supporters of the Japan mission were much heartened when Yoshimura had visited the United States in the winter of 1897–98 under the auspices of the trustees of the General Convention. Here was living proof that the far-off mission was accomplishing part of its purpose. Yoshimura was warmly received, spoke in several churches, and appeared in native dress at the General Convention in Chicago; Perin acted as interpreter when needed during the address Yoshimura delivered in halting English.[114] Judging from all accounts, the visitor was a charismatic figure who was described as "the native leader of Universalism in Japan."[115]

Japanese students preparing for work in the mission were also brought to the United States from time to time at denominational expense to receive religious training. Among the first were Tame Imai and Kiyoshi Satoh, both of whom attended Lombard College and Tufts College as special students.

One of the most successful and enduring parts of the Japan mission was the girls' home established in 1896 at the instigation of Osborn only a year after her arrival. It was not primarily a school, although English and music were taught, or a "rescue home" for unfortunates, as some Universalists thought. It was "simply a Christian home where girls may live under its helpful influence while attending school."[116] The home, which was intended to provide a training ground for future workers in the church, began with one girl, Masu Hirima, who lived in Osborn's residence. Two more were ready to enter if facilities could be provided. Temporary quarters were secured in 1896 when a four-room house was rented for $3.50 a month.[117] By 1900 there were five girls in residence.

While on furlough to America, Osborn was commissioned to raise funds for a permanent building, and interested Lucian Blackmer of St. Louis in the idea of a girls' home; he became its ardent and life-long supporter. His initial donation of $2,000 in 1897 was augmented by later gifts. It was estimated that $8,000 would be needed to acquire a site and erect a building.[118] In the fall of 1902 Blackmer offered an additional $1,500 on a matching basis.[119] With this encouragement, property for what became the Blackmer Universalist Girls' Home was acquired in 1902 and a structure with a capacity for about twenty girls was erected a year later and survived until the Second World War. An estimated 110 girls had resided in the home for varying periods by 1915. A kindergarten was opened on the grounds of the Home in 1907 and in 1908 a Sunday school (actually meeting on Saturdays) was established. Teachers were usually selected from girls in the Home, as originally planned.[120] Eight of the twenty girls in residence in 1912 were sponsored by such church agencies in the United States as Mission Circles.

By 1902 the Universalists had another project under way in Tokyo besides the regular work of the mission and planning for the Blackmer Home. The wooden central church was replaced by a one-story brick edifice seating 200.[122]

In the meantime, the convention trustees, who were taking on more and more of the responsibility for the mission, were struggling with the problem of how to fill contractual arrangements with the missionaries, pay the bills, and make up the difference between the $10,000 needed for 1902, and the less than $7,500 available.[123] In 1903 the trustees were forced to request authorization to draw up to $1,000 from general funds for each of two years to assist the mission, but fortunately were not required to expend all of the money requested. A similar contingency was avoided in 1905 when $1,400 was raised by pledges made on the floor of the convention.[124] Such a hand-to-mouth existence for the mission had spurred a motion on the floor of the General Convention in 1903 to undertake no new missionary efforts abroad until its resources justified it, but the attempt was swept aside.[125] What had probably prompted the motion was talk about establishing outposts on the Asian mainland, a possibility held out by Perin many years before. Universalist activities in China and Korea were to come later.

With the opening of the Blackmer Home an enlarged staff was immediately needed, and the WCA set out to find a qualified person and to be responsible for providing the annual salary of $1,000. After a prolonged search Miss Claudia E. Schrock of Akron, Ohio, was recruited. But after

Tenth anniversary celebration of the graduates of the Midori kindergarten, 1918

arrangements had been made for her training she announced plans to marry which would have precluded any long-term commitment. The disappointment was "too deep for expression," for the WCA had to begin the search all over again.[126]

M. Agnes Hathaway was the individual finally selected; she entered upon her duties in the winter of 1904–1905. A native of Bristol, New York, she was a graduate of the Genesee Valley Wesleyan Seminary in Lima, New York, and had several years' experience as a public school teacher. At the time she accepted the missionary post she had been Dean of Women for three years at Lombard College and then had become an instructor in history in the fall of 1903. She completed the requirements for the AB degree before leaving for Japan.

The mission was considerably strengthened when Nelson L. Lobdell (1876–1964), who was engaged by the General Convention, arrived in 1905. He was born 30 June 1876 on a farm near the village of Victor (Ontario County), New York, and was a member, in 1894, of the first graduating class of the local high school.[128] After completing his sophomore year at St. Lawrence he taught in country schools for two years and then returned to St. Lawrence, from which he received an AB in 1900. He served as a teacher and assistant principal in the Clifton Springs High School in New York State for three years; after resigning in 1903 he completed two years of the three-year curriculum of the Tufts Divinity School and was ordained in 1905.

Hathaway had arrived at her post just when what Cate described as "our educational crisis in Japan" had arisen.[129] The school facilities near the church in Tokyo had to be relinquished because the land was being taken over for street improvements. The alternatives were to abandon school work altogether or to carry it on separately from the church. This involved the larger question of whether the work of general education was to be part of the mission system. Up to this point the school work for the boys had been confined to rather narrow limits, consisting largely of offering instruction in English. The lack of facilities for offering a comprehensive educational program which could in part serve as a feeder for a theological school had been one of the reasons for the abandonment of systematic theological instruction. The best solution, in Cate's estimation, was the establishment of a permanent residential school for boys which would involve an expenditure in the neighborhood of $15,000. This proposal to establish the Perin-Cate Home for Boys in Tokyo was never carried out. It was to have been supervised by Sempo Ito from the Shizuoka church.

One idea which was never acted on was the establishment of a Universalist college in Japan to appeal to liberal Christians.[130] There were thousands of students in Tokyo and many seemed to be anti-creedal. Those who became converts to various orthodox Protestant denominations considered themselves Christians rather than Methodists, Baptists, or the like, and could not understand the splintered religion they observed.[131] This might have been a great opportunity for the Universalists, so the argument went, to teach "pure Christianity" without the encumbrance of narrow sectarianism. The convention trustees, in another context, made the same point about the nature of the Universalist mission. The philosophy behind it was not so much "ecclesiastical aggrandizement [as] spiritual leadership passing from old to new religious experience"; namely, to Christianity, the exact form of which no one could foresee.[132]

Without realizing the magnitude of what they would be undertaking, the Universalist missionaries in 1906 outlined a grand scheme for establishing strategic centers the entire length of Japan, with outposts on three of the four main islands that comprised the empire, and extending on a north-south axis more than 600 miles, from Sendai and Akita to Fukuoka on the island of Kyushu.[133] There was some degree of activity at twelve different points, five of them auxiliary preaching stations. But there was simply neither the staff nor the money to operate on such a scale, and many of the stations offered religious services to less than ten individuals.

When the annual convention of the Japanese Universalists met in Tokyo in 1906, only four of the stations were represented.[134] The Tokyo church continued to be the largest part of the mission, with a membership of sixty-five and a Sunday school in excess of 100. The Nagoya church, headed by N. Nagano, had thirty-six names on its roll, but the average attendance was only seventeen. A Sunday school with sixteen pupils had recently been organized, and a number of social and religious clubs existed. The Shizuoka church, headed by Ito, had a "book list" of thirty-nine members and a Sunday school of sixty, with average attendance of twenty. The Akita mission, which had arisen by "spontaneous combustion," had been organized in 1904 through the efforts of a layman and one of several Japanese who had withdrawn from the Disciples church. The mission had a membership of twenty-three, all of whom were professional men, and their families. It had no regular pastor.

The Japan mission at its greatest extent, 1906

Under the circumstances, the better part of wisdom was to retrench and to concentrate on three main stations: Tokyo, Shizuoka, and Nagoya. It was finally realized that the mission had been overextended and spread too thin. The decision came none too soon, for the entire mission came perilously close to collapsing during 1907. Everything seemed to have gone wrong. Catherine Osborn had been offered an important supervisory and educational position in the Women's University of Tokyo in the fall of 1906.[135] She was to have continued in an advisory position in the mission. Arrangements were made for her to take her leave a year earlier than called for by her contract, so she returned to the United States early in 1907. But illness intervened, and she was unable either to assume her new duties or to make personal appearances at various denominational gatherings to bring first-hand reports of the mission and its work.

Then, to make matters worse, it was mistakenly reported in the press that because the mission had not fulfilled expectations, it was to be abandoned. This, together with strained relations between the United States and Japan which threatened the existence of all foreign missions, added to the doubt and uncertainty. The consequence was a noticeable hesitancy on the part of Universalists to support the effort, and contributions plummeted. Convincing the denomination to support the mission seemed to have failed, including the salesmanship effort represented by *Our Word and Work for Missions,* edited by Rugg. By 1905 only half of the original press run in 1894 had been disposed of, so the price of $1.00 was halved to encourage sales.[136]

In the decade from 1897 to 1907 annual contributions to the mission had averaged $6,000, considerably short of the $10,000 usually requested. Only small comfort could be taken from the fact that in 1903 more money was contributed to the mission than to any other special church activity that year; the same situation occurred in 1909.[137] In 1907 the contributions dropped to less than $4,500.

The trustees had no solution to offer. Even though the churches had been made aware of the critical state of affairs for most of the year, they had not felt moved to come to the rescue. The deficiency by 1908 had become "alarming," with scarcely 100 churches responding to appeals. Even attempting to make Universalists feel guilty about their poor record was not completely effective. It was estimated that members of Protestant churches in the United States gave an annual average of $1.00 to foreign missions. The Universalists gave less than 15 cents, and in 1909 contributed less than 11 cents for such purposes.[138] There was great rejoicing in 1913, when for the first time in memory the income for the mission exactly matched expenditures; the WNMA contributed the final $75 needed.[139]

Some Universalists began to talk about abandoning the mission altogether, but the convention trustees adamantly refused even to consider the possibility although they admitted in 1908 that it never enjoyed the confidence and support of the entire denomination. Almost twenty years later the editor of the *Leader* observed that "explaining the Japan mission to Universalists often is harder than explaining Universalism to the Japanese."[140]

The situation in Japan was complicated in 1908 by the illness and death on shipboard of Cate while en route to the United States. This left only Lobdell and his wife, Hathaway, and Osborn. Because of her work in the Women's University, Osborn could devote only part of her time to the mission. Arrangements were made for the return of Keirn, who had served between 1899 and 1901. Having been established as pastor of the church in Muncie, Indiana, for seven years, he had planned never again to visit Japan. His reappearance infused new life into the faltering mission.

Mrs. Ella Cate, widow of the former missionary, also elected to return to Japan, in 1909, with her three younger children, to teach English at Waseda University and at a Baptist school.[141] The trustees tried unsuccessfully to persuade her to remain in the United States to work among the churches on behalf of the mission. She did not serve the mission in any official capacity after her return to Japan, although the WNMA considered her as one of the teachers.[142]

The staff was strengthened in 1909 when Osborn resigned from the Women's University and resumed her place in the mission.[143] Morale was raised also by the determination of the WNMA to disregard all talk about closing the mission, and to continue supporting the Blackmer Home for which they had been taking increased responsibility. In 1907 they undertook to raise an endowment of $20,000 for the Home, accomplished in 1911. In 1909 the organization provided funds for a small building on the grounds of the Home to serve as a free kindergarten for poor children in the neighborhood.[144]

The Japan mission was given special attention by the convention trustees between 1910 and 1915. In 1912 a five-person Commission on Foreign Missions was created in accordance with a vote of the biennial denominational meeting the previous year, and in 1913 became the Board of Foreign Missions. With this step the work of the mission was accepted as a part of the permanent work of the General Convention. This meant ultimate financial responsibility. Simultaneously the WNMA, which had completely supported only one missionary (Hathaway) up to 1913, agreed to support Osborn and take over entire responsibility for staffing and maintaining the Blackmer Home and its kindergarten.[145] In the meantime the YPCU had begun (in 1905) to make financial contributions to the mission, and in 1914 the General Sunday School Association had decided to sponsor one of the women who staffed the Blackmer Home.

It was all very fine to have so many organizations interested and involved in the mission, but there was a minimum of coordination, and whoever happened to be in charge of the mission at any given time reported to the various organizations rather than directly to the trustees. Centralized management and oversight and a coherent chain of command were finally provided in 1915. The Board of Foreign Missions was reorganized in order to provide representation to the three organizations cooperating in the mission and to unify and systematize their work.[146] As reconstituted, the board consisted of two convention trustees, two representatives from the WNMA, and one from the YPCU, together with the convention secretary who served also as secretary of the board. The specific responsibilities of the superintendent of the mission, as the office in Japan came to be called, was spelled out in 1917, calling for responsibility for administration of the mission as a whole.

The year 1915 was important for the Japan mission in another respect. Keirn, as superintendent, prepared a pamphlet intended for American Universalists (printed in English in Japan), reviewing the experience of the first twenty-five years. It gave Universalists some much-needed perspective, and was by no means a glowing story of unadulterated success, as he saw it.

Keirn divided the history of the mission into four distinct periods. The first five years had been dominated by high hopes, much idealism and enthusiasm, and had been characterized by simultaneous establishment and extension. Keirn was very critical of the latter policy, considering it to have been unwise as well as unrealistic. There had been no thought given as to how outposts were to be staffed or financed. The Japanese converts placed in the field were inadequately trained, in spite of the short-lived theological school; met indifference or hostility; and had to make do with temporary rented quarters or none at all. The results were "nothing worthy the name of a church" as Universalists in America understood the term.

What had caused this unhappy situation? The missionaries were not wholly to blame. There was great pressure from American Universalists to expect immediate and measurable results which were just not forthcoming and which should not have been expected. It was a period of inflated ideas and unjustified expectations in both the United States and Japan.

Then came the next five years (1895–1900) which Keirn called a period of "testing," of "confusion of ideas." Universalism in Japan did not expand with the great rapidity expected by many; the mission churches did not immediately become self-supporting; and calls for money to support them became both numerous and insistent. This was followed, until 1909, by a policy of contraction and discouragement. One by one, mission stations were closed — Fukuoka, Osaka, Sendai. The Japanese Universalist clergy failed to realize both the inevitability and desirability of this step in view of the previous over-expansion, and saw only closed churches and dismissed clergy. This had created a morale problem which Keirn believed was finally being overcome.

The true situation was ultimately grasped by Universalists back home, who began to realize that "mushroom growth" was neither possible nor wise. This was reflected in a more positive and pragmatic attitude beginning in 1910. The General Convention had stood firmly behind the mission throughout its stage of trial and tribulation. Mistakes had been made and corrected so far as possible. Universalists were learning from experience. The past quarter-century was "a closed book." It was the future that beckoned.

At the time Keirn outlined the history of the mission there were three missionaries besides himself (Osborn, Lobdell, and Hathaway) and four Japanese ministers (Hoshino, Nagano, Ito, and Midzuhira).[147] In addition, O. Matsuo served as a lay preacher as well as interpreter at the central church in Tokyo. The Shizuoka mission became second only to the Tokyo church in importance, largely through the leadership of Lobdell, and in 1917 sufficient funds had been accumulated to make possible the building of a church.

The Blackmer Home was prospering sufficiently in 1914 to justify the addition of a third woman missionary to the staff, financed to a great extent by Sunday school offerings channelled through the WNMA. Miss Louise Klein, a native of Plainfield, New Jersey, and a graduate of the Department of Domestic Science at the Pratt Institute in Brooklyn, New York, and with two years' experience in settlement house work, was chosen.[148] Klein, a Presbyterian turned Universalist, completed her studies at St. Lawrence in 1915 and was fellowshipped there. She prepared for her assignment in Japan under the auspices of the WNMA and attended courses in California at Berkeley and San Francisco, and served as a student teacher under the founder of the so-called Montessori system of pedagogy, about which Klein was most enthusiastic.[149]

Keirn greeted the expansion of the staff of the Blackmer Home with mixed feelings, believing that too much attention was paid to this part of the mission and not enough to direct missionary endeavor; but he accepted the situation with good grace. The entire operation looked so much more promising in 1915 than when he had rather reluctantly agreed to return to Japan in 1909. It appeared that the struggle to survive had been successful.

Chapter 24

The Japan Mission Between Two Wars

The outbreak of the Great War in Europe in 1914 had but a minimal effect on the Universalist mission in Japan. About the only visible action was a law enacted by the Japanese government prohibiting all foreign organizations from holding property.[1] Keirn, head of the mission, had suggested that a "holding association" *(Zaidan)* be created to serve the purpose, and the General Convention had complied by authorizing the creation of a corporation in Japan to hold mission property in trust for it.

The mission had, in fact, not only survived for a quarter of a century but had begun to show signs of positive future development. The findings of a comparative study made in 1916 with the mission a decade earlier seemed to be proof positive that it was at least a modest success.[2] The amount raised to support it had almost doubled ($14,000 compared to $8,500), and the reported membership in the four churches had grown from 207 to 503. Nearly $8,000 was pledged by 1917 toward the construction of a church building in Shizuoka.[3]

There were also significant changes in the staff of the mission, but they did not disrupt its activities unduly. Osborn had resigned in 1916 for reasons of health while on a vacation in the United States.[4] But her work in Japan was not actually over until 1919, for she agreed to serve while Hathaway was on furlough. Osborn was considered by Lobdell as "by far the ablest missionary that our Church has ever sent to Japan."[5] Klein, after a relatively brief stay, left the mission in 1917 to be married. Keirn, after many years of service extending over two tours of duty, departed in 1917. After serving a year in the United States as a money-raiser for the mission he accepted the pastorate of the Universalist-Unitarian church in Atlanta. He died in 1922.

The mission was supervised temporarily by Lobdell until a successor to

Keirn could be found in the person of Samuel G. Ayres (1870–1955), pastor in Woonsocket, Rhode Island. He arrived with his wife in 1919 and remained until 1925. Mrs. Minnie J. Ayres, an enthusiastic supporter of missions, had been active in the affairs of the WNMA, having served as its president for four years. One of the contributions of the Ayres was the building of a mission home for the staff, opened in 1920 and financed largely by them.[6] One of Ayres' experiences was to realize that Universalists were only on the fringe of Japanese missionary activities. He found himself rebuffed by the Federated Missions of Japan, which allowed him to attend its meetings but prohibited him from voting or even speaking.[7]

Mrs. Ayres was pessimistic and sorely disappointed by what she found in Japan. After thirty years the Universalists had all too little to show for their efforts. The entire history of the mission had been one of "lost opportunities."[8] The only bright spot in her estimation was the Blackmer Home, and the only one that kept the denominational experience in Japan from being a complete "tragedy."

In his final report in 1917 Keirn had called attention to the fact that the entire expense of the Japan mission for the twenty-seven years of its history had been $275,000 and that, overall, it had been a wise investment.[9] He repeated his conviction expressed in 1915, that missionary activity should be greatly expanded, and suggested the exploration of possibilities in Korea. The WNMA considered a similar suggestion, made in 1919 by the Massachusetts Women's Missionary Association, that work in China should be started.[10]

The WNMA continued its responsibility for maintaining the Blackmer Home. Between 1915 and 1938 all of its American personnel were selected and paid by them. Hazel Ida Kirk was appointed in 1918. Her services had to be lent to the Shizuoka parish when a new church was dedicated in 1920. Mrs. Alice G. Rowe; Miss Bernice Kent, who was added to the staff in 1922; and Miss Ruth G. Downing, were among those furnished by the WNMA.

Overall administration and coordination in America of the Japan mission was continued by the Board of Foreign Missions, whose responsibilities were clarified in 1917. The Mission Council in Japan was enlarged in 1918 to include not only the American missionaries and their wives but the pastors of any Japanese church that became self-supporting.[11] One of the stateside activities of the Board of Foreign Missions was to support briefly a Japanese Universalist church organized in Boston in 1915.[12] Among those who worked among the Japanese in Boston was J. C. Orito, a student at Crane, who moved to Washington State, edited a Japanese newspaper in Seattle, and founded a Japanese Universalist church before returning to his native land.[13]

Two Japanese students sponsored by American Universalists in the early 1920s were Tame Imai, who attended both Lombard and Tufts; and

The Shizuoka Church in 1920

K. Satoh, who also attended Tufts and was ordained in the Every Day Universalist Church in Boston. The Illinois Convention sponsored C. Kawabata, who studied at the Ryder Divinity School of the University of Chicago and returned to Japan, his salary paid by the convention.[14]

The General Convention, determined to provide at least the semblance of a regular income for the Japan mission, introduced a state quota system in 1921.[15] The system worked at least for a while, for by 1923 receipts were in excess of $12,000 from that source alone.[16] One potential source of competition in Japan was removed in 1922 when the AUA decided to withdraw and transfer the responsibility for Unitarian missionary activity to the Liberal Christian Association which had changed its name from the Japanese Unitarian Association in 1921.[17]

Clifford R. Stetson and his family replaced Ayres and remained until 1933. They arrived on the eve of a disastrous earthquake which destroyed one-third of Tokyo. News of the disaster arrived in the United States just as the General Convention trustees were prepared to report that in 1922–23, for the first time in the history of the Japan mission, there was a balance in its favor ($191.96) and that there was a waiting list of those wishing to serve there. The Universalist church in the city was totally destroyed by fire; the missionary residence there, and the Blackmer Home, were damaged but repairable, but the Midori kindergarten was levelled.

It was fortunate that neither the persons nor the personal property of Universalists was damaged. The Shizuoka church, where the Stetsons were located, and which was the newest and best of the equipment in Japan, escaped damage.[18] The total cost of rebuilding in Tokyo, including the proposed Perin-Cate Home for Boys projected for many years but never constructed, was estimated at $100,000. There was the opportunity after the earthquake to settle on a quieter and less congested location. In the interim, temporary wooden structures (known as "The Barracks") were erected with the aid of the Japanese government. Until these were provided, services were held in the damaged Blackmer Home and the missionary residence.[19] The WNMA immediately pledged to contribute their proportionate share in the cost of rebuilding.

The Board of Foreign Missions decided to appeal for funds to rebuild, but complications developed immediately. A campaign had already been announced to raise an even larger sum to build a national memorial church in Washington, D.C. Where should the priorities lie? A mutually unsatisfactory decision was made to raise both funds simultaneously, although the original plan had been to give the Japan mission first place.[20] The result was that neither fund was completed as planned.

By 1924–25 there had been a complete turnover of American personnel in the Tokyo mission. Hathaway retired after a record sojourn of twenty years.[21] She served after her return to the United States as a field secretary for Japanese work and as Home Missionary.[22] The Ayres family returned to the United States and were replaced by Henry Montfort Cary (1878–1936) and Maude Simonton Lyon Cary (1878–1937).

Cary had been born on 14 February 1878 and died in Tokyo on 30 April 1936. He was the son of a "liberal-minded" Roman Catholic father and a Methodist mother.[23] Cary was reared as a Catholic and was prepared for the priesthood in which he was ordained. In 1902 he volunteered to serve with the American Catholic Mission in Argentina and spent five years there as a monastic librarian. After his return to the United States he broke with the church and while in New York City took courses at Union Theological Seminary. He was befriended by the president of the Bible Teachers' Training School, served as "literary secretary," and was assigned to a mission in the city. He attracted the attention of Mrs. George Inness, Jr., a supporter of the Universalist church in Tarpon Springs, Florida, and through her became minister in an interdenominational church in New York State. He was then employed by the Congregational Home Missionary Society of New York State. He married Maude S. Lyon in 1907.

Cary's varied experiences were extended even farther when, through the influence of Frederick W. Betts, pastor of the Universalist church in Syracuse, New York, he entered the Universalist ministry in which he was ordained in 1916. After serving churches in Auburn and Little Falls, Cary was selected for the Japan mission by Fred C. Leining, chairman of the Board of Foreign Missions. The missionary received an honorary DD from Lombard in 1926.

Maude Cary, likewise an ordained minister (1919), with two college

Georgene Bowen teaching a men's Bible class in 1926

degrees, held several pastorates before departing for Japan.[24] She had been active as an officer in the WNMA and in promoting mission work. Cary and his wife were accompanied by their six children who returned to the United States one by one. Their son Henry (Harry) M. Cary, Jr., after attending the Tufts School of Religion, returned to Japan in 1935 and was there when his father died in 1936. The son then became a representative of the General Convention in Japan. After the senior Cary's death the widow elected to stay in Japan and continue the work whether or not financial support came from America.[25]

The Carys arrived in Japan at a particularly tense period in Japanese-American relations, precipitated by the Immigration Exclusion Act of 1924 legislated by the American Congress which barred further immigration to the United States. Both Stetson and Cary reported that, much to the relief of the American missionaries, they were not harassed because the Japanese made a distinction between "the people of America" and the politicians responsible for the legislation.[26]

The entire Cary family was very popular with the Japanese and their home became itself a social center. It was estimated that in 1925 more than 2,700 guests were entertained. One appreciative Universalist in the United States observed that the family "would be a bargain at double the salary" in terms of the good will they generated.[27] Cary and his energetic wife infused a new vitality into the mission, and among their other activities distributed thousands of tracts and pamphlets.[28]

Further personnel changes in the 1920s brought Georgene E. Bowen to Japan. A native of Bellows Falls, Vermont, she had been suggested as a candidate by Stetson and had been a leader in the Camp Murray summer missionary training program in Western Massachusetts.[29] The WNMA furnished $600 so that she could enter Boston University for special training. Bowen sailed for Japan in 1925 and remained until 1937. After her return to America she served for a time on the staff of Hull House in Chicago.[30] She made two subsequent visits, one in 1958 and another in 1964. Long since retired, she wrote in warm terms in January 1983 of the lasting friendships and associations she had made as she continued to correspond with former Blackmer Home "girls," by then in their fifties and sixties.

The Japan mission entered a period not only of reconstruction but of expansion in the 1920s. A site was secured in 1925 for a new church in Tokyo to replace the one destroyed by the 1923 earthquake. Dojin House, a multi-purpose building, was constructed in 1924 with funds obtained from the Million Dollar Drive of 1919 and was connected with the Blackmer Home. The Iidomachi (Ohayo) Kindergarten, financed by $110,000 from the Ohio State Association of Universalist Women and named for its sponsors, was flourishing by 1927. The rebuilt Midori Kindergarten operated double sessions. Alice G. Rowe, who had been in Japan since 1922, succeeded Hathaway as head of the Blackmer Home in 1925.[31] After Bernice Kent returned to the United States in 1928 Agnes Hathaway was persuaded to return to Japan for service on a part-time basis for three years.[32] After her final retirement the veteran Universalist remained in Japan on half salary.[33]

Miss Ruth Downing, after a tour of duty at Friendly House in Western North Carolina, joined the staff in 1929. A grand total of seven missionaries, including both husbands and wives, were serving in Japan, with five native pastors.[34] Ishi Tarasawa, serving in Shizuoka in the mid-1920s, was in the anomalous position of serving as president of the local Sunday School Union while simultaneously his colleagues from other denominations refused to recognize him as a Christian minister.[35]

There were five "centers of influence" in Tokyo by 1927, with churches also in Shizuoka, Nagoya, Osaka, and Kyoto. All of this activity cost money, and expenditures exceeded income by $5,000 in 1926–27, made up out of the funds of the General Convention.[36] A plea was made that state conventions pay the salaries of missionaries from their states, such as the Carys from New York. Extension of Universalist work into Palestine was suggested in 1927 but was ruled out because of the continued deficits in the Japan mission.[37]

Cary did get a Universalist outpost under way in Korea by depending on recruits from Doshisha University, operated by the Congregationalists. Ryongki Jio (Cho or Dzo), a Korean, had started preaching in 1926 while still a student. He was fellowshipped as a Universalist in 1928 and established his headquarters at first in Seoul.[38] He and a fellow graduate of Doshisha named Pak then acquired a run-down old wrestling hall in Taiku where they organized a Sunday school using adult volunteers.[39]

Mrs. Pak was the first Korean known to have been trained in the

Blackmer Home; she conducted a sewing school. Jio and Pak worked also in the neighboring villages of Wulchon and Kumpo, assisted by a Mr. Yee. Activities were extended to include medical service and the operation of a farm some twenty-five miles from Taiku.[40] Jio had made a plea in 1931 for $1,000 to purchase the property which was acquired after a last-minute collection was taken up in 1932.[41]

There was never any systematic financial support for the Korean mission, and much of the little that could be raised came from Cary's own pocket until the International Church Extension Board provided a small subsidy which ended in 1939.[42] The Universalist church in Joliet, Illinois, had agreed to pay Jio's salary in 1932, but whether this was done is not clear from the records.

An attempt was made in 1933 by Jio to organize a Federation of the Free Churches of Korea, but nothing is known of the result.[43] Little more was heard regarding Universalist activities in Korea until 1955, when a request for help in organizing a Univeralist movement there was made as an outgrowth of denominational participation in UNESCO relief and rehabilitation programs.[44]

American Universalists tried throughout the history of the Japan mission to strengthen the sense of responsibility among the Japanese for the support of Universalist work. One of Ayres' accomplishments had been to secure a pledge from them to contribute the equivalent of $1.00 for every $10 furnished from American sources for such special projects as the construction of the Tokyo church.[45] Another device was the creation of a cooperative board, organized in 1925 with an equal number of Japanese and Americans, to provide an enlarged voice for native Universalists in the conduct of their activities. A Japanese Convention of Universalist Churches was organized in 1932 as the governing body, with all the offices to be held by native Universalists. Fifteen delegates from all five Universalist centers then in existence attended the first meeting of the Japan Convention.[46] Although all of the American missionaries were present all decisions were made by the Japanese.

A policy statement had been issued by the Board of Foreign Missions in 1926 reiterating the often-expressed idea that the goal of Universalists in Japan was neither selfish nor sectarian nor to build a strong proselytizing organization for its own sake. It was to further "the good of the Japanese people, as well as . . . the good of humanity."[47] The church was the instrumentality for service which transcended narrow (and to the Japanese, inexplicable) denomination divisions. The organization of the Japanese Convention was intended to be a step in that direction although it was clear that the Universalist connection was not to be completely lost.

One of the positive accomplishments of the Universalists in Japan in the

1920s was their growing acceptance by other denominations. They were admitted to the National (Japan) Christian Church Council in 1928, largely through the influence of the Congregationalists.[48] The next year they became full members in the Alliance of Protestant Churches in Japan.[49] Cary attended a meeting of the Federation of Missions in Japan in 1932 and assisted in drafting an eleven-point program which called for a common name for all Christian churches in that nation.[50]

There was a grim as well as a bright side to the Japan mission by the late 1920s and early 1930s. Income to support it fell off sharply and even the revival of the state quota system in 1929 which had been used earlier, failed to solve the problem.[51] Only $5,500 was raised for the 1929–30 fiscal year and John van Schaick, editor of the *Leader,* told its readers bluntly that "our plain duty is to support the missionaries or recall them."[52] Some considered the continuation of the Japan mission to be "absurd" while churches in America were "going on the rocks in all directions."[53] But a poll of 100 Universalists indicated such overwhelming support that the Carys continued their work.

One partial solution to the financial problem was worked out in 1930, when a combination of state conventions, local parishes, and organizations took over responsibility for providing the money for specific parts of the mission.[54] The New York Convention agreed to pay Cary's salary, while other state conventions took on other obligations.

Even that expedient proved insufficient, and in 1933 Universalists found they could no longer support their own missionary in Shizuoka. The Stetsons returned to the United States and the church was left in the hands of Tarasawa, a graduate of Doshisha University who had been fellowshipped in 1923.[55] Services had ceased there by 1935, so the church building was disassembled and moved to Tokyo where it was christened "The House of Friendship" and was used primarily as a student center as a substitute for the unbuilt Perin-Cate Home.[56] The Carys volunteered to come home in order to reduce expenses but their services were considered too important to be terminated.[57]

The church at Osaka was continued under the supervision of Keijiro Mizumakai, who had been fellowshipped in 1926.[58] Masao (John) Shidara, who had become interested in the Universalist church through the efforts of Georgene Bowen, served the Central Church in Tokyo.[59] The Universalist center in Nagoya was still operated by Naoichiro Nagano, the only minister remaining in Universalist fellowship who had been trained in the theological school established by George Perin.[60] Nagano used a tea room as its meeting place.

There was recurring talk of closing the entire Japan mission. Sheldon Shepard, pastor of the Universalist church in Los Angeles, and a longtime opponent of all such overseas activities, insisted that the Universalists, in conducting the mission, were merely aping other denominations;

were almost always on the defensive about it; and were complaining constantly about the lack of a "missionary spirit" which had to be revived periodically.[61] Why go so far afield to do so little good when so much needed to be done at home? Shepard's argument bore a striking resemblance to that used so frequently in the late nineteenth century to oppose missions. He interpreted missionary activity, worthy as it might seem to be, as an "invasion" of another country based on an "unbecoming assumption of superiority."

There was so much doubt expressed about the mission and its worth that in 1934 Roger Etz, the General Superintendent, made a one-month visit to Japan, the first officer of the General Convention to have visited the mission.[62] He recommended that it be continued, but that all subsidies be phased out over a four-year period.[63] "Our mission, small as it has always been, has made a decided contribution to Japan, and has an influence far out of proportion to its size. . . . its influence should be carried on."[64] Vincent Tomlinson, a long-time supporter of the mission, also visited Japan in 1934 and was much impressed by what he saw.[65]

The last missionary sponsored by the WNMA was Miss Martha Stacy, a native of Haverhill, Massachusetts, who joined Downing in 1938. Although she had been an employee of the American Board of Foreign Missions (Congregational) in Japan, Stacy was fellowshipped as a Universalist while in Tokyo. The junior Cary resigned late in 1938 because of ill health and Darley Downs, a Congregationalist who had served in Japan for the American Board since 1919, supervised the upkeep of Universalist property.[66] He was at the same time admitted to dual fellowship. The extension board was unsuccessful in its efforts to have the Stetsons return to Japan.[67]

With the administration of the mission in other hands, contributions for its support fell to less than $2,000 in 1939. One of the last remaining direct American links with the mission was broken with the death of Agnes Hathaway in Japan in 1939. She had retired from active service in 1932.[68]

No foreign currency was allowed to enter Japan after 1940, so what little money still trickled in from the United States for the mission was diverted to aid Chinese refugees.[69] The Koishikawa church, one of the five Universalist centers in Tokyo, had been organized in 1930 by Georgene Bowen but had been disbanded after her departure in 1937. The Japanese Convention came to an end that year because there were insufficient churches to maintain it. The Nagoya center under Nagano had become a hospice rather than a church by the late 1930s and the small church at Isaka had withered away almost completely because funding was not sufficient to support a full-time minister.

A government enactment (the Japan Religious Organization Bill) in 1940 stipulated that foreign missionaries were to be replaced with Japanese, and that only denominations having at least fifty churches were to be recognized. The Blackmer Home was classified as a social service rather than as a religious agency so that the Universalist connection could still be maintained although under Japanese supervision.[70] The last vestiges of official connection between Universalism and the mission came to an end in 1940 when the Japan Council (Universalist) voted to merge its few remaining churches with the *Kumai* (Congregational churches in Japan).[71] The action took place on the fiftieth anniversary of the establishment of the Japan mission, which went almost unnoticed in the United States.[72]

After war was declared, Martha Stacy, who had relinquished her executive duties at the Blackmer Home to the Japanese and to the Congregationalists, returned to the United States in 1942 and then joined the Grenfell mission in Labrador.[73] Ruth Downing was interned in a Roman Catholic convent and later became a nun.

The destruction wrought by World War II shattered the physical side of the remnants of the Japan mission. Only the Ohayo Kindergarten building remained standing. The Blackmer Home and Dojin House which contained the Midori Kindergarten were torn down in order to create a fire break for a nearby hospital.[74] Charles E. Hersey salvaged what mementos he could from the cornerstone of the wrecked Blackmer Home and brought them to the United States.

After the war there was much discussion about whether to resume work in Japan or to allow the mission to retreat into history and concentrate on projects in China already under way through the church extension board and the AUW.[75] The AUW had become involved in 1943 in supporting a seven-year rural service project near Nanking, established under the supervision of Ginling College in China. It included a nursing school, health training, classes in reading, writing, and crop improvement, and playground and nursery activities. By 1947 the Association was contributing $3,000 a year.[76] Mrs. Regina Cary Lapoint, with vivid memories of her parents' activities and contributions in Japan, and her own residence there, was ready to resume the work in Japan, starting with relief and rehabilitation and continuing with more permanent activities as emergency needs were met and as resources permitted.[77] She was "heartsick" at the general apathy of Universalists toward the mission.[78]

The obstacles to rebuilding the mission were indeed formidable. It was estimated in 1949 that there were no more than 1,000 Universalists scattered throughout Japan.[79] There had been no direct denominational identification or connection since 1940. Yet there were remnants that could be reassembled. An Association of Japanese Religious Liberals had been established by J. C. Orito in 1949. It was an offshoot of a church established by Michio Akashi, of the Japan Free Religious Association, who attended the General Assembly in 1951.[80]

Universalist properties in Japan may have been almost totally destroyed by World War II, and the few Universalists dispersed far and wide, but the spirit that lay behind them and animated them was not. It was a far cry from the ten churches and half a dozen educational institutions which the Universalists had established in the previous half-century, but a small band led by the AUW and the Universalist Service Committee headed by Carleton M. Fisher determined to carry on. The AUW assisted in financing a survey trip by Fisher in 1950 to assess the situation.

But more than physical property had been destroyed by war. The conflict had brought to an end the well-intentioned but somewhat old-fashioned and imperfectly realized goal of converting Orientals to Christianity. Fisher reported that a new intercultural approach was needed which called for the exchange of shared insights of both East and West. The Order of the New Day, as it was labelled, called for both financial assistance and the exchange of personnel and ideas, and a partnership rather than imposition from outside, benevolent as it might have been.

The AUW was the first to respond. Trust funds it held specifically for the Blackmer Home, which no longer existed, were freed in 1949 to be used for the training of young people, with preference to be given to Japanese girls. The AUW provided scholarships in America, one for Aiko Onishi who studied at the Eastman School of Music in Rochester, New York, beginning in 1950. The organization also assisted in financing the construction of the Koishikawa Universalist Center in 1950 on the site of the former Blackmer Home, and contributed to the support of its kindergarten, temporarily housed in a Quonset hut allotted by the American occupying forces in 1948. One reminder of the lasting influence of AUW efforts in Japan was the pledge by Prime Minister Hatoyama (a Universalist) of 100,000 yen toward the building of the center.[81] His great-granddaughter was enrolled in the kindergarten and his wife had lived in the Blackmer Home, where she had received instruction in English and music.

A two-year construction program was planned after Fisher's visit, to be a joint project with the Unitarians in cooperation with the Japan Free Religious Association.[82] Among the plans was the building of two new churches in Tokyo besides the Koishikawa Universalist Center, opened in 1952. It housed the revived Midori Kindergarten and all church activities except the Dojin (Ohayo) public kindergarten and church school.

Mrs. Mitsuko Ike and her husband Shigeo had managed to carry on the kindergarten on a greatly reduced scale, even during the rigors and disruptions of war. She had a staff of six and an enrollment aproaching 100 by 1952. The AUW financed a new annex to the kindergarten in 1953 and a year later the UCA likewise paid for the construction of the office and headquarters *(Shadan)* of the Universalist Church of Japan.

The new program continued to take shape in 1951 when the UCA financed a meeting house in Nagano (Komagone City) Prefecture, ninety miles northwest of Tokyo, and a day care center for children in 1952. Both were established by John Shidara and his wife. He was a former minister who had agreed after the war to rejoin the Universalist movement.

Development of ministerial leadership was one of the most urgent needs in post-war Japan. So, with the assistance of the AUW, Toshio Yoshioka was brought to the Canton Theological School at St. Lawrence for a three-year period of study. During his last year he was joined by Satoshi Arai, a former Buddhist and protege of Shidara; Arai was then serving as minister of the Tokyo Universalist Center and was replaced by an orthodox minister, much to the distress of the Universalists. So Yoshioka and Arai, after consultation with Dana Klotzle, director of the Universalist Service Committee, decided to return to Japan immediately. Yoshioka received a certificate of religious education in 1954.

After consultation with members of the board of the Universalist Church of Japan it was agreed that Yoshioka would serve as its executive director and minister and as representative of the Service Committee in the Far East. Arai returned to his post as minister of the Tokyo Center. It was due to the efforts of these two young men that the Universalist movement in Tokyo was literally reborn. By 1959 the legal adult membership of the church had exceeded 130.

Among other service projects under the direct control of the Japanese Universalist organization (the *Shadan*) were the Komagane Universalist Center serving five rural villages; and a weekly program for 200 students at Showa Women's University, conducted by Arai, as well as the Koishikawa Center and another kindergarten program.

The Universalist Church of Japan took another step in strengthening liberal religion in that nation when in 1954 it joined the Japan Free Religious Association. The latter had been organized in 1948 after Universalist and Unitarian representatives had met with Hideo Kishomoto, a leading religious liberal. The Free Christian Church and the Unity Church (both in Tokyo) had cooperated to organize formally the Free Religious Association. It was thought necessary to form a separate organization because none could conscientiously become members of the United Church of Japan *(Kyodan)* which was dominated by orthodox Protestant groups. Thus was created the Far Eastern counterpart of the Council of Liberal Churches in America. The Universalist Service Committee provided $8,000 to assist in the building program.

As small and even as insignificant as the Japan mission conducted by the Universalists since 1890 might have seemed especially to those outside the denomination, it was indeed an "investment in Universal Brotherhood" of which Universalists could justifiably be proud. Always under-financed, usually understaffed, and suffering from the slights and barbs of other denominations for most of its history, the Japan mission doggedly held on. The fruits of its efforts are difficult to measure, but at least to some Universalists they were worth all the effort and even sacrifice that had been expended. Their work was not only continued but much strengthened after resources were augmented by consolidation with the Unitarians. The existence of a Unitarian Universalist Fellowship in Tokyo many decades after the horrors of war had faded away was but a small reminder of not only the persistence of liberal religion in Japan but of the Universalist contribution to it.

Section VII

Universalism, Social Issues, and Social Service

Chapter 25

Facing A World of Change

Although Universalists were not always in a position, as a denomination, to carry out extensive programs to ameliorate or solve the multitude of problems they discerned as American society underwent a series of revolutionary changes after the Civil War, they often expressed their sensitivity and some even engaged in humanitarian and philanthropic projects individually, usually with official denominational backing or support. Most of the expressions of sympathy and concern had a long history, extending far back into pre–Civil War days, and were quite in harmony with Universalist principles. Cast in twentieth-century language, the facts of denominational history seemed to one Universalist to demonstrate "a great tradition of courageous and forthright ethical liberalism" which few could challenge.[1] Often the reach and the grasp failed to coincide, but at least the vision of a better world was there.

The Massachusetts State Convention expressed the enthusiasm and optimism of the nineteenth century with the wording of a resolution adopted by acclamation in 1860, taking virtually all of humankind into its province. They affirmed "a lively interest in the cause of education, temperance, freedom, purity, prison discipline, juvenile reformation, homes for the destitute, and whatever tends in any way to the progress of society, the reclamation of the wandering, the welfare of youth, or the amelioration of man's earthly condition."[2] The social mission of Universalism was defined much more bluntly by a leading Universalist in the 1930s who told his audience that, "having got the people out of hell we must now turn ourselves to the task of getting hell out of the people."[3]

A social program almost as broad as that proposed by the Massachusetts Convention in 1860 for "bettering the lot of humanity" had been drawn up by the Universalist General Reform Association, which lasted from

1847 until 1862. A short-lived post–Civil War organization which was intended to carry on the same tradition was the Universalist Reform League, organized in Boston in 1874, complete with a constitution. Its purpose was to establish "a free platform for the discussion of such reforms in social, economic and civic life as the evolution of time may bring to the surface, the discussion to be in the light of the fundamental principles of the Universalist Church."[4]

The first meeting of the Reform League was addressed by Adin Ballou on "The Christian Basis of Reform," and there were speeches on temperance; promotion of world peace, by Julia Ward Howe; and on women's role in reform by Mary A. Livermore, vice-president of the League. Among the speakers at the second (and last) meeting in 1875 was Mrs. Elizabeth M. Bruce, an ordained Universalist minister who had long championed rights for women, including their admission in the 1870s to (then) all-male Tufts College. She made a plea for a larger number of women in the Universalist ministry, pointing out that there were only 10 among almost 700 preachers in the denomination.[5]

The *Universalist* took a very cautious position about whether the entrance of women into the ministry would be successful. Referring in 1873 to Olympia Brown's ordination a decade earlier, it was noted that "ten years and ten examples hardly approach, much less answer, the question."[6] Bruce attended the first Woman's Ministerial Conference in Boston in 1873, organized as an interdenominational (Protestant) group, as did Mrs. Ada C. Bowles, another ordained Universalist minister, who served as recording secretary.[7] The organization did not have a continuous history; an attempt was made in 1910 by another Universalist minister, Mrs. Florence K. Crooker, to revive it.

The question of the appropriateness of women in the ministry continued to remain unanswered throughout the remaining history of the Universalists as a separate denomination. One individual unalterably opposed sought refuge in Biblical history and precedent. Jesus had included no women among those he sent forth as apostles, and he ordained no women "for any purpose whatever."[8] The individual felt that it was fortunate that the number of women attempting to take over men's jobs and professions was so small.

On the more positive side, the Maine Convention in 1874 recommended that its Committee on Fellowship, Ordination, and Discipline be authorized to ordain candidates "without regard to sex." It was intended that "the question of ordaining a woman may not be left for . . . decision to the personal coinvictions or caprices of the persons who may happen to constitute the committee."[9] On the other hand, such veteran Universalists as T. J. Sawyer were not so entranced by the idea of female ministers. He introduced a resolution adopted by the Massachusetts Convention in 1881 urging the General Convention to appoint a committee "to inquire into the expediency of encouraging the continuance of a women ministry in our church."[10]

Alonzo A. Miner, another representative of an earlier generation, objected when, at the General Convention meeting in 1883, an attempt was made to amend a call for "renewed and untiring efforts" to fill ministerial ranks with promising young men, to include women.[11] This would, in his view, commit the denomination to a "woman ministry" for which he insisted it was not ready. A compromise was worked out by substituting the word "youth." In the course of the discussion it was pointed out that, according to the literary canons of the day, the words "man" and "mankind" were generic terms which included women. If interpreted otherwise, the Winchester Profession of 1803 would need rewriting because the word "mankind" or "man" appeared at least once in every one of the three articles — a fact no one could deny. When Ada C. Bowles objected to the reference exclusively to men in ministerial recruitment she was told that, unless specific individuals were identified by name, the word "men" always referred to the entire human race and not to males alone.[12]

One female correspondent in the *Leader* alleged with indignation that some Universalist churches discriminated against women as late as 1925 and refused to employ them as ministers.[13] She called for a general airing of the problem at the General Convention meeting that year. The editor of the *Leader,* commenting on the ordination of fifty-four year old Jennie Lois Ellis in 1925, state superintendent in Pennsylvania, noted the persistence of prejudice against women clergy. He called attention to the fact that such prejudice was outmoded. Women were, in fact, "the backbone of the church." Such male clergy as Levi Powers and Arthur M. Soule had obviously not suffered because women had preached their ordination sermons — the former by Augusta Chapin and the latter by Eleanor Forbes.[14]

Complaints continued to be heard after World War II about the paucity of women in the Universalist ministry, but nothing was done officially to alleviate the situation. When the question was raised in 1946 about the small number of women ministers, Editor Lalone of the *Leader* responded somewhat defensively by calling attention to the presence of nine living ordained women clergy.[15] It was as much a matter of individual choice as it was of prejudice that governed the number of women in the ministry.

It was in another area of activity that Universalist women were most visible and influential after the Civil War. In 1867 Olympia Brown delivered an address to the alumna of her *alma mater* (Antioch College) when she received an MA degree. The *Star in the West* acknowledged the occasion by pointing with pride that the denomination was "in the van of the ranks moving forward in the cause of woman [and that] we ought to be proud and glad" to occupy such a place.[16] The paper was referring not so much to the work of women in the ministry or even to the unusually large number of "estimable female writers" like Mrs. Julia Scott who had earlier been a "matter of pride and admiration to all Universalists." It was in other fields of endeavor that they had become increasingly involved.[17]

A few women, like Mrs. Hattie Tyng Graham, daughter of a Universalist minister and both a poetess and a prose writer of some note, had continued to be published in the 1870s in such journals as *Grahams*, *Harper's Weekly*, and *Scribner's*.[18] However, such prominent Universalist authors as John Greenleaf Adams noted in the early 1880s that the women were making less of a contribution to literature than thirty years earlier and were expending their efforts on more "practical" concerns and in a more organized fashion than heretofore.[19] Instead of continuing the impressive pace of literary production set before the Civil War, Universalist women after 1870 turned more and more of their attention to developing their political power in the secular as well as the religious realm.

By the 1870s women were in the voting majority in almost all parishes, and they were urged to make even greater use of their potential to influence church affairs.[20] Mrs. M. Louise Thomas, a founding member of the Woman's Centenary Association, recommended that at least half the trustees of the General Convention should be women, a policy with which Augusta Chapin completely agreed.[21] The editor of the *Universalist* strongly disagreed, not because he opposed feminine participation but because the recommendation sounded too much like the establishment of a quota system. Women were already eligible to hold all offices in the denomination but were hesitant to come forward because they lacked administrative experience. Women should become trustees because they were qualified for the office, not because they were women.

As to equal rights for women in secular affairs, the General Convention first went on record against sex discrimination in general in 1874. It was not until 1905 that there was a call specifically for equal suffrage with men. Three justifications were offered: It was compatible with the democratic idea; in harmony with the logic of Universalism; and furthered "the interests of humanity."[22] A similar resolution in 1907 failed of adoption because it was considered an inappropriate subject for a religious body to consider.[23] Resolutions calling for enfranchisement of women met defeat in 1909 and again in 1911, both offered by Henry M. Metcalf. The resolution of 1909 was tabled, and the one in 1911 was defeated by a vote of 59 to 74. It was clear that, as a denomination, Universalists were more ambivalent than forward-looking, in the eyes of those advocating suffrage for women.

It was in the resolutions of state conventions that the most forthright statements about suffrage rights for women were to be found. The New Hampshire Convention in 1890 called not only for extension of the franchise to women in municipal, state, and national elections but their unqualified eligibility for any and all public offices on the same conditions as for men. This rationale was very simply stated: It was "very evident that women have as much knowledge, capacity and character for the conduct of public business as men, while their God-given rights are undeniably the same."[24]

Universalist women such as Mary A. Livermore, Olympia Brown, and Ada C. Bowles were active participants in the suffrage movement — lecturing, writing, campaigning, and admonishing their male colleagues for not being sufficiently supportive of efforts in behalf of women's rights in general.[25] It was Bowles who presented a resolution adopted by "a large majority" at the Massachusetts Convention in 1890 which stated that "the exclusion of women from direct representation in the government of our state, while taxed for its support, is unjust in principle, and therefore unwise in policy."[26]

There were other men besides Metcalf who championed rights for women. One of the most outspoken supporters and prolific writers in the Midwest was John Wesley Henley (1832–1902), a native of Ohio, and a Universalist minister converted from Methodism.[27] He made a great point of the fact that only two groups had been excluded from full participation in American society in spite of the rhetoric of the Declaration of Independence. They were black men, and women regardless of color. Except for Negro slavery, legal until after 1865, the white woman's position was no better than that of "her colored brother."[28] He considered the denial of equality to women as a direct contradiction of the American principle of equality and listed eight presumed arguments for keeping women in subservience. He then proceeded to demolish each one, pointing out that any intellectual shortcomings detected in women were the fault of males who had thwarted the development of the feminine mind. There was no reason why a woman could not be elected President of the United States if she received the requisite number of votes.

Henley was active in organizations promoting women's rights and for a time served as chaplain of the National Woman Suffrage Association founded in 1869. He was certain that the "woman question" would remain "until it is disposed of by the complete liberation of women, and her recognition as man's equal before the law, possessing all civil rights that man does." But even the ratification of the Nineteenth Amendment to the United States Constitution in 1920, greeted enthusiastically by most Universalist women, was no guarantee that the "liberation" called for by Henley had been automatically achieved.

The health and welfare of the American family were also matters to which Universalists paid official attention. Concern was voiced in 1883 over the rapidly mounting divorce rate as a threat to the solidarity of the family and home life.[29] The denomination called for the enactment of uniform divorce laws and reaffirmed "the supreme importance of the home as the safe-guard of our national and religious life" and the sanctity of marriage as proclaimed in the New Testament.[30]

The matter of artificial birth control had become a sensitive issue of nationwide proportions by the 1920s, and at the General Convention meeting in 1927 Universalists tackled the subject. The trustees were authorized to appoint a committee to collaborate with other denominations in investigating "the bearing of the practice of Birth Control upon the institution of marriage, and the welfare of the race."[31] This action grew out of a speech advocating birth control made on the convention floor by L. Griswold Williams.

There was considerable agitation at the biennial meeting in 1929 after the committee (consisting of four men and two women) appointed two years earlier made its report. Their resolution favoring birth control came up for a vote after an attempt had been made, first not to report it at all, and another to table it. But it was presented from the floor and adopted by a vote of 97 to 62. The resolution called for the immediate repeal of all federal and state laws which in any way interfered with the prescription or dissemination of birth control devices or information by physicians, or prevented the establishment of birth control clinics where not illegal. Universalists claim that they were the first denomination in the United States to go on record in favoring birth control.[32] By an interesting coincidence the Universalist action took place the very year that Margaret Sanger's birth control clinic in New York City was raided by police on complaint of the Daughters of the American Revolution.

The convention reporter commented wryly that while the vote was being taken "a hasty glance around the room . . . did not suggest that the families of those who voted against the resolution were any larger than the families of those who favored it."[33] Universalists continued to support the principle and practice of birth control, and after World War II favored the work of the Planned Parenthood organization.[34]

Universalists continued also, in the tradition of such individuals as Charles and John Murray Spear of an earlier day, to oppose the death penalty and to advocate an enlightened penal system. The General Convention adopted unanimously in 1882 a resolution condemning capital punishment as "barbarous, revolting, demoralizing, contrary to the spirit of the Christian religion, and unnecessary."[35] A resolution reaffirming the sanctity of life and opposing the death penalty "for any crime whatsoever" was adopted in 1927, just as the controversial trial and execution of Sacco and Vanzetti took place in Boston.[36] A year later Victor Friend, Greater Boston businessman and a trustee of the General Convention, the Massachusetts Convention, and the Universalist Publishing House, testified against capital punishment in a hearing regarding a bill pending before the state legislature. He, like the General Convention itself, was opposed to "the taking of human life for any cause whatsoever."[37] In every instance resolutions opposing the death penalty were adopted by the General Convention by substantial if not overwhelming majorities.

Universalists took the same unflinching stand regarding penal reform that they did with capital punishment, and linked the two together. They uniformly opposed the punishment of convicted criminals and called instead for reform and rehabilitation of the individual. Q. H. Shinn was responsible for the presentation of a series of resolutions at the General Convention meeting in 1897 calling for an enlightened penal system and the abolition of the death penalty, and served on a special committee on Penology and Capital Punishment established by the denomination.[38] Shinn was also responsible, beginning in 1899, for making the fourth Sunday in October "Prison Sunday" in order to keep the problem at the forefront of Universalist consciousness.[39]

Mrs. Ellen C. Johnson, a member of one of the Universalist churches in Boston, was active in penal reform in the late nineteenth century and had the opportunity to put her ideas into practice when she was not only appointed a member of the Massachusetts Board of Commissioners of Prisons but served in the 1880s as superintendent of the Reformatory Prison for Women in Sherborn, Massachusetts. She remained in that position for fifteen years, until her death in 1899. She died only one day after making a major address in London at the international Woman's Congress.

While serving the Church of Our Father in Detroit, Lee S. McCollester was active in the operation of the Home of Industry for released prisoners which became the Ford Boys Republic, supported by many Universalists.[40] Orlando F. Lewis, an historian of the American prison system, was involved in the Charity Organization of New York City and served as secretary of the New York State Prison Society. Any organization or activity promoting prison reform attracted the attention of Universalists, and the General Convention supported the work of the American Prison Congress.[41] In fact, Universalists lent a sympathetic ear to any call that would better the lot of humanity on earth and promote human brotherhood, including the organization of interracial congregations in the South, even when such moves brought the threat of punitive action.

One area of concern was the plight of the American Indian at the hands of the white man, a concern voiced by L. F. W. Andrews, itinerant Universalist in the South in the 1830s. Missionaries of orthodox denominations had replaced the Indians' benevolent "Great Spirit" and their "centuries of peace and innocence" with a vengeful and vindictive Christian deity.[42] The Universalist General Reform Association in the 1850s was distressed at the degradation of the Indian wrought by rum, gunpowder, smallpox, and the white man's avarice.⁴³ The Rhode Island Convention was told in 1870 that "humanity, justice, and sound economy demanded that we shall respect the rights of the Indian, and open before him the prospect of citizenship."⁴⁴ Another Universalist called for atonement by whites for "many a wrong" done the Indian.⁴⁵ A policy of humanity rather than cruelty should be followed. "Blood enough is on our hands already." Still another noted that the record of the Canadians was much better than that of Americans, and made an eloquent plea for justice for the Indian as a fellow member of the human race.⁴⁶

Universalists expressed the same concern for the immigrants who flooded into America in a series of waves in the 1830s and thereafter. Those members of the denomination who left a record of their opinions were very much committed to the historic national policy of the "open door" and of welcoming "the virtuous from every part of the globe." Even before the intensification of urbanization after the Civil War, Edwin H. Chapin, popular minister in New York City, dealt with some of the problems of the urban dweller in *Moral Aspects of City Life,* published in 1853.

Even when numbers of the "criminal classes" seemed to be pouring into America, the task of government was not to stop the arrival of immigrants but to sift them carefully.⁴⁷ President Rutherford B. Hayes' veto of a bill to exclude the Chinese was hailed as a victory for human rights.⁴⁸ In a few instances Universalists, like most other Americans, felt somewhat overwhelmed by the torrents of immigrants pouring in after the Civil War and expressed a bit of nostalgia for the "old days," when "the people were almost wholly Americans," and the owners and operators of businesses and industries were of "New England stock."⁴⁹

Americanization of the immigrant as promptly and as completely as possible was thought to be the best way to handle the situation. Sylvanus Cobb, the reform-minded editor of the *Christian Freeman,* warned against allowing "nations within our nation" to develop; "let them come to *be* Americans."⁵⁰ In 1907, the year that immigration reached the highest peak in American history, the General Convention appointed a committee to investigate ways of reaching urban immigrant groups.⁵¹ Their recommendation was not to treat them as foreigners at all, but as "new Americans." One concession was made, however, to the linguistic handicap of the recent arrival. The trustee Committee on Missions arranged in 1909 to issue a series of tracts in the "leading language of the immigrants" and at least one was published in Italian.⁵²

The "first attempt in any large way to take the ministers of our faith to the foreigners at our doors" was made between 1907 and 1909 by Galusha A. King, pastor of the Universalist church in Wichita, Kansas.⁵³ It was estimated that at least 1,600 employees in the packing house district of the city were recent immigrants representing a dozen nationalities, and with no YMCA or church or recreational facilities.⁵⁴ King was able to interest local business, civic, and religious leaders in organizing the Wichita Manual Training Association, and the General Convention appropriated $1,000 to assist. A building was started in the winter of 1911–12, but was not opened as a Universalist-sponsored facility until the spring of 1915 because of a shortage of funds.⁵⁵ King had an ambitious plan to establish a settlement house with complete services, including a gymnasium, library, and equipment to teach both domestic science courses and conduct classes in manual training. But the denomination was unable to contribute even $1,500 toward the estimated $3,500 annual operating expenses, and the project fell into other hands.

With the end of the Civil War came a burst of technological innovation and industrialization and an upsurge of urban population concentration which brought to the fore a new set of relations between capital and labor characterized by tensions which frequently erupted into strikes, various outbreaks of violence, and attempts at unionization on a scale unprecedented in American labor history. It was natural that Universalists, many of whom were themselves industrialists and businessmen as well as skilled workmen and clerks, should respond in some manner. The common denominators of the denominational press were calls for moderation and the application of the principles of Christian stewardship, particularly by the employer.

Much attention was paid to economic and social questions by the *Universalist Quarterly* between 1875 and the date it ceased publication (1891). George Emerson, editor of the *Leader* in the 1880s, wrote many an editorial calling for industrial justice for laboring men, arguing that they had the same right to combine to keep wages up that the profit-minded employers had to keep wages down.⁵⁶ Picketing and any form of violence were opposed because the laborer had an independent right to work. The *Leader* was, however, generally circumspect in treating economic issues, and was chided for not devoting sufficient space to such labor upheavals as the famous Homestead steel strike of 1892. Readers had to be reminded that the paper was a religious publication and not part of the secular press.⁵⁷ Alonzo A. Miner devoted several sermons in the 1880s to social problems, arguing the right of employees to organize but frowning on strikes because they were as damaging to employees as they were to employers.⁵⁸ He called for laborers to recognize the problems of the employer as well as their own interests.

Another Universalist clergyman, George Hill, offered advice to laboring men which counseled moderation and the use of peaceful means in achieving their goals.⁵⁹ Neither violence nor the use of extravagant and intemperate language would accomplish their purposes. They had a "perfect right" to unionize and to use "fair and reasonable methods." They did indeed deserve a greater voice than then prevailed in establishing reasonable hours of labor or improving their wage scales. Such matters were neither self-regulating nor the exclusive province of the employer. Hill called for "a new departure . . . a friendly and equitable partnership" between capital and labor, with a fair share for each. The time had come as major material improvements were being completed, immigrants were arriving by the thousands, and labor-saving machinery was being introduced.

Hill argued that, relatively, it was labor rather than capital that was falling behind; so a renewed determination to forge ahead had to surface. This should be manifested, among other things, in the accumulation of savings and the elevation of moral character. Money should not be squandered on strong drink; over half of the money spent each year on intoxicating liquors was from the pockets of the laboring man. The formation of industrial and consumer cooperatives and credit unions was listed as another means of adding to the strength of the laboring man.

One of the industries in which technological developments were most evident was shoe manufacturing. New inventions enabled the work previously done by four individuals to be accomplished by one person. This threat to job security brought the possibility of boycott of any shoemaking firm using such new devices, but the *Leader* discouraged such activity. Resistance was unwise in both policy and principle because labor-saving machinery was in reality "a providential device for the emancipation of labor."[60] In spite of exceptions, labor would ultimately benefit by reduced hours and increased wages. No factual support or proof was offered for this optimistic assertion.

Henry Blanchard, pastor in Portland, Maine, delivered an address in 1887 on "The Future of Workingmen" on the invitation of the Knights of Labor. He made an earnest appeal that they "should study, should be patient, should be considerate, and, above all, should see how large a part they have to perform in bringing a bright, happy, noble future for workingmen."[61] The average Universalist seems to have accepted this simplistic advice without question or even hesitation.

Universalists clothed much of their language about difficulties in capital-labor relations in moralistic garb and blamed much of the trouble on foreign agitators. When longshoremen and other laborers in New York City struck for higher wages in 1887 and appeals were made on behalf of their "ragged and starving children," the *Leader* conjectured that their plight was due more to the frequenting of saloons by their fathers than to inadequate wages.[62] It was claimed that "nine-tenths of our labor troubles are imported, and all of that part of the agitation that is false and disruptive is led by men who can with difficulty articulate the English language."[63]

The General Convention, preoccupied with internal denominational concerns for many years after the Civil War, was slow to take any official stand on social and economic problems and did not express itself officially on capital-labor relations until 1889. In that year it adopted a vague and mildly worded resolution calling for self-restraint by the laborer and a spirit of "Christian charity" by the employer.[64] Even though a legislative attempt had been made in Massachusetts to regulate child labor as early as 1879, it was not until 1907 that the practice was first condemned by the General Convention. As had been the case with the treatment of social and economic issues before the Civil War, there was still a wide difference of opinion in the late nineteenth century over the appropriateness of bringing them into the deliberations of an ostensibly religious body.

Isaac M. Atwood devoted a long article to the subject of "The Church and the Labor Question," published in 1893.[65] He called for an augmented role for the church in general on behalf of the individual laborer who had found himself caught in the toils of modern technology which had diminished his power as a person and had transformed him from a craftsman into a machine tender. His personality, individuality, and independence were reduced, and his identity diminished. It was the church's responsibility to assist the faceless worker in restoring his "moral resources," cultivating his independence, and strengthening "the inner and real man," without reference to artificial class distinctions. Church leaders must recognize the inherent dignity of labor.

Universalists had just as much to say on behalf of the industrialist as in criticism, and called in general for an attitude of "paternalistic benevolence" in relations with the employees. One of the most widely advertised events in labor history was the Pullman strike of 1894. George M. Pullman (1831–1897), a Universalist layman, had perfected the "railroad palace sleeping car" which bore his name, and he had created by the early 1890s a huge industrial empire. By 1889 there were 2,000 cars in the Pullman system, operating on almost 100,000 miles of track and serving nearly 100 railroad systems, large and small.[66]

Pullman had built a model city to house his thousands of employees.[67] The site, located ten miles south of Chicago, had been open prairie in 1880. Three thousand acres were purchased by the Pullman Company and a decade later a complete city had been created, with a total investment approaching $7,000,000. Streets and parks were laid out in advance, and the factory buildings were planned carefully, as was the housing (built exclusively of brick) for the workers. A church, a school, a bank, a library, and other amenities required for a self-contained community of 10,000 had been provided by 1889. Rentals ranged from $4.00 to $100 per month. No house within the city limits could be purchased, but if a worker wished to own property he could buy freehold rights from the company in a belt of land outside the city and could construct his own home. There were such added features as playgrounds, macadam roads, an amphitheater beside Lake Calumet, a theater, and a water tower disguised to resemble a Florentine baptistery. There were no saloons within the city limits.

Pullman's experiment was described enthusiastically by one awe-struck visitor as "the most perfect city in the world."[68] After talking to the founder he had decided to visit "the great industrial experiment which [was] being tested on the western prairies" and find out for himself "if philanthropy can exist without paternalism, order without tyranny, and economy without meanness." He found that "the highest wages [were] paid consistent with the competition of the market" and that the city represented the ideal blending of the efforts of capital and labor. It was "philanthropy based on common sense, a recognition of the rights of labor, and the obligations of wealth."

But this presumably idyllic picture was rudely shattered in 1894. Economic depression had struck the previous year, resulting in wage cuts, irregular employment, and layoffs, first among those outside the community boundaries who did not pay rent to the company. The Pullman Company refused to reduce rents or utility prices, left the salaries of its executives intact, and continued to pay dividends (8 percent) to its stockholders. These and other grievances were presented to the company which not only rejected various demands and refused to submit them to arbitration, but laid off three members of the grievance committee for being so audacious as to make any demands at all. Some 3,000 workers then went on strike, necessitating the suspension of plant operations. The destitution of the workers was only partially alleviated by public and private charity. Even the sympathetic strikes and boycotts of other employees were ineffective, and after federal troops were called in, the strike collapsed completely; none of the workers' demands were met, and their plight became even worse than before.

The *Leader* had no sympathy whatever for the strikers, calling the work stoppage "as unjust as it is imbecile. . . . labor must suffer in common with other interests."[69] The strike was "an act of ingratitude as well as folly."

Shortly after Pullman's death in 1897 a correspondent in the *Leader* came to the industrial tycoon's defense.[70] Although he had not known Pullman personally, he considered the widespread criticism of the industrialist for his reputedly high-handed actions to be quite unfounded. He noted that Pullman was not only a brother of two prominent Universalist ministers but "a friend and generous benefactor of our church" as well as the founder of an industrial community. It was "intended and adapted to promote the comfort and elevation of a large number of working men" and was considered a model "in its moral and sanitary aspects, where workingmen had good wages, comfortable dwellings, at reasonable expense for lights and fuel, free from the temptations and dangers of saloons, with free option to live inside or outside of the city."

The intervention of a third party to arbitrate the dispute would have been "unnecessary and unsatisfactory" and would have been equally unacceptable to the workers if they had struck for higher wages and Pullman had proposed arbitration. It would have been "absurd" to have reduced house rents in the same way that he reduced wages. Wage reduction was necessitated in order to reduce company expenses and to have reduced rents would have been self-defeating and inconsistent. The gas plant was part of the working capital of the company and the stockholders were fully entitled to receive regular dividends. As to giving preference to residents of the Pullman community in employment, it would have been "unnatural and suicidal" to have done otherwise from a business point of view. The correspondent implied further that men who chose not to live within the community may have done so because no saloons were allowed inside, and such men would automatically be less desirable workers.

In sum, Pullman was "a noble and useful, unjustly censured man." His "true character" was best portrayed in the memorial sermon delivered in the Pullman Memorial Church in Albion, New York, in 1897. In characterizing the life and accomplishments of Pullman, Almon Gunnison insisted that there was neither paternalism nor philanthropy involved in the establishment of the model industrial city. It was "an honest attempt to bring large capital and corporate ability to the increasing of the comfort of men's living, to give to men's work a finer touch, by giving to their lives a finer quality."[71]

Levi M. Powers, an outspoken Universalist clergyman and critic of the concentration of wealth in private hands, did not agree. On the very eve of the Pullman strike Powers had warned against the "wage slavery" practiced by insensitive industrial leaders such as Pullman.[72] Very few Universalists were as critical of Pullman as was Powers. They were too enamored with his contributions to American industrial progress to support the cause of the strikers.

Not nearly as well known an entrepreneur as Pullman, Arthur Nash (1870–1927), another Universalist lay person, very self-consciously attempted to apply Christian religious principles to industry and attracted considerable attention, both favorable and otherwise, with his self-styled application of the Golden Rule to labor-management relations. A former Seventh Day Adventist, he had become a convert to Universalism and had determined to put the concept of brotherhood into practice in the treatment of his workers.

During the nation-wide labor upheavals of 1919, employees in thirty of the thirty-one clothing manufacturers in Cincinnati, Ohio, went out on strike for higher wages. The strike lasted fourteen weeks and was settled when the workers won a wage increase of 20 percent. But the employees of A. Nash Co. neither ceased work nor demanded an increase beyond the $12 a week earned by learners and the $16 a week received by skilled and experienced workers. Nash triumphantly offered the explanation for this unusual phenomenon: "Applied Universalism — Be human with human help."[73]

Nash had incorporated his company in 1916 with $60,000 in stock to manufacture cheap men's clothing. By the mid-1920s he had turned his venture into a business grossing $14,000,000 annually.[74] Much of the stock was held by the workers themselves, and profit sharing had been introduced in 1920 for his 400 employees. In the same year he introduced a five-day week for the men without reducing wages, and three years later extended the plan to women whose weekly working hours were reduced from forty to thirty-five, with minimum hourly pay set at 50 cents.[75] The number of employees had grown to 900 by 1921, and he had opened a factory in Chattanooga, Tennessee.[76]

Nash shocked his fellow businessmen by defending the right of labor to organize. He not only created an employee advisory group to offer suggestions on improving the manufacturing process and working conditions, but actually encouraged them to unionize by joining the Amalgamated Clothing Workers of America.[77] He even went so far as to encourage his workers to invite Sidney Hillman, the first president of the union, to address them (which he did). This unconventional employer attracted national attention in 1925 by contributing to a strike fund in case his own workers went out on the picket line.[78] Nash's argument was simplicity itself: The practice of true human brotherhood would make unnecessary the traditional protagonist-antagonist relationship which had seemed always to have created tension between capital and labor.[79]

Nash spread his version of welfare capitalism as widely as he could, with numerous speaking appearances before church, business, and labor groups, and at such educational institutions as Harvard.[80] In 1923 he published *The Golden Rule in Business*, written with the aid of Philip I. Roberts of New York City.[81] The work was even translated into Japanese and run serially in the leading newspaper in Nagoya, Japan, through the efforts of Nagano, a native Universalist missionary.[82] Nash also started a weekly, the *Nash Journal*, which he edited, and which was intended "to promote the ideals of brotherhood" in the business community.[83]

Nash's attempt to apply Christian principles to industry brought not only skepticism from the business community as to its workability but unfavorable comments from religious bodies. He was accused by the secretary of the Church League for Social Democracy of using religion for advertising purposes and of "degrading" the Golden Rule by making it "a mere business slogan."[84] It was also suggested that, despite all his professions to the contrary, he was following a policy of thinly disguised paternalism which furthered his own self-interest primarily. After interviewing Nash the author of an article in the *New Republic* entitled "An Eight-Carat Golden Rule" still doubted the idealistic conditions he described and accused him of a basically anti-union stance in spite of all his protestations to the contrary.[85] Whether or not he deserved the criticism levelled at him, there is no gainsaying the fact that his approch was unusual if not almost unique for his day.

Nash's desire to promote brotherhood extended considerably beyond labor-management relations. He was active in promoting the Five Year Program sponsored by the denomination after World War I to raise $1,000,000, part of which was to be spent beyond both Universalist and American boundaries to promote "a world church for world service." He offered to contribute $100,000 over a five-year period but his death within two years prevented him from carrying out his plan.[86] The General Convention trustees designated the program in his honor as the "Golden Rule Service Fund," but enthusiasm for it was short-lived, and with inadequate financing the project collapsed.[87] The denomination did, however, appropriate $7,000 to be used by the Federal Council of Churches to promote harmonious industrial relations.[88]

One of the questions which troubled some Americans in the 1880s was whether the wealthy industrialist had any obligation to share with society any of the riches he had accumulated. By and large, the answer was in the affirmative, and Universalists fully supported what became known as the Gospel of Wealth enunciated by Andrew Carnegie who had made his fortune in steel and had earlier introduced Pullman's sleeping cars on the Pennsylvania Railroad.

Elmer H. Capen, president of Tufts College, delivered an address at the Massachusetts State Convention in 1890 entitled "Responsibilities of Wealth."[89] He offered several guidelines. Wealth should be used productively, for the benefit of society, and not be expended on such selfish items as private yachts. Charity in the narrow and literal sense, good as it might be, was not enough; mere giving for its own sake was insufficient. It was more important to expend money to get at the root causes of misery and poverty than only to feed the hungry. Wealth was best distributed through institutions such as hospitals or the endowment of academic chairs that continue after donors have passed away, so that several generations might benefit.

Capen's advice bore a distinct resemblance to Carnegie's philosophy which Carnegie himself outlined in Charles H. Eaton's Church of the Divine Paternity in New York City in 1892 as part of a Sunday evening lecture series.[90] Isaac M. Atwood was another believer in the Gospel of Wealth. He commended Samuel J. Tilden, wealthy lawyer and presidential candidate in 1876, who left four million of his five million dollar fortune to establish free public libraries. This policy was much to be preferred over that followed by such millionaires as A. T. Stewart, the pioneer department store owner in Chicago, and the Vanderbilts and others who "sought to perpetuate their name by keeping their dead hand on their cash" or leaving their fortunes to their families.[91] Men such as Tilden "gave back to the world what the world had given them," and thus well illustrated the principle of Christian stewardship.

Some Universalists justified business consolidation resulting from successful competition and supported the then-popular theory of Social Darwinism which applied the biological theory of natural selection and survival of the fittest to economic and social life. One such person was Henry B. Metcalf, himself a successful businessman and philanthropist. He admitted that competition was sometimes ruthless but indispensable to social progress.[92]

Simultaneously, a few Universalists refused to support the dog-eat-dog competitiveness characteristic of American *laissez faire* capitalism after the Civil War, and advocated cooperation and a socialistic economy instead. Warren S. Woodbridge, on the faculty of the Tufts Divinity School, was one of these.[93] Much more of an activist than Woodbridge was Henry C. Ledyard (1880–1950), a Universalist clergyman, Christian socialist and pacifist, and labor organizer.[94]

Regardless of their personal convictions, it was the better part of wisdom for most Universalists not to risk their reputations and careers by abandoning the capitalistic ethos to which the great majority of Americans subscribed. Ledyard antagonized several congregations with his socialistic ideas and finally resigned from the Universalist ministry, in part because the church, in his view, failed to practice what it preached about human brotherhood. C. B. Rheiner, pastor of the church in Norway, Maine, was condemned by the Norway Shoe Comany because he supported workers protesting a wage cut and was ousted by his Universalist congregation as a result.[95] Taken as a whole, it is probably safe to say that Universalists in both the nineteenth and twentieth centuries who addressed themselves to social and economic issues elected to stay within the capitalistic mainstream. Those who did not were the exceptions, not the rule.

The issues of war and peace had always been uppermost in the minds of some Universalists but by no means all. There had been but few written expressions of sentiment regarding these questions until after 1830 either individually or denominationally, when peace organizations began to appear.

A few scattered Universalists had objected to the Mexican-American conflict in the 1840s as a war of aggression on the part of the United States. Caveats about the fighting of the Civil War in the 1860s were scarcely to be heard. And Universalists overwhelmingly supported American efforts in 1898 to "liberate" the Cubans from "the atrocities of Spanish misrule."[96] The *Leader* at first took a cautious "wait and see" attitude toward the growing tension between the United States and Spain, but the blowing up of the battleship *Maine* settled the matter. After the ship's destruction the paper gave unqualified support to the decision of "a patriotic president and Congress" to go to war. The *Leader* doubted the real necessity of war and admitted that much war fever was stirred up by a jingoistic press, a bellicose pulpit, and those "spoiling for a fight," but thought that war was still probably the best solution. Universalists were undoubtedly influenced in their enthusiasm for war by the vivid description by the Red Cross leader, Clara Barton, who was in Havana at the time the *Maine* was destroyed.[97] The consensus of Universalists was probably accurately reflected in a resolution of the Franklin County (Maine) Association rejoicing "in the rekindling of the fires of patriotism in the hearts of our countrymen."[98]

After war broke out in Europe in 1914 the vast majority of Universalists supported Woodrow Wilson's policy of neutrality in 1915; wholeheartedly (but not unanimously) supported American preparations for war in 1916 and involvement in 1917; and enthusiastically called for enduring peace after the conclusion of hostilities and for the creation of a federation of nations. The year 1917 brought pledges of devotion to American ideals from the General Convention and state conventions alike, pledging "loyal support in making the world safe for democracy."[99]

American entrance into the conflict was preceded by some uncertainty and even confusion among a few Universalists. F. O. Hall opposed American involvement and in 1915 called for support of international peace even though the stand might be unpopular.[100] Clinton Lee Scott, pastor in Buffalo, New York, recalled that the majority of his congregation was for the war in Europe. He was not, and said so. Anticipating a request for his resignation, he prepared a letter to that effect but it was never acted on.[101] On the other hand, Marion D. Shutter, pastor of the largest Universalist church in Minneapolis, expressed his willingness in 1916 to march in a preparedness parade. "I am a Christian because I am a patriot, and patriotism is the path to true and lasting peace."[102] Simultaneously, the Massachusetts Convention protested the militarism which accompanied preparedness and announced that the goal should not be 'America first' but 'humanity first.'[103] There was distress that clergy were willing to take part in preparedness parades, and one Universalist called for support of the slogan "I am a pacifist because I am a Christian."

T. Andrew Caraker, ministering to the Universalist Church of Our Father in Baltimore, told members of the American Legion at a banquet that "had Jesus lived in 1917 he would have been the first to volunteer in the American Army, to wear a gas mask, shoulder a rifle and enter the trenches."[104] Bisbee, editor of the *Leader,* greeted the onset of war in Europe with doubts and hesitation about American participation but by the spring of 1917 he admitted reluctantly that the battle between democracy and aristocracy had to be fought. "It is an awful price to pay, and a foolish, criminal way to get it, but if it can not be won in any other way, it is worth the price."[105] The tragedy of it all was that the talk of human brotherhood "for centuries" had to be sacrificed to war. He wrote very little about the military aspects of the conflict but instead concentrated on the role that civilians could play in supporting the war effort by conservation and frugality.

Lee S. McCollester, president of the General Convention in 1917, called for renewed efforts to spread the ideas and principles of the church. "If Universalism had been practiced there would have been no war, and, after the guns are stacked, if the philosophy of Universalism shall not spread, there shall be no permanent peace."[106]

Hundreds of Universalists enrolled for both domestic and overseas service in the military or some related activity, and support for the war effort replaced efforts at social service and reform at home. In the course of gathering data for his book on Universalist social attitudes and action, Emerson H. Lalone sent out questionnaires to all ministers about the nature and extent of their participation in the conflict. Of the fifty-five who replied, ten had been in military service, six had served in the Red Cross, four were chaplains, and twenty-six were on "home service" as Liberty Bond salespeople, workers in relief agencies, and the like. Only six reported no war service of any kind, and three were pacifists.[107] Many returned from the war disillusioned, experiencing the let-down that thousands of others underwent as they lived through post-war readjustments and watched with foreboding the rise of totalitarianism in the 1930s.

But even the dislocations of World War I and the disillusionment following it failed to dampen the Universalist desire to do their part in healing its wounds and bringing about a better world. Best known of all was George E. Huntley; through his leadership of the General Sunday School Association almost $75,000 was raised between 1918 and 1921 for the relief of Armenian war victims. He had visited the Near East as part of an American interchurch delegation and had returned more convinced than ever that links could be forged between the children of America and those of another part of the world.

Other Universalists who did their part in the Near East Relief organization until it officially came to an end in 1929 were Ruth Woodis of Worcester, Massachusetts, the first to answer the appeal for assistance and who worked in Harpoot, central Turkey; Inez Webster of Galesburg, Illinois, who spent three years in Syria and worked at Sidon in an orphanage for girls; and Henry Murphy of Lawrence, Massachusetts, who directed young people's work in Beirut.[108] Little more than a decade later, Universalists were appealing for aid to relieve the plight of Jewish refugee children.[109]

It was estimated that in the thirteen years between 1916 and 1929

Universalists contributed *almost a quarter of a million dollars* to Near East Relief alone.¹¹⁰ Much came from Sunday school offerings and collections from "orphan's plates" in which contributions were made in Universalist homes at mealtime. A contribution of $60 a year provided for the "adoption" of an orphan.

The decade after World War I was a tumultuous one in American history, marked by a shift from idealism to disillusionment, a resurgence of isolationism and nationalism which took the form of super-Americanism, a renewed drive for conformity, a fear of radicalism in any guise, and a growing disparity in American values. This was illustrated by an upsurge of political and religious fundamentalism as a counterbalance to liberalism, progressivism, the findings of Darwinian science, and modernism in religion.¹¹¹ This was the decade of the most restrictive immigration legislation in American history, the Red Scare, the Sacco-Vanzetti case, the revival of the Ku Klux Klan, and the Scopes trial in Tennessee. The last mentioned event, which took on many aspects of a circus, pitted William Jennings Bryan, personifying the traditional allegiance to a Biblically-centered Protestantism, against Clarence Darrow, apostle of intellectual freedom and champion of the findings of modern science (and of Unitarian heritage).

One of the better known social and religious phenomena of the post-World War I period was the revival of the Ku Klux Klan, a secret organization which had been organized originally in Tennessee in 1866 to combat Northern-dominated political power in the South during the period following the Civil War and to restore white supremacy. Although the organization was formally dissolved in 1869, the anti-Negro feeling on which the Klan capitalized had continued to exist, and it had been revived in 1915 and had reached its maximum numerical strength during the early 1920s, claiming more than 4,000,000 members. By then it had become widely known for its crusades not only against Negroes but against Roman Catholics, Jews, and liberal immigration policies. It had become a full-fledged nativist movement.

Universalists in general opposed both its principles and its practices, which included intimidation and acts of violence as well as anti-internationalism and anti-Darwinism. The Klan had become such a controversial subject by 1924–25 that almost an entire issue of the *Leader* was devoted to a discussion of it.¹¹² Some recommended ignoring the organization; a few defended it; the overwhelming majority of Universalists who expressed their views unalterably opposed the Klan and the ideas for which it stood. The Klan was particularly strong in Indiana, and Harry A. Hersey, pastor in Muncie, was horrified to discover Klansmen in his own congregation.

The presence of the Klan was brought directly home to Boston-area Universalists when the pastor of the Medford Hillside Universalist Church, Charles E. Clark, welcomed a contingent of robed and hooded Klansmen to a Sunday evening service in the fall of 1924. The event was greeted with a sarcastic editorial in the *Leader*, based on an account in a Boston newspaper, labelling the Klansmen's appearance as a publicity stunt in the poorest of taste.[113]

The eipsode elicited several defenses of Clark for having put into practice "the love, tolerance, charity and Christian kindness" so much emphasized by Universalists. One correspondent demanded an apology from the *Leader* for impugning the pastor, and another felt that he had been dealt with unjustly.[114] One indignant woman cancelled her subscription because of the "hateful" way the paper had attacked the Klan.[115] To her way of thinking, the rules of the organization were "clean, good, and based upon the eternal verities of nature and revelation." Most of the members of the Boston Universalist Ministers Association felt quite differently, and met a few weeks after the appearance of the Klan in Medford to act on a resolution condemning the spirit and actions of the organization as "diametrically opposite to that of the Universalist Church in its endeavor to serve the common welfare in the spirit of Jesus."

Clark, who was present at the meeting, vigorously defended the Klan, insisting that the accusations levelled at it as anti-Catholic, anti-Semitic, and anti-Negro were not true, and were based on ignorance and misunderstanding. Instead, he insisted that it was "a great Christian Crusade. It has brought more men to the cross of Christ in the last four years than all the evangelists combined."[116] He carefully refrained from indicating whether or not he himself belonged to the Klan but did aver that it was "a good enough organization for hundreds of members of the Universalist Church in New England." Clark admitted that he had joined the church only recently and might be considered an "alien" because he had not grown up in a Universalist family or been educated in a denominational school. He had, in fact, been originally fellowshipped in 1919 by the Alabama Convention and had transferred to the Massachusetts jurisdiction in December 1922 from Camp Hill.[117]

The pastor in question had also anticipated the possibility that he might "be turned out of the Universalist Church" although he would always remain a Universalist in sympathy and belief. His arguments in favor of the Klan were sufficiently persuasive to result in a postponement of action on the condemnatory resolution until more information could be obtained about the Klan and its "actual social effects." At the next meeting of the ministers the topic for discussion was the educational level of Universalist clergy; no mention was recorded about the matter of the Klan and the proposed resolution condemning it.

But the episode at the church was far from over. At its annual meeting in the spring of 1925, with approximately 125 persons present, a substantially new slate of officers was elected, many of whom were either members of the Klan or sympathetic to Clark.[118] The congregation was so badly divided that some of the older members who had participated in the establishment of the church in 1896, announced their intention of attending elsewhere but retaining their voting membership in case the church was forced to disband. Clark was reported by a Boston newspaper to have said that "A man who is eligible for membership in the Ku Klux Klan and does not join is not a good American." Such assertions soon brought an end to Clark's pastorate and the church recovered its equilibrium without disbanding.[119]

In an address delivered at the Community Church in 1927 entitled "The Drive Against Liberalism in America," Clarence R. Skinner cited some of the more obvious and graphic examples of the anti-liberal hysteria which swept over America in the 1920s and which occurred specifically within the Greater Boston area.[120] He singled out particularly the attacks on efforts to achieve world peace and internationalism, and the allegations that various individuals and organizations were communistic, communist-inspired by Russia, or otherwise subversive. Among the examples he listed were the attempt to discredit the Fellowship of Youth for Peace in Concord; the attempt of the Veterans of Foreign Wars to silence Mrs. Lucia Ames Mead, a speaker in the interests of world peace and member of the Woman's International League for Peace and Freedom; the labelling of the Boston building which housed the offices of the Community Church and other organizations as the Communist headquarters in Massachusetts; the work of the Industrial Defense Association organized 'to inculcate the principle of Americanism' which charged some 250 societies and organizations with "such diverse crimes as pacifism and communism"; and attacks on Jane Addams and on the American Civil Liberties Union for alleged subversion of one kind or another. It was high time, said Skinner, for liberals "to stand and fight together for justice and truth."

In the 1950s and 1960s, more than a quarter of a century after Skinner had cited these examples, the same battle had to be fought again "for justice and truth." After World War II the "battle for the maintenance of traditional civil liberties and the protection of the dignity and freedom of the individual citizen [was] second in importance only to the international struggle of the cold war."[121] It was "a critical testing period for . . . democratic idealism," and religious liberals were among the casualties.

This time the setting was what has been called the McCarthy Era in which attacks on Russian communism and those thought to be associated with or sympathetic to it in the United States reached hysterical proportions. The word "McCarthyism" even entered the American language and the dictionary, which described it as "the political practice of publicizing accusations of disloyalty or subversion with insufficient regard to evidence."

Among the numerous government organizations associated with

McCarthy's probes into alleged communist (subversive) influences were a series of Congressional investigating committees intended to root out threats to patriotism and national security. One crusade to save America was conducted by the Velde Committee which, among other things, attacked Protestant clergy for having communist connections of some sort. Five ministers in the Boston area, three of whom had either Universalist or Unitarian associations, were singled out for special attention. They were suspected of subversion, with no evidence to support the allegation, but were nonetheless identified in the public press. None was ever offered the opportunity to defend himself. To make matters worse, the heads of neither the Universalist nor Unitarian denominations came to the defense of the individuals suspected. This was, in the eyes of Kenneth Patton, minister of the Charles Street Universalist Meeting House in Boston, evidence of "the bankruptcy of leadership in the liberal church."[122] Sometimes Universalists had difficulty in living up to the ideals they professed.[123]

Arbitration of disputes among nations rather than resort to war was advocated by most Universalists and was reflected over many decades in resolutions adopted by the denomination. One of the first such expressions had come in 1875, a few years after political unification had been accomplished in both Germany and Italy, accompanied by a resurgence of nationalism over most of Europe.[124] Universalists encouraged the United States government in 1889 not only to negotiate treaties with other nations to settle or prevent disputes, but to build into such treaties a provision for arbitration of differences.[125] In the same year, Alonzo A. Miner attended the International Peace Congress in Paris which had as its theme the use of arbitration, and Mrs. Amanda Deyo of Oxford, New York, attended as a representative of both the Union for Universal Peace and the Woman's Centenary Association (Universalist).[126]

The denomination joined with others in a petition in 1893 addressed to world leaders on behalf of world peace, and there were three Universalist representatives appointed to a peace conference held in connection with the World's Columbian Exposition that year.[127] When the Senate Committee on Foreign Relations was considering a treaty providing for unlimited arbitration, Universalists gave their "unqualified approval" and were urged to write their senators accordingly.[128]

After World War I was over, Universalists engaged, together with other denominations, in a renewed effort to secure world peace.[129] There was such a feeling of revulsion against war that the *Leader* recommended that new hymnbooks omit the widely used "Onward Christian Soldiers" because its militaristic title and wording were completely inappropriate for a denomination standing for peace and brotherhood.[130]

The General Convention called for Senate ratification of United States membership in the League of Nations. The convention repeatedly urged American entrance into the World Court and the support of "every effort towards causing war to be recognized as a crime in international law." War was declared to be "a denial of the basic principles of the fatherhood of God and the brotherhood of man. . . . a violation of the Christian religion."[131]

The Christ Crusade undertaken by Universalists after World War I was intended, besides strengthening the denomination, "to promote peace, outlaw war, exact respect for law and secure through co-operation with other religious forces throughout the world a nobler brotherhood."[132] A denominational Commission on World Peace was authorized by the General Convention in 1923. However, instead of creating yet another agency, the name of the existing Commission on Foreign Affairs was enlarged to include "World Peace."[133] The commission was given a mandate to adopt "a ringing resolution" against war and was urged to put the denomination "in the lead in the movement sweeping the country for peace."[134]

Shortly after the commission was created the General Conference of the Methodist Church adopted a peace platform which the members of the Universalist commission considered "perhaps the most comprehensive platform upon which all Christians can enthusiastically unite."[135] The newly created commission announced their acceptance of the Methodist platform "as their own" and urged the trustees of the General Convention to respond to the invitation extended by the Methodists to participate in a world-wide conference 'to consider the best plans and methods for making the impact of united Christendom against the evils we deplore.' The Methodist peace platform expressed the determination to 'outlaw the whole war system' and challenged the nation to lead the way in a 'crusade for peace.'

When a statement renouncing war as an instrument of national policy (which became the Kellogg-Briand Pact of 1928) was under discussion, the General Convention memorialized both the president of the United States and the Senate by not only supporting the proposed pact but by urging that the words "except for defense in case of attack" be stricken out.[136] In short, even defensive war was renounced.

Even though the General Convention admitted that its attempts seemed "very small and our efforts futile," the ends sought were considered so desirable and vital that the agitation should be continued; even a "Universalist Statement Concerning World Peace" was suggested.[137] Unfortunately, the Commission on Foreign Affairs and World Peace could actually do little in a tangible way because it was unable to hold meetings. On a budget of $100 in 1928, correspondence was the only possible medium of communication.[138]

Universalists did, however, send as many representatives as they could afford to meetings promoting world peace. F. O. Hall attended a conference in Prague, Czechoslovakia, of the World Alliance for Promoting International Friendship from the Church as well as a meeting of the Church Peace Union in Geneva, Switzerland, to plan for a Universal Religious Peace Conference in 1930.[139] Universalists were among the representatives from some twenty denominations who attended a series of study conferences on the Churches and World Peace held at various locations in the United States.[140]

The General Convention urged Senate ratification, without reservations, of the General Treaty of Inter-American Arbitration (the Pan American Arbitration Treaty) signed in 1929. The central denominational body likewise supported international disarmament conferences, arguing that nations should "gradually cease reliance upon instruments of war to promote peace."[141]

When news of the persecution of Jews in Germany began to filter in, the General Convention expressed sympathy for the "unfortunate victims of racial and economic prejudice," condemned totalitarianism, and reaffirmed faith in democracy.[142] At the 1941 meeting a strong resolution was unanimously adopted opposing anti-Semitism in the name of world brotherhood and the principles of Universalism.

During the 1930s a wave of anti-war sentiment swept over the nation, generally supported by the churches. In a nationwide questionnaire circulated in 1931 more than 200 Universalist and Unitarian clergy recorded their belief that churches should refuse to sanction or support any future war or participate individually as combatants.[143] Another poll of clergy was taken in 1934 to which 35 percent of the Universalist and Unitarian clergy responded. The great majority supported the League of Nations in spite of the fact that by the early 1930s it had faltered badly in achieving the purposes for which it had been created. More than 80 percent opposed compulsory military training in public high schools and colleges.[144]

At the height of the anti-war movement Universalists pledged to present, with other denominations, "a common front [to] outlaw and banish war."[145] But when it came down to specifics, Universalists themselves were unable to agree. There was a split vote at the 1939 convention over whether it was the duty of individual Universalists to go to war. Should or should not they have a part "in the killing of our brother men"?[146] Many persons had to wrestle with their consciences over this.

The first official action taken by the denomination after war broke out in Europe in 1939 was to create an Emergency War Relief Committee in 1940 in order to cooperate with existing agencies such as the Red Cross, and to donate $1,000.[147] Between 1941 and 1943 the Universalists managed to contribute slightly more than $10,000; even that amount was less than half of what had been requested.[148]

Isolationist sentiment among Universalists was undeniably present, but it played no key role in determining official policy. In fact, J. M. Atwood, dean of the Canton Theological School, took the opposite stand. Even before the Japanese attack on Pearl Harbor, Hawaii, in December 1941, he denounced isolationism as "the most selfish, contemptible kind of nationalism" and told the 1941 General Convention that it was the Christian duty of Americans to employ force if necessary to stop Nazi aggression.[149] This rather bellicose statement reflected a complete reversal of Atwood's earlier position — that he would "never sanction or support any war in which America might be engaged." When confronted with this obvious turn-about in his thinking, he explained that "duty is always relative, with reference to some particular problem — not absolute."

Just as soon as war had been declared against Japan and the existence of a state of war with Germany and Italy had been recognized, the trustees of the General Convention issued a statement pledging loyalty and "unswerving support . . . to the winning of the war."[150] A service flag flew from denominational headquarters in Boston, beginning in 1943, and before the end of hostilities more than 5,000 Universalist men and women were known to have been in the armed forces.[151] A total of approximately thirty clergy served as chaplains in the army and navy, some holding dual fellowship.[153] There was much discussion about the advisability of holding the biennial meeting at all in 1943 in view of travel and other wartime restrictions, but government permission was obtained and the sessions took place in New York City.[154]

Determined to do what they could to promote a durable peace after World War II was over, Universalists established a Commission on World Order in 1947 and pledged cooperation with the parallel Unitarian commission and any other such agency, regardless of denominational connection.[155] However, the Commission's duties overlapped those of the existing Peace Committee (a sub-committee of the Commission on Social Action), so all related activities were consolidated and reorganized as the World Order Commission under three divisional heads: Peace Action, Inter-Faith, and Human Rights.[156] The denomination continued to participate in the meetings of the International Association for Religious Freedom and official delegates were sent to the meetings in Oxford, England in 1952 and in Belfast, Ireland, in 1954.[157]

Resolutions were adopted supporting the United Nations. The federal government was urged to admit up to 400,000 displaced persons over a four-year period. Universalists were the first American denomination to make an offer of assistance in the resettlement and rehabilitation of Jewish refugees from Egypt and Eastern Europe.[158]

Adopting resolutions outlawing war and promoting world peace, and attending and participating in organizations to further such ends were all very well. But taking a personal stand as a pacifist or conscientious objector was quite another matter. It was very much an individual decision that might and could bring blanket condemnation, even social ostracism, and a curbing of civil rights.[159] And then there was the problem of defining and setting the boundaries and limits of pacifistic thought and action.[160] Was it "pure, absolute, and uncompromising," as was the case with Clarence R. Skinner, Universalist social thinker and reformer, and William W. Rose, prominent pastor of the Universalist church in Lynn, Massachusetts?[161] Would opposition to war extend to all circumstances, including participation in a war to defend one's homeland? There were all gradations of pacifism.

Almost as soon as the determination had been made in the early 1920s to outlaw "the whole war system," a related question arose. Should opposition to war be carried a step further by committing either churches or individuals to a stand against participation in any war under any circumstances, whether aggressive or defensive? The result was a difference of opinion among Universalists, as indicated at the General Convention meeting in 1923, when an unsuccessful attempt was made to secure, for the first time, official endorsement and protection for conscientious objectors.

One of the first prominent Universalists to express himself on the entire subject was Shutter, who offered the judgment that the committing of any denomination to an all-or-nothing stand would be divisive if not fatal.[162] Shutter flatly disavowed any linkage between non-resistance and Christianity as propounded by the Unitarian Universalist Adin Ballou in 1846.[163] They were in no sense synonymous. Refusal of the call to service by the state was an individual matter in which the church should not be used as a defense merely because it had committed itself in advance. Further, there were too many kinds of wars to justify an uncompromising commitment for the future, and no unilateral declaration would guarantee that all others would do likewise.

Defenders of conscientious objection were more successful in 1925 than they had been two years earlier. At the General Convention meeting a resolution was presented from the floor by L. Griswold Williams of Reading, Pennsylvania, which elicited considerable reaction. It called for a recognition that, in accord with its fundamental principles, members of the Universalist Church had "the right to refuse on conscientious grounds to participate in any warfare."[164] This was based on an interpretation of Universalist allegiance to the 'spiritual authority and leadership of Jesus' to mean "a complete condemnation and renunciation of violence between nations as well as between individuals, operative even in time of warfare itself." After a series of parliamentary maneuvers, the convention supported the resolution by a vote of 80 to 53 after an unsuccessful attempt was made to refer it to the trustees for consideration.

The resolution recognized the right of every Universalist "to follow the voice of conscience" regarding participation in future wars.[165] The fight on behalf of the resolution was led by Richard McLaughlin of Hartford, Connecticut, a veteran of World War I and a member of the Officers Reserve Corps.

One indignant Universalist who had sold Liberty Bonds during World War I and who misunderstood the General Convention resolutions, condemned as "yellow" all objectors to war on grounds of conscience.[166] The editor of the *Leader* made haste to point out that the resolution did not commit the denomination to a pacifist position at all, but only affirmed the right of all individuals to follow their own conscience. "No Protestant Christian body can take any other attitude." Edwin C. Sweetser said that he would "never lift a hand in war" although his own son had served as an aviator in Italy during World War I. Sweetser disagreed with his son but supported "his right and every man's right to follow his own sense of duty."[167] The perturbation that had resulted from the adoption of the resolution was the very reason that the same resolution had been voted down in 1923; many feared that, if adopted, it would be misinterpreted as denominational endorsement of non-resistance.

The question of the status of conscientious objectors within the denomination did not surface again until 1931. An effort was made that year to turn the resolution of 1925 into an amendment to the church's constitution in order to make the official support of Universalists available to conscientious objectors in time of war.[168] The General Convention did not follow precisely that course but, instead, referred the matter to the Committee on Revision of the Laws of Fellowship for later report. But it did approve the principle that the "allegiance to the spiritual authority and leadership of Jesus [was] to be interpreted by its members as their consciences may direct with particular reference to refusal of military service at any time on conscientious grounds."[169] The General Convention also sided with Douglas Macintosh, on the faculty of the Yale Divinity School, who brought suit in the federal courts because he was denied naturalized citizenship for refusal to bear arms in any war declared by Congress.[170]

Conscientious objectors were again given official recognition by the denomination when a new Article XIII was added to the Laws of Fellowship in 1933. It provided that "fellowship in this Convention shall confer the right to interpret the general purpose and spirit of the Universalist faith as sanctioning refusal of all forms of military service if such refusal be based on conscientious grounds."[171] The secretary of the General Convention was then instructed to request the federal government to hand down an interpretation which would safeguard the conscientious objector in this position; and if not to ask what action was necessary to create such safeguards. The purpose was to give them the same legal status as afforded to Quakers, and was strongly supported by Lalone, who had himself served in the military during World War I.[172]

There ensued a prolonged and inconclusive correspondence between the Universalists and the federal government, which refused to make any commitment or give any assurance to protect conscientious objectors during wartime.[173] The Universalists even appealed directly to President Roosevelt but were merely referred to other federal agencies. After an unsuccessful appeal to the office of the Attorney General, the War Department finally responded (in 1935) that "while the Constitution of the United States guarantees every citizen certain liberties, it also gives the Congress the right to raise armies and to prescribe the rules and conditions under which voluntary or compulsory service are [sic] to be rendered by citizens." Hence, in the event of a national emergency, the War Department would be governed by whatever laws were enacted by Congress. The General Secretary concluded that the matter could be settled only by court decision in case of war.[174]

But the Universalists were not satisfied with such an ambivalent reply, and in 1939 asserted that "the Christian's highest allegiance is to the law of God and not to the decrees of man."[175] It followed, by this reasoning, that the rights of the conscientious objector should be reaffirmed, and the General Convention instructed its secretary "to so inform the President and the Secretary of State of the United States." General Superintendent Robert Cummins called for "a ringing pronouncement telling the world that, should the United States be dragged into this heinous war, a Universalist refusing to take up arms against a fellow being shall remain a member of the Universalist Church *in good standing*."[176] Students at the Canton Theological School, by "a large majority," voted that they would "not support any war engaged in by the United States."[177]

The outbreak of World War II precipitated a lively debate among Universalists over preparedness, the legitimacy of war, and the role of the individual in it. A small but active group of pacifists emerged. Emerson S. Schwenk, pastor in Bridgeport, Connecticut, made his pacifist views abundantly clear to his congregation in 1940, announcing that he would register as the Selective Service Act required, but would refuse to participate in any military activity in any form.[178] He considered the placing of a service flag in the church to be a symbol of war which he abhorred, and resigned in protest when one was installed.[179] A register of conscientious objectors was established in 1940 at denominational headquarters at the request of the Vermont and Quebec Unitarian Universalist Ministers' Association, and within three months twenty-two were on the list.[180]

After the Selective Service Act was enacted in 1940 eight theological students at Union Theological Seminary refused to register, even though their status would have exempted them from military service. Each was sentenced to a prison term of a year and a day. Two of the eight were from Tufts, although neither was a student in the Crane Theological School.[181] However, Universalist theological students at Tufts did organize an Adin

Ballou Pacifist Fellowship in 1941; fifteen had signed up by the fall of 1941.[182] The Fellowship disappeared temporarily when the war was over but was reactivated in 1946.[183] During the General Convention meeting in 1941 thirty ministers and their wives drew up and signed a pledge "to refuse to participate in or give moral support to war."[184] Several other Universalist clergy and/or ministerial students were also affiliated with the Fellowship of Reconciliation, an interdenominational peace organization.

At the 1941 General Convention meeting there was much debate over a recommendation that would have not only reaffirmed the right of conscientious objectors to denominational fellowship but would have provided financial assistance to those enrolled in work camps as an alternative to regular military service.[185] When the revised Laws of Fellowship were adopted in 1943 the provision granting full fellowship to conscientious objectors in time of war was unanimously adopted (129-0), and some financial support was provided.[186]

Conscientious objectors had to pay $35 a month while serving in work camps, and in 1943 the Social Service Commission requested the General Assembly to appropriate up to $500 for a two-year period to assist those unable to pay.[187] There was some bitterness expressed by those who had sons and relatives in regular military service, but the recommendation was adopted.[188] Until the General Assembly took action, some financial aid had been rendered by the Adin Ballou Fellowship.

Robert T. Dick was among those clergy and theological students who waived the deferment or exemption available to them and took his stand as a conscientious objector. Fully cognizant of the consequences, he participated in a variety of non-military assignments, some of which exposed him to considerable risk to his health and general welfare. After serving in a facility for the mentally ill in Brattleboro, Vermont, he completed a ten-month voluntary experiment in dieting at a hospital in Rochester, New York, for the Office of Scientific Research and Development; spent two months in a heat and dehydration experiment; and volunteered for tests at the University of Rochester on the effects of high altitude on the human system.[189]

The General Assembly continued long after 1945 to express anti-military and anti-war views, and to defend conscientious objectors. It protested the fact that the latter were being held in service for many months after the cessation of hostilities, and called for immediate, blanket amnesty for the estimated 900 still in federal prisons. It urged the restoration of the full civil rights of those already released.[190] The General Assembly called for resistance to all threats to personal liberty because of individual conscience, claiming that conscience was superior to the demands of the state.[191] The denomination opposed the continuation of the Selective Service Act in peacetime as "an extension of militarism into the post war life of the United States."[192] Sometimes the resolutions were inadvertently quite contradictory. In 1946 it opposed military training in peacetime but in the very next declaration demanded that military strength be "maintained commensurate with our world responsibility and leadership."[193]

Not one of the resolutions condemning universal peacetime military service was ever passed unanimously, although the proportion was usually about 2 to 1.[194] The Universalists likewise opposed the government practice of employing "belief in a Supreme Being" as a test of religious objection to military training or service. This was challenged on the ground that it was an exclusive test of religious conviction. The legislative body called, instead, for the recognition of "the broadly religious implications of social and philosophical objections to war."[195]

The devastation wrought by the atomic bombs dropped on Japan and the potential for even greater destruction on a world-wide scale brought one resolution after another from the General Assembly calling for cancellation of tests and for the international control of atomic energy.[196] A Liberal Religious Peace Fellowship opposing the testing of atomic bombs was organized in the 1950s, appealing primarily to Universalists and Unitarians. After Unitarian-Universalist consolidation had taken place another registry for conscientious objectors was established at national headquarters by trustee action.[197] Thus the denominational commitment to world brotherhood rather than to fratricide continued to be confirmed, whether the rest of the world adhered or not.

Chapter 26

Clarence R. Skinner and the Social Gospel

Much of the social concern felt by Universalists was embodied in the "Social Gospel" movement which appeared in America at the end of the nineteenth century and reached its fullest expression on the eve of World War I. Although never formally organized, lacking a progammatic base, and exhibiting a wide variety of forms and expression, it originated as an attempt, basically among Protestant churches, to ameliorate the lot of the industrial wage-earner in a rapidly urbanizing nation, and to attempt to attract them to churches ostensibly dominated by the employing classes. By heightening both individual and social conscience and creating awareness of the social and economic evils of the day, the movement was intended to bring about a bright, new, and untarnished civilization. Sometimes known as "applied" or "social" Christianity, many of its proponents veered off into a version of Christian (non-Marxist) socialism, at the heart of which was an attempt to mitigate some of the rigors of what was conceived to be exploitative capitalism.

Social Christianity was premised on the assumption, articulated by Universalist clergyman A. B. Hervey in the early 1880s, that poverty and other social ills were not misfortunes without a remedy but the result of ascertainable causes which could be identified and removed by human effort.[1] Moral judgments played no major part if needs were to be met, and theological considerations were to be subordinated to social action. It was an eminently optimistic movement, replete with confidence in human ability to solve social, economic, and political problems.[2]

Among the leaders of the Social Gospel movement were Washington Gladden (1836–1918), minister of the First Congregational Church in Columbus, Ohio; and Walter Rauschenbusch (1861–1918), a Baptist who became nationally prominent with three major works: *Christianity and the*

Social Crisis (1907), *Christianizing the Social Order* (1812), and *A Theology for the Social Gospel* (1917). Christian socialism was advocated by such individuals as George D. Herron (1862–1926), an Episcopal minister in Boston.

In order to educate middle- and upper-class Americans who usually had no direct contact with or knowledge of the problems of the industrial laborer, churches all over the nation organized study groups to discuss industrial problems, created committees or commissions to deal with social issues, and produced, besides great quantities of literature dealing with such questions, platforms and statements of principles and policy. They frequently dealt with much broader issues than those of the industrial laborer alone.

The Federal (later National) Council of Churches was organized in 1908, with its primary concern the problem of how to deal most effectively with urban and industrial problems. The Methodist Episcopal Church was one of the earliest religious bodies to formulate a social service platform. In 1907 it presented an eleven-point statement of principles which was adopted by the thirty-four member Federal Council the following year without a dissenting vote and with only minor verbal changes.[3] The declaration was further refined, developed, and adopted by the Baptist, Presbyterian, and Unitarian churches in 1910 and 1911. The AUA had already established in 1908 both a Department of Social Reform and Public Service, and a Fellowship for Social Justice. The Universalist General Convention recommended at its biennial session in 1909 the creation of a Commission on Social Service to act on behalf of the entire church. The commission was made permanent in 1911. The trustees initially chose Frank Oliver Hall of New York City as Chairman, and he, together with Frederic W. Perkins and O. P. Briggs, immediately set about the complex task of educating themselves and the denomination regarding the best means by which Universalists could contribute to social reform and social betterment on many fronts.

Because none of the committee appointed in 1911 considered themselves sufficiently knowledgeable on the subject, they turned to those with both expertise and practical experience. They soon discovered that the work contemplated was altogether too large to be undertaken by a single committee.[4] They therefore enlisted the support of others and worked out a rough division of labor. They obtained the volunteer services of Levi M. Powers of Haverhill, Massachusetts, a layman at the time, to review the rapidly proliferating professional literature and to make recommendations. Powers was described "not so much a book worm as a boa-constrictor, who swallows books by the shelf full and has a supernormal faculty of digesting them, contents, paper, ink, binding and date of publication." Powers used both personal correspondence and the columns of the *Leader* to recommend background sources, particularly for ministers in the field.[5]

Levi M. Powers (1864-1920) at his desk in Somerville, Massachusetts in the 1890s

For those preparing for the ministry L. M. Bristol, on the faculty of Tufts College, inaugurated two courses in sociology for theological students which became a regular part of the curriculum. He also arranged a course of lectures on "Social Christianity and the Development of Scientific Christian Philanthropy" which would contribute to the training of prospective ministers for service in their communities.

Another resource tapped by the commission comprised the numerous men's clubs and Laymen's Leagues which had been organized in churches and which had heretofore performed, like many church women's organizations, mostly social functions. They were encouraged to support special projects in their communities; e.g., the establishment of "a more just relationship between employers and employed." Personnel were recruited by the commission for both men's and women's organizations. Mrs. Marion D. Shutter of Minneapolis was delegated to carry the message to women in the denomination. There were also opportunities for cooperation through the YPCU, which had a commission of its own. Individual churches and Sunday schools were also encouraged to discuss social questions. John van Schaick of the Washington, D.C. church was put in charge of coordinating those activities in special fields in which Universalists were already engaged, such as the problems of child labor, temperance, and tenement house conditions. The *Leader* devoted an entire issue in 1911 to the theme of social action, and Social Service Sunday was added that year to the church calendar.⁶ Arrangements were also made to have the denomination represented at national conferences dealing with such social issues as charities and prison reform.

The commission never lacked grist for its mill. The General Convention in 1911 was flooded with all kinds of resolutions bearing on such issues as temperance, women's suffrage, scientific agriculture as a part of the training of country ministers, the single tax espoused by Henry George, and innumerable organized charities. They were all referred to the Commission on Social Service for consideration.⁷

The momentum generated by the creation of the commission was immediately sustained. Walter Rauschenbusch of New York, the most prominent exponent of the Social Gospel, spoke at the meeting of the General Convention in 1913 on "The Christianizing of the Social Order," a theme adopted for the next session in 1915. Jane Addams of Chicago, well known for her settlement work at Hull House, was another speaker in 1913.⁸ Several state commissions were created, and parishes were encouraged to do likewise; they were urged to hold "social forums" to discuss public questions. Even the creation of a national Secretaryship for Social Service was recommended.

The year 1915 was a busy one for the Commission on Social Service, operating as it did with voluntary participation and without a paid representative in the field. A Forum Bureau with headquarters in Boston under the chairmanship of Harold Marshall coordinated speaking engagements.⁹ The problem of international peace was uppermost in most people's minds as war spread in Europe, and several Universalists rendered what services they could. Among them was Powers, who journeyed to Europe as a representative of the Society for Removing the Economic Causes of War.

The problem of unemployment was addressed by a Universalist layman on the Mayor's Committee on Unemployment in New York City, and by two Universalist clergymen: Perkins, who was president of the Charity Organization of Lynn, Massachusetts, which contributed extensively to local relief; and Charles Conklin, Massachusetts state superintendent, who served as chairman of the legislative committee of the Federation of Churches in Massachusetts. But of all the members of the Social Service Commission it was the secretary, appointed in 1910, who became best known as an exponent of the Social Gospel in its broadest reaches, and within the context of the church to which he belonged. It was Clarence Russell Skinner who took the Social Gospel beyond the bounds of Protestantism and attempted to apply its precepts to all of humankind.

Skinner (1881–1949) was born in Brooklyn, New York, on 23 March 1881, with a long line of Universalist clergy and laity in his religious background.¹⁰ His father was Charles M. Skinner, editor of the *Brooklyn*

Clarence Russell Skinner (1881-1949), prophet of the social gospel

Eagle and his mother was Ada Blanchard Skinner. He was the grandson of Charles Skinner; great-grandson of Warren Skinner; and the great-nephew of Dolphus Skinner — all clergymen. Another clerical relative had been Otis Ainsworth Skinner, who had been the agent to raise the first $100,000 to establish Tufts; and in a later day, Otis Augustus Skinner, a Universalist layman and actor of some renown to whom Tufts awarded an honorary degree in 1895.[11]

He attended public schools in Brooklyn, where he was interested particularly in public speaking, debating, and dramatics, all of which remained lifetime interests. He enrolled in 1900 in St. Lawrence University and remained a campus leader throughout his undergraduate years. He attended that institution not only because it had Universalist origins and long-standing associations, but because the president, Almon Gunnison was a close friend of the family. Immediately after his graduation in 1904 Skinner became assistant to Hall, pastor of the Church of the Divine Paternity in New York City. Skinner was ordained to the Universalist ministry in 1905 without having sought a theological degree although he subsequently took graduate courses at both Columbia and Harvard, attended the Boston School of Social Workers, and received an MA from his alma mater in 1910.

It was during his first pastorate, in Mount Vernon, New York, beginning in 1906, that he became involved in settlement house work in metropolitan New York. In that year he married Clara L. Ayres of Stamford, Connecticut. While ministering to the Mount Vernon church he organized the first meeting of New York City clergy; the group eventually became the Church Peace Union. He moved in 1910 to Grace Universalist Church in Lowell, Massachusetts, where he organized a successful forum on public issues. It was from this post that he was called to the Crane Theological School faculty at Tufts in 1914 as Professor of Applied Christianity, at the age of thirty-three. While serving on the Tufts faculty he was also involved in denominational affairs in Massachusetts. He served in 1918 as chairman of the Commission on Social Welfare of the state convention, followed by two years as its president.

From 1933 until his retirement in 1945 he was dean of the theological school and carried an exceptionally heavy teaching load in addition to his administrative duties. His educational and religious leadership was recognized beyond the Tufts campus. A year after his appointment to the deanship he became a candidate for the presidency of St. Lawrence but withdrew his name from consideration.[12]

Controversy swirled about Skinner during his long tenure at Tufts, and relations were often strained with the majority of his colleagues for his determined and unrelenting pacifism and his support of unpopular causes. With few exceptions they shunned him, as did most of his fellow clergy. McCollester, dean of the theological school, was one of Skinner's strongest supporters and defenders — not because he agreed with all of Skinner's ideas, but because he respected Skinner's integrity and honesty. In the course of recommending Skinner as his successor to the deanship, McCollester called him "a natural crusader [who] has been criticized at times because he set his lance at too many lost causes" but defended his colleague for his unswerving devotion to high social ideals.[13]

President John A. Cousens of Tufts quietly supported Skinner during both world wars, not so much because he agreed with Skinner but because he respected a person of conviction and because he believed strongly in the principle of freedom of speech and expression. In the summer of 1918 Skinner was even grilled by six of his senior colleagues who called upon him to defend himself and to explain and justify his various pronouncements and actions, many of which were thought to be an embarrassment to the college and prejudicial to its interests. He made it clear that he was not a Marxian socialist but a believer in "collective democracy" who deprecated the socialist appeal to class consciousness and class antagonism. As to his pacifism, he insisted that he greatly admired President Woodrow Wilson for keeping the ideals of war aims "on a high plane" but refused to accept war as a means of achieving these ideals. He pointed to the influence of his mother who had a Quaker's hatred of war. Skinner vehemently denied any attempt on his part to dissuade any individual from obeying the government during wartime, and willingly supported such measures as food conservation and the sale of Liberty Bonds.

Even before he had joined the Tufts faculty he had made his views crystal clear on peace, civil liberties, and the prevailing economic and social system, and maintained them throughout his life. As a confirmed pacifist he had already, by 1910, expressed his opposition to war. In that year he called on Universalists to spearhead "an almighty crusade by the Christian Church against war" and recommended that a "Peace Day" be observed in all churches. Those who wanted war were only "a few benighted legislators and soldiers."[14] By the end of 1915 he had delivered a lecture on the evils of militarism some fifty times before all kinds of church, school, and general audiences.[15] The failure of the United States Senate to approve unlimited arbitration treaties in 1912 he considered "a shameful, treacherous defeat," and the legislative body "un-Christian and unsocial."[16] Skinner supported the right of any Universalist to refuse military service "on the Christian grounds of conscientious objection."[17]

In 1919 he delivered an address at the American Forum in Faneuil Hall in Boston called "America in Crisis." It upset so many that the state attorney general wrote to Cousens calling it to his attention. Skinner had approved the strike of the radical International Workers of the World in Centralia, Illinois, and had called the members of the American Legion "anarchists." Skinner spoke in 1920 at the First Congregational Church in Lynn, Massachusetts, on "Industrial Democracy" and predicted that the continued exploitation of labor by employers would bring a class struggle that would eclipse that of the recent war against Germany. Arthur W. Newhall, a Tufts alumnus and officer of the Hood Rubber Company, much upset by the account of Skinner's speech in a local newspaper, objected strenuously to the "stuff" that Skinner was irresponsibly spreading, and expressed doubt that such individuals should be on the Tufts faculty.[18]

Skinner, active in the American Civil Liberties Union which had been founded in 1920, became much interested in the case of Nicola Sacco and Bartolomeo Vanzetti, two immigrant anarchists who were accused of murdering a paymaster and guard at a shoe factory in South Braintree, Massachusetts. They were convicted in 1921 on what some thought was flimsy evidence, and by 1927, when they were executed as convicted criminals, had become a center of national controversy. When the case first attracted public attention in 1921 Skinner called for dispassionate consideration of all the facts rather than following the sensationalism of an inflamed public opinion exacerbated by the press.[19] Before the prolonged trial was over, Skinner became convinced of the innocence of the two men, and never retreated. One of his many arguments against capital punishment was the potential danger of executing the innocent.[20] To the very end he maintained his faith in "rational humanity" and his confidence in the American legal tradition of presumption of innocence until proved otherwise.

A dedicated and enthusiastic teacher, Skinner magnetized and inspired generations of students and created a large and loyal following probably unmatched by any other individual in the history of the theological school. His contributions were recognized by an honorary D.Litt. awarded by Tufts in 1945. This degree took its place beside an honorary DD from the Meadville Theological School in 1926 and a second DD in 1933 which he received from his alma mater, of which he had been a trustee for five years.

When his retirement in 1945 was announced the Crane Alumni Association immediately determined to have a portrait painted in his honor. Joseph B. Kahill, a Universalist artist from Portland, Maine, executed the work, unveiled in December 1948. Literally hundreds flocked in from far and near to witness the ceremony. John Haynes Holmes, lifelong friend and colleague and co-founder with Skinner of the Community Church in Boston, was the principal speaker. When Skinner died on 27 August 1949 at the age of sixty-eight it was also Holmes who was one of the four selected to pay tribute to him at memorial services at Tufts.

The denomination paid tribute to him by the creation in 1958 by the Massachusetts Convention of the Skinner Award for the most significant sermon of social concern, the idea of Robert Wolley.[21] In 1962 the Unitarian Universalist Ministers Association initially assumed the responsibility for administering the award.[22] One of the buildings comprising the complex of denominational headquarters in Boston was named Skinner House in his honor. These were all indeed tokens of recognition of an individual described as "the most influential Universalist minister of his generation."

Skinner had already begun to earn a name for himself in the denomination at the time of his appointment as secretary of the Social Service Commission in 1910, and as the years went by, with his prolific writings and his passion for social justice, he became the representative, as his bibliographer has stated, of "the best of modern Universalism."[23] Skinner propagated his ideas not only in sermons, addresses, and in the classroom but in seven books of which he was the author, co-author, or editor. He was a constant contributor to the religious press, notably to the denominational *Leader* (first in 1908) and to *Unity*, on the executive board of which he served, beginning in 1921.

The groundwork for Skinner's first book, published in 1915, had been laid by F. O. Hall in *Common People,* which had appeared in 1901;[24] in an occasional sermon in 1909, "The Gospel for an Age of Indifference"; and in an address entitled "A Social Program for the Universalsit Church," delivered in 1911. However, it was Skinner who most fully developed the Universalist version of the Social Gospel.

Feeling that "one of the deepest needs of the denomination" was a statement of the social responsibilities of Universalists, Skinner wrote a series of articles for the *Leader* which were revised and enlarged, and published in book form in 1915 as *The Social Implications of Universalism* which contained most of the elements of Skinner's religious and social philosophy.[25]

After a lapse of more than twenty years Skinner's second book appeared in 1937: *Liberalism Faces the Future.*[26] His third, *Human Nature and the Nature of Evil,* appeared in 1939, and *A Religion for Greatness* was published in 1945 and reprinted in 1958.[27] The final work, *Worship and the Well Ordered Life,* appeared posthumously, comprising three manuscripts which were edited for publication by various colleagues.[28] He was also co-author, with Alfred S. Cole, of *Hell's Ramparts Fell,* a brief biography of John Murray based largely on his autobiography.[29]

Stated as concisely as possible, the Social Gospel "involved a criticism of conventional Protestantism, a progressive theology and social philosophy, and an active program of propagandism and reform."[30] The basic ideas which dominated the movement were the immanence of God, an organic (unified) view of society, a progressive realization of the kingdom of God, and the social teachings of Jesus. Each of these was reflected in Skinner's thought to a striking degree, and the outlines of all of these are discernible in his *Social Implications of Universalism.* The very first sentence summed up the purpose of the Social Gospel movement: "How to transform this old earth into the Kingdom of Heaven — that's the primal question."

Several corollaries or auxiliary themes were imbedded in the whole concept of the Social Gospel: a strong ethical strain; a realistic appraisal of the task of religion in sociological terms which included an awareness of "social sin," most thoroughly developed in Skinner's *Human Nature and the Nature of Evil;* the persistence of crisis and challenge in the environment; and a critique (sometimes severe) of capitalism. Again, Skinner's ideas paralleled these themes to a remarkable degree.

Religion, to Skinner, went far beyond the confines of traditional Christianity to become "a spiritual interpretation of the whole of life," providing "insight into the unities and universals" — the true meaning of Universalism. Skinner's expression of the unity of all humankind sometimes reached mystical proportions. "We are of the substance of all that is or ever has been, of ancient stars, of living soils, and immortal spirits . . . All that prophets have dreamed, that poets have seen, that builders have wrought have come to us in this hour of life."[31]

A truly universal religion meant a religion "founded upon a twentieth century psychology and theology, a religion which is throbbing with the dynamics of democracy, a spirituality which expresses itself in terms of humanism, rather than in terms of individualsm." Skinner believed that "the sciences of psychology and sociology will replace the dogmatism of theology in the New Religion."[32] Religion served no real purpose or had no real vitality if it was encrusted with formalism, imprisoned by the past, and did not meet the contemporary needs of humanity. The church, only one organized expression of religion, "must take sides on every question which involves right or wrong."

With an optimism scarcely borne out by world events after 1914, he proclaimed that the Universalism which he envisioned would break down barriers among and between nations and allow humankind the fullest possible expression of individual personality enveloped by a social consciousness based on brotherhood in its widest sense. A "true" religion such as Universalism opposed a theological conservatism which called for the perpetuation of the *status quo* and blind obedience to authority, and had been "the foe to the intellectual, political and social progress of humanity."

The ideal was the free church in its broadest possible reach, unshackled by tradition, custom, and inertia, willing to experiment without the limitations imposed by a creed. The social implications of a "free religion" followed logically. Dissatisfaction with the *status quo* in society paralleled dissatisfaction with that in theology, whether it be the prevalence of war, corruption in politics, or "the tyrannies of the commercial oligarchies." But mere recognition of social evils was not enough. Using the literary device of aphorism which is to be found frequently in his writings, Skinner summed up his philosophy of dynamism: "Belief without action is sterile! Action without belief is unintelligent."[33] If humanity were to achieve the goals which Skinner sought for it, thought had to be translated into something more effective than mere words. The result would be "a radical reformation of society."

Skinner was no supporter of secular humanism in the sense that the signatories of the Humanist Manifesto of 1933 proclaimed. Theologically, according to Skinner, the Universalist idea of God was "of a universal, impartial, immanent spirit whose nature is love. It is the largest thought the world has ever known; it is the most revolutionary doctrine ever proclaimed; it is the most expansive hope ever dreamed. This is the God of the modern man, and the God who is in modern man." Above all, it was a democratic God, embracing all. But this did not mean equality within humankind; the universal fatherhood of God meant recognition of the differences and diversities which called for "mutual respect and mutual self-fulfillment" rather than arbitrary social division and economic exploitation.

The universe of God meant, additionally, "the innate spirituality and worth of man." It was "the consciousness of his divineness" which underlay the determination to "fight the wrong and build the right." One of the "supreme contributions of Jesus to the world" was the fact that "his sympathies reached out beyond narrow ethnic boundaries and included all humanity in his vision of a unified world under God." It was the attainment of this vision that Skinner sought to achieve, insisting that "no social problem can ever be completely solved until it is spiritually solved, for every social problem involves a spiritual content. It was in this way that Skinner gave an enlarged dimension to the reform impulse inherent in the Social Gospel movement by calling for "a religion of greatness" (Universalism) which would transcend all creeds and all parochialisms.

The first official expression of denominational social policy, which stood for a quarter of a century, was largely Skinner's handiwork in his capacity as secretary of the Social Service Commission. The Declaration of Social Principles was adopted in 1917 as part of the biennial report of the commission.[34] It was both a restatement of "the essential principles of the Universalist faith" and an affirmation of its social goals "in relation to modern life." The specific program offered in the Declaration was clearly modeled on the Social Creed of the Federal Council of Churches.

Unfortuntely, the involvement of the nation in World War I and the readjustments which followed, brought an untimely although temporary end to the implementation of such expressions of social idealism as the Declaration signified. The best that could be done was to reaffirm the principles of the social service program on 1917 every two years. The idea of appointing a full-time Social Service secretary was considered in 1919, but no one could be spared, so a group effort was attempted. Sixteen persons had been selected by 1921, each to head one department of a newly designated Committee on Public Welfare. Skinner was to prepare a booklet on the subject.[35] But the responsibility was so diffused and the efforts so infrequently recognized or supported that the idea was abandoned. Universalists were warned that, once a program was adopted, it would not "enact itself."[36]

An eleven-point social service program was adopted by the ministers meeting preceding the General Convention assembled in 1921 which provoked much debate.[37] The argument over the release after World War I of such individuals as the labor leader Eugene Debs from federal prison was so heated that the tumultuous proceedings had to be halted by an impromptu prayer by one of the clergy "asking that the spirit of harmony prevail."[38] There was so much attention being paid to social issues that one Universalist clergyman warned his colleagues not to become "community errand boys" instead of attending to their religious responsibilities.[39]

In 1923 the General Convention authorized the creation of a Department of Social Welfare, with Charles H. Pennoyer (1978–1963) as the full-time director.[40] He prepared a "Declaration of Social Faith" consisting of thirty-eight "beliefs" on almost every conceivable subject, including "sexual reform." It called for medical certificates as prerequisites for marriage licenses, sterilization of the feeble-minded, and "supervised information" on birth control. He travelled extensively both in the United States and abroad, attending meetings and promoting his social platform.[41] But he was so discouraged by the failure of churches to become involved in any activities outside their own bailiwicks that his efforts were allowed to lapse by 1927. The Committee on Public Welfare disappeared.

The Department (Commission) on Social Welfare continued to exist but its effectiveness was seriously weakened by lack of resources; it had to struggle on an annual budget of $100 during the period of economic depression in 1930–31.[42] Despite such a severe financial restriction the commission held on, and Skinner served as its chairman during much of the 1930s.

The Federal Council of Churches adopted in 1932 an updated and revised version of the Social Creed of the Churches which they had adopted almost a quarter of a century earlier and which had in turn been adopted by the Universalists.[43] Skinner's recommendation that the Federal Council statement be again adopted as also that of the Universalists was approved.[44] Copies of the Federal Council program were distributed to all Universalist churches with the recommendation that each appoint a standing Committee on Social Action.[45]

Perkins succeeded Skinner as chairman of the Social Welfare Commission and in 1939 recommended that a Committee on Social Action be created that would be more effective than the existing committee.[46] He complained that for too long the Social Welfare Commission had been "chiefly a symbolic recognition of an unmet need," showing a distressing lack of creativity and originality in merely adopting the programs of other churches and failing for the most part to carry them out.[47] Among the difficulties were that the existing Universalist commission was staffed with individuals whose primary duties lay elsewhere and that it operated with virtually no funds even for clerical expenses. The entire situation seemed to Perkins to be nothing less than "humiliating."

But the collective conscience of Universalism was only submerged — not completely abandoned. It was in 1943, again in the context of world conflict even more extensive and destructive than between 1914 and 1918 that the second major statement of social policy was issued by the denomination. The Declaration of Social Principles and Objectives, entitled "Our Task," and prepared jointly by the Commission on Social Welfare and International Relations, and the International Church Extension Board, was presented to the General Assembly in New York City. It was unanimously adopted.[48]

At the very same session in 1943 a six-member Commission on Social Action was created, combining the two committees which had submitted a draft of the document for denominational approval.[49] The first task of the new commission was to edit the statement for publication. It appeared shortly thereafter as "The Affirmation of Social Principles."[50] It was supplemented and updated in 1946, 1951, and 1953.[51]

There was great difficulty in staffing the Commission on Social Action, and only two of the original six members were serving a year later.[52] Skinner was given the responsibility in 1945 as chairman of the commission for organizing its activities, and he immediately plunged into the work.[53] Each member was assigned a special field of social endeavor: data gathering, international relations, peace work (through the Federal Council of Churches), race relations, economic and labor relations, rural church problems, public health, delinquency, community resources, and women's organizations. Each individual was to prepare pamphlets outlining a special sphere of action.

A committee or commission was to be established in each church which was to serve as "the conscience of the community." The goal was "to make an aggressive and organized attack upon poverty, war, sickness, crime, ignorance, intolerance, prejudice, and human misery." Mere talk and the passage of resolutions were not sufficient. One of the first steps taken by those responsible for various assignments was to prepare articles which appeared in the *Leader*.

The results were far from encouraging. The extensive community involvement which Skinner urged was not forthcoming except in isolated instances. A widely circulated study manual, "Our Faith Demands...," prepared by the commission, received only minimal attention. A questionnaire was sent out in 1946 to 450 churches to inventory their social action programs. Only seventy-one active churches responded, and only eighteen of them had social action committees.[54] A questionnaire to the approximately sixty Universalist churches in Massachusetts in 1947 brought about thirty responses; only three had social action committees.[55]

Whether successful or not in its efforts, the Social Action Commission continued to sponsor one resolution after another calling attention to pressing social problems. Typical was one in 1947 calling for the extension of public health services and the formation of comprehensive health insurance plans.[56]

The third and final Declaration of Social Principles drawn up by Universalists while still a separate denomination was adopted in 1957. It was drawn up by a five-member Commission of Social Concern authorized in 1955 and given the charge of seeking a consensus on social problems.[57] The hoped-for consensus was difficult to achieve but the resulting document bore witness to continuing concern by Universalists for the welfare of all human beings. In spite of all their failures, frustrations, and unfulfilled aspirations they clung to their faith in their social mission which could in no way be separated from their religious beliefs, translated over the years from salvation in another world to salvation in this one.

The Community Church of Boston

On 11 January 1920 between 150 and 200 individuals met in Steinert Hall in the center of Boston to attend the first service of the Community Church in that city and to hear John Haynes Holmes, founder and leader of the Community Church of New York City. What had prompted such a gathering?

According to Holmes, the original members of the church were in large part men and women who had opposed World War I and, as pacifists, had suffered the consequences. It attracted likewise those who believed that the mission of the church, writ large, was to unite all humankind regardless of racial, national, or creedal differences and put an end to all sectarian and class divisions which had split the religious world into warring factions over the centuries. Denominationalism based on theological, social, and economic differences had to give way to a sense of community overreaching all lines of demarcation. Above all it had to be a church imbued with both social idealism and social action beyond its own boundaries.

The first challenge to such a conception of the church had been the ending of war; then its aims widened to fight poverty, defend civil liberties, bring about prison reform, end capital punishment, and assail militarism, political corruption, economic exploitation, racial discrimination, and religious bigotry. It should, in short, set out to help reform the world, in the tradition of those who lived and worked in the Jacksonian period before the Civil War.[58]

The Community Church of Boston was co-founded by Skinner and Holmes (1879–1964), the latter having already established a similar church in New York City. Skinner's ministry in the Boston church extended over sixteen years, as its president until 1932 and as its "leader" (executive director) until 1936.[59] It was Skinner's way of advocating a universalized religion on a one-world basis of brotherhood — a philosophy completely shared by Holmes.

Holmes had been pastor of the Unitarian Church of the Messiah in New York City for twelve years and had, in 1919–1920, refashioned it into the nondenominational Community Church. His *New Churches for Old*, published in 1922 and in which the idea of community churches was outlined, was enthusiastically endorsed by Skinner. He called the book the herald of "the New Reformation."[60] Holmes remained the leader of the Community Church in New York City until his retirement in 1949. He had offered to resign in 1941 so that no odium would be attached to it because of his pacifism.[61]

There was an interesting historical precedent in Universalism for the idea of a community church. The Universalist Free Church Association of the City of Boston had been organized in 1845 largely through the efforts of Otis A. Skinner. The object of the church, which held it first public worship service in 1844 in Fort Hill Temperance Hall, was to provide spiritual sustenance to all who wished to attend, churched and unchurched alike.[62] It was intended especially for the poor, who were unable or unwilling to rent or purchase pews elsewhere, or did not feel welcome at other churches. A nominal membership fee of $1.00 was charged for those who could pay. Services were conducted by Asa P. Cleverly who also organized a Sunday school which by 1846 was attended by sixty-five children.[63] In 1845 a small room was rented, known as Samaritan Chapel, dedicated in November of that year.[64]

This missionary attempt was never adequately supported, despite the efforts of Edwin H. Chapin, William H. Ryder, and other Universalists. A Free Church Union conference meeting was held at the Fifth Universalist (Warren Street) Church in 1846 to solicit contributions, but the results were disappointing. Cleverly received only $200 for two years of clerical labor, and the chapel was forced to close early in 1847.[65] But the idea of a church for all people did not die.

In the very year (1845) that a constitution was drafted for the Universalist Free Church Association, Theodore Parker (1810–1860), the Unitarian publicist and social reformer considered by Holmes to have been the "spiritual ancestor" of the Community Church, was installed in a Boston pulpit.[66] After Parker's death in 1860, the cause of free religion was taken up by the Free Religious Association which had been formed in 1867 and of which Holmes was the last president in 1919. It was out of the continued need for such an organization that the Community Church in New York had been born.[67] Holmes made much of the fact that the Community Church was in fact a continuation and lineal descendent of both the traditions and principles of the Free Religious Association.

The movement which resulted in the establishment of the Community Church of Boston began in the fall of 1919 when a call for a meeting was issued; Skinner was one of the signatories. There was sufficient interest to justify a series of experimental services, and the first meeting took place early the next year. The church was formally organized later in 1920. A Statement of Purpose was adopted which described the Community Church as "a free fellowship of men and women united for the study of universal religion, seeking to apply ethical ideals to individual life and the co-operative principle to all forms of social and economic life." A Bond of Union was also adopted, subscription to which was the only condition of membership. It called for mutual assistance and fellowship which would promote "the cause of truth, righteousness and love in the world."

Interest in the church increased steadily, with an average attendance of 175 each Sunday in 1921, and a membership of 206. The church was incorporated in 1922, bylaws were drafted, a charter was obtained, and a downtown headquarters was opened. The speakers included such prominent individuals, besides Holmes, as Rabbi Stephen S. Wise (1874–1949), internationally known religious leader; Scott Nearing (1883–1983), controversial socialist and pacifist; James Harvey Robinson (1863–1936), nationally known exponent of the "New History;" and Bertrand Russell (1872–1970), British philosopher and mathematician.

The speakers attracted such sizable audiences that larger quarters than Steinert Hall had to be obtained, and the meetings were moved to the Copley Theater. Symphony Hall, even more commodious, was then used, beginning in 1926, with an attendance of 1,800 on opening day. High rental costs and speakers' fees created some financial strain in a church with no endowment; this difficulty was surmounted by Sunday morning collections, membership pledges, and some gifts. Educational work was carried on also through weekday lectures and forums as well as Sunday services, supper conferences, and various social occasions. A young people's organization was formed in 1923.

In order to translate into action the social idealism for which the church stood, a Social Justice Committee was organized in 1926. The church took a particular interest in the controversial Sacco-Vanzetti case, with meetings and the distribution of literature between 1921 and 1927, when the death sentences were carried out. There was also a Civil Liberties Council which, together with the Social Justice Committee, participated in a campaign to free the nine Scottsboro boys in Alabama charged with rape whose convictions were reversed by the Supreme Court in 1935. The committee also furnished aid to the Loyalists during the Spanish civil war of the 1930s. Skinner was especially active in the work of the Peace Action Council, another church agency. A twelve-point Social Program was adopted in 1935 which embodied most of Skinner's ideas. The Community Church, in brief, took an active role in politial, social, and economic affairs, usually supporting the losing side — a stance which took the courage of conviction and commitment.

Liturgy, symbolism, and other traditional outward marks of religiosity were minimized and much emphasis was put during the Skinner period on "rational worship" freed from "superstition." Although the forms and orders of service might have been traditional, the content was far from that. There was no invocation of a deity, and although the familiar practice of a "lesson" or "reading" was retained, selections from Abraham Lincoln, Walt Whitman, Edwin Markam, and Robert Ingersoll and the writings of such ancient religious leaders as Confucius and Buddha took their places beside the Bible. A forum for free and wide-ranging discussion, a staple item in Skinner's approach, was scheduled after almost all services. Here, in the Community Church, Skinner had the opportunity to put into practice the ideas which he espoused in his writings and promoted in his classroom in the Crane Theological School.

The tradition of championing unpopular causes was carried on by the church long after Skinner had ceased to be its leader. It experienced its share of difficulty even in obtaining places to meet, in the absence of a regular church building. In 1953-54, at the height of the so-called McCarthy era, the John Hancock Insurance Company of Boston, in whose auditorium the church met after many years in Symphony Hall, refused to renew the lease held by the church for its Sunday services. The action took place presumably because the church had been accused of communist leanings and had opened it pulpit to some who were sympathietic to Russia. The company was accused of bowing to public pressure and their action raised the larger question of freedom of expression and of religion, long-cherished American ideals. All protests against the company's action were unavailing, and the Community Church was forced to find other quarters.[68]

Operating always as a maverick organization, the Community Church's unorthodoxy was intensified by the national drive for conformity during the 1950s. Skinner, had he still been living, would undoubtedly have stood up for the principles he believed in, regardless of the consequences for him. His faith in the Universalist version of a better world, to be brought about by a combination of enlightened human effort and an ever-present spark of divinity in all, remained unshaken. It was a never-ending "struggle to emancipate mankind from ignorance, slavery, injustice, and war."[69]

Lalone had written in 1939 that "he only deserves the honor . . . to stand in the line of this noble tradition . . . of universal human brotherhood . . . who, like his spiritual fathers, accepts the responsibility of loving his neighbor as himself."[70] This accolade could well be applied to Clarence Russell Skinner, "prophet of twentieth century Universalism."

Chapter 27

"Not Your Creed, But Your Need:" Social Service and Benevolences

A goodly proportion of Universalists had a strong sense of stewardship, as befitted a denomination with the ideals they professed, and their numerous benevolences, which took a wide variety of forms throughout the nation, bore witness to this.[1] The settlement house movement, especially popular in the nineteenth century, was one in which Universalists had a significant share.

One of the first and most successful settlement houses established in New York City was the Brevoort Mission, begun by Universalists in 1858 as the First Universalist Mission Society of the City of New York, and incorporated in 1869. The founder had been Elisha Hebbard, a member of T. J. Sawyer's Orchard Street Church. Until Brevoort Hall was purchased the mission had been operated in his home.[2] During its existence it changed both location and name several times. When it moved to a building on East 53d Street between Second and Third Avenue, and was dedicated in 1919, it became the Prescott Mission, named after the building in which it was located. Until 1926 it was known simply as "the Mission." It was also referred to for some time as Divine Paternity House, after the Universalist church which sponsored it. The acquisition of the property had been made possible by two gifts totalling $40,000.

The settlement house met an immediate need. It was particularly valuable for first- and second-generation immigrants who at first made up as much as nine-tenths of its patronage. It served a congested tenement area of more than 25,000 inhabitants and operated seven days a week.[3] At first it reflected its religious sponsorship and identification, with a Sunday school and both a senior and junior Young Peoples Christian Union. George G. Needham, one of the incorporators, was superintendent of the Sunday school for half a century. The kindergarten was sponsored by a woman's group in the church.

Settlement house activities soon extended far beyond religious boundaries, providing facilities for industrial education, recreation, and health services, with concentration by the 1920s on the welfare of children up to the age of thirteen. In 1907 the 100-acre Chestnut Hill Farm near Boonton, New Jersey, was purchased by funds supplied by the Church of the Divine Paternity, and used as a fresh-air camp for both children and adults.

Brevoort Hall, the designation most familiar to Universalists in the early days of the mission, was a strictly cooperative project, involving the entire neighborhood and attracting personnel from such organizations as the New York School of Social Work. The settlement house was a member of United Neighborhood Houses comprising fifty leading organizations, such as the well known Henry Street Settlement which attracted national attention.

By the time of the outbreak of World War II the mission had lost most of its original religious association, and was known as Prescott Neighborhood House. Even though one of the smaller such organizations in New York City, in 1940 it was serving almost 300 families, most of which were American-born and more than half Roman Catholic.[4] It was able to provide numerous valuable services with an annual budget of less than $6,000. When the property was sold by the Church of the Divine Paternity in 1946 it had become largely a nursery for children of working parents. All Universalist association with it ceased and a new corporation was formed involving the neighborhood and financed increasingly by government subsidies.[5] The Universalists had most assuredly done their part in establishing what was a pioneer in its field.

Among Universalist benevolences in the Midwest were those associated with the Church of the Redeemer in Minneapolis. The first was the Washburn Memorial Home, established in 1887. It was the gift of General Cadwallader C. Washburn, one-time governor of Wisconsin, on behalf of the numerous Washburn brothers, in memory of their mother; it was his way of doing 'something for mankind.'[6] He communicated his plans to James H. Tuttle (1824–1903), pastor of the church for twenty-five years, proposing to erect a building costing about $100,000, with an endowment sufficient to support about 100 occupants.

It was intended for orphans and children of broken homes having a legal residence in Minnesota and was open to children under fourteen who were to be discharged at the age of fifteen.[7] They were to be admitted, "nurtured and trained for usefulness in life . . . without any question as to . . . sex, color, or religion." The brick and stone building which was financed out of what became a $375,000 bequest, was located in the center of Washburn Park, a twenty-six acre area donated by another brother and member of the Church of the Redeemer, W. D. Washburn.[8] Although it bore no distinctive denominational name, the majority of the trustees were members of the church.

Marion Shutter, who had arrived in Minneapolis as Tuttle's assistant pastor in 1886 and who had succeeded him in 1891, was a strong advocate of applied Christianity and made his church's influence in the city even stronger than had Tuttle. Among his activities was the founding in 1897 of the Unity Settlement House, the first such agency of is kind in Minneapolis. He was president of it until his death in 1939.[9]

The settlement house was the first attempt to found an urban residential facility under the auspices of religious liberals in the Midwest. Known at first as the "Unity-House Social Settlement," it was initially under the charge of Howard McQueary, a controversial Universalist clergyman who had come to grief theologically in the Episcopal Church.[10] It was established in a run-down section of the city and was at first located in a rented house in which McQueary and his family resided together with two young men who served as assistants.

The settlement house was organized along the same lines as Jane Addams' Hull House in Chicago and was to be a center of educational and humanitarian work. The plan included a kindergarten, a day nursery, a savings bank, and evening Americanization classes for recently-arrived immigrants, economics, bookkeeping, mechanical drawing, and other studies. Social hours were scheduled each weekend, with addresses and talks on topics of current interest. The agencies were intended to assist the large population of Swedes, Norwegians, and other foreign nationalities who needed "to be assimilated to our American ways of thinking on social problems and instructed in our history and principles of government." In addition, the settlement house was to improve the environment of the recently-arrived immigrants and alleviate some of the harshness of life they experienced.

The Church of the Redeemer, under Shutter's leadership, immediately gave "cordial support." While strictly non-sectarian, with cooperation from Lutherans and Methodists, it was Universalists and Unitarians who took the lead in the management of the settlement house. In addition to a multitude of other activities, the organization sponsored, beginning in 1906, a series of summer "Unity camps" in rural locations for urban youngsters. The camp in 1909 provided facilities for more than 100 children over the age of twelve.[11]

The activities of the settlement house soon attained such proportions that a series of enlarged facilities had to be provided, including a gymnasium (1909) and a main structure (1912). Before World War I a resident director was provided, with half a dozen paid staff members, and a number of volunteers. After the war the settlement house became a public as well as a church responsibility, receiving support not only from endowment but from the Community Fund through the Minneapolis Council of Social Agencies, to which members of the Church of the Redeemer contributed $31,000 in 1925.[12] By the mid-1920s student assistants from the University of Minnesota were receiving academic credit for social service work at Unity House.[13] The administration was still in the hands of the Unity Settlement Association, created earlier by the church, and headed for many years by Shutter.[14] In 1929 a one-story building to house the day nursery and dental clinic was added to the three-story brick building which housed the other activities. Like so many other Universalist social service projects Unity House served in its early days as the prototype for others with possibly greater renown but much shorter histories.

Among Universalist benevolent organizations in which the denomination was a pioneer and in which it attained a deservedly wide reputation was the so-called "institutional church" which offered a wide range of important services not strictly religious in nature. The precedent had been set in 1837 when Otis A. Skinner opened an "Every Day Church" in Boylston Hall in Boston to serve the needs of transients and rootless people who had no church home or even any other home to call their own. It lasted into the late 1850s and attempted to meet to a limited extent the material needs of those who sought its services even though its primary mission was religious in the conventional sense.[15]

Universalists in Boston were faced, in the 1890s, like members of other denominations, with a gradual but inexorable shift in both the character and location of the urban inhabitants their churches traditionally served. Population shifted, and the original constituency of the churches moved for the most part to the suburbs. The resident population had not necessarily decreased, but its makeup underwent a significant change. Year by year the congregations diminished and the resources of most of the churches declined correspondingly. The alternative was clear: Abandon the churches or alter the nature and scope of their activities to meet changed conditions and retain their vitality.

The Shawmut Avenue Universalist Church chose the latter route, under the dynamic leadership of George L. Perin, its former pastor. He had returned in 1894 from Japan where he had set up the first denominational foreign mission addressed to non-Christians. He determined to give the church a new and broadened dimension. It was transformed into an "institutional," or as it was popularly known, an "Every Day Church," offering a wide range of services to the neighborhood and operating seven days a week.

Perin's first step was to acquire a vacant sixteen-room house next door to the church which became the headquarters for day and evening classes in stenography, drawing, dressmaking, and cooking as well as church school activities. One especially popular feature was a day nursery for children of working mothers.[16] Free legal services were provided by an attorney who donated his services, and summer outings were enjoyed by more than 100 children in 1895.[17]

The combination of philanthropy and religion was an instant success and attracted much favorable attention — so much that Perin was forced to depend on a large corps of volunteer lay assistants as well as the services of fellow clergy. After almost a decade of activity the Shawmut society was merged with the First Universalist Parish in neighboring Brookline and continued to be a "family" church while retaining many institutional features, although on a greatly reduced scale.[18]

A score of institutional churches and non-sectarian community centers was being operated by the denomination in urban centers all over the nation by the time of World War I. Some were as elaborate as the programs of the Church of the Redeemer in Minneapolis and St. Paul's Universalist Church in Chicago, while others were as small and as frugally operated as Goddard House in Boston's North End, begun in the 1890s and conducted for several years by Irving C. Tomlinson.[19]

One of the most valuable social services growing out of Perin's long association with the Every Day Church was the Franklin Square House in Boston's South End. Hundreds of young women flocked into the area in the late nineteenth century to find employment. The vast majority lived in lodging and boarding houses, many of which not only lacked amenities but earned unsavory reputations and collected what seemed to Perin to be unnecessarily high fees for their services. He therefore offered the proposition that the old quarters of the New England Conservatory of Music in Franklin Square (East Newton and St. James Streets) be converted into a non-profit, self-supporting, non-sectarian facility for young working women and students who lived on modest incomes.[20] The intent was to provide as homelike an atmosphere and as many services as possible for more than 250 individuals and to provide for transients.

A corporation was formed in 1901 to purchase the property; the remodelled structure was occupied the following year. There was so much demand for rooms that adjoining property was acquired almost immediately, raising the total capacity to more than 400.[21] A new wing was added in 1914, and by the end of World War I the enlarged quarters served 900 young women.[22] It was estimated that by 1922 some 75,000 had used the services of the Franklin Square House, an enduring monument to Perin and Universalist philanthropy.[23] It was still in operation in the 1980s, although not by Universalists, providing housing for the elderly.

Another residence for women in Boston had been provided by Universalists in 1889, the idea of John D. W. Joy, a member of Perin's Shawmut Universalist Church.[24] He and forty-nine others incorporated the Bethany Home for Young Women which was formally opened in 1890, under the auspices of the Massachusetts Convention.[25] Joy had earlier been involved in operating a home in the city for aged men. Financing for

Bethany Union, Boston

the Bethany Home was provided through a network of Bethany Sister Circles, each member of which contributed sixty cents annually. A few of the Circles, which were organized in almost every Massachusetts Universalist church, were still in existence in the 1940s.

The Bethany Home in Boston was the second one bearing that name and founded by members of the denomination. The first had been opened as a home for "fallen women" by a member of the Church of the Redeemer in Minneapolis.[26]

In spite of its name the Bethany Home was intended by its original charter to provide a non-denominational refuge for women aged twenty to forty who were unable to support themselves because of 'general disability or inability to work.' The charter was revised in 1898, when it became the Bethany Union and a residence primarily for young working women who paid for its services on a sliding scale, depending on their income. This urban benevolent agency served hundreds of women, and in the day before Franklin Square House was in full operation (1902) and before the present organization of the YWCA was perfected (1906).

Bethany Union expanded rapidly and by 1910 was occupying three adjoining buildings. The Union moved in 1941 to new quarters on Newbury Street, where it was still operating in the 1980s as an independent affiliate of the Unitarian Universalist Association. Two Universalists who had unusually long associations with Bethany Union were Miss Ruth Hersey, who served as its superintendent from 1915 to 1939, and Frank A. Dewick, who resigned as president in 1948 after thirty-one years of service but continued as treasurer until the time of his death.[27]

Among the many benevolences organized or operated by Universalists were four facilities intended for the aged and infirm. Although each originated under somewhat different circumstances and sponsoring agencies, they were all intended primarily for members of the denomination but were basically nonsectarian in their philosophy and frequently served others besides Universalists.

The first was founded by the widow of Edwin H. Chapin (1814–1880) as a memorial to her husband, acknowledged to be one of the outstanding pulpit orators of his day, a prolific hymn writer, and a much sought-after lecturer on temperance, urban problems, and world peace. He served from 1848 until his death as pastor of the Fourth Universalist Society in New York City, better known as the Church of the Divine Paternity.

The Chapin Home for the Aged and Infirm was incorporated by the New York state legislature on 19 May 1869, The twenty-one corporators were all Universalist women, including Mrs. Chapin and Mrs. Caroline M. Sawyer. No less than fifteen nor more than forty trustees were to be elected by members of the corporation annually by ballot. The corporation was authorized to hold real estate up to $100,000 and personal property up to $500,000. Except for the name of the institution and the names of the corporators, there was nothing to suggest its connection with any denomination. The word "Universalist" was nowhere in evidence.

By another act, of 12 May 1869, the State Commissioners of the sinking fund were authorized to lease to the corporation lots belonging to New York City north of 66th Street for the erection of the home under such conditions as provided for charitable institutions. A lease at nominal rent authorized by this act the use of twelve lots between 66th and 67th Street, and Third and Lexington Avenues. The home, for both men and women, was to be open to all who applied, irrespective of "birth, creed, or denomination." The constitution of the Home, however, provided that officers were to be chosen from women of the Universalist denomination.[28] Mrs. Chapin served as the first chairperson of the board of trustees, and the Church of the Divine Paternity provided the operating expenses.[29]

The cornerstone of the building to house the Chapin Home was laid on 24 October 1871 and when completed the structure was valued at $83,000.[30] Other assets were more than thirty-five acres in Franklin County, New York.[31] There were almost sixty in residence by 1888, and a new wing was needed. Between the date of its opening and 1911, more than 300 individuals had been cared for, less than a third of whom were Universalists. Among the eighteen religious faiths represented were Roman Catholics.

As a result of growing pressure for larger quarters, in 1909 a plot of almost five acres in Jamaica, Queens (Long Island) was secured and the cornerstone of a complex of new buildings was laid in October 1910; the new facility was occupied within a year. Among the benefactors were Mrs. Andrew Carnegie and Mrs. Washington L. Cooper, who furnished funds for the chapel and infirmary.[32]

The Chapin Home continued to operate at or near its capacity of about 100, and to disregard religious boundaries. Of the five admissions in 1929, only one was a Universalist.[33] By 1933 the endowment had risen to almost a quarter of a million dollars. The only requirements for entrance were attainment of the age of sixty-five and payment of a $1,000 entrance fee.[34] The bylaws were amended in 1947 to admit women of other denominations as trustees.[35] The tradition of nonsectarianism in the Chapin Home was an integral part of a long-standing Universalist tradition evident in other denominational institutions as well.

One of the best known benefactions sponsored by Universalist churches was the Messiah Home, incorporated in Philadelphia in 1900. It lasted as a separate entity until after the consolidation of the Universalist and Unitarian denominations, when it was merged with the Joseph Priestley House (Unitarian) into a new corporation known as the Unitarian-Universalist House of the Joseph Priestley District; court approval was

The Chapin Home on Long Island, New York

given in 1964. The property of the old Messiah Universalist Home was sold for $50,000 to an organization of Ukrainians in Philadelphia in 1963.[36]

The Home was the creation of the Church of the Messiah which was noteworthy in the nineteenth century for its charities. The church membership had voted in 1878 to establish a Permanent Charity Fund, the proceeds of which would be used to assist hospitals and other institutions for the relief of the sick and the poor. It had also become evident that existing homes for the aged in the Philadelphia area discriminated against professed Universalists and that provision was needed for such individuals.

In 1885 the congregation resolved to establish a charitable institution directly under the control of the church to be opened as soon as sufficient funds became available. A minimum of $25,000 was considered necessary, and a home for the aged, to be opened to both sexes, was determined to be the greatest need. Preference was to be given to Universalists, although others were to be welcomed if facilities permitted. Its nonsectarian character was stressed throughout its history; in 1912 only three of the eleven occupants were members of the Church of the Messiah and many of the others were from other denominations such as the Baptists. Pastors from different churches were invited to conduct religious services.

The principal of the fund had reached the hoped-for amount in 1889 and steps were taken to carry out the announced plan. At least $1,000 was thought to be necessary to supplement revenue from the interest on the $25,000 and other sources such as gifts in order to provide $2,500 a year to operate the facility. Actually, when the $1,000 was raised it was immediately set aside as a permanent contingency fund. It was drawn upon many times when deficits occurred, and top priority was given to replenish it whenever part of it had to be used.

Circular letters were sent to a large number of Universalists in Pennsylvania soliciting funds; contributions were at first intended to be for one year only. The appeal was so successful that a charter was obtained in 1900 and the governance of the institution was placed in the hands of a fifteen-person board of managers, all of whom were required to be male. Two-thirds were to be members of the Church of the Messiah, but other Universalist churches in Philadelphia, including primarily the Church of the Restoration, could and did have a voice in the management. An all-woman auxiliary board was selected to share in the processing of applications and admissions and to oversee housekeeping matters and the choice of a matron.

A house was rented in the suburb of Germantown in 1901 and the Home was formally opened in January 1902 and dedicated a few weeks later with three occupants already installed. Donations of all kinds were sought, from cash gifts to furniture, kitchen utensils, and food. Among the early contributions from one woman were a barrel of flour, twenty-five pounds of sugar, a carpet sweeper, and copies of the *Christian Leader*. It was on such donations, miscellaneous as they might have been, that the Home depended for most of its life.

The Home was an immediate success and obviously met a long-felt need. The number of occupants (originally all women) increased from three to seven in 1902. The principal of the charities fund exceeded $30,000 within a year, and the treasury for operating expenses was more than $3,000 at the end of the first year. Contributing memberships of various categories were also established to encourage monetary gifts.

The need for larger quarters was evident almost immediately, so a building fund was created in 1903. By 1906 sufficient money had become available to purchase property in Logan, a suburban section of Philadelphia, and to erect a substantial three-story brick building of Georgian-style architecture with facilities for about fifteen individuals. The new building was dedicated in May 1906 although actually occupied several months earlier. There were ten occupants in 1907, with a waiting list. Such a list existed throughout the history of the Home.

A concerted effort was made to bring the Home to the attention of the entire denomination. Photographs and literature were displayed at the General Convention in 1911, and the hope was expressed that the charities of the Philadelphia church would be given a place in the work of the convention at least to the extent of "endorsement and moral support."

Prudent use of resources, numerous fund-raising activities, and donations of all kinds enabled the Home to operate without a deficit until 1914. The failure to balance the budget that year and the next was blamed on a generally depressed economy and pleas for aid for those who suffered from the German invasion of Belgium and the rigors of the Great War. The number of occupants never dropped below thirteen after 1915. The

Home was endorsed by the Philadelphia Chamber of Commerce in 1919 as a worthy charity of a nonsectarian nature and hence could appeal to all for assistance. By the end of that year the impressive sum of more than $100,000 had been contributed since the opening of the Home, largely from denominational sources, and included a permanent fund in excess of $30,000. The new official status brought prompt results. More than 60 percent of the increased contributing membership roll in 1920 came from non-Universalists. Among the donations that year were seventy-five hymnbooks from the Logan Methodist Episcopal Church. A bequest of $10,000 in 1927 came from outside the denomination.

Of all the names associated with the Home, that of William R. Lyman (1854–1928) was probably the most familiar. He was a member of the board of managers during the first years of the Home's existence, and from 1903 until his death in 1928 was its president. During his lifetime he served as local manager of William Skinner & Sons Company, silk manufacturers, but he found time to take the leading part in the affairs of the Home. It was described as "a monument to his zeal and untiring spirit." He left a bequest of $2,700 to the Home.

The year 1928 was significant for the Home because the first (and only) male, Harry A. Albright, was admitted, making a temporary total of sixteen in residence. He was described as a "model member of the family." Another milestone in the history of the Home was reached in 1929 with the death of Edwin C. Sweetser, pastor of the Church of the Messiah and long active in the administration of the Home.

The assets of the Home rose steadily after 1920. Permanent endowment had reached $50,000 in 1927, and had exceeded $95,000 in 1940, and when the fiftieth anniversary of the occupation of the second headquarters of the Home was celebrated in 1956, the funds totalled more than $250,000. The Church of the Messiah, which had for so long sponsored the Home, closed its doors in 1958. Its Permanent Charities Fund, the entire proceeds of which had been devoted to this benevolence, was administered thereafter by the Pennsylvania Universalist Convention.

The Association of Universalist Women of the Church of the Restoration assumed many of the responsibilities previously met by the Church of the Messiah.[37] After merger with the Joseph Priestley House, which became the new residence, the assets were used to assist in improving recreational and dining facilities and in building a nursing wing named in honor of Benjamin Rush — a facility lacking in the former Messiah Home.

On the eve of denominational consolidation a new constitution and bylaws were adopted, effective in 1960. The board of managers was enlarged from fifteen to twenty-one, on which women were for the first time authorized to serve, as well as on all committees, some of which were restructured. The changing character of the American economy and actuarial statistics was reflected as the Home was about to close its highly successful institutional life as a Universalist agency. In 1903 the per capital cost of maintenance had been $266; in 1960 it was $2,138. The average age of the occupants had risen from sixty-six to eighty-three during the same period.

Although never a nursing facility in the usual sense, the Messiah Home had been the recipient of thousands of dollars of free medical service by the staff of the Temple University Hospital.[38] It was indeed a truly cooperative project from which all benefited.

The Thompson Home for Aged and Indigent Women, in Waldron, Indiana, was the third institution of this nature established by Universalists. Located in a rural community southeast of Indianapolis, it was the result of a bequest by Delos H. Thompson, a Universalist who in 1909 willed his twelve-room home and a forty-three acre farm to the state convention through the efforts of Marion Crosley, one-time pastor of the Central Universalist Church in Indianapolis.[39] It was opened and dedicated in 1913, with a capacity of twelve occupants, and by 1928 had an endowment exceeding $30,000.[40] It was intended for women sixty years of age or over and was completely nonsectarian, with no political or religious test for admission. By 1933 it was forced to levy an admission fee of $2,000 and always remained a very small operation.[41]

The last of the retirement facilities established under Universalist auspices was the Doolittle Universalist Home for Aged Persons in Foxboro, Massachusetts, incorporated in 1915 and still in operation in the 1980s. Behind it was an interesting story.[42] In the fall of 1911, Massachusetts State Superintendent Charles Conklin had temporary charge of the neighboring Mansfield parish which had among its members an impoverished elderly man without a family. Universalists in the parish furnished him with food, clothing, and shelter, at Conklin's suggestion, and the plight of the indigent individual became widely known locally. The idea occurred to Conklin that there should be a permanent refuge for such unfortunate individuals. He presented the proposal at the state convention in 1913 and Miss Sarah Billings Doolittle (1840–1927) took up the challenge. She offered her twenty-seven room house left by her parents as a gift to the convention, and for her remaining fifteen years lived in Mansfield.

A corporation was authorized in 1914 to hold and administer the property, with occupant preference to be given to Universalists, both men and women. The house, built by Allen C. Doolittle in 1850, stood opposite the town Common and near the Universalist church. The property, comprising an acre, made later enlargement possible. Seven applicants were immediately accepted, the first resident being Ira P. Whittlesey. Annual memberships at $1.00 each were sold to finance the operation and drive for an endowment was begun which amounted to $30,000 in 1925.[43]

The Doolittle Home

The Doolittle Home proved so popular that by 1930 the capacity of thirteen occupants had been reached, and there were twenty-seven on the waiting list.[44] It was decided to raise $50,000 to enlarge the Home, with the understanding that construction would not take place until 1933, when it was anticipated that the full amount would be raised. But by 1931 $40,000 was in hand; so, in spite of severe economic depression, it was decided to go ahead with the addition.[45] The enlarged facilities accommodated twenty-one residents, served by a staff of four.

Income from the permanent funds of $65,000 by 1933 was inadequate, even though supplemented by many individual gifts, and a series of emergency drives had to be conducted periodically to keep the Home out of debt. The admission fee in the 1930's was a modest $750; however, it was stipulated that each applicant accepted was required to give to the Home all moneys and property. Conklin had hoped that the endowment would be increased to $100,000; by the mid-1930's it was slightly over $70,000, and before the end of the decade the permanent fund had exceeded $130,000.[47] Although the Home was operating with a small deficit in the late 1950's its value to the denomination far outweiged the expenses incurred, and the permanent funds had reached almost $1,000,000 by 1962.

The administrative base of the Home was extended in 1959 by increasing the number of trustees to twenty-five.[48] It was truly, as its advertising proclaimed, "A Home — Not an Institution." That was the spirit that governed all of the facilities set up by Universalists to care for their own as well as those of other faiths.

The Universalist Service Committee

It was "that valiant little unarmed army who, by their deeds, wrote this shining chapter of Universalist concern for persons both in lands beyond the seas and in areas of human need in this land." These words were written by Emerson H. Lalone in the introduction to his updated version of his brief history of Universalist social action.[49] His reference was to the Universalist Service Committee of which he was chairman for six years, in its period of most dramatic activity as a contributor to post-World War II relief and rehabilitation work.

The Service Committee had its origins in a War Relief Fund created by the denomination in 1940 after the outbreak of hostilities in Europe and placed in the hands of a supervisory committee in 1943.[50] The UCA had started the fund with an appropriation of $1,000, with solicitations from individual Universalists. The plan was to disburse money to approved war relief organizatons. But the results were so meager that Ellsworth C. Reamon, president of the UCA, told the 1943 convention that 'We ought to hang our heads in shame over what we give to this cause.'[51] There was sufficient response this time to prompt Carleton M. Fisher, minister of the First Universalist Church in Buffalo, New York, to resign his pastorate late in 1944 and enter war relief work. During the next year he participated in a post-war relief and rehabilitation training program conducted at the Pacific School of Religion in Berkeley, California.

In mid-1945 the Unitarian Service Committee announced that it would welcome cooperation with Universalists in its European work which had been under way since 1938. The Unitarian gesture had resulted from an inquiry from Robert Cummins, the General Superintendent, about the possibility of a joint relief project. Fisher agreed to be the Universalist representative. He was commissioned by a group of Universalist clergy and lay persons from various organizations in the denomination in October of that year, at a meeting in Williamstown, Massachusetts, and a month later journeyed to France. For two months he familiarized himself with the work of the Unitarian Service Committee at their headquarters in Paris and Geneva, the latter having been set up in 1942.

In the United States the War Relief Committee was succeeded by the Universalist Service Committee consisting of Roger D. Bosworth, Mrs. J. Russell Bowman, and John van Schaick, who had been the American Red Cross Commissioner in Belgium during World War I. In their first public announcement the commitee explained that it was not intended to serve primarily as a social service agency but, by furnishing food, clothing, and shelter to those in distress, "to help restore a faith in love and good will by means of a practical demonstration of human brotherhood." It was a commitment that went to the heart of Universalist philosophy expressed in the name of the committee's bulletin, *One Humanity*, which reached a circulation of 3,500 in 1952. The power of good could indeed "create a better world" for all. This nonsectarian and nonpolitical policy in human relations was consistently followed, and to that end the denomination committed $10,000 a year.[52]

Fisher's first assignment, which lasted a year, was in devastated Holland. A collection headquarters for goods was established in New York City, and by December 1946 Fisher and a local committee that he organized had distributed thousands of pounds of food, articles of clothing, and pairs of shoes. Hungary, another area in crisis, was the next stop, beginning in 1947. Provision of food to starving children during a bitterly cold winter was the first priority, all carried out in cooperatin with the Ministry of Public Welfare. The communist-controlled government in Budapest became more and more difficult to work with. In the summer of 1947, after being decorated by the government "for meritorious service to the Republic," Fisher and two other Americans were given a one-way visa out of the country.[53]

Fisher returned to the United States and his report at the General Assembly in the fall of 1947 brought forth not only an enthusiastic response but cash contributions of almost $2,000 for a new service project which he outlined. Response to a request for financial support of a Unitarian Service Committee project for housing displaced children and war orphans in Germany in 1947 had been so poor that its abandonment seemed to be the only choice. But the Universalists agreed to furnish the supervisory personnel of the four homes then being operated, and the project was rescued. From this point on, the overseas program changed from emergency relief to rehabilitation. Fisher was made full-time director of all Universalist service projects in 1947.[54]

In 1947 the International Church Extension Board of the church, which was merged with the Service Committee, commissioned Cummins and Lalone, chairman of the committee, to visit Western Europe and ascertain where they could be of the greatest assistance. They found the most need to be the establishment of a separate center for displaced adolescents so that they would not be intermixed with youngsters in the child care centers. The individual selected to direct this new facility was Gustav H. Ulrich, who went to Germany in the spring of 1948 as senior representative of the joint child care team, and worked under the International Refugee Organization in the British zone and with several bureaucratic agencies. A shelter was established at Verden. Ulrich was assisted for a brief time in 1948 by David H. Cole, later the minister of the First Universalist Church in Chicago.

The International Refugee Organization, one of the many agencies operating in West Germany, was much impressed with the work done by Ulrich and his team, considering the youth shelter 'the most important single project in the British Zone.'[55] It became, in fact, a model for other such homes.

Award to the Universalist Service Committee by the Dutch government, 1947

Charles N. Vickery, a Universalist minister and executive director of the Columbia Street Community Center in Bangor, Maine, replaced Ulrich in 1949. He assisted Helen MacKenzie, director of the Verden home, and Helen French became senior representative on the joint staff.

The activities of the Service Committee between 1947 and 1949 extended in other directions besides the care of displaced children and adolescents. Summer work camps were established both in the United States and abroad. The first attempt had been made in Holland in 1946, where six European youth enlisted to assist three Universalist adults.[56] In the same year Ann Postma, the president of the Universalist Youth Fellowship, was a member of a youth camp in Stalingrad, in the Soviet Union. Ten Universalist young people participated in a Unitarian-sponsored camp in Prague, Czechoslovakia, in the summer of 1947. One of these, a young minister named George Niles, headed a group of ten young people who had volunteered at their own expense to work in the first Universalist-sponsored camp in Europe in 1949. It was located at Druhwald, a camp for displaced boys, including refugees from East Germany. It had been set up in the ruins of a Nazi arsenal partially destroyed in the course of the war. The German sponsoring agency was the *Arbeiter Wohlfahrt*. The camp was so successful that it was reopened in the summer of 1950 and continued for over a decade.

Work camps were also established in the United States, the first during the summer of 1948, in such widely separated locations as Ohio, New Hampshire, and New Jersey (Murray Grove). A total of about fifty Universalists, both lay and clerical, were involved that summer in such domestic projects as repairing church buildings and operating recreational and educational centers. There were six summer projects in operation by the summer of 1949.[57] The first Institutional Service Unit was conducted by Robert T. Dick at the Danvers State Hospital in Massachusetts that summer. Little more than a decade later, twelve-week periods of service were being provided by students from all denominations at mental hospitals in Minnesota, Ohio, and New Hampshire.[58]

When the Universalist Church was reorganized in 1949 on a departmental basis the functions of the Service Committee were taken over by the Department of Service Projects. However, the old name was still used, partly because it was so widely known by that designation, and partly because it was so registered with the State Department and changing it would have been too complex a procedure.

The Service Committee conducted four surveys in 1950 in order to determine its future activities and policies in regard to its broadened jurisdiction and responsibilities. The joint program of the two service committees in West Germany between 1947 and 1949 involved ten different homes for displaced persons, and in the latter years their administration was consolidated at Bad Rothenfelde and continued as part of an interdenominational effort staffed by large numbers of volunteers.

The International Refugee Organization had originally intended to close out its work by the end of 1950 but the need for its services was so great that much of it continued. Vickery, after coming home to the United States in December 1950, returned to West Germany early the next year and stayed until 1952. Resettlement and medical aid were two of the most urgent problems needing attention. A series of training institutes for home nursing was held in 1951 to meet one of these needs, the candidates selected by the *Arbeiter Wohlfahrt*.

Another activity which increased Universalist participation was the outgrowth of a recommendation made by the General Assembly in 1949 that each church sponsor at least one displaced person or family.[59] Twenty-four families totalling fifty-one individuals had been sponsored by Universalists by the close of 1950, and within a year the number had risen to more than 100. Arrangements were under way by 1951 for the relocation of dozens of others who had lost their homes, their property, and their livelihood.

Fisher resigned from the directorship of the Service Committee in 1953 to return to the parish ministry and was replaced by Dana E. Klotzle, with a smooth transition period in the interim. Thus another stage ended of what was described as "the most shining chapter in the story of American Universalism."[60]

The work continued without major interruption, both in the United States and in other parts of the world. Assistance went in the 1950s and early 1960s to the victims of a flood in Holland (1953), and in the case of Hungary was expanded to meet the human emergencies created by the abortive revolt of 1956-57. Projects were administered through the International Association for Religious Freedom (IARF) secretariat based in Amsterdam. The Ulrichs were replaced in 1959 by the Donald Lombards and by Janet Stover, a registered nurse from Maine.[61] At the same time the Service Committee was registered as an authorized voluntary agency with the International Cooperation Administration of the Department of State. When a United Nations resolution declared 1959-1960 as World Refugee Year, Universalists recruited and assigned twenty-three college students as volunteers in West Germany. The Lombards and Stover worked without salary, with only their expenses paid by the Service Committee.[62]

In 1953 the Ryder Community Center in Chicago joined Jordan Neighborhood House in Virginia and the center in Nagano, Japan as one of the three institutions sponsored by the Department of Service Projects. Located in a public housing project on the South Side of Chicago known as LeClaire Courts, it served some 3,000 individuals (650 families), two-thirds of whom were under eighteen years of age, and 90 percent of whom were low-income Blacks. It was an enclave surrounded by an all-white population, and racial tensions were endemic.

Life for the Universalists who leased the community center from the

Carleton Fisher, associated with the Universalist Service Committee from 1944-1953

Chicago Housing Authority was made no easier by their effort to serve all, without regard for race, color, nationality, or religious preference. In spite of difficulties the center, offering a wide variety of services for young and old, was expanded to two buildings in 1960 and was renamed the Clarence Darrow Community Center for a Unitarian famous in American legal and social history.

One administrative problem which troubled the Universalists in the 1950s in carrying out their service projects was the status of the Service Committee. There was a movement on foot to make it a separate corporate entity independent of the UCA, comparable to the position of the Unitarian Service Committee which had become an independent agency in 1948 in order to raise its own funds without a formal religious connection. The proposal was to have been made at the 1957 General Assembly to make the Service Committee autonomous because it was feared that no money would be provided to support the committee's work. Resolutions to that effect were withdrawn when the crisis over money was averted and the committee was included in the 1957-58 budget. Klotzle was much opposed to the idea of independence, thinking it very unwise at the very time the denomination was attempting to solidify and concentrate its strength.[63]

The Unitarian Service Committee remained an independent agency for two years after denominational consolidation, so the Unitarian Universalist Service Committee within the UUA remained until 1963 a basically Universalist body.[64] It was not until the General Assembly of that year that the Unitarian Service Committee voted to merge functionally with the other service units; but even then it retained its separate corporate identity rather than become a department of the UUA.[65] Although the members of the corporation were to be elected by Unitarian Universalist churches and fellowships, the reconstituted Unitarian Universalist Service Committee was to be only an associate member of the UUA. Its reports to the General Assembly were to be for informational purposes only.[66]

However, the administrative arrangements were much less important than the motivating force and philosophy behind the entire history of the Universalist Service Committee. During its first decade it had posted a remarkable record of achievement. Its first task had been to assist in healing the wounds of war in Holland, and then in Hungary, with emergency relief services. It then helped to develop and operate pilot homes for displaced children and youth, all in cooperation with the Unitarian Service Committee and the International Refugee Organization. The committee organized in 1948 its first overseas international work camp, and in the United States created its first institutional service unit in a mental hospital. A year later it established an intercultural and interracial World Camp for junior high school youth.

In 1950 it planned a five-year assistance program for Japanese Universalists and other religious liberals whose lives had been shattered by war. Simultaneously it assisted in Germany to train social service workers. On the home front it became responsible for the administration of Jordan Neighborhood House. It assisted the victims of a disastrous flood in Holland and of political upheaval in Hungary. Operating through UNESCO and the Brittish relief organization UNKRA, it provided educational, medical, and scientific equipment for Korea and India.

The second decade of service was somewhat less dramatic but just as important in numerous ways. It continued and expanded its work in both the Middle and Far East as well as in the United States. Work in Korea and India was maintained, the latter concentrated at the Purdah Park Education Center in Delhi, and expanded to include the Philippines as well as assistance to the school at Bir-Zeit in Jordan (1960). The Ryder Community Center had been opened to further intercultural relations, with its services later expanded.

Wherever the need existed for bettering the human condition, whether to assist Blacks in Virginia to accomplish the delicate task of complying with court-ordered desegregation or to assist underdeveloped countries to combat illiteracy, starvation, or disease, and recover from emergencies, the Service Committee was at hand, depending for much of its work on unpaid, volunteer support. It was, as Lalone had expressed it, a "valiant little unarmed army" who put "need before creed" on its banner and did what it could to make the word "Universalism" more than an empty abstraction.

Section VIII

Interdenominational Relations

Chapter 28

Edging Closer Together: Universalist-Unitarian Relations, 1870-1925

On the eve of the Civil War, Moses Ballou, staunchly Universalist to the core, produced probably as vitriolic a diatribe against Unitarians as came from any pen in the nineteenth century. He averred that "from all the facts of my experience and observation . . . [Unitarian] treatment of Universalists and Universalism, has been characterized by more that is offensive, than that which we have received from any other sect in Christendom. They have shown traits of illiberality which have frequently amounted to downright meanness."[1]

Ballou reported that the range of Unitarian behavior was a wide one. Some followed a policy of studied neglect, refusing to recognize that there were such people as Universalists. When recognized at all, Universalists were greeted with an "exceedingly patronizing air and manners which rendered such recognition "really more offensive than any downright abuse would be." Universalists were considered as mere plebians, while Unitarians were "proud, exclusive, and insufferably arrogant."

Ballou had served in five Universalist churches by 1860, extending over a quarter of a century, in communities in all of which a Unitarian church also existed. When he had arrived at each post, he had received courtesy calls from all other denominations, but only two from Unitarian clergy, both of whose churches were a "humble minority." The same pattern was seen in pulpit exchanges; if the Unitarians were a distinct minority, they were willing to tolerate a Universalist preacher; otherwise, exchanges were a rarity. In short, Unitarians regarded Universalists as *"poor relations."* To add insult to injury, "after stealing the leading principles of our faith, they would be very glad to get rid of our company."

Much the same spirit, although not as extremely stated, was reflected in a sarcastic editorial which appeared in the Universalist press a year after

Edward Everett Hale and Charles Lowe had extended officially the greetings of the Unitarians at the centennial celebration of 1870.

> Our Unitarian friends... constitute a model 'happy family,' a grand, consolidated, 'mutual admiration society.' Every thing Unitarian is perfect and divine. For talents, learning, taste, and all other human excellence, gifts and grace, they stand of course at the head, as they gravitate about the hub of the universe. What they do not know is undoubtedly not worth knowing. What they cannot do, and do better than any other mortals, must of necessity be set down in the narrow category of the impossible.[2]

If these two expressions of sentiment regarding Unitarians had prevailed, relations between the two denominations would never have progressed beyond the stage of antagonism, and the gradual and sometimes faltering steps to coexistence and even to gestures of fraternity would never have taken place. Despite all the roadblocks in the way of increased harmony and cooperation between Universalists and Unitarians, the two denominations had edged closer together by the mid-1920s and had proved wrong Moses Ballou's judgment that Unitarians should "go their own way, and we will go ours."

Until near the turn of the twentieth century it was difficult to discern a prevailing theme in Universalist-Unitarian relations. There were numerous instances of friendliness, cooperation among individuals of the two denominations, and even federation or union of local churches and parishes which sometimes attracted considerable attention but often went almost unnoticed, while at the same time there were outbursts of hostility which made the supporters of ultimate coalescence or even of more cordial relations fearful that such movements would never take place. Some Universalists were stubbornly resistant to any move that would bring the two denominations closer together, and remained suspicious and unsympathetic, if not actually hostile, to the very end. Simultaneously, others tried in various ways to break down barriers, real or imagined, and promote a feeling of identity as well as harmony. Much the same could be said for Unitarians, although it was they who took most of the initiatives in fostering improved relations.

One device was to attempt to link Universalists with religious liberalism and thus to underline their affinity with Unitarians. One of the principal subjects of discussion at the meeting of the Illinois Convention in 1878 was their standing among Christian denominations. The editor of *Unity* chided them for their timidity, arguing that they should stand up and be counted and reassert their "heroic old-time Universalist spirit" as champions of "the grand principles of Liberal Christianity for which they have so long battled."[3]

When fraternal greetings from the Unitarian NationaL Conference were sent to the General Convention meeting in 1874, Universalists were identified as promoters of liberal Christianity and were thus to be considered akin to the Unitarians.[4] But G.H. Emerson, editor of the *Universalist*, consistently and strongly opposed the terminology as ambiguous and even misleading, insisting that Universalists should always be identified with the larger Christian community by their denominational name and not buried in the broader designation.[5] This fear of losing identity was a persistent theme throughout Universalist history and did much to delay or prevent the possibility of union with any other denomination.

The 100th anniversary of the birth of William Ellery Channing was celebrated widely in 1880 among Unitarians, and was noted by several Universalists. It gave Isaac M. Atwood, at the time president of the Canton Theological School, an excellent opportunity to point up the comparisons and contrasts between the two denominations. He contributed an article entitled "Channing's Influence on Universalism" to a special memorial issue of *Unity*.[6] In it he compared Channing and Hosea Ballou as fellow New Englanders and as "providential men." Aside from the similar role that each played, Atwood found it much easier to see the differences in the two men than the similarities, even in age and physical appearance. Ballou was ten years older than Channing, tall and stalwart, while the younger Channing was short and slight. Channing had both the educational and social advantages which Ballou lacked.

Although both rebelled against their Calvinistic heritage, Ballou considered Calvinism a caricature of God while Channing was particularly offended because Calvinism "maligned human nature and extinguished the hope of human improvement." Ballou was a thinker and logician, a theologian and a controversialist, while Channing was a philosopher and a poet, a reformer and a philanthropist.

The characteristics of the two men were, in a broad sense, mirrored in the two denominations with which they were respectively associated. In its early days Universalism appealed to the common people while Unitarians addressed a much smaller and more select class. The number of college graduates in the Universalist ministry during the lifetimes of the two men could be counted on the fingers of one hand, but almost every Unitarian preacher was a graduate of Harvard College. Universalists lacked the exceptional culture, wealth, and social position of the Unitarians.

It might be noted parenthetically that the socio-economic differences between Universalists and Unitarians were recurrent themes in Atwood's writings, and one he considered paramount in keeping the two denominations apart.[7] This explanation had become something of a fixture in the projection of the Universalist self-image by the 1880s, and was repeated by Unitarians. In the same year that Atwood's article was published, Henry W. Bellows, in addressing the General Convention on behalf of Unitarians, called attention to the fact that Universalists had "reached the common people... even more successfully than we [Unitarians] can claim to have done."[8]

According to Atwood, as changes gradually came over both denominations over the years, they became less unlike than early in the nineteenth century. They inevitably affected each other, standing as they did in such close fellowship of thought and competing for much the same territory. Atwood found Channing's contribution to Universalism to be not so much in anything new as in his reinforcement and articulation of ideas held in common — "moral discernment, moral conviction, moral enthusiasm, raised to the highest power in a character of unique moral elevation." Channing's ability to universalize any topic or idea had made his name a household word in denominational circles, orthodox and liberal alike. Universalism had been touched in many ways by the influence of Channing — from its "improved literary taste and graces,... its growing disposition to identify the improvement of mankind with their salvation, [to] its enriched moral life."

Were there any caveats? There were but few, and Atwood called particular attention to one, which reflected his own bias. Channing was so fearful of "the repressing power of pledges and organizations" and was so much a champion of liberty, that it had become not only a source of disorder among religious liberals in general, but had provoked Unitarian criticism of the narrow denominationalism and sectarianism which was allegedly beginning to prevail among Universalists. Such an atomistic approach to religion as Channing stood for at the individual level could be carried too far and could threaten churchly solidarity.

J. G. Townsend, for more than twenty years a Methodist Episcopal clergyman, withdrew from that church in 1885 and organized the Independent Congregational Church in Jamestown, New York.[9] He proclaimed what was referred to as the "New Theology" which was actually a version of liberal Christianity recognizable by and familiar to both Universalists and Unitarians. Taking a leaf from the Chautauqua movement then popular, Townsend sponsored a two-week conference of public lectures and discussions in the summer of 1886 known as the "Lakewood School of the New Theology" at Chautauqua Lake. The announced aim was to unite all liberal Christians in one common effort to disseminate their ideas. Among the participants were two Unitarian and two Universalist educators: A. A. Livermore, president of Meadville Theological School; Harvard ex-President Thomas Hill; Orello Cone, president of Buchtel College; and Isaac M. Atwood, president of the Canton Theological School. For the first time in anyone's recollection, Universalists and Unitarians shared the same lecture platform.

Livermore's discourse, published in pamphlet form under the title "Liberal Christianity, Its Fruits," identified two of the "fruits": an improved theology; and leadership in humanitarian, philanthropic, educational, and social reform efforts. Under the first heading he defined the word "liberal" to mean "to be free from the hindrances and corruptions to which other forms of Christianity are subject, to be charitable in its fellowship, to be large-minded in its plans and purposes, to be inclusive rather than exclusive in its spirit, to hold the unity of spirit in the bond of peace." The "New or Liberal Theology" rejected the concept of the Trinity, total depravity, original sin, eternal punishment, predestination, particular grace, the Godship of Christ, and miraculous conversion. In their places were "one God our Father in Heaven and one Beloved Son of the Father, whom to know is life eternal and the capacity of all men to be sons of God; sin its own hell and goodness its own heaven, life an education, the supreme end of our being service to God and man."

The second fruit of liberal Christianity was its practical application to human affairs, a carrying out of the principle of "the great philanthropist Christ and the greater philanthropist God." Livermore identified no less than twenty-four "philanthrophies" which had originated in or were associated in some way with the liberal churches and their members. He led off with the peace movement in America in which Noah Worcester was a pioneer. Livermore listed nine men (all Unitarians) who were associated with "the first decided *temperance* movement in America" and close to a dozen professors of religious liberalism, including Adin Ballou, who participated in the anti-slavery cause. Then there was the part played by such men as Joseph Tuckerman in preaching to and ameliorating the lot of the poor in Boston, out of which arose the principle of the "Ministry at Large" which he outlined in 1838 after over a decade of activity.[10] There were among liberal Christians active agitators for public hospitals for the insane, the establishment during the Civil War of the United States Sanitary Commission and its branches, to aid soldiers, and scores of other movements and organizations to better the lot of humanity.

In commenting briefly on Livermore's discourse, the *Leader* drew attention to two points: the impressively long list of Unitarians eminent in philanthropic and reform movements; and the conspicuous absence of a similar array of Universalist names.[11] Of the dozens of reformers mentioned by name, only a scattering with direct Universalist association were mentioned; two of them (Adin Ballou and Thomas Starr King) were professed Unitarians in their formal religious connections during much of their ministerial careers. Mary A. Livermore was mentioned in connection with the Sanitary Commission as one who "hailed from the faith of Channing and Ballou," but was not identified as a Universalist.

There were, of course, numerous examples of denominational crossovers in the nineteenth century between Universalists and Unitarians. In 1880 Henry Blanchard, ordained as a Universalist in 1857, who had later switched to Unitarianism, elected to return to Universalism. In announcing this the *Christian Register* noted that 'the step from the pulpit of one of these denominations to that of the other is so short and easy that we wonder it is not oftener taken both ways."[12]

Such was the case also with Adin Ballou and Amory D. Mayo (1823–1907), listed by Livermore as a Unitarian pioneer in educational missions in the South. Mayo had studied for the ministry under Hosea Ballou 2d and had served his first pastorate in a Universalist church in Gloucester. Mary A. Livermore was listed by some authors as a Unitarian, although she was officially a Universalist.[13] Livermore made no mention of Clara Barton's contributions to the Red Cross; instead, he cited the less familiar name of George E. Gorton, a Unitarian clergyman and president of the American Humane Society, described as "the most active promoter" of the Red Cross.

Livermore did call attention to the fact that "the Universalist brethren have a brilliant record in philanthropy," attributed in part to the fact that "their doctrine of the Love of God is fitted to make philanthropists." Charles Spear, George W. Quinby, Edwin H. Chapin, "and others, God bless their memories," were recognized for their efforts to abolish capital punishment. In the field of literature the Cary sisters were enumerated among those of "the liberal christian faith," which in turn was part of "the church Universal."

The president of Meadville made no claim that his list of reformers and literary leaders was complete, as the *Leader* pointed out. Further, he was, it was noted, an eminently fair and courteous person. Yet, on balance, the sad fact seemed to be that the roster of Universalists would be shorter than Unitarians in any case. The editors also noted, with a touch of asperity, that Livermore would naturally be more familiar with the names of "his own people" than with those of "foreigners." Mutual knowledge of and communication between Universalists and Unitarians still left something to be desired.

The defensive position of the Universalists regarding their contributions was reminiscent of the complaint of Thomas B. Thayer several years earlier that the Unitarians had never acknowledged Hosea Ballou's key role in offering and defending the central doctrine of Unitarianism almost a quarter of a century before Channing preached his famous Baltimore sermon.[14]

Bisbee was much more assertive in a speech on behalf of the International Congress of Religious Liberals in 1909. He claimed that Universalists were the first "to bring into existence the Unitarian movement in this country. The Unitarian Church is the child of the Universalist Church and we are proud of our offspring."[15]

In the very same year that Livermore had talked about liberal Christianity and its contributions, Unitarian clergy in the Greater Boston area invited their Universalist colleagues to a "union meeting" to achieve better mutual understanding and greater cooperation.[16] The consensus was that, despite "so many things in common," sufficient differences existed between the two denominations to make "full affiliation," at least at the time, "impracticable."

One of the factors keeping Universalists and Unitarians apart in the 1880s was the growing rationalist wing within Unitarianism with which many Universalists refused to sympathize. John Greenleaf Adams was one of these. He blamed Theodore Parker, who had earlier left Unitarians without a "positive and united stand in regard to the divine authority of Christianity, as made known in the Scriptures."[17] The diversity of opinion within Unitarian ranks lacked a "theological base of Christian fellowship" such as the one holding Universalists together.

In the 1880s a split threatened to develop in the Western Unitarian Conference which had been organized in 1852 and at the time of its annual meeting in Cincinnati in 1886, comprised sixty-one churches.[18] Only twenty-one were represented at the meeting. One of the most important items on the agenda was the formulation of an acceptable definition of the aims and purposes of the Conference which would define Unitarian belief without imposing the constrictions of a creed. One resolution which declared the purpose of the Conference to be 'the promotion of a religion of love to God and love to man' was defeated, as was one referring to the diffusion of 'pure Christianity.' After four sessions, the Conference, by a vote of 34 to 10, rejected all proposals which included any reference to divine authority or revealed religion, and 'welcomed all who wish to join it to help establish Truth, Righteousness and Love in the world.'[19]

Universalists who reacted to this refusal to commit at least one segment of Unitarians to any theistic position at all, interpreted the action as a rejection of "God, Christianity and the immortal life as realities to be formally affirmed by a Unitarian body."[20] This left the Unitarians with no more than a vaguely worded ethical ideal which bore but slight resemblance to their historical roots. The editors of the *Leader* made haste to inform their readers that they were "wholly and thoroughly" on the side of those Unitarians who protested the action of the Conference. There was sufficient opposition among the more conservative western Unitarian churches to precipitate a secession which resulted in a split in 1886.

Five years earlier, Alonzo A. Miner, representing an older generation of Universalists, had delivered a sermon in which he had cast his lot with the conservative wing of Unitarianism which he hoped would some day triumph. So long as they adhered to their "historic foundation of Christianity, recognizing the special mission of Christ, from God," he could support Unitarians wholeheartedly and without reservation.[21] But until then, Universalists and Unitarians had to pursue their separate ways.

Opposition from conservative Universalists to what they perceived to be a "dangerous" tendency among Unitarians continued unabated. The

Leader was distressed that some Unitarians were turning rationalism into a religion itself, and had scarcely retained even "the aroma of that devout Christian sentiment" which had formerly characterized the denomination.[22] J. W. Hanson, a conservative Universalist and editor of the *New Covenant* in Chicago, accused the Western Unitarian Conference of emasculating the Bible, and announced that Universalists would cooperate only with *Christian* Unitarians.[23] John Coleman Adams was positive that any idea of uniting the Universalists and Unitarians had to be abandoned if the latter persisted in moving away from their historic Christian moorings.[24]

To make matters worse, some Unitarian spokesmen insisted on either implying or even stating explicitly that Universalists were riding too much on their history, were behind the times, and were either unwilling or unable to look to the future. When Hanson announced a plan to publish a series of biographies of early Universalist clergy, the reaction of *Unity* was not likely to endear Universalists to the Unitarian cause. "This is well, but 'tis better to let the 'dead past bury its dead,' and devote ourselves to the making of fresh heroes."[25]

Charles W. Wendte, superintendent of Unitarian work on the West Coast, was even more forthright in criticizing Universalists. He reviewed the comparative progress and strength of Universalism and Unitarianism on the Pacific Slope, and particularly in California, and saw no future for Universalism unless it rejected "the old, outworn, denominational, doctrinal Universalism. . . . There is simply no call in California for the old type of Universalist gospel, with its incessant polemic against hell-fire, its literal interpretation of Scripture, its supernaturalism, and other primitive features."[26]

Wendte found cooperation between Universalists and Unitarians minimal in spite of his efforts. A major reason was the fact that Universalists were about half a century behind in their intellectual outlook. Hence the missionary efforts of such men as Quillen H. Shinn were likely to be wasted, because he worked "on the old denominational lines." There were strong implications that the Universalists had better reconcile themselves to joining forces with the Unitarians and bringing themselves up to date. Ada C. Bowles immediately challenged Wendte as to his authority to serve as the spokesman for Unitarians.[27]

Relations had become so strained by 1889 that they appeared in the uppermost echelon of Universalism. The General Convention defeated a resolution to send three "fraternal delegates" to the National Unitarian Conference which convened a week after the Universalist meeting.[28] A recommendation by the same Unitarian body in 1891 for combining efforts in their Japan missions and otherwise promoting enlarged cooperation, although favored by the Universalist missionary George L. Perin, was summarily rejected. It was stipulated that merger was not to be approved, and that the Universalist mission was to retain its distinctive identity.[29] The fact that some Unitarians did not consider themselves "distinctly Christian" certainly contributed to the Universalist opposition to consolidation of missionary activities.[30]

At the same meeting in 1891 the General Convention refused to endorse a proposal to establish an interdenominational international journal devoted to "rational Christianity" — probably because it had been endorsed by the National Unitarian Conference.[31]

T. J. Sawyer, like Miner a spokesman for an earlier generation of Universalists, objected to the title *Liberal Christian,* the newspaper issued by Perin for the Japan mission. It should have been called the *Universalist Christian.* The word "liberal" was associated in Sawyer's mind with Unitarians. They were "quite too *liberal* for any intelligent Universalist to accept."[32]

Even a resolution offered at the General Convention in 1895 looking to "closer union" of Universalist and Unitarian churches was tabled, as was one which would have authorized a committee to consider "securing harmony and mutual help in Church extension."[33]

The same argument that had been used regarding denominational cooperation in the Japan mission was used by adults to oppose closer relations between the YPCU and the equivalent Unitarian youth group. After the Universalist young people had solidly endorsed closer relations with their Unitarian counterparts at their national meeting in 1897, Edwin C. Sweetser warned that "For Christ and his Church," the YPCU motto, could and would never be accepted by Unitarian youth.[34] The *New Unity* had then accused Sweetser of attempting to set the clock back.[35] Shinn, who had been a moving force in the YPCU and had been responsible for its slogan, agreed with Sweetser that Universalists and Unitarians could never be "natural" co-workers at any level so long as Unitarians possessed no system of Christian theology. The gap between the two denominations was unbridgable.[36]

Even as many Universalists looked askance at the idea of building interdenominational bridges, talk even of formal consolidation of Universalists and Unitarians was heard from time to time. In 1891 "a slight fit of proposed affliation" seized a few individuals, including some from within the Universalist ranks. Isaac M. Atwood, a contributing editor of the *Leader* and an opponent of formal union, took pen in hand and produced a long editorial on the subject.[37] After reviewing the general theological and ethical similarities, he found the differences in the particulars the deciding factors at the time, precluding the merging of the identity of either denomination into that of the other.

He singled out four differences: Neither denomination desired it; he failed to find twenty influential Universalists or Unitarians who favored consolidation. Logic may have justified it, but history and tradition did not. Neither group was "prepared to cut from its distinctive past." But even if all parties were agreed, there was no convincing evidence that union was desirable. There was virtue and merit in diversity as such. Let the Unitarians put their emphasis on Biblical criticism and the ethical elements in political and social problems and the Universalists on divine goodness and the gospel of Christ. Each could make its own contribution. Further, the Unitarians conceived their mission to be "with the scholarly and the elite." Unitarianism had "never taken hold of the common people." Conversely, Universalism from the beginning had won its converts in the main from the middle class, from neither the rich nor the poor. Neither denomination felt at home in the camp of the other. The logic of events, circumstances, and even of Providence, had made each group what it was. These alone would make formal affiliation impossible. And finally, the rationalism which was expressed in "pale negation" of the uniqueness of a revealed Christianity, which apparently dominated Unitarian thought, could not be accepted by the majority of Universalists.

The most concrete step yet taken toward Universalist-Unitarian cooperation was the provision for a joint committee in 1899. The idea had originated with the Unitarians who had formally proposed closer relationships in 1891, as already indicated, and again in 1895. But the timing had been unfortunate. No positive action had been taken by Universalists. The General Convention had engaged in a long and exhausting debate over the revision of the Winchester Profession of Faith and was in no mood to tackle another proposal which would have undoubtedly encountered opposition and precipitated another debate.[38]

In May 1899 it was Samuel A. Eliot, then secretary of the AUA, who renewed the proposal in his annual report. In his opinion, it was time that Unitarians extended their activities beyond their own borders. He suggested that "the time has come for a closer and more cordial co-operation with our brethren of the Universalist fellowship."[39] He told his fellow Unitarians that "compromise which rests upon the sandy foundation of merely verbal agreements" was not enough; "nor do I advocate any organic union of these distinct Christian bodies. Each has its own work to do, each has its honorable traditions to preserve; but I hold that it ought to be possible for these two organizations to work side by side with heartier good will and with mutual helpfulness." Close cooperation based on "a recognition of the intellectual agreements and the deep faiths of the heart which, beneath all diversity of gifts, bind together the Unitarian and Universalist fellowships."

A resolution to this effect was then adopted by the AUA in which the General Convention was invited to appoint five representatives who would serve with an equivalent group from the Unitarians as a "conference committee." Their responsibility would be to consider and devise means of closer cooperation and make a report to their respective constituencies.

There was lively discussion on the floor of the General Convention when the Unitarian proposal was introduced. Atwood, among others, urged that Universalists welcome "this overture of our sister church" and appoint such a committee. Edward Everett Hale, Francis G. Peabody, and Eliot were present on invitation to speak on behalf of the Unitarians. The invitation was accepted and a joint committee was authorized by a vote of 101 to 26, but not until after Sweetser had attempted to block the move by trying to have the matter of cooperation left in the hands of local churches.[40]

Press coverage of the Universalist-Unitarian discussions and actions at the 1899 General Convention distressed many Universalists, for it was erroneously reported that the two denominations had been amalgamated. Much of the responsibility for the mistake was placed on the Boston correspondents of the Associated Press.[41] Atwood tried to set the record straight. He pointed out that anyone who knew anything about the histories of the two denominations would never have made such a mistake.[42] He explained to the general public in an article in the *Independent* that the appointment of a joint committee was in no way to be construed as part of an attempt to unite Universalists and Unitarians. He made haste to point out that "nothing of the sort was intended. So long as the Orthodox churches exclude them both from Christian fellowship, they inevitably are driven to make alliance."[43] Aside from the immediate aim of closer cooperation, it was hoped by "the more catholic spirits in both groups" that this would lead in turn to eventual alliance among "all liberal Christians, in all denominations that are so fortunate as to possess such a saving remnant."

To further clarify and set to rest the matter of "the new relations" between Universalists and Unitarians, the trustees of the General Convention issued a circular in 1900 which they requested be read in all churches. "What both parties seek, is not union but unity; it is not consolidation, but co-operation; it is not to merge, but to fraternize; it is not identity but alliance."[44]

The joint Committee of Conference held its first meeting at AUA headquarters in Boston in January 1900, with all Universalist representatives present, and four of the five Unitarians.[45] They drew up a four-point platform, prefaced by a statement in which the committee went on record as "not desiring nor expecting to disturb in any way the separate organic autonomy of the two denominations. We seek co-operation, not consolidation; unity, not union."[46]

The plan called for the creation of a permanent consultative committee with two-year terms, meeting at least twice a year. The committee was to consider any matter in which the two denominations were jointly interested. This included opportunities for instituting churches or missions in new fields; circulation of tracts; and resolution of cases of conflict or duplication of missionary efforts. Regarding the latter, the committee would recommend appropriate action to the organization having jurisdiction. Clergy and churches were also encouraged to hold occasional joint meetings.

The Conference Committee requested that it be authorized to discharge the functions agreed upon until such time as their successors could be appointed, but the Universalist trustees declined to concur on the ground that they had no authority to do so. The 1901 convention did approve the biennial appointment of a committee of five to work with a Unitarian committee, but specified that the General Superintendent be a member and that the committee should not have, or exercise, joint missionary functions.[47] Further, its responsibilities were to be confined to cases where there might be conflict of interest, duplication of missionary efforts, or where friction might arise among the representatives of the two bodies. In short, the committee's prerogatives were to be carefully delimited.

Eliot greeted the creation of the committee with great satisfaction. Here was an effective way of showing "that federation in Christian work is not incompatible with distinction of organization." But many Universalists were not as sanguine. The Unitarian proposal, and the committee that had resulted, were warmly debated both before and after the General Convention took action. After Frederic W. Perkins had greeted with favor the idea of closer relations, Hanson vehemently disagreed. He saw "no advantage whatever" in closer cooperation.[48] Universalists should avoid "entangling alliances" of all kinds. The two denominations were not interchangeable.

But it was Sweetser, implacable foe of the Unitarians, who was most vociferous and persistent in leading the opposition to more than token cooperation with the Unitarians.[49] He used almost every conceivable argument he could muster, repeating them, with minor variations, time and time again, updating them and adding fresh examples as Universalist-Unitarian negotiations progressed.

Sweetser's major indictment of the Unitarians rested on his assumption that they were no longer a Christian denomination.[50] Did Universalists want to associate in any way with an ostensibly religious body that had become "scarcely anything but an ethical culture society."? He put part of the blame for the perilous state of Unitarianism which he saw in perceptible decline, on the lowered quantity and quality of leadership and pictured the Unitarian overture toward greater cooperation as a curious combination of desperation aimed toward survival and a nefarious scheme to worm their way into Universalist ranks. It was all a conspiracy to take over the Universalists.

The allegations about the Unitarians were considered so extreme by F. O. Hall, pastor of the church in Cambridge, Massachusetts, that he undertook to refute them, feeling that Sweetser had not only exaggerated the implication that amalgamation was imminent, but that Sweetser had done Unitarians a grave injustice on several counts. To Hall, all that seemed to be requested was to systematize the cooperation that already existed on a completely informal and uncoordinated basis.[51] No sinister conspiracy existed among Unitarians to take over the Universalist denomination. One of the prime functions of the proposed committee would be to see to it that neither church gained at the expense of the other. As to Sweetser's allegation that the Unitarians had abandoned Christianity, Hall called attention to the fact that in their formal resolution they were calling for a joint committee to serve 'the interests of pure Christianity.' That did not sound to him like the entrance into a post-Christian era.

Hall considered Sweetser's assertion that the Unitarians were on the verge of disappearing as a denomination to be not only a misstatement of fact but misleading as compared with Universalists. Hall granted that neither denomination had much to brag about in terms of increasing the number of churches organized on a self-supporting basis, but that the Unitarians had the better record of the two. As to the Unitarian propensity for stealing Univeralist churches, alleged constantly by Sweetser, there seemed to be evidence enough that the Universalists had done the same, although probably not as frequently. If Unitarian clergy were willing to subscribe to Universalist principles as a condition of fellowship, why should this not be accepted and encouraged? And Universalist clergy had exactly the same choice.

All of this discussion had taken place before the General Convention had acted on the Unitarian recommendation. The creation of the joint committee in 1899 and its first report (in 1900) brought forth another torrent from Sweetser, matched by another reply from Hall.

Sweetser had prepared a detailed article published in two parts in advance of the biennial meeting of the General Convention in Buffalo in 1901, entitled "Shall We Ally Outselves with the Unitarians?" His answer was a resounding "No."[52] The implications of the entire arrangement were, in Sweetser's view, extremely hazardous to the health of the Universalist denomination. The proposals of the joint committee, if adopted, would represent, in political phraseology, an "offensive and defensive alliance" in which the Unitarians could and would be the chief beneficiaries. Although formal union was not spelled out in the proposal, the consequence would be "an inevitable and constant tendency toward unification of the bodies themselves." In the meantime, attempts at union movements at the local level would result in either Universalist or Unitarian churches, probably the latter.

Regarding theology, Sweetser went over the same ground he had covered many times before; to wit, Unitarians, with all their talk about 'pure Christianity,' had for the most part rejected the Christhood of Jesus and had limited him to 'the natural order of humanity.' Sweetser could not accept this, and refused to approve a linkage, no matter how tenuous, with any denomination that took such a stand.

Did Universalists want to cooperate in missionary work in Japan with a denomination whose work there was at one time headed by Clay Mac-Cauley, who told the Japanese people that Unitarianism had outgrown Christianity and was better than any of the historic religions? The answer again — from Sweetser — was a decisive "No." The Unitarian denomination, taken as a whole, had, as Atwood had expressed it, 'ceased to be Christian in any but the hereditary and statistical sense.' Unitarians were not even committed to a belief in universal salvation. Universalists could not, in Sweetser's view, cooperate with the Unitarians in the manner proposed without violating their own principles.

He focused also on the tendency he perceived of Unitarians to object to the Universalist presence in many communities where Unitarian churches already existed, and cited a number of specific instances, some of which were intended to show Unitarian efforts to undermine Universalists and even to alienate them from their own denomination. Dredging Universalist churches out of financial difficulties seemed to be a favorite occupation among Unitarians. Among the examples cited were Duluth, Minnesota; Erie, Pennsylvania; Lincoln, Nebraska; Richmond, Virginia; and Schenectady, New York. In almost every instance cited by Sweetser, the churches eventually carried the word "Unitarian" in their titles.[53]

The tenor of Sweetser's arguments was clear. Whether viewing the matter doctrinally or operationally, the General Convention should not adopt the report of the joint committee. "To do so would be to invite a calamity."

The *Leader* reacted to Sweetser's articles by expressing regret that he had devoted so much space (over half) to showing the "unchristian" character of Unitarianism.[54] While the majority of Unitarians were undoubtedly more radical in their beliefs, theological speaking, than the majority of Universalists, whether they were less Christian was a matter of opinion; further, there was as much diversity of views among Unitarians as among Universalists. The principal quarrel with the Unitarian church was that "it does not stand for anything or anywhere."

The *Leader* felt that Sweetser made a better case for his other major point; namely, the tendency of Unitarians toward "benevolent assimilation" of Universalists. But, on balance, the *Leader* believed that the overtures toward closer cooperation were sincere and were offered in good faith. For the most part, excluded as they were from other churches, Universalists and Unitarians were naturally thrown together; hence the plan of more formal consultation was in part a legitimate defense mechanism, provided the limits and obligations of cooperation were clearly defined. The proposed commission therefore had the blessing of the denomination's leading publication.

Furthermore, the *Leader* did not look upon the proposal as either intending or involving the sort of alliance defined by Sweetser.[55] Neither did they see inevitable conflict between the two denominations, as predicted by Sweetser. Although the *Leader* did have qualms about some of the conflicts that had occurred, and raised the question of who really spoke for the Unitarians, it had no really serious doubts about proceeding in the fashion outlined by the Unitarians.

Hall added his voice to the pre-convention debate over the report of the joint committee by criticizing Sweetser for his extremism and strongly urging adoption of the report. Its rejection would mean, "once and for all time," the only offer of fellowship ever received from the approximately 150 Christian religious bodies in existence in the United States.[56] No less than 149 of them had either ignored or repudiated the Universalists.

Closer home, if Sweetser's bitterness and his accusations of "dishonorable conduct and crafty motives" were taken to represent the feelings of the entire denomination, then Hall would not be surprised if the Unitarian church withdrew its proposition of cooperation and refused to consider the matter further. Inspection of the records of the joint committee would indicate that almost every proposition presented in the report had come from the Universalist representatives. The only opposition in the committee came from one Universalist who doubted the practicability (not the desirability) of closer cooperation.

The alleged takeover of Universalist churches by the Unitarians did not bother Hall. After all, cooperation was a two-way street, and was it not better to have a Unitarian church with Universalists in it than no church at all? The Unitarians were spending more money, founding more churches, and circulating more literature than the Universalists. Who would fault them for that? It was time the Universalists were up and doing.

As to the purportedly unchristian character of Unitarianism, Hall considered this argument largely irrelevant. Sweetser was both ignoring the recent scholarship on the divinity of Christ and applying a doctrinal test to another denomination which would never be put to a vote among Universalists themselves. The argument that the Unitarians were insincere in their proffered hand of fellowship was in no way proven. Hall then proceeded to challenge the accuracy and/or credibility of almost every example Sweetser cited of religious kleptomania on the part of the Unitarians.[57] Here, thought Hall, were some excellent case studies for the proposed joint committee to investigate and to which appeals could be made when conflicts did in fact develop. If no such machinery were established, "we shall go on indefinitely nagging, bickering and working at cross purposes. . . . Let us have done with fighting."

Since the indictment by Sweetser was so severe, J. T. Sunderland, a leading and highly respected Unitarian, felt constrained to reply.[58] He felt that Sweetser's strong language would alienate members of both denominations at the very time when cooperation was needed. The Unitarian pastor was particularly upset by Sweetser's characterization of Unitarians as conspirators who deliberately set out to sabotage Universalist efforts and hence were not to be trusted. This was a serious charge, and the condemnation of an entire denomination was not only unfair but completely wrong.

Sunderland then responded to the charge that Unitarians were not Christians and that the radical wing had captured the denomination. Sweetser had no authority to set up any particular Christology as a test of Christianity or even of Universalism. Unitarians had as much right to establish their own interpretation as did Universalists. In addition, the wording of the Universalist Declaration of 1899 regarding the leadership of Christ as the son of God was quite in harmony with Unitarian belief.

The Unitarian responded regarding radical-conservative issues by citing chapter and verse, as it were, to show that Sweetser had taken the refusal in 1886 of the most radical wing within the Western Unitarian Conference to adopt a Christian or even a theistic basis, as the stand of the entire denomination. The recalcitrant Universalist had failed to point out that the Conference had modified its statement in 1892 and that two years later the National Conference had, by unanimous vote, taken an unequivocally Christian position not only by taking the Christian name but by accepting 'the religion of Jesus.' What could be more Christian than that? Sweetser had conveniently failed to mention this. Sunderland triumphantly concluded his article with the uncompromising statement that "the Unitarian body shows no signs of moving away from Christianity." The *Leader*, in commending the article to its readers, felt tht the author had "placed the whole matter in the right light."

Between 1900 and 1905 the record indicated only minimal activity by the Universalist-Unitarian committee. In 1900 Eliot suggested to Atwood that in such places as Schenectady and Albany, New York, where there were both Universalist and Unitarian churches, parishes should have the fellowship of both denominations. The Albany churches were finally federated thirty years later. But Atwood vetoed that idea. He thought it would be wiser for "every church to be distinctively one thing or the other."[59] The policy that each should still fly its own flag would be the best way to escape the "*entangling* alliances" of which so many Universalists were so afraid.

The joint committee appointed in 1901, with severely circumscribed powers, did in fact meet at irregular intervals and serve as a sort of arbitration committee in the case of half a dozen churches and/or communities where both Universalists and Unitarians were to be found. The committee investigated problems in Wichita, Kansas; Schenectady; and Erie, in 1901–1902, with inconclusive results.[60]

The comparative silence was finally broken by Sweetser on the eve of the General Convention meeting in Minneapolis in 1905.[61] Jealous guardian that he was of Universalist beliefs and denominational autonomy, and suspicious as he always was of Unitarian motives, Sweetser forewarned Universalists that the Unitarians were about to present another scheme for closer cooperation. What put him on his guard was a questionnaire sent in 1904 by the Unitarian Committee on Comity and Fellowship to Universalist clergy, of whom some 200 responded. The thrust of the inquiry was to determine their views as to the possibility and desirability of enhanced interchange. Slightly over 100 were in favor of increased "interdenominational activity" of some kind, but Sweetser interpreted the failure of the great majority of the more than 700 Universalist clergy to reply as proof positive that there was no real sentiment in favor of closer relations. Even more telling to Sweetser was the fact of the questionnaire itself; to him it represented an underhanded attempt to bypass the expressed will of the General Convention or actually to overturn the decision not to become deeply involved with the Unitarians.

A review of the state of the Unitarians, as reported in their official documents for 1905, convinced Sweetser that their denomination was still in serious trouble, and would grasp at any straw to survive. It was a matter of self-preservation to court the Universalists. So far as the joint committee was concerned, it was accomplishing nothing anyway. In view of the fact that Unitarians had drifted so far away from the Christocentric and theocentric principles of Biblical Universalism, it would be nothing less than folly for Universalists to consort with them ecclesiastically. Let each group "go its own way, doing its own work and submitting to the law of the survival of the fittest." The General Convention thought otherwise, and voted to continue the joint committee. It continued to meet until 1907 and saw to it that new missionary movements of the two denominations did not occupy the same ground or engage in any "injurious and wasteful competition."[62]

Official relations between Universalists and Unitarians remained much as they had before 1900, with occasional bursts of enthusiasm for merger and just as many evidences of retreat or of maintenance of the *status quo*. In 1909 the Missouri Convention memorialized the General Convention, calling for efforts "in every possible way in starting merger movements."[63] The Committee on Official Reports, to whom the memorial was referred, refused to endorse it, leaving the matter of organic union "to make its own way."

Nothing more than fraternization and some vague form of "federation" seemed to be appropriate, as Eliot told a joint meeting at the Universalist Club in New York City in 1906.[64] Henry Wilder Foote brought Unitarian greetings to the General Convention meeting in Detroit in 1909, and compared the two denominations to "twin brothers," closely related but still retaining their individual identities.[65]

There were indeed examples of the merger of local groups in all parts of the nation. In 1878 the Universalist and Unitarian societies in Englewood, a suburb of Chicago, caused quite a stir by dropping their old names and combining as the Christian Union Society.[66] Augusta Chapin and J. T. Sunderland, the respective pastors, preached on alternate Sundays.

Unity Church (Temple) in Oak Park, Illinois, another Chicago suburb, was dedicated in 1909 as an interesting example of Universalists-Unitarian cooperation. The history of the church was unusual in several respects. It had been organized in 1871 by joint effort, as an independent entity. Johonnot, the pastor since 1892, held fellowhip in both denominations. After the original edifice burned in 1905 a new structure was designed by Frank Lloyd Wright, nephew of Jenkin Lloyd Jones. The church was built of reinforced concrete poured on the site and was completely fireproof.[67] The dedicatory sermon was preached by Eliot, who had been a classmate of Johonnot at the Harvard Divinity School.

Such mergers were by no means confined to the Midwest. All Souls' Unitarian-Universalist Church in New London, Connecticut, and All Souls' Universalist-Unitarian Church in Waterbury, both dedicated in 1909–1910, were experiments sponsored by the Connecticut Convention to test the feasibility of union.[68] Eliot, representing the Unitarians, and John Coleman Adams the Universalists, gave addresses at the dedicatory ceremonies at each church.

While the Unitarian leadership was cultivating a wider fellowship after 1900, Universalists were adamant about retaining their denominationalism and their Christian orientation. At the meeting of the National Conference of Unitarians and other Christian Churches in Chicago in 1909, a proposal was made to drop the word "National" in order to include Canadian Unitarians.[69] Another possibility was to change the name of the Conference to "Unitarians and Kindred Churches" so that Jews would not be excluded from fellowship. The debate among Unitarians over a possible change of name was resumed in 1922–1923, all with the intent of appealing to liberals outside the denomination. The suggestion was made that even the word "Unitarian" might be dropped, on the ground that it was a handicap and was too confining.[70]

The editor of the *Leader* saw no objection to deleting "National" but he dissented sharply from the proposal to drop the word "Christian."[71] That was carrying the idea of larger fellowship entirely too far and would obliterate all church boundaries. Friendliness and cooperation were all very well, but such a move would rule out anything more than that so far as Universalists were concerned. They were "*Christian,* first, last, and all the time." He warned that the Unitarians would lose their denominational integrity by attempting to become "everything to every body in [the] search for companionship." Such gratuitous advice was probably not fully appreciated. To the end of his career, Editor Bisbee opposed merger, and used the columns of the *Leader* to say so.[72]

Little was either said or done about promoting closer relations for several years after 1910, and the nation's involvement in the First World War brought movement in that direction almost to a halt. One of the few attempts to keep the question of interdenominational relations alive was made at a joint meeting of Universalist and Unitarian clergy in the Greater Boston area in 1916.[73] The chief speakers were McCollester and Eliot. The Universalists called for closer working relationships with liberal Congregationalists as well as Unitarians, but Eliot went much farther, addressing himself primarily to relations with his own denomination. He considered duplication of effort as a "scandal" and announced somewhat dramatically that the state of the nation threatened the very existence of liberal churches. "We must get together. . . . Unless something is done we shall all go to the scrap-heap." The encroachments of materialism, "the onward march of the disciplined order of the Romish church," and the outburst of interest in the brand of "reactionary theology" being spread by the Billy Sunday crusade, were among the threats to the very existence of the kind of liberalism for which Unitarians and Universalists stood. He called for the multiplication of joint conferences, union Sunday school meetings, greater use of "common instrumentalities of public worship," consolidation of divinity schools, more union churches, and the updating of church laws to provide for dual fellowship (aimed at the Universalists).

Bisbee, present at the meeting, saw fit to say that if all this meant looking toward amalgamation it was unwise. He was positive that, in nine cases out of ten, union churches turned out to be Unitarian, no matter what the sign in front might say. A hyphenated church was "an ecclesiastical Siamese twin" which could be "but little more than a curiosity, and its perpetuation and multiplication but a tragic disaster!" No matter who "won," the other would experience a sense of loss. Each had a different mission to fulfill, the Unitarians appealing to the aristocratic, the "cultural," the "trained mind" — the Universalists to the democratic, the "spiritual," to "warmth and fervor." Bisbee was but repeating what had become an almost endless litany.[74]

One attempt at local Universalists-Unitarian merger which attracted some attention and was pronounced a success was the creation in 1918 of the Liberal Christian Church in Atlanta, Georgia, largely through the efforts of the Universalist pastor, Gideon I. Keirn, who had served twice in the Japan Mission. He could see no reason why the "Atlanta Plan" could not be applied on a larger scale to unite the denominations and enhance both their power and influence. He even offered a revised Five Points of Fellowship which incorporated both Universalist and Unitarian wording that included a "liberty clause."[75]

But such talk of the desirability of unification was counterbalanced by

Eugene Rodman Shippen, a Unitarian clergyman, who argued that a unified denomination would in no way mean a doubling of strength as proponents of union argued. "Arithmetic is a poor guide in ecclesiastical affairs."[76] And so the debate went on, back and forth, seemingly both interminable and without resolution.

After the First World War there was renewed attention to interdenominational affairs. Eliot gave an address at the installation of John Sayles (Universalist) in the newly federated First Liberal Church of Mt. Vernon, New York, in 1923, in which he announced that "the time is ripe for [a] constructive federated movement. There is no valid reason for the continued separation of the people of the Universalist and Unitarian traditions."[77] He sidestepped the question of organic union by stating that "real unity is in the wealth of co-operating diversities." George H. Baxter, the Unitarian pastor in Orlando, Florida, admitted that Unitarians had to give up their historic preoccupation with their pedigree and pay more attention to their neighbors.[78]

Universalists were simultaneously warming a bit to the desirability of greater cooperation, although as a whole they were certainly not ready to follow the advice of one who said that it was time "to forget old feuds, old fights, old differences, old names, and resolve to bring to pass a new and greater Church."[79] Perkins addressed the Unitarian General Conference just before the General Convention met in 1927, and devoted much of his presentation to the "close spiritual relations between the two denominations and the bonds which were "drawing them closer together."[80]

There was indeed among some Universalists a "longing for a larger fellowship," at least among the clergy. Nearly every minister, man or woman, had "borne the brunt of isolation and know what it means."[81] Yet, paradoxically, much of the isolation was self-imposed, so far as relations with the Unitarians were concerned; the fierce determination of the Universalists to maintain their own independence had brought from a Unitarian clergyman, Augustus P. Reccord, this plaintive comment: "Unfortunately the attempt to cooperate with our Universalist brethren has so often proved abortive that I have lost faith in it. Perhaps we are 'too near akin.' "[82]

If any steps toward a new alignment were ever taken, the initiative had to come from outside the denomination to be effective, and there could be no sense of supplication on the part of Universalists. As Atwood told a meeting of Massachusetts Universalist clergy in the fall of 1924, if a new relationship ever did come to pass, it could do so "whenever doors open so we can — not to lose our faith or Church or go out of business, but to make both mightier in a new union."[83] Less than a year after these words were uttered, the doors did actully open, but on the initiative of two other denominations rather than one.

Chapter 29

An Enlarged "Household of Faith?" Aborted Union with the Congregationalists

Two interlocking events occurred at the General Convention meeting in Syracuse, New York, in 1925 which stirred the denomination and created a complex triangle of Universalists-Congregational-Unitarian relations which occupied much of the attention of all three denominations for almost five years. Universalists found themselves wooed simultaneously by the other two groups, an occurrence unprecedented in the history of the denomination.

The first was a communication from the American Unitarian Association, worded as follows:

> Whereas it has come about in the Providence of God, and through the deepening insight and enlarging experience of men, that the principles of religious thought and conduct long cherished in lonely fortitude by the churches of the Universalist and Unitarian Fellowships, have now become the conviction and possession of many minds and hearts, and
>
> Whereas in every Christian Communion there are now men and women of progressive spirit who increasingly affirm that Christianity is a way of life rather than a conformity to creed, and
>
> Whereas the challenge to leadership in the cause of a free and spiritual religion comes with a peculiar significance to our Free churches, be it
>
> Resolved that this Association respectfully requests the Universalist General Convention to authorize its President to appoint a Commission of not less than three or more than five representatives to meet with a similar Commission to be appointed by the President of the American Unitarian Association, with a view to inviting and organizing a Council of representative liberal Christians for the purpose of promoting sympathy and co-operation among them, furthering their common aims and uniting them for the advancement of the Kingdom of God.[1]

Judge Roger S. Galer of Iowa promptly moved that the convention receive the communication "with an expression of appreciation" and authorize the president to refer the matter to an appropriate committee to consider it.

The second event was a telegram from the National Council of the Congregational Churches of the United States reporting a similar resolution adopted by that body, with the full text to follow. President Atwood announced that when received it would be referred to the same committee. The National Council directed its Commission on Interchurch Relations "to express to the General Convention its sincere desire to welcome to its fellowship all churches which can find freedom and satisfaction on the general basis of the Kansas City Statement of 1913, and it invites the General Convention to appoint a corresponding Commission to consider with more care what is practicable."[2]

To those who had kept abreast of Universalist-Unitarian relations over previous decades, the Unitarian overture probably came as no great surprise. But with the Congregationalists the situation was somewhat different. Until the eve of the First World War relations with them had been generally harmonious but not unusually close. Clergy of each denomination had more and more frequently participated on invitation in programs sponsored by the other. William E. Barton, minister of the largest Congregational church in Illinois, in suburban Oak Park (Chicago), had given one of the addresses in 1920 at the celebration in Gloucester, Massachusetts, of the 150th anniversary of the founding of Universalism in America.[3]

The Congregational overture to the Universalists was no isolated move. It was both part of a great surge of ecumenism on a national and international scale, among largely Protestant religious bodies after the First World War; and at the same time the reflection of a long-standing desire on the part of Congregationalists to unite all Christians. This resulted in a series of attempts at cooperation in some degree, from closer fellowship to complete merger, with other Protestant groupings.

The year 1927 saw a World Conference on Faith and Order in Lausanne, Switzerland, with some 500 delegates representing most Protestant churches as well as the Eastern Orthodox. In the United States, Christian Unity conferences were held in the 1920s all over the nation in metropolitan centers. In Canada, Congregationalists, Methodists, and Presbyterians joined forces to create the United Church of Canada which attracted much attention and was often cited as a model for cooperation among American churches. There was much talk of a "United Church of America" to match it. Plans for union, federation, or some other form of inter-church cooperation seemed to be in the air everywhere.

The Congregational drive for church unity could be traced as far back as 1871, with the founding of the National Council, which in turn had established in 1886 a Commission on Church Unity to further the idea of a federation of "all bodies of Christian churches."[4] In 1920 a plan had been put forward for the unification of some eighteen denominations in which the Congregationalists had been in the forefront. They endorsed it overwhelmingly at their meeting in 1923. But the idea had been advanced too rapidly, and supporters of the Federal Council of Churches had opposed it. The National Council had expressed a willingness even to surrender the name "Congregational" if this would advance Christian unity.

At the very same time that the Congregationalists approached the Universalists in 1925, the former were negotiating with both the Presbyterian and Christian churches. This effort resulted in the ratification in 1931 of merger with the latter, voted two years earlier. The result was the Congregational Christian Church.

When the General Convention and the National Council had met simultaneously in 1913 in Chicago and Kansas City, respectively, something had taken place at the Congregational meeting which was to have a direct bearing on relations with the Universalists and bring the two denominations closer together than ever before. The National Council had adopted a new constitution, and a statement concerning "faith, polity and fellowship" had been included as a preamble, with only one dissenting vote among the nearly 600 delegates.[5]

The so-called "Kansas City Platform" affirmed or reaffirmed, in very generalized terms, belief in a God "infinite in wisdom, goodness and love"; the mission of "laboring for the progress of knowledge, the promotion of justice, and the reign of peace and the realization of human brotherhood"; belief in "the freedom and responsibility of the individual soul and the right of private judgment . . . [and] the autonomy of the local church." It also called for "hearty co-operation" with all branches of the Christian church.

Frederick A. Bisbee, then editor of the *Leader,* had reported that the new Congregational profession of faith, "in spirit, and almost in letter, was simply an enlargement of our own Five Principles of Fellowship. It was read with astonishment and delight by our people, and everywhere the question was raised as to what there was to keep Universalists out."[6] He went on to say that "not a few discerned an invitation to come in! We do not anticipate an immediate amalgamation, but it was felt very profoundly . . . that this greatest step towards Christian and even church unity had been taken."

Not all Universalists agreed with Bisbee. One minister had reservations and doubts about the new Congregational statement. It lacked a definite, straightforward, clear-cut affirmation of Universalist principles and was merely a glossing over of part of the Five Principles; he was not sure either that it was truly representative of most Congregational thought.[7] Neither did he find an explicit repudiation of the Congregational creed of 1883 which referred to the Final Judgment and "everlasting punishment."[8] Regardless of that, the 1913 statement was still a "creed," new or not, and was therefore not acceptable to most Universalists.

Frank Oliver Hall, speaking before the New England Congregational Conference in 1914, emphasized the common structure of the two denominations and indicated that it might be the destiny of the Universalist church to be "reabsorbed" into the older organization.[9] If the Congregationalists had stood a century earlier on the platform adopted in 1913 "there would never have been a Universalist church." Personally, he would rejoice if the denomination could join the Congregationalists; Hall was "tired of being separated from my brethren."

More and more attention was paid to the question of increased Universalist-Congregational cooperation, if the amount of space devoted to the subject in the columns of the *Congregationalist* and at meetings of Congregational bodies are accurate gauges. At the meeting of the National Council in 1923, the moderator (Barton) devoted much of his opening address to the position of the church in the larger Christian world. In an historical review he paid particular attention to the contributions of the Universalists who had come into being as a denomination largely to offer a new conception of the benevolent character of God which had long needed adequate expression.[10] The Universalists had contributed to a cleavage in the established (Congregational) church which both sides acknowledged, but why should it continue to exist? "Is not modern Congregationalism broad enough and inclusive enough to set about an effort for the healing of these old divisions of misunderstanding? The time has long since passed when this or any other orthodox communion believes that a man's fitness for heaven depends upon his opinion of hell." Barton also put much stress on the "creedless" character of Congregationalism, and described the Kansas City statement as a declaration of faith, "not as a test but as a testimony." It seemed that some kind of action was imminent on the part of the Congregationalists in their relations with Universalists; the way was being prepared.

The atmosphere at the General Convention meeting in Providence in 1923 was strongly conducive to furthering inter-denominational cooperation; J. C. Adams, L. B. Fisher, and L. S. McCollester were among those who spoke strongly in favor. Prominent among the recommendations of the trustees, as part of a document entitled "Present Day Objectives of the Universalist Church," which was adopted as read, was a statement on Christian unity. It called for seeking "closer relations with all liberal Christians."[11] At the same meeting the Universalists were informed that the Congregationalists were prepared to discuss with other denominations "such plans as seemed practicable and wise for a unification of liberal religious forces." An Associated Press report of the convention proceedings left the impression that the Universalists were deliberately splitting the ranks of the Congregationalists by attempting to appeal to their liberal wing. This was emphatically denied.[12]

With the Congregational offer in mind, a seven-person special Commission on Comity and Church Unity was appointed by the Universalist trustees "to enter into correspondence and conference with other similar bodies" and to report to the next meeting. Formal machinery for interdenominational cooperation was thus created; a reconstituted commission was authorized in 1925 to carry on the work.

The first commission, headed by Harold Marshall, met in January 1924, and by consensus affirmed that "the time had come when we ought to seek closer relations with other groups of liberal Christians."[13] Their first action was to make a survey of religious liberalism to see what progress had been made and what needed to be done to carry out the resolution of Christian unity adopted by the convention in 1923. The chairman traveled nearly 20,000 miles and held conferences with more than 100 individuals and groups representing "many denominations." Other members of the commission did likewise. Over 14,000 letters were sent out and 25,000 pieces of literature were distributed. Judging from the results, the commission concluded that the time was ripe for efforts at "Christian union as well as Christian unity."[14]

While the commission was doing its work, the *Congregationalist* was busy courting Universalists. In the summer of 1925 the editor had observed that there were many Universalists who would welcome union with the Congregationalists.[15] Admittedly there might be some objection among the more conservative, but "it would be folly to assert that the Universalists today in religious views, temper and outlook, differ in any radical way from large numbers who are now within the Congregational fellowship."

The development which had made visible the emerging Congregational interest in the Universalists was a resolution in 1925 from the Northern California Congregational Conference requesting the National Council to appoint at its forthcoming meeting in Washington, D.C., a special committee to explore the possibilities of closer relationships with the Universalists. At almost the same time the Maine Universalists Convention had urged the forthcoming General Convention to seek "cooperation, unity, and a fellowship of common service" with other denominations.[16]

The Congregational Commission on Interchurch Relations had met preceding the October meeting of the National Council in 1925, and Frank K. Sanders, the chairman of the commission, had made his report.[17] He acknowledged receipt of the request from California and noted, regarding the resolution of the Maine Universalists, that although the Congregationalists had not been mentioned by name, it was "understood that they were in the mind of the Maine Convention." He further reported that the commission, in attempting to establish good relations with "all those denominations of reasonably Congregational type," had received "informal proposals [and] indirect approaches had been made by the Universalist Church." This presumably referred to the inquiries about religious liberalism that had been made by the Commission on Comity and Church Unity after its creation in 1923, and to informal conferences, principally among officers of the respective commissions prior to the fall meeting of the General Convention.

The Congregational commission had been "truly responsive" and had expressed the hope "that a way may soon eventuate for such fellowship." Congregationalists were informed, possibly as much for their benefit as for the Universalists who read their paper, that the "expressed basis of fellowship" would be the Kansas City Platform, which was emphatically not a creed. The National Council had thereupon voted unanimously, on recommendation of the commission, to extend the invitation to the Universalists at their convention then in progress in Syracuse.

Much of the cultivation of increasingly cordial relations between the Universalists and the Congregationalists was the result of the longstanding journalistic friendship of the editors of the leading religious paper in each denomination. Both John van Schaick *(Leader)* and William E. Gilroy *(Congregationalist)* were ardent proponents of interdenominational cooperation and Christian unity, and had nothing but compliments for each other and the churches they represented. They comprised, in short, a two-person mutual admiration society. Nothing more laudatory could probably have been written than the editorial by Gilroy when van Schaick received an honorary Litt. D. from Tufts College at its 1927 Commencement.[18] When the Congregationalists held their biennial convention in Detroit in 1929 which van Schaick attended as an honorary delegate, Gilroy gave a luncheon in his honor.[19] They frequently exchanged items for publication, and the *Leader* and the *Congregationalist* each carried a column which appreared regularly, entitled "Safed the Sage," written by the prominent Congregationalist William E. Barton.[20]

When the Northern California Congregationalists called for an exploratory conference with the Universalists about closer relationships, Gilroy had thoroughly approved and thought that no harm could come to "talk things over"; he looked forward "with pleasure and confidence" to closer relations.[21] The editor of the *Leader* prepared, at Gilroy's request, an article on Universalism published a week before the National Council meeting in 1925.[22] Gilroy prefaced the article with the observation that "probably no two groups anywhere in the religious world today are more similar in temper and spirit than the Universalists and Congregationalists." The Congregational editor stood "squarely and firmly" with van Schaick in all of his ideas.[23]

Beginning with the first issue in January 1926, van Schaick changed the name of the *Universalist Leader* to the *Christian Leader* — a return to the one abandoned in 1897. He offered several reasons, among them his intention to reaffirm that Universalists were still Christians, especially at a time "when some so-called liberals" were urging that they abandon that name;

and his desire to play down denominational labels and emphasize the more inclusive and broader field in which the church was engaged.[24] Reactions to this unilateral act on the part of the editor were by no means all favorable among Universalists. The letters to the editor were full of protests, which were of no avail.

Between 1925 and 1927, while the Congregational and Universalist commissions were negotiating (in executive session), the two editors reprinted from the other's columns every document, speech, or discussion that had any bearing on the subject. There was no question that the readers of each paper were kept fully informed, even if they did not always understand exactly what was going on. Both editors capitalized on every indication, no matter how small and localized, that Universalists and Congregationalists were drawing closer together, but had very little to say about the Unitarians. The *Leader* reported as another "step forward" the fact that the Monday Ministers Club, composed of Congregational clergy in the San Francisco Bay area, had elected to membership the pastor of the Universalist church in Oakland.[25]

A joint meeting of Universalist and Congregational ministers in the Boston area in 1926 was described as a "love feast" at which Daniel Evans, Abbott Professor of Theology in the Harvard Divinity School, and Perkins, delivered papers stressing the common history of the two denominations and "the pleasant prospect of the reunion in the not distant future."[26] The *Congregationalist* took pains to point out that the meeting had been the fulfillment of a wish expressed in 1916 by the Universalist Ministers Association to meet with the Fortnightly Club (Congregational) not only for fellowship but for "a frank discussion" of the possibilities of closer relations. It had never been held because of the intervention of war and changes of personnel. The meeting in 1926 was described as, in spirit, "unanimous for union."

From the time of the adjournment of the General Convention in 1925, and even before, the discussions and actions that took place regarding denominational relations inevitably involved the Unitarians as well as the Congregationalists. In 1922 there had been much informal Universalist-Congregational-Unitarian intermingling and discussion regarding closer cooperation. When the Universalist Club of Boston had met in the winter of 1922 the speakers had been McCollester (Universalist), Eliot (Unitarian), and Samuel H. Woodrow (Congregationalist). The editor of the *Leader* speculated that the meeting might be the forerunner of a united liberal church of some kind, but he admitted that his conjecture had been off base. Instead, all three "extolled the beauties of separation and diversity and kept away from any talk of organic union."[27] There was a note of wistfulness in this statement, for in 1924 van Schaick had written: "I hope to live to see Congregationalists, Unitarians, and Universalists all in one free Church."[28]

Sheldon Shepard, the associate pastor of the Universalist church in Los Angeles, introduced a motion at the California Convention in 1927 to present to the General Convention a memorial requesting that it "endeavor to bring about the establishment of a permanent joint commission of the Congregational, Unitarian, and Universalist denominations for the purpose of carrying on cooperative education, propaganda and crusade for liberalism and modernism in religion."[29] The primary idea was to increase visibility for liberal churches while still retaining separate denominations.

The Iowa Convention called for inclusion of the Unitarians in any arrangements for interdenominational cooperation. They had issued an invitation to the state Unitarian organization (which had been accepted) to hold a joint meeting in 1928.[30]

The question was immediately raised of why the Unitarians had neither received in 1925 a similar overture from the Congregationalists nor had been specifically included in the invitation to the Universalists. One explanation which had an important bearing on the question was doubt among Congregationalists about the Christian character of Unitarianism. Some kind of union with the Universalists was thought to be more "feasible" because they and the Congregationalists had "everything in common" while the Congregationalists and the Unitarians did not.[31]

Some Congregationalists were much disturbed when A. Wakefield Slaten, the pastor of the West Side Unitarian church in New York City, had delivered a series of sermons arguing that the name "Christian" was a handicap; the use of the term "God" was unnecessary; and personal immortality was a delusion. Even though the minister might have been very much in a minority in expressing such ideas, he was still within the Unitarian fellowship. Unitarians as a group were also considered too aloof and too critical of ecumenical efforts by other denominations.

Curtis W. Reese, editor-in-chief of the *Western Unitarian* and an editor of *Unity*, explained bluntly and at some length why Unitarians should not have been included in the proposed entente, even if an offer had been made. The reasons given for the presumed affinity of Universalists and Congregationalists did not apply to the Unitarians. The former were "intellectually cautious; we are intellectually venturesome. They are temperamentally evangelical; we are temperamentally rationalistic. They are doctrinally Christian; we are doctrinally universalist."[32] Congregationalism was too confining. Unitarians should not 'fall victim to the paralyzing tendency to merge things that are essentially different.' Unitarians had much more in common with liberal Judaism, Ethical Culture, Rationalism, and various independent movements both inside and outside of Christianity than with Congregationalism. Any attempt to engineer closer relations would mean a completely unacceptable sacrifice of these broader associations and would curtail the intellectual independence for which Unitarianism had always stood. The editor of the *Congregationalist* was positive that such "separatist" views as Reese expressed were not propitious for any kind of union.

The Congregational Commission on Interchurch Relations apparently had had no advance knowledge that the Unitarian resolutions were going to be presented to the Universalist convention in 1925. Congregationalists were told by Editor Gilroy that "a new and important factor, not apparently contemplated in the mutual overtures . . . [had] arisen."[33] He wondered whether the Unitarian action had been taken spontaneously or under the stimulation of the Congregational move. Gilroy emphasized the fact that the implications of the Congregational invitation to the Universalists should not be "misunderstood or minimized"; the offer was more than a mere friendly gesture or even a preliminary attempt to close an historic breach. It was to be interpreted as part of a broader alignment that might evolve eventually into a tripartite union of all three denominations. If such were the case, it had to be accomplished on the basis of "good will, mutual recognitions, and good understandings, and not upon the basis of some vague and sentimental 'liberalism' " One of the first steps was to obtain a better knowledge of each other than then existed.

The simultaneous action of the Unitarians and Congregationalists in 1925 in extending a cordial hand to Universalsits was immediately construed by many as a stage in developing Christian unity and cooperation on an unprecedented scale, and to the promotion of which, Universalists had officially committed themselves in 1923. Among the speakers at the 1925 convention was Richard Roberts, pastor of the American Presbyterian Church in Canada.[34] The burden of his address was a call for the unity of Protestant Christendom. Sherwood Eddy, well-known Congregationalist layman, world traveller, and public speaker, who gave the closing address at the 1925 Universalist convention, placed his stamp of approval on the Unitarian and Congregational actions and saw in them hope for a common ground to halt the "Balkanizing" of the Christian church.[35]

However, the two overtures were just as promptly interpreted to mean more than closer fellowship. It seemed to be assumed that the Universalists would eventually join either of the two other denominations, or both, creating in that case some kind of united liberal church. It was this assumption that a merger of some kind was in the offing that was to create no end of discussion and some misunderstanding in the next few years. The words "unity," "union," "reunion," "amalgamation," and "merger" were used so indiscriminately, so interchangeably, so frequently, and so loosely by the secular press, the editors of the denominational papers, and by individual members of the three religious groups most directly involved, that it was no wonder that intentions were not always clear.

One thing, however, was clear to Universalists: Whatever the outcome, it was they who were being approached by others; it was they who were being sought, and not the reverse. In fact, they had to be warned not to be "undignified and over-anxious" during the courtship.[36] One Universalist summed up the situation by noting with delight the distance they had travelled from the days when they had been classed "with atheists, free thinkers, Mohammedans, Saracens, Antinomians, and what not."[37]

The Universalist commission created in 1925 was much larger than its predecessor, consisting of sixteen members. Perkins, who had been a member of the earlier commission, served as chairman and took the lead and acted as its spokesman in its deliberations. Among the other members were the officers of the General Convention; the president of Tufts College; and one lone woman, from Brewton, Alabama.[38] At its first meeting, in January 1926, a seven-person executive committee was appointed and the commission voted to accept the invitations for further conferences proffered by the Congregationalists and Unitarians. As was the case at the first meeting, the commission, in its annual report in 1926, indicated its positive response, but only in the most generalized way. Neither of the two denominations with which negotiations had commenced were mentioned by name. The Universalists negotiators committed themselves publicly only to "unity and fraternity."

The fact that the Congregational and Unitarian overtures had come at the same time created a dilemma. So the first action was to ask the chairmen of the other two commissions if a conference among representatives of the three could be arranged. Perkins conferred with Eliot, president of the AUA and chairman of its commission, in the late fall of 1925. The Unitarian spokesman exressed his willingness to do so if it could be arranged, and agreed that meetings between the Unitarian and Universalist commissions should be postponed until the question of a three-party conference had been decided. Sanders, chairman of the Congregational commission, decided that it would be inadvisable to hold such a conference because it would have exceeded its charge. The Congregationalists had been instructed to negotiate only with the Universalists. So the three-way conference was never held and discussions were conducted at first only between the Congregationalists and the Universalists.

Many months of delicate negotiations followed. The closest possible communication was maintained by the parties involved. Contacts were complicated to some extent by the fact that although the majority of the commission members of both denominations were concentrated in the East, communication had to be maintained also with other members who were scattered all over the country. This necessitated much correspondence and voting by mail as well as meetings of both the two commissions and of their respective executive committees in various combinations. It was reported that "much of the action" was unanimous, and that the two commissions had no trouble reaching an agreement either among themselves or in joint conference. The basis for what became known as the Joint Statement was a document drawn up by the Universalist commission.[39]

The statement, as eventually hammered out, carried the signatures of all twenty-three members of the Congregational commission, which included fourteen clergy and four women. It was then approved unanimously by the executive committee of the National Council. All but one of the Universalist commission affixed their signatures, and all but one of the trustees of the General Convention approved the document when they met in January 1927. The single abstainer in both groups was Judge Galer. The long-awaited Joint Statement on Interchurch Relations was published simultaneously by the two denominations in February 1927.[40]

The editor of the *Leader* greeted the Joint Statement with jubilation, calling it "a remarkable document" and the efforts of the two commissions "an epoch-marking achievement" which heralded "a new and better day."[41] Regardless of how the delegate bodies voted on the report at their respective meetings, it marked "a forward step in Christian unity which never can be retraced." Gilroy was just as elated. The editorials written by each editor were captioned "Progress Towards a Practicable Union" and "Free Churches Move Toward Union," and were reprinted in each other's papers.[42] The statement was of course not yet an official document of either denomination as a whole. The National Council, to meet in Omaha, Nebraska, in May, and the General Convention, to meet in Hartford, Connecticut, in October, had yet to act.

Before presenting seven specific recommendations, the two sets of commissioners prefaced them with general remarks in which they emphasized the desirability of Christian unity and Christianity as a way of life; the leadership of Christ; and the non-essentiality of creeds and the unimportance of complete theological agreement. The fact that both denominations were "only branches of the same parent stock" was underlined, as was the argument that the justifications for union were much stronger than the historic reasons for their separateness. They now differed "in no essential respects." In spirit of use of the word "union," that step was not included as such in the recommendations. The goal was, instead, the seeking of "the closest practicable fellowship." No one could foresee what form that might take.

The proposed cooperative arrangement was elaborated as follows:

> *First:* That the ministers and representatives of each denomination be invited to sit as corresponding members in the local, state, and national associations of the other denomination and to participate in their deliberations.
>
> *Second:* That the agencies of each denomination in the realms of religious educa-

tion, social service, evangelism, rural church development and similar problems, be urged to arrange for joint programs for promotion so far as practicable.

Third: That in each community where churches of both denominations are found they be urged to study what they can do together with mutual profit by way of union services, the interchange of pulpits and the promotion of common enterprises.

Fourth: That there be a mutual interchange of representative speakers at national, state and local gatherings.

Fifth: That the denominational journals be urged to make the largest practicable interchange of editorials and of printed matter of common interest, in order that each constituency may be kept fully informed regarding the other and of the progress made in the direction of a closer fellowship.

Sixth: That, in order to secure more thoroughly coordinated movements, no actual steps toward the organic union of local Congregational and Universalist churches be made without consulting their respective Commission.

Seventh: Whenever the problem of an adequate church constituency presses for solution, and in any community where denominational divisions work for wastefulness, those responsible are urged to cooperate in organizing for more effective service.

The Joint Statement was released to the Associated Press on 17 February 1927 and thereby obtained national publicity; the response from the religious press was overwhelmingly favorable.[43] Albert Dieffenbach, editor of the *Christian Register,* wrote a lead editorial praising the statement, and comments from both the *Leader* and the *Congregationalist* were quoted extensively. Harold E. B. Speight, Unitarian minister of King's Chapel in Boston, and a strong advocate of Christian unity, greeted the statement with enthusiasm and hoped for its prompt acceptance by the two denominations involved. In 1925 he had begun a well-attended series of noonday services, with speakers from a wide variety of denominations. Both van Schaick and Perkins had been among them.[44]

Zion's Herald (Methodist Episcopal) published the statement in full and called it 'one of the most significant steps toward Christian unity attempted in recent years.' It expressed some surprise that a move for unity had not come first from the Unitarians but presumed that this was due to a split between the theists and the "materialistic humanists" and the resulting lack of unified leadership.

The Quaker *Friends' Intelligencer* in Philadelphia called it 'a wonderful beginning' and expressed its delight that such a movement was under way. John Haynes Holmes, editor of *Unity* and pastor of the Community Church in New York City, wrote directly to the *Leader* that the news was "one of the most heartening things I have heard in a long time." However, this long-time foe of denominationalism in any form thought the Universalists and Congregationalists should have gone "a good deal farther" and, following the Canadian model, ought to have "ended their separate sectarian organizations, and established a 'United Church.' "[45]

The Salem, Massachusetts *Evening News,* a secular paper, carried a long news story; an interview with Judge Hill, a member of the Universalist commission; and an editorial heartily endorsing the action. The

Waltham, Massachusetts *News-Tribune,* another secular organ, remarked cautiously that should the two groups be "absolutely united, no harm would be done.' It went so far as to suggest a name for the new combination: The "Universal Congregational Church."

The *Christian Century* devoted a long editorial to the statement under the heading "Two Great Churches Face Toward Union," reproduced the Joint Statement, and called it "the most promising and significant movement toward union between two important denominations that has occurred in this country in a generation." The journal, which gave its unqualified approval to the proposal of closer cooperation, went on to declare that Universalists were "no longer outcasts from good religious society," and that their cardinal principle of the salvation of all had become so widely accepted that Universalists could very well do without their own separate organization. The assumption throughout was that ultimate organic union was a foregone conclusion; it would come "naturally and inevitably." It was the harbinger of the day when "many more of the artificial divisions which now weaken Protestantism have been wiped out." The *Christian Century,* in underlining the similarities between Universalists and Congregationalists, even defined the Universalists as "an evangelical group, within any defensible meaning of that term."

The editor of the *Presbyterian Advance* (Nashville, Tennessee) used the announcement of the Joint Statement as an opportunity to criticize fellow Presbyterians for the lack of unity in their own ranks. The Christian Church, themselves in the midst of negotiations with the Congregationalists, had nothing but good to say about the Joint Statement.

The reactions of the Universalists to the Joint Statement were naturally much more diverse and complex than the presses of other denominations would have one believe. There were also all kinds of questions and speculations raised, both while the two commissions had been negotiating and after the document had been made public.

One of the first tasks was to inform the denomination of the existence of the Joint Statement, and van Schaick undertook to assume this responsibility as well as to act as one of its chief propagandists. In fact he devoted so much space and attention to it in the *Leader* that Vincent Tomlinson, for one, complained that reportage of other denominational affairs was being neglected, and that Universalists were not being properly informed of other issues that had to be confronted and discussed. There was more than the Joint Statement to be considered at the forthcoming convention.

There is no doubt that widespread interest was expressed in the Joint Statement. It was the major topic of discussion at numerous gatherings. In Bangor, Maine, fifty-five Universalists and Congregationalists assembled in the Universalist church to hear it read by Stanley Manning, then secretary of the Maine Convention. It was reported to have been received with evident approval.[46]

A fractional minority saw in it an opportunity for complete union. One individual, the son of a pioneer Universalist preacher, welcomed the idea, even though it might mean that the name of the denomination might become "only a cherished memory."[47] Here was not only the possibility of a larger fellowship but a way of ridding the denomination of the word "Universalist" which unfortunately served as "a red flag in an arena."

Tomlinson came out at first for complete consolidation, on purely pragmatic grounds. It was he who, at the 1913 convention, had made the motion in response to Congregational greetings by expressing the hope that "closer unity" would eventually be achieved.[48] By 1927, after earlier service on the convention finance committee while it struggled every year with deficits, he had come to the unhappy conclusion that Universalists were always operating beyond their means, with "large plans and small performance."[49] He cited what he considered the "ridiculous" example of trying to operate three theological schools with a grand total of only sixty-two students. On economic grounds alone, the Universalists should throw in their lot with the Congregationalists. However, he later modified his ideas about union and supported the principle of denominationalism.

The vast majority of Universalists who spoke or wrote on the subject shied away from any idea of integral union and expressed varying degrees of skepticism about the real meaning of the Joint Statement. Editor van Schaick forewarned that both Universalists and Congregationalists would also cite examples of lack of agreement and would find fault with individuals in the other denomination.[50] Such individuals, he wrote, were being excessively conservative and were unwilling to see beyond the confines of their own group. His prediction was indeed borne out. A scattering of Congregationalists expressed their dislike or suspicion of Universalists because they paid insufficient attention to "the judgments of God upon sinners" or because they were "wanting in religious virility."[51] One veteran Congregational minister, with a Vermont background and a partly Universalist heritage, registered his "intensest opposition" to the possibility of union because Universalists were not Christians in the Congregational sense.[52]

The crux of the matter, so far as it affected Universalists, was whether or not the document meant eventual merger, as was clearly implied in the sixth point and as almost unanimously assumed by the religious press in general. Several months before the Joint Statement had appeared, there had been considerable talk, and even some action, indicating the possibility of merger. In 1926 Alfred V. Bliss, the Congregational state superintendent in Maine, reported a joint meeting of twenty-seven Universalist and Congregational clergy held at Hallowell to confer on possible union of the churches in that state.[58]

Almost as soon as the Joint Statement had been made public, inquiries began to be received by the chairman of the Universalist commission about its bearing on the question of possible mergers of local Universalist and Congregational churches. Perkins promptly responded by pointing out that such actions, so far as the Joint Statement was concerned, would be premature and inappropriate.[54] The statement had yet not even been approved by either denomination. If no reason for merger had existed before, none had been created by the issuance of the statement. Even if approval were forthcoming, and fusion were effected at some time in the future, this would not itself justify merging local churches. Acknowledgement of closer fellowship than existed before in no way required union at the local level.

Much of the responsibility for the constant talk about complete amalgamation with the Congregationalists was laid at the door of van Schaick, who for more than two years had talked and written about the desirability of Christian unity without making a clear distinction between that and union. As a consequence, he had left such a strong impression that many were unable to put church union out of their minds and were unable to assess the Joint Statement on its own merits. Hence, ironically, van Schaick had inadvertently stirred up opposition to the very thing he so vigorously supported.[55]

Galer, as the only individual who had refused to sign the Joint Statement or to concur with the other Universalist trustees in approving it, gave his reasons in detail in the *Leader*.[56] He had been quite upset when van Schaick, in reporting the commission's vote, had failed to make clear Galer's opposition. The editor had merely listed those who favored it and had not mentioned Galer at all.[57] He was "profoundly convinced" that the action taken so far was unwise, in a document "loudly heralded and carefully press-agented" and containing lofty sentiments couched in felicitous and largely meaningless language. It was merely an exercise in rhetoric.

It was obvious to Galer that although the Joint Statement did not openly propose eventual organic union, that intent was the "ulterior purpose." The "proclamation," as he called it, was only the first step. He vigorously denied that 'these two branches of Protestantism differ now in no essential respects,' and that the Kansas City platform and the Universalist Five Principles could be made to harmonize. He was convinced that, whatever the leaders might believe, rank-and-file Congregationalists were far from accepting essential Universalist doctrines.

Mutual acceptance of " 'Christianity as a way of life' might be a beautiful sentiment," but unless made explicit, it was mere verbiage, subject to endless and undoubtedly differing interpretations that at best would be valueless and at worst would lead to discord and division. If some species of religious unity could be achieved either voluntarily arrived at or imposed, it would be at the sacrifice of intellectual freedom for Universalists, which Galer argued was more important than unity as such. In fact, religious pluralism was not only the reality but the ideal. Denominational unity was "highly illusory," and creeds and denominations were not only unavoidable but necessary.

Universalism, wrote Galer with passionate intensity, was more than "a specific doctrine as to future punishment." It represented "a whole philosophy of life and religion, differing radically from that of traditional Orthodoxy." The Universalist denomination had been and still was a pioneer. With merger "it would lose its leadership, its ability to blaze the way in the immense and as yet untrodden fields that lie before us. . . . To merge with another denomination of more conservative tendencies would only result in swallowing up our organization and submerging our peculiar traditions."

Galer considered the failure of the Congregationalists to make the same offer to the Unitarians — "those who have always been our religious allies" — as a device for weakening religious liberalism by dividing its forces. Besides the practical problems of merging subsidiary organizations, budgets, and other such housekeeping matters, there was the fact that, above all, merger would mean "the obliteration of the Universalist Church, leaving not a trace behind." He suggested, knowing full well that the Congregationalists would reject the idea, that the Universalists make a counter-offer inviting them to join on the platform of the Five Principles. This would be the "acid test," as he expressed it, of how far the Congregationalists had advanced theologically.

The response of the editor of the *Leader* was both immediate and predictable; van Schaick identified ten points made by Galer and commented on each, making it emphatic that he had consulted no member of either commission before writing the editorial, and was expressing his own views only.[58]

As to the invidiousness implied in the expression 'ulterior object,' the Joint Statement, while indicating that 'something larger and more inclusive than anything that now exists' might come in the future, van Schaick made it clear that organic union was not being sought or expected in 1927. The present alternative was to work more closely with "our Congregational brethren" or "to stand off at arms length." The discord and unhappiness predicted by Galer was not inevitable; in fact, it was the very purpose of the preliminary steps outlined in the Joint Statement to see if such were going to be the case. The matter of both the Kansas City Declaration and the Five Principles was irrelevant because the Joint Commission dropped all questions about creedal statements and agreed that "true fellowship" rested on other considerations.

One of the basic principles back of the proposal was to find out pragmatically whether Universalists and Congregationalists were "much the same kind of people." If not, no harm had been done. The Universalist editor saw no threat whatever to the independence of intellectual convictions even if union did take place at some time in the future. There was room enough for all. And why should the distinctive philosophy of Universalism be automatically lost in a larger framework? There might even be an expanded platform from which to speak and be heard, and an enlarged opportunity for spreading Universalist ideas. The matter of relations with the Unitarians gave van Schaick no great cause for concern. Nothing in the Joint Statement asked Universalists to be less friendly with Unitarians, and nothing in the statement excluded them.

The Universalist editor concluded his defense of the Joint Statement by pointing out that Galer, in the very act of criticizing it, had unwittingly "rendered the largest possible service" to the support of the statement. With a confidence certainly not shared by everyone, van Schaick asserted that Galer, by speaking to the issue, had "made it absolutely sure that every Univeralist in the land will read what is proposed" and act intelligently on it at the forthcoming meeting in Hartford. A defeat for the statement, said van Schaick, "would be going back on our Universalism as it has been proclaimed throughout our history." There would be no further need even to consider a future for the church, for it would have none.

Lewis R. Lowry, pastor of the church in Blanchester, Ohio, added his voice of opposition to the Joint Statement.[59] First of all, it was evident to him that, in spite of all protestations to the contrary, especially by the editor of the *Leader,* union was the ultimate object and was so interpreted by the vast majority of those that had paid any serious attention to the whole subject. It was patently a case of allowing the stronger to absorb the weaker, of a majority to swallow up a minority.

If purely quantitative criteria were used, there was no question that Lowry was correct. The federal religious census of 1926 (published in 1928) indicated that there were 498 Universalist churches, 244 of which were classified as urban, with three-fourths of the total membership of 54,957, excluding those in federated churches in which Universalists were involved.[60] The National Council (Congregational) represented 5,636 churches with 901,660 members, and 3,244 clergy in active service. Approximately half of the churches were in rural areas or villages but more than half the membership was urban.[61]

Further, union whenever it might occur and regardless of the form it might take, would be a tacit recognition that Universalism had fulfilled its mission and there was no longer any work for it to do. Lowry disagreed, and argued that if Universalists wanted to perpetuate the tradition of religious liberalism for which they had stood for so long, union with the Unitarians rather than with the Congregationalists was the best alternative.

C. Ellwood Nash, writing from Los Angeles, tentatively approved the Joint Statement and, if he had been able to be there, would probably have voted with the majority in favor of the adoption which he predicted at the forthcoming Hartford convention.[62] As a step toward comity he favored the principles expressed in the document, but he had reservations about both its wording and its implications. His objections to the ambiguously worded "Christian way of life" echoed those offered by Galer. What on earth did the expression mean? There were as many or more disagreements and divisions about this among both individuals and denominations as there were about theology. It was a case of fuzzy thinking that Nash thought might have serious consequences.

McCollester was "unalterably opposed" to a merger with the Congregationalists and inquired why the Unitarians had not been included in the discussions about cooperation.[63] "Why should we now form an alliance with a former opponent which excludes our faithful ally?" The editor of the *Christian Register* reported that, according to "representative Universalist ministers," four-fifths of the preachers and administration of the Universalist church supported McCollester in arguing that, if union were ever to take place, it would and should be with the Unitarians.[64] Why not "a new Liberal Christian Church" with the Universalists blazing the trail? McCollester challenged van Schaick to provide answers to these and related questions. The *Leader* editor reiterated the often-made point that no actual consolidation had been provided or was under consideration. Further, Unitarians had as much freedom of action as Universalists, and van Schaick saw no reason whatever why increased cooperation with Congregationalists should jeopardize good relations with Unitarians.

Samuel A. Eliot, outgoing president of the AUA, took up the challenge posed by McCollester and replied to it at great length in a letter to van Schaick.[65] He prefaced his remarks with the note that the Universalist editor's construction of the Universalist-Congregational negotiations did not accord with popular understanding. It was assumed by the Unitarians and a large number of both Universalists and Congregationalists that the probability of an eventual merger was at least implied. Otherwise, if the Joint Statement were merely one of many gestures of fraternal greeting customary among Christian communions at the time, then the whole matter was being taken too seriously.

McCollester's query had been headed "Where Are the Unitarians?" Eliot's answer was, in effect, that they had been unceremoniously pushed into the background by the enticements offered to the Universalists by the Congregationalists and that the Unitarian overture, made in the fall of 1925, had been shunted aside because the Universalists had become so enamored of the Congregational offer of fellowship. Eliot noted tartly that after the Universalist-Unitarian commissions had been appointed, he had spent no less than fourteen months, on no less than eight occasions, attempting to convene the two commissions. Perkins, chairman of the Universalist commission, kept putting him off. They finally found a mutually acceptable time and place to meet, coinciding with Perkins' installation in the Washington, D.C. church in January 1927. When Perkins read the manuscript of the Joint Statement, not yet published, to the two commissions, and asked for Unitarian comment, the reaction had been "a rather painful surprise." It was then decided that it would be futile to proceed any further with discussion looking to closer fellowship until the two other denominations had concluded their conferences.

Eliot had attended Perkins' installation ceremonies, but noted that there were no Congregational representatives present to extend greetings. At the same service Eliot had read a letter from All Souls Unitarian Church in Washington not only welcoming Perkins but offering the use of the parish house for Universalist gatherings while their Memorial Church was under construction. Eliot did not recall a similar invitation from the Congregationalists.

In reply, Perkins pointed out that Eliot had been mistaken in several respects and had not been aware of all the facts. The Congregationalists had indeed conferred with the Universalists regarding Perkins' installation and had not offered use of their facilities because the First Congregational Church in Washington was temporarily without a home and had none to offer.[66]

The AUA president concluded his letter with assurance that the Unitarian overture was "not a mere gesture." Everything seemed to point to the desirability of consolidating "the vanguard of the Christian army and promoting a 'United Liberal Church.'" However, if the Universalists preferred "to turn backward and fall in with the main body of the Christian army that is slowly and hesitantly coming along the roads that the Universalists and Unitarians had blazed, then the Unitarians will have to go ahead alone." When the Universalists had finished "making their polite bows to Orthodoxy," Unitarians would be glad to welcome them back, even though Universalists might "have to run a little to catch up" with the Unitarian pioneers who had been "steadily on the march." It was statements such as this that irritated many Universalists and seemed to confirm the criticism Speight had made about self-proclaimed Unitarian superiority.

One Unitarian minister, who remained unidentified, wrote to the *Leader* that Eliot's letter filled him with "shame and indignation," and was sorry that it had been dignified by publication.[67] Eliot's petty and self-righteous attitude was not to be taken as representative of Unitarians. The Eliot letter was reproduced in the *Congregationalist* and his remark about the alleged "backwardness" of Congregationalists elicited an indignant editorial.[68] The letter was described as "amazing" and a "left-hand slap" which demonstrated "querulousness and self-complacency." Editor Gilroy was also mystified at Eliot's references to historic Universalist-Unitarian friendship in view of the fact that although the two denominations had existed side by side for a full century, he had observed no effective movements towards either unity of organization or "effective alliance."[69] Why the sudden discovery of affinity just at the time of the Congregational overture? Gilroy informed his readers, under the heading "We Stand Committed," that the Congregationalists would continue along the same path of cooperation with the Universalists as already worked out, and "regardless of what others may determine as the course for themselves."

Editor van Schaick's reply to Eliot was courteous but pointed. Universalists took up the Congregational overture first because Universalists believed that it was the better part of wisdom to take up one thing at a time; further, the Congregationalists and Universalists had authorized joint conferences before the Unitarians had officially acted. More important and more serious was Eliot's allegation that the Universalists were taking "a backward step." Neither they nor the Congregationalists were presented in a favorable light, and van Schaick took umbrage at this. He further protested the implication that the Universalist-Congregational negotiations meant that Universalists were turning their backs on Unitarians.

Perkins immediately replied to Eliot's criticisms and emphatically disavowed any deliberate intent to procrastinate in meeting with the Unitarian commission and "unqualifiedly" denied any insinuation that he "was blocking the way to conference with our Unitarian friends in order to enter into preferred negotiations with the Congregationalists."[70] The simultaneous overture of the Unitarians and Congregationalists had indeed created a problem which he had explained to Eliot, who had agreed to postpone further Universalist-Unitarian discussions until the matter of the three-way conference could be settled. It was the Congregationalists, not the Universalists, who had declined to hold the proposed conference, and for very good reason. So the Universalists had had no other choice than to conduct separate negotiations with the Congregationalists.

Perkins found quite incomprehensible Eliot's assertion that the Joint Statement, if not interpreted as a proposition for immediate merger, was not to be taken seriously. It was to be taken exactly as stated, and was to be considered an ideal that might become a model for efforts at cooperation for other denominations. Certainly the document was the expression of a goal so worthy and so significant that "all of us will have to do some running to keep abreast of it," Unitarians and Universalists alike.

The strained relations between Perkins and Eliot had a certain irony about them. Perkins' friendship with Eliot, which had extended over almost thirty years, had started when Eliot, then the newly elected secretary of the AUA, had proposed closer fellowship between Universalists and Unitarians, and Perkins had written an article published in the *Leader* strongly endorsing the idea.

In July 1927 the trustees of the General Convention issued their interpretation of the Joint Statement which they had already adopted. They emphasized that no question of merger or consolidation was contained in it, and its ratification in no way committed either denomination to such a plan. There was complete freedom of choice as to what the next step would be, if any.

Galer was somewhat mollified, although by no means satisfied. He had not, despite the fact that he was a trustee, been consulted as to the precise language used, and did not know of its exact content until its publication. At the April meeting of the trustees he had offered a resolution to the effect that the Joint Statement was not to be in any way interpreted as contemplating a merger. Perkins had agreed in principle with the idea but not to Galer's exact wording and therefore had withheld his approval, but with the understanding that "some statement to that effect" would be issued.

The explanatory statement, in Galer's opinion, went "far beyond what was contemplated." He wanted "a positive declaration against merger." There should have been absolutely nothing in the statement to lead anyone to believe that merger was even a remote possibility; yet the trustees' statement encouraged that very possibility. If persisted in, he predicted that it would split the Universalists into two camps and catastrophe would result.

It was inconceivable that two bodies as diverse in theology, tradition, and temperament as the Universalists and Congregationalists could ever "happily coalesce." In order to avoid the unhappy consequences of such an ill-advised attempt, an unequivocal assertion by Universalists was needed that neither the Joint Statement, in whole or in part, should be construed as contemplating merger or organic union. One possible way to solve the problem might be the formation of a "liberal bloc" representing like-minded individuals from all denominations to act as a clearing-house but not as a formal union. In this way the Unitarians, who were otherwise being unjustly excluded, could be given an opportunity to participate; they were, after all, "the largest and most important single group of liberals."

Regardless of the doubts and opposition raised when the Joint Statement was published, there was a great flurry of Universalist-Congregational interchange and gestures of cooperation and good will on the eve of the meetings of the two denominations. Shutter, pastor of the Universalist church in Minneapolis, was invited to address the Conference of Congregationalists which met in St. Paul.[72] Union services were held widely, such as those conducted in Lansing, Michigan, which were reported to be a complete success.[73] A mass meeting was held in a Congregational church in Beverly, Massachusetts by members of four Congregational churches and the Universalist church, at which the Joint Statement was printed on the back of the program and the editors of the *Congregationalist* and the *Leader* gave addresses.[74]

When the National Council assembled in Omaha in May, Perkins was the Universalist fraternal delegate and gave an address entitled "An Adventure in Spiritual Unity," reproduced in the press. He received a "prolonged ovation."[75] The Congregational commission made its report and recommendtions, from which all reference to the Kansas City statement of 1913 had been deleted at the last moment by "a large majority vote" in order to remove any lingering doubts that anyone (particularly Universalists) might have had about the requirements of a creedal test. In recommending adoption of the Joint Statement the commission believed "that the breach of more than five generations should rapidly be forgotten" and called for "the closest practicable union of our separate interests."[76]

In its report the commission went a step further and recommended that "the National Council again place itself on record as being willing for the sake of promoting the larger unities which our churches earnestly desire even to surrender its historic name, or to return to its historic designation (Churches of Christ) which is still largely used among us."[77]

The entire report was approved with "unanimity and enthusiasm." The commission, in making its report, went even further than the Joint Statement by calling for a "very compact federal union" as the next possible step which would involve no changes in existing organizations but encouraged conferences with such churches as were willing to participate. The commission was also instructed to confer with the Universalist commission and present at the next National Council meeting in 1929 a plan for closer cooperation. The next move was up to the Universalists.

Even before either denomination had met, van Schaick was confident that if the National Council approved the Joint Statement the Universalists meeting at Hartford would ratify the document by an "overwhelming vote."[78] He could see no other possibility unless they went "back on their professions by churlishly taking an attitude of aloofness." He was nothing short of ecstatic when the results of the Omaha meeting were known.

Discussion and debate over the Joint Statement continued at an accelerated pace between the time the Congregationalists had acted and the convening of the Universalists. Others joined him in a chorus of approval. Willard C. Selleck addressed the California convention on "The Approachment [sic] of Universalists, Unitarians, and Congregationalists" in which he favored the Joint Statement and interpreted it literally as evidence of "mutual recognition, affiliation, and co-operation," and not as a step toward organic union, which he opposed.[79]

J. M. Atwood, president of the General Convention, agreed with those who felt that the question of merger (which he also opposed) had unfortunately overshadowed "the essential element" of the Joint Statement;

namely, that it would be a great forward step toward eliminating the sectarianism which was "the great foe within the Christian church to progress and efficiency."[80] It was not denominationalism that was at fault; that was a sign of religious vitality and should be maintained. It was that the numerous denominations could not or would not work together. It was sectarianism that excluded Universalists and Unitarians from the Federal Council of Churches. The tendency toward narrow partisanship was the great evil to be eliminated. He lauded the Joint Statement for playing down the importance of doctrine and creeds and stressing a cooperative spirit. He claimed to have been caught by surprise by the action of the Congregationalists at Omaha in view of the conservatism of many of their churches and clergy but hoped that the Universalists would be "as broad-minded, as forward-looking and as united in spirit."

There appears to have been so much confusion in the minds of so many about the intent of the Joint Statement that Isaac Smith, pastor of Grace Universalist Church in Lowell, Massachusetts, suggested the holding of a popular referendum because he estimated that those who voted at the General Convention meeting would probably represent no more than 10 percent of the denomination.[81] He phrased two direct questions: "Do you favor cooperation with the Congregationalists but retention of Universalism as a denomination? or, Do you favor organic union between the two?" The proposal was never acted on.

Because of the importance of the issues involved and what van Schaick interpreted as "the widespread interest throughout the church," the report of the Commission on Unity and Comity was published several weeks in advance of the Hartford convention. It was an extensive document detailing the chronology of events beginning in 1925 when the simultaneous overtures had been received, and including a copy of the Joint Statement. Included also was a detailed exposition of its meaning and significance as well as a correction and clarification of some of the misunderstandings that had arisen, notably the allegedly shabby treatment of the Unitarians and the possibility of organic union, both of which were emphatically denied. Perkins, the chief author, repeated substantially all of the points he had already made in numerous articles in the *Leader*.

The commission made three recommendations: Approval of the Joint Statement; reaffirmation of Universalist approval of the closer fellowship proposed by the Unitarians and the working out of practical ways of furthering it; and continued conferences with not only the Congregationalists and Unitarians but with "other like-minded Christians who also seek a wider liberal fellowship" in harmony with the principles in the Joint Statement.

When the commission drafted its report in final form, it had amended the first recommendation, on Galer's insistence, by adding the following statement: "The adoption of this recommendation is to be interpreted in the light of the assertion in the Report of the Commission that nothing in the Joint Statement commits us to organic union or restricts in any degree our freedom or independent action with reference to other liberals either persons or denominations." This reaffirmation, redundant as it might have been, was made to allay fears and to reassure such individuals as Galer and such bodies as the Church of the Messiah (Philadelphia). The latter had adopted resolutions opposing merger and calling for independent action on the part of state conventions and churches if such should ever take place.[82]

The commission had already stated in the body of their report that adoption of the Joint Statement meant exactly what it said and nothing more. The commission emphatically pointed out that to read into it some commitment to union would be to read something that simply was not there. The addition of Galer's amendment had accomplished another very significant thing: It had made possible a unanimous report.

The real test of what all the rhetoric, paper, and printer's ink expended on Christian cooperation and unity really meant, came in October 1927, when the report of the commission came up for consideration at the convention. This was preceded by two extended and rather effusive greetings furnished respectively by Charles R. Joy of Lowell, Massachusetts, representing the Unitarians, and by Frank K. Sanders of New York City, chairman of the Congregational Commission on Interchurch Relations. They paved the way and set the stage for the convention action to follow. Joy was, he said, not troubled because Unitarians were not mentioned in the body of the Joint Statement, for it was "the Christian way of life" that was at stake, not mere denominationalism.[83] He had nothing but praise for the Joint Statement, considering it to be a model if Universalists and Unitarians were ever to come together on a common platform. He, as well as the Unitarian circles with which he was familiar, saw nothing whatever in the statement that indicated any intention on the part of Universalists to abandon the Unitarians, their "old religious allies." With Eliot's earlier remark obviously in mind about the "backward step" presumably being taken by Universalists in establishing closer relations with the Congregationalists, Joy firmly denied that such an allegation had any merit. The three denominations, and all others who were committed to freedom "from dogma of conformity," had to stand or fall together.

Sanders, whose address was even lengthier than Joy's, stressed the desirability of Christian unity and the graitfying decline of denominational particularism which the Joint Statement represented. He called for federation, not the merging into one body, although he did leave the door ajar to that eventual possibility. The advantage of federation was, however, too restricted if confined to only two denominations. Federation had to open the way to the inclusion of other religious units, such as the Christian Church, with whom federation had already been achieved by a joint statement prepared in 1926. Sanders made no mention of the Unitarians by name in any part of his address, although at one point he alluded to the Congregational desire for "a liberal evangelism" in preference to "a segregated liberalism."

The report, distributed to the delegates in printed form, was first read to the convention without comment by Perkins. After he moved adoption, F. O. Hall seconded it, accompanied by an address in which he announced that in the forty-four years of his ministry the report was "the most important piece of business that had come before the General Convention in all that time." Much of his presentation consisted of quotations from a long editorial in the *Christian Century* expressing its unqualified approval of the Joint Statement.

The editorial, entitled "Universalists Face a Test," called the Joint Statement "a crucial moment in the history of the Christian union movement," and saw "no reason in the world why the step should not be taken."[84] There were no two denominations that could better lead the way, "one an evangelical body which is also liberal in its best traditions, the other a liberal body which is evangelical in the sanest sense of that word." The absence of the Unitarians from the negotiations was in no sense to be interpreted as a defection of Universalists from "an ancient alliance."

Hall also called attention to the groundwork for cooperation between Universalists and Unitarians laid in 1901, when he had served on the commission appointed that year and which had resulted in increased friendship between the two groups. He considered the Joint Statement quite in keeping with that effort, although this time it concerned another religious body.

Galer then made a speech full of good will and support of "the splendid statement of a faith and a policy upon which we may all stand and for which we may all labor." The Universalists, he said, were too small a body to fight among themselves and the cause for which they stood too great to let division occur. The report, as presented (with his amendment included), now fairly met the objections which he and others had raised, and which he still felt were "fully justified." Many of his fears about relations with the Unitarians — "the oldest and closest and the staunchest of our allies" — had been quieted by the second and third recommendations, so he would no longer dissent. Universalist principles and identity had been adequately protected.

Then followed speeches of varying lengths, most of them far exceeding the three-minute limit agreed upon. McCollester, who had previously voiced many objections, reported that he was now satisfied, and announced that he would vote with "all the rest" in supporting the report.

So did Lowry, who had earlier opposed part of it. Carl F. Henry, a delegate from the Throop Memorial Church in Pasadena, California, read telegrams supporting the Joint Statement. The support of the previous doubters and objectors like Galer and McCollester doubtless helped swing the vote to the affirmative.

A sort of climax was achieved when, after a short speech by Perkins, he read a series of resolutions from the General Conference of the AUA then meeting in Washington, D.C., urging the continuation of conversations between the two denominations and offering congratulations and good wishes on the progress of Universalist-Congregational cooperation. The Universalist commission's report and recommendations were "most heartening to all followers of the ideal of inclusive and undogmatic religious fellowship."[85] The Unitarians had put into official form what Joy had already said on behalf of the Unitarians. Whatever doubts the Universalists had had about Unitarian reaction to the Joint Statement and the circumstances surrounding its negotiation and adoption had finally been put to rest.

The vote to adopt the commission report and its recommendations was all but unanimous. There was but one in the negative. Sweetser, defiantly opposed to the idea of closer fellowship with the Unitarians under any conditions, refused to accept the report and the three recommendations because they were included.[86] He made a determined effort to have the recommendations voted on separately, but was ruled out of order. The "remarkable demonstration" of unity sought for in the report was marred only, as van Schaick reported, by Sweetser's "discordant note."

The *Christian Century*, disregarding the single dissenting vote, carried a follow-up editorial to the one appearing on the eve of the Hartford convention, entitled this time "Universalists Stand the Test."[87] Christian unity had taken a significant step forward.

General Superintendent Lowe, who had served on the Universalist commission, was even more sweeping in his assessment of the convention's action. He considered the Joint Statement "one of the most significant, vital statements, edicts, or utterances put out by any religious body of men and women since the days of the Reformation."[88] Even the triumphant editor of the *Leader* did not claim quite as much. He did, however, call the adoption of the Joint Statement "a story which will live in Universalist annals and in the history of the Christian church."[89]

The momentum created by the adoption of the Joint Statement did, in fact, continue, although at a somewhat reduced rate. Even before the Hartford convention, Universalists had been invited to a conference between representatives of the Congregational and Christian churches. It was held just a few weeks after the Hartford convention, with three members of the Universalist commission present.[90] Two things were made clear at the conference. The eventual and complete union with other Protestant denominations was the long-range aim of the Congregationalists, preceded by two preliminary stages of closer fellowship and then by a federation comparable to the United Church of Canada. The Christian Church had taken the first two steps and was in the midst of negotiating the third. It was also evident that the Universalists were willing to take the first step, and might consider the second, but refused absolutely to go the entire way.

There was no discussion of Universalist-Congregational relations at the biennial meeting of the National Council held in Detroit in 1929, and no action taken except to accept the report of their Committee on Interchurch Relations which was concerned primarily with working out the procedural details of the merger with the Christian church. Editor van Schaick, who was present when the report was made, noted that there was not "the slightest doubt" that the Congregationalists had in mind merger with the Universalists at some time, but that, to Congregationalists, it meant union only at the top of the church bureaucracy. The independency of local congregations would be retained, and in such matters as property interests a federation rather than a literal merger would take place.[91] This rather technical distinction would probably not have been understood by most rank-and-file Universalists.

The Congregational commission reported that at the earlier meeting the Universalist representatives "deemed themselves restrained from any discussion of merger by the vote of their Convention. . . . Farther [sic] negotiations regarding the organic unity of the Universalist Churches with our own, however much desired, must await their initiative."[92] That initiative never came, and there the matter rested.

Vincent Tomlinson, who was much fonder of his fellow Universalists than of either the Unitarians or the Congregationalists, concluded that all of the time, energy, and wordage expended on relations with the Congregationalists had resulted only in "a house of cards."[93] He believed that most of the interest had been "manufactured" by a few, and that the entire idea had garnered but little sympathy from Universalists at large. It was a manifestation of the efforts of a minority in a denomination depending for its very existence on majority support from the bottom up — and even that did not come easily. It was, in short, a movement lacking the grassroots momentum which the leadership alone could not furnish.

Congregationalist editor Gilroy, speaking to the Boston Universalist Club in 1930, came to precisely the same conclusion. He admitted that the great difficulty in bringing Universalists and Congregationalists closer together in the 1920s had been that both groups were working "from the top down" without any real comprehension by the rank and file of what was involved.[94] But surely the effort had been worth it.

Behind it all was the ever-present and pervasive fear by Universalists that their identity would be irretrievably lost, and that the denomination and its traditions would cease to exist. Absorption by another denomination was too high a price to pay for whatever advantages there might be.

A conference was held between representatives of the Universalist and Unitarian commissions in February 1928. The principles of the Joint Statement were affirmed and methods of achieving closer alignment were discussed. In addition, the Unitarians agreed to participate in a larger but unofficial conference which would include representation of both liberal and conservative denominations. This proposal had come out of the earlier Universalist-Congregational-Christian meeting and was intended to see how far the principles of the Joint Statement could be carried out in a broader context.[95] The conference was duly held in the spring of 1928 in Washington, D.C., with twenty-five individuals from twelve denominations; three Universalists were among them. No resolutions were offered or votes taken; there was consensus that "common loyalty to the Christian way of life" was a sufficient bond of unity.

At the regional level there was considerable informal discussion among clergy. An annual retreat was established in 1928 for New England ministers known as the Idlewild Fellowship, meeting in Dunstable, Massachusetts, and including preponderantly Universalist, Unitarian, and Congregational clergy.[96] The executive committees of the Universalist and Congregational commissions held their last meeting in the fall of 1929 to take stock of what had happened in the past few years; general satisfaction with the results was relayed by the Universalist commission in its final report to the General Convention, which was accepted unanimously and without discussion.[97] The spirit of the Joint Statement was being carried out exactly as hoped, with an evident move toward local federated and even union churches; at least six denominations were involved, in various combinations. Ninety interdenominational churches had been created in Massachusetts alone, two-thirds of them within ten years.[98]

So many local federations and unions had taken place by 1929 that the Massachusetts Universalist Convention established procedures for all such actions involving Universalist churches. Each was to receive the approval of the executive committee; secure or retain fellowship with the convention, as were also the pastors; continue to pay appropriate quotas; and provide that all Universalist property be held in trust by the state convention, or revert to it.[99]

The Universalist commission, during the immediate post-Joint Commission period, scrupulously avoided any discussion of merger with any denomination and received no proposals for such action. But talk about such would not be downed. At a meeting of the Laymen's League in Detroit in the spring of 1928 which included Frank D. Adams, president of the General Convention; Alexander M. Meikle, superintendent of the

Congregational churches in Detroit; and Augustus P. Reccord, pastor of the First Unitarian Church in Detroit, a consensus was reported, expressed in a romantic metaphor: "After years of flirtation, during which there had not even been approximated a companionate marriage, something ought to be done with a view to matrimony. The churches are waiting for someone to propose."[100] Fellowship might suffice for the immediate future, but the ultimate goal should be "a merger of the liberal churches into one great liberal fellowship."

The three clergymen who led the various discussions spent considerable time debating a possible name for the proposed combination. Adams suggested "The United Free Church of America" and insisted that the chief obstacle to closer fellowship in the past had been "a combination of pride and prejudice." He believed that the leadership of all three denominations was ready for complete union but that it was those in the pews who were holding back. His remedy was an aggressive educational campaign. Meikle recommended "The American Church" (amended to read "American Liberal Church"). Reccord preferred the name "United Congregational Church of America" because it would reflect the commonly held historical principle of complete freedom of private judgment and local autonomy of churches.

Cooperation among the three denominations was, with but few exceptions, agreed upon. Merger was, however, quite another matter. A conference on denominational comity had been held in Lowell, Massachusetts, in the fall of 1927 at which the editors of the *Leader,* the *Congregationalist,* and the *Christian Register* unanimously agreed that closer understanding and more effective cooperation among denominations was a much more urgent need and a more reasonable expectation than any amalgamation.[101] The progress made by the 1930s certainly seemed to bear this out, although the emphasis had begun to shift. Talk of enhanced formal ties with Congregationalists faded away, but cordial relations continued to exist, and there was much evidence of cooperation. Congregationalist representatives were included in the Council of the Free Church Fellowship organized in 1934, and both Universalists and Unitarians assisted the Congregational Education Society in the publication of the periodical *Church and Society.*

In 1947, many years after he had relinquished the editorship of the *Congregationalist,* Gilroy recalled the offer of his denomination to affiliate with the Universalists twenty years earlier, and put the blame for the failure squarely on "the action of the Unitarian headquarters in Boston ... [who] played an unworthy, dog-in-the-manger policy in that situation."[102]

Gilroy considered it more than coincidence that official Unitarianism suddenly became very active when a Universalist-Congregationalist affiliation seemed imminent. The effect was "to create a diversion that upset any plans that were in formulation and nullified any action," without at the same time drawing Universalists and Unitarians closer together. They were, so far as Gilroy could observe, as far apart in 1947 as they had ever been. He insisted that "in the whole range of denominations today the Universalists and the Congregational Christians are most akin. . . . If a practical movement to revive the project were made, a strong argument for it would be the fact that there are among our million or more Congregational Christians today probably more members who hold essentially Universalist views than there are members in the entire official Universalist denomination."

George N. Marshall, describing himself in 1948 as a "Unitarian-Universalist" and later serving as head of the Church of the Larger Fellowship, considered Gilroy's allegations about the Unitarians to be a "scandalous charge" which historically were "not accurate."[103] But he concentrated instead on a more recent development — the union of the Congregationalists and the Evangelical and Reformed Church then under discussion, in a proposed United Church of Christ.[104] The Congregationalist had veered away from the liberalism of the 1920s and had taken a different (and much less desirable) road. If merger of the Universalists and Congregationalists were to take place under these circumstances, "the entire genius of Universalism [would] be sacrificed."

Increasing concentration on Universalist-Unitarian relations replaced the attention paid to the Congregationalists. The Commission on Comity and Unity disappeared and in 1931 was replaced by a "Commission to confer with the Unitarian Commission regarding closer co-operation." Victor A. Friend served as chairman, with Perkins as one of the members. Another stage in the evolution of Universalist-Unitarian comity was about to be reached.

Chapter 30

Half-way Steps Toward Union: Universalist-Unitarian Relations, 1927–1937

The first meeting of the eleven-member Universalist-Unitarian commission which had been agreed upon in 1925 to consider the Unitarian resolutions calling for closer relations had been delayed for more than a year because of Universalist involvement in negotiations with the Congregationalists. It had finally met in mid-January 1927, but at Eliot's suggestion had confined its discussions to "practical matters of cooperation" instead of taking up larger measures concerned with interdenominational relationships.

The specific problems discussed included a proposed course of action for the several Universalist and Unitarian churches in Florida which were engaged in establishing closer ties. It had all begun when clergy and lay delegates from both denominations had met in Jacksonville and had agreed to try an experiment in federation.[1] The churches would be fellowshipped in both, and all new missions were to be developed cooperatively. They were requested by the commission to defer choosing names until after conferences with them regarding "a distinctive title which might be acceptable to all." Among those suggested as possibilities were "All Souls," "Liberal Christian," "United Free," and "United Liberal."

The idea of establishing joint missions in "centers of influence" in which no liberal churches existed was endorsed, as was a nation-wide exchange of Universalist and Unitarian ministers on a specified date, which did in fact take place to a limited extent, mostly in the Boston area. Other ways of furthering cooperation were considered "in a general way" but no action was taken. The fact that no reference at all of the meeting appeared in the *Leader* and that it was relegated to a back page of the *Christian Register* almost two months later might indicate that the editor of neither paper had expected much to be accomplished.

The federation of churches in Florida did take place. Both Eliot and Lowe made separate trips there later in 1927 and approved the idea. The first step actually taken was the combination of the Jacksonville congregations as the United Liberal Church (Unitarian-Universalist).[2] By the end of 1927 the churches in St. Petersburg and Miami had followed suit. Only the churches in Tarpon Springs and Orlando had yet to act.[3] The state convention also went on record as favoring complete merger of the two denominations.

Considerable time and attention were paid to inter-denominational relations at the May meetings of the AUA in 1927.[4] Stanard D. Butler, a Unitarian, not only endorsed the Joint Statement but took the position that the Universalists and Unitarians should be federated immediately. Lon Ray Call of Louisville, Kentucky, in an elaborate disquisition in which he drew up a balance sheet of the arguments for and against merger, concluded that the next logical step was complete union. "We are like two great rivers having their rise in different parts of the country which have now come near together and are flowing in parallel lines. The natural thing for them to do is to join and flow together."

Call had distributed a questionnaire to both organizations and individual clergy in each fellowship, to which fifty-seven replies were received. Thirty-six were "emphatically in favor of organic union," twelve were opposed, and nine were "conditional." All of Call's arguments in favor of union had been stated before by someone at some time: Theological differences were no longer relevant; both denominations were agreed on the principle of brotherhood, and at least preached it if they did not always practice it; union would add prestige as well as numbers, particularly effective in missionary work; temperamentally, "the Unitarian head and the Universalist heart would make a good combination, [and] the social radicalism of the Universalists and the theological radicalism of the Unitarians would be blended into a balanced radicalism"; organization would be simplified and economies could be effected; the two constituencies would become more aware than ever that, as religious liberals, they had a distinctive message, and there would be "a rededication to the principle of freedom" as a result.

On the negative side, Unitarians would be handicapped by "the orthodoxy of the conservative element among the Universalists"; this was demonstrated by their very flirtation with the Congregationalists. Further, Univeralists were "almost entirely Bible Christians," while the Unitarians were not; this was in itself a curb on freedom of thought. Then there were practical difficulties, such as the readjustment of trust funds. There might even be an aggregate loss of combined membership, although the counter-argument could be used that the Unitarian church was blessed by its very smallness, and the resulting spirit of fraternity might be weakened by consolidation and enlargement. And then there was the "awful fear" of loss of identity on the part of both Universalists and Unitarians. But all of these arguments against union were, in Call's estimation, overbalanced by the advantages.

Harold E. B. Speight's emphatic endorsement at the AUA meeting of the Joint Statement was reported to have "made something of a sensation." The reasons were not difficult to ascertain. He took issue with the warning in the *Western Unitarian* that the arguments in support of the contemplated rapprochement between Universalists and Congregationalists did not apply to Unitarians.[5] The idea was clearly expressed that Unitarians were the only true religious liberals and, if for no other reason, were somehow superior to everyone else. Speight much preferred the attitude expressed in a "Fraternal Letter to the Churches" signed in 1924 by twenty-seven Unitarian ministers calling for a more generous and charitable spirit toward others than they believed existed in most Unitarian circles. Unitarians did not have a monopoly on liberalism. Neither did the barrenness of a purely intellectual approach so characteristic of Unitarianism meet the needs of the time. Unitarians should realize that they had something to learn from those (especially the Universalists) who had been "more closely attached to the historic Christian tradition."

The Unitarian press, represented by the *Christian Register* and Albert C. Dieffenbach, its editor, naturally watched the Universalist-Congregationalist negotiations with deep interest, and kept readers informed of almost every step. Dieffenbach denied the implication that there was a rift within Unitarianism between a right and left wing — a consideration which had supposedly made Congregationalists hesitant to approach the Unitarians — and insisted that they were a united denomination.[6] This was reinforced by the fact that the National (General) Conference and the parent AUA had been merged in 1925, after four years of deliberation, although they continued to hold separate meetings. Dieffenbach's reaction to the adoption of the Joint Statement was completely favorable. So far as the Unitarians were concerned, cooperation with the Universalists should and would continue undiminished. The Universalists had achieved the best of both worlds — a "double entente."

The only basis of unity between Universalists and Unitarians, according to the Unitarian editor, whether "in local parish arrangements or in the ultimate uniting of denominations," was "perfect spiritual freedom." Any united movement that could endure had to "include with mutual respect the extremes of doctrinal belief, like that of the Fundamentalist Congregationalist, the evangelical Universalist, and the humanist Unitarian."[7]

In the late 1920s and early 1930s the editors of the *Leader* and the *Register* engaged in a prolonged editorial exchange over the nature and extent of the concept of liberty as it applied to the two denominations they represented. Specifically, were Universalists and Unitarians obligated to receive into membership any individuals, regardless of their religious ideas? Did, for example, professed atheists have the right to join? Editor van Schaick argued that there were indeed limits to liberty which could conceivably keep people out of the Universalist church on the basis of belief (or non-belief), while Editor Deiffenbach recognized no such restriction for Unitarians. The key question seemed to be the presence or absence of a statement of belief.

The closest approximation to a Unitarian creed was the principle embodied in the so-called "Five Points" outlined by James Freeman Clarke in a sermon delivered at the Church of the Disciples in Boston on 10 May 1885.[8] They were as follows: "The Fatherhood of God; the Brotherhood of Man; the Leadership of Jesus; Salvation by Character; and the Continuity of Human Development in all worlds, or the Progress of Mankind onward and upward forever." Clarke suggested that these five points might "constitute the theology of the future" as distinguished from Calvin's theology. So far as is known, the Five Points were never formally adopted by any official body of the AUA but became generally accepted as expressing the common denominators of Unitarian belief; in some instances they were displayed in Unitarian churches.

The absence of an official Unitarian statement was underlined by Norman D. Fletcher, who had been born to Unitarians, was trained for the ministry of the Universalist church, ordained as a Unitarian in a Universalist church, held dual fellowship, and was in 1930 the minister of the Universalist church in Haverhill, Massachusetts, which included Unitarian members.[9] He argued that the question of how far the interpretation of liberty could be carried was an overlooked but vital difference between the two denominations. Universalists limited liberty by a statement of belief (1899 version) to which adherence, at least in spirit, was expected by the General Convention. There was no such limit imposed by the AUA on its constituency, for it had no statement of belief to which either churches or their members were expected to subscribe. If there were any limits, in practice, they were to be found in the local church. This was the principle of congregationalism carried to its "logical extremity." If the rather basic denominational difference between Universalists and Unitarians were to disappear, it would be more likely, according to Fletcher, that the former would dispense entirely with its statement of belief, liberal as it was, than that the Unitarians would adopt one.

It was inevitable that all the talk and action about Christian unity so prevalent in the 1920s would bring a corresponding discussion and debate over the merits and demerits of denominationalism. The editor of the *Leader* greeted with unqualified approval the union in 1928 of three of the five churches in Walpole, Massachusetts (Congregational, Methodist, and Unitarian) as a United Church by means of an "Agreement of Association."[10] But Tomlinson was skeptical. He saw great merit in denominationalism and feared that individuals like van Schaick, with their intense commitment to Christian unity, were overdoing the desirability of actual union. The editor, put on the defensive, argued that denominations were not at all necessary merely to accommodate differences; such could and would be respected if churches were only sufficiently broadminded.[11] He denied that the union of two or more denominations somehow put individuality in jeopardy or that people would be required to relinquish their church homes.

It was not the dissolution of all denominations for which van Schaick was arguing, but the coalesence of those which had broken apart for "trivial" reasons or were continuing to exist separately long after the original cause of division had disappeared; or if they had natural affinities. He cited as examples the long-continued splintering within the Methodists, Baptists, and Presbyterians. Why should not the liberal churches, "those nearest together . . . get together"? He appreciated the reluctance of committed Universalists to approve any change that might endanger their religious identity or security but saw no reason why they could not have them or keep them "in a new federation or even union."

However, when it came to union with Unitarians, he backed himself into a corner. At an all-day meeting in Lowell, Massachusetts, in January 1929, of Universalists representing the Merrimac Valley Conference, and Unitarians, representing the North Middlesex Conference, the delegates unanimously voted "that the time has arrived when steps should be taken with a view to the organic union of these two liberal communions."[12] F. O. Hall was the principal spokesman for the Universalists and Eliot for the Unitarians.

Both men had been on their respective commissions in 1901. Hall regretted that they had not insisted at the time on union, but admitted that, given the circumstances then, three denominations rather than one would probably have resulted. But now the situation was different. Each denomination was better acquainted with the other. Cooperation had replaced competition in small communities. Dual fellowship was becoming increasingly popular. There was no real distinction between the Five Principles of the Universalists and those of the Unitarians. Religious liberals had to stand together, united, and what better way than by merging the two denominations? Eliot's remarks were in the same vein. It was only "inconsequentials" that kept them apart. Forget the dissensions of the past and "wipe the slate clean." Universalists and Unitarians needed each other, and much could be accomplished through combination rather than by wasteful competition.

Then Editor van Schaick, in reporting the meeting, dropped a bombshell (or so it was interpreted) when he opposed the merger of the two denominations; his argument was that such action would further isolate the two groups from the larger movement of unity with liberals of other denominations.[13] What he wanted was a "United Liberal Church" of much broader dimensions than would be represented by a mere Universalist-Unitarian fusion. The latter move would not only cut them off even farther from "liberal orthodoxy" but would result merely in "another sect bent on spreading its own kind of sectarianism."

Dieffenbach had for many years been critical of van Schaick, and the Universalist editor had reciprocated. Although both had publicly professed personal friendship, they differed so widely editorially that it was assumed that a feud existed between the two. To this allegation van Schaick, with elaborate sarcasm, issued a denial and commented that, "except for being mistaken most of the time . . . the *Christian Register* and its dynamic editor are perfect."[14]

The Unitarian editor professed to be completely taken aback at what he interpreted as van Schaick's "abrupt reversal" in opposing Universalist-Unitarian union.[15] It seemed to him that the Universalist editor was turning his back on liberalism and embracing orthodoxy, which was anathema to Unitarians. For that reason it was impossible for them to have more than minimal fellowship with denominations other than Universalists, who had been their greatest hope. The religious liberty for which both had stood for a century was being repudiated. The "leaning toward orthodoxy" which had always been present among some Universalists had now gotten the upper hand, and as long as that prevailed, union with the Unitarians was out of the question. Such far-sighted Unitarians as Dieffenbach (in his own estimation) had been aware of this for some time; this accounted for the apparent lack of enthusiasm for union on their part and went far to explain their cautious attitude. Unitarians would continue to move ahead of other movements, regardless of what the Universalists might choose to do.

The *Leader* editor responded to what he called the "slashing attack" by Dieffenbach; van Schaick called the *Register* editorial a "grotesque description" of the Universalist position and considered the Unitarian editor's distrust of all groups outside his own and the Universalists as an exhibition of prejudice bordering on paranoia rather than of true liberality.[16] The assumption that true liberalism and freedom were confined to the small, closed circles of Universalists, Unitarians, and possibly a few Jews and Quakers, was not only excessively narrow but naive.

Charles R. Joy (Unitarian), pastor of All Souls Church in Lowell where the meeting had been held urging merger, read van Schaick's editorial "with a sinking heart."[17] As an individual strongly committed to Christian unity, Joy, who held both Unitarian and Congregational fellowship, preached in a church which itself had been formed by a combination of two such churches and which had a dozen other denominations represented in it. He found in the resolutions absolutely none of the "dogmatic and sectarian liberalism" of which van Schaick complained. And why would not a Universalist-Unitarian merger be a long step toward the creation of a unified Christendom so much talked about?

There was no question that van Schaick found himself very much in the minority in opposing Universalist-Unitarian union. The resolutions at the Lowell meeting had met with approval by both McCollester and Atwood. Lorenzo D. Case, pastor of the Universalist church in Lowell, had presided at the meeting and had thoroughly approved the idea of merger. At the meeting of the Merrimac Valley Conference of Universalist Churches held in Nashua, New Hampshire, following the Lowell meeting, the resolutions adopted earlier at the joint conference were unanimously endorsed.[18]

Galer, unenthusiastic about merger of the Universalists with any other group, accused van Schaick in 1929 of disrupting the denomination with his refusal to join the Unitarians.[19] All this talk about union with anybody was "only a passing wave of hysteria." When talk of that died down, as it inevitably would, there would probably be some other panacea offered. But if federation or union of some kind did ever take place, it should be with the Unitarians. Protestant denominations, said Galer, fell into only two groups, evangelical and liberal. Universalists and Unitarians might sometime unite, as liberal denominations. But union with any other group, including the Congregationalists, was impossible, for the gulf was too wide and too deep.

Galer seems to have reconciled himself to the possibility of Universalist-Unitarian union later in the same year that he had attacked van Schaick. In bringing the greetings of the midwestern Universalists to a Unitarian meeting in Chicago in 1929 he voiced the hope that their ranks would "melt into each other [and] proceed as one body."[20] By 1931, as a trustee, Galer was considered a strong supporter of union.[21]

The Merrimac Valley Conference (Universalist) and the North Middlesex Conference (Unitarian) met again in Lowell exactly one year after their joint meeting in 1929. This time, however, the Andover Association of Congregational Churches was included. Those present unanimously voted in favor of union of all three denominations.[22] The time seemed propitious for yet another attempt at union of Universalists and Unitarians at least. It was the Unitarians who again took the initiative.

The Free Church Fellowship

Two resolutions addressed to the General Convention recommending merger came from Unitarians in 1931, one from the annual May meeting of the AUA held in Boston, and the other from the biennial meeting of the General Conference in Philadelphia.[23] Although the latter resolution referred to the fact that Universalists and Unitarians were "now walking a common road and fronting a common destiny," the end-product in the 1930s was not merger but a federation lasting less than six years — the Free Church Fellowship.

The resolution from the annual meeting read as follows:

> WHEREAS, For many years and in many meetings of the respective constituencies of the Universalists and Unitarians, resolutions have been unanimously adopted expressing utmost friendliness and comradeship in the common work of liberal religion and a looking forward to closer affiliation,
>
> THEREFORE, RESOLVED, That the President of the American Unitarian Association is hereby requested, if he finds it advisable after conference with officials of the Universalist General Convention, to appoint a Commission of such numbers as he may designate, whose duty it will be to look into the practicability of uniting these two communions for the common good; this Commission to meet with any similar commission that may be appointed by the Universalists and report at the next Annual meeting of the American Unitarian Association.[24]

The resolution had been presented to the Unitarians by Carlyle Summerbell, a frequent contributor to the *Leader*. Three amendments had been made from the floor of the Unitarian meeting before being passed unanimously. In the original version the Unitarian commission was to have consisted of no more than fifteen nor less than nine members, but it was thought inadvisable to bind or limit the president in making his choice. The clause "after conference with officials of the Universalist General Convention" was "included to avoid any embarrassment about withdrawal and waiting a little longer" rather than putting Universalists in the position of having flatly to refuse. And a time limit was imposed on the commission's report in order to avoid prolonged delay.

Although the text of the AUA resolution was promptly made public, it did not appear in the *Leader* for two weeks after its adoption, and was then quoted without comment, tucked away near the end of the thirty-two page issue.[25] No mention, editorial or otherwise, was made by van Schaick for almost a month, and even then in the context of a report that the Ohio Convention had endorsed the idea of appointing a Universalist commission looking to merger.[26] Almost two months passed before van Schaick published an editorial response, when he suggested that some kind of federation was probably desirable, provided an "open door" policy regarding the earlier Joint Statement was maintained.[27] The Unitarian proposal had to be at least considered.

The reaction to the Unitarian resolutions on the floor of the General Convention at its meeting in Buffalo was mixed.[28] Thirty seconds after the motion was made to appoint the commission suggested by the Unitarians, G. H. Leining was on his feet, calling for a prompt decision on whether to remain a distinctive denomination or to join forces with the Unitarians. Richard H. McLoughlin supported the motion as not only desirable but something already far advanced. "There is no way to stop our uniting with the Unitarians, regardless of what motion is passed."

Arthur W. Peirce of Dean Academy spoke in opposition. When put on the level of individuals and local churches, "you cannot unite two opposite things; that is against human nature." His attempt to substitute the word "co-operating" for "uniting" was defeated by "an overwhelming vote." True merger, he said, arranged by "the higher-ups" in the denomination, could never take place without local church assent. H. C. Ledyard contended that union was impossible. After all, "the humanists in the Unitarian Church have thrown God and Jesus over as junk." Tomlinson and others supported the idea of appointing a commission, Asa Bradley pointing out that the motion was not binding. Outgoing convention President Frank D. Adams said that failure to honor the Unitarian recommendation would sweep Universalists "into the backwash of this current of religious progress." It would be little short of tragic to let the opportunity go by default. Clinton Lee Scott was in favor of the motion and believed that the Unitarians "meant what they said" when they used the word "unite."

Before a commission was appointed, Victor Friend, incoming president of the convention, and General Secretary-General Superintendent Etz were instructed to confer with their Unitarian counterparts, AUA President Louis Cornish (who had replaced Eliot in 1927) and Secretary Walter R. Hunt, to work out strategy. A difference of opinion developed immediately over the procedure to be followed.[29] Cornish favored small commissions of not more than five members from each denomination to work out plans to be submitted to a larger representative group. Etz and Friend argued for large commissions, their recommendations to be submitted to a small joint executive committee and re-submitted after consideration. A third possibility was to have small commissions hold hearings in various centers about the country.

A compromise was finally worked out, with a nine-person commission from each. All of the Universalists were trustees and/or officers of the General Convention.[30] The joint commission held its first meeting, lasting two days, in December 1931 at Brown University, with Friend as chairman. An executive committee, with three individuals from each denomination, was selected to draft plans and make a report to the full commission in February 1932.

The editor of the *Leader* was solicited to write an article on the objectives of the proposed union, but refused to do so until the commission had one or more proposals to offer.[31] He was not reluctant, however, to make predictions. He thought that anything that came to pass would take the form of federation rather than union, with each denomination retaining its corporate existence. There might, however, be merger of some subsidiary bodies. Local churches would have freedom to have as much or as little to do with such a federation (if it came about) as they wished. And neither commission wanted prolonged negotiations in view of the long history of previous efforts. Most of the ground had already been covered many times before.[32]

A preliminary statement from the commission was made available in May 1932, co-signed by Friend and Cornish. Various plans and alternatives had been discussed, including merger, which had been endorsed by the Western Unitarian Conference.[33] But that was discarded in favor of an umbrella organization to be known as the "Free Church of America" which would include not only the two denominations but would leave the way open for others to unite in "a larger fellowhsip which all desire."[34] Union was not recommended for Universalsits and Unitarians because it would have meant the sacrificing of "historic values" and the "impoverishing of American religious influences." So it was recommended that "each denomination preserve its own organization and honored name." Under this arrangement, for example, the Church of the Redemption (Second Universalist Society) in Boston would be designated as "The Church of the Redemption, Universalist (Free Church of America)."

The commissioners voted to designate themselves as "The Council for the Establishment of the Free Church of America." According to this plan, they would "interview confidentially members and leaders of other free independent churches" to sound them out as to whether they would be interested in cooperating or joining.

The proposal included also recommendations for elimination of duplicated efforts among similar departments, and heightened cooperation in such efforts as church extension, social amelioration and reform, and recruitment for the liberal ministry. A tentative draft of a constitution was also accepted by the self-appointed Council, to be submitted in more complete form as part of the entire plan of the two denominations.

After a series of meetings the joint commission made its final report in December 1932, subject to the approval of the Unitarians at their May meeting in 1933 and the Universalists at their biennial meeting in the fall. The report was mainly an elaboration of why they were not recommending merger.

The commission had considered three alternatives: maintenance of the *status quo;* i.e., "friendly relationship without definite plan." All members considered this "inadequate." The second alternative, complete merger, was considered but discarded on two grounds: Many constituencies in each denomination, both ministers and local churches, were not yet ready; and it would not strengthen "the larger cause of liberalism," for the same barriers that already existed to prevent other like-minded liberals from joining forces with their Universalist or Unitarian brethren still existed. Therefore the third alternative was the one agreed upon — a larger and inclusive fellowship of *all* liberals. The proposed Free Church of America would, in the view of the commission, include all the advantages of merger with none of the complications such action would entail.

The proposed constitution provided "entire freedom in matters of religious belief and statement of faith" and left it up to local circumstances as to whether churches at the community level would merge. Local consolidation was not the objective of the Free Church movement, but enlargement of the work of the constituent fellowships. The commission identified nineteen areas of activity that might be carried on in common among participating churches. Eight areas were listed in which cooperation already existed among liberals (including Congregationalists). There were already under way conversations looking to cooperation or even merger of major religious publications (the *Leader* and the *Register*), as well as closer relations between the Universalist and Unitarian publishing houses.

The commission went on record with the belief that the plan of the Free Church provided "the foundation for the final union of the forces of liberal religion in the United States and Canada." It was confidently described as "a venture of faith which once undertaken will be abundantly justified."

According to the records, both the idea and the organizational form of the Free Church were the work of Cornish, who became the first president.[35] Over two-thirds of the constitution dealt with the mechanics and framework of the organization, with only a brief and generalized statement of purpose; namely. "to bring about closer relationship and greater co-operation among liberal denominations, churches, parishes and societies; to establish other liberal movements wherever possible; to spread the knowledge of and to deepen devotion to the ideals of liberal religion."[36]

Membership was to comprise "such religious denominations and such churches, parishes or societies as may be admitted to membership in it." This included individual groups, "whether or not members of any denomination which is a member of this Fellowship."[37]

What became the most controversial section in the constitution was the Preamble which stated that

> We, representatives of churches of the free spirit, unite ourselves in the Fellowship of the Free Church of America. We affirm our faith that unity of purpose is the bond of highest religious fellowship. We seek closer co-operation with others of like purpose, recognizing that, in accordance with congregational polity, the members of this Fellowship have entire freedom in matters of religious belief and statements of faith, and holding that, if we are controlled by a purpose to serve mankind in a spirit of mutual good-will, differing statements of faith may enrich our common life.

Many Universalists, notably Tomlinson, who served on the Council, were upset because there was not even an allusion to Christianity, or any statement of faith.[38] The latter was uppermost in the minds of some Universalists because ratification of a revised statement of belief was on the agenda of the very same meeting at which they were being asked to join the Free Church. The Rhode Island Convention, insistent on some positive statement of faith, voted that the Preamble should include a provision making it "forever impossible for any individual or group professing atheism or indifference to the personality of Jesus Christ... to become or remain constituent members."[39]

Concern over the absence of any reference to Christianity and a "declaration of spiritual principles" was not limited to Universalists. William L. Sullivan, distinguished and influential minister of the Unitarian church in Germantown, Pennsylvania, noted the absence with much regret.[40] Sullivan, ordained in the Catholic priesthood in 1899, became a Paulist father. In 1909 he left the church to become a Unitarian minister, and served the Germantown church from 1929 until his death in 1935.[41] In reply to Sullivan's objection, the original constitution of the AUA was quoted to affirm its Christian origins.[42]

The AUA, at its 107th annual meeting in Boston in 1932, heard a forceful presentation in favor of the Free Church concept by President Cornish. A resolution was adopted not only endorsing the report of the Council but hailing the birth of the new organization as a step leading "to the early and effective union of the forces of liberal religion."[43] Endorsement of the Free Church at the annual meeting in 1933, following a presentation by Frederick R. Griffin as a Unitarian representative on the commission, was a foregone conclusion. A resolution calling for immediate merger with the Universalists was postponed for one year. To table it might be construed as hostility; passing it might be interpreted as a lack of confidence in the Free Church.[44] The Free Church faced a much less enthusiastic reception among Universalists.

Printed copies of the report of the joint commission were circulated, together with the proposed constitution, at the General Convention meeting in Worcester in the fall of 1933. Adams and Hill, both members of the Universalist commission, made the presentation, followed by an endorsement by Owen D. Young read in his absence by Max Kapp. The plan for the Free Church of America was endorsed. It had been approved by the trustees the preceding year.[45]

When the proposal to adhere to the fellowship of the Free Church came up for discussion and vote, the opposition that had developed suddenly evaporated. One after the other, those who had been critical of the idea for some reason, such as Tomlinson, rose to second the motion to join, and it passed almost unanimously, with only two or three negative votes, and without amendment from the floor.[46]

What had happened? It was disclosed prior to the vote that Hall intended to offer two motions if the convention would agree first to join the Free Church. One would ask for an amendment to the Preamble to the Free Church constitution testifying to its Christian character and the other was a request for a change of name.[47] One delegate, Ledyard of Brockton, Massachusetts, who was among the handful voting against joining the Free Church, insisted that the two amendments be voted by the convention immediately, without referring them to the full commission, but he received no support.

Only a matter of hours before the vote was taken, the opposition had conferred with Universalist members of the commission and had decided not to argue against the Free Church principle on the floor. Two weeks earlier, they had drafted the two resolutions offered by Hall, but had withheld their contents because the atmosphere had become so tense that they might not have received a fair hearing if divulged too far in advance. Together, they satisfied those who had fought against the proposal, and a lengthy and undoubtedly unpleasant debate had been avoided.

The two changes that had resulted in an about-face of the opposition to the Free Church and were recommended for consideration by the entire commission were, first, that the sentence in the Preamble indicating "We seek closer co-operation with others of like purpose. . . ." be modified to read "with others who would work for the Kingdom of God in the spirit of Jesus."[48] Universalists insisted on retaining their Christian commitment and refused to compromise on that, regardless of what Unitarians did or did not believe. There was a strong implication that they would refuse to join if this change were not made.

The other recommendation was that another name for the new organization be found that "may be more truly descriptive of the nature of the Fellowship." The proposed constitution had, in actuality, created a federation of existing religious bodies rather than a new denomination or church. It represented merely a council of existing liberal churches, not a new organization. The argument was offered that the word "church" in the constitution merely confused the situation, particularly because the organization had already been incorporated under Massachusetts law in the spring of 1933, before either denomination had even approved the constitution or had voted to join.

The first amendment was passed overwhelmingly, although there were more negative votes than for the motion to endorse the Free Church. Scott, who had signed the Humanist Manifesto not long before, opposed the amendment because of its ambiguity as a theistic statement. The second amendment passed without debate, and the Universalist Church had become officially a member of the Free Church.

After the Worcester meeting a Boston newspaper carried the misleading headline "Universalists, Unitarians Unite." A church spokesman hastened to correct the error, explaining that the two denominations had voted not for union but "for a co-operative working organization."

At a meeting in the fall of 1933 the General Convention's request for the two changes was presented to the executive committee of the Council.

Both were voted, although one Unitarian member (Percy W. Gardner) "wished to be recorded as prophesying that the future historian will record that in adopting this amendment [reference to God and Jesus].... the Free Church of America took a step backward."[49] An *ad hoc* committee was appointed to solicit suggestions for a new name. All three Universalist members of the Council executive committee agreed upon "Free Church Fellowship." Tomlinson, however, still had his doubts about the Free Church, preferring outright merger with the Unitarians.[50]

The two commissions agreed to both changes at a joint meeting in January 1934. A place for both God and Jesus was found in the organization, which was redesignated as the Free Church Fellowship at the same meeting. The majority of the Universalists who had served on the original joint commission became members of its Council, and the same proportion of clerical to lay (6 to 3) was continued.[51]

It was obvious that the negotiations inaugurated in 1931 by the Unitarians had not achieved the purpose intended, and supporters of merger (mostly Unitarians) were visibly disappointed. Augustus P. Reccord, a Unitarian strongly in favor of merger, read the report of the commission and its accompanying constitution "with disappointment and chagrin. Verily the mountain hath labored and brought forth a very diminutive rodent."[52] Everything that had been proposed was already provided by the National Federation of Religious Liberals. Why the duplication?

Gordon Kent, of the Unitarian church in Sioux City, Iowa, wondered "if there is as much indignation among Universalists as among Unitarians at the abortiveness of that committee on the merger of the two denominations. I'm for one headquarters, one paper, one hymn book."[53]

After the preliminary report of the commission had been released in 1932, *Onward,* the YPCU publication, reacted angrily by calling its recommendations 'an emasculated relic of a robust movement' to join the two denominations.[54]

Stanard D. Butler (Unitarian) was positive that the preliminary report could not possibly have been unanimous. Where was the minority report?[55] The editor of the *Leader* greeted the report with resignation, if not enthusiasm, but defended it against its critics. Joy, a member of the Unitarian commission who had attended every meeting, insisted that all decisions had been unanimous.[56]

Judge Hill, a lay member of the Universalist commission, tried to explain to a meeting in Salem, Massachusetts, of representatives of the ten Universalist and twelve Unitarian churches in Essex County, why merger had not been recommended. The desire to carry all elements of the two denominations — from conservative to radical — into the Free Church, precluded such a step. They needed time to be persuaded.[57]

There was support as well as criticism of the Free Church. The New York Convention endorsed the work of the commission, as did the

Southwestern Federation of Religious Liberals meeting in Hutchinson, Kansas.[58] Early in 1933 the *Leader* carried reactions from some ten sources which were generally positive in tone.[59]

Unitarians, both before and after the report of the commission had been made public, continued to urge merger. Ulysses S. Milburn, president of the Boston Ministers group, at which Cornish had been the speaker in the fall of 1931, had doubts if as many as 2 percent of the population were religiously liberal. "if we are to make any impression on the Orthodoxy even of New England, it behooves all liberals to come together and work together."[60] The Western Unitarian Conference, which had officially supported merger earlier, on learning that the commission had "abandoned all efforts to unite said communions," determinedly went again on record as favoring "an actual merger . . . on a basis of unlimited freedom."

In accordance with the decision to appeal to liberals everywhere, the commission had voted that at least four of the Council members were to be from outside the Universalist and Unitarian denominations. William E. Gilroy, Dwight Bradley, and Russell J. Clinchy were the Congregational representatives; the fourth was John Haynes Holmes, pastor of the Community Church in New York City. Representatives of the Council had also immediately entered into conversations with leaders in other churches and had compiled a long list of "independent thinkers" who might endorse the Free Church idea. The results were almost completely disappointing.

John H. Lathrop, pastor of the First Unitarian Congregational Society in Brooklyn, New York, discussed the idea of the Free Church with Harry Emerson Fosdick, the nationally known Baptist preacher who occupied the pulpit of the Park Avenue Baptist Church (later Riverside Church) from 1930 in New York City. Lathrop met with "complete failure," according to his report to Cornish in December 1931. Fosdick had said, in substance, that he had no faith in "organizations at the top," was not himself an "organization man," and shunned, wherever possible, conferences of such groups which usually included "a lot of speech making that I feel is a waste of time." The Free Church was "in danger of becoming just another denomination."

Etz and Joy attended the General Conference of the Society of Friends in the summer of 1932. The Quakers expressed interest, but "certain difficulties" stood in the way of their active participation in the Free Church. Their greatest concern was that affiliation would jeopardize the attempts by the Hicksite (liberal) wing represented by the General Conference, to heal the historic breach with the orthodox (Philadelphia) Friends which extended back into the early nineteenth century. Etz and Joy, accepting this situation, pursued the matter no farther. Cornish had substantially the same experience when he explained the Free Church to the president of the Friends' University in Wichita, Kansas, the same year.

Holmes of the Community Church reacted quite differently. He cordially endorsed the Council's plan as "statesmanlike," with significance far beyond Universalist-Unitarian boundaries. He suggested that the Congregationalists "could not long remain outside, for their freedom is a boasted heritage."[61] He was likewise sure that the Society for Ethical Culture would accept an offer of fellowship. However, Holmes' predictions were over-optimistic. The Committee on Inter-Church Relations of the Congregational Church considered Free Church membership "impracticable" and refused in 1933 to commit its membership to the Free Church, although a few individual parishes joined. No progress was reported in bringing the Ethical Culture Society into the federation. The Universalist insistence on writing Christianity into the constitution, if nothing else, made their membership unlikely at best.

Holmes, as well as several others, borrowed terminology from the business community by describing the proposed Free Church as "a sort of holding company" for Universalists and Unitarians. But those less sanguine noted that, despite the change of name, the two commissions had actually created a third liberal denomintion which would do no more than complicate an already complex situation. Even more disturbing to supporters of complete union was the refusal of the two commissions to go the whole way, although some Universalist churches opposed any such move at all. The Church of the Messiah in Philadelphia used the well-worn argument that consolidation "would prove detrimental to the future interests and existence of the Universalist Church at large" because it would disappear as a separate denomination.[62]

The proposal of the joint commission to stop short of merger was met not only with words like "disappointment," "chagrin," and "disapproval" but with such stronger expressions as "breach of faith" and "betrayal of trust."[63] The Ohio Convention, which had supported merger, felt that the preliminary report 'practically nullifies the purpose for which the joint commission was created.'[64] A total of only twenty-one votes had been cast — clearly unrepresentative of Universalist opinion in the state.[65] One individual characterized the creation of the Free Church as "a futile gesture" and wanted to know why it had been attempted in the first place.[66]

There was also recurrent criticism of the word "Free" in the title. Both the Norwegian-Danish and the Swedish Evangelical churches objected to use of the term on the ground that the word was included in both their official names, and that misunderstanding and confusion would result if used also by another body. Reccord considered the name "Free Church" unfortunate, smacking of presumptuousness.[67] The *Christian Century* also raised the question of the appropriateness of the terminology. Use of the expression might "promote the illusion that no other churches are free."[68]

More inclusive wording than that was needed if true comprehensiveness were to be achieved. Hall hastened to explain that the title was "the best we could invent. Give us a better one and we will organize around that." The terms "Council of Liberals" or "Liberal Churches" were among those offered.

There was some effort to gauge sentiment about the Free Church from both denominations at large but the results were inconclusive. After the subject had been discussed at great length at the Michigan Universalist Convention meeting in 1932, with Unitarians as invited guests, "everybody talked about church union — but not all were for it — that is, among the Universalists."[69] A straw ballot was conducted by Leining, editor of *Team Work*, with 207 replies. Of that number, 58 percent were in favor of merger while 42 percent were not.[70] There was so much uncertainty about how Pennsylvania Universalists would react that it was thought inadvisable even to consider putting the question of the Free Church on the agenda for the 1932 meeting. At a conference of forty Universalists and Unitarians in Cleveland, Ohio, an informal poll indicated that although seventeen were in favor of merger and eleven in favor of the Free Church, twelve did not even vote. A referendum of all Universalists as to their views about the Free Church had been suggested prior to the General Convention meeting in Worcester in 1933, but nothing was done to carry it out.[71]

While arguments continued over such matters as the prospects for merger, and terminology, there was at first a considerable flurry of activity. The Council of the Free Church of America in Southern California was organized in the summer of 1933 and held an Institute of Liberal Religion early in 1934 in a Unitarian church opened for the occasion.[72] The Pacific Coast Conference-Free Church Fellowship was created by the Unitarians later that year, with Universalist representatives on the board of directors; and the four Universalist churches in southern California had voted to join the Conference.[73] When it met in 1936 it was attended by twenty-one Unitarian ministers and representatives of three of the four Universalist churches, including Robert Cummins, pastor in Pasadena.[74]

An unprecedented joint meeting of the Minnesota Unitarian Conference and the Universalist state convention took place in Unity Church in St. Paul in the fall of 1933.[75] Even a Universalist state convention (North Carolina) applied for membership, in 1934, although there was no provision in the Free Church constitution for such a body.[76]

In the spring of 1934 twenty-one churches were voted into the Fellowship — nine Universalist, nine Unitarian, and three community churches. The greatest feather in the cap of the Free Church supporters was the addition in 1934 to the Council of former Bishop Frederick B. Fisher, pastor of the Central Methodist Episcopal Church in Detroit, with a large and flourishing congregation. His church joined the Fellowship in 1935, and at the same meeting he was elected president, a post which he assumed with the greatest reluctance.

But Joy was not satisfied with the progress being made. Part of the difficulty was "the spirit of caution and denominational conservatism" among both Universalists and Unitarians.[77] Griffin, who had made such an effective presentation at the Unitarian annual meeting in 1933 on behalf of the Free Church, had become less and less enthusiastic in a matter of only a few months. There was constant bickering about the presence or absence of a theological statement in the constitution. Some Universalists became jittery when the Unitarian Commission of Appraisal, created in 1933 to assess the state of that denomination, reported in 1935 the wish of many "to restore the original and more inclusive wording" of the Preamble by deleting all references to Christianity.[78] Tomlinson adamantly opposed the Unitarian recommendation, noting that Universalists could be as tenacious as Unitarians. It brought to mind the generation gap that Max Kapp discerned within Universalist ranks. Younger clergy like himself failed to understand the qualms of veteran Universalists who were engaging in a "rumpus of controversy [that] is slightly wearisome, and slightly ludicrous."[79]

By the close of 1934 individuals like Holmes were becoming increasingly restive and impatient about the lack of a concrete program to pin down the vague rhetoric enunciated in the constitution. Earlier that year representatives from several organizations and departments in both denominations had met with the Council executive committee to offer suggestions and work out a program. Out of it had come a Declaration of Principles and a Statement of Immediate Aims, adopted in 1935, which had been both masterpieces of high-flown language and sufficiently ambitious in aims to have engaged the attention and committed the potential financial resources of a national legislative body for decades to come.

Declaration of Principles

1. We believe that religion is ethical, that ethics is social, and that the church is the organized conscience of society.
2. We conceive our task to be: first, the cultivation of excellence, the promotion of character, the encouragement of the individual in his endeavor to realise through all his relationships, the principles of integrity and honor; and second, the uniting of individuals and churches for the upbuilding of human welfare.
3. We propose that the Free Church Fellowship shall be a union of religious liberals, a home for the emancipated spirit of man, whatever the forms of religious faith and worship.

Statement of Immediate Tasks

1. The preparation of a social platform which shall crystallize and enunciate the great social ideals which we recognize and the immediate concrete objectives for which we would now strive.

2. The organization of liberal ministers' conferences in areas of possible or actual industrial unrest.
3. The formation of a board of social strategy to mobilize the churches of America for united social action.
4. The formation in our churches of study groups for the consideration of selected social problems and problems of personal religion, these groups to promote cooperation and understanding between clergy and laity, and wherever possible, to translate conviction into action.
5. The preparation of a book of personal spiritual guidance as a suggested way of life for the individual.
6. The promotion of regional and local conferences of the Free Church Fellowship.
7. The closest relations and wherever possible, the merging of departmental enterprises in member and cooperating denominations; for example, in denominational publications, young people's organizations, departments of religious education and social relations.
8. The rounding out of the Free Church Fellowship by securing the adherence of many more of the Universalist and Unitarian Churches and of the ministers and churches of other denominations.

The Unitarian Commission of Appraisal, in its second preliminary report delivered to the May 1935 annual meeting, called the Declaration of Principles "an epoch-making event in the struggle for a united liberal fellowship."[80] Universalists were much less lyrical in their praise. Their representatives on the Council were more interested in insisting on inserting the adjective "Christian" at every opportunity, a tactic which helped delay the distribution of the material for almost six months.[81] The board of social strategy provided by the third item in the Statement of Immediate Aims was actually appointed in 1935 "to seek to unify the efforts of all denominations engaged in social movements and in efforts to secure world peace."[82] This was the climactic statement of a truly grand design.

Joy, who had become secretary of the Council in 1935, warned Fisher, the new president, that the Fellowship was "far too big as to purposes and methods of action at the present time to be very effective."[83] One social service project was to have been assistance in relocating some of the approximately 5,000 people to be displaced by the building of a series of reservoirs planned by the Tennessee Valley Authority. This met the same fate as most of the other projects envisioned by the Statement of Immediate Tasks—nothing was ever done.

The first annual meeting of the Free Church Fellowship was held in the Church of Our Savior (Unitarian) in Brooklyn in January 1935, with seventy-three delegates and about twenty-five others present. All but nine of the delegates were Universalists or Unitarians, eight of the others being representatives of community churches. Fisher, the sole Methodist delegate, addressed an audience of about thirty. The small attendance was attributed in large part to the weather. Fisher spoke during the worst blizzard since 1888.[84]

Only eighty-one churches had joined the Fellowship by early 1935, a source of much discouragement to its advocates. This poor showing was blamed on lack of publicity, and on the mistaken assumption by many Unitarian churches that membership in the AUA meant automatic Free Church membership and therefore did not bother to apply.[85] Even then, there were almost twice as many Unitarian as Universalist churches in the membership.

The second annual meeting, adjourned from Boston in 1936 to meet with Fisher's church in Detroit, was only an appendage to an Institute on Religion and Social Reconstruction already planned by Fisher. When publicity was being prepared, there was no mention at all of the participation or co-sponsorship of the Fellowship in the preliminary printed program. When the Council met in Detroit, only five were present, with Adams as the sole Universalist.

The situation was even more demoralizing at the third (and final) annual meeting of the Fellowship, held in Chicago in 1937 at the People's Church (Unitarian). The program, for which Lon Ray Call of the Western Unitarian Conference was largely responsible, dealt with such social and political issues as the threat of Fascism, and was declared to have been "excellent." So far as Free Church involvement was concerned, the Institute was "a miserable failure."[86] Registration was "negligible," with speakers and officers of the Fellowship (including less than half the Council), making up the bulk of the attendance. Kapp, who had been elected secretary of the Council, was the only Universalist member present. At the first session the tactical error of charging 50 cents admission had resulted in over 200 being turned away. This policy was abandoned the second day of the Institute but the damage had been done. To make matters worse, the church in which the Institute was held was more interested in making plans to celebrate the twenty-fifth anniversary of its pastor's tenure than in playing host to a group of outsiders.

The Free Church came to an ignominious end in the fall of 1937, after an unsuccessful appeal for funds.

The failure of the Free Church Fellowship was not difficult to explain. It had been created as a half-way house which satisfied very few, as a step toward merger which the Unitarians were much more willing to push than were the Universalists. It had attempted both too little and too much, with resources which in no way matched the idealistic, not to say grandiose, plans for the future. The motive power had come from a small band of denominational leaders, without grass-roots support, to appeal to a larger fellowship among religious liberals. Instead, it had become entangled with a continuing internal squabble between Universalists and Unitarians over their relationships. Men like Fisher felt themselves to be outsiders who were witnessing a strictly family quarrel. Arthur C. McGiffert of the Chicago Theological Seminary was mildly interested in the Free Church movement, but quickly perceived that excessive attention was being paid to Universalist-Unitarian matters and that the movement of the Free Church was suffering from schizophrenia.[87]

Joy was intent on using the Fellowship as a vehicle for uniting the two denominations, which he considered a matter of survival for both. Their decline might "continue until nothing but our endowments are left."[88] But the accomplishment of his goal met with one frustration after another. He felt that the merger of the two youth groups would be one of the easiest steps to take, and as early as 1932 had suggested that the YPCU and the YPRU be represented on the commission.[89] The YPRU had actually voted for merger in 1935, but when the Universalist youth group approached the General Convention for advice, they were dissuaded from taking any such step.

Attempts to consolidate the *Leader* and *Register* had been effectively opposed by van Schaick, knowing well that the Unitarian publication was in serious financial difficulty, with a subscription list below 3,700. An effort to combine them with the monthly *Advance,* the successor to the weekly *Congregationalist and Herald of Gospel Liberty* in 1934, also failed, as did a suggestion that *Unity* be made the journalistic organ for the Free Church.[90]

Adequate financing for the Fellowship had likewise never been furnished, especially difficult to acquire in a period of national economic depression. No provision whatever for paying bills for such mundane items as postage, letter-head stationery, and certificates of membership had been made when the organization was formed. As a consequence, Unitarian headquarters footed most of the bills and furnished most of the secretarial services until a plea for funds was issued requesting a $10 minimum contribution from all participating churches. The plea for 1935 brought one response. Eleven members of the Council then made personal pledges ranging from $25 to $50. Much of the treasury, amounting to $113.27 in 1935, was the residue of the funds contributed by Fisher's church toward paying his travel expenses.

Disregarding the sorry plight of the treasury, the Council drew up a budget of $6,000 for 1935, with $1,500 each to be requested from the AUA and the General Convention, the balance to be raised "as best it could." This generous figure was arrived at in order to pay for a full-time executive officer (secretary) authorized by the constitution, as well as for other operating expenses.

The AUA actually appropriated $400 and the General Convention $200, lamentably short of the target. So the plans for an executive officer had to be abandoned. The pledges of several members of the Council had been contingent upon employing one, so some were never paid. Fisher, busy in Detroit with a mutitude of parish activities, took time to suggest a candidate, but was greatly disappointed at the inability or unwillingness of the Universalists and Unitarians to raise the necessary funds for a post that they themselves had authorized.

Fisher had also taken some risk in associating himself wih the Free Church. His name had been omitted from the list of Methodist delegates to the World Conference on Faith and Order to meet in 1937, presumably because of his "extremely liberal tendency."[91] He had already written Joy in 1935 that he could not devote sufficient attention to Free Church matters to continue to serve as president. A Unitarian member of the Council considered this "a calamity of the first order," and the loss of his leadership "just short of disastrous."[92] Joy himself was so discouraged that he threatened to resign. All the talk about church unity was getting nowhere, and the Universalists were becoming more uncooperative than ever. Holmes blamed both Universalists and Unitarians for continuing their "traditional denominational way, just as though nothing had happened, and are thus leaving the Fellowship to perish.[93]

The Free Church, by the time of a Council meeting early in 1936, was admittedly "devoid of accomplishment," and had failed either to interest those outside Universalism and Unitarianism, or even to obtain the necessary support from within them. In a questionnaire answered by 269 Unitarian clergy in 1936 as to their priorities for the denomination, based on a nine-point ranking, the Free Church had ranked eighth.[94] Typical of the Universalist criticism of the organization was that of William Couden, pastor of the First Universalist Church in Providence, who requested that his name be removed from the mailing list. The Fellowship was nothing more than another social action group which was "dabbling too much in the materialistic and social problems of the times" and had abandoned the true mission of the church - "the promulgation of a real Christian personal religion."[95]

The lack of any constructive action by the Fellowship was a recurring theme by 1936. Tomlinson was so discouraged that he was ready to disband the entire organization, which had "*done absolutely nothing . . . . we should make application for membership in the 'Sounding Brass & Tinkling Cymbal Union.*" Snow, president of Meadville Theological School and elected secretary of the Council in 1936, resigned that fall and asked that his action not be reconsidered.[96] Hill, who had been a leading layman on the Universalist commission and was reelected in 1937 for a six-year term even though he had ceased to attend most Council meetings, had given up in disgust. After almost two years of participation without any real action, he considered the Fellowship "wholly visionary" and lacking in direction.[97]

Much to the surprise of his listeners at the General Convention meeting in the nation's capital in 1935 Tomlinson, instead of making one of his customary denominational loyalty speeches, spoke fervently on behalf of the Free Church.[98] But it was too late even then. The prevailing mood had been distinctly otherwise. To the extent that the Universalists had to take major responsibility for the collapse of the Free Church movement, the basic explanation could be found in the great revival of denominational morale at the convention. Kapp, in reporting the meeting, had observed that "Universalists are rather decided that their destiny in the future lies in being a separate denomination rather than being a part of a larger liberal movement."[99] This had been frankly stated by the editor of the *Leader* in reporting a Free Church Council meeting later that year, when Unitarians had been "saddened [by] the fact that official Universalism blocks every movement toward union . . . and that even cooperative movements have to happen through the action of interested individuals only." The Fellowship had become merely "a department of the AUA," not even the true Broad Church movement so hoped for by its founders.

Clinton Lee Scott, looking back on the brief history of the Free Church Fellowship, called it "a contrivance . . . a bastard third ecclesiastical organization" which signalled a failure of the Universalist and Unitarian commissions to carry out their mandate to explore the practicability of union.[100] He described it as a "debacle" whose "lingering death . . . came with less resistance and less attention than was accorded its birth."[101] Yet, while Universalist-Unitarian movements toward merger appeared to be stymied at the national level in the 1930s, discernible progress in cooperation, if not actual consolidation, was being made elsewhere.

Horace Westwood, who held dual fellowship and was mission preacher for the Unitarian Laymen's League, became in 1930 the first such person known to have conducted a preaching mission in a Universalist church (in Kent, Ohio).[102] In 1933 the Universalist trustees appointed Westwood minister-at-large for the church in recognition of the services he was rendering.[103]

Many of the steps taken were the direct result of a series of recommendations made by the executive committee of the joint commission after a meeting in December 1931. Two officers of the Universalist General Sunday School Association were serving on the curriculum committee of the Unitarian Department of Religious Education in 1932.[104]

Of even broader import than this was a decision of the two denominations to produce a joint hymnal acceptble to both. In the first flush of enthusiasm over the Free Church in 1933 two new hymns celebrating its creation had been offered, intended to transcend denominational lines. One was introduced at a conference of Universalist and Unitarian churches in northeastern Maine by its author, Louis Walter Sanford, pastor of the Unitarian church in Eastport, entitled "Free Church of America."[105] The second, composed by Marion Franklin Ham, bore the title "Hymn to the Free Church of America."[106]

Prior to 1932 Universalists and Unitarians had been engaged in compiling new hymnals for their separate use. As early as 1912 a project had been conceived to prepare a joint hymnal, and committees had been appointed by the Universalist trustees and the Universalist Publishing House to confer with a committee of the AUA regarding the preparation of such a hymnal, but nothing had resulted.[107] Twenty years later the idea was revived, this time successfully. In 1932 authorization was given by the Universalist trustees to proceed with their part of the plan, and questionnaires were sent out to clergy by a joint commission on hymnals. By the spring of 1933 it had held six meetings.[108] The project was a complex and laborious one, and the finished product, *Hymns of the Spirit for Use in the Free Churches of America,* finally appeared in 1937. While the new hymnal was being prepared, most Universalist churches continued to use *Hymns of the Church, with Service and Chants,* an all-purpose compilation first published in 1907 and reprinted numerous times.[109]

Another indication of closer identification between the two denominations was the appearance, by 1932, of the term "Uni-Uni" as a form of conversational shorthand in youth groups.

Universalist and Unitarian churches also continued to combine as well as to associate closely, although many, such as the churches in Melrose, Massachusetts, considered union "impracticable."[110] But merger did take place in Cleveland, Ohio, in 1932. The pastor who took charge (Dilworth Upton) held dual fellowship.[111]

When the West Side Unitarian Church in New York City found itself in serious financial difficulty, it worked out an arrangement of "association" offered by F. O. Hall, pastor of the Church of the Divine Paternity, to use their building and to hold union services until the Unitarians could lease or sell their property.[112]

At the annual meeting of the National Federation of Religious Liberals in Joliet, Illinois, in 1931, the proposed union of the two denominations was the principal topic, with Galer, ex-president of the General Convention, and Snow, president of Meadville Theological School, as the main speakers.[113]

It was suggested the same year that the *Leader* and the *Register* be merged, not only for reasons of economy but as a way of bringing the two denominations closer together.[114] This was not yet to be achieved, but one step was taken in 1933, when the Universalist Publishing House assumed responsibility for printing the Unitarian paper as well as the *Leader;* eight pages of material considered common to both denominations were included.[115]

One of the early by-products of the interdenominational planning of the Free Church in 1932 was the consolidation of two outdoor bulletin boards intended to provide "educational and inspirational service" for each denomination. The editors of the *Wayside Pulpit* (Unitarian) and the

Universalist Community Pulpit, C. R. Joy and C. H. Pennoyer respectively, agreed in 1932 to combine the two projects as the *Wayside Community Pulpit* which appeared in 1933.[113]

Consideration was also being given in 1932 to having the Department of Social Relations (Unitarian) serve both denominations.[117] This suggestion had been made by the executive committee of the joint commission the previous year.[118] The pastor of the Universalist church in Santa Barbara, California, suggested in 1934 that a combined Universalist-Unitarian headquarters be established for the Pacific coast.[119]

So, little by little, the two denominations were coming closer together in spite of the failure of the Free Church to accomplish the purposes intended.

Chapter 31

"God's Stepchildren:" The Rebuffs of the Federal Council of Churches, 1939–1947

"Following several years of negotiations, the Federal Council of Churches of Christ in America on two occasions, first at its meeting in Pittsburgh in November 1944 and again in Seattle in December 1946, voted to bar from its membership The Universalist Church of America."[1] Behind this barebones statement lay a long and complex history of relations with other Protestant denominations going back into the nineteenth century and bringing into bold relief the basic and ultimate failure of the Universalist Church to obtain firm and unquestioned acceptance into the family of American Protestant churches.

Much of the difficulty centered on the term "evangelical," a word used loosely to embrace a wide variety of meanings and connotations. To most Universalists in the latter half of the nineteenth century it was used synonymously with "orthodox"; namely, those denominations which held to the doctrine of endless punishment except for selected individuals who would be saved by faith and divine grace rather than by good works and observation of the sacraments alone. Grace was to be acquired through belief in Christ as Lord and Savior, the recognition of whose divinity was indispensable to salvation. This meant emphasis on the unquestioned authority of the Gospels, particularly as outlined in the four key books of the New Testament. In practice, an evangelist was one fired with missionary zeal to preach and disseminate said Gospels, often associated with individual conversion, and accompanied by emotional fervor and what was generally known as revivalism, the excesses of which represented to most Universalists an unworthy retreat from reason.

The *Leader* reported in full the revivals conducted by Dwight L. Moody (1837-1899) and Ira D. Sankey (1840-1908) in the 1870s. Their activities were looked at askance by Universalists like Isaac M. Atwood and W. H.

Ryder, although they admitted that some good could result from the heightened religious interest, provided it did not become overly emotional and promote undue sectarianism.[2]

To thoughtful Universalists the flamboyant career of William Ashley ("Billy") Sunday (1862-1935) represented evangelism at its worst, and they reacted accordingly. The editor of the *Leader* complained that Sunday had "turned the Christian pulpit into a vaudeville show."[3] He was "a caricature of the Christian ministry . . . a ministerial calamity." When Sunday conducted a seven-week series of revival meetings in Syracuse, New York, most churches were closed for the occasion. F. W. Betts, the Universalist pastor, was shocked, disgusted, and generally aghast at Sunday's performance, calling him "arrogant, egotistical, [and] intolerant."[4] Betts was thoroughly repelled by his "slaughterhouse and barroom approach" and noted that the evangelist used the same hell-fire-and-damnation theology always exploited by revivalists. When Sunday descended on Boston to lead a ten-week revival in 1917, Universalist clergy decided to remain aloof and neither to mount a counterattack nor to join other Protestant churches in cooperating with Sunday.[5]

Even though Universalists were sometimes temporarily accepted into the Protestant mainstream, there was always likely to be raised at least a shadow of doubt about their legitimacy as a completely Christian denomination. Consequently it was often a special local circumstance that allowed them to move from the periphery to full participation in a given organization or activity. There was more than a shadow of doubt raised in 1902, when a Baptist publication in Cincinnati had condemned Universalists in language reminiscent of the battles fought in an earlier day. 'Today the most depraved, the most vicious, the most daring sinner, is a believer in a future probation, to be followed by deliverance and bliss. Universalism is the religion of the gambling-room, the race-track, the theater, the brothel, the saloon, the den of infamy.'[6]

In the fall of 1873 New York City played host to a series of meetings of the International Evangelical Alliance, an organization founded in London in 1846, with an American branch established in 1867. It was intended to unify all Protestant Christians in a campaign to evangelize the world. One of its leaders, who became an eminent church historian, was Philip Schaff, who at the World's Parliament of Religions in 1893 urged the formation of a federation of Protestant denominations. Another was Josiah Strong, for many years secretary of the Evangelical Alliance, who called not only for interdenominational cooperation but for increased attention to the social responsibilities of Christianity.[7]

The Universalists greeted the ideas behind the Evangelical Alliance with favor and chose three representatives to attend the organization meeting in 1873: J. H. Chapin, Alonzo A. Miner, and W. H. Ryder.[8] But they were excluded from participation because the Universalists were not considered a truly evangelical denomination and therefore not a *bona fide* Christian body, because they did not subscribe to the doctrine of endless punishment.[9] Further, one of the delegates made a violent attack on Universalists and charged them not only with infidelity but held them largely responsible for the irreligion which allegedly existed extensively in the post-Civil war period.

A. St. John Chambré, a Universalist preacher, devoted an entire sermon to refuting the charges and claiming that "we can do without the Evangelical Alliance, but it cannot do without us."[10] He recognized that the word "evangelical" had usually been associated with denominations not sympathetic to Universalism, but insisted that Universalists were nonetheless evangelical in the historic sense of the term because the words "gospel" and "evangelism" were synonymous. It was the misuse of the word by the orthodox that caused the difficulty. Chambré did not himself "propose to be cut off from the communion of the Church Universal, the church of the ages, by giving up this word." That would be equivalent to giving up the Universalist faith as he understood it. He dispensed with the allegation of infidelity in short order. The Scriptures were still accepted by Universalists "as final authority in all matters of religious faith and life." Without the Bible and without Christ as made known in it, Universalists would have nothing on which to build.

As to the sufficiency of Universalism, Chambré had no doubts. Other Protestant churches, including all of those represented in the Evangelical Alliance, taught only variations of the same doctrine of endless punishment as did the Roman Catholic church, the most powerful of all. Therefore "the only power that can meet Romanism, and successfully resist its claims, is Universalism." So why worry about the Evangelical Alliance? The ultimate success of Christianity itself depended on the elimination of the doctrine of endless punishment. He was confident that the time would come, and that not far distant, when the power of the Universalist idea would become pervasive. A common bond between Universalists and other Protestant Christians, including those in the Evangelical Alliance, already existed. They were already "brethren in Christ Jesus." The next logical step was to extend the idea of the Church Universal to embrace the Roman Catholic church, for were not the words "Universal" and "Catholic" one and the same?

Universalists were included in the "Council of Twenty-five" when an American Congress of Churches met in Hartford, Connecticut, in May 1885.[11] James M. Pullman, then pastor in Lynn, Massachusetts, participated in a symposium on "The Attitude of the Secular Press towards Religion," led by Washington Gladden, the well-known Protestant social reformer. W. H. Dearborn, pastor of the Hartford parish, served on the local arrangements committee. The meeting was intended "to promote Christian union, and to advance the kingdom of God, by a free discussion of the great religious, moral and social questions of the time." There was no intention of creating a society, organizing a plan of union, or of establishing a creed, but of holding public discussions of theological questions and social questions with a religious bearing, particularly those on which Christians disagreed.

Willingness on the part of Universalists to cooperate with other denominations at the local level was evident in 1895, when Gideon I. Keirn represented the denomination at a series of meetings to promote Christian unity sponsored by the rector of the Episcopal church in Charlestown, Massachusetts.[12] Not much was accomplished. Even though there were admitted to be many experiences and goals held in common, the churches were too deeply divided by doctrine and dogma to make much progress. The Unitarians declined to participate.

Neither Universalists nor Unitarians were invited to an ecumenical missionary conference held in New York City in 1900.[13] There was considerable stir in religious circles when in 1905 the executive committee of the National Federation of Churches and Christian Workers, the immediate predecessor of the Federal Council of Churches, excluded from their annual meeting the delegates provided by the American Unitarian Association.[14] It was assumed that the publicly announced meeting of the "Federation of All Christian Churches" meant general participation, and the Unitarians proceeded accordingly without receiving a formal invitation. As it happened, the committee, in issuing special invitations, omitted also the Universalists and the Roman Catholics.

Keirn, then the Universalist pastor in Muncie, Indiana, was excluded in 1902 from membership in the local ministerial association because he served an "unevangelical" church.[15] He was finally accepted five years later when the restriction was waived in his case because of his great popularity and the high esteem in which he was held.[16]

It took no less than thirty years of controversy before the Universalist church was declared to be "evangelical" by the Sunday School Union in Brooklyn, New York, and hence eligible for full fellowship the same year.[17] It was not until 1920 that the state Sunday School Association in Massachusetts formally admitted Universalists, although they had participated anyway by mutual consent. The constitution of the organization was revised by striking out the term "evangelical" and substituting "Protestant Christian."[18]

The status of Universalists in their relations with the Young Men's Christian Association (YMCA) was another question of long standing which indicated lack of full acceptance. For many years Universalists were completely excluded. A proposal was made in the 1880s to establish a branch in Waltham, Massachusetts, and an invitation was sent out to all Protestant clergy to attend an organization meeting. The local Universalist clergyman received his, and duly appeared, only to witness a vote (22 to 9) of those present not to include Universalists because they were not an evangelical denomination.[19] They were officially excluded from full membership in the entire YMCA until 1906, when membership was left up to local decision.[20]

Excluded or not, Universalists made significant financial contributions to the organization. The two Ball brothers of Muncie, Indiana, wealthy manufacturers of home canning equipment, and "loyal and generous" members of the local Universalist church, gave $150,000 to the YMCA.[21] To Universalists, the social service provided by the YMCA overrode its restrictions concerning theology. This was precisely the same stance that the denomination took regarding the work of the Federal Council of Churches, even though rejected twice in their bid for membership.

The Federal Council of Churches of Christ in America, an outgrowth of the National Federation of Churches and Christian Workers, met in 1905 in Carnegie Hall in New York City, convened as the Inter-Church Conference on Federation, with delegates from thirty Protestant denominatons. The ratifications of the plan in 1908 by thirty-three formally brought the Council into existence.[22] Its primary purpose was to achieve, so far as possible, a unified front of all Protestant denominations interested in the solution of social and economic problems without interfering in any way with the autonomy of the member churhes, "preserving liberty and diversity in theology, polity and worship of the constituent denominations."

The preamble to the constitution expressed the hope that the member denominations might "more fully manifest the essential oneness of the Christian churches of American in Jesus Christ as their divine Lord and Savior, and to promote the spirit of fellowship, service and cooperation among them." According to one historian of the Federal Council, when the preamble was being considered prior to adoption, there was a "lively discussion" on the question of including the word "divine" before "Lord and Savior."[23] That descriptive but limiting adjective, voted unanimously, was to become the key factor in the discussions over the admission of Universalists almost forty years later.

The Unitarians never applied for membership, and the Universalists not until 1942. Up to that time both denominations were simply not invited to join. There was to be no commingling of the orthodox and the liberal. Unitarian leaders had urged the formation of the Council in the first place, and in 1908 Charles W. Eliot; John D. Long, governor of Massachusetts; and Edward Everett Hale were in New York City, expecting to be invited to help form the Council — an invitation that was never extended.[24]

Universalists, even though not for many decades invited to participate officially, supported the idea of Protestant unity propagated by the Federal Council. Even more appealing to them was its social program, embodied in "The Social Creed of the Churches," endorsed by the Universalists in 1913.[25] Step by step the denomination became involved in Federal Council activities over the years. Its Social Service Department and Department of International Justice and Good Will particularly appealed to Universalists. They greeted with approbation the hopeful spirit and social consciousness of the Council when it met in Boston in 1920 to plan for post-war reconstruction.[26]

A vast Interchurch World Movement was organized among major Protestant denominations in 1919 and 1920, with the goal of raising 330 million dollars (later increased to 500 million and then to one billion) to evangelize the entire world.[27] The Universalist trustees voted to participate and even appointed a committee to see what the denomination could contribute. But they soon discovered that they would not be welcome because, as a liberal rather than orthodox church, they were not eligible for membership in the Federal Council of Churches and were therefore excluded from the Interchurch World Movement.[28]

One of the money-raising strategies employed by the Interchurch Movement was a general campaign to solicit funds from public-spirited individuals who either had no denominational connection or did not belong to an "approved" denomination. Universalists were solicited, but were advised by their trustees not to contribute to an organization which not only excluded them but used high-pressure tactics to raise money.[29] Ironically, one of the five-person committee organized in Springfield, Massachusetts, to raise a working force for the Movement was Clarence E. Rice, pastor of St. Paul's Universalist Church.[30]

As it turned out, the Interchurch World Movement was an abysmal failure, and had for the most part collapsed in 1922. Part of the difficulty was getting denominations to commit unrealistically large sums of money. Only thirty actually participated, and expenses far exceeded revenues. Of the nearly eight million dollars expended before the end of 1920, only three million had been collected from "friendly citizens."

The fact that the Interchurch World Movement did not succeed was not of as much concern to Universalists as that they had been excluded from it. But even that could be rationalized. Clarence J. Harris, pastor of the Washington Heights Universalist Church in New York City, noted that some Universalists were too easily seduced by the desire to join and hence be popular like other Christians by losing their distinctive identity. Joining the evangelical majority would mean in effect that their work was over, and that they would probably disappear, in time, as a separate denomination.[31] They were told not to feel disappointed or humiliated because they had been frozen out. Instead, Universalists should take pride in being "the advance guard of religious pioneers. Many

Universalists forget that they are heretics, they are 'come-outers,' they are radicals." The very act of excluding them was recognition of their distinctiveness. "If we have been quarantined, it is evidence that we are still thought to be contagious."

Rebuffed in their efforts to join officially the larger Protestant religious family, Universalists followed two courses of action: They created their own crusade under the banner of "A World Church for World Service"; and they continued to cooperate unofficially with the Federal Council. Regarding the first, one of the things they accomplished was to contribute amost $75,000 on behalf of the "starving children of Armenia" orphaned by the destruction wrought within the Ottoman Empire before and during World War I. The sum amounted to the equivalent of "adopting" more than 1,000 homeless victims.[32] As to the Federal Council, they became more and more deeply involved. In the mid-1920s General Superintendent Lowe was designated by the trustees to serve as the Universalist representative on its Social Welfare Commission; during the same decade the denomination contributed toward the salary of James Myer, executive secretary of the Council's Commission on the Church and Social Service.[33] During the 1930s Herbert E. Benton served for a time as chairman of the Commission on International Relations, of which Frank O. Hall and Stanley Manning were also members. After Benton resigned, Manning replaed him as chairman. Benton and Manning were also active in the Department of International Justice and Good Will. Hall expressed his exuberance in another context at the growing favor with which the Universalists were being greeted and what appeared to be "a new friendship between the churches.... If the time has come when some of the barbed wire fences between denominations are to go down, then let us take off our coats and go to work."[34]

Increased participation in the work of the Federal Council was one indication that "there is a new spirit in the air." When the Council was subjected to a Congressional investigation in 1930 the editor of the *Leader* lent his complete support to the organization.[35] Nine Universalists represented the denomination at a conference on the international situation sponsored by the Federal Council in 1940.[36] All in all, the circumstances seemed to favor a formal application for membership in the organization in which Universalists had been so active, and the social principles of which they wanted so much to support.

It was General Superintendent Cummins who assumed the principal role in the negotiations. His motives in pushing for membership were based not so much in attempting to win acceptance in the family of Christians as "just another Protestant denomination" as on his commitment to translating the One World concept into religious life by propagating the idea of "a more universal Universalism." Healing the wounds of war and thus promoting international brotherhood by furthering good works would be best accomplished, he thought, by linking up with an organization much better equipped than were the Universalists acting alone. Theological similarities and/or differences with other denominations were strictly secondary to the main task of building a better world. Here was the great opportunity "to establish a sound understanding of Universalist purpose."[37]

Cummins thought he had a point in his favor in gaining admission because of his strong personal friendship with George A. Buttrick (a Presbyterian), who was president of the Federal Council in 1940, and who invited him to be his personal guest at the forthcoming biennial meeting of the Council that winter. Cummins was unable to go, and by mutual agreement F. W. Perkins took his place. Two other Universalists were also present.[38] Perkins participated in the program and was given a most cordial reception. In an address to the Council he assured his listeners of his belief in the divinity of Christ.[39]

Before taking any formal action Cummins discussed the matter at length with colleagues both inside and outside the denomination. The editor of the *Leader* had warned him in 1939 that Cummins' insistence on a Universalism that included "Humanists, Christocentrics, and all others" would probably not sit well with some members of the Council; and the president of the AUA "looked with strong disfavor upon any possible relationship we might achieve with the Council." On the other hand, the secretary of the Massachusetts Council of Churches (a Baptist) and a member of the Federal Council's advisory committee, encouraged Universalists to consider making application, as did the bishop of the Methodist Church and the editor of the (Methodist) *Zion's Herald*. Even more strongly supportive were Douglas Horton and Frederick L. Fagley, Congregational leaders. They advised that Cummins confer with Samuel M. Cavert, a Presbyterian and executive secretary of the Federal Council.

Cummins' first intimation that Universalist theology might become an issue came with his conference in 1940 with Cavert, who suggested the possibility of associate or affiliate rather than full membership. Universalists were apparently not sufficiently Christocentric to merit full membership.

At the General Convention sessions in 1941 Cummins called in the strongest possible terms for cooperation with all denominations, especially with those considered religiously liberal. "The time has come for us to co-operate in all practical ways with the free churches — Unitarians, Congregationalists, Quakers, Reform Jews. Parochialism is a sin."[40] He called as well for membership in the Federal Council, a recommendation approved by the assemblage "if, after careful exploration, [the trustees] deem such action advisable." The conditional form of the resolution was intended to avoid embarrasment if for any reason the application was not welcomed. Donald F. Hoyt, pastor of the Congress Square Church in

616 / Interdenominational Relations

Robert Cummins, leader in Universalist affairs, with his son John, also a Universalist minister

Portland, Maine, who was clerk of the Committee on Recommendations and Official Reports at the 1941 convention, noted later the delegates were told that some of the officers of the Federal Council had sought out and encouraged Universalists to apply, though the application would probably not receive unanimous endorsement.[41]

The trustees responded by appointing a committee consisting of Perkins, Manning, and Cummins to explore the possibilities. The application was to be made "solely on the basis of our Avowal."[42] The meaning of the first statement in the 1935 Bond of Fellowship would be settled once and for all; namely, "a common purpose to do the will of God as Jesus revealed it and to co-operate in establishing the Kingdom for which he lived and died." Evidence of the willingness of the denomination to cooperate in good works, which was the point that Cummins wanted to make, seemed to be abundant and unquestioned. He, as well as other Universalists, assumed that this coincided exactly with the whole purpose of the Federal Council.

While Perkins drafted an application, Cummins conferred with the officers of the various denominations in the Council. Personal contacts were at first made with representatives of the Congregational, Methodist, Baptist, and Episcopal churches which brought pledges of support. This included Bishop G. Bromley Oxnam (Methodist), the incoming president of the Council. Additional contacts were made at Cavert's suggestion, and the results were most encouraging. The Universalists were told informally that "a considerable opinion" prevailed in favor of their admission — an estimated twenty out of the twenty-three churches then members of the Council.[43]

The next task was to meet with those known to be either undecided or opposed to Universalist membership; the results were far from happy. The leading opponent was Lewis S. Mudge, a Presbyterian and member of the Council's executive committee. He read from the preamble to the Council's constitution, putting all the emphasis on the necessity of belief "in Jesus Christ as . . . divine Lord and Savior," and disregarding completely the part calling for the promotion of "the spirit of fellowship, service and cooperation," on which the Universalists had been prepared to report their impressive record. It was clear that good works were to be subordinate to the uniformity of belief which the preamble professed not to require.

There was still sufficient hope that membership could be achieved, and the committee recommended formal application. They were encouraged especially by the Congregationalists who were willing "to stand up and be counted" on the issue of "Christian inclusiveness or . . . sectarian prejudice." Even though it was given "full power to complete negotiations if they deem it wise to do so," the committee felt that the application should be made in the name of the full board of trustees as the official representatives of the church. This was done.[44]

The Universalists applied for membership on 2 November 1942, a month prior to the meeting of the Council. Following customary procedure, the application was presumably reviewed by its executive committee prior to submission to the full body. But instead of transmitting it to the plenary body for action, the committee did nothing. The Universalists waited in vain for an invitation to attend and to explain their position. At the last minute Cummins attended the sessions without invitation as the only member of the denomination present. His existence was never acknowledged; there was no mention made of the application and no explanation was given for the lack of action.

It was only after the Council sessions were over that the Universalists were informed that their application had not been presented for delegate consideration because it was too brief. More conferences were called for.[45]

Cummins persisted in his attempt to obtain additional information, and was informed by the executive secretary of the Council that the Universalist application would be likely to be accepted only if two conditions were met: The denomination, by convention, needed to vote approval of the action their trustees had taken; and there had to be a clear statement that they were "in full accord" with the evangelical position of the Council as defined in its constitution.[46]

The *Christian Century* speculated that the real reason for bypassing the application was doubt about the theological orthodoxy of the applicants.[47]

The journal came to the conclusion that the Universalists were worthy of defense and argued that, so far as the specifications stated in the preamble to the Council's constitution applied, a brief review of Universalist history indicated that the denomination amply met the definitions laid down. There should consequently have been no hesitation in welcoming Universalists into the circle of fellow Christians.

When the General Assembly (a new name for the meetings of the General Convention as a legislative body) met in the fall of 1943, the Universalists again voted (92 to 18) to submit their application for membership with full standing.[48] Opposition from within the denomination came on several grounds. Tracy M. Pullman argued that the denomination had departed so far from the Christian tradition that membership in the Federal Council was inappropriate. Clinton L. Scott, who had sought to have the application tabled, believed the entire idea to be ill-conceived, and ought to be abandoned. The ignoring by the Council of the application in 1942 had been a serious blow to Universalist self-respect.[49]

Even though ostensibly snubbed in 1942 the Universalists strongly endorsed interdenominational cooperation at the General Assembly the next year, and voted to omit all reference to the "apparent refusal" of the Federal Council to admit them.[50] The denominational Commission on Foreign Relations continued to serve as the connecting link between Universalists and the Council's Department of International Justice and Good Will, including attendance at its meetings and distribution of its literature.[51]

Universalists were further assured that all was well when it was divulged that the Congregational Christian Churches, at their General Council session in the summer of 1944, had voted unanimously in favor of the admission of the Universalist church to the Federal Council.[52] At the same time, Universalists were sobered by the report that the Lutheran Church was opposing Universalist entrance until they changed their "official confessional statement to conform to the evangelical basis of the Federal Council as set forth in the preamble to its constitution."[53] Niceties of theology were apparently going to be a persistent stumbling-block.

As soon as it was made known to Universalists that the next meeting of the Federal Council would convene in Pittsburgh in November 1944, they filed application with the expectation that they would be invited to send fraternal delegates who would be available to answer questions. No such invitation was ever proffered. Cummins protested that when the Council had met in 1942, when it admitted the Church of the Nazarene, the latter had been represented by a full delegation. Why were the Universalists not accorded the same treatment in 1944?

The receipt of the Universalist application was merely acknowledged by the executive committee and was referred, without discussion, for action by the Council. The following statement accompanied the application:

> The primary motive that prompts this action is genuine sympathy with the avowed purpose of the council 'more fully to manifest the essential oneness of the Christian churches of America in Jesus Christ as their Divine Lord and Savior, and to promote the spirit of fellowship, service and cooperation among them.' That sense of oneness in Christ as the basis of Christian fellowship is thrown to the fore in the official declaration of the Universalist Church as follows: 'The bond of fellowship in this convention shall be a common purpose to do the will of God as Jesus revealed it and to cooperate in establishing the Kingdom for which he lived and died.' It is in that spirit that we are moved to apply for membership in the Federal Council.

Horton made the motion on the floor to accept the Universalists and spoke in their behalf, as did Theodore F. Herman of the Evangelical and Reformed Seminary in Lancaster, Pennsylvania, even though the church he represented was against admission.

The Universalist church was refused membership on 29 November 1944 by a vote of 6 in favor and 12 opposed.[54] The opposition of the Presbyterian Church USA and the Lutheran Church was expected. The Presbyterians added a political note by threatening to resign from the Council if the Universalists were admitted.[55] The Methodists cast a negative vote in the belief that the admission of Universalists might split the Council just as their Bishop Oxnam was about to become its president.[56]

The Universalist leadership immediately cast about for the reasons for their overwhelming rejection. According to Cummins, Horton, in supporting his motion to admit the Universalists, committed a tactical error, although presumably "with the best of intentions." The Congregationalist, instead of citing more recent authors in support of Universalist theology, had quoted from such eighteenth-century Universalists as George DeBenneville and John Murray, many of whose ideas were by then far out of date.[57]

Another explanation of probably greater consequence was reported by the *Christian Century*. One of the statements furnished by the secretary of the Universalist trustees for the *Yearbook of American Churches* and which undoubtedly led to the negative decision was that 'Universalists as a body are now practically Unitarians so far as the person, nature, and work of Christ are concerned.'[58] The journal commented that "Unitarianism has been historically regarded as one of the antitheses of evangelism." The Universalists were thus "put in a bad light" by apparently contradicting the wording in the preamble to the Council's constitution and thus casting doubt on the good faith of the Universalists or at least raising the question of ambiguity. The paper called the whole matter "a regrettable action" and an "unhappy episode," and felt that if any criticism were to be levelled, it should have been at the separate denominations and not at the Federal Council as a whole. The way was still open for Universalists to reapply, but with "greater candor, a more orderly procedure, and ... with better understanding [by] their brethren of other churches."[59]

As soon as the decision of the Council had been made known, a statement was released to the press which indicated the official reaction of the denomination.[60] It asserted that the vote had been a test of the Council, not of the Universalists. They were saddened that any body calling itself Christian would take such a stand on such narrow grounds. Universalists had a clear conscience and no regrets, and would try "to live our faith . . . and serve our fellows when we can." Manning issued a plea for Universalists not to withdraw into their shells, but to continue to cooperate with the Federal Council agencies committed to social amelioration and reform.[61] And cooperate they did, to the best of their ability. They expressed full sympathy with the Federal Council's report on economic and racial tensions adopted early in 1946.[62]

The editor of the *Leader* brought together numerous comments on the rebuff by the Federal Council under the heading "Universalists Who are Glad, Who are Sorry, Who are Hurt, Who are Mad," and added his own."[63] In attempting to explain what had happened, van Schaick attributed the negative vote to a change in the character of the Council, which had "ceased to be a federation with no doctrinal test for admission [and had] become a superchurch — a kind of holding corporation for the churches, with the doctrinal views of the conservatives controlling."

Cummins, who had become deeply involved emotionally in the whole affair, was angry, hurt, and frustrated, but in his public announcement of the action of the Federal Council, showed careful restraint. He issued a brief report of what had happened and urged that "the . . . rehearsal of facts be read from every Universalist pulpit in the land, and, further, that it be printed in every parish bulletin." The General Superintendent was somewhat less restrained when, at the request of the editor of *Zion's Herald,* he prepared a feature article for that publication which appeared in their issue of 17 January 1945, headed "God's Stepchildren."[64] Cummins told its readers that, although quite within their legal right to act as they did, the members of the Council voting against admission of Universalists had imposed "a creedal definition of Christianity" against which Universalists were protesting. The trustees agreed.[65] The action of the Council raised questions that needed answers. "What is it that makes a man or a church Christian? Is a Christian one who tries to follow the teaching of Jesus, or one who holds certain beliefs about him? It was clear to Cummins that belief (in the divinity of Jesus Christ) was paramount in the minds of the Council, while following his precepts should have been the prime consideration, especially in a period of "world upheaval, bloodshed, sorrow and suffering." Willingness "to conform to some prescribed theological tenet is a thing difficult to comprehend and not very commendable."

After their rejection by the Federal Council there was some talk in the denomination about establishing a Council of Liberal Churches as a counterbalance to the Federal Council, but Cummins opposed the idea.⁶⁶ Such an organization would, in his view, be just as creedal and therefore just as exclusive in its own way as was the Federal Council. Universal Universalism was much more to be desired than mere liberalism.

Scott applauded the Council's action in rejecting the Universalists. "We simply do not belong with the denominations that dominate the Federal Council."⁶⁷ The rejection on theological grounds manifested "a moral insensitiveness reminiscent of sixteenth-century horse-trading."⁶⁸

Reaction to the Council's decision outside the denomination was immediate and overwhelmingly sympathetic to the Universalists if the excerpts in the *Leader* are assumed to be representative. It was estimated that the denomination received one million dollars worth of free publicity by way of the extensive comments in both the religious and secular press.⁶⁹ Even more important were the expressions of support from members of churches which had voted in opposition as well as from those who had favored the Universalists.

The ministerial council of the Jefferson County Council of Churches in Watertown, New York, relayed to the Federal Council a series of resolutions expressing 'spiritual and ecclesiastical bafflement . . . and very deep sorrow and profound regret, not unmixed with astonishment.' Individual Presbyterian, Baptist, and Methodist clergy expressed their concern and voiced their protest at the Council's decision. *Zion's Herald* considered the action a "mistake" and called upon it to change its vote. Harry Emerson Fosdick reported that 'My blood boils at this nonsensical obscurantism' and offered to 'do anything within my power to break the deadlock.'⁷⁰ Universalists were undoubtedly gathering "a vast reservoir of good will."⁷¹

There was much doubt in the minds of many Universalists about the advisability of reapplying in 1946, in spite of all the encouragement from other denominations. They had been warned that their application would receive about the same treatment as had the effort two years earlier. Postponement of action until 1948 was considered, when there might be a softening of the theological position of the opponents. But the General Assembly voted by a margin of more than twelve votes (65-50) to reapply, stressing the Universalist conviction that "concerted Protestant action is urgently needed" to meet world problems.⁷² In preparing the application, Cummins and Manning, who were delegated the responsibility by the trustees, disregarded the suggestion made privately by a member of the Federal Council that some modifications be made in the supporting statement in order to "dilute" the Universalist position and make it more acceptable. But this Cummins refused to do; there would be no compromise, and the Universalists would stand on their record and on their previous statements.

Again, as in 1940 when preparations were being made to submit the first application, Cummins relied in part on personal connections to carry the Universalist application to a successful conclusion. Charles P. Taft, son of the former President of the United States and the new head of the Council, had been a fraternity brother during their undergraduate days, had cooperated in civic affairs, and they had together received honorary degrees from Miami University. Taft was also a layman and hence presumably not as subject to "theological quibblings" as were his clerical colleagues. But Cummins was greatly disappointed when he sounded out Taft, who replied that Universalist chances were slim. "If we let in the Unitarians [read Universalists], we let out the Lutherans." Further, the body of Lutherans was large and influential, while the Universalists were neither. Cummins replied rather sarcastically that he assumed "the Federal Council was organized to serve religious purposes, not on the basis of numbers and financial worth."[73]

The application of the Universalists was rejected a second time in 1946, both in the vote of the Council as a whole (sixty in favor and seventy opposed) and in the separate vote by denominations (four in favor, eight opposed, three deferring judgment, and one abstaining).[74]

The delegation representing the Disciples of Christ, which had voted for admission, proposed that a seven-person committee be appointd to confer with the Universalists 'to clarify the position of that church regarding its theological qualifications, and then to report to the next biennial meeting of the Federal Council.'[75] The apparent motive was to clear up once and for all the ambiguity about Universalist theology, and to give that denomination a further opportunity to state its position. The president of the Council was authorized to appoint such a committee to confer, if they so desired. The Universalists, expecting to meet the committee, prepared by appointing their own, consisting of Ellsworth Reamon, president of the General Assembly; Emerson Lalone, editor of the *Leader*; and Cummins. They were never contacted. It was obvious that the possibility of Universalist membership was no greater than before; in fact, they had lost ground so far as the vote was concerned, as compared to that of 1944.

Cummins gave up as almost a lost cause the effort to join the Federal Council, considering the organization "a theological closed shop."[76] But he predicted (erroneously) that the vote of the Council would eventually be rescinded when "self-accusing consciences [replaced] arrogance in the name of Christ." At the meeting of the General Assembly in 1947 the last section of a resolution supporting the work of the Federal Council but providing that no further application for membership be made, was stricken out.[77] The door was left ajar if not fully open, for further action by the Universalists in seeking membership, but they never attempted again to enter it. Instead, they concentrated on simultaneously continuing cooperation with the larger body and with promoting their own distinctiveness. It should be noted that Universalists and Unitarians were often accepted as members or even as officers of state councils.

Chapter 32

Universalism at the Crossroads

A Temporary Reprieve

It was at a critical stage in denominational affairs, when there was serious doubt whether the church could survive, that a personality appeared on the scene in the 1930s who reversed, at least temporarily, the visible decline of Universalism in numbers, strength, and morale, and infused new life and hope into it. That personality was Robert Cummins (1897-1982), who served as the dynamic and untiring General Superintendent from 1938 to 1953. He was forty years of age at the time of his appointment, and was full of vigor and determination. Above all, he was a devoted convert to Universalism.

Cummins had been born in 1897 in Sidney, Ohio; his father was a banker. The son enrolled in Miami University but left in his junior year to enlist during World War I and returned and completed his degree requirements in 1919. After graduation he was secretary of the local YMCA for three years, during which time he also served as a track coach at local schools. He became a licensed Methodist minister, although reared as a Presbyterian, and married Alice Elizabeth Guinn, granddaughter of a Methodist circuit rider. He had earlier spent more than two years as head of the Boon-it Institute in Bangkok, Siam (Thailand), an educational institution for young men, as a representative of the Presbyterian Board of Foreign Ministers.

He became interested in Universalism while YMCA secretary, and was ordained in 1926. After serving five years in the First Universalist Church in Cincinnati, Ohio, and from 1932 to 1938 in the Throop Memorial Church in Pasadena, he was called to assume the General Superintendency. After his resignation he headed the International Cooperation division of the State Department during the Eisenhower period.

Full of determination to rebuild the denomination and to restore the strength and unity which he perceived had been lost, as well as to interpret Universalism in the broadest possible terms, he went to work on every front. He spent much of his first year on the road, looking into every nook and cranny of denominational activity, and was much disturbed by what he found.

Cummins devoted much space in his early reports to grim recitals of the shortcomings of the denomination, of which he identified all too many. The presentations were replete with statistics, a device which he used time and time again to support his arguments. He bombarded the General Convention repeatedly with figures to document the shrinkage in recent decades of both the total constituency and the number of churches. In 1910 there had been forty-three state conventions; in 1939 there were twenty-four. There were 52,272 Universalist family units reported in 1910; in 1939 the number had declined to 39,827. There had been 819 Universalist churches in 1910 but only 544 in 1939, and of those only 71 had resident ministers, supported themselves, and contributed financially to denominational purposes. Only 171 met the first two specifications, although not the third; 99, although unaided, were unable to support both a full-time resident minister and the denomination; and 100 received aid. Of the 544, 97 were dormant.

It was a sorry sight to behold, and the fact that a total of $40,000 a year from all sources was being poured into churches from outside seemed to make no real difference. The church in Denver, Colorado, had received $35,000 in the last fifteen years and was still not self-supporting. A policy of allowing such chronic dependency had to come to an end. The denomination was in "no position to function as a glorified kind of ecclesiastical PWA."[1]

Cummins placed the low-point in recent denominational history at the time of the poorly attended General Convention sessions in Chicago in 1937.[2] Pessimism amounting to despair had seemed to permeate the Universalist community, with a combination of factors rather than any one of them responsible. There were serious losses in both personnel and churches, accountable at least partly to the ravages of the Great Depression and inability or unwillingness to provide adequate financial support. Some saw with sorrow the decline of the YPCU, as youth drifted into other churches or into none at all. Others blamed the gloomy state of affairs on clergy of low caliber, lacking in missionary zeal and a spirit of sacrifice. Some blamed lack of leadership at the top, with domination by the "Boston crowd." Projects were formulated and then abandoned. There were "too many organizations working independently at cross purposes or with overlapping programs." The Universalist Church had "undertaken too many projects for [its] size.... some of these are needless duplications, poorly supervised, and inadequately financed."

Cummins made his first formal presentation to the General Convention in 1939, supplemented by a printed report. It was an eminently practical presentation, with the theme of "A United Church," and with what he conceived to be a realistic set of solutions. He called for "a renewed consciousness of worth, dignity, and confidence" to replace the sense of defeatism, indifference, and separatism that had enveloped Universalism in a time of frustration, economic depression, and the onset of war in Europe. It was time to recapture a lost *esprit de corps;* to cease looking nostalgically to a past which the passage of time had glorified; had to be done with such uninspiring activities as "bean suppers and fourth-rate speakers."

He outlined a four-point set of objectives, all of which had been previously approved by the trustees: A rigorous evaluation of the entire program of the church based on a comprehensive survey of where matters stood; a plan for aggressive general field work; the integration of denominational programs based on a sense of common mission as a church unified in fact as well as in theory; and the commitment of sufficient funds to accomplish the other objectives. It was all presented under the slogan "Forward Together."

A systematic inventory needed to be made first of every aspect of activity so that intelligent decisions could be made. He had listed no less than twenty-two suggestions in his printed report as a starting-point. He called, in effect, for a thorough system of social engineering to pull the church out of its doldrums.

Cummins' second objective was a consolidation of field work into one agency rather than such separate yet overlapping organizations as the WNMA, the GSSA, and the YPCU. All phases of a local program should be served by general field workers rather than splintered among several special and semi-autonomous interests. This meant, in the third place, an integration of denominational programs, operating as a unit rather than as disparate parts. The "solo habit" had operated too long, with near-disastrous results. Cummins identified at least eight regional publications costing thousands of dollars, not to mention a myriad of organizational papers, all struggling for their financial existence, capped by the *Leader* which was itself facing "possible extinction."

The multiplicity of financial appeals for special projects, often competing for Universalist dollars, and frequently a source of both embarrassment and irritation, should be integrated into a single budget. The General Convention was not merely another auxiliary body but the church itself, operating ideally through a series of departments; e.g., youth, religious education, and publications. No one agency had, for example, the responsibility for distributing denominational literature; it was split haphazardly among half a dozen uncoordinated jurisdictions, all with special axes to grind.

The Universalist Church in Hollywood, California

The final objective was the commitment of $100,000 over a four-year period to accomplish the other three. Cummins volunteered to raise half that amount himself; a start of more than $800 had already been made. He boldly recommended that $50,000 of the more than $500,000 of unrestricted funds held by the General Convention be used instead of hoarded by the church. A contribution of $1.00 from each Universalist for four years would more than suffice. As for the matter of supporting dependent churches, he recommended that a ten-year limit be placed on such aid, with 10 percent less each year until either self-support was achieved or the church closed and the property deeded to the General Convention. A building and loan fund of $25,000 was authorized in 1947 to encourage church extension, with a goal of $100,000 (never achieved).[3]

As one way of promoting denominational unity Cummins pushed for a change in the corporate name of the church. The idea was not his, for it had been suggested in 1937 as a means of more clearly defining the role and responsibilities of the General Convention, but he eagerly supported it because it fitted in so well with his goal of a truly unified church. Authority to seek a revised charter from New York State was granted at the General Convention sessions in 1941 and in February 1942 the governor of New York signed into law the change which transformed the

Universalist General Convention into the Universalist Church of America.[4]

The new name cleared up much confusion, particularly for those outside the denomination, for the term "Universalist General Convention" had not meant a national church but a delegate body meeting periodically to transact business rather than the denomination itself. The heretofore ambiguous use of the term was removed, and the legislative body of the church became the General Assembly.

The constitution and by-laws of the Universalist Church of America were overhauled at the biennial meeting in 1943 to harmonize with the new charter. The changes were mostly mechanical and editorial in nature, representing the tidying up of loose ends; neither the basic organization nor the powers of the central body was altered.[5] The constitution as a separate document was abolished and consolidated as bylaws, thus making possible immediate adoption without the customary waiting period of two years for ratification.

The bylaws were next revised in 1951. The most significant change was the omission, in the statement of purposes of the church, of any reference to furthering "the Kingdom of God"; and the substitution, "to propagate the teachings of Jesus" for "propagate the Christian faith."[6] This was consistent with the wording of the revised charter which had called for "harmony among adherents of all religious faiths, whether Christian or otherwise."

By the end of the second year of his administration (in 1940) Cummins reported "genuine progress on all fronts."[7] The watchword was "centralization," the goal "efficiency." He was, among other things, in the process of organizing all headquarters activities into a series of departments, finally authorized in 1949.[8] A Department of General Field Work had been created temporarily early in 1940 as part of the Forward Together program under Miss Harriet G. Yates. She resigned because of her marriage, and was replaced by Edna P. Bruner who had been ordained in 1930.[9] Within a year she had visited more than forty parishes throughout the nation, and had supplied numerous pulpits.[10]

One of Cummins' disappointments was the failure to establish a consolidated Department of Finance. As part of his plan of centralization he wanted to create a Department of Publications of which the Universalist Publishing House would be a part. He was also unhappy because the denominational theological schools were not directly under the supervision or control of the church but had worked out their own relationships with the institutions to which they were attached.[11] The closest he came to realizing that wish was the creation of a Department of Education in 1946, recommended by the Central Planning Council, and including representation of the theological schools as well as the GSSA, the youth group, and AUW, each of which had its own educational program. Angus H. MacLean, dean of the Canton Theological School, was the first chairman.[12]

If the denomination were to be consolidated as Cummins wished, a central headquarters was indispensable. The problem of an adequate location had plagued the denomination from the very start, and a reasonably satisfactory one had not been obtained until only five years before he became General Superintendent. Because the General Convention was chartered in New York State the trustees usually met in New York City, while the majority of auxiliary agencies were concentrated in Boston, but in scattered locations.[13] There was no central point where the General Superintendent, the General Secretary, and the president could confer, and they often had to conduct their business hurriedly before or after General Convention meetings. Those having business with the denomination had no single place to come, and commissions and committees, because of the scattered locations of their membership, were forced to resort to the mails to get their work done. The General Convention voted in 1917 to establish a central office "as soon as possible," and in 1918 Boston was made the temporary official headquarters by trustee vote.[14] But very few individuals paid any attention to this action, and continued to debate the question as though the trustees did not exist.

The Unitarians did not experience this problem, for they had always been chartered in Massachusetts and located in Boston and in 1927 moved their headquarters into their new building at 25 Beacon Street, marked by a celebration in the Arlington Street Church.[15] The Universalists, meanwhile, were still debating the question of their own location. Thomas E. Potterton thought that the choice of Boston as a permanent headquarters would be a mistake. "Are we to dwindle to a New England denomination?"[16] Universalists needed "to get the provincial out of our system." He persisted in his opposition to Boston and suggested in 1927 that headquarters be located either in New York City, in that state in which the denomination had been chartered, or in Washington, D.C. "Sometimes a change of climate proves beneficial."[17]

Executive Secretary Roger Etz suggested in 1930 that two lots owned by the church in Washington, D.C., be used on which to build a national headquarters.[18] This would serve the double purpose of quieting those who criticized the denomination for being controlled by the so-called "Boston crowd," and locating in proximity to the Universalist National Memorial Church, a visible symbol of the denomination just completed in the nation's capital.

One native New England clergyman (from Maine) who favored the Washington location, used the same argument as had Potterton, noting that such a move would stir the denomination out of its provincialism. After all, Boston was "the logical center of nothing save New England, which in some parts of our land would not be regarded as [even] a very large state."[19]

The possibility of locating in Washington, D.C., was discussed by the trustees in 1931 but no action was taken until 1933, and involved Boston rather than Washington.

In the summer of 1933 Universalist headquarters were moved from Newbury Street to 16 Beacon Street, the quarters vacated by the Unitarians and donated by them.[20] It had been unoccupied for some two years, and was an historic building, the last of the private residences in that part of Beacon Hill. It had been built a century earlier and its last resident, Mrs. Martha B. Angell, had bequeathed it to the Unitarians who had taken possession in 1919.[21]

The Universalists, still beset with financial difficulties in the 1940s, investigated several times whether a move from Beacon Street would result in greater economies.[22] The property on Newbury Street had been put up for sale and a return to it was considered when it failed to be sold promptly. A site in Kenmore Square (Boston) was also considered but abandoned.[23]

Technically, the title to Beacon Street address was held in the name of the Universalist Publishing House because it was incorporated in Massachusetts and the Universalist Church was still chartered in New York State. Under Massachusetts law it was considered a "foreign" corporation and hence subject to much higher taxes."[24] A reversionary clause left the property to the AUA.

In 1949 a study was initiated to investigate reincorporation in Massachusetts to save taxes and, if necessary, to relocate, but it was not followed through. The problem of relocation was finally resolved in 1961 when the single headquarters of the combined denominations were located at 25 Beacon Street, and there they remained. Offices for the trustees were established there in 1961 — the first time that the governing board had their own offices in one place; but that situation did not last, for they immediately found themselves part of the Unitarian Universalist Association.[25] The former Universalist headquarters at 16 Beacon Street were retained temporarily to house the publications office and the bookstore, and later in the year the property was sold to the Boston Bar Association.[26] A former private dwelling at 8 Mt. Vernon Place, abutting an alley to the rear of No. 25, was purchased from the estate of Mrs. Fiske Warren and named Skinner House in honor of Clarence R. Skinner, the well known Universalist leader. Skinner House was dedicated in 1963 and was used as headquarters for the Department of Publications. The sum of $118,000 was the estimated cost for purchase and remodelling, the proceeds from the sale of the old Beacon Street property being used to assist in financing it.[27] A third building nearby, Eliot House, was already owned by the AUA.

By the time the "United General Convention" met at Tufts in 1941 — the first time it had been convened on a college campus — Cummins had to face a rising chorus of opposition to his policy of consolidation. Many Universalists were aghast at what Frank D. Adams, two-time president of the General Convention and in 1941 president of the Illinois Convention, called "the fatal policy of centralization" which was sapping the strength and resources of local and state organizations.[28] Always sensitive to criticism and interpreting it as a personal affront, Cummins delivered a hard-hitting report which startled many and angered some. He vigorously defended his program and insisted that the denominational unity for which he fought was being sabotaged by "the stealthy, persistent, barbed opposition of a handful of those from whom one might rightfully hope to receive only the finest team-play."[29]

Without naming individuals he launched a tirade against those who, because they had their own selfish interests to protect or their own pet projects to further, or were fearful that he was upsetting unduly the *status quo*, were weakening the solidarity of the church. The "cruel and destructive practice of 'knifing' each other" had to cease. "It is a poor time, indeed, for self-appointed individuals to picture themselves in the role of having been divinely commissioned to save the rest of us from some imagined archbishop who secretly cherishes the pontificate." Cummins not only defended his program but went over the heads of Universalist officialdom and appealed directly for support from the entire denomination, in effect asking for a vote of confidence. This he received, at least from the General Convention, when it voted to continue the Forward Together program.[30]

Attempting to overlook the criticisms levelled at him, and impatient at the slow progress being made, Cummins continued to stress the importance of organization. He told fellow Universalists that "we have bungled wretchedly."[31] The denomination had a structure at the top that would not be "tolerated by the business community." It was "a hodge-podge of independent corporations known as 'denominational auxiliaries.'" Mere federalism was not the solution. The General Superintendent needed additional authority and involvement, and obtained at least involvement in 1949 when he was made an *ex officio* non-voting member of all of the twenty committees, commissions, and boards appointed by the trustees.[32]

Finances continued to be a serious problem, for Cummins' ambitious program cost money which the denomination felt it could not afford. Budgets showed continued deficits, so a special drive known as "Volunteers for Universalism" was started in 1942 to make up an anticipated deficit that year.[33] The quota system was abolished, as was the Loyalty Fellowship, the Cent-a-Day plan, and all other special fund-raising programs. They were consolidated into a "Unified Appeal" which Cummins designated as "Fair Share."[34] Altogether, ten separate and piecemeal channels of contributions to most organizations were replaced with one, to be allocated from central headquarters.[35]

Even that expedient did not work with complete success. In 1943 a deficit exceeding $40,000 had to be charged to unrestricted funds.[36] Harry Adams Hersey, reputed to have made more speeches at denominational gatherings than any other individual in Universalist history, summed it all up by noting that "we are trying to run a high-geared automobile on a wheelbarrow budget." All the while, to use his self-description, Cummins "blasted away, shamed, cajoled, ridiculed, threatened and begged," and had made himself "a source of serious irritation."[37] He did it all for the sake of the church "and its rightful place in the scheme of things." How could this be accomplished when only one Universalist in seven contributed anything? The denominaton stood at the bottom of the list of per capita giving among all Protestants in 1948.[38]

Even the appointment in 1949 of Philip Randall Giles, highly successful pastor of the White Memorial Universalist Church in Concord, New Hampshire, as director of the Unified Appeal, worked no financial miracles.[39] His service had to be terminated in 1951 because he was ordered to active duty as a chaplain in the United States Air Force.[40] A professional fund-raising analyst (John Hansen) was hired in 1954 to direct the Unified Appeal, but with less than dramatic results.

When Cummins resigned from the General Superintendency in 1953, after fifteen years of arduous effort, he left a mixed record of achievement, both inside and outside the denomination. Within its confines Cummins had at least momentarily stirred Universalists to action. At the 1943 General Assembly he had reviewed with enormous satisfaction the progress of the denomination in the first five years of his administration which the *Leader* characterized as nothing short of "spectacular." In sharp contrast to the decade preceding, church membership had increased significantly. A Central Planning Council had replaced the Council of Executives in 1941, the national youth fellowship had been reinvigorated, general and regional field work had either begun or had been expanded, a united appeal for funds had been introduced, the deficit had been reduced (temporarily) by more than $10,000, and a general reorganization had taken place or was in the planning stage. It seemed as though a sense of unity in the church comparable to the anticipated and highly publicized post-war "One World" concept was about to be achieved. Cummins was, in fact, described as "the modern architect of organized Universalism."[41]

Yet most of the problems facing the denomination remained for others to solve. By 1953 the momentum for increasing membership had been lost. The financial situation had not only deteriorated but was reaching a critical stage to be confronted by Cummins' successor. His reorganization plan remained only partially fulfilled, hobbled by lack of funds and shortages of personnel. Doubts were raised about whether organization, as such, was the key to denominational success.

Relations with other denominations were far from ideal, due in part to Cummins' fierce denominationalism. A speech made at the Boston Universalist Club in 1939 had caused dismay and consternation among some Congregationalists. In it he had ridiculed and denounced the idea of church federation then under discussion, and had declared that such a movement in Massachusetts was nothing short of "vicious."[42] One Congregationalist official was so distressed at this uncooperative attitude that he complained through the columns of the *Leader*. He saw no reason why Universalists, Unitarians, and Congregationalists could not pool their resources in areas like the South and Southwest, where there was so much to be done by liberal churches. Trying to go it alone was not only the least effective route but smacked of "an intolerant superiority complex" on the part of the leadership of the Universalist Church."[43] It was admittedly a harsh indictment.

The continued refusal of the Federal Council of Churches to accept Universalists into full membership had been a serious personal blow to Cummins, who had become deeply involved in negotiations extending through almost the entire decade of the 1940s. The Federal Council, in his estimation, was too tradition-bound to respond positively to the "new Universalism" for which he professed to stand. Perhaps the rejection was all to the good. The denomination for which he had fought so valiantly for fifteen years as General Superintendent would not be circumscribed by the limits of any one religion. "'Christian Universalism' is partialism and a contradiction of terms."[44] In 1951 he told the General Assembly that "our Universalism has been too Bible-centered, appallingly parochial." There was need to grow, for "our generation's interpretation is rarely the interpretation of the next."[45]

But Americans were not yet prepared or willing to accept such an enlarged view of religion. There were less than 350 active Universalist parishes remaining two years after Cummins left office, and the membership had dropped to less than 42,000. Had all his hopes and efforts been in vain? The Universalist Church had become only a barely distinguishable dot on the American religious horizon.

Beyond Christianity

By the late 1940s a clear conflict had developed within Universalism over its nature and its destiny. As a denomination it was in the midst of a serious crisis of identity. Mason F. McGinness, pastor of the First Universalist Church in Lowell, Massachusetts, delivered to the state convention in 1947 a hard-hitting keynote sermon, described as "realistic but not pessimistic."[46] Entitled "The Universalist Crisis," McGinness raised in it the question of whether the Universalists were justifying their existence as a denomination.

> In our insistence upon freedom of individual belief, we Universalists have too often ended up with no religious philosophy, no religious point of view toward life. In many ways, it appears that we have no Universalist movement but rather a conglomeration of churches calling themselves Universalist, the programs and emphases of which very often bear no resemblance to each other. The conglomeration of theological and social ideas held in the name of Universalism is confusing enough to stump even the wisest sage. The truth is that, in many instances, the only thing that distinguishes the Universalist church from the neighboring Congregational, Baptist, or Methodist church in some communities is the name, not the gospel that is preached, nor the program of education.... If the Universalist Church has no message, no program that is different from other churches in the community, nothing that is distinctive, then let's unite with some other church quickly.... We have been drifting and disintegrating.

Brainard F. Gibbons, pastor of the First Universalist Church in Wausau, Wisconsin, delivered the occasional sermon at the General Assembly in Rochester, New York, the very same year, and confronted the very same issue.[47] Entitling his presentation "New Wine and Old Bottles," he posed a question that went to the heart of the problem.

> Is Universalism a Christian denomination, or is it something more, a truly universal religion? This issue is the most vital Universalism has ever faced, striking at the very base of its religious foundation, for Christianity and this larger Universalism are irreconcilable. A momentous decision must be made, and soon! Unless Universalism stands for something distinctive and affirmative, it falls in indistinguishable, negative nothingness — neither loved nor hated, just ignored!

Gibbons believed that the spirit of inquiry inherent in Universalism had carried it beyond Christianity. It was no longer "simply a Christian sect whose central doctrine is universal salvation ... [or] merely a rationalized interpretation of Christianity." It was "a new type of Universalism ... boundless in scope, as broad as humanity, and as infinite as the universe. ... a synthesis of all religious knowledge." In reaching beyond the confines of Christianity the "old bottles" were inadequate for Universalists. New wines required new containers. Such a new and different conception of Universalism would be unpopular both inside and outside the denomination. But Gibbons threw down the challenge without equivocation: "It is better to risk hate now for the love of future generations than to court respectable oblivion."

Gibbons' call for "a clean break with the exclusive claims and pretensions of orthodox and historic Christianity" and his attempt to build "a universal religious fellowship" brought diverse reactions from Universalists, extending over many years. He startled some, antagonized some, and elicited strong support from still others. Fred C. Leining, editor of the *Empire State Universalist* (New York), accused him of disrupting the denomination and declared rather dramatically that 'the house is divided.'[48] Others came to Gibbons' defense and declared that he had articulated what many Universalists actually believed but had not expressed.

He was by no means alone in issuing his ultimatum to the denomination and in expressing his determination to put new meaning into Universalism and "religious liberalism." It was voiced most noticeably among young and newly ordained ministers in several Massachusetts churches, and in the ideas especially of Albert F. Ziegler, then pastor in Wakefield; Dana E. Klotzle, in the newly opened church in Wellesley Fells; and John E. Wood of the Murray Universalist Church in Attleboro. They were joined by Clinton L. Scott and Carleton M. Fisher in an issue of the *Leader* devoted to their common "one religious world" concept.[49]

Each used a different emphasis and approach but all aimed at a common denominator: a world-wide religious fellowship which, while recognizing the Christian origins of Universalism, called for a rejection of the traditional idea that any one religion had an exclusive claim to truth. Editor Emerson Lalone, now in charge of the *Leader,* supported the general theme expressed by Ziegler, Wood, and Klotzle, but added cautionary remarks about the potential difficulties and dangers of such an approach. One was the obstacle of surmounting the barrier of language and of understanding the complex cultural patterns of religious traditions other than one's own. It was deceptively easy to become superficially eclectic. "He who believes everything ends up by believing nothing." A second danger was to fall prey to "spiritual eccentricity" and religious faddism by subscribing to some form of culture which seemed to offer a simplistic, monistic solution to humankind's religious searching. "There is no easy route to world religious fellowship."

Ziegler argued that a truly satisfying religion had to be "life centered," an integral part of human experience, not compartmentalized or isolated and bound by outworn tradition, but receptive to change. To him, religious liberalism meant "a confidence in the divinity of man and the validity of his needs." Klotzle called for a religious foundaton which went beyond the limits of Christianity, to "a new sense of universalism" (with a small letter). "There can be no common ground for any of us to stand upon unless Christians are willing to grant the worth of non-Christian beliefs." This did not mean that Jesus should be rejected; as described in the New Testament he was in actuality "a universal figure who is not confined to a sectarian or particularistic approach to God." It was his followers who had turned a cosmic figure into a narrowly Christian one; the concepts of love and brotherhood were not the monopoly of a small minority of believers labelled Christian.

Less than a year after his article appeared, Klotzle carried his argument even farther by asserting that "the Universalist Church is doomed to ultimate extinction if it continues to be only an echo for a decadent Christianity instead of a vital voice for a universal religion."[50]

Wood based his argument for freedom of the spirit on the "liberty clause" in the Avowal of Faith adopted in 1935 and in the fact that Universalism was a series of non-creedal beliefs larger than either a church or denomination, the uniqueness of which was its inclusiveness.

This was the theme of the meeting, the first since the war, of thirty-seven delegates from free Christian churches held in Cambridge, England, in 1946, attended by Fisher.[51] Although the International Association for Religious Freedom took no action in that direction, there was much discussion of associating with such non-Christian groups as "liberal Mohammedans and liberal Jewish fellowships." Fisher heartily concurred in furthering such cooperation and cited the non-sectarian work of the Universalist and Unitarian Service Committees in Holland as a practical application of the "One World" idea. Scott's major theme was the inclusiveness of Universalism, outlined in an article presented originally as a radio address.[52]

Only a few weeks before the symposium on One-World Religion was published in the *Leader* an apparently unrelated event had taken place in Foxboro, Massachusetts. Earle T. McKinney had been ordained, and part of the ceremony had upset a number of Universalists, including Wood.[53] He was offended in particular by a stole which was used as a symbol of ordination without any definition of meaning or any official approval by any agency of the church. The color (red) was "a most unfortunate choice from a liturgical, symbolic, or artistic point of view," and the stole was tawdry in appearance. It was decorated at both ends with a "strange device" — a circle enclosing an off-center cross — which Ziegler explained during the service as the symbol of Universalism. What did it all mean?

Both Ziegler and McKinney were members of a small group of students and alumni of the Tufts School of Religion known as the *Humiliati*. Smarting from the rejection of the Universalist Church in its bid for membership in the Federal Council of Churches, concerned over the blanket of lethargy which seemed to have settled over a denomination declining in numbers, strength, and fervor, and convinced that a combination of highly personal spiritual renewal and a new and distinctive Universalism apart from the Protestant mainstream were the keys to survival, they created a fraternal order. Although it reached a maximum membership of only ten and existed barely a decade, it sent ripples throughout the denomination that lasted much longer.[54]

The idea was conceived by Gordon McKeeman and Albert Ziegler who, with graduation imminent and placement in parishes that might be widely separated, wished to create some basis for continued contact with a larger group similarly interested in both personal religious experience and denominational revival.[55] They realized that the intellectual stimulation and friendships they had experienced as students should not be lost when they scattered after graduation. It was intended also as a mutual support group for those about to enter the active ministry, somewhat unsure of what parish responsibilities might be facing them.

An annual meeting for study and discussion was decided upon, modelled on the Fraters of the Wayside Inn for an older generation of

Universalist clergy. A group of five students and young clergy met informally at Tufts in the spring of 1945, and the idea was so well received that a more formal meeting was held. It was decided that the group be kept relatively small at first, for practical reasons. Compatibility was an important requirement, for they intended to live, work, and study closely together for as much as a week at a time.[56]

A set of rules was adopted to govern the *Humiliati*, which was in no sense to be a secret society. Its purpose was "in humble spirit to promote the religious and intellectual growth of the undersigned, united in their desire to be better servants in their ministry. It is hoped that there will grow among the brethren a fellowship and feelings of mutual responsibility so genuine that it will seek expression outside as well as in the activities of the group."[57] Membership was by invitation, and only after attendance as an invited guest at one convocation, and unanimous election. The organization was headed by an abbot, whose office would rotate annually, and whose authority was to be unquestioned. Lists of basic readings were prepared, and the books were to serve as a basis for discussion. It was the task of at least one member to present a book review at each convocation.

At their annual meetings the *Humiliati* usually took a different theological or philosophical question as a theme for each session and wrestled, very much at the personal level, with such issues as free will, the format and content of worship, and the meaning of the Communion service. In order to appeal to diverse needs in their congregations and to reaffirm individual faith on a participatory rather than spectator basis, a creed was thought to be essential. The one adopted, to be recited on appropriate occasions such as Communion, admittedly bore an interesting resemblance to Roman Catholic liturgy. The *Humiliati* believed also that there had to be more "ecclesiasticism" in Universalism, such as a rather elaborate liturgy, vestments, and other visual symbols of religion, for true worship was itself an emotional experience.

The *Humiliati* were of course running completely counter to traditional Universalism, which scrupulously avoided anything partaking of creedalism and made minimal, if any, use of the outward signs of religiosity. Here was an unabashed return to the pomp and pageantry associated with medievalism, except that its exclusively Christian emphasis was conspicuously missing.

In accord with their insistence on symbolism the *Humiliati* offered a new design to represent the denomination. It was very simple, consisting of an unbroken circle with a small off-center cross inside it. It was created as a result of informal discussions at the General Assembly in 1946 by a group of young clergy which included members of the *Humiliati*. The first public use of the symbol was made at the ordination of McKinney that year. The circle represented a single, unified, and all-embracing humanity, and the cross as only one (Christian) expression of it. There was room for other religions besides Christianity. Universalism, it was argued, had been associated too long with a provincial and limiting religion to which less than one-third of the world adhered. Here was a distinctive emblem to represent the new Universalism, part of a larger whole that could in time become the whole itself, embracing all.

The symbol was never adopted by the denomination, although it appeared on some church calendars and the letterhead stationery of churches whose pastors were member of the *Humiliati*. It was used on the masthead of the *Bay State Universalist*, the organ of the Massachusetts Convention, which also adopted it for optional use. It appeared even on watch charms. The symbol was prominently displayed on the new building of the South Weymouth church in Massachusetts, occupied in 1954 and replacing one destroyed by fire.[58] The off-center cross within the circle was joined in the Murray Universalist Church in Attleboro, Massachusetts by the Unitarian symbol, a flaming chalice, on the eve of the consolidation of the two denominations.[59]

Stanley Manning suggested that there be two symbols — the one used by the *Humiliati* and the one with a cross at the center for those who believed that the teachings of Jesus were at the heart of Universalist tradition.[60] Mrs. Rosalie A. West, prominent in denominational affairs and future pastor of the church in Halifax, Nova Scotia, suggested, possibly with a trace of irony, that perhaps there should be no symbol at all. "A 'cross' symbol should go into the discard, along wih litanies, the ordinances of Baptism and Communion, the Christian shepherds, the Easter angels, and all the other mouldy heirlooms."[61]

On the surface the membership of the group seemed to be rather heterogeneous, with widely varying backgrounds. The oldest member and its principal spokesman and formulator of its theology, was Albert Ziegler, born in 1911.[62] A former Methodist, he had earned a degree in business in 1935 from Northeastern University in Boston and had been a junior executive in the John Hancock Mutual Life Insurance Company before deciding to prepare for the ministry.[63] His BD thesis, completed in 1945, was entitled "A Functional Theology for Liberal Religion" which served as the main topic for discussion at the first convocation, held at Tufts in 1946, and convened by McKeeman.

Like Ziegler, Frederick Libby Harrison (1912-1962) was older than most of his fellow students. A life-long Universalist, he had entered Tufts at the age of thirty-one, after a career as a railroad accountant, and received his AB in 1948 and was ordained in 1949 without completing the requirements for the STB for which he was a candidate.

Charles N. Vickery (1920-1972) likewise came with a Universalist background and completed his theological training with an STB in 1945. David H. Cole, born in 1921 and reared in the Universalist church in

Lynn, Massachusetts, received an AB from Tufts in 1946 and an STB in 1948, and caused considerable debate in 1947 when he insisted on being ordained in the Universalist rather than the Christian ministry as provided in the UCA bylaws. He also broke precedent by delivering the sermon at his own ordination in 1947. His efforts to make a distinction between Universalism and Christianity were finally successful when an option was written into the revised laws of fellowship in 1951.

Raymond C. Hopkins, born in 1919, also had a Universalist background. He received his AB from Tufts in 1947 and his STB in 1949. McKeeman, like Cole, was a member of the Lynn church, and received his theological degree in 1945. Keith C. Munson, born in 1922 and a Universalist from Caribou, Maine, was not a charter member, and was the youngest of the group. He received his AB from Tufts in 1944 and his STB in 1946. Earle McKinney, born in 1920, whose ordination ceremony in 1946 raised some eyebrows, had begun his academic career at Tufts as an engineering student (and as an Episcopalian); by way of friendship with some members of the *Humiliati* he transferred to the School of Liberal Arts and received his AB in 1943 and his STB in 1946.

The other two members were not as active in the organization as those mentioned previously. Albert Harkins, who died in 1976, came from an Evangelical Lutheran background and was the only member not a Tufts student or alumnus. He became acquainted with the membership through ministerial activities. Leon C. Fay, born in 1913, was a Unitarian who graduated from Tufts in 1945 and received his STB later the same year. He joined the *Humiliati* in 1947 but dropped out.

The *Humiliati* averred that it was time that Universalists ceased to remain silent on theological questions, for their failure to speak out gave the impression that they believed such "outmoded dogmas of the orthodox Christian Church as the Trinity, the Deity of Jesus, the validity of petitionary prayer, the existence of heaven and hell, the validity of the division of the world between good and evil, [and] the existence of 'free will.' This outmoded theology failed to meet the needs of the day; "the old answers simply will not do." The conflict between "dead dogma" and their own intellectual conclusions created uncertainty and confusion in people's minds. What they needed, above all, was "confidence in the supreme worth of every human being" and "a rational and understandable concept of God." This necessitated "an emotional basis for action" as well as a new theology.

The character and status of Jesus were likewise targeted by the *Humiliati*. They challenged the "blind assumption of his spiritual superiority" and argued that the multiplicity of values attributed to him was excessive; they were actually derived culturally from numerous sources, not from Jesus alone. It was nothing short of ridiculous to extend his teachings to labor-management relations in the mid-twentieth century when they might have been appropriate for the first century of the Christian calendar. Modern scholarship had even made him only a "semi-historical figure."

Hopkins, at the time pastor of the church in Brockton, Massachusetts, delivered the sermon at Harrison's ordination in 1949.[65] Entitled "Emergent Universalism," it summarized the leading beliefs of the *Humiliati*. He noted that Universalists, by tradition as well as official statement, had identified themselves as Christian — not separate and distinct — but "merely one of the more liberal of the some two hundred and eighty-seven differing Protestant interpretations and explanations." But an increasing number of Universalists believed that their denomination was emerging as much more than this — a religion that "transcends and goes beyond Christianity." It was naturalistic, with its faith in science and its rejection of supernaturalism; humanistic in its belief in mankind as not only basically good but capable of directing itself and determining its own destiny; and theistic because of faith in the reality of God as a force, "creative, omnipotent, purposive, impersonal and imminent."

From what sources had the ideas of the *Humiliati* been derived, apart from their own thinking? Most of the members acknowledged to some degree the influence of individuals who had contributed essays to a small volume entitled *Tufts Papers on Religion,* issued by the Universalist Publishing House in 1939.[66] The two who were particularly influential were Skinner, whose inspirational teaching and social idealism fired many of the group; and Bruce W. Brotherston (1877-1947), Fletcher Professor of Philosophy at Tufts who also held a professorship in Philosophy of Religion in the theological school and was the author of *A Philosophy of Liberalism.*[67]

Brotherston had stressed the universal impulse of individuals to seek unity, integration, and wholeness which the *Humiliati* thought was expressed most fully in the Communion service, with which they experimented.[68] Discipline, involving total commitment, was a response to impulse, often difficult to achieve in order to obtain "the greater good."

Skinner's influence could be seen in the theme of the 1949 convocation, at which the use of worship as a way of expressing *Humiliati* ideas was discussed; and in Hopkins' STB thesis, "A Functional Philosophy of Worship for the Liberal Church" (1949). Skinner's emphasis on the social responsibility of Universalists, and on the Social Gospel, played a diminishing part in the thinking of Ziegler, who by 1948 was emphasizing personal renewal and individual commitment rather than social action.[69]

The *Humiliati,* referred to by an older Universalist as "this insurrectionary group," were accused of arrogance and a dogmatism which belied their name, "excommunicating those who do not hold to our theology."[70] They were sufficiently sensitive to that charge to make self-discipline and self-inventory the theme of their 1948 convocation. They were faulted for their tendency to believe that "all the rest of us are all wrong all of the time."[71] They were pictured as a group of delayed, immature, and rebellious adolescents, denominationally "a joke" and not to be taken seriously. Their ideas were replete with logical inconsistencies and even contradictions. They might even become a pressure group and not only divide the denomination but try to take it over.[72] The *Humiliati* were out of their depth, for it was too much to expect youth to think philisophically; and, after all, they represented only a squabble among "professionals," a "tempest in a teapot" about which the denomination as a whole should have little or no concern. The *Humiliati* were criticized for overdoing the non-Christian element and making unacceptably disparaging remarks about the tradition out of which the denomination had come.

The proposed new symbol for Universalism came in for its share of criticism. The retired editor of the *Leader,* van Schaick, a confirmed theist, vigorously denied the allegation that there was no such thing as superhuman help, and asked why people had to be confused, needlessly shocked, and alienated "by putting the cross off in a corner."[73] He also attacked the *Humiliati* for their "bizarre ritualism and half truths stated as if they were new discoveries." One irritated correspondent in the *Leader* referred to "the New (off-center) Universalism" in contemptuous terms, and accused the group of "transforming the church into a sort of Free Liberal Miscellaneous Cultural Anthropological Society whose object is to promote the worship of the human race."[74]

The *Humiliati* attracted sufficient attention to have been mentioned by General Superintendent Cummins in his report to the denomination in 1949. He defended not only their right to belong to the Universalist family but to air their views freely.[75] This stance was quite consistent with Cummins' often-repeated conception of an all-embracing denomination that encouraged diversity of thought as well as unity. Gibbons, who startled many Universalists with his occasional sermon that same year, touched on many of the points made by the *Humiliati,* indicating general acceptance of their main arguments, notably the need to recognize religious traditions other than Christianity.

Lalone also came to their defense, arguing that the *Humiliati,* in spite of frequent over-statement, were sincerely "wrestling with a problem of conscience," even though at times they did sound dogmatic.[76] When five of the group consulted with Lalone in 1951 about the possibility of having Hopkins' thesis on worship prepared for publication, he read the manuscript and offered encouragement and assistance.[77] One layman, seventy-eight year old Frank Blackford, cast his lot with the "adolescents."[78] They should be allowed to express their ideas, not because they were completely in the right but because their elders had not done a very effective job of renewing the denomination. Another commentator congratulated the *Humiliati* for attempting to bring "their theology into line with modern scholarship and to give intellectual content to their ministry."[79]

Clinton L. Scott was one of their most consistent defenders. He applauded their attempt to revitalize a Universalism that "shall make demands upon the conscience, lead to personal commitment, and to a sacrificial consecration."[80] If the denomination were to evolve into a truly world-wide religion it had to get away from an "ambiguous Protestantism" by reinforcing both faith and discipline and taking "a more definitive and more positive theological position."[81]

Although they were considered as mavericks by many of their contemporaries and even as subversives by some older Universalists, the *Humiliati* were all ordained in and became pastors in Universalist churches at one time or another. The majority were not only sympathetic to Unitarianism but favored denominational merger, and several served in Unitarian churches. Many of them held positions of prestige and/or responsibility in the church or in the UUA. Harrison served as superintendent of the Massachusetts and Connecticut state conventions. Vickery worked on behalf of the Universalist Service Committee in West Germany, beginning in 1949, and was director of Unitarian Universalist Service Committee international programs between 1962 and 1968. Cole became prominent as a social activist in Chicago while pastor of the Universalist church there. Hopkins played an active part as a member of the Unitarian Universalist merger commission, served as Acting Administrator of the Council of Liberal Churches, and was the first executive vice-president of the UUA in 1961. McKeeman was one of three candidates for the presidency of the combined denominations in 1977, and was chosen in 1983 to head the Starr King School in California. Fay was in the AUA Department of the Ministry from 1957 to 1961 and became the first director of the consolidated department (1961-1966). Ziegler held pastorates in Massachusetts, served as state superintendent in Rhode Island, and in the 1970s was minister of the First Unitarian Church in Shaker Heights, Ohio. He received an honorary DD from Meadville/ Lombard in 1971. Munson chaired the joint Universalist-Unitarian Interim Committee which had recommended merger in the mid-1950s. He was also chairman of the Department of Church Extension of the Massachusetts Convention and, after serving for six years (1950-1955) in the Universalist church in Palmer, Massachusetts, helped organize, with three other ex-*Humiliati*, a new fellowship in a suburb of Springfield.[82]

The *Humiliati* held nine annual meetings (1946-1954) before they disbanded, and continued their efforts in individual capacities.[83] Hopkins had suggested in 1949 that the group be dissolved because it was creating discord and division within the denomination, but the majority view prevailed until after 1953; by then, fervor had diminished, and what one critic called "armchair verbalization" had been replaced by the realities of parish administration.

The *Humiliati* had set out to counteract the inertia and complacency which they perceived to be smothering post-1945 Universalism. The "emergent Universalism" which they espoused was a curious and sometimes contradictory blend of religion that was "functional, naturalistic, theistic, and humanistic," simultaneously invoking the past and projecting the future. From an individual point of view the *Humiliati* felt by 1954 that one of their original missions — personal spiritual renewal — had been accomplished, however imperfectly. Theologically, they represented at one and the same time a casting back to the historic role of Universalism as interpreted by Hosea Ballou and a call for a new and bold cutting edge for religion in which a new, enlarged, and eclectic Universalism would be the moving force.

Toward a World Religion

In the midst of a soul-searching called for by Gibbons and the controversy provoked by the *Humiliati*, General Superintendent Cummins unburdened himself about his own religious philosophy, centering on the meaning of Universalism. Buried in the middle of his long report in 1947 to the General Assembly was a plea to universalize Universalism, to make it a religion synonymous with the One World concept then being so much talked about in the international realm. One of the trends greatly disturbing him was the rise of the belief that Universalist fellowship was to be limited "to form of racially exclusive and sectarian Christianity." True Universalism could be limited neither to Protestantism nor to Christianity, or it would be denying its very name. Universalism was "a world fellowship, not a Christian sect." It was "the religion and philosophy of the all-inclusive, [it] levels all barriers, embraces all religions, demands whole-souled consecration, under God's fatherhood, to the task of building on earth a brotherhood universal. Any Universalism worthy of its name cannot recognize divisions between people on the basis of race or class or religion or nationality. . . . all are welcome . . . unitarian or trinitarian, white or colored, theist or humanist, so that whatever exclusion there may be is self-exclusion. A circumscribed Universalism is unthinkable."[84]

The transformation of Universalism into a world religion was an old idea. It was first expressed within a Christian context and later without Christian limits, as called for by such denominational leaders as Cummins.[85] One of the first pleas for a world religion divorced from exclusive attachment to Christianity had been made by Elbert Whippen in 1919. It should, he said, be "large enough to include the Jew, the Christian, the Catholic, the Protestant, the Mohammedan, the Buddhist — in short, all who aspire to learn Truth and live lives of character."[86] This was very much in line with the vision of the "World Soul" expressed by Clarence R. Skinner the very same year in a prose-poem. In it he referred to the "international mind" and "the universal self."[87] It was premised on a brotherhood of love that transcended all boundaries.

The idea of a truly "universal Universalism" was carried to its ultimate

The historic Charles Street Meeting House in Boston

in the person of Kenneth L. Patton, controversial pastor of the Charles Street meeting house in Boston between 1949 and 1964. Universalists had faced a paradoxical situation after World War II. Although Boston was the headquarters of both the national and state organization and the center of denominational activity in general, there was no Universalist church in the entire city by 1948.[88] Twenty-two churches in Greater Boston, including those in the city itself, had disappeared. So the state convention, under the leadership of Superintendent Clinton L. Scott, decided to establish a new church as a pilot project where experiments in organization, religious art, services, and programs, might attract Greater Bostonians. The basic purpose would be "to find a religious setting for a religion of one humanity and one world." None would be excluded; all activities were to be open to everyone, regardless of age, sex, or ethnic background. It would be a bold attempt to establish "an idealistic world community in miniature."

The historic Charles Street meeting house, in downtown Boston, was acquired by the state convention in 1948 as the locale of this experiment in world-wide religious expression. The building, constructed in 1807 and designed by Asher Benjamin for the use of the Third Baptist Church, had changed hands many times.[89] Among its occupants had been the African Methodist Episcopal Church and the Albanian Orthodox Church of St. John the Evangelist.

Patton, with a Unitarian background, was selected as the first minister, and was supported by the *Humiliati*. He had for six years been the very successful leader of the First Unitarian Society in Madison, Wisconsin, and had had great results with students attending the state university.[90] He had been an outspoken champion of intercultural and interracial cooperation, and had attracted national attention when he "resigned from the white race" as a protest against discrimination aimed at Blacks. He was also an openly avowed naturalistic (non-theistic) humanist, a fact which disturbed more conservative Universalists so much that the state convention, although it granted $8,000 in aid to the church, at first denied fellowship to it.[91] A resolution to grant fellowship was tabled in 1951 and was not passed until 1953.

The unconventional minister, whose special interest was religion and the arts, proceeded to decorate the interior of the meeting house with no less than sixty-five symbols from the world's religions, and wrote extensively on the subject.[92] One much earlier and much more modest attempt to express Universalism graphically had been a mural panel executed for the church in Peoria, Illinois, in 1920. Called "The Apotheosis of Man," it had been painted by Joseph G. Cowell and was exhibited at the Boston Architectural Club.[93]

Patton also expressed himself so unreservedly about the theological school curricula that he antagonized many. He advocated a complete

The interior of the Charles Street Meeting House

overhaul in order to dispense with programs "still ridden by the biblialatry of Protestantism."[94] Curricula were overloaded with courses on Christian church hisory, the Bible, and Christian theology, and made only passing reference to the cultures of other traditions. This situation he considered "shameful," and asserted that prospective clergy were not only uneducated but miseducated.

Almost as soon as he had taken charge of the Charles Street meeting house he found himself in the midst of a storm of controversy over free speech. The Massachusetts Universalist Convention had contracted and paid for a series of twenty-six broadcasts. Among those to have been carried by radio station WLAW (Lawrence) was one on Easter Sunday in 1949 on the theme "The Risen Christ." The station, in an unprecedented action, requested a copy of Patton's manuscript several days before its scheduled delivery, and refused to broadcast it. In the sermon Patton was sufficiently ambivalent about belief in immortality to cast serious doubt on it.[95] The state convention brought suit against the radio station in the Federal District Court on the ground of denial of free speech, and the General Assembly promised financial support.[96] The court upheld the radio station's decision, as did the United States District Court of Appeals.[97] The *Leader* urged that the issue be carried all the way to the United States Supreme Court, but this was not done.

Some of the old-line Universalists sympathized with the court's decision. Edson R. Miles, retired from the Canton Theological School faculty, claimed that Patton had, without justification, negated the doctrine of immortality while attempting to speak under denominational auspices, and that Patton's views did not represent the thinking of most Universalists.[98]

Paralleling in some ways Patton's career in Boston at the same time was that of Leland Perry Stewart on the West Coast. He organized in Claremont, California, a Center for Universal Religion, and used as his symbol the circle favored by the *Humiliati*, but without even their off-center cross within it.

It was evident that the soul-searching among some Universalists as to their beliefs in the post-World War II period had yet to reach final solution. The problem of denominational identity had yet to be completely resolved and a consensus had yet to be reached.

Chapter 33

"And Flow on Together:" Universalist-Unitarian Consolidation, 1937-1961

Between the time of the collapse of the Free Church Fellowship in 1937 after a life of less than three years, and the conclusion of World War II in 1945, no steps of any significance were taken toward furthering the consolidation of the Universalist and Unitarian denominations.[1] They were both occupied with internal matters, battling with the Great Depression, and were undergoing a surge of denominational fervor sharpened in part among Universalists by the series of rebuffs in their efforts in the 1940s to become a member of the Federal Council of Churches.

It was probably as much the weight of indifference of the majority of Universalists to the idea of joining hands with the Unitarians as any outright antagonism which dulled the impulse toward closer relations. There was seldom heard in the 1930s and 1940s such blasts against Unitarians as those attributed to Isaac M. Atwood in the 1890s. He was described as "a narrow-minded hater of Unitarians" who, according to Universalist E. C. Bolles, would 'rather affiliate with the devil any time than with the Unitarians.'[2]

The Unitarians who became the leading exponent of merger in the 1930s was Frederick May Eliot. He had become president of the AUA in 1937 and two years later, as the guest of the General Convention, had told the assemblage that he hoped to see union achieved "in the not too distant future" as the United Liberal Church of America.[3] "The era of divided endeavor" was nearing an end.

There seems to be some indication by 1945 that joint rather than "divided endeavor" might indeed take place. In an unprecedented move the Universalist trustees voted to request the AUA to appoint members to a committee "in connection with our joint interests . . . to consider problems of concern to both denominations."[4] The committee was created but at first its accomplishments were considerably less than dramatic. It did approve the merger of the publications of the respective youth groups as the *Young Liberal.* In 1947 Max Kapp recommended that the existence of the committee be given increased publicity and that it be encouraged to take on such far-ranging projects as considering "the possibility of bringing into existence the United Liberal Church."[5]

However, this was considered premature and Kapp's recommendation was withdrawn. There were still too many Universalists who felt ill at ease in the presence of Unitarians. One Universalist wrote to Kapp, in response to his recommendation, that the two groups were still on different wavelengths. Unitarians, with their cold intellectuality, seemed to be more interested "in analyzing the nature of infinity . . . than in the [Universalist] spirit of love. I . . . feel that I ought to put on my company manners when I go into a Unitarian church."[6]

"Union by Installments:" The Council of Liberal Churches

Still, Eliot continued to hammer away at the idea of the "ultimate unity of all religious liberals."[7] He felt sure in 1947 that Universalists and Unitarians would lead the way, and that the new religious configuration would be extended to those with other than a Christian heritage. Eliot's persistence paid off, for a Universalist committee of ten was appointed in 1948 to meet with a similar Unitarian group, this time to study the possibilities of union.[8] It found "no insuperable obstacles" and recommended a federalized arrangement based on "freedom of faith and congregational polity." Debate over the proposal was lengthy and intense at the General Assembly in 1949 but a joint resolution was eventually approved unanimously (189-0) by the Universalists.[9]

The Universalist and Unitarian legislative bodies voted officially to submit to each of their local churches the question of "whether they even wish to study and consider the possibilities of federal union of their two national bodies." General Superintendent Cummins for the Universalists and President Eliot for the Unitarians issued a joint statement explaining and clarifying the nature and intent of the action taken.[10] The cautious wording was intended unmistakably to avoid the error made in past attempts of giving the impression that the proposals for closer relations emanated exclusively from denominational officialdom and were somehow being hastily imposed on the local churches without their knowledge or consent.

The first provision of the resolution sought merely to sound out the two constituencies as to their desire to study the possibilities; nothing could have been more tentative than that. If the initial vote were affirmative, the resolution called only for drawing up a plan looking toward federal union, not merger. Even then, it would affect the two denominations only at the administrative, service, and affiliated agency level, and not at the local church or parish level. Even if the votes were all affirmative, it would take several years to put the plan into operation. There was also the mandate "to explore the interest of other churches and associations of churches in forming a wider and more inclusive federal union of churches." Interim Universalist-Unitarian commissions were charged also to conduct an educational campaign and to supervise the entire project.

The first of several steps was to ascertain reaction at the grass roots. If a minimum of 51 percent of church members voted in favor in both denominations, Universalists and Unitarians would each appoint a representative Commission on Church Union of seven members; they, in cooperation with officers of both denominations and affiliated organizations, would then draw up a plan and submit it to both denominations in 1951 for official action. If approved, the final plan would be submitted to each church, to be voted on within two years. An affirmative vote of 75 percent of the eligible members present in each church would be required; in turn, 75 percent of the churches voting affirmatively would be necessary to put the plan into effect. Those abstaining were counted as negatives.[11] Ratification of the action by each denomination would then be necessary before federal union became binding. No plan had yet been worked out, although it was evident that some surrender of denominational sovereignty and autonomy was presupposed.

The showing of the Universalists when the first set of returns was tabulated was very poor. By mid-1950 only ninety-seven churches had responded; ninety were in favor, six were negative, and the vote of one was tabled. When the final vote was taken, of the 304 certified Universalist churches, 220 voted affirmatively — 72.3 percent.[12] There was so much doubt that the requisite number could be obtained that at their meetings in 1951 the two denominations had voted to reduce the necessary proportion of churches favoring the plan from 75 percent to 60 percent.[13] According to the rather complex formula agreed upon, the downward revision meant that, in theory, less than half (45.6 percent) of each constituency was necessary to vote federal union — a source of much objection.[14]

It was difficult to imagine a more complicated arrangement than the one provided. It was made even more so when the Joint Commission on Church (Federal) Union established a grand total of fifteen subcommittees through which to operate.[15] A joint board of administration was created as a temporary organization to provide combined services in religious education, public relations, and publications.

There was so much complaint that the two denominations were not being kept adequately informed of what was going on that the commission prepared a pamphlet ("Twenty Questions on Unitarian-Universalist Federal Union") to educate both constituencies.[16] The editor of the *Leader* conducted a symposium on federal union in 1952 which included both clerical and lay representatives. The consensus seemed to be generally favorable, but the greatest hurdle was a blanket of indifference which seemed to overspread the entire denomination.[17]

There was also a vague aura of restlessness. Nothing tangible seemed to have been accomplished in the fields of publication and public relations — two of the three areas in which joint operation was to take place. There was questioning about why such subjects as ministerial federation had not been included. The lowering in mid-stream of the percentage of church assent required for the system to go into effect seemed to indicate to some that neither denomination was ready even for federation, not to mention union.[18] Some churches, such as the one in Stafford, Connecticut, had refused to vote at all until a specific plan of organization was available.[20] The number of Universalist churches which had voted by the spring of 1953 (seventy-two) was considered "alarmingly low." Eventually, 88 percent of all accredited Universalist churches voted, and 79 percent voted in the affirmative. The Unitarian percentages were 92 and 94 respectively.[21]

The next step was a prcedent-setting one. In the summer of 1953, at a joint assembly in Andover, Massachusetts, both bodies adopted the by-laws prepared by the Joint Commission and the By-Laws Committee, and the Council of Liberal Churches (Universalist-Unitarian) came into existence.[22] There was a myriad of names suggested by the Universalists for the new organization. Among them were United Liberal Church Council, Association of Religious Liberals, Church of the Universals, Council of Federated Liberal Churches, Council of Religious Liberals, Federated Liberal Church Council, Federation of Free Churhes, Free Church Council, and Free Church Union. A suggestion (no doubt semi-facetious) was made that members of the two denominations thereafter be known as "Univsitarians" and the denomination be designated as "Universitianism."[23] The Universalist vote was 257 to 12 and the Unitarian vote was unanimous.[24]

The Council of Liberal Churches (CLC) was incorporated on 8 October 1953 and a charter obtained from the state of Delaware. It was claimed, with some exaggeration, that the new organization brought together more than 175,000 Universalists and Unitarians.[25] The total number of churches was 900 at the time the CLC was created. An interim six-member board of administrators (reduced to four in 1955) was provided, with a director for each of the three joint activities. The overall administration was to be in the hands of an eighteen-member governing board, with nine from each denomination, including the head of each who served *ex officio* without vote.[26] The Universalist headquarters in Boston was designated as the legal home of the Council, although shortage of

Newly elected members of the Council of Liberal Churches in 1957

space necessitated the use also of the Unitarian headquarters a few doors down Beacon Street.

The Andover meeting also authorized the appointment of a twelve-member Joint Interim Commission which would review the working of federal union and make a report at the second biennial joint meeting in 1955. One of their responsibilities was to consider the feasibility of extending joint activities to such areas as the ministry and church extension.[27]

The CLC held its first meeting in Boston in the fall of 1953, elected officers, provided the administrative board, and appointed committees in the three designated fields of activity. For several months they were involved in drafting plans, formulating policies, and working on staff and budgetary requirements. Ernest Kuebler served as executive director of the Division of Education and doubled as acting administrator of the Council in 1954, but served for less than a year because of other demands.[28] The original plan called for six professional educators, with associate directors to cover the areas of church school, youth, and adult religious education. William Y. Bell, a Black with considerable professional training and experience, was placed in charge of the programs in adult education and social relations.[29] The preliminary annual budget was set at $85,000 for the Education Division but almost immediately had to be reduced to $72,500 and the professional staff from six to four. There was also the problem at first of overlapping functions, for the UCA Department of Education continued to exist until mid-1954, with George M. Lapoint as chairman. Frances Wood and Edna P. Bruner served as educational consultants and as field workers under the new arrangement.[30]

The denominational Department of Public Relations was not transferred to the CLC's Department of Public Information until January 1955. It was headed by Roland Gammon, with headquarters in New York City. He was forced to raise part of his own salary.[31] The transfer of the

"And Flow on Together:" Universalist-Unitarian Consolidation, 1937-1961 / 653

Robert Cummins (Universalist) and Frederick May Eliot (Unitarian) in 1953

denominational Publications Department was never accomplished during the life of the CLC. By 1956 the educational activities were still split among the General Alliance of Unitarian and other Liberal Christian Women, the Association of Universalist Women, and the UCA Service Department. The unified program so optimistically dreamed of had failed to develop.

The problem of financing the work of the Council appeared almost immediately. A budget of $111,304 was adopted for the 1954-1955 fiscal year.[32] Assurances were given by both the Universalist and Unitarian boards that this was a guaranteed total. The formula announced for the first year was to have all budgeted income except that for the Education Department shared equally; for that department, each body was to contribute the same amount as was budgeted by each denomination the previous year. Such nicely laid plans soon went glimmering. Universalist commitment to support of the CLC amounted to $68,000 but had to be reduced to little more than $45,000 before the end of the first year.[33] The Unitarian experience was similar. The AUA had expected to allocate $102,000 but was barely able to provide $80,000. There were complaints that denominational interests were being subordinated to those of the CLC. This helped account for the greatly reduced contributions by both denominations.³⁴ It was clear that the whole matter of the CLC had to be reviewed and a decision made as to its future.

The financial implications of attempting to make workable the Council of Liberal Churches bore heavily on the Universalist Church. The creation of yet another administrative superstructure occurred at the very same time that the denomination was struggling with mounting dissatisfaction with its own internal administration and what had become chronic deficit financing.³⁵

These were among the challenges facing Brainard F. Gibbons, who was elected to the General Superintendency in 1951, took office in 1952, and was formally installed in 1953.³⁶ He held the position until 1956. A native of New York City, he had earned a law degree in 1926 from New York University and had practiced for ten years. He became interested in the Universalist ministry and attended the Canton Theological School, from which he received a BD in 1939. After service in several Massachusetts churches he accepted a pastorate in Wasau, Wisconsin. After one year there he served as chaplain in the United States Navy until 1945, after which he returned to a highly successful pastorate in Wisconsin. He attracted widespread attention in the denomination with his occasional sermon, delivered at the General Assembly in 1949, entitled "New Wine and Old Bottles." In it he called for "a universal religious fellowship" that went beyond the "pretensions of orthodox and historic Christianity."³⁷ He became president of the Universalist Church in 1951, from which position he was elected General Superintendent. He received an honorary DD from Tufts in 1952.

At the very meeting of the General Assembly in 1955 where the Joint Interim Commission of the CLC made its report, Gibbons told Universalists that they did not have a true denomination because they had neither delegated sufficient authority to their central body to allow it to act like one, nor supported it with either work or money.³⁸ In a blunt nuts-and-bolts report he told the denomination that its financial and administrative affairs had to be put on a much sounder basis than then prevailed if it were not to be hopelessly outdistanced by the Unitarians and fall by the wayside.

There had always been some grumbling about the operation of denominational headquarters. It was considered by rank-and-file Universalists as a remote bureaucracy which had little or nothing to do with local churches or even state conventions, let alone individuals. Some, always distrustful of centralized authority, however minimal it might have been, were suspicious of what went on in Boston. Others felt that the limited financial resources of the denominations were being improperly handled by headquarters, and that its operations were not businesslike. Increasing inability to match actual income with budgeted expense finally brought some action after it was realized that, between 1948 and 1956, expenditures had exceeded income every single year. Revenue in 1955 was less than $126,000 and even the deficit budget that year was exceeded by over $140,000. Such a situation could not continue indefinitely.

There were also other sources of dissatisfaction. The centralizing policies of General Superintendent Cummins had been criticized; there was disgruntlement over one or another of the programs and/or the priorities which were set in doling out money. Some were unhappy with the departmental organization which Cummins had promoted. It seemed to be time to engage in a general stocktaking.

It was the Council of Superintendents who first suggested in 1956 to the trustees that an objective review be made of the entire headquarters operation. To that end the board held a special meeting during the summer and decided to employ a professional outside consulting firm to make a thorough study and assessment of the situation. The organization selected was the Institutional Consulting Associates of Englewood, New Jersey, who advertised themselves as "management analysts and counsellors."

The confidential 152-page report of their finding was transmitted to Alan F. Sawyer, president of the UCA, early in January 1957. It covered in detail the organization, personnel, finance, and operation of headquarters, including the physical plant. The critique was not only exhaustive but went considerably beyond the technical aspects of management. It touched on everything from the duties of the General Superintendent to the advisability of purchasing floor wax in quantity as an economy measure. The comments and recommendations ran the entire gamut of the denomination, with attention particularly to weaknesses, worded diplomatically but leaving no room for doubt as to either seriousness or the need to take corrective action.

Four time schedules were set up to implement the recommendations and two received immediate attention. The authority of the General Superintendent was increased when the department boards established by Cummins became advisory bodies instead of separate policy-making agencies. The financial resources of the denomination were inventoried and some attempt was made to centralize and simplify them. The greatest resistance came from the state conventions which still jealously guarded their own treasuries. Some progress had been made by 1955 to arrange for the merger of some state conventions with the UCA, an effort encouraged by the Universalist half of the Joint Interim Commission of the CLC.

The Joint Merger Commission

The Joint Interim Commission met twice preceding the 1955 biennial CLC meeting and prepared a brief and general report. It then proceeded to consider three possibilities: total merger (consolidation) of the two denominations; extension of the existing federal union to such additional areas as the ministry; and the financial problems faced by both denominations and reflected in the precarious state of the CLC.[39]

The commission made its report, as scheduled. To the surprise of some, instead of making only a progress report, it recommended that a twelve-member joint merger commission be established to prepare plans for consolidation, to be voted on through a series of plebiscites by local churches. The report was signed by all members of the commission.[40] They asserted that "the Unitarian and Universalists hold enough in common to become one people" and proceeded to line out their specific arguments in favor of merger. Too many serious difficulties were being experienced in working out the CLC arrangement. Adding more functions and responsibilities would merely aggravate the problems. Attempting to finance three organizations was too great a task to be carried out successfully.

There was sharp debate among Universalists over the commission's recommendation to appoint another body to consider merger. A scattering of individuals felt that the interim commission had exceeded its mandate, and that considering merger had not been part of its responsibility. Ziegler opposed the whole idea because Universalists could not "obtain the kind of democracy we want in entering another denomination."[41] Sawyer made a motion in favor of merger, to be ratified by three-fourths of all Universalist churches, but it was withdrawn after much discussion.[42] General Superintendent Gibbons was convinced that there were so many differences of polity and organization between Universalists and Unitarians that the CLC was not a workable plan for union.[43] In his estimation, the only alternative was to merge outright or to withdraw from the CLC. Simultaneously, some Unitarias believed that the idea of merger was premature, and felt that the CLC should be given more time to prove itself rather than precipitately voting for total merger.[44] But the arguments of the Universalists on the commission were so persuasive that the vote in the General Assembly to recommend appointment of a joint merger commission was 133 to 15. The commission was instructed to make a further report in 1957.

Between the 1955 meeting and the one scheduled two years later there was a small flurry of Universalist-Unitarian church consolidation about which Lalone was very concerned. He believed that the creation of the CLC had resulted in a misapprehension within several churches. Consolidation was not called for by the federal arrangement. The result would be a reduction in the number of liberal churches. "Union by subtraction equals extinction."[45] A species of chaos could conceivably be created if most Universalist and Unitarian churches united while at the national level only a federated relationship existed. Ellsworth Reamon, pastor in

Syracuse, New York, felt even more strongly. He believed that further talk of merger would be "suicide" and in any case would mean absorption of the Universalists by the Unitarians rather than a real consolidation.[46]

With the approval of a joint commission on merger each denomination selected its six representatives and the work began in the fall of 1956, with William B. Rice of Wellesley Hills, Massachusetts, as chairman.[47] The lack of coordination within the denomination had become embarrassingly evident by 1957. No meeting had ever been held between the Universalist members of the Interim Commission and the trustees of the denomination.[48] A similar lack of communication and integration existed between the Joint Merger Commission and the trustees in 1957.

Just as the Joint Merger Commission began its work, the UCA elected a new General Superintendent. Philip R. Giles served until consolidation was finally achieved in 1961 and the office was abolished. He took office on his birthday (23 January), and had been born in Haverhill, Massachusetts, in 1917. He had received his undergraduate degree from Tufts and his BD from the Crane Theological School in 1942, the year of his ordination at Southbridge.

Giles held a variety of pastorates in New England and, like Gibbons, had been a chaplain during World War II, although he served in the Air Corps rather than in the Navy. Between 1949 and 1951 he had been director of the denominational Unified Appeal but had been called back to active service as a chaplain during the Korean conflict. He had had considerable additional experience in denominational headquarters, for he served as assistant to Cummins and since 1954 had been director of the Departments of the Ministry and Church Extension. He received an honorary DD from Tufts in 1958.

Giles had immediately outlined a forward-looking practical three-pronged program for the denomination which he called "Operation Bootstrap." It involved evaluation, study, and implementation. He stressed the importance of the local church in increasing denominational effectiveness. The role of headquarters was to furnish written guidelines and aids in regard to membership and finances, but was in no sense to be dictatorial. When differences arose among churches he much preferred that leading churches rather than national headquarters serve as "peacemakers."[49]

From 1957 through 1959 one poll after another was taken to obtain the views of local churches regarding consolidation. Lalone selected a dozen lay persons to get their views on merger in 1958 and published the results in the *Leader*. Those in favor edged out those opposed by a substantial margin, but with a small but vociferous opposition led by Cornelius Greenway, a Universalist since 1920 and pastor of All Souls Church in Brooklyn, New York.[50] Robert M. Bowman, editor of *Teamwork*, the Universalist publication for ministers, favored merger and argued that a combination of fear and pride rather than any fundamental differences between the denominations was responsible for the persistent debate.[51] Frederick L. Harrison cautioned against setting up splinter groups if a clear majority favored consolidation.[52] Throughout the discussion the *Leader* took a position of "organizational neutrality" which endeared the editor to neither supporters nor opponents. Lalone was criticized especially for refusing to commit himself to consolidaton, as the majority clearly wished.[53] He kept reminding readers that merger was not inevitable, and that no such commitment had yet been made.[54]

By 1958 the word "consolidation" was being substituted for "merger" in order to avoid the legal and technical implication that one of the parties would lose its identity if "merger" were employed.[55] Hence, when the final votes were taken the substituted terminology was employed.

The Joint Merger Commission was instructed to suggest one or more outline plans and submit them to member churches. A manual on "Merger and Alternatives," together with a study guide, was made available to all Universalist and Unitarian churches in the fall of 1958. Then the churches were asked to participate in a plebescite by indicating a preference as between two plans and four alternatives. Plan No. 1 called for a complete functional consolidation and Plan No. 2 for an enlarged Council of Liberal Churches.

A preliminary report was made to the Universalist trustees in May 1959. Approximately 600 churches and fellowships of the 930 total in both denominations had voted by then, with 75 percent in favor.[56] A complete final report was made on 1 July. By a vote of approximately 3 to 1 the churches favored Plan No. 1. This was interpreted by the commission as authorizing it to move to the next step; namely, to prepare a detailed plan (a constitution and bylaws) which the churches would then have the opportunity to consider before the next joint biennial assembly.

A total of 41,000 copies of the condensed version of the proposed plan, together with revisions, was prepared by the commission and distributed in 1959 to all ministers and presidents or clerks of churches one month preceding the biennial meeting. Delegates were, after discussion and further amendment if necessary, to "approve a definite plan or reject all plans." The editor of the *Leader* kept insisting that merger was not yet an accomplished fact.[57]

The commission presented its final report and a proposed constitution and bylaws at the Joint UCA-AUA meeting in Syracuse, New York, in October 1959. Almost 1,000 individuals, both delegates and visitors, jammed into Betts Memorial Universalist Church. The Universalist vote in favor of the report and adoption of the constitution was 238 to 33 and that of the Unitarians 518 to 43, with three abstentions.[58] During the joint session, which lasted five hours, there were "frequent moments of great tension," and "intense differences of opinion" within both groups. Greenway left the General Assembly meeting completely disgruntled, complaining about the "steam-roller tactics [used] by the higher-ups" to promote merger.[59] On a more positive note Paul Carnes, later to become president of the combined denominations, noted that "Something happened to the Universalists. They met the Unitarians and found that Unitarians are, more or less, just like Universalists except there are more of them and they make more noise."[60]

The "enabling resolution," as the vote was described, was next subject to a final plebiscite by the churches, and that in turn to ratification by separate special meetings of each denomination in 1960. On the final plebiscite an affirmative vote of 60 percent of the eligible voting units (churches and fellowships) was required for adoption, and 70 percent of the units voting in each denomination had to vote favorably to assure adoption.

If the plan had not been approved, General Superintendent Giles recommended that the General Assembly declare a moratorium of at least ten years on any further discussion of the subject.[61] He further recommended that, in such an eventuality, the Council of Liberal Churches be continued only in the field of joint educational effort, acknowledged to have been the most successful of the three areas of Council operation. Instead, the CLC came unofficially to an end in 1959, when Plan No. 2 was rejected, and officially a year later, with the acceptance of the new constitution and bylaws. It was to be merger or nothing. "Union by Installments" was no longer a viable alternative.

The name "Unitarian Universalist Association" was adopted with minimal discussion and by "a resounding majority."[62] The greatest debate was over whether to refer to the Judeo-Christian tradition and to "truths taught by Jesus" in Article II which outlined the purposes and objectives of the new UUA. At first, references to both were omitted; the next day, reference to the Judeo-Christian tradition was restored, but without reference to Jesus. In the final version adopted by the joint session there was reference only to "universal truths taught by the great prophets and teachers of humanity in every age and tradition."[63]

The organizational plan included no surprises, and embraced features and characteristics already familiar to both Universalists and Unitarians. The policy of congregational autonomy and the non-creedal nature of both denominations were both affirmed in the new organization. The consolidation required no internal changes of any kind in individual churches and fellowships, and they were left to conduct affairs as they saw fit. This included freedom to adopt any name they wished; consequently, the bewildering variety of church and fellowship designations which already existed was continued. Annual meetings of the General Assembly were substituted for the biennial meetings to which the Universalists had been accustomed since 1889.

One of the first steps taken by the Universalists on the Joint Merger Commission in 1955 had been to arrange for the merger of state conventions into the UCA, and fellowship functions in four were immediately turned over to the central committee.[64] The regional arrangement of conferences or councils long followed by the Unitarians rather than the system of state conventions used by the Universalists was provided in the constitution, but the continued existence of state conventions was recognized. Two decades after consolidation there were still five "intermediate organizations" (conventions) still in existence: The Georgia Universalist Convention, the New York State Convention of Universalists, the Universalist Convention of North Carolina, Inc., the Pennsylvania State Convention, and the Vermont and Quebec Universalist Unitarian Convention. Regional organization was nothing new to Universalists, many such having existed in the past.

Associate membership for auxiliary and support groups, with voting privileges for delegates, was provided on application. The procedural details for consolidation of parallel groups in the two denominations were left to the groups concerned, on a completely voluntary basis and with the timetable left open. As a consequence, the dates of consolidaton varied widely. The last to merge were the Universalist and Unitarian historical societies, accomplished in 1978. One of the first was the Unitarian Church of the Larger Fellowship which had been organized in 1944 and the Larger Fellowship of the Universalists, organized in 1945 but without a denominational identification.[65] Their purposes were identical: To provide religious materials for isolated members who did not have a church of their denomination accessible.

A precedent of sorts for such an organization among Universalists had been created in 1921. Known as the "Convention Church," it had been intended for those without a church home and was part of the Murray Crusade to increase membership.[66] Enrollees were members of either the General Convention or state conventions, and the respective superintendents were to serve as ministers. The plan was never fully developed and disappeared.

The organization created by Universalists in 1945 had originally been a project of the Massachusetts State Convention under the leadership of State Superintendent Clinton L. Scott, but was later taken over by the UCA. Both the programs and membership of the Universalist group were expanded under the leadership of Cummins, Giles, and Wolley, the last minister-at-large. It was considered part of the denominational church extension department. It was never as large as its Unitarian counterpart, with a membership never exceeding 1,000, but it performed a valuable service, especially for shut-ins unable to attend regular church services. Some members of this "church by mail" belonged to and supported both Universalist and Unitarian fellowships. The merger of the two was planned even before denominational consolidation was formally voted, and was accomplished in 1961.

Some differences between parallel organizations obviously needed to be resolved, as was the case with the two women's groups. The Unitarian Alliance was organized into eight regions while that of the AUW followed state lines. The Universalist women used an organization of three departments while the Unitarian women used a system of six committees. At their national meetings the Unitarian women acted as a delegate body while in their meetings all Universalist women had voting rights.[67] It was a multitude of such differences that had to be ironed out before consolidation actually took place in 1963.

The Final Steps

The fate of the proposed plan for Universalist-Unitarian consolidation was in no sense a foregone conclusion in spite of the substantial majorities already in favor. The vote of the churches and fellowships was absolutely crucial to the success of the plan over which so many individuals had struggled for so long. The plebescite was scheduled to extend from 1 December 1959 to 31 March 1960. If the decision were in favor of consolidation that plan would be presented to each denomination at separate but concurrent meetings in May 1960 for adoption. If the plan were approved it would be effective in May 1961 with final acceptance of the constitution and bylaws. All efforts would cease immediately if the vote in either the UCA or AUA were unfavorable. If favorable, the new Association would begin functioning and the two denominations would cease to exist in May 1961. If adopted, five special bilateral commissions would work out the details of consolidation, including procedures for nomination and election of officers.

Almost as soon as the meetings at Syracuse were concluded in 1959 the parties opposing consolidation were mobilized and made their views known in an *ad hoc* organization known as "Universalists and Unitarians for Cooperation Without Consolidation" (UUCC) which issued its first brochure on 25 January 1960 under the heading "Unity Without Union." They took as their slogan the aphorism of Unitarian Samuel A. Eliot: "We seek cooperation, not consolidation; unity, not union." J. Ray Shute was the chairman and Reamon, an unyielding enemy of consolidation, was the vice-president. He had argued for a federation of liberal churches with the resources of each left intact. He thought that there was too much attention being paid to science and reason by the Unitarians. "When reason alone becomes God the people in the pews suffer from frostbite."[68]

There were at first twenty-one members of the organizing committee by early 1960. Among them were such names especially familiar to Universalists as Seth R. Brooks, Cornelius Greenway, Alan F. Sawyer, and Alfred Ziegler, who later dropped out. The First Parish Church (Universalist) in Malden, Massachusetts, of which Richard W. Knost was minister, served as headquarters. Their plea for "ideas and money" was to mount and sustain a campaign against consolidation.

After much more than the required percentage of churches had voted for consolidation in the spring of 1961, the UUCC changed its name to "Universalists for Universalism" in a last-ditch effort to salvage what they conceived to be the crux of the Universalist message — the doctrine of universal salvation and specific recognition of its Christian heritage.[69]

The voice of the headquarters staff was heard through "The Report," a mimeographed weekly fact sheet charting the progress of the plebiscite. The chairman of the plebiscite committee, a subcommittee of the merger commission, was Raymond C. Hopkins of Brockton, Massachusetts. There was a total of 899 eligible voting units (later reduced to 895) on which to report. The principal function of the subcommittee was to "get out the vote," with the assistance of thirteen area captains. Less than 40 percent of Universalist ballots had been received by mid-February 1960, little more than five weeks before the deadline.

Thanks to the efforts of the area captains and constant reminders to the churches of the importance of the plebiscite to the future of both denominations, a rush of votes was turned in at almost the last minute. Participation in the plebiscite "exceeded the predictions of even the most optimistic."[70] A total of 183 Universalist churches and fellowships with a legal membership of 28,922 cast affirmative votes; 49 churches with a membership of 6,533 cast negative votes.[71] Twelve churches with a membership of 1,409 did not participate. A total of 232 (95 percent) participated and 183 (79 percent) voted affirmatively.

Among the Unitarians, of the 651 units eligible to participate, 609 (94 percent) voted, and 555 (91 percent) voted affirmatively.[72] Of the grand total of 895 churches and fellowships, 841 (94 percent) participated and 738 (88 percent) voted affirmatively. The returns far exceeded the minima of 60 percent participation of all accredited units and a 70 percent affirmative vote among those participating. The Unitarian membership was 104,821 and the Universalist membership was 36,864, making a grand total of 141,685. The final step of ratification was ready to be taken.

The culminating event in the history of both denominations, after more than a century of discussion, took place on 23 May 1960 in John Hancock Hall in Boston, preceded by simultaneous special sessions of each denomination in adjoining rooms connected with a public address system that broke down in the midst of proceedings.[73] Of the 430 Universalist delegates, the largest ever to attend an assembly, 365 voted to ratify and 65 were opposed. The record turnout was accounted for in part because

Universalists had been forcefully reminded by the General Superintendent that the vote was no mere perfunctory fulfillment of certain legal requirements. The plebiscite had had no legal standing whatever. The key question of whether consolidation actually took place depended on the votes of delegates.

Among the Unitarians the vote was 725 to 143. The usual variety of views could be heard in the Universalist gathering. Albert Q. Perry, who had served in 1960 on the organizing committee of the group calling for 'unity without union,' raised the question of what would happen to the Universalist faith. Greenway acknowledged that "my heart is heavy." Reamon claimed that the vote for consolidation really meant absorption of the Universalists and a step toward oblivion.[74]

But these were only scattered voices of dissent drowned out by a vast chorus favoring consolidation. An estimated 2,000 gathered in Symphony Hall for a service of celebration. Two pulpits were used: that of the Oxford church in which Hosea Ballou had been ordained; and that of the Federal Street Church in Boston from which William Ellery Channing had preached. Donald S. Harrington, minister of the Community Church, proclaimed the creation of "a new world faith" to stand beside the three major religions on the American continent — Catholic, Protestant, and Jewish.[75] The ceremony was concluded in an emotionally charged pledge of allegiance to the new organization.

The Unitarian Universalist Church of Silver Spring, Maryland, the newest member of the old UCA, was the first to adopt the new constitution in 1960, even before it had been finally ratified.[76] In the one-year transition period before ratification was complete the two denominations continued to operate separately while five study committees established earlier, plus a coordinating committee on consolidation, worked out the administrative details.[77] It issued a 119-page report in 1961 entitled "The Free Church in a Changing World."

The last formal act consolidating the two denominations took place at the first annual meeting of the UUA in Boston on 12 May 1961, with more than 1,000 present, when the constitution and bylaws were ratified. Those who tallied the vote heard about a dozen "noes."[78] The next task was to put the new organization into operation, with a host of decisions to be made and differences to be resolved.

Proposals for no less than twenty-three changes had already been made a month before the meeting, some made in the committee reports, and some involving the necessity of amending the constitution which had just been ratified.[79] There were debates over the regional organization provided in the constitution; the trustees finally settled the question by recognizing eleven in 1962.[80] There was continuing debate over the name of the Association. Should it have been hyphenated? Or should a less awkward name have been chosen? "Liberal Church of America" was heard so frequently as a possibility that it became an agenda item for the 1962 General Assembly, where it was voted down.[81]

There was one unforeseen complication in the election of the first president of the UUA. There had been an expectation that the heads of neither previously separate denomination would become a candidate, but Dana Greeley, president of the old AUA, was nominated and there was immediate protest. There were also many who felt that democratic procedures required more than one candidate for such an important post at such a critical juncture, and persuaded William Rice to run for the office. He was widely known, and had played a key role in the entire merger proceedings. Four months of intense campaigning ensued, with two managers selected for each of the rivals. Jack Mendelsohn and Max Kapp served for Greeley and H. Clay Burkholder and Carleton Fisher for Rice.[82] Greeley won the election by a vote of 1,135 to 980 and was installed as the first president of the UUA on 22 October 1961 at the Community Church in Boston.[83] All other offices were uncontested.

The decision to consolidate the UCA and AUA had been by no means unanimous. A "Committee for Continuing (Christian) Universalist Churches" was organized in the spring of 1961, with considerable strength in Pennsylvania and parts of the South.[84] Elmo Robinson reacted to the creation of the committee by explaining that he had no objection to keeping the Christian origins of Universalism alive, and pointed out that he belonged simultaneously to the Unitarian Christian Fellowship and the American Humanist Association. They each reflected some facet of truth.[85] In 1964 the organization became the short-lived Christian Universalist Church of America.[86] Thirty-seven Unitarian churches had voted negatively in the final plebiscite, as had forty-nine Universalist churches.

Greenway's Universalist church in Brooklyn, New York, refused to participate in UUA affairs and was not represented at the 1962 General Assembly. In 1963 the church voted to "renounce all connection with the new Unitarian Universalist Association" and became an associate member of the National Association of Congregational Christian Churches, a group of congregations which had not accepted membership in the United Church of Christ.[87] By the end of the 1970s all Universalist churches had joined the UUA, so no congregations were lost as a result of consolidation.

Carnes, who served as secretary of the coordinating committee for the five study committee established in 1961 to work out the details of consolidation, had his moments of discouragement about the future of the new Association. "It is time we stopped kidding ourselves: We are all but irrelevant in the religious life and thought of our nation.... Today we are easily tolerated and almost as easily dismissed. We are scarcely taken seriously by anyone, except perhaps ourselves — and even here one may question the health and depth of our sincerity."[88] Kapp, who delivered the sermon at Greeley's installation, was realistic but not as pessimistic as

Carnes. Unitarian Universalists, said Kapp, were marching "into perilous and untried tomorrows . . . in a bold, fresh enterprise of the liberal spirit [and] the splendid expectancy of a significant future." He offered no guarantees, only hope.[89]

What that future would bring, no one could really know. But the pledge of allegiance to which some 2,000 Unitarian Universalists had enthusiastically subscribed at the service of celebration stood as an affirmation of the Larger Hope on the threshold of another era yet to unfold.

> We, Unitarians and Universalists, children of the Judeo-Christian heritage, inheritors of the wisdom of the universal prophets, eager to experience the insights of the great faiths of the world, open to all sources of inspiration ancient and modern, determined to explore the boundless ocean of truth which lies about on every hand and on before, and welcoming into fellowship all men of whatever background of faith, here together on this night of Consolidation, conscious of the presence of the past, and of our urgent tasks, dedicate ourselves anew to the free and universal fellowship of all mankind that is the church to be.
>
> We declare our allegiance to the new Unitarian Universalist Association, and pledge our lives, our fortunes and our faith to its high purposes and sure upbuilding.[90]

Notes

Chapter 1: THE EVOLUTION OF AN ORGANIZATION: A RETROSPECTIVE GLANCE

1. "Universalism in America: Its Centenary Year, 1870" (Boston: J. S. Spooner, n.d.), p 11. The pamphlet consisted of a feature article published originally in the *New York Tribune*, of which Horace Greeley (a Universalist) was the editor; the article was published under the auspices of the Women's Centenary Association.

2. *Universalist* 51 (23 October 1869): [2].

3. *Universalist Leader* 11 (25 July 1908): 939-42.

4. Proceedings, General Convention, 1879, p. 25.

5. Ibid., p. 26.

6. *Universalist Leader* 4 (5 January 1901): 14.

7. See *The Life-Work of Elbridge Gerry Brooks, Minister in the Universalist Church* (Boston: Universalist Publishing House, 1881), by his son Elbridge Streeter Brooks.

8. For a critical review of the book, see the *Universalist Quarterly* 11 n.s. (January 1874): 117-21.

Chapter 2: INVENTORY AND SELF-ASSESSMENT

1. The article was reprinted in the *Christian Leader* 51 (20 January 1881): 3.

2. Both were reprinted in the *Christian Leader* in the same issue as the original article.

3. *Christian Leader* 51 (27 January 1881): [4].

4. In 1870 there were, according to his reckoning, 602 preachers; a decade later there were approximately 800, and the number of parishes in the period had risen from 1,000 to 1,200.

5. The address was reproduced in the *Christian Leader* 65 (14 November 1895): 2.

6. *Universalist* 54 (6 July 1872): [2]; *Christian Leader* 53 (19 October 1882): 1, and the *Universalist Leader* 9 (21 April 1906): 486. In compliance with its Portland Declaration of 1869, members of Universalist churches were excluded from the YMCA because they denied everlasting punishment for part of the human race — a condition for membership. *Christian Leader* 64 (8 March 1894): 8.

7. *Universalist Leader* 9 (2 June 1906): 686.

8. The convention proceedings were reported in detail in the *Christian Leader* 67 (28 October 1897): 4 ff.

9. *Universalist Leader* 7 (30 April); 7, 14 May 1904): 555-57, 487-89, 619-21.

10. Proceedings, General Convention, 1871, pp. 26-27.

11. "Introductory," *A Century of Universalism in Philadelphia and New-York* (Philadelphia: published by the author), p. vii.

Chapter 3: "THAT LITTLE COMPANY CALLED UNIVERSALISTS": THE STATISTICAL RECORD

1. *Universalist Leader* 4 (January 1901): 71. The quotation in the chapter title comes from a letter to the editor of the *Christian Leader* 33 (5 July 1930): 854.

2. There was for 1870, however, a single alphabetical listing, for the first time, of all known clergy, totalling 625.

3. *A Compendium of the Ninth Census, 1870* (Washington: Government Printing Office, 1872), pp. 514, 523-24.

4. Trustee Report, 1871; Proceedings, General Convention, 1871, p. 17.

5. *Universalist Register*, 1881, p. 66; Proceedings, General Convention, 1880, pp. 44-46.

6. *Christian Leader* 50 (15 April 1880): 2 n.

7. Ibid. 61 (6 November 1890): 2.

8. Ibid. 65 (14 November 1895): 2.

9. *Universalist Leader* 3 (12 May 1900): 587.

10. *Independent* 52 (4 January 1900): 119-64.

11. *Universalist Leader* 2 (13 January 1900): 38-39.

12. Ibid. 4 (23 March 1901): 365.

13. Ibid. 3 (15 September 1900): 1156.

14. Trustee Report, 1909; Proceedings, General Convention, 1909, pp. 30-31.

15. See H. K. Carroll, *The Religious Forces of the United States* (N.Y.: Christian Literature Co., 1893).

16. *Universalist Leader* 13 (24 September 1910): 1069.

17. Trustee Report, 1910, 1911; Proceedings, General Convention, pp. 51, 23-24.

18. This was done, for example, when the *Register* was abandoned, after no issue was published for 1921-22 because of a printers' strike. A Year Book was substituted in 1922 which lasted until 1934. There was none published in 1935; and in 1936, the annual trustee report became biennial to coincide with the meetings of the General Convention, and covered the years 1933-1935. The incongruity of continuing to call the publication a "Year Book" resulted in a change to the title *Universalist Biennial Reports and Directory,* covering 1937-38. It became simply a *Directory* after 1941, and minutes of national meetings were published only erratically thereafter — presumably for financial reasons.

19. Trustee Report, 1909; Proceedings, General Convention, pp. 30-31.

20. *Universalist Leader* 20 (11 August 1917): 522.

21. Trustee Report, 1917; Proceedings, General Convention, p. 13.

22. *Universalist Leader* 10 (20 April 1907): 510.

23. *Christian Register* 107 (1 November 1928): 879-80.

24. *Universalist Leader* 8 (23 February 1905): 238.

25. *Christian Leader* 31 (25 August 1928): 1079.

26. Ibid. 31 (29 December 1928): 1645, 1647; 32 (5 January 1929): 24.

27. David H. MacPherson, "Trends in Universalist Churches in Massachusetts in the First Half of the Twentieth Century" (unpublished STB thesis, Crane Theological School, Tufts College, Medford, Mass., 1952); and Richard M. Woodman, "An Evaluation of Data Relevant to the Decreasing Number of Churches in the New York State Convention of Universalists, 1900-1954" (unpublished BD thesis, Canton Theological School, St. Lawrence University, Canton, N.Y., 1954). Both studies included extensive statistics, maps, and other graphic aids. Both appeared in abridged form, edited by James D. Hunt, in the *Annual Journal of the Universalist Historical Society* 6 (1966): 5-45. The MacPherson study has been supplemented in the present study with additional details, and covers a somewhat longer period of time.

28. *Christian Leader* 62 (1 October 1891): 1.

29. The statistics cited are a composite derived from the two works mentioned, and from official Universalist statistics.

30. In his analysis of church closings in Massachusetts, MacPherson lists the reasons as "unknown" for the vast majority.

31. The editor of the *Leader* was skeptical, and called attention to "many who doubted the accuracy of his [Cummins'] statistics, questioned the wisdom of some of his plans, and could not approve his disparagement of everything that happened before 1938." *Christian Leader* 125 (6 November 1943): 653.

32. This sobering picture was painted by Cummins himself, in his report for 1946, p. 4.

33. *Directory and Biennial Reports, 1948,* pp. 11, 124. Typical of this situation was John A. Cousens, president of Tufts College from 1920 to 1937, who was active in the parish affairs of the church in Brookline, Massachusetts, but who apparently never became a member.

34. *Christian Leader* 123 (1 February 1941): 107–108.

35. Final Report, Joint Merger Commission, 22 April 1960.

Chapter 4: ADMINISTERING AND FINANCING THE DENOMINATION

1. Trustee Report, 1872; Proceedings, General Convention, p. 18; 1877, p. 20.

2. Ibid. 1873, pp. 23–24.

3. Proceedings, General Convention, 1879, pp. 14–16.

4. Minutes, *Christian Leader* 63 (5 October 1893): 1.

5. Proceedings, General Convention, 1897, pp. 14, 77–78.

6. *Christian Leader* 120 (26 November 1938): 1439–40. It was an expanded version of a paper given previously at a Boston ministers' meeting, entitled "The Organized Church," and published in the *Gospel Banner* (Maine).

7. *Universalist Leader* 1 (3 September 1898): 8.

8. Ibid. 1 (29 October 1898): 12–13.

9. Proceedings, General Convention, 1899, p. 19.

10. *Universalist Leader* 1 (29 October 1898): 6.

11. Trustee Report, 1898, Proceedings, General Convention, p. 9.

12. Much of the biographical information included here was derived from Robert Cummins, "The General Superintendency of the Universalist Church of America," *Annual Journal of the Universalist Historical Society* 3 (1962): 14–29.

13. *Universalist Leader* 1 (22 October 1898): 18.

14. This was the evaluation made by Robert Cummins in 1962; he himself assumed the office in 1938. He had intended to write the entire history of the General Superintendency after he retired from it, but it was never completed.

15. *Universalist Leader* 2 (4 November 1899): 6; for his first annual report, see Proceedings, General Convention, 1899, pp. 100–103.

16. Trustee Report, 1899; Proceedings, General Convention. p. 35.

17. Report, in Proceedings, General Convention, 1901, p. 100.

18. *Universalist Leader* 3 (24 March, 13 October 1900): 357, 1285.

19. Ibid. 5 (11 October 1902): 1286.

20. Its duties and responsibilities were set forth in a sixteen-page booklet prepared by William H. McGlauflin and published as "The Place of the Superintendency in the Universalist Church" in 1908. The publication was discovered in the central files in 1956. *Universalist Leader* 138 (December 1956): 275.

21. Proceedings, General Convention, 1903, p. 18; Trustee Report, 1907, ibid., p. 22.

22. *Universalist Leader* 4 (31 August 1901): 1102.

23. Ibid. 4 (5 October 1901): 1263.

24. Ibid. 4 (21 September 1901): 119.

25. Ibid. 4 (28 September 1901): 1222.

26. Ibid. 4 (14 September 1901): 1170.

27. Proceedings, General Convention, 1903, pp. 12–13; 1905, pp. 15–16.

28. Ibid. 1903, p. 19; Trustee Report, 1904, ibid., pp. 18–19.

29. *Onward* 5 (6 May 1898): 53.

30. *Universalist Leader* 9 (10 November 1906): 1433.

31. Ibid. 8 (4 November 1905): 1381.

32. Proceedings, General Convention, 1905, p. 12.

33. Ibid., pp. 97–100.

34. For a tribute and a summary of his activities as General Superintendent, see Trustee Report, 1916, Proceedings, General Convention, pp. 17–21.

35. Ibid., 1909, p. 31.

36. Committee on Official Reports, Proceedings, General Convention, 1915, pp. 35, 64.

37. *Universalist Leader* 14 (30 September 1911): 1222.

38. Ibid. 14 (14 October 1911): 1287.

39. President's Report, 1917, Proceedings, General Convention, pp. 5–8.

40. *Universalist Leader* 20 (20 January 1917): 86.

41. Ibid. 20 (17 February 1917): 102.

42. *Universalist Expositor* 1 n.s. (July 1833): 279.

43. *Universalist Leader* 23 (16 October 1920): 955–56.

44. See the review and analysis of denominational finance prepared by Isaac M. Atwood, the General Secretary, and published in the *Leader* 7 (6, 13 August 1904): 1002, 1034.

45. Report of the General Secretary, *The Universalist Centennial* (Boston: Universalist Publishing House, 1870), pp. 7–8.

46. Trustee Report, 1915, Proceedings, General Convention, p. 11.

47. Proceedings, General Convention, 1873, p. 16.

48. Quoted in the *Universalist* 53 (9 December 1871): [1].

49. Trustee Report, 1871, Proceedings, General Convention, p. 12.

50. Abstract of Trustee Minutes, 10 April 1872, *Universalist* 53 (27 April 1872): [2].

51. Proceedings, General Convention, 1872, pp. 18–19.

52. Ibid., 1875, p. 14.

53. Trustee Report, 1873, Proceedings, General Convention, pp. 22–23.

54. Ibid., 1871, p. 12.

55. Proceedings, General Convention, 1889, pp. 21–23.

56. Ibid., 1899, p. 116.

57. *Universalist* 57 (22 January 1876): [2].

58. Ibid. 57 (12 February 1876): [2].

59. Proceedings, General Convention, 1876, pp. 16–17.

60. Ibid., 1878, pp. 41–42.

61. Ibid., 1880, p. 21.

62. Ibid., 1883, pp. 17, 18; 1887, p. 27.

63. Richard Eddy, *Universalism in America: A History*, 2 vols. (Boston: Universalist Publishing House, 1884, 1886) 2: 360.

64. Biennial Report, 1892, Proceedings, General Convention, p. 12.

65. Proceedings, General Convention, 1889, p. 73.

66. Trustee Report, 1890, Proceedings, General Convention, p. 8.

67. Trustee Report, 1892, Proceedings, General Convention, p. 7.

68. Minutes, *Christian Leader* 63 (5 October 1893): 8.

69. Trustee Report, 1894, Proceedings, General Convention, pp. 7–8.

70. Proceedings, General Convention, 1895, pp. 65-66.

71. Ibid., 1899, p.15.

72. *Universalist Leader* 1 (3 December 1898): 7; 3 (3 November 1900): 1377; Proceedings, General Convention, 1899, pp. 14-15.

73. *Universalist Leader* 2 (4 November 1899): 8-9.

74. Trustee Report, 1900, Proceedings, General Convention, p. 9.

75. Ibid, 1905, p. 36.

76. Ibid., 1900, p. 3; *Universalist Leader* 9 (3 February 1906): 140.

77. Trustee Report, 1901, Proceedings, General Convention, p. 36.

78. Ibid., 1903, p. 19.

79. Ibid., 1905, pp. 37-38.

80. Ibid., 1907, pp. 38, 42; 1908, p. 7.

81. Ibid., 1911, pp. 11, 87.

82. Report, 1911, ibid., p. 113.

83. *Universalist Leader* 18 (6 February 1915): 137.

84. Ibid., 18 (25 September 1915): 918-20.

85. Proceedings, General Convention, 1915, pp. 8, 10.

Chapter 5: FROM EXPANSION TO CONTRACTION

1. Report of the General Superintendent, 1925, Universalist Year Book, 1926, p. 58.

2. *Christian Leader* 31 (8 September 1928): 1126-30.

3. *Universalist Leader* 22 (15 November 1919): 1084.

4. Trustee Report, 1920, Proceedings, General Convention, p. 4.

5. Trustee Report, 1923, Year Book, 1924, pp. 19-20.

6. *Universalist Leader* 28 (31 October 1925): 18. His company was famous for preparing and marketing "Friend's Baked Beans."

7. Minutes, Year Book, 1924, p. 61.

8. *Universalist Leader* 24 (15 January 1921): 58.

9. A detailed record of the two celebrations was prepared by Frederick A. Bisbee, editor of the *Leader,* and was published in book form under the title *From Good Luck to Gloucester* (Boston: Murray Press, 1920).

10. Trustee Report, 1920, p. 35.

11. *Universalist Leader* 23 (21 February 1920): 190-92.

12. Year Book, 1922, p. 72-73.

13. Ibid., 1924, pp. 11, 59-60.

14. Ibid., 1922, pp. 82-83.

15. *Universalist Leader* 22 (22 November 1919): 1133.

16. Proceedings, ibid. 22 (15 November 1919): 1097.

17. Year Book, 1922, p. 71.

18. Ibid., pp. 82-83.

19. Trustee Report, 1923, Year Book, 1924, pp. 21-25.
20. *Universalist Leader* 22 (20 September 1919): 853.
21. Trustee Report, 1925, Year Book, 1926, pp. 30-31.
22. *Christian Leader* 29 (3 April 1926): 20.
23. Ibid. 30 (3 September 1927): 1133-34.
24. Year Book, 1928, p. 20.
25. Report of the Secretary-General Superintendent, 16 April 1931; Trustee Report, 1931, Year Book, 1932, p. 23.
26. Minutes, General Convention, 1929, Year Book, 1930, pp. 21-22.
27. *Christian Leader* 34 (31 October 1931): 1390.
28. Ibid. 35 (14 May 1932): 619.
29. Trustee Report, 1933, Year Book, 1934, pp. 15, 25.
30. *Christian Leader* 36 (28 October 1933): 1359.
31. Trustee Report, 1935, Year Book, 1936, pp. 17, 20.
32. Report, General Convention, 1929, Year Book, 1930, p. 56.
33. *Christian Leader* 35 (7 May 1932): 579.
34. *Universalist Leader* 16 (8 November 1913): 1304.
35. A somewhat similar Council of Executives had been created in 1921, with its functions limited to coordinating the various fund drives in which the denomination became simultaneously engaged. Trustee Report, 1921, Year Book, 1922, pp. 28-29.
36. *Christian Leader* 131 (November 1949): 383.
37. Ibid. 119 (6 November 1937): 1427.
38. Ibid. 32 (11 May 1929): 582 ff.
39. *Universalist Leader* 24 (5 November 1921): 1174.
40. Until January 1922, when John van Schaick became the interim pastor, the pulpit had been supplied by more than thirty visiting clergy. Ibid. 25 (29 April 1922): 5.
41. *Universalist Leader* 25 (11 February, 4 March 1922): 17, 9-10.
42. Ibid. 25 (30 December 1922), facing p. 16.
43. Ibid. 26 (21 April 1923): 14-15.
44. Ibid. 26 (29 September 1923): 19-20.
45. Ibid. 26 (6 October 1923): 6.
46. Ibid. 28 (8 August 1925): 5.
47. Year Book, 1924, p. 12.
48. *Universalist Leader* 27 (8 November 1924): 6.
49. *Christian Leader* 31 (7 April 1928): 440.
50. Ibid. (14 April 1928): 451.
51. Trustee file, 28 April 1930.
52. *Christian Leader* 33 (14 June 1930); 740.
53. Ibid. 126 (18 November 1944): 687.
54. WNMA Records.
55. Year Book, 1928, p. 100.
56. This organization had also designed new buildings for the Hartford Theological Seminary and the Church of the Redemption (Universalist) in Boston. Year Book, 1928, p. 82.
57. *Christian Leader* 32 (10 August 1929): 101.
58. For a detailed description of the stained glass windows, see the *Christian Leader* 33 (29 March 1930): 400-401. A complete list of memorials received by 1930 was included in ibid. 33 (3 May 1930): 549; see also the pamphlets prepared by the church.
59. *Christian Leader* 32 (26 October 1929): 1377.
60. Ibid. 33 (19 April, 3 May 1930): 492-93, 558-61.
61. Ibid. 32 (5 January 1929): 19.
62. Minutes, Year Book, 1930, pp. 15-16.
63. *Christian Leader* 32 (26 October 1929): 1380.
64. Ibid. 32 (14 December 1929): 1588.
65. Ibid. 34 (12 December 1931): 1576-77.
66. William Lloyd Fox (ed.), *Recollections and Reflections of Seth R. Brooks and Corinne H. Brooks* (Washington, D.C.: Universalist National Memorial Church, 1977), pp. 46-47.
67. Ibid., p. 47; *Christian Leader* 120 (3 December 1938): 1459.
68. *Universalist Leader* 135 (October 1953): 249.
69. *Christian Leader* 122 (7 December 1940): 1087.
70. *Universalist Leader* 137 (October 1955): 225.
71. Ibid. 138 (June 1956): 140.

72. *Recollections,* pp. 50-51.
73. *Universalist Leader* 16 (18 October 1913) 1213-15.
74. *Boston Herald,* 22 February 1914.
75. *Universalist Leader* 17 (7 March 1914): 233.
76. Ibid. 17 (30 May 1914): 541.
77. Ibid. 18 (4 December 1915): 1159-60.
78. Ibid. 19 (1 January 1916): 14.
79. Ibid. 19 (19 February 1916): 185.
80. Ibid. 22 (13 September 1919): 831-32.
81. Ibid. 23 (12 June 1920): 573.
82. *Christian Leader* 32 (2 November 1929): 1391-95.
83. Ibid., p. 1381.

Chapter 6: TESTING THE WINCHESTER PROFESSION

1. The addresses were published in a volume entitled *The Winchester Centennial, 1803-1903* (Boston and Chicago: Universalist Publishing House, 1903).
2. *Universalist* 57 (29 April 1876): [1].
3. Appendix, Proceedings, General Convention, 1867, pp. 58-59.
4. Records, Vermont State Convention, 1868, 1: 172.
5. *Universalist* 51 (8 May 1869): [1].
6. Proceedings, General Convention, 1873, p. 44. The individual was not identified.
7. Cantwell, *Winchester Centennial,* p. 33.
8. *Beliefs Commonly Held Among Us* (Boston: Universalist Church of America), pp. 43-44.
9. The most complete record of Bisbee, his relations with the denomination, and his trial and disfellowshipping, is "The Minneapolis Radical Lectures and the Excommunication of the Reverend Herman Bisbee," *Journal of the Universalist Historical Society* 7 (1967-68): 3-69. Mary Florensia Bogue, granddaughter of Bisbee and daughter of Mabel Bisbee Bogue, reproduced in whole or in part several original documents possessed by her mother, as well as extracts from the denominational press, and added connective passages and her own commentary.
10. See Herman Bisbee, *Memoir of Rev. Seth Barnes* (Cincinnati: Williams & Cantwell, 1868).
11. *Universalist* 52 (8 April 1871): [3].
12. Ibid. 52 (29 April 1871): [2].
13. Ibid. 53 (17 February 1872): [2].
14. Ibid. 53 (9 March 1872): [2].
15. Ibid. 54 (2 November 1872): [2].
16. Italics in the original.
17. These are presented in some detail in Miss Bogue's account.
18. It should be noted that in his autobiography Tuttle mentions Bisbee only once, merely identifying him as one of a succession of pastors of the St. Anthony church.
19. A complete transcript of the proceedings of the board was appended to the annual report of the trustees and was printed in the Proceedings, Appendix, pp. 42-54.
20. The information recorded below was overlooked by Miss Bogue and those who assisted her in gathering the documentation for the article on her grandfather.
21. *Christian Leader* 51 (19 September 1880): 5.
22. *Universalist Leader* 10 (14 September 1907): 1168.
23. *Universalist* 57 (4 December 1875): [3].
24. Proceedings, General Convention, 1877, pp. 7, 15; 1878, p. 6.
25. *Christian Leader* 59 (16 October 1879): 1.
26. Ibid. 59 (23 October 1879): 8; 60 (8 January, 5 February 1880): 3, 2.
27. Proceedings, General Convention, 1880, p. 52.
28. *Christian Leader* 52 (13 October 1881): 1.
29. When the *Universalist* and the *Christian Leader* (New York) were consolidated in January 1879, the Winchester statement was carried on the front page of every issue. However, it was called the "Confession" rather than the historically proper "Profession." A few readers raised the question of when and why the change had taken place, but no one seemed to know. The words "Confession" and "Profession" were used interchangeably in denominational literature. The *Christian Leader* continued to use the word "Confession" which had come

into widespread usage after the centennial meeting of the General Convention. It apparently made the Winchester Profession somehow more "creedal," a fact which many Universalists thought quite appropriate since the denomination had become by 1870 a full-fledged church. When the *Universalist* (Chicago), the *Gospel Banner* (Maine), and the *Christian Leader* (Boston) were consolidated in 1897 as the *Universalist Leader,* the Winchester statement was still carried in each issue, but was designated "Profession."

30. *Christian Leader* 52 (3 November 1881): 2.

31. Ibid. 53 (26 October 1882): 4. This motion, which was defeated, was omitted from the official printed minutes.

32. *Christian Leader* 54 (8 November 1883): 4.

33. Ibid. 55 (13 November 1884): 5.

34. Proceedings, General Convention, 1887, p. 52.

35. For an abstract of the discussion, which was not included in the official minutes, see the *Christian Leader* 58 (27 October 1887): 4.

36. Ibid. 62 (9 July 1891): 2.

37. Ibid. 64 (12 October 1893): 2.

38. *New World* 3 (March 1894): 42.

39. *Christian Leader* 64 (20 July 1893): 5.

40. Ibid. 67 (1 July 1897): 8.

41. Ibid. 64 (27 September 1894): 4.

42. *Bibliotheca Sacra* 40 (July 1883): 473 n.

43. *Christian Leader* 65 (14, 21 November 1895): 4, 4.

44. Ibid. 67 (1 October 1896): 17.

45. The latter reference was to the third article alluding to things that were "profitable unto men." Sweetser had also deplored the utilitarian and materialistic philosophy which he thought was implied in the wording.

46. *Christian Leader* 66 (24 September 1896): 5.

47. Ibid. 66 (18 June 1896): 13.

48. Ibid. 67 (1 July 1897).

49. Proceedings, General Convention, 1897, pp. 79-81.

50. *Christian Leader* 67 (28 October, 4 November 1897): 10, 16. The story circulated that Sweetser merely said "here" rather than vote "yes," thus making the tally unanimous.

51. Ibid. 67 (25 February 1897): 13.

52. Ibid. 67 (29 April, 1 July 1897): 5, 3-5.

53. *New Unity* 4 (11 November 1897): 808.

54. Ibid. 4 (3 February 1898): 1100.

55. *Universalist Leader* 2 (7 October 1899): 5. The *Christian Leader* had become the *Universalist Leader* beginning with the issue of 4 December 1897.

56. *Universalist Leader* 2 (14 October 1899): 4.

57. Ibid.

58. Proceedings, General Convention, 1899, p. 20.

59. *Universalist Leader* 2 (16 September 1899): 14.

60. *Christian Leader* 67 (28 October 1897): 1.

61. *Universalist Leader* 2 (16 September, 11 November 1899): 14, 1.

62. Minutes, Year Book, 1924, p. 15.

63. *Universalist Leader* 23 (29 May 1920): 526.

64. Ibid. 2 (25 November 1899): 5.

65. For samples, see ibid. 2 (18 November 1899): 1.

66. Ibid. 3 (17 February 1900): 206.

67. Ibid. 6 (16 May 1903): 614.

68. *Winchester Centennial,* p. 42. An entire issue of the *Universalist Leader* (17 October 1903) was devoted to the Winchester celebration, including photographs and sketches.

69. "The Universalists," *The Religious History of New England: King's Chapel Lectures* (Cambridge: Harvard University Press: 1917), p. 310.

70. *Which Way? A Study of Universalists and Universalism* (Boston: Universalist Publishing House, 1921), p. 18.

71. *Universalist Leader* 26 (8 December 1923): 6-7.

72. The address, "And Practice Good Works," appeared in *Progress* 17 (November 1978): 5-8, published by the New Hampshire-Vermont District of Unitarian Universalist Societies.

73. See Elmo A. Robinson, "Universalism, A Changing Faith," *Annual Journal of the Universalist Historical Society* 2 (1960-61): 1-21.

Chapter 7: SCIENCE AND RELIGION: A DEBATE AVOIDED

1. Whitney R. Cross, *The Burned Over District: The Social and Intellectual History of Enthusiastic Religion in Western New York, 1800-1860* (Ithaca, N.Y.: Cornell University Press, 1950), p. 324. The Universalist publication cited by Cross was the *Evangelical Magazine* (Utica, New York).

2. *Our New Departure*, p. 38.

3. For a summary of early attempts by New England divines to reconcile Genesis and geology, see Conrad Wright, "The Religion of Geology," *New England Quarterly* 14 (1941): 335-58.

4. *Universalist Union* 8 (22 April 1843): 363-66.

5. *Universalist Quarterly* 2 (October 1845): 349-84. The author, identified only as "W. F.," might have been William Fishbough, a Universalist clergyman who was attacked by a fellow Universalist for having been a "rationalist."

6. "Beauty and Religion," *Rose of Sharon* (1847), pp. 9-32.

7. *Universalist Quarterly* 8 (October 1851): 329-49. The essay was written by "J. S. L.," probably John Stebbins Lee (1820-1902), a clergyman active in several Universalist educational projects.

8. Ibid. 14 (October 1857): 373-89.

9. *Christian Freeman* 21 (24 June 1859): 31.

10. Arthur M. Schlesinger, "A Critical Period in American Religion, 1875-1900," *Proceedings*, Massachusetts Historical Society 44 (June 1932): 523-47.

11. For the backgrond of this movement, see Jerry Wayne Brown, *The Rise of Biblical Criticism in America, 1800-1870: The New England Scholars* (Middletown, Conn.: Wesleyan University Press, 1969).

12. *The Ten Great Religions: An Essay in Comparative Theology* (Boston: James R. Osgood & Co., 1871). See the favorable review by Thomas B. Thayer, editor of the *Universalist Quarterly* 8 n.s. (October 1871): 494-98.

13. An intervening work, offering a provisional hypothesis of the inheritance of acquired characteristics, later discredited, was published in 1868.

14. *Universalist Quarterly* 11 (January 1854): 2. The article was signed only by the initials "W. S.," so the authorship is uncertain. Three Universalist clergy bore those initials in 1854: William Spaulding of West Haverhill, Massachusetts; William Sias of Plainfield, Vermont; and Warren Skinner of Proctorsville, Vermont.

15. *Christian Leader* 60 (25 July 1889): 2.

16. Ibid.

17. "Scripture and Science," *Trumpet* 45 (11 July 1863): 45.

18. *Moses and Modern Science* (Cincinnati, Ohio: Williamson & Cantwell Publishing Co., 1872).

19. Ibid., p. 87.

20. Ibid., pp. 99, 102, 104.

21. Ibid., p. 139.

22. For a brief analysis, based on articles and reviews appearing in the *Universalist Quarterly*, see Ernest Cassara, "The Effect of Darwinism on Universalist Belief, 1860-1900," *Annual Journal of the Universalist Historical Society* 1 (1959): 32-42. He discerned four stages of reaction: a brief period of hostility, followed by a decade of "cautious consideration," then a period of "growing sympathy," and finally, "joyful acceptance."

23. *Universalist Quarterly* 17 (April 1860): 127.

24. Ibid. 10 n.s. (April 1871): 259.

25. Ibid. 15 n.s. (April 1878): 186-98.

26. "The Human Race," ibid. 20 (October 1863): 347-67.

27. *Universalist Quarterly* 1 n.s. (January 1864): 67.

28. Ibid. 1 n.s. (October 1864): 414.

29. *Universalist* 55 (17 May 1873): 2 ff.

30. *Universalist Quarterly* 13 n.s. (January 1876): 114-18; 4 (October 1867): 486.

31. *Universalist* 57 (7 August 1875): [2].

32. Draper's work was first published in 1874 and went through several reprintings. It was first reviewed in the *Quarterly* in 1875 and again two years later, the second by Druley. *Universalist Quarterly* 12 n.s. (April 1875): 251-53; 14 n.s. (January 1877): 91-102.

33. *Universalist* 58 (9 December 1876): [3].

34. "Ethics and Evolution," *Universalist Quarterly* 17 n.s. (April 1880): 175-87.

35. *Universalist Quarterly* 22 (October 1885): 461.

36. *Christian Leader* 58 (5 January 1887):1.

37. Ibid. 62 (10 March 1892): 2.
38. Cone to Eliot, 12 October 1899, AUA Letterbooks.
39. *Universalist Leader* 8 (1 July 1905): 818.
40. Schlesinger "Critical Period," p. 526.
41. *Christian Leader* 57 (16 September 1886): 4.
42. *Universalist* (Chicago), cited in the *New Unity* 1 (30 May 1895): 202.
43. *New Unity* 1 (20 June 1895): 253.
44. "Science and Religion," *Universalist Quarterly* 19 n.s. (January 1882): 84-92.
45. *Christian Leader* 52 (27 October 1881): 4.
46. See his "Evolution and Revelation," *Universalist Quarterly* 22 n.s. (July 1885): 342-58.
47. *Christian Leader* 64 (22 February 1894): 4.
48. *Applied Evolution* (Boston: Eugene F. Endicott, 1900).
49. Ibid., p. 180.
50. Ibid., p. 248.
51. The sermon was reproduced in the *Christian Leader* 30 (12 February 1927): 207-208.
52. *Universalist Leader* 28 (3 October 1925): 14-15.
53. Quoted in ibid. 25 (1 April 1922): 4.
54. Rollin Lynde Hartt, "Down with Evolution!," *World's Work* 46 (October 1923): 607-608.
55. See Norman F. Furniss, *The Fundamentalist Controversy, 1918-1931* (New Haven: Yale University Press, 1954).
56. For a lively account, see Ray Ginger, *Six Days or Forever? Tennessee v. John Thomas Scopes* (Boston: Beacon Press, 1958; reprinted by Quadrangle Books, 1969).
57. Minutes, Year Book, 1924, pp. 64-65.
58. Ibid., 1926, pp. 62-63.
59. *Universalist Leader* 27 (9, 16 February 1924): 19-20, 13-16.
60. *Christian Leader* 29 (24 April 1926): 18.
61. *Universalist Leader* 27 (8 March 1924): 3-4.
62. Ibid. 27 (31 May 1924): 18.
63. Ibid. 26 (8 September 1923): 5-8.
64. Ibid. 26 (6 October 1923): 18-19.
65. *Christian Leader* 33 (17 May 1930): 615.

Chapter 8: THE BOND OF FELLOWSHIP AND STATEMENTS OF FAITH (1935)

1. For a leading statement by a Unitarian of the humanist position, see Curtis W. Reese, *Humanist Religion* (N.Y.: Macmillan, 1931).
2. For his ideas, see *Religion Can Make Sense* (Boston: Universalist Publishing House, 1949).
3. For his views, see *Humanism States Its Case* (Boston: Beacon Press, 1933).
4. This fact was called to the attention of the editor of the *Leader* by Potter after van Schaick had claimed that Scott had been the only Universalist on the list. *Christian Leader* 36 (27 May 1933): 661.
5. *Christian Leader* 35 (9 January 1932): 53-54.
6. Ibid., p. 53.
7. Ibid. 36 (29 April 1933): 532.
8. Ibid. 33 (1 February 1930): 131.
9. Ibid. 125 (17 April 1943): 246.
10. *Some Things Remembered*, p. 49.
11. *Christian Leader* 35 (17 December 1932): 1493.
12. Quoted in Scott, *Universalist Church*, p. 43.
13. For the complete text and a list of the first 114 individuals to sign it, see *The Humanist* 33 (September-October 1973): 4-9. For a negative critique, see Robert W. Haney, " 'Humanist Manifesto II ': A Personal Response," *Unitarian Universalist Christian* 30 (Autumn 1975): 39-48.
14. Minutes, Year Book, 1924, p. 63.
15. Ibid., 1928, p. 56.
16. *Christian Leader* 30 (17 December 1927): 1618.
17. An unsuccessful attempt was made in 1947 to remove this last vestige of restrictiveness. (Minutes, General Assembly, 1947, p. 5.) It was finally accomplished in 1953.
18. Minutes, Year Book, 1930, p. 27.
19. *Christian Leader* 34 (26 September 1931): 1236.
20. Ibid. 34 (10 October 1931): 1302-1303.

21. Quoted in ibid. 34 (25 July 1931): 944.

22. Ibid. 34 (7 November 1931): 1418.

23. The other members were Arthur W. Peirce, Charles Neal Barney, Leroy W. Coons, and L. S. McCollester.

24. *Christian Leader* 36 (11 March 1933): 295.

25. The editor of the *Leader* immediately suggested the following abbreviated declaration: "We believe in the Fatherhood of God, the Responsibility of Man, the Leadership of Jesus, the Victory of Good, and the Life Everlasting."

26. Minutes, Year Book, 1934, pp. 6, 8.

27. *Christian Leader* 38 (2 November 1935): 1386.

28. Ibid. 36 (28 January 1933): 115.

29. Ibid. 36 (1 April 1933): 405.

30. Minutes, General Assembly, 1946, p. 11.

31. Superintendent's Report, 1946, p. 11.

32. *Universalist Leader* 28 (24 October 1925): 9.

33. *Which Way? A Study of Universalists and Universalism* (Boston: Universalist Publishing House), p. 13.

34. Robinson, "Universalism, A Changing Faith," p. 16.

35. Minutes, General Convention, 1935; Year Book, 1936, p. 17.

36. *Beliefs Commonly Held Among Us* (Boston: Universalist Publishing House, 1940, 1945). The pamphlet had appeared originally in the *Helper* as "The Faith of a Free Church." A third printing in the form of a memorial edition, with a new Foreword, was published in 1945, two years after Perkins' death.

Chapter 9: THE INTERNATIONAL SCENE

1. See David Burg, *Chicago's White City* (Lexington, Ky.: University Press of Kentucky, 1976): Rossiter Johnson (ed.), *A History of the World's Columbian Exposition*. 4 vols. (N.Y.: D. Appleton & Co., 1897-1898); and Reid Badger, *The Great American Fair: The World's Columbian Exposition and American Culture* (N.Y.: Nelson-Hall, 1979).

2. *The World's Congress of Religions*, with an Introduction by Rev. Minot J. Savage (Boston: Arena Publishing Co., 1893), p. 3. This volume comprises verbatim addresses representing various religions, and includes a paper delivered by the Universalist clergyman Everett L. Rexford (pp. 237-44): and the address of welcome by Augusta J. Chapin, another Universalist minister (pp. 17-19). For the texts of the complete proceedings of the World's Parliament, see John Henry Barrows (ed.), *The World's Parliament of Religions: An illustrated and popular story of the World's First Parliament of Religions, held in Chicago in connection with the Columbian Exposition of 1893*. 2 vols. (Chicago: The Parliament Publishing Co., 1893). See also J. W. Hanson (ed.), *The World's Congress of Religions: The Addresses and Papers delivered before the Parliament, and an Abstract of the Congresses ... under the Auspices of the World's Columbian Exposition* (Chicago: W. B. Conkey Co., 1894); and Charles C. Bonney and Paul Carus, *The World's Parliament of Religions and the Religious Parliament Extension* (Chicago: Open Court Publishing Co., 1896).

3. Barrows, *World's Parliament* 1:38.

4. Ibid. 1:37.

5. Reproduced in ibid. 1: 509-22.

6. Reproduced in ibid. 1: 1076-78.

7. *Christian Leader* 65 (4 July 1895): 5.

8. For summaries of the Universalist Church Congress, see Barrows, *World's Parliament* 1: 1531-35; and Hanson, *World's Congress*, pp. 1078-98. The most detailed account is to be found in the *Universalist* (Chicago) (23 September 1893); reprinted in the *Christian Leader* 63 (28 September 1893): 1, 8. Twenty-five of the papers were reprinted in the *Columbian Congress of the Universalist Church* ... (Boston: Universalist Publishing House, 1894). Verbatim transcripts of many of the papers were also published from time to time in the denominational press, but not necessarily in the order in which they were originally presented. Unless otherwise noted, the account given here was derived from the *Christian Leader*.

9. Barrows, *World's Parliament* 1: 1531.

10. Proceedings, 1905, p. 9.

11. *Universalist Leader* 9 (13 October 1906): 1285.

12. Ibid. 10 (5 October 1907): 1256.
13. Ibid. 10 (12 October 1907): 1290-92; the address was reproduced in its entirety.
14. Proceedings, 1909, p. 94.
15. For a brief biography, see Hitchings, "Unitarian and Universalist Women Ministers," *Journal of the Universalist Historical Society* 10 (1975): 92-93.
16. *Universalist Leader* 13 (17 September, 31 December 1910): 1030-31, 1516-17.
17. Ibid. 16 (14 June, 16 August 1913): 755, 985; Trustee Report, 1913, p. 35.
18. Proceedings, 1913, p. 98.
19. Report of the Commission on Foreign Relations, Proceedings, 1915, p. 58.
20. *Christian Leader* 30 (5 November 1927): 1420.
21. Trustee files, Andover-Harvard Theological Library; Trustee Report, Year Book, 1931, p. 7.
22. *Universalist Leader* 13 (12 February 1910): 198.
23. Report of the Commission on Foreign Relations, Proceedings, 1911, pp. 103-105.
24. Proceedings, 1917, p. 67; *Universalist Leader* 28 (26 September 1925): 11-13.
25. *Christian Leader* 32 (30 November 1929): 1527.
26. Ibid. 34 (23 May 1931): 662.
27. Ibid. 34 (27 June 1931): 817.
28. Proceedings, Year Book, 1930, p. 27; *Christian Leader* 33 (15 November 1930): 1460, 1462.
29. Proceedings, Year Book, 1930, p. 26.

Chapter 10: THE NATIONAL SCENE

1. *Unity* 31 (22 June, 3 August 1893): 171, 269.
2. *Christian Leader* 65 (6 June 1895): 5.
3. See Charles H. Lyttle, *Freedom Moves West* (Boston: Beacon Press, 1952), especially Chapter 9.
4. Despite its subtitle, it was at first a bimonthly and became a weekly in mid-1885. The subtitle subsequently went through several changes.
5. See Thomas Graham, "Jenkin Lloyd Jones and the World's Columbian Exposition of 1893," *Collegium Proceedings* (Collegium: Association for Liberal Religious Studies) 1 (1979): 61-81.
6. The other publication was the *Non-Sectarian*, published in St. Louis, Missouri. The *Universalist Record*, first published in 1878 and renamed the *Universalist Monthly* in 1891, originated as a local church paper edited by W. S. Crowe in Newark, New Jersey. The paper was merged with the *Non-Sectarian* in 1894. *Unity* 33 (1 March 1894): 2-3. After publication of five volumes the *Non-Sectarian* was in turn merged in January 1896 with *To-Day*, edited by Frederick A. Bisbee, a Universalist clergyman in Philadelphia. This short-lived journal, begun in 1894, came to an end in March 1896. Thereupon the *Non-Sectarian*, still in need of a home, merged with the *New Unity* a month later. *New Unity* 3 (9 April 1896): 99.
7. *New Unity* 1 n.s. (7 March 1895): 2.
8. *Unity* 32 (1 February 1894): 340.
9. For a copy of the call and names of respondents, see *Unity* 33 (12 April 1894): 76-78.
10. *New Unity* 1 (27 June 1895): 257.
11. Proceedings, *New Unity* 4 (27 October 1898): 134.
12. Proceedings, *Unity* 33 (27 September 1894): 435.
13. *New Unity* 1 (7 March 1895): 16.
14. *Christian Leader* 64 (21 June 1894): 5.
15. *To-Day* 2 (April 1895): 207.
16. *New Unity* 1 n.s. (21 March 1895): 33.
17. Ibid. 4 n.s. (21 January 1897): 327.
18. It was reproduced in *Unity* 48 (28 November 1901): 199-202 (first version); and in the *Universalist Leader* 10 (12 October 1907): 1290-92 (second version).
19. Among the Unitarians he cited, with direct quotation, were Minot J. Savage, Brooke Hereford, and Charles Wendte; and for the Universalists, Asa Saxe, Orello Cone, and George H. Emerson.
20. After a thirteen-year pastorate in Newark, New Jersey, in 1897 Crowe became pastor of the Church of Eternal Hope (New York City); he died in 1914. *Universalist Leader* 17 (26 December 1914): 1262.
21. *Unity* 33 (11 October 1894): 457.
22. *Universalist Monthly*, quoted in *Unity* 31 (31 August 1893): 333.
23. The twelve lectures were published under the title *Phases of Religion in America* (Newark, N.J.: Ward and Tichenor, 1893).

Notes for Chapter 10

24. Ibid., p. 40.
25. *New World* 3 (March 1894): 180; this publication was the successor to the *Unitarian Review*.
26. *Unity* 3 (29 March 1894): 55-56.
27. *The Unitarian: A Magazine of Liberal Christianity* 9 (May 1894): 206.
28. See Alcott, "Universalism a Progressive Faith," *New World* 3 (March 1894): 38-55.
29. The letter from the convention committee on fellowship was reproduced, together with Alcott's reply, in *Unity* 33 (21 February 1895): 693-94.
30. *New Unity* 1 n.s. (4 July 1895): 273.
31. Ibid. 1 n.s. (28 November 1895): 611.
32. Ibid.
33. The documents mentioned here are to be found in the *New Unity* 1 n.s. (28 March, 18 April 1895): 54, 108-10.
34. Ibid. 1 n.s. (13 June 1895): 230.
35. *Unity* 33 (25 October 1894): 481-82.
36. *Christian Leader* 62 (8 October 1891): 4; 65 (26 September 1895): 2; *Universalist Register*, 1892, pp. 35, 106.
37. *Christian Leader* 64 (20 September 1894): 1.
38. *New Unity* 5 n.s. (29 April 1897): 163.
39. Ibid. 2 n.s. (15 October 1896): 97, 101-102.
40. Proceedings, *New Unity* 4 n.s. (26 November 1896): 200-201.
41. *New Unity* 4 n.s. (23 September 1897): 641.
42. White to the editor, 20 December 1894, reprinted in *Unity* 33 (17 January 1895): 634-35.
43. Lyttle, *Freedom Moves West*, p. 241.
44. *New Unity* 4 n.s. (5 May 1898): 228.
45. *Christian Leader* 61 (11 March 1880): 4.
46. *Unity* 32 (23 November 1893): 177-78.
47. Quoted in the *New Unity* 1 n.s. (27 June 1895): 257.
48. *Universalist Leader* 3 (24 March 1900): 365, 367.
49. It was reprinted in *Unity* 33 (31 January 1895): 651-53.
50. *Universalist Leader* 4 (15 June 1901): 744.
51. Ibid. 10 (21 December 1907): 1610.
52. Extract from Proceedings, *New Unity* 3 n.s. (15 October 1896): 108-109.
53. *New Unity* 3 n.s. (19 November 1896): 188.
54. *Universalist Leader* 4 (15 June 1901): 747.
55. Ibid., pp. 747-48.
56. Minutes, Board of Directors, *New Unity* 1 n.s. (11 April 1895): 90.
57. *New Unity* 1 n.s. (13 June 1895): 228 ff.
58. The remark is supposed to have been made by Stephen Pearl Andrews to P. T. Barnum. *New Unity* 1 n.s. (19 December 1895): 661.
59. For the text of Cone's address, see the *New Unity* 1 n.s. (18 July 1895): 307-10.
60. For an elaboration of his plans, see ibid. 1 n.s. (12 July 1895): 291-93.
61. Minutes, in ibid. 1 n.s. (13 June 1895): 235.
62. *Christian Register* 74 (13 June 1895): 373-74.
63. *New Unity* 1 n.s. (20 June 1895): 241.
64. Ibid. 1 n.s. (27 June 1895): 268.
65. Ibid. 1 n.s. (11 July 1895): 295.
66. Ibid. 1 n.s. (4 July 1895): 283-84.
67. *To-Day* 2 (September 1895): 460-62.
68. For the proceedings, see the *New Unity* 4 (26 November 1896): 195-96. The complete record was never published in pamphlet form because of lack of funds.
69. *New Unity* 4 (3 December 1896): 211.
70. *Universalist Leader* 3 (6 January 1900): 8.
71. Proceedings, *New Unity* 4 (28 October 1897): 768-69.
72. The paper was reproduced in the *New Unity* 4 (18 November 1897): 836-40.
73. *New Unity* 4 (3 March 1898): 2-18.
74. *Universalist Leader* 3 (14 April 1900): 477.
75. Proceedings, *Unity* 45 (17 May 1900): 180.
76. Ibid., p. 177.
77. In ibid. 47 (4 July 1901): 277.
78. Lyttle, *Freedom Moves West*, p. 223.
79. *Universalist Leader* 6 (5 December 1903): 1541.
80. Ibid. 8 (25 February 1905): 244.
81. Ibid. 12 (2 June 1909): 25.
82. Ibid. 12 (20 February 1909): 238.
83. This plan was modified in 1915, providing for two official representatives

from each denomination as well as individual membership. Hall and Lee were the representatives of the General Convention that year. *Universalist Leader* 18 (3 July 1915): 645-46.

84. In ibid. 12 (8 May 1909): 590-92.

85. Universalist Church general files, Andover-Harvard Theological Library.

86. *Universalist Leader* 16 (22 February 1913): 236-39.

87. Ibid. 14 (13, 20 May, 10 June 1911): 592-93, 627, 720.

88. This organization, which had maintained an erratic existence since 1867, met in Boston in 1916, with John Haynes Holmes as president. Plans were made to celebrate its fiftieth anniversary in 1917. *Universalist Leader* 19 (10 June 1916): 573.

89. *Universalist Leader* 16 (22 February 1913): 236-39.

90. Ibid. 18 (20 March 1915): 267.

91. Ibid. 20 (8 December 1917): 878.

92. Ibid. 20 (17 February 1917): 101.

93. Ibid. 22 (13 December 1919): 1231.

94. *Christian Leader* 32 (30 November 1929): 1521.

95. Ibid. 35 (20 February 1932): 240.

96. Ibid. 36 (8 July 1933): 860-61.

Chapter 11: INSTITUTIONAL ACTIVITIES AND ORGANIZATIONS

1. Records, Washington Association, August 1874.

2. Theological education is treated separately; see Chapters 16 and 17.

3. Proceedings, General Convention, 1880, pp. 45-47.

4. *Universalist Register*, 1874, p. 24.

5. *Universalist Leader* 24 (5 February 1921): 155.

6. *Christian Leader* 128 (18 May 1946): 239.

7. See the Year Book, 1922, p. 74.

8. Ibid., 1924, pp. 72 ff.

9. United States Department of Commerce, Bureau of Statistics, *Census of Religious Bodies, 1906, 1916* (Washington, D.C.: Government Printing Office, 1910, 1919), pp. 96-97, 72, 73.

10. *Universalist Leader* 15 (20 April 1912): 499.

11. Ibid. 20 (27 January 1917): 57.

12. Ibid. 21 (21 December 1918): 983.

13. *Christian Leader* 39 (18 January 1936): 66.

14. Ibid. 119 (6 November 1937): 1415.

15. Report of the General Superintendent, 1946, p. 7; *Christian Leader* 129 (4 October 1947): 438.

16. Report of the General Superintendent, 1947, p. 10.

17. *Chrstian Leader* 129 (4 October 1947): 437-41.

18. MacPherson, "Universalist Churches," p. 79.

19. *Universalist Leader* 3 (5 September 1900): 1137.

20. Trustee Report, 1917.

21. Proceedings, 1911, pp. 14, 90.

22. Ibid., 1913, p. 6.

23. *Universalist Leader* 19 (1 April 1916): 329.

24. Ibid. 20 (14 July 1917): 457.

25. Ibid. 22 (15 November 1919): 1095; Year Book, 1921, p. 67.

26. Ibid., 1921, pp. 58-59.

27. Proceedings, Year Book, 1924, p. 15.

28. *Universalist Leader* 27 (24 May 1924): 23.

29. Trustee Report, 1925, Year Book, 1926, p. 33.

30. Ibid., 1927, Year Book, 1928, p. 32; *Christian Leader* 30 (22 October 1927): 1374.

31. *Christian Leader* 31 (19 May, 9 June, 8 September 1928): 636-37, 730, 1122; Year Book, 1929, pp. 7-8.

32. *Christian Leader* 119 (6 November 1937): 1438.

33. Ibid. 37 (6 January 1934): 4.

34. Brooks, *Recollections*, p. 35.

35. Minutes, 1939, Biennial Reports, p. 9.

36. *Christian Leader* 121 (15 April 1939): 345.

37. Ibid. 122 (21 December 1940): 1151.

38. Trustee Report, 1943, p. 37.

39. Ibid., 1946, Directory and Biennial Reports, 1948, pp. 17, 37; Report of the General Superintendent, 1946, p. 6.

40. *Christian Leader* 130 (5 June 1948): 244; Report of the General Superintendent, 1949; *Christian Leader* 131 (November 1949): 419.
41. Report, Department of the Ministry, 1951.
42. *Universalist Leader* 140 (June 1958): 144.
43. Proceedings, 1911, pp. 14, 86.
44. Trustee Report, *Universalist Leader* 20 (10 February 1917): 87.
45. Proceedings, 1917, pp. 19, 37-38; *Christian Leader* 31 (26 May 1928): 645.
46. *Universalist Leader* 20 (15 September 1917): 605.
47. *Christian Leader* 30 (13 August 1927): 1036.
48. Ministerial fellowship records, Andover-Harvard Theological Library.
49. Minutes, Year Book, 1924, p. 12. Neither the reports of the committee which was responsible for drafting revisions nor the revised version was included in either the minutes or supporting documents.
50. *Universalist Leader* 27 (3, 24 May 1924): 4, 23.
51. Year Book, 1926, p. 77.
52. *Universalist Leader* 27 (12 December 1924): 8.
53. Trustee Report, 1925; Year Book, 1926, pp. 34-35; *Christian Leader* 36 (29 July 1933): 958.
54. Proceedings, Year Book, 1926, p. 35.
55. *Universalist Leader* 28 (26 September 1925): 14-15.
56. Trustee Report, 1929; Year Book, 1930, p. 34.
57. *Christian Leader* 31 (7 July 1928): 851.
58. Ibid. 36 (14 January 1933): 39.
59. Minutes, General Convention, 1939; Directory and Biennial Reports, p. 14. They were listed separately in the 1939-1940 Directory, pp. 124-27.
60. *Christian Leader* 38 (25 May 1935): 665; Directory, 1936.
61. Ibid. 134 (September 1952): 218; Minutes, General Assembly, 1957, 1959.
62. *Universalist Leader* 137 (May 1955): 115.
63. *Christian Leader* 33 (19 July 1930): 920.
64. For Rice's own explanation of his action, see the *Christian Leader* 32 (10 August 1929): 998-1000.
65. *Christian Leader* 33 (12 April 1930): 473-74.
66. The text of the revised laws was included as part of the minutes in the Year Book, 1934, pp. 10-13, 14.
67. *Christian Leader* 36 (28 October 1933): 1354.
68. Ibid. 119 (30 October 1937): 1390.
69. One issue the Central Fellowship Committee was called upon to settle in 1936 involved Elmo A. Robinson (1887-1972), for eight years on the faculty of San Jose State (Teachers) College in California. He had been suspended by the fellowship committee of the state convention because the General Convention fellowship laws made mandatory the dropping of any Universalist clergyman engaged in secular business not connected with denominational interests. Robinson appealed, and as a result the dropping of fellowship because of involvement in secular business was made "permissive" rather than mandatory when the laws of fellowship were again revised in 1937. *Christian Leader* 119 (30 October 1937): 1390. Robinson encountered the same difficulty with the Unitarians, with whom he also held fellowship. He was dropped completely in 1945 after a long and generally inconclusive correspondence with AUA headquarters. After his retirement from teaching he became minister of the Unitarian church in Los Alamos, New Mexico, and was restored to full fellowship.
70. *Christian Leader* 122 (6 April 1940): 318.
71. Louis C. Cornish, Presidential Address, AUA Annual Meeting, 19 May 1931.
72. *Christian Leader* 35 (29 October 1932): 1269-70.
73. For the constitution and bylaws, see the *Christian Leader* 32 (9 November 1929): 1427; Year Book, 1933, pp. 34-35.
74. Records, General Assembly, 1951.
75. Annual Report, Massachusetts Bay District Executive Director, 1964-65.
76. Unless otherwise noted, all information regarding this organization was derived from its records.
77. As originally planned, those too distant to attend regularly were to be considered "honorary" members. The only exception ever made to this rule in the first half-century of the Fraters was the election of John A. Cousens to honorary membership;

he was a layman and president of Tufts College at the time.

78. *Christian Leader* 32 (23 February 1929): 230.

79. For a selected list of individual lay contributors, see Scott, *The Universalist Church of America*, pp. 62-63.

80. *Trumpet* 11 (24 April 1830): 170.

81. *Universalist Leader* 9 (10, 17 February 1906): 185, 209.

82. Ibid. 9 (1 December 1906): 1517-18.

83. Correspondence, Universalist Club of Boston.

84. *Universalist Leader* 10 (11, 25 May 1907): 582-83, 645.

85. Ibid. 10 (9 November 1907): 1415, 1418.

86. Ibid. 23 (28 August 1920): 799-800.

87. Ibid. 24 (5 November 1921): 1174.

88. Ibid. 26 (3 November 1923): 18.

89. Trustee Report, 1920, pp. 30-31.

90. *Universalist Leader* 24 (19 February 1921): 213-15.

91. Year Book, 1923, p. 40.

92. Ibid., 1926, p. 30.

93. Trustee Report, 1926, pp. 30-31.

94. Year Book, 1926, p. 108.

95. *Christian Leader* 29 (13 March 1926): 4-5.

96. Year Book, 1932, p. 14; 1934, p. 45.

97. *Christian Leader* 38 (3, 31 August 1935): 989, 1110-11.

98. Ibid. 125 (6 February 1943): 91.

99. Ibid. 132 (November 1950): 367-68; 133 (February 1951): 70.

100. Ibid. 134 (February 1952): 40.

101. *Universalist Leader* 138 (September 1956): 192.

102. Ibid. 141 (June 1959): 150.

103. Minutes, Joint Meeting, October 1936, pp. 13-14.

Chapter 12: THE CHURCH AND ITS YOUTH

1. *Gospel Banner*, 31 October 1889, quoted in the *Christian Leader* 121 (8 July 1939): 635.

2. This was the name under which the organization was incorporated under Massachusetts law in 1893; it was reincorporated in 1898 in order to hold property and receive bequests, and to conduct its business outside the state. After local unions were organized in Canada and Japan the national body was known as the Central Union, but the word "National" was officially retained until the YPCU became the Universalist Youth Fellowship in 1941. There have been several historical sketches prepared at various stages in its evolution. The first, published in 1893, was in the form of an "historical souvenir" pamphlet edited by Carl F. Henry and Herbert B. Briggs. It was followed by one prepared by Clara B. Adams as a preface to the report of the Decennial Anniversary Convention held in Lynn in 1889, 1,000 copies of which were printed. In 1900 Lewis B. Fisher prepared *A Brief History of the Universalist Church* by direction of the YPCU, but its publication was delayed for a year because of lack of funds; the work included a chapter-length history of the youth organization in which the author had himself played a part during its preliminary stages. A fourth edition appeared in 1913, with updated material included as footnotes. A "miniature history" was prepared in 1914 by Frederick A. Bisbee as part of the celebration of the twenty-fifth anniversary of the YPCU. Yet another, "A Brief History of the Young People's Christian Union, 1889-1939," by Harry Adams Hersey, was published to celebrate the fiftieth anniversary, and appeared in the *Christian Leader* 121 (8 July 1939): 634-51. Hersey was exceptionally well qualified to prepare a complete history, for by 1939 he had held continuous membership for forty-five years. He was not only the national secretary for a time, but edited its paper for seven years and was present at twenty-six of its annual conventions. He had gathered and organized great quantities of material, but the uncertain financial status of the YPCU had frustrated his original intent to publish a detailed and comprehensive history. A more recent work by Wayne B. Arnason, *Follow the Gleam*, was published in 1980 as a comparative study of the Universalist and Unitarian youth movements. Unless otherwise indicated, all material in the present account is derived from these sources, and from the official records, including *Onward*, its chief publication.

3. There is a minor discrepancy in statistics, repeated by various sources. The YPCU Handbook (1935 edition) indicated 133 delegates from 62 societies, but the number of states represented seemed not to have been in question.

4. Hersey, "Brief History," p. 635.

5. Stanley Manning, Director of Young People's Work, who addressed the annual meeting of the Unitarian youth group in 1920, found them very different from the Universalists. Little was said that "suggested devotional and missionary activity." *Universalist Leader* 23 (12 June 1920): 587.

6. Proceedings, 1884, p. 13.

7. *Christian Leader* 65 (17 April 1884): 5.

8. For a critical view of such church-sponsored, adult-dominated, and paternalistically operated youth organizations in the late nineteenth century as Christian Endeavor, see Joseph F. Kett, *Rites of Passage: Adolescence in America, 1790 to the Present* (N.Y.: Basic Books, 1977), especially pp. 189-211.

9. *Christian Leader* 50 (23 October 1884): 1.

10. Proceedings, General Convention, 1885, pp. 10-11.

11. Much of the biographical information given here was derived from the reminiscences of James D. Tillinghast and Walter Stuart Kelley, published in the *Christian Leader* 36 (1 July, 2 September 1933): 821, 1110. Kelley, who was superintendent of the Sunday school at the First Universalist Church in Lowell, Massachusetts, had organized a Christian Endeavor society there early in 1888 and was chairman of the committee that drew up the YPCU constitution.

12. This publication should not be confused with a denominational paper of the same title published in New York City between 1835 and 1847.

13. Constitutional amendments were proposed recurrently, the first in 1901, to provide for biennial meetings alternating with those of the General Convention, but no such action was ever taken.

14. Reproduced in *Onward* 1 (19 July 1894): 6.

15. *Christian Leader* 61 (4 December 1890): 2.

16. Ibid. 66 (25 June 1896): 1.

17. The hymn was never officially adopted. Repeated attempts were made by numerous individuals to compose an original song, but the organization was unable to agree on one.

18. *Christian Leader* 61 (30 October 1890): 1.

19. Bisbee, "Miniature History," p. 22.

20. YPCU Handbook, 1935, p. 5.

21. This was the first national convention held under the revised charter, which allowed freedom of choice as to meeting place. Previously, at least seven members of the executive board were required to be residents of Massachusetts.

22. Annual conventions held outside metropolitan areas were at Murray Grove (New Jersey), Turkey Run State Park (Indiana), and Camp Hill (Alabama).

23. *Christian Leader* 34 (18 April 1931): 502.

24. Of the sixty-two youth groups represented at the first convention, thirty-two were so designated. Somewhat ironically, the Christian Endeavor society in Lynn, where the YPCU had been organized, did not change its name until 1896.

25. Year Book, 1936, p. 36.

26. *Onward* 2 (26 July 1895): 103. There is no documentation for this in YPCU records. Their decision to hold their own meeting in Boston had been many months earlier.

27. *Christian Leader* 66 (25 July 1895): 1.

28. *Onward* 1 (29 March 1894): 3.

29. Ibid. 1 (27 September 1894): 3.

30. Ibid. 1 (7 June 1894): 5.

31. Hersey, "Brief History," p. 643.

32. *Universalist Register,* 1891, p. 66.

33. *Encyclopedia of Associations* (Detroit, Mich.: Gale Research Co.), 18th ed. (1984), p. 14241.

0. 34. *Universalist Leader* 14 (2 September 1911): 114-15.

35. Ibid. 15 (10 February 1912): 192.

36. *Onward* 1 (26 April 1894): 5.

37. Ibid. 1 (7 June 1894): 6.

38. Ibid. 2 (29 March 1895): 33.

39. Ibid. 2 (1 November 1895): 159.

40. *Christian Leader* 65 (17 January 1895).

41. *Universalist Leader* 25 (4 March 1922): 17.

42. *Christian Leader* 123 (25 October 1941): 855.

43. Ibid. 123 (17 May 1941): 437.

44. *Universalist Leader* 14 (28 January 1911): 114.

45. Ibid. 18 (5 June 1915): 538-39.

46. Ibid. 19 (26 February 1916): 205.

47. *Christian Leader* 39 (25 January 1936): 111.

48. Proceedings, 1895, pp. 9, 64.

49. The Unitarian youth group received national publicity by way of an Associated Press dispatch when its first woman president was elected in 1944 and took office the following year.

50. *Praise and Thanks: A Hymn Book for the Young People's Christian Union of the Universalist Church* (Boston: Universalist Publishing House) was published in 1895 and went through several editions. It was followed by *Praise and Thanks No. 2*, and still later by *Songs of Work and Worship*.

51. *Universalist Leader* 24 (5 November 1921): 1180.

52. Annual Report, Universalist Publishing House, 1896, *Christian Leader* 66 (4 June 1896): 17.

53. Mrs. Bruce is also known for the Wayside Chapel built near her home in Malden, Massachusetts. For over twenty years she conducted daily services there. It has been estimated that at least 80,000 people attended over the years. Fisher, *Brief History*, p. 169 n.

54. *Christian Leader* 1 (3 December 1898): 9.

55. *Universalist Leader* 4 (5 October 1901): 1255.

56. YPCU Report, 1929; Year Book, 1930, p. 113.

57. See *Onward* 2 (17 May 1895): 61; and George W. Knepper, *New Lamps for Old: One Hundred Years of Urban Higher Education at the University of Akron* (Akron: University of Akron, 1970), pp. 45-46.

58. *Onward* 2 (31 May 1895): 71.

59. *Christian Leader* 62 (14 April 1892): 2-3.

60. Ibid. 62 (5 November 1891): 2-3.

61. *Universalist Register*, 1885, p. 95.

62. *Onward* 1 (10 May 1894): 8.

63. *Christian Leader* 61 (4 December 1890): 1.

64. Ibid. 64 (31 August 1893): 5.

65. Knepper, *New Lamps for Old*, p. 23.

66. *Onward* 1 (10 May 1894): 8.

67. *Christian Leader* 61 (30 October, 13 November 1890): 4, 5.

68. Hersey, "Brief History," p. 635.

69. *Christian Leader* 62 (14 April, 20 October 1892): 2-3, 1.

70. *Onward* 1 (10 May 1894): 8.

71. *Christian Leader* 65 (25 July 1895): 2.

72. McGlauflin considered Knoxville the second YPCU mission project and Atlanta the third. *Onward* 4 (6 August 1897): 106.

73. *Christian Leader* 65 (25 July 1895): 2.

74. Trustee Report, *Universalist Leader* 6 (6 June 1903): 722.

75. *Universalist Leader* 7 (19 March 1904): 383.

76. Ibid. 3 (28 July 1900): 934, 945-50.

77. One of the first pledges made by the YPCU had been $100 to assist in constructing a church for Negroes in Norfolk, Virginia, but there is no indication that it was ever paid.

78. *Onward* 4 (6 August 1897): 107.

79. *Universalist* 47 (19 August 1865): [1].

80. Ibid. 54 (2 November 1872): [2].

81. *Christian Leader* 62 (25 June 1891): 2.

82. *Universalist Leader* 8 (15 April 1905): 468.

83. *Christian Leader* 65 (18 April 1895): 5.

84. Ibid. 33 (15 March 1930): 336.

85. Ibid. 119 (28 August 1937): 1103.

86. Ibid. 127 (20 January 1945): 31.

87. *Onward* 1 (January 1894): 4.

88. Ibid. 27 (17 September 1920): 218.

89. *Christian Leader* 38 (31 August 1935): 1105.

90. Ibid. 39 (29 August 1936): 1094-95; Year Book, 1936, p. 12.

91. Year Book, 1937-38, p. 31.

92. *Christian Leader* 120 (17 September 1938): 1123.

93. Minutes, General Assembly, 1946; Directory and Biennial Reports, 1948, p. 20.

94. *Christian Leader* 38 (17 August 1935): 1045-47.

95. YPCU Report, Year Book, 1936, p. 36.

96. Year Book, 1934, p. 41.

97. *Christian Leader* 30 (19 November 1927): 1495.

98. Year Book, 1933, p. 21.

99. *Christian Leader* 32 (27 July 1929): 937-39.

100. Ibid. 29 (14 August 1926): 20.

101. The most detailed account, largely a summary of the minutes of annual meetings and board sessions, is Frances Bradley Morrison, "The Young People's Christian Union of Massachusetts and Rhode Island from June 1889 to March 1939" (Norwood, Mass.: Fiftieth Anniversary Committee [1939], mimeographed). Unless otherwise noted, the material on the state organization included here was derived from this source.

102. *Christian Leader* 32 (5 January 1929): 26.

103. Trustee Minutes, ibid. 32 (11 May 1929): 599.

104. *Christian Leader* 33 (22 November 1930): 1488-89.

105. Ibid. 126 (1 January 1944): 11.

106. Annual Report, YPCU, 1905; Proceedings, General Convention, pp. 76-77.

107. *Christian Leader* 126 (1 January 1944): 7.

108. Ibid. 67 (3 June 1897): 4-5.

109. *Universalist Leader* 28 (28 February 1925): 27.

110. Ibid. 27 (12 July 1924): 21.

111. Proceedings, 1899, p. 97.

112. *Christian Leader* 36 (12 August 1933): 1014-15.

113. Free Church Fellowship files, Andover-Harvard Theological Library.

114. *Christian Leader* 37 (10 March 1934): 293.

115. Ibid. 37 (9 June 1934): 725-26. Extracts from the diary kept jointly by John Brigham and Homer Thomas of an eight-week tour of Indiana were published in installments in the *Leader*.

116. *Christian Leader* 38 (16 November 1935): 1458-59.

117. Report of Advisory Committee, YPCU files.

118. *Christian Leader* 120 (15 October 1938): 1248-51.

119. Proceedings, General Convention, 1891, p. 56.

120. Fisher, *Brief History*, p. 128.

121. Proceedings, 1899, pp. 90-92; 1900, p. 4.

122. Official Reports, Proceedings, 1909, pp. 91-93.

123. Proceedings, 1911, pp. 11, 88.

124. *Universalist Leader* 16 (8 November 1913): 1314.

125. For the constitution and bylaws, see the Proceedings, 1913, pp. 99-102. The word "National" in the title was considered but abandoned because there were Universalist Sunday schools in both Canada and Japan.

126. Proceedings, General Convention, 1914, pp. 36-37.

127. Trustee Report, 1917, p. 17.

128. *Christian Leader* 31 (28 July 1928): 942-45.

129. *Universalist Leader* 26 (3 November 1923): 18; Year Book, 1928, pp. 98-99.

130. Year Book, 1934, p. 38.

131. GSSA Report, ibid., 1933, p. 17.

132. Trustee Report, 1873, pp. 29-30.

133. Proceedings, General Convention, 1879, p. 39; 1880, p. 61.

134. Trustee Report, Year Book, 1923, p. 33.

135. GSSA Report, 1933; *Christian Leader* 36 (21 October 1933): 1330-33.

136. *Christian Leader* 36 (16 December 1933): 1587.

137. They were for Asian relief, refugee children, and for the community center for Blacks in Suffolk, Virginia.

138. *Christian Leader* 128 (18 May 1946): 236.

Chapter 13: SUMMER INSTITUTES: COMBINING RELIGION AND RECREATION

1. *Christian Leader* 59 (13 September 1888): 5.

2. See Victoria and Robert Ormond Case, *We Called It Culture: The Story of Chautauqua* (Garden City, N.Y.: Doubleday, 1948), a popular treatment.

3. *Universalist* 59 (6, 13 April 1878): [2], [3].

4. Ibid. 60 (3, 24 August 1878): [3], [2].

5. *Universalist Leader* 9 (14, 21 April 1906): 476-77, 508.

6. McGlauflin, *Faith With Power*, p. 73.

7. *Universalist Leader* 9 (28 April 1906): 542.

8. *Christian Leader* 57 (9 September 1886): 4.

9. *Trumpet* 5 n.s. (1 June 1833): 195.

10. *Christian Leader* 52 (15 December 1881): 2.

11. *Universalist* 60 (27 July 1878): [3].

12. *Universalist Leader* 1 (8 January 1898): 5.

13. Report of the Murray Grove Association.

14. *Universalist Leader* 8 (16 September 1905): 1169.

15. Ibid. 12 (4 December 1909): 1549-50; 13 (12 February 1910): 207-208.

16. Ibid. 15 (7 September 1912): 1130-31; 16 (27 December 1913): 1498.

17. Samples are in the files of the Andover-Harvard Theological Library.

18. *Universalist Leader* 18 (24 July 1915): 708-709.

19. Ibid. 25 (17 June 1922): 20.

20. Year Book, 1934, p. 50.

21. *Universalist Leader* 140 (January 1958): 30.

22. Barbara L. Harwi to Carl Seaburg, 23 February 1970. The typescript draft of the book is in the Andover-Harvard Theological Library.

23. See Louis C. Cornish, *The Story of the Isles of Shoals* (Boston: Beacon Press, 1916, 1936) and Lyman V. Rutledge, *Ten Miles Out: Guide Book to the Isles of Shoals* (Boston: Isles of Shoals Association, 5th ed., 1972).

24. *Universalist Leader* 8 (5 August 1905): 975-77.

25. *Christian Leader* 66 (11 June 1896): 17.

26. Ibid. 64 (24 August 1893): 2.

27. Ibid. 30 (16 July 1927): 925.

28. Universalist Register, 1908, p. 28.

29. *Universalist Leader* 9 (30 June 1906): 828.

30. Ibid. 1 (11 June 1898): 18.

31. Ibid. 1 (20 August 1898): 15.

32. *Christian Leader* 49 (7 August 1879): 8.

33. The definitive history, published by the denomination in 1948, is *Universalists at Ferry Beach: A History,* prepared by Katharine Augusta Sutton, Professor of History and Government at Teachers College, Danbury, Connecticut from 1921 to 1945; and Robert Francis Needham, secretary of the Ferry Beach Park Association from 1932 to 1944.

34. *Christian Leader* 119 (13 February 1937): 207-10.

35. Ibid. 123 (11 October 1941): 830.

36. Ibid. 126 (3 June 1944): 350.

37. Ibid. 125 (18 September 1943): 573.

38. Ibid. 124 (16 May 1942): 312.

39. Ibid. 126 (5 February 1944): 93.

40. Sutton and Needham, "Preface," *Ferry Beach.*

41. *Christian Leader* 35 (12 March 1932): 346.

42. Ibid. 120 (28 May 1938): 688-89.

Chapter 14: PUBLICATIONS AND SCHOLARSHIP

1. "One Hundred Years of Universalist Journalism," *Universalist Leader* 22 (4 January 1919): 11-12.

2. *Christian Leader* 65 (18 April 1895): 4.

3. Ibid. 65 (2 May 1895): 1.

4. Ibid. 127 (20 October 1945): 476.

5. *Universalist Leader* 135 (October 1953): 258.

6. *The Edge* 1 (Issue No. 3), [n.d.].

7. For a detailed and appreciative review of the first volume by Eddy's mentor, T. J. Sawyer, see the *Universalist Quarterly* 22 n.s. (April 1885): 222-36. The second volume was never reviewed in the *Quarterly,* probably for two reasons. Sawyer was undoubtedly the best qualified person in the denomination to have done so, but he would have been put in an awkward position, for the volume was dedicated to him in fulsome language. In addition, Eddy himself had become editor of the *Quarterly* the same year the second volume appeared, following the death of Thayer, and it might have seemed self-serving under the circumstances. Instead, the volume was frequently mentioned in the columns of the *Leader,* and excerpts or summaries based on the work appeared frequently in the fall and winter of 1886-87.

8. Annual Report, Universalist Publishing House, *Christian Leader* 51 (1 July 1880): 3.

9. *Christian Leader* 55 (13 November 1884): 5; 57 (18 November 1886): 8.

10. For a recent study see Kenneth M. Johnson, "The Doctrine of Universal Salvation and the Restorationist Controversy in

Early Nineteenth Century New England" (unpublished PhD dissertation, University of Ottawa, 1978).

11. However, Eddy did fill in many of the gaps later, with detailed histories of such topics as Sunday schools, temperance, and the evolution of Universalist theology and the organizational development of the denomination. The articles appeared in such publications as the *Universalist Quarterly* and the *Leader*.

12. For biographical sketches and memorials, see the *Universalist Register*, 1907, pp. 103-107; *Universalist Leader* 9 (1 September 1906): 1105; and the *Tufts College Graduate* 4 (October 1906): 12-22. In 1980 the Andover-Harvard Theological Library acquired two of Eddy's scrapbooks, but his notes and other papers have not yet come to light.

13. Eddy served as Sawyer's biographer after the latter's death, at the request of the Sawyer family. See *The Life of Thomas J. Sawyer, S.T.D., LL.D and of Caroline M. Sawyer* (Boston: Universalist Publishing House, 1900).

14. Eddy dedicated the first volume of his history to John A. McAllister of Philadelphia, who had assisted him in collecting material.

15. *Universalist* 57 (22 January 1876). Whittemore's history had first appeared in 1830; in the 1850s he had undertaken to expand and update it, but only the first of the two volumes planned was actually published (1860), a year before Whittemore's death, and covered the European origins of Universalism. The second volume was to have covered Universalism in America.

16. *Universalist Leader* 27 (5 January 1924): 3.

17. Trustee Minutes, *Christian Leader* 37 (29 September 1934): 1236.

18. *Christian Leader* 122 (25 May 1940): 491-92.

19. *The Universalist Church of America: A Short History* (Boston: Universalist Historical Society, 1957).

20. *Universalist Leader* 137 (April 1957): 97.

21. See the critical review of the book in the *Tar Heel Universalist* 40 (November 1971).

22. Another newspaper, the *Harbinger*, although a Universalist publication, was not associated with the denominational press. It was first published as a semi-monthly in St. Louis, Missouri, beginning in 1872, and was edited by Thomas Abbott. It ceased publication in 1876 after it had become a monthly in 1873 and had been moved to Paducah, Kentucky, two years later. A general-interest publication, *Manford's Monthly Magazine*, was published from 1854 until 1884 by Erasmus Manford, a Universalist, first in St. Louis and then in Chicago. It was continued for some years thereafter by his widow.

23. Of the two newspapers, only one, the *Leader*, was truly national in coverage. The other, the *Universalist Herald*, published in Georgia, was basically regional in nature and appeal.

24. *Christian Leader* 58 (3 November 1887): 1, 8.

25. *Universalist* 54 (16 November 1872): [2].

26. Annual Report, ibid. 56 (13 June 1874): [2].

27. *Christian Leader* 51 (1 July 1880): 3.

28. *Universalist Quarterly* 12 (April 1875): 259.

29. *Universalist* 57 (2 October 1875): [2].

30. *Christian Leader* 62 (2 June 1892): 5.

31. Ibid. 61 (21 August 1890): 5; 63 (8 June 1893): 4.

32. The only reasonably complete run of the fourteen volumes of this paper is to be found in the Indiana State Library in Indianapolis.

33. Extract from Minutes, Universalist Publishing House, 22 June 1908.

34. *Universalist Leader* 13 (8 January 1910): 48.

35. Extract from Minutes, Board of Directors, 19 December 1910.

36. *Universalist Leader* 13 (19 February 1910): 233.

37. Proceedings, General Convention, 1871, pp. 7, 25.

38. Ibid., 1889, p. 31.

39. *Christian Leader* 65 (31 October 1895): 1.

40. Proceedings, General Convention, 1897, p. 10.

41. Ibid., 1913, p. 8.

42. Trustee Report, 1914, pp. 5-6; extract from Minutes, 3 May 1914.

43. *Universalist Leader* 3 (6 January 1900): 2.

44. *Universalist Register*, 1874, pp. 93-97.

45. *Christian Leader* 32 (9 November 1929): 1432.
46. *Universalist Leader* 23 (12 June 1920): 579-81.
47. Year Book, 1922, p. 84.
48. *Universalist Register*, 1899, p. 96.
49. See the *Universalist Leader* 26 (1 December 1923): 6-11, for a brief biographical sketch. For a more detailed biography, see Dorothy and Frank Oliver Hall, *Handicapped: Being the Life Story of Frederick A. Bisbee* (Boston: Universalist Publishing House, [n.d.]. One-half of the book is devoted to selected speeches and essays.
50. *Universalist Leader* 1 (4 June 1908): 4.
51. Opening Address, Twenty-fifth Anniversary Convention of the Young Peoples Christian Union, 8 July 1914.
52. *Universalist Leader* 21 (1 June 1918): 457.
53. Ibid. 16 (5 July 1913): 841-42.
54. Extract from Minutes, Universalist Publishing House, 25 January 1915.
55. *Universalist Leader* 23 (12 June 1920): 579-80.
56. Ibid. 24 (11 June 1921): 625-27.
57. Ibid. 27 (24 May 1924): 3.
58. See "Strong Son of God: A Memoir of John van Schaick, Jr.," *Christian Leader* 131 (July 1949): 241-54.
59. The work in Belgium is related by van Schaick in *The Little Corner Never Conquered* (N.Y.: Macmillan 1921).
60. Boston: Universalist Publishing House, 1939.
61. *Christian Register* 110 (23 July 1931): 588. The *Register* finally abandoned the historic adjective in its title in mid-1957 and became the *Unitarian Register* by a vote of 266 to 205 at the annual meeting of the denomination that year. See ibid. 136 (Mid-Summer 1957): 2 ff.
62. *Christian Leader* 34 (23 May 1931): 659.
63. Annual Report, Universalist Publishing House, in ibid. 29 (9 January, 12 June 1926): 5, 16-17.

64. *Christian Leader* 32 (29 June, 13 July 1929): 805, 868; 121 (10 June 1939): 541.
65. Ibid. 35 (25 June 1932): 803.
66. Minutes, Universalist Council, 24 May 1935. Full responsibility for the *Register* was assumed by the AUA in 1932.
67. *Christian Leader* 25 (30 July 1932): 899.
68. Ibid. 39 (6 June 1936): 707-708.
69. Ibid. 130 (July 1948): 323.
70. Ibid. 126 (17 June 1944): 359.
71. Ibid., pp. 359-60.
72. Ibid. 127 (3 February 1945): 60-61.
73. Ibid. 133 (May 1951): 162.
74. Ibid. 128 (15 June 1946): 289-90.
75. *Universalist Leader* 135 (April 1953): 117.
76. Minutes, General Assembly, 1949.
77. *Universalist Leader* 137 (April 1955): 89.
78. Memorandum to UCA [n.d.].
79. Report, Department of Business Administration, 1951.
80. *Universalist Leader* 137 (April 1955): 88-89.
81. Ibid. 138 (June 1956): 134.
82. Minutes, Board of Directors, 16 February 1961.
83. *Unitarian Register-Universalist Leader*, January, February 1962, pp. 25, 3.
84. *UUA Now*, Summer I, 1968, p. 16.
85. Cummins to Ziegler [n.d.].
86. Minutes, Board of Directors, 9 March, 11 May 1960.
87. Reports, Commission on Literature, 1946 *et seq.*
88. Memorandum of Agreement, 21 November 1961.
89. Records, Universalist Publishing House.
90. Balance Sheet, Universalist Publishing House, 31 March 1961.
91. *Christian Leader* 126 (1-15 July 1944): 413.

Chapter 15: SECULAR EDUCATION IN OTHER HANDS

1. *Christian Leader* 35 (5, 19 November 1932): 1285, 1348.
2. Adams to Acting President Hooper, 17 November 1914. Adams was both an alumnus (1870) and a graduate of the divinity school (1872).
3. The recipient was Peter Noel Knost, who came from a Universalist background,

received his undergraduate degree at Tufts in 1958, and his theological degree from Crane in 1961. At the time he received his honorary degree he was minister of a Congregational church in California.

4. *Universalist Leader* 15 (10 February 1912): 176.

5. Ibid. 15 (10 August 1912): 1004-1005.

6. Ibid. 17 (7 November 1914): 1073-74.

7. Ibid. 18 (12 June, 7 August 1915): 566, 766-67.

8. For a biographical sketch, see the *Christian Leader* 31 (3 March 1928): 273; for tributes, see ibid. (10 March 1928): 301-302.

9. *Universalist Leader* 19 (10 June 1916): 564.

10. Ibid. 19 (15 July 1916): 685, 730-31.

11. Ibid. 22 (18 January 1919): 57-58.

12. Ibid. 20 (13 October 1917): 679.

13. Ibid. 25 (20 May 1922): 10-11.

14. Ibid.

15. Ibid. 22 (22 November 1919): 1130.

16. Ibid. 26 (3 November 1923): 18.

17. Ibid. 26 (9 June 1923): 13-14.

18. Ibid. 26 (3 November 1923): 23.

19. Biennial Report, Year Book, 1924, p. 24.

20. Galer to Etz, 31 March 1926.

21. *Christian Register* 107 (5 April 1928): 275-77.

22. *Christian Leader* 31 (31 March 1928): 386, 400-401.

23. *Christian Register* 107 (5 April 1928): 275-77.

24. Ibid. 107 (26 April 1928): 342.

25. Ibid. 107 (5 April 1928): 278.

26. Ibid. 107 (11 October 1928): 815.

27. Ibid. 107 (5 April 1928): 276.

28. Ibid. 108 (31 January 1929): 99.

29. Ibid. 107 (11 October 1928): 823.

30. Ibid. 107 (5 July 1928): 567.

31. Ibid. 108 (31 January 1929): 99.

32. Ibid. 108 (20 June 1929): 535.

33. *Christian Leader* 32 (22 June 1929): 786-87.

34. *Christian Register* 108 (24 October 1929): 872.

35. Year Book, 1930, pp. 24, 140.

36. This information is based largely on an article in the *Voice of Fellowship* (McCordsville, Indiana), 8 February 1978, prepared by David More Maynard, minister of the Universalist Unitarian Church in Peoria.

37. Extract from Proceedings, *Christian Freeman* 22 (16 November 1860): 114.

38. Proceedings, General Convention, 1861, p. 32.

39. *Christian Leader* 61 (8 May 1890): 4.

40. Proceedings, General Convention, 1862, pp. 1, 9.

41. *Christian Leader* 61 (17 July 1890): 4.

42. Throop to Shinn, 24 January 1889; 3 May 1892, in McGlauflin, *Faith with Power,* pp. 45-46, 57.

43. *Christian Leader* 39 (27 June 1936): 816.

44. *Universalist Register,* 1892, p. 79; *Christian Leader* 62 (3 December 1891): 1.

45. *Christian Leader* 62 (17 September 1891): 4, 5.

46. *Universalist Register,* 1893, pp. 80, 89.

47. *Christian Leader* 64 (21 September 1893): 5.

48. *Universalist Register,* 1894, pp. 81, 91.

49. *Christian Leader* 64 (20 July 1893): 5.

50. Proceedings, General Convention, 1895, p. 69.

51. Trustee Report, 1896, pp. 11-12.

52. *Christian Leader* 61 (8 May 1890): 4.

53. *Universalist Leader* 26 (15 December 1923): 28.

54. McGlauflin, *Faith with Power,* pp. 90-91.

55. Ibid., p. 92.

56. *Universalist Leader* 1 (22 January 1898): 12.

57. Unless indicated otherwise, biographical details were derived from the Lyman Ward file, Andover-Harvard Theological Library.

58. See Ward's reminiscences in the *Christian Leader* 34 (21 March 1931): 369-70.

59. *Universalist Leader* 1 (26 March 1898): 5.

60. Neither Mississippi nor Louisiana was represented. Among the trustees were Mrs. Athalia J. Irwin of Columbia, South Carolina, one of the few Universalist women to serve in the ministry in the South; Thomas Chapman, a clergyman who was then serving as the Georgia state superintendent; and Daniel B. Clayton, a veteran itinerant clergyman.

61. *Universalist Leader* 2 (6 May 1899): 6.

62. Ibid. 1 (17 September 1898): 4.

63. Ibid. 2 (24 June 1899): 18.
64. Ibid. 1 (3 December 1898): 18; *Report of the Commissioner of Education for the Year 1898-99* (Washington, D.C.: Government Printing Office, 1900): 2: 2143.
65. *Universalist Register*, 1900, p. 94.
66. *Universalist Leader* 3 (24 February 1900): 254.
67. *Universalist Register*, 1901, p. 86.
68. Ibid., 1901, pp. 86-87.
69. These details were derived from Dorothy Cleaveland Salisbury, "They Builded Better Than They Knew," pp. 7-8.
70. *Universalist Leader* 28 (4 July 1925): 28-29.
71. Ibid. 3 (17 March 1900): 331.
72. For a tribute by Ward, who attended Washington's funeral in 1915, see ibid. 18 (4 December 1915): 1161-62.
73. Ibid. 3 (29 December 1900): 1642.
74. Ibid. 4 (22 June 1901): 771.
75. Ibid. 4 (31 August 1901): 1094-95.
76. Ibid. 4 (14 September 1901): 1154-55.
77. There were actually some exceptions to this assertion by Shinn. Tufts College was never officially sponsored by or supported by the Massachusetts Convention, but received general denominational support instead.
78. *Universalist Leader* 4 (14 September 1901): 1157.
79. Church Record Book, Camp Hill Universalist Church.
80. *Report of the Commissioner of Education*, 1906, 2: 1058-59.
81. WNMA Records, 1905.
82. *Universalist Leader* 15 (4 May 1912): 560.
83. Ibid. 17 (28 February 1914): 223.
84. Ibid. 8 (6 May 1905): 560.
85. Ibid. 33 (12 July 1930): 893.
86. *Christian Leader* 124 (6 June 1942): 348.
87. Ibid. 33 (12 July 1930): 893.
88. For an appreciation of his life and work, see the *Southern Quarterly* (Camp Hill, Alabama), 3 March 1949; and the *Sentinel* (Lyman Ward Military Academy, Camp Hill, Alabama), April 1968.

Chapter 16: THEOLOGICAL EDUCATION: RYDER AND CANTON

1. Precise statistics for Ryder were not available.
2. Report of Acting Dean Eugene S. Ashton, Crane Theological School, 1953.
3. *Universalist Leader* 27 (27 December 1924): 8.
4. Ibid. 15 (11 May 1912): 590.
5. Ibid. 15 (27 January 1912): 102-103.
6. Ibid. 16 (8 November 1913): 1313.
7. Ibid. 18 (11 September 1915): 875-76.
8. Ibid. 16 (8 November 1913): 1313.
9. Ibid. 20 (10 February 1917): 86.
10. Ibid. 20 (31 March 1917; 2 February 1918): 203-204, 86.
11. Buchtel had severed its official ties with the denomination in 1907, although there were still many Universalists in the student body.
12. Year Book, 1922, p. 162; 1923, p. 100.
13. *Universalist Leader* 18 (11, 18 September 1915): 875-76, 900 ff.
14. Ibid. 18 (2 October 1915): 945-47.
15. Ibid. 19 (13 May 1916): 472.
16. Minutes, General Convention, 1923; Year Book, 1924, p. 62.
17. Ibid., 1925, p. 71.
18. *Christian Register* 107 (25 October 1928): 864-65.
19. *Christian Leader* 32 (23 February 1929): 252-53.
20. *Christian Register* 107 (5 April 1928): 277.
21. Year Book, 1930, p. 151.
22. *Christian Leader* 123 (8 February 1941): 141.
23. Ibid. 126 (19 February 1944): 111. The federation was dissolved in 1959.
24. Records, General Assembly, 1959.
25. Dorothy Tilden Spoerl, "Lombard Remembered" (typescript). She delivered the address in 1980 at the fiftieth anniversary of the closing of the college.
26. *Trumpet* 29 (6 September 1856): 54.
27. There are three brief published histories of the school. The earliest comprises two chapters in *Sixty Years of St. Lawrence,* a collaborative work edited by Malcolm S. Black and published by the Class of 1916

(Canton, N.Y.: St. Lawrence University, 1916). The book, intended originally to have marked the fiftieth anniversary of the institution in 1906, did not appear until a decade later, when the Class of 1916 completed the manuscript. A second collaborative work, *Candle in the Wilderness: A Centennial History of the St. Lawrence University, 1856-1956* (N.Y.: Appleton-Century-Crofts, 1957), edited by Louis H. Pink and Rutherford E. Delmage, contains one chapter devoted to the history of the theological school. The most recent history is *109 Years: An Account of the Theological School of St. Lawrence University, 1856-1965* [n.p., n.d.], written and edited jointly by Max A. Kapp and David B. Parke. A second edition entitled *120 Years* was published in 1976. There is in this edition an elaboration of the history of the St. Lawrence Foundation for Theological Education which represents a continuation of the theological school after it closed in 1965. None of these three works is documented, but *109 Years* has a brief note on sources. Most of the records (either originals or copies) of the Canton Theological School in the twentieth century are available in the Andover-Harvard Theological Library.

28. For a biography, published a year after his death, see George H. Emerson, *Memoir of Ebenezer Fisher, D.D.* (Boston: Universalist Publishing House, 1880) and Volume I of the present work.

29. *Universalist Register*, 1871, pp. 88-89.

30. *Trumpet* 45 (24 October 1863): 107.

31. *Sixty Years of St. Lawrence*, p. 34.

32. Ibid., pp. 22-23.

33. Extract from Proceedings, *Universalist* 51 (24 July 1869): [3].

34. See the *Christian Leader* 49 (10 July 1879): 2 for his inaugural address.

35. *Sixty Years of St. Lawrence*, p. 25.

36. *Candle in the Wilderness*, p. 51.

37. Ibid., p. 50.

38. *Universalist Leader* 13 (4 June 1910): 707.

39. Minutes, Regents of New York State, 1901.

40. Ibid., 7 March 1907.

41. Treasurer's Report, Clinton Liberal Institute, 1935.

42. *Universalist Leader* 14 (23 September 1911): 1202.

43. *Trumpet* 46 (1 October 1864): [2].

44. *Christian Leader* 53 (15 June 1882): 4.

45. Proceedings, *Christian Leader* 53 (26 October 1882): 4.

46. *Christian Leader* 134 (March 1952): 82-83.

47. Atwood to Roger Etz, 12 November 1930.

48. *Christian Leader* 33 (2 August 1930): 964.

49. Ibid. 34 (10 January 1931): 36.

50. Ibid. 121 (4 November 1939): 1046.

51. Minutes, General Assembly 1946, 1947; Trustee Report, 1946, p. 35.

52. Trustee files, 1950.

53. *Empire State Universalist*, February 1951, p. 65.

54. *Universalist Leader* 135 (December 1953): 309.

55. Fred Leining to MacLean and Kapp, 22 January 1952.

56. Report of the Committee on Theological Schools, UCA, 1949.

57. *Universalist Leader* 135 (April 1953): 106.

58. Ibid. 136 (December 1954): 296-97, 301.

59. *Christian Leader* 134 (July 1952): 180.

60. Records, General Assembly, 1949.

61. Annual Report, Dean Kapp, 9-10 October 1961.

62. Report of the General Superintendent, *Christian Leader* 131 (November 1949): 418.

63. Massena Goodrich had been employed in 1860 and had departed after two years; and E. Parl Welch, employed in 1939 to teach History and Philosophy of Religion, remained only one year.

64. *Universalist Leader* 134 (July 1952): 180.

65. Ibid. 136 (July 1954): 174.

66. Ibid. 133 (December 1951): 353. Among MacLean's autobiographical writings are *The Galloping Gospel* (Boston: Beacon Press, 1966); *God and the Devil at Seal Cove* (Halifax, N.S.: Patheric Press, 1976); and *I Began in Cape Breton* (Cleveland, Ohio: The First Unitarian Church, 1969).

67. *Universalist Leader* 140 (January 1959): 14.

68. "The Education of a Universalist Minister," *Christian Leader* 35 (9 January 1932): 41 ff.

69. *Christian Leader* 133 (December 1951): 355-56.

70. *The Candle* 1 (April 1959): 3.
71. *Empire State Universalist,* Winter 1961, p. 7.
72. Ibid., Autumn 1960, p. 3.
73. Annual Report, Dean Kapp, 31 March 1961.
74. Secretary, UUA, to Albert C. Niles, 8 February 1961. Niles was director of the Develoment Office but was let go at the end of the next year.
75. Dean's Report, 1962.
76. Ibid.
77. Trustee Minutes, 15 October 1962.
78. The Institute finally came to an end in 1973 when its separate board of trustees was abolished and its funds added to those of the St. Lawrence Foundation which administered the assets of the old Clinton school.
79. Trustee Minutes, 24 October 1963.
80. Ibid., 1 June 1962.
81. Dean's Report, 1962.
82. Trustee Minutes, 26 November 1962.
83. Dean's Report, 1963.
84. Secretary of the Fisher Society to the Chairman of the Trustees, 7 March 1963.
85. Trustee Minutes, 31 May 1963.
86. Dean's Report, 1963.
87. Ibid., January, June 1964.
88. Trustee Minutes, 26 November 1962.
89. Ibid., 24 October 1963.
90. Ibid., 25-26 March 1963.
91. Ibid., 18 July 1963.
92. Ibid., 14 November 1963.
93. Kapp to Hersey, 17 December 1963.
94. Trustee Minutes, 31 May 1963.
95. Treasurer's Reports, 1950-1962; Dean's Report, 1963.
96. *Empire State Universalist,* August 1964, [n.p.].
97. Trustee Minutes, 5 June 1964. The vote was 7-2-2.
98. Kapp to Hersey, 21 October 1965.
99. *Unitarian Register-Universalist Leader,* December 1964, p. 13.
100. Jeffries to William Rice, 16 November 1964; Denominational Affairs Committee, First Universalist Church of Syracuse, to Ministers and Board Chairmen, December 1964.
101. Trustee Minutes, 15-16 October 1964.
102. Bertram A. Stroock to Rice, 24 November 1964.
103. Treasurer's Report, 1965-1967.
104. Rice to the New York Convention, 11 February 1966.
105. Kapp to Hersey, 5 August 1965.

Chapter 17: THEOLOGICAL EDUCATION: CRANE

1. Unless otherwise indicated, all information presented here was derived from material in the Tufts University Archives, including the records of the Crane Theological School.
2. Trustee Minutes, 29 May 1866.
3. Ibid., 2 November 1866, 7 February 1867.
4. *Universalist* 51 (8 November 1869): [2].
5. Trustee Minutes, 7 February 1867, 25 May 1869.
6. Sawyer to Alonzo A. Miner, 25 February 1869.
7. Trustee Minutes, 16 August 1869.
8. Trustee Records, 1870; Trustee Minutes, 15 December 1870.
9. Trustee Minutes, 11 March 1889, 4 December 1893.
10. Tufts Catalogue, 1869-70.
11. Trustee Minutes, 15 June 1883.
12. Ibid., 13 June 1884.
13. Annual Report, C. H. Leonard, 17 June 1872.
14. Trustee Minutes, 16 October 1871.
15. *Christian Leader* 58 (9 June 1887): 5.
16. Trustee Minutes, 30 November 1896.
17. Ibid.
18. Proceedings, General Convention, 1883, pp. 53-57.
19. Trustee Report, General Convention, 1890, p. 38.
20. *Christian Leader* 51 (3 February 1881): 8.
21. Trustee Minutes, 29 May 1877.
22. Ibid., 6 March 1883.
23. Sawyer to Trustees, 26 December 1883.
24. Trustee Report, Centennial Convention, 1870, p. 5.
25. Tufts Catalogue, 1871-72.
26. Proceedings, General Convention, 1889, p. 21.

27. President Capen to T. H. Armstrong, 14 March 1882.
28. Trustee Minutes, 6 February 1894.
29. Ibid., 29 June 1891.
30. Paige had been compelled in 1829 "by the feebleness of his health" to suspend temporarily his ministerial activities. *Trumpet* 11 (3 October 1829): 54. He lived to be ninety-five.
31. For an account of the introduction of coeducation at Tufts and President Frederick Hamilton's opposition to it, see Russell E. Miller, *Light on the Hill: A History of Tufts College, 1852-1952* (Boston: Beacon Press, 1966).
32. *Universalist Leader* 137 (March 1955): 68.
33. Ibid. 3 (10 November 1900): 1424.
34. Hamilton to Gunnison, 22 October 1910.
35. President's Report, 1901-1902, pp. 15-16.
36. Gunnison to Hamilton, 25 October 1910.
37. *Christian Leader* 65 (1 August 1895): 5.
38. President's Report, 1882-83.
39. Ibid., 1892-93.
40. Ibid., 1907-1908.
41. Trustee Minutes, 26 May 1908.
42. The course was listed as "Philosophy 18" and was described as "Psycho-Pathology — the mental and moral origin of functional nervous disorders, and their treatment by methods of suggestion."
43. Extract from will; Trustee Finance Committee Records, 14 November 1899.
44. Finance Committee Report; Trustee Minutes, 9 October 1900.
45. Trustee Minutes, 20, 29 June 1906.
46. *Universalist Leader* 9 (7, 21 July 1906): 849, 906.
47. President's Report, 1876-77.
48. William G. Tousey, "Introductory Address," in E. G. Brooks, *Universalism, and the Ministry to Make It Effective* (Boston: Wright and Potter, 1874), p. 3. Brooks' address was delivered to the divinity school alumni, who had organized their own association the previous year. It was the first public exercise under their sponsorship.
49. Minutes, College of Letters, 31 October, 3 November 1902.
50. President's Report, 1901-1902.
51. As part of the reorganization the divinity degree (BD) was redesignated temporarily as Bachelor of Sacred Theology (STB) in 1903, but again became BD two years later, as an undergraduate professional degree. With another reorganization during World War I the STB was restored and the dean reported in 1917 that "it stands as a graduate degree." McCollester Report, 1916-17. The exact status of the STB apparently remained in question, for in 1920 the catalogue statement provided that holders of such degrees were eligible to apply for admission to the Master's program. The last STB degrees were awarded in 1959.
52. President's Report, 1906-1907.
53. As an economy measure the trustees had reduced Woodbridge's salary by limiting it to the income from the endowment of the chair which paid only one-third of his stipend. At the same time, he took on additional teaching duties at the dean's request. By the time Woodbridge had protested to the trustees and they had responded by reducing both his teaching load and salary for 1909-10, he departed. Woodbridge to Trustees, 4 December 1908.
54. For an appreciation of Leonard and his work, written after his death, see the *Tufts College Graduate* 17 (September 1918–August 1919): 14-17.
55. Trustee Minutes, 12 April 1910.
56. Ibid., 7 June 1910.
57. Hall to Hamilton, 11 January 1910.
58. Cushman to Hamilton, 4 February 1908.
59. Gunnison to Hamilton, 25 October 1910.
60. Harold Marshall to Hamilton, 1 February 1912.
61. Hamilton to Marshall, 3 February 1912.
62. Aldred S. Cole, Memorandum of conversation with Lee S. McCollester, 16 March 1937.
63. Vincent E. Tomlinson to Hamilton, 25 March 1911.
64. President's Report, 1910-11.
65. Hamilton to McCollester, 29 February 1912.
66. President's Report, 1911-12.
67. *Christian Leader* 35 (6 February 1932): 170-73.
68. William Leslie Hooper, who had served as Acting President (1912-1914) after Hamilton's resignation, was a Universalist layman. All of the previous presidents had been Universalist clergymen.

69. Skinner to Bumpus, 14 July 1917.
70. McCollester Report, 7 October 1917.
71. Trustee Minutes, 10 December 1925.
72. Annual Report, Visiting Committee, 9 October 1924.
73. Dean McCollester, President's Report, 1923-24, Trustee Minutes.
74. Skinner to Murray Kenney, 1, 9 February 1943.
75. Skinner to Carmichael, 8 June 1942.
76. McCollester Annual Report, 8 October 1924.
77. Trustee Executive Committee Minutes, 24 October 1930.
78. Trustee Minutes, 31 October 1929.
79. President's Report, 1928-29, Trustee Minutes.
80. Trustee Executive Committee Minutes, 31 January 1930.
81. McCollester to Cousens, 22 April 1932. The letter of resignation was reproduced in the *Christian Leader* 34 (5 November 1932): 1302-1303.
82. Trustee Executive Committee Minutes, 16 May 1940.
83. McCollester to Carmichael, 26 April 1940.
84. The arcade was the gift of Theodore A. and Mrs. Fischer of New Haven, Connecticut; he was a divinity school alumnus (1896). The chapel building was the gift of Mrs. Albert Crane, widow of the individual who had given the largest single benefaction to the school, in the name of his father.
85. *Christian Register* 108 (14 February 1929): 138.
86. Trustee Minutes, 31 October 1935.
87. Trustee Executive Committee Minutes, 14 December 1937.
88. This was part of a statistical report prepared by Ratcliff; Dean Skinner sent a copy of it with his annual report to the president on 28 September 1935.
89. President's Report, 1941-42.
90. Report of the Committee of Visitors, 20 October 1937, Trustee Minutes.
91. Cole, "History," p. 54.
92. Trustee Executive Committee Minutes, 30 June 1943.
93. Alumni Association to Trustees, 25 October 1944.
94. Ibid., 19 May 1945.
95. President's Report, 1943-44.
96. Minutes, General Assembly, 1947, p. 8.
97. President's Report, 1949-50.
98. Trustee Executive Committee Minutes, 13 December 1943.
99. Isaiah J. Domas, "A Study of the School of Religion Alumni" (unpublished STB thesis, Tufts College School of Religion, 1941).
100. For purposes of the questionnaire, the definitions were as follows: deistic — "having faith in God as the source of all finite existence, but this on the basis of the testimony of reason rather than revelation"; theistic — "having faith in a God who has been personally and supernaturally self-revealed to man"; humanistic — "agnostic with regard to deity and confident of man's capacity for self-realization independent of the supernatural or the divine."
101. Trustee Executive Committee Minutes, 24 November 1952.
102. Ibid., 30 March 1953.
103. Report, Acting Dean Ashton, 17 August 1953.
104. Provost's Report, 1956.
105. Hersey to Wessell, 18 October 1957.
106. President's Report, 1957.
107. Hersey to Robert H. Barber, 11 February 1957.
108. See the final report of the Study Committee for the Crane Theological School (Tufts-Carnegie Self Study, 1 July 1958), pp. 864-76.
109. President's Report, 1959.
110. Ibid., 1963-64.
111. Mead to Crane Faculty, 15 January 1965. Unlike the Canton Theological School, the Crane School sponsored briefly a scholarly journal, the *Crane Review*. The publication, of serious intent and generally high quality, carried articles by scholars from outside the University as well as from within. The journal lasted for a decade (1958-1968) and had a press run of about 600 copies.
112. President's Report, 1961.
113. Ibid., 1962.
114. Ibid., 1963-64.
115. Faculty Minutes, Crane School, 3 May 1961.
116. *Unitarian Register-Universalist Leader*, June 1962, p. 27.
117. The Tufts allocation of 15 percent of the total was $6,297 for 1963 and $5,844 a

year later. Hersey to Vice-President Frank A. Tredinnick, 29 July 1963, 26 June 1964.

118. The two reports, published in two parts but under one cover, entitled *A Plan of Education for the Unitarian Universalist Ministry*, were distributed in both typescript and printed form.

119. Taylor Report, pp. 121-22.

120. Greeley to Wessell, 29 January 1964.

121. Wright to Greeley, 7 February 1963.

122. Report of Meeting, 11 February 1964.

123. Taylor Report, p. 44.

124. *Unitarian Register-Universalist Leader*, October 1962, pp. 14-15.

125. Only nine of the signatories were full-time students and hence the manifesto was far from representing the consensus of the entire student body. Ibid., January 1963, p. 18.

126. Starr King did not participate because it was the only school that came out relatively unscathed. Even Harvard, although not a denominational school, came in for its share of criticism.

127. Hersey to Wessell, 11 March 1963; Hersey served as secretary at the meeting.

128. Charles N. Vickery to Wessell, 29 October 1963.

129. Kapp to Hersey, 17 December 1963.

130. *Unitarian Register-Universalist Leader*, January 1963, p. 30.

131. The Senexet Conference, composed of about twenty-five individuals, included heads of the theological schools, with usually a faculty member from each; the staff of the Department of Ministry; representatives of the ministerial association; and other invited participants.

132. Memorandum of telephone conversation with William Rice, 24 November 1964. Rice was a member of the Canton Theological School board of trustees.

133. Memorandum to Trustees, 13 November 1964.

134. Annual Report of Executive Director, 1964-65.

135. Trustee Finance Committee Minutes, 1 March 1966.

136. See, for example, the long and enthusiastic letter of 1 December 1964 from Wallace W. Robbins, an alumnus.

137. Miller to Mead, 5 February 1965.

138. Mead to Wessell, 23 October 1964.

139. Trustee Educational Policy Committee Minutes, 1 December 1965, 20 January 1966.

140. Wessell Memorandum to Trustees, 13 November 1964.

141. Patton to Hersey, 29 June 1964.

142. Cole to Wessell, 1 January 1965.

143. Alumni Newsletter, 15 June 1964.

144. Trustee Executive Committee Minutes, 17 April 1967.

145. Trustee Minutes, 3 June 1967.

146. Dean's Report, President's Report, 1968.

147. Trustee Minutes, 3 June 1967.

148. Hersey to Mead, 22 April 1968.

149. Trustee Minutes, 26 October 1967. Hallowell, who was not a member of the Universalist denomination, had no involvement in any of the proceedings concerning the school which had preceded his election to the presidency.

150. The total endowment intended exclusively for Crane was about $400,000 (market value) as of 1964. If land and buildings were included as assets, the total exceeded $600,000, but this was largely an internal bookkeeping matter. The buildings were immediately put to other uses.

151. "The Crane Program" (pamphlet), 11 February 1968.

152. Dean's Report, President's Report, 1968.

153. Mead to Theodore Webb, 26 June 1964.

154. Trustee Minutes, 4 June 1966.

155. Greeley to UUA Trustees, 23 November 1964.

Chapter 18: QUILLEN HAMILTON SHINN: THE "GRASSHOPPER MISSIONARY"

1. *Universalist Leader* 10 (14 September 1907): 1160.

2. Trustee Report, 1901, pp. 23-24.

3. This was the subtitle of a brief biography of Shinn published in pamphlet form by Athalia L. J. Irwin, who spent much of her ministerial life in the South.

4. *Universalist Leader* 5 (11 October 1902): 1299-1300; Anson Titus, "Quillen Hamilton Shinn, D.D.," *To-Day* 2 (August 1895): 401.

5. The fullest biography, by William H. McGlauflin, *Faith with Power: A Life Study of Quillen Hamilton Shinn, D.D.* (Boston and Chicago: Universalist Publishing House, 1912), was commissioned by the General Convention in 1911, at McGlauflin's suggestion. Proceedings, 1911, p. 16. A long-time friend and associate of Shinn, McGlauflin was General Superintendent of the Universalist Church at the time. Roughly one-half of the book comprises excerpts from Shinn's sermons and other writings. His frequent letters to the denominational press were collected in four scrapbooks. See also Titus's biography, referred to above, and another by the same author in the *Universalist Leader* 10 (14 September 1907): 1168-69.

6. *Universalist Leader* 9 (28 April 1906): 542.

7. *Christian Leader* 29 (3 July 1926): 23.

8. This episode, not to be found in the official records, was related in the two biographical sketches prepared by Anson Titus.

9. *Universalist* 54 (25 January 1873): [2].

10. *Christian Leader* 53 (8 June 1882): 5.

11. The letter of invitation is reproduced in McGlauflin, *Faith with Power*, pp. 45-46.

12. *Christian Leader* 53 (22 February 1883): 8.

13. Ibid. 60 (23 January 1890): 5.

14. Ibid. 29 (3 July 1926): 20.

15. Shinn published selected addresses delivered at summer meetings held in Saratoga, New York, 1898-1900, under the title *Good Tidings* (Boston and Chicago: Universalist Publishing House, 1900).

16. *Universalist Leader* 1 (18 December 1897): 3.

17. Ibid. 3 (15 December 1900): 1599.

18. *Christian Leader* 54 (14 June 1883): 4.

19. *Universalist Leader* 10 (29 June 1907): 828-29.

20. Ibid. 10 (30 November 1907): 1521.

21. Ibid. 11 (11 April 1908): 455.

22. The trip was reported in detail in ibid. 15, beginning with the issue of 16 March 1912.

23. Trustee Report, 1909, p. 30.

24. The plans were discussed in detail in a special missionary issue of the *Universalist Herald* 18 n.s.; 30 o.s. (6 May 1911) dedicated to Shinn's memory.

25. Proceedings, 1911, pp. 14, 91; *Universalist Leader* 15 (13 July 1912): 880.

26. Proceedings, 1913, pp. 12, 79.

27. Trustee Report, 1916, p. 20.

28. *Universalist Leader* 20 (11 August 1917): 19-20.

29. Trustee Report, 1920, p. 33.

30. *Christian Leader* 33 (12 July 1930): 866, 893.

31. Toward the end of his life, Shinn left a partially autobiographical 500-page manuscript entitled "The Optimist."

32. *Universalist Leader* 4 (13 July 1901): 894.

33. *Christian Leader* 65 (18 April 1895): 5.

34. *Universalist Leader* 1 (1 January 1898): 3; 5 (1 November 1902): 1398.

35. Ibid. 5 (15 November 1902): 1470.

36. McGlauflin, *Faith with Power*, pp. 64-65.

37. *Universalist Leader* 5 (19 April 1902): 510.

38. *Christian Leader* 65 (14 November 1895): 8.

39. Ibid. 67 (28 October 1897): 9-10.

40. Biennial Report, 1905, pp. 101-102.

41. *Christian Leader* 60 (28 November 1889): 1.

42. McGlauflin, *Faith with Power*, p. 124.

43. *Universalist Leader* 10 (20 April 1907): 509.

44. *Christian Leader* 63 (18 May 1893): 5.

45. *Universalist Leader* 1 (4 December 1897): 3.

46. Ibid. 2 (15 July 1899): 18.

47. Ibid. 3 (24 February 1900): 254.

48. Andover-Harvard Theological Library, Shinn file.

49. Proceedings, 1897, pp. 16-17.

50. *Universalist Leader* 2 (25 February 1899): 18.

51. McGlauflin, *Faith with Power*, p. 109.

52. Ibid., p. 120.

53. Biennial Report, 1899, pp. 111-12.

54. *Christian Leader* 62 (9 June 1892): 1.

55. Goddard to Shinn, 30 March 1894, in McGlauflin, *Faith with Power*, pp. 58-59.

56. Quoted in ibid., p. 117.

57. *Universalist Leader* 5 (13 September 1902): 1163-65. Bilkovsky added the surname Beresford in 1907 from a collateral branch of his maternal ancestry. *Universalist Leader* 10 (19 January 1907): 79; Proceedings, General Convention, 1907, p. 17.

58. *Universalist Leader* 5 (27 September 1902): 1228.

59. Ibid. 5 (4 October 1902): 1278.

60. Ibid. 5 (6 December 1902): 1567.

61. Ibid. 5 (25 October 1902): 1355-56.

62. Ibid. 5 (8 November 1902): 1422.

63. *Christian Leader* 64 (14 September 1893): 1.

64. *Universalist Leader* 6 (28 March 1903): 398.

65. Ibid. 13 (15 October 1910): 1163.

66. Irwin, "Rev. Quillen Hamilton Shinn, D.D.," [n.d., n.p.]; the pamphlet was distributed by the Post Office Mission, one of Shinn's many projects.

67. Biennial Report, 1901, pp. 105-106.

68. *Universalist Leader* 18 (25 September 1915): 915.

69. *Christian Leader* 29 (24 April 1926): 18.

70. *Universalist Leader* 28 (7 November 1925): 11.

71. Proceedings, 1899, p. 15.

72. *Universalist Leader* 2 (4 November 1899): 6; Trustee Report, 1899, p. 35.

73. *Christian Leader* 62 (6 August 1891): 1.

74. Proceedings, 1901, p. 12.

75. Ibid., 1903, pp. 69-70.

76. Trustee Report, 1908, p. 6.

77. *Universalist Leader* 23 (2 October 1920): 909-10.

Chapter 19: THE NORFOLK AND SUFFOLK MISSIONS IN THE SOUTH

1. Maine Convention Records, 1866.

2. See George R. Bentley, *A History of the Freedmen's Bureau* (Philadelphia: University of Pennsylvania, 1955).

3. *Universalist Herald* 15 (15 June 1867): 25.

4. *Christian Leader* 61 (18 September 1890): 1.

5. Ibid. 61 (4 December 1890): 2.

6. *Universalist* 48 (4 May 1867): [2].

7. *Christian Leader* 52 (7 December 1882): 1.

8. Ibid. 63 (26 October 1893): 1.

9. McGlauflin, *Faith with Power*, p. 86.

10. Proceedings, General Convention, 1889, p. 11.

11. *Christian Leader* 61 (23 April 1891): 5.

12. Proceedings, General Convention, 1893, pp. 3-4.

13. WCA Records, 1893.

14. *Christian Leader* 64 (29 November 1894): 8.

15. *Universalist Leader* 1 (15 January 1898): 7.

16. Biennial Report, Q. H. Shinn, Proceedings, General Convention, 1901, pp. 92-93.

17. *Universalist Leader* 7 (30 April 1904): 559.

18. Ibid., p. 93.

19. Ibid. 8 (18 February 1905): 209.

20. Trustee Report, Proceedings, General Convention, 1913, pp. 19, 33.

21. Much of the biographical information about Jordan was derived from Henry L. and Mary Grace Canfield, "History of Universalism in North Carolina" (typescript, n.d.); for a photo see the *Christian Leader* 32 (15 May 1929): 634; and McGlauflin, *What the Universalist Church is Doing* (Boston and Chicago: Universalist Publishing House, 1909), p. 49.

22. *Universalist Leader* 6 (24 January 1903): 126-27.

23. No copies of this paper have come to light.

24. *Universalist Leader* 7 (30 April 1904): 559.

25. Ibid. 8 (18 February 1905): 209.

26. Ibid. 12 (18 September 1909): 1209.

27. Ibid. 9 (17 November 1906): 1450.

28. Ibid. 10 (9 March 1907): 303.

29. W. H. McGlauflin, "Our Mission to the Colored People" (pamphlet, Universalist Publishing House, 1911).

30. *Universalist Leader* 18 (13 February 1915): 161.

31. Proceedings, General Convention, 1911, p. 10.

32. *Universalist Register*, 1913, p. 102; Trustee Report, Proceedings, General Con-

vention, 1912, p. 5. The idealized sketch of the proposed new building for the "Universalist Normal Training School" bore but little resemblance to the actuality. *Universalist Leader* 15 (6 January 1912): 37.

33. *Universalist Leader* 18 (13 February 1915): 161.

34. Ibid. 14 (9 December 1911): 1580.

35. Ibid. 23 (10 July 1920): 678.

36. *Christian Leader* 33 (11 January 1930): 56.

37. McGlauflin, *Faith with Power*, p. 88 n.

38. Trustee Report, Proceedings, General Convention, 1917, p. 17.

39. Trustee Report, 1920, p. 11.

40. McGlauflin, *Faith with Power*, p. 88.

41. *Universalist Leader* 20 (10 February 1917): 86.

42. McGlauflin, "Our Mission," p. 4.

43. *Universalist Leader* 17 (19 September 1914): 917.

44. *Christian Leader* 32 (15 May 1929): 634.

45. *Universalist Leader* 5 (26 April 1902): 542.

46. Ibid. 1 (15 January 1899): 7.

47. Biennial Report, Q. H. Shinn, Proceedings, General Convention, 1901, pp. 104-105.

48. The last report concerning the church was made in the Year Book, 1929, p. 121.

49. The average salary in 1922 was $60 a month. Annual Report, J. F. Jordan, 1922.

50. *Christian Leader* 121 (14 January 1939): 47.

51. Trustee Report, 1939, p. 30; Minutes, General Convention, 1939, p. 18. The school had abandoned attempts many years earlier to offer instruction beyond the eighth grade, having met problems of accreditation in instruction beyond that point.

52. Minutes, General Convention, 1941, p. 11.

53. *Christian Leader* 126 (2 December 1944): 728.

54. Ibid. 124 (5 September 1942): 533.

55. Report, Department of Service Projects, 1951.

56. For this information as well as some other facts dealing with the most recent history of Jordan Neighborhood House, the writer is indebted to Prof. Willard C. Frank, Jr., of Old Dominion University, Norfolk, Virginia.

Chapter 20: IN THE MOUNTAINS OF WESTERN NORTH CAROLINA

1. *Christian Leader* 38 (25 May 1935): 668.

2. The most comprehensive history of the Pigeon River settlement in its early days was written by John van Schaick, who visited there in the fall of 1928 and published an account in the *Christian Leader* 31 (8 December 1928): 1542-44; it was incorporated into H. L. and Mary Grace Canfield's unpublished "Universalism in North Carolina, 1896-1938." Mrs. Verna Mitchell Taylor of Jacksonville, North Carolina, has done considerable research on the settlement and particularly its leading individual, Hannah Jewett Powell, with whom she was acquainted after the latter's retirement. The writer is indebted to Mrs. Taylor, who generously shared her extensive knowledge.

3. Two constitutions were adopted, the second more elaborate than the first, and signed by seventeen individuals. *Christian Leader* 40 (30 January 1937): 141-42. Both constitutions were reproduced in John E. Williams (comp.), *A History of Universalism in North Carolina* ([n.p.]: Universalist Convention of North Carolina, 1968), pp. 113-17.

4. Burruss to Inman, 6 October 1867, in Williams, *North Carolina*, p. 113.

5. *Universalist Leader* 5 (1 February 1902): 158.

6. Ibid. 6 (5 September, 7 November 1903): 1150, 1438-39.

7. WNMA Records.

8. Trustee Report, *Universalist Leader* 18 (30 October 1915): 1049.

9. *Christian Leader* 121 (10 January 1939): 44.

10. *Universalist Leader* 24 (5 November 1921): 1161; 25 (21 October 1922): 17.

11. *Christian Leader* 37 (22 December 1934): 1626.

12. WNMA Records.

13. *Christian Leader* 31 (17 November 1928): 1444-45.

14. Ibid. 34 (3 January 1931): 27.

15. Emerson Lalone, *And Thy Neighbor as Thyself: A Story of Universalist Social Action* (Boston: Universalist Publishing House, enlarged edition, 1959).

16. *Christian Leader* 33 (19 April 1930): 509. Among them was Mrs. Annie Maxwell Outlaw, who before her marriage spent parts of seven years at Pigeon River. For her reminiscences, see the *Tar Heel Universalist* 40 (May 1971).

17. *Christian Leader* 29 (11 December 1926): 28.

18. Ibid. 124 (19 September 1942): 570.

19. Ibid. 123 (28 June 1941): 532; 124 (18 April 1942): 250.

20. Ibid. 126 (1 April 1944): 219.

21. Ibid. 126 (3, 17 June 1944): 324, 357.

22. Ibid. 126 (2 December 1944): 732.

23. Verna Mitchell Taylor, "Hannah Jewett Powell" (typescript, 1979), p. 14.

24. *Christian Leader* 128 (2 March 1946): 122.

25. *Youth Leader* (December 1947), pp. 4-5.

26. *Christian Leader* 128 (3 August 1946): 364, 368.

27. Report of the Committee on Official Business, AUW, *Christian Leader* 129 (July, 2 August 1947): 334, 352.

28. *Christian Leader* 129 (6 September 1947): 405.

29. Secretary's Report, General Convention, 17 January 1927; Minutes, Fifty-Second North Carolina Convention, 11-13 October 1957, in Williams, *Universalism in North Carolina*, Appendix, p. A-34.

30. UCA Personnel Files.

31. *Christian Leader* 31 (17 March 1928): 337.

Chapter 21: THE ASSOCIATION OF UNIVERSALIST WOMEN

1. Besides the minute books and other records, see *Centenary Voices: or, a Part of the Work of the Women of the Universalist Church from its Centenary Year to the Present Time* (Philadelphia: Woman's Centenary Association, 1886); and Mary Shaw Attwood, "Half a Century of Progress," *Universalist Leader* 22 (6 December 1919): 1198-99. For more comprehensive treatments, see *Seventy-five Years... Onward: A History of the Work and Progress of Universalist Women between the Years 1869 and 1945* (Boston: The Association of Universalist Women, 1945); updated and edited by Ida M. Folsom in 1955 as *A Brief History of the Work of Universalist Women, 1869-1955* (Boston: The Association of Universalist Women). This edition contains photographs of all presidents of the Association through the election of Mrs. Laura Hersey in 1953.

2. She requested that "no other words [be] chiseled upon my gravestone save only these: First President of the Woman's Centenary Association." WCA Records, January 1874.

3. WCA Records, 1882. Aid to Canadian Universalists averaged less than $100 a year in the late nineteenth century, but the very fact that it existed is the significant point.

4. WCA Records, 1874.

5. *Christian Leader* 52 (15 December 1881): 2.

6. WCA Records, 1891.

7. Attwood, "Half a Century of Progress," pp. 1198-99.

8. *Christian Leader* 52 (15 December 1881): 2.

9. Ibid. 56 (14 January 1886): 5.

10. Ibid. 58 (8 March 1888): 1.

11. Ibid. 59 (29 November 1888): 5.

12. Ibid. 59 (14 March 1889): 1.

13. *Universalist Leader* 5 (31 May 1902): 687.

14. WCA Records, 1903.

15. Biennial Report, Proceedings, General Convention, 1909, p. 78; WNMA Records, 1914.

16. WCA Records, 1893.

17. Proceedings, General Convention, 1874, p. 9.

18. WCA Records, 1874.

19. Trustee Report, Proceedings, General Convention, 1874, pp. 17-18.

20. *Christian Leader* 55 (23 October 1884): 1.

21. Proceedings, General Convention, 1879, p. 23. Soule was the first woman to contribute a tract during the early years, followed by Mrs. Maude A. Adams.

22. WCA Records, 1879.

23. WNMA Records, 1906.

24. WCA Records, 1894.
25. Ibid., 1898.
26. WNMA Records, 1915, 1917.
27. Ibid., 1921.
28. Ibid., 1911.
29. Ibid., 1921-22.
30. Biennial Report, AUW, 1949.
31. *Universalist Leader* 3 (6 January 1900): 16.
32. WCA Records, 1899.
33. WNMA Records, 1907.
34. *Universalist Leader* 14 (15 July 1911): 883.
35. Minutes, North Carolina Convention, 1916.
36. WNMA Records, 1920, 1921, 1923.
37. *Christian Leader* 124 (4 April 1942): 204.
38. WNMA Report, *Universalist Leader* 28 (7 November 1925): 7-8.
39. *Christian Leader* 122 (13 January 1940): 48.
40. Ibid. 126 (4 March 1944): 152.
41. See *Tar Heel Universalist* 49 (December 1982-January 1983): [1].
42. *Christian Leader* 35 (12 March 1932): 346.
43. Annual Report, North Carolina Convention, 1923.
44. Minutes, North Carolina Convention, 1924.
45. For a detailed analysis, see Jessie Marvin Ormond, *The Country Church in North Carolina* (Durham, N.C.: Duke University Press, 1931).
46. Ibid., pp. 193-95.
47. WNMA Records, 1934.
48. Alice E. Taylor to Ellsworth C. Reamon, 2 May 1939.
49. Gustav Ulrich to Reamon, 24 May 1939. Ulrich, who was minister of the Outlaw's Bridge church, felt that the Association had made some errors of judgment in selecting personnel, and that the administrative work could be better accomplished by the General Superintendent. Ulrich to Reamon, 26 April 1939.
50. *Universalist Leader* 24 (5 November 1921): 1161; *Christian Leader* 119 (30 October 1937): 1394.
51. *Universalist Leader* 28 (7 November 1925): 7.
52. WNMA Records, 1926-27.

53. Biennial Report, 1939, pp. 43-44.
54. Report of the General Secretary, 1943.
55. Report of the Biennial Session, 1943, p. 26.
56. Trustee Report, 1947, p. 5.
57. Ibid., 1941, p. 6.
58. *Christian Leader* 129 (7 June 1947): 256.
59. For the history of the involvement of the women's organization in Japan and elsewhere in the Far East, see the chapters on the Japan mission.
60. *Universalist Leader* 19 (17 June 1916): 592.
61. Some Universalists served on the original board of directors, and by the end of 1919 had contributed about $5,000. *Universalist Leader* 22 (6 December 1919): 1200. Powers' aim was to establish a "Universalist Room" or a "Murray Room," to contain, among other things, a portrait of Murray painted by Edwin Bacon and donated by E. M. Grant; and the papers of Richard Eddy, the denominational historian. Ibid. 23 (3 May 1919): 426.
62. WNMA Records, 1920, 1921.
63. *Universalist Leader* 24 (16 April 1921): 429-30.
64. WNMA Records, 1923.
65. *Christian Leader* 29 (3 July 1926): 16.
66. Ibid. 38 (7 September 1935): 1138.
67. Ibid. 120 (2 July 1938): 842-43.
68. *Universalist Leader* 137 (January 1955): 14-15.
69. *Christian Leader* 35 (2 April 1932): 431.
70. Ibid. 125 (3 July, 4 December 1943): 409, 730.
71. Ibid. 38 (21 December 1935); 1609-10.
72. Ibid. 119 (23 October 1937): 1361.
73. Ibid. 129 (4 October 1947): 443.
74. Ibid. 130 (August 1948): 350-53.
75. Ibid. 131 (January 1949): 10; *Universalist Leader* 137 (November 1955): 272-73.
76. *Universalist Leader* 135 (October 1953): 254-55; Biennial Report, AUW, 1959. A popular and appealing device to encourage individual contributions from children was the use of Clara Barton cardboard stockings and baseballs for the Joslin boys' camp into which coins could be inserted.
77. *Universalist Leader* 137 (May 1955): 126.

Chapter 22: THE SCOTTISH MISSION

1. The writer is indebted for this information to the Reverend Andrew M. Hill, minister of the church, secretary of the Unitarian Historical Society, and author of "The Successors of the Remnant: A Bicentary Account of St. Mark's Unitarian Church, Edinburgh," *Transactions of the Unitarian Historical Society* 16 (September 1977, September 1978): 101-23, 149-75. For the early history of Universalism in Scotland, see Geoffrey Rowell, "The Origins and History of Universalist Societies in Britain, 1750-1850," *Journal of Ecclesiastical History* 22 (January 1971): 35-36; see also Thomas Whittemore, *Modern History of Universalism, from the Era of the Reformation to the Present Time* (Boston: published by the author, 1830), pp. 173-77; and T. J. Sawyer, "Universalism in Great Britain and Ireland," *Expositor and Universalist Review* 4 n.s. (May 1840): 183-212.

2. *Universalist Leader* 19 (12 August 1916): 775-76. See the biographical sketch written in 1852 by John Fraser, reproduced in the *Universalist* 56 (14, 21 November 1874): [1], [1]; Fraser was the last surviving member of Douglas' congregation. See also the brief biography by J. W. Hanson, *Christian Leader* 57 (10 March 1887): 5; and R. S. Bowie, *Some Stray Jottings about Universalism and its Preachers, in the West of Scotland during the Past Eighty Years* (Glasgow: Andrew Wilson, [n.d.]).

3. Smith, *Historical Sketches and Incidents* (Buffalo: James S. Leavitt, 1848) 2: 201-203.

4. *Christian Leader* 57 (30 September 1886): 5.

5. Bowie, *Stray Jottings*, pp. 14-15.

6. Report of the Committee on Foreign Relations, Proceedings, General Convention, 1913, pp. 96-97. The organization was originally known as the "Larbert Kirk." The community of Larbert later became part of Stenhousemuir, and the church was referred to interchangeably under either name.

7. *Universalist Register*, 1874, p. 68; 1875, p. 79.

8. *Universalist* 55 (21 March 1874): [3].

9. Ibid. 53 (27 May, 17 June 1871): [2], [3].

10. Cantwell, *Thirty Days over the Sea* (Cincinnati: Williamson & Cantwell, 1873), cited in *Fifty Years of Universalism: Jubilee of the Universalist Church, Stenhousemuir, Larbert,* *Scotland, 1867-1917* (Falkirk, Scotland, 1917), pp. 17-18.

11. WCA Records, 1874.

12. *Universalist Leader* 28 (31 January 1925): 30.

13. *Universalist* 57 (15 April 1876): [1].

14. For a biographical sketch and bibliography, see Catherine F. Hitchings, "Universalist and Unitarian Women Ministers," *Journal of the Universalist Historical Society* 10 (1975): 134-36; see also Alan Seaburg, "Missionary to Scotland: Caroline Augusta Soule," *Transactions of the Unitarian Historical Society* 14 (October 1967): 28-41; and Ida M. Folsom, *History of the Association of Universalist Women, 1869-1955* (Boston: The Association, 1955).

15. WCA Records, 1875.

16. *Christian Leader* 57 (24 February 1887): 5.

17. Ibid. 51 (16 September 1880): 5.

18. *Universalist* 53 (5 August 1871): [1].

19. Bowie, *Stray Jottings*, p. 11.

20. *Universalist* 60 (10 August 1878): [3].

21. Unidentified ms history of the Scottish mission, Andover-Harvard Theological Library.

22. *Christian Leader* 53 (26 October 1882): 5.

23. *Universalist* 60 (16 November 1878): [2].

24. *Centenary Voices* (Philadelphia: Woman's Centenary Association, 1886), p. xxxi.

25. *Christian Leader* 51 (27 January 1881): 3.

26. Ibid. 51 (1 July 1880): 2-3.

27. Ibid. 55 (13 November 1884): 5.

28. Ibid. 49 (3 April 1879): 4.

29. Ibid. 49 (15 January 1880): 1.

30. Ibid. 54 (13 September 1883): 5.

31. Ibid. 49 (27 March 1879): 1.

32. Proceedings, General Convention, 1879, p. 5.

33. Ibid., 1880, p. 1; 1887, p. 63.

34. *Christian Leader* 52 (15 December 1881): 2.

35. *Universalist Register*, p. 42.

36. *Christian Leader* 53 (13 July 1882): 3.

37. Ibid. 55 (28 August 1884): 5.

38. Ibid. 55 (25 September 1884): 1.

39. Ibid. 55 (16 October 1884): 1.
40. Ibid. 55 (23 October 1884): 1.
41. Ibid. 56 (14 January, 11 February 1886): 5, 5.
42. Seaburg, "Missionary to Scotland," pp. 38-39.
43. Douglas Webster, "The Williamson Memorial Unitarian Church," in *Scottish Unitarian Churches* (London: Lindsey Press, 1963).
44. *Universalist Register*, 1892, p. 60.
45. *Christian Leader* 62 (28 May 1891): 5.
46. Ibid. 62 (18 June 1891): 5.
47. See ibid. 62 (31 March 1892): 5 for a view of the church.
48. Ibid.
49. Ibid. 65 (24 January 1895): 8.
50. WCA Records, 1894.
51. *Universalist Register*, 1895, p. 61.
52. WCA Records, 1897.
53. *Universalist Quarterly* 25 n.s. (July 1888): 373.
54. *Christian Leader* 55 (13 November 1884): 5.
55. *Universalist Leader* 8 (16 September 1905): 1173.
56. Trustee Report, General Convention, 1904, p. 61.
57. *Universalist Leader* 9 (3 February 1906): 144.
58. *Fifty Years of Universalism in Scotland*, pp. 17-18.
59. *Christian Leader* 30 (17 December 1927): 1616-17; the details were recounted in an article in a Scottish newspaper, reprinted in the *Leader*.
60. *Christian Leader* 32 (28 December 1929): 1661.
61. *Universalist Leader* 4 (10 August 1901): 1005.
62. Ibid. 20 (10 November 1917): 785.
63. Ibid. 5 (15 November 1902): 1458; for a brief biographical sketch, see Hitchings, "Unitarian and Universalist Women Ministers," pp. 140-41.
64. *Universalist Leader* 5 (5 July 1902): 847.
65. Ibid. 7 (2 January, 12 November 1904): 14, 1452-53.

Chapter 23: "THE FIELD IS THE WORLD:" THE ESTABLISHMENT OF THE JAPAN MISSION, 1890-1915

1. *Universalist Magazine* 3 (3 November 1821): 75.
2. *Trumpet* 27 (25 October 1845): 72.
3. *Christian Freeman* 23 (5 July 1861): 38.
4. *Trumpet* 44 (16 August 1862): 66.
5. Extract from Proceedings, *Universalist* 51 (15 May 1869): [2].
6. *Christian Leader* 49 (2 January 1879): 4.
7. Ibid. 49 (20 March 1879): 8.
8. *Universalist Quarterly* 18 n.s. (January 1881): 114-16.
9. See Spencer Lavan, *Unitarianism and India: A Study in Encounter and Response* (Boston: Skinner House, Beacon Press, 1977).
10. See Clifton Jackson Phillips, *Protestant America and the Pagan World: The First Half Century of the American Board of Commissioners for Foreign Missions, 1810-1860* (Cambridge, Mass.: Harvard University Press, 1969).
11. *Universalist Quarterly* 25 n.s. (January 1888): 98-99.
12. Ibid. 18 n.s. (January 1881): 114-16.
13. *Christian Leader* 53 (29 June 1882): 8; WCA Records, 1891.
14. *Christian Leader* 56 (27 May 1886): 5.
15. *Universalist Leader* 1 (30 July 1898): 4.
16. *Christian Leader* 61 (6, 27 November 1890): 5, 5; 62 (6 August 1891): 3; *Universalist Leader* 7 (4 June 1904): 715-16.
17. Proceedings, *Christian Leader* 53 (5 October 1882): 4.
18. Ibid. 53 (19 October 1882): 8.
19. Ibid. 53 (21 December 1882): 1.
20. Proceedings, 1882, p. 18.
21. Ibid., 1883, p. 11.
22. *Christian Leader* 54 (14 June 1883): 1.
23. The sermon was reproduced in ibid. 57 (28 April 1887): 2.
24. Ibid. 54 (14 June 1883): 4.
25. *Universalist Leader* 69 (24 November 1887): 1.
26. Proceedings, 1886, pp. 53-54.
27. Ibid., 1887, p. 6.

28. *Independent,* June 1887.
29. *Christian Leader* 58 (30 June 1887): 1.
30. Ibid. 59 (24 January 1889): 1.
31. *Trumpet* 42 (8 December 1860): 110.
32. Proceedings, 1887, p. 26.
33. Chapin's account of his trip is to be found in *Japan to Granada: Sketches of Observation and Inquiry in a Tour Round the World in 1887-8* (New York: G. P. Putnam's Sons, 1889).
34. *Christian Leader* 58 (24 November 1887): 5.
35. Ibid. 58 (1, 22 September 1887): 1, 1.
36. Proceedings, 1888, p. 24.
37. Ibid., p. 11.
38. For excerpts from his speech, see the *Universalist Quarterly* 25 n.s. (January 1888): 106-107.
39. K. Asakawa, "Christianity in Japan," *Atlantic* 99 (May 1907): 656.
40. *Christian Leader* 60 (19 September 1889): 1.
41. *Universalist Quarterly* 26 n.s. (July 1880): 348 ff.
42. Ibid. 25 n.s. (January 1880): 106-107.
43. *Universalist Leader* 10 (7 December 1907): 1543.
44. Asakawa, "Christianity in Japan," p. 659.
45. The exact figures for Protestants, Roman Catholics, and Greek Orthodox, derived from Japanese official sources based on religious censuses, are cited by Asakawa, p. 660.
46. *Christian Leader* 59 (31 January 1889): 1.
47. *Univesalist Quarterly* 26 n.s. (July 1889): 353.
48. "The Underlying Principle of Missions," *Universalist Quarterly* 27 n.s. (January 1890): 5-15.
49. The history of the Japan mission is among the most fully documented of Universalist activities. Aside from plentiful manuscript records and correspondence, the missionaries prepared frequent and detailed reports published in the denominational press, and many made their written reminiscences available. For many years the *Universalist (Christian) Leader* published an annual "Japan Number," usually in the fall preceding a "Japan Day" which all parishes and churches were urged to hold. For a collection of articles on the early history of the mission, and the justifications for it, see Henry W. Rugg (ed.), *Our Word and Work for Misssions* (Boston and Chicago: Universalist Publishing House, 1894). See also G. I. Keirn, *1890-1915: Twenty-five Years of the Universalist Japan Mission* (Tokyo: [n.p.], 1915). For a brief illustrated history of the mission, see Carl Seaburg, *Dojin Means All People: The Universalist Mission to Japan, 1890-1942* (Boston: for the Universalist Historical Society, 1978); this work was also translated into Japanese.

50. See Anson Titus, "George Landor Perin, D.D.," *To-Day* 2 (April 1895): 178-82.
51. Proceedings, General Convention, 1893, p. 19.
52. *Christian Leader* 60 (13 March 1890): 4.
53. Ibid. 2.
54. Ibid. 60 (6 February 1890): 4.
55. Ibid. 61 (29 January 1891): 1.
56. Ibid. 63 (19 January 1893): 2.
57. Ibid. 62 (28 May 1891): 2.
58. *Universalist Leader* 9 (27 October 1906): 1356.
59. *Christian Leader* 61 (16, 23 October 1890): 4, 1.
60. Keirn, *Japan Mission,* p. 6.
61. *Christian Leader* 60 (19 December 1889): 5.
62. Ibid. 61 (30 October 1890): 4.
63. *Universalist Leader* 9 (27 October 1906): 1356.
64. *Christian Leader* 64 (2 August 1894): 1.
65. *Universalist Leader* 6 (4 July 1903): 850.
66. *Christian Leader* 61 (16 October 1890): 4.
67. *Universalist Leader* 12 (27 November 1909): 1515-16.
68. *Christian Leader* 62 (28 May 1891): 2.
69. Ibid. 61 (10 July 1890): 1.
70. *Universalist Leader* 9 (2 June 1906): 685.
71. Ibid. 3 (15 December 1900): 1575.
72. *Christian Leader* 61 (1 January 1891): 5.
73. Keirn, *Japan Mission,* p. 18; Trustee Report, 1916, p. 26.
74. *Chrstian Leader* 63 (5 January 1893): 1.
75. *Universalist Leader* 9 (27 October, 17 November 1906): 1356, 1358, 1453.
76. *Christian Leader* 62 (14 July 1892): 2.

77. Ibid. 62 (23 June 1892): 5.
78. Ibid. 61 (26 February 1891): 1.
79. Ibid. 61 (26 June 1890): 1.
80. Ibid. 62 (23 June 1892): 4.
81. Ibid. 62 (3 December 1891): 2.
82. Ibid. 61 (31 July 1890): 1.
83. Ibid. 62 (29 October 1891): 4.
84. The complete proceedings of the conference also accompanied the annual report of the trustees in 1894.
85. *Christian Leader* 63 (10 August 1893): 1.
86. Biennial Report, 1892, p. 11.
87. *Christian Leader* 62 (3 December 1891): 2.
88. The papers were published under the title *Our Word and Work for Missions*. Substantially the same article appeared as Paper No. 18 of the *Columbian Congress of the Universalist Church* issued by the Universalist Publishing House in 1894.
89. *Christian Leader* 65 (17 October 1895): 1.
90. Ibid. 63 (10 August 1893): 1.
91. Ibid. 65 (17 October 1895): 2.
92. Keirn, *Japan Mission*, p. 17.
93. *Universalist Leader* 1 (4 December 1897): 12.
94. Ibid.
95. Ibid. 3 (15 December 1900): 1578.
96. Ibid. 5 (29 November 1902): 1520.
97. Ibid. 12 (27 November 1909): 1510.
98. Ibid. 17 (3 January 1914): 11.
99. Ibid. 1 (28 May 1898): 6.
100. Ibid. 2 (9 December 1899): 14.
101. Ibid. 2 (11 November 1899): 2.
102. Ibid. 5 (1 November 1902): 1388.
103. *Christian Leader* 65 (1 August 1895): 1.
104. *Universalist Leader* 1 (4 December 1897): 12-13.
105. Keirn, *Japan Mission*, p. 8.
106. *Universalist Leader* 1 (30 April 1898): 6-7.
107. Proceedings, 1913, p. 85.
108. Trustee Report, 1897, pp. 24-25.
109. *Universalist Leader* 1 (19 February 1898): 5.
110. *Christian Leader* 33 (19 July 1930): 920.
111. *Universalist Leader* 2 (28 January 1897): 1.
112. Trustee Report, 1900, pp. 9-10.
113. Ibid., 1901, pp. 24-25.
114. *Christian Leader* 67 (28 October 1897): 10.
115. *Universalist Leader* 1 (4 December 1897): 1.
116. Keirn, *Japan Mission*, pp. 9-10.
117. *Universalist Leader* 15 (9 November 1912): 1433.
118. Ibid. 4 (6, 20 July 1901): 850, 907.
119. Ibid. 5 (11 October 1902): 1291.
120. Ibid. 9 (27 October 1906): 1358.
121. Ibid. 15 (9 November 1912): 1414.
122. Ibid. 5 (6 September 1902): 1139; for an etching and description of the proposed building, see ibid. 6 (3 January 1903): 14-15.
123. Trustee Report, 1902, pp. 7, 8.
124. *Universalist Leader* 8 (4 November 1905): 1382.
125. Proceedings, 1903, p. 105.
126. *Universalist Leader* 7 (13 August 1904): 1042; WCA Records, 1905.
127. *Universalist Leader* 7 (17 December 1904): 1617.
128. Ibid. 8 (25 March 1905): 368-69.
129. Ibid. 7 (6 August 1904): 1006.
130. Trustee Report, 1905, p. 43.
131. *Universalist Leader* 9 (27 October 1906): 1356.
132. Trustee Report, 1917, p. 19.
133. *Universalist Leader* 9 (27 October 1906): 1356.
134. Ibid. 9 (17 November 1906): 1452-53.
135. Trustee Report, 1907, p. 20.
136. *Universalist Leader* 8 (20 May 1905): 635.
137. Ibid. 6 (5 December 1903): 1546; 2 (23 October 1909): 1369.
138. Ibid. 13 (8 January 1910): 47.
139. Ibid. 16 (15 November 1913): 1350.
140. Ibid. 11 (7 November 1908): 1424; Trustee Report, 1911, pp. 27-28; *Christian Leader* 29 (30 October 1926): 3.
141. *Universalist Leader* 12 (16 October 1909): 1337.
142. WNMA Records, 1911; the Woman's Centenary Association (WCA) had been renamed in 1905.
143. Trustee Report, 1909, pp. 28-29.
144. Biennial Report, WNMA, 1909, pp. 78-79.

704 / Notes for Chapter 24

145. Trustee Report, 1915, p. 88.
146. Ibid., pp. 14, 56-57.
147. For brief biographies of the Japanese clergy, see Keirn, *Japan Mission*, pp. 13-15.
148. *Universalist Leader* 17 (4 July 1914): 647.
149. Ibid. 18 (6 November 1915): 1068.

Chapter 24: THE JAPAN MISSION BETWEEN TWO WARS

1. *Universalist Leader* 18 (30 January 1915): 111.
2. *Census of Religious Bodies, 1906, 1916*. United States Department of Commerce, Bureau of Statistics (Washington, D.C.: Government Printing Office, 1910, 1919).
3. *Universalist Leader* 20 (3 November 1917): 760.
4. Ibid. 19 (23 September 1916): 874. After her return she wrote *From Dream to Reality*, issued in 1918 by the WNMA and based on her diary kept while in Japan. *Universalist Leader* 21 (30 November 1918): 928.
5. *Universalist Leader* 22 (13 December 1919): 1230-31.
6. Ibid. 22 (27 September 1919): 877-78.
7. Ibid.
8. Ibid. 23 (27 March 1920): 315.
9. Ibid. 20 (24 November 1917): 825-26, 827.
10. WNMA Records.
11. *Universalist Leader* 21 (2 February 1918): 89.
12. Ibid. 19 (5 February 1916): 136.
13. Ibid. 24 (10 September 1921): 947.
14. Year Book, 1922, p. 72.
15. Ibid., p. 68.
16. Trustee Report, 1923, ibid., 1924, p. 20.
17. *Unity* 89 (11 May 1922): 166.
18. Trustee Report, Year Book, 1924, p. 20.
19. *Universalist Leader* 26 (8 December 1923): 18.
20. Minutes, Year Book, 1924, p. 12.
21. For her reminiscences, see the *Universalist Leader* 27 (19 April 1924): 10-13.
22. WNMA Records.
23. For biographical sketches, see the *Universalist Leader* 27 (7 June 1924): 15 and the *Christian Leader* 39 (16 May 1936): 619-20.
24. For a biographical sketch, see the *Christian Leader* 120 (8 January 1938): 45-46.
25. Ibid. 39 (7 November 1936): 1422.
26. *Universalist Leader* 27 (1 November 1924): 6, 14.
27. *Christian Leader* 29 (13 March 1926): 20.
28. For samples of his infectious enthusiasm for the mission and its work, see the *Christian Leader* 30 (19 November 1927): 1490-91.
29. WNMA Records.
30. *Christian Leader* 119 (19 June 1937): 773.
31. *Universalist Leader* 28 (5 December 1925): 12.
32. WNMA Records; Year Book, 1929, p. 21.
33. Year Book, 1933, p. 20.
34. Ibid., 1926, p. 65.
35. *Universalist Leader* 28 (5 December 1925): 13.
36. Report of the Board of Foreign Missions, Year Book, 1928, pp. 65-66.
37. Trustee Report, 1928, Year Book, 1929, p. 9.
38. *Christian Leader* 31 (12 May 1928): 594.
39. Year Book, 1933, p. 60.
40. *Christian Leader* 37 (17 November 1934): 1453.
41. Ibid. 34 (7 November 1931): 1429.
42. Ibid. 32 (4 May 1929): 566; Report, International Church Extension Board, in ibid. 123 (27 September 1941): 780.
43. *Christian Leader* 36 (4 November 1933): 1397.
44. Report, Universalist Service Committee, 1955.
45. *Universalist Leader* 27 (1 November 1924): 3.
46. *Christian Leader* 35 (31 December 1932): 1552.
47. Ibid. 29 (10 April 1926): 4.
48. Year Book, 1929, p. 20.
49. *Christian Leader* 33 (25 October 1930): 1349.
50. Ibid. 35 (19 November 1932): 1365.
51. Ibid. 32 (25 May 1929): 661.
52. Ibid. 33 (1 November 1930): 1381.
53. Ibid. 35 (30 April 1932): 557-58.
54. Ibid. 33 (22 February 1930): 229.

55. Year Book, 1934, p. 26.
56. *Christian Leader* 38 (8 June, 16 November 1935): 13-14, 1461.
57. Ibid. 36 (7 October 1933): 1265-66.
58. Ibid. 37 (10 November 1934): 1418-19.
59. Ibid., p. 1417.
60. Ibid. 37 (11 August 1934): 1002.
61. Ibid. 36 (25 March 1933): 363-65.
62. Ibid. 37 (21 July 1934): 921.
63. Ibid. 37 (29 September 1934): 1236.
64. Ibid. 37 (1 September 1934): 1096.
65. Ibid. 37 (22 December 1934): 1630.
66. Ibid. 120 (22 October 1938): 1266.
67. Ibid. 122 (15 June 1940): 558.
68. WNMA Report, General Convention, 1939, p. 43.
69. *Christian Leader* 123 (27 September 1941): 776.
70. Ibid. 123 (18 January 1941): 51.
71. Report, International Church Extension Board, 1939-40, p. 83.
72. *Chistian Leader* 122 (30 November 1940): 1062.
73. Ibid. 124 (6 June 1942): 349.
74. Ibid. 128 (5 January 1946): 24.
75. Trustee Report, 1946, Directory and Biennial Reports, 1948, p. 37.
76. *Christian Leader* 129 (4 October 1947): 442.
77. Ibid. 128 (19 January 1946): 45.
78. Ibid. 129 (July 1947): 321.
79. Ibid. 131 (April 1949): 135-36.
80. General Assembly Records, 1951.
81. *Universalist Leader* 138 (August 1956): 182.
82. Report, Department of Service Projects, 1951.

Chapter 25: FACING A WORLD OF CHANGE

1. Lalone, *And Thy Neighbor as Thyself*, p. 3.
2. Proceedings, *Christian Freeman* 22 (26 October 1860): 102.
3. Frank Oliver Hall, pastor emeritus, Church of the Divine Paternity, New York City. *Christian Leader* 120 (12 November 1938): 1369.
4. *Universalist* 45 (6 June 1874): [2].
5. Ibid. 46 (5 June 1875): [2].
6. Ibid. 44 (26 July 1873): [2].
7. *Universalist Leader* 13 (30 April 1910): 560.
8. *Universalist* 41 (23 July 1870): [1].
9. Maine Convention Records, 1874.
10. Proceedings, General Convention, 1881, *Christian Leader* 52 (6 October 1881): 5.
11. Ibid. 54 (1 November 1883): 4.
12. Ibid. 61 (2 October 1890): 5.
13. *Universalist Leader* 28 (8 August 1925): 18.
14. *Christian Leader* 30 (12 February 1927): 212.
15. Ibid. 128 (16 March 1946): 144.
16. Quoted in the *Ladies' Repository* 38 (September 1867): 230.
17. *Universalist Miscellany* 1 (January 1844): 235.
18. *Universalist Repository* 51 (February 1874): 153-54.
19. *Fifty Notable Years*, p. 80.
20. *Universalist* 44 (20 December 1873): [2].
21. Ibid. 44 (20, 27 December 1873): [2], [3].
22. Proceedings, General Convention, 1905, p. 17.
23. *Universalist Leader* 10 (16 November 1907): 1454.
24. Proceedings, *Christian Leader* 61 (9 October 1890): 1, 8.
25. A review of the biographical sketches in Catherine F. Hitchings' "Universalist and Unitarian Women Ministers" reveals the strikingly large number who were involved in one or more aspects of the women's rights movement.
26. Proceedings, *Christian Leader* 61 (20 October 1890): 5.
27. His extensive papers, covering the period 1848-1900, and including a diary and many of his sermons and speeches, are available in the Manuscript Division of the Ohio Historical Library, Columbus, Ohio.
28. "Shall Women Vote?" Henley Papers, ibid.
29. Proceedings, General Convention, 1883, p. 8.
30. Ibid., 1903, p. 19.
31. Proceedings, Year Book, 1928, p. 25.
32. Lalone, *And Thy Neighbor as Thyself*, p. 89.

33. *Christian Leader* 32 (9 November 1929): 1422.
34. Minutes, General Assembly, 1946, p. 23.
35. Proceedings, General Convention, 1882, p. 5.
36. Minutes, Year Book, 1928, p. 24.
37. *Christian Leader* 31 (3 March 1928): 271.
38. Proceedings, General Convention, 1897, pp. 16-17.
39. Ibid., 1899, p. 17.
40. Lalone, *And Thy Neighbor as Thyself*, pp. 72-73.
41. Minutes, Year Book, 1932, p. 20.
42. *Southern Pioneer* 3 (15 February 1834): 71.
43. Proceedings, *Christian Freeman* 20 (4 June 1858): 18.
44. Extract from Proceedings, *Universalist* 52 (25 June 1870): [2].
45. *Universalist* 55 (10 May 1873): [1].
46. *Christian Leader* 54 (28 June 1883): 2-3.
47. Ibid. 62 (11 June 1891): 4.
48. Ibid. 49 (6 March 1879): 4.
49. Mary A. Livermore, *The Story of My Life* (Hartford, Conn.: A. D. Worthington & Co., 1897), p. 398.
50. *Christian Freeman* 15 (27 January 1854): 154.
51. Proceedings, 1909, pp. 99-103.
52. Ibid., 1909, p. 97; William H. McGlauflin, *What the Universalist Church is Doing*, p. 83.
53. *Universalist Leader* 15 (13 January 1912): 50.
54. Ibid. 15 (17 August 1912): 1036-38.
55. Ibid. 18 (12 June 1915): 565.
56. *Christian Leader* 54 (31 May 1883): 4.
57. Ibid. 63 (5 January 1893): 4.
58. Ibid. 56 (23 July 1885): 5; (25 February 1886): 4.
59. Ibid. 55 (12 February 1885): 1.
60. Ibid. 57 (16 September 1886): 4.
61. Ibid. 57 (3 February 1887): 5.
62. Ibid. 57 (10 February 1887): 1.
63. Ibid. 57 (13 January 1887): 4.
64. Minutes, General Convention, 1889, p. 8.
65. *Christian Leader* 63 (5 January 1893): 1.
66. Ibid. 60 (11 July 1889): 5.
67. See Stanley Buder, *Pullman: An Experiment in Industrial Order and Community Planning, 1880-1930* (N.Y.: Oxford University Press, 1967). For a contemporary defense of Pullman by a Universalist clergyman, see Charles H. Eaton, "Pullman, a Social Experiment," *To-Day* 2 (January 1895): 1-9.
68. *Christian Leader* 60 (11 July 1889): 5.
69. Ibid. 64 (5 July 1894): 4.
70. *Universalist Leader* 68 (4 December 1897): 9.
71. *Christian Leader* 67 (4 November 1897): 4.
72. Ibid. 64 (May 1894): 2.
73. *Universalist Leader* 22 (29 November 1919): 1154-57.
74. *Congregationalist* 112 (10 November 1927): 580-81.
75. *Universalist Leader* 23 ((26 June, 3 July 1920): 625-26, 652-53; 26 (27 July 1923): 8-9.
76. Ibid. 24 (2 July 1921): 702-703.
77. Ibid. 28 (19 December 1925): 15-16.
78. *Christian Leader* 29 (30 January 1926): 6-8.
79. *Universalist Leader* 28 (19 December 1925): 16-17.
80. Ibid. 26 (7 July 1923): 3.
81. N.Y.: Fleming H. Revell Co. In 1930, three years after Nash's death, Roberts published a new edition. The book was originally published as a pamphlet by the Murray Press in 1920 and later expanded. Part of the book comprised a series of lectures which Nash delivered at the Massachusetts Institute of Technology, published as *An Industrial Miracle and How It Happened*. *Christian Leader* 38 (5 October 1935): 1272.
82. *Christian Leader* 29 (10 April 1926): 22. Nash also wrote an article entitled "The Organized Church and Organized Labor," published in Jerome Davis (ed.), *Business and the Church* (N.Y.: Century Co., 1926), pp. 333-44.
83. *Christian Leader* 29 (18 December 1926): 5.
84. *Congregationalist* 110 (27 August 1925): 262.
85. *New Republic* 29 (22 February 1922): 364-66.
86. *Universalist Leader* 28 (24 January 1925): 6.

87. Ibid. 28 (23 May 1925): 18.

88. Ibid. 28 (31 January 1925): 12.

89. *Christian Leader* 61 (2 October 1890): 5.

90. The address, entitled "Young Men and Business Life; or, The Gospel of Wealth," was reproduced in the *Christian Leader* 62 (25 February 1892): 2.

91. *Christian Leader* 57 (26 August 1886): 1.

92. Ibid. 57 (15 July 1886): 1.

93. *Universalist Leader* 1 (29 October 1898): 9-10.

94. For a study of his career and ideas, see James D. Hunt, "The Social Gospel as a Way of Life: A Biography of H. C. Ledyard, Universalist Minister and Labor Leader, 1880-1950," *Journal of the Universalist Historical Society* 5 (1964-65): 31-63.

95. *Christian Leader* 36 (29 April 1933): 532-33.

96. *Universalist Leader* 1 (30 April 1898): 5.

97. See Percy H. Epler, *The Life of Clara Barton* (N.Y.: Macmillan, 1915).

98. Records, Franklin County Association, 1898.

99. Proceedings, General Convention, 1917, pp. 64-65.

100. Ibid., 1915, pp. 75-81.

101. *Some Things Remembered* (Boston: Church of the Larger Fellowship, 1976), p. 36.

102. *Universalist Leader* 19 (8 July 1916): 653.

103. Ibid. 19 (27 May 1916): 516.

104. *American Mercury* 25 (March 1932): 290.

105. *Universalist Leader* 20 (7 April 1917): 214.

106. Trustee Report, 1917, p. 10; ibid. 20 (3 November 1917): 750.

107. *And Thy Neighbor as Thyself*, p. 79.

108. *Universalist Leader* 28 (5 September 1925): 3; *Christian Leader* 30 (3 December 1927): 1539-40.

109. *Christian Leader* 121 (15 April 1939): 343, 353.

110. Report, Committee on National and International Relief, Year Book, 1930, p. 71.

111. For a documented account of the battle of religious conservatives against evolutionary science and modernism in theology, see Norman F. Furniss, *The Fundamentalist Controversy, 1918-1931* (New Haven, Conn.: Yale University Press, 1954).

112. *Universalist Leader* 28 (17 January 1925).

113. Ibid. 27 (8 November 1924): 3-4.

114. Ibid. 27 (22 November 1924): 20-21.

115. Ibid. 28 (11 April 1925): 21.

116. Ibid. 28 (13 December 1924): 12.

117. Letter of Transfer, UCA Personnel Records.

118. *Universalist Leader* 28 (30 May 1925): 29.

119. Clark was listed as pastor of the Medford Hillside church for only one year, and his name did not appear at all in the official directory of Universalist clergy.

120. The address was reprinted in *Unity* 99 (7 March 1927): 10-15.

121. Kenneth L. Patton, "The Bankruptcy of Leadership in the Liberal Church," delivered at the Charles Street Meeting House, Boston, 23 May 1954.

122. Ibid.

123. The continuing Cold War frame of mind spawned dozens of private organizations, often described as part of the Radical Right. Universalists and Unitarians were often among the targets. See Harry and Bonaro Overstreet, *The Strange Tactics of Extremism* (N.Y.: W. W. Norton, 1964), especially pp. 157-69.

124. Proceedings, General Convention, 1875, p. 10.

125. Ibid., 1889, p. 8.

126. *Christian Leader* 60 (1, 15 August 1889): 1, 1.

127. Proceedings, General Convention, 1911, pp. 14, 89.

128. Ibid., 1911, pp. 14, 89.

129. For a general review which includes references to Universalist contributions, see Walter Van Kirk, *Religion Renounces War* (Chicago: Willett, Clark & Co., 1934); and Charles DeBenedetti, *Origins of the American Peace Movement, 1915-1929* (Millwood, N.Y.: KTO Press, 1978).

130. *Universalist Leader* 23 (16 October 1920): 948-49.

131. Minutes, General Convention, 1923, Year Book, 1924, p. 66.

132. Trustee Minutes, *Universalist Leader* 27 (19 January 1924): 8.

133. *Christian Leader* 29 (30 October 1926): 10-11.

134. *Universalist Leader* 27 (17 May 1924): 4.

135. Ibid. 27 (7 June 1924): 23.

136. Year Book, 1928, pp. 15, 24.

137. Ibid., p. 69.

138. Ibid., 1929, p. 23.

139. *Christian Leader* 31 (29 September, 6 October 1928): 1222-23, 1263.

140. *Universalist Leader* 28 (19 December 1925): 9; *Christian Leader* 32 (30 March 1929): 401-403.

141. Minutes, General Convention, 1931, Year Book, 1932, p. 17.

142. Ibid., 1936, p. 17.

143. *Christian Leader* 34 (27 May 1931): 644-45.

144. Ibid. 37 (2 June 1934): 687-89.

145. Minutes, Year Book, 1936, p. 13.

146. Ibid., 1939, pp. 21-22; *Christian Leader* 121 (28 October 1939): 1041-42.

147. *Christian Leader* 122 (8, 29 June 1940): 535, 605.

148. Ibid. 123 (1 March 1941): 195; Report, Emergency War Relief Committee, 1943.

149. Minutes, General Convention, 1941; *Commercial Advertiser* (Canton, N.Y.), 16 September 1941.

150. *Christian Leader* 124 (20 June 1942): 353.

151. So far as is known, no complete statistics were ever published. There were 2,320 individuals recorded on the service flag in 1943; a service roster was attempted by the youth department of the church, but the totals were incomplete. *Christian Leader* 125 (6 February 1943): 79-80; 126 (17 June 1944): 376.

153. Report of the General Superintendent, 1943, p. 6; *Christian Leader* 126 (4 March 1944): 135, 156. For accounts of some of their experiences, see ibid. 127 (3 November 1945): 489-96.

154. *Christian Leader* 125 (20 March, 3 April 1943): 163-64, 183, 196.

155. Minutes, General Assembly, 1947.

156. *Christian Leader* 130 (20 March 1948): 134.

157. Ibid. 134 (November 1952): 269; Trustee Report, 1954.

158. General Assembly Records, 1957.

159. See Mulford Q. Sibley and Philip E. Jacob, *Conscription and Conscience: The American State and the Conscientious Objector, 1940-1947* (Ithaca, N.Y.: Cornell University Press, 1952).

160. For a summary of the various types and degrees of pacifism, see the *Christian Leader* 121 (30 December 1939): 1244-45.

161. *Christian Leader* 34 (14 November 1931): 1462.

162. *Universalist Leader* 27 (14 June 1924): 9.

163. *Christian non-resistance, in all of its important bearings, illustrated and defended* (Philadelphia: J. Miller McKim).

164. Minutes, Year Book, 1926, p. 13.

165. *Universalist Leader* 28 (31 October 1925): 10.

166. Ibid. 28 (19 December 1925): 19.

167. Ibid. 28 (31 October 1925): 10.

168. *Christian Leader* 34 (7 November 1931): 1420.

169. Minutes, Year Book, 1932, p. 12.

170. Ibid., pp. 19-20.

171. Ibid., 1934, p. 13.

172. *Christian Leader* 34 (31 October 1931): 1380.

173. The correspondence is reproduced in Lalone, *And Thy Neighbor as Thyself,* Appendix.

174. Trustee Report, Year Book, 1935.

175. Minutes, General Convention, 1939, p. 21.

176. *Christian Leader* 121 (4 November 1939): 1054.

177. Minutes, General Convention, 1939, p. 21; *Christian Leader* 121 (4 November 1939): 1046.

178. *Christian Leader* 122 (26 October 1940): 958.

179. Ibid. 126 (15 April 1944): 227.

180. Ibid. 122 (3 August 1940): 695.

181. Milton R. Konvitz, "The Case of the Eight Divinity Students," *Bill of Rights Review* 1 (Spring 1941): 196-205. Both received degrees from the Chicago Theological Seminary.

182. *Christian Leader* 123 (20 September 1941): 749.

183. Ibid. 128 (7 December 1946): 544.

184. Ibid. 123 (2 August, 4 October 1941): 611, 806.

185. Proceedings, General Convention, 1941, p. 12.
186. Conscientious objectors were again recognized when the Laws of Fellowship were revised in 1953.
187. Report, Biennial Session, General Assembly, 1943, p. 26. The UCA trustees had earlier refused to allow funds contributed for war relief to be used for the support of Universalists in civil and public service camps. *Christian Leader* 125 (17 July 1943): 442.
188. *Christian Leader* 125 (6 November 1943): 652.
189. Ibid. 126 (1 April 1944): 223; 127 (15 September 1945): 410.
190. Minutes, General Assembly, 1946, p. 8; 1947, p. 25.
191. Ibid., p. 27.
192. Minutes, General Assembly, 1946, p. 24.
193. Ibid., p. 27.
194. See the *Christian Leader* 109 (20 September 1947): 422.
195. This resolution was never actually adopted by the General Assembly but by the UCA trustees to whom the resolution was referred in 1959.
196. Minutes, General Assembly, 1946, pp. 24-25.
197. *Unitarian Register-Universalist Leader*, October 1961, p. 27.

Chapter 26: CLARENCE R. SKINNER AND THE SOCIAL GOSPEL

1. *Christian Leader* 54 (19 July 1883): 1.
2. For the background, character, and leadership of the Social Gospel movement, see Aaron I. Abell, *The Urban Impact on American Protestantism, 1865-1900* (Cambridge, Mass.: Harvard University Press, 1943); Henry F. May, *Protestant Churches and Industrial America* (N.Y.: Harper, 1949); and Charles H. Hopkins, *The Rise of the Social Gospel in American Protestantism, 1865-1915* (New Haven, Conn.: Yale University Press, 1940).
3. *Universalist Leader* 14 (23 December 1911): 1631-32.
4. Commission Report, Proceedings, General Convention, 1911, pp. 96-101.
5. For a bibliography which he prepared, see the *Universalist Leader* 14 (8 April 1911): 432-33.
6. Ibid. 14 (23 September 1911).
7. Proceedings, General Convention, 1911, p. 14, 89.
8. Ibid., 1913, pp. 15, 16.
9. Report of the Commission on Social Service, Proceedings, General Convention, 1915, p. 54.
10. There are several brief biographies available, as well as a chronology of his life and a bibliography of his extensive writings prepared by Alan Seaburg and published in the *Annual Journal of the Universalist Historical Society* 5 (1964-65): 65-77. One of the most extensive biographical treatments is Charles A. Gaines, "Clarence R. Skinner, Image of a Movement" (unpublished special BD thesis, Crane Theological School, Tufts University, 1961), to whom the author is indebted both for giving access to the thesis and to related materials. Gaines based much of his study on interviews with Skinner's colleagues and former students. One chapter was edited as an article in the *Annual Journal of the Universalist Historical Society* 3 (1962): 1-13, entitled "Clarence R. Skinner: The Dark Years." Among the briefer treatments are Alfred S. Cole, "Clarence R. Skinner, Prophet of Twentieth Century Universalism," first delivered as an address before the Universalist Historical Society in 1955 and reprinted by it in pamphlet form the following year. For a later account by the same author, see "Clarence R. Skinner, Prophet of the Larger Faith," *Universalist Leader* 143 (April 1961): 75 ff. For a critique of the relation between Skinner's religious and social thought, see James D. Hunt, "The Liberal Theology of Clarence R. Skinner," *Journal of the Universalist Historical Society* 7 (1967-68): 102-20. Hunt believed that Skinner's "outstanding qualities were personal rather than intellectual" and that he achieved his reputation in the denomination for leadership, courage, and imagination rather than for scholarship. Hunt to Gaines, 3 August 1960.
11. Another member of the family, Cornelia Otis Skinner, a first cousin, also received an honorary degree from Tufts (in 1935).
12. Skinner to Cousens, 5 March 1934, Tufts University Archives.
13. Annual Report to the President of Tufts College, 1931-32, pp. 44-45.
14. *Universalist Leader* 13 (26 March 1910): 401.

15. See his "Militarism or Christianity?" in ibid. 14 (29 April 1911): 526-28.

16. *Universalist Leader* 15 (6 April 1912): 435.

17. Ibid. 26 (17 November 1922): 3.

18. Newhall to Cousens, 15 January 1920.

19. See his article in the *Survey,* 25 June 1921. G. Louis Joughin and Edmund M. Morgan, in *The Legacy of Sacco and Vanzetti* (N.Y.: Harcourt, Brace, 1948), pp. 226-27, considered Skinner's analysis of the early period of the trial "the soundest discussion of the case" that had yet appeared, but it was too late to have much influence.

20. *Unity* 100 (26 December 1927): 249-50.

21. *Universalist Leader* 140 (September 1958): 220; 142 (July 1960): 164.

22. *Unitarian-Universalist Register-Leader,* December 1962, p. 31.

23. Seaburg, "Bibliography," p. 66.

24. Boston: James H. West Co.

25. Boston: Universalist Publishing House. The articles which form the core of the book appeared originally as seven articles in February and March 1915. The expanded essays (eleven in all) were reprinted, accompanied by a brief analysis by James D. Hunt in the *Annual Journal of the Universalist Historical Society* 5 (1964-65): 79-122. Skinner's essays were again reprinted as the Beacon Reference Series No. 4, in 1966.

26. N.Y.: Macmillan.

27. Boston: Universalist Publishing House.

28. Boston: Universalist Historical Society, 1955. The manuscripts were originally entitled "Living an Ordered Life in a Disordered World." *Christian Leader* 132 (August 1950): 262.

29. Boston: Universalist Publishing House, 1941.

30. Hopkins, *Social Gospel,* p. 3.

31. *Christian Leader* 128 (10 January 1946): 37.

32. *Unity* 83 (31 July 1919): 259.

33. Unpublished manuscript, Skinner Papers.

34. See Appendix A for the complete text. The text was not included in the printed proceedings of the General Convention meeting when it was adopted, but was reproduced in the *Universalist Leader* 20 (3 November 1917): 759-60 and in the appendix of Lalone's *And Thy Neighbor as Thyself.*

35. Report, Committee on Public Welfare, Year Book, 1922, pp. 83-84.

36. Year Book, 1924, pp. 77-78.

37. Ibid., 1922, pp. 76-78.

38. Ibid., pp. 14-16.

39. *Universalist Leader* 26 (3 November 1923): 10.

40. Trustee Minutes, ibid. 27 (19 January 1924): 8.

41. Report, Year Book, 1928, pp. 70-71; 1929, pp. 24-26.

42. Pennoyer to Etz, 6 February 1931.

43. *Christian Leader* 36 (14 January 1933): 51-52.

44. Minutes, Year Book, 1936, p. 6.

45. Ibid., pp. 13-14.

46. *Christian Leader* 121 (28 October 1939): 1039.

47. Ibid. 123 (27 September 1941): 790.

48. It was reproduced in ibid. 125 (2 October 1943): 582-83. See Appendix A for the complete text.

49. The previous Commission on International Relations became a subcommittee.

50. Minutes, General Assembly, 1943, pp. 30-32.

51. See Appendix A.

52. *Christian Leader* 126 (6 May 1944): 278.

53. The preliminary program was outlined in the *Christian Leader* 127 (3 February 1945): 61-62.

54. Commission Report, April 1946.

55. *Christian Leader* 129 (7 June 1947): 247.

56. Minutes, General Assembly, 1947, p. 8.

57. Ibid., 1955. One of their tasks was to compile and publish all statements of social principles adopted by the denomination up through that of 1957. An incomplete set appeared in the *Universalist Leader* in February 1954, pp. 47-49. The pioneer statement of 1917 was omitted for some inexplicable reason. The most recent statement (1957) was to have been published in 1959 but never appeared in print. See Appendix A for the complete text of the 1957 statement.

58. Holmes, address on the 20th anniversary of the first service of the Community Church of Boston, 7 January 1940, *Christian*

Leader 122 (13 January 1940): 34-37. The commemorative address was also published in pamphlet form as "The Community Church of Boston After Twenty Years, 1920-1940."

59. For representative addresses delivered in the church, see *A Free Pulpit in Action* (N.Y.: Macmillan, 1931), edited by Skinner.

60. *Unity* 89 (6 April 1922): 85-87.

61. *Christian Leader* 124 (3 January 1942): 5.

62. *Trumpet* 26 (8 February 1845): 135; for a draft of the constitution, see ibid., 22 March 1845, p. 158.

63. Ibid. 28 (2 January, 29 May, 1847): 115, 199.

64. Ibid. 27 (8 November 1845): 83.

65. Ibid. 28 (8 August 1846): 30; *Christian Freeman* 8 (1 January 1847): 142-43.

66. "The Community Church of Boston: History and Principles" (n.p., n.d.), p. 3.

67. *Christian Leader* 122 (13 January 1940): 35.

68. The Community Church of Boston continued to exist into the 1980s, located on Boylston Street, in the center of the city. Skinner's successors were Donald Lothrop (1936-1974), Philip Zwerling (1974-1978), and William Alberts (1978-   ).

69. Minutes, Year Book, 1934, p. 23.

70. *And Thy Neighbor as Thyself*, p. 98.

Chapter 27: "NOT YOUR CREED, BUT YOUR NEED": SOCIAL SERVICE AND BENEVOLENCES

1. The motto in the chapter title was adopted in 1874 for the Chapin Home for the Aged, a Universalist-sponsored facility located in Jamaica, Long Island, New York. See the *Christian Leader* 33 (29 March 1930): 389.

2. *Universalist Leader* 22 (15 February 1919): 149-51.

3. *Christian Leader* 29 (17 April 1926): 9-11.

4. Ibid. 123 (22 March 1941): 266.

5. Ibid. 129 (15 March 1947): 134.

6. Marion D. Shutter, *Rev. James Harvey Tuttle, D.D.: A Memoir* (Boston: Universalist Publishing House, 1905), p. 170.

7. *Christian Leader* 61 (21 August 1890): 5.

8. The Home was built in Richfield township, south of Minneapolis, later incorporated into the city.

9. Descriptive pamphlet, [1959], p. 3.

10. *Universalist Leader* 68 (4 December 1897): 4.

11. McGlauflin, *Universalist Church*, p. 57.

12. Year Book, 1926, pp. 153-54.

13. For an enthusiastic description by a visitor in 1926, see the *Christian Leader* 29 (17 April 1926): 12-13.

14. At the time of World War I Shutter had also served as president of the trustees of the Sheridan Cobb Hospital in St. Paul, established by a Universalist physician. Most of the other officers were also Universalists. Trustee Report, 1914, Proceedings, General Convention, 1915, p. 13.

15. *Universalist Leader* 7 (16 January 1904): 80-81.

16. *Christian Leader* 65 (4 July 1895): 4.

17. Ibid. 66 (11 June 1896): 17.

18. *Universalist Leader* 7 (7 May 1904): 596.

19. *Christian Leader* 66 (11 June 1896): 17.

20. *Universalist Leader* 5 (31 May 1902): 685.

21. Ibid. 15 (27 April 1912): 527.

22. Ibid. 17 (11 April 1914): 367.

23. Year Book, 1923, p. 52; *Universalist Leader* 25 (7 January 1922): 9.

24. *Christian Leader* 122 (13 April 1940): 356-58.

25. Ibid. 61 (27 November 1890): 4.

26. Ibid. 61 (11 December 1890): 4.

27. Ibid. 125 (3 April 1943): 221; 130 (15 May 1948): 237.

28. *Universalist* 52 (15 April 1871): [2].

29. *Universalist Leader* 14 (18 November 1911): 1156, 1469-72.

30. *Christian Leader* 59 (27 September 1888): 1.

31. *Universalist Register*, 1880, p. 8.

32. *Universalist Leader* 14 (18 November 1911): 1469-72.

33. *Christian Leader* 33 (1 March 1930): 261.

34. Ibid. 36 (30 December 1933): 1647.

35. Ibid. 129 (6 September 1947): 395.

36. The complete records of the Home, comprising sixty printed annual reports

beginning in 1902, and a typescript summary, were made available through the Andover-Harvard Theological Library by the generosity of Mrs. Louise Greene through Miss Georgene Bowen, who also wrote a brief history of the Home.

37. Georgene E. Bowen, "Messiah Universalist Home: Its Birth, Life, and Merger, 1900-1964" (multilithed typescript), (n.p., n.d.) p. 15.

38. Ibid., pp. 11-12.

39. *Christian Leader* 29 (14 August 1926): 16; McGlauflin, *Universalist Church,* p. 55.

40. Year Book, 1929, pp. 102-103.

41. *Christian Leader* 36 (30 December 1933): 1647.

42. See the *Universalist Leader* 19 (29 January 1916): 110-111.

43. Ibid. 28 (12 December 1925): 29.

44. *Christian Leader* 33 (3 May 1930): 547.

45. Ibid. 34 (23 May 1931): 642.

46. Ibid. 36 (27 May 1933): 668.

47. Ibid. 121 (29 July 1939): 728.

48. *Universalist Leader* 141 (March 1959): 87.

49. *And Thy Neighbor as Thyself,* first published in 1939 and appearing in an enlarged edition twenty years later.

50. *Christian Leader* 37 (1 January 1944): 28.

51. Quoted in Lalone, *And Thy Neighbor,* p. 102.

52. *Christian Leader* 127 (20 October 1945): 465-67.

53. Ibid. 129 (16 August 1947): 363.

54. Ibid. 129 (20 September 1947): 412.

55. Quoted in Lalone, *And Thy Neighbor,* p. 111.

56. *Christian Leader* 128 (July 1946): 322.

57. Report, Universalist Service Committee, 1949.

58. *Universalist Leader* 142 (August 1960): 200.

59. Records, General Assembly, 1949.

60. *Universalist Leader* 135 (June 1953): 165.

61. Report, Universalist Service Committee, 1959.

62. *Universalist Leader* 141 (September 1959): 205.

63. Klotzle to Mrs. Dudley King, 17 September 1957.

64. *Unitarian-Universalist Register-Leader,* May 1963, p. 3.

65. Ibid., Mid-Summer 1963, p. 10.

66. Ibid., January 1963, p. 20.

Chapter 28: EDGING CLOSER TOGETHER: UNIVERSALIST-UNITARIAN RELATIONS, 1870-1925

1. *Christian Ambassador* 10 (21 April 1860): 62.

2. *Universalist* 53 (15 July 1871): [2].

3. *Unity* 2 (1 October 1878): 71.

4. Proceedings, 1874, p. 8.

5. *Universalist* 59 (16 November 1878): [2].

6. *Unity* 5 (1 April 1880): 41-42.

7. See his *Walks About Zion: Ten Lectures* (Boston: Universalist Publishing House, 1882), Lecture No. 8 ("The Unitarians").

8. Proceedings, 1880, p. 43.

9. *Christian Leader* 68 (9 September 1886): 1.

10. See George W. Cooke, *Unitarianism in America* (Boston: American Unitarian Association, 1902), pp. 247 ff.

11. *Christian Leader* 68 (16 September 1886): 1.

12. *Christian Register,* quoted in the *Christian Leader* 61 (11 March 1880): 4.

13. See, for example, Cooke, *Unitarianism in America,* p. 368.

14. *Universalist Quarterly* 19 n.s. (1882): 505.

15. *Universalist Leader* 12 (13 November 1909): 1460.

16. *Christian Leader* 68 (9 December 1886): 4.

17. *Fifty Notable Years,* pp. 45-46.

18. See Lyttle, *Freedom Moves West.*

19. Quoted in ibid., p. 185.

20. *Christian Leader* 68 (15 July 1886): 4.

21. Ibid. 62 (20 January 1881): 2.

22. Ibid. 65 (19 July 1883): 1.

23. *Unity* 13 (16 June 1884): 169.

24. *Christian Leader* 73 (12 November 1891): 1.

25. *Unity* 9 (1 May 1882): 81.
26. *Christian Register* 72 (11 May 1893): 298.
27. *Christian Leader* 63 (15 June 1893): 5.
28. Proceedings, 1889, pp. 4-5, 72.
29. Ibid., 1891, pp. 7, 8.
30. *Christian Leader* 67 (2 September 1897): 2.
31. Proceedings, 1891, p. 75.
32. *Christian Leader* 63 (5 October 1893): 1.
33. Proceedings, 1895, p. 69.
34. *Christian Leader* 67 (2 September 1897): 2; *Universalist Leader* 2 (7 October 1899): 2.
35. *New Unity* 4 n.s. (23 September 1897): 641.
36. *Universalist Leader* 1 (22 January 1898): 9.
37. *Christian Leader* 62 (3 December 1891): 4.
38. *Universalist Leader* 2 (1 July 1899): 2.
39. Annual Report, AUA, 1899, p. 22.
40. Proceedings, 1899, p. 11.
41. *Universalist Leader* 3 (17 February 1900): 200.
42. Ibid. 2 (11 November 1899): 1.
43. *Independent* 52 (4 January 1900): 58.
44. *Universalist Leader* 2 (3 February 1900): 134.
45. The Universalist representatives were Isaac M. Atwood, John Coleman Adams, Henry I. Cushman, Henry B. Metcalf, and Frederick A. Winkleman.
46. The minutes of the meeting were reproduced in the *Universalist Leader* 3 (16 June 1900): 750.
47. The Universalist committee consisted of Atwood (chairman), F. O. Hall, Hosea S. Ballou, L. S. McCollester, and John Coleman Adams.
48. *Universalist Leader* 2 (19 August 1899): 3.
49. His views were embodied in an extensive series of long articles in the *Leader*, beginning in 1897 and extending into 1901. They were reprinted in whole or in part in such widely separated papers as the *Gospel Banner* (Maine) and the *Universalist Herald* (Georgia) and many of them appeared in a twenty-four page pamphlet which was published in 1901. The *Leader* refused to publish one article which Sweetser submitted which criticized the paper for not reporting completely the actions taken at the convention session in 1901. He thereupon published the rejected letter in an eight-page pamphlet which he called "How the Matter Now Stands in Regard to the Unitarian Overture" (20 November 1901).

50. *Universalist Leader* 2 (7 October 1899): 2, 8.
51. Ibid. 2 (14 October 1899): 4.
52. Ibid. 4 (28 September, 5 October 1901): 1227-30, 1259 ff.
53. Much of the documentation for this activity came from Shinn, who saw it happen first-hand as part of his extensive field work. Theological considerations aside, these experiences help explain Shinn's dislike of the Unitarians which sometimes amounted to antipathy.
54. *Universalist Leader* 4 (5 October 1901): 1254.
55. Ibid. 4 (19 October 1901): 1319.
56. Ibid. 4 (12 October 1901): 1290.
57. Hall's judgment was confirmed by the findings of a member of the joint committee (a Unitarian) who investigated Sweetser's repeated allegations of Unitarian "aggression." He found that the great majority of them were either without any foundation at all, were grossly distorted, or were exaggerated. Samuel A. Eliot files, Andover-Harvard Theological Library.
58. *Universalist Leader* 4 (19 October 1901): 1323-24.
59. Atwood to Eliot, 12 October 1900; AUA Letterbooks.
60. *Universalist Leader* 5 (8 February 1902): 178-79.
61. Ibid. 8 (16 September 1905): 1163-66.
62. Ibid. 8 (24 June 1905): 781. Among the purported conflicts between Universalist and Unitarian church interests investigated by the committee were: A complaint by the Pennsylvania Universalist Convention of the "take-over" of the closed Universalist church in Erie, in which the right of the Unitarians to establish their own churches was confirmed; presumed competition between churches of the two denominations in Wichita, Kansas, Milwaukee, Wisconsin, and the Flatbush section of New York City, with the finding that there was room for both in each.
63. Proceedings, 1909, p. 95.
64. *Universalist Leader* 9 (3 February 1906): 138.

65. Ibid. 12 (13 November 1909): 1449.
66. *Unity* 1 (1 March 1878): xi.
67. *Universalist Leader* 12 (16 October 1909): 1323-26; *Christian Register* 88 (14 October 1909): 1107.
68. *Universalist Leader* 13 (5, 26 February 1910): 170, 269.
69. *Christian Register* 88 (21 October 1909): 1123-26.
70. Ibid. 101 (16 November 1922): 1092.
71. *Universalist Leader* 12 (16 October 1909): 1318-19.
72. See, for example, the *Universalist Leader* 13 (24 September 1910): 1068-69.
73. *Universalist Leader* 19 (8 April 1916): 344-46.
74. For an elaborate review of the distinctive character of Universalism, see John Coleman Adams' address as one of the King's Chapel lectures in 1916 sponsored by the Lowell Institute.
75. *Universalist Leader* 23 (25 December 1920): 1217-18.
76. Ibid. 23 (23 October 1920): 983-84.
77. Ibid. 26 (24 November 1923): 17-18.
78. *Christian Leader* 29 (2 January 1926): 16.
79. *Universalist Leader* 26 (3 February 1923): 19.
80. The address was reproduced in the *Christian Register* 106 (3 November 1927): 865.
81. *Universalist Leader* 28 (17 January 1925): 3.
82. Reccord to Samuel A. Eliot, 26 February 1912.
83. *Universalist Leader* 27 (8 November 1924): 6.

Chapter 29: AN ENLARGED "HOUSEHOLD OF FAITH"? ABORTED UNION WITH THE CONGREGATIONALISTS

1. Minutes, Universalist Year Book, 1926, p. 15.
2. The text of the Congregational overture was never written into the official records of the convention. However, it was reproduced in its entirety in the *Leader* and in the minutes of the National Council.
3. Bisbee (ed.), *From Good Luck to Gloucester*, p. 73.
4. Manfred Waldemar Kohl, *Congregationalism in America* (Oak Creek, Wisconsin: Congregational Press, 1977), p. 45. For a summary of the various initiatives and their results, see also Gaius Glenn Atkins and Frederick L. Fagley, *History of American Congregationalism* (Boston and Chicago: Pilgrim Press, 1942), pp. 340-59.
5. The statement was reproduced in the *Congregationalist* 98 (6 November 1913): 643; see also Atkins and Fagley, *Congregationalism*, pp. 404-405.
6. *Universalist Leader* 16 (8 November 1913): 1305.
7. Ibid. 17 (5 December 1914): 1176-78.
8. For the text, see Atkins and Fagley, *Congregationalism*, pp. 402-404.
9. *Universalist Leader* 17 (5 November 1914): 854-55.
10. *Congregationalist* 108 (18 October 1923): 524.
11. Minutes, Year Book, 1924, pp. 15, 63.
12. *Universalist Leader* 26 (27 October 1923): 3-4.
13. Minutes, Year Book, 1926, p. 76.
14. Ibid., p. 77.
15. *Congregationalist* 110 (16 July 1925): 71.
16. All relevant documents referred to here were reproduced in the *Universalist Leader* 28 (7 November 1925): 3-5.
17. *Congregationalist* 110 (5 November 1925): 619.
18. Ibid. 112 (30 June 1927): 836.
19. *Christian Leader* 32 (15 June 1929): 743-44.
20. *Universalist Leader* 28 (21 November 1925): 3.
21. *Congregationalist* 110 (3 September 1925): 292.
22. Ibid. 110 (15 October 1925): 523-24.
23. Ibid. 114 (7 March 1929): 302.
24. *Christian Leader* 29 (2 January 1926): 3.
25. *Universalist Leader* 28 (26 December 1925): 12-13.
26. *Congregationalist* 111 (20 May 1926): 618. Both addresses were reproduced.
27. *Universalist Leader* 25 (23 December 1922): 7.
28. Ibid. 27 (8 March 1924): 19.

29. *Christian Leader* 30 (10 September 1927): 1166-67.

30. Ibid. 106 (13 October 1927): 811.

31. *Congregationalist* 111 (14 January 1926): 37.

32. Quoted in ibid. 112 (12 May 1927): 612-13; a copy of the *Western Unitarian* was not available.

33. *Congregationalist* 110 (12 November 1925): 655.

34. *Universalist Leader* 28 (14 November 1925): 11.

35. Ibid. 28 (21 November 1925): 6-9.

36. *Christian Leader* 29 (6 February 1926): 4.

37. *Universalist Leader* 28 (31 October 1925): 11-12.

38. The complete membership was as follows, exclusive of the chairman: James F. Albion, A. Ingham Bicknell, John A. Cousens, Roger F. Etz, George F. Fortier, Roger S. Galer, Carl F. Henry, Robert W. Hill, John Smith Lowe, Harold Marshall, Mrs. T. R. Miller, B. C. Ruggles, H. E. Simmons, S. D. Tilney, and G. D. Elbert Walker.

39. *Christian Leader* 30 (23 July 1927): 947.

40. Ibid. 30 (19 February 1927): 230-31; *Congregationalist* 112 (17 February 1927): 202-203. Each paper also carried photographs of the members of the two commissions, with brief biographical sketches.

41. *Christian Leader* 30 (19 February 1927): 227.

42. *Congregationalist* 112 (17 February 1927): 198, 202-203; *Christian Leader* 30 (19 February 1927): 233-34.

43. Excerpts were reproduced for several weeks in the *Leader*, beginning 5 March.

44. One series was published as *Week Day Sermons in King's Chapel* (N.Y.: Macmillan, 1925); one by Perkins was included.

45. *Unity* 99 (14 March 1927): 21; *Christian Leader* 30 (2 April 1927): 429.

46. *Congregationalist* 112 (3 March 1927): 280.

47. *Christian Leader* 30 (9 April 1927): 467.

48. Minutes, General Convention, 1913, p. 4.

49. *Christian Leader* 30 (23 April 1927): 532-33.

50. Ibid. 30 (26 February 1927): 260-61.

51. *Congregationalist* 111 (3, 24 June 1927): 691, 792.

52. Ibid. 112 (24 March 1927): 371.

53. Ibid. 111 (16 December 1926): 803; *Christian Leader* 29 (18 December 1926): 13.

54. *Christian Leader* 30 (19 March 1927): 365.

55. Ibid. 30 (23 July 1927): 949.

56. Ibid. 30 (12 March 1927): 328-30.

57. Ibid. 30 (5 March 1927): 291.

58. His response appeared as the lead editorial in the same issue in which Galer's article was published. The van Schaick editorial (but not Galer's article) was also reprinted in the *Congregationalist*.

59. *Christian Leader* 30 (4 June 1927): 722-23.

60. Urban communities were defined as those with 2,500 or more inhabitants. The number of active clergy in 1926 was listed in neither the religious census nor the denominational yearbook. The statistics for 1927 listed more than 500 in fellowship, but only 283 as active.

61. *Christian Leader* 30 (11 June 1927): 743, 744.

62. Ibid. 30 (23 July 1927): 948-49.

63. Ibid. 30 (9 July 1927): 867.

64. *Christian Register* 108 (14 March 1929): 214.

65. Eliot's letter was reproduced in the *Christian Leader* 30 (23 July 1927); and in both the *Christian Register* and the *Congregationalist*.

66. *Christian Leader* 30 (6 August 1927): 1011.

67. Ibid., p. 1012.

68. *Congregationalist* 112 (4 August 1927): 145-46.

69. Ibid. 114 (7 March 1929): 301-302.

70. *Christian Leader* 30 (30 July 1927): 972.

71. Ibid. 30 (13 August 1927): 1030-31.

72. Ibid. 30 (26 March 1927): 403.

73. *Congregationalist* 112 (14 April 1927): 451-52.

74. *Christian Leader* 30 (23 April 1927); *Congregationalist* 112 (5 May 1927): 598.

75. *Congregationalist* 112 (9 June 1927): 740.

76. Minutes, Twenty-second Regular Meeting, National Council of the Congregational Church of the United States (N.Y.: Office of the National Council, 1927), p. 86.

716 / Notes for Chapter 30

77. Ibid., p. 231.
78. *Christian Leader* 30 (5 March 1927): 291.
79. Ibid. 30 (20 August 1927): 1062-64.
80. Ibid. 30 (13 August 1927): 1031.
81. Ibid. 30 (17 September 1927): 1204.
82. Ibid. 30 (11 June 1927): 741.
83. The official minutes contained none of the many speeches given on the Joint Statement; they were reproduced in the *Leader*.
84. *Christian Century* 44 (20 October 1927): 122-23.
85. *Christian Leader* 30 (29 October 1927): 1395.
86. Ibid., p. 1388.
87. *Christian Century* 44 (3 November 1927): 1287-88.
88. *Christian Leader* 30 (22 October 1927): 1346.
89. Ibid. 30 (29 October 1927): 1379.
90. Ibid. 31 (3 March 1928): 281.
91. Ibid. 32 (15 June 1929): 742.
92. Minutes, Twenty-third Regular Meeting, 1929, p. 78.
93. *Christian Leader* 32 (16 February 1929): 206.
94. Ibid. 33 (20 December 1930): 1628.
95. Report of the Commission on Comity and Unity, Universalist Year Book, 1929, pp. 28-29.
96. *Christian Leader* 31 (5 May 1928): 557-58.
97. Ibid. 32 (9 November 1929): 1413.
98. Report of the Commission on Comity and Unity, Year Book, 1930, p. 64.
99. *Christian Leader* 32 (25 May 1929): 658.
100. *Christian Register* 107 (12 April 1928): 313.
101. Ibid. 106 (17 November 1927): 904-905.
102. *Christian Leader* 129 (1 November 1947): 493.
103. Ibid. 130 (21 February 1948): 89.
104. Marshall pointed out that the Evangelical and Reformed Church had voted against admission of the Universalist Church to the Federal Council of Churches on theological gounds.

Chapter 30: HALF-WAY STEPS TOWARD UNION: UNIVERSALIST-UNITARIAN RELATIONS, 1927-1937

1. *Christian Register* 106 (10 March 1927): 190.
2. *Christian Leader* 30 (17 December 1927): 1618.
3. Ibid. 30 (26 November 1927): 1533-34.
4. These were reported in detail in both the *Christian Register* and the *Leader*.
5. Speight's address was reproduced in the *Christian Leader* 30 (11 June 1927): 750-52.
6. *Christian Register* 106 (28 July 1927): 606-607.
7. Ibid. 106 (10 November 1927): 882.
8. The sermon was published as a twelve-page pamphlet entitled "The Five Points of Calvinism and the Five Points of the New Theology" (Boston: George H. Ellis, 1885).
9. *Christian Leader* 33 (14 June 1930): 751-52.
10. Ibid. 31 (18 February 1928): 212.
11. Ibid. 31 (3 March 1928): 259-60.
12. Ibid. 32 (2 February 1929): 145.
13. Ibid., pp. 131-32.
14. Ibid. 32 (5 October 1929): 1252.
15. *Christian Register* 108 (14 February 1929): 130-31.
16. *Christian Leader* 32 (2 March 1929): 259-60.
17. Ibid. 32 (16 February 1929): 206-207.
18. Ibid. 32 (8 June 1929): 720-21.
19. Ibid. 32 (6 April 1929): 423-26.
20. Ibid. 32 (26 October 1929): 1366.
21. Ibid. 34 (31 October 1931): 1379.
22. Ibid. 33 (8 February 1930): 176.
23. Minutes, Year Book, 1932, p. 9.
24. Minutes, Annual Meeting of the American Unitarian Association, 19 May 1931, pp. 123-25.
25. *Christian Leader* 34 (6 June 1931): 732.
26. Ibid. 34 (4 July 1931): 835.
27. Ibid. 34 (29 August 1931): 1090-91.
28. Ibid. 34 (7 November 1931): 1415.
29. Etz Report, 10 November 1931; Universalist Trustee files.
30. The original Universalist members were Victor A. Friend, F. D. Adams, Louis

A. Ames, A. Ingham Bicknell, Roger Etz, Robert W. Hill, Walter H. Macpherson, Frederic W. Perkins, and Clinton Lee Scott.

31. *Christian Leader* 35 (2 January 1932): 19.

32. Ibid. 35 (14 May 1932): 613.

33. *Christian Register* 111 (9 June 1932): 381.

34. Unless otherwise indicated, all information regarding the history of the Free Church was derived from the records of the commission and the officers of the Free Church. Much of it was, of course, published in the denominational presses.

35. Hall claimed in 1933 that the idea came from Tomlinson, who at the time opposed actual union.

36. The tentative draft, which became the final draft without revision, was reproduced in the *Christian Leader* 36 (25 March 1933): 370-71.

37. The constitution was soon interpreted to allow membership of individuals as well as organizations. A few were admitted under this ruling and were placed on the "Roll of Fellows."

38. *Christian Leader* 36 (11 March 1933): 339.

39. Proceedings, in ibid. 36 (8 July 1933): 851.

40. *Christian Leader* 36 (6 May 1933): 550-51.

41. See Max F. Daskan (ed.), *The Flaming Spirit: Meditations and Prayers of William L. Sullivan* (Nashville, Tenn.: Abingdon Press, 1961).

42. *Christian Leader* 36 (3 June 1933): 674.

43. Proceedings, *Christian Register* 111 (2 June 1932): 349.

44. *Christian Leader* 37 (2 June 1932): 684.

45. Ibid. 35 (5 November 1932): 1284. The exact vote of the convention was not recorded in the printed minutes. The only indication of a specific vote was that of C. H. Pennoyer, who insisted that he be placed on record as favoring the plan but wished that "it might go on as a complete merger between the denominations."

46. Among the others voicing opposition who had come around sufficiently to second the motion to adopt were John Sayles and John Smith Lowe. Bets on the outcome had been made by representatives of the secular press who were present; they were paid as soon as Tomlinson had been heard.

47. The details of the convention action were given in the *Christian Leader* 36 (28 October 1933): 1347-48.

48. Minutes, Year Book, 1934, pp. 8-9.

49. Council Minutes, 14-15 November 1933.

50. *Christian Leader* 36 (16, 30 December 1933): 1589, 1634.

51. Louis A. Ames, W. H. Macpherson, and Scott were replaced by Lowe, H. W. Reed, and Tomlinson, none of whom consistently favored merging.

52. *Christian Register* 111 (16 June 1932): 394.

53. *Christian Leader* 35 (16 July 1932): 886.

54. Quoted in ibid. 35 (17 December 1932): 1491.

55. *Christian Leader* 35 (8 October 1932): 1172.

56. *Christian Register* 111 (27 October 1932): 621.

57. Ibid., p. 619.

58. *Christian Leader* 35 (14 October, 12 November 1932): 1296, 1327.

59. Ibid. 36 (11 February 1933): 177-78.

60. Ibid. 34 (14 November 1931): 1442.

61. *Unity* 109 (20 June 1932): 245.

62. *Christian Leader* 35 (23 April 1932): 540.

63. See, for example, the reportage in ibid. 35 (13 August 1932): 949.

64. Quoted in ibid.

65. Memo, Joy to Unitarian Administrative Council, 9 November 1932.

66. *Christian Leader* 35 (8 October 1932): 1172.

67. Ibid. 36 (1 April 1933): 399-401.

68. *Christian Century* 50 (25 January 1933): 111.

69. George F. Patterson to Cornish, 14 October 1932.

70. Memo, Joy to Unitarian Administrative Council, 9 November 1932.

71. *Christian Leader* 36 (27 May 1933): 661.

72. Julia N. Budlong to Frederick B. Fisher, 17 October 1935.

73. Berkeley B. Blake to Etz, 23 November 1934.

74. *Christian Leader* 39 (9 May 1936): 594-96.

718 / Notes for Chapter 31

107. Trustee Minutes, *Universalist Leader* 15 (3 February 1912): 145.

108. *Christian Leader* 36 (4 March 1933): 277.

109. Ibid. 36 (15 April 1933): 478.

110. *Christian Register* 111 (20 October 1931): 607.

111. Ibid. 111 (5 May 1932): 291; *Christian Leader* 35 (7 May 1932): 583.

112. *Christian Leader* 34 (14 March 1931): 338.

113. *Christian Register* 111 (28 January 1932): 61.

114. *Christian Leader* 35 (30 July 1932): 917.

115. Year Book, 1934, pp. 41-42.

116. There had been an earlier "Wayside Pulpit" sponsored by Universalists, and of a somewhat different character. It had consisted of a series of publications of selected sermons preached in Universalist pulpits. It had been started in 1899, the idea of Charles Conklin, the Massachusetts state superintendent, and lasted for several years. See the *Universalist Leader* 10 (11, 25 May 1907): 583, 669; and McGlauflin, *Universalist Church*, p. 25.

117. *Christian Register* 111 (6 October 1932): 565.

118. Minutes, 29 December 1931.

119. Etz Report, 4 December 1934, Trustee files.

75. Ibid. 36 (28 October 1933): 1346.

76. Extract from Minutes in ibid. 37 (3 November 1934): 1395.

77. Memo to Unitarian Administrative Council, 10 April 1934.

78. *Christian Leader* 38 (1 June 1935): 686-87.

79. Ibid. 36 (30 September 1933): 1236.

80. Ibid. 38 (16 November 1935): 1458.

81. For example, "promotion of character" in the second item of the Declaration of Principles would have become "promotion of Christian character."

82. Minutes, First Annual Meeting, 24 January 1935.

83. Joy to Fisher, 8 February 1935.

84. *Christian Leader* 38 (2 February 1935): 137.

85. Memo, Walter Hunt to Cornish, 27 February 1935.

86. Call, Report of Chicago Institute, [n.d.].

87. McGiffert to Joy, 10 October 1935.

88. Joy to Kapp, 5 September 1935.

89. Memo, Joy to Cornish, 14 January 1932.

90. Holmes to Joy, 12 July 1935.

91. Fisher to Cornish, 30 September 1936.

92. Herbert Parsons to Joy, 18 December 1935.

93. Holmes to Joy, 24 December 1935.

94. Free Church files.

95. Couden to Joy, 20 February 1936.

96. Snow to Joy, 19 October 1936.

97. Hill to Fisher, 14 May 1935.

98. *Christian Leader* 38 (2 November 1935): 1388.

99. *Christian Register* 114 (7 November 1935): 654.

100. Scott, *Some Things Remembered*, p. 49.

101. Scott, *Universalist Church*, p. 112.

102. *Christian Leader* 34 (17 January 1931): 78.

103. Ibid. 35 (11 March 1933): 290.

104. Trustee Report, Year Book, 1933, pp. 6, 19.

105. *Christian Leader* 36 (20 May 1933): 624.

106. The words were reproduced in the *Christian Register* 112 (28 December 1933): 843.

Chapter 31: "GOD'S STEPCHILDREN": THE REBUFFS OF THE FEDERAL COUNCIL OF CHURCHES, 1939-1947

1. Robert Cummins, *Excluded: The Story of the Federal Council of Churches and the Universalists* (Boston: Beacon Reference Series No. 3, 1966). This thirty-page pamphlet comprises the most detailed, documented account, written by the General Superintendent at the time, and one of the three members originally appointed by the trustees in 1941 to conduct negotiations.

2. *Universalist* 58 (13 January, 3 February 1877): [2], [1].

3. *Universalist Leader* 18 (8 May 1915): 436-37.

4. Ibid. 19 (22 January 1916): 79-80.

5. Ibid. 20 (10 February 1917): 82.

6. Quoted in ibid. 6 (3 January 1903): 7.

7. See Ruth Rouse and S. C. Neill (eds.), *A History of the Ecumenical Movement, 1517-1948* (Philadelphia: Westminster Press, 1954).

8. Proceedings, General Convention, 1873, pp. 12-13.

9. The creedal statement of the Evangelical Alliance which served as a guide for determining eligibility for membership included belief in "the utter depravity of human nature in consequence of the fall" as well as others such as "the eternal punishment of the wicked." John A. Hutchison, *We Are Not Divided* (N.Y.: Round Table Press, 1941), pp. 14-15.

10. The sermon was reproduced in the *Universalist* 55 (1 November 1873): [1].

11. *Christian Leader* 55 (7 May 1885): 4, 5.

12. Ibid. 65 (11 July 1895): 1.

13. *Universalist Leader* 3 (5 May 1900): 553.

14. Ibid. 8 (21 October 1905): 1318. The National Federation had been projected in 1900 and organized in Philadelphia the following year.

15. Ibid. 6 (3 January 1903): 5-6.

16. Ibid. 10 (2 February 1907): 134.

17. Ibid.

18. Ibid. 24 (1 January 1921): 4.

19. *Christian Leader* 57 (25 November 1886): 4.

20. *Universalist Leader* 9 (10 March 1906): 294-95; 20 (3 November 1917): 759.

21. Ibid. 23 (31 January 1920): 115.

22. When the Syrian Antiochian Orthodox Church became a member in 1938 the Council lost its exclusively Protestant character. The membership fluctuated, consisting of twenty-two denominations in 1940, representing almost 25 million individuals. Hutchison, *We Are Not Divided*, p. 56. The Federal Council became the National Council in 1950.

23. Hutchison, *We Are Not Divided*, pp. 36-37.

24. Cummins, *Excluded*, p. 7.

25. Proceedings, General Convention, 1913, pp. 12, 78-79. The document, together with the report of the Federal Council's Commission on the Church and Social Service, was reproduced in the *Universalist Leader* 16 (18 January 1913): 69, 74, 76-80.

26. *Universalist Leader* 23 (25 December 1920): 1219-20.

27. See Donald B. Meyer, *The Protestant Search for Political Realism, 1919-1941* (Berkeley, Calif.: University of California Press, 1960).

28. *Universalist Leader* 23 (7 February, 6 March 1920): 149, 236.

29. Ibid. 23 (24 April 1920): 401, 404.

30. Ibid. 23 (15 May 1920): 482.

31. Ibid. 23 (19 June 1920): 598-99.

32. Ibid. 24 (22 January 1922): 76.

33. Etz to Worth M. Tippy, 30 October 1928, Trustee files.

34. *Universalist Leader* 28 (31 October 1925): 1.

35. *Christian Leader* 33 (12 August 1930): 965.

36. Ibid. 122 (16 March 1940): 254 ff.

37. Cummins took issue with Scott on this point. In his brief history of the church the latter had written that the expectation of membership was based on the Christian character of Universalism. Cummins thought otherwise. It was the enlarged opportunity to be of service that prompted the application for membership.

38. Mrs. Irving L. Walker, representing the Rochester (New York) Council of Church Women; and Manning, active in the Council's Department of International Justice and Good Will.

39. *Christian Leader* 122 (28 December 1940): 1166-67.

40. Directory and Biennial Reports, 1941, p. 5.

41. *Christian Leader* 127 (6 January 1945): 13.

42. Trustee Minutes, 27-29 October 1941, pp. 11, 13.

43. Report of the General Superintendent, 1943, pp. 7-8.

44. Trustee Minutes, 21-23 September 1942.

45. The Universalist committee had struggled valiantly with the exact form the application should take and how detailed it should be, and had settled on a brief statement on the advice of Council officials themselves. The Universalist commitee had furnished the Council with a much more detailed version to be used if thought desirable. Officials of the Council later denied, after Manning inquired, that they had ever seen such a document. Perkins, who had conducted the preliminary negotiations, had died in 1943, so there was no way to verify the Universalist claim to have submitted a detailed application.

46. Report of the General Superintendent, 1943, pp. 7-8.

47. *Christian Century* 60 (27 January 1943): 102-104, reproduced in the *Christian Leader* 125 (20 February 1943): 116-17.

48. Minutes, General Assembly; Directory and Biennial Reports, 1943, p. 22-25.

49. *Christian Leader* 125 (6 November 1943): 650.

50. Minutes, 1943, pp. 20, 28-29.

51. Report of the Commission on International Relations, 1943.

52. *Christian Leader* 126 (5 August 1944): 451.

53. Ibid. 126 (2 December 1944): 726.

54. According to the rules of the Council, a vote of two-thirds of the denomination, voting separately, was necessary to approve an application before being submitted to the full body, where a two-thirds majority was again required for final acceptance. Of the twenty-five denominations then members of the Council, two abstained and five either were not represented or did not vote. Those who voted were lined up as follows: For: Congregational Christian, Disciples of Christ, the Society of Friends (Quakers), Seventh-Day Baptists, Colored Methodist Episcopal in America, and African Methodist Episcopal; provisionally against, unless Universalists accepted 'Jesus Christ as Divine Lord and Savior ': Northern Baptist, and Protestant Episcopal; and against: National Baptist Convention, Church of the Brethren, Evangelical and Reformed in America, Reformed Episcopal, Lutheran, Methodist, United Brethren, United Presbyterian, Presbyterian USA, and United Church of Canada.

55. *Christian Leader* 126 (17 June 1944): 370.

56. Cummins, *Excluded*, p. 22.

57. Ibid., p. 21.

58. Quoted in the *Christian Century* 61 (13 December 1944): 1440.

59. Ibid., p. 1441.

60. *Christian Leader* 126 (16 December 1944): 757.

61. Ibid., pp. 746-47.

62. Ibid. 128 (20 April 1946): 193-94.

63. Ibid. 127 (6 January 1945): 4, 6.

64. It was reprinted in ibid. 127 (3 February 1945): 53-56.

65. Trustee Report, 1946, p. 35.

66. Report of the General Superintendent, 1946, p. 4.

67. *Christian Leader* 127 (6 January 1945): 7.

68. In his account of his experiences with the Federal Council, Cummins backdated the matter even farther. "The great bulk of the Christian church finds itself in the second half of the 20th century with a 4th century theology." *Excluded*, p. 29.

69. Ibid., p. 24.

70. Quoted in ibid.

71. Report of the General Superintendent, 1947, p. 3.

72. Minutes, General Assembly, 1946, Directory and Biennial Reports, 1948, p. 21. A motion to table was lost.

73. *Excluded*, p. 27.

74. All four who voted in favor had also done so in 1944. They were African Methodist Episcopal, Congregational Christian, Disciples of Christ, and the Society of Friends.

75. Quoted in the *Christian Leader* 129 (4 January 1947): 4.

76. Report of the General Superintendent, 1947, pp. 3-4.

77. Minutes, General Assembly, 1947, p. 8.

Chapter 32: UNIVERSALISM AT THE CROSSROADS

1. Public Works Administration, a New Deal relief agency in the 1930s.

2. *Christian Leader* 125 (6 November 1943): 647.

3. Report of the Department of Church Extension, 1955.

4. *Christian Leader* 124 (21 March 1942): 163.

5. The report of the committee responsible for drawing up the new document (A. Ingham Bicknell, Fred B. Perkins, and Frederic W. Perkins) and the draft of the revisions were published in the *Christian Leader* 125 (5 June 1943): 332-35.

6. Records, General Assembly.

7. *Christian Leader* 122 (14 December 1940): 1114-15.

8. Ibid. 131 (October, November 1949): 343, 397. They were Education, (Social) Service, Ministry, Finance, Publications, Public

Relations, Church Extension, and Survey and Evaluation. The first five were to be organized immediately. In order to improve communication, a trustee was to serve as chairman of each department.

9. This department became part of the Department of Church Extension.

10. Trustee Report, Proceedings, General Convention, 1941, pp. 26-27.

11. Report of Trustee meeting, *Christian Leader* 126 (5 August 1944): 466.

12. Minutes, 1946, Directory and Biennial Reports, 1948, p. 16.

13. Both the national and the state women's groups, and the state convention, were all headquartered in 1909 at 361 Boylston Street, the building having been erected that year; their headquarters were subsequently moved to Newbury Street.

14. Proceedings, General Convention, 1917, p. 60; *Universalist Leader* 21 (2 February 1918): 93.

15. *Christian Leader* 30 (7 May 1927): 595-96.

16. *Universalist Leader* 21 (16 February 1918): 122.

17. *Christian Leader* 30 (10 September 1927): 1167.

18. Secretary's Report, 28 April 1930, Trustee files.

19. *Christian Leader* 33 (28 June 1930): 821.

20. Year Book, 1934, p. 26.

21. *Christian Leader* 36 (15 April 1933): 462.

22. Report of the Biennial Meeting, 1943, p. 25.

23. *Christian Leader* 125 (6 November 1943): 651.

24. Report of Consultants, 1956, Section 5, p. 18.

25. *Unitarian Register-Universalist Leader*, November 1961, p. 25.

26. Ibid., April 1962, p. 23.

27. Ibid., January 1963, p. 23.

28. *Christian Leader* 123 (12 July 1941): 555.

29. Report of the General Superintendent, 1941, p. 4. It was mimeographed and distributed at the General Convention meeting, but was not published in the *Leader* on the ground that it was too lengthy to be printed. Editor van Schaick was one of Cummins' main targets. The latter failed to make clear in his allegations against the *Leader* that most of the critical comment which he quoted in his report was to be found in the "Letters to the Editor" section, and not in the newspaper's own editorials.

30. Proceedings, 1941, p. 12.

31. Report of the General Superintendent, 1947, pp. 6-7.

32. Trustee Report, 1949, p. 4.

33. *Christian Leader* 124 (18 April 1942): 249.

34. Ibid. 125 (6 February 1943): 69.

35. This did not apply to such semi-autonomous organizations as the AUW and the Universalist Publishing House, but the denominational youth group was the first to join. Trustee Report, 1943, p. 36.

36. *Christian Leader* 125 (6 November 1943): 649.

37. Report of the General Superintendent, 1947, p. 14.

38. *Christian Leader* 131 (January 1949): 7.

39. Ibid. 131 (March 1949): 100.

40. Report, Department of Business Administration, 1951.

41. *Unitarian Universalist World*, June 1982, p. 7.

42. *Christian Leader* 121 (23 December 1939): 1219-20.

43. Ibid. 122 (13 January 1940): 31-32.

44. Ibid. 128 (2 March 1946): 110.

45. Biennial Report, 1951, p. 4.

46. The sermon was reproduced in the *Christian Leader* 129 (7 June 1947): 247-48.

47. *Christian Leader* 131 (November 1947): 403-404.

48. Quoted in ibid. 132 (March 1950): 94.

49. Ibid. 128 (19 October 1946): 471 ff.

50. Ibid. 129 (16 August 1947): 368.

51. Ibid. 128 (19 October 1946): 480-81.

52. Entitled "Universalism, a Philosophy for Living," it had been delivered over station WMEX in September 1946. Ibid., pp. 483-84.

53. Ibid. 128 (2 November 1946): 510.

54. The definitive work is "The *Humiliati* of Tufts: A Model for Renewal in Religion," by Patricia McClellan Bowen (unpublished Doctor of Ministry thesis, Chicago: Meadville/Lombard Theological School, 1978). It is a thoroughly documented study, including interviews, correspondence, and tran-

scriptions of the reminiscences of the surviving members of the group. A briefer treatment prepared in 1952 by Raymond C. Hopkins, one of the members, is located in the Tufts University Archives.

55. Hopkins, "The *Humiliati*" (typescript).

56. The name was derived from a twelfth-century association of "the humble ones," lay-penitents who combined "the prosecution of gospel ideals with the avowed Christian principles to economic practices [and] frequently gathered in common assembly for mutual edification, social and spiritual." Vergius T. A. Ferm (ed.), *An Encyclopedia of Religion* (N.Y.: Philosophical Library, 1945), p. 350.

57. Several variants of this statement of purpose were proposed by the members, but the idea of "a real and lasting fellowship and comradeship," an outgrowth of the camaraderie developed while students, was a basic motivation for organizing.

58. *Universalist Leader* 136 (September 1954): 199.

59. Ibid. 143 (January 1961): 18.

60. *Christian Leader* 129 (16 August 1947): 369.

61. Ibid., p. 371.

62. According to one member, Ziegler was the only "original thinker" in the group; the others were mere "shadows."

63. The writer is indebted to Bowen's thesis for much of the biographical material concerning the individuals comprising the *Humiliati;* it was supplemented by information from the files of the Tufts School of Religion.

64. *Theologically Speaking,* No. 2 [n.d., n.p.].

65. The sermon was reprinted in the *Christian Leader* 131 (July 1949): 256-57.

66. The evidence of this influence was obtained by Bowen in the course of her interviews and correspondence with members. The five authors were all members of the School of Religion faculty — Skinner, Brotherston, Ratcliff, Rolland E. Wolfe, Alfred S. Cole, J. A. C. Fagginger Auer, and McCollester.

67. Boston: Beacon Press, 1934. Brotherston also developed many of his ideas in the annual Russell Lecture which he delivered on the campus in 1945, a year after his retirement from the faculty; the lecture was reproduced in two parts in the *Christian Leader* 128 (19 January, 2 February 1946): 38 ff, 63 ff.

68. When David Cole suggested the publication of a newspaper to spread the ideas of the *Humiliati,* one title considered was *The Impulse.*

69. *Christian Leader* 130 (3 April 1948): 150. When a bibliography comprising twenty-seven titles was recommended by the *Humiliati* for professional reading, Brotherston was included but Skinner was omitted.

70. *Christian Leader* 129 (6 September 1947): 397.

71. Ibid. 132 (March 1950): 93.

72. Ibid. 131 (November 1949): 420-21.

73. Ibid. 129 (2 August 1947): 341-42.

74. Ibid. 131 (December 1949): 448.

75. Ibid. 131 (November 1949): 420-21.

76. Ibid. 131 (December 1949): 448.

77. *Humiliati Epistle,* 1951.

78. *Christian Leader* 129 (16 August 1947): 371-72.

79. Ibid., p. 377.

80. Ibid. 131 (March 1949): 89.

81. Although not intended to be a denominational "political action group," there is evidence that the *Humiliati* supported the election of Scott as Massachusetts State Superintendent in 1946 and that of his wife, Mary Slaughter Scott, as a UCA trustee in 1947. See Bowen, *"Humiliati,"* pp. 112, 116 n.

82. *Universalist Leader* 137 (August 1955): 187-89.

83. For several months the *Leader* carried a column called "Plumb Line," by "Criterious," who was identified by Bowen as Ziegler.

84. Biennial Report of the General Superintendent, 1947, p. 12.

85. For a brief historical review of the concept, extending back to the end of the nineteenth century, see the concluding pages of George H. Williams, *American Universalism* (Boston: Universalist Historical Society, revised edition, 1976), pp. 82-85.

86. *Universalist Leader* 22 (20 September 1919): 854.

87. Ibid. 22 (11 January 1919): 40-41.

88. Ibid. 138 (October 1956): 219-24.

89. *Christian Leader* 130 (August 1948): 338.

90. Ibid. 130 (December 1948): 519.

91. Ibid. 132 (July, August 1950): 232, 275-77.

92. See his "Art and Symbols for a Universal Religion" (illustrated), *Universalist Leader* 138 (October 1956): 219-24, expanded as *A Religion for One World: Art and Symbols for a Universal Religion* (Boston: Beacon Press and Meeting House Press, 1964). Among Patton's other contributions to worship were new hymns and readings, incorporated into a hymnbook in 1964, as well as such innovations as flexible seating and full participation of the congregation in services.

93. *Universalist Leader* 23 (12 June 1920): 582.

94. Ibid. 139 (February 1957): 48.

95. *Christian Leader* 131 (June 1949): 224, 226; 132 (September 1950): 295-96, 301-303. The sermon was printed in *Zion's Herald*, the Methodist paper. The sermon was originally entitled "Up-a-daisy!" It was probably the title as much as the contents that offended sensibilities.

96. Records, General Assembly, 1949.

97. *Christian Leader* 132 (August 1950): 265.

98. Ibid. 131 (July 1949): 255.

Chapter 33: "AND FLOW ON TOGETHER": UNIVERSALIST-UNITARIAN CONSOLIDATION, 1937-1961

1. The quotation in the chapter title was taken from a speech made by Lon Ray Call (a Unitarian) at the May meeting of the AUA in 1927.

2. D. W. Morehouse to [Grindall] Reynolds, 2, 5 February 1892, AUA Letterbooks. Morehouse was superintendent of the AUA Department of the Middle States and Canada and Reynolds was secretary of the AUA.

3. *Christian Leader* 121 (11 November 1939): 1078-79.

4. Ibid. 127 (19 May 1945): 222-23.

5. Minutes, General Assembly, 1947, p. 7.

6. Clement F. Robinson to Kapp, 4 September 1947.

7. Minutes, General Assembly, 1947, p. 9; *Christian Leader* 129 (20 September 1947): 418.

8. *Christian Leader* 130 (5 June 1948): 251.

9. Ibid. 131 (November 1949): 395-96.

10. Ibid. 132 (January 1950): 25-26.

11. Ibid. 132 (August 1950): 265.

12. Ibid. 132 (May 1950): 149; Trustee Biennial Report, 1951.

13. Minutes, General Assembly, 1949.

14. *Christian Leader* 133 (October 1951): 288.

15. Ibid. 133 (May 1951): 159-60.

16. Ibid. 134 (September 1952): 214.

17. Ibid., pp. 211-18.

18. Ibid., pp. 219-20.

19. No constitution was ever adopted; that device was dispensed with and bylaws only were adopted in 1953.

20. *Universalist Leader* 135 (February 1953): 60.

21. Report, Council of Liberal Churches, 1953, p. 6.

22. William W. Lewis, chairman of the Universalist half of the commission, presented the report and plan of federal union to his constituency.

23. *Universalist Leader* 136 (March 1954): 80.

24. Minutes, General Assembly, 1953. The parenthetical description in the name was added as the result of a separate preferential ballot by the Universalists and was accepted by the Unitarians.

25. *Universalist Leader* 137 (March 1955): 70.

26. Two of the Universalist appointees had to be replaced because, as paid staff members, they were prohibited by the bylaws from serving. The two denominational youth groups, which had just merged by an "overwhelming vote," requested membership on the board but failed to receive it.

27. Minutes, General Assembly, 1953.

28. *Universalist Leader* 136 (July 1954): 168.

29. Ibid. 136 (December 1954): 290.

30. Report, Department of Education, 1955.

31. Minutes, General Assembly, 1955.

32. The Council specified 1 July to 30

June, disregarding completely Article V, Section 5 of its own bylaws which provided that "the fiscal year . . . shall be the calendar year."

33. *Universalist Leader* 137 (June 1955): 141.

34. General Assembly files, 1955.

35. *Christian Leader* 134 (September 1952): 215.

36. *Universalist Leader* 136 (January 1954): 4.

37. *Christian Leader* 131 (November 1949): 384.

38. Biennial Report, General Superintendent, 1955.

39. *Universalist Leader* 137 (May 1955): 113-14.

40. The Universalist members were Keith C. Munson, Mrs. Anne Bowman, Kapp, Scott, Carol J. Westman, and Robert C. Wolley.

41. Minutes, General Assembly, 1955.

42. Ibid.

43. *Universalist Leader* 137 (June 1955): 141.

44. Ibid. 137 (July 1955): 159-61.

45. Ibid. 138 (December 1956): 277.

46. Reamon to Kapp, 12 April 1956.

47. The Universalists on the commission were Carleton M. Fisher, Kapp, Wilson C. Piper, Sawyer, Westman, and Wolley. *Universalist Leader* 139 (April 1957): 109.

48. *Universalist Leader* 139 (July 1957): 164.

49. Giles' first report as General Superintendent was reproduced in the *Universalist Leader* 139 (November 1957): 267-71.

50. Ibid. 141 (January, February 1959): 40-46, 47 ff.

51. Ibid. 141 (March 1959): 72-74.

52. Ibid. 141 (May 1959): 126.

53. Ibid. 141 (October 1959): 234.

54. Ibid. 140 (October 1958): 238.

55. Ibid. 141 (December 1959): 272.

56. Ibid. 141 (June 1959): 147.

57. The full plan was published in 6,600 "green books" and contained fourteen recommendations from the commission. Ibid., p. 148.

58. Minutes, General Assembly, 1959; *Universalist Leader* 141 (December 1959): 271.

59. *Universalist Leader* 142 (January 1960): 24.

60. Ibid., p. 23.

61. Report of the General Superintendent, 1959.

62. See Appendix B for the complete text of the constitution and bylaws adopted in 1959 which went into effect after final ratification in 1961. No subsequent amendments have been included.

63. Three reports were made by the commission at the Syracuse meeting. It was the "Third Syracuse Report," including all amendments, that was finally adopted, and is reproduced in the Appendix.

64. Minutes, General Assembly, 1955; Trustee Report, 1955.

65. CLF files.

66. *Universalist Leader* 24 (26 March 1921): 363.

67. *Christian Leader* 134 (September 1952): 216.

68. *Universalist Leader* 142 (January 1960): 14.

69. The undated publication announcing the change carried the names of Brooks, Henry H. Schooley, Albert Q. Perry, John M. Schofield, and Reamon.

70. Final Report, Joint Merger Commission, 22 April 1960.

71. There were nine Universalist fellowships in 1960.

72. There were 269 Unitarian fellowships in 1960.

73. *Universalist Leader* 142 (July 1960): 163-67.

74. Ibid., p. 165.

75. Ibid., pp. 166-67.

76. Ibid. 142 (August 1960): 199.

77. Ibid., p. 201.

78. *Unitarian Register-Universalist Leader*, Mid-Summer 1961, p. 10.

79. Ibid., p. 12.

80. Ibid., Mid-Summer 1962, p. 31.

81. Ibid., p. 3.

82. Ibid., May 1961, p. 27.

83. Ibid., Mid-Summer 1961, p. 11.

84. Ibid., Mid-Summer 1962, p. 4.

85. Ibid., February 1962, p. 18.

86. A. C. Piepkorn, *Profiles in Belief: The Religious Bodies of the United States and Canada* (N.Y.: Harper & Row, 4 vols., 1977-1979) 4: 178-79.

87. *Unitarian-Universalist Register-Leader*, November 1963, p. 41.

88. *Unitarian Register-Universalist Leader,* Mid-Summer 1961, pp. 15-16.

89. Ibid., December 1961, p. 23.

90. *Universalist Leader* 142 (July 1960): 163.

Selected Bibliography
Works Consulted and Cited

Collections and Depositories

Andover-Harvard Theological Library, Harvard Divinity School, Cambridge, Massachusetts
Department of Special Collections and Archives, Nils Y. Wessell Library, Tufts University, Medford, Massachusetts
Indiana State Historical Library, Indianapolis, Indiana
Ohio Historical Society Library, Columbus, Ohio
Work Projects Administration, Division of Community Service Programs. *An Inventory of Universalist Archives in Massachusetts.* Boston: Historical Records Survey, 1942.

Newspapers, Magazines, and Journals

American Mercury
(Annual) Journal of the Universalist Historical Society
Bibliotheca Sacra
Boston Herald
Christian Ambassador
Christian Century
Christian Freeman
Christian Leader
Christian Register
Commercial Advertiser (Canton, New York)
Congregationalist
Crane Review
The Edge
Empire State Universalist
The Humanist
Independent
Ladies' Repository
New Republic
New Unity
New World
Onward
Rose of Sharon
Sentinel (Lyman Ward Military Academy, Camp Hill, Alabama)
Southern Pioneer
Tar Heel Universalist
Theologically Speaking
To-Day
Trumpet and Universalist Magazine
UUA Now
The Unitarian
Unitarian Register
Unitarian Register-Universalist Leader

Unitarian Universalist Christian
Unitarian-Universalist Register-Leader
Unitarian Universalist World
Unity
Universalist (Boston)
Universalist (Chicago)
Universalist Expositor
Universalist Herald
Universalist Leader
Universalist Magazine
Universalist Miscellany
Universalist Quarterly and General Review
Universalist Register
Universalist Repository
Universalist Union
Voice of Fellowship
Youth Leader

Denominational History

Adams, John Greenleaf. *Fifty Notable Years*. Boston: Universalist Publishing House, 1882.

Arnason, Wayne B. *Follow the Gleam*. Boston: Skinner House, Beacon Press, 1980.

Atwood, Isaac M. *Walks About Zion: Ten Lectures*. Boston: Universalist Publishing House, 1882.

Barnum, P[hineas] T[aylor]. "Why I Am a Universalist." Universalist Leaflet series No. 1. Boston: Universalist Publishing House, 1891.

Betts, Frederick W. *Forty Fruitful Years: An Autobiography*. Boston: Murray Press, Universalist Publishing House, 1929.

Bisbee, Frederick A. *Beliefs Commonly Held Among Us*. Boston: Universalist Church of America, 1940.

Bisbee, Frederick A. *From Good Luck to Gloucester*. Boston: Murray Press, Universalist Publishing House, 1920.

Bisbee, Frederick A. *A Miniature History of the YPCU*. Boston: [n.p.], 1914.

Bisbee, Herman. *Memoir of Reverend Seth Barnes*. Cincinnati: Williams and Cantwell, 1868.

Bogue, Mary F. "The Minneapolis Radical Lectures and the Excommunication of the Reverend Herman Bisbee," *Journal of the Universalist Historical Society* (1967-68): 3-69.

Bowen, Georgene E. "Messiah Universalist Home: Its Birth, Life, and Merger, 1900-1964." Typescript, [n.d.]

Bowen, Patricia McClellan. "The *Humiliati* of Tufts: A Model for Renewal in Religion." Unpublished Doctor of Ministry thesis. Chicago: Meadville/Lombard Theological School, 1978.

Bowie, R. S. *Some Stray Jottings about Universalism and its Preachers in the West of Scotland during the Past Eighty Years*. Glasgow, Scotland: Andrew Wilson, [n.d.].

Bradley, Asa Mayo. "History of Universalism on the Pacific Coast." Typescript, 1910.

Brooks, Elbridge Gerry. *Our New Departure*. Boston: Universalist Publishing House, 1874.

Brooks, Elbridge Gerry. *Universalism, and the Ministry to Make It Effective*. Boston: Wright & Potter, 1874.

Brooks, Elbridge Streeter. *The Life-Work of Elbridge Gerry Brooks*. Boston: Universalist Publishing House, 1881.

Canfield, H. L. & Mary Grace. *Universalism in North Carolina*. Typescript, [n.d.].

Cassara, Ernest, "The Effect of Darwinism on Universalist Belief, 1860-1900," *Annual Journal of the Universalist Historical Society* 1 (1959): 32-42.

Cassara, Ernest (ed.). *Universalism in America: A Documentary History*. Boston: Beacon Press, 1971.

Centenary Voices; or, a Part of the Work of the Woman of the Universalist Church from its Centenary Year to the Present Time. Philadelphia: Woman's Centenary Association, 1886.
Chapin, Eben H. *Japan to Granada: Sketches of Observation and Inquiry in a Tour Round the World in 1887-8.* N.Y.: G. P. Putnam's Sons, 1889.
Cole, Alfred S. "Clarence R. Skinner, Prophet of Twentieth Century Universalism." Boston: Universalist Historical Society, 1956.
Cole, Alfred S. *Our Liberal Heritage.* Boston: Beacon Press, 1951.
The Columbian Congress of the Universalist Church . . . . Boston: Universalist Publishing House, 1894.
Commission of Appraisal of the American Unitarian Association. *Unitarians Face a New Age.* Boston: American Unitarian Association, 1936.
Cone, Orello. "Evolution and Revelation." *Universalist Quarterly* 22 n.s. (July 1885): 342-58.
Cone, Orello. *Gospel Criticism and Historical Christianity.* N.Y.: G. P. Putnam's Sons, 1891.
Cone, Orello. "Is the Higher Criticism Destructive?" *To-Day* 1 (January 1894): 5-8.
Cone, Orello. "Science and Religion," *Universalist Quarterly* 19 n.s. (January 1882): 84-92.
Cooke, George Willis. *Unitarianism in America.* Boston: American Unitarian Association, 1902.
Cornish, Louis C. *The Story of the Isles of Shoals.* Boston: Beacon Press, 1916, 1936.
Cummins, Robert. *Excluded. The Story of the Council of Churches and the Universalists.* Boston: Beacon Reference series No. 3, 1966.
Cummins, Robert. "The General Superintendency of the Universalist Church of America," *Annual Journal of the Universalist Historical Society* 3 (1962): 14-29.
Daskan, Max F. (ed.). *The Flaming Spirit: Meditations and Prayers of William L. Sullivan.* Nashville, Tenn.: Abingdon Press, 1961.
Domas, Isaiah J. "A Study of the School of Religion Alumni." Unpublished STB thesis. Medford, Mass.: Tufts College School of Religion, 1941.
Eddy, Richard. *Universalism in America: A History.* 2 vols. Boston: Universalist Publishing House, 1884-1886.
Emerson, George H. *Memoir of Ebenezer Fisher, D.D.* Boston: Universalist Publishing House, 1880.
Fifty Years of Universalism: Jubilee of the Universalist Church, Stenhousemuir, Larbert, Scotland, 1867-1917. Falkirk, Scotland: [n.p.], 1917.
Final Report, Joint Merger Commission, Universalist Church of America and American Unitarian Association, 1961.
Fisher, L[ewis] B[eals]. *A Brief History of the Universalist Church for Young People.* 4th edition. Boston: Prepared by the Director of the Young People's Christian Union, 1913.
Fisher, Lewis B. *Which Way? A Study of Universalists and Universalism.* Boston: Universalist Publishing House, 1921.
Folsom, Ida M. (ed.). *A Brief History of the Work of Universalist Women, 1869-1955.* Boston: The Association of Universalist Women, 1955.
Fox, William Lloyd (ed.). *Recollections and Reflections of Seth R. Brooks and Corinne H. Brooks.* Washington, D. C.: Universalist National Memorial Church, 1977.
Gaines, Charles A. "Clarence R. Skinner: The Dark Years," *Annual Journal of the Universalist Historical Society* 3 (1962): 1-13.
Gaines, Charles A. "Clarence R. Skinner: Image of a Movement." Unpublished BD thesis. Medford, Mass.: Crane Theological School, Tufts University, 1961.
Graham, Thomas. "Jenkin Lloyd Jones and the World's Columbian Exposition of 1893," *Collegium Proceedings.* [n.p.]: Association for Liberal Religious Studies 1 (1979): 61-81.
Hall, Dorothy and Frank Oliver Hall. *Handicapped: Being the Story of Frederick A. Bisbee.* Boston: Universalist Publishing House, [n.d.].
Haney, Robert W. " 'Humanist Manifesto II:' A Personal Response," *Unitarian Universalist Christian* 30 (Autumn 1975): 39-48.
Hill, Andrew M. "The Successors of the Remnant: A Bicentenary Account of St.

Mark's Unitarian Church, Edinburgh," *Transactions of the Unitarian Historical Society* 16 (September 1977, September 1978): 101-103, 149-75.

Hitchings, Catherine F. "Universalist and Unitarian Women Ministers," *Journal of the Universalist Historical Society* 10 (1975).

Hunt, James D. (ed.). "Clarence R. Skinner: The Social Implications of Universalism," *Annual Journal of the Universalist Historical Society* 5 (1964-65): 79-122.

Hunt, James D. "The Social Gospel as a Way of Life: A Biography of H. C. Ledyard, Universalist Minister and Labor Leader, 1880-1950," *Annual Journal of the Universalist Historical Society* 5 (1964-65):31-63.

Irwin, Athalia L. J. "Rev. Quillen Hamilton Shinn, D.D." [n.p., n.d.].

Johnson, Kenneth M. "The Doctrine of Universal Salvation and the Restorationist Controversy in Early Nineteenth Century New England." Unpublished PhD dissertation. Ottawa, Canada: University of Ottawa, 1978.

Kapp, Max and David B. Parke. *109 Years: An Account of the Theological School of St. Lawrence University, 1856-1965*. [n.p., n.d.]. 2d edition, *120 Years* [n.p.], 1976.

Keirn, Gideon Isaac. *1890-1915: Twenty-five years of the Universalist Japan Mission*. Tokyo, Japan: [n.p.], 1915.

King, Thomas Starr. "Beauty and Religion," *Rose of Sharon* (1847), pp. 9-32.

Lalone, Emerson. *And Thy Neighbor as Thyself: A Story of Universalist Social Action*. Enlarged edition. Boston: Universalist Publishing House, 1939.

Lavan, Spencer. *Unitarianism in India: A Study in Encounter and Response*. Boston: Skinner House, Beacon Press, 1977.

Livermore, Mary A. *The Story of My Life*. Hartford, Conn.: A. D. Worthington & Co., 1897.

Lyttle, Charles Harold. *Freedom Moves West*. Boston: Beacon Press, 1952.

MacLean, Angus. *The Galloping Gospel*. Boston: Beacon Press, 1966.

MacLean, Angus. *God and the Devil at Seal Cove*. Halifax, N.S.: Patheric Press, 1976.

MacLean, Angus. *I Began in Cape Breton*. Cleveland, Ohio: The First Unitarian Church, 1969.

MacPherson, David Hicks. "Trends in Universalist Churches in Massachusetts in the First Half of the Twentieth Century." Unpublished STB thesis. Medford, Mass.: Crane Theological School, Tufts College, 1952.

McGlauflin, William H. *Faith With Power: A Life Story of Quillen Hamilton Shinn, D.D.* Boston and Chicago: Universalist Publishing House, 1912.

McGlauflin, William H. "Our Mission to the Colored People." Boston: Universalist Publishing House, 1911.

McGlauflin, William H. *What the Universalist Church is Doing*. Boston and Chicago: Universalist Publishing House, 1909.

Morrison, Francis B. "The Young People's Christian Union of Massachusetts and Rhode Island from June 1889 to March 1939." Norwood, Mass.: Fiftieth Anniversary Committee, [1939].

Patton, Kenneth L. "The Bankruptcy of Leadership in the Liberal Church." Mimeographed. Delivered at the Charles Street Meeting House, Boston, 23 May 1954.

Patton, Kenneth L. *A Religion for One World: Art and Symbols for a Universal Religion*. Boston: Beacon Press and Meeting House Press, 1964.

Perkins, Frederic W. *Beliefs Commonly Held Among Us*. Boston: Universalist Church of America, 1945.

A Plan for Education for the Unitarian Universalist Ministry. Boston: Unitarian Universalist Association, 1962.

Praise and Thanks: A Hymn Book for the Young People's Christian Union of the Universalist Church. Boston: Universalist Publishing House, 1895.

Records, Canton Theological School, St. Lawrence University, Canton, New York.

Records, Crane Theological School, Tufts University, Medford, Massachusetts.

Records, General Convention and General Assembly, Universalist Church of America.

Records, Local Societies, Churches, and Associations (see footnotes).

Records, Maine State Convention.

Records, Massachusetts Bay District, Universalist Church of America.

Records, Vermont State Convention.

Records, Universalist Convention of North Carolina.
Records, Women's National Missionary Association (Universalist).
Records, Young People's Christian Union (Universalist).
Robinson, Elmo Arnold. *American Universalism.* N.Y.: Exposition Press, 1970.
Robinson, Elmo A. "Universalism, A Changing Faith," *Annual Journal of the Universalist Historical Society* 2 (1960-61): 1-21.
Rowell, Geoffrey. "The Origins and History of Universalist Societies in Britain, 1750-1850," *Journal of Ecclesiastical History* 22 (January 1971): 35-56.
Rugg, Henry W. *Our Word and Work for Missions.* Boston and Chicago: Universalist Publishing House, 1894.
Rutledge, Lyman V. *Ten Miles Out: Guide Book to the Isles of Shoals.* 5th edition. Boston: Isles of Shoals Association, 1972.
Salisbury, Dorothy Kendall Cleaveland. "They Builded Better Than They Knew: The Universalist Church and Its Concern for Education." Boston: Association of Universalist Women, 1957.
Sawyer, Thomas J. "Universalism in Great Britain and Ireland," *Expositor and Universalist Review* 4 n.s. (May 1840): 183-212.
Scott, Clinton Lee. *Religion Can Make Sense.* Boston: Universalist Publishing House, 1949.
Scott, Clinton Lee. *Some Things Remembered.* Boston: Church of the Larger Fellowship, Unitarian Universalist, 1976.
Scott, Clinton Lee. *The Universalist Church of America: A Short History.* Boston: Universalist Historical Society, 1957.
Scott, Peter Lee. "A History of the Attempts of the Universalist and Unitarian Denominations to Unite." Unpublished BD thesis. Canton, N.Y.: St. Lawrence University Theological School, 1957.
Seaburg, Alan. "Clarence Russell Skinner: A Bibliography," *Annual Journal of the Universalist Historical Society* 5 (1964-65): 65-77.
Seaburg, Alan. "Missionary to Scotland: Caroline Augusta Soule," *Transactions of the Unitarian Historical Society* 14 (October 1967): 28-41.
Seaburg, Alan. "Recent Scholarship in American Universalism: A Bibliographical Essay," *Church History* 41 (December 1972): 513-23.
Seaburg, Carl. *Dojin Means All People: The Universalist Mission to Japan, 1890-1942.* Boston: Universalist Historical Society, 1978.
Shinn, Quillen Hamilton. *Good Tidings.* Boston and Chicago: Universalist Publishing House, 1900.
Shutter, Marion D. *Rev. James Harvey Tuttle, D.D.: A Memoir.* Boston: Universalist Publishing House, 1905.
Skinner, Clarence R. and Alfred S. Cole. *Hell's Ramparts Fell: The Life of John Murray.* Boston: Universalist Publishing House, 1941.
Skinner, Clarence R. *A Religion for Greatness.* Boston: Murray Press, Universalist Publishing House, 1945.
Skinner, Clarence R. *The Social Implications of Universalism.* Boston: Universalist Publishing House, 1915.
Skinner, Clarence R. *Worship and the Well Ordered Life.* Boston: Universalist Historical Society, 1955.
Smith, Stephen Rensselaer. *Historical Sketches and Incidents.* Vol. 2. Buffalo: James S. Leavitt, 1848.
Spoerl, Dorothy Tilden. "And Practice Good Works," *Progress* 17 (November 1978): 5-8.
Spoerl, Dorothy Tilden. "Lombard Remembered." Typescript. 1980.
Sutton, Katherine Augusta and Robert Francis Needham. *Universalists at Ferry Beach: A History.* Boston: Universalist Publishing House, 1948.
Swanson, James Arthur. "A History of Lombard College, 1851-1930." Macomb, Ill.: Western Illinois State College, 1955.
Taylor, Verna Mitchell. "Hannah Jewett Powell." Typescript. 1979.
Thomas, Abel C. *A Century of Universalism in Philadelphia and New York.* Philadelphia: Published by the author, 1872.
Titus, Anson. "George Landor Perin, D.D.," *To-Day* 2 (April 1895): 178-82.

Titus, Anson. "President Isaac Morgan Atwood, D.D.," *To-Day* 3 (January 1896): 23-26.
Titus, Anson. "Quillen Hamilton Shinn, D.D.," *To-Day* 2 (August 1895): 401-406.
Tuttle, James H. *The Field and the Fruit.* Boston: Universalist Publishing House, 1891.
Universalism in America: Its Centennial Year, 1870. Boston: J. S. Spooner, [n.d.].
Universalist Biennial Reports and Directory.
The Universalist Centennial. Boston: Universalist Publishing House, 1870.
Universalist Year Book.
"The Universalists," *The Religious History of New England: King's Chapel Lectures.* Cambridge, Mass.: Harvard University Press, 1917.
Vickery, Charles Nelson. "A Century of Attempted Rapprochement between the Universalist Church of America and the American Unitarian Association." Unpublished STB thesis. Medford, Mass.: Crane Theological School, Tufts College, June 1945.
Webster, Douglas. "The Williamson Memorial Unitarian Church," *Scottish Unitarian Churches.* London: Lindsey Press, 1963.
Whittemore, Thomas. *Modern History of Universalism, from the Era of the Reformation to the Present Time.* Boston: Published by the author, 1830.
Williams, George Huntston. *American Universalism.* Boston: Universalist Historical Society, 1971; Skinner House, Beacon Press, 1976.
Williams, John E. and others. *A History of Universalism in North Carolina.* [n.p.]: Universalist Convention of North Carolina, 1968.
The Winchester Centennial, 1803-1903. Boston: Universalist Publishing House, 1903.
Woodman, Richard M. "An Evaluation of Data Relevant to the Decreasing Number of Churches in the New York State Convention of Universalists, 1900-1954." Unpublished BD thesis. Canton, N.Y.: St. Lawrence University Theological School, 1954.

General References

Abell, Aaron, I. *The Urban Impact on American Protestantism, 1865-1900.* Cambridge, Mass.: Harvard University Press, 1943.
Asakawa, K. "Christianity in Japan," *Atlantic* 99 (May 1907): 652-57.
Atkins, Gaius Glenn and Frederick L. Fagley. *History of American Congregationalism.* Boston and Chicago: Pilgrim Press, 1942.
Auer, J. A. C. Fagginger. *Humanism States Its Case.* Boston: Beacon Press, 1933.
Badger, Reid. *The Great American Fair: The World's Columbian Exposition and American Culture.* N.Y.: Nelson-Hall, 1979.
Barrows, John Henry (ed.). *The World's Parliament of Religions: An Illustrated and Popular Story of the World's First Parliament of Religions, held in Chicago in Connection with the Columbian Exposition of 1893.* 2 vols. Chicago: The Parliament Publishing Co., 1893.
Bentley, George R. *A History of the Freemen's Bureau.* Philadelphia: University of Pennsylvania Press, 1955.
Black, Malcolm S. (ed.). *Sixty Years of St. Lawrence.* Canton, N.Y.: St. Lawrence University, 1916.
Bolles, E. C. "Contributions of Science to Religion," *Universalist Quarterly* 1 n.s. (January 1864): 61-71.
Bonney, Charles C. and Paul Carus. *The World's Parliament of Religions and the Religious Parliament Extension.* Chicago: Open Court Publishing Co., 1896.
Brock, Peter. *Pacificism in the United States: From the Colonial Era to the First World War.* Princeton, N.J.: Princeton University Press, 1968.
Brown, Jerry Wayne. *The Rise of Biblical Criticism in America 1800-1870: The New Scholars.* Middletown, Conn.: Wesleyan University Press, 1969.
Buder, Stanley. *Pullman: An Experiment in Industrial Order and Community Planning, 1880-1930.* N.Y.: Oxford University Press, 1967.
Burg, David. *Chicago's White City.* Lexington, Ky.: University Press of Kentucky, 1976.
Carroll, H. K. *The Religious Forces of the United States.* N.Y.: Christian Literature Co., 1893.
Case, Victoria and Robert O. Case. *We Called It Culture: The Story of Chautauqua.* Garden City, N.Y.: Doubleday, 1948.

Clarke, James Freeman. *The Ten Great Religions: An Essay in Comparative Theology.* Boston: James R. Osgood & Co., 1871.
Cross, Whitney R. *The Burned Over District: The Social and Intellectual History of Enthusiastic Religion in Western New York, 1800-1860.* Ithaca, N.Y.: Cornell University Press, 1950.
Curti, Merle. *Peace or War: The American Struggle, 1636-1936.* N.Y.: Norton, 1936.
DeBenedetti, Charles. *Origins of the Modern American Peace Movement, 1915-1929.* Millwood, N.Y.: KTO Press, 1978.
Eaton, Charles H. "Pullman, a Social Experiment," *To-Day* 2 (January 1895): 1-9.
Epler, Percy H. *The Life of Clara Barton.* N.Y.: Macmillan, 1915.
Furniss, Norman F. *The Fundamentalist Controversy, 1918-1931.* New Haven: Yale University Press, 1954.
Ginger, Ray. *Six Days or Forever? Tennessee v. John Thomas Scopes.* Boston: Beacon Press, 1958; reprinted by Quadrangle Books, 1969.
Hall, Frank Oliver. *Common People.* Boston: James H. West Co., 1901.
Hanson, J. W. (ed.). *The World's Congress of Religions.* Chicago: W. B. Conkey Co., 1894.
Holmes, John Haynes. "The Community Church of Boston: History and Principles." [n.p., n.d.]
Hopkins, Charles H. *The Rise of the Social Gospel in American Protestantism, 1860-1915.* New Haven, Conn.: Yale University Press, 1940.
Hutchison, John A. *We Are Not Divided.* N.Y.: Round Table Press, 1941.
Johnson, Rossiter (ed.). *A History of the World's Columbian Exposition.* 4 vols. N.Y.: D. Appleton & Co., 1897-1898.
Joughin, G. Louis and Edmund M. Morgan. *The Legacy of Sacco and Vanzetti.* N.Y.: Harcourt, Brace, 1948.
Kett, Joseph F. *Rites of Passage: Adolescence in America, 1790 to the Present.* N.Y.: Basic Books, 1977.
Knepper, George W. *New Lamps for Old: One Hundred Years of Urban Higher Education at the University of Akron.* Akron, Ohio: University of Akron Press, 1970.
Kohl, Manfred Waldemar. *Congregationalism in America.* Oak Creek, Wisconsin: Congregational Press, 1977.
Konvitz, Milton R. "The Case of the Eight Divinity School Students," *Bill of Rights Review* 1 (Spring 1941): 196-205.
May, Henry F. *Protestant Churches and Industrial America.* N.Y.: Harper, 1949, 1958.
Meyer, Donald B. *The Protestant Search for Political Realism, 1919-1941.* Berkeley, Calif.: University of California Press, 1960.
Miller, Russell E. *Light on the Hill: A History of Tufts College, 1852-1952.* Boston: Beacon Press, 1966.
Nash, Arthur. *The Golden Rule in Business.* N.Y.: Fleming H. Revell Co., 1923.
Nash, Arthur. "The Organized Church and Organized Labor," in Jerome Davis (ed.). *Business and the Church.* N.Y.: Century Co., 1926.
Ormond, Jessie Marvin. *The Country Church in North Carolina.* Durham, N.C.: Duke University Press, 1931.
Overstreet, Harry and Bonaro. *The Strange Tactics of Extremism.* N.Y.: W. W. Norton, 1964.
Phillips, Clifton Jackson. *Protestant America and the Pagan World: The First Half Century of the American Board of Commissioners for Foreign Missions, 1810-1860.* Cambridge, Mass.: Harvard University Press, 1969.
Piepkorn, Arthur Carl. *Profiles in Belief: The Religious Bodies of the United States and Canada.* 4 vols. N.Y.: Harper & Row, 1977-1979.
Pink, Louis Heaton and Rutherford E. Delmage (eds.). *Candle in the Wilderness: A Centennial History of the St. Lawrence University.* N.Y.: Appleton-Crofts, 1957.
Reese, Curtis W. *Humanist Religion.* N.Y.: Macmillan, 1931.
Rouse, Ruth and S. C. Neill (eds.). *A History of the Ecumenical Movement, 1517-1948.* Philadelphia: Westminster Press, 1954.
Schlesinger, Arthur M. "A Critical Period in American Religion," *Proceedings, Massachusetts Historical Society* 44 (June 1932): 523-47.
Shutter, Marion D. *Applied Evolution.* Boston: Eugene F. Endicott, 1900.
Sibley, Mulford Q. and Philip E. Jacob. *Conscription and Conscience: The American State and the Conscientous Objector, 1940-1947.* Ithaca, N.Y.: Cornell University Press, 1952.

Skinner, Clarence R. (ed.). *A Free Pulpit in Action.* N.Y.: Macmillan, 1931.
Skinner, Clarence R. *Human Nature and the Nature of Evil.* Boston: Universalist Publishing House, 1939.
Skinner, Clarence R. *Liberalism Faces the Future.* N.Y.: Macmillan, 1937.
Skinner, Clarence R. "The Sacco-Vanzetti Case," *Survey* 46 (25 June, 16 August 1921): 431-32, 584.
United States Commissioner of Education. Reports. Washington, D. C.: Government Printing Office.
United States Department of Commerce, Bureau of the Census. *Census of Religious Bodies: 1906, 1916, 1926, 1936.* Washington, D. C.: Government Printing Office, 1910, 1919, 1929, 1940.
United States Government. *A Compendium of the Ninth Census, June 1, 1870.* Washington, D. C.: Government Printing Office, 1872.
Van Kirk, Walter. *Religion Renounces War.* Chicago: Willett, Clark & Co., 1934.
Van Schaick, John. *The Little Corner Never Conquered.* N.Y.: Macmillan, 1921.
Warne, Colston E. (ed.). *The Pullman Boycott of 1894.* Boston: D. C. Heath, 1955.
Weaver, George S. *Moses and Modern Science.* Cincinnati, Ohio: Williamson & Cantwell Publishing Co., 1872.
White, Ronald C., Jr. and C. H. Hopkins. *The Social Gospel: Religion and Reform in Changing America.* Philadelphia: Temple University Press, 1976.
The World's Congress of Religions. Boston: Arena Publishing Co., 1893.
Wright, Conrad. "The Religion of Geology," *New England Quarterly* 14 (1941): 335-58.

Appendix A
Universalist Declarations of Social Principles

A Declaration of Social Principles, 1917[1]

"In the present general confusion of thought we deem it wise to restate the essential principles of the Universalist faith and their social implications in relation to modern life.

We proclaim the doctrine of the essential divinity of man, of God's universal Fatherhood, and of man's universal brotherhood. Upon this we build our claims to the divine and inherent right of democracy, which does not mean the pulling down of the few to the level of the many, but implies the giving to the many the culture, the responsibilities which beget self-restraint and rulership, and the arts and refinement of life which are now the possession of the few.

While in no wise minimizing the responsibility of the individual for his own life, we denounce as superstition the teaching that men are led into sin by inherent depravity and by devils of an unseen world; but we hold it to be self-evident that mankind is led into sin by evil surroundings, by the evils of unjust social and economic conditions, which condemn one to be born in the squalor and filth of the slums, and another amidst the equally demoralizing influences of unearned luxury. We hold, therefore, that all systems that attempt to load the blame on Adam, upon Satan, or upon human depravity, tend to weaken human self-respect, and to lead men away from the discovery and cure of the real causes of human sin and misery.

In view of these conclusions, which we believe were plainly taught by the great Founder of Christianity, we insist that we should not judge one another any more, but rather, that we should remove the stumbling blocks and the barriers to the kingdom of heaven out of our brother's way.

We conclude also that democracy is not only an inherent right, but also a divinely imposed duty. We find that none of us liveth or dieth to himself, and that true men and women should consider nothing foreign to them which is common to humanity.

Specifically, therefore, we urge that a full and free democracy be set up in our country, and that every man and woman be allowed to exercise the divine right and duty of personal responsibility in the acts of government, first, by the full extension of the franchise to women, and second, by granting to each citizen a direct voice in the vital affairs of his own government.

We brand as infamous the practice of subordinating human interests to "business interests," and we urge that the National Government should not hesitate to assume immediate control of the management of the production and distribution of the necessaries of life to prevent want and starvation and the economic enslavement of the people to predatory interests in time of a crisis.

We assert that the claims of the religion of Jesus, the religion of democracy and of international brotherhood, transcend all the claims of race and of nationality, and that the highest form of patriotism demands that we endeavor to place our nation in the position of one that seeks its permanent glory in subordinating selfish interests to those of the coming Federation of the World, in which "the common sense of most shall hold a fretful realm in awe."

We confidently affirm our faith in God with us and in us, the assurance of the ultimate triumph of good. As our great Teacher has taught us to respect and reverence him in the very lowliest of humanity, and as one of his disciples wrote that love of God is shown in love of man, so we urge a higher and better morality than that based upon escaping hell and winning a heaven. We assert the old maxim, "Whatsoever ye do, whether ye eat or drink, do all to the glory of God" — the welfare of His children. We believe it to be the duty and the privilege of each one to be a co-worker with God towards that "long desire of the nations." It is our duty, and our privilege, to keep ourselves at our best in body, mind, and spirit for the sake of the service which it is ours to give. In this faith and in this service we invite the co-operation of all.

Program

The Universalist Church recognizes the fact that no individual and no nation can live a completely effective Christian life in an unchristian social order. We therefore declare the primal task of the church of to-day to be the reconstruction of the world's civilization in terms of justice, peace and righteousness, so that the spiritual life of all may develop to its fullest capacity.

To this end we submit the following working program:

> Through all the agencies of the church we shall endeavor to educate and inspire the community and the nation to a keener social consciousness and a truer vision of the kingdom of God on the earth.
>
> We want to safeguard marriage so that every child shall be born with a sound physical, mental and moral heritage.
>
> We want to guarantee to every child these conditions of housing, education, food and recreation which will enable him to become his best.
>
> The standard and plane of living for all should be such that deterioration becomes impossible and advancement becomes limited only by capacity.

Democracy, in order to be complete, must be economic and social as well as political. We therefore declare for the democratization of industry and of land, and for the establishment of co-operation.

We would condemn those forms of private monopoly which make it difficult or impossible for men to attain their common share of the common heritage of earth, and especially do we condemn those forms of exploitation which in time of national stress and suffering make the few wealthy at the cost of the many.

No democracy can be real which shuts out half the people. Women should therefore have equal economic, social and political rights with men.

Free discussion is the soul of democracy and the guarantee of our liberties. It should therefore be maintained in our churches, colleges, and public platforms, and limited only by mutual self-respect and courtesy.

We recognize in the use of narcotic habit-forming drugs an imminent peril to social welfare, and we are particularly alarmed at the extent to which tobacco, in the form of cigarettes, is undermining the health and character of American youth. We therefore recommend action toward securing national prohibition of the manufacture and sale of alcoholic liquors, and such progress in restriction of the manufacture of cigarettes and the sale of tobacco as public welfare shall require and public sentiment support. We particularly commend the tobacco laws of Kansas as a model for all the states.

While co-operating to the fullest extent possible with the various forms of charity, relief and correction, we recognize that they do not eradicate fundamental causes. We would mobilize the forces of our church against the causes which create misery, disease, accidents, ignorance and crime, and summon all our strength to the establishment of justice, education and social righteousness.

Some form of social insurance should gradually replace the present individualistic and inadequate methods of charitable relief.

War is brutalizing, wasteful, and ineffective. We therefore pledge ourselves to work for the organization and federation of the world, that peace may be secured at the earliest possible date consistent with justice for all.

The Universalist Church offers a complete program for completing humanity:

First: An Economic Order which shall give to every human being an equal share in the common gifts of God, and in addition all that he shall earn by his own labor.

Second. A Social Order in which there shall be equal rights for all, special privileges for none, the help of the strong for the weak until the weak become strong.

Third. A Moral Order in which all human law and action shall be the expression of the moral order of the universe.

Fourth. A Spiritual Order which shall build out of the growing lives of living men the growing temple of the living God."

Affirmation of Social Principles, 1943[2]

"We Universalists avow our faith in the supreme worth of every human personality, and in the power of men of good will and sacrificial spirit to overcome all evil and progressively establish the Kingdom of God. This faith is being challenged on every side. We therefore reaffirm our historic stand and call upon our people to think through and act upon that faith.

Now is the time for greatness. There have been few if any periods in the entire history of the human race when men have had such an opportunity to mold the future. We stand at the great divide. On one side lies a land of promise, an unprecedented opportunity to build a better world than has ever been known. On the other side lies a return to the old order with its greed, poverty and war.

The hour for decision is at hand. We must move backward toward the old or forward toward the new. It is a fateful decision to make, for destiny will be determined by it; but we cannot and would not escape the responsibility.

Partialism cannot solve the problems of today and tomorrow. Partialism limits, divides and excludes. It emphasizes nationalism, racism, classism, sectarianism, caste and privilege, and it inevitably issues in conflict. Partialism is the underlying philosophy of an old order which was founded on a technological and sociological isolationism which no longer exists. It is discredited and impotent. It cannot construct a unified and universalized civilization, but will lead us backward to the past. [In] that way lies disaster.

The peoples of the world have built an interdependent and integrated culture. Nations, races, classes share a common heritage of science. Airplanes have abolished boundaries. Radios have brought the voice of every people into our homes. Industry has distributed far and wide the commodities of inventive genius. Music, art and education speak a common language.

The only possible philosophy for a better world is universalism. It alone is realistic and creative. In it lies the hope of mankind; without it we are doomed.

This faith means that the whole is greater than the parts. It is the philosophy and the religion of the all-inclusive. It interprets life in terms of the universals and the unities. It levels barriers, abjures prejudice, and renounces all that sets man against his fellow man. It endeavors to integrate humanity into one harmonious co-operating unity.

This faith demands that the common humanity of all races be recognized.

This faith demands that all men of all classes, races, creeds, shall abjure war as a method of solving international disputes and shall affirm their faith in the possibility of progressively building a lasting peace.

This faith demands that we must build an international order in which the sovereign power to settle international disputes resides in a league or assembly of all peoples.

This faith demands that the physical resources of the earth be so used that all men everywhere shall have the essentials of a good life.

This faith demands that we must build an economic order based on the abundant life for all rather than upon the acquisitive power of the few.

This faith demands that the human resources of society, such as education, culture, the arts, be made progressively available to all.

We here and now call upon all fellow Universalists to unite in a great and consecrated movement to make these things come to pass.

In the field of social welfare:

1. We must acquaint ourselves with the faith and practice of other religionists that we may help to overcome the destructive force of religious prejudice.

2. We must recognize that today Americans of Negro, Indian and Oriental descent, and many not yet citizens, are suffering from unjust forms of discrimination. We must combat every such form of race prejudice by practical steps which shall achieve a just status for these our brethren.

3. We must work for such forms of social betterment and security as will enable the American family to provide conditions of housing, food, education and recreation consistent with constructive religious living.

4. We must work for the strengthening of the spiritual foundations of the American home that all members of the family may be growing Christian persons.

5. We must engage in sacrificial and informed community activity which will produce wholesome and progressive results in the areas of planning, relief, reconstruction and recreation.

6. We must study the complex problems of labor, management and capital so that we can intelligently bring the insights of Christian ethics to bear on the problems of economic justice for all members of society.

7. We must recognize the importance of a strong, independent, land-owning farm folk to the future health and well-being of a growing democracy. To this end we recommend support of such legislation and other organized activities as help to increase the number of family-sized and family-owned farms.

8. We must welcome and encourage the growth of the co-operative movement as a check on unwholesome economic practices and a service to producers and consumers alike.

9. We must work for improved educational opportunities for young and old and for a freedom in teaching which will put no restriction upon the authority of truth known or to be known.

10. We must condemn as destructive to the best interests of society all forms of gambling and small games of chance which are an attempt to get something for nothing, and we must work for more stringent laws governing such practices.

11. We must advance the cause of temperance through wise legislation pertaining to the manufacture, distribution, advertising and sale of alcoholic beverages and we must promote a sustained and scientific educational program dealing with the personal and social effects of intemperance.

12. We must avoid both sentimentality and vindictiveness in our attitudes toward criminals. To this end we must give enlightened support to penologists, jurists and trained social workers who seek to develop scientific, humane and ethical treatment of actual and potential criminals and so promote the cause of corrective penology.

13. We must commit ourselves and encourage others to consistent obedience to law lest we and all our society suffer the consequences of disorder and unrestraint.

14. We must recognize the fact that there is no common judgment among Christians as to one's personal duty when called for military service and we call our people to be true in policy and action to a basic law of our church, Article XII of the Laws of Fellowship, which grants full fellowship to conscientious objectors in time of war.

15. We must increase our participation in government as individuals and as representatives of groups of citizens, and must as a denomination and as local churches know and speak our mind on significant public questions.

In the field of international relations:

16. We must inform ourselves concerning the problems of today's world.

17. We must co-operate in establishing an international organization which shall be truly democratic and all-inclusive. In this world organization there must be some internationally organized power to restrain those who threaten the peace of mankind; there must be provision for peaceful change, for the regulation of currencies, tariffs, and other economic concerns by international agreement, and for equal opportunity for all to share the natural resources of the earth.

18. We must be prepared to continue in a spirit of self-sacrifice after the fighting ends to provide food, medical care, and the materials and leadership for reconstruction in all devastated lands.

In the field of international church extension:

19. We must evaluate the work which we have done in Japan and Korea and decide whether or not to re-establish any or all of it, and we must study opportunities offered in the postwar period for new approaches to the Japanese through educational and social work.

20. We must consider new opportunities in world mission, and take our share in the responsibility of Christians for relief, reconstruction and education.

We, therefore, consecrate ourselves to the task of building, under God, a universal brotherhood."

Opposition to Continuation of the Selective Service Act; International Control of Atomic Energy; Compulsory Peace Time Military Training[3]

Opposition to Continuation of Selective Service Act

Resolved, that we oppose the continuation of the Selective Service Act as an extension of militarism into the postwar life of the United States.

International Body for Control of Atomic Energy

Resolved, that this General Assembly approves the setting up of an international body for control of atomic energy, and that we are in complete harmony with the conclusion of the Acheson report wherein it is stated that "there can be no international co-operation which does not presuppose an international community of knowledge."

Support in Conflicts of Conscience

Resolved, that we adopt a positive policy, consistent with the highest ethical insights of religion, of resistance to any and all invasions of the personal liberty of the individual conscience, and in all cases of conflict between the demands of the state and the demands of conscience, we pledge our support to those individuals whose consciences lead them into such a conflict.

Compulsory Peace Time Military Training

Whereas, compulsory military training is a denial of the rights of the individual, and *Whereas*, it is detrimental to the Christian education of our youth, and, *Whereas*, it is an historical fact that military conscription has never prevented war, we *Resolve*, that the delegates to the General Assembly of the Universalist Church of America go on record as being opposed to compulsory peace-time military training.

Be It Further

Resolved, that a copy of this resolution be sent to the President of the United States, to Representative Joseph Martin, Republican minority leader in the House, and to the leader of the opponents of this measure in the Senate.

Support of the United Nations, 1951[4]

Whereas, we, as church people, believe that the only ultimate solution of our world problems lies in the practice of universal brotherhood, *Be It Resolved* that we urge the support of all those commissions of the United Nations which seek and promote world unity and cooperation. *Therefore, Be It Resolved* that the Universalist Church of America in General Assembly convened at Portland, Maine, August 29–September 2, 1951, affirm its own loyalty to the freedom of the mind to believe and of the tongue to speak what the mind believes; and *Be It Further Resolved* that it condemn all persecution of persons for belief without evidence of treason, all enforced submission to doctrine, religious or political; and
Be It Further Resolved that it assert its confidence that national security is guarded more through freedom and constructive criticism than it could ever be through the silence of conformity and fear.

Rights of Conscientious Objectors

Be It Resolved that the Universalist Church of America, in General Assembly convened at Portland, Maine, August 29–September 2, 1951, hereby reaffirm our position as a religious fellowship regarding the right of members and ministers to affirm their convictions as conscientious objectors to war on religious grounds as stated in our Laws of Fellowship (Art. XII).

Civil Liberties

Whereas, we of the Universalist Church of America share with all liberty-loving people the solemn responsibility for preserving and extending freedom in a world threatened by totalitarianism, and *Whereas,* the moral law applied to nations no less than to individuals, and no nation can violate the laws of justice, mercy, equality and freedom of thought and conscience without incurring spiritual and material penalties, and *Whereas,* the McCarran Act and Section 2 and 3 of the Smith Act are representative of present-day legislation which violates these principles in the following ways:

> 1. It destroys equality before the law by imposing harsh penalties on unpopular minorities who are innocent of any criminal act.
> 2. It destroys the civil liberties of *all* Americans by placing in the hands of government officials arbitrary power by which they can proscribe almost any organization peaceably agitating for social, economic or political changes.
> 3. It invokes intimidation, intolerance and persecution to stifle the discussion and dissent without which democracy cannot function.
> 4. By intimidating the citizen against supporting unpopular civic movements of which his conscience approves, it robs him of his moral and intellectual integrity.

Therefore, Be It Resolved that all Universalists be alerted to the danger of current national, state and local legislation aimed at subverting our traditional civil liberties; and
Be It Further Resolved that we urge our several churches through their study groups and social action committees, to make known to their elected governmental representatives their opposition to all legislation which would sacrifice our freedom to totalitarian pressures."

Civil Liberties, 1953[5]

"*Whereas,* Universalists profess to believe in the supreme worth of every human personality, as expressed in the historic Washington avowal of faith; and *Whereas,* persons of various ethnic and religious backgrounds seek the fellowship of the Liberal church; and
Whereas, persons of these ethnic and religious backgrounds may from time to time wish to enter the ministry of the Universalist Church;
Therefore, Be It Resolved that we reaffirm our historic position by urging our several churches and peoples to extend a warm welcome to both potential members and potential clergy regardless of race or color.
Whereas, the Universalist Church has cherished and championed the cause of spiritual freedom throughout its history, and
Whereas the dignity of the human soul requires and deserves the fullest measure of that liberty which has been won in the age-long struggle for emancipation and enlightenment

Be It Therefore Resolved that this Assembly re-assert its allegiance to the principles of human freedom which are implicit in the professions and traditions of our faith and which are in part embodied in the Bill of Rights of the Constitution of the United States

And Be It Further Resolved that while we recognize the obligation of responsible government to take reasonable and orderly measures to make secure its traditions and institutions, we strongly deplore any tendency, governmental or non-governmental, which would curtail freedom of speech, freedom of the press, freedom of worship, freedom of conscience and those other liberties which give character to citizenship in a free society. Especially would we deplore the use or approval of all measures of coercion, intimidation, irresponsible accusation of individuals, groups and professions, which would foster authoritarian control and tyrannical repression, and result at length in the destruction of civil and spiritual freedom;

And Be It Further Resolved that this Assembly call upon all Universalists so to employ and defend the privileges of freedom with reason and love, that we may further the Kingdom of God and the Brotherhood of Man."

Declaration of Social Principles, 1957[6]

"Universalists have from their earliest beginnings, recognized the social implications of religion. They have prided themselves upon the freedom from dogma found in their religious community and have, from time to time, sought publicly to express those value which they hold in common.

Since they believe that religion and life must be made one, Universalists do not support any concept of religion which ignores social and human values. For them, ethical awareness is at once the foundation and flower of vital faith. Nor can they agree that religious faith must be grounded in some supernatural revelation. For them, the common experiences of men, evaluated by reason and the tradition of religious liberalism, provide ethical guidance. To them, the test of ethical principles lies in their ability to create and sustain the goods of life for all men and in this world.

Three basic beliefs characterize the Universalist fellowship and provide the basis for personal and social values. These are, first the worth of the person regardless of race, creed or standing, second the commitment to developing truth and third that men of good will and sincere purpose can overcome evil and transform it into good.

Earlier Universalists were not content to rest upon a simple statement of these general principles. Nor are we. In voicing this consensus of our social principles, we recognize that they must be continually reinterpreted and this in a manner appropriate to our fellowship and consistent with the democratic process. Through worship, study, discussion, resolving and acting we deepen the sensitivity of the liberal church. Our social concern is part of the very dynamics of our faith. As we apply our principles to today's problems, a number of agreements emerge:

1. Relations with other religions.

In our relations with other religious groups, we have tried to avoid two extremes. There is an arrogant assumption that all virtue and truth have been given only to members of one particular sect. Many groups have made this claim and it cannot stand up under reasonable examination. On the other hand is an easy sentimentality which assumes the sameness and equality of all religions. Both of these positions reveal a lack of knowledge of man's history. We believe in sharing what we have learned of truth with others while at the same time correcting our vision with their insights. Such mutuality is the best path to a common understanding that will unite mankind.

2. Freedom of the pulpit and pew.

Every congregation is a community dedicated to seeking and serving truth. Since we know that further knowledge must be gained by devoted inquiry, we believe in freedom of pulpit and pew.

3. Church and state.

We hold the American tradition of the separation of the church and state to be a crucial bulwark against ecclesiastical and political tyranny. If sectarian influences remain removed from our schools, courts and common life, both our churches and our society will be freer and healthier. For this reason we stand against religious instruction in the public schools on released time and against other efforts to make sectarian definitions of religion a basis of law.

4. Conscientious objectors.

We recognize that some Universalists, by reason of their religious training and conviction, cannot conscientiously serve in the armed forces. Because of our respect for individual conscience, we stand ready to support them as well as those who conscientiously choose to bear arms.

5. Civil liberties.

Because respect for personality must include support of those conditions under which personality can best grow, we champion the cause of civil liberties, free speech, petition and assembly being the conditions of such growth.

6. Civil rights.

All citizens should have equal access to educational, vocational, recreational and residential opportunity. Knowing the blighting effects of segregation, discrimination and prejudice, we support all responsible defenses of civil rights when these have been denied on the basis of race, creed, national origin or otherwise.

7. Public education.

Good public schools are essential to our society and to the development of personality. We dedicate ourselves to work in our communities to protect our schools from unwarranted and uninformed criticisms and to cooperate with school personnel and others in raising standards.

8. School integration.

We hold the public schools to be a crucial training ground of democracy and therefore support efforts to effect integration in those areas where race or other irrelevant factors have defeated democracy.

9. Penal reform.

Believing in the redemptive principle as a genuine goal of life, and recognizing that society as well as the offender stands in need of such redemption, we support such procedures in the penal system as will tend to undo the physical, moral and spiritual estrangement of the criminal from his fellows in the human community. We strenuously oppose capital punishment as a total denial of this principle, and as a crime inflicted by society against itself. Likewise we oppose any employment of physical or psychological abuse against the imprisoned. We endorse the principle of probation and parole which gives offenders an opportunity with guidance to relate themselves honorably to society. And we advocate such procedures in prisons and corrective institutions as will enable even those who must remain incarcerated permanently, to enter into creative relationships within the prison community, and to have such contact with the outside world as may be consistent with the necessary precautions of the institution.

10. Political duty.

In affirming the common nature and destiny of all men, we have become conscious of our common responsibility for our mutual welfare. Since enlightened democracy is the best way of insuring continuing justice and flexibility to change, we educate and encourage all Universalists to participate in political life, as voters, party members and office-holders.

11. United Nations.

Universalists deny that force and violence are desirable methods of resolving differences among nations. We instead support free exchange of ideas and persons, mutual respect and discussion, and a system of international law and arbitration. So we now support the United Nations as the potential organization of world peace.

12. Foreign aid.

In viewing the differences of living standards enjoyed by various countries, we are well aware of the claims made to justify a particular nation's position and wealth. But we are also aware that men are brothers who are, by pure chance, born in one or another area. This fact places an obligation upon a wealthy nation to share skills and abundance with underdeveloped nations. To this end we support all reasonable efforts to achieve the elimination of poverty.

13. Temperance.

Recognizing that neither the attempt at absolute prohibition represented by the 18th amendment, nor its subsequent repeal, have solved the continuing problems arising from the unwise or excessive use of alcohol in beverages, we reaffirm our historic position that this is a matter of grave concern to all. We support such studies as will enable us to understand and treat chronic alcoholism, and all democratic efforts to guard against excessive or unwise drinking.

1. *Universalist Leader* 20 (30 November 1917): 759-60.
2. *Christian Leader* 125 (2 October 1943): 582-83.
3. Extract from Resolutions adopted by the General Assembly, April 1946.
4. Extract from Resolutions Adopted by the General Assembly, 1951.
5. Extract from Resolutions Adopted by the General Assembly, 1953.
6. Adopted by the General Assembly, 1957.

Appendix B
Constitution and By-Laws of the Unitarian Universalist Association Ratified in 1961

ARTICLE I
Name

The name of this organization shall be the Unitarian Universalist Association.

ARTICLE II
Purpose and Objectives

Section 1. The Unitarian Universalist Association is an incorporated organization which by consolidation has succeeded to the charter powers of the American Unitarian Association, incorporated in 1847, and the Universalist Church of America, incorporated in 1866, by virtue of legislation enacted by The Commonwealth of Massachusetts and the State of New York, respectively.

"The Unitarian Universalist Association is empowered to, and shall devote its resources to and exercise its corporate powers for, religious, educational and charitable purposes. It is further empowered: to solicit and receive funds separately or with others to support its work; to make appropriations to carry on its work including appropriations to its members and to other organizations to enable them to assist the Unitarian Universalist Association in carrying on its work; and without limitation as to amount, to receive, hold, manage, invest and reinvest and distribute any real and personal property for the foregoing purposes."

Section 2. In accordance with these corporate purposes, the members of the Unitarian Universalist Association, dedicated to the principles of a free faith, unite in seeking:

1. To strengthen one another in a free and disciplined search for truth as the foundation of our religious fellowship;

2. To cherish and spread the universal truths taught by the great prophets and teachers of humanity in every age and tradition, immemorially summarized in their essence as love to God and love to man;

3. To affirm, defend and promote the supreme worth of every human personality, the dignity of man, and the use of the democratic method in human relationships;

4. To implement our vision of one world by striving for a world community founded on ideals of brotherhood, justice and peace;

5. To serve the needs of member churches and fellowships, to organize new churches and fellowships, and to extend and strengthen liberal religion;

6. To encourge cooperation with men of good will of all faiths in every land.

Section 3. The Unitarian Universalist Association hereby declares and affirms the independence and autonomy of local churches, fellowships, and associate members; and nothing in this Constitution or By-Laws of the Association shall be deemed to infringe upon the congregational polity of churches and fellowships, nor upon the exercise of direct control by their memberships of associate member organizations, nor upon the individual freedom of belief, which are inherent in the Universalist and Unitarian heritages. No minister shall be required to subscribe to any particular interpretation of religion, or to any particular religious belief or creed to obtain and hold Fellowship with the Unitarian Universalist Association.

ARTICLE III
Membership

Section 1. All churches and fellowships which are members of the American Unitarian Association and all churches and fellowships which are members of or in full fellowship with The Universalist Church of America on the effective date of this Constitution shall be members of the Unitarian Universalist Association.

Section 2. Those individuals who, on the effective date of this Constitution, were Life Members of the American Unitarian Association and were so constituted on or before May 1, 1925, shall be Life Members of the Unitarian Universalist Association and shall have all the rights and privileges of membership, including the right to vote at meetings of the Association.

Section 3. A church or fellowship may become a member of the Association upon acceptance by the Board of Trustees of the Association of a written application for membership stating that it subscribes to the purposes and objectives of the Association and pledges itself to support the Association. Those individuals who, on the effective date of this constitution have served as Presidents of the Universalist Church of America shall have all the rights and privileges of membership, including the right to vote at meetings of the Association.

Section 4. Any church or fellowship which is a member shall have the right through delegates to vote at meetings of the Association, during the fiscal year in which it becomes a member and thereafter, provided such church or fellowship has met the following conditions in the next preceding fiscal year:
   A. Made a financial contribution to the Association.
   B. Conducted regular religious services.
   C. Maintained a regularly constituted organization with adequate records of membership, with elected officers and with provisions for annual meetings of members.
   D. Furnished the Association with requied reports on church statistics and activities.

Churches and fellowships which do not comply with these requirements in one fiscal year shall not have their delegates accredited in the next fiscal year nor until the beginning of the fiscal year next following their compliance therewith. The Board of Trustees shall have the duty of determining compliance or non-compliance with these requirements and it shall make rules to carry out the intent of this Section.

Section 5. The Board of Trustees may admit to associate membership any other organization the purposes and programs of which, in the Board's judgment and discretion, are auxiliary to and support the purposes and objectives of the Association, upon a written application from such organization stating that it subscribes to the purposes and objectives of the Association and pledging itself to support the Association. Such membership shall continue so long as in the Board's judgment and discretion such organization's purposes and programs continue to be auxiliary to and in support of the purposes and objectives of the Association. Each associate member, through delegates, shall have the right to vote at each meeting of the Association during the fiscal year in which it becomes an associate member and thereafter provided such associate member has made a financial contribution to the Association in the next preceding fiscal year.

ARTICLE IV
Conduct of the Association's Affairs

Section 1. Delegates and individuals having the right to vote shall constitute the General Assembly of the Association. The General Assembly shall be the overall policy making body for carrying out the purposes and objectives of the Association and shall direct and control its affairs. The Board of Trustees shall conduct the affairs of the Association and subject to the provisions of its Constitution and By-Laws, shall carry out the policies and directives of the General Assembly and shall have all the usual powers of corporate directors as provided by law. The Officers of the Association, including those elected by the General Assembly and those appointed by the Board, shall be subject to the direction and control of the Board and shall have all the usual powers of such officers as provided by law.

Section 2. The responsibility for investment of funds of the Association is vested in the Board which may from time to time delegate these powers to its Investment Committee, but no such delegation shall relieve the Board of its overall responsibility in this respect.

Section 3. The Association, as of the effective date of this Constitution, hereby assumes all financial obligations and debts of the American Unitarian Association and The Universalist Church of America and agrees to pay and discharge the same. Funds and assets held prior to said effective date for the benefit of any church, fellowship or organization by either the American Unitarian Association or The Universalist Church of America shall be held by the Unitarian Universalist Association upon the same conditions and obligations, so far as required by law. If, after the effective date of this Constitution, the Association shall consolidate, merge with, or become the successor of any organization (other than the American Unitarian Association or the Universalist Church of America) which holds funds or assets for the benefit of any church, fellowship or organization, any such assets and funds thus acquired by the Association shall be held under the same conditions and obligations, so far as required by law. Unless subject to specific restrictions, such funds or assets may be invested in the General Investment Fund of the Association.

Section 4. The Association shall raise capital and operating funds to carry out its purposes and objectives and also may raise capital and operating funds for the use of its associate members and others as provided in Article II, Section 1.

ARTICLE V
Regions

Section 1. In order to provide for the services and work which can best be accomplished through regional organizations, the Association shall support areas of regional responsibility to be known as Regions, the same to be established in such number and with such geographical location as the General Assembly, following consultation with authorized representatives of the churches and fellowships concerned, shall from time to time determine. Recognizing that prior to the formation of the Association, Conferences and Councils of Unitarian churches and fellowships, and State Conventions of Universalist churches and fellowships had been created by groups of churches and fellowships and vested with certain duties and powers, independent in whole or in part from the jurisdiction of the American Unitarian Association or The Universalist Church of America, respectively, and recognizing that the Boards of Trustees and Officers of these units and their successors can continue to contribute a major part of the direction and operation of regional services and work, and recognizing also that the development of the pattern of the cooperation of these Conferences, Councils and Conventions with the Association will not be necessarily contemporaneous or in identical form, such Regions shall make use of a system having regional organization based on the principle of local autonomy, consistent with the promotion of the welfare and interests of the Association as a whole and of its member churches and fellowships.

ARTICLE VI
The Ministry

Section 1. Ministers having Ministerial Fellowship with the American Unitarian Association or The Universalist Church of America on the effective date of this Constitution shall thereby have Ministerial Fellowship with the Unitarian Universalist Association. Other ministers may be admitted to Ministerial Fellowship upon filing an application with the Association and meeting its requirements as set forth in its By-Laws and Rules made pursuant thereto. The Association recognizes and affirms that member churches alone have the right to call and ordain their ministers. The Association alone shall have the right to grant Ministerial Fellowship with the Association.

Section 2. The Association shall establish and maintain a pension system for ministers having full Ministerial Fellowship with the Association. Ministers who, on the effective date of this Constitution, have pension rights and benefits theretofore conferred by the American Unitarian Association or The Universalist Church of America shall not have those rights or benefits abridged without their written consent insofar as the same are at that time vested rights and benefits which constitute legal obligations.

ARTICLE VII
Financial Services to Churches and Fellowships

Section 1. The Association may receive funds and other assets for investments and hold the same for the benefit of member churches, fellowships and other organizations subject in each instance to the approval of the Board of Trustees. The Board of Trustees shall establish rules to carry out the intent of this Section and such rules shall include the right of withdrawal of such funds and assets on reasonable notice.

ARTICLE VIII
Seal

The Association shall have a corporate seal which shall be in such form as the Board of Trustees shall approve.

ARTICLE IX
Rules Under This Constitution

Rules made under the authority of this Constitution shall take effect upon adoption but may be amended or repealed by vote of the General Assembly.

ARTICLE X
Amendments

This Constitution may be amended or repealed by the General Assembly at a regular meeting of the Association at which a quorum is present if two-thirds of those present and voting so order, but the General Assembly shall act on any proposed amendment or repeal only when the same has been submitted in accordance with the By-Laws and read at the previous regular meeting.

BY-LAWS
ARTICLE I
Meetings

Section 1. Regular meetings of the General Assembly of the Unitarian Universalist Association shall be held annually in April or May at such time and place in the United States of America or in Canada as the Board of Trustees from time to time shall determine.

Section 2. A special meeting of the General Assembly of the Association may be called by the Board of Trustees at any time, and a special meeting shall be called by the Board of Trustees upon petition of not less than three hundred legal members or not less than one hundred of the member churches and fellowships in at least ten different states and provinces. Such a meeting shall be held at such time and place in the United States of America or in Canada as the Board from time to time shall determine.

Section 3. A quorum at any meeting of the General Assembly shall be not less than three hundred accredited delegates representing among them not less than one hundred of the member churches or fellowships located in at least ten different states or provinces.

Section 4. The Board of Trustees from time to time shall prescribe the form and manner of giving notice of all meetings of the General Assembly, such notice to be given not less than 60 days before the date thereof.

ARTICLE II
Fiscal Year

Section 1. The fiscal year of the Association shall be from April 1 to March 31.

ARTICLE III
Officers and Trustees

Section 1. The elected Officers of the Association shall be a Moderator, a President, two Vice Presidents, a Secretary and a Treasurer. These Officers shall be members of the Board of Trustees and they and twenty other persons shall constitute the Board of Trustees of the Association. Neither the President nor the Treasurer, as members of the Board of Trustees, shall have the right to vote at meetings of the Board.

Section 2. The Board of Trustees may from time to time appoint such executive and administrative officers of the Association as it shall determine.

Section 3. No Trustee who is not also an elected officer may serve more than two successive terms of four years each. However, a Trustee may at any time become one of the elected Officers of the Association and serve the full term of such office. No person who has served as an elected Officer for a full term shall thereafter be elected a Trustee without an interim of four years.

Index

Abbott, A R, 98
Abbott, Thomas, 193, 686 n
Abe, Yasujiro, 431
Achenbach, Lyman I, 377
Adams, Clara B, 178
Adams, Frank D, 58, 60, 203-204, 259, 580, 591, 602, 716 n
Adams, John Coleman, 21 *illus*, 92, 101, 121, 123, 126, 215, 255, 424, 540, 550, 556, 713 n
Adams, John Greenleaf, 67, 415, 466, 539
Adams, Maude A. 699 n
Adin Ballou Pacifist Fellowship, 491
Adler, H, 121
Advance, 249, 603
Affirmation of Social Principles, 505
African Methodist Episcopal Church in America, 720 n
Akashi, Michio, 456
Alabama State Conference, 266, 269, 388
Albion, James F, 165, 715 n
Albright, Harry A, 520
Alcott, A N, 84, 124, 143, 137
Allen, Ethel M, 391 *illus*, 393
Alliance of Unitarian Women, 398, 661
Allin, Thomas, 428
American Association of Theological Schools, 275, 293, 325, 327-328
American Board of Commissioners for Foreign Missions, 413
American Civil Liberties Union, 499
American Congress of Liberal Religion (Religious Socities), 131
American Friends Service Committee, 210
American Friendship offering, 368
American Temperance University, 194
Ames, Louis Annan, 170, 198, 716-717 n
Anderson, J W, 354
Andrews, Charles F, 165
Andrews, L F W, 469
Andrews, Mary Garard, 142
Andrews, Stephen Pearl, 678 n
Andrews, Susan M, 216
Angell, Martha B, 630
Arai, Satoshi, 458
Arisian, Khoren, 112
Arkansas, Little Rock, Universalism in, 198-199
Ashton, Eugene S, 322, 324, 325
associations, 6
Attwood, Luther Weston, 437

Atwood, Isaac Morgan, 7, 22, 33, 36, 42, 60, 81, 125, 140, 149, 177-178, 182, 197, 218, 228 *illus*, 231, 241, 279, 284, 287 *illus*, 288, 289-290, 358-359, 362, 367, 406, 410, 473, 535-536, 541-542, 543, 548, 608-609, 648, 713 n
Atwood, John Murray, 33, 112, 113, 286, 287 *illus*, 288, 487, 552, 574-575, 713 n
Atwood Memorial Hall, 292
AUA (American Unitarian Association), 210, 237, 238, 252, 449, 494, 542-543, 553, 578, 585, 611, 630
Auer, J A C Fagginger, 110, 128, 317, 322
AUW (Association of Universalist Women), 333, 371, 379, 394 *illus*, 395, 398, 399, 456, 457, 661, 721 n
AUY (American Unitarian Youth) 208
Averill, George C, 398
Avowal of Faith; see Washington Declaration of 1935
Ayres, Clara L, 498
Ayres, Minnie J, 373, 387 *illus*, 448, 450
Ayres, Samuel G, 448, 450

Babcock, Clara Maria, 75
Bailey, Emma E, 347
Balch, William S, 6, 66, 281
Baldwin, Peter A, 335
Ball brothers, 612
Ballard, T E, 87, 89, 144
Ballou, Adin, 464, 537, 538
Ballou, Hosea, 8, 9, 11, 137, 535
Ballou, Hosea 2d, 6, 11
Ballou Hosea Starr, 713 n
Ballou, Latimer W, 354
Ballou, Moses, 533, 534
Ballou, Mary L, 215
Ballou, Russell A, 244
Baptists, 21, 175, 413,
Barnes, Gilbert W, 221
Barnes, Seth, 69
Barney, C Neal, 213
Barnum, P T, 223, 237, 419, 428
Barrows, John Henry, 121
Barth, Joseph, 332
Barton, Clara, 354, 538
Barton, Ralph M, 256
Barton, William E, 554, 556, 558
Baughan, Raymond J, 251
Baxter, George H, 552
Bay State Universalist, 638

Beachcomber Society, 180
Beacon Press, 251, 252
Beem, A K, 143
Bell, William Y, 652
Bellows, Henry W, 535-536
Bennet, Gertrude Estelle, 257
Bennett, Frank P, 169
Benton, Herbert E, 614
Berle, Adolph A, 310
Bethany Home (Boston), 514-515, 515 *illus*
Bethany Home (Minneapolis), 516
Betts, Frederick W, 149, 219, 450, 609
Bewkes, Eugene G, 291
Bicknell, A Ingham, 52, 208, 249, 715 n, 717 n, 720 n
Bilkovski (Beresford), Anthony, 14-15, 355-356, 696 n
Billings, James, 200, 385
Billings, Mary, 200, 385
Bir-Zeit, Jordan, 529
birth control, 468
Bisbee, Eleanor, 186
Bisbee, Frederick A, 43, 50, 54, 126, 127, 140, 149, 213, 222, 242-244, 243 *illus*, 314, 479, 538, 551, 555
Bisbee, Frederick A (Mrs), 222, 347
Bisbee, Herman, 68 ff, 69 *illus*, 672 n
Bisbee heresy trial, 68 ff
Bishop, Francis B, 229, 360, 392
Blackford, Frank, 641
Blackmer, Lucian, 437, 439
Blackmer Home for Girls, 55, 439, 444, 446, 448, 449, 456
Blackmer Home Fund, 200
Blackwell Antoinette Brown, 122
Blakely, Russell, 73
Blalock, Ira Jr, 331
Blanchard, Henry, 124, 131, 132, 142, 142 *illus*, 472, 537
Bliss, Alfred V, 566
Board of Foreign Missions, 444, 445, 448, 450, 453
Bodell, Willard O, 389, 390
Bogue, Mary Florensia, 672 n
Bolles, Edwin C, 100, 223, 648
Bond of Fellowship and Statements of Faith; see Washington Declaration of 1935
Bonney, Charles Carroll, 120
Boorn, George, 376
Boston Association
Boston Ministers Association, 88
Boston Declaration (Plan), 87-88
Boston Sunday Herald, 9
Boston Tuberculosis Association, 398
Boston Universalist Ministers Association, 482
Bosworth, Roger D, 523
Bovee, Victor, 251
Bowen, Georgene, 451, 451 *illus*, 454, 455

Bowen, Henry, 412
Bowers, J M, 267
Bowie, R S, 401, 404
Bowles, Ada C, 147, 357, 389, 395, 464, 465, 467, 540
Bowles, B F, 78
Bowman, Anne, 724 n
Bowman, J Russell (Mrs), 523
Bowman, Robert M, 657-658
Bowser, B, 412
Boys Battalions (Brigades), 183, 184
Bradley, Asa M, 385-386, 591
Bradley, Dwight, 597
Bradley, Hannah, 243
Bradley, Lydia Moss, 261
Bradley University, 261
Brevoort Mission, 510
Briggs, Samuel A, 214
Brigham, John, 684 n
Brigham, L Ward, 150, 279
Bristol, Lucius M, 319, 495
Brittain, S B, 97
Brooks, Elbridge Gerry, 6, 8, 13, 30, 94, 230
Brooks, Phillips, 10
Brooks, Seth R, 58, 159, 662, 724 n
Brotherhood of Christian Unity, 123
Brotherhood of St Andrew, 184
Brotherston, Bruce W, 293, 317, 322, 640, 722 n
Brown, "Aunty" Lucinda, 191-192, 192 *illus*
Brown, Olympia, 122, 124, 282, 464, 465
Bruce, Elizabeth M, 464, 683 n
Brummit, Lillie Belle, 377
Bruner, Edna P, 628
Bryant, Ordell E, 377, 390
Buchtel, John R, 191
Buchtel College, 40, 103, 253, 254, 689 n
budget, 52
"Buds of Promise," 183
Bumpus, Hermon C, 316
Burkholder, H Clay, 664
Burnell, Maria S, 344
Burnham, Daniel H, 119
Burruss, John C, 372
Butler, Stanard D, 584, 596
Butler, Thomas, 235
Buttrick, George A, 615

California Institute of Technology, 263
California State Convention, 103, 263-264
Call, Lon Ray, 584-585, 602, 723 n
Camp Hill, Alabama, 199, 267
Camp (grove) meetings, 218 ff
Camp Kenmore, 229
Camp Murray, 388, 451
Campbell, Jeffrey W, 202
Canada, Universalism in, 356
Canfield, A J, 120, 123, 124

Canfield, Harry L, 113, 182 *illus*, 185, 373, 390
Canfield, Mary Grace, 182*illus*, 182-183, 373,390
Canton Theological School, 33, 113, 274, 275, 281 ff, 287 *illus*, 291 *illus*, 490
Cantwell, J S, 65, 68, 92, 140, 402
Capen, Elmer H, 10, 80, 123, 310, 311, 423, 477
capital and labor, Universalist attitude toward, 471 ff
capital punishment, 468-469
Caraker, T Andrew, 479
Cardall, Alfred J, 176
Carlson, Carl O, 396
Carmichael, Leonard, 321, 398
Carnegie, Andrew, 377
Carnegie, Andrew (Mrs), 517
Carnes, Paul, 659, 664-665
Carrier, F L, 198
Cary, Henry (Harry), Jr, 451, 455
Cary, Henry Montfort, 450
Cary, Maude Simonton Lyon, 450-451
Case, Lorenzo D, 589
Cassara, Ernest, 335
Cate, Ella, 444
Cate, Isaac Wallace, 421, 423, 424, 426 *illus*, 432, 435, 437, 444
Caverly, Charles, 81, 244
Cavert, Samuel M, 615
Cent-a-Day plan, 43, 631
centennial celebration, 3-4
Central Conference of American Rabbis, 150
Central Planning Council, 54, 632
Chambré, A St John, 10, 610
Chaney, J C, 73
Channing, William Ellery, 237, 535-536
Channing-Murray Sunday School Union, 215
Chapin, Augusta J, 120, 122, 123, 147, 465, 466, 550, 676 n
Chapin, Edwin Hubbell, 9, 10, 13, 418, 470, 516, 538
Chapin, Edwin H (Mrs), 516-517
Chapin, James H. 25, 418, 421, 423, 609
Chapin Home, 516-517, 518 *illus*
Chapman, Thomas, 155, 271, 359, 389, 688 n
Charles Street Meeting House (Boston), 111, 231-232, 644 *illus*, 645, 646 *illus*
Chattanooga, Tennessee, 199, 228
Chautauqua movement, 183
Chicago Declaration of 1899, 86-89, 114
Chicago World's Fair of 1893; see World's Columbian Exposition
Christ Crusade, 49, 485
Christian Century, 565, 577, 578, 598, 617-618, 619
Christian Endeavor, 175, 181-182, 682 n
Christian Freeman, 236

Christian Leader, 20, 85, 133, 237, 242, 248, 249, 558, 606
Christian Register, 24, 145, 259, 585, 687 n
Christian Repository, 236
Christian socialism, 493, 494
Christian Universalists, 111, 664
Church Extension Fund, 191
Church of the Brethren, 720 n
Church of the Divine Paternity (New York City), 510, 511
Church of the Larger Fellowship (Universalist), 660
Church of the Messiah (Philadelphia), 518, 576, 598
Church of the Redeemer (Minneapolis), 511
Church of the Restoration (Philadelphia), 519, 520
civil liberties, 740 (Appendix A)
Clara Barton camp, 201, 396, 396 *illus*
Clara Barton Guilds, 388, 396, 397
Clara Barton Memorial Association, 396
Clarence Darrow Community Center; see Ryder Community Center
Clark, Charles, E, 482-483
Clark, Francis E, 175
Clark, Walter H, 335
Clarke, E Palmer, 335
Clarke, James Freeman, 96, 134, 586
Clayton, D B, 193, 359, 688 n
clergy, 154 ff; economic status, 154 ff; fellowship rules, 160; pensions, 156
Cleveland, Grover, 180
Cleverly, Asa P, 507
Clinchy, Russell J, 597
Clinton Liberal Institute, 253, 289, 301, 691 n
Cobb, Sylvanus, 236, 237, 412, 470
Cohen, Beryl D, 322, 323
Cole, Alfred S, 235, 318, 334-335, 501
Cole, David H, 524, 638-639, 642, 722 n
Collens, Charles, 57
Colored Methodist Episcopal Church in America, 720 n
Colored Universalist, 366
Columbus Avenue Church (Boston), 59
Commission on Comity and Church Unity, 161
Commission on Foreign Relations, 125, 127
Commission on Social Action, 505
Commission on Social Service, 494, 496
Commission on World-Wide Free Religious Fellowship, 129
Committee on Survey and Reorganization, 54
Community Church (Boston) 483, 500, 506 ff, 711 n
Community Church (New York), 29, 506
compulsory military training, 486, 738-739 (Appendix A)

Cone, Orello, 83, 102 ff, 102 *illus*, 132, 140, 145, 147, 231, 282, 284-285, 536
Conger, E L, 78
Congregational Christian Churches, 618, 720 n
Congregational-Unitarian relations, 560-561
Congregationalist, 556, 557
Congregationalists, 61, 413-414, 554 ff
Congress of Liberal Religions, 89
Congress of Religion; see American Congress of Religion (Religious Societies)
Connecticut State Convention, 31-32
conscientious objectors, 487-491, 499, 709 n, 739 (Appendix A)
Convention Church, 660
Convention of the New England States, 5
Coons, Leroy, 50
Cooper, Washington L (Mrs), 517
Cope, Robert L, 295
Cornish, Louis C, 259, 591, 593, 597
Cotton States and International Exposition (1895), 187
Couden, H N, 424, 604
Council of Executives, 54, 671 n
Council of Liberal Churches (CLC), 651, 652 *illus*, 659
Council of Free Churches of America, 599
Cousens, John A, 498, 668 n, 680-681 n, 715 n
Craig, John, 283
Crane, Albert (Mr & Mrs), 310, 693 n
Crane, Stephen, 125
Crane, Thomas, 310
Crane Program Fund, 337
Crane Review, 231
Crane Theological School, 254, 274-275, 302 ff, 310, 321 *illus*, 692 n, 694 n
Cromie, William Wesley, 200
Crooker, Florence Kollock, 141, 147, 464
Crooker, Joseph H, 141
Crosely, Marion, 35, 407, 437, 521
Crowe, Winfied Scott, 75, 132, 135, 139, 677 n
Cummins, John, 616 *illus*
Cummins, Robert, 28, 115, 211, 252, 370, 490, 523, 524, 599, 614 ff, 616 *illus*, 620 ff, 631 ff, 641, 643, 649, 653 *illus*, 655, 660, 668 n, 669 n, 718 n, 719 n, 720 n
Cunningham, J M, 404-405
Currie, James F, 409
Curtis, Anson B, 140, 304
Cushing, Stella Marek, 129, 201
Cushman, Henry I, 83, 312, 713 n
Cutler, Julian S, 84

Danforth, Abbie E, 424
Danforth, Vinnie, 424
Darrow, Clarence, 481
Darwin, Charles R, 96, 97, 99, 674 n
Davis, Andrew Jackson, 97
Dean Academy, 254
Dearbon, W H, 610
Debs, Eugene V, 58, 503
Declaration of 1899; see Chicago Declaration
Declaration of Social Faith, 504
Declaration (Affirmation) of Social Principles (1943), 504, 735-738 (Appendix A)
Declaration of Social Principles (1957), 505, 741-744 (Apendix A)
Demarest, G L, 30, 36, 90, 419
Dennis, J S, 74
Denton, William, 69
Department of Church Extension, 191
Department of Service Projects; see Universalist Service Committee
Department of Social Welfare, 503-504
Dewick, Frank A, 516
Deyo, Amanda, 484
Dick, Robert T, 491, 526
Dieffenbach, Albert C, 248, 259, 564, 585, 588
Dinsmore, L J, 147
Disciples of Christ, 720 n
displaced families, 527
Divine Paternity House; see Brevoort Mission
Dockstader, George A, 283-284, 307
Dodge, Henry Nehemiah, 427
Dodge, J Smith, 124, 231
Dojin House, 452, 456
Dolbear, Amos E, 147, 309-310
Dole, Walter, 83
Doolittle, Allen C, 521
Doolittle, Sarah Billings, 521
Doolittle Home, 26, 521, 522, 522 *illus*
Douglas, Neil, 400-401
Downing, Ruth G, 374-375, 448, 452, 456
Downs, Darley, 455
Dowson, J Lonsdale, 148
Drake, Franklin J, 256
Druley, T C, 101
dual fellowship, 160, 163

Earle, Augusta Gertrude, 308
East, Charles R, 196
East Tennessee Land Company, 193, 194
Eaton, Charles H, 124, 132, 242, 245, 477
Eberhart, Isa B, 267
Eddy, Richard, 6, 21, 42-43, 86, 88, 181, 232 ff, 236, 420, 422-423, 686 n
Eddy, Sherwood, 561
Eliot, Charles W, 612
Eliot, Frederick May, 211, 648, 649, 653 *illus*

756 / Index

Eliot, Samuel A, 14, 542, 543, 544, 548, 550, 551, 552, 559, 570-571, 584, 587, 661
Eliot House, 630
Eliot P. Joslin Camp for Diabetic Boys, 200, 398, 699 n
Ellis, Jennie Louis, 465
Emergency War Relief Committee, 486
Emerson, George H, 11, 124, 231, 241-242, 471, 535
Emmons, Charles H, 57
Empire State Universalist, 634
Endicott, Eugene F, 244
Enslin Morton S, 295
Essential Principles of the Universalist Faith; see Chicago Declaration of 1899
Ethical Culture Society, 598
Etz, Roger F, 24, 25, 53, 128, 202, 208, 455, 591, 597, 629, 715 n, 717 n
Evangel, 432
Evangelical and Reformed Church in America, 720 n
Evans, Daniel, 559
Evening News (Salem, Massachusetts), 564
Everton, J L, 373
Every-Day Church, 513
evolution, debate over, 106 ff, 674 n

Fagley, Frederick L, 615
"Fair Share" plan, 631
Fay, Leon C, 639, 642
Federal Council of Churches, 52, 494, 504, 612 ff, 719 n
Federation of Religious Liberals; see National Federation of Religious Liberals
Feehan, Patrick A, 122
Fellowship of Youth for Peace, 483
Ferris, Walter, 88
Ferry Beach, Maine, 180, 224, 224 *illus*, 226, *illus*, 227 ff, 228 *illus*
Ferry Beach Park Association, 225, 226
Field, Brayton A, 213
finances, denominational, 38 ff
Fischer, Theodore A (Mr & Mrs), 226, 693 n
Fishbough, William, 97, 674 n
Fisher, Carleton M, 457, 523 ff, 527, 528 *illus*, 635, 636, 664, 724 n
Fisher, Ebenezer, 72, 242, 287 *illus*, 282, 284
Fisher, Frederick B, 599-600, 601, 602, 604
Fisher, Lewis B, 93, 115, 176, 256, 277, 278, 279, 286, 556,
Fisher Hall, 285 *illus*, 291
Fisher Society, 298
Fisk, Richmond, Jr, 74, 76, 147
Fiske, H S, 219
Fiske, John, 104
Fiske, Wallace, 299
"Five Points" (Unitarian), 586
"Five Principles" (Universalist), 89, 91, 93, 112

Five Year (Fund) Program, 51, 52
Flanders, G T, 97-98
Fletcher, L J, 80
Fletcher, Norman D, 161, 586
Fluhrer, Charles, 132
Folsom, Ida M, 395
Foote, Henry Wilder, 549
Forbes, Eleanor, 465
Forbes, Henry Prentiss, 285, 286, 287 *illus*
Ford, Addie B, 288
Ford, Henry, 167, 315
foreign missions, 14
Fortier, George F, 715
Fortney, Jacob H, 341
Fosdick, Harry Emerson, 597, 621
Foster, Emma, 387 *illus*
Franklin Square House, 201, 514
Fraser, Donald, 402
Fraters, 165 ff, 166 *illus*, 636
Frazier, Douglas, 185
Free Church Fellowship, 111, 581, 590 ff, 660-602
Free Church of America; see Free Church Fellowship
Free Religious Association, 139, 149, 507, 679 n
Free Religious Movement, 69
French, Helen, 526
French, M E (Mrs), 365
Friedrich, George A, 222-223
Friend, Victor A, 48, 171, 172 *illus*, 249, 468, 582, 591, 716 n
"Friendly House" (North Carolina), 374, 375 *illus*
Friends' Intelligencer, 564
Fukuzawa, Stejiro, 419

Gage, Sarah, A, 286
Gaines, Absalom, G, 284
Galer, Roger S, 150, 258, 553, 563, 567-568, 573, 575, 577, 589, 715 n
Gally, Matty, 243
Gammon, Ronald, 652
Gardiner, Robert W, 331
Gardner, Percy W, 596
Garst, Charles A C, 409
Gaskins, Ora Cox, 376
Gay, George A, 208, 348
Gaylord, John D, 103
General Aid Association, 39
General Assembly, 5, 618, 621, 628, 659
General Field (Financial) Secretary, 31, 35-36, 44-45
General Missionary, 188
General Secretary, office of, 30, 54
General Superintendent, office of, 31 ff, 54, 669 n
Georgia, Atlanta, 197
Georgia State Convention, 87, 660

Gibb, Sophie S, 142
Gibbons, Brainard F, 634, 641, 654, 656, 657
Gibbons, James Cardinal, 122
Giles, Philip Randall, 632, 657, 659, 660
Gilman House Association; see Sargent-Murray Gilman House
Gilroy, William E, 558, 561, 579, 581-582, 597
Gladden, Washington, 493, 610
Goddard, Mary T, 238, 310, 354, 355
Goddard House, 514
Goddard Seminary, 254
Golden Rule World Service Fund, 52, 477
Goodrich, Massena, 124, 282, 690 n
Goodrich, Moses, 73
Gorton, George E, 538
Gospel Banner (Maine), 174, 244, 266, 344, 419, 669 n
Gospel of Wealth, 477-478
Graham, Hattie Tyng, 466
Grant, Ulysses S, 217
Graves, Bibb, 272
Greeley, Dana M, 210, 300, 664
Greeley, Horace, 13, 97, 667 n
Green Mountain Liberal Institute, 253-254

Harris, Clarence J, 197, 613
Harris, Thomas L, 97
Harrison, Alice, 207
Harrison, Frederick Libby, 638, 640, 642, 658
Harsen Fund, 156
Harvard Divinity School, 319
Haskell, William G, 69
Hathaway, M Agnes, 440, 450, 452, 455
Hebberd, Elisha 510
Helper; see *Sunday School (Universalist) Helper*
Henley, John Wesley, 467
Henry, Carl, F, 578, 715 n
Herman, Theodore F, 619
Herron, George D, 494
Hersey, Benjamin B, 202, 208, 295, 325, 337
Hersey, Charles E, 456
Hersey, Harry Adams, 178, 179 *illus*, 183, 185, 207, 208, 215, 481, 632, 681 n
Hersey, Laura S, 325, 394 *illus*
Hersey, Ruth, 516
Hervey, A B, 286, 493
Hicks, Granville, 209
Higher (Biblical) Criticism, 104, 108, 130
Hill, Andrew M, 700 n
Hill, George, 471-472
Hill, Robert W, 53, 171, 564, 596, 604, 715 n, 717 n
Hill, Thomas, 536
Hirima, Masu, 439
Historical Society of Pennsylvania, 233
Holden, D L, 221

Holleroth, Hugo J, 296
Hollywood Universalist Church (California), 627 *illus*
Holmes, Henry, 369
Holmes, John Haynes, 500, 506-507, 564, 597, 598, 604
Hooper, William L. 692 n
Hopkins, Raymond C, 639, 640, 642, 662
Horton, Douglas, 615, 619
Hosely, Lillian, 183, 200
Howe, Julia Ward, 120, 464
Hoyt, Donald F, 615-616
Humanism, 109 ff
Humanist Manifesto (1933), 109
Humanist Manifesto II (1973), 112, 675 n
Humiliati, 636 ff, 722 n
Hunt, James D, 334, 709 n
Hunt, Walter R, 591
Hunter, Howard E, 328
Hunter, John, 128
Huntley, George E, 213, 213 *illus*, 214, 216, 286, 386, 480
Hurt, H W, 256
Hurtado, Evaristo, 414
Hutchinson, Charles L, 87
hymnology, 238, 605-606, 723 n

IARF (International Association for Religious Freedom), 128, 201, 527, 636
Idlewild Fellowship, 164, 580
Iidomachi (Ohayo) Kindergarten, 452
Ike, Mitsuko (Mrs), 457
Ike, Shigeo, 457
Illinois State Convention, 138, 144, 241, 260
Imai, Tame, 201, 431, 438, 448
immigration, 470-471
Independent, 21 ff, 417, 543
India, 529
Indian (American), 469-470
Indiana State Convention, 87, 143
Industrial Defense Association, 483
Industrial Student, 268
Inman, James Anderson, 372
Inman, James Ballou, 376
Inman's Chapel (North Carolina), 373, 375 *illus*
Inness, George Jr (Mrs), 450
Interchurch World Movement, 613
international arbitration, 484
Institute of Churchmanship, 227
Institute of International Relations, 227
Institute of World Affairs, 227
institutional churches; see Every-Day Church
International Association of Free Christian and Free Religious Youth; see International Religious Fellowship
International Congress of Religious Liberals, 125-126, 127, 148

International Evangelical Alliance, 609
International Religious Fellowship, 201, 202
International Uniform Sunday School-Lessons, 214
International Youth Fellowship, 202
Iowa Liberal Congress, 142
Iowa State Convention, 560
Irwin, Athalia L J, 198, 354, 357, 359, 688 n
Isles of Shoals, 223
Ito, Sempo, 201, 441

Japan Free Religious Association, 456, 457, 458
Japan mission, 14, 200, 201, 412 ff, 426 *illus*, 440 *illus*, 442 *illus*, 449 *illus*, 451 *illus*
Japan Mission Board, 433
Japanese Universalist Convention, 453
Jefferson Liberal Institute, 254
Jeffrey, Caroline M, 222
Jeffries, Robert J, 300
Jenison, Nannie, 186
Jews, 486, 487
Jio, Ryongki, 452, 453
John Hancock Insurance Company, 509, 662
John Murray Atwood Fund, 290, 299
John Muray Lectureship, 49, 50
Johnson, Ellen C, 469
Johnson, Ellen O, 354
Johnson, Raymond B, 330
Johnson Report, 330
Johonnot, Rodney F, 89, 136, 145-146, 357, 550
Joint Commission on Church Union, 650
Joint Interim Commission, 652
Joint Merger Commission, 656, 658
Joint Statement of the Universalists and Congregationalists, 112, 563 ff
Joint UCA-AUA meeting (1959), 658
Jones, C W, 365
Jones, Effie McCollum, 126-127
Jones, Jenkin Lloyd, 89, 131, 133, 145, 148, 550
Jones, Leon P, 390
Jones, Martha G, 390
Jordan, Joseph, 362
Jordan, Joseph Fletcher, 365-367, 369
Jordan Neighborhood House, 371, 527, 529
Joseph Priestley House, 517
Joslin, Elliot P, 397
Joslyn, Lee E, 177
Journal of Liberal Religion, 231
Journal of the Universalist Historical Society, 231
Joy, Charles R, 576, 588, 596, 600, 601, 603, 604, 607
Joy, John D W, 514, 597
Jubilee Fund Drive, 386

Judy, Arthur M, 145

Kahill, Joseph B, 500
Kansas City Platform (Congregational), 555, 574
Kapp, Max Adolph, 113, 210, 287 *illus*, 295, 331-332, 600, 602, 605, 649, 664-665, 724 n
Kawabata, Chujiro, 201, 449
Keirn, Gideon, I, 434, 437-438, 444, 445-446, 447, 551, 611
Kellerman, R S, 28
Kelley, Walter Stuart, 682 n
Kent, Alexander, 144
Kent, Bernice, 448, 452
Kent, Gordon, 111, 596
Keyes, Charles H, 263
Kidwell, Jonathan, 97
King, Galusha A, 470-471
King, Thomas Starr, 95, 537
King's Daughters and Sons, 183
Kirk, Hazel Ida, 208, 391 *illus*, 448
Kirkland, Joseph B, 272
Klein, Louise, 446, 447
Klotzle, Dana E, 458, 527, 528, 635
Knapp, Arthur M, 419, 425
Knight, George T, 88, 230-231, 303
Knost, Peter Noel, 687-688 n
Knost, Richard W, 662
Knowlton, Isaac C, 99-100
Knox College, 255, 256, 261
Koppeis, Francis, 168
Korea, 201, 529
Ku klux Klan, 481-483
Kuebler, Ernest, 652

laity, Universalist, 169 ff
Lake Winnepesaukee (New Hampshire), 219 ff
Lalone, Emerson, Hugh, 159, 249, 250, 250 *illus*, 251, 465, 480, 489, 509, 523, 524, 529, 622, 635, 641, 656, 657, 658
Lapoint, George M, 652
Lapoint, Regina Cary, 456
Latham, Harold S, 171
Lathrop, John H, 597
Laurence, W I, 430
Laymen's League, 49, 169, 495
Laymen's Sunday, 170
League of Universalist Men, 171
Leavitt, Edgar, 31, 32, 431-432, 437
Ledyard, H C, 199, 478, 591, 595
Lee, J C, 49, 148
Lee John Stebbins, 282, 286, 674 n
Lee S. McCollester Professorship, 320
LeFevre, C F, 405
Legion of the Cross, 191, 204
Leining, Fred C, 164, 168, 208, 450, 634
Leining, G H, 590

Index / 759

Leonard, Charles H, 10, 57, 303, 309, 310
Lewis, Orlando F, 469
Lewis, William W, 723 n
Liberal Christian, 428
Liberal Religious Peace Fellowship, 492
"liberty clause," 66, 91, 112
Libby, Emilie F, 57
Liberal Congress; see American Congress of Liberal Religion (Religious Societies)
Livermore, A A, 536-537
Livermore, Mary A, 131, 223, 464, 537, 538
Lobdell, Nelson L, 440, 446, 447-448
Lombard, Donald (Mr & Mrs), 527
Lombard, University (College), 253, 255 ff
Long, John D, 612
Longbrake, George R, 163-164
Longfellow, Henry Wadsworth, 165
Lowe, Charles, 534
Lowe, John Smith, 47, 57, 157, 208, 578, 584, 614, 715 n, 717 n
Lowry, Lewis Roy, 158, 569, 578
LRY (Liberal Religious Youth), 208
Luden, W H, 178
Lumsen, Harold A, 206
Lutheran Church, 618, 720 n
Lyman, William R, 520
Lyman Ward Military Academy, 272-273
Lyon, W H, 136

MacCauley, Clay, 430, 546
MacDuff, Isabella Stirling, 308
MacIntosh, Douglas, 489
MacKenzie, Helen, 526
MacLean, Angus Hector, 287 *illus*, 293-294, 629
MacPherson, David, 25
MacPherson, Robert H, 211
MacPherson, Walter H, 128, 129, 717 n
Macrae, David, 406
Maine State Convention, 464, 557
Manford, Erasmus, 686 n
Manning, Stanley, 50, 129, 184, 203, 208, 565, 614, 616, 638, 682 n, 719 n
Marsh, George B (Mrs), 175, 384
Marshall, George N, 582
Marshall, Harold, 244, 245, 249, 260, 314, 496, 557, 715 n
Marvin, Thomas O, 255
Mary Louise Lisbon Fund, 368
Massachusetts, Gloucester, 3, 48, 49
Massachusetts, Universalism in, 25-27
Massachusetts Council of Churches, 615
Massachusetts State Convention, 31, 43, 57, 111, 155, 157, 158, 414-415, 416, 463, 464-465, 467, 479, 580, 645, 647, 660
Massachusetts Woman's Missionary Society, 270, 448
Masseck, Frank L, 24
Matsuo, O, 446

Maynard, David More, 688 n
Mayo, Amory D, 538
Mayo, Ann Maria, 257
Mayo, Clara, 212
Mayo Clinic, 52
McCallister, John A, 686 n
McCarthy Era, 483
McCollester, Lee S, 13, 37-38, 46, 49, 50, 108, 127, 148, 150, 154, 234, 256, 279, 314, 319 *illus*, 319-320, 322, 323 *illus*, 469, 479, 498, 551, 556, 559, 570, 577, 713 n
McCollester, Sullivan H, 305, 406
McQueary, Howard, 140, 146, 512
McGiffert, Arthur C, 602
McGlauflin, Lucy, 194
McGlauflin, William H, 36, 45, 127, 187-188, 194 ff, 197, 265, 347, 360, 695 n
McKeeman, Gordon, 636, 639, 642
McKinney, Earle T, 636, 637, 639
McLoughlin, Noble E, 410
McLoughlin, Richard H, 489, 590
Mead, Leonard C, 332
Mead, Lucia Ames, 483
Meadville/Lombard Theological School, 261, 280
Medford Hillside Universalist Church (Massachusetts), 482
Meikle, Alexander M, 580-581
Melhuish, Rowena, 376
Mendelsohn, Jack, 664
Merrick, Frank W, 52
Messiah Home, 517, 521
Metcalf, Henry B, 13, 90, 354, 466, 478, 713 n
Methodists, 21, 175, 414, 430, 494, 615
Meyer, Eugene (Mrs), 335
Miami Association (Ohio), 81
Michigan State Convention, 599
Mid-Southern Federation of Religious Liberals, 150
Middlesex Sabbath School Union (Massachusetts), 96
Midori Kindergarten, 440 *illus*, 449, 452, 456, 457
Milburn, Ulysses S, 50, 597
Miles, Edson Russell, 288, 647
Millen, Edmund, 169
Miller, Etta Wallace, 184
Miller, Lewis, 217
Miller, O D, 97
Miller, Robert L'H, 333
Miller, T R (Mrs), 715 n
Milligan, Charles S, 328
Millikan, Robert Andrews, 263
Million Dollar (Campaign) Drive, 47
Miner, Alonzo A, 11, 12, 13, 32, 82, 85, 101, 125, 230, 236, 242, 308, 415-416, 465, 471, 484, 539, 609
Ministerial Association, 113
Minister's Covenant (1897), 14

Ministers' Fellowship, 157
Minnesota, Fort Snelling, 52
Minnesota, St. Paul, Universalism in, 198
Minnesota State Convention, 70, 73, 599
Mission Brotherhood, 165
Mission Circles, 395
missionary boxes, 41
"Missionary Day," 380
"Missouri Plan," 349-350
Missouri State convention, 549
Mitchell, Hinckley G, 312
Mitchell, James Ure, 401-402, 404, 409
Mitchell, John, 401
Mitchell Seminary, 254
Mizumakai, Keijiro, 454
Moody, Dwight L, 98, 608
Moore, John, 99
Morehouse, D W, 723 n
Morrell, Herbert Philbrick, 286
Mudge, Lewis S, 617
Mulford, Jeannette C, 394 *illus*
Munson, Keith C, 639, 642, 724 n
Murphy, J A, 369
Murray, John, 3, 4, 5, 9, 183
Murray Anniversary Crusade, 48 *illus*, 49
Murray Centenary Fund, 39, 40, 42, 45, 175, 379
Murray Crusade, 660
Murray Foundation, 185
Murray Graded Lessons, 215
Murray Grove, 183, 220
Murray Grove Association, 183, 220, 221
Murray Grove Memorial Church, 221 *illus*
Murray Press, 240, 250
Murray Universalist Church (Washington, D C), 55
Myer, James, 614
Myrtle, 187, 189

Nagano, Naoichiro, 441, 454, 455
Nash, Arthur, 52, 475-477
Nash, C Ellwood, 35, 125, 185, 190, 193-194, 195, 569-570
Nash, Melville S, 244
National Association of Universalist Men, 171
National Capitol Choir, 58
National Council of Superintendents, 34, 155
National Council of Women, 386
National Federation of Religious Liberals, 149 ff, 596, 606
National Laymen's Committee, 52, 171
National League of Universalist Laymen, 169
National Prison Association, 354
National Unitarian Conference, 540, 541, 548, 585
Nearing, Scott, 508

Needham, George G, 510
Negroes, Universalism and, 197-198, 361-362
New Beacon Series in Religious Education, 215
New Covenant (Chicago), 40, 72
New England Conference of Ministers (1896), 86
New England Convention, 39
New Hampshire State Convention, 466-467
New Jersey, Good Luck, 220
New Jersey State Convention, 33, 144, 221
New Radical Society, 70
"New Theology", 536-537
New Unity; see *Unity*
"New" Universalism, 130, 135-136, 141
New World, 678 n
New York, Universalism in, 25, 27-28
New York Age, 366
New York State Conventionctarian, 677 n
Norfolk Mission, 362 ff, 683 n
North Carolina, Universalism in 357, 372 ff, 388 ff
North Carolina State Convention, 389, 393, 599, 660
Northern Baptist Church, 720 n
Noyes, Arthur Amos, 263
Non-Sectarian, 677 n
Norfolk Mission, 362 ff, 683 n
North Carolina, Universalism in 357, 372 ff, 388 ff
North Carolina State Convention, 389, 393, 599, 660
Northern Baptist Church, 720 n
Noyes, Arthur Amos, 263

Ocean Home Association, 218
off-center cross, 637-638
Ohio State Convention, 40, 115, 155, 241, 424, 590, 598
Ohio Universalist and Literary Companion, 241
Olmsted, Frederic Law, 119
Onishi, Aiko, 457
Onward, 113, 187, 189, 190, 202, 203, 204, 209, 211, 596
Order of Universal Brotherhood, 185
Order of Universalist Comrades, 169-171
Orito, J C, 201, 448, 456
Orleans Liberal Institute, 254
Osborn, Catherine M, 431, 437, 443, 444, 447
Outlaw, Annie Maxwell, 698 n
Oxford, Massachusetts, 4, 5
Oxnam, G Bromley, 616

Pacific Coast Conference - Free Church Fellowship, 599

Pacific Unitarian School of the Ministry; see Thomas Starr King School
pacifism, 487 ff, 708 n
Packard, Silvanus, 302
Paige, Lucius R, 308, 692 n
Palmer, J H, 142
Pan American Exposition, 148
Parke, David B, 296
Parker, Hosea W, 124
Parker, Theodore, 507
Pasadena Convention (1915), 45-46
Paterson, James, 405
Patterson, A J, 12, 219, 343
Patton, Kenneth L, 232, 334, 484, 645
Pauline Brotherhood, 184
Peabody, Francis G, 543
Peirce, Arthur W, 591
Pelletrau, M K, 237
penal reform, 468-469
Pennoyer, Charles H, 504, 607, 717 n
Pennsylvania State Convention, 161, 520, 660, 713 n
Perham, Sidney, 384
Perin, George L, 43, 124, 141, 147, 180, 200, 423, 425 ff, 426 illus, 513, 540
Perin-Cate Home for Boys, 55, 441
Perkins, Charles E, 102, 136
Perkins, Florida (Mrs), 376
Perkins, Fred B, 720 n
Perkins, Frederic W, 56, 58, 60, 68, 91, 93, 113, 113 illus, 114, 115, 116, 149, 168, 240, 494, 496, 504, 544, 552, 559, 562, 567, 570-571, 572, 574, 577, 615, 616, 717 n, 720 n
Permanent Church Extension Fund, 191
Perry, Albert Q, 663, 724 n
Peshdrimaljian, B M, 414
Peterson, Thomas F, 296
Petrie, Omer G, 189
Petty, Charles E, 222
Phillips, T Glenn, 222
Pierce, Ellis E, 295
Pigeon River Mission, 372 ff, 275 illus
Piper, Wilson C, 724 n
Pizzo, William C, 288
Plott, Donald (Mrs), 377
Plott, Jonathan, 372
Poor, Charles M, 259
Pope, Frederick A, Jr, 333
Porter, John William, 106
Post Office Mission, 187
Postma, Ann 186, 202, 526
Potter, Charles Francis, 110
Potter, Thomas, 220
Potter homestead, 222
Potter meeting house, 395
Potter Memorial Fund, 220-221
Potterton, Thomas E, 629
Powell, Hannah J, 208, 358, 373-374, 375-376, 377, 378, 390

Powers, Levi M, 167, 396, 465, 475, 494, 495 illus, 496, 699 n
Prater, Leonard D, 271
Prendergast Preventorium, 398
Presbyterian Advance (Nashville, Tennessee), 565
Presbyterian Church (United), 720 n
Presbyterian Church USA, 619, 720 n
Presbyterians, 413, 414, 430
Prescott Mission; see Brevoort Mission
Prescott Neighborhood House; see Brevoort Mission
Prince, Morton, 310
Protestant Episcopal Church, 720 n
Pullman, George M, 217, 473-475
Pullman, James M, 125, 131, 144, 145, 383, 610
Pullman, Royal H, 30, 42, 74, 384
Pullman, Tracy M, 618
Pullman Strike, 474-475
Purves, James, 400

"Quillen" (Ferry Beach, Maine), 224 illus, 225
Quinby, Cordelia A, 125, 381 illus, 382, 386, 388
Quinby, George W, 342, 538
quota system, 39, 48, 53, 449, 631

radio station WMEX, 721 n
Rasnake, J M, 196
Ratcliff, John M, 214, 317, 322, 324
Rauschenbusch, Walter, 60, 493-494, 496
Red Horse Tavern; see Wayside Inn
Reamon, Ellsworth C, 523, 622, 656-657, 661, 663
Reccord, Augustus P, 552, 582, 596, 598
Reed, H W, 717 n
Reese, Curtis W, 259, 260, 675 n
Reeves, Gene A, 328
Reformed Episcopal Church, 720 n
regional (district) superintendents, 34
Restorationist controversy, 685-686 n
Rexford, Everett, L, 74, 76, 79, 122, 124, 132, 140, 143, 147, 148, 424, 676 n
Rheiner, C'B, 478
Rhode Island State Convention, 416, 419, 594
Rice, Clarence E, 56, 163, 426, 431, 433, 434, 437, 613
Rice, Jonah F, 188
Rice, Luther, 431
Rice, William B, 657, 664
Richardson Hall, 284
Robbins, C Guy, 127
Roberts, Richard, 561
Robinson, Elmo A, 235, 664, 680 n
Robinson, James Harvey, 508
Robinson, Luther R, 208
Roblin, Stephen H, 176, 341

Rodehaver, Myles W, 295
Rogers, A G, 8
Romaine, Julia Asenath, 246
Roman Catholics, 21
Rose, Henry R, 150
Rose, Louie, 190
Rose, William Wallace, 159, 488
Rowe, Alice G, 448, 452
Rugg, Henry W, 43, 80, 177, 219, 415, 516, 422, 431, 443
Ruggles, B C, 715 n
Russell, Bertrand, 508
Russell, E T, 410
Ryder, William H, 6, 10, 13, 30, 74, 76 ff, 80, 131, 277, 286, 608-609
Ryder Community Center (Chicago), 527-528
Ryder Divinity School, 261, 274, 275, 277 ff, 278 *illus*

Sacco and Vanzetti case, 499-500
Sagara, Takeo, 429, 431
Sahlin, G A, 124
St Lawrence Foundation for Theological Education, 300, 301
St Lawrence University, 253, 281
St Paul's Universalist Industrial School, 362
Sanders, Frank K, 557, 562, 576
Sanford, Louis Walter, 605
Sankey, Ira D, 608
Sargent, John G, 56
Sargent, Judith
Sargent-Murray-Gilman House, 49, 396
Satoh, Kiyoshi, 201, 427, 438, 448-449
Sawyer, Alan F, 655, 656, 662, 724 n
Sawyer, Thomas J, 6, 11, 83, 124, 281, 283, 302, 306, 401, 417, 464, 541
Saxe, Asa, 30, 40, 123, 177
Sayles, John, 552, 717 n
Schaff, Philip, 609
Schofield, John M, 724 n
Schooley, Henry H, 724 n
Schouler, Margaret C, 423-424, 425
Schrock, Claudia E, 439, 440
Schumacher, Ferdinand, 194
Schwenk, Emerson S, 490
Scotland, Universalism in, 400 ff
Scott, Clinton Lee, 110, 110 *illus*, 111, 112, 235, 479, 591, 595, 605, 618, 635, 636, 641-642, 645, 660, 717 n, 719 n, 724 n
Scott, Julia, 466
Scott, Mary Slaughter, 722 n
Scottish Universalist Convention, 402
Seaburg, Alan, 328, 334
Seaburg, Carl, 227, 232
Selleck, Willard C, 31, 127, 574
Senexet, 164-165
Seventh-Day Baptists, 720 n
Shakamak State Park (Indiana), 229

Shawmut Avenue Universalist Church (Boston), 513-514
Shealey, William R Jr, 334
Shelter Neck, North Carolina, 228, 229, 390-391
Shepard, Sheldon, 454-455, 560
Sheridan, Philip H, 217
Shidara, Masao (John), 454, 458
Shigataro, Akashi, 427
Shinn, Quillen Hamilton, 23, 32, 34, 153, 184, 185, 186, 187, 198, 218-219, 223, 228 *illus*, 262, 264 ff, 341 ff, 343 *illus*, 345 *illus*, 351 *illus*, 363, 364, 373, 416, 469, 540, 541, 713 n
Shinn Memorial Church, 199, 199 *illus*, 348
Shinn Memorial Fund, 199, 347
Shinn Memorial Lectureship, 347
Shippen, Eugene Rodman, 552
Shipler, Guy Emery, 248
Shizuoka Church, 449 *illus*
Shrigley, James, 178, 418
Shutter, Marion D, 37, 46, 104 ff, 105 *illus*, 126, 127, 132, 133, 150, 479, 488, 512, 573, 711 n
Shutter, Marion D (Mrs), 386, 495
Sias, Mary Phelps, 69
Simmons, H E, 715 n
Skeels, W H, 60, 155
Skinner, Ada Blanchard, 497
Skinner, Charles M, 496
Skinner, Clarence R, 58, 250, 316, 318-319, 323 *illus*, 483, 488, 496 ff, 497 *illus*, 540, 643
Skinner, Cornelia Otis, 709 n
Skinner, Dolphus, 103, 497
Skinner, Otis Ainsworth, 497, 507
Skinner, Otis Augustus, 497
Skinner, Warren, 497
Skinner Award, 500
Skinner House, 630
Slaten, A Wakefield, 560
Slaughter, George M, 266
Smith, Benton, 244
Smith, Isaac, 51, 575
Smith, Mary Louise, 265
Smith, Nancy Wiley Paine, 308
Smith, Richard M, 265, 267
Smith, Stephen R, 401
Smithson College, 253
Snow, J C, 310
Social Christianity; see Social Gospel
Social Darwinism, 101, 478
Social Gospel, 246, 493, 501, 709 n
Social Principles, Declaration of, 503, 504, 505
Society for Ethical Culture, 148
Society of Friends (Quakers), 150, 597, 720 n
Sorosis, 380
Soule, Arthur M. 465

Soule, Caroline A, 220, 379, 383-384, 381 *illus*, 400, 403 ff, 698 n
South, Universalism in the, 197
Southern Industrial Institute, 264 ff, 688 n
Southern Missionary, office of, 34, 187-188, 190, 346
Southern Religious Young People's Federation, 200
Southern Universalist Association, 348
Southwestern Federation of Religious Liberals, 597
Southworth, Franklin C, 126, 280
Spear, Charles, 538
Special Gifts Fund, 52
Speight, Harold E B, 564, 585
Spoerl, Dorothy (Tilden), 93, 186, 204, 206
Springall, Marjorie L, 394 *illus*
Stacy, Martha, 455, 456
Stanford University, 264
Star and Covenant, 238
Star in the West, 74, 218, 465
Star Island, 223, 227
Start, William A, 26, 218
state conventions, 6, 660
state superintendents, 34
Stearns, Charles E, 336
Stebbins, Livingston, 252
Stetson, Clifford R, 201, 449, 454
Stetson, Margaret, 201, 454
Stewart, A T, 477
Stewart, Leland Perry, 647
Stiernotte, Alfred B, 296
Stimson, Ella, 431
Stover, Janet, 527
Strain, A G, 272
Strain, Benjamin F, 372
Straub, Jacob, 410-411
Straub, Mary A, 410
Street, J K, 362
Student Religious Liberals, 185
Strong, Josiah, 609
Suffolk mission, 363 ff, 365 *illus*, 371; see also Jordan Neighborhood House
suffrage movement, 467
Sullivan, William L, 594
Summer, Henry, 361
summer institutes, 228-229
Summerbell, Carlyle, 590
Sunday, William Ashley ("Billy"), 609
Sunday School Association (Massachusetts), 611
Sunday School (Universalist) Helper, 214, 237, 249
Sunday School Union (Brooklyn, N Y), 611
Sunderland, J T, 547-548, 550
Suye Fund, 200
Swan, James H, 124
Sweet, Joseph L, 213
Sweetser, Edwin C, 58, 78 ff, 85, 87, 90, 100, 124, 126, 160-162, 177, 209, 222, 489, 520, 541, 543, 544-546, 549, 578, 673 n, 713 n
Taft, Charles P
Taft, William Howard, 127
Tanner, Frank J, 169
Tapp, Robert B, 295
Tar Heel Universalist, 390
Tarasawa, Ishi, 452, 454
Taylor, Alice Enbom, 397
Taylor, Harold, 297, 330
Taylor, Henry B, 198
Taylor Report, 297-298, 330, 331
Teamwork, 165, 599
Tennessee, Universalism in, 193 ff
Texas, Universalism in, 200, 204, 385
Thayer, Thomas B, 10, 99, 100, 230, 234, 237, 342, 413, 414, 415, 538
Thayer, William M, 342
The Edge, 231-232
"The Report," 662
The Weirs (New Hampshire), 219, 223
Thomas, Homer, 684 n
Thomas, M. Louise, 380, 381 *illus*, 407, 414, 466
Thomas Starr King School, 264
Thompson, Delos H, 521
Thompson, Zenas, 431
Thompson Home, 521
Throop, Amos G, 262-263, 344
Throop Polytechnic Institute, 262 ff
Tilden, Charles H, 257
Tilden, Joseph M, 47, 150, 256-258, 259
Tilden, Samuel J, 477
Tillinghast, James D, 176, 188, 207, 308
Tilney, S D, 715 n
Titus, Anson, 230
To-Day, 101, 242
Todd, William E Manning, 196
Tomlinson, Charles W, 85, 416
Tomlinson, D C, 383
Tomlinson, Irving C, 514
Tomlinson, Vincent E, 50, 52, 163, 165, 168, 415, 455, 565, 566, 579, 586-587, 591, 593, 596, 600, 604, 717 n
Tompkins, Abel, 236
Tousey, William G, 242, 303
Townsend, Eleanor P, 354
Townsend, J G, 536
Trimble, L Andrews, 267
Trumpet and Christian Freeman, 238, 242
Trumpet and Universalist Magazine, 236
Tucker, John G, 267
Tufts College, 3, 253, 254, 490, 689 n
Tufts Divinity School; see Crane Theological School
Tufts Papers on Religion, 640, 722 n
Tufts School of Religion; see Crane Theological School

764 / Index

Turkey Run State Park (Indiana), 229
Tuskegee Institute, 382
Tuskegee Negro Conference, 269
Tuttle, James Harvey, 32, 69, 263, 511
Twentieth Century Fund, 45
"Two-Cents-a-Week for Missions," 190, 191

UCA (Universalist Church of America), 290, 457
Ulrich, Gustav H, 524, 699 n
Underwood, Carrie P, 225
"Uni-Uni," 606
Union Association (Massachusetts), 86
Union for Universal Peace, 484
Unirondack, 229
Unitarian Church of the Larger Fellowship, 660
Unitarian Commission of Appraisal, 660, 601
Unitarian Laymen's League, 50, 173
Unitarian Register, 687 n
Unitarian Register-Universalist Leader, 251
Unitarian Review; see *New World*
Unitarian Service Committee, 523, 524, 528
Unitarian Universalist Ministers Association, 500
Unitarian-Universalist Register-Leader, 251
Unitarian Universalist Service Committee, 528-529
Unitarian Universalist World, 112, 252
Unitarians, 21, 23-24
United Brethren Church, 720 n
United Christian Adult Movement, 227
United Church of Canada, 554, 720 n
United Liberal Churches (Florida), 113, 130, 584
United Nations, 739 (Appendix A)
United States Census, 19, 23
United States Sanitary Commission, 537
Unity, 131, 132, 133, 147, 148, 249
Unity Settlement House, 201, 512-513
Universalism and science, 94 ff
Universalist (Boston), 70 ff, 236, 237, 464
Universalist (Chicago), 75, 133, 238
Universalist (Japan), 428, 436
Universalist Biennial Reports and Directory; see *Universalist Directory*
Universalist Chautauqua, 223
Universalist Church, headquarters, 629, 721 n
Universalist Church, organization, 5 ff, 626 ff, 628 ff, 720-721 n
Universalist Church, publications, 235 ff
Universalist Church, statistics, 19 ff, 625, 667 n, 668 n, 708 n, 715 n
Universalist Church of America (UCA), 5, 58, 252, 523, 627-628
Universalist Church of Japan, 457, 458
Universalist Club (Boston), 169, 559

Universalist Community Pulpit, 607
Universalist Comrades, 55
Universalist Congress, 123
Universalist Directory, 668 n
Universalist Free Church Association, 507
Universalist General Convention, 5, 6-7, 13, 14, 37, 45, 74, 235, 240, 383-384, 430, 485, 486, 487, 628
Universalist General Reform Association, 463-464, 469-470, 494
Universalist Herald, 201, 241, 361, 686 n
Universalist Historical Society, 234, 235, 328, 334
Universalist Leader, 248, 250, 558, 673 n
Universalist League, 130-131, 142
Universalist Loyalty Fellowship, 53
Universalist Magazine, 412
Universalist Ministerial (Ministers) Association, 165, 231, 559
Universalist Ministers Retirement Society, 159
Universalist National Cemetery, 222
Universalist National Convention (Japan), 432
Universalist National Memorial Church, 54, 55 ff
Universalist Publishing House, 8, 90, 138, 232, 236 ff, 239 *illus*, 251, 252, 606, 630, 721 n
Universalist Quarterly, 95, 100, 103, 231, 234, 236, 242, 471
Universalist Reform League, 464
Universalist Register, 19 ff, 77, 181, 234, 237, 249, 269, 271, 668 n
Universalist Retirement Service Society, 159
Universalist Service Committee, 457, 458, 523 ff, 525 *illus*, 526, 527
Universalist Union, 176, 188
Universalist-Unitarian consolidation, 661 ff
Universalist-Unitarian relations, 126, 130 ff, 134-135, 136-137, 215, 223, 533 ff, 583 ff
Universalist Year Book, 668 n
Universalist Youth Fellowship (UYF), 209 *illus*,
Upson, Josiah, 97
Upton, Dilworth, 606
Ure, Andrew, 409-410
Ure, George, 409-410
Usher, James M, 236
UU Church of the Larger Fellowship, 660-661
UUA (Unitarian Universalist Association), 252, 289, 300, 659
UUA, constitution and bylaws (1961), 745-751 (Appendix B), 724 n
UUA, pledge of allegiance, 665
UUA Now, 251
UUCC (Universalists and Unitarians for Cooperation Without Consolidation), 661, 662

UUWF (Unitarian Universalist Women's Federation), 379, 398, 399
UYF (Universalist Youth Fellowship), 208, 721 n

Vail, W S, 198
Valentyne, Grace, 391 *illus*
van Schaick, John, 111, 163, 232, 245 ff, 246 *illus*, 454, 495, 523, 548, 559-560, 565, 566, 568-569, 572, 579, 587-588, 603, 620, 641
van Schaick, John (Mrs), 247
Vannevar, John, 307
Veazey, Harry Lawrence, 196
Velde Committee, 484
Vermont and Quebec Convention, 31-32, 87, 660
Vermont Quebec Unitarian Universalist Ministers Association, 490
Veterans of Foreign Wars, 483
Vickery, Charles N. 526, 527, 638, 642
Vincent, John H. 217
Voice of Fellowship, 688 n
Voss, Carl H, 296

Waddell, P H, 401
Waka, R John, 329
Walker, Alice T, 391 *illus*
Walker, G D Elbert, 715 n
Walker, George D, 28
Walker, Irving L (Mrs), 719 n
Wallace, M R M (Mrs), 74, 124
Ward, Lyman, 265 ff, 388
Warren, Fiske (Mrs), 630
Washburn, Cadwallader C, 511
Washburn, Israel, Jr, 13, 79, 81, 406
Washburn, L K, 70
Washburn, W D, 511
Washburn Memorial Home, 511
Washington, Booker T, 269, 347, 689 n
Washington, Tacoma, Universalists in, 218 *illus*
Washington Association (Ohio), 153
Washington, Declaration of (1935), 11, 115
Watson, George W, 365
Wayside Chapel (Malden, Massachusetts), 683 n
Wayside Community Pulpit, 607
Wayside Inn, 165 ff
Wayside Pulpit (Unitarian), 606
WCA (Woman's Centenary (Aid) Association), 40, 379, 380-381, 381 *illus*, 382 ff, 400, 402 ff, 484, 677 n, 703 n
Weaver, George S, 98
Webb, Alexander Russell, 122
Webster, Inez, 480
Welch, E Parl, 690 n
Wendte, Charles, 149, 540
Wessell, Nils Y, 185, 299, 326
West, Rosalie A, 377, 638

Westbrook Seminary, 253
Western Association of New York State, 5
Western Unitarian, 560, 585
Western Unitarian Conference, 131, 539, 597
Western Universalist Conference, 144
Westman, Carol J, 724 n
Westwood, Horace, 605
Whack, Ethel, 370
Whippen, Elbert, 643
Whitcomb, Merrick, 243
White, Nehemiah, 125
White, Rufus A, 124, 132, 139, 141, 147, 183-184
White, William Allen, 245
Whitman, H S, 242
Whittemore, Thomas, 38, 236
Whittlesey, Ira P, 521
Wilkins, Marietta B, 387 *illus*, 388, 396, 397
Williams, L Griswold, 468, 488
Williams, Theresa A, 387 *illus*
Williamson, Henry, 408, 410
Willis, Annie B, 370, 371
Willson, Andrew, 342
Wilson, J W, 367
Winchester, Margaret, 216
Winchester Profession of Faith (1803), 3, 65 ff, 78 ff, 92, 114, 137, 672 n
Winkleman, Frederick A, 713 n
Winter, Charles, 107
Wisconsin Liberal Congress, 142
Wisconsin State Convention, 142
Wise, Stephen S, 508
Wise, Thomas E, 350, 363, 364 *illus*
WNMA (Women's National Missionary Association), 57, 169, 196, 227, 270, 272, 373, 379, 386 ff, 387 *illus*, 389 *illus*, 391 *illus*, 394 *illus*, 396, 443, 444, 450, 451
WNMA Bulletin, 388
WNMA Yearbook, 388
Wolfe, Rolland Emerson, 320, 322
Wolley, Robert C, 500, 660, 724 n
Woman's International League for Peace and Freedom, 483
women, Universalist, 464 ff, 705 n
Women's Universalist Missionary Society (Massachusetts), 381-382
Wood, George, 390
Wood, John E, 635
Wood, Madelyn H, 391 *illus*, 394 *illus*
Woodbridge, Samuel F, 304
Woodbridge, Warren S, 242, 304, 478, 692 n
Woodin, Ruth, 480
Woodman, Richard, 25
Woodrow, Samuel H, 559
"World Church for World Service" (Universalist), 614
World Federation of Democratic Youth, 202
world peace, 484, 486, 487
World's Columbian Exposition, 119 ff
World's Congress of Religion, 120

World's Parliament of Religions, 96, 119-120
Worrall, William, 401
Wright, C Conrad, 330
Wright, Daniel, 184
Wright, Frank Lloyd, 550
Wright, Nathaniel R, 344
Wyatt, William, F, 317
Wyman, Charles A, 249

Yates, Harriet G, 214, 628
YMCA (Young Men's Christian Association), 13, 52, 611-612, 677 n
Yoshimura, Hizedo, 425, 429, 431, 438
Yoshioka, Toshio, 458
Young, Owen D, 52, 57, 170 *illus*, 594
Young Liberal, 211, 649
Young People's Sunday, 187

Young Tower of World Peace, 57
Youth Day, 180
Youth for Action, 211
YPCU (Young Peoples Christian Union), 113, 174 ff, 179 *illus*, 220, 227, 348, 444, 681 n, 682 n, 683 n
YPCU (Japan), 200
YPCU (Massachusetts), 204 ff
YPCU (Rhode Island), 177, 205-206
YPCU (Vermont), 182
YPRU (Young People's Religious Union (Unitarian), 203, 208 ff, 603, 683 n
YRUU (Young Religious Unitarian Universalists), 208, 209

Ziegler, Albert F, 251, 635, 636, 638, 642, 656, 662, 722 n
Zion's Herald, 564, 615